Genetic Technologies and the Law

Genetic Technologies and the Law

Cases and Materials

Patricia Kuszler
Charles I. Stone Professor of Law
University of Washington

Kathryn Battuello
Research Assistant Professor of Law
University of Washington

Sean O'Connor
Associate Professor of Law
University of Washington

Carolina Academic Press
Durham, North Carolina

ISBN 10: 0-89089-621-6, ISBN 13: 978-0-89089-621-1
LCCN: 2006936997

Carolina Academic Press
700 Kent Street
Durham, North Carolina 27701
Telephone (919) 489-7486
Fax (919) 493-5668
www.cap-press.com

Printed in the United States of America

Contents

Table of Cases

Preface

Without question, rapidly progressing scientific, technological and clinical developments in the field of genetics are revolutionizing our approach to clinical medicine, research and development, agricultural production, and public health. Increasingly, attention is shifting to the law, with inquiring minds speculating about the role genetics and genetics-based technologies will play in framing and resolving lawsuits and other forms of dispute under the law. Although the introduction of genetics-based evidence in the courtroom is still a relatively rare occurrence, the role genetics and genetics-based technologies could play in influencing legal rights and remedies is becoming increasingly clear. So too are questions regarding the extent to which genetics should influence the framework for and resolution of cases and controversies arising under constitutional, statutory or common-law precedents. This book will introduce students in law, medicine, public health and public policy to the many ways in which genetics is, or is about to, intersect with law, and assist them in addressing the complex legal, ethical and social policy issues that come into play when considering the extent to which genetics should play a role in shaping—or reshaping—our laws.

Because the role of genetics in law is evolving, this casebook incorporates a wide range of materials, in addition to relevant judicial opinions from federal and state courts. Our materials include statutes, administrative regulations, proposed federal and state legislation, professional medical guidelines, public policy statements and advisory opinions, and relevant analyses and commentary drawn from leading legal, medical, and scientific scholars who are studying the many issues that attend the intersection of law and genetics. One prevailing theme throughout these materials is the important role that scientific understanding plays in achieving an appropriate application of genetics-based knowledge to issues of law, and an appropriate application of law to disputes involving the application, interpretation or ownership of genetics-based information and technologies. Throughout this book the authors either provide students with an introduction to the relevant scientific principles, or refer them to reliable sources for the scientific background that is critical to a comprehensive understanding of the legal issues under study.

Consistent with our emphasis on multidisciplinary understanding, Chapter 1 provides students with a brief historical overview of the science of genetics. Chapters 2, 3 and 4 introduce students to relevant cases and materials bearing on the controversial issues of genetic privacy and genetic discrimination. Chapter 2 focuses primarily on legal rights, responsibilities and remedies surrounding access to and dissemination of genetic information. Chapters 3 and 4 analyze the myths and realities underlying public and political concerns about genetic discrimination in both the workplace and the insurance context. Chapter 5 provides an introduction and overview of increasingly visible and disputed issues arising in genetics research involving human subjects. Chapter 6 moves students from the laws regulating research, to those that govern the commercialization of—and ownership rights in—the products of genetics-based research. Chapters 7, 8 and 9 address the legal issues that surround three of the most well-known and established areas of application for genetics-based technologies: clinical medicine, agricultural biotechnology and forensic evidence. Chapter 10 completes our overview of genetic technologies and the law with an in-depth review of relevant cases and materials outlining the role of genetics in public health, moving from the eugenics movement in the early 1900s to issues underlying contemporary public health programs promoting prenatal and newborn screening.

The authors wish to acknowledge and thank the many law, public health, and public affairs students at the University of Washington whose contributions helped with the development and ultimate publication of this book. Special recognition is due to Nora Beidler Hendrickson who was a contributing author on Chapters 2 and 10. In addition, we would like to offer a very special thank you to Katherine Mary Van Maren, who was our principal editor and oversaw all aspects of the final compilation and editing of this book. We also wish to specifically recognize the following University of Washington law students, reference librarians, and staff who helped to research and edit this book: Ruth Beardsley, Cynthia Fester, Megan Grembowski, Cory Johnson, Christina Latta, Nancy McMurrer, Heather Meade, Jeri Miles, Cheryl Nyberg, Victoria Parker, Josh Piper, Kaye Reiter, Jennifer Snider, and Mary Whisner. Finally, we extend a well-deserved thank you to our families for their ongoing support throughout the process.

Kate Battuello
Patricia Kuszler
Sean O'Connor

Acknowledgments

American Academy of Pediatrics, Committee on Bioethics, *Ethical Issues With Genetic Testing in Pediatrics*, 107 PEDIATRICS 1451 (2001). Used with permission from American Academy of Pediatrics. Copyright © 2001 American Academy of Pediatrics.

American Academy of Pediatrics, Task Force on Newborn Screening, *Serving the Family from Birth to the Medical Home*, 107 PEDIATRICS 389 (2000). Copyright © 2000 American Academy of Pediatrics. Reprinted with permission from American Academy of Pediatrics.

American Society of Human Genetics/American College of Medical Genetics, *Points to Consider: Ethical, Legal, and Psychosocial Implications of Genetic Testing in Children and Adolescents*, 57 AMERICAN JOURNAL OF HUMAN GENETICS 1233 (1995). Reprinted with permission of the University of Chicago Press, excerpts from the American Society of Human Genetics and American College of Medical Genetics. Copyright © 1995 American Society of Human Genetics. All rights reserved.

Adrienne Asch, *Prenatal Diagnosis and Selective Abortion: A Challenge to Practice and Policy*, 89 AMERICAN JOURNAL OF PUBLIC HEALTH 1649 (1999). Copyright © 1999 American Public Health Association. Reprinted with permission from the American Public Health Association.

Eric Beckenhauer, Note, *Redefining Race: Can Genetic Testing Provide Biological Proof of Indian Ethnicity?*, 56 STANFORD LAW REVIEW 161 (2003). Copyright © 2003 Stanford Law Review. Reprinted with permission.

Paul W. Brandt-Rauf & Sherry I. Brandt-Rauf, *Genetic Testing in the Workplace: Ethical, Legal and Social Implications*, 25 ANNUAL REVIEW OF PUBLIC HEALTH 139 (2004). Reprinted, with permission, from the Annual Review of Public Health Volume 25 © 2004 by Annual Reviews www.annualreviews.org.

Wylie Burke, *Genomic Medicine: Genetic Testing*, 347 NEW ENGLAND JOURNAL OF MEDICINE 1867 (2002). Copyright © 2002 Massachusetts Medical Society. Reprinted with permission. All rights reserved.

Ellen Wright Clayton, *Genetics, Public Health, and the Law* in GENETICS AND PUBLIC HEALTH IN THE 21ST CENTURY: USING GENETIC INFORMATION TO IMPROVE HEALTH AND PREVENT DISEASE (M.J. Khoury, W. Burke & E.J. Thomson eds. 2000). Reprinted by permission of Oxford University Press, Inc. www.oup.com.

Francis S. Collins, Eric D. Green, Alan E. Guttmacher & Mark S. Guyer, *A Vision for the Future of Genomics Research: A Blueprint for the Genomic Era*, 422 NATURE 835 (2003). Copyright © 2003 Macmillan Publishers Ltd. Reprinted with permission.

James P. Evans, Cecile Skrzynia & Wylie Burke, *The Complexities of Predictive Genetic Testing*, 322 British Medical Journal 1052 (2001). Copyright © 2001 BMJ Publishing Ltd. Reprinted with permission.

Stanley Fields, *Proteomics in Genomeland*, 291 Science 1221 (2001). Reprinted with permission from the American Association of the Advancement of Science. Copyright © 2001 American Association of the Advancement of Science.

Mark A. Hall, *Legal Rules and Industry Norms: The Impact of Laws Restricting Insurers' Use of Genetic Information*, 40 Jurimetrics Journal 93 (1999). Copyright © 1999 American Bar Association. Reprinted with permission.

Gary E. Marchant, *Genetic and Toxic Torts*, 31 Seton Hall Law Review 949 (2001). Copyright © 2001 Seton Hall University School of Law. Reprinted with permission.

Paul Steven Miller, *Genetic Discrimination in the Workplace*, 26 American Journal of Law, Medicine and Ethics 189 (1998). Copyright © 1998 American Society of Law, Medicine and Ethics. Reprinted with permission from the American Society of Law, Medicine and Ethics.

Martin S. Pernick, *Eugenics and Public Health in American History*, 87 American Journal of Public Health 1767 (1997). Copyright © 1997 American Public Health Association. Reprinted with permission from the American Public Health Association.

Thomas Parker Redick, *Twenty-First Century Toxicogenomics Meets Twentieth Century Mass Tort Precedent: Is There a Duty to Warn of a Hypothetical Harm to an "Eggshell" Gene?*, 42 Washburn Law Journal 547 (2003). Copyright © 2003 Washburn University School of Law. Reprinted with permission.

Robert F. Rich & Julian Ziegler, *Genetic Discrimination in Health Insurance for a (Not So) Special Problem?*, 2 Indiana Health Law Review 5 (2005). Copyright © 2005 Indian Health Law Review. Reprinted with permission granted by Indiana Health Law Review.

Mark A. Rothstein, *Genetics and the Work Force of the Next Hundred Years*, 2000 Columbia Business Law Review 371 (2000). Copyright © 2000 Columbia Business Law Review; Mark A. Rothstein. Reprinted with permission from the Columbia Business Law Review.

Mark A. Rothstein, *Should Genetic Information Be Used to Predict Life Expectancy of Plaintiffs in Tort Cases?*, Houston Lawyer, Sept.–Oct. 1996, at 49. Copyright © 1996 Houston Bar Association. Excerpt reprinted with permission.

Mark A. Rothstein & Mary R. Anderlik, *What Is Genetic Discrimination and When and How Can It Be Prevented?*, 3 Genetics in Medicine 354 (2001). Reprinted with permission from Lippincott, Williams & Wilkins.

Mark A. Rothstein, Betsy D. Gelb & Steven G. Craig, *Protecting Genetic Privacy by Permitting Employer Access Only to Job-Related Employee Medical Information: Analysis of a Unique Minnesota Law*, 24 American Journal of Law and Medicine 399 (1998). Copyright © 1998 American Society of Law, Medicine and Ethics. Reprinted with permission from the American Society of Law, Medicine and Ethics.

Susan Soble & C. Brookes Cowan, *Ambiguous Loss and Disenfranchised Grief: The Impact of DNA Testing on the Family as a System*, 42 Family Process 47 (2003). Copyright © 2003 Blackwell Publishing-Journals. Reprinted with permission.

Deborah Spar, *Reproductive Tourism and the Regulatory Map,* 352 NEW ENGLAND JOURNAL OF MEDICINE 351 (2005).

Alexandra Minna Stern, *Sterilized in the Name of Public Health,* 95 AMERICAN JOURNAL OF PUBLIC HEALTH 1128 (2005).

Kathy Swedlow, *Don't Believe Everything You Read: A Review of Modern "Post-Conviction" DNA Testing Statutes,* 38 CALIFORNIA WESTERN LAW REVIEW 355 (2002).

Hilary Vallance & Jason Ford, *Carrier Testing for Autosomal-Recessive Disorders,* 40 CRITICAL REVIEWS IN CLINICAL LABORATORY SCIENCES 473 (2003).

Note on Editing

The student's ability to easily read the material was a guiding principle when editing the text. Cases, statutes and other sources are edited to a reader-friendly format. Deleted material is generally denoted by the use of ellipses which serve to indicate an undetermined amount of omitted text. When footnotes and citations, including parallel citations, are omitted there is no indication.

Note on Extramural Funding

The authors' work on Chapters 3, 7 and 10 was supported in part through grants from the National Human Genome Research Institute (P50 HG003374 and HG02263). Ms. Hendrickson's work on Chapters 2 and 10 was supported by the National Cancer Institute through the Biobehavioral Cancer Prevention and Control Training Program (R25 CA92408).

Genetic Technologies and the Law

Chapter 1

Overview of Genetic Science

Genetic science and its advancing technologies present law and society with ever-increasing challenges. This book introduces the reader to the interface between genetics, medicine, and the law. This chapter provides a brief historical overview of the science of genetics and serves as the backdrop to the issues covered in the other chapters. Later chapters delve into some of the most controversial, and often unsettled questions, of genetics and the law including the following: Should genetic information be treated differently from other medical information and be subject to greater privacy protections under the law? What right, if any, might an employer or insurer have to an individual's genetic information? What protections should be in place with respect to research and development of genetic tests and therapies and how should the burdens and benefits of research be shared? What impact will genetics have on clinical medicine, on social and legal constructs of "family," and on public health practice? How is genetics revolutionizing criminal law and what changes is it bringing to the determination of civil liability? This book explores these questions and the role law and policy play and will play as genetic science brings opportunities and risks to medicine and society. But first, this chapter chronicles the evolution of genetics from Mendel's experiments on garden peas to the recent sequencing of human DNA and scientists' quest to more fully understand the role of genetics in human health, behavior and disease.

A. Mendel, Galton, and Genetics in the Nineteenth Century

Although interest in and theories about heredity date back to the ancient Greeks, the modern history of genetics is rooted in the nineteenth century. In the eighteenth century, the microscope first allowed scientists to look closely at cells and tissues. Anton van Leeuwenhoek (1632–1723) used the microscope he invented to visualize bacteria, cells and sperm. This led to increased interest in the science and mechanisms of heredity. Medical studies began to consider the pattern of heredity and the pedigrees of disease. Notably, a British scientist, Joseph Adams (1756–1818), postulated that hereditary disease was more common when the parents were closely related or were members of an isolated, inbred population group. He also was a proponent of what we now know as gene-environment interaction, in that he believed that environmental stresses might cause a genetic disease to become manifest, when, absent those stresses, the disease might remain latent and unexpressed.

By the mid-nineteenth century, interest in heredity and evolution was piqued by Charles Darwin's theory of evolution and natural selection. Shortly after Darwin's theory shook the scientific world, two scientists further stimulated interest in the science of heredity: Francis Galton (1822–1911), a British scientist and distant cousin of Darwin's, and Gregor Mendel (1822–1884), a monk working and living in what is now the Czech Republic.

Francis Galton studied inheritance statistically, looking at human physical traits, such as height and skin color. He essentially founded the "biometric" approach to genetics. Galton was a man of many accomplishments. In his early career, he was as an explorer and geographer studying Africa. He then became engaged in bioscience, psychology, and statistics and studied inherited traits in humans. His work in tracking traits led Galton to analyze pedigrees and determine that certain beneficial traits were more common in eminent persons who were leaders in politics, business and science. Through his pedigree studies, Galton became more closely linked to the controversial Darwinism. He also became the father and leading proponent of "eugenics," a term he coined.

Gregor Mendel explored the science of heredity through his garden. Over a period of several years, he studied, examined, and cataloged the physical traits of pea plants. By choosing seven separate traits and their variants, Mendel was able to posit a theory by which traits were passed from generation to generation. He discerned that certain pea characters had two variants and that inheritance of one character over the other could be explained using a theory of paired characters that would separate during reproduction and then recombine in the progeny to produce the final physical trait. This conclusion resulted in Mendel's law of segregation. Moreover, Mendel determined that each of the physical traits he was studying segregated independently of the others. This led to Mendel's law of independent assortment. He went on to develop the concept of dominant and recessive traits to account for the absence of a given trait in one generation and its reappearance in a later generation. Mendel's meticulous work was presented in 1865 and published in 1866. However, it would not be fully recognized until the dawn of the twentieth century.

B. Genetics in the Twentieth Century: DNA and the Discovery of the Double Helix

Mendel's work did not receive the recognition it deserved until his work was "rediscovered" in 1900. In 1902, Mendel's scientific contribution was republished and heralded by William Bateson (1861–1926), who prefaced the publication with the following:

> In the Study of Evolution, progress had well-nigh stopped. The more vigorous, perhaps also the more prudent, had left this field of science to labour in other where the harvest is less precarious or the yield more immediate. Of those who remained some still struggled to push towards truth through the jungle of phenomena: most were content supinely to rest on the great clearing Darwin made long since.
>
> Such was our state when two years ago it was suddenly discovered that an unknown man, Gregor Johann Mendel, had, alone and unheeded, broken off from the rest—in the moment that Darwin was at work—and cut a way through.
>
> This is no mere metaphor, it is simple fact. Each of us who now looks at his own patch of work sees Mendel's clue running through it: whither that clue will lead we dare not yet surmise.

William Bateson, Mendel's Principles of Heredity: A Defense (1st ed. 1902), *available at* http://www.esp.org/books/bateson/mendel/facsimile/. The rediscovery of Mendel's work occurred at a propitious time coinciding with other advances in science related to heredity. In the same decade, Karl Landsteiner (1868–1943) discovered ABO blood types, and in 1924, Felix Bernstein furthered understanding of blood typing by determining that three alleles coupled with Mendelian genetic patterns could explain blood types. Another scientist, Archibald Garrison (1857–1936), applied Mendel's theories to inborn errors of metabolism, demonstrating that alkaptonuria conformed to autosomal recessive inheritance. Meanwhile, research in cytogenetics had revealed the presence of chromosomes. These and other discoveries set the stage for the discovery of DNA, its structure and mechanism.

Genetics took another leap forward in the post-World War II era. In 1944, Alfred Day Hershey (1908–1997) and Martha Chase (1928–2003) determined that nuclear deoxyribonucleic acid (DNA) was the biochemical agent of heredity. However, how DNA worked biochemically and structurally remained unclear. It was not until 1953 that scientists James Watson (1928–) and Francis Crick (1916–2004), working at the Cavendish Laboratories at Cambridge University, suggested "a radically different structure for the salt of deoxyribose nucleic acid" comprised of two helical chains coiled around the same axis. Their work was founded on the work of several other scientists trying to characterize the biochemical basis for genetics, notably that of Rosalind Franklin (1920–1958) and Maurice Wilkins (1916–2004), two scientists at Kings College who had determined the helical structure of DNA using X-ray diffraction patterns. Watson's and Crick's seminal article described DNA as follows:

> The novel feature of the structure is the manner in which the two chains are held together by the purine and pyrimidine bases. The planes of the bases are perpendicular to the fibre axis. They are joined together in pairs, a single base from the other chain, so that the two lie side by side with identical z-co-ordinates. One of the pair must be a purine and the other pyrimidine for bonding to occur. The hydrogen bonds are made as follows: purine position 1 to pyrimidine position 1; purine position 6 to pyrimidine position 6.
>
> If it is assumed that the bases only occur in the structure in the most plausible tautomeric forms (that is, with the keto rather than the enol configurations) it is found that only specific pairs of bases can bond together. These pairs are: adenine (purine) with thymine (pyrimidine), and guanine (purine) with cytosine (pyrimidine).
>
> In other words, if an adenine forms one member of a pair, on either chain, then on these assumptions the other member must be thymine; similarly for guanine and cytosine. The sequence of bases on a single chain does not appear to be restricted in any way. However, if only specific pairs of bases can be formed, it follows that if the sequence of bases on one chain is given, then the sequence on the other chain is automatically determined.
>
> It has been found experimentally that the ratio of the amounts of adenine to thymine, and the ration of guanine to cytosine, are always very close to unity for deoxyribose nucleic acid.
>
> ...
>
> It has not escaped our notice that the specific pairing we have postulated immediately suggests a possible copying mechanism for the genetic material.

James D. Watson & Francis H. Crick, *A Structure for Deoxyribose Nucleic Acid*, 117 Nature 737 (1953). Because Watson and Crick determined that DNA was a double intertwined helix, they were able to posit a replication method. Watson and Crick would go on to further elucidate the nature and structure of DNA and win the Nobel Prize.

Building on their knowledge of DNA, Crick went on to posit the Central Dogma of Molecular Biology in 1958, a theory which was subject to much discussion and elaboration over the next several years but ultimately stood the test of time.

Francis H. Crick, *Central Dogma of Molecular Biology*

227 Nature 561 (1970)

...

The central dogma was put forward at a period when much of what we now know in molecular genetics was not established. All we had to work on were certain fragmentary experimental results, themselves often uncertain and confused, and a boundless optimism that the basic concepts involved were rather simple and probably much the same in all living things. In such a situation well constructed theories can play a really useful part in stating problems clearly and thus guiding experiment.

The two central concepts which had been produced, originally without any explicit statement of the simplification being introduced, were those of sequential information and of defined alphabets. Neither of these steps was trivial. Because it was abundantly clear by that time that a protein had a well defined three dimensional structure, and that its activity depended crucially on this structure, it was necessary to put the folding-up process on one side, and postulate that, by and large, the polypeptide chain folded itself up. This temporarily reduced the central problem from a three dimensional one to a one dimensional one. It was also necessary to argue that in spite of the miscellaneous list of amino-acids found in proteins, (as then given in all biochemical textbooks) some of them, such as phosphoserine, were secondary modifications; and that there was probably a universal set of twenty used throughout nature. In the same way minor modifications to the nucleic acid bases were ignored; uracil in RNA was considered informationally analogous to thymine in DNA, thus giving four standard symbols for the components of nucleic acid.

The principal problem could then be stated as the formulation of the general rules for information transfer from one polymer with a defined alphabet to another. This could be compactly represented by the diagram of Fig. 1 (which was actually drawn at that time, though I am not sure that it was ever published) in which all possible simple transfers were represented by arrows. The arrows do not, of course, represent the flow of matter but the directional flow of detailed, residue-by-residue, sequence information from one polymer molecule to another.

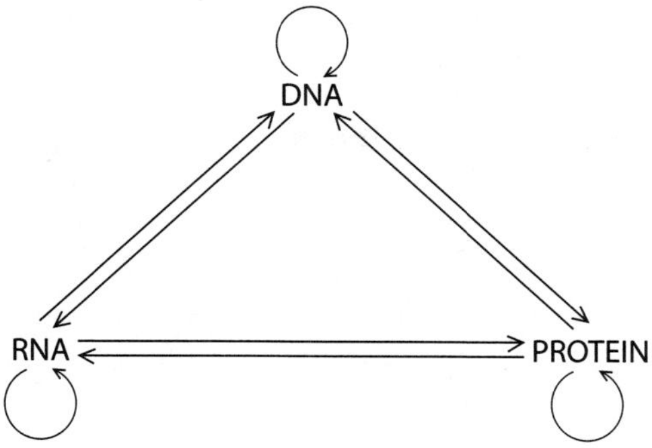

Fig. 1. The arrows show all the possible simple transfers between the three families of polymers. They represent the directional flow of detailed sequence information.

Now if all possible transfers commonly occurred it would have been almost impossible to construct useful theories. Nevertheless, such theories were part of our everyday discussions. This was because it was being tacitly assumed that certain transfers could not occur. It occurred to me that it would be wise to state these preconceptions explicitly.

A little analysis showed that the transfer could be divided roughly into three groups. The first group was those for which some evidence, direct or indirect, seemed to exist. These are shown by the solid arrows in Fig. 2.

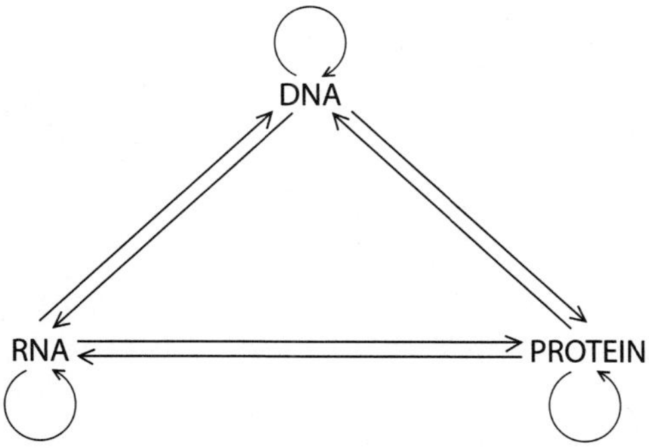

Fig. 2. The arrows show the situation as it seemed in 1958. Solid arrows represent probable transfers, dotted arrows possible transfers. The absent arrows (compare Fig. 1) represent the impossible transfers postulated by the central dogma. They are the three possible arrows starting from protein.

They were:

I (a) DNA —> DNA

I (b) DNA —> RNA

I (c) RNA —> Protein

I (d) RNA —> RNA

The last of these transfers was presumed to occur because of the existence of RNA viruses.

Next there were two transfers (shown in Fig. 2 as dotted arrows) for which there was neither any experimental evidence nor any strong theoretical requirement. They were[:]

II (a) RNA —> DNA (see the reference to Temin's work)

II (b) DNA —> Protein

The latter was the transfer postulated by Gamow, from (double stranded) DNA to protein, though by that time his particular theory had been disproved.

The third class consisted of the three transfers the arrows of which have been omitted from Fig.2. These were the transfers:

III (a) Protein —> Protein

III (b) Protein —> RNA

III (c) Protein —> DNA

The general opinion at the time was that class I almost certainly existed, class II was probably rare or absent, and that class III was very unlikely to occur. The decision had to be made, therefore, whether to assume that only class I transfers occurred.

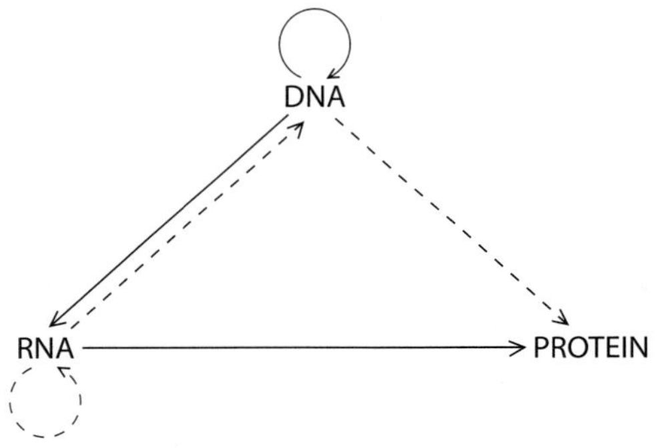

Fig. 3. A tentative classification for the present day. Solid arrows show general transfers; dotted arrows show special transfers. Again, the absent arrows are the undetected transfers specified by the central dogma.

There were, however, no overwhelming structural reasons why the transfer in class II should not be impossible. In fact, for all we knew, the replication of all RNA viruses could have gone by way a DNA intermediate. On the other hand, there were good general reasons against all the three possible transfers in class III. In brief, it was most unlikely, for stereochemical reasons, that protein —> protein transfer could be done in the simple way that DNA —> DNA transfer was envisaged. The transfer protein —> RNA (and the analogous protein —> DNA) would have required (back) translation, that is the transfer from one alphabet to a structurally quite different one. It was realized that forward translation involved very complex machinery. Moreover, it seemed unlikely on general grounds that this machinery could easily work backwards. The only reasonable alternative was that the cell had evolved an entirely separate set of complicated machinery for back translation, and of this there was no trace, and no reason to believe that it might be needed.

I decided, therefore, to play safe, and to state as the basic assumption of the new molecular biology the non-existence of transfers of class III. Because these were all the possible transfers from protein, the central dogma could be stated in the form "once (sequential) information has passed into protein it cannot get out again." About class II, I decided to remain discreetly silent.

At this stage I must make four points about the formulation of the central dogma which have occasionally produced misunderstandings. . . .

(1) It says nothing about what the machinery of transfer is made of, and in particular nothing about errors. (It was assumed that, in general, the accuracy of transfer was high.)

(2) It says nothing about control mechanisms—that is, about the rate at which the processes work.

(3) It was intended to apply only to present-day organisms, and not to events in the remote past, such as the origin of life or the origin of the code.

(4) It is not the same, as is commonly assumed, as the sequence hypothesis, which was clearly distinguished from it in the same article. In particular, the sequence hypothesis was a positive statement, saying that the (overall) transfer nucleic acid —> protein did exist, whereas the central dogma was a negative statement, saying that transfers from protein did not exist.

In looking back I am struck not only by the brashness which allowed us to venture powerful statements of a very general nature, but also by the rather delicate discrimination used in selecting what statements to make. Time has shown that not everybody appreciated our restraint.

So much for the history of the subject. What of the present? I think it is clear that the old classification, though useful at the time, could be improved, and I suggest that the nine possible transfers be regrouped tentatively into three classes. I propose that these be called general transfers, special transfers and unknown transfers.

General and Special Transfers

A general transfer is one which can occur in all cells. The obvious cases are[:]

DNA —> DNA

DNA —> RNA

RNA —> Protein

Minor exceptions, such as the mammalian reticulocyte, which probably lacks the first two of these, should not exclude.

A special transfer is one which does not occur in most cells, but may occur in special circumstances. Possible candidates are[:]

RNA —> RNA

RNA —> DNA

DNA —> Protein

At the present time, the first two of these have only been shown in certain virus-infected cells. . . .

Unknown Transfers

These are the three transfers which the central dogma postulates never occur:

Protein —> Protein

Protein —> DNA

Protein —> RNA

Stated in this way it is clear that the special transfers are those about which there is the most uncertainty. It might indeed have "profound implications for molecular biology" if any of these special transfers could be shown to be general, or—if not in all cells—at least to be widely distributed. So far, however, there is no evidence for the first two of these except in a cell infected with an RNA virus. In such a cell the central dogma demands that at least one of the first two special transfers should occur—this statement, incidentally, shows the power of the central dogma in making theoretical predictions. Nor, as I have indicated, is there any good theoretical reason why the transfer RNA —> DNA should not sometimes be used. I have never suggested that it cannot occur, nor, as far as I know, have any of my colleagues.

Although the details of the classification proposed here are plausible, our knowledge of molecular biology, even in one cell—let alone for all the organisms in nature—is still far too incomplete to allow us to assert dogmatically that it is correct.... Nevertheless, we know enough to say that a non-trivial [] example showing that the classification was wrong could be an important discovery. It would certainly be of great interest to find a cell (as opposed to a virus) which had RNA as its genetic material and no DNA, or a cell which used single-stranded DNA as messenger rather than RNA. Perhaps the so-called repetitive DNA is produced by an RNA —> DNA transfer. Any of these would be of the greatest interest, but they could be accommodated into our thinking without undue strain. On the other hand, the discovery of just one type of present day cell which could carry out any of the three unknown transfers would shake the whole intellectual basis of molecular biology, and it is for this reason that the central dogma is as important today as when it was first proposed.

* * *

The "Central Dogma" essentially held that DNA could replicate to form new DNA or, alternatively, transcribe messenger RNA, which in turn would code for proteins. During the later part of the twentieth century, scientists increasingly became involved in the study of DNA, RNA, and chromosomes, studying their role in human characteristics, physiology, and pathology. In 1964, scientists proved that the central dogma was not the only way by which DNA could be replicated. David Baltimore and Howard Temin discovered reverse transcriptase, an enzyme that allows RNA to be used in replicating DNA. Additional enzymes were discovered that had the ability to isolate and analyze fragments of DNA. In 1978, scientists discovered restriction-fragment-length polymorphisms (RFLP) that allowed characterization and matching of segments of DNA. This allowed scientists to map genes to certain chromosomes and find the genes responsible for certain disorders. In the late 1980s, both the gene and some of the key mutations responsible for cystic fibrosis, an autosomal recessive disorder, were identified. In 1983, the polymerase chain reaction (PCR) method was developed; this innovation allowed amplification of a small amount of DNA to be increased millions of times to create a sufficient quantity of DNA for study. PCR technology allowed scientists to contemplate the possibility of sequencing the entire human genome.

In 1990, the Human Genome Project was launched with the goal of sequencing the entire human genome. Over the next few years, the goals of the project became both more defined and ambitious. By 1998, the goals were as follows:

Goal 1: Provide a complete high-quality sequence of human genomic DNA to the research community as a publicly available resource.

Goal 2: Develop increasingly efficient, economic and effective methods of sequencing technologies.

Goal 3: Continue to develop understanding of human genome sequence variations and their relationship to disease. This requires study and understanding of single-nucleotide polymorphisms (SNPs) and their relationship to complex disorders (i.e. cancer, diabetes) on the genetic map.

Goal 4: Lay the foundation for technologies to explore functional genomics—the interpretation of the function of DNA on a genomic scale

Goal 5: Further Comparative Genomics by studying the relationship between the human genomes and those of other organisms and mammals.

Goal 6: Examine the ethical, legal and social implications of advances in genetics and genomics

See Francis S. Collins et al., *New Goals for the U.S. Human Genome Project: 1998–2003*, 282 Science 682 (1998). Moreover, the Project had grown to become an international collaboration of twenty scientists and several governments.

C. Genetics in the New Millennium

In 2001, two years ahead of schedule, a draft of the human genome sequence was announced by the National Human Genome Research Institute and their many collaborators. Since completion of the genome sequencing, scientists have begun to research gene function. The HapMap Project seeks to enhance the ability to identify genetic variations responsible for common, but complex, medical disorders. There is also increasing research on the end result of the genetic coding, the proteins prescribed by mRNA; this new area of study, proteomics is essentially functional genomics.

Press Release, National Human Genome Research Institute International Human Genome Sequencing Consortium Publishes Sequence and Analysis of the Human Genome

(Feb. 12, 2001), http://www.genome.gov/10002192

The Human Genome Project international consortium today announced the publication of a draft sequence and initial analysis of the human genome—the genetic blueprint for a human being....

The draft sequence, which covers more than 90 percent of the human genome, represents the exact order of DNA's four chemical bases—commonly abbreviated as A, T, C and G—along the human chromosomes. This DNA text influences everything from eye color and height, to aging and disease.

The consortium's initial analysis of this text represents scientists' first global view of the human genomic landscape, with its extraordinary trove of information about human development, physiology, medicine and evolution.

The results reported in this week's *Nature* represent major progress for the human genome consortium. On June 26, the consortium announced that it had collected roughly 90 percent of the letters of the text for the "Book of Life." The consortium's new achievement represents a further compilation of these letters into the first draft of a readable text.

There are small gaps still remaining in this text, but scientists are already getting a good sense of what the genome landscape looks like and the surprising stories it has to tell. Below are highlights:

- The distribution of genes on mammalian chromosomes is striking. It turns out that our chromosomes have crowded urban centers with many genes in close proximity to one another and also vast expanses of unpopulated desert where only non-coding "junk" DNA can be found. This distribution of genes is in marked contrast to the genomes of many other organisms, such as the mustard weed, the worm and the fly. Their genomes, more closely resemble uniform, sprawling suburbs, with genes relatively evenly spaced throughout.
- Though a definitive count of human genes must await further experimental and computational analysis, scientists now estimate that humans have some 30,000 to 35,000 genes in their genomes. This new estimate indicates that humans have only about twice as many genes as the worm or the fly. How can human complexity be explained by a genome with such a paucity of genes? It turns out that humans are very thrifty with their genes, able to do more with what they have than other species. Instead of producing only one protein per gene, the average human gene produces three different proteins.
- The full set of proteins (the proteome) encoded by the human genome is more complex than those of invertebrates because humans and other vertebrates have rearranged old protein domains into a rich collection of new architectures. In other words, humans have for the most part achieved innovations by rearranging and expanding tried-and-true strategies from other species, rather than by developing novel strategies of their own.
- Scientists have identified more than 200 genes in the human genome whose closest relatives are in bacteria. Analogous genes are not found in invertebrates, such as the worm, fly and yeast. This suggests that these genes were acquired at a more recent evolutionary past, perhaps after the emergence of vertebrates. Scientists didn't find any single bacterial source for the transferred genes, indicating that several independent gene transfers from different bacteria occurred.
- Our junk DNA, characterized by long stretches of repeating sequences, represents a rich fossil record of clues to our evolutionary past. It is possible to date groups of so-called "repeats" to when in the evolutionary process they were "born" and to follow their fates in different regions of the genome and in different species. The HGP scientists used 3 million such repeating elements as dating tools. Based on such "DNA dating," scientists can build family trees of the repeats, showing exactly where they came from and when. These repeats have reshaped the genome by rearranging it, creating entirely new genes, and modifying and reshuffling existing genes.
- We have a greater percentage of junk DNA in our genomes—50 percent—than the mustard weed (11 percent), the worm (7 percent) or the fly (3 percent). Also, shockingly, there seems to have been a dramatic decrease in the activity of repeats in the human genome over the past 50 million years—as if the human species decided 50 million years ago to stop collecting junk. In contrast, there seems to be no such decline in repeats in rodents.
- Ordinarily, repeat elements land in inhospitable regions of the genome—regions that are A,T rich and G,C poor. But mysteriously, one type of repeat called "SINE elements" has found a way to take up residence in the GC-rich neighbor-

hoods of the genome. Over the years, SINE elements have acquired a bad reputation among scientists for what looked like parasitic behavior. But this bad reputation is unjustified. We now see that SINE elements may by helpful symbionts that earn their keep in the genome.

- By dating the 3 million repeat elements and examining the pattern of interspersed repeats on the Y chromosome, scientists estimated the relative mutation rates in the X and the Y chromosome and in the male and female germ lines. They found that the ratio of mutations in males versus females is 2:1. Scientists point to several possible reasons for the higher mutation rate in the male germ line, including the fact that there are a greater number of cell divisions involved in the formation of sperm than in the formation of eggs.
- In a companion volume to the Book of Life, scientists have created a catalogue of 1.4 million single-letter differences, or single nucleotide polymorphisms (SNPs)—and specified their exact location in the human genome. This SNP map, the word's largest publicly available catalogue of SNPs, promises to revolutionize both mapping diseases and tracing human history.

The sequence information from the consortium has been immediately and freely released to the world, with no restrictions on its use or redistribution. The information is scanned daily by scientists in academia and industry, as well as by commercial database companies, providing key information services to biotechnologists. Already, many tens of thousands of genes have been identified from the genome sequence, including more than 30 that play a direct role in human disease.

The scientific work reported here will serve as a basis for research and discovery in the coming decades. Such research will have profound long-term consequences for medicine. It will help elucidate the underlying molecular mechanisms of disease. This in turn will allow researchers to design better drugs and therapies for many illnesses.

But, as the authors of the *Nature* paper write, "the science is only part of the challenge. We must also involve society at large in the work ahead. We must set realistic expectations that the most important benefits will not be reaped overnight. Moreover, understanding and wisdom will be required to ensure that they are implemented broadly and equitably."

"We are standing at an extraordinary moment in scientific history. It's as though we have climbed to the top of the Himalayas. We can for the first time see the breathtaking vista of the human genome," said Eric Lander, director of the Whitehead Institute Center for Genome Research." For many years to come, we will be exploring the intricate details of the terrain ahead. We've got a long way to go before we will ultimately understand all the secrets that the genome has to tell us."

"This remarkable achievement is a clear testament to the hard work of the hundreds of scientists in the sixteen genome centers that make up the Human Genome Project consortium," said Francis Collins, director of the National Human Genome Research Institute. "These scientists have proved to the world that they can work together toward a common human good. For, with the human genome sequence in hand, we can begin to build the tools we need to conquer the host of illnesses that cause untold human suffering and premature death."

What's Next?

The consortium's ultimate goal is to produce a completely "finished" sequence with no gaps and 99.99 percent accuracy. Although the near-finished version is adequate for most biomedical research, the HGP has made a commitment to filling all gaps and resolving all ambiguities in the sequence by 2003.

Production of genome sequence has skyrocketed over the past year, with more than 90 percent of the sequence having been produced in the past 15 months alone. Because of this increased capacity, the next phase is expected to move much more rapidly than previously expected.

The HGP also plans to sequence the genomes of many other species, because comparing genomes across species will provide researchers key tools for understanding the essential elements that evolution has designated as important to survival. This information will in turn translate into practical knowledge toward developing better therapies in the future.

As the authors of the *Nature* paper point out, the draft genome sequence has provided an initial look at the human gene content, but many ambiguities remain. One of the HGP's priorities will be to refine the data to accurately reflect every gene and every alternatively spliced form.

Several steps are needed to reach this ambitious goal, they report. Finishing the human sequence will help, but in addition, scientists will need cross-species comparisons to achieve this goal. A newly formed public-private consortium is speeding this effort, producing freely accessible data that can be readily used for cross-species comparison.

Comparative genomics will also offer scientists insights into important regions in the sequence that perform regulatory functions. Also among the future plans for HGP scientists is the sequencing of other large genomes, such as primates. Scientists also plan to complete the catalogue of human variations in the population and identify the genes that predispose individuals to risk for common diseases.

Finally, the sequence will serve as a foundation for a broad range of functional genomic tools to help biologists to probe the function of the genes in a more systematic manner. Development of such post-genomic tools will be one of the major thrusts for biologists in the next decade, according to the scientists.

...

* * *

By 2003, full sequencing of the human genome was completed and scientists at the National Human Genome Research Institute and around the globe began to ponder the future of genetic research.

Francis S. Collins, Eric D. Green, Alan E. Guttmacher & Mark S. Guyer, *A Vision for the Future of Genomics Research: A Blueprint for the Genomic Era*

422 Nature 835 (2003)

The completion of a high-quality, comprehensive sequence of the human genome, in this fiftieth anniversary year of the discovery of the double-helical structure of DNA, is a landmark event. The genomic era is now a reality.

In contemplating a vision for the future of genomics research, it is appropriate to consider the remarkable path that has brought us here. [A] timeline of landmark accomplishments in genetics and genomics, beginning with Gregor Mendel's discovery of the laws of heredity and their rediscovery in the early days of the twentieth century.

Recognition of DNA as the hereditary material, determination of its structure, elucidation of the genetic code, development of recombinant DNA technologies, and establishment of increasingly automatable methods for DNA sequencing set the stage for the Human Genome Project (HGP) to begin in 1990. Thanks to the vision of the original planners, and the creativity and determination of a legion of talented scientists who decided to make this project their overarching focus, all of the initial objectives of the HGP have now been achieved at least two years ahead of expectation, and a revolution in biological research has begun.

The project's new research strategies and experimental technologies have generated a steady stream of ever-larger and more complex genomic data sets that have poured into public databases and have transformed the study of virtually all life processes. The genomic approach of technology development and large-scale generation of community resource data sets has introduced an important new dimension into biological and biomedical research. Interwoven advances in genetics, comparative genomics, high-throughput biochemistry and bioinformatics are providing biologists with a markedly improved repertoire of research tools that will allow the functioning of organisms in health and disease to be analysed and comprehended at an unprecedented level of molecular detail. Genome sequences, the bounded sets of information that guide biological development and function, lie at the heart of this revolution. In short, genomics has become a central and cohesive discipline of biomedical research.

The practical consequences of the emergence of this new field are widely apparent. Identification of the genes responsible for human mendelian diseases, once a herculean task requiring large research teams, many years of hard work, and an uncertain outcome, can now be routinely accomplished in a few weeks by a single graduate student with access to DNA samples and associated phenotypes, an Internet connection to the public genome databases, a thermal cycler and a DNA-sequencing machine. With the recent publication of a draft sequence of the mouse genome, identification of the mutations underlying a vast number of interesting mouse phenotypes has similarly been greatly simplified. Comparison of the human and mouse sequences shows that the proportion of the mammalian genome under evolutionary selection is more than twice that previously assumed.

Our ability to explore genome function is increasing in specificity as each subsequent genome is sequenced. Microarray technologies have catapulted many laboratories from studying the expression of one or two genes in a month to studying the expression of tens of thousands of genes in a single afternoon. Clinical opportunities for gene-based pre-symptomatic prediction of illness and adverse drug response are emerging at a rapid pace, and the therapeutic promise of genomics has ushered in an exciting phase of expansion and exploration in the commercial sector. The investment of the HGP in studying the ethical, legal and social implications of these scientific advances has created a talented cohort of scholars in ethics, law, social science, clinical research, theology and public policy, and has already resulted in substantial increases in public awareness and the introduction of significant (but still incomplete) protections against misuses such as genetic discrimination.

These accomplishments fulfill the expansive vision articulated in the 1988 report of the National Research Council, *Mapping and Sequencing the Human Genome*. The successful completion of the HGP this year thus represents an opportunity to look forward and offer a blueprint for the future of genomics research over the next several years.

The vision presented here addresses a different world from that reflected in earlier plans published in 1990, 1993 and 1998. Those documents addressed the goals of the

1988 report, defining detailed paths towards the development of genome-analysis technologies, the physical and genetic mapping of genomes, and the sequencing of model organism genomes and, ultimately, the human genome. Now, with the effective completion of these goals, we offer a broader and still more ambitious vision, appropriate for the true dawning of the genomic era. The challenge is to capitalize on the immense potential of the HGP to improve human health and well-being.

The articulation of a new vision is an opportunity to explore transformative new approaches to achieve health benefits. Although genome-based analysis methods are rapidly permeating biomedical research, the challenge of establishing robust paths from genomic information to improved human health remains immense. Current efforts to meet this challenge are largely organized around the study of specific diseases, as exemplified by the missions of the disease-oriented institutes at the U.S. National Institutes of Health (NIH) and numerous national and international governmental and charitable organizations that support medical research. The National Human Genome Research Institute (NHGRI), in budget terms a rather small (less than 2 percent) component of the NIH, will work closely with all these organizations in exploring and supporting these biomedical research capabilities. In addition, we envision a more direct role for both the extramural and intramural programmes of the NHGRI in bringing a genomic approach to the translation of genomic sequence information into health benefits.

...

The vision for genomics research detailed here is the outcome of almost two years of intense discussions with hundreds of scientists and members of the public, in more than a dozen workshops and numerous individual consultations. The vision is formulated into three major themes—genomics to biology, genomics to health, and genomics to society—and six crosscutting elements.

We envisage the themes as three floors of a building, firmly resting on the foundation of the HGP. For each theme, we present a series of grand challenges, in the spirit of the proposals put forward for mathematics by David Hilbert at the turn of the twentieth century. These grand challenges are intended to be bold, ambitious research targets for the scientific community. Some can be planned on specific timescales, others are less amenable to that level of precision. We list the grand challenges in an order that makes logical sense, not representing priority. The challenges are broad in sweep, not parochial—some can be led by the NHGRI alone, whereas others will be best pursued in partnership with other organizations. Below, we clarify areas in which the NHGRI intends to play a leading role.

The six critically important crosscutting elements are relevant to all three thematic areas. They are: resources; technology development; computational biology; training; ethical, legal and social implications (ELSI); and education. We also stress the critical importance of early, unfettered access to genomic data in achieving maximum public benefit. Finally, we propose a series of 'quantum leaps', achievements that would lead to substantial advances in genomics research and its applications to medicine. Some of these may seem overly bold, but no laws of physics need to be violated to achieve them. Such leaps would have profound implications, just as the dreams of the mid-1980s about the complete sequence of the human genome have been realized in the accomplishments now being celebrated.

I. Genomics to Biology[:] Elucidating the structure and function of genomes

The broadly available genome sequences of human and a select set of additional organisms represent foundational information for biology and biomedicine. Embedded within this as-yet poorly understood code are the genetic instructions for the entire repertoire of cellular components, knowledge of which is needed to unravel the complexities of biological systems. Elucidating the structure of genomes and identifying the function of the myriad encoded elements will allow connections to be made between genomics and biology and will, in turn, accelerate the exploration of all realms of the biological sciences.

For this, new conceptual and technological approaches will be needed to:

- Develop a comprehensive and comprehensible catalogue of all of the components encoded in the human genome.
- Determine how the genome-encoded components function in an integrated manner to perform cellular and organismal functions.
- Understand how genomes change and take on new functional roles.

Grand Challenge I-1 Comprehensively identify the structural and functional components encoded in the human genome.

Although DNA is relatively simple and well understood chemically, the human genome's structure is extraordinarily complex and its function is poorly understood. Only 1–2 percent of its bases encode proteins, and the full complement of protein-coding sequences still remains to be established. A roughly equivalent amount of the non-coding portion of the genome is under active selection, suggesting that it is also functionally important, yet vanishingly little is known about it. It probably contains the bulk of the regulatory information controlling the expression of the approximately 30,000 protein-coding genes, and myriad other functional elements, such as non-protein-coding genes and the sequence determinants of chromosome dynamics. Even less is known about the function of the roughly half of the genome that consists of highly repetitive sequences or of the remaining non-coding, non-repetitive DNA.

The next phase of genomics is to catalogue, characterize and comprehend the entire set of functional elements encoded in the human and other genomes. Compiling this genome 'parts list' will be an immense challenge. Well-known classes of functional elements, such as protein-coding sequences, still cannot be accurately predicted from sequence information alone. Other types of known functional sequences, such as genetic regulatory elements, are even less well understood; undoubtedly new types remain to be defined, so we must be ready to investigate novel, perhaps unexpected, ways in which DNA sequence can confer function. Similarly, a better understanding of epigenetic changes (for example, methylation and chromatin remodelling) is needed to comprehend the full repertoire of ways in which DNA can encode information.

Comparison of genome sequences from evolutionarily diverse species has emerged as a powerful tool for identifying functionally important genomic elements. Initial analyses of available vertebrate genome sequences have revealed many previously undiscovered protein-coding sequences. Mammal-to-mammal sequence comparisons have revealed large numbers of homologies in non-coding regions, few of which can be defined in functional terms. Further comparisons of sequences derived from multiple species, especially those occupying distinct evolutionary positions, will lead to significant refinements in our understanding of the functional importance of conserved sequences. Thus, the generation of additional genome sequences from several well-chosen species is crucial to the functional characterization of the human genome. The generation of such large sequence data sets will benefit from further advances in sequencing technology that yield significant cost reductions. The study of sequence variation within species will also be important in defining the functional nature of some sequences (see Grand Challenge I-3).

Effective identification and analysis of functional genomic elements will require increasingly powerful computational capabilities, including new approaches for tackling ever-growing and increasingly complex data sets and a suitably robust computational infrastructure for housing, accessing and analysing those data sets. In parallel, investigators will need to become increasingly adept in dealing with this treasure trove of new information. As a better understanding of genome function is gained, refined computational tools for de novo prediction of the identity and behaviour of functional elements should emerge.

Complementing the computational detection of functional elements will be the generation of additional experimental data by high-throughput methodologies. One example is the production of full-length complementary DNA (cDNA) sequences, for example at the Mammalian Gene Collection and Expressed Sequence Tag Projects. Major challenges inherent in programmes to discover genes are the experimental identification and validation of alternate splice forms and messenger RNAs expressed in a highly restricted fashion. Even more challenging is the experimental validation of functional elements that do not encode protein (for example, regulatory regions and non-coding RNA sequences). High-throughput approaches to identify them will be needed to generate the experimental data that will be necessary to develop, confirm and enhance computational methods for detecting functional elements in genomes.

Because current technologies cannot yet identify all functional elements, there is a need for a phased approach in which new methodologies are developed, tested on a pilot scale and finally applied to the entire human genome. Along these lines, the NHGRI recently launched the Encyclopedia of DNA Elements (ENCODE) Project to identify all the functional elements in the human genome. In a pilot project, systematic strategies for identifying all functionally important genomic elements will be developed and tested using a selected 1% of the human genome. Parallel projects involving well-studied model organisms, for example, yeast, nematode and fruitfly, are ongoing. The lessons learned will serve as the basis for implementing a broader programme for the entire human genome.

Grand Challenge I-2 Elucidate the organization of genetic networks and protein pathways and establish how they contribute to cellular and organismal phenotypes.

Genes and gene products do not function independently, but participate in complex, interconnected pathways, networks and molecular systems that, taken together, give rise to the workings of cells, tissues, organs and organisms. Defining these systems and determining their properties and interactions is crucial to understanding how biological systems function. Yet these systems are far more complex than any problem that molecular biology, genetics or genomics has yet approached. On the basis of previous experience, one effective path will begin with the study of relatively simple model organisms, such as bacteria and yeast, and then extend the early findings to more complex organisms, such as mouse and human. Alternatively, focusing on a few well-characterized systems in mammals will be a useful test of the approach.

Understanding biological pathways, networks and molecular systems will require information from several levels. At the genetic level, the architecture of regulatory interactions will need to be identified in different cell types, requiring, among other things, methods for simultaneously monitoring the expression of all genes in a cell. At the gene-product level, similar techniques that allow in vivo, real-time measurement of protein expression, localization, modification and activity/kinetics will be needed. It will be important to develop, refine and scale up techniques that modulate gene expression, such as conventional gene-knockout methods, newer knock-down approaches and small-molecule inhibitors to establish the temporal and cellular expression pattern of individual proteins and to determine the functions of those proteins. This is a key first step towards assigning all genes and their products to functional pathways.

The ability to monitor all proteins in a cell simultaneously would profoundly improve our ability to understand protein pathways and systems biology. A critical step towards gaining a complete understanding of systems biology will be to take an accurate census of the proteins present in particular cell types under different physiological conditions. This is becoming possible in some model systems, such as microorganisms. It will be a major challenge to catalogue proteins present in low abundance or in membranes. Determining the absolute abundance of each protein, including all modified forms, will be an important next step. A complete interaction map of the proteins in a cell, and their cellular locations, will serve as an atlas for the biological and medical explorations of cellular metabolism. These and other related areas constitute the developing field of proteomics.

Establishing a true understanding of how organized molecular pathways and networks give rise to normal and pathological cellular and organismal phenotypes will require more than large, experimentally derived data sets. Once again, computational investigation will be essential, and there will be a greatly increased need for the collection, storage and display of the data in robust databases. By modelling specific pathways and networks, predicting how they affect phenotype, testing hypotheses derived from these models and refining the models based on new experimental data, it should be possible to understand more completely the difference between a 'bag of molecules' and a functioning biological system.

Grand Challenge I-3 Develop a detailed understanding of the heritable variation in the human genome.

Genetics seeks to correlate variation in DNA sequence with phenotypic differences (traits). The greatest advances in human genetics have been made for traits associated with variation in a single gene. But most phenotypes, including common diseases and variable responses to pharmacological agents, have a more complex origin, involving the interplay between multiple genetic factors (genes and their products) and non-genetic factors (environmental influences). Unravelling such complexity will require both a complete description of the genetic variation in the human genome and the development of analytical tools for using that information to understand the genetic basis of disease.

Establishing a catalogue of all common variants in the human population, including single-nucleotide polymorphisms (SNPs), small deletions and insertions, and other structural differences, began in earnest several years ago. Many SNPs have been identified, and most are publicly available. A public collaboration, The International HapMap Project, was formed in 2002 to characterize the patterns of linkage disequilibrium and haplotypes across the human genome and to identify subsets of SNPs that capture most of the information about these patterns of genetic variation to enable large-scale genetic association studies. To reach fruition, such studies need more robust experimental and computational methods that use this new knowledge of human haplotype structure.

A comprehensive understanding of genetic variation, both in humans and in model organisms, would facilitate studies to establish relationships between genotype and biological function. The study of particular variants and how they affect the functioning of specific proteins and protein pathways will yield important new insights about physiological processes in normal and disease states. An enhanced ability to incorporate information about genetic variation into human genetic studies would usher in a new era for investigating the genetic bases of human disease and drug response (see Grand Challenge II-1).

Grand Challenge I-4 Understand evolutionary variation across species and the mechanisms underlying it

The genome is a dynamic structure, continually subjected to modification by the forces of evolution. The genomic variation seen in humans represents only a small glimpse through the larger window of evolution, where hundreds of millions of years of trial-and-error efforts have created today's biosphere of animal, plant and microbial species. A complete elucidation of genome function requires a parallel understanding of the sequence differences across species and the fundamental processes that have sculpted their genomes into the modern-day forms.

The study of inter-species sequence comparisons is important for identifying functional elements in the genome (see Grand Challenge I-1). Beyond this illuminating role, determining the sequence differences between species will provide insight into the distinct anatomical, physiological and developmental features of different organisms, will help to define the genetic basis for speciation and will facilitate the characterization of mutational processes. This last point deserves particular attention, because mutation both drives long-term evolutionary change and is the underlying cause of inherited disease. The recent finding that mutation rates vary widely across the mammalian genome raises numerous questions about the molecular basis for these evolutionary changes. At present, our understanding of DNA mutation and repair, including the important role of environmental factors, is limited.

Genomics will provide the ability to substantively advance insight into evolutionary variation, which will, in turn, yield new insights into the dynamic nature of genomes in a broader evolutionary framework.

Grand Challenge I-5 Develop policy options that facilitate the widespread use of genome information in both research and clinical settings

Realization of the opportunities provided by genomics depends on effective access to the information (such as data about genes, gene variants, haplotypes, protein structures, small molecules and computational models) by a wide range of potential users, including researchers, commercial enterprises, health-care providers, patients and the public. Researchers themselves need maximum access to the data as soon as possible. Use of the information for the development of therapeutic and other products necessarily entails consideration of the complex issues of intellectual property (for example, patenting and licensing) and commercialization. The intellectual property practices, laws and regulations that affect genomics must adhere to the principle of maximizing public benefit, but must also be consistent with more general and longer-established intellectual property principles. Further, because genome research is global, international treaties, laws, regulations, practices, belief systems and cultures also come into play.

Without commercialization, most diagnostic and therapeutic advances will not reach the clinical setting, where they can benefit patients. Thus, we need to develop policy options for data access and for patenting, licensing and other intellectual property issues to facilitate the dissemination of genomics data.

II. Genomics to Health[:] Translating genome-based knowledge into health benefits

The sequencing of the human genome, along with other recent and expected achievements in genomics, provides an unparalleled opportunity to advance our understanding of the role of genetic factors in human health and disease, to allow more precise definition of the non-genetic factors involved, and to apply this insight rapidly to the prevention, diagnosis and treatment of disease. The report by the US National Research Council that originally envisioned the HGP was explicit in its expectation that the human genome sequence would lead to improvements in human health, and subsequent five-year plans reaffirmed this view. But how this will happen has been less clearly articulated. With the completion of the original goals of the HGP, the time is right to develop and apply large-scale genomic strategies to empower improvements in human health, while anticipating and avoiding potential harm.

Such strategies should enable the research community to achieve the following:

- Identify genes and pathways with a role in health and disease, and determine how they interact with environmental factors.
- Develop, evaluate and apply genome-based diagnostic methods for the prediction of susceptibility to disease, the prediction of drug response, the early detection of illness and the accurate molecular classification of disease.
- Develop and deploy methods that catalyse the translation of genomic information into therapeutic advances.

Grand Challenge II-1 Develop robust strategies for identifying the genetic contributions to disease and drug response

For common diseases, the interplay of multiple genes and multiple non-genetic factors, not a single allele, usually dictates disease susceptibility and response to treatments. Deciphering the role of genes in human health and disease is a formidable problem for many reasons, including impediments to defining biologically valid phenotypes, challenges in identifying and quantifying environmental exposures, technological obstacles to generating sufficient and useful genotypic information, and the difficulties of studying humans. Yet this problem can be solved. Vigorous development of crosscutting genomic tools to catalyse advances in understanding the genetics of common disease and in pharmacogenomics is needed. Prominent among these will be a detailed haplotype map of the human genome (see Grand Challenge I-3) that can be used for whole-genome association studies of all diseases in all populations, as well as further advances in sequencing and genotyping technology to make such studies feasible.

More efficient strategies for detecting rare alleles involved in common disease are also needed, as the hypothesis that alleles that increase risk for common diseases are themselves common will probably not be universally true. Computational and experimental methods to detect gene-gene and gene-environment interactions, as well as methods allowing interfacing of a variety of relevant databases, are also required. By obtaining unbiased assessments of the relative disease risk that particular gene variants contribute, a large longitudinal population-based cohort study, with collection of extensive clinical information and ongoing follow-up, would be profoundly valuable to the study of all common diseases. Already, such projects as the UK Biobank, the Marshfield Clinic's Personalized Medicine Research Project and the Estonian Genome Project seek to provide such resources. But if the multiple population groups in the United States and elsewhere in the world are to benefit fully and fairly from such research (see Grand Challenge II-6), a large population-based cohort study that includes full representation of minority populations is also needed.

Grand Challenge II-2 Develop strategies to identify gene variants that contribute to good health and resistance to disease.

Most human genetic research has traditionally focused on identifying genes that predispose to illness. A relatively unexplored, but important, area of research focuses on the role of genetic factors in maintaining good health. Genomics will facilitate further understanding of this aspect of human biology and allow the identification of gene variants that are important for the maintenance of health, particularly in the presence of known environmental risk factors. One useful research resource would be a 'healthy cohort', a large epidemiologically robust group of individuals with unusually good health, who could be compared with cohorts of individuals with diseases and who could also be intensively studied to reveal alleles protective for conditions such as diabetes, cancer, heart disease and Alzheimer's disease. Another promising approach would be rigorous examination of genetic variants in individuals at high risk for specific diseases who do not develop them, such as sedentary, obese smokers without heart disease or individuals with HNPCC mutations who do not develop colon cancer.

Grand Challenge II-3 Develop genome-based approaches to prediction of disease susceptibility and drug response, early detection of illness, and molecular taxonomy of disease states.

The discovery of variants that affect risk for disease could potentially be used in individualized preventive medicine—including diet, exercise, lifestyle and pharmaceutical intervention—to maximize the likelihood of staying well. For example, the discovery of variants that correlate with successful outcomes of drug therapy, or with unfortunate side effects, could potentially be rapidly translated into clinical practice. Turning this vision into reality will require the following: (1) unbiased determination of the risk associated with a particular gene variant, often overestimated in initial studies; (2) technological advances to reduce the cost of genotyping; (3) research on whether this kind of personalized genomic information will actually alter health behaviours (see Grand Challenge II-5); (4) oversight of the implementation of genetic tests to ensure that only those with demonstrated clinical validity are applied outside of the research setting; and (5) education of healthcare professionals and the public to be well-informed participants in this new form of preventive medicine.

The time is right for a focused effort to understand, and potentially to reclassify, all human illnesses on the basis of detailed molecular characterization. Systematic analyses of somatic mutations, epigenetic modifications, gene expression, protein expression and protein modification should allow the definition of a new molecular taxonomy of illness, which would replace our present, largely empirical, classification schemes and advance both disease prevention and treatment. The reclassification of neuromuscular diseases and certain types of cancer provides striking initial examples, but many more such applications are possible.

Such a molecular taxonomy would be the basis for the development of better methods for the early detection of disease, which often allows more effective and less costly treatments. Genomics and other large-scale approaches to biology offer the potential for developing new tools to detect many diseases earlier than is currently feasible. Such 'sentinel' methods might include analysis of gene expression in circulating leukocytes, proteomic analysis of body fluids, and advanced molecular analysis of tissue biopsies. An example would be the analysis of gene expression in peripheral blood leukocytes to predict drug response. A focused effort to use a genomic approach to characterize serum proteins exhaustively in health and disease might also be highly rewarding.

Grand Challenge II-4 Use new understanding of genes and pathways to develop powerful new therapeutic approaches to disease.

Pharmaceuticals on the market target fewer than 500 human gene products. Even though not all of the 30,000 or so human protein-coding genes will have products targetable for drug development, this suggests that there is an enormous untapped pool of human gene-based targets for therapeutic intervention. In addition, the new understanding of biological pathways provided by genomics (see Grand Challenge I-2) should contribute even more fundamentally to therapeutic design.

The information needed to determine the therapeutic potential of a gene generally overlaps heavily with the information that reveals its function. The success of imatinib mesylate (Gleevec), an inhibitor of the BCR-ABL tyrosine kinase, in treating chronic myelogenous leukaemia relied on a detailed molecular understanding of the disease's genetic cause. This example offers promise that therapies based on genomic information will be particularly effective. Grand Challenge I-1 describes the 'functionation' of the genome, which will increasingly be the critical first step in the development of new therapeutics. But stimulating basic scientists to approach biomedical problems with a genomic attitude is not enough. A therapeutic mindset, lacking in much of academic biomedical research and training, must be explicitly encouraged, and tools developed and provided for its implementation.

A particularly promising example of the gene-based approach to therapeutics is the application of 'chemical genomics'. This strategy uses libraries of small molecules (natural compounds, aptamers or the products of combinatorial chemistry) and high-throughput screening to advance understanding of biological pathways and to identify compounds that act as positive or negative regulators of individual gene products, pathways or cellular phenotypes. Although the pharmaceutical industry applies this approach widely as the first step in drug development, few academic investigators have access to this methodology or are familiar with its use.

Providing such access more broadly, through one or more centralized facilities, could lead to the discovery of a host of useful probes for biological pathways that would serve as new reagents for basic research and/or starting points for the development of new therapeutic agents (the 'hits' from such library screens will generally require medicinal chemistry modifications to yield therapeutically usable compounds).

Also needed are new, more powerful technologies for generating deep molecular libraries, especially ones tagged to allow the ready determination of precise molecular targets. A centralized database of screening results should lead to further important biological insights. Generating molecular probes for exploring the basic biology of health and disease in academic laboratories would not supplant the major role of biopharmaceutical companies in drug development, but could contribute to the start of the drug development pipeline. The private sector would doubtless find many of these molecular probes of interest for further exploration through optimization by medicinal chemistry, target validation, lead compound identification, toxicological studies and, ultimately, clinical trials.

Academic pursuit of this first step in drug development could be particularly valuable for the many rare mendelian diseases, in which often the gene defect is known but the small market size limits the private sector's motivation to shoulder the expense of effective pharmaceutical development. Such translational research in academic laboratories, combined with incentives such as the US Orphan Drug Act, could profoundly increase the availability of effective treatments for rare genetic diseases in the next decade. Further, the development of therapeutic approaches to single-gene disorders might provide valuable insights into applying genomics to reveal the biology of more common disorders and developing more effective treatments for them (in the way that, for example, the search for compounds that target the presenilins has led to general therapeutic strategies for late-onset Alzheimer's disease).

Grand Challenge II-5 Investigate how genetic risk information is conveyed in clinical settings, how that information influences health strategies and behaviours, and how these affect health outcomes and costs.

Understanding how genetic factors affect health is often cited as a major goal of genomics, on the assumption that applying such understanding in the clinical setting will improve health. But this assumption actually rests on relatively few examples and data, and more research is needed to provide sufficient guidance about how to use genomic information optimally for improving individual or public health.

Theoretically, the steps by which genetic risk information would lead to improved health are: (1) an individual obtains genome-based information about his/her own health risks; (2) the individual uses this information to develop an individualized prevention or treatment plan; (3) the individual implements that plan; (4) this leads to improved health; and (5) healthcare costs are reduced. Scrutiny of these assumptions is needed, both to test them and to determine how each step could best be accomplished in different clinical settings.

Research is also required that critically evaluates new genetic tests and interventions in terms of parameters such as benefits, access and cost. Such research should be interdisciplinary and use the tools and expertise of many fields, including genomics, health education, health behaviour research, health outcomes research, healthcare delivery analysis, and healthcare economics. Some of these fields have historically paid little attention to genomics, but high-quality research of this sort could provide important guidance in clinical decision-making as the work of several disciplines has already been helpful in caring for people with an increased risk of colon cancer as a result of mutations in *FAP* or *HNPCC*.

Grand Challenge II-6 Develop genome-based tools that improve the health of all.

Disparities in health status constitute a significant global issue, but can genome-based approaches to health and disease help to reduce this problem? Social and other environmental factors are major contributors to health disparities; indeed, some would question whether heritable factors have any significant role. But population differences in allele frequencies for some disease-associated variants could be a contributing factor to certain disparities in health status, so incorporating this information into preventive and/or public-health strategies would be beneficial. Research is needed to understand the relationship between genomics and health disparities by rigorously evaluating the diverse contributions of socioeconomic status, culture, discrimination, health behaviours, diet, environmental exposures and genetics.

It is also important to explore applications of genomics in the improvement of health in the developing world, where both human and non-human genomics will play significant roles. If we take malaria as an example, a better understanding of human genetic factors that influence susceptibility and response to the disease, and to the drugs used to treat it, could have a significant global impact. So too could a better understanding of the malarial parasite itself and of its mosquito vector, which the recently reported genome sequences should provide. It will be necessary to determine the appropriate roles of governmental and non-governmental organizations, academic institutions, industry and individuals to ensure that genomics produces clinical benefits for resource-poor nations, and is used to produce robust local research expertise.

To ensure that genomics research benefits all, it will be critical to examine how genomics-based health care is accessed and used. What are the barriers to equitable access, and how can they be removed? This is relevant not only in resource-poor nations, but also in wealthier countries where segments of society, such as indigenous populations, the uninsured, or rural and inner city communities, have traditionally not received adequate health care.

III. Genomics to Society[:] Promoting the use of genomics to maximize benefits and minimize harms

Genomics has been at the forefront of giving serious attention, through scholarly research and policy discussions, to the impact of science and technology on society. Although the major benefits to be realized from genomics are in the area of health, as described above, genomics can also contribute to other aspects of society. Just as the HGP and related developments have spawned new areas of research in basic biology and in health, they have also created opportunities for research on social issues, even to the extent of understanding more fully how we define ourselves and each other.

In the next few years, society must not only continue to grapple with numerous questions raised by genomics, but must also formulate and implement policies to address many of them. Unless research provides reliable data and rigorous approaches on which to base such decisions, those policies will be ill-informed and could potentially compromise us all. To be successful, this research must encompass both 'basic' investigations that develop conceptual tools and shared vocabularies, and more 'applied', 'translational' projects that use these tools to explore and define appropriate public-policy options that incorporate diverse points of view.

As it has in the past, such research will continue to have important ramifications for all three major themes of the vision presented here. We now address research that focuses on society itself, more than on biology or health. Such efforts should enable the research community to:

- Analyse the impact of genomics on concepts of race, ethnicity, kinship, individual and group identity, health, disease and 'normality' for traits and behaviours.
- Define policy options, and their potential consequences, for the use of genomic information and for the ethical boundaries around genomics research.

Grand Challenge III-1 Develop policy options for the uses of genomics in medical and non-medical settings

Surveys have repeatedly shown that the public is highly interested in the concept that personal genetic information might guide them to better health, but is deeply concerned about potential misuses of that information. Topping the list of concerns is the potential for discrimination in health insurance and employment. A significant amount of research on this issue has been done, policy options have been published, and many US states have now passed anti-discrimination legislation. The US Equal Employment Opportunity Commission has ruled that the Americans with Disabilities Act should apply to discrimination based on predictive genetic information, but the legal status of that construct remains in some doubt. Although an executive order protects US government employees against genetic discrimination, this does not apply to other workers. Thus, many observers have concluded that effective federal legislation is needed, and the US Congress is currently considering such a law.

Making certain that genetic tests offered to the public have established clinical validity and usefulness must be a priority for future research and policy making. In the

United States, the Secretary's Advisory Committee on Genetic Testing extensively reviewed this area and concluded that further oversight is needed, asking the Food and Drug Administration to review new predictive genetic tests prior to marketing. That recommendation has not yet been acted on; meanwhile, numerous websites offering unvalidated genetic tests directly to the public, often combined with the sale of 'nutraceuticals' and other products of highly questionable value, are proliferating.

Many issues currently swirl around the proper conduct of genetic research involving human subjects, and further work is needed to achieve a satisfactory balance between the protection of research participants from harm and the ability to conduct clinical research that benefits society as a whole. Much effort has gone into developing appropriate guidelines for the use of stored tissue specimens, for community consultation when conducting genetic research with identifiable populations, and for the consent of non-examined family members when conducting pedigree research, but confusion still remains for many investigators and institutional review boards.

The use of genomic information is not limited to the arenas of biology and of health, and further research and development of policy options is also needed for the many other applications of such information. The array of additional users is likely to include the life, disability and long-term care insurance industries, the legal system, the military, educational institutions and adoption agencies. Although some of the research informing the medical uses of genomics will be useful in broader settings, dedicated research outside the healthcare sphere is needed to explore the public values that apply to uses of genomics other than for health care and their relationship to specific contextual applications. For example, should genetic information on predisposition to hyperactivity be available in the future to school officials? Or should genetic information about behavioural traits be admissible in criminal or civil proceedings? Genomics also provides greater opportunity to understand ancestral origins of populations and individuals, which raises issues such as whether genetic information should be used for defining membership in a minority group.

Because uses of genomics outside the healthcare setting will involve a significantly broader community of stakeholders, both research and policy development in this area must involve individuals and organizations besides those involved in the medical applications of genomics. But many of the same perspectives essential to research and policy development for the medical uses of genomics are also essential. Both the potential users of non-medical applications of genomics and the public need education to understand better the nature and limits of genomic information and to grasp the ethical, legal and social implications of its uses outside health care.

Grand Challenge III-2 Understand the relationships between genomics, race and ethnicity, and the consequences of uncovering these relationships.

Race is a largely non-biological concept confounded by misunderstanding and a long history of prejudice. The relationship of genomics to the concepts of race and ethnicity has to be considered within complex historical and social contexts.

Most variation in the genome is shared between all populations, but certain alleles are more frequent in some populations than in others, largely as a result of history and geography. Use of genetic data to define racial groups, or of racial categories to classify biological traits, is prone to misinterpretation. To minimize such misinterpretation, the biological and sociocultural factors that interrelate genetics with constructs of race and ethnicity need to be better understood and communicated within the next few years.

This will require research on how different individuals and cultures conceive of race, ethnicity, group identity and self-identity, and what role they believe genes or other biological factors have. It will also require a critical examination of how the scientific community understands and uses these concepts in designing research and presenting findings, and of how the media report these. Also necessary is widespread education about the biological meaning and limitations of research findings in this area, and the formulation and adoption of public-policy options that protect against genomics-based discrimination or maltreatment (see Grand Challenge III-1).

Grand Challenge III-3 Understand the consequences of uncovering the genomic contributions to human traits and behaviours.

Genes influence not only health and disease, but also human traits and behaviours. Science is only beginning to unravel the complicated pathways that underlie such attributes as handedness, cognition, diurnal rhythms and various behavioural characteristics. Too often, research in behavioural genetics, such as that regarding sexual orientation or intelligence, has been poorly designed and its findings have been communicated in a way that oversimplifies and overstates the role of genetic factors. This has caused serious problems for those who have been stigmatized by the suggestion that alleles associated with what some people perceive as 'negative' physiological or behavioural traits are more frequent in certain populations. Given this history and the real potential for recurrence, it is particularly important to gather sufficient scientifically valid information about genetic and environmental factors to provide a sound understanding of the contributions and interactions between genes and environment in these complex phenotypes.

It is also important that there be robust research to investigate the implications, for both individuals and society, of uncovering any genomic contributions that there may be to traits and behaviours. The field of genomics has a responsibility to consider the social implications of research into the genetic contributions to traits and behaviours, perhaps an even greater responsibility than in other areas where there is less of a history of misunderstanding and stigmatization. Decisions about research in this area are often best made with input from a diverse group of individuals and organizations.

Grand Challenge III-4 Assess how to define the ethical boundaries for uses of genomics.

Genetics and genomics can contribute understanding to many areas of biology, health and life. Some of these human applications are controversial, with some members of the public questioning the propriety of their scientific exploration. Although freedom of scientific inquiry has been a cardinal feature of human progress, it is not unbounded. It is important for society to define the appropriate and inappropriate uses of genomics. Conversations between diverse parties based on an accurate and detailed understanding of the relevant science and ethical, legal and social factors will promote the formulation and implementation of effective policies. For instance, in reproductive genetic testing, it is crucial to include perspectives from the disability community. Research should explore how different individuals, cultures and religious traditions view the ethical boundaries for the uses of genomics—for instance, which sets of values determine attitudes towards the appropriateness of applying genomics to such areas as reproductive genetic testing, 'genetic enhancement' and germline gene transfer.

...

In conclusion, the successful completion this month of all of the original goals of the HGP emboldens the launch of a new phase for genomics research, to explore the remarkable landscape of opportunity that now opens up before us. Like Shakespeare, we are inclined to say, "what's past is prologue" (The Tempest, Act II, Scene 1). If we, like bold architects, can design and build this unprecedented and noble structure, resting on the firm bedrock foundation of the HGP, then the true promise of genomics research for benefiting humankind can be realized.

Press Release, U.S. Department of Health & Human Services, National Institutes of Health, International Consortium Completes Map of Human Genetic Variation: New Tool Speeding the Discovery of Genes for Common Diseases

(Oct. 26, 2005),
http://www.genome.gov/17015412

The International HapMap Consortium today published a comprehensive catalog of human genetic variation, a landmark achievement that is already accelerating the search for genes involved in common diseases, such as asthma, diabetes, cancer and heart disease.

In a paper in the Oct. 27 issue of the journal *Nature*, more than 200 researchers from Canada, China, Japan, Nigeria, the United Kingdom and the United States describe the initial results from their public-private effort to chart the patterns of genetic variation that are common in the world's population. The results provide overwhelming evidence that variation in the human genome is organized into local neighborhoods, called haplotypes, that usually are inherited as intact blocks of information.

At the project's outset in October 2002, the consortium set an ambitious goal of creating a human haplotype map, or HapMap, within three years. The *Nature* paper marks the attainment of that goal with its detailed description of the Phase I HapMap, consisting of more than 1 million markers of genetic variation, called single nucleotide polymorphisms (SNPs). The consortium is also nearing completion of the Phase II HapMap that will contain nearly three times more markers than the initial version and will enable researchers to focus their gene searches even more precisely on specific regions of the genome.

"This represents a milestone for medical research. Built upon the foundation laid by the human genome sequence, the HapMap provides a powerful new tool for exploring the root causes of common diseases. Such understanding is required for researchers to develop new and much-needed approaches to prevent, diagnose and treat diseases, such as diabetes, bipolar disorder, cancer and many others," said David Altshuler, M.D., Ph.D., of the Broad Institute of Harvard and MIT in Cambridge, Mass., who along with Peter Donnelly, Ph.D., of the University of Oxford in England are the paper's corresponding authors.

Any two unrelated people are 99.9 percent identical at the genetic level. However, it is important to understand the 0.1 percent difference because it can help explain why one person is more susceptible to a disease or responds differently to a drug or an environmental factor than another person.

The HapMap shows the boundaries of neighborhoods of correlated genetic variation, or haplotypes, across the entire human genome. With these haplotypes defined, HapMap provides an efficient method for choosing "tag SNPs" that capture the genetic variation in each neighborhood with a minimum amount of work. By using HapMap data to compare the SNP patterns of people affected by a disease with those of unaffected people, researchers can survey genetic variation across the whole genome and identify genetic contributions to common diseases far more efficiently than is possible with traditional approaches.

"The HapMap is a phenomenal tool that is making possible research that was impractical, if not unimaginable, only a few years ago," said Yusuke Nakamura, M.D., Ph.D., director of the University of Tokyo's Human Genome Center, as well as leader of the RIKEN SNP Center and the Japanese group working on the HapMap." It offers the scientific community an enormous savings, reducing the expense of searching the genome for hereditary factors in common disease by a factor of 10 to 20."

Gene hunters around the world have been quick to recognize the potential of the HapMap, tapping into its publicly available SNP datasets even before the first draft of the map was completed. For example, in studies published in March in the journal Science, scientists used HapMap data to uncover a genetic variation that substantially increases the risk of age-related macular degeneration, the leading cause of severe vision loss in the elderly. The discovery of this single spelling variant out of the 3 billion letter DNA instruction book for humans, which affects a gene that codes for a protein involved in inflammation, points the way for development of better diagnostic tests and treatments for this debilitating disease.

Many other discoveries lie on the horizon as the HapMap empowers studies of other common diseases, including diabetes, Alzheimer's disease, cancer, schizophrenia, asthma, hypertension and heart disease. In fact, more than 70 papers and presentations related to the HapMap are on the program for this week's meeting of the American Society of Human Genetics in Salt Lake City.

In addition to assisting in the identification of genetic factors involved in disease, the HapMap can help to pinpoint genetic variations that may affect the response of people to medications, toxic substances and environmental factors. Such information can be used to help doctors prescribe the right drug in the right dose for each patient, as well as recommend prevention strategies that take into account individuals' varying responses to environmental factors, such as diet. Also, the HapMap may be used to find genetic factors that contribute to good health, such as those protecting against infectious diseases or promoting longevity.

Still, the consortium members caution the research community not to jump to conclusions too quickly when using HapMap data to facilitate their genome-wide searches for genes associated with human health and disease. "Rigorous standards of statistical significance will be needed to avoid a flood of false positive results," they write in their paper. To avert such problems, they urge their scientific colleagues to confirm any gene "discovery" by replicating the findings in independent studies that use the same set of SNP markers in different groups of people with the same disease or condition.

Researchers produced the HapMap using DNA from blood samples collected from 269 volunteers from widely distributed geographic regions. Specifically, the samples came from Yoruba in Ibadan, Nigeria; Japanese in Tokyo, Han Chinese in Beijing and Utah residents with ancestry from northern and western Europe. No medical or personal identifying information was obtained from the donors. However, the samples are identified by the population from which they were collected.

"We have devoted much effort to making sure this project is done as ethically and transparently as possible. Following the precedent set by the Human Genome Project, we have weighed the ethical, legal and social implications of this research from the outset," said Bartha M. Knoppers, J.D., Ph.D., of the University of Montreal. "For example, we developed a very careful community engagement and sampling strategy to ensure that participants from all the different population groups could give full informed consent. Still, we know our job is far from over and we stand ready to address whatever ethical, legal and social issues may arise in the future."

In addition to its intended function as a resource for studies of human health and disease, the Phase I HapMap has yielded fascinating clues into how our species evolved over time and specific forces that were important as the human population spread around the globe.

Genetic diversity in humans is increased by recombination, which is the swapping of DNA from the maternal and paternal lines. It has been recently realized that in humans, most such swapping occurs primarily at a limited number of "hotspots" in the genome. By analyzing the HapMap data, the researchers have produced a genome-wide inventory of where recombination takes place. This will enable more detailed studies of this fundamental property of inheritance, as well as serve to improve the design of genetic studies of disease.

The HapMap consortium found that genes involved in immune response and neurological processes are more diverse than those for DNA repair, DNA packaging and cell division. Researchers speculate the difference might be explained by natural selection shaping in the human population in ways that favor increased diversity for genes that influence the body's interactions with the environment, such as those involved in immune response, and that do not favor changes in genes involved in core cellular processes.

As expected, the vast majority of both rare and common patterns of genetic variation were found in all of the populations studied. However, the consortium did find evidence that a very small subset of human genetic variation may be related to selection pressures related to geographic or environmental factors, such as microorganisms that cause infectious diseases. This evidence appears as significant differences in genetic variation patterns in particular genomic regions among the populations studied. While more follow-up study is needed to explore the differences, researchers say some of the most striking examples merely serve to confirm well-known genetic differences among populations, such as the Duffy blood group, which plays a role in response to malaria, and the lactase gene, which influences the ability to digest milk products.

All in all, across the 1 million SNPs surveyed, researchers found only five exclusive, or "fixed," differences on human's 22 pairs of non-sex (autosomal) chromosomes between the Yoruba samples and the Japanese and Han Chinese samples; 11 between the Yoruba samples and the samples from Utah residents of northern and western European ancestry; and 21 between the Utah samples and the Japanese and Han Chinese samples.

The International HapMap Consortium is a public-private partnership of scientists and funding agencies from Canada, China, Japan, Nigeria, the United Kingdom and the United States. The U.S. component of the $138 million international project is led by National Human Genome Research Institute (NHGRI) on behalf of the 20 institutes, centers and offices of the National Institutes of Health (NIH) that contributed funding.

"Like the Human Genome Project before it, the key to the International HapMap Project's success lies in the shared vision and hard work of hundreds of researchers from many different nations and many different disciplines," said NHGRI Director Francis S. Collins, M.D., Ph.D., who led the U.S. component of the Human Genome Project and served as the project manager for HapMap." Each member of the consortium is to be commended for helping to create this outstanding public resource for exploring the genetic components of human health and disease."

As was the case with all of the data generated by the Human Genome Project, HapMap data are being made swiftly and freely available in public databases. Researchers can access this data through the HapMap Data Coordination Center (www.hapmap.org), the NIH-funded National Center for Biotechnology Information's dbSNP (http://www.ncbi.nlm.nih.gov/SNP/index.html) and the JSNP Database in Japan (http://snp.ims.u-tokyo.ac.jp).

Phase II of the HapMap, for which the data has already been generated and analysis is getting underway, will be an even more powerful tool than the Phase I version described in the Nature paper. Taking advantage of the high-throughput genotyping capacity of Perlegen Sciences, Inc., of Mountain View, Calif., Phase II is adding 2.1 million additional SNPs to the HapMap by testing virtually the entire known catalog of human variation on the HapMap samples.

"Our participation in this collaborative effort underscores the private sector's enthusiasm for the HapMap and its potential as a tool for the understanding of disease. The Phase II map will make it even easier for researchers to correlate genetic variation with gene function, which is crucial for developing therapies tailored to each person's genetic make-up," said Kelly A. Frazer, Ph.D., vice president of genomics at Perlegen.

For more information on the ethical, legal and social implications of the International HapMap Project, see www.genome.gov/17015413. For more details on the project's scientific design and rationale, see www.genome.gov/11511175. For a complete list of participating research organizations and funders, see www.genome.gov/17915414.

...

Stanley Fields, *Proteomics in Genomeland*

291 SCIENCE 1221 (2001)

If the architect you hired to design your home brought you a blueprint that solely consisted of a long list of parts that began "windowwabeborogovestaircasedoorjubjub...," you might start to wonder if and when you will see your new house. Some people have similar reservations about the recently "completed" human genome sequence, heralded as the "genetic blueprint" that will revolutionize biology and medicine. Deciphering how a mere 107 nucleotides result in a yeast cell—let alone how 3 x 109 nucleotides result in Tiger Woods or Britney Spears—cannot begin until the genes have been annotated. This step includes figuring out the proteins that these genes encode and what they do for a living. But understanding how all of these proteins collaborate to carry out cellular processes is the real enterprise at hand.

In the wonderland of complete sequences, there is much that genomics cannot do, and so the future belongs to proteomics: the analysis of complete complements of proteins. Proteomics includes not only the identification and quantification of proteins, but also the determination of their localization, modifications, interactions, activities, and, ultimately, their function. Initially encompassing just two-dimensional (2D) gel electrophoresis for protein separation and identification, proteomics now refers to any procedure that characterizes large sets of proteins. The explosive growth of this field is driven by multiple forces—genomics and its revelation of more and more new proteins; powerful protein technologies, such as newly developed mass spectrometry approaches, global two-hybrid techniques, and spin-offs from DNA arrays; and innovative computational tools and methods to process, analyze, and interpret prodigious amounts of data.

The shift in thinking from genomics to proteomics comes with an appreciation of the difficulty of the task: Proteins are much more complicated than nucleic acids. Unlike the decoratively challenged DNA, proteins get phosphorylated, glycosylated, acetylated, ubiquitinated, farnesylated, sulphated, linked to glycophosphatidylinositol anchors, and embellished in numerous other ways. A single gene can encode multiple different proteins—these can be produced by alternative splicing of the mRNA transcript, by varying translation start or stop sites, or by frameshifting during which a different set of triplet codons in the mRNA is translated. All of these possibilities result in a proteome estimated to be an order of magnitude more complex than the genome. (So it may be fortunate for proteomicists that humans might have as few as six times the number of genes that yeast have!) What is more, proteins respond to altered conditions by changing their location within the cell, getting cleaved into pieces, and adjusting their stability as well as changing what they bind to (other proteins, nucleic acids, lipids, small molecules, or other ligands). Protein levels often do not reflect mRNA levels and even the presence of an open reading frame does not guarantee the existence of a protein. Lastly, a single protein may be involved in more than one process, and conversely, similar functions may be carried out by different proteins.

Where We Are

It's worth noting that in the pre-proteomic era, thousands of proteins were exquisitely characterized—those in metabolic and signaling pathways; in the replication, transcription, and translation machinery; in secretory and cytoskeletal networks; and in a host of other cellular complexes. These functional assignments came from efforts to understand specific cellular processes, with three major factors fueling progress in the last two decades. First, a confluence of geneticists, cell biologists, biochemists, and structural biologists arrived to tackle the same problems from different directions. Second, the extraordinary conservation of fundamental cellular mechanisms enabled insights garnered from the study of one organism to be immediately applied to all others—what's true for the walrus is true for the carpenter. Third, developments in technology—the now-standard tools of molecular biology such as DNA sequencing, recombinant DNA, and the polymerase chain reaction—sparked new experimental strategies.

With the emergence of proteomics, additional proteins are now pouring in to join those already implicated in some process or other. This extra information, however, derives not from continued small-scale analysis of a biological activity, but from much larger and more systematic studies. Proteomics, like its precursor genomics, thus represents the emergence of a new way of doing research that is not dependent on the testing of specific models of cellular behavior. This style of science obviously does not replace, but rather will increasingly operate in tandem with, traditional biological research methods.

One general principle is that proteins prefer to hang out in the cell with others that they work with; thus, the identity of new proteins in the complexes left intact after cell lysis often provides clues to function. A big boost has come from recent advances in mass spectrometry that allow the rapid identification of proteins separated in a 2D gel or by chromatography. The mass spectrometer measures the masses of peptides (typically derived from a trypsin digestion), which are then compared to the predicted masses of peptides from in silico digestions of sequences in genomic databases. Although unambiguous identification of a protein cannot always be derived from the masses of a few of its peptides, in the tandem mass spectrometer, peptide ions from the first mass spectrometer run are fragmented and identified in a second run to yield the more valuable commodity of a peptide sequence. A single peptide sequence usually identifies a protein. Advances in automation, increased sensitivity, and higher throughput, combined with improved biochemical fractionations and the availability of vastly expanded databases, have extended the application of mass spectrometry to ever bigger jobs. For example, megadalton protein complexes can be purified, often with a single tagged component, and their constituents can be identified after gel electrophoresis. Such analyses have been performed on, among other complexes, the human spliceosome, the yeast nuclear pore complex, and the pea chloroplast. Bypassing even gel separation, the direct analysis of protein complexes identifies components of heterogeneous protein mixtures, often using 1D or 2D chromatography for fractionation before analysis by mass spectrometry. Application of this procedure to a whole-cell yeast lysate identified 189 proteins and more recently 1484 proteins, including integral membrane proteins and those of low-abundance in the cell.

The complement to mass spectrometry, the yeast two-hybrid system, has been increasingly "genomicized." From its initial application to finding protein partners that interact with just one protein, the assay has been scaled up to handle, for example—15 proteins implicated in yeast mRNA splicing, 29 proteins involved in *Caenorhabditis elegans* development, the ~55 proteins of bacteriophage T7, 266 proteins of vaccinia virus, and even 5345 proteins of *Saccharomyces cerevisiae*. For yeast, more than 2700 putative interactions involving at least 2000 different proteins have been identified, mostly through two-hybrid experiments. This set of interaction data can be visualized as protein networks, with one analysis yielding a network that encompasses over 2300 links. The validity of many of the links in this network is supported by database annotations. More than 70% of characterized proteins with partners that have also been described could be assigned a correct functional category according to the properties of these partners (compared with only 12% if the proteins in the network are kept constant and the links are scrambled). Thus, a protein of unknown function that binds to one of known function can be tentatively assigned to the same cellular category as its partner.

Protein localization within the cell can now be addressed at a genomic level. In a tour de force of transposon tagging and analysis, over 11,000 yeast strains were generated with more than 2000 *S. cerevisiae* genes affected; indirect immunofluorescence was then used to determine subcellular localizations for over 1300 of the tagged proteins. Biochemistry, too, is feeling the impact of complete sequence information. The entire set of predicted yeast proteins has been fused to the "purification hook" of glutathione S-transferase. This set enables a biochemical genomics strategy in which the fusions are purified as 64 pools of 96 proteins each. The pools can be assayed for any biochemical activity, and the protein responsible for the activity in a pool can be quickly identified. Because the pools are derived from an array of yeast strains harboring a single gene, the gene encoding the activity is immediately known.

For the expanding number of genome sequences available, clever algorithms have been developed that assign functions to previously unknown proteins that do not rely on amino acid similarity. One approach scores the presence or absence of a given protein in all sequenced genomes, revealing sets of proteins that have co-evolved (that is, all members of a set are either present or absent in an organism), and are therefore likely to act in the same cellular process. A second approach is based on the observation that many proteins consist of two domains in one organism, whereas the domains are two separate proteins in another organism. The existence of the fusion, in which the two domains clearly interact, suggests that in the second organism the two separate proteins also interact. A third approach identifies cases in which multiple genomes harbor the same set of neighboring genes, a situation implying that each set encodes proteins of related function. Such operons in prokaryotes typically specify functionally linked proteins, but some examples are also found in eukaryotes.

Although strictly speaking not a proteomics technique, DNA arrays often provide insight into the functions of sizable collections of proteins. Genes that are transcriptionally co-regulated generally code for proteins that act in the same process, as demonstrated by yeast genes that operate in the cell division cycle, sporulation, and the diauxic shift. Expression profiles reveal up- or down-regulated mRNAs (and thus, presumptively, their protein products) in disease processes such as cancer, and consequently can be used to classify tumors. Microarray technology can identify classes of proteins—for example, membrane-bound and secreted proteins have been identified through the localization of their mRNAs, and proteins that bind to a DNA sequence have been identified by their interaction with a double-stranded DNA array. Microarray-based assays can also be used to detect polymorphisms (variations in the DNA), thereby associating protein variants with a disease state. An early application of this approach correctly identified 14 of 15 patients carrying known mutations in the hereditary breast and ovarian cancer gene *BRCA1*.

Given the current genomic and proteomic commotion, we should keep in mind that a protein found to be "in the spliceosome complex," "interacting with actin," "co-evolving with a prion protein," or "up-regulated in leukemia" has not been functionally characterized in the traditional sense to which biologists are accustomed. Instead, these types of results often serve only to place a protein in the appropriate bailiwick for follow-up analysis.

Where We're Heading

So far, most proteomic measurements have been performed in a cataloging mode, but the future will see more studies that address the dynamics of cellular processes. The protein composition of a cell is not static, therefore, it is crucial to obtain quantitative comparisons after a cell's environment changes. Proteomic strategies increasingly allow such quantitative analyses to be carried out. For example, stable isotopes enable two protein populations to be labeled with either a heavy or a light affinity tag, then mixed, trypsinized, and fractionated to enrich for subsets of proteins. Because the peptides in the two populations are identical except for the defined mass difference of the two tags, quantitation by mass spectrometry is possible. These studies are in their early stages and their potential is tremendous. Increasingly, proteins will undergo wholesale analyses to probe for their various modifications. Affinity purification approaches using specific antibodies, metals, lectins, or other reagents allow enrichment for modified proteins, which then can be detected by mass spectrometry. These types of strategies should make it feasible to follow, at the level of the proteome, a series of complicated cellular events such as those that ensue after a T cell encounters an antigen. Advances in direct analysis by mass spectrometry of peptide mixtures generated by the digestion of complex protein samples will lead to an escalating number of protein identifications in one experiment. This procedure may allow human tissues to be used as the protein source and renders feasible the discovery of early disease markers (through the comparison of the protein content of pathogenic cells with that of their normal counterparts).

Protein expression and purification technologies will continue to improve. The biochemical genomics strategy of purifying pools of tagged proteins will be particularly suitable for the many bacteria that have had their genomes sequenced, but it can be applied to multicellular organisms as well. These and other procedures that make use of protein arrays will become commonplace. The arrays may be generated by in vivo expression of tagged proteins, in vitro translation, peptide synthesis, or protein capture by antibodies or oligonucleotide aptamers. Their potential applications include: revealing interactions among proteins and between proteins and small molecules (drugs) or other ligands, identifying substrates for a modifying enzyme such as a protein kinase, and searching for enzymatic activities. A harbinger of the promise of this approach is the recent demonstration of proteins in nanoliter droplets immobilized by covalent attachment to glass slides; more than 10,000 samples could be spotted onto each slide with this technique. The few test proteins in this array format were assayed for interactions with another protein or a small molecule, and for their phosphorylation by a protein kinase. Targeted arrays will allow the identification of all of the enzymes in an organism that are able to carry out a specific modification of a substrate; for example, protein arrays have tested nearly the entire set of the predicted protein kinases in yeast for their activity on 17 substrates.

Protein databases will need to become much more sophisticated if they are to help scientists make sense of the staggering number of experimental measurements that will soon emerge. Demands range from tracking all of the ligands for each analyzed member of a protein family (such as the SH3 domain) to cataloging all of the known substrates of each protein kinase, protein phosphatase, or other modifying activity. In addition, protein data will need to be integrated with results from expression profiling, genome-wide mutation or antisense analyses, and polymorphism detection. As proteomic data accumulate, we will become better at triangulating from multiple disparate bits of information to gain a bearing on what a protein does in the cell. Proteomics will come of age when its revelations about formerly uncharacterized proteins directly drive imaginative hypotheses about their functions.

What We Need

For a field so laden with razzmatazz methods, it is striking that the number one need in proteomics may be new technology. There are simply not enough assays that are sufficiently streamlined to allow the automation necessary to perform them on a genome's worth of proteins. Those currently available barely scratch the surface of the thousands of specialized analyses biologists use every day on their favorite proteins. What we need are experimental strategies that could be termed cell biological genomics, biophysical genomics, physiological genomics, and so on, to provide clues to function. In addition, a protein contains so many types of information that each of its properties needs to be assayed on a proteome-wide scale, ideally in a quantitative manner.

As we have argued, existing technology—and more importantly, the reagents (sets of genes, plasmids, strains, proteins, and the like) and equipment to handle these reagents—must rapidly spread from the specialized genomic and proteomic centers to the rest of the community. Only when every laboratory is comfortable doing proteomics will its power be exploited fully. Moreover, the likelihood of new approaches increases in proportion to the number of investigators participating in the field.

An interdisciplinary spirit will come to guide those excited by the global analysis of protein function. Geneticists need to talk to chemists, physiologists to physicists, cell biologists to computer scientists. With questions so grand, the expertise to answer them requires the entire spectrum of science. This combination of new technology and its widespread dispersion together with broad-ranging collaborative projects will culminate in the fabulous day when the undertaking that began with genome sequencing reaches fruition.

* * *

For additional reading and references on genetic science and its evolution to the present day, see the following:

Cindy Pham Lorentz, et al., *Primer on Medical Genomics: History of Genetics and Sequencing of the Human Genome*, 77 Mayo Clin. Proc. 773 (2002).

William Bateson, Mendel's Principles of Heredity: A Defence (1902), *available at* http://www.esp.org/books/bateson/mendel/facsimile.

James D. Watson & Francis H. Crick, *Molecular Structure of Nucleic Acids: A Structure for Deoxyribose Nucleic Acid*, 171 Nature 737 (1953).

James D. Watson, The Double Helix: A Personal Account of the Discovery of the Structure of DNA (1968).

James D. Watson & Andrew Berry, *DNA*: The Secret of Life (2003).

U.S. Department of Energy, The Human Genome Project: 1990–2003, http://www.ornl.gov/sci/techresources/Human_Genome/publicat/primer2001/2.shtml.

U.S. Department of Energy, Human Genome Project Information, http://www.ornl.gov/sci/techresources/Human_Genome/publicat/publications.shtml.

J. Christopher Post & Garth D. Ehrlich, *The Impact of the Polymerase Chain Reaction in Clinical Medicine*, 283 J. Am. Med. Assoc. 1544 (2000).

James D. Watson & Robert M. Cook-Deegan, *Origins of the Human Genome Project*, 5 FASEB J. 8 (1991).

Francis Collins & David Galas, *A New Five-year Plan for the U.S. Human Genome Project*, 262 Science 43 (1993).

International Human Genome Sequencing Consortium, *Initial Sequencing and Analysis of the Human Genome*, 409 Nature 860 (2001).

J. Craig Venter, et al., *The Sequence of the Human Genome*, 291 Science 1304 (2001).

Stacey B. Gabriel, et al., *The Structure of Haplotype Blocks in the Human Genome*, 296 Science 2225 (2002).

The International HapMap Consortium, *The International HapMap Project*, 426 Nature 789 (2003).

The International HapMap Consortium, *Integrating Ethics and Science in the International HapMap Project*, 5 Nature Reviews: Genetics 467 (2004).

The ENCODE Project Consortium, *The ENCODE (ENCyclopedia Of DNA Elements) Project*, 306 Science 636 (2004).

The International HapMap Consortium, *A Haplotype Map of the Human Genome*, 37 Nature 1299 (2005).

Chapter 2

Access to and Disclosure of Genetic Information: Rights, Duties, and Liabilities

The integration of genetics into medical research, clinical medicine, and public health promises to significantly improve health care and health outcomes by enhancing individual and population-based techniques for screening, diagnosis, prevention, and treatment. It also promises to significantly increase the volume of individual genetic information that is collected, stored, and available for dissemination, giving rise to concerns regarding privacy and confidentiality.

As with all medical information, genetic information provides insights into an individual's present and future health that are highly personal and entitled to protection under existing laws regarding the privacy and confidentiality of medical information. Proponents of genetic exceptionalism, who view genetic information as uniquely predictive and revealing compared to other medical information, are advocating with some success for laws that afford greater protection for "genetic privacy" than the protection given to general health care information. Underlying the genetic exceptionalism debate is a general recognition of the highly personal nature of health care information; the potential for that information to be misused in a way that stigmatizes, discriminates against, or otherwise disadvantages individuals whose health profile, genetic or otherwise, connotes risk for disease or disability; and the need for the law to protect and promote privacy and confidentiality.

The cases and materials in this chapter outline the sources of protection the law currently provides for health care information generally and for genetic information in particular. As you review these materials, think about the differences between privacy and confidentiality, the nature and extent of protection each is afforded under the law, and how the law balances individual rights against competing interests of the general public, including health care delivery, public health, law enforcement, and research. Consider also the extent to which genetic information is, or should be, treated differently from other health care information and the individual and social costs associated with each perspective on the genetic exceptionalism debate.

A. Privacy and Confidentiality: Sources of Protection

1. Constitutional Rights to Privacy

Whalen v. Roe

429 U.S. 589 (1977)

Mr. Justice Stevens delivered the opinion of the Court.

The constitutional question presented is whether the State of New York may record, in a centralized computer file, the names and addresses of all persons who have obtained, pursuant to a doctor's prescription, certain drugs for which there is both a lawful and an unlawful market.

The District Court enjoined enforcement of the portions of the New York State Controlled Substances Act of 1972 which require such recording on the ground that they violate appellees' constitutionally protected rights of privacy. We noted probable jurisdiction of the appeal by the Commissioner of Health and now reverse.

Many drugs have both legitimate and illegitimate uses. In response to a concern that such drugs were being diverted into unlawful channels, in 1970 the New York Legislature created a special commission to evaluate the State's drug-control laws. The commission found the existing laws deficient in several respects. There was no effective way to prevent the use of stolen or revised prescriptions, to prevent unscrupulous pharmacists from repeatedly refilling prescriptions, to prevent users from obtaining prescriptions from more than one doctor, or to prevent doctors from over-prescribing, either by authorizing an excessive amount in one prescription or by giving one patient multiple prescriptions. In drafting new legislation to correct such defects, the commission consulted with enforcement officials in California and Illinois where central reporting systems were being used effectively.

The new New York statute classified potentially harmful drugs in five schedules. Drugs, such as heroin, which are highly abused and have no recognized medical use, are in Schedule I; they cannot be prescribed. Schedules II through V include drugs which have a progressively lower potential for abuse but also have a recognized medical use. Our concern is limited to Schedule II which includes the most dangerous of the legitimate drugs.

With an exception for emergencies, the Act requires that all prescriptions for Schedule II drugs be prepared by the physician in triplicate on an official form. The completed form identifies the prescribing physician; the dispensing pharmacy; the drug and dosage; and the name, address, and age of the patient. One copy of the form is retained by the physician, the second by the pharmacist, and the third is forwarded to the New York State Department of Health in Albany. A prescription made on an official form may not exceed a 30-day supply, and may not be refilled.

The District Court found that about 100,000 Schedule II prescription forms are delivered to a receiving room at the Department of Health in Albany each month. They are sorted, coded, and logged and then taken to another room where the data on the forms is recorded on magnetic tapes for processing by a computer. Thereafter, the forms are returned to the receiving room to be retained in a vault for a five-year period and then destroyed as required by the statute. The receiving room is surrounded by a locked wire fence and protected by an alarm system. The computer tapes containing the prescription data are kept in a locked cabinet. When the tapes are used, the computer is run "off-line," which means that no terminal outside of the computer room can read or record any information. Public disclosure of the identity of patients is expressly prohibited by the statute and by a Department of Health regulation. Willful violation of these prohibitions is a crime punishable by up to one year in prison and a $2,000 fine. At the time of trial there were 17 Department of Health employees with access to the files; in addition, there were 24 investigators with authority to investigate cases of over dispensing which might be identified by the computer. Twenty months after the effective date of the Act, the computerized data had only been used in two investigations involving alleged overuse by specific patients.

A few days before the Act became effective, this litigation was commenced by a group of patients regularly receiving prescriptions for Schedule II drugs, by doctors who prescribe such drugs, and by two associations of physicians....

Appellees contend that the statute invades a constitutionally protected "zone of privacy." The cases sometimes characterized as protecting "privacy" have in fact involved at least two different kinds of interests. One is the individual interest in avoiding disclosure of personal matters, and another is the interest in independence in making certain kinds of important decisions. Appellees argue that both of these interests are impaired by this statute. The mere existence in readily available form of the information about patients' use of Schedule II drugs creates a genuine concern that the information will become publicly known and that it will adversely affect their reputations. This concern makes some patients reluctant to use, and some doctors reluctant to prescribe, such drugs even when their use is medically indicated. It follows, they argue, that the making of decisions about matters vital to the care of their health is inevitably affected by the statute. Thus, the statute threatens to impair both their interest in the nondisclosure of private information and also their interest in making important decisions independently.

We are persuaded, however, that the New York program does not, on its face, pose a sufficiently grievous threat to either interest to establish a constitutional violation.

Public disclosure of patient information can come about in three ways. Health Department employees may violate the statute by failing, either deliberately or negligently, to maintain proper security. A patient or a doctor may be accused of a violation and the stored data may be offered in evidence in a judicial proceeding. Or, thirdly, a doctor, a pharmacist, or the patient may voluntarily reveal information on a prescription form.

The third possibility existed under the prior law and is entirely unrelated to the existence of the computerized data bank. Neither of the other two possibilities provides a proper ground for attacking the statute as invalid on its face. There is no support in the record, or in the experience of the two States that New York has emulated, for an assumption that the security provisions of the statute will be administered improperly. And the remote possibility that judicial supervision of the evidentiary use of particular items of stored information will provide inadequate protection against unwarranted disclosures is surely not a sufficient reason for invalidating the entire patient-identification program.

Even without public disclosure, it is, of course, true that private information must be disclosed to the authorized employees of the New York Department of Health. Such disclosures, however, are not significantly different from those that were required under the prior law. Nor are they meaningfully distinguishable from a host of other unpleasant invasions of privacy that are associated with many facets of health care. Unquestionably, some individuals' concern for their own privacy may lead them to avoid or to postpone needed medical attention. Nevertheless, disclosures of private medical information to doctors, to hospital personnel, to insurance companies, and to public health agencies are often an essential part of modern medical practice even when the disclosure may reflect unfavorably on the character of the patient. Requiring such disclosures to representatives of the State having responsibility for the health of the community, does not automatically amount to an impermissible invasion of privacy.

Appellees also argue, however, that even if unwarranted disclosures do not actually occur, the knowledge that the information is readily available in a computerized file creates a genuine concern that causes some persons to decline needed medication. The record supports the conclusion that some use of Schedule II drugs has been discouraged by that concern; it also is clear, however, that about 100,000 prescriptions for such drugs were being filled each month prior to the entry of the District Court's injunction. Clearly, therefore, the statute did not deprive the public of access to the drugs.

Nor can it be said that any individual has been deprived of the right to decide independently, with the advice of his physician, to acquire and to use needed medication. Although the State no doubt could prohibit entirely the use of particular Schedule II drugs, it has not done so. This case is therefore unlike those in which the Court held that a total prohibition of certain conduct was an impermissible deprivation of liberty. Nor does the State require access to these drugs to be conditioned on the consent of any state official or other third party. Within dosage limits which appellees do not challenge, the decision to prescribe, or to use, is left entirely to the physician and the patient.

We hold that neither the immediate nor the threatened impact of the patient-identification requirements in the New York State Controlled Substances Act of 1972 on either the reputation or the independence of patients for whom Schedule II drugs are medically indicated is sufficient to constitute an invasion of any right or liberty protected by the Fourteenth Amendment....

... A final word about issues we have not decided. We are not unaware of the threat to privacy implicit in the accumulation of vast amounts of personal information in computerized data banks or other massive government files. The collection of taxes, the distribution of welfare and social security benefits, the supervision of public health, the direction of our Armed Forces, and the enforcement of the criminal laws all require the orderly preservation of great quantities of information, much of which is personal in character and potentially embarrassing or harmful if disclosed. The right to collect and use such data for public purposes is typically accompanied by a concomitant statutory or regulatory duty to avoid unwarranted disclosures. Recognizing that in some circumstances that duty arguably has its roots in the Constitution, nevertheless New York's statutory scheme, and its implementing administrative procedures, evidence a proper concern with, and protection of, the individual's interest in privacy. We therefore need not, and do not, decide any question which might be presented by the unwarranted disclosure of accumulated private data whether intentional or unintentional or by a system that did not contain comparable security provisions. We simply hold that this record does not establish an invasion of any right or liberty protected by the Fourteenth Amendment....

Mr. Justice Brennan, concurring.

... The New York statute under attack requires doctors to disclose to the State information about prescriptions for certain drugs with a high potential for abuse, and provides for the storage of that information in a central computer file. The Court recognizes that an individual's "interest in avoiding disclosure of personal matters" is an aspect of the right of privacy, but holds that in this case, any such interest has not been seriously enough invaded by the State to require a showing that its program was indispensable to the State's effort to control drug abuse.

The information disclosed by the physician under this program is made available only to a small number of public health officials with a legitimate interest in the information. As the record makes clear, New York has long required doctors to make this information available to its officials on request, and that practice is not challenged here. Such limited reporting requirements in the medical field are, and are not generally regarded as an invasion of privacy. Broad dissemination by state officials of such information, however, would clearly implicate constitutionally protected privacy rights, and would presumably be justified only by compelling state interests. *See, e. g.*, *Roe v. Wade*, 410 U.S. 113 (1973).

What is more troubling about this scheme, however, is the central computer storage of the data thus collected. Obviously, as the State argues, collection and storage of data by the State that is in itself legitimate is not rendered unconstitutional simply because new technology makes the State's operations more efficient. However, as the example of the Fourth Amendment shows the Constitution puts limits not only on the type of information the State may gather, but also on the means it may use to gather it. The central storage and easy accessibility of computerized data vastly increase the potential for abuse of that information, and I am not prepared to say that future developments will not demonstrate the necessity of some curb on such technology.

In this case, as the Court's opinion makes clear, the State's carefully designed program includes numerous safeguards intended to forestall the danger of indiscriminate disclosure. Given this serious and, so far as the record shows, successful effort to prevent abuse and limit access to the personal information at issue, I cannot say that the statute's provisions for computer storage, on their face, amount to a deprivation of constitutionally protected privacy interests, any more than the more traditional reporting provisions.

In the absence of such a deprivation, the State was not required to prove that the challenged statute is absolutely necessary to its attempt to control drug abuse. Of course, a statute that did effect such a deprivation would only be consistent with the Constitution if it were necessary to promote a compelling state interest. *Roe v. Wade*, *supra*; *Eisenstadt v. Baird*, 405 U.S. 438 (1972).

Mr. Justice Stewart, concurring.

In *Katz v. United States*, 389 U.S. 347, the Court made clear that although the Constitution affords protection against certain kinds of government intrusions into personal and private matters, there is no "general constitutional 'right to privacy.'... [T]he protection of a person's general right to privacy his right to be let alone by other people is, like the protection of his property and of his very life, left largely to the law of the individual States."

Mr. Justice Brennan's concurring opinion states that "[b]road dissemination by state officials of (the information collected by New York State) ... would clearly implicate constitutionally protected privacy rights." ... The only possible support in his opinion for this statement is its earlier reference to two footnotes in the Court's opinion. The footnotes, however, cite to only two Court opinions, and those two cases do not support the proposition advanced by Mr. Justice Brennan....

Norman-Bloodsaw v. Lawrence Berkeley Laboratory

135 F.3d 1260 (9th Cir. 1998)

Reinhardt, Circuit Judge.

This appeal involves the question whether a clerical or administrative worker who undergoes a general employee health examination may, without his knowledge, be tested for highly private and sensitive medical and genetic information such as syphilis, sickle cell trait, and pregnancy.

Lawrence Berkeley Laboratory is a research institution jointly operated by state and federal agencies. Plaintiffs-appellants, present and former employees of Lawrence, allege that in the course of their mandatory employment entrance examinations and on subsequent occasions, Lawrence, without their knowledge or consent, tested their blood and urine for intimate medical conditions—namely, syphilis, sickle cell trait, and pregnancy. Their complaint asserts that this testing violated ... their right to privacy as guaranteed by both the United States and State of California Constitutions. The district court granted the defendants-appellees' motions for dismissal, judgment on the pleadings, and summary judgment on all of plaintiffs-appellants' claims. We ... reverse as to the ... state and federal privacy claims.

Plaintiffs ... are current and former administrative and clerical employees of defendant Lawrence Berkeley Laboratory ("Lawrence"), a research facility operated by the appellee Regents of the University of California pursuant to a contract with the United States Department of Energy (the Department).... The named defendants are sued in both their official and individual capacities.

The Department requires federal contractors such as Lawrence to establish an occupational medical program. Since 1981, it has required its contractors to perform "preplacement examinations" of employees as part of this program, and until 1995, it also required its contractors to offer their employees the option of subsequent "periodic health examinations." The mandatory preplacement examination occurs after the offer of employment but prior to the assumption of job duties. The Department actively oversees Lawrence's occupational health program, and, prior to 1992, specifically required syphilis testing as part of the preplacement examination.

With the exception of Ellis, who was hired in 1968 and underwent an examination after beginning employment, each of the plaintiffs received written offers of employment expressly conditioned upon a "medical examination," "medical approval," or "health evaluation." All accepted these offers and underwent preplacement examinations, and Randolph and Smith underwent subsequent examinations as well. In the course of these examinations, plaintiffs completed medical history questionnaires and provided blood and urine samples. The questionnaires asked, inter alia, whether the patient had ever had any of sixty-one medical conditions, including "[s]ickle cell anemia," "[v]enereal disease," and, in the case of women, "[m]enstrual disorders."

The blood and urine samples given by all employees during their preplacement examinations were tested for syphilis; in addition, certain samples were tested for sickle cell trait; and certain samples were tested for pregnancy....

Following receipt of a right-to-sue letter from the EEOC, plaintiffs filed suit in September 1995 on behalf of all past and present Lawrence employees who have ever been subjected to the medical tests at issue. Plaintiffs allege that the testing of their blood and urine samples for syphilis, sickle cell trait, and pregnancy occurred without their knowledge or consent, and without any subsequent notification that the tests had been conducted. They also allege that only black employees were tested for sickle cell trait and assert the obvious fact that only female employees were tested for pregnancy. Finally, they allege that Lawrence failed to provide safeguards to prevent the dissemination of the test results. They contend that they did not discover that the disputed tests had been conducted until approximately January 1995, and specifically deny that they observed any signs indicating that such tests would be performed....

We first examine [the district court's] ruling with respect to the claim for violation of the federal constitutional right to privacy. While acknowledging that the government had failed to identify any "undisputed legitimate governmental purpose" for the three tests, the district court concluded that no violation of plaintiffs' right to privacy could have occurred because any intrusions arising from the testing were de minimis in light of (1) the "large overlap" between the subjects covered by the medical questionnaire and the three tests and (2) the "overall intrusiveness" of "a full-scale physical examination." We hold that the district court erred.

The constitutionally protected privacy interest in avoiding disclosure of personal matters clearly encompasses medical information and its confidentiality. *Doe v. Attorney General of the United States*, 941 F.2d 780, 795 (9th Cir. 1991) (citing *United States v. Westinghouse Elec. Corp.*, 638 F.2d 570, 577 (3d Cir. 1980)); *Roe v. Sherry*, 91 F.3d 1270, 1274 (9th Cir. 1996); *see also Doe v. City of New York*, 15 F.3d 264, 267–69 (2d Cir. 1994). Although cases defining the privacy interest in medical information have typically involved its disclosure to "third" parties, rather than the collection of information by illicit means, it goes without saying that the most basic violation possible involves the performance of unauthorized tests—that is, the non-consensual retrieval of previously unrevealed medical information that may be unknown even to plaintiffs. These tests may also be viewed as searches in violation of Fourth Amendment rights that require Fourth Amendment scrutiny. The tests at issue in this case thus implicate rights protected under both the Fourth Amendment and the Due Process Clause of the Fifth or Fourteenth Amendments. *Yin v. California*, 95 F.3d 864, 870 (9th Cir. 1996), *cert. denied*, 519 U.S. 1114 (1997).

Because it would not make sense to examine the collection of medical information under two different approaches, we generally "analyze [medical tests and examinations] under the rubric of [the Fourth] Amendment." 95 F.3d at 871 & n. 12. Accordingly, we must balance the government's interest in conducting these particular tests against the plaintiffs' expectations of privacy. 95 F.3d at 873. Furthermore, "application of the balancing test requires not only considering the degree of intrusiveness and the state's interests in requiring that intrusion, but also 'the efficacy of this [the state's] means for meeting' its needs." *Id.* (quoting *Vernonia Sch. Dist. 47J v. Acton*, 515 U.S. 646, 660 (1995)).

The district court erred in dismissing the claims on the ground that any violation was de minimis, incremental, or overlapping....

One can think of few subject areas more personal and more likely to implicate privacy interests than that of one's health or genetic make-up. Furthermore, the facts revealed by the tests are highly sensitive, even relative to other medical information. With respect to the testing of plaintiffs for syphilis and pregnancy, it is well established in this circuit "that the Constitution prohibits unregulated, unrestrained employer inquiries into personal sexual matters that have no bearing on job performance." The fact that one has syphilis is an intimate matter that pertains to one's sexual history and may invite tremendous amounts of social stigma. Pregnancy is likewise, for many, an intensely private matter, which also may pertain to one's sexual history and often carries far-reaching societal implications. Finally, the carrying of sickle cell trait can pertain to sensitive information about family history and reproductive decision making. Thus, the conditions tested for were aspects of one's health in which one enjoys the highest expectations of privacy.

As discussed above, with respect to the question of the statute of limitations, there was little, if any, "overlap" between what plaintiffs consented to and the testing at issue here. Nor was the additional invasion only incremental. In some instances, the tests related to entirely different conditions. In all, the information obtained as the result of the testing was qualitatively different from the information that plaintiffs provided in their answers to the questions, and was highly invasive. That one has consented to a general medical examination does not abolish one's privacy right not to be tested for intimate, personal matters involving one's health—nor does consenting to giving blood or urine samples, or filling out a questionnaire. As we have made clear, revealing one's personal knowledge as to whether one has a particular medical condition has nothing to do with one's expectations about actually being tested for that condition. Thus, the intrusion was by no means de minimis. Rather, if unauthorized, the testing constituted a significant invasion of a right that is of great importance, and labeling it minimal cannot and does not make it so.

Lawrence further contends that the tests in question, even if their intrusiveness is not de minimis, would be justified by an employer's interest in performing a general physical examination. This argument fails because issues of fact exist with respect to whether the testing at issue is normally part of a general physical examination. There would of course be no violation if the testing were authorized, or if the plaintiffs reasonably should have known that the blood and urine samples they provided would be used for the disputed testing and failed to object. However, as we concluded in Section I, material issues of fact exist as to those questions. Summary judgment in the alternative on the merits of the federal constitutional privacy claim was therefore incorrect....

To assert a cause of action under Article I, § 1 of the California Constitution, one must establish three elements: (1) a legally protected privacy interest; (2) a reasonable expectation of privacy under the circumstances; and (3) conduct by the defendant that amounts to a "serious invasion" of the protected privacy interest. These elements must be "viewed simply as 'threshold elements,' "after which the court must conduct a balancing test between the "countervailing interests" for the conduct in question and the intrusion on privacy resulting from the conduct. A showing of "countervailing interests" may, in turn, be rebutted by a showing that there were "feasible and effective alternatives" with a "lesser impact on privacy interests."

For much the same reasons as we have discussed above with respect to the statute of limitations and federal privacy claims, the district court erred in dismissing the state constitutional privacy claim. The only possible difference between the state claim and the federal claim is the threshold requirement that the invasion be serious, and for purposes of summary judgment, that requirement has been more than met. For the reasons discussed above, we find that material issues of fact exist with respect to whether the defendants had any interest at all in obtaining the information and whether plaintiffs had a reasonable expectation of privacy under the circumstances. Both these questions involve a factual dispute regarding the ordinary or accepted medical practice regarding general or pre-employment medical exams. Accordingly, the district court also erred in dismissing the state constitutional privacy claims....

Sherman v. Jones

258 F. Supp. 2d 440 (E.D. Va. 2003)

ELLIS, DISTRICT JUDGE.

Plaintiff, a Virginia inmate proceeding pro se, filed this complaint pursuant to 42 U.S.C. § 1983, alleging that the remaining defendant, Deputy Jones ("Jones"), violated his constitutional right to privacy by revealing his HIV status in the presence of other inmates.... For the following reasons, plaintiff's claim must be dismissed for failure to state a claim upon which relief may be granted.

In his complaint, plaintiff alleges that on September 16, 2002, he approached Jones, a deputy sheriff at the Arlington Detention Facility, to ask her about receiving a "snack bag." Plaintiff further alleges that Jones responded by stating loudly, "Get away from the desk," and "I'm not scared of you or your AIDS." Plaintiff also alleges that Jones' loud statement was overheard by other inmates in the vicinity at the time. Plaintiff's claim is that by making public plaintiff's HIV status, Jones violated plaintiff's constitutional right to privacy and is accordingly liable to plaintiff under § 1983.... Accordingly, the sole question presented is whether plaintiff has a constitutional right to privacy with respect to his HIV status that was violated by Jones' conduct....

The Supreme Court has never proclaimed a "general constitutional right to privacy." *Whalen v. Roe*, 429 U.S. 589, 607–08 (1977) (Stewart, J., concurring) (quoting *Katz v. United States*, 389 U.S. 347, 350 (1967)). It is also true that the Constitution nowhere explicitly mentions such a fundamental privacy right.

Yet, the Supreme Court, to be sure, has found a constitutional right to privacy lurking in various amendments to the Constitution and, in this respect, it is clear that the Supreme Court has extended that constitutional right to certain "zones of privacy," including private decisions involving marriage, procreation, contraception abortion, and child raising and education. But significantly, the Supreme Court has carefully avoided creating a broad, fundamental privacy right, noting that the matter of general individual privacy rights is an issue that should be "left largely to the law of the individual States." *Katz*, 389 U.S. at 351.

Consistent with this principle, there is no Supreme Court declaration that an individual's confidential medical information falls within a constitutionally protected "zone of privacy." Particularly instructive in this regard is *Whalen v. Roe*, 429 U.S. 589 (1977). There, doctors and patients challenged the constitutionality of a New York statute that required disclosure to the state of the names and addresses of individuals who received prescriptions for Schedule II drugs. Plaintiffs in Whalen argued that the patients had a constitutional right to privacy in their medical information and that the law "invade[d] a constitutionally protected 'zone of privacy.'" ... [J]ustice Stevens elected not to adopt this principle, choosing instead to hold simply that "neither the immediate nor the threatened impact of the patient-identification requirements in the [state law] ... is sufficient to constitute an invasion of any right or liberty protected by the Fourteenth Amendment." Thus, Justice Stevens, speaking for the Court, declined the opportunity to label any privacy interest in medical records as a fundamental constitutional right, focusing instead on the fact that the New York statute would not likely result in the public dissemination of patients' medical information. It is clear, however, a different result would have obtained had the Supreme Court found a fundamental constitutional right to privacy in an individual's medical information, for in that circumstance, the statute would have contravened that right because it required the release of presumably protected personal medical information. Thus, Whalen points persuasively to the conclusion that there is no general fundamental constitutional right to privacy in personal medical information.

Authority in this circuit is to the same effect. Thus, the Fourth Circuit has also declined invitations to declare a constitutional right to privacy in one's personal medical information. *See Watson v. Lowcountry Red Cross*, 974 F.2d 482, 487–89 n. 9 (4th Cir. 1992); *Taylor v. Best*, 746 F.2d 220, 225 (4th Cir. 1984)....

In the instant case, plaintiff is alleging that Jones violated his constitutional right to privacy by stating within earshot of other inmates that plaintiff has HIV. Yet, it appears that viewing the facts in the light most favorable to plaintiff, plaintiff is claiming the violation of a privacy right that has not been recognized by either the Supreme Court or the Fourth Circuit. Nor does the privacy right claimed by plaintiff fall within the ambit of any of the various "zones of privacy" recognized by the Supreme Court. Accordingly, it follows that defendant's conduct did not violate any constitutional right. Hence, this complaint must be dismissed pursuant to § 1915A(b)(1) for failure to state a claim upon which relief may be granted....

It may well be sensible public policy to provide legal protection to ensure the privacy of medical records. Indeed, most persons would so conclude, although perhaps not in all circumstances or for all kinds of medical information. Yet, even assuming that privacy protection should be accorded to an individual's medical information, the nature and scope of that protection is more sensibly determined by elected legislators via state or federal statute, rather than by judicial stretching of the constitutional text to reach a subject not explicitly treated in the text. This is so because "[i]nferring very broad 'constitutional' rights where the Constitution itself does not express them is an activity not appropriate to the judiciary." ...

Notes & Questions

1. *Whalen v. Roe* is considered by many to be the leading case on the constitutional dimension of medical privacy. To what extent does the Court's opinion recognize a constitutional right to medical privacy? How is the Court's opinion interpreted and applied in *Sherman v. Jones*? In the *Bloodsaw* case, although the Ninth Circuit recognizes a constitutionally protected privacy interest in medical information, it does not cite to the *Whalen* opinion. Why might this be? The *Sherman* and *Bloodsaw* opinions highlight the split among the circuit courts regarding the existence and extent of a constitutional right to medical privacy. Additional authorities on this issue include: *Tokar v. Armontrout*, 97 F.3d 1078 (8th Cir. 1996) (inmates do not have a clearly established constitutional right to privacy in their HIV status); *Doe v. Wigginton*, 21 F.3d 733 (6th Cir. 1994) (there is no general constitutional right to nondisclosure of private information); *Doe v. City of New York*, 15 F.3d 264 (2d Cir. 1994) (recognizing a constitutional right to privacy regarding HIV status); *A.L.A. v. West Valley City*, 26 F.3d 989 (10th Cir. 1994) (recognizing the existence of constitutional privacy protection for confidential medical information).

2. Medical privacy is generally thought to encompass four dimensions, which Anita Allen has summarized and applied to genetics: informational privacy, decisional privacy, physical privacy, and proprietary privacy.

> "Genetic privacy" is no less rich in ambiguity than "privacy." Although the expression "genetic privacy" is a product of recent developments in science, it

> does not stand for a wholly new concept. "Genetic privacy" signifies applications of the familiar concept of privacy to genetic-related phenomena.
>
> When used to label issues that arise in contemporary bioethics and public policy, "privacy" generally refers to one of four categories of concern. They are: (1) informational privacy concerns about access to personal information; (2) physical privacy concerns about access to persons and personal spaces; (3) decisional privacy concerns about governmental and other third-party interference with personal choices; and (4) proprietary privacy concerns about the appropriation and ownership of interests in human personality. "Genetic privacy" typically refers to one of these same four general categories."

Anita L. Allen, *Genetic Privacy: Emerging Concepts and Values*, *in* GENETIC SECRETS: PROTECTING PRIVACY AND CONFIDENTIALITY IN THE GENETIC ERA 31, 33–34 (Mark A. Rothstein ed. 1997). Which of these privacy dimensions are implicated in the three cases featured in this section? How might issues surrounding access to and disclosure of genetic information trigger privacy concerns in each of these dimensions?

What are the privacy concerns that attend storage of biologic samples collected in the course of medical care and treatment or for purposes of medical research? What types of privacy protections do the featured cases suggest need to be in place to withstand a constitutional challenge to centralized computer-based storage of individual health or health care data and under what circumstances might state interests take precedence? What if, as in the *Whalen* case, the data is stored for law enforcement purposes? For a more in-depth look at issues pertaining to DNA databanks *see* Chapter 9.

3. The three featured cases discuss the scope of constitutional protections for medical privacy, considering the issue from the individual, fundamental rights perspective. Some advocate for the recognition of property rights in genetic information as another way to control access. *See* George J. Annas, *Genetic Privacy: There Ought to Be a Law*, 4 TEX. REV. L. & POL. 9 (1999); Sonia M. Suter, *Disentangling Privacy from Property: Toward a Deeper Understanding of Genetic Privacy*, 72 GEO. WASH. L. REV. 737 (2004). In the leading court case on this issue, the California Supreme Court declined to recognize a patient's conversion claim arising from the alleged unauthorized use of genetic tissue for biomedical research and ultimate entrepreneurial activity. The court described a number of policy reasons for its decision, including the observation that existing laws protecting individual privacy and autonomy provided adequate remedies for the patient's claimed injuries. In the final analysis, the court deferred the ownership issue to the legislature, *Moore v. The Regents of the Univ. of Cal.*, 793 P.2d 479 (Cal. 1990), cert. denied, 499 U.S. 936 (1991). Relevant portions of the court's opinion appear in Chapter 5. A number of state legislatures have adopted genetic privacy legislation that afford individuals property rights in their DNA (ALASKA STAT. §18.13.010(a)(2); COLO. REV. STAT. ANN. §10-3-1104.7(1)(a); FLA. STAT. ANN. §760.40(2)(a); GA. CODE ANN. §33-54-1(1)). The Oregon legislature initially passed, but ultimately repealed, legislation establishing property rights in both genetic samples and genetic information (OR. REV. STAT. §659.715(1)(1999)). Somewhat similarly, the New Jersey legislature passed a genetic privacy bill that included provisions recognizing a private property interest in individual genetic information, but then-Governor Whitman vetoed the bill. *N.J. Governor Vetoes Genetic Privacy Act*, EMP. TESTING L. & POL'Y REP., October 1996, at 160. An excerpt from the New Jersey Genetics Privacy Act appears at p. 56 *infra* in this chapter. Does the property rights model offer additional or enhanced privacy protections for genetic information and, if so, at what cost? How might the property rights model impact the delivery of health care or the progress of medical research?

4. The excerpt from the *Bloodsaw* case features the court's opinion regarding plaintiffs' state and federal privacy claims. The privacy threat in this case arose in the context of an employer-directed medical screening examination. Why might employers be interested in accessing employees' genetic information? Can you think of instances when workplace genetic screening might be potentially beneficial to employees? Plaintiffs in this case also pursued claims under Title VII of the Civil Rights Act of 1964 and the Americans with Disabilities Act (ADA). The court's opinion on these claims is discussed in Chapter 3, which is focused on genetic discrimination in the workplace. In addition, Chapter 3 summarizes the relevant federal and state laws that permit employer access to employee health care information (*see* Part B, Note 2).

2. Statutory Privacy Protections

The protection afforded to the privacy of individual health care information through federal and state constitutions is limited to incursions by the government or its agents and has no impact on the conduct of non-governmental entities that interface with health care information, including health plans, insurers, employers, and private health research enterprises. A patchwork of federal and state laws attempt to fill this void and, with increasing frequency, genetic information is subject to special statutory recognition and privacy protections. The primary public concerns are that insurers will access and use genetic information to deny, limit, or cancel insurance and employers will do the same to limit employment opportunities or benefits. Hence, privacy protections are often incorporated into legislation seeking to prevent or limit genetic discrimination, although several states have enacted specific "genetic privacy" laws. The following materials provide an introduction to relevant federal and state statutory materials.

Genetic Information Nondiscrimination Act of 2005

S. 306, 109th Congress, (1st Sess. 2005)

Sec. 102. Amendments to PUBLIC HEALTH SERVICE ACT.

...

(4) Definitions— ...

(15) Family Member.—The term 'family member' means with respect to an individual—

- (A) the spouse of the individual;
- (B) a dependent child of the individual, including a child who is born to or placed for adoption with the individual; and
- (C) all other individuals related by blood to the individual or the spouse or child described in subparagraph (A) or (B).

(16) Genetic Information.—

- (A) In General.—Except as provided in subparagraph (B), the term 'genetic information' means information about—(i) an individual's genetic tests; (ii) the genetic tests of family members of the individual; or (iii) the occurrence of a disease or disorder in family members of the individual.
- (B) Exclusions.—The term 'genetic information' shall not include information about the sex or age of an individual.

(17) GENETIC TEST.—

(A) IN GENERAL.—The term 'genetic test' means an analysis of human DNA, RNA, chromosomes, proteins, or metabolites, that detects genotypes, mutations or chromosomal changes.

(B) EXCEPTIONS.—The term 'genetic test' does not mean—

(i) an analysis of proteins or metabolites that does not detect genotypes, mutations or chromosomal changes; or

(ii) an analysis of proteins or metabolites that is directly related to a manifested disease, disorder, or pathological condition that could reasonably be detected by a health care professional with appropriate training and expertise in the field of medicine involved.

(18) GENETIC SERVICES.—The term 'genetic services' means—

(A) a genetic test;

(B) genetic counseling (such as obtaining, interpreting, or assessing genetic information); or

(C) genetic education".

SEC. 104. PRIVACY AND CONFIDENTIALITY.

(a) APPLICABILITY.—Except as provided in subsection (s), the provisions of this section shall apply to group health plans, health insurance issuers (including issuers in connection with group health plans or individual health coverage), and issuers of Medicare supplemental policies....

(b) COMPLIANCE WITH CERTAIN CONFIDENTIALITY STANDARDS WITH RESPECT TO GENETIC INFORMATION.—

(1) IN GENERAL.—The regulations promulgated by the Secretary of Health and Human Services under part C of title XI of the Social Security Act (42 USC 1320d et sep.) and section 264 of the Health Insurance Portability and Accountability Act of 1996 (42 U.S.C. 1320d-2 note) shall apply to the use or disclosure of genetic information.

(2) PROHIBITION ON UNDERWRITING AND PREMIUM RATING.—Notwithstanding paragraph (1) a group health plan, a health insurance issuer, or issuer of a medicare supplemental policy shall not use or disclose genetic information (including information about a request for or a receipt of genetic services by an individual or family member of such individual) for purposes of underwriting, determinations of eligibility to enroll, premium rating or the creation, renewal or replacement of a plan, contract or coverage for health insurance or health benefits.

(c) PROHIBITION ON COLLECTION OF GENETIC INFORMATION.—

(1) IN GENERAL.—A group health plan, health insurance issuer, or issuer of a medicare supplemental policy shall not request, require, or purchase genetic information (including information about a request for or a receipt of genetic services by an individual or family member of such individual) for purposes of underwriting, determinations of eligibility to enroll, premium rating, or the creation, renewal or replacement of a plan, contract or coverage for health insurance or health benefits.

(2) Limitation Relating to the Collection of Genetic Information Prior to Enrollment.—A group health plan ... shall not request, require, or purchase genetic information (including information about a request for or a receipt of genetic services by an individual or family member of such individual) concerning a participant, beneficiary, or enrollee prior to the enrollment, and in connection with such enrollment, of such individual under the plan, coverage or policy.

(3) Incidental Collection.—Where a group health plan ... obtains genetic information incidental to the requesting, requiring, or purchasing of other information concerning a participant, beneficiary, or enrollee, such request, requirement or purchase shall not be considered a violation of this subsection if—(A) such request, requirement, or purchase is not in violation of paragraph (1); and (B) any genetic information (including information about a request for or receipt of genetic services) requested, required, or purchased is not used or disclosed in violation of subsection (b).

(d) Application of Confidentiality Standards.—The provisions of subsections (b) and (c) shall not apply—

...

(2) to genetic information that is not considered to be individually-identifiable health information under the regulations promulgated by the Secretary ... under ... section 264 of the Health Insurance Portability and Accountability Act of 1996....

(e) Enforcement.—A group health plan, health insurance issuer ... that violates a provision of this section shall be subject to the penalties described in sections 1176 and 1177 of the Social Security Act (42 U.S.C. 1320d-5 and 1320d-6) I the same manner and to the same extent that such penalties apply to violations of part C of title XI of such Act.

(f) Preemption.—

(1) In General.—A provision or requirement under this section or a regulation promulgated under this section shall supersede any contrary provision of State law unless such provision of State law imposes requirements, standards, or implementation specifications that are more stringent than the requirements, standards or implementation specifications imposed under this section or such regulations. No penalty, remedy, or cause of action to enforce such a State law that is more stringent shall be preempted by this section.

(2) Rule of Construction.—Nothing in paragraph (1) shall be construed to establish a penalty, remedy, or cause of action under State law if such penalty, remedy, or cause of action is not otherwise available under such State law.

(g) Coordination With Privacy Regulations.—The Secretary shall implement and administer this section in a manner that is consistent with the implementation and administration by the Secretary of the regulations promulgated by the Secretary ... under ... the Social Security Act ... and ... the Health Insurance Portability and Accountability Act of 1996....

(h) Definitions.—In this section:

(1) GENETIC INFORMATION; GENETIC SERVICES.—The terms "family member", "genetic information", "genetic services", and "genetic test: have the meanings given such terms in section 2791 of the Public Health Service Act (42 U.S.C. 300 gg-91) as amended by this act....

* * *

The Genetic Information Nondiscrimination Act of 2005 (S. 306) is representative of the types of genetic privacy and genetic discrimination legislation under consideration at the federal level. Senate Resolution 306 was approved in the U.S. Senate on February 17, 2005 (98–0). At the end of 2005 its counter part in the U.S. House of Representatives (H.R. 1227) had not been voted on. A similar chronology occurred in 2003 when the Senate passed a comparable bill, S. 1053, only to have it languish in the House. The National Human Genome Research Institute (NHGRI) at the National Institutes of Health maintains a legislative database with a comprehensive listing of relevant bills introduced into the U.S. Congress and relevant state laws, with links to full text of proposed legislation and current statutes, http://www.genome.gov.

The privacy provisions of S. 306 expressly incorporate the privacy and confidentiality standards of the Health Insurance Portability and Accountability Act of 1996 (HIPAA) Pub. L. No. 104-191, §264, 110 Stat. 1936 (1996). HIPAA authorized the Secretary of Health and Human Services Services to promulgate federal regulations protecting the privacy and confidentiality of individual health care information. The resulting "HIPAA Privacy Rule" (45 C.F.R. Parts 160, 164) became effective in April, 2001 following extensive public comment (over 52,000 comments).

The Privacy Rule addresses the use and disclosure of individually identifiable health information by health plans, health care clearinghouses, and health care providers (both individual and institutional providers) who transmit health information in electronic form. In general, these "covered entities" may not use or disclose an individual's protected health information without their written authorization except for purposes of treatment, payment, health care operations, or public health and safety purposes including state public health reporting laws and law enforcement. Protected health care information (PHI) is defined as all individually identifiable information that is transmitted or maintained by a covered entity in any form or medium. Thus PHI includes an individual's entire medical and mental health care history, along with information regarding payment for that care. The Privacy Rule also contains specific provisions relating to the use and disclosure of protected health care information in research.

A complex regulatory framework, the HIPAA Privacy Rule represents the first comprehensive effort of the federal government to set national standards for health information privacy. By its terms it is intended to set the floor, explicitly permitting states to enact more protective rules, CFR § 160.203, which many states have done or are in the process of considering. The enforcement provisions do not establish a private cause of action or remedy but rather contemplate administrative enforcement with significant civil penalties and/or criminal liability. Information on the HIPAA Privacy Rules is available at http://www.hhs.gov/ocr/hipaa and Georgetown's Health Privacy Project, http://www.healthprivacy.org. For a comprehensive discussion of the regulations and how they compare with common law protections *see* Peter Winn, *Confidentiality in Cyberspace: The HIPAA Privacy Rules and the Common Law*, 33 RUTGERS L.J. 617 (2002). Additional references include Arthur S. Di Dio, *The Hype About HIPAA: Standards for Privacy of Individually Identifiable Health Information*, 6 PERSPECTIVES ON LEGISLATION, REGULATION, & LITIGATION 1 (2002); Lawrence O. Gostin & James G. Hodge, Jr., *Per-*

sonal Privacy and Common Goods: A Framework for Balancing Under the National Health Information Privacy Rule, 86 MINN. L. REV. 1439 (2002); Peter D. Jacobson, *Medical Records and HIPAA: Is It Too Late To Protect Privacy?* 86 MINN. L. REV. 1497 (2002); James G. Hodge, Jr., *Health Information Privacy and Public Health*, 31 J.L. MED. & ETHICS 663 (2003); Mark A. Rothstein, *Research Privacy Under HIPAA and the Common Rule*, 33 J.L. MED. & ETHICS 154 (2005). For a discussion of other federal legislation that relates to health information privacy generally *see* Lawrence O. Gostin, *Health Information Privacy*, 80 CORNELL L. REV. 451 (1995).

HIPAA does not offer extraordinary protection to genetic information; it is afforded the same protection as medical information generally and subject to the same exceptions permitting disclosure without a patient's consent. What are costs associated with treating genetic information differently? What are the benefits? If you were a member of the U.S. House of Representatives, how would you vote on the pending federal legislation (H.R. 1227) and why?

Notes & Questions

1. Why has the U.S. Congress been slow to adopt legislation relating specifically to the privacy of genetic information? It may relate in part to ongoing debate about the need for or wisdom of affording extraordinary protection to genetic information as distinct from health care information generally. While not opposed to genetic privacy, the opponents of exceptional treatment for genetic information focus on the need to strike the appropriate balance between individual interests in controlling access to genetic information and broader social interests in law enforcement, public health, and efficient, effective health care delivery. *See* Sonia M. Suter, *The Allure and Peril of Genetics Exceptionalism: Do We Need Special Genetics Legislation?* 79 WASH. U. L.Q. 669 (2001); Henry T. Greely, *Genotype Discrimination: the Complex Case for Some Legislative Protection*, 149 U. PA. L. REV. 1483 (2001); Martin Richards, *How Distinctive is Genetic Information?* 32 STUD. HIST. PHIL. BIOL. & BIOMED. SCI. 663 (2001); Lawrence O. Gostin & James G. Hodge, Jr. *Genetic Privacy and the Law: An End to Genetics Exceptionalism*, 40 JURIMETRICS J. 21 (1999); George J. Annas, *Genetic Privacy: There Ought to be a Law*, 4 TEX. REV. L. & POL. 9 (1999); Thomas H. Murray, *Genetic Exceptionalism and "Future Diaries": Is Genetic Information Different from Other Medical Information? in* GENETIC SECRETS: PROTECTING PRIVACY AND CONFIDENTIALITY IN THE GENETIC ERA 60–73 (M.A. Rothstein ed. 1997); Lawrence O. Gostin, *Genetic Privacy*, 23 J.L. MED. & ETHICS 320 (1995).

Executive Order No. 13145, 65 FED. REG. 6877, To Prohibit Discrimination in Federal Employment Based on Genetic Information

February 8, 2000

By the authority vested in me as President of the United States by the Constitution and the laws of the United States of America, it is ordered as follows:

Section 1. Nondiscrimination in Federal Employment on the Basis of Protected Genetic Information.

1-101. It is the policy of the Government of the United States to provide equal employment opportunity in Federal employment for all qualified persons and to prohibit discrimination against employees based on protected genetic information, or information about a request for or the receipt of genetic services. This policy of equal opportunity applies to every aspect of Federal employment....

1-201. Definitions.

...

(c) Genetic services means health services, including genetic tests, provided to obtain, assess, or interpret genetic information for diagnostic or therapeutic purposes, or for genetic education or counseling.

(d) Genetic test means the analysis of human DNA, RNA, chromosomes, proteins, or certain metabolites in order to detect disease-related genotypes or mutations. Tests for metabolites fall within the definition of "genetic tests" when an excess or deficiency of the metabolites indicates the presence of a mutation or mutations....

(e) Protected genetic information.

(1) In general, protected genetic information means:

(A) information about an individual's genetic tests;

(B) information about the genetic tests of an individual's family members; or

(C) information about the occurrence of a disease, or medical condition or disorder in family members of the individual.

(2) Information about an individual's current health status (including information about sex, age, physical exams, and chemical, blood, or urine analyses) is not protected genetic information unless it is described in subparagraph (1).

1-202. In discharging their responsibilities under this order, departments and agencies shall implement the following nondiscrimination requirements.

...

(c) The employing department or agency shall not request, require, collect, or purchase protected genetic information with respect to an employee, or information about a request for or the receipt of genetic services by such employee.

(d) The employing department or agency shall not disclose protected genetic information with respect to an employee, or information about a request for or the receipt of genetic services by an employee except:

(1) to the employee who is the subject of the information, at his or her request;

(2) to an occupational or other health researcher, if the research conducted complies with the regulations and protections provided for under part 46 of title 45, of the Code of Federal Regulations;

(3) if required by a Federal statute, congressional subpoena, or an order issued by a court of competent jurisdiction, except that if the subpoena or court order was secured without the knowledge of the individual to whom the information refers, the employer shall provide the

individual with adequate notice to challenge the subpoena or court order, unless the subpoena or court order also imposes confidentiality requirements; or

(4) to executive branch officials investigating compliance with this order, if the information is relevant to the investigation.

(e) The employing department or agency shall not maintain protected genetic information or information about a request for or the receipt of genetic services in general personnel files; such information shall be treated as confidential medical records and kept separate from personnel files.

Sec. 3. Exceptions.

1-301. The following exceptions shall apply to the nondiscrimination requirements set forth in section 1-202.

(a) The employing department or agency may request or require information defined in section 1-201(e)(1)(C) with respect to an applicant who has been given a conditional offer of employment or to an employee if:

(1) the request or requirement is consistent with the Rehabilitation Act and other applicable law;

(2) the information obtained is to be used exclusively to assess whether further medical evaluation is needed to diagnose a current disease, or medical condition or disorder, or under the terms of section 1-301(b) of this order;

(3) such current disease, or medical condition or disorder could prevent the applicant or employee from performing the essential functions of the position held or desired; and

(4) the information defined in section 1-201(e)(1)(C) of this order will not be disclosed to persons other than medical personnel involved in or responsible for assessing whether further medical evaluation is needed to diagnose a current disease, or medical condition or disorder, or under the terms of section 1-301(b) of this order.

(b) The employing department or agency may request, collect, or purchase protected genetic information with respect to an employee, or any information about a request for or receipt of genetic services by such employee if:

(1) the employee uses genetic or health care services provided by the employer ... ;

(2) the employee who uses the genetic or health care services has provided prior knowing, voluntary, and written authorization to the employer to collect protected genetic information;

(3) the person who performs the genetic or health care services does not disclose protected genetic information to anyone except to the employee who uses the services for treatment of the individual; pursuant to section 1-202(d) of this order; for program evaluation or assessment; for compiling and analyzing information in anticipation of or for use in a civil or criminal legal proceeding; or, for payment or accounting purposes, to verify that the service was performed (but in such cases the genetic information itself cannot be disclosed);

(4) such information is not used in violation of sections 1-202(a) or 1-202(b) of this order....

(d) Genetic monitoring of biological effects of toxic substances in the workplace shall be permitted if all of the following conditions are met:

(1) the employee has provided prior, knowing, voluntary, and written authorization;

(2) the employee is notified when the results of the monitoring are available and, at that time, the employer makes any protected genetic information that may have been acquired during the monitoring available to the employee and informs the employee how to obtain such information;

(3) the monitoring conforms to any genetic monitoring regulations that may be promulgated by the Secretary of Labor; and

(4) the employer, excluding any licensed health care professionals that are involved in the genetic monitoring program, receives results of the monitoring only in aggregate terms that do not disclose the identity of specific employees....

Notes & Questions

1. President Clinton's Executive Order of February 8, 2000, was issued to protect employees and applicants for employment in the executive branch of the federal government from discrimination on the basis of protected genetic information and to challenge, by way of example, all employers in America to adopt genetic nondiscrimination policies. EEOC Policy Guidance on Executive Order 13145, http://www.lawmemo.com/eeoc/genetic.htm. It incorporates strong privacy protections for employees' and applicants' genetic information, which are set forth in the featured excerpt (the remaining provisions are excerpted in Chapter 3). For example, it precludes employer access to an employee's protected genetic information and prohibits disclosure of this information, with very limited exceptions. What are the exceptions and how do they compare with the exceptions outlined in the HIPPA Privacy Rules? Additionally, the Order requires employers to assure the confidentiality of protected genetic information, in part by maintaining the information in confidential files that are separate from the employee's personnel files. One of the challenges for compliance with this or any genetic privacy or genetic discrimination legislation is deciding what falls under the ambit of "genetic information." How does the Executive Order define "protected genetic information"? Is the definition limited to genetic test results or does it encompass other indicia of the presence of inherited traits that may be associated with disease or disability? What role does "family history" play in the definition of "protected genetic information"? Look at the Executive Order's definition of a "genetic test": what is the difference between analyses of human DNA, RNA, and chromosomes on the one hand and proteins or metabolites on the other hand? In fact, the Order defines "protected genetic information" rather broadly. What are the implications of this approach compared with a definition that is focused solely on the results of tests that identify individual genotype? For a discussion of the challenges associated with developing an appropriate "working definition" of genetic information, *see* Mark A. Rothstein, *Why Treating Genetic Information Separately Is a Bad Idea*, 4 Tex. Rev. L. & Pol. 33 (1998).

New Jersey Genetic Privacy Act, N.J. Stat. Ann. §§ 10:5-43 to 5-49

(West 2005) (enacted in 1997)

10:5-43. Short title; Genetic Privacy Act Sections 1 through 10 of this act shall be known and may be cited as the "Genetic Privacy Act."

10:5-44. Legislative findings and declarations

The Legislature finds and declares:

a. The DNA molecule contains information about an individual's probable medical future. This information is written in a code that is rapidly being broken.

b. Genetic information is personal information that should not be collected, retained or disclosed without the individual's authorization.

c. The improper collection, retention or disclosure of genetic information can lead to significant harm to the individual, including stigmatization and discrimination in areas such as employment, education, health care and insurance.

d. An analysis of an individual's DNA provides information not only about an individual, but also about the individual's parents, siblings and children, thereby impacting family privacy, including reproductive decisions.

e. Current legal protections for medical information, tissue samples and DNA samples are inadequate to protect genetic privacy.

f. Laws for the collection, storage and use of identifiable DNA samples and private genetic information obtained from those samples are needed both to protect individual privacy and to permit legitimate genetic research.

g. Progress in mapping the genes that cause breast cancer and other diseases has far outpaced the development of a legal and ethical context in which genetic information can be properly evaluated.

h. Effective tests to determine the presence of genes that cause breast cancer and other diseases carry with them the devastating potential for discrimination against carriers of these genes.

10:5-45. Informed consent required to obtain genetic information

No person shall obtain genetic information from an individual, or from an individual's DNA sample, without first obtaining informed consent from the individual or the individual's representative ...

a. The requirements of this section shall not apply to genetic information obtained:

(1) By a State, county, municipal or federal law enforcement agency for the purposes of establishing the identity of a person in the course of a criminal investigation or prosecution;

(2) To determine paternity in accordance with the provisions of section 11 of P.L.1983, c.17 (C.9:17-48);

(3) Pursuant to the provisions of the "DNA Database and Databank Act of 1994," P.L.1994, c.136 (C.53:1-20.17 et seq.);

(4) To determine the identity of deceased individuals;

(5) For anonymous research where the identity of the subject will not be released;

(6) Pursuant to newborn screening requirements established by State or federal law; or

(7) As authorized by federal law for the identification of persons.

b. In the case of a policy of life insurance or a disability income insurance contract, informed consent shall be obtained pursuant to the provisions of P.L.1985, c.179 (C. 17:23A-1 et seq.)

10:5-46. Authorization to retain genetic information

a. No person shall retain an individual's genetic information without first obtaining authorization under the informed consent requirement of section 6 of P.L.1996, c.126 (C.10:5-45) from the individual or the individual's representative, unless:

(1) Retention is necessary for the purposes of a criminal or death investigation or a criminal or juvenile proceeding;

(2) Retention is necessary to determine paternity in accordance with the provisions of section 11 of P.L.1983, c.17 (C.9:17-48);

(3) Retention is authorized by order of a court of competent jurisdiction;

(4) Retention is made pursuant to the provisions of the "DNA Database and Databank Act of 1994," P.L.1994, c.136 (C.53:1-20.17 et seq.); or

(5) Retention of information is for anonymous research where the identity of the subject will not be released.

b. The DNA sample of an individual from which genetic information has been obtained shall be destroyed promptly upon the specific request of that individual or the individual's representative, unless:

(1) Retention is necessary for the purposes of a criminal or death investigation or a criminal or juvenile proceeding; or

(2) Retention is authorized by order of a court of competent jurisdiction.

c. A DNA sample from an individual who is the subject of a research project shall be destroyed promptly upon completion of the project or withdrawal of the individual from the project, whichever occurs first, unless the individual or the individual's representative directs otherwise by informed consent.

d. A DNA sample from an individual for insurance or employment purposes shall be destroyed promptly after the purpose for which the sample was obtained has been accomplished unless retention is authorized by order of a court of competent jurisdiction.

e. An individual or an individual's representative, promptly upon request, may inspect, request correction of and obtain genetic information from the records of the individual unless the individual directs otherwise by informed consent....

10:5-47. Conditions for disclosure of genetic information

a. Regardless of the manner of receipt or the source of genetic information, including information received from an individual, a person may not disclose or be compelled, by subpoena or any other means, to disclose the identity of an individual upon whom a genetic test has been performed or to disclose genetic information about the individual in a manner that permits identification of the individual, unless:

(1) Disclosure is necessary for the purposes of a criminal or death investigation or a criminal or juvenile proceeding;

(2) Disclosure is necessary to determine paternity ...

(3) Disclosure is authorized by order of a court of competent jurisdiction;

(4) Disclosure is made pursuant to the provisions of the "DNA Database and Databank Act of 1994," P.L.1994, c.136 (C.53:1-20.17 et seq.);

(5) Disclosure is authorized by the tested individual or the tested individual's representative by signing a consent which complies with the requirements of the Department of Health and Senior Services;

(6) Disclosure is for the purpose of furnishing genetic information relating to a decedent for medical diagnosis of blood relatives of the decedent;

(7) Disclosure is for the purpose of identifying bodies;

(8) Disclosure is pursuant to newborn screening requirements established by State or federal law;

(9) Disclosure is authorized by federal law for the identification of persons; or

(10) Disclosure is by an insurer pursuant to the requirements of P.L.1985, c.179 (C.17:23A-1 et seq.)....

10:5-49. Violations, penalties for unlawful disclosure of genetic information

a. Any person violating the provisions of sections 6 through 9, inclusive, of P.L.1996, c.126 (C.10:5-45 through C.10:5-48) shall be a disorderly person and shall be punished by a fine of $1,000, a prison term of six months, or both.

b. Any person who willfully discloses an individual's genetic information to any third party in violation of P.L.1996, c.126 shall be punished by a fine of $5,000, a prison term of one year, or both.

c. Any person who discloses an individual's genetic information in violation of P.L.1996, c.126, shall be liable to the individual for all actual damages, including damages for economic, bodily, or emotional harm which is proximately caused by the disclosure.

Notes & Questions

1. The New Jersey Genetic Privacy Act is an example of state legislation that pertains specifically to genetic information. The majority of state legislatures have adopted laws providing privacy protections for genetic information. As of 2005, sixteen states require informed consent for a third party to perform or require a genetic test or obtain genetic information; twenty-four states require informed consent to disclose genetic information, and two of these require written authorization (Washington and Rhode Island); four states mandate individual access to personal genetic information; and eighteen states impose civil and/or criminal penalties for violating genetic privacy laws. In addition, Alaska, Colorado, Florida, Georgia, and Louisiana explicitly define genetic infor-

mation as personal property. (Oregon repealed its statute affording property rights in DNA and genetic information in 2001.) The National Conference of State Legislatures maintains a complete and up-to-date listing of all state genetic privacy laws, http://www.ncsl.org.

2. State laws generally protect the privacy and confidentiality of health care information through a variety of legislative approaches. These include comprehensive medical or health care information privacy statutes; specific disease statutes such as those protecting the confidentiality of HIV information or mental health information; and, in the case of Washington and Montana, the Uniform Health Care Information Act, Wash. Rev. Code § 70.02 ; MONT. CODE ANN. § 50.16. In addition, professional licensing or practice statutes often impose standards for confidentiality. *See, e.g.*, 225 ILL. COMP. STAT. 135/1-99 (2004). Finally, statutes defining a testimonial or evidentiary physician-patient privilege generally limit the extent to which health care providers can be compelled to disclose a patient's medical information in the context of court proceedings. *See Fairfax Hospital v. Curtis,* 492 S.E.2d 642 (1977), *infra*; Lawrence O. Gostin, *Health Information Privacy,* 80 CORNELL L. REV. 451 (1995); Joy L. Pritts, *Altered States: State Health Privacy Laws and the Impact of the Federal Health Privacy Rule,* 2 YALE J. HEALTH POL'Y L. & ETHICS 325 (2002). For an example of a disease specific statutory mandate regarding confidentiality and its application *see Doe v. Marselle,* 675 A.2d 835 (Conn. 1996), defining the elements of a cause of action for violation of laws protecting the confidentiality of medical information regarding AIDS testing and treatment.

3. The push to implement genetic privacy legislation across the U. S. and at the federal level begs consideration of "genetic exceptionalism"—whether, in fact, there is anything extraordinary about genetic information compared with other types of health information that warrants special protection under the law. George Annas characterizes human DNA as a "future diary" that has a unique ability to predict the future health of an individual and his or her biologic family and create the potential for stigmatization and discrimination based upon genetic labels. George J. Annas, *Privacy Rules for DNA Databanks Protecting Coded Future Diaries,* 270 J. AM. MED. ASS'N 2346 (1993). Larry Gostin, Mark Rothstein, and others dispute the extent to which genetic information is unique from other types of medical information, particularly in its potential to stigmatize or effect discriminatory treatment. They also argue that affording genetic information special treatment under the law unfairly discriminates against people whose similar health conditions have a different pathogenesis. Lawrence O. Gostin & James G. Hodge, Jr., *Genetic Privacy and the Law: An End to Genetic Exceptionalism,* 40 JURIMETRICS J. 21 (1999). To illustrate, Mark Rothstein points out how genetic privacy and nondiscrimination laws could result in different social outcomes for the patient with hereditary breast cancer associated with mutations in the BRCA1 and BRCA2 genes compared to the patient whose breast cancer is sporadic or idiopathic in origin. Mark A. Rothstein, *Genetic Privacy and Confidentiality: Why They are so Hard to Protect,* 26 J.L. MED. & ETHICS 198 (1998).

3. Common Law Rights, Duties, and Liabilities

The types of statutory protections reviewed above vary across jurisdictions with respect to enforcement. For example, the New Jersey Genetic Privacy Act recognizes a private right of action for damages, whereas HIPAA's enforcement provisions are administrative in nature. As the following cases indicate, most jurisdictions recognize common law claims for invasion of privacy and breach of confidentiality in the context of unauthorized access to or disclosure of health care information.

Doe v. High Tech Institute, Inc.

972 P.2d 1060 (Colo. 1999)

Opinion by JUDGE DAVIDSON.

This action concerns the unauthorized testing of a blood sample and the subsequent publication of the results of that test. In his complaint against defendant, High-Tech Institute, Inc., d/b/a Cambridge College (Cambridge), plaintiff, John Doe, brought several claims for relief including, as relevant here, two claims for invasion of privacy, one premised on a theory of intrusion upon seclusion for the improper appropriation of private information, and another premised on public disclosure of private facts for the improper publication of that information. He appeals from the judgment entered against him by the trial court dismissing the claim for intrusion upon seclusion pursuant to C.R.C.P. 12(b)(5). We reverse and remand.

According to his complaint, plaintiff was a student in Cambridge's medical assistant training program. Shortly after the beginning of a class, he informed the instructor that he had tested positive for human immunodeficiency virus (HIV) as the result of an anonymous blood test and requested the instructor to treat that information as confidential.

That same month, the instructor informed the class that all students at Cambridge were required to be tested for rubella. Each student was given a consent form indicating that such test would be performed on a blood sample. Plaintiff signed and returned the consent form with the understanding that his blood sample would be tested only for rubella. Without plaintiff's knowledge, the instructor requested the laboratory doing the testing also to test plaintiff's blood sample for HIV. She did not request this test for any other student. The test yielded a positive result for HIV. The laboratory, as required under § 25-4-1402, C.R.S.1997, reported plaintiff's name, address, and positive HIV status to the Colorado Department of Health and informed Cambridge of the test results.

As a result of these events, plaintiff filed suit against Cambridge and the laboratory asserting several claims, including those described above. The laboratory moved for and was granted dismissal of the claim for intrusion upon seclusion....

In addressing the merits of this appeal, we must answer two questions: (1) Does an unreasonable intrusion upon seclusion constitute a cognizable claim for relief in Colorado; and (2) if so, has plaintiff here stated such a claim. We answer both in the affirmative....

[T]he vast majority of courts in other jurisdictions which have recognized other types of common law privacy claims, without significant debate, also have recognized the existence of a discrete claim for invasion of privacy based on intrusion upon seclusion. Although using slightly varying terms, those jurisdictions describe this claim as an intentional tort in which a plaintiff must establish that: (1) another person has intentionally intruded, physically or otherwise; (2) upon the plaintiff's seclusion or solitude; and (3) such intrusion would be offensive or objectionable to a reasonable person. This is consistent with the common law definition of invasion of privacy by intrusion upon seclusion as set forth under the Restatement (Second) of Torts § 652B (1981) which provides that: One who intentionally intrudes, physically or otherwise, upon the solitude or seclusion of another or his private affairs or concerns, is subject to liability to the other for invasion of his privacy, if the intrusion would be highly offensive to a reasonable person....

Thus, consistent with prior recognition of such claims, and in accordance with the views expressed in other jurisdictions, we see no reason in law or policy not to recognize a claim of invasion of privacy by intrusion upon one's seclusion....

Accordingly, here, the facts as alleged in plaintiff's complaint, taken as true, must show that he had a privacy interest in the seclusion of his blood sample and that the unauthorized additional test performed upon the sample was an offensive intrusion.

There are very few reported cases which involve factual circumstances similar to those presented here. However, in *Doe v. Dyer-Goode*, 566 A.2d 889 (Pa. 1989), upon considering an intrusion upon seclusion claim, the court determined that a plaintiff, by consenting to a premarital blood test, voluntarily relinquished the blood sample and, therefore, no longer held the sample in private seclusion. That court further determined that the defendant would be liable to the plaintiff only if the additional test unreasonably invaded the plaintiff's private seclusion. The court concluded that, because the plaintiff did not hold the blood sample in private seclusion, the test could not be considered an invasion.

Here, the trial court, relying on *Doe v. Dyer-Goode, supra*, similarly determined that plaintiff's act of relinquishing the blood sample with permission to conduct a specific test extinguished any seclusion plaintiff may have had in his blood sample prior to its being taken.

Cambridge argues that the trial court was correct and that a person's privacy interest ends once the blood is removed from the body and that, therefore, here, plaintiff had no reasonable expectation of privacy in his blood sample once it was drawn. We disagree. Instead, we conclude that a person has a privacy interest in his or her blood sample and in the medical information that may be obtained from it. We further conclude that an additional, unauthorized test, such as alleged here, can be sufficient to state a claim for relief for intrusion upon seclusion.

Although intrusion upon seclusion clearly encompasses an intrusion upon a physical space held in seclusion by a person, the element of seclusion also encompasses intrusions into a person's private concerns based upon a reasonable expectation of privacy in that area....

We note first that there is a generally recognized privacy interest in a person's body. Because personal information concerning a person's health may be obtained through one's blood, urine, and other bodily products, such products cannot be extracted from a person or initially tested without either consent or proper authorization. *See Skinner v. Railway Labor Executives' Ass'n*, 489 U.S. 602 (1989).

Similarly, there is a generally recognized privacy interest in information concerning one's health. *Norman-Bloodsaw v. Lawrence Berkeley Laboratory*, 135 F.3d 1260 (9th Cir.1998) (few matters are quite so personal as the status of one's health). Health records, which are compiled on the basis of tests and other examinations, generally are considered as confidential, and information contained in such records cannot be released or disclosed without a patient's consent and authorization....

Moreover, most information placed in these files is controlled by a person's consent, or withholding of permission, for certain tests. And, the mere act of placing information in these files does not make that information available to the public. Instead, there are strictly controlled, limited circumstances under which a person may obtain another's health records. *See* generally § 25-4-1404, C.R.S.1997 (prohibiting release of certain health care reports except in specified circumstances); § 10-3-1104.7(3), C.R.S.1997 (information derived from genetic testing is confidential and privileged requiring written consent of person tested for disclosure of such information).

We see little difference between a person's objectively reasonable expectation to keep in seclusion the medical information that may be obtained from a blood sample and his or her expectation to keep in seclusion information in medical files. Thus, we conclude, there is a recognizable privacy interest in a person's blood sample and the medical information that may be derived from it.

Cambridge argues that, even if plaintiff holds his blood sample in seclusion and has an expectation of privacy in such sample, here, the additional, unauthorized test conducted on his relinquished blood was so minimal, it cannot be considered an offensive intrusion as a matter of law. We disagree.

An offensive intrusion requires an unreasonable manner of intrusion or an intrusion for an unwarranted purpose. It is the degree of intrusion that determines whether such intrusion is offensive.

Here, contrary to Cambridge's assumption, the act of extracting a blood sample and the tests performed upon the sample are separate intrusions, requiring separate inquiries into a balancing of interests to determine whether each intrusion is reasonable. *Cf. Skinner v. Railway Labor Executives' Ass'n, supra* (blood draw and blood test are separate searches subject to separate analyses under the Fourth Amendment).

Simply because a blood test is unauthorized does not, of course, necessarily compromise privacy rights; the question must be whether the nature of the intrusion was such so that it can be considered unwarranted or offensive under the circumstances.

Thus, in determining if the unauthorized performance of an HIV test, such as alleged here, would be offensive or objectionable to a reasonable person, we note first that what may be unreasonably intrusive is not the physical test of a blood sample itself. Instead, it is because particular, highly personal medical information may be obtained from such test that this intrusion may be offensive to a reasonable person. Indeed, "the most basic violation [of one's right to privacy] possible involves the performance of unauthorized tests—that is, the non-consensual retrieval of previously unrevealed medical information that may be unknown even to [plaintiff]." ... *Norman-Bloodsaw v. Lawrence Berkeley Lab., supra*, 135 F.3d at 1269 (determining that testing for syphilis, pregnancy, and sickle cell trait, conducted without plaintiffs' knowledge or consent, was unreasonable).

The intrusion to be evaluated is, in this regard, the interference with a person's autonomy, that is, the right of an individual to control important health decisions, such as whether to have one's blood tested for a particular disease, condition, or genetic trait.

And, simply because at some time such condition may be known publicly does not change the fact that, by removing from an individual the decision whether to have a blood test that would make such information known—to oneself as well as to anyone else—an unwarranted test intrudes upon that person's control over decisions concerning his or her health status.

The question then becomes whether the ramifications of that loss of autonomy are serious enough so that such intrusion would be considered offensive by a reasonable person. This depends, in turn, on the nature of the specific blood test and the circumstances under which it was performed.

Importantly, then, we note that the diagnosis of HIV, the result of the unauthorized test here, carries with it a strong social stigma against the infected person. Thus, such information is unquestionably very highly sensitive, and accordingly, there is a heightened need for an individual to hold such information in seclusion, that is, to decide whether to have a blood test performed and whether to do so anonymously. *See Norman-Bloodsaw v. Lawrence Berkeley Lab., supra*, (highest expectations of privacy attach to those medical conditions which carry far-reaching social implications).

Also, the General Assembly, by providing that a person's blood may be tested for HIV only with a person's consent, tacitly has acknowledged the existence of a significant privacy interest in one's blood, and the information so derived, by enacting legislation encouraging voluntary and confidential testing for HIV.

Furthermore, we note that these statutory provisions do not require testing for HIV under any of the circumstances alleged in the complaint here. Consequently, under the circumstances here, Cambridge was not required by reason of public policy to seek an HIV test of plaintiff's blood. It remained with plaintiff to choose when, and under what conditions, his blood would be so tested.

For these reasons, we conclude that an unauthorized HIV test, under the circumstances as set forth in plaintiff's complaint, would be considered by a reasonable person as highly invasive, and therefore, such is sufficient to constitute an unreasonable or offensive intrusion.

To summarize, plaintiff's complaint alleges that Cambridge's conduct was intentional. And, unlike in *Doe v. Dyer-Goode, supra*, plaintiff gave only limited consent to the testing of his blood and asserted his desire to hold in seclusion his blood sample and the information contained in it. Plaintiff here has alleged that he specifically asserted his desire to keep in seclusion his HIV status as revealed through his blood sample. He asserted this desire to his instructor by questioning the purpose of the blood test to which his blood sample would be subjected and, only after being assured that the blood test would be for rubella only, did plaintiff give his limited consent.

In contrast, Cambridge has asserted no public policy or private interest that would warrant the need to determine the HIV status of the students in its program. And, absent a need to identify persons with HIV, Cambridge, under these circumstances, had no reason to order the blood test required to obtain such information.

We conclude that this assertion—that Cambridge, by its unauthorized request to test plaintiff's blood sample for HIV, unreasonably intruded upon his privacy—is sufficient to state a claim for relief based on invasion of privacy by intrusion upon seclusion....

Notes & Questions

1. The excerpt from *Doe v. High Tech* focuses on one of two common law claims for invasion of privacy and that is a claim for intrusion upon seclusion. What are the elements of this claim and which facts did the Colorado appellate court rely on to support its conclusion that the plaintiff had sufficiently established a *prima facie* case? The second claim, for invasion of privacy based upon public disclosure of private facts, was settled. The elements of this claim (under Colorado law) are (1) the fact disclosed was private in nature; (2) the disclosure was made to the public; (3) the disclosure was one which would be highly offensive to a reasonable person; (4) the disclosed fact was not of legitimate concern to the public; and (5) the one who disclosed the fact did so in reck-

less disregard of the private nature of the fact disclosed. One of Cambridge's arguments on appeal was that any damages the plaintiff might receive would duplicate the settlement recovery. The court disagreed. Considering the facts, why do you think the court concluded the two invasion of privacy claims were "distinct," "discrete," and "established by different facts"? Consider again the facts in the *Norman-Bloodsaw* case. Could the plaintiffs have pursued either of the two common law invasion of privacy claims involved in the *Doe v. High Tech* case? If so, which facts would you rely on to establish the elements of the claim(s)?

2. The specific type of test involved in the case and the type of personal information it revealed was critical to the court's ruling in *Doe v. High Tech*. Assume the unauthorized test had been a genetic test looking for the specific gene mutation associated with Huntington disease, that the test result was positive, and that instead of reporting the result to the health department, the instructor made a note of the result in the medical student's file. Huntington disease is an incurable neurodegenerative disease that generally manifests after age forty with uncontrolled involuntary movements, intellectual decline, depression, and psychiatric disturbance, progressing toward early death. This test is highly accurate and the gene mutation is highly penetrant, which means that if the genetic test is positive for the mutation the affected individual is nearly certain to develop this devastating disease for which there is no current treatment or cure. Would this change in facts impact the court's ruling and why?

McCormick v. England

494 S.E.2d 431 (S.C. 1998)

ANDERSON, JUDGE:

Sally McCormick filed a complaint alleging that her physician, Kent England, breached a duty of confidentiality by disclosing information about her emotional health during a divorce proceeding involving her former husband. The special circuit court judge struck the allegation from the complaint, finding it did not state a cause of action. McCormick appeals. We hold South Carolina shall recognize a cause of action for a physician's breach of a duty of confidentiality. Accordingly, we reverse and remand.

Dr. England was the family physician for McCormick, her former husband, and their children. McCormick and her husband became involved in a divorce action in which custody of the children was at issue. In support of his Motion for Emergency Relief and a Restraining Order, McCormick's husband submitted two letters to the family court regarding McCormick's emotional status. One letter was from a licensed social worker, defendant Michael Meyers, who alleged that McCormick had a severe drinking problem which caused her to be a danger to herself and to her family. The other letter was prepared by Dr. England and was addressed "To Whom It May Concern." In his letter, Dr. England diagnosed McCormick as suffering from "major depression and alcoholism, acute and chronic." Further, Dr. England stated the children had experienced school difficulties due to the family discord caused by McCormick's drinking. He stated it was his medical opinion that McCormick was "a danger to herself and to her family with her substance abuse and major depressive symptoms," and concluded that she required hospitalization. There is no indication in the record that the letter was prepared under court order....

Whether a separate tort action for a physician's breach of a duty of confidentiality exists under the common law is a novel issue in this state....

A person who lacks medical training usually must disclose much information to his or her physician which may have a bearing upon diagnosis and treatment. Such disclosures are not totally voluntary; therefore, in order to obtain cooperation, it is expected that the physician will keep such information confidential.

The belief that physicians should respect the confidences revealed by their patients in the course of treatment is a concept that has its genesis in the Hippocratic Oath, which states in pertinent part: "Whatever, in connection with my professional practice, or not in connection with it, I see or hear, in the life of men, which ought not to be spoken of abroad, I will not divulge as reckoning that all such should be kept secret." Taber's Cyclopedic Medical Dictionary 902 (17th ed., 1993).

The modern trend recognizes that the confidentiality of the physician-patient relationship is an interest worth protecting. A majority of the jurisdictions faced with the issue have recognized a cause of action against a physician for the unauthorized disclosure of confidential information unless the disclosure is compelled by law or is in the patient's interest or the public interest.

In the absence of express legislation, courts have found the basis for a right of action for wrongful disclosure in four main sources: (1) state physician licensing statutes, (2) evidentiary rules and privileged communication statutes which prohibit a physician from testifying in judicial proceedings, (3) common law principles of trust, and (4) the Hippocratic Oath and principles of medical ethics which proscribe the revelation of patient confidences. The jurisdictions that recognize the duty of confidentiality have relied on various theories for the cause of action, including invasion of privacy, breach of implied contract, medical malpractice and breach of a fiduciary duty or a duty of confidentiality....

We find the reasoning of the cases from other jurisdictions persuasive on this issue and today we join the majority and hold that an actionable tort lies for a physician's breach of the duty to maintain the confidences of his or her patient in the absence of a compelling public interest or other justification for the disclosure.

In the order from the motion for reconsideration, the trial court rejected the common law tort of breach of confidence, explaining, "I do not tarry too long with concern because in my opinion any damages which might be recovered if such a cause of action existed can here be recovered in the invasion of privacy cause of action." Although there may be some overlap between the two, we find the existence of a cause of action for invasion of privacy should not preclude our recognition of an independent tort for a physician's breach of confidence because the actions are distinguishable.

Invasion of privacy consists of the public disclosure of private facts about the plaintiff, and the gravamen of the tort is publicity as opposed to mere publication. The defendant must intentionally reveal facts which are of no legitimate public interest, as there is no right of privacy in public matters. In addition, the disclosure must be such as would be highly offensive and likely to cause serious mental injury to a person of ordinary sensibilities. *Snakenberg v. Hartford Cas. Ins. Co.*, 383 S.E.2d 2 (Ct.App.1989).

Thus, an invasion of privacy claim narrowly proscribes the conduct to that which is "highly offensive" and "likely to cause serious mental injury." This standard is not consistent with the duty attaching to a confidential relationship because it focuses on the content, rather than the source of the information. The unauthorized revelation of confidential medical information should be protected without regard to the degree of its offensiveness. The privacy standard would not protect information that happens to be very distressing to a particular patient, even though the individual would likely not have revealed it without the expectation of confidentiality.

Further, the requirement of "publicity" is a limitation which would preclude many cases involving a breach of confidentiality. Publicity involves disclosure to the public, not just an individual or a small group. However, where the information disclosed is received in confidence, "one can imagine many cases where the greatest injury results from disclosure to a single person, such as a spouse, or to a small group, such as an insurance company resisting a claim. A confidential relationship is breached if unauthorized disclosure is made to only one person not a party to the confidence, but the right of privacy does not cover such a case." Alan B. Vickery, Note, *Breach of Confidence: An Emerging Tort*, 82 Colum. L. Rev. 1426, 1442 (1982). The Note distinguished invasion of privacy from an action for breach of confidentiality: Privacy is a right against the public at large. Its doctrinal limits narrowly circumscribe the zone of proscribed conduct in order to prevent hindrance of public expression. In contrast, a right to confidentiality exists against a specific person, who, by virtue of his relationship to the confider, has notice of the duty to preserve the secrecy of clearly identifiable information. Privacy's doctrinal limits are thus unnecessary in breach-of-confidence situations, and should not bar recovery to plaintiffs deserving of a remedy. Id. at 1440.

...

For the foregoing reasons, we hold South Carolina should recognize the common law tort of breach of a physician's duty of confidentiality. Patients have the right to be candid in their disclosures of private information to their physicians without fearing this information will be disseminated throughout the community. However, this right is not absolute and must give way when disclosure is compelled by law or is in the best interest of the patient or others....

Notes & Questions

1. *McCormick v. England* introduces the common law action for breach of a duty of confidentiality and distinguishes this claim from an invasion of privacy claim. What is the difference between the two claims: what are the interests each seeks to protect or the harms each seeks to redress? Do the facts in *Doe v. High Tech supra* give rise to a breach of confidentiality claim? Why or why not? As noted in the *McCormick* opinion, a majority of jurisdictions recognize a tort claim for breach of a physician's duty to maintain confidentiality. *See* Judy E. Zelin, Annotation, *Physician's Tort Liability for Unauthorized Disclosure of Confidential Information About Patient*, 48 A.L.R. 4th 668 (1986); Allan B. Vickery, Note, *Breach of Confidence: An Emerging Tort*, 82 Colum. L. Rev. 1426 (1982). Generally the duty arises only with respect to information disclosed in the context of a physician-patient relationship where there is an assumed expectation of confidentiality by the patient. *Berger v. Sonneland*, 26 P.3d 257 (Wash. 2001). In some jurisdictions, state privacy laws may trigger liability for disclosures outside of the treatment relationship. *Washburn v. Rite Aid Corp.*, 695 A.2d 495 (R.I. 1997).

Biddle v. Warren General Hospital

715 N.E.2d 518 (Ohio 1999)

Alice Robie Resnick, J.

The third issue, as framed by the law firm, "is whether the duty to hold this patient information confidential is absolute ... or, whether, and under what circumstances the hospital may disclose the confidential information to others and for what purpose." In particular, appellants and their amici argue that a privilege should attach in this case under which a hospital may disclose confidential medical information to its attorney without obtaining prior patient authorization to do so.

We do not interpret the court of appeals' decision to provide for an absolute duty of confidentiality, but it does contain some language suggesting that a disclosure may be privileged only if mandated by statute. Disclosures of otherwise confidential medical information made pursuant to statutory mandate are certainly privileged, such as occupational diseases, diseases which are infectious, contagious, or dangerous to public health, medical conditions indicative of child abuse or neglect, and injuries indicative of criminal conduct. Otherwise, a physician would be forced into the dilemma of violating a statute for failing to report a medical condition to the appropriate state agency or incurring civil liability for disclosing it. Thus, when a physician's report "is made in the manner prescribed by law, he of course has committed no breach of duty toward his patient and has betrayed no confidence, and no liability could result." *Simonsen v. Swenson* 177 N.W. 831, 832 (Neb. 1920).

The physician also has certain duties under the common law to disclose otherwise confidential medical information concerning the public health or safety to third persons, the breach of which can result in civil liability. If a privilege to disclose were held not to attach under these circumstances, the physician would be placed in the untenable position of incurring civil liability for breaching one of two opposing common-law duties.

More important, the privilege to disclose is not necessarily coextensive with a duty to disclose.... As one court explained, the duty of confidentiality "is not absolute, and its breach is actionable only if it is wrongful, that is to say, without justification or excuse. Although public policy favors the confidentiality described herein, there is a countervailing public interest to which it must yield in appropriate circumstances." *MacDonald v. Clinger*, 84 A.D.2d 482, 487 (N.Y. 1982). Thus, special situations may exist where the interest of the public, the patient, the physician, or a third person are of sufficient importance to justify the creation of a conditional or qualified privilege to disclose in the absence of any statutory mandate or common-law duty.

We hold that in the absence of prior authorization, a physician or hospital is privileged to disclose otherwise confidential medical information in those special situations where disclosure is made in accordance with a statutory mandate or common-law duty, or where disclosure is necessary to protect or further a countervailing interest which outweighs the patient's interest in confidentiality....

It is appropriate at this point to step back for a moment and review the facts of this case. A hospital hands over to a law firm thousands of patient registration forms containing information about the medical condition of each patient, including diagnoses of alcohol and drug abuse, mental illness, and sexually transmitted diseases. The law firm reviews these forms for the sole purpose of finding amongst them potential Social Security claimants. The firm then calls these potential claimants and gives them unsolicited advice that they should take legal action in the form of obtaining SSI. In so doing, the law firm either conceals its legal identity or, according to one account, directly asked the potential claimant to engage Attorney Heller to represent her regarding a potential Social Security claim. Those who show interest are scheduled for an appointment with Heller, which is the admitted purpose of making the calls, and the law firm ultimately accepts employment (which Elliott testified was contemplated from the outset).

We can find no interest, public or private, that would justify the recognition of a privilege under these circumstances. Thus, we agree with the court of appeals that "[i]f hospitals wish to engage in this type of procedure in the future, liability can be avoided [only] by obtaining clear patient consent for this type of informational release." ...

For all the foregoing reasons, the judgment of the court of appeals is affirmed, and the cause is remanded to the trial court for further proceedings consistent with this opinion.

...

Fairfax Hospital v. Curtis

492 S.E.2d 642 (Va. 1997)

HASSELL, JUSTICE.

In this appeal we consider, among other things, whether a patient has a cause of action against a health care provider which voluntarily disseminated the patient's medical records to third parties without the patient's authorization....

Plaintiff received prenatal care at Fairfax Hospital beginning in July 1988. She was admitted to Fairfax Hospital in January 1989, and gave birth to a child, Jessie Curtis, on February 13, 1989. During the course of such treatment, she communicated personal information, including her medical history, to Fairfax Hospital's employees. Jessie later suffered a cardiopulmonary arrest and died.

In March 1990, Patricia Curtis, in her capacity as administrator of the estate of Jessie Curtis, filed a notice of claim against Fairfax Hospital System, Linda Beckett, and others, pursuant to the Virginia Medical Malpractice Act. Beckett was a nurse in the Hospital's neonatal intensive care unit at the time of Jessie's birth.

Following receipt of the notice of claim, Nancy Perrelli, INOVA Health System Foundation's Director of Legal Affairs, requested that the Hospital provide a complete copy of Patricia Curtis' medical records to Gerald R. Walsh, an attorney for the Hospital. Subsequently, Walsh directed "that a copy of the medical records be provided to Nurse Beckett." Perrelli complied with Walsh's directive.

The plaintiff's counsel learned during a discovery deposition of Beckett that she "had possession of, and had reviewed three to four days before the deposition, the medical records obtained from Perrelli, pursuant to the direction of defense counsel Walsh. Beckett brought a copy of the medical records to the deposition." The medical records contained very personal information about plaintiff's medical history before and after her pregnancy with Jessie Curtis....

In our jurisprudence, a health care provider owes a duty of reasonable care to the patient. Included within that duty is the health care provider's obligation to preserve the confidentiality of information about the patient which was communicated to the health care provider or discovered by the health care provider during the course of treatment. Indeed, confidentiality is an integral aspect of the relationship between a health care provider and a patient and, often, to give the health care provider the necessary information to provide proper treatment, the patient must reveal the most intimate aspects of his or her life to the health care provider during the course of treatment.

We hold that in the absence of a statutory command to the contrary, or absent a serious danger to the patient or others, a health care provider owes a duty to the patient not to disclose information gained from the patient during the course of treatment without the patient's authorization, and that violation of this duty gives rise to an action in tort. We observe that our holding today is consistent with decisions of most jurisdictions which have considered this issue.

The defendants suggest that even if the plaintiff has a cause of action for the wrongful disclosure of her medical records, she is not entitled to recover against them because she placed her medical condition "at issue" when she filed the notice of medical malpractice against the Hospital and others to recover damages for the death of her daughter. The plaintiff responds that she did not waive her right to the confidentiality of her medical records by ... filing, an action against the Hospital and others in her capacity as administrator for her deceased daughter's estate.

Code § 8.01-399, in effect when the wrongful disclosures were made, and which we have described as "merely a rule of evidence," *Pierce v. Caday*, 422 S.E.2d 371, 373 (Va. 1992) stated: "Except at the request of, or with the consent of, the patient, no duly licensed practitioner of any branch of the healing arts shall be required to testify in any civil action, respecting any information which he may have acquired in attending, examining or treating the patient in a professional capacity if such information was necessary to enable him to furnish professional care to the patient; provided, however, that when the physical or mental condition of the patient is at issue in such action ... no fact communicated to, or otherwise learned by, such practitioner in connection with such attendance, examination or treatment shall be privileged and disclosure may be required."

...

This statute did not automatically compel disclosure of a patient's confidential medical information in all instances, but permitted a court, in the exercise of its discretion, to require disclosure of such information. We hold that if the patient did not manifestly place his or her medical condition at issue in a civil proceeding, then the statute required a determination by a judicial officer whether the patient's condition was at issue in the civil action before the health care provider was entitled to disseminate the patient's confidential communications to third persons.

The notice of claim that the plaintiff forwarded to the Hospital and others, in her capacity as administrator of her daughter's estate, simply did not manifestly place Curtis' medical condition at issue. Thus, before disseminating such information, the Hospital was required, in accordance with the aforementioned version of Code § 8.01-399, to obtain permission from either a court or the patient. The defendants concede that they unilaterally disseminated the plaintiff's confidential medical records to an attorney and a nurse without the requisite consent from the patient or determination from a judicial officer....

The defendants assert that the trial court erred by ruling that the plaintiff was entitled to recover for emotional distress caused by the defendants' negligent acts. We disagree.

As a general rule, in tort cases, absent accompanying physical harm or wanton and willful conduct, emotional distress damages are not recoverable. However, as we noted in *Sea-Land v. O'Neal*, 297 S.E.2d 647 (Va. 1982), there are exceptions to this general rule: "[W]e have approved the recovery of damages for humiliation, embarrassment, and similar harm to feelings, although unaccompanied by actual physical injury, where a cause of action existed independently of such harm." 297 S.E.2d at 653.

Here, we are of opinion that the plaintiff's cause of action falls within the exception to the general rule because her cause of action is independent of the humiliation, embarrassment, and harm to feelings that she suffered. Without question, a patient, whose intimate personal medical information is wrongfully disseminated to third parties, will experience some degree of humiliation, embarrassment, and hurt. Under these circumstances, we perceive no logical reason to refuse recovery of emotional distress damages....

Notes & Questions

1. The featured excerpts from the courts' opinions in *Biddle v. Warren General Hospital* and *Fairfax Hospital v. Curtis* describe the many exceptions to a health care provider's duty to protect patient confidences. Under what circumstances might a provider have a competing duty to disclose and how high is the threshold for establishing that a particular disclosure is, in fact, privileged or immune from liability? What were the circumstances surrounding the contested disclosures in each of these cases and what did the court conclude regarding whether the disclosures were privileged? At the close of the opinion in the *Fairfax* case, the court turns to the issue of damages and the extent to which a plaintiff can recover damages for emotional distress associated with the alleged disclosure of confidential health care information. What does the court conclude and why?

B. Duty to Breach Confidentiality: The Evolving Duty to Warn

As the foregoing cases and materials demonstrate, the law generally recognizes and seeks to protect individual privacy rights surrounding medical information. These rights, which encompass the right to informed autonomous decision-making regarding access to personal data are not, however, absolute. Indeed the law also recognizes several exceptional circumstances in which health care providers have a competing obligation to disclose otherwise confidential information in an effort to protect third parties from harm. In this section we review the evolution of a provider's common law duty to warn third parties when her patient's health presents a risk. We end by reviewing the cases that are shaping the duty to warn family members regarding genetic risk factors.

1. Evolution of the Psychiatrist's Duty to Warn

Tarasoff v. The Regents of the University of California

551 P.2d 334 (Cal. 1976)

TOBRINER, JUSTICE.

On October 27, 1969, Prosenjit Poddar killed Tatiana Tarasoff. Plaintiffs, Tatiana's parents, allege that two months earlier Poddar confided his intention to kill Tatiana to Dr. Lawrence Moore, a psychologist employed by the Cowell Memorial Hospital at the University of California at Berkeley. They allege that on Moore's request, the campus police briefly detained Poddar, but released him when he appeared rational. They further claim that Dr. Harvey Powelson, Moore's superior, then directed that no further action be taken to detain Poddar. No one warned plaintiffs of Tatiana's peril....

We shall explain that defendant therapists cannot escape liability merely because Tatiana herself was not their patient. When a therapist determines, or pursuant to the standards of his profession should determine, that his patient presents a serious danger of violence to another, he incurs an obligation to use reasonable care to protect the intended victim against such danger. The discharge of this duty may require the therapist to take one or more of various steps, depending upon the nature of the case. Thus it may call for him to warn the intended victim or others likely to apprise the victim of the danger, to notify the police, or to take whatever other steps are reasonably necessary under the circumstances.

...

... As a general principle, a 'defendant owes a duty of care to all persons who are foreseeably endangered by his conduct, with respect to all risks which make the conduct unreasonably dangerous.' As we shall explain, however, when the avoidance of foreseeable harm requires a defendant to control the conduct of another person, or to warn of such conduct, the common law has traditionally imposed liability only if the defendant bears some special relationship to the dangerous person or to the potential victim. Since the relationship between a therapist and his patient satisfies this requirement, we need not here decide whether foreseeability alone is sufficient to create a duty to exercise reasonably care to protect a potential victim of another's conduct....

...

Defendants contend, however, that imposition of a duty to exercise reasonable care to protect third persons is unworkable because therapists cannot accurately predict whether or not a patient will resort to violence.... We recognize the difficulty that a therapist encounters in attempting to forecast whether a patient presents a serious danger of violence. Obviously we do not require that the therapist, in making that determination, render a perfect performance; the therapist need only exercise 'that reasonable degree of skill, knowledge, and care ordinarily possessed and exercised by members of (that professional specialty) under similar circumstances.' Within the broad range of reasonable practice and treatment in which professional opinion and judgment may differ, the therapist is free to exercise his or her own best judgment without liability; proof, aided by hindsight, that he or she judged wrongly is insufficient to establish negligence.

...

The risk that unnecessary warnings may be given is a reasonable price to pay for the lives of possible victims that may be saved. We would hesitate to hold that the therapist who is aware that his patient expects to attempt to assassinate the President of the United States would not be obligated to warn the authorities because the therapist cannot predict with accuracy that his patient will commit the crime.

Defendants further argue that free and open communication is essential to psychotherapy; that 'Unless a patient ... is assured that ... information (revealed by him) can and will be held in utmost confidence, he will be reluctant to make the full disclosure upon which diagnosis and treatment ... depends.' (Sen.Com. on Judiciary, comment on Evid.Code, § 1014.) The giving of a warning, defendants contend, constitutes a breach of trust which entails the revelation of confidential communications.

...

We realize that the open and confidential character of psychotherapeutic dialogue encourages patients to express threats of violence, few of which are ever executed. Certainly a therapist should not be encouraged routinely to reveal such threats; such disclosures could seriously disrupt the patient's relationship with his therapist and with the persons threatened. To the contrary, the therapist's obligations to his patient require that he not disclose a confidence unless such disclosure is necessary to avert danger to others, and even then that he do so discreetly, and in a fashion that would preserve the privacy of his patient to the fullest extent compatible with the prevention of the threatened danger.

The revelation of a communication under the above circumstances is not a breach of trust or a violation of professional ethics; as stated in the Principles of Medical Ethics of the American Medical Association (1957), section 9: 'A physician may not reveal the confidence entrusted to him in the course of medical attendance ... Unless he is required to do so by law or unless it becomes necessary in order to protect the welfare of the individual or of the community.' We conclude that the public policy favoring protection of the confidential character of patient-psychotherapist communications must yield to the extent to which disclosure is essential to avert danger to others. The protective privilege ends where the public peril begins....

Notes & Questions

1. Justice Tobriner's opinion in the *Tarasoff* case is generally recognized as the classic case defining the scope of a health care provider's duty to warn a third party regarding confidential patient information that poses a risk to that third party. When does the duty arise and how is it to be discharged? What are the limits of a health care provider's duty to warn under Justice Tobriner's framework? Relying on this opinion, how would you counsel physician clients regarding when their duty to maintain patient confidentiality gives way to a competing duty to protect others from harm?

2. Duty to Warn in the Infectious Disease Context

Bradshaw v. Daniel

854 S.W.2d 865 (Tenn. 1993)

ANDERSON, JUSTICE.

We granted this appeal to determine whether a physician has a legal duty to warn a non-patient of the risk of exposure to the source of his patient's non-contagious disease—Rocky Mountain Spotted Fever....

On July 19, 1986, Elmer Johns went to the emergency room at Methodist Hospital South in Memphis, Tennessee, complaining of headaches, muscle aches, fever, and chills. He was admitted to the hospital under the care and treatment of the defendant, Dr. Chalmers B. Daniel, Jr. Dr. Daniel first saw Johns on July 22, 1986, at which time he ordered the drug Chloramphenicol, which is the drug of choice for a person in the latter stages of Rocky Mountain Spotted Fever. Johns' condition rapidly deteriorated, and he died the next day, July 23, 1986. An autopsy was performed, and the Center for Disease Control in Atlanta conclusively confirmed, in late September 1986, that the cause of death was Rocky Mountain Spotted fever. Although Dr. Daniel communicated with Elmer Johns' wife, Genevieve, during Johns' treatment, he never advised her of the risks of exposure to Rocky Mountain Spotted Fever, or that the disease could have been the cause of Johns' death.

A week after her husband's death, on August 1, 1986, Genevieve Johns came to the emergency room of Baptist Memorial Hospital in Memphis, Tennessee, with similar symptoms of chills, fever, mental disorientation, nausea, lung congestion, myalgia, and swelling of the hands. She was admitted to the hospital and treated for Rocky Mountain Spotted Fever, but she died three days later, on August 4, 1986, of that disease. It is undisputed that no patient-physician relationship existed between Genevieve Johns and Dr. Daniel.

The plaintiff, William Jerome Bradshaw, is Genevieve Johns' son. He filed this suit alleging that the defendant's negligence in failing to advise Genevieve Johns that her husband died of Rocky Mountain Spotted Fever, and in failing to warn her of the risk of exposure, proximately caused her death. The defendant filed a motion to dismiss for failure to state a cause of action on the grounds that the physician owed Genevieve Johns no legal duty because of the absence of a patient-physician relationship. The trial judge denied the motion.

Later, the defendant filed a motion for summary judgment on the same grounds, supported by the affidavit of Dr. Michael S. Gelfand. Dr. Gelfand testified that the medical standard of care did not require a physician treating a patient infected with, or suspected of being infected with, Rocky Mountain Spotted Fever to treat the family of the patient in contact with him, or to warn them of the risk of exposure to the disease or the risk of exposure to ticks or tick bites. The plaintiff responded with the affidavit of Dr. Burt Prater. Dr. Prater testified that because of the clustering effect of the disease, the medical standard of care required that a physician treating a patient with symptoms of Rocky Mountain Spotted Fever advise the family of the patient as to the incubation period, the symptoms of the disease, and the need for immediate medical attention upon manifestation of the symptoms. Dr. Prater further testified that the defendant, Dr. Daniel, negligently failed to diagnose Elmer Johns' fatal disease of Rocky Mountain Spotted Fever and failed to warn his wife, Genevieve Johns, of the incubation period of the disease, the symptoms, and the need to seek medical treatment upon manifestation of the symptoms. He also testified that the disease, if untreated, has a 40 percent mortality rate, but if treated promptly, has a 4 percent mortality rate. Based on the affidavits, the defendant's motion for summary judgment was denied.

The case was then ... tried before a jury, which returned a verdict of $50,000 against the defendant....

The defendant physician argues that he owed his patient's wife no legal duty because first, there was no physician-patient relationship, and second, Rocky Mountain Spotted Fever is not a contagious disease and, therefore, there is no duty to warn of the risk of exposure.

We begin our analysis by examining how we determine when a legal duty may be imposed upon one for the benefit of another. While duty was not part of the early English common law jurisprudence of tort liability, it has since become an essential element in negligence cases.... The existence or nonexistence of a duty owed to the plaintiff by the defendant is entirely a question of law for the court.... [T]he imposition of a legal duty reflects society's contemporary policies and social requirements concerning the right of individuals and the general public to be protected from another's act or conduct. Indeed, it has been stated that "'duty' is not sacrosanct in itself, but is only an expression of the sum total of those considerations of policy which lead the law to say that the plaintiff is entitled to protection." W. Keeton, *Prosser and Keeton on the Law of Torts*, §53 at 358 (5th ed. 1984).

The defendant contends that the absence of a physician-patient relationship negates the existence of a duty in this case. While it is true that a physician-patient relationship is necessary to the maintenance of a medical malpractice action, it is not necessary for the maintenance of an action based on negligence, and this Court has specifically recognized that a physician may owe a duty to a non-patient third party for injuries caused by the physician's negligence, if the injuries suffered and the manner in which they occurred were reasonably foreseeable. *Wharton Transport Corp. v. Bridges*, 606 S.W.2d 521, 526 (Tenn. 1980) (physician owed duty to third party injured by disabled truck driver's negligence, where the physician was negligent both in his physical examination and certification of the truck driver for the employer).

Here, we are asked to determine whether a physician has an affirmative duty to warn a patient's family member about the symptoms and risks of exposure to Rocky Mountain Spotted Fever, a non-contagious disease. Insofar as we are able to determine, there is no reported decision from this or any other jurisdiction involving circumstances exactly similar to those presented in this case.

We begin by observing that all persons have a duty to use reasonable care to refrain from conduct that will foreseeably cause injury to others. In determining the existence of a duty, courts have distinguished between action and inaction. Professor Prosser has commented that "the reason for the distinction may be said to lie in the fact that by 'misfeasance' the defendant has created a new risk of harm to the plaintiff, while by 'nonfeasance' he has at least made his situation no worse, and has merely failed to benefit him by interfering in his affairs." Prosser, §56 at 373.

Because of this reluctance to countenance nonfeasance as a basis of liability, as a general rule, under the common law, one person owed no affirmative duty to warn those endangered by the conduct of another. To mitigate the harshness of this rule, courts have carved out exceptions for cases in which the defendant stands in some special relationship to either the person who is the source of the danger, or to the person who is foreseeably at risk from the danger. Accordingly, while an actor is always bound to prevent his acts from creating an unreasonable risk to others, he is under the affirmative duty to act to prevent another from sustaining harm only when certain socially recognized relations exist which constitute the basis for such legal duty. Harper & Kime, *The Duty to Control the Conduct of Another*, 43 Yale L.J. 886, 887 (1934).

One of the most widely known cases applying that principle is *Tarasoff* [*v. Regents of the Univ. of Cal.*, 551 P.2d 334 (Cal. 1976)], in which the California Supreme Court held that when a psychotherapist determines or, pursuant to the standards of his profession, should determine that his patient presents a serious danger of violence to another, the therapist has an affirmative duty to use reasonable care to protect the intended victim against such danger, and the duty may require the physician to warn the intended victim of the danger. The special relationship of the patient to his psychotherapist supported imposition of the affirmative duty to act for the benefit of third persons....

Decisions of other jurisdictions have employed the same analysis and held that the relationship of a physician to his patient is sufficient to support the duty to exercise reasonable care to protect third persons against foreseeable risks emanating from a patient's physical illness. Specifically, other courts have recognized that physicians may be liable to persons infected by a patient, if the physician negligently fails to diagnose a contagious disease, or having diagnosed the illness, fails to warn family members or others who are foreseeably at risk of exposure to the disease. *[S]ee generally* Bateman, Annotation, *Liability of Doctor or Other Health Practitioner to Third Party Contracting Contagious Disease from Doctor's Patient,* 3 A.L.R.5th 370 (1992)....

Returning to the facts of this case, first, it is undisputed that there was a physician-patient relationship between Dr. Daniel and Elmer Johns. Second, here, as in the contagious disease context, it is also undisputed that Elmer Johns' wife, who was residing with him, was at risk of contracting the disease. This is so even though the disease is not contagious in the narrow sense that it can be transmitted from one person to another. Both Dr. Daniel and Dr. Prater, the plaintiff's expert, testified that family members of patients suffering from Rocky Mountain Spotted Fever are at risk of contracting the disease due to a phenomenon called clustering, which is related to the activity of infected ticks who transmit the disease to humans. Dr. Prater also testified that Dr. Daniel negligently failed to diagnose the disease and negligently failed to warn his patient's wife, Genevieve Johns, of her risk of exposure to the source of disease. Dr. Daniel's expert disputed these conclusions, but Dr. Daniel conceded there is a medical duty to inform the family when there is a diagnosis of the disease. Thus, this case is analogous to the Tarasoff line of cases adopting a duty to warn of danger and the contagious disease cases adopting a comparable duty to warn. Here, as in those cases, there was a foreseeable risk of harm to an identifiable third party, and the reasons supporting the recognition of the duty to warn are equally compelling here.

We, therefore, conclude that the existence of the physician-patient relationship is sufficient to impose upon a physician an affirmative duty to warn identifiable third persons in the patient's immediate family against foreseeable risks emanating from a patient's illness. Accordingly, we hold that under the factual circumstances of this case, viewing the evidence in a light most favorable to the plaintiff, the defendant physician had a duty to warn his patient's wife of the risk to her of contracting Rocky Mountain Spotted Fever, when he knew, or in the exercise of reasonable care, should have known, that his patient was suffering from the disease. Our holding here is necessarily limited to the conclusion that the defendant physician owed Genevieve Johns a legal duty. We express no opinion on the other elements which would be required to establish a cause of action for common-law negligence in this case....

Reisner v. The Regents of the University of California

37 Cal. Rptr. 2d. 518 (Cal. Ct. App. 1995)

Miriam A. Vogel, Associate Justice.

The day after 12-year-old Jennifer Lawson received a transfusion, her doctor discovered the blood was contaminated with HIV antibodies. Although the same doctor continued to treat Jennifer, he never told her or her parents about the tainted blood. Three years later, Jennifer started dating Daniel Reisner and they became intimate. Two years later, the doctor told Jennifer she had AIDS and Jennifer told Daniel. A month later, Jennifer died. Shortly thereafter, Daniel discovered he was HIV positive. Daniel sued Jennifer's doctor and others for negligence. The defendants moved for judgment on the pleadings, claiming they owed no duty to Daniel, an unidentified third person. The motion was granted. We reverse....

When the avoidance of foreseeable harm to a third person requires a defendant to control the conduct of a person with whom the defendant has a special relationship (such as physician and patient) or to warn the person of the risks involved in certain conduct, the defendant's duty extends to a third person with whom the defendant does not have a special relationship. *Tarasoff v. Regents of Univ. of Cal.* (1976) 17 Cal. 3d 425. Dr. Fonklesrud and UCLA concede as much but contend this rule does not create a duty where, as here, the third person is both unknown and unidentifiable. We disagree.

...

First, Tarasoff dictates the result in our case by holding that the doctor's duty includes the duty to warn "others likely to apprise the victim of the danger ... or to take whatever ... steps are reasonably necessary under the circumstances." *Tarasoff, supra*, 17 Cal. 3d at p. 431. Daniel does not claim Defendants had to warn him, only that they had to warn Jennifer or her parents, "others [who were] likely to apprise [him] of the danger" (and, of course, did just that when they learned of it).

Second, there is the case of *Myers v. Quesenberry* (1983) 193 Cal.Rptr. 733. In *Myers*, two physicians (Quesenberry and Beaumont) were treating a pregnant patient (Hansen) for diabetes. During an examination at Quesenberry's office, the doctor concluded the fetus had died. When Quesenberry told Hansen to have the dead fetus removed within 18 hours, Hansen became emotionally upset. "The doctors then directed Hansen to drive immediately to [a local hospital] for preliminary laboratory tests. Hansen lost control of her car due to a diabetic attack and struck Myers as he was standing by the side of the road." (*Id.* at 733.) Myers sued the doctors.... [T]he issue on appeal was whether they owed a duty to Myers, with whom they had no relationship, for failing to warn their patient of the foreseeable and dangerous consequences of engaging in the conduct which caused Myers's injuries.

The Court of Appeal reversed, holding (among other things) that "the fact that Myers was a foreseeable but not a readily identifiable victim of Hansen's driving does not preclude him from stating an action against the doctors for negligently failing to warn her not to drive in an irrational and uncontrolled diabetic condition. As a practical matter, the doctors here could not have effectively warned Myers of the danger presented by Hansen's driving....

"However, they could easily have warned Hansen not to drive because of her irrational and uncontrolled diabetic condition. Under the facts as alleged here, this probably would not have been a futile act. Having otherwise complied with her doctors' professional recommendations, Hansen presumably would have continued to follow their advice had they warned her not to drive.... On these pleadings, we cannot factually presume Hansen would have ignored the doctors' warning. Thus, under these circumstances where warning the actor is a reasonable step to take in the exercise of the standard of care applicable to physicians, liability is not conditioned on potential victims being readily identifiable as well as foreseeable." (*Myers v. Quesenberry, supra*, at p. 735.)

Similarly, on the pleadings before us, ... Defendants' liability is not conditional upon Daniel's identity being known or ascertainable, and we cannot factually presume Jennifer or her parents would have ignored Defendants' warning. According to Daniel's complaint, as soon as Jennifer and her parents discovered Jennifer had AIDS, Daniel was immediately notified. As a result, it appears a timely warning to Jennifer probably would have prevented Daniel's injury....

Third, the facts of this case compel a conclusion designed to encourage the highest standard of care concerning communicable and infectious diseases, and Defendants' arguments to the contrary are red herrings.

In *DiMarco v. Lynch Homes-Chester Cty.* (1990) 583 A.2d 422, the Supreme Court of Pennsylvania considered this issue on facts strikingly similar to those of our case. In DiMarco, a blood technician (Viscichini) was accidentally punctured while taking a blood sample from a patient. When Viscichini learned the patient had hepatitis, she immediately sought treatment from two physicians, both of whom told her that, if she remained symptom free for six weeks, it would mean she had not been infected by the hepatitis virus. Although she was not told to refrain from sexual relations for any period of time, she did so until eight weeks after exposure. As she had remained symptom free during that time, she then resumed sexual relations with her boyfriend (DiMarco). Three months after exposure, Viscichini developed Hepatitis B and, three months after that, DiMarco was diagnosed as having the same disease. (*Id.*, 583 A.2d at p. 423.)

DiMarco sued Viscichini's doctors, claiming they were negligent in not warning Viscichini that if she had sexual relations within six months of exposure she could infect her sexual partner. In affirming the existence of a duty owed to DiMarco, the court explained that when "a physician treats a patient who has been exposed to or who has contracted a communicable and/or contagious disease, it is imperative that the physician give his or her patient the proper advice about preventing the spread of the disease. Communicable diseases are so named because they are readily spread from person to person. Physicians are the first line of defense against the spread of communicable diseases, because physicians know what measures must be taken to prevent the infection of others. The patient must be advised to take certain sanitary measures, or to remain quarantined for a period of time, or to practice sexual abstinence or what is commonly referred to as 'safe sex.'

"Such precautions are taken not to protect the health of the patient, whose well-being has already been compromised, rather such precautions are taken to safeguard the health of others. Thus, the duty of a physician in such circumstances extends to those 'within the foreseeable orbit of risk of harm.'... If a third person is in that class of persons whose health is likely to be threatened by the patient, and if erroneous advice is given to that patient to the ultimate detriment of the third person, the third person has a cause of action against the physician, because the physician should recognize that the services rendered to the patient are necessary for the protection of the third person." (*DiMarco v. Lynch Homes-Chester County*, *supra*, 583 A.2d at pp. 424–425, some emphasis added.)

Defendants contend we should find they owed no duty to Daniel because the imposition of liability on these facts would not prevent future harm.... Defendants miss the point. Civil liability for a negligent failure to warn under the circumstances of this case may not hasten the day when AIDS can be cured or prevented but it may, in the meantime, protect one or more persons from unnecessary exposure to this deadly virus.

We summarily reject Defendants' alternative suggestion that a physician ought not to owe any duty to a third person because such a duty could adversely affect the doctor's treatment of his patient, to whom his primary duty is owed. As explained above, existing California law already imposes a duty to third persons and the only arguably "new" issue in this case is whether that duty is the same when the third person's identity is unknown to the physician and not readily ascertainable. And, contrary to Defendants' contention, the duty involved in this case—a duty to warn a contagious patient to take steps to protect others—has nothing to do with a physician's decision about how to treat his patient or with a physician's potential liability for the unauthorized disclosure of AIDS test results. Once the physician warns the patient of the risk to others and advises the patient how to prevent the spread of the disease, the physician has fulfilled his duty—and no more (but no less) is required.

We also reject Defendants' suggestion that we ought not to find a duty is owed to Daniel because it would necessarily follow that a duty would be owed to "other persons with whom [Daniel] had sex, and the persons with whom they had sex," and so on ad infinitum.... There are at least two reasons for rejecting this argument.

First, it presumes too much.... To actually recover in this case, Daniel will be required to prove that a physician and a teaching hospital, knowing they had inadvertently infected a patient with a contagious disease that is almost always deadly, failed to tell her what had happened and failed to warn her about the danger in infecting her loved ones. Daniel will also have to prove causation—not just that Jennifer would have told him about her illness and that he would then have refrained from intimate contact with her but also that he could not have acquired the disease elsewhere....

Second, the argument goes too far.... However, the possibility of such an extension does not offend us, legally or morally. Viewed in the abstract ... we believe that a doctor who knows he is dealing with the 20th Century version of Typhoid Mary ought to have a very strong incentive to tell his patient what she ought to do and not do and how she ought to comport herself in order to prevent the spread of her disease. In any event, the doctor's liability to fourth and fifth persons would by its nature be limited by traditional causation principles....

Notes & Questions

1. The court's rationale in finding a duty to warn in *Bradshaw* closely follows the *Tarasoff* framework: an identifiable victim is at risk for a foreseeable and serious injury that can be avoided (or at least the risk can be minimized) by breaching confidentiality and warning the victim. In addition, to what extent does the court appear to rely on expert testimony regarding the standard of care? Could the court (would this court) have found a duty to warn solely on the basis of expert testimony about the degree of risk to the wife and other members of the family?

2. In *Reisner v. Regents of the Univ. of Cal.*, there was no identifiable or known potential victim at the time the doctors determined their patient suffered from HIV/AIDS. On what basis did the court justify the imposition of a duty to warn third parties and how did it propose that the duty be discharged? Given this opinion, how might your advice to clients regarding the nature and scope of their obligations to protect confidentiality versus their obligations to warn third parties change from what you outlined based upon your reading of the *Tarasoff* case?

3. Duty to Warn in the Context of Inherited Conditions

Like all medical information, genetic information is entitled to a presumption of confidentiality. However, unlike much of a patient's medical history, the implications of genetic information are simultaneously uniquely personal and necessarily familial. This "dual ownership" aspect of genetic information poses unique challenges for physicians as they attempt to reconcile competing duties to safeguard patient confidentiality and promote the welfare of others.

An identifiable—or at least foreseeable—victim is a critical element of the common law duty to warn. Because genetic information can be informative regarding disease risks for both the patient and her first-degree relatives, the existence of foreseeable victims is essentially a given, although actual identification and contact may be difficult to accomplish, depending upon the extent of contact between a patient and his or her family. Two other key assumptions in the foregoing cases finding a duty to warn are the likelihood and seriousness of the potential harm (in essence, a significant risk of death or profound disability) and the availability of an intervention to minimize or avoid that harm. Yet the ambiguous nature of many genetic diagnoses and the technological gap between our rapidly expanding ability to identify genetic risk factors and our limited options for treatment, prevention, or cure for a majority of genetically mediated diseases make it difficult to assess these two elements in the *Tarasoff* framework.

In reviewing the following cases addressing the duty to warn family members regarding hereditary disease risks, consider how uncertainties regarding the identity of first-degree relatives, the nature or extent of the genetic risk, or the likelihood of interventions might impact a court's analysis. What is the scope of the duty to warn family members regarding hereditary disease risk? How would you define the limits of this duty?

Pate v. Threlkel

661 So. 2d 278 (Fla. 1995)

WELLS, JUSTICE.

We have for review the following question certified to be of great public importance: Does a physician owe a duty of care to the children of a patient to warn the patient of the genetically transferable nature of the condition for which the physician is treating the patient? We answer the question in the affirmative provided the children of the patient first establish that pursuant to the prevailing standard of care set forth in section 766.102, Florida Statutes (1989), a reasonably prudent physician would give such warning to his or her patient in light of all relevant circumstances.

In March 1987, Marianne New received treatment for medullary thyroid carcinoma, a genetically transferable disease. In 1990, Heidi Pate, New's adult daughter, learned that she also had medullary thyroid carcinoma. Consequently, Pate and her husband filed a complaint against the physicians who initially treated New for the disease as well as the physicians' respective employers. Pate and her husband alleged that the physicians knew or should have known of the likelihood that New's children would have inherited the condition genetically; that the physicians were under a duty to warn New that her children should be tested for the disease; that had New been warned in 1987, she would have had her children tested at that time; and if Pate had been tested in 1987, she would have taken preventative action, and her condition, more likely than not, would have been curable. Pate claimed that as a direct and proximate cause of the physicians' negligence, she suffers from advanced medullary thyroid carcinoma and its various damaging effects.

The respondent health care providers moved to dismiss the complaint for failure to state a cause of action.... The trial court granted the motion.... The district court affirmed the trial court's dismissal....

We conclude that to answer the certified question we must consider two questions related to duty. First, we must determine whether New's physicians had a duty to warn New of the genetically transferable nature of her disease. We find that to make this determination we must apply section 766.102, Florida Statutes (1989), which defines the legal duty owed by a health care provider in a medical malpractice case.... In applying this statute to the instant case, we conclude that a duty exists if the statutory standard of care requires a reasonably prudent health care provider to warn a patient of the genetically transferable nature of the condition for which the physician was treating the patient.

In medical malpractice cases, the standard of care is determined by a consideration of expert testimony. Because this case comes to us on appeal from an order granting the physicians' motion to dismiss, the record has yet to be developed in respect to such testimony. However, the court's dismissal requires us to assume that the factual allegations in the complaint are true. Accordingly, we must accept as true the Pates' allegations that pursuant to the prevailing standard of care, the health care providers were under a duty to warn New of the importance of testing her children for medullary thyroid carcinoma....

The second question we must address in answering the certified question is to whom does the alleged duty to warn New of the nature of her disease run? The duty obviously runs to the patient who is in privity with the physician. In the past, courts have held that in order to maintain a cause of action against a physician, privity must exist between the plaintiff and the physician. In other professional relationships, however, we have recognized the rights of identified third party beneficiaries to recover from a professional because that party was the intended beneficiary of the prevailing standard of care. In such cases, we have determined that an absence of privity does not necessarily foreclose liability.... We conclude that this analysis recognizing that privity is not always needed to establish liability should apply to the professional relationship between a patient's child and a health care provider.

Here, the alleged prevailing standard of care was obviously developed for the benefit of the patient's children as well as the patient. We conclude that when the prevailing standard of care creates a duty that is obviously for the benefit of certain identified third parties and the physician knows of the existence of those third parties, then the physician's duty runs to those third parties....

Though not encompassed by the certified question, there is another issue which should be addressed in light of our holding. If there is a duty to warn, to whom must the physician convey the warning? Our holding should not be read to require the physician to warn the patient's children of the disease. In most instances the physician is prohibited from disclosing the patient's medical condition to others except with the patient's permission. Moreover, the patient ordinarily can be expected to pass on the warning. To require the physician to seek out and warn various members of the patient's family would often be difficult or impractical and would place too heavy a burden upon the physician. Thus, we emphasize that in any circumstances in which the physician has a duty to warn of a genetically transferable disease, that duty will be satisfied by warning the patient.

Accordingly, we conclude that the trial court erred by dismissing the complaint with prejudice. Whether the Pates can recover for medical malpractice depends upon the prevailing standard of care pursuant to section 766.102.... We ... remand for further proceedings in accord with this opinion.

Safer v. Pack

677 A.2d 1188 (N.J. 1996)

KESTIN, J.A.D.

Plaintiffs appeal from the trial court's order dismissing their complaint and denying their cross-motion for partial summary judgment as to liability only. We reverse that portion of the order dismissing the complaint and affirm the denial of plaintiffs' motion.

Donna Safer's claim arises from the patient-physician relationship in the 1950s and 1960s between her father, Robert Batkin, a resident of New Jersey, and Dr. George T. Pack, also a resident of New Jersey, who practiced medicine and surgery in New York City and treated Mr. Batkin there. It is alleged that Dr. Pack specialized in the treatment and removal of cancerous tumors and growths.

In November 1956, Mr. Batkin was admitted to the hospital with a pre-operative diagnosis of retroperitoneal cancer. A week later, Dr. Pack performed a total colectomy and an ileosigmoidectomy for multiple polyposis of the colon with malignant degeneration in one area. The discharge summary noted the finding in a pathology report of the existence of adenocarcinoma developing in an intestinal polyp, and diffuse intestinal polyposis "from one end of the colon to the other." Dr. Pack continued to treat Mr. Batkin postoperatively.

In October 1961, Mr. Batkin was again hospitalized. Dr. Pack performed an ileoabdominal perineal resection with an ileostomy. The discharge summary reported pathology findings of "ulcerative adenocarcinoma of colon Grade II with metastases to Levels II and III" and "adenomatous polyps." Dr. Pack again continued to treat Mr. Batkin postoperatively. He also developed a physician-patient relationship with Mrs. Batkin relative to the diagnosis and treatment of a vaginal ulcer.

In December 1963, Mr. Batkin was hospitalized once again at Dr. Pack's direction. The carcinoma of the colon had metastasized to the liver with secondary jaundice and probable retroperitoneal disease causing pressure on the sciatic nerve plexus. After some treatment, Mr. Batkin died on January 3, 1964, at forty-five years of age. Donna was ten years old at the time of her father's death. Her sister was seventeen.

In February 1990, Donna Safer, then thirty-six years of age and newly married, residing in Connecticut, began to experience lower abdominal pain. Examinations and tests revealed a cancerous blockage of the colon and multiple polyposis. In March, Ms. Safer underwent a total abdominal colectomy with ileorectal anastamosis. A primary carcinoma in the sigmoid colon was found to extend through the serosa of the bowel and multiple polyps were seen throughout the entire bowel. Because of the detection of additional metastatic adenocarcinoma and carcinoma, plaintiff's left ovary was also removed. Between April 1990 and mid-1991, Ms. Safer underwent chemotherapy treatment.

In September 1991, plaintiffs obtained Robert Batkin's medical records, from which they learned that he had suffered from polyposis. Their complaint was filed in March 1992, alleging a violation of duty (professional negligence) on the part of Dr. Pack in his failure to warn of the risk to Donna Safer's health.

Plaintiffs contend that multiple polyposis is a hereditary condition that, if undiscovered and untreated, invariably leads to metastatic colorectal cancer. They contend, further, that the hereditary nature of the disease was known at the time Dr. Pack was treating Mr. Batkin and that the physician was required, by medical standards then prevailing, to warn those at risk so that they might have the benefits of early examination, monitoring, detection and treatment, that would provide opportunity to avoid the most baneful consequences of the condition.

The summary judgment proceeding in the trial court was based upon a scanty record, largely comprised of hospital records. Dr. Pack himself had died in 1969; none of his individual records were before the court. The reports of the parties' medical experts and a deposition of plaintiffs' expert were submitted. Ida Batkin, Donna Safer's mother, had also given a deposition in which she testified, among other details, that neither her husband nor Dr. Pack had ever told her that Mr. Batkin suffered from cancer; and that, throughout the courses of surgery and treatment, Dr. Pack advised her that he was treating a "blockage" or an unspecified "infection". On the one or two occasions when Mrs. Batkin inquired of Dr. Pack whether the "infection" would affect her children, she was told not to worry....

Whether a legal duty exists is ... a matter of law. We see no impediment, legal or otherwise, to recognizing a physician's duty to warn those known to be at risk of avoidable harm from a genetically transmissible condition. In terms of foreseeability especially, there is no essential difference between the type of genetic threat at issue here and the menace of infection, contagion or a threat of physical harm. The individual or group at risk is easily identified, and substantial future harm may be averted or minimized by a timely and effective warning.

The motion judge's view of this case as one involving an unavoidable genetic condition gave too little significance to the proffered expert view that early monitoring of those at risk can effectively avert some of the more serious consequences a person with multiple polyposis might otherwise experience. We cannot conclude either, as the trial court did, that Dr. Pack breached no duty because avoidable harm to Donna was not foreseeable.... Such a determination would ignore the presumed state of medical knowledge at the time. It would also tend to undervalue the concepts that inform our case law establishing a cause of action for increased risk of harm, as well as the underlying rationale of our rules of law on foreseeability, heretofore held to be specifically applicable in professional negligence cases involving genetic torts. *See Schroeder v. Perkel*, [432 A.2d 834 (1981)].

Although an overly broad and general application of the physician's duty to warn might lead to confusion, conflict or unfairness in many types of circumstances, we are confident that the duty to warn of avertible [sic] risk from genetic causes, by definition a matter of familial concern, is sufficiently narrow to serve the interests of justice. Further, it is appropriate ... that the duty be seen as owed not only to the patient himself but that it also "extend[s] beyond the interests of a patient to members of the immediate family of the patient who may be adversely affected by a breach of that duty." We need not decide, in the present posture of this case, how, precisely, that duty is to be discharged, especially with respect to young children who may be at risk, except to require that reasonable steps be taken to assure that the information reaches those likely to be affected or is made available for their benefit. We are aware of no direct evidence that has been developed concerning the nature of the communications between physician and patient regarding Mr. Batkin's disease: what Dr. Pack did or did not disclose; the advice he gave to Mr. Batkin, if any, concerning genetic factors and what ought to have been done in respect of those at risk; and the conduct or expressed preferences of Mr. Batkin in response thereto. There may be enough from Mrs. Batkin's testimony and other evidence for inferences to be drawn, however.

We decline to hold as the Florida Supreme Court did in *Pate v. Threlkel*, *supra*, 661 So.2d [278, 282 (Fla. 1995)], that, in all circumstances, the duty to warn will be satisfied by informing the patient. It may be necessary, at some stage, to resolve a conflict between the physician's broader duty to warn and his fidelity to an expressed preference of the patient that nothing be said to family members about the details of the disease. We cannot know presently, however, whether there is any likelihood that such a conflict may be shown to have existed in this matter or, if it did, what its qualities might have been. As the matter is currently constituted, it is as likely as not that no such conflict will be shown to have existed and that the only evidence on the issue will be Mrs. Batkin's testimony, including that she received no information, despite specific inquiry, that her children were at risk. We note, in addition, the possible existence of some off-setting evidence that Donna was rectally examined as a young child, suggesting that the risk to her had been disclosed.

This case implicates serious and conflicting medical, social and legal policies, many aptly identified in Sonia M. Suter, *Whose Genes Are These Anyway? Familial Conflicts Over Access to Genetic Information*, 91 Mich. L.Rev. 1854 (1993).... Some such policy considerations may need to be addressed in ultimately resolving this case. For example, if evidence is produced that will permit the jury to find that Dr. Pack received instructions from his patient not to disclose details of the illness or the fact of genetic risk, the court will be required to determine whether, as a matter of law, there are or ought to be any limits on physician-patient confidentiality, especially after the patient's death where a risk of harm survives the patient, as in the case of genetic consequences. See generally Janet A. Kobrin, *Confidentiality of Genetic Information*, 30 UCLA L.Rev. 1283 (1983).

Issues of fact remain to be resolved, as well. What was the extent of Donna's risk, for instance? We are led to understand from the experts' reports that the risk of multiple polyposis was significant and that, upon detection, an early full colectomy, i.e., an excision of her entire colon, may well have been the treatment of choice to avoid resultant cancer—including metastasis, the loss of other organs and the rigors of chemotherapy. Full factual development may, however, cast a different light on these issues of fact and others.

Difficult damage issues portend also. Not the least of these will involve distinguishing between the costs of the medical surveillance that would have followed a timely and effective warning, and the costs of medical care attributable to any breach of duty that may be found to have occurred....

The order of the trial court dismissing the complaint is reversed.... The matter is remanded to the trial court for further proceedings....

Notes & Questions

1. To what extent do the courts' opinions in *Pate* and *Safer* incorporate the *Tarasoff* framework? What are the underlying facts in each case regarding the severity of the risk and the availability of interventions? In other words, what was the nature and significance of the hereditary risk in each case and what difference would early identification of the risk make in the outcome for the affected family member?

2. The *Pate* court concluded that a physician could discharge his or her duty to warn potentially affected family members regarding hereditary disease risks by counseling the patient and encouraging that patient to discuss the hereditary implications of his diagnosis with his family: "Thus, we emphasize that in any circumstances in which the physician has a duty to warn of a genetically transferable disease, that duty will be satisfied by warning the patient." 661 So. 2d at 282. What are the costs and benefits associ-

ated with this approach and which of the physician's twin duties does it favor—confidentiality or disclosure to protect third parties? On the other hand, what advantages and disadvantages flow from the more open-ended limits of the duty to warn that are suggested in the *Safer* court's opinion: "We need not decide, in the present posture of this case, how, precisely, that duty is to be discharged, especially with respect to young children who may be at risk, except to require that reasonable steps be taken to assure that the information reaches those likely to be affected or is made available for their benefit.... We decline to hold as the Florida Supreme Court did in *Pate v. Threlkel*, that, in all circumstances, the duty to warn will be satisfied by informing the patient." 677 A.2d at 282. What guidance do the *Safer* and *Pate* opinions provide to the physician whose patient, after being appropriately warned of the inherited nature of her disease and the need to advise potentially affected family members regarding their potential genetic risk, refuses to disclose any information about her medical condition to her family and directs her physician not to make any disclosures?

3. The New Jersey Genetic Privacy Act, N.J.S.A. 10:5-43 to 5-49 (p. 56), was passed subsequent to the court's ruling in *Safer v. Pack*. How does the Act impact the *Safer* ruling? Assuming that Dr. Pack were treating Mr. Safer today, under what circumstances would he be permitted to inform family members of Mr. Safer's genetic disease? For a more in-depth discussion of the passage of the New Jersey Privacy Act, *see* Natalie Anne Stepanuk, *Genetic Information and Third Party Access to Information: New Jersey's Pioneering Legislation as a Model for Federal Privacy Protection of Genetic Information*, 47 CATH. U. L.R. 1105 (1998).

4. The HIPAA privacy rules specifically address the duty to warn in 45 C.F.R. § 164.512(j), which states in pertinent part: "A covered entity may, consistent with applicable law and standards of ethical conduct, use or disclose protected health information, if the covered entity, in good faith, believes that the use or disclosure ... [i]s necessary to prevent or lessen a serious and imminent threat to the health or safety of a person or the public; and ... [is] to a person or persons reasonably able to prevent or lessen the threat, including the target of the threat...." How does this federal regulation, which permits a covered health care provider to disclose protected health care information without a patient's consent in circumstances where the disclosure is likely to prevent harm to others, affect the court opinions in *Safer* and *Pate*?

5. The public generally associates genetic disease with single gene disorders, such as Huntington disease, which have a predictable, severe impact on patient health. However, single gene disorders are relatively rare. The most common and least understood of human genetic diseases are multifactorial, resulting from the interaction of multiple genes with each other and the environment. Outcomes for these diseases depend upon the ways in which the interactive effects of many genes create a predisposition to disease, which in turn requires certain environmental triggers to become manifest. Thus, with multifactorial diseases determining that an individual carries the genetic traits associated with the disease of interest only suggests that they have an enhanced susceptibility toward that disease. Even for single gene disorders, clinical manifestation of disease can be variable because of incomplete penetrance, phenocopies, genetic heterogeneity, and variable expressivity. E. Lander & N. Schork, *Genetic Dissection of Complex Traits*, 265 SCIENCE 2037 (1994). A positive genetic diagnosis is not always a certain or even very clear predictor of the onset or nature and extent of genetic disease in family members who carry a similar genetic abnormality. N. Holtzman, et al., *The New Genetics: Genetic Testing and Public Policy*, 316 BRITISH MED. J. 852 (1998). The public and many physicians also misunderstand the therapeutic value of genetic diag-

noses. Conditions such as Huntington disease, Tay-Sachs disease, cystic fibrosis, hemophilia A, and sickle cell disease can be identified, but there remains no meaningful treatment or cure for the afflicted. On the other hand, knowledge of risk for these diseases can positively influence lifestyle decisions regarding employment, leisure, finances, and reproductive planning. Knowledge regarding disease susceptibility can trigger environmental or lifestyle changes that might minimize the risk of developing the disease. Given the evolution of case law surrounding the physicians' duty to warn regarding familial risk, what do you think the outcome would be in a case involving hereditary risk for a multifactorial disease in which the likelihood of occurrence was difficult to predict, there were no therapeutic interventions that would change the health outcome for a family member who inherited the genetic risk factor, but the plaintiff contended that forewarning would have influenced decisions regarding employment or reproductive planning? Would it make any difference in your analysis if the physician's patient expressly refused to share the genetic diagnosis with his or her family members and specifically asked the physician not to disclose any genetic information to anyone, including potentially affected first-degree relatives?

6. The preceding notes and questions are intended to focus your attention on the factual circumstances that trigger a duty to warn, as well as on the implications of different approaches for discharging such a duty once it arises. The potential for conflicts between competing duties to protect confidentiality and to prevent harm to third parties is real in these circumstances, and a review of the ethical, legal, and professional medical literature reveals several alternative recommendations for how these conflicts might be minimized or avoided. *See, e.g.* PRESIDENT'S COMMISSION FOR THE STUDY OF ETHICAL PROBLEMS IN MEDICINE AND BIOMEDICAL AND BIOBEHAVIORAL RESEARCH, SCREENING AND COUNSELING FOR GENETIC CONDITIONS: THE ETHICAL, SOCIAL AND LEGAL IMPLICATIONS OF GENETICS SCREENING, COUNSELING, AND EDUCATION PROGRAMS, (1998); INSTITUTE OF MEDICINE COMMITTEE ON ASSESSING GENETIC RISKS, ASSESSING GENETIC RISKS IMPLICATIONS FOR HEALTH AND SOCIAL POLICY, (1994); The American Society of Human Genetics Social Issues Subcommittee on Familial Disclosure, *Professional Disclosure of Familial Genetic Information*, 62 AM. J. HUM. GENET. 474 (1998). For an in-depth review and analysis of the legal issues, *see* Ellen Wright Clayton, *What Should the Law say about Disclosure of Genetic Information to Relatives?* 1 J. HEALTH CARE L. & POL'Y 373 (1998); Michelle R. King, *Physician Duty to Warn a Patient's Offspring of Hereditary Genetic Defects: Balancing the Patient's Right to Confidentiality Against the Family Member's Right to Know—Can or Should Tarasoff Apply?* 4 QUINNIPIAC HEALTH L.J. 1 (2000); Sonia M. Suter, *Whose Genes are these Anyway? Familial Conflicts over Access to Genetic Information*, 91 MICH. L. REV. 1854 (1993). For a recent review written from the medical perspective, *see* Kenneth Offit, et al., *The "Duty to Warn" a Patient's Family Members About Hereditary Disease Risks*, 292 J. AM. MED. ASS'N 1469 (2004).

7. The underlying assumption in the *Safer* and *Pate* cases was that the deceased defendant physician had been aware of the hereditary nature of his patient's disease at the time the diagnosis was made and elected, either independently or after discussion with his patient, not to disclose the presence of hereditary risk to potentially affected family members. The following case arises from an alleged failure to diagnose Fragile X Syndrome, a hereditary syndrome associated with developmental delays and other abnormalities in growth and development. The plaintiff's claims included breach of the duty to warn regarding a familial hereditary risk for Fragile X.

Molloy v. Meier

679 N.W.2d 711 (Minn. 2004)

MEYER, JUSTICE.

...

This case arises out of the medical treatment of S.F., the daughter of Kimberly Molloy and her ex-husband, Robert Flomer. As a young girl, S.F. was treated by appellant Dr. Diane M. Meier.... When S.F. was three years old, Dr. Meier noted during a check-up that S.F. was developmentally delayed. Dr. Meier ordered a number of tests, but the results did not reveal the source of S.F.'s difficulties. On May 18, 1992, Dr. Meier met with Molloy, Robert Flomer, and S.F. to discuss the possible causes for S.F.'s developmental delays, including the possibility of a genetic cause. Molloy told Dr. Meier about Molloy's mentally retarded half-brother and asked Dr. Meier to conduct genetic tests on S.F. to determine whether S.F. had inherited any abnormalities from Molloy.

In her notes from the May 18 visit, Dr. Meier wrote "? chromosomes + fragile X," which meant she intended to order chromosomal testing and testing for Fragile X syndrome. In May of 1992, a Fragile X chromosomal test capable of diagnosing the disorder with 70 to 80 percent accuracy was in widespread use.... Dr. Meier conceded that "it was appropriate to test [S.F.] for [F]ragile X in keeping with accepted standards of pediatric practice on May 18, 1992." ...

On June 17, 1992, the chromosome testing ordered by Dr. Meier was performed at North Memorial Medical Center.... Dr. Meier received the test results, telephoned the Flomers and informed them that the test results were negative; i.e., normal. However, Dr. Meier failed to mention that Fragile X testing had not been performed. The Flomers then informed Molloy that the test results were "normal." Based on the fact that Dr. Meier had mentioned Fragile X in her discussion of chromosomal testing, Molloy assumed that the negative test results included a negative result for Fragile X.

... [O]n June 23, 1992, S.F. was referred by Dr. Meier to the Minneapolis Clinic of Neurology where she was seen by Dr. Reno Backus.... Molloy inquired about her chances of conceiving another child with S.F.'s defect. According to Molloy, Dr. Backus responded that S.F.'s problems were not genetic in origin and the risk that Molloy might give birth to another child like S.F. was extremely remote, especially with a father other than Robert Flomer. Dr. Backus was aware that chromosomal testing had been done but he made his assessment before the test results were known.

Several years later S.F. was referred to Dr. Kathryn Green.... Dr. Green did not order or recommend Fragile X testing. Dr. Green testified that she recognized the importance of Fragile X testing in general, but she assumed such tests had already been performed on S.F. and had come back negative, as S.F. had already seen three physicians.

In the meantime, Molloy remarried and gave birth to M.M. on June 30, 1998. M.M. showed signs of the same developmental difficulties as S.F., so his pediatrician, Dr. David Tilstra, ordered Fragile X testing for him. The Fragile X test results were positive ... When Dr. Tilstra received the positive results, he counseled Kimberly and Glenn Molloy about Fragile X syndrome and recommended that they and other potentially affected family members receive testing. Based on Dr. Tilstra's recommendation, S.F. and Kimberly Molloy were tested for Fragile X, and it was discovered that they both carried the genetic disorder.

Molloy commenced this lawsuit on August 23, 2001, alleging that Drs. Meier, Backus, and Green and their employers were negligent in the care and treatment rendered to S.F., Kimberly Molloy, and Glenn Molloy by failing to order Fragile X testing on S.F., failing to properly read those lab tests that were performed, mistakenly reporting that S.F. had been tested for Fragile X, and failing to provide counseling to Kimberly and Glenn Molloy regarding the risk of passing an inheritable genetic abnormality to future children. Molloy claimed she would not have conceived M.M. if Drs. Meier, Backus, and Green had correctly diagnosed S.F. with Fragile X and informed Molloy of the diagnosis.

... Molloy presented expert testimony of a pediatrician and a pediatric neurologist who described the prevailing standard of care in the medical community with respect to testing and counseling for genetic disorders. The experts indicated that a patient who exhibits the symptoms of this disorder with a family history of mental retardation should be tested for Fragile X. Further, a physician who identifies the possibility of Fragile X has a responsibility to follow up to confirm that the tests are performed. Finally, the physician of a child with Fragile X has an obligation to provide genetic counseling to the child's family.

...

Molloy advances two legal theories. She first argues that a physician-patient relationship existed between her and the appellants that gave rise to a legal duty to warn her about the risks of becoming pregnant as a carrier of Fragile X. Additionally ... Molloy urges this court to hold that even if a physician-patient relationship cannot be established, a physician's duty to warn others of a patient's genetic disorder arises from the foreseeability of injury.

The appellants argue that their duty is owed only to S.F., the person with whom they had a physician-patient relationship. The appellants claim that they met with S.F. solely for S.F.'s own benefit and not for the benefit of her family. If any duty extended beyond the minor patient, the appellants argue that it should reach only those parties who have a contractual relationship with the physician, in this case the Flomers, S.F.'s custodial parents.

...

Our decision today is informed by the practical reality of the field of genetic testing and counseling; genetic testing and diagnosis does not affect only the patient. Both the patient and her family can benefit from accurate testing and diagnosis. And conversely, both the patient and her family can be harmed by negligent testing and diagnosis. Molloy's experts indicate that a physician would have a duty to inform the parents of a child diagnosed with Fragile X disorder. The appellants admit that their practice is to inform parents in such a case. The standard of care thus acknowledges that families rely on physicians to communicate a diagnosis of the genetic disorder to the patient's family. It is foreseeable that a negligent diagnosis of Fragile X will cause harm not only to the patient, but to the family of the patient as well. This is particularly true regarding parents who have consulted the physicians concerning the patient's condition and have been advised of the need for genetic testing.

We therefore hold that a physician's duty regarding genetic testing and diagnosis extends beyond the patient to biological parents who foreseeably may be harmed by a breach of that duty. In this case, the patient suffered from a serious disorder that had a high probability of being genetically transmitted and for which a reliable and accepted test was widely available. The appellants should have foreseen that parents of childbearing years might conceive another child in the absence of knowledge of the genetic disorder. The appellants owed a duty of care regarding genetic testing and diagnosis, and the resulting medical advice, not only to S.F. but also to her parent.... [W]e ... conclude that the duty arises where it is reasonably foreseeable that the parents would be injured if the advice is negligently given.

...

Appellants suggest that recognizing a duty to Molloy would extend a physician's duty to an unreasonable extent, requiring the physician to seek out and inform distant relatives.... [W]e need not, and do not, address whether the duty recognized here extends beyond biological parents who foreseeably will rely on genetic testing and diagnosis and therefore foreseeably may be injured by negligence in discharging the duty of care.

Notes & Questions

1. How does the application of a duty to warn in this case fit with the *Tarasoff* framework? Consider how it meshes with the following recommendations from the American Society for Human Genetics, outlined in the ASHG 1998 Statement on Professional Disclosure of Familial Genetic Information:

I. Points to Consider

A. *The General Rule of Confidentiality.* Genetic information, like all medical information, should be protected by the legal and ethical principle of confidentiality that exists within the patient-physician relationship....

B. *Exceptional Circumstances that Permit Disclosure.* (1) Disclosure should be permissible where attempts to encourage disclosure on the part of the patient have failed; where the harm is highly likely to occur and is serious and foreseeable; where the at-risk relative(s) is identifiable; and where either the disease is preventable/treatable or medically accepted standards indicate that early monitoring will reduce the genetic risk.... (2) The harm that may result from failure to disclose should outweigh the harm that may result from disclosure....

C. *Ethical Duty to Inform Patients about Familial Implications.* At a minimum, health-care professionals should be obliged to inform patients about the implications of their genetic test results and about the potential risks to their family members....

ASHG Statement, *Professional Disclosure of Familial Genetic Information*, 62 AM. J. HUM. GENET. 474 (1998).

Was Dr. Meier aware of a serious risk that was both foreseeable and highly likely to occur? At the time she was considering the Fragile X diagnosis, was there an identifiable at-risk relative? What opportunities for prevention or treatment would have attended a warning in that case? Would it make any difference in your analysis if Molloy had already conceived her second child? Whose interests in privacy and confidentiality are at stake in this case? Does the fact the patient is a child and the "third party" is that child's parent have any impact on your assessment? Was it necessary to include a claim for "breach of duty to warn" to recover damages associated with the birth of a second child affected with Fragile X? *See Harbeson v. Parke Davis*, 656 P.2d 483 (Wash. 1983).

2. The *Molloy* case illustrates a fact pattern that is becoming more frequent in medical malpractice litigation—the failure to diagnose a genetic condition. These cases, and some of the unique damages theories that have arisen from them, are discussed in greater detail in Chapter 7.

Chapter 3

Genetic Discrimination in the Workplace

In this chapter we begin to consider the non-clinical ramifications of genetic testing and the information such testing reveals, focusing on the potential for discrimination as employers begin to consider whether and how individual genetic information could inform decisions regarding the terms and conditions of employment. Chapter 4 will continue the genetic discrimination discussion, shifting focus to another area of significant public concern—the impact of genetic information on access to health care coverage and life and disability insurance.

Part A of this chapter introduces and discusses the general concept of genetic discrimination, challenging the reader to consider the range of criteria that can and should be used to define appropriate and inappropriate uses of genetic information in the employment context. Part B provides an introduction and historical overview of the genetic discrimination issue as it applies to decisions affecting hiring, firing, and the terms and conditions of employment. Part C reviews the legislative response to the perceived threat of genetic discrimination in the workplace, beginning with a review of state legislative approaches and then moving to the federal government's response. In Part D we turn to case law for insight on how the courts view the nature and scope of protection against genetic discrimination offered under the ADA and Title VII of the Civil Rights Act.

A. Defining Genetic Discrimination

Mark A. Rothstein & Mary R. Anderlik, *What Is Genetic Discrimination, and When and How Can It Be Prevented?*

3 GENET. IN MED. 354 (2001)

...

The two most common uses of the term discrimination differ dramatically in the degree of disapproval they connote. On the one hand, the term discrimination may be used to indicate a type of distinction that invariably is or should be socially unacceptable. We refer to this as the civil rights definition. For example, the Council for Responsible Genetics position paper on genetic discrimination does not define the term discrimination, but the negative connotation is clear from its use. Discrimination is linked to evaluating people based on "questionable stereotypes" rather than their individual merits and abilities, invading people's privacy, the morally and publicly unacceptable stratification of the community into "haves" and "have-nots," and the punishment of people for characteristics over which they have no control in violation of cherished beliefs in justice and equality. The proper response to discrimination is legal prohibition.

On the other hand, the term discrimination may be used as an all-purpose descriptor for the practice of making distinctions. Further, some individuals and entities link social unacceptability with irrationality, that is, they believe that only irrational distinctions should be socially unacceptable. We refer to this as the actuarial definition. For example, in the insurance industry, the term discrimination is considered neutral and simply refers to classification for purposes of underwriting. On the industry view, discrimination only becomes problematic where there is no sound actuarial basis for the manner in which risks are classified, or individuals with equivalent risks are treated differently. Often, in the business context, "irrational" means that the distinction cannot be defended in economic terms or, in the case of insurance, by reference to sound actuarial principles.

For both definitions, the term genetic discrimination also conveys that adverse treatment is based solely on the genotype of asymptomatic individuals. Differential treatment on the basis of phenotype is frequently rational and accepted as a social necessity, such as where an employer bases a hiring decision on a job-related need for visual acuity. Cases of adverse treatment based on the phenotypic expression of a genetic characteristic fit well within the analytical framework of laws dealing with disability-based or health status-based discrimination generally. The most important of these laws is the Americans with Disabilities Act. To the contrary, cases of adverse treatment of phenotypically "normal" individuals fit poorly within the disability discrimination framework. A large majority of the public considers discrimination against these individuals as unfair because current opportunities are being denied to seemingly unaffected individuals merely because a genetic test or assessment indicates an increased risk of future incapacity.

We define discrimination as drawing a distinction among individuals or groups plus an element of either irrationality or social unacceptability or both. Our definition draws upon elements of both the civil rights and actuarial definitions. When discrimination is defined in this way, the term clearly has a negative connotation; discrimination is a bad thing. Even so, legal proscription of the classification may not be warranted. The appropriate legal and policy response to social unacceptability—a widely shared sense within a polity that some activity or state of affairs is "wrong"—will depend on the circumstances.... Our definition recognizes that some forms of irrational discrimination are accepted, or at least tolerated, by society and some forms of discrimination are socially unacceptable, despite the fact that they are rational.

Table 1 illustrates the application of our definition of discrimination by indicating how a sample of selection criteria for employment would be arrayed along dimensions of social acceptability and rationality. Note that standards for judging social acceptability will vary according to the context. While employers are generally not prohibited from basing hiring decisions on Zodiac signs, even though this is clearly irrational, an insurer would have to offer some actuarial basis for the distinction in order to meet the requirements of state insurance laws. One justification or differences in the law of employment and insurance is that, in our society, there is no history of systematic mistreatment of Virgos relative to Capricorns in employment, and the costs of policing idiosyncratic factors in isolated hiring decisions would be very high. On the other hand, risk classification in insurance involves assigning individuals to risk pools; hence, insurance practices have the potential to create systematic mistreatment. Insurance underwriting policies also are more amenable to regulation than hiring decisions.

Table 1. Categories of discrimination

	Rational	Irrational
Acceptable	• Choosing an employee based on relative skill or other job-related criteria	• Choosing an employee based on Zodiac sign
	• Choosing an employee based on medical assessment of ability to perform the job	• Choosing an employee based on a coin toss
Unacceptable	• Excluding a person with cancer from consideration for employment based on concerns about health care costs	• Excluding a person from consideration for employment based on religion (in a secular enterprise)
	• Excluding a pregnant woman from consideration for employment because she may soon go on maternity leave	• Excluding a person from consideration for employment based on national origin.

Historically, in insurance underwriting the law has mirrored the industry view that rational distinctions are acceptable. More recently, however, at least with respect to health insurance, this view is changing. In the United States, state laws prohibiting health insurers from gaining access to or using genetic information, and provisions of the Health Insurance Portability and Accountability Act (HIPAA) prohibiting employer-sponsored group health plans from using genetic information and other health-status related factors in underwriting, mark a significant expansion of the category of "rational but unacceptable." The change likely reflects consensus about the importance of access to health care. Proposals to restrict or eliminate genetic discrimination in other insurance products do not yet enjoy the same degree of support. In countries that have universal access to health care, life insurance is now at the center of debate.

...

There are good ethical reasons for preventing genetic discrimination. On the other hand, considerations of justice weigh against treating genetic discrimination differently from other forms of health status-based discrimination. There are also many practical considerations that weigh against separate treatment of genetic information. Three have become increasingly obvious over time: (1) We can't define "genetic"; (2) Even if we could define genetic, it is not feasible to separate genetic information from other health information; (3) Separate treatment increases the stigma attached to genetic conditions and lends legitimacy to genetic reductionism and determinism.

We can't define genetic

Discussions of genetic discrimination often note the line drawing problems associated with the word "genetic." Is family medical history "genetic" information? Is breast cancer a "genetic" disease? Is a sweat chloride test for cystic fibrosis a "genetic" test? A great deal of information concerning inherited genetic disorders can be derived from family history. Yet, state laws may define genetic information as including only information derived from laboratory tests. Narrow definitions also fail to protect information about genetic services, for example, whether an individual has ever undergone genetic testing or has participated in genetic research.

Monogenic disorders, in which the condition is caused by a single gene, are certainly genetic conditions. However, it is less clear that diagnostic tests analyzing proteins and other gene products are genetic tests under laws that apply to "direct" tests for abnormalities, defects, or deficiencies in genetic material, and expressly exclude tests for indirect manifestations of genetic disorders (e.g., Colorado, Indiana, Kansas, Ohio). Problems of definition will be exacerbated as genetic research turns increasingly to complex disorders. Scientists can be expected to identify a genetic component of numerous health problems. Researchers have already discovered a genetic contribution to some forms of diabetes, hypertension, hypercholesterolemia, epilepsy, osteoporosis, and various cancers. Because these and similar complex or multifactorial disorders are likely to be the main focus of future genetic inquiries in clinical and other settings, a DNA-based definition of "genetic" would be demonstrably under inclusive. Yet a more comprehensive definition would include virtually all medical conditions.

Even if we could define genetic, it is not feasible to separate genetic information from other health information

In most medical records, information about family history and similar matters is interspersed with other kinds of information. Editing or otherwise expunging genetic information from the patient's medical record before releasing it to authorized third parties would be burdensome and impractical. (By comparison, the results of HIV testing are fairly easy to isolate in the medical record.) Attempting to isolate genetic information so that, for example, only nongenetic information is maintained in patient records, might also compromise the quality of patient care, by impeding the access of health care professionals to this clinically significant information. Third parties such as employers and insurers will not be the only ones affected.

Separate treatment increases the stigma attached to genetic conditions and lends legitimacy to genetic reductionism and determinism

Separate treatment increases the stigma of genetic conditions. People may believe that because genetic conditions are singled out for protection, they must be particularly shameful. Separate treatment also encourages genetic reductionism, whereby all traits, health problems, and behaviors are attributed to genes, without regard to other factors. Genetic determinism is the belief that an individual's future "is defined and predicted by genetic make up and cannot be changed." Separate treatment suggests that genetic information is wholly unlike other kinds of health information and that genetic conditions are wholly unlike other kinds of health conditions....

Notes & Questions

1. Rothstein and Anderlik draw a distinction between *genotype* (the specific DNA sequence for a gene) and *phenotype* (the expression of a particular genotype by a cell or an individual), suggesting that decisions based upon the latter are "frequently rational and accepted as a social necessity." Do you agree? Why might decisions based upon genotype alone be more likely to be discriminatory in a socially unacceptable way than decisions based upon phenotype? What other factors might bear on your assessment of the rationality and/or social acceptability of an adverse decision regarding insurability or employment that is based upon an individual's genotype? Should it make a difference

whether the genetic trait of interest (the genotype) is associated with a single-gene or multifactorial disorder?

Single-gene disorders result from the inheritance of either a single mutant copy of the gene from one parent (autosomal dominant disorders); two mutant copies of the gene, one from each parent (autosomal recessive disorders); or a mutant copy of an X-chromosome-linked gene from the mother (X-linked disorders). These disorders are highly penetrant, which means they are almost certain to occur, although the degree of expression and the age of onset may vary. Multifactorial disorders, on the other hand, are associated with genetic mutations that significantly increase the risk for disease but are not sufficient, standing alone, to cause disease. These disorders, which include such common but complex diseases as cancer, heart disease, and diabetes, are triggered by an interaction between one or more genetic variations and one or more environmental exposures. By way of analogy, the individual's genetic makeup may be thought of as the gun and the environment as the trigger: a gun presents a certain risk of harm, but the harm is realized only if the trigger is pulled. Kenneth Olden & S.H. Wilson, *Environmental Health and Genomics: Visions and Implications*, 18 NAT. REV. GENET. 91 (2000).

To what extent should genetic factors such as *penetrance*, variable *expressivity*, *pleiotropy*, *heterogeneity*, or variable *age of onset* influence your assessment of the social acceptability of a discriminatory employment decision? For a good introduction to the meaning and significance of these scientific factors, see Richard R. Sharp, *The Evolution of Predictive Genetic Testing: Deciphering Gene-Environment Interaction*, 41 JURIMETRICS J. 145 (2001); Thomas D. Gelehrter, Francis S. Collins & David Ginsburg, PRINCIPLES OF MEDICAL GENETICS (2d ed. 1998); The New York State Task Force on Life and the Law, GENETIC TESTING AND SCREENING IN THE AGE OF GENOMIC MEDICINE (2000); Eric S. Lander & Nicholas J. Schork, *Genetic Dissection of Complex Traits*, 265 SCIENCE 2037 (1994).

To illustrate how these variables may influence the assessment of whether a decision to distinguish treatment based upon genetic traits is rational or socially acceptable, consider the following three case scenarios. How would you characterize the employer's decision in each case: is it rational and socially acceptable under the facts of the case? (You will be asked to return to these three case scenarios at the end of the chapter and reanalyze them in light of the court cases and statutory materials covered in the chapter's remaining sections.)

> (1) Sam, a twenty-five-year-old engineer learns that his father (aged sixty) has been diagnosed with Huntington disease (HD). HD is a highly penetrant, autosomal dominant disorder. HD is associated with progressive deterioration of mental and neurologic function over a ten-to-twenty-year period and reduced life expectancy. It typically manifests in the fifth decade, although age of onset has varied between the third and seventh decades. Medical care, which is expensive, is largely symptomatic since there is currently no cure. Sam's father first began to show signs of neurologic difficulties in his mid-fifties. Realizing that he has a 50% likelihood of having inherited the HD gene from his father, Sam decides to undergo genetic testing. Unfortunately, the tests are positive. Sam is currently healthy, is fully capable of performing his job and, given his age, will likely remain symptom free for at least the next fifteen-to-twenty years. When Sam's employer learns of the diagnosis, Sam is fired. *See* M. Bloch, S. Adam, S. Wiggins, M. Huggins & M.R. Hayden, *Predictive Testing for Huntington Disease in Canada: The Experience of those Receiving an Increased Risk*, 42 AM. J. MED. GENET. 499 (1992).

(2) Sally is a twenty-six-year-old university graduate with a master's degree in special education. She suffers from cystic fibrosis (CF), an autosomal recessive disorder associated with a range of respiratory and gastrointestinal problems, as well as sterility in males. Unfortunately Sally's CF significantly limits her respiratory capacity and renders her exceptionally susceptible to infections. In other words, Sally's disease is both symptomatic and physically limiting. Sally has received a conditional offer of employment with her local public school district for a teaching position in an inner city high school that has an established record of significant problems with student discipline, drugs, and violence. During the required pre-placement medical screening examination Sally's employer learns of her CF and her extensive medical history involving ongoing hospitalizations and therapy. The offer of employment is withdrawn. *See* Julian Zielenski & Lap-Chee Tsui, *Cystic Fibrosis: Genotypic and Phenotypic Variations*, 29 ANN. REV. GENET. 777 (1995).

(3) Ted is a forty-two-year-old emergency room physician who is employed by an HMO. Ted has a long family history of heart disease, and his primary care physician recommends he undergo genetic testing to see if he has inherited any of the ApoE gene variants that are linked to increased risk for some cardiovascular disorders (CVD). The testing reveals that Ted has one copy of the ApoE e4 variant, which, in addition to indicating increased risk for CVD is also associated with an increased risk for late-onset familial Alzheimer disease. Alzheimer disease (AD) is characterized by adult-onset dementia. Disease onset manifests with a subtle memory failure that slowly progresses until it is incapacitating. Other symptoms include confusion, language disturbance, agitation, withdrawal, and occasionally seizures, tremors, increased muscle tone, and incontinence. In late-onset disease symptoms appear after age sixty to sixty-five, and the typical duration of the disease ranges from eight to ten years. While inheritance of one copy of the ApoE e4 gene has been shown to increase individual risk over that of the general population, it is not considered necessary or sufficient to cause late-onset AD; many individuals with one APOE4 variant do not develop the disease, and research is ongoing to identify relevant cofactors that contribute to disease onset. Ted does not have a family history of dementia and is currently symptom free. His employer expresses concern about his ongoing ability to manage patient care and proposes early retirement. *See* American College of Medical Genetics/American Society of Human Genetics Working Group on ApoE and Alzheimer's Disease, *Statement on the Use of Apolipoprotein E Testing For Alzheimer Disease,* 247 J. AM. MED. ASS'N 1627 (1995).

2. There appears to be a growing consensus that "genetic discrimination" is discrimination based upon the genotype of a presently healthy individual, *i.e.,* discrimination on the basis of genetic traits that predict future risk for disease or disability but are, as yet, unexpressed. To what extent did your analysis of the rationality or social acceptability of the three case scenarios reflect this definition? Can you think of circumstances in which this definition would be underinclusive or overinclusive?

3. The Rothstein and Anderlik article points out that one of the challenges facing lawmakers seeking to protect against genetic discrimination is deciding how to define "genetic." A definition limited to information about genotype that comes from laboratory examinations of genes or chromosomes includes a much narrower range of information bearing upon an individual's genetic make-up than one that includes tests for

metabolites or other biomarkers for genetic traits or one that encompasses family history. The former offers protection to designated carriers of known genetic traits associated with single-gene disorders (*e.g.*, Huntington disease) or increased susceptibility to multifactorial gene-environment diseases such as hereditary breast and ovarian cancer (carriers of relevant mutations in the BRCA1 and BRCA2 genes are at increased risk for this condition). The latter definition expands the reach of protection to cover individuals whose family history suggests risk for certain conditions, regardless of whether the specific genetic contributors have yet been characterized (*e.g.*, alcoholism, depression, Parkinson disease). For additional commentary on and proposed solutions to the challenges associated with defining "genetic," *see, e.g.*, Thomas H. Murray, *Genetic Exceptionalism and "Future Diaries": Is Genetic Information Different from Other Medical Information? in* GENETIC SECRETS: PROTECTING PRIVACY AND CONFIDENTIALITY IN THE GENETIC ERA (Mark A. Rothstein, ed. 1997); Henry T. Greely, *Genotype Discrimination: The Complex Case for Some Legislative Protection*, 149 U. PA. L. REV. 1483 (2001).

The following two state statutory excerpts illustrate the two ends of the definition spectrum. As you review them, think about the scope of protection offered under each. How are they different? Are they overinclusive, underinclusive, or appropriately balanced? Would either statute offer protection against genetic discrimination as it is defined in the Rothstein article?

Arizona Revised Statutes

Sec. 20-1051. Definitions.

In this article, unless the context otherwise requires:

. . .

4. "Genetic information" means information about genes, gene products and inherited characteristics that may derive from the individual or a family member, including information regarding carrier status and information derived from laboratory tests that identify mutations in specific genes or chromosomes, physical medical examinations, family histories and direct analysis of genes or chromosomes.

. . .

8. "Health status-related factor" means any factor in relation to the health of the individual or a dependent of the individual enrolled or to be enrolled in a health care services organization including:

(a) Health status.

(b) Medical condition, including physical and mental illness.

(c) Claims experience.

(d) Receipt of health care.

(e) Medical history.

(f) Genetic information.

Alaska Statutes

A.S. 18.13.100. Definitions.

In this chapter,

(1) "DNA" means deoxyribonucleic acid, including mitochondrial DNA, complementary DNA, and DNA derived from ribonucleic acid;

(2) "DNA analysis" means DNA or genetic typing and testing to determine the presence or absence of genetic characteristics in an individual, including tests of nucleic acids or chromosomes in order to diagnose or identify a genetic characteristic; "DNA analysis" does not include a routine physical measurement, a test for drugs, alcohol, cholesterol, or the human immunodeficiency virus, a chemical, blood, or urine analysis, or any other diagnostic test that is widely accepted and in use in clinical practice;

(3) "genetic characteristic" includes a gene, chromosome, or alteration of a gene or chromosome that may be tested to determine the existence or risk of a disease, disorder, trait, propensity, or syndrome, or to identify an individual or a blood relative; "genetic characteristic" does not include family history or a genetically transmitted characteristic whose existence or identity is determined other than through a genetic test.

Notes & Questions

1. In a position statement advocating greater legislative protection against genetic discrimination, the American College of Medical Genetics acknowledged the difficulty legislators face in defining "genetic test," "genetic information," and "genetic services" and offered the following recommendations:

- Definitions must be sufficiently broad to accommodate the wide range of what is known about classical single-gene disorders and the contribution of multiple genes to common, complex diseases.
- Definitions must be sufficiently flexible to avoid becoming rapidly outdated by new developments.
- Definitions must be sufficiently narrow and clear to avoid confusion in application of statutory protection in the current system of health delivery.
- Definitions must avoid creating arbitrary distinctions that unfairly exclude some individuals from protections afforded to others.
- Protected genetic information must include that based on evaluation, testing and family histories of individuals and their family members.

M.S. Watson & C.L. Greene, *Points to Consider in Preventing Unfair Discrimination Based on Genetic Disease Risk: A Position Statement of the American College of Medical Genetics*, 3 GENET. IN MED. 436 (2001). To what extent do the Alaska and Arizona statutes satisfy the ACMG recommendations? If you were responsible for drafting proposed genetic discrimination legislation for your state, how would you draft a definitions section that met the ACMG criteria?

2. How real is the problem of genetic discrimination? Obviously the answer to this question is going to depend, in part, upon how genetic discrimination is defined. Regardless, as the cases and materials in this chapter and Chapter 4 demonstrate, there is considerable public concern and substantial legislative and policy activity around this issue. Yet the data substantiating a risk of genetic discrimination are largely anecdotal.

See, e.g., Margaret Otlowski, et al., *Genetic Discrimination: Too Few Data,* 11 EUROPEAN J. HUM. GENET. 1 (2003); P. Billings, et al., *Discrimination as a Consequence of Genetic Testing,* 50 AM. J. HUM. GENET. 476 (1992); L. Geller, et al., *Individual, Family and Societal Dimensions of Genetic Discrimination: A Case Study Analysis,* 2 SCIENCE AND ENGINEERING ETHICS 71 (1996); E. Lapham, et al., *Genetic Discrimination: Perspectives of Consumers,* 274 SCIENCE 62 (1996).

What robust research has been done suggests public fears may be misplaced. *See* M.A. Hall & S.S. Rich, *Laws Restricting Health Insurers' Use of Genetic Information: Impact on Genetic Discrimination,* 66 AM. J. HUM. GENET. 293 (2002). With this in mind consider the following questions as you review the cases and materials in this chapter and Chapter 4. To what extent are there data establishing that genetic discrimination is indeed a sufficient problem to warrant affording genetic information extraordinary protection under the law? To what extent does existing law discourage or preclude genetic discrimination? Does genetic discrimination legislation pose a significant risk for reverse discrimination, particularly when dealing with predictive genetic information regarding risk for multifactorial disease? Should an individual with genetic susceptibility to breast cancer receive greater protection under the law against discrimination than the individual who faces the general population risk for idiopathic breast cancer? Why or why not? *See* Mark A. Rothstein, *Genetic Privacy and Confidentiality: Why They are so Hard to Protect,* 26 J.L. MED. & ETHICS 198 (1998).

B. Genetic Testing and the Workplace: Problems, Perceptions, and Policy Proposals

Paul Steven Miller, *Genetic Discrimination in the Workplace*

26 J.L. MED. & ETHICS 89 (1998)

The surge in genetic research and technology, fueled in large part by the Human Genome Project, has resulted in the continuing expansion of the range of genetic tests and other genetic information available to physicians, insurance companies, employers, and the general public. Genetic tests can provide presymptomatic medical information about an individual, including information about an individual's increased risk of future disease, disability, or early death. These tests can reveal information about an individual's carrier status, that is, the likelihood of parents passing on to their children a genetic condition, and about the health of the individual's family members. Although genetic information provides the promise of early detection and treatment of certain illnesses and disorders, it also poses risks. As a result of the increase in genetic testing and information, legal issues regarding employment discrimination on the basis of genetic information are emerging. These issues are important to all working Americans because genetic testing is becoming more prevalent. If employers are permitted to base personnel decisions on genetic information, people will be unfairly barred or removed from working for reasons that are unrelated to their ability to perform their jobs. In addition, people will be reluctant to take advantage of the growing array of genetic tests that can identify their vulnerability to specific diseases and possibly permit early treatment because of a fear that the information, or inferences drawn from the fact that an individual has sought to be tested, will be misused....

Workers' fears and the reality of genetic discrimination

Although little systematic data gauging the extent of actual genetic discrimination in the workplace are available, workers clearly fear that employers will use genetic information to lower their insurance and sick leave costs by weeding out individuals who have traits linked to inherited medical conditions. A 1997 national survey of 1,000 people conducted by the federally funded National Center for Genome Resources found that nearly two-thirds of respondents would not take a genetic test if employers and health insurers could see the results, and 85 percent felt that employers should be prohibited from obtaining information about an individual's genetic conditions and predispositions. Similarly, a 1995 poll of the general public found that over 85 percent of survey respondents were very concerned or somewhat concerned about access to and use of genetic information by insurers and employers. Researchers at Georgetown University conducted a survey of 332 individuals with one or more family members with a genetic disorder who were affiliated with genetic support groups. The vast majority, 87 percent, said that they would not want their employers to know if they were tested and found to be at high risk for a genetic disorder with serious complications. Seventeen percent of respondents said that they have not revealed known genetic information to their employers for fear of losing their jobs or insurance coverage.

Individuals' fears of workplace discrimination could keep them from being tested and learning whether they have genetic traits linked to breast cancer, cystic fibrosis (CF), Huntington disease, colon cancer, or other conditions, even though early detection and treatment could extend their lives. The Georgetown study (cited above) also revealed that, as a result of fears of discrimination, nearly one in ten persons surveyed chose not to undergo genetic tests. The Clinton administration has noted findings that many women have refused to take advantage of genetic screening to determine the likelihood of breast cancer because they fear that the information might be made available to employers or insurers. Individuals' refusals to get genetic tests because they fear genetic discrimination have negative consequences not just for those individuals, but also for scientific research in this area. Some medical researchers have voiced concerns because individuals are refusing to participate in long-term medical studies to assess their risk of developing genetically linked diseases, such as various forms of cancer, because these individuals believe that involvement in such studies would be a red flag on their medical records that could subject them to genetic discrimination.

Workers' fears of genetic discrimination are not baseless. Although no statistically representative studies measuring the extent of actual genetic discrimination have been conducted to date, and those studies that have been conducted rely in large part on individuals' perceptions of discrimination, anecdotal evidence of genetic discrimination in employment has been compiled. A 1996 study conducted by a team of medical researchers documented more than 200 cases of individuals with a genetic predisposition to certain diseases, but who were asymptomatic at the time, who reported a range of discriminatory actions, made on the basis of genetic information, by insurance companies, employers, and others. A 1989 survey of 400 employers by Northwest Life Insurance found that, by the year 2000, 15 percent of employers plan to check the genetic status of prospective employees and their dependents before making job offers. In the Georgetown study, 15 percent of respondents said that they or affected family members had been asked questions about genetic diseases or disabilities on job applications (although it is not clear how often this information was used subsequently to deny jobs to applicants). Thirteen percent of respondents reported that they or another family member had been denied a job or terminated from a job because of a genetic condition in the family. In a recent survey that attempted to assess the extent of discrimination against individuals with genetic abnormalities who were otherwise healthy, genetic services providers and primary care physicians who were surveyed reported knowing of 582 people who were refused employment or insurance based on a genetic predisposition. Although the study's authors regarded this number as small in relation to the total number of patients seen by the surveyed professionals, they concluded that genetic discrimination does in fact exist.

...

Although advances in genetic research and technology portend tremendous benefits for humankind in medicine and science, adequate protections need to be in place to ensure that such technology will not be used for the wrong reasons. The use of genetic testing and/or genetic information to exclude qualified individuals from the workplace should be illegal. The ADA provides protection from workplace discrimination against individuals with disabilities and individuals who are regarded as disabled, including people with genetic predispositions. And yet, to date, no court has ruled on this issue. Moreover, genetic information is a very powerful tool that can be used by employers to preclude an otherwise qualified individual from getting or holding a job.

A job action based on a genetic predisposition is rooted in an employer's fears, myths, and stereotypes, rather than in an employee's ability to do the job, and therefore constitutes unlawful discrimination. As developing technology is increasingly able to reveal individuals' genetic predisposition for mental and physical disabilities and disorders, additional protections will be necessary to ensure that genetic information is not misused in the workplace. In the area of genetic technology, we are traveling down an unknown road. As new situations are posed by the rapid development of genetic technology, a flexible approach must be adopted to ensure that civil rights will continue to be protected. Courts will need to utilize the flexible structure of the ADA to apply its protections to those who are deprived of employment opportunities and regarded as disabled simply on the basis of genetic markers. In addition, state and federal legislation should be adopted to provide additional protections in this ever expanding area. In this way, one's genotype will not substitute for one's qualifications.

Paul W. Brandt-Rauf & Sherry I. Brandt-Rauf, *Genetic Testing in the Workplace: Ethical, Legal, and Social Implications*

25 Ann. Rev. of Pub. Health 139 (2004)

On February 9, 2001, the Equal Employment Opportunity Commission filed suit in federal district court in Sioux City, Iowa, challenging the genetic testing program of the Burlington Northern Railway Company as a violation of the Americans with Disabilities Act (ADA). The Commission asked the court to order the railroad to end its policy of requiring all union members who claim work-related carpal tunnel syndrome to provide blood samples for DNA analysis for a genetic marker that may be related to some forms of carpal tunnel syndrome. The court papers alleged that employees were asked for blood samples but were not told the sample's purpose was genetic testing and that at least one individual who refused to provide a sample because he suspected it would be used for genetic testing was threatened with discharge if he did not submit. In the face of a legal challenge, Burlington Northern agreed to halt genetic testing of its employees.

The Burlington Northern case is only the most recent example of the contested use of genetic testing in the workplace, but it will likely not be the last. Now that the Human Genome Project is complete, it can be anticipated that the application of new genetic information and technologies that have emerged from this project will greatly expand in society in general and in the workplace, raising significant ethical, legal, and social issues. The use of emerging genetic information and technologies in the workplace has the potential to benefit worker health and safety, but their misapplication could equally work to the detriment of employees in many different ways. As is true with all applications of genetics, the current challenge in the workplace is to realize the potential benefits for workers in a manner that is ethically, legally, and socially acceptable and that minimizes the potential risks.

The roots of these issues in genetic testing are many and complex. It has been recognized for some time that the phenotypic expression of disease represents an interaction between an individual's genetic makeup and various factors in the environment, including the work environment, to which the individual is exposed over his/her lifetime. The contributions of genotype and environment to the phenotypic expression will vary depending on the particular disease state. The more common human diseases, such as coronary artery disease and cancer, are believed to reflect the interaction of multiple genes with a significant environmental component. In some cases, the genetic component of these complex but common disorders represents an inherited susceptibility to the development of the disease, which may emerge only in interaction with necessary environmental factors. In other cases (cancer, for example), part of the genetic component is contributed by somatic genetic changes acquired after birth, usually owing to environmental factors, including those in the workplace; these genetic alterations indicate acquired susceptibility (as opposed to inherited susceptibility) to these disorders. Of course, in all these cases it is important to recognize that the particular genetic alterations usually only indicate susceptibility for disease, not the certainty of disease, and the degree of certainty (or, in other words, the predictive value of testing for the genetic alterations) varies widely. Even in the case of the less common, single gene inherited disorders, where we have the most experience with genetic testing and often more certainty in the test results' predictive value for revealing disease development, many different ethical, legal, and social issues have arisen. By mapping and sequencing the entire human genome through the Human Genome Project, which will allow the detection of genetic alterations for more single-gene disorders as well as for inherited and acquired genetic susceptibility for common disorders, these issues will undoubtedly expand.

Although it is hoped that the ability to determine the genetic component of many diseases will ultimately lead to better treatment and prevention, effective curative or prophylactic interventions have generally lagged behind detection ability. The identification of the genetic basis for disease may have value for individuals with disease or with a carrier status or susceptibility for disease. For example, with appropriate counseling, individuals who wish to know their genetic status can use the knowledge to make significant life decisions such as whether or not to reproduce. However, also important is to realize the grave potential for misuse of the ability to detect the genetic components of disease or susceptibility, both in the application of the technology and in the handling of the resulting information. The growth of the biotechnology industry increases the probability that with little forethought and few precautions experimental scientific advances will be rapidly translated into easily accessible, commercial genetic tests. We have already seen heated debate over the availability of testing for the breast cancer susceptibility gene BRCA 1, which some believe was offered prematurely and resulted in more harm than good. Inappropriate genetic testing can threaten individual autonomy, privacy, and confidentiality and lead to various types of genetic stigmatization and discrimination without any commensurate benefit for the individual tested.

As the Burlington Northern case illustrates, one venue where genetic testing is already being subject to such misuse is the workplace. Employers may have several reasons for interest in the genetic information of current or prospective employees. First, as already noted, disease expression represents the interaction between genotype and environmental exposures, including those in the workplace. In order to minimize the potential health effects of adverse workplace exposures, employers could have an interest in identifying individuals who have a particular genetic susceptibility to such interactions to avoid placing them in jobs that might put them at risk from those exposures. The expansion in genetic knowledge will allow increasing ability to detect such genetic susceptibilities to particular exposures. In addition, since many employers subsidize the health insurance of employees either indirectly or directly (in the case of some large companies that self-insure), employers have a financial interest in the health status of employees and thus in their risk for the development of disease. The financial incentives for employers in this area are further compounded by the fact that the health of employees is increasingly found to be a major contributor to worker productivity. Together these factors contribute to the expansion of health screening and health risk assessment programs for employees, particularly with the escalation of health care costs over the past years and the recent economic downturn, which has served to emphasize the need for increased worker productivity. As noted above, the expansion of genetic knowledge will allow increasing ability to detect inherited and acquired genetic alterations that increase the risk of development of the more common diseases, greatly enhancing the power of such health screening and risk assessment. Thus, misuse of genetic testing in the employment setting could have direct adverse impacts on an individual's insurability and employability, as well as their privacy and confidentiality, personal autonomy, stigmatization, and quality of life.

Background of the Problem

Although the recent advances in genetics will certainly greatly expand its potential applications in the workplace, concern over the use and misuse of genetic information in the employment setting has a long history. Since the early writings about occupational disease by Paracelsus, Agricola, and Ramazzini in the 1500s and 1600s, it has been known that people who have particular workplace exposures develop much higher rates of certain diseases than the rest of the population, and that even within the same worker groups, certain individuals seemed more susceptible to disease than others. For example, Ramazzini suggested that it was "not improbable that some morbid constitution proved to be more injurious" in certain cases. The possibility that such a "morbid constitution" might have a genetic basis and that genetic testing might be useful in identifying susceptible individuals in the workplace was first explicitly posited by the British geneticist J.B.S. Haldane in his book Heredity and Politics. Haldane noted:

> The majority of potters do not die of bronchitis. It is quite possible that if we really understood the causation of this disease we should find out that only a fraction of potters are of a constitution which renders them liable to it. If so, we could eliminate potters' bronchitis by regulating entrants into the potters' industry who are congenitally disposed to it.

In Haldane's time, physicians had little way, other than perhaps family history, gender, or some other phenotypic marker of susceptibility, to determine if a worker might be of such a constitution. For example, at one point, some tar and creosote makers denied employment to fair-skinned workers, using skin color as a phenotypic marker for a certain genetic composition, because they thought such individuals would be more susceptible to skin cancer in conjunction with exposure to the known carcinogens in coal tar. However, in the intervening years since Haldane's observation, scientific advances in the ability to test various aspects of genetic susceptibility have led to increasingly more sophisticated ways to try to implement his suggestion.

Based on observations of acute hemolytic anemia among military personnel in Korea who received the antimalarial primaquine and were also heterozygous for glucose-6-phosphate dehydrogenase (G6PD) deficiency, beginning in the 1960s it was hypothesized that workers who were similarly G6PD deficient might also develop anemia under oxidant stresses from a variety of chemical exposures such as aromatic nitro and amino compounds, metal hydrides, and dyes. In 1963, Herbert Stokinger and John Mountain were among the first to propose the use of genetic testing for G6PD deficiency to eliminate susceptible individuals from work with such chemicals....

By 1973, various other genetic conditions were identified for potential workplace screening including: alpha-1-antitrypsin deficiency, sickle cell trait, and sensitivity to carbon disulfide and organic isocyanates. Applications in the workplace soon followed. In 1978, DuPont reported using preemployment blood testing of African Americans on a routine basis for sickle cell trait and restricting individuals who tested positive for the trait and who had low hemoglobin levels from work with nitro and amino compounds. Similarly, in the 1970s, the Air Force excluded African Americans with sickle cell trait from Academy admission and flight training because of presumed risk in hypoxic atmospheres. At the same time, over a ten-year period, the Dow Chemical Company engaged in experimental studies of cytogenetic abnormalities, using them as genetic markers of acquired susceptibility for presumed future risk of cancer and reproductive problems among workers exposed to benzene and epichlorohydrin, although the information was not used in making employment decisions; as noted below, these studies at Dow have recently led to a new twist to the ethical, legal, and social implications of workplace genetic testing. Over the years, other examples of genetic testing in the workplace have been noted, including N-acetylation ability, paraoxonase activity, nicotine-adenine dinucleotide dehydrogenase deficiency, and various cytochrome P450 variants, and new possibilities continue to emerge. For example, it has become possible recently to test for an inherited variation in HLA-DPB1 that may contribute to susceptibility to the development of berylliosis in some workers exposed to beryllium; however, the predictive value of the test is weak as up to 30% of unaffected individuals also carry this variant.

However, it has really been the Burlington Northern case that has brought the controversy over genetic testing back into the spotlight. As noted above in relation to this case, it is now possible to test for an inherited genetic predisposition to carpal tunnel syndrome (CTS): hereditary neuropathy with liability to pressure palsies (HNPP), a demyelinating neuropathy caused by deletion of the peripheral myelin protein-22 (PMP-22) gene. Although up to 90% of HNPP cases develop carpal tunnel syndrome, HNPP is not common, affecting only 1 in 2500–5000 individuals, and thus contributes negligibly to the incidence of carpal tunnel sundrome, making detection of PMP-22 deletion a very inefficient way to screen for carpal tunnel genetic susceptibility. Besides failing to meet the minimal scientific basis for a testing program, the program failed minimal ethical, legal, and social standards in neglecting informed consent, failing to provide genetic counseling, and threatening employees with dismissal for failure to comply.

On the other hand, in some instances employees may come to expect that employers will perform genetic tests for their protection from workplace hazards, arguably making the employer legally liable if it fails to conduct appropriate genetic testing.... In fact, Dow Chemical Company has recently been sued by the widow of a deceased employee for failure to include the employee in the aforementioned cytogenetic testing program, which might have detected early biological indications of his development of leukemia from his workplace exposure to benzene. The plaintiff's argument is strengthened by several studies that have demonstrated predictive value of certain cytogenetic changes for the subsequent development of cancer. Although the Dow program predated these results, the case raises the concern that employers, motivated by fears of legal liability, may well be encouraged to do genetic testing in cases in which the utility for workers' health has not been well established. It also underlines the critical importance that testing can have for workers health in appropriate cases....

Mark A. Rothstein, *Genetics and the Work Force of the Next Hundred Years*

2000 Colum. Bus. L. Rev. 371 (2000)

...

The answer [to the question of whether some genetic information may be job-related] is almost certainly yes. There is little doubt that exposures to certain environments have markedly different effects on individuals based on their genotype. Indeed, this is the premise underlying the Environmental Genome Project coordinated by the National Institute of Environmental Health Sciences, which is attempting to identify the thousands of polymorphisms associated with variations in response to environmental stimuli. The scientific fact of variations in response based on genotype, however, does not resolve the ethical and legal issues of how, if at all, this information should be used by employers, employees, and regulators.

There are two ethical cross-currents in the laws regulating the workplace: paternalism and autonomy. The legal framework of employment in the United States is based, quite literally, on the paternalism of feudal England, where servants were under the direction and control of a master whose legal duties included providing for the safety, health, and well-being of the servant. In the nineteenth century, the master-servant model gave way to the contractual, laissez-faire model of employment at will, in which the law would not regulate the presumed arms-length transactions of employers and employees. Because of an inequality in bargaining power, the effect of the at-will rule was to continue a corporate paternalism that, in industrial America, was often less benign than the manor-based, individual, feudal paternalism. Even our current regulatory regime, from minimum wage and maximum hour laws to child labor laws and the Occupational Safety and Health Act are based on paternalism, albeit a governmental paternalism intended to compensate for the inequality in bargaining power between employers and employees.

Legally protected employee autonomy in the workplace is represented by the National Labor Relations Act, which allows workers the right to organize and bargain collectively, while leaving the terms of the negotiations to the parties. Another example is the ADA, which seeks to prohibit employers from relying on paternalistic myths and stereotypes of what work is suitable for people with various disabilities....

Autonomy and paternalism conflict in the area of genetic predisposition to occupational disease. Should workers be screened for polymorphic markers of varied sensitivity to toxic chemicals and other hazards in some workplaces? One view is that workers should not be screened; instead, the employer should be required to make the workplace safe and healthful for all workers. The problem is that reducing exposures to levels where even the most sensitive individual can work safely is neither technologically nor economically feasible because of the wide variability among individuals and because the difficulty and cost of reducing exposure levels increases exponentially as exposures are reduced to very low levels. The opposite view is that employers should be free to use genetic screening as a way of protecting the health of employees and their own financial interests. This approach, however, shifts the economic burden of working with dangerous substances from the employer to the worker, removes an important incentive to clean up workplaces for the benefit of even 'low-risk' workers, and runs counter to the notion of autonomy embraced in Johnson Controls [*International Union v. Johnson Controls, Inc.*, 499 U.S. 187 (1991)] as well as the ADA.

A middle position is that a worker who is currently capable of performing the job should have the option of learning whether he or she is at increased risk of occupational disease based on genetic factors. This information should not be available to the employer, but should be used by the employee in deciding whether to accept or continue in the position. A threshold issue is whether a scientific test has sufficient analytical and clinical utility to be used as a screening device for individuals, as opposed to a research tool for population studies. Another issue is what criteria should be used in evaluating whether there is scientific justification for the individual to avoid a job with a certain exposure. Finally, other logistical questions include how individuals get referred for genetic testing, who pays for the testing, and who has access to test results.

. . .

Notes & Questions

1. As the preceding articles discuss, employer interest in workplace genetic testing is motivated by a variety of factors, including a desire to minimize the expense and potential liability exposure associated with occupational illness. Occupational illness resulting from exposure to workplace chemicals and other hazards increases production costs because of time loss from work and expenditures for health insurance, health care, and worker compensation. The ability to screen out at-risk workers is seen as a means for reducing the incidence of occupational illness, injury, and associated costs without having to modify workplace conditions. For a review of current evidence regarding the burden of occupational injury and illness, *see* Paul A. Schulte, *Characterizing the Burden of Occupational Injury and Disease*, 47 J. EXPERIMENTAL MED. 607 (2005). For a review of data documenting employer interest in and use of genetic testing to screen and/or monitor workers, *see* U.S. Congress Office of Technology Assessment (OTA), *The Role of Genetic Testing in the Prevention of Occupational Disease* (1983); U.S. Congress Office of Technology Assessment (OTA), *Genetic Monitoring and Screening in the Workplace* (1990); American Management Association Survey Regarding Medical Testing of Employees (2001), http://www.amanet.org.

Although genetic screening could potentially benefit highly susceptible workers by enabling them to minimize hazardous exposures, workers are generally inclined to oppose genetic screening programs because of concerns about job reassignment or loss. Workers also express concerns that genetic screening programs may divert scarce resources and attention from occupational health practices that more effectively protect all workers and the environment. Finally, workers share the concern articulated by Professor Miller that employers will use genetic screening as a pretext to obtain information that has no bearing on the present ability to do the job or on an individual's risk of illness in response to work-site exposures, but instead is suggestive of future health problems that may result in time loss and health care expenses for non-occupational related illness or injury. For a good discussion of the various stakeholder perspectives on the benefits and costs of workplace genetic screening, *see* Elaine Draper, *The Screening of America: The Social and Legal Framework of Employer's Use of Genetic Information,* 20 Berkeley J. Emp. & Lab. L. 286 (1999).

2. Concerns about the potential for genetic discrimination in employment assume that employers can request or otherwise access individual genetic information. In fact, the law does permit employers to access employee genetic information according to established procedures for medical screening of prospective employees to determine their fitness to work and for medical monitoring of existing employees to assess their ongoing health and ability to perform. Relevant federal laws overseeing the medical screening and medical monitoring processes include the Americans with Disabilities Act (ADA), 42 U.S.C. § 12112 and Rehabilitation Act of 1973, 29 U.S.C. § 794. The ADA divides the employment process into three stages: (1) application ("pre-employment"); (2) conditional offer ("pre-placement"); and (3) employed. (42 U.S.C.A. § 12112(d)) At the application stage employers cannot make any inquiries regarding a prospective employee's health or medical history and cannot require any medical screening. Once an offer of employment is extended, employers can require medical screening. The scope of the screening process can be as comprehensive as the employer desires and may include genetic testing. However, the information obtained during this process cannot be used to discriminate in job placement or benefits unless the discriminatory action is job related or dictated by business necessity. 29 C.F.R. § 1630.14(b)(3). The ADA does not permit genetic testing of existing employees unless the testing is performed with their knowledge and consent and is directly related to their qualifications to complete the job or is otherwise necessary for employee safety. 42 U.S.C.S. § 12112(d)(4). Although the ADA's protection against discrimination in employment extends only to qualified persons with a disability (*see* discussion in Part C, *infra.*), the courts have held that a plaintiff need not prove that he or she is a qualified individual with a disability in order to bring a claim challenging the scope of a medical examination under the ADA. *See, e.g., Fredenburg v. Contra Costa County Dep't of Health Servs.*, 172 F.3d 1176 (9th Cir. 1999); *Cossette v. Minnesota Power & Light,* 188 F.3d 1176 (8th Cir. 1999); *Griffin v. Steeltek, Inc.*, 160 F.3d 591 (10th Cir. 1998); *Conroy v. N.Y. State Dep't of Corr. Servs.*, 333 F.3d 88 (2d. Cir. 2003); *Green v. Joy Cone Co.*, 278 F. Supp. 2d 526 (W.D. Pa. 2003). The Rehabilitation Act of 1973 essentially mirrors the ADA but is limited in scope to federal employers.

State laws prohibiting genetic discrimination in employment also impose varying degrees of limits on employers' ability to access or use genetic information to screen, monitor, or diagnose workers. For example, genetic nondiscrimination laws in Iowa, New Hampshire, New York, Rhode Island, Texas, and Wisconsin prohibit employers from soliciting, requiring, or administering a genetic test in either the application process or as a condition of employment. *See* Iowa Code § 729.6; New Hampshire Rev. Stat. Ann. 141-H:3; New York Exec. Law § 296 (19)(a); Rhode Island Gen. Laws § 28-6.7-1; Texas Lab. Code Ann. § 21.402; Wisconsin Stat. § 111.372. However, in Iowa, New Hampshire, New York, and Wisconsin an exception exists for voluntary genetic testing for the purposes of investigating workers' compensation claims or for determining and monitoring worker susceptibility to workplace toxins. New York laws permit employers to require genetic testing for traits that indicate increased risk of disease as a result of workplace exposures. New York Exec. Law §296 (1999). For a good review of state legislative approaches to this issue, *see* Mark A. Rothstein, *Genetics and the Work Force of the Next Hundred Years*, 2000 Colum. Bus. L. Rev. 371 (2000); Michael S. Yesley, *Genetic Differences in the Workplace*, 40 Jurimetrics J. 129 (1999); Mark A. Rothstein, *Protecting Genetic Privacy by Permitting Employer Access Only to Job-Related Employee Medical Information: Analysis of a Unique Minnesota Law*, 24 Am. J. L. & Med. 399 (1998). For examples of how genetics might enter in to a dispute over a worker compensation claim, *see EEOC v. Burlington Northern Santa Fe Railway Co.*, 5:01-cv-04013-MWB (N.D. Iowa. 2001) (discussed in greater detail in Note 4 *infra*) and *Batt v. Workers' Compen. App. Bd.*, 2003 WL 1931923 (Cal. App. 2 Dist.).

The ADA, the Rehabilitation Act of 1973, and HIPAA (Health Insurance Portability and Accountability Act) privacy regulations, 45 C.F.R. Parts 160 and 164, along with the various state genetic privacy and nondiscrimination laws, contain provisions intended to protect the confidentiality of employees' genetic information. Generally these provisions require that any genetic information obtained by employers be maintained with the employee's medical information and that release of that information requires written employee consent. For a more in-depth discussion of law as it pertains to the privacy and confidentiality of genetic information, refer to Chapter 2.

3. The Occupational Safety and Health Act of 1970 (OSHA), 29 U.S.C. §651 *et seq.* (1970) arguably obliges employers to incorporate genetic susceptibility screening into their medical screening and monitoring programs. OSHA is a federal mandate to employers to provide a safe and healthy workplace. Its regulatory framework, which imposes civil penalties on employers for safety and health violations, is particularly relevant to work sites that present significant risks for occupational disease or injury. Indeed, OSHA encourages—and for some industries mandates—employer-conducted medical examinations that encompass periodic biological monitoring of employees to measure the impact of chemical exposures and assess health risks. 29 U.S.C. §655(c)(7)(1994). To date none of the mandates require genetic-based testing or monitoring, although such worksites are precisely the settings where predictive genetic testing might prove beneficial in identifying highly susceptible workers. For a more in-depth discussion of the extent to which OSHA encourages or obliges employers to use genetic susceptibility screening to promote or protect worker health and safety, *see* Gary E. Marchant, *Genetics in the Courtroom: Genetics and Toxic Torts*, 31 Seton Hall L. Rev. 949 (2001); Mark A. Rothstein, *Genetics and the Work Force of the Next Hundred Years*, 2000 Colum. Bus. L. Rev. 371 (2000); Melinda B. Kaufmann, *Genetic Discrimination in the Workplace: An Overview of Existing Protections*, 30 Loy. U. Chi. L.J. 393 (1999).

The prospect of using predictive genetic testing to ameliorate occupational health risks for the genetically susceptible raises several issues with somewhat unique legal implications. To what extent should current environmental standards be further tightened to protect those members of society whose genetic makeup confers heightened susceptibility to environmental agents, and should it make a difference how large in number the group of highly susceptible individuals is? If environmental standards cannot be further tightened without effectively ending the production process involved, what alternative measures can or should be undertaken to minimize the risk of exposure for the genetically susceptible? Who should bear the responsibility (and expense) for protecting the genetically at risk? Should the responsibility to intervene rest with the "polluter," the government, or the individual? Does it make a difference whether the toxic exposure is associated with a recognized social benefit? Consider, for example, pesticide workers. Society generally benefits from the widespread use of pesticides yet many of these agents are demonstrated neurotoxins. If a genetic test were available to accurately predict risk for agricultural workers exposed to pesticides, who should be responsible for providing the testing? How should the costs associated with minimizing risk for the genetically susceptible worker be allocated among the worker, his or her employer, and the greater community that relies on the crops the worker is maintaining with pesticides?

4. Although predictive genetic testing offers the potential for improvements in environmental health and safety, a dynamic tension exists between the potential for health benefits and the risks associated with premature applications of genetic tests that have uncertain or limited predictive value for disease onset. As outlined in the excerpted article by Paul and Sherry Brandt-Rauf, historical experience with workplace genetic testing demonstrates that premature use of genomic advances can have a stigmatizing and discriminatory impact on individuals who are labeled as genetically susceptible. For example, workplace applications of genetic testing for sickle cell trait, glucose-6-dehydrogenase deficiency, and alpha1-antitrypsin deficiency—genetic variations that, at the time of application, had a poorly defined impact on worker risk for anemia, hemolytic crisis, emphysema, and other health problems associated with exposure to workplace chemicals—unnecessarily excluded individuals from the workplace. For additional commentary on the historical background for workplace genetic testing, *see* Elaine Draper, RISKY BUSINESS: GENETIC TESTING AND EXCLUSIONARY PRACTICES IN THE HAZARDOUS WORKPLACE (Cambridge University Press 1991); and U.S. Congress Office of Technology Assessment (OTA), *The Role of Genetic Testing in the Prevention of Occupational Disease* (1983).

These historical experiences occurred in part because of premature applications of genetic technologies that had yet to demonstrate their accuracy in predicting risk for disease. Two critical scientific considerations bear on the predictive value of a positive genetic susceptibility test result. First, the tests predict genetic risk for multifactorial disease, that is, disease triggered by an interaction between one or more genetic variations and one or more environmental factors. Second, the predictive value of a positive test result is dependent on a series of established epidemiologic parameters, notably: the population frequency of the genetic marker, the cumulative incidence of the disease outcome of interest, and the strength of the association between the marker and the disease. For a good review of the scientific considerations that influence predictive value of genetic susceptibility tests, *see, e.g.*, C.A. Newill, Muin J. Khoury & Gary A. Chase, *Epidemiological Approach to Evaluation of Genetic Screening in the Workplace*, 28 J. OCCUP. MED. 1108 (1986); K.V. Van Damme, et al., *Individual Susceptibility and Prevention of Occupational Diseases: Scientific and Ethical Issues*, 37 J. Experimental Med. 91 (1995). Because experience with the application and outcomes of genetic susceptibility testing in populations is limited, our ability to define these parameters—and therefore the predictive value of these tests—is largely untested. Because the law will be used, increasingly, as a tool to define socially acceptable practices in the development and application of workplace genetic testing, lawyers and others in the legal system must grapple with the challenge of understanding the scientific basis of this technology. Additionally, they must identify and understand when the relevance, reliability, and utility of given applications have been sufficiently demonstrated to render them appropriate for use in a clinical, commercial, or occupational setting.

Leading scholars in the fields of occupational medicine, environmental health, epidemiology, law, and bioethics have proposed criteria for assessing the merits of occupational screening tests. *See, e.g.*, Gilbert S. Omenn, *Predictive Identification of Hyper Susceptible Individuals*, 24 J. OCCUP. MED. 369 (1982); Gilbert S. Omenn, *Predictive and Workplace Testing*, ENCYCLOPEDIA OF BIOETHICS (Warren T. Reich, ed. 1995); Marc

Lappe, *Ethical Issues in Testing for Differential Sensitivity to Occupational Hazards*, 25 J. Occup. Med. 797 (1983); Paolo Vineis & Paul A. Schulte, *Scientific and Ethical Aspects of Genetic Screening of Workers for Cancer Risk: The Case of the N-acetyltransferase phenotype*, 48 J. Clin. Epi. 189 (1995); Task Force on Genetic Testing, Promoting Safe and Effective Genetic Testing in the United States (1998); Mark A. Rothstein, *Genetics and the Work Force of the Next Hundred Years*, 2000 Colum. Bus. L. Rev. 371 (2000). Omenn's guidelines in particular emphasize the need to consider both the state of scientific evidence and the ethical, legal, and social implications of testing: (1) the prevalence of the predisposing trait must be high enough to be detected in the usual size of worker population, taking into account ethnic and geographic differences in prevalence; (2) the relative risk for a significant adverse outcome must be at least three, and preferably should exceed ten, so as to enhance the likelihood that the particular tested predisposition is, indeed, putting those workers at a significantly higher risk than other workers with other non-testable predispositions; (3) the test must be reliable, inexpensive, and well characterized with respect to sensitivity, specificity, and predictive value; and (4) there must be a clear understanding with management and unions and their workers about how test results are to be utilized, what actions might be taken on the basis of the results, and who would have access to the information.

In addition there is a considerable body of policy guidance available to assist legislators, regulatory agencies, and the courts in the development and application of laws bearing on workplace genetic testing. *See, e.g.*, American Public Health Association (APHA), *Guidelines for Genetic Testing in Industry*, 74 Am. J. Public Health 281 (1984); U.S. Department of Labor (DOL), *Genetic Information and the Workplace,* Joint Memorandum of DOL, Dep't of Health & Human Servs., Equal Employment Opportunity Comm'n, Dep't of Justice (January 20, 1998), http://www.dol.gov/dol/asp/public/programs/history/herman/reports/genetic; Karen Rothenberg, et al., *Genetic Information and the Workplace: Legislative Approaches & Policy Challenges*, 275 Science 1755 (1997) (report of The Hereditary Susceptibility Working Group of the National Action Plan on Breast Cancer (NAPBC) and the National Institutes of Health, Department of Energy Working Group on Ethical, Legal and Social Implications of Human Genome Research); American College of Occupational and Environmental Medicine (ACOEM), *Position Statement on Genetic Screening in the Workplace* (1994); American Medical Association (AMA) Council on Ethical and Judicial Affairs, *Opinion 2.131: Genetic Testing by Employers*, 266 J. Am. Med. Ass'n 1827 (1991). These guidelines suggest consensus on several important issues. First, employers' use of genetic tests and genetic information should be limited to those few instances in which the need for genetic information is job-related, of business necessity, and would assist in preventing significant risks for the employee or for public safety. Second, the assessment of whether the genetic testing in question meets these standards should be based on scientific evidence of the test's predictive value and the ability to use positive test results to prevent or minimize occupational illness. Third, genetic screening programs should be voluntary, tests should not be performed without the employee's informed consent, there should be strict procedures in place for protecting confidentiality, and employers should not disclose an employee's genetic information without the employee's written informed consent. Finally, current federal and state regulations regarding genetic privacy, confidentiality, and discrimination are viewed as providing inadequate protections for workers.

For additional materials and perspectives regarding genetic testing in the workplace, *see, e.g.*, Paul S. Miller, *Is There a Pink Slip in my Genes? Genetic Discrimination in the*

Workplace, 3 J. Health Care L. & Pol. 225 (2000); Lori B. Andrews & Ami S. Jaeger, *Confidentiality of Genetic Information in the Workplace*, 17 Am. J. L. & Med. 75 (1991); Lawrence O. Gostin, *Genetic Discrimination: The Use of Genetically Based Diagnostic and Prognostic Tests by Employers and Insurers*, 17 Am. J. L. & Med. 109 (1991); Henry Greely, *Health Insurance Employment Discrimination and the Genetics Revolution*, *in* The Code of Codes: Scientific and Social Issues in the Human Genome Project 264 (Daniel Kevles & Leroy Hood, eds. 1992); David Orentlicher, *Genetic Screening by Employers*, 263 J. Am. Med. Ass'n 1005 (1990).

5. The excerpted article by Paul and Sherry Brandt-Rauf begins with a discussion of the EEOC's case against Burlington Northern Santa Fe Railway, *EEOC v. Burlington Northern Santa Fe Railway Co.*, 5:01-cv-04013-MWB (N.D. Iowa 2001). This is the first, and to date only, EEOC lawsuit asserting claims of genetic discrimination in violation of the ADA. The case was initiated when the EEOC filed a Petition for a Preliminary Injunction against Burlington Northern Santa Fe Railroad (BNSFR) to halt genetic testing of employees who had filed worker compensation claims for carpal tunnel syndrome. The lawsuit alleged that genetic testing was performed on blood samples of thirty-six employees without their knowledge or consent and that, in at least one instance, a claimant who refused to provide a blood sample was threatened with termination. The blood samples were collected as part of the medical evaluation BNSFR initiated to evaluate the employees' compensation claims. The EEOC claimed that the surreptitious use of predictive genetic testing violated the ADA. The case was quickly settled for $2.2 million. BNSFR denied that it violated the ADA or otherwise engaged in workplace discrimination but did agree to cease requiring employees to submit blood samples for genetic testing, absent employee notice and consent.

The primary focus of the BNSFR case was the surreptitious use of genetic testing to inform employment-related decisions. However, the speculative nature of the genetic tests that were used was also of concern. These tests identified variations in the PMP22 gene and the gene for the protein transtyretin that are associated with two very rare genetic conditions thought to enhance susceptibility to carpal tunnel syndrome in some cases, Hereditary Neuropathy with Liability to Pressure Palsies (HNPP) and Familial Amyloidotic Polyneuropathy (FAP). At the time of testing neither the scientific basis nor the population validity of these genetic tests as predictors for enhanced susceptibility to carpal tunnel syndrome had been established. In short, their validity in identifying the cause of carpal tunnel syndrome was unproven. For a discussion of the scientific merits of BNSFR's decision to use these tests, *see* Paul A. Schulte & Geoffrey P. Lomax, *Assessment of the Scientific Basis for Genetic Testing of Railroad Workers with Carpal Tunnel Syndrome*, 45 J. Experimental Med. 592 (2003).

6. In contrast to the BNSFR experience with genetic testing, certain industrial employers whose employees are exposed to beryllium have collaborated with their workers and the federal government to develop a genetic screening program that identifies workers with genetic susceptibility to chronic beryllium disease (CBD). For a discussion of the science surrounding genetic susceptibility testing for CBD and the research and development efforts surrounding this program, *see, e.g.*, Centers for Disease Control and Prevention, National Institute for Occupational Safety and Health, NIOSH Board of Scientific Counselors, *Report from the Subcommittee on Beryllium Research* (October 29, 2002); E.C. McCanlies, K. Kriess, et al., *HLA-DPB1 and Chronic Beryllium Disease: a HUGE Review*, 157 Am. J. Epidemiol. 388 (2003); A. Weston, J. Ensey, K. Kriess, et al., *Racial Differences in Prevalence of Supratypic HLA-genetic Marker Immaterial to Pre-employment Testing for Susceptibility Testing for Chronic Beryllium Dis-*

ease, 41 Am. J. Ind. Med. 457 (2002); Scott M. Bartell, Rafael A. Ponce, Timothy K. Takaro, et al., *Risk Estimation and Value of Information Analysis for Three Proposed Genetic Screening Programs for Chronic Beryllium Disease Prevention*, 20 Risk Anal. 87 (2000). How does this case example differ from the program involved in the BNSFR case? What difference, if any, does the state of scientific evidence regarding the genetics of CBD susceptibility play in your assessment of the merits of these two different programs?

7. How might the law be used to prevent workplace applications of genetic technologies that are unproven or, worse yet, predicated upon bad science? To what extent can or should the law embrace and/or enforce the policy guidelines for workplace genetic tests outlined in Note 4, *supra*? Keep these questions in mind as you review the cases and materials in Sections C and D and, in particular, consider what role the quality of the scientific evidence surrounding a workplace genetic testing application should play in assessing whether an employment decision based upon the results of that test is in violation of the ADA or other relevant state and federal antidiscrimination laws.

C. Genetic Discrimination in the Workplace: Legislative Response

1. State Legislation

Mark A. Rothstein, Betsy D. Gelb, & Steven G. Craig, *Protecting Genetic Privacy by Permitting Employer Access Only to Job-Related Employee Medical Information: Analysis of Unique Minnesota Law*

24 Am. J.L. & Med. 399 (1998)

...

In the 1970s, as a response to irrational discrimination against heterozygous carriers of the sickle cell trait, state legislatures started enacting laws prohibiting genetic discrimination in employment. The first type of law, such as those enacted in Florida, Louisiana and North Carolina, establish a pattern of limited statutory prohibitions. New Jersey and New York also adopted laws based on this model of prohibiting discrimination against the unaffected carriers of recessive disorders. New Jersey's law, until amended and broadened significantly in 1996, prohibited discrimination against individuals with sickle cell, hemoglobin C, thalassemia, Tay-Sachs or cystic fibrosis traits. New York's law, also amended and broadened in 1996, prohibited discrimination against individuals possessing sickle cell, Tay-Sachs or—thalassemia traits.

In 1989, Oregon became the first state to enact a second type of genetic discrimination statute. This law prohibits employers from requiring applicants or employees to undergo a "genetic test," although the term was undefined until subsequent amendments. The state legislatures in Arizona, California, Connecticut, Delaware, Iowa, New Hampshire, New Mexico, New York, North Carolina, Oklahoma, Rhode Island, Texas, Vermont and Wisconsin enacted laws of this general type in their respective states. Most of the statutes prohibit employers from performing genetic tests on applicants or employees or conditioning employment on the results of a genetic test. The statutes generally define "genetic test" as a test analyzing human DNA.

In 1996, the New Jersey legislature enacted the third type of genetic discrimination statute. The law prohibits discrimination based on genetic test results or the refusal to take a genetic test. Additionally, it disallows discrimination based on genetic information. New Jersey statutory law defines genetic information as "information about genes, gene products or inherited characteristics that may derive from an individual or family member." The New Jersey law is valuable because, unlike the other states' laws, it prohibits discrimination based on a family's history of genetic disease. Its strength, however, is also its weakness. The law prohibits discrimination based on inherited characteristics derived from an individual. Because new discoveries have identified associations between genes and common disorders, such as cancer, heart disease, epilepsy, diabetes and hypertension, it is possible that an employer could be prevented from considering an individual's history of such a disorder, which may be relevant to the ability to perform a job, because it is "genetic" information. In addition, the New Jersey law, like other state laws, does not prohibit employers from gaining access to an individual's complete medical history, which may contain genetic information.

These state laws fail to effectively protect employees and, conversely, may even expose the public to unintended risks. Stated simply, legislators need to develop other criteria besides "genetic" test results or information to determine whether an employer may gain access to or rely on an employee's medical information. The most promising approach to preventing genetic discrimination involves restricting employer access only to an employee's "job-related" medical information. Thus, coupling a job-relatedness limitation on access to medical information with the general antidiscrimination provisions of disability discrimination laws is a more promising approach than using specific genetic discrimination laws. The proposal eliminates the need to stipulate what constitutes genetic information, a seemingly impossible task, and it restricts employer access to employee medical records that could contain the results of genetic tests and other sensitive, but non-job-related, medical information. It also avoids further stigmatizing genetic conditions by treating them differently from other medical conditions.

...

Similar to virtually every other state, Minnesota has a state law prohibiting discrimination in employment on the basis of various criteria including disability. The MHRA [Minn. Stat. Ann. §363.01-.20. (West 1991 & Supp. 1998)], as amended, is the only state or federal law to require that all medical examinations, including post-placement medical examinations, be strictly limited to measuring the individual's ability to perform job-related functions. The MHRA provides that it is not an unfair employment practice for an employer to require or request a person to undergo physical examination, which may include medical history, for the purpose of determining the person's capability to perform available employment, provided: (a) that an offer of employment has been made on condition that the person meets the physical or mental requirements of the job ... [and] (b) that the examination tests only for essential job-related abilities....

The scope of this provision has not been litigated, but members of the Minnesota bar and officials at the Minnesota Department of Human Rights (MDHR) generally agree that the provision prevents employers from requiring "blanket releases" of medical records in the possession of employees' personal physicians.

...

Notes & Questions

1. In the foregoing article, Rothstein, *et al.*, point out that state legislatures first began to consider the use of genetic information in employment decisions in the 1970s when they passed laws protecting employees from discrimination based upon sickle cell trait. More general restrictions regarding the use of genetic testing to inform employment decisions did not begin to surface until the early 1990s when concerns about the potential for widespread genetic discrimination began to capture state legislatures across the country. By 2005, 33 states had genetic nondiscrimination laws in place, although the scope and function of these laws varied widely. Current compilations of these laws, by state, are maintained by the National Human Genome Research Institute (www.genome.gov); the National Conference of State Legislatures (www.ncsl.org); and the Council for Responsible Genetics (www.gene-watch.org).

2. Although a majority of the states have adopted genetic discrimination legislation there is a striking dearth of activity in the courts seeking to enforce, define or test these laws. Similarly, a review of published appellate court decisions issued before the wave of genetic discrimination legislation that occurred over the past decade suggests little activity on the part of workers seeking compensation for perceived or actual genetic discrimination. Does the absence of litigation suggest public fears are grounded more in myth than reality? Or, is it the case that genetic discrimination laws are actually deterring a previously latent but real problem in the workplace? Are there other barriers to genetic discrimination litigation that could explain the apparent absence of lawsuits?

2. Federal Legislation

The federal government has yet to pass legislation specifically addressing genetic discrimination in the workplace, although several bills have been introduced over the past ten years which seek, in part, to limit the prerogative of employers to use genetic information to impact decisions regarding the terms, conditions, and benefits of employment. The Genetic Information Nondiscrimination Act of 2005, passed by a unanimous vote of the U.S. Senate on February 17, 2005, is illustrative of the nature and scope of regulation under consideration. As you review the following excerpts pay particular attention to how genetic information is defined. In addition, consider the extent to which the provisions address the policy concerns identified and discussed in Part B. Finally, to what extent do legislative efforts at the federal level mirror the approach taken in the Minnesota Human Rights Act? What policy considerations might be influencing the scope of protection proposed at the federal level? How might they differ from the forces at play when the MHRA provisions regarding employer access to employee medical information were adopted?

Genetic Information Nondiscrimination Act of 2005

S. 306, 109th Congress, (1st Sess. 2005)

Title II—Prohibiting Employment Discrimination on the Basis of Genetic Information

Sec. 201 Definitions

(4) Genetic Information—

(A) In General—Except as provided in subparagraph (b), the term ‘genetic information’ means information about—(i) an individual’s genetic tests; (ii) the genetic tests of family members of the individual; or (iii) the occurrence of a disease or disorder in family members of the individual.

(B) Exceptions—The term 'genetic information' shall not include information about the sex or age of an individual.

(5) Genetic Monitoring—The term "genetic monitoring' means the periodic examination of employees to evaluate acquired modifications to their genetic material, such as chromosomal damage or evidence of increased occurrence of mutations, that may have developed in the course of employment due to exposure to toxic substances in the workplace, in order to identify, evaluate, and respond to the effects of or control adverse environmental exposures in the workplace.

...

(7) Genetic Test—

(A) In General—The term 'genetic test' means the analysis of human DNA, RNA, chromosomes, proteins or metabolites that detects genotypes, mutations or chromosomal changes.

(B) Exception—The term 'genetic test' does not mean an analysis of proteins or metabolites that does not detect genotypes, mutations, or chromosomal changes.

Sec. 202. Employer Practices

(a) Use of Genetic Information—It shall be an unlawful employment practice for an employer—

(1) to fail or refuse to hire or to discharge ay employee, or otherwise to discriminate against any employee with respect to the compensation, terms conditions, or privileges of employment of the employee, because of genetic information with respect to the employee (or information about a request for or the receipt of genetic services by such employee or family member or such employee); or

(2) to limit, segregate, or classify the employees of the employer in any way that would deprive or tend to deprive any employee of employment opportunities or otherwise adversely affect the status of the employee as an employee, because of genetic information with respect to the employee (or information about a request for or the receipt of genetic services by such employee or family member of such employee).

(b) Acquisition of Genetic Information—It shall be an unlawful employment practice for an employer to request, require, or purchase genetic information with respect to an employee or a family member of the employee (or information about a request for the receipt of genetic services by such employee or a family member of such employee) except—

(1) where an employer inadvertently requests or requires family medical history of the employee or family member of the employee;

(2) where—

(A) health or genetic services are offered by the employer....

(B) the employee provides prior, knowing, voluntary and written authorization;

(C) only the employee ... and the licensed health care professional or board certified genetic counselor involved in providing such services receive individually identifiable information concerning the results of such services; and

(D) any individually identifiable genetic information provided under subparagraph (C) ... is only available for purposes of such services and shall not be disclosed to the employer except in aggregate terms that do not disclose the identity of specific employees;

(3) where an employer requests or requires family medical history from the employee to comply with the certification provisions of section 103 of the Family and Medical Leave Act ...

(4) where an employer purchases documents that are commercially and publicly available ... that include family medical history; or

(5) where the information involved is to be used for genetic monitoring of the biological effects of toxic substances in the workplace, but only if—

(A) the employer provides written notice of the genetic monitoring to the employee;

(B) (i) the employee provides prior, knowing, voluntary, and written authorization; or (ii) the genetic monitoring is required by Federal or State law;

(C) the employee is informed of individual monitoring results;

(D) the monitoring is in compliance with—[federal or state genetic monitoring regulations]

(E) the employer, ... excluding any licensed health care professional ... involved in the genetic monitoring program, receives the results of the monitoring only in aggregate terms that do not disclose the identify of specific employees

...

* * *

In contrast to the U.S. Congress, the executive branch of the federal government has taken action to address concerns regarding the potential for genetic discrimination in the workplace, as illustrated by the following excerpt from President Clinton's February 8, 2000 Executive Order to Prohibit Discrimination in Federal Employment Based on Genetic Information (portions of the Executive Order dealing with privacy and confidentiality protections for genetic information are featured in Chapter 2).

Executive Order No. 13145, 65 Fed. Reg. 6877, To Prohibit Discrimination in Federal Employment Based on Genetic Information

February 8, 2000

...

Section 1. Nondiscrimination in Federal Employment on the Basis of Protected Genetic Information.

1-101. It is the policy of the Government of the United States to provide equal employment opportunity in Federal employment for all qualified persons and to prohibit discrimination against employees based on protected genetic information, or information about a request for or the receipt of genetic services. This policy of equal opportunity applies to every aspect of Federal employment....

Section 2. Requirements Applicable to Employing Departments and Agencies.

1-201. Definitions.

(a) The term "employee" shall include an employee, applicant for employment, or former employee covered by section 717 of the Civil Rights Act of 1964, as amended (42 U.S.C. 2000e-16).

(b) Genetic monitoring means the periodic examination of employees to evaluate acquired modifications to their genetic material, such as chromosomal damage or evidence of increased occurrence of mutations, that may have developed in the course of employment due to exposure to toxic substances in the workplace, in order to identify, evaluate, respond to the effects of, or control adverse environmental exposures in the workplace.

(c) Genetic services means health services, including genetic tests, provided to obtain, assess, or interpret genetic information for diagnostic or therapeutic purposes, or for genetic education or counseling.

(d) Genetic test means the analysis of human DNA, RNA, chromosomes, proteins, or certain metabolites in order to detect disease-related genotypes or mutations. Tests for metabolites fall within the definition of "genetic tests" when an excess or deficiency of the metabolites indicates the presence of a mutation or mutations. The conducting of metabolic tests by a department or agency that are not intended to reveal the presence of a mutation shall not be considered a violation of this order, regardless of the results of the tests. Test results revealing a mutation shall, however, be subject to the provisions of this order.

(e) Protected genetic information.

  (1) In general, protected genetic information means:

    (A) information about an individual's genetic tests;

    (B) information about the genetic tests of an individual's family members; or

    (C) information about the occurrence of a disease, or medical condition or disorder in family members of the individual.

  (2) Information about an individual's current health status (including information about sex, age, physical exams, and chemical, blood, or urine

analyses) is not protected genetic information unless it is described in subparagraph (1).

1-202. In discharging their responsibilities under this order, departments and agencies shall implement the following nondiscrimination requirements.

(a) The employing department or agency shall not discharge, fail or refuse to hire, or otherwise discriminate against any employee with respect to the compensation, terms, conditions, or privileges of employment of that employee, because of protected genetic information with respect to the employee, or because of information about a request for or the receipt of genetic services by such employee.

(b) The employing department or agency shall not limit, segregate, or classify employees in any way that would deprive or tend to deprive any employee of employment opportunities or otherwise adversely affect that employee's status, because of protected genetic information with respect to the employee or because of information about a request for or the receipt of genetic services by such employee.

(c) The employing department or agency shall not request, require, collect, or purchase protected genetic information with respect to an employee, or information about a request for or the receipt of genetic services by such employee.

(d) The employing department or agency shall not disclose protected genetic information with respect to an employee, or information about a request for or the receipt of genetic services by an employee except:

(1) to the employee who is the subject of the information, at his or her request;

(2) to an occupational or other health researcher, if the research conducted complies with the regulations and protections provided for under part 46 of title 45, of the Code of Federal Regulations;

(3) if required by a Federal statute, congressional subpoena, or an order issued by a court of competent jurisdiction, except that if the subpoena or court order was secured without the knowledge of the individual to whom the information refers, the employer shall provide the individual with adequate notice to challenge the subpoena or court order, unless the subpoena or court order also imposes confidentiality requirements; or

(4) to executive branch officials investigating compliance with this order, if the information is relevant to the investigation. The receipt of genetic services in general personnel files; such information shall be treated as confidential medical records and kept separate from personnel files.

Section 3. Exceptions.

1-301. The following exceptions shall apply to the nondiscrimination requirements set forth in section 1-202.

(a) The employing department or agency may request or require information defined in section 1-201(e)(1)(C) with respect to an applicant who has been given a conditional offer of employment or to an employee if:

(1) the request or requirement is consistent with the Rehabilitation Act and other applicable law;

(2) the information obtained is to be used exclusively to assess whether further medical evaluation is needed to diagnose a current disease, or medical condition or disorder, or under the terms of section 1-301(b) of this order;

(3) such current disease, or medical condition or disorder could prevent the applicant or employee from performing the essential functions of the position held or desired; and

(4) the information defined in section 1-201(e)(1)(C) of this order will not be disclosed to persons other than medical personnel involved in or responsible for assessing whether further medical evaluation is needed to diagnose a current disease, or medical condition or disorder, or under the terms of section 1-301(b) of this order.

(b) The employing department or agency may request, collect or purchase protected genetic information with respect to an employee, or any information about a request for or receipt of genetic services by such employee if:

(1) the employee uses genetic or health care services provided by the employer (other than use pursuant to section 1-301(a) of this order);

(2) the employee who uses the genetic or health care services has provided prior knowing, voluntary, and written authorization to the employer to collect protected genetic information;

(3) the person who performs the genetic or health care services does not disclose protected genetic information to anyone except to the employee who uses the services for treatment of the individual; pursuant to section 1-202(d) of this order; for program evaluation or assessment; for compiling and analyzing information in anticipation of or for use in a civil or criminal legal proceeding; or, for payment or accounting purposes, to verify that the service was performed (but in such cases the genetic information itself cannot be disclosed);

...

(c) ...

(d) Genetic monitoring of biological effects of toxic substances in the workplace shall be permitted if all of the following conditions are met:

(1) the employee has provided prior, knowing, voluntary and written authorization;

(2) the employee is notified when the results of the monitoring are available and, at that time, the employer makes any protected genetic information that may have been acquired during the monitoring available to the employee and informs the employee how to obtain such information;

(3) the monitoring conforms to any genetic monitoring regulations that may be promulgated by the Secretary of Labor; and ults of the monitoring only in aggregate terms that do not disclose the identity of specific employees.

...

Notes & Questions

1. At the end of 2005 the U.S. Congress had not passed the Genetic Information Nondiscrimination Act of 2005, or any other comparable genetic discrimination legislation. For an in-depth analysis of the arguments both for and against federal genetic discrimination legislation, *see, e.g.*, Susan M. Wolf, *Beyond "Genetic Discrimination": Toward the Broader Harm of Geneticism*, 23 J.L. Med. & Ethics 345, 347 (1995); Colin S. Diver & Jane Maslow Cohen, *Genophobia: What is Wrong with Genetic Discrimination?* 149 U. Pa L. Rev. 1439, 1445–446 (2001); Sonia M. Suter, *The Allure and Peril of Genetics Exceptionalism: Do We Need Special Genetics Legislation*? 79 Wash. U. L.Q. 669 (2001); Henry T. Greely, *Genotype Discrimination: The Complex Case for Some Legislative Protection*, 149 U. Pa. L. Rev. 1483 (2001); Martin Richards, *How Distinctive is Genetic Information?* 32 Stud. Hist. Phil. Biol. & Biomed. Sci. 663 (2001); Lawrence O. Gostin & James G. Hodge, Jr., *Genetic Privacy and the Law: An End to Genetics Exceptionalism*, 40 Jurimetrics J. 21 (1999); George J. Annas, *Genetic Privacy: There Ought to be a Law*, 4 Tex. Rev. L. & Pol. 9 (1999); Thomas H. Murray, *Genetic Exceptionalism and "Future Diaries": Is Genetic Information Different from Other Medical Information? in* Genetic Secrets: Protecting Privacy and Confidentiality in the Genetic Era (Mark A. Rothstein, ed. 1997).

2. The scope and application of Executive Order 13145 has yet to be tested in the courts. However the plain language of the Order suggests an effort to limit federal employers' ability to use genetic information that does not implicate a worker's present ability to perform essential job functions. While the Order appears to prohibit federal employers from requiring or requesting genetic tests as a condition of being hired or receiving benefits, it does permit them to inquire into family medical history to the extent necessary to determine if further medical evaluation is needed to diagnose a condition that could prevent the employee from performing an essential function of their job. The issue of qualification to perform essential job functions must be decided, however, on the basis of present ability to safely perform. How might the distinction between how genetic tests and family history information are treated impact the scope of protection the Executive Order affords?

The EEOC views the Executive Order as a clear statement that it is inappropriate to use genetic information to make employment decisions based upon a predisposition to disease, medical condition or disorder that has no bearing on the workers present ability to do the job, EEOC Policy Guidance on Executive Order 13415 (2000), *available at* www.eeoc.gov/policy/docs/guidance-genetic.html. This interpretation, if upheld by the courts, would significantly restrict the ability of federal employers to use predictive genetic information in employment decisions regarding prospective or current employees who are phenotypically normal or asymptomatic and are presently able to perform essential job functions.

3. While not specifically addressing genetic discrimination, a number of federal laws do influence the extent to which employers can acquire and use employee genetic information. Notable among these are the Rehabilitation Act of 1973, 29 U.S.C. §§701–796, which prohibits federal employers from discriminating on the basis of a qualifying disability; the Americans with Disabilities Act, 42 U.S.C. §12101 *et seq.*, which extends the Rehabilitation Act's prohibitions to all non-federal employers of 15 or more full time employees; and Title VII of the Civil Rights Act of 1964, 42 U.S.C. §2000 *et seq.*, which prohibits discrimination on the basis of race, ethnicity, gender, or religion. The extent to which these laws effect and, more importantly, proscribe ge-

netic discrimination has yet to be definitively addressed in the courts, although the Ninth Circuit Court of Appeals concluded that Title VII prohibits workplace genetic testing that has a disparate impact on the terms or conditions of employment for members of a protected group. *Norman-Bloodsaw v. Lawrence Berkeley Lab.*, 135 F.3d 1260 (9th Cir. 1998).

A critical issue that has yet to reach the courts is the scope of protection provided under the ADA and its federally focused counterpart, the Rehabilitation Act of 1973. The ADA prohibits employers of fifteen or more employees from discriminating against a "qualified individual with a disability because of the disability" in hiring, promotion, discharge, compensation, and other terms/conditions of employment. To be "qualified" an individual must demonstrate that he or she has, has had, or is regarded as having one or more physical impairments that substantially limit a major life activity. 42 U.S.C. § 12102. Employers must make reasonable accommodations in the workplace for qualified individuals. The Act does permit employers to discriminate if they can establish that the adverse employment action is job-related, a business necessity or required because of a direct threat to the health or safety of individuals in the workplace.

The statutory language of the ADA does not reference genetic traits or genetic information; however the legislative history suggests that the intent of at least some members of Congress was to afford protection against genetic discrimination. For example, Rep. Owens stated:

> [T]he protections of the ADA will also benefit individuals who are identified through genetic tests as being carriers of a disease-associated gene. There is a record of genetic discrimination against such individuals, most recently during sickle cell screening programs in the 1970's. With the advent of new forms of genetic testing, it is even more critical that the protections of the ADA be in place. Under the ADA, such individuals may not be discriminated against simply because they may not be qualified for a job sometime in the future. The determination as to whether an individual is qualified must take place at the time of the employment decision, and may not be based on speculation regarding the future. Moreover, such individuals may not be discriminated against because they or their children might incur increased health care costs for the employer.

136 Cong. Rec. H4623 (daily ed. July 12, 1990) (remarks of Rep. Owens). The EEOC's interpretation of the Act is that it does prohibit employers from discriminating against employees on the basis of predictive genetic information because employers who do so "regard" a worker's predisposition or susceptibility to illness as a disability. 2 EEOC Compliance Manual, § 902, order 915.002, 902-45 (1995). The EEOC used the following example to illustrate its application of the "regarded as" prong of the ADA's definition of disability:

> CP's genetic profile reveals an increased susceptibility to colon cancer. CP is currently asymptomatic and may never in fact develop colon cancer. After making CP a conditional offer of employment, R learns about CP's increased susceptibility to colon cancer. R then withdraws the job offer because of concerns about matters such as CP's productivity, insurance costs and attendance. R is treating CP as having an impairment that substantially limits a major life activity. Accordingly CP is covered by the third part of the definition of disability.

2 EEOC Compliance Manual, § 902.8 (1995). The EEOC's interpretation has yet to be tested in the courts. Consider the likelihood its position will be adopted as you review the collection of ADA cases in Part D.

The remaining materials in this chapter introduce you to court cases that are relevant to an assessment of the nature and scope of protection against genetic discrimination available under current federal antidiscrimination laws. As you review these cases consider the extent to which existing federal laws provide an adequate framework for addressing genetic discrimination in the workplace.

D. Genetic Discrimination in the Workplace: The Courts' Application of Existing Law

1. Title VII of the Civil Rights Act

International Union, United Automobile, Aerospace and Agricultural Implement Workers of America, UAW v. Johnson Controls, Inc.

499 U.S. 187 (1991)

Justice Blackmun.

In this case we are concerned with an employer's gender-based fetal-protection policy. May an employer exclude a fertile female employee from certain jobs because of its concern for the health of the fetus the woman might conceive?

Respondent Johnson Controls, Inc., manufactures batteries. In the manufacturing process, the element lead is a primary ingredient. Occupational exposure to lead entails health risks, including the risk of harm to any fetus carried by a female employee.

... Between 1979 and 1983, eight employees became pregnant while maintaining blood lead levels in excess of 30 micrograms per deciliter. This appeared to be the critical level noted by the Occupational Safety and Health Administration (OSHA) for a worker who was planning to have a family. See 29 CFR §1910.1025 (1990). The company responded by announcing a broad exclusion of women from jobs that exposed them to lead.... The policy defined "women ... capable of bearing children" as "[a]ll women except those whose inability to bear children is medically documented." It further stated that an unacceptable work station was one where, "over the past year," an employee had recorded a blood lead level of more than 30 micrograms per deciliter or the work site had yielded an air sample containing a lead level in excess of 30 micrograms per cubic meter.

In April 1984, petitioners filed in the United States District Court for the Eastern District of Wisconsin a class action challenging Johnson Controls' fetal-protection policy as sex discrimination that violated Title VII of the Civil Rights Act of 1964, as amended, 42 U.S.C. §2000e *et seq.* Among the individual plaintiffs were petitioners Mary Craig, who had chosen to be sterilized in order to avoid losing her job, Elsie Nason, a 50-year-old divorcee, who had suffered a loss in compensation when she was transferred out of a job where she was exposed to lead, and Donald Penney, who had been denied a request for a leave of absence for the purpose of lowering his lead level because he intended to become a father.... The District Court granted summary judgment for defendant-respondent Johnson Controls.... The Court of Appeals for the Seventh Circuit, sitting en banc, affirmed the summary judgment by a 7-to-4 vote.

The bias in Johnson Controls' policy is obvious. Fertile men, but not fertile women, are given a choice as to whether they wish to risk their reproductive health for a particular job. Section 703(a) of the Civil Rights Act of 1964, 78 Stat. 255, as amended, 42 U.S.C. § 2000e-2(a), prohibits sex-based classifications in terms and conditions of employment, in hiring and discharging decisions, and in other employment decisions that adversely affect an employee's status. Respondent's fetal-protection policy explicitly discriminates against women on the basis of their sex. The policy excludes women with childbearing capacity from lead-exposed jobs and so creates a facial classification based on gender. Respondent assumes as much in its brief before this Court.

The [Court of Appeals] assumed that because the asserted reason for the sex-based exclusion (protecting women's unconceived offspring) was ostensibly benign, the policy was not sex-based discrimination. That assumption, however, was incorrect.

... Johnson Controls' policy is not neutral because it does not apply to the reproductive capacity of the company's male employees in the same way as it applies to that of the females. Moreover, the absence of a malevolent motive does not convert a facially discriminatory policy into a neutral policy with a discriminatory effect. Whether an employment practice involves disparate treatment through explicit facial discrimination does not depend on why the employer discriminates but rather on the explicit terms of the discrimination.... We hold that Johnson Controls' fetal-protection policy is sex discrimination forbidden under Title VII unless respondent can establish that sex is a "bona fide occupational qualification."

Under § 703(e)(1) of Title VII, an employer may discriminate on the basis of "religion, sex, or national origin in those certain instances where religion, sex, or national origin is a bona fide occupational qualification reasonably necessary to the normal operation of that particular business or enterprise." 42 U.S.C. § 2000e-2(e)(1).... The wording of the BFOQ defense contains several terms of restriction that indicate that the exception reaches only special situations. The statute thus limits the situations in which discrimination is permissible to "certain instances" where sex discrimination is "reasonably necessary" to the "normal operation" of the "particular" business. Each one of these terms ... prevents the use of general subjective standards and favors an objective, verifiable requirement. But the most telling term is "occupational"; this indicates that these objective, verifiable requirements must concern job-related skills and aptitudes.

... Johnson Controls argues that its fetal-protection policy falls within the so-called safety exception to the BFOQ. Our cases have stressed that discrimination on the basis of sex because of safety concerns is allowed only in narrow circumstances. In *Dothard v. Rawlinson* [433 U.S. 321 (1977)], this Court indicated that danger to a woman herself does not justify discrimination. 433 U.S., at 335. We there allowed the employer to hire only male guards in contact areas of maximum-security male penitentiaries only because more was at stake than the "individual woman's decision to weigh and accept the risks of employment." *Ibid.* We found sex to be a BFOQ inasmuch as the employment of a female guard would create real risks of safety to others if violence broke out because the guard was a woman. Sex discrimination was tolerated because sex was related to the guard's ability to do the job—maintaining prison security. We also required in *Dothard* a high correlation between sex and ability to perform job functions and refused to allow employers to use sex as a proxy for strength although it might be a fairly accurate one.

... We considered safety to third parties in *Western Airlines, Inc. v. Criswell* [472 U.S. 400 (1985)], *supra*, in the context of the ADEA. We focused upon "the nature of the flight engineer's tasks," and the "actual capabilities of persons over age 60" in relation to those tasks. 472 U.S., at 406. Our safety concerns were not independent of the individual's ability to perform the assigned tasks, but rather involved the possibility that, because of age-connected debility, a flight engineer might not properly assist the pilot, and might thereby cause a safety emergency. Furthermore, although we considered the safety of third parties in *Dothard* and *Criswell,* those third parties were indispensable to the particular business at issue. In *Dothard,* the third parties were the inmates; in *Criswell,* the third parties were the passengers on the plane. We stressed that in order to qualify as a BFOQ, a job qualification must relate to the "'essence,'" *Dothard,* 433 U.S., at 333, (emphasis deleted), or to the "central mission of the employer's business," *Criswell,* 472 U.S., at 413.

... We have no difficulty concluding that Johnson Controls cannot establish a BFOQ. Fertile women, as far as appears in the record, participate in the manufacture of batteries as efficiently as anyone else. Johnson Controls' professed moral and ethical concerns about the welfare of the next generation do not suffice to establish a BFOQ of female sterility. Decisions about the welfare of future children must be left to the parents who conceive, bear, support, and raise them rather than to the employers who hire those parents. Congress has mandated this choice through Title VII, as amended by the PDA [Pregnancy Discrimination Act, 42 USC Sec. 2000e(k)]. Johnson Controls has attempted to exclude women because of their reproductive capacity. Title VII and the PDA simply do not allow a woman's dismissal because of her failure to submit to sterilization.

Nor can concerns about the welfare of the next generation be considered a part of the "essence" of Johnson Controls' business. Judge Easterbrook in this case pertinently observed: "It is word play to say that 'the job' at Johnson [Controls] is to make batteries without risk to fetuses in the same way 'the job' at Western Air Lines is to fly planes without crashing." 886 F.2d, at 913.

A word about tort liability and the increased cost of fertile women in the workplace is perhaps necessary. One of the dissenting judges in this case expressed concern about an employer's tort liability and concluded that liability for a potential injury to a fetus is a social cost that Title VII does not require a company to ignore. 886 F.2d, at 904–905. It is correct to say that Title VII does not prevent the employer from having a conscience. The statute, however, does prevent sex-specific fetal-protection policies. These two aspects of Title VII do not conflict.

More than 40 States currently recognize a right to recover for a prenatal injury based either on negligence or on wrongful death. According to Johnson Controls, however, the company complies with the lead standard developed by OSHA and warns its female employees about the damaging effects of lead. It is worth noting that OSHA gave the problem of lead lengthy consideration and concluded that "there is no basis whatsoever for the claim that women of childbearing age should be excluded from the workplace in order to protect the fetus or the course of pregnancy." 43 Fed.Reg. 52952, 52966 (1978). See also *id.,* at 54354, 54398. Instead, OSHA established a series of mandatory protections which, taken together, "should effectively minimize any risk to the fetus and newborn child." *Id.,* at 52966. See 29 CFR § 1910.1025(k)(ii) (1990). Without negligence, it would be difficult for a court to find liability on the part of the employer. If, under general tort principles, Title VII bans sex-specific fetal-protection policies, the employer fully informs the woman of the risk, and the employer has not acted negligently, the basis for holding an employer liable seems remote at best.

... The tort-liability argument reduces to two equally unpersuasive propositions. First, Johnson Controls attempts to solve the problem of reproductive health hazards by resorting to an exclusionary policy. Title VII plainly forbids illegal sex discrimination as a method of diverting attention from an employer's obligation to police the workplace. Second, the specter of an award of damages reflects a fear that hiring fertile women will cost more. The extra cost of employing members of one sex, however, does not provide an affirmative Title VII defense for a discriminatory refusal to hire members of that gender....

We, of course, are not presented with, nor do we decide, a case in which costs would be so prohibitive as to threaten the survival of the employer's business. We merely reiterate our prior holdings that the incremental cost of hiring women cannot justify discriminating against them.

Our holding today that Title VII, as so amended, forbids sex-specific fetal-protection policies is neither remarkable nor unprecedented. Concern for a woman's existing or potential offspring historically has been the excuse for denying women equal employment opportunities....

It is no more appropriate for the courts than it is for individual employers to decide whether a woman's reproductive role is more important to herself and her family than her economic role. Congress has left this choice to the woman as hers to make.

The judgment of the Court of Appeals is reversed, and the case is remanded for further proceedings consistent with this opinion.

Norman-Bloodsaw v. Lawrence Berkeley Laboratory

135 F.3d 1260 (9th Cir. 1998)

Reinhardt, Circuit Judge:

This appeal involves the question whether a clerical or administrative worker who undergoes a general employee health examination may, without his knowledge, be tested for highly private and sensitive medical and genetic information such as syphilis, sickle cell trait, and pregnancy.

Lawrence Berkeley Laboratory is a research institution jointly operated by state and federal agencies. Plaintiffs-appellants, present and former employees of Lawrence, allege that in the course of their mandatory employment entrance examinations and on subsequent occasions, Lawrence, without their knowledge or consent, tested their blood and urine for intimate medical conditions—namely, syphilis, sickle cell trait, and pregnancy. Their complaint asserts that this testing violated Title VII of the Civil Rights Act of 1964, the Americans with Disabilities Act (ADA), and their right to privacy as guaranteed by both the United States and State of California Constitutions. The district court granted the defendants-appellees' motions for dismissal, judgment on the pleadings, and summary judgment on all of plaintiffs-appellants' claims. We affirm as to the ADA claims, but reverse as to the Title VII and state and federal privacy claims.

Plaintiffs Marya S. Norman-Bloodsaw, Eulalio R. Fuentes, Vertis B. Ellis, Mark E. Covington, John D. Randolph, Adrienne L. Garcia, and Brendolyn B. Smith are current and former administrative and clerical employees of defendant Lawrence Berkeley Laboratory ("Lawrence"), a research facility operated by the appellee Regents of the University of California pursuant to a contract with the United States Department of Energy (the Department). Defendant Charles V. Shank is the director of Lawrence, and defendants Henry H. Stauffer, Lisa Snow, T.F. Budinger, and William G. Donald, Jr., are all current or former physicians in its medical department. The named defendants are sued in both their official and individual capacities.

The Department requires federal contractors such as Lawrence to establish an occupational medical program. Since 1981, it has required its contractors to perform "preplacement examinations" of employees as part of this program, and until 1995, it also required its contractors to offer their employees the option of subsequent "periodic health examinations." The mandatory preplacement examination occurs after the offer of employment but prior to the assumption of job duties. The Department actively oversees Lawrence's occupational health program, and, prior to 1992, specifically required syphilis testing as part of the preplacement examination.

With the exception of Ellis, who was hired in 1968 and underwent an examination after beginning employment, each of the plaintiffs received written offers of employment expressly conditioned upon a "medical examination," "medical approval," or "health evaluation." All accepted these offers and underwent preplacement examinations, and Randolph and Smith underwent subsequent examinations as well. In the course of these examinations, plaintiffs completed medical history questionnaires and provided blood and urine samples. The questionnaires asked, inter alia, whether the patient had ever had any of sixty-one medical conditions, including "[s]ickle cell anemia," "[v]enereal disease," and, in the case of women, "[m]enstrual disorders."

The blood and urine samples given by all employees during their preplacement examinations were tested for syphilis; in addition, certain samples were tested for sickle cell trait; and certain samples were tested for pregnancy. Lawrence discontinued syphilis testing in April 1993, pregnancy testing in December 1994, and sickle cell trait testing in June 1995. Defendants assert that they discontinued syphilis testing because of its limited usefulness in screening healthy populations, and that they discontinued sickle cell trait testing because, by that time, most African-American adults had already been tested at birth. Lawrence continues to perform pregnancy testing, but only on an optional basis. Defendants further contend that "for many years" signs posted in the health examination rooms and "more recently" in the reception area stated that the tests at issue would be administered.

Following receipt of a right-to-sue letter from the EEOC, plaintiffs filed suit in September 1995 on behalf of all past and present Lawrence employees who have ever been subjected to the medical tests at issue. Plaintiffs allege that the testing of their blood and urine samples for syphilis, sickle cell trait, and pregnancy occurred without their knowledge or consent, and without any subsequent notification that the tests had been conducted. They also allege that only black employees were tested for sickle cell trait and assert the obvious fact that only female employees were tested for pregnancy. Finally, they allege that Lawrence failed to provide safeguards to prevent the dissemination of the test results. They contend that they did not discover that the disputed tests had been conducted until approximately January 1995, and specifically deny that they observed any signs indicating that such tests would be performed. Plaintiffs do not allege that the defendants took any subsequent employment-related action on the basis of their test results, or that their test results have been disclosed to third parties.

On the basis of these factual allegations, plaintiffs contend that the defendants violated the ADA by requiring, encouraging, or assisting in medical testing that was neither job-related nor consistent with business necessity.... Finally, plaintiffs contend that Lawrence and the Regents violated Title VII by singling out black employees for sickle cell trait testing and by performing pregnancy testing on female employees generally.

...

IV. Title VII Claims

The district court ... dismissed the Title VII counts on the merits on the ground that plaintiffs had failed to state a claim because the "alleged classifications, standing alone, do not suffice to provide a cognizable basis for relief under Title VII" and because plaintiffs had neither alleged nor demonstrated how these classifications had adversely affected them.

Section 703(a) of Title VII of the Civil Rights Act of 1964 provides that it is unlawful for any employer:

> (1) to fail or refuse to hire or to discharge any individual, or otherwise to discriminate against any individual with respect to his compensation, terms, conditions, or privileges of employment, because of such individual's race, color, religion, sex, or national origin; or
>
> (2) to limit, segregate, or classify his employees or applicants for employment in any way which would deprive or tend to deprive any individual of employment opportunities or otherwise adversely affect his status as an employee, because of such individual's race, color, religion, sex, or national origin.

42 U.S.C. §2000e-2(a). The Pregnancy Discrimination Act further provides that discrimination on the basis of "sex" includes discrimination "on the basis of pregnancy, childbirth, or related medical conditions." 42 U.S.C. §2000e(k). "In accordance with Congressional intent, the above language is to be read in the broadest possible terms. The intent of Congress was not to list specific discriminatory practices, nor to definitively set out the scope of the activities covered." EEOC Compliance Manual (CCH) §613.1, at ¶2901 (citing *Rogers v. EEOC*, 454 F.2d 234 (5th Cir.1971)).

Despite defendants' assertions to the contrary, plaintiffs' Title VII claims fall neatly into a Title VII framework: Plaintiffs allege that black and female employees were singled out for additional nonconsensual testing and that defendants thus selectively invaded the privacy of certain employees on the basis of race, sex, and pregnancy. The district court held that (1) the tests did not constitute discrimination in the "terms" or "conditions" of plaintiffs' employment; and that (2) plaintiffs have failed to show any "adverse effect" as a result of the tests. It also granted the plaintiffs leave to amend their complaint to show adverse effect.

Under §2000e-2(a)(1), supra, an employer who "otherwise ... discriminate[s]" with respect to the "terms" or "conditions" of employment on account of an illicit classification is subject to Title VII liability. It is well established that Title VII bars discrimination not only in the "terms" and "conditions" of ongoing employment, but also in the "terms" and "conditions" under which individuals may obtain employment. See, e.g., *Griggs v. Duke Power Co.*, 401 U.S. 424, 432–36 (1971) (facially neutral educational and testing requirements that are not reasonable measures of job performance and have disparate impact on hiring of minorities violate Title VII). Thus, for example, a requirement of preemployment health examinations imposed only on female employees, or a requirement of preemployment background security checks imposed only on black employees, would surely violate Title VII.

In this case, the term or condition for black employees was undergoing a test for sickle cell trait; for women it was undergoing a test for pregnancy. It is not disputed that the preplacement exams were, literally, a condition of employment: the offers of employment stated this explicitly. Thus, the employment of women and blacks at Lawrence was conditioned in part on allegedly unconstitutional invasions of privacy to which white and/or male employees were not subjected. An additional "term or condition" requiring an unconstitutional invasion of privacy is, without doubt, actionable under Title VII. Furthermore, even if the intrusions did not rise to the level of unconstitutionality, they would still be a "term" or "condition" based on an illicit category as described by the statute and thus a proper basis for a Title VII action. Thus, the district court erred in ruling on the pleadings that the plaintiffs had failed to assert a proper Title VII claim under § 2000e-2(a)(1).

The district court also erred in finding as a matter of law that there was no "adverse effect" with respect to the tests as required under § 2000e-2(a)(2). The unauthorized obtaining of sensitive medical information on the basis of race or sex would in itself constitute an "adverse effect," or injury, under Title VII. Thus, it was error to rule that as a matter of law no "adverse effect" could arise from a classification that singled out particular groups for unconstitutionally invasive, non-consensual medical testing, and the district court erred in dismissing the Title VII claims on this ground as well.

...

Conclusion

... [B]ecause the tests were a separate and more invasive intrusion into their privacy than the aspects of the examination to which they did consent, the district court erred ... in dismissing the federal and state constitutional privacy claims and the Title VII claims on the merits. The district court's dismissal of the ADA claims was proper....

Notes & Questions

1. Promoting individual worker safety has been offered as one of the principal justifications for employers' consideration of genetic tests to screen and/or monitor workers. *Johnson Controls* suggests that the individual worker's right to autonomy takes precedence over the employers' desire to protect its workers. The court's decision to overturn a fetal protection policy, which excluded fertile women from relatively high-paying jobs involving lead exposure, rested in part on the conclusion that employers should not unilaterally decide that fetal health takes priority over women's right to equal employment opportunity. In other words, the decision whether to take on the health risks associated with lead exposure should be left up to the worker. Additionally, the court's reasoning arguably suggests that in attempting to protect workers the employer should not discriminate against one of many possible high-risk groups (in this case removing fertile women—but not fertile men—from the job) but instead should undertake workplace protections that benefit all exposed workers. To be sure, the excluded workers in this case were members of a class that Title VII of the Civil Rights Act protects from employment discrimination. However, some have argued that the court's reasoning suggests there could be limits to an employer's ability to use individual worker safety as a grounds for excluding genetically susceptible workers in situations where the workplace exposure at issue is potentially harmful to all workers. *See, e.g.*, Elaine Draper, *Genetic Secrets: Social Issues of Medical Screening in a Genetic Age*, 22 Hastings Center Report S15 (1992).

2. The genetic discrimination claim in the *Norman-Bloodsaw* case was specifically predicated upon a workplace genetic testing program. On what facts regarding the application of these tests did the Court of Appeals focus in deciding that the district court's decision to dismiss plaintiffs' Title VII claims was in error? The outcome of the Court of Appeals opinion was that the plaintiffs' Title VII and privacy claims survived

summary judgment (the relevant excerpts of the court's opinion on the privacy claims appear in Chapter 2). In other words, the court's opinion is not a finding that prohibited discriminatory conduct did in fact occur, but instead is a conclusion that there are sufficient factual issues to withstand summary judgment. The case did not go on to a full trial and disposition on the merits, but instead settled.

3. To successfully defend a Title VII claim predicated on a genetic testing program, an employer would have to show that its program is job-related and consistent with business necessity. This is a difficult defense to make in the context of a hazardous workplace because the alternative of cleaning up the workplace for all workers—which would not have a disparate impact on a protected group—always exists. Moreover, the courts have set a high threshold for business necessity. For example, saving money is not an adequate justification for discriminatory conduct. *See, e.g. Chrapliwy v. Uniroyal, Inc.*, 458 F. Supp. 252 (N.D. Ind. 1977). Similarly, as evidenced by the court's ruling in *Johnson Controls*, trying to avoid financial risks associated with the employer's liability exposure do not satisfy the "business necessity" exception.

2. The ADA

Bragdon v. Abbott

524 U.S. 624 (1998)

JUSTICE KENNEDY.

We address in this case the application of the Americans with Disabilities Act of 1990 (ADA), 104 Stat. 327, 42 U.S.C. § 12101 *et seq.*, to persons infected with the human immunodeficiency virus (HIV). We granted certiorari to review, first, whether HIV infection is a disability under the ADA when the infection has not yet progressed to the so-called symptomatic phase; and, second, whether the Court of Appeals, in affirming a grant of summary judgment, cited sufficient material in the record to determine, as a matter of law, that respondent's infection with HIV posed no direct threat to the health and safety of her treating dentist.

Respondent Sidney Abbott (hereinafter respondent) has been infected with HIV since 1986. When the incidents we recite occurred, her infection had not manifested its most serious symptoms. On September 16, 1994, she went to the office of petitioner Randon Bragdon in Bangor, Maine, for a dental appointment. She disclosed her HIV infection on the patient registration form. Petitioner completed a dental examination, discovered a cavity, and informed respondent of his policy against filling cavities of HIV-infected patients. He offered to perform the work at a hospital with no added fee for his services, though respondent would be responsible for the cost of using the hospital's facilities. Respondent declined.

Respondent sued petitioner under state law and § 302 of the ADA, 104 Stat. 355, 42 U.S.C. § 12182, alleging discrimination on the basis of her disability. The state-law claims are not before us. Section 302 of the ADA provides:

> "No individual shall be discriminated against on the basis of disability in the full and equal enjoyment of the goods, services, facilities, privileges, advantages, or accommodations of any place of public accommodation by any person who ... operates a place of public accommodation."

The term "public accommodation" is defined to include the "professional office of a health care provider." A later subsection qualifies the mandate not to discriminate. It provides:

> "Nothing in this subchapter shall require an entity to permit an individual to participate in or benefit from the goods, services, facilities, privileges, advantages and accommodations of such entity where such individual poses a direct threat to the health or safety of others." ...

We first review the ruling that respondent's HIV infection constituted a disability under the ADA. The statute defines disability as:

> "(A) a physical or mental impairment that substantially limits one or more of the major life activities of such individual;"(B) a record of such an impairment; or "(C) being regarded as having such an impairment."

We hold respondent's HIV infection was a disability under subsection (A) of the definitional section of the statute. In light of this conclusion, we need not consider the applicability of subsections (B) or (C).

...

The ADA's definition of disability is drawn almost verbatim from the definition of "handicapped individual" included in the Rehabilitation Act of 1973, 87 Stat. 361, as amended, 29 U.S.C. §706(8)(B) (1988 ed.), and the definition of "handicap" contained in the Fair Housing Amendments Act of 1988, 102 Stat. 1619, 42 U.S.C. §3602(h)(1) (1988 ed.). Congress' repetition of a well-established term carries the implication that Congress intended the term to be construed in accordance with pre-existing regulatory interpretations. In this case, Congress did more than suggest this construction; it adopted a specific statutory provision in the ADA directing as follows:

> "Except as otherwise provided in this chapter, nothing in this chapter shall be construed to apply a lesser standard than the standards applied under title V of the Rehabilitation Act of 1973 (29 U.S.C. §790 *et seq.*) or the regulations issued by Federal agencies pursuant to such title." 42 U.S.C. §12201(a).

The directive requires us to construe the ADA to grant at least as much protection as provided by the regulations implementing the Rehabilitation Act.

The first step in the inquiry under subsection (A) requires us to determine whether respondent's condition constituted a physical impairment. The Department of Health, Education and Welfare (HEW) issued the first regulations interpreting the Rehabilitation Act in 1977.... The HEW regulations, which appear without change in the current regulations issued by the Department of Health and Human Services, define "physical or mental impairment" to mean:

> "(A) any physiological disorder or condition, cosmetic disfigurement, or anatomical loss affecting one or more of the following body systems: neurological; musculoskeletal; special sense organs; respiratory, including speech organs; cardiovascular; reproductive, digestive, genito-urinary; hemic and lymphatic; skin; and endocrine; or
>
> "(B) any mental or psychological disorder, such as mental retardation, organic brain syndrome, emotional or mental illness, and specific learning disabilities." 45 CFR §84.3(j)(2)(i) (1997).

In issuing these regulations, HEW decided against including a list of disorders constituting physical or mental impairments, out of concern that any specific enumeration might not be comprehensive. 42 Fed.Reg. 22685 (1977), reprinted in 45 CFR pt. 84, App. A, p. 334 (1997). The commentary accompanying the regulations, however, contains a representative list of disorders and conditions constituting physical impairments, including "such diseases and conditions as orthopedic, visual, speech, and hearing impairments, cerebral palsy, epilepsy, muscular dystrophy, multiple sclerosis, cancer, heart disease, diabetes, mental retardation, emotional illness, and ... drug addiction and alcoholism." *Ibid.*

In 1980, the President transferred responsibility for the implementation and enforcement of §504 to the Attorney General. *See, e.g.*, Exec. Order No. 12250, 3 CFR §298 (1981). The regulations issued by the Justice Department, which remain in force to this day, adopted verbatim the HEW definition of physical impairment quoted above. 28 CFR §41.31(b)(1) (1997). In addition, the representative list of diseases and conditions originally relegated to the commentary accompanying the HEW regulations were incorporated into the text of the regulations. Ibid.

HIV infection is not included in the list of specific disorders constituting physical impairments, in part because HIV was not identified as the cause of AIDS until 1983. HIV infection does fall well within the general definition set forth by the regulations, however.

The disease follows a predictable and, as of today, an unalterable course.... The initial stage of HIV infection is known as acute or primary HIV infection. In a typical case, this stage lasts three months. The virus concentrates in the blood. The assault on the immune system is immediate. The victim suffers from a sudden and serious decline in the number of white blood cells. There is no latency period. Mononucleosis-like symptoms often emerge between six days and six weeks after infection, at times accompanied by fever, headache, enlargement of the lymph nodes (lymphadenopathy), muscle pain (myalgia), rash, lethargy, gastrointestinal disorders, and neurological disorders. Usually these symptoms abate within 14 to 21 days. HIV antibodies appear in the bloodstream within 3 weeks; circulating HIV can be detected within 10 weeks.

After the symptoms associated with the initial stage subside, the disease enters what is referred to sometimes as its asymptomatic phase. The term is a misnomer, in some respects, for clinical features persist throughout, including lymphadenopathy, dermatological disorders, oral lesions, and bacterial infections. Although it varies with each individual, in most instances this stage lasts from 7 to 11 years. The virus now tends to concentrate in the lymph nodes, though low levels of the virus continue to appear in the blood. It was once thought the virus became inactive during this period, but it is now known that the relative lack of symptoms is attributable to the virus' migration from the circulatory system into the lymph nodes. The migration reduces the viral presence in other parts of the body, with a corresponding diminution in physical manifestations of the disease. The virus, however, thrives in the lymph nodes, which, as a vital point of the body's immune response system, represents an ideal environment for the infection of other CD4+ cells.

A person is regarded as having AIDS when his or her CD4+ count drops below 200 cells/mm3 of blood or when CD4+ cells comprise less than 14% of his or her total lymphocytes. During this stage, the clinical conditions most often associated with HIV, such as pneumocystis carninii pneumonia, Kaposi's sarcoma, and non-Hodgkins lymphoma, tend to appear. In addition, the general systemic disorders present during all stages of the disease, such as fever, weight loss, fatigue, lesions, nausea, and diarrhea, tend to worsen. In most cases, once the patient's CD4+ count drops below 10 cells/mm3, death soon follows.

In light of the immediacy with which the virus begins to damage the infected person's white blood cells and the severity of the disease, we hold it is an impairment from the moment of infection. As noted earlier, infection with HIV causes immediate abnormalities in a person's blood, and the infected person's white cell count continues to drop throughout the course of the disease, even when the attack is concentrated in the lymph nodes. In light of these facts, HIV infection must be regarded as a physiological disorder with a constant and detrimental effect on the infected person's hemic and lymphatic systems from the moment of infection. HIV infection satisfies the statutory and regulatory definition of a physical impairment during every stage of the disease.

The statute is not operative, and the definition not satisfied, unless the impairment affects a major life activity. Respondent's claim throughout this case has been that the HIV infection placed a substantial limitation on her ability to reproduce and to bear children. Given the pervasive, and invariably fatal, course of the disease, its effect on major life activities of many sorts might have been relevant to our inquiry. Respondent and a number of amici make arguments about HIV's profound impact on almost every phase of the infected person's life. In light of these submissions, it may seem legalistic to circumscribe our discussion to the activity of reproduction. We have little doubt that had different parties brought the suit they would have maintained that an HIV infection imposes substantial limitations on other major life activities.

From the outset, however, the case has been treated as one in which reproduction was the major life activity limited by the impairment. It is our practice to decide cases on the grounds raised and considered in the Court of Appeals and included in the question on which we granted certiorari. We ask, then, whether reproduction is a major life activity.

We have little difficulty concluding that it is. As the Court of Appeals held, "[t]he plain meaning of the word 'major' denotes comparative importance" and "suggest[s] that the touchstone for determining an activity's inclusion under the statutory rubric is its significance." Reproduction falls well within the phrase "major life activity." Reproduction and the sexual dynamics surrounding it are central to the life process itself.

While petitioner concedes the importance of reproduction, he claims that Congress intended the ADA only to cover those aspects of a person's life which have a public, economic, or daily character. The argument founders on the statutory language. Nothing in the definition suggests that activities without a public, economic, or daily dimension may somehow be regarded as so unimportant or insignificant as to fall outside the meaning of the word "major." The breadth of the term confounds the attempt to limit its construction in this manner.

. . .

The final element of the disability definition in subsection (A) is whether respondent's physical impairment was a substantial limit on the major life activity she asserts....

Our evaluation of the medical evidence leads us to conclude that respondent's infection substantially limited her ability to reproduce in two independent ways. First, a woman infected with HIV who tries to conceive a child imposes on the man a significant risk of becoming infected. The cumulative results of 13 studies collected in a 1994 textbook on AIDS indicates that 20% of male partners of women with HIV became HIV-positive themselves, with a majority of the studies finding a statistically significant risk of infection. Second, an infected woman risks infecting her child during gestation and childbirth, i.e., perinatal transmission. Petitioner concedes that women infected with HIV face about a 25% risk of transmitting the virus to their children....

The Act addresses substantial limitations on major life activities, not utter inabilities. Conception and childbirth are not impossible for an HIV victim but, without doubt, are dangerous to the public health. This meets the definition of a substantial limitation. The decision to reproduce carries economic and legal consequences as well. There are added costs for antiretroviral therapy, supplemental insurance, and long-term health care for the child who must be examined and, tragic to think, treated for the infection. The laws of some States, moreover, forbid persons infected with HIV to have sex with others, regardless of consent. Iowa Code §§139.1, 139.31 (1997); Md. Health Code Ann. §18-601.1(a) (1994); Mont. Code Ann. §§50-18-101, 50-18-112 (1997); Utah Code Ann. §26-6-3.5(3) (Supp.1997); id., §26-6-5 (1995); Wash. Rev. Code §9A.36.011(1)(b) (Supp.1998); see also N.D. Cent. Code §12.1-20-17 (1997).

... Notwithstanding the protection given respondent by the ADA's definition of disability, petitioner could have refused to treat her if her infectious condition "pose[d] a direct threat to the health or safety of others." 42 U.S.C. §12182(b)(3). The ADA defines a direct threat to be "a significant risk to the health or safety of others that cannot be eliminated by a modification of policies, practices, or procedures or by the provision of auxiliary aids or services." Ibid....

The existence, or nonexistence, of a significant risk must be determined from the standpoint of the person who refuses the treatment or accommodation, and the risk assessment must be based on medical or other objective evidence. As a health care professional, petitioner had the duty to assess the risk of infection based on the objective, scientific information available to him and others in his profession. His belief that a significant risk existed, even if maintained in good faith, would not relieve him from liability....

Our conclusion that courts should assess the objective reasonableness of the views of health care professionals without deferring to their individual judgments does not answer the implicit assumption in the question presented, whether petitioner's actions were reasonable in light of the available medical evidence. In assessing the reasonableness of petitioner's actions, the views of public health authorities, such as the U.S. Public Health Service, CDC, and the National Institutes of Health, are of special weight and authority. The views of these organizations are not conclusive, however. A health care professional who disagrees with the prevailing medical consensus may refute it by citing a credible scientific basis for deviating from the accepted norm....

Our evaluation of the evidence is constrained by the fact that on these and other points we have not had briefs and arguments directed to the entire record. In accepting the case for review, we declined to grant certiorari on question five, which asked whether petitioner raised a genuine issue of fact for trial. As a result, the briefs and arguments presented to us did not concentrate on the question of sufficiency in light all of the submissions in the summary judgment proceeding....

We conclude the proper course is to give the Court of Appeals the opportunity to determine whether our analysis of some of the studies cited by the parties would change its conclusion that petitioner presented neither objective evidence nor a triable issue of fact on the question of risk. In remanding the case, we do not foreclose the possibility that the Court of Appeals may reach the same conclusion it did earlier. A remand will permit a full exploration of the issue through the adversary process.

The determination of the Court of Appeals that respondent's HIV infection was a disability under the ADA is affirmed. The judgment is vacated, and the case is remanded for further proceedings consistent with this opinion.

It is so ordered.

Laws v. Pact, Inc.

2000 WL 777926 (N.D. Ill. 2000)

Gettleman, J.

Plaintiff Patricia Laws has brought a two count amended complaint against her former employer, Pact, Inc., alleging violations of § 504 of the Rehabilitation Act, 29 U.S.C. § 794 (Count I), and the Americans With Disabilities Act ("ADA"), 42 U.S.C. § 12101 *et seq* and 42 U.S.C. § 1981 (Count II). Defendant has moved for summary judgment on both counts. For the reasons set forth below, defendant's motion is granted.

Facts

Defendant is a non-profit agency that assists developmentally disabled clients and their families in locating residential, vocational, recreational and day program options, and links clients with funding sources. Plaintiff was employed by defendant in a variety of positions from September 1990 until her termination in May 1997. Plaintiff's last position with defendant was as an Individual Service Coordinator ("ISC") in the Case Coordination Unit ("CCU").

In August 1996 plaintiff's mother died, leaving plaintiff as executor of the estate and sole guardian of her disabled sister. Around that time, plaintiff was suffering from depression and began to experience some symptoms of what she later learned to be Huntington's Disease, which is an "inherited progressive degenerative disease of cognition, emotion, and movement." It "affects men and women equally and is transmitted by a single autosomal dominant gene on the short arm of chromosome 4. The disease is usually diagnosed in the late 30s to early 40s but may begin as early as age 4 in the juvenile form or as late as 85 years in the late-onset form. The onset of the disease is often heralded by insidious changes in behavior and personality, including depression, irritability and anxiety." American Psychiatric Association: *Diagnostic and Statistical Manual of Mental Disorders,* Fourth Edition, p. 149, 294.1.

On February 21, 1997, plaintiff asked for a one month leave of absence to deal with her family affairs. The request did not mention either her depression or any other medical condition, nor did it indicate in any way an inability to handle her work load. That request was denied based on staffing problems, but defendant suggested an alternative of five days leave.

One week later, February 28, 1997, plaintiff submitted another request, this time seeking at least 2 1/2 weeks leave, based on recommendations of her therapist and psychiatrist who were treating her for depression. That request was granted. On March 4, 1997, plaintiff informed defendant that "under no circumstances am I able to continue to perform in my present position as Individual Service Coordinator at this time." Plaintiff therefore requested a disability leave without pay, from March 8, 1997, through April 11, or 15, 1997. Submitted with her March 4, 1997, letter was a letter from her primary care physician, requesting that plaintiff be put on disability leave for 25 to 30 days, based on her depression. Again, nothing in either of plaintiff's memos or the doctor's letter mentioned Huntington's Disease.

Around the same time, plaintiff apparently informed Karen Delhotal, whom plaintiff calls her immediate supervisor, that she had been diagnosed with Huntington's Disease. Plaintiff had not yet actually been formally diagnosed with Huntington's, but was undergoing testing. Plaintiff asked Delhotal not to reveal the diagnosis to anyone, but plaintiff has presented evidence that Delhotal told a co-worker that plaintiff had Huntington's. There is no evidence, however, that Delhotal told either Steve Boisse, Associate Director, or Dr. Joseph Straka, the Executive Director, the ultimate decision makers on personnel matters.

Plaintiff was told that her position might be filled while she was on leave, due to staffing problems. The position was filled shortly after her leave began. On April 2, 1997, Boisse wrote to plaintiff informing her that her position had been filled and that there were no positions currently available, but that she would be given preference should any position for which she was qualified open. On May 5, 1997, the date plaintiff was finally medically cleared to return to work, there were no such positions available. Boisse informed plaintiff of that in a letter dated May 5, 1997, in which he terminated her employment and informed her that pursuant to company policy she would be given preference for any opening in a similar position.

Defendant had an employee policy in effect which provided that "every attempt will be made to reinstate those employees who have been granted an authorized leave of absence in the same, similar, or vacant position for which they are qualified." Pursuant to that policy, on June 2, 1997, Boisse spoke with plaintiff and offered her a position similar to her previous position. According to plaintiff, the position offered was in the Bogard Department, for which she was qualified but would need additional training. According to defendant, the offer was for an ISC position, although it is unclear whether that position was in the Bogard Unit. Plaintiff considered the offer for two days then rejected it because of a slightly lower salary and because the Bogard Unit had an aging, dying population which plaintiff and her doctor decided would be difficult for her to handle.

Discussion

Defendant has moved for summary judgment on a number of grounds: 1) plaintiff is not now, and was not disabled at the time of her termination; 2) the claims are time barred; and 3) the actions are not discriminatory.

Defendant first argues that plaintiff can not establish that she was disabled. To establish a claim of discriminatory treatment under the ADA or the Rehabilitation Act, plaintiff must demonstrate that she suffers from a disability as defined in those statutes. Disability is defined as: a) a physical or mental impairment that substantially limits one or more of the major life activities of an individual; b) a record of such impairment; or c) being regarded as having such an impairment. 22 U.S.C. § 12102(2). EEOC regulations define major life activities to include "functions such as caring for one self, performing manual tasks, walking, seeing, hearing, speaking, breathing, learning and working." 29 C.F.R. § 1630.2(i). Substantially limited means that the person is either "unable to perform in a major life activity or is significantly restricted as to the condition, manner or duration under which the individual can perform a major life activity as opposed to the average person in the overall population. *Id.* at § 130.2(j)(i).

In the instant case, it is undisputed that at the time of the actions in question, plaintiff was not yet substantially limited in her ability to care for herself, perform manual tasks, walk, see, speak, breath, learn, or work. Although she may have begun to exhibit early signs of Huntington's Disease, her own testimony established that it had only minor effects on her activities. Plaintiff argues that once she told Delhotal that she had been diagnosed with Huntington's, defendant perceived her as disabled, but she has no evidence to support that theory. Although Delhotal may have known that plaintiff had the disease, knowing that plaintiff was ill and perceiving her as disabled are different matters. To perceive plaintiff as disabled, Delhotal (who arguably was not plaintiff's supervisor) must have perceived plaintiff as substantially limited in a major life activity, and there is no evidence to support that theory.

Plaintiff also argues, however, that Huntington's Disease substantially limits reproduction, which *Bragden v. Abbott*, 524 U.S. 624 (1998), holds is a major life activity. A person with Huntington's Disease has a 50% risk of passing the disease on to a child, a risk certainly substantial enough to control a decision. Plaintiff testified that she elected not to have a child based on this risk. Plaintiff had not yet be diagnosed with Huntington's when she made her decision, however, leaving open the question as to whether the *Bragden* holding is applicable. The court need not reach the complicated issue of whether plaintiff's decision not to reproduce because she might have had Huntington's Disease constitutes a disability, because even if plaintiff was disabled, her claim of disability discrimination fails. Plaintiff's claim is for discriminatory treatment based on her disability. Therefore, she must establish that her disability impacted on defendant's decisions. She has not done so.

Plaintiff's theory of the case is that once learning of her disease, defendant began to scheme to terminate her. Thus, plaintiff argues that there was no need to immediately replace her, and that her replacement was hired simply to assure that there would be no position for her to return once being medically cleared for work. This argument is negated by plaintiff's own original request for leave, however, in which she acknowledged that "I realize that this is not the best time for the Case Coordinator Department, in terms of staff availability and caseload...."According to plaintiff, once defendant learned of her illness, it wanted her out to reduce its health insurance costs. Her only evidence to support this theory is that once plaintiff's replacement transferred to a new position, Boisse recommended that plaintiff's former position be eliminated. Straka's memorandum to Boisse accepting the recommendation listed a number of factors, including keeping down rising health insurance costs.

The problem with plaintiff's theory is that it is undisputed that plaintiff was offered a position that was substantially similar to the one she vacated. Had plaintiff accepted the position, defendant's health insurance costs would not have been reduced, destroying her theory. She argues that defendant (Boisse and Straka) knew that she could not take the position, but has no evidence to support that claim. Indeed, plaintiff took several days to determine that she did not want the position. Even under a reasonable accommodation theory, plaintiff does not have the right to pick and choose her position among reasonable accomodations. Plaintiff elected not to take the position offered by defendant. There is no evidence that Boisse and Straka based their decisions to offer her that particular position based on her condition. Indeed, there is no evidence to suggest that Boisse or Straka even knew of her condition. Absent such knowledge, plaintiff could not have been terminated "because of" her disability as required by the ADA. Accordingly, because there is no evidence of a causal connection between plaintiff's alleged disability and defendant's decisions, and because plaintiff turned down a position that constituted a reasonable accommodation, defendant's motion for summary judgment is granted.

Conclusion

For the reasons set forth above, defendant's motion for summary judgment is granted.

Notes & Questions

1. In *Bragdon v. Abbott* the Supreme Court concluded that Sidney Abbott's asymptomatic HIV infection met the statutory and regulatory definition of a disability, defined as "a physical or mental impairment that substantially limits one or more of the major life activities of such individual." To what extent did established scientific knowledge regarding the pathophysiology and natural history of HIV infection and the likelihood it would progress to AIDS influence the Court's determination? What characteristics of this viral process did the court focus on? To what extent did established scientific knowledge contribute to the court's conclusion regarding the impact of HIV on the major life activity of reproduction?

How might a genetic discrimination claim advanced on behalf of a carrier of the relevant mutations in the BRCA1 and BRCA2 genes (conferring increased risk for breast and ovarian cancer) compare with a claim advanced by an HIV patient? (For additional background information regarding hereditary breast cancer, *see, e.g.* A. Antoniou, et al., *Average Risk of Breast and Ovarian Cancer Associated with BRCA1 or BRCA2 Mutations Detected in Case Series Unselected for Family History: A Combined Analysis of 22 Studies*, 72 Am. J. Hum. Genet. 1117 (2003). Assume both individuals are asymptomatic at the time an adverse employment decision is made. Applying the Court's analysis in *Bragdon*, do both employees have a qualifying disability under the ADA? Why or why not? For a more in-depth discussion of the impact of *Bragdon* on discrimination claims advanced by individuals with asymptomatic disease, including genetic susceptibilities, *see* Laura F. Rothstein, *Genetic Discrimination: Why Bragdon Does Not Ensure Protection*, 3 J. Health Care L. & Pol'y 330 (2000); Roger Clegg, *Commentary, Bragdon v. Abbott, Asymptomatic Genetic Conditions, and Antidiscrimination Law: a Conservative Perspective*, 3 J. Health Care L. & Pol'y 409 (2000); Wendy E. Parmet, *The Supreme Court Confronts HIV: Reflections on Bragdon v. Abbott*, 26 J.L. Med. & Ethics 225 (1998).

Sutton v. United Air Lines, Inc.

527 U.S. 471 (1999)

Justice O'Connor.

The Americans with Disabilities Act of 1990 (ADA or Act), 104 Stat. 328, 42 U.S.C. § 12101 *et seq.*, prohibits certain employers from discriminating against individuals on the basis of their disabilities. See § 12112(a). Petitioners challenge the dismissal of their ADA action for failure to state a claim upon which relief can be granted. We conclude that the complaint was properly dismissed. In reaching that result, we hold that the determination of whether an individual is disabled should be made with reference to measures that mitigate the individual's impairment, including, in this instance, eyeglasses and contact lenses. In addition, we hold that petitioners failed to allege properly that respondent "regarded" them as having a disability within the meaning of the ADA.

...

Petitioners are twin sisters, both of whom have severe myopia. Each petitioner's uncorrected visual acuity is 20/200 or worse in her right eye and 20/400 or worse in her left eye, but "[w]ith the use of corrective lenses, each ... has vision that is 20/20 or better." Consequently, without corrective lenses, each "effectively cannot see to conduct numerous activities such as driving a vehicle, watching television or shopping in public stores," but with corrective measures, such as glasses or contact lenses, both "function identically to individuals without a similar impairment."

In 1992, petitioners applied to respondent for employment as commercial airline pilots. They met respondent's basic age, education, experience, and Federal Aviation Administration certification qualifications. After submitting their applications for employment, both petitioners were invited by respondent to an interview and to flight simulator tests. Both were told during their interviews, however, that a mistake had been made in inviting them to interview because petitioners did not meet respondent's minimum vision requirement, which was uncorrected visual acuity of 20/100 or better. Due to their failure to meet this requirement, petitioners' interviews were terminated, and neither was offered a pilot position.

In light of respondent's proffered reason for rejecting them, petitioners filed a charge of disability discrimination under the ADA with the Equal Employment Opportunity Commission (EEOC). After receiving a right to sue letter, petitioners filed suit in the United States District Court for the District of Colorado, alleging that respondent had discriminated against them "on the basis of their disability, or because [respondent] regarded [petitioners] as having a disability" in violation of the ADA. Specifically, petitioners alleged that due to their severe myopia they actually have a substantially limiting impairment or are regarded as having such an impairment, and are thus disabled under the Act.

...

The ADA prohibits discrimination by covered entities, including private employers, against qualified individuals with a disability. Specifically, it provides that no covered employer "shall discriminate against a qualified individual with a disability because of the disability of such individual in regard to job application procedures, the hiring, advancement, or discharge of employees, employee compensation, job training, and other terms, conditions, and privileges of employment." 42 U.S.C. § 12112(a); see also § 12111(2) ("The term 'covered entity' means an employer, employment agency, labor organization, or joint labor-management committee"). A "qualified individual with a disability" is identified as "an individual with a disability who, with or without reasonable accommodation, can perform the essential functions of the employment position that such individual holds or desires." § 12111(8). In turn, a "disability" is defined as:

> "(A) a physical or mental impairment that substantially limits one or more of the major life activities of such individual;
>
> "(B) a record of such an impairment; or
>
> "(C) being regarded as having such an impairment."

Accordingly, to fall within this definition one must have an actual disability (subsection (A)), have a record of a disability (subsection (B)), or be regarded as having one (subsection (C)).

...

[W]e turn first to the question whether petitioners have stated a claim under subsection (A) of the disability definition, that is, whether they have alleged that they possess a physical impairment that substantially limits them in one or more major life activities. See 42 U.S.C. § 12102(2)(A). Because petitioners allege that with corrective measures their vision "is 20/20 or better," they are not actually disabled within the meaning of the Act if the "disability" determination is made with reference to these measures. Consequently, with respect to subsection (A) of the disability definition, our decision turns on whether disability is to be determined with or without reference to corrective measures.

Petitioners maintain that whether an impairment is substantially limiting should be determined without regard to corrective measures. They argue that, because the ADA does not directly address the question at hand, the Court should defer to the agency interpretations of the statute, which are embodied in the agency guidelines issued by the EEOC and the Department of Justice. These guidelines specifically direct that the determination of whether an individual is substantially limited in a major life activity be made without regard to mitigating measures. See 29 CFR pt. 1630, App. § 1630.2(j); 28 CFR pt. 35, App. A § 35.104 (1998) 28 CFR pt. 36, App. B § 36.104.

Respondent, in turn, maintains that an impairment does not substantially limit a major life activity if it is corrected. It argues that the Court should not defer to the agency guidelines cited by petitioners because the guidelines conflict with the plain meaning of the ADA. The phrase "substantially limits one or more major life activities," it explains, requires that the substantial limitations actually and presently exist. Moreover, respondent argues, disregarding mitigating measures taken by an individual defies the statutory command to examine the effect of the impairment on the major life activities "of such individual." And even if the statute is ambiguous, respondent claims, the guidelines' directive to ignore mitigating measures is not reasonable, and thus this Court should not defer to it.

We conclude that respondent is correct that the approach adopted by the agency guidelines—that persons are to be evaluated in their hypothetical uncorrected state—is an impermissible interpretation of the ADA. Looking at the Act as a whole, it is apparent that if a person is taking measures to correct for, or mitigate, a physical or mental impairment, the effects of those measures—both positive and negative—must be taken into account when judging whether that person is "substantially limited" in a major life activity and thus "disabled" under the Act....

Three separate provisions of the ADA, read in concert, lead us to this conclusion. The Act defines a "disability" as "a physical or mental impairment that *substantially limits* one or more of the major life activities" of an individual. § 12102(2)(A) (emphasis added). Because the phrase "substantially limits" appears in the Act in the present indicative verb form, we think the language is properly read as requiring that a person be presently—not potentially or hypothetically—substantially limited in order to demonstrate a disability. A "disability" exists only where an impairment "substantially limits" a major life activity, not where it "might," "could," or "would" be substantially limiting if mitigating measures were not taken. A person whose physical or mental impairment is corrected by medication or other measures does not have an impairment that presently "substantially limits" a major life activity. To be sure, a person whose physical or mental impairment is corrected by mitigating measures still has an impairment, but if the impairment is corrected it does not "substantially limi[t]" a major life activity.

The definition of disability also requires that disabilities be evaluated "with respect to an individual" and be determined based on whether an impairment substantially limits the "major life activities of such individual." § 12102(2). Thus, whether a person has a disability under the ADA is an individualized inquiry. See *Bragdon v. Abbott,* 524 U.S. 624, 641–642 (1998) (declining to consider whether HIV infection is a *per se* disability under the ADA); 29 CFR pt. 1630, App.§ 1630.2(j) ("The determination of whether an individual has a disability is not necessarily based on the name or diagnosis of the impairment the person has, but rather on the effect of that impairment on the life of the individual").

The agency guidelines' directive that persons be judged in their uncorrected or unmitigated state runs directly counter to the individualized inquiry mandated by the ADA. The agency approach would often require courts and employers to speculate about a person's condition and would, in many cases, force them to make a disability determination based on general information about how an uncorrected impairment usually affects individuals, rather than on the individual's actual condition. For instance, under this view, courts would almost certainly find all diabetics to be disabled, because if they failed to monitor their blood sugar levels and administer insulin, they would almost certainly be substantially limited in one or more major life activities. A diabetic whose illness does not impair his or her daily activities would therefore be considered disabled simply because he or she has diabetes. Thus, the guidelines approach would create a system in which persons often must be treated as members of a group of people with similar impairments, rather than as individuals. This is contrary to both the letter and the spirit of the ADA.

The guidelines approach could also lead to the anomalous result that in determining whether an individual is disabled, courts and employers could not consider any negative side effects suffered by an individual resulting from the use of mitigating measures, even when those side effects are very severe. *See, e.g.,* Johnson, Antipsychotics: Pros and Cons of Antipsychotics, RN (Aug. 1997) (noting that antipsychotic drugs can cause a variety of adverse effects, including neuroleptic malignant syndrome and painful seizures); Liver Risk Warning Added to Parkinson's Drug, FDA Consumer (Mar. 1, 1999) (warning that a drug for treating Parkinson's disease can cause liver damage); Curry & Kulling, Newer Antiepileptic Drugs, American Family Physician (Feb. 1, 1998) (cataloging serious negative side effects of new antiepileptic drugs). This result is also inconsistent with the individualized approach of the ADA.

Finally, and critically, findings enacted as part of the ADA require the conclusion that Congress did not intend to bring under the statute's protection all those whose uncorrected conditions amount to disabilities. Congress found that "some 43,000,000 Americans have one or more physical or mental disabilities, and this number is increasing as the population as a whole is growing older." § 12101(a)(1). This figure is inconsistent with the definition of disability pressed by petitioners.

...

[N]onfunctional approaches to defining disability produce significantly larger numbers. As noted above, the 1986 National Council on Disability report estimated that there were over 160 million disabled under the "health conditions approach." Toward Independence, *supra,* at 10; see also Mathematica Policy Research, *supra*, at 3 (arriving at similar estimate based on same Census Bureau data). Indeed, the number of people with vision impairments alone is 100 million. See National Advisory Eye Council, U.S. Dept. of Health and Human Services, Vision Research—A National Plan: 1999–2003, p. 7 (1998) ("[M]ore than 100 million people need corrective lenses to see properly"). "It is estimated that more than 28 million Americans have impaired hearing." National Institutes of Health, National Strategic Research Plan: Hearing and Hearing Impairment V. (1996). And there were approximately 50 million people with high blood pressure (hypertension). Tindall, Stalking a Silent Killer; Hypertension, Business & Health 37 (August 1998) ("Some 50 million Americans have high blood pressure").

Because it is included in the ADA's text, the finding that 43 million individuals are disabled gives content to the ADA's terms, specifically the term "disability." Had Congress intended to include all persons with corrected physical limitations among those covered by the Act, it undoubtedly would have cited a much higher number of disabled persons in the findings. That it did not is evidence that the ADA's coverage is restricted to only those whose impairments are not mitigated by corrective measures.

... The use of a corrective device does not, by itself, relieve one's disability. Rather, one has a disability under subsection (A) if, notwithstanding the use of a corrective device, that individual is substantially limited in a major life activity. For example, individuals who use prosthetic limbs or wheelchairs may be mobile and capable of functioning in society but still be disabled because of a substantial limitation on their ability to walk or run. The same may be true of individuals who take medicine to lessen the symptoms of an impairment so that they can function but nevertheless remain substantially limited. Alternatively, one whose high blood pressure is "cured" by medication may be regarded as disabled by a covered entity, and thus disabled under subsection (C) of the definition. The use or nonuse of a corrective device does not determine whether an individual is disabled; that determination depends on whether the limitations an individual with an impairment *actually* faces are in fact substantially limiting.

Applying this reading of the Act to the case at hand, we conclude that the Court of Appeals correctly resolved the issue of disability in respondent's favor. As noted above, petitioners allege that with corrective measures, their visual acuity is 20/20, and that they "function identically to individuals without a similar impairment." In addition, petitioners concede that they "do not argue that the use of corrective lenses in itself demonstrates a substantially limiting impairment." Accordingly, because we decide that disability under the Act is to be determined with reference to corrective measures, we agree with the courts below that petitioners have not stated a claim that they are substantially limited in any major life activity.

Our conclusion that petitioners have failed to state a claim that they are actually disabled under subsection (A) of the disability definition does not end our inquiry. Under subsection (C), individuals who are "regarded as" having a disability are disabled within the meaning of the ADA. See § 12102(2)(C). Subsection (C) provides that having a disability includes "being regarded as having," § 12102(2)(C), "a physical or mental impairment that substantially limits one or more of the major life activities of such individual," § 12102(2)(A). There are two apparent ways in which individuals may fall within this statutory definition: (1) a covered entity mistakenly believes that a person has a physical impairment that substantially limits one or more major life activities, or (2) a covered entity mistakenly believes that an actual, nonlimiting impairment substantially limits one or more major life activities. In both cases, it is necessary that a covered entity entertain misperceptions about the individual—it must believe either that one has a substantially limiting impairment that one does not have or that one has a substantially limiting impairment when, in fact, the impairment is not so limiting. These misperceptions often "resul[t] from stereotypic assumptions not truly indicative of ... individual ability." See 42 U.S.C. § 12101(7). See also *School Bd. of Nassau Cty. v. Arline*, 480 U.S. 273, 284 (1987) ("By amending the definition of 'handicapped individual' to include not only those who are actually physically impaired, but also those who are regarded as impaired and who, as a result, are substantially limited in a major life activity, Congress acknowledged that society's accumulated myths and fears about disability and disease are as handicapping as are the physical limitations that flow from actual impairment"); 29 CFR pt. 1630.

There is no dispute that petitioners are physically impaired. Petitioners do not make the obvious argument that they are regarded due to their impairments as substantially limited in the major life activity of seeing. They contend only that respondent mistakenly believes their physical impairments substantially limit them in the major life activity of working. To support this claim, petitioners allege that respondent has a vision requirement that is allegedly based on myth and stereotype. Further, this requirement substantially limits their ability to engage in the major life activity of working by precluding them from obtaining the job of global airline pilot, which they argue is a "class of employment." In reply, respondent argues that the position of global airline pilot is not a class of jobs and therefore petitioners have not stated a claim that they are regarded as substantially limited in the major life activity of working.

Standing alone, the allegation that respondent has a vision requirement in place does not establish a claim that respondent regards petitioners as substantially limited in the major life activity of working. See Post-Argument Brief for Respondent 2–3 (advancing this argument); Post-Argument Brief for United States et al. as *Amici Curiae* 5–6 ("[U]nder the EEOC's regulations, an employer may make employment decisions based on physical characteristics"). By its terms, the ADA allows employers to prefer some physical attributes over others and to establish physical criteria. An employer runs afoul of the ADA when it makes an employment decision based on a physical or mental impairment, real or imagined, that is regarded as substantially limiting a major life activity. Accordingly, an employer is free to decide that physical characteristics or medical conditions that do not rise to the level of an impairment—such as one's height, build, or singing voice—are preferable to others, just as it is free to decide that some limiting, but not *substantially* limiting, impairments make individuals less than ideally suited for a job.

Considering the allegations of the amended complaint in tandem, petitioners have not stated a claim that respondent regards their impairment as *substantially limiting* their ability to work. The ADA does not define "substantially limits," but "substantially" suggests "considerable" or "specified to a large degree." See Webster's Third New International Dictionary 2280 (1976) (defining "substantially" as "in a substantial manner" and "substantial" as "considerable in amount, value, or worth" and "being that specified to a large degree or in the main"); see also 17 Oxford English Dictionary 66–67 (2d ed.1989) ("substantial:" "[r]elating to or proceeding from the essence of a thing; essential"; "of ample or considerable amount, quantity or dimensions"). The EEOC has codified regulations interpreting the term "substantially limits" in this manner, defining the term to mean "[u]nable to perform" or "[s]ignificantly restricted." See 29 CFR §§ 1630.2(j)(1)(i),(ii) (1998).

When the major life activity under consideration is that of working, the statutory phrase "substantially limits" requires, at a minimum, that plaintiffs allege they are unable to work in a broad class of jobs. Reflecting this requirement, the EEOC uses a specialized definition of the term "substantially limits" when referring to the major life activity of working:

> "significantly restricted in the ability to perform either a class of jobs or a broad range of jobs in various classes as compared to the average person having comparable training, skills and abilities. The inability to perform a single, particular job does not constitute a substantial limitation in the major life activity of working." § 1630.2(j)(3)(i).

The EEOC further identifies several factors that courts should consider when determining whether an individual is substantially limited in the major life activity of working, including the geographical area to which the individual has reasonable access, and "the number and types of jobs utilizing similar training, knowledge, skills or abilities, within the geographical area, from which the individual is also disqualified." §§ 1630.2(j)(3)(ii)(A), (B). To be substantially limited in the major life activity of working, then, one must be precluded from more than one type of job, a specialized job, or a particular job of choice. If jobs utilizing an individual's skills (but perhaps not his or her unique talents) are available, one is not precluded from a substantial class of jobs. Similarly, if a host of different types of jobs are available, one is not precluded from a broad range of jobs.

Because the parties accept that the term "major life activities" includes working, we do not determine the validity of the cited regulations. We note, however, that there may be some conceptual difficulty in defining "major life activities" to include work, for it seems "to argue in a circle to say that if one is excluded, for instance, by reason of [an impairment, from working with others] ... then that exclusion constitutes an impairment, when the question you're asking is, whether the exclusion itself is by reason of handicap." Indeed, even the EEOC has expressed reluctance to define "major life activities" to include working and has suggested that working be viewed as a residual life activity, considered, as a last resort, *only* "[i]f an individual is not substantially limited with respect to *any other* major life activity." 29 CFR pt. 1630, App. § 1630.2(j) (1998) (emphasis added) ("If an individual is substantially limited in *any other* major life activity, no determination should be made as to whether the individual is substantially limited in working" (emphasis added)).

Assuming without deciding that working is a major life activity and that the EEOC regulations interpreting the term "substantially limits" are reasonable, petitioners have failed to allege adequately that their poor eyesight is regarded as an impairment that substantially limits them in the major life activity of working. They allege only that respondent regards their poor vision as precluding them from holding positions as a "global airline pilot." Because the position of global airline pilot is a single job, this allegation does not support the claim that respondent regards petitioners as having a *substantially limiting* impairment. See 29 CFR § 1630.2(j)(3)(i) (1998) ("The inability to perform a single, particular job does not constitute a substantial limitation in the major life activity of working"). Indeed, there are a number of other positions utilizing petitioners' skills, such as regional pilot and pilot instructor to name a few, that are available to them. Even under the EEOC's Interpretative Guidance, to which petitioners ask us to defer, "an individual who cannot be a commercial airline pilot because of a minor vision impairment, but who can be a commercial airline co-pilot or a pilot for a courier service, would not be substantially limited in the major life activity of working." 29 CFR pt. 1630, App. § 1630.2 (1998).

Petitioners also argue that if one were to assume that a substantial number of airline carriers have similar vision requirements, they would be substantially limited in the major life activity of working. Even assuming for the sake of argument that the adoption of similar vision requirements by other carriers would represent a substantial limitation on the major life activity of working, the argument is nevertheless flawed. It is not enough to say that if the physical criteria of a single employer were *imputed* to all similar employers one would be regarded as substantially limited in the major life activity of working *only as a result of this imputation.* An otherwise valid job requirement, such as a height requirement, does not become invalid simply because it *would* limit a person's employment opportunities in a substantial way *if* it were adopted by a substantial number of employers. Because petitioners have not alleged, and cannot demonstrate, that respondent's vision requirement reflects a belief that petitioners' vision substantially limits them, we agree with the decision of the Court of Appeals affirming the dismissal of petitioners' claim that they are regarded as disabled.

For these reasons, the judgment of the Court of Appeals for the Tenth Circuit is affirmed.

Chevron U.S.A., Inc. v. Echazabal

536 U.S. 73 (2002)

Justice Souter.

A regulation of the Equal Employment Opportunity Commission authorizes refusal to hire an individual because his performance on the job would endanger his own health, owing to a disability. The question in this case is whether the Americans with Disabilities Act of 1990, 104 Stat. 328, 42 U.S.C. § 12101 *et seq.* (1994 ed. and Supp. V), permits the regulation. We hold that it does.

Beginning in 1972, respondent Mario Echazabal worked for independent contractors at an oil refinery owned by petitioner Chevron U.S.A. Inc. Twice he applied for a job directly with Chevron, which offered to hire him if he could pass the company's physical examination. Each time, the exam showed liver abnormality or damage, the cause eventually being identified as Hepatitis C, which Chevron's doctors said would be aggravated by continued exposure to toxins at Chevron's refinery. In each instance, the company withdrew the offer, and the second time it asked the contractor employing Echazabal either to reassign him to a job without exposure to harmful chemicals or to remove him from the refinery altogether. The contractor laid him off in early 1996.

Echazabal filed suit, ultimately removed to federal court, claiming, among other things, that Chevron violated the Americans with Disabilities Act (ADA or Act) in refusing to hire him, or even to let him continue working in the plant, because of a disability, his liver condition. Chevron defended under a regulation of the Equal Employment Opportunity Commission (EEOC) permitting the defense that a worker's disability on the job would pose a "direct threat" to his health, see 29 CFR § 1630.15(b)(2) (2001).

Section 102 of the ADA, 104 Stat. 328, 42 U.S.C. § 12101 *et seq.*, prohibits "discriminat[ion] against a qualified individual with a disability because of the disability ... in regard to" a number of actions by an employer, including "hiring." 42 U.S.C. § 12112(a). The statutory definition of "discriminat[ion]" covers a number of things an employer might do to block a disabled person from advancing in the workplace, such as "using qualification standards ... that screen out or tend to screen out an individual with a disability." § 12112(b)(6). By that same definition, as well as by separate provision, § 12113(a), the Act creates an affirmative defense for action under a qualification standard "shown to be job-related for the position in question and ... consistent with business necessity." Such a standard may include "a requirement that an individual shall not pose a direct threat to the health or safety of other individuals in the workplace," § 12113(b), if the individual cannot perform the job safely with reasonable accommodation, § 12113(a). By regulation, the EEOC carries the defense one step further, in allowing an employer to screen out a potential worker with a disability not only for risks that he would pose to others in the workplace but for risks on the job to his own health or safety as well: "The term 'qualification standard' may include a requirement that an individual shall not pose a direct threat to the health or safety of the individual or others in the workplace." 29 CFR § 1630.15(b)(2) (2001).

Chevron relies on the regulation here, since it says a job in the refinery would pose a "direct threat" to Echazabal's health. In seeking deference to the agency, it argues that nothing in the statute unambiguously precludes such a defense, while the regulation was adopted under authority explicitly delegated by Congress, 42 U.S.C. § 12116, and after notice-and-comment rulemaking. Echazabal, on the contrary, argues that as a matter of law the statute precludes the regulation, which he claims would be an unreasonable interpretation even if the agency had leeway to go beyond the literal text.

As for the textual bar to any agency action as a matter of law, Echazabal says that Chevron loses on the threshold question whether the statute leaves a gap for the EEOC to fill. Echazabal recognizes the generality of the language providing for a defense when a plaintiff is screened out by "qualification standards" that are "job-related and consistent with business necessity" (and reasonable accommodation would not cure the difficulty posed by employment). 42 U.S.C. § 12113(a). Without more, those provisions would allow an employer to turn away someone whose work would pose a serious risk to himself. That possibility is said to be eliminated, however, by the further specification that "'qualification standards' may include a requirement that an individual shall not pose a direct threat to the health or safety of other individuals in the workplace." § 12113(b); see also § 12111(3) (defining "direct threat" in terms of risk to others). Echazabal contrasts this provision with an EEOC regulation under the Rehabilitation Act of 1973, 87 Stat. 357, as amended, 29 U.S.C. § 701 *et seq.*, ante dating the ADA, which recognized an employer's right to consider threats both to other workers and to the threatening employee himself. Because the ADA defense provision recognizes threats only if they extend to another, Echazabal reads the statute to imply as a matter of law that threats to the worker himself cannot count....

Since Congress has not spoken exhaustively on threats to a worker's own health, the agency regulation can claim adherence under the rule in *Chevron Inc. v. Nat'l Res. Def. Council, Inc.* 467 U.S. 837, 843 (1984), so long as it makes sense of the statutory defense for qualification standards that are "job-related and consistent with business necessity." 42 U.S.C. § 12113(a). Chevron's reasons for calling the regulation reasonable are unsurprising: moral concerns aside, it wishes to avoid time lost to sickness, excessive turnover from medical retirement or death, litigation under state tort law, and the risk of violating the national Occupational Safety and Health Act of 1970, 84 Stat. 1590, as amended, 29 U.S.C. § 651 *et seq.* Although Echazabal claims that none of these reasons is legitimate, focusing on the concern with OSHA will be enough to show that the regulation is entitled to survive.

Echazabal points out that there is no known instance of OSHA enforcement, or even threatened enforcement, against an employer who relied on the ADA to hire a worker willing to accept a risk to himself from his disability on the job. In Echazabal's mind, this shows that invoking OSHA policy and possible OSHA liability is just a red herring to excuse covert discrimination. But there is another side to this. The text of OSHA itself says its point is "to assure so far as possible every working man and woman in the Nation safe and healthful working conditions," § 651(b), and Congress specifically obligated an employer to "furnish to each of his employees employment and a place of employment which are free from recognized hazards that are causing or are likely to cause death or serious physical harm to his employees," § 654(a)(1). Although there may be an open question whether an employer would actually be liable under OSHA for hiring an individual who knowingly consented to the particular dangers the job would pose to him, there is no denying that the employer would be asking for trouble: his decision to hire would put Congress's policy in the ADA, a disabled individual's right to operate on equal terms within the workplace, at loggerheads with the competing policy of OSHA, to ensure the safety of "each" and "every" worker. Courts would, of course, resolve the tension if there were no agency action, but the EEOC's resolution exemplifies the substantive choices that agencies are expected to make when Congress leaves the intersection of competing objectives both imprecisely marked but subject to the administrative leeway found in 42 U.S.C. § 12113(a).

Nor can the EEOC's resolution be fairly called unreasonable as allowing the kind of workplace paternalism the ADA was meant to outlaw. It is true that Congress had paternalism in its sights when it passed the ADA, see § 12101(a)(5) (recognizing "overprotective rules and policies" as a form of discrimination). But the EEOC has taken this to mean that Congress was not aiming at an employer's refusal to place disabled workers at a specifically demonstrated risk, but was trying to get at refusals to give an even break to classes of disabled people, while claiming to act for their own good in reliance on untested and pretextual stereotypes. Its regulation disallows just this sort of sham protection, through demands for a particularized enquiry into the harms the employee would probably face. The direct threat defense must be "based on a reasonable medical judgment that relies on the most current medical knowledge and/or the best available objective evidence," and upon an expressly "individualized assessment of the individual's present ability to safely perform the essential functions of the job," reached after considering, among other things, the imminence of the risk and the severity of the harm portended. 29 CFR § 1630.2(r) (2001). The EEOC was certainly acting within the reasonable zone when it saw a difference between rejecting workplace paternalism and ignoring specific and documented risks to the employee himself, even if the employee would take his chances for the sake of getting a job.

Finally, our conclusions that some regulation is permissible and this one is reasonable are not open to Echazabal's objection that they reduce the direct threat provision to "surplusage". The mere fact that a threat-to-self defense reasonably falls within the general "job related" and "business necessity" standard does not mean that Congress accomplished nothing with its explicit provision for a defense based on threats to others. The provision made a conclusion clear that might otherwise have been fought over in litigation or administrative rulemaking. It did not lack a job to do merely because the EEOC might have adopted the same rule later in applying the general defense provisions, nor was its job any less responsible simply because the agency was left with the option to go a step further. A provision can be useful even without congressional attention being indispensable.

Accordingly, we reverse the judgment of the Court of Appeals and remand the case for proceedings consistent with this opinion.

Notes & Questions

1. The Supreme Court's rulings in *Sutton* and *Echazabal* have raised concern about the Court's willingness to extend ADA protection to workers who claim discrimination on the basis of predictive genetic test results. Why? How does the Court's ruling in *Toyota v. Williams*, 534 U.S. 184 (2002), suggesting that to qualify for protection the claimed disability must limit activities that are of central importance to daily life in a considerable way and on a permanent or long-term basis, affect your analysis?

2. Compare the Court's ruling in *Echazabal* with its earlier opinion in the *Johnson Controls* case. Does the result strike a different balance between worker autonomy and

employer paternalism? How do you explain the difference in outcome? What if, instead of Hepatitis C, Echazabal carried the genetic trait that increases risk for hereditary non-polyposis colon cancer (HNPCC): how might that diagnosis change the result in the case? For background regarding this condition *see, e.g.*, G. Marra & C.R. Boland, *Hereditary Nonpolyposis Colorectal Cancer: The Syndrome, the Genes and Historical Perspectives*, 87 J. NATL. CANCER INST. 1114 (1995).

3. Reconsider each of the three case studies presented in Part A. Evaluate the strength of each employee's potential genetic discrimination claims in light of the legislation and court opinions outlined above. What claims, if any, might be available to each of the aggrieved workers, and what would be their likely outcome?

Chapter 4

Genetic Discrimination in Health Care

Accompanying the promise of genetic science is the concomitant fear that this uniquely private information will be abused. In Chapter 3, Rothstein and Anderlik argue that discrimination based on genotype should be preemptively routed out by legislation to prevent the stratification of society into the "haves" and the "have nots." Nowhere is this issue more volatile than in the context of access to health care coverage and employment. Numerous surveys and public polls have documented public fears that undergoing genetic testing or participating in genetic research studies will result in inability to get insurance or employment. For example, a 1995 Harris Poll found that over 85% of those surveyed were concerned that insurers or employers might have access to and use genetic information. Similarly, in a 1997 national telephone survey of more than 1000 people, 63% reported that they would not take genetic tests for diseases if health insurers or employers had access to the results; 85% felt employers should be prohibited from obtaining information about an individual's genetic information.

Public perception aside, little data quantifying or validating the incidence and range of actual discrimination exists. The little empirical research that has been conducted does not demonstrate evidence of genetic discrimination. The few isolated cases that have been reported to date seem to illustrate a misunderstanding of genetics, more than a movement toward systematic use of genetic discrimination. Despite lack of data substantiating significant discrimination, state and federal legislators have responded to their constituents' concerns with a flood of legislation focusing on genetic privacy and discrimination.

This chapter considers the risk of genetic discrimination in access to health care coverage and life, disability, and long-term care insurance. Part A focuses on access to health care and genetics in the context of health care coverage and reimbursement. It also reviews the scope of state and federal legislation seeking to deter genetic discrimination. Part B focuses on life, disability, and long-term care insurance. Unlike health care coverage, these products have not engendered a wellspring of antidiscrimination legislation. As you read the materials in this chapter, you should consider the aims and purposes of health, life, disability, and long-term care insurance and the reasons why the legislative response has differed.

A. Genetic Discrimination and Access to Health Care

Access to health care is a fundamental and contentious issue in the United States, and the panoply of public and private health plans is daunting. Pivotal to understanding the health care market is recognition of the fact that health care, although rooted in the concept of insurance and frequently referred to as such, has moved substantially away from insurance principles and practices. At present, our health care market is comprised of several different health plan models, nearly all of which, although responsive to economic drivers, do not engage in individual underwriting or individual risk assessment.

1. Health Care Coverage in America

Americans obtain coverage for health care services from several different public and private sources; they include the public programs of Medicare, Medicaid, and the State Children's Health Insurance Program (SCHIP), and the private plans offered by employers or purchased by individuals.

On the public side of the health care equation, our elderly population (over age 65) enjoys a public entitlement for hospital coverage through Medicare Part A and federally subsidized coverage plans for physician services and prescriptions through Medicare Parts B and D. People who are elderly, disabled, in end-stage renal failure, or diagnosed with amyotrophic lateral sclerosis are also eligible for the federally funded Medicare programs. A combination of federal and state public dollars funds the Medicaid and SCHIP programs. These public plans provide comprehensive health care coverage for those eligible by virtue of poverty and medical need. The majority of those eligible for Medicaid are single women with children, although Medicaid is also the safety net for poor elderly people needing nursing home care. In 2003, 12% of non-elderly Americans were covered by Medicaid and SCHIP, an increase from only 9% in 2001. None of the publicly funded programs use individual underwriting or risk adjustment in determining access to health care coverage.

On the private side of the health care equation, many employers provide health care coverage to their employees. In 2003, 63.4% of non-elderly Americans received health care coverage through their employer; although this number has decreased over the last few years from a high in 2001 of 67%. *See* Bradley C. Struck & James D. Reschovsky, *Trends in U.S. Health Insurance Coverage 2001–2003*, Center for Studying Health System Change: Tracking Report, Aug. 2004, *available at* http://hschange.org/CONTENT/694/.

Fifty-two percent of these workers are covered through employers who choose to self-insure or self-fund the health care needs of their employees. *See* Kaiser Family Foundation, 2003 Employer Health Benefits Survey Charts, http://profile.kff.org/insurance/ehbs2003-12-chart.cfm. Such self-insured plans are governed by the federal Employee Retirement Income Security Act of 1974 (ERISA). Under ERISA, the employer carries the risk for the health care costs of the employee group, is not susceptible to state coverage mandates, and has substantial flexibility in designing and modifying the coverage parameters of the plan. Eligibility would be extended to all employees regardless of individual health care profiles.

Employers who do not self-insure typically purchase group coverage for their employees. Premiums for such coverage are based on overall health care costs of the employee group and are not individually underwritten. Such purchased health care insurance plans are regulated by the state, are susceptible to all state mandates, and cannot be changed substantially without approval of the state insurance commissioner.

Unfortunately, employers are not required to provide health care coverage to their employees and, with the increasing costs of health care, more employers are declining to provide such coverage. Some of these workers (about 15%) may be of such low income that they will qualify for Medicaid; this accounts for some of the increased percentage in Medicaid spending. About 5% will purchase health care coverage as an individual, even though such coverage is generally expensive and limited. Although individual underwriting may be done by the firms offering individual coverage, this market is known for volatility and the health plans are interested primarily in the health care costs associated with an individual's already manifested disease and its sequelae. Most of these workers will join the 45 million (15%) non-elderly Americans who have no health care coverage.

In sum, the 85% of non-elderly Americans who have health care coverage obtain it from a variety of public and private sources. Most (approximately 65%) obtain it through employer-provided group health plans, approximately half of which are ERISA plans. Of those not covered through their employer, approximately 15% will qualify for Medicaid. Only the 5% who purchase health care coverage on an individual basis will be subject to individual underwriting.

2. Genetics and Access to Health Care Coverage

Despite the sparse use of individual underwriting by public and private health plans, there has been a plethora of state legislation addressing genetic discrimination over the last decade. The legislative remedy for perceived genetic discrimination is detailed in Section 4, *infra*. Most state statutes forbid health plans from using genetic information in determining eligibility. The following excerpted article documents one of the few studies that have empirically assessed the use of genetic information by health plans in their decisions to offer coverage to individuals seeking health care coverage.

Mark A. Hall, *Legal Rules and Industry Norms: The Impact of Laws Restricting Insurers Use of Genetic Information*

40 Jurimetrics J. 93 (1999)

...

Findings on the Extent of Genetic Discrimination by Health Insurers

For purposes of this study, genetic discrimination is defined as the denial, limitation, or increased price of health insurance based on the results of presymptomatic genetic information....

A. The View from the Medical Genetics Community

Early published reports that insurers discriminate based on genetic information have been criticized for overstating the extent of discrimination and for using imprecise definitions or criteria for what constitutes discrimination. Therefore, we conducted in-depth interviews with genetic counselors to make our own assessment of the extent of insurance discrimination. Genetic counselors are in an excellent position to report on insurance discrimination. Discrimination concerns are frequently a focus of counselors' discussions with patients and families, and their clients readily report troubles they face with health insurance at the time of testing. Most counselors said they stay in touch with their clients following testing that shows positive (adverse) results, and their clients are prone to contact them even several years later if they encounter difficulties as a consequence of test results. A few counselors, however, said they would not have reason to know if clients experienced discrimination after leaving the clinic.

Of the twenty-nine counselors and five patient advocates we spoke to, the great majority said they believe or they have read or heard that insurance discrimination occurs to a significant extent for adult patients with presymptomatic adverse genetic profiles. They characterize insurance discrimination as a matter of great concern, which they think is widespread or not at all uncommon. They base this view on what they hear at professional meetings or what they read in professional journals. When asked about instances of insurance discrimination with their own clients or those of their colleagues, however, almost every counselor and every patient advocate said they knew of no actual cases of health insurance discrimination, classified as we have for purposes of this study.

About half had no examples to offer of any type of insurance discrimination, however defined or classified, and said this simply had not been an issue for their clients. Four counselors and one physician with considerable experience said they think the concern over genetic discrimination is greatly exaggerated. One experienced counselor, for instance, explained:

> None of my patients have had problems with [insurance discrimination].... I think that it is an artificial fear and I think that the Huntington's patients are a classic example of that. There is no proof [of discrimination]. That is why I am very curious to know what your conversations with the insurance side of things reveal. There is no proof that this is really a problem.... I have people that will give me a false name or are so paranoid about [discrimination], but there is really no foundation in reality for it. I think it is something that we have been conditioned to be fearful of, but that there is no proof of it.... I really think [the fear] is out of proportion to what we are seeing in practice.

Some counselors gave examples of patients who had trouble getting insurance because of a family history of genetic disease, but, as noted above, most states with these laws do not prohibit using family history, or genetic tests. As noted below, genetic testing is as, or more, likely to help than to hurt patients with an adverse family history. Also, as noted by these two counselors, genetic discrimination based on family history is not widespread:

> Counselor 1: [After describing a case of a person whose health insurance rates increased because of a family history of Huntington's, turns to Counselor 2, and says:] you don't have any cases that you know of?

Counselor 2: No, I don't have any. It's a concern that has been brought up in our counseling, but I do not have any documented cases such as that.

Counselor 1: The deal is, other than this one case, there really aren't any, I don't think it is a really big problem. I think it's an issue, but I think on the scale of all of the things that people have to deal with, I don't think it's rampant. I don't know if that is because insurance companies haven't figured it out or if it really isn't a big problem. I'm unclear about that. I think it's a hot topic and that's where that is. [Counselor 2 has] had more experience. Cancer is different.

Counselor 2: ... It hasn't been documented for cancer anywhere, I'm not aware of any documentation in the medical literature for a cancer family that has been discriminated against.

Most of these family history examples, and some of the genetic testing examples, also involved situations where there were other clinical indications of existing genetic disease and so were not presymptomatic or purely predictive, as explained by this counselor:

Q: Have any of the patients that you have dealt with or any others in your direct knowledge personally experienced discrimination in terms of health insurance: either their rates have been raised, or they have lost coverage or have been refused coverage because of the results of a genetic test?

A: Not that I know of, but when we ask the question on this survey [in our clinic], "Have you had any negative experiences as a result of seeking genetic counseling?," fifteen percent said yes and then "Have you in any way been discriminated against in health insurance or employment?," twenty-one percent [answer] yes. Now, we didn't say "because of genetic testing," we just said that in general, and some of these people have cancer, so because they are affected they would have been discriminated against. So, kind of what I tell my patients is that if they already have a diagnosis of cancer then the fact that they are going to get genetic testing probably won't mean much to them unless we are saying that they need further procedures because they are at risk for other types of cancers, and so they have already gone through not being able to get insurance because they've been diagnosed with cancer.... But, no one has ever said to me I've had a problem getting insurance because of a genetic test.

Many counselors could only give examples of patients who had trouble getting their insurer to pay for genetic counseling, testing, or preventative services. This was the dominant focus of concern in many of our interviews, such as the following:

A: [After describing a case of a patient who couldn't get life insurance based on their family history,] we have not heard of any discrimination from health insurance. We have people who've tried to have their insurance companies pay for the testing, in particular women who have had breast cancer or have a family history of breast or ovarian cancer and they want the testing to know if they have a higher risk for ovarian and they want to know if they should have their ovaries out and that kind of a thing. One patient I'm thinking about had breast cancer at a young age, early forties, and her health insurance company denied paying for the test even though the doctor recommended it, he wrote a letter saying that this is important in her upcoming surveillance and reducing her risk for ovarian cancer and they came back saying no, they would not pay for it. They are not discriminating and saying that she cannot have it done, but they are not going to pay for it. That is the kind of thing that we have heard.

Q: That is certainly not unimportant, but in this case we are more interested in not the [payment] question, but whether people have been denied coverage or their rates have gone up.

A: Have not heard of that yet.

Q: None except this life insurance case, and this includes your experience with Huntington's Disease as well?

A: Yes.... From my knowledge there has not been a documented case of discrimination of an individual who has had cancer genetic testing [either]. It's more of the fear of the population.

Finally, we were given examples of discrimination relating to life, disability, or long-term care insurance, or to employment, but not to health insurance.

We heard of only two examples that are somewhat close to the type of genetic discrimination addressed by the health insurance laws. In both instances, a patient asked the insurer to pay for genetic counseling (for cancer testing in one case and Huntington's Disease in the other), and the insurer subsequently raised its rates, based merely on the suspicion of a genetic disorder or the possibility of increased monitoring costs, without regard to the actual presence of the disease. Whether this runs afoul of state law depends on the statute's wording, but it appears to be more akin to discrimination based on family history, which none of the states in our study prohibit, rather than discrimination based on genetic *testing*, since family history was the reason for requesting genetic tests and the insurance rates were increased without regard to the results of the test. This does not lessen the impact of the discrimination, but it means that we were not able to document from genetic counselors that there was any occurrence before or after the laws' enactment of the type of discrimination prohibited by most state laws.

Narrowing our focus to precisely this type of discrimination might be criticized for missing the fact that these laws are allowing other types of genetic discrimination to continue that are more prevalent. However, most of the instances of discrimination in underwriting that we documented either do not relate to health insurance (three cases) or are based on symptoms of existing disease (six cases). Only the presymptomatic family history cases are fairly classified as discrimination based solely on genetic information. We heard of four such cases, two of which were just described. In the other two, discussed below, health insurers' initial adverse use of family history was *corrected* with genetic test results that showed absence of the genetic defect. Thus, even when the definition of genetic discrimination is expanded to include family history cases, we were able to document only two such cases, and we observed an equal or greater number of cases discussed below in which genetic test results were used to resolve health insurance problems based on family history.

If health insurers were using presymptomatic genetic test information against applicants or subscribers to any significant extent, it would mostly likely show up in this sample of twenty-nine genetic counselors. Almost all of these were experienced genetic counselors with three or more years of clinical practice, and many with five or more years. Included are the directors of genetic counseling at some of the largest, most established, and most prominent centers of medical genetics and research in country. Although this is the same community that provided information for the earlier published reports of genetic discrimination by insurers, our interviews are not necessarily in flat contradiction, since we heard a number of examples of adverse insurance consequences for people with genetic conditions. But our more detailed evaluation indicates that, in the vast majority of cases, these most likely are based more on existing symptoms than on predictive genetic information, relate to other types of insurance besides health, or are concerned with coverage of genetic services rather than the availability and pricing of health insurance. These are certainly issues of concern, but they are not the kinds of adverse effects that these laws attempt to address.

B. The View from the Insurance Industry

This view is confirmed by multiple credible sources in the insurance industry. None of these sources said that genetic discrimination of the sort just defined has ever occurred or is occurring. Health insurers do not require genetic tests, they do not seek the results of genetic test information, and they have no track record of finding and using presymptomatic, predictive genetic information. This is the consistent report from regulators, independent agents, and reliable sources with insurance companies.

1. Regulators

All of the regulators we spoke to said they could remember no complaints or documented instances of genetic discrimination by health insurers, either narrowly or broadly defined. These were not technical or defensive responses. These subjects genuinely conveyed the attitude that genetics simply is not on their radar screen of significant issues in health insurance. Most regulators were completely puzzled why this is an issue of public concern. Many had no idea what the impetus for the legislation was in their state. Others said the legislation was prompted by a generalized concern to avoid possible discrimination and not in response to any actual cases of discrimination. One regulator said this is a "stupid issue," a "big waste of time," in which public policy got way ahead of the technology. Another said he felt "burned" and "frustrated" by having to spend $250,000 on a task force looking for evidence of genetic discrimination, without finding a single case. "We scoured the earth," "looking everywhere we could" to find a "bad case scenario" involving health insurers' use of genetic information, but found nothing. A group of advocates for the law in New Mexico also reported failing to find any actual examples of genetic discrimination in that state, despite considerable searching and widespread discussion throughout the state.

2. Agent Interviews

Insurance agents are another highly credible source. They are independent brokers, paid by commission, who are well situated and highly motivated to advocate for coverage of their clients and detect any adverse insurer behavior. None of the thirty agents we interviewed could recall any instances of health insurers using genetic test information. Several commented that insurers sometimes use family history information to interpret diagnoses of current conditions, or they remembered instances where clients were treated as having a genetic disease based on their symptoms. But none could remember genetic test results ever having played a role in an underwriting decision. Here are typical exchanges with these interview subjects:

Iowa agent

Q: Have you had any experience of anyone who has been turned down for coverage because of information from a genetic test?

A: No....

Q: Have you had any experience of someone who was turned down because of a genetic condition that was either suspected or known for some reason but the person had no symptoms?

A: Not that I can recall.

Q: So in your experience, you haven't found any case where either of those, a person has been turned down, either because they've had a genetic test or because they've had a family history of it.

A: No. And again, we work with a number of carriers and it's never come up from any of the carriers that we've done business with.

New Mexico agent

A: I have never had a discussion with a client about their specific gene situation as it relates to underwriting health problems. I had a couple of discussions as it relates to underwriting life products. Never had one with respect to health care, ... other than as a casual comment. A new story will come out like this breast cancer thing and ... they think that they may have identified a gene propensity for this cancer or that cancer. If that was the same day I came by to talk to somebody about health insurance, they might say "are you guys going to start underwriting based on genes." I say "no I think that's about twenty-five years down the road maybe." It's just so impractical with respect to health insurance.

Q: Nobody's come in and said, "look I've got this deep dark family secret or genetic history. Do we have to report this? Is it going to get me in trouble?"

A: No, no. I have lots of discussions like that, but not related to genes.... I have to be perfectly frank and straight forward about it, I have never had a discussion with anybody about gene pools or the potential for [being declined for genetic information].

This same agent went on to say that the new law is "administrative overkill," "asinine," and a "stupid liberal knee-jerk reaction." Another New Mexico agent gave a personal illustration relating to her own health insurance. Her grandmother died of cancer and her mother had a mastectomy. She applied for an individual policy from a commercial indemnity insurer known for careful underwriting. The insurer requested her medical records and she felt it was clear from the records that she has a family history of cancer. She was also at the average age of disease onset. But, the insurer sold her the policy without any exclusions, at the standard rate.

These are not randomly selected insurance agents but mostly ones who have years of specializing in individual or small group health insurance. In many cases, they are leaders in their professional circles and so come in contact with many of their peers.

3. Industry Self-Reports

Credible subjects with health insurers also consistently confirm these accounts. We spoke to actuaries and underwriters who work with individual and small group products, which are the products that require the most intensive examination of medical records. Uniformly, we heard that all branches of the industry—Blue Cross plans, HMOs, and commercial indemnity plans—do not inquire about genetic test results, do not use this information if they come across it in the medical record, and do not include this type of information in their underwriting guidelines. This was the case both before and after these laws were enacted, and in states both with and without these laws. No insurer subject said that its medical underwriting practices relating to genetics were in any way different prior to these laws. The following is a typical exchange, with an underwriter at a New Mexico HMO:

Q: Have you changed any of your practices in response to the [new] law?

A: No, because we never ask those questions to begin with. We've never medically underwritten based on genetic testing....

Q: Again, on the genetics when the law came out it wasn't like you had to go back to the manual and take a bunch stuff out because you were underwriting for that already?

A: Oh no. I've never used it, it doesn't apply. It might be an issue for life insurance....

Subjects with other insurers, including some Blue Cross plans and indemnity insurers, were even more vehement. They insisted that, for both business and moral reasons, they are firmly opposed to using presymptomatic genetic test information. Several said this is flatly contrary to their philosophy of proper medical underwriting, which is to focus only on conditions that presently or previously existed, or that it would be ethically wrong to penalize people for genetic defects that haven't yet manifested. Others said they are concerned about the political or public relations backlash that would result from using this type of information, which would be hard to justify because of others' understandable moral or philosophical objections. Still others said the issue simply has not come up in any discussions, at any level they are aware of within the company.

Because of the suspicion with which many people view the insurance industry, it is important to verify the credibility of these potentially self-serving accounts. First, these subjects were interviewed at length by researchers with knowledge and expertise in underwriting practices who were able to probe for more detail and look for possible contradictions or confirmations. Second, we judged these subjects to be candid and credible. On other points, many of these subjects were willing to admit policies and behaviors that put them in somewhat negative light. Very few were defensive or evasive, and many were extraordinarily forthcoming and helpful; the remainder appeared to answer carefully but somewhat guardedly all the questions put to them. Also, these were not subjects selected as spokespeople for their companies, who regularly do public relations or lobbying work. They were career professional actuaries and underwriters who approach these issues in a disciplined and objective fashion and who subscribe to a widely regarded standard of professional integrity, much like certified public accountants.

How, then, do we reconcile these reports from the industry with the contrary reports from the medical genetics community and patient advocates? First, it requires careful scrutiny of the facts to determine whether cases are properly classified as genetic discrimination in health insurance underwriting. If these more detailed facts were known, it is likely that most of the initial reports from the genetics and patient community, like those discussed above from the genetic counselors we interviewed, would constitute some other type of discrimination or would be based on something other than purely genetic information. Second, the few instances of genetic discrimination more precisely defined that might be documented for health insurance might well be isolated instances that occurred because of lower level decisions by insurers that do not reflect deliberate corporate policy. We heard of several instances of patients who experienced initial insurance problems that were later resolved favorably. The institutional inertia or legal defensiveness that often results from justifying an initial decision may make these isolated examples appear more purposeful and insistent than is actually the case in established corporate policy or regular practice.

4. Industry Practices and Sources of Information

The strongest confirmation of the credibility of these industry sources comes from two other directions: a review of the sources and types of information actually collected by insurers, and a convincing explanation of why it is not cost-effective to use genetic test results in underwriting.

We gathered from agents and insurers a selection of application forms from fifty insurers for individual and small group health insurance. We examined these to determine both the level of compliance with genetic discrimination laws and the level of inquiry about genetic information in states without these laws and prior to having these laws. We found only two instances (4%) of insurers potentially asking specifically for genetic test results. One was a commercial indemnity insurer with an extremely detailed application form, which includes one question that reads:

> Do you have a mental or physical impairment or deformity, or a congenital or hereditary abnormality, disease or trait not previously disclosed?

We observed this insurer using this question mainly in states without a genetic discrimination statute at the time, although the form appeared to be in use in one state, New Mexico, shortly after the law was enacted there. On its surface, this question is ambiguous as to whether it requires the disclosure of presymptomatic, predictive genetic test results. "Congenital or hereditary abnormality or disease" clearly speaks to existing conditions, such as birth defects. However, "trait" conceivably refers to mere carrier status or unexpressed disease potential. It is debatable whether this is the necessary meaning. If not, an applicant might be justified in not disclosing such test results, even in response to this question. Several agents said they are very careful to not disclose damaging information unless it is clearly required. As one explained:

> I have lots of discussions about "yeah I kind of [had this medical problem] but it wasn't really anything," how would I put that down? The art of underwriting in the individual marketplace based on a medical questionnaire is trying to accurately represent what the underwriter has interest in without (A) telling the client that's it's okay to leave anything off; or (B) putting down what literally could be expected with a question that said "have you ever sought consultation advice or treatment for anything?" I took an application this morning for individual health with a lady who has a fairly—there's two kinds of people out there, there are ones that want to tell you everything and there are those who just say no, no, no when you know for a fact that it could possibly be the case—she was one of those let-me-tell-you-everything kinds, and so what would normally take thirty to forty minutes ends up taking an hour.... You know, she's in the legal business, and I certainly don't want to be talking to a paralegal and giving them advice "oh no let's leave this off." It's a matter of trying to accurately reflect information that's pertinent to underwrite the case. There were some particulars about her history, I mean when you underwrite business every day there are certain types of conditions that you know, gosh, if we write that, that's ridiculous, if we write that down we're declined and it ain't that big of a deal, like marriage counseling.... From my perspective, if a guy goes to a marriage counselor that's an effort to try and improve his relationship with his wife, it has nothing to do with health.... So, if the question on the ap-

> plication said counseling, and the guy said "yeah I went to a marriage counselor," I would say "well was the guy a degreed medical professional," we are going to get right down here to see if there is any way that we are not going to have to disclose that because all of my underwriting slack is going to be taken up by something that I don't see as pertinent to whether or not this guy's got health insurance.

Another reason these two instances of genetic-specific questions do not refute the indications above that insurers do not seek out or use this information is that knowledgeable and credible sources at these two organizations, when asked, were not aware these questions were on their application forms, and did not think the information gathered would be used to predict future health problems. In their view, the questions were included only to help diagnose present conditions, consistent with practices in the rest of the industry.

If application forms do not ask about genetic test results, and agents know not to volunteer them, then it is unlikely that insurers will learn about them. If insurers order complete copies of medical records, they might come across references to genetic testing, but this is rarely done because of the expense. As explained by this Iowa agent, rather than order complete medical records, insurers typically send specific queries to the applicant's physician, and only in cases where doubts are raised by the application form:

> They probably aren't going to have much of that [genetic] information coming available to them. And I'm not sure on a medical record [how much] of that information is actually disclosed.... A lot of times they're getting abbreviated medical records based off of what they found out that you disclosed on the application. They're typically not going out today and asking for all your medical records because the typical medical records charge these days is like a $25 fee to initiate the record, $2.50 a page, $10 processing fee; they've segmented it out into all these charges.... I mean here in the last two years, you know, we've just seen medical records costs go through the ceiling. I mean $25 was a big cost two years ago. Now $25 doesn't cover hardly anybody's medical records.... If you [use] me for example and ask for my medical history, it's ... 490 pages. So they're going to go ask about specifically [my] current status, [my] blood pressure, specifics, and you're going to get an abridged physician statement. So they typically today just don't get that broad-based medical record. They're keying in on a specific and since they're not asking any questions related to genetics, they're typically not going to be writing saying "any genetic testing that you've done."

This New Mexico agent confirmed that same point and also spoke to the concern that health insurers might conduct their own genetic tests:

> I think this movement across the country on the part of reform-minded individuals to get genetic information laws passed nationwide is about fifteen years in front of any possible, practical or affordable useful information.... People who don't underwrite health [insurance] on a day-to-day basis ... just flat don't understand that in the health business, companies cannot afford to spend two months worth of premium trying to decide whether to write a risk or not. In the life [insurance] business they take this fairly exhaustive medical questionnaire on the front end, they send out a paramedic, they might do an EKG, they always require blood and urine [tests], and it's very common for them to pay $90 a pop for three or four attending physician statements where they can

> review the guy's complete medical file. In the health [insurance] business, if a company has a fairly liberal underwriting policy they might take the time to review records that the applicant submitted at his own expense, but most companies don't even do that. It's pretty much, here's our decision....

Also, physicians and medical geneticists are careful about how they document these evaluations so as to avoid unnecessarily calling attention to the genetic component. Insurers might learn of genetic testing for those they currently cover if policyholders submit the testing and counseling for reimbursement under their policy. However, insurers are not entitled to learn of the tests results, only the fact of testing. Similarly, neither the fact of a genetic test being done, nor its result, is recorded in the Medical Information Bureau, we were told by several sources. Instead, that data bank reflects only the general nature of the medical diagnosis and procedure, such as evaluation for cancer, or neurological evaluation.

These barriers to information are not insurmountable, however. Applicants might feel compelled to volunteer information about genetic testing in response to generic questions about any medical visits or tests of any kind. The insurer whose form is quoted above, for instance, asks "During the past five years have you visited a medical doctor ... for diagnosis, advice, treatment, ... or consultation not previously explained?" Learning the mere fact of testing or evaluation can itself be very damaging or prompt an insurer to make further inquiry, even if the results are not initially revealed. If not prohibited by law, once an insurer is put on notice, it might ask an applicant or her physician a pointed question about genetic information, which must be answered truthfully to avoid insurance fraud. Also, some forms are designed for both life and health insurance, when companies sell both, and life insurers are more likely to ask about genetic testing. Therefore, it is important to consider further whether, if health insurers do come across genetic tests results, what use are they likely to make of them.

We heard repeatedly from agents, insurers, and regulators that using genetic information to predict future health conditions makes no sense for health insurance because of the short time-frame of reference that typically is used in medical underwriting. Underwriters try to assess only existing or prior health problems based on recent health care utilization because these are the most predictive of likely health care costs in the immediate future. A Colorado agent explained that, for small group insurance, "they do a cursory review and they'll look for something that's a full-blown case of AIDS or somebody who's got something that's obviously ongoing and a current concern. They don't try to predict like Methuselah what kind of health care utilization you're going to have in the future."

Near-term medical expenses are the dominant focus because these can be predicted with more certainty, because over time those who begin as higher or lower risks tend to "regress to the mean" by operation of natural laws of probability, and because few people keep the same health insurance for extended periods of time. On the latter point, both individual and small group insurers reported a very rapid turnover in enrollment. Virtually every insurer subject estimated the average or predicted length of enrollment to be only two to three years, and most said that twenty-five to thirty-five percent of new subscribers drop their coverage after only one year. This short duration is most prominent for individual coverage, which is frequently kept for only a few months, when someone is in between jobs or school. Half of insurers estimated that ninety percent or more of subscribers will change coverage within five to eight years; the other half estimated near-total turnover in about ten years. For these reasons, insurers do not consider it very relevant or worth the effort to predict health expenditures five, ten or more years into the future for specific enrollees. This is especially true for relatively rare conditions, as this New Mexico agent explains:

> You are talking about 1 person out of 1000, even if you took 1000 women with your breast cancer gene, ... which is more than you would see in a town the size of Albuquerque. Let's assume that there are 1000 people in Albuquerque that have this preponderance gene and they aware of it, so out of 500,000 there's 1000 out there, there might be one that 10 years from now could be negatively impacted, because 80% of them would be covered on group contracts where there are no medical questions. So when you start chopping down how many of these applications would have questions that would lead the company to suspect that would be the case, you are talking about a person who potentially happens to be self-employed and has some other medical condition for which the company is willing to review her medical records and without a guideline specifically relating to this gene deal, an underwriter who makes maybe $30,000 a year, if it's not a guideline, it's not going to be acted on. You could have a medical record that says due to a family history of chronic alcoholism, blah, blah, blah; they're not looking for that. Underwriters look at stuff from blinders. Here is the issue, what's our guideline, what do these records say that is relevant to that particular guideline, here's our decision. They don't take extraneous stuff and include it in [their decision].

These basic economic and statistical facts differ significantly from the situation with life insurance. It is much more typical to hold onto a life insurance policy for a long time. If changes are made, it is usually to add additional life coverage on top of older policies, rather than to replace them. Also, life insurance underwriting is all about predicting future mortality, so genetic issues are much more relevant to the life underwriting frame of mind. And, the potential is much greater with life insurance for an adverse genetic test to prompt someone to apply for more insurance coverage. Therefore, other studies indicate that life insurers have a stronger interest in knowing genetic test results.

Further confirmation comes from the fact that most health insurers do not inquire about or consider family history of major diseases, and when they do, they use this information only to help interpret other indicators of existing disease, rather than to predict future problems. This explanation was heard consistently throughout all parts of the industry and from many credible sources. It was also confirmed by regulators and agents, and by our inspection of application forms. These sources also said that fewer insurers are asking for this information, and it is being used somewhat less often, so the trend is toward diminished use. This is occurring mainly for pragmatic, not legal reasons. One knowledgeable agent explained why:

> Q: Why aren't [insurers] doing this [using family history information]? Is it because it isn't very useful? ... Or is it because it's a fear that if they ask this question where it's legal to do so, that they'll have such an outrage in the part of the public that it's politically not wise to do?
>
> A: Well, my opinion is I think is probably a couple of reasons. One, ... what do they do with it? They probably don't have an underwriting department that's been trained, at this point in time, since it's not something they've used in the past or are currently using, that would really know what to do with it. And we probably as an industry don't have much resource information that tells us probabilities and occurrence and cost and all that kind of stuff. So it's probably a knowledge issue.... Then too if we do do it, is it valuable enough informa-

> tion that it's going to be worth the cost and the time.... Paramed exams are the other ones that carriers have been toying with, and a number of carriers have discontinued paramed exams because as they look at their block of business and they look at the information they've gathered, you know, was it worth the additional three to four weeks of underwriting time, the cost to have it done, and the information you got back, is all of that stuff worth the investment for the return that you got? And for the majority of the carriers over the last couple of years, they've started to say well no, it's really not. And as companies look at cost in that range to run those types of things, ... companies have to start looking at do we give up writing the business ... or do we figure out another way to handle those.

One contrary indication, however, suggests that health insurers are interested in predicting future health problems. They do consider cholesterol levels and tobacco use, and sometimes these factors will increase rates. However, it was observed that both of these indicators are very common and easy to evaluate, and tobacco use has systemic effects on a broad range of health conditions, both in a near and far time span. Also, cholesterol levels predict current as well as future medical costs because of the cost of drugs prescribed to control cholesterol levels and the increased doctor visits to monitor cardiac health for high risk patients. And, high cholesterol, like high blood pressure, is a diagnosable disease category and so can be viewed as an existing condition rather than purely presymptomatic prediction. Naturally, the same is potentially true for genetic conditions. Thus, we do not entirely dismiss the possibility that health insurers might use predictive genetic information. Although it appears convincing that they are not now doing so, in the following section, we look at indications and speculation that this situation might soon change.

5. The Potential for Genetic Discrimination

As noted above, it is perfectly possible, unless prohibited by law, for health insurers to obtain information about genetic testing. Although they do not now ask for this information directly, they could learn about it from more generic questions about medical visits and diagnostic testing, or from examining medical records or claims for reimbursement. Therefore, we asked health insurers whether, if they happen to learn of positive (adverse) genetic test results, would they use this information in medical underwriting in any fashion, even if the information is entirely presymptomatic or predictive and not diagnostic of current symptoms or conditions. We sometimes asked this question in a general fashion, but we also frequently posed a specific hypothetical, involving breast cancer. We asked what insurers would do if legally permitted to consider information that a woman tested positive for the breast cancer gene and she was fifteen years younger than the average age of onset.

About half of insurers who responded to the general inquiry (eight of seventeen) and about two-thirds of those who responded to the breast cancer example (ten of fourteen) conceded that they might or probably would use such information in some fashion, if legally permitted to do so. Also, four of six insurer subjects said that in the future it is likely that so much more genetic information will exist and predictive data will be so much more precise that genetic test results probably will be much more relevant to medical underwriting. These subjects thought that, whether this information will be used is largely a cost-benefit business decision, in response to market forces. Agents gave similar responses. Ten of fifteen agents said insurers might or would use genetic information in some fashion if legal and it came to their attention, and two of four said use of this information is likely some time in the future. The following exchange with underwriters in New Mexico is typical of these opinions and impressions:

Q: Another question is how relevant would it be, if [genetic information] did come up? So, understanding that you have never looked for it, it's never come up and it's not considered to be legal, what if you could consider it or it did come up? Let's take for example, the gene for breast cancer, would that be potentially relevant, or a family history of breast cancer?

A: If we could? Yeah. From a business standpoint yes. Strictly from a business standpoint. If it was legal, yes.

Q: What decision might you make based on that? Would you potentially decline somebody simply because they have a future potential for breast cancer?

A: Yeah, if for instance you had first-degree relatives and you also had the gene, ... and they wanted to submit that kind of information and if it were legal, sure.

Q: Because one response I've heard is it all depends. It depends in part on the age. So, if it's let's say a forty-year-old woman, and the average age of onset is fifty-five, just to pick a number, the odds are that [sic]

A: Breast Cancer could happen at any time, so there is no sort of safe age for that.... I've never used [information like this], it doesn't apply.... Could it potentially? Sure. In fifty more years when they can test for three dozen things instead of just a handful of things, sure that would be an issue.... And who knows if we'll even have insurance in the form that we know it. By the time that technology is available, we may [have] a more socialized National Health Insurance. We just keep evolving.

Here is the same view expressed by an Iowa agent:

> You know, I think insurance companies are ... set up to make a profit and if laws allow them to, I think that they would use what information the laws would permit. I think on the genetic side though, just because there is such an outcry in the country from voters to protect medical records and to protect some of that information, I think it's going to be tough for them to ever get to a point where they're actually using it. But at the same time, if it's perfectly legal to do so and there are some studies done and some more information, provided that there are some realistic results by looking at it, I'm sure they probably would fit it into their underwriting scheme.

Many of the insurer subjects were much more tentative, saying they were not sure whether any genetic information would be relevant now, and they would consult their medical director and legal department first before using it. Others said the breast cancer information would have only marginal impact, for instance, raising rates only one to two percent, depending on the probabilities indicated by existing data. Of the eight agents who were asked the breast cancer question, only two thought insurers would find this genetic information relevant. However, some underwriters said the breast cancer example would be a basis for "ridering out" or "waivering" that condition, not as a generic pre-existing condition, but through a specific contractual exclusion of that particular condition. This is usually permissible for individual insurance.

In justifying their possible use of presymptomatic genetic test results, several insurers noted that even the breast cancer example is not wholly irrelevant to current health care costs. Someone with the breast cancer gene is certain to receive more intensive cancer screening, and may well be a candidate for prophylactic mastectomy. If subscribers expect to be reimbursed for these costs, some insurers insisted that it is only fair they be allowed to consider the results of the genetic tests that prompt these medical costs, even though the person does not currently have the condition. It was also noted that obtaining reimbursement for these preventative services places physicians and patients in a bind. Under conventional indemnity insurance, only existing medical conditions are covered, and not preventative services. Therefore, it is necessary to declare that a genetic predisposition is an existing condition, much like high blood pressure or cholesterol levels, to claim reimbursement. But, once doing this, it is inconsistent to say that no condition exists for underwriting purposes.

This led us to ask some insurer subjects a difficult, borderline hypothetical involving a blood condition known as hemochromatosis. This is the accumulation of excess iron in the blood due to liver insufficiency. Some cases are genetic, some are not, and severity varies widely. We asked whether, if a patient were found to have elevated iron levels but at a level that does not require clinical treatment, only monitoring, could the patient be regarded as having a pre-existing condition based on a genetic test that confirmed that the cause of the elevated iron is hemochromatosis. All five insurers consistently said yes, especially if the physician diagnoses the patient as now having hemochromatosis rather than simply being at risk for the condition. The two regulators who were asked this question puzzled over it and considered it to be a close call that requires further deliberation, but they seemed to lean in favor of the insurers' view.

A final indication of the potential for health insurers to use genetic information, now or in the future, is the strong reaction of fear that two genetic counselors reported from their clients who work in the insurance or health care industry:

> [It] has happened to me with at least three or four families where at least one family member worked in the insurance industry and said absolutely not, we are not giving you our names or any identifying information. I know how the insurance industry works and you would not believe the exchange of information that occurs. Anybody can get anything. That has happened to me more than once. It is amazing to me and it always gets my attention that people that work in that industry are really the most paranoid. I just really wonder why people that work in the industry are so much more concerned about it than people that are not. That makes me wonder if there is some reality or basis for [the concern]. I've had a patient who is someone that really understands the health care field, say for example this person is in health administration, and that person requested that I destroy all of the records after the testing is done. They also went under an anonymous name, they went to the bank and got a check with the anonymous name on it. I've had several people do that and ... most of the time they are people that are in the medical field or they are maybe legal people or just very highly educated people. They are the ones that are saying to me "I want to be an anonymous name, I want to have records destroyed or how do you keep your records, I'm concerned about that, what are the laws?" When I tell them about the laws in Colorado they tend to settle down a little bit, even though I explain that there are loopholes in it.

Thus, there is ample reason to take seriously the concern that health insurers might begin to use presymptomatic genetic testing results. As one genetic counselor noted, the fact that such results have not been used much to date fails to recognize how recently these tests have come into clinical use and how rapidly clinical use might grow in the near future. Still, it is notable how disconnected these indications of potential use are from the pattern of state laws that currently exists. Insurers' and agents' responses to the various hypothetical questions and general attitudes just described bear no relationship to the pattern of laws across our study states, nor are they related to the type of insurer represented. This mix of positive and negative views is remarkably consistent or evenly scattered across all study states and all segments of the insurance industry.

6. Knowledge of and Attitudes About the Law

A final way to assess the impact of these laws on the extent of genetic discrimination is to determine insurers' and agents' awareness of the law and its perceived impact on underwriting practices. All of the state insurance regulators we spoke to were well aware of the relevant state and federal laws. Although they sometimes stumbled on questions about the laws' details, this is because no enforcement issues have arisen under these laws and so they have not been required to look at them closely. In our interviews, regulators were able to quickly locate and examine the state laws when we asked them to consider more subtle or detailed questions.

In contrast, both agents and insurer subjects had only spotty knowledge of these laws. Only forty-two percent of agents (ten of twenty-four) had any awareness there is any genetic-specific law, either state or federal, and almost none had basic, accurate understanding of what state and federal laws say about genetic discrimination in health insurance. Insurance underwriters and actuaries did only slightly better. Fifty percent (ten of twenty) knew there was some genetic-specific legal restriction on underwriting, but most of these had an imprecise or inaccurate understanding of what the law said. However, their understanding typically was overbroad. For instance, many assumed that the federal law has a broad prohibition, or incorrectly thought that state law prohibits the use of family history.

None of these subjects believed the genetic discrimination laws have changed underwriting practices for health insurance. As noted above, we detected no changes or differences in application forms for health insurance, either before or after these laws, or between states with and without the laws. Also, none of the national insurers said that their underwriting practices varied among states according to these laws. Instead, they all consistently decline to seek or use genetic test information in any state. Only one subject suggested that, if genetic information were to be used under the various hypotheticals we presented, this use might differ among states according to what the law allows.

This does not mean that these laws have had no effect on insurers' attitudes and policies about the use of genetic information. Subjects with five insurers said their company's practice of not using genetic information was in part a response to a hostile legal environment. These subjects have a general sense there are legal problems with using genetic information, and this reinforced their decision not to use this information or "go down that path." However, these perceptions and reactions are undifferentiated among the states, and, as noted above, insurers often overestimate the prohibitive impact of these laws.

Thus, to the extent these laws have had any impact, they appear to have deterred health insurers that might be inclined to use genetic information from even considering doing so. As noted above, insurers are divided on the legitimacy of using this information. Some believe that this is not morally or philosophically acceptable; others simply see it as a business judgment of whether the economic and political costs of acquiring and using the information are outweighed by the actuarial benefits. Several subjects said they hold both attitudes, and they take different views depending on whether they are thinking like an actuary or instead like an ordinary person. Thus, these laws appear to have had some impact in reinforcing the industry's more socially oriented instincts. Health insurers that might be tempted to consider using genetic information have stayed far clear of this arena because of an undifferentiated and imprecise sense that it is legally problematic, and insurers that are more philosophically committed to not using this information are not placed in the dilemma of having to respond to competitors that might do so.

C. Potential Harms from Banning the Use of Genetic Information

We now consider whether laws prohibiting health insurers' use of genetic information have had any negative impact. There are two primary negative effects of potential interest. One is whether barring insurers from using potentially relevant or important underwriting information causes adverse selection. The other is whether these laws make it more difficult for people to purchase insurance by preventing them from using favorable genetic test results to establish their good health.

Adverse selection is a technical term used to describe a situation where insurers do not know as much as applicants do about their risk status. In this situation, high risk people will purchase a disproportionate amount of insurance. "Disproportionate" here means out of proportion to what they would be willing to buy if their risk status were accurately known. The problem this creates is not simply a threat to insurers' profits. Adverse selection forces insurers to raise rates across the board to anticipate it, since they are not able to identify those at higher risk whose rates they should selectively increase. Raising everyone's rates compounds the problem, however, by making insurance less attractive to lower risks. If they drop coverage, average rates go even higher. In the most extreme cases, adverse selection can cause rates to spiral so high that no one wants to purchase the insurance, and the market for that product entirely collapses. More commonly, the market reaches an equilibrium in which insurers can earn a reasonable return even with higher risks in the pool, yet the price remains sufficiently attractive to keep medium or lower risks in the pool. However, even moderate adverse selection will inevitably increase prices somewhat and therefore deter at least some purchasers.

It is impossible to avoid all aspects of adverse selection, since there are always some aspects of risk that motivate insurance purchase yet that insurers cannot feasibly or affordably discover. Low level adverse selection is no more problematic for successful markets than are any number of other minor market imperfections, such as transaction costs and deficiencies in consumer knowledge. However, any level of adverse selection will inevitably increase prices somewhat and therefore deter at least some purchasers.

It is clear from our interviews that serious adverse selection has not resulted, and is not likely to result any time soon, from the genetic discrimination laws that restrict health insurers. This conclusion follows from the prior observations that insurers do not consider this information important or useful. Barring insurers from using information they do not consider important for underwriting obviously cannot significantly undermine their ability to counter adverse selection. What is more telling is that most health underwriters and actuaries seem perfectly content to accept this ban, both now and far into the future. Many observed that these risks are already in the market, so keeping things the way they are now is not likely to harm the market. The implication is that there is not a large number of people without insurance and at high genetic risk waiting to enter the market as soon as they learn their genetic status. In contrast, the potential for adverse selection in life insurance is much greater. Many more people lack substantial life insurance, and those with life insurance are able to buy much more coverage if they learn they are at increased health risk. There is only so much health insurance coverage any one person can buy, and most people are already fully covered or unable to afford coverage regardless of their health status.

Another indication of the lack of concern over adverse selection is that none of the insurers that indicated possible interest in genetic information raised adverse selection as the main reason for this interest. Instead, they said they would use genetic information only if doing so would give them a competitive advantage, or if this were necessary to respond to their competitors. This is a much milder response than saying that this information is vital to a well-functioning market. Our subjects appeared to have full confidence that health insurance would remain a viable product even if insurers were prohibited from using genetic information, as long as the prohibition is applied equally to their competitors. This is a classic "collective action" situation in which everyone agrees that not using genetic information is economically acceptable, but if any one firm starts to use the information effectively, all the others will be forced to do likewise.

The other potential harm of prohibiting the use of genetic testing information is that it may prevent people with favorable results from using them to their advantage. For instance, a person with a family history of Huntington's Disease has a fifty percent chance of having a debilitating degenerative neurological disease. This individual may have great difficulty obtaining both life and health insurance because of the clinical record of their first degree relatives. A genetic test that shows they in fact have the gene and so increases the probability to 100% would not make them much worse off, but a test that shows the opposite would reduce their risk to virtually nothing and so could greatly benefit their insurability. Would these laws bar such favorable use? If so, have they had that effect?

None of the few insurer subjects we asked had given these issues any thought, so it appears that favorable use of genetic test results has not arisen very often. But, the few insurer subjects and regulators who addressed this issue all agreed that, logically, if the law prohibits adverse use of genetic information, it should also prohibit favorable use. Underwriters cannot look only at the positive side of a potential source of information. They must either consider both sides, or disregard it altogether. This is not only dictated by insurers' notions of what is fair, but by practical realities. Consider, for instance, allowing younger applicants to disclose their age but prohibiting insurers from inquiring about age. Insurers would simply assume that anyone who does not volunteer the information is not young. Therefore, to preclude age discrimination in rating, states must prohibit any consideration of age, both positive and negative.

This logic may not apply with the same force to risk factors that only a few applicants have, such as a single, rare gene defect. Considering the Huntington's Disease example above, it may in fact be feasible for only those with favorable test results to reveal them to insurers since those with a family history who do not reveal their results are already regarded as being at greatly increased insurance risk based merely on family history. Thus, a few states explicitly allow insurance applicants to voluntarily submit favorable genetic test results, or they ban only adverse use. But as more and more genetic conditions become identifiable, it is more likely that greater portions of the population will be able to demonstrate that they are genetically favored, and so allowing favorable use would undermine the goal of preventing wide scale genetic discrimination.

Regardless of logic, most of the laws enacted so far do not differentiate favorable from unfavorable use, but instead prohibit any use of genetic information. This is also how regulators and underwriters appear to interpret the law, although we only asked a few of them. But how great is the potential for favorable use? None of our insurer or agent subjects knew of genetic information being used in this way, but the several insurers who spoke to the issue said that favorable use of genetic information is possible and plausible, just as much as the possibility of unfavorable use. The strongest confirmation came from genetic counselors. They gave several instances of clients who had been able to counter adverse family history or misleading clinical indicators by using genetic tests to show the absence of suspected genetic disease.

Three counselors gave examples almost exactly like the Huntington's Disease illustration above, one for life insurance and two for health insurance, where favorable genetic testing results either enabled clients to get insurance, or possibly had that effect. Another counselor had a client who used favorable genetic test results for ataxia to help obtain both health and life insurance. Yet another counselor recalled a client with a family history for VHL (Von Hippel Lindau) disease, which causes noncancerous tumors. This client's favorable genetic test result allowed him to stop undergoing annual screenings to check for tumors. The counselor wrote the health insurer with this favorable news so this would be on the patient's record and perhaps help him obtain a better rate. Two other counselors explained that they routinely advise patients that favorable genetic test results can help them with insurance, and they write letters to insurers to facilitate this favorable use:

> I've told people who get negative results that this is a good thing.... I tell them it may be viewed in a positive manner. People that are true negatives, I let them know that this is a positive thing for you in terms of insurance and if you ever have any problems because someone does anything about family history stuff, you can tell them that you were negative.

It is interesting to note that, from their experience with their own patients, genetic counselors were able to give as many or more examples of favorable use as they were of unfavorable use of genetic testing results by health insurers.

D. Conclusion: Legal Influence on Industry Norms

What does one make of a set of laws that respond to a problem that does not exist, that are widely misunderstood or not known at all within the industry, and that have little or no discernible effect. One is tempted to conclude, in the words of Shakespeare, that genetic discrimination laws are full of sound and fury signifying nothing, or, in reference to the children's story, are the result of a Chicken Little syndrome by medical geneticists and advocacy groups. A more positive view is also justified, however. There is some potential for health insurers to use genetic information. These laws have solidified the industry's more socially constructive instincts and guarded against socially destructive competitive forces, by reinforcing an industry norm that opposes the use of predictive, presymptomatic information in general, and genetic information in particular.

A useful theoretical framework to evaluate and explain the more psychological impact of these laws comes from a growing body of work by prominent legal scholars on the relationship between law and social norms. Professor Robert Ellickson has explained why social and commercial systems often follow informal norms that completely ignore, contradict, or markedly differ from prevailing law and why this displacement of law by social norms should usually be encouraged rather than criticized. He observes that social norms often reach a superior substantive result than do legal rules and that they activate informal enforcement mechanisms that are cheaper and more effective than legal enforcement. Professor Cass Sunstein has explained how laws and norms interact rather than displace or compete with each other. He observes that laws often express social values contained in informal norms and that law can shape, create, or fortify norms. He gives as an example laws that prohibit various types of discrimination:

> A society might identify the norms to which it is committed and insist on those norms via law, even if the consequences of the insistence are obscure or unknown. A society might, for example, insist on an anti-discrimination law for expressive reasons even if it does not know whether the law actually helps members of minority groups.... If the Supreme Court holds that segregation is unlawful, ... the real-world consequences may be much smaller than is conventionally thought. But the close attention American society pays to the Court's pronouncements is connected with the expressive or symbolic character of those pronouncements. When the Court makes a decision, it is often taken to be speaking on behalf of the nation's basic principles and commitments. This assumption is a matter of importance quite apart from its consequences as conventionally understood.

This explanation assumes in part that law has little actual effect on social behavior, but, as Professor Shapiro explains, laws that communicate values can have educative or attitudinal effects that alter behavior by changing individual preferences or social norms. A good example is laws requiring the use of seat belts. Seat belt use has increased significantly following these laws, but this is likely due more to the educative or norm-altering impact of these laws than to simply their legal threat. Although people are occasionally cited for not buckling up, it seems likely that most people who comply do so because the new law helped to educate people about safety concerns, or because the legal prohibition helped to shape a social norm that rejects the prior libertarian attitude in favor of one that regards failure to use seatbelts as socially irresponsible. Thus, compliance occurs, not simply because of the legal threat, but because individual and social attitudes now view not buckling up as wrong—wrong not just under the law but according to social norms.

An apt example of these interactions that relates to insurance is the discrediting of racial classification in all lines of insurance, including health. Widespread condemnation this practice in the 1970s led to rapid and widespread change in industry practices, followed by a spate of state legislation in the early 1980s. One attempting to measure the impact of these laws might find almost none, since the insurance industry had voluntarily ceased using racial classifications prior to many of these laws. However, almost no one would say these laws were unwise or unjustified. They express social condemnation of racial factors in underwriting, and they help to ensure that such practices are not revived. Thus, the push for legislation helped to quickly reshape industry norms, and widespread enactment of these laws fortified the new industry norm.

These examples and explanations apply to much of what we have observed about genetic discrimination laws. In this instance, there has not been a change in industry behavior, but the law has helped to preserve the status quo. The insurance industry struggles with competing norms of actuarial fairness and social fairness. Actuarial fairness says that insurers not only may, but should, use the best available information about risk to determine each person's risk status. Social fairness says that certain types of risk classification unfairly penalize people for factors they cannot control or for which they should not be held responsible. Usually in these debates the industry is univocal in defending the norm of actuarial fairness; this occurred, for instance, with AIDS testing. But, in this instance, as with racial discrimination, laws prohibiting health insurers from using genetic information have helped move the industry norm toward social fairness. Having done so, these laws operate more effectively and with broader sweep than if they had to be actively enforced against a reluctant industry looking for ways to circumvent them.

Rather than criticizing these laws for responding to a problem that does not exist, one can maintain that the law has a legitimate function in simply expressing the social judgment that it is wrong to use genetic information in health underwriting. Even though insurers and agents do not have widespread and accurate knowledge of these laws, these laws have fortified their impression of social disapproval by creating a general climate of legal condemnation. Health insurers avoid the use of genetic information not so much because of the specific threat of law but because the law reinforces the instinct that doing otherwise would be socially wrong. To this extent, they have been effective. However, the expressive effect of the law can also have unintended negative consequences. It may be that, rather than calming fears about genetic discrimination and therefore encouraging more people to undergo beneficial genetic testing, these laws have heightened fears without substantial justification by calling undue attention to a problem that, in large measure, does not exist.

Whether these laws, on balance, are a success depends also on an appreciation of their potential harms. Although the harms are not great, that is because genetic information simply is not much used by health insurers, for either adverse or favorable purposes. But, once adverse uses become possible, so too do favorable ones. At that point, the potential for inhibiting favorable use by those who wish to clear up a suspect family or medical history becomes real, and this potential seems to be roughly as great as the potential for these laws to protect against adverse use. The difficult judgment social policy makers must make is whether this trade-off is socially desirable.

Schmidt v. Fortis Insurance Co.

349 F. Supp. 2d 1171 (N.D. Iowa 2005)

A. Factual Background

1. General Background

The plaintiffs, Karen Schmidt and Daniel Schmidt ("Schmidts"), are husband and wife. Karen is a self-employed business owner and is currently the owner/operator of several businesses including a video rental and tanning business (known as "Home Video" and "The Sun Tanner"), a payday loan business housed near the video and tanning business, Hampton Home Store and the Coonley apartment building.... From approximately 1990 through August 2001, Daniel Schmidt was employed by the Hampton-Dumont Community School District as the director of maintenance. In approximately 1988, prior to Daniel obtaining his position with the Hampton-Dumont Community School District, the Schmidts purchased a family health insurance policy from Blue Cross Blue Shield ("BCBS"). The Schmidts were covered by the BCBS policy when Karen was diagnosed with breast cancer and underwent a mastectomy followed by chemotherapy in 1989. When Daniel began his employment with the Hampton-Dumont Community School District, and secured health insurance for his family via that employment, the Schmidts terminated their BCBS policy on the basis of cost and duplication of benefits. At no point did the Schmidts have health insurance coverage through any of the businesses that they owned.

In the summer of 2001, the Schmidts were anticipating the purchase of the Hampton Home Store—a major appliance retail store which also services appliances. At this time, the Schmidts were considering the possibility of Daniel ending his employment with the Hampton-Dumont Community School District and co-operating the Hampton Home Store with Karen. The sale of the Hampton Home Store to the Schmidts was to be completed on August 13, 2001. At this time, the Schmidts had health insurance through the Hampton-Dumont Community Schools under a self-funded plan—but, this coverage would lapse following the termination of Daniel's employment with the school district.[1] Therefore, obtaining replacement health care insurance prior to the completion of the sale of the Hampton Home Store to the Schmidts became a priority. Karen was particularly concerned with obtaining replacement coverage in light of her breast cancer history, which is explained in great detail below. When Daniel expressed an interest in leaving his position at the school district in favor of co-operating the Hampton Home Store with Karen, Dr. Lee Morrison, the superintendent of the school district, recommended that the Schmidts contact the school district's insurance agent, Loren Kiel, at Midwest Group Benefits, Inc. in Decorah, Iowa, to discuss their options for purchasing replacement health care insurance.

2. Pertinent medical background

Dr. Keith Hansen, D.O., has been Karen's primary care physician since 1973. On March 21, 1989, a mammogram performed on Karen revealed the presence of a mass in her right breast. A biopsy of the mass was conducted on that same day. The biopsy revealed a medullary carcinoma and Karen was diagnosed with stage II breast cancer, with one of eighteen lymph nodes positive. On March 29, 1989, Karen underwent a radical partial mastectomy with axillary dissection. The surgery was performed by Dr. Hansen and Dr. Richard Francis, M.D. The last time Karen had detectable residual cancer was at the time of her mastectomy on March 29, 1989.

Following the surgery, Karen began seeing Dr. Peter Silberstein, M.D., who at the time was an oncology/hematology specialist at The Park Clinic in Mason City, Iowa. Karen's first visit with Dr. Silberstein was on April 20, 1989. Under Dr. Silberstein's supervision, Karen underwent six months of chemotherapy—from approximately April 1989 through September 1989. In approximately November of 1989, following the completion of the chemotherapy regimen and after finding that the tumor was estrogen and progesterone receptor positive, Dr. Silberstein prescribed the prescription drug tamoxifen for Karen—which Karen then began taking.... Following December 1990, Dr. Hansen continued to renew Karen's original tamoxifen prescription initiated by Dr. Silberstein, and Karen remained on a daily tamoxifen regiment through 1996. Dr. Hansen's progress notes throughout this time period contain numerous references to Karen's tamoxifen prescription and usage.... Karen took tamoxifen for approximately seven years. Karen was not participating in a clinical trial at the time she used tamoxifen.

Dr. Hansen's medical records in the years following Karen's mastectomy and chemotherapy treatment contain numerous references to her history of breast cancer.... Karen's medical records also indicate that in the years following her mastectomy and chemotherapy treatment, she had the following procedures performed: (1) twelve blood panels; (2) ten blood chemistry analyses; (3) three bone scans; (4) four chest x-rays; and (5) eleven mammograms Of the contralateral breast.

...

In August 2002, Karen was seen in the Hereditary Cancer Prevention Clinic at Creighton University in Omaha, Nebraska "for evaluation and counseling related to her risk for hereditary breast ovarian cancer." Given Karen's own breast cancer at age 35,

1. The Schmidts were aware that COBRA continuation coverage was available to them following the termination of Daniel's employment with the school district, but they did not believe it was a viable option as they were seeking long-term health coverage.

and the fact that her sisters and mother had experienced either breast or ovarian cancer, Karen underwent genetic testing to determine whether she had a BRCA1/2 mutation. Genetic testing revealed that Karen did have a BRCA 1 mutation, putting her at a high risk of cancer in the contralateral breast and ovarian cancer. In light of testing positive for the BRCA 1 mutation, in January 2003, Karen consulted with Dr. Thoo H. Tan, D.O., at the Hampton Clinic, and Dr. Harsha U. Jayawardena, M.D., at the Mason City Clinic, about a prophylactic mastectomy of the left breast and a prophylactic hysterectomy. Both Dr. Tan and Dr. Jayawardena agreed that due to her breast cancer history and positive test for the BRCA 1 mutation that the prophylactic mastectomy and hysterectomy should be scheduled.

3. The search for health insurance

...

As described above, in the summer of 2001 the Schmidts were in search of replacement health insurance so that Daniel could transition out of his job with the Hampton-Dumont Community School District, and into a position as an active co-owner of the various businesses owned by the Schmidts. On the advice of the school superintendent, Dr. Lee Morrison, Karen contacted the school district's insurance agent, Loren Kiel ("Kiel"). In 2001, Kiel was the president of Midwest Benefits, Inc. ("Midwest Benefits"), in Decorah Iowa.... In 2001, Kiel worked with an assistant, Karla Baumler ("Baumler"). At that time, Baumler had obtained her insurance license for health care products, and worked on individual quotes and applications, small group quotes and applications, and some customer service work.

Karen first contacted Midwest Benefits by telephone sometime in June 2001. Karen discussed the fact that Daniel was intending to leave his employment with the school district and transition into co-ownership of their small businesses, and that hopefully this transition would be complete by the time the sale of the Hampton Home Store to the Schmidts was finalized. Karen also indicated that Daniel's transition was contingent on the Schmidts obtaining replacement health insurance coverage as close to the closing date on the Hampton Home Store sale as possible. Given Karen's history of breast cancer, described in detail above, she was concerned over whether they would be able to obtain health insurance coverage.

After her initial contact, Karen conversed with Kiel and Baumler on a number of occasions before any application for insurance was submitted. According to Kiel, the conversations were generally about "what the benefits were of the various plans that were available and the different ... deductibles and premium rates and so forth for each plan, somewhat about how that compared to current coverage that they had under the group plan, what might be good, in terms of coverage." Other than a comparison of the options available, another key topic of conversation was Karen's concern over obtaining coverage due to her breast cancer history. *See id.* ("we talked about—The concern was about the prior history back a number of years"). The parties agree that Karen told Kiel and Baumler that she had breast cancer and a mastectomy in 1989—however, what additional details, if any, Karen told Kiel and Baumler about her medical history is hotly contested by the parties.

...

Kiel recommended that the Schmidts first submit an application for health insurance coverage to Life Investors Insurance Company of America ("Life Investors"). Kiel recommended Life Investors first because he felt it offered the best coverage, was a quality company, had the best rates, and was most likely to offer coverage to someone who had a past medical history. On the advice of Kiel, the Schmidts decided to submit an application to Life Investors. In preparation for the submission of the Life Investors application, Karen compiled some of her medical records surrounding her cancer treatment and provided them to Kiel and Baumler. While these records were not exhaustive, they did contain portions of Dr. Silberstein's progress notes, portions of Dr. Hansen's progress notes, some mammogram results, and some blood test results. Karen also procured a letter from Dr. Hansen for submission with her application which [summarized Karen's lack of cancer recurrence].

...

Sometime in July 2001, Midwest Benefits mailed the Life Investors application to Karen and Daniel to fill out. The Schmidts filled out, signed and dated the Life Investors application on July 26, 2001, and mailed it back to Midwest Benefits with a packet of Karen's medical records and the July 17, 2001, letter from Dr. Hansen. On the application, Karen and Daniel checked "Yes" in response to Questions 2(k), which asked: "Has any person listed in question number 1 EVER had or to the best of your knowledge now have: ... Disorder of skin, cyst, tumor or any cancer?" In the following section which required details regarding "yes" answers, the Schmidts identified Karen as the family member associated with the "yes" answer to Question 2(k), and there is a handwritten notation to "see Dr's reports attached" where it asks for details. Karen and Daniel also checked "Yes" in response to Question 4(a) which asked: "Has anyone above, within the past 5 years: ! ... Had a check-up, consultation, lab test, illness, injury, surgery?" In the section that asks for details, the Schmidts again identified Karen as the family member associated with the "yes" answer, and in the box for providing details wrote "yearly mamogram (sic)—see attached reports." ... Baumler testified that this additional documentation was submitted because the application asked if any proposed insured had *ever* had cancer and asked for details regarding her cancer history.

...

Kendy Robinson, of the Health Service Unit at Live Investors, sent Kiel a letter dated August 10, 2001, regarding the underwriting status of the Schmidts' application. It is characterized as an "Agent Action Report" and states:

> For Your Action:
>
> • Karen will be denied due to health history of Breast cancer.
>
> • Shall we continue?
>
> • This is your second request.
>
> Comments: Certificate will be pending until information is received.

Kiel does not recall when this letter was received. On August 28, 2001, Baumler sent a fax to Linda Smith of the Health Service Unit at Live Investors. The fax stated:

> Please discontinue the request for a new individual policy on Daniel Schmidt and daughter Kathy.... This application was sent in and due to Daniel's spouse Karen being denied the whole family has decided to get a policy elsewhere....

Sometime after Kiel and Karen became apprised that there was a problem with the Life Investors application, it was decided that the Schmidts should submit an application for health insurance to Fortis Insurance Company ("Fortis"). Part of the rationale behind submitting an application to Fortis was the fact that the application only asked for medical history for the past ten years.

...

Baumler mailed a Fortis individual medical insurance application to Karen on August 8, 2001. Daniel and Karen Schmidt completed and signed the application on August 9, 2001 and mailed the application back to Midwest Benefits. The Schmidts checked "No" in response to Question 15, which asked: "Have any of the proposed insureds ever been declined, postponed, charged an extra premium or had a portion of coverage excluded for life, disability, or medical insurance or had such coverage rescinded?" In response to Question 18(k), the Schmidts also checked "No." The Schmidts left page 5 of the application, which allotted space for applicants to provide additional medical details, blank.... At the end of the application, directly above the signature block where the Schmidts signed and dated the application, the following appears:

> I represent to the best of my knowledge and belief, that all statements and answers on this enrollment form are complete and true. The enrollment form and any amendments shall be the basis for the contract. I also agree that:....
>
> We, the undersigned Proposed Insured(s) and agent acknowledge that the Proposed Insured(s) has read the completed enrollment form. We understand and acknowledge that any fraudulent statement or material misrepresentation on the enrollment form and/or any amendments may result in claim denial or contract rescission, subject to the time limit on certain defenses or incontestability provisions of the contract.

...

The application was subsequently mailed ... on August 13, 2001. The packet of medical records that Karen provided to Midwest Benefits, and that had been submitted with the Life Investors application, was not submitted with the Fortis application.... Fortis notified Midwest Benefits that coverage had been extended to the Schmidts in a correspondence dated August 20, 2001. The policy that Fortis issued to the Schmidts had an effective date of September 1, 2001.

4. Fortis's rescission

As discussed above, in August 2002, Karen went to the Hereditary Cancer Prevention Clinic at Creighton University in Omaha, Nebraska in order to undergo genetic testing to determine if she had a BRCA1/2 mutation. Dr. Henry Lynch, M.D., the physician overseeing Karen's genetic testing, wrote Fortis a letter dated August 13, 2002, requesting preauthorization for the proposed testing. Amongst other information, the letter noted that "Karen has a history of breast cancer at 35." Receipt of this letter by Fortis triggered an investigation in Karen's medical history. In a letter dated September 14, 2002, and addressed to Daniel Schmidt, Fortis indicated that it had received a statement of expense from Dr. Hansen, and indicated that more information regarding Karen's medical history would be necessary before Fortis's liability could be determined. In the letter, Fortis asked that Karen provide the name and address of any doctors or hospitals by who she had been treated in the past 11 years, and the name and address of any pharmacies where she purchased prescription medication within the past 11 years. In addition, Fortis asked Karen to sign a medical records release. LeeAnn Szopinski, Senior Individual Medical Underwriter for Fortis, wrote the following letter, dated March 12, 2003, to the Schmidts:

> During the course of your recent claim for benefits under the above policy, we received information regarding Karen Schmidt. This prompted a review of Karen's medical history and medical records were obtained from Dr. Hanson.

> In reviewing these medical records, we discovered medical information that was not disclosed on your application for insurance. As you know, at the time you applied for coverage, we asked you to complete an application/enrollment form.
>
> Karen's eligibility for insurance coverage with our company was based on the information included in the application/enrollment form. We found misrepresentation on questions (sic) 18K of the application/enrollment form. Had our Underwriting Department been aware of this medical history at the time the application/enrollment form was approved, Karen's eligibility for insurance coverage with our company would have been affected.
>
> In light of this additional information, the following adverse action would have been required at the time that your policy was issued. We are enclosing an Amendment of Application that excludes coverage for Karen Schmidt from the effective date of the policy.
>
> If you choose to accept the above Amendment of Application, please sign, date and return it to Fortis in the enclosed envelope. Your policy will remain in force, limited by the Amendment of Application.
>
> If you choose not to accept and sign the Amendment of Application, you will leave us no alternative except to rescind the entire policy back to the effective date of September 1, 2001. We require notification within 30 days of receipt of this letter of your intentions. Fortis will arrange for any appropriate refund of premium, less any claims, which may have already been paid.
>
> If you have any new information that may impact this decision please submit this information in writing.

At this point the Schmidts obtained counsel, through whom they appealed this decision internally with Fortis and filed a complaint with the Iowa Insurance Commissioner....

...

A May 22, 2003, letter from Michael Prudlow, Individual Medical Underwriting Correspondent for Fortis, to counsel for the Schmidts, indicated that "[a]fter careful review, we find that our actions have been appropriate." The letter states the basis for Fortis's decision as follows:

> Despite the fact that Ms. Schmidt's diagnosis and primary treatment occurred in 1989, she did continue the use of Tamoxifen until 1995. Additionally, Ms. Schmidt underwent follow-up visits with the doctor(s) to be screened for any recurrence of the cancer, well after 1989.
>
> The Enrollment Form completed by the Schmidts asks: "*Within the last 10 years has any proposed insured: Had any diagnosis of, received treatment for, or consulted with a physician concerning:*" The Schmidts answered "no" to all of the health statement questions despite the fact that Ms. Schmidt took prescription medication and underwent follow-up exams within the ten years prior to the application date. Had we been aware of this information at the time of application, an offer of coverage would not have been extended to Ms. Schmidt.

([E]mphasis in original). A June 2, 2003, letter from Margaret Chase ("Chase"), Market Conduct Analyst for Fortis, to the Iowa Insurance Commission indicates the following as the basis for Fortis's decision:

> The Enrollment Form completed by the Schmidts asks: "*Within the last 10 years has any proposed insured: Had any diagnosis of, received treatment for, or*

> *consulted with a physician concerning:*" The Schmidts answered "no" to all of the health statement questions on the Enrollment Form....
>
> On or about February 19, 2003, a routine claims investigation was conducted. As a result, medical records were requested from Dr. Peter Silberstein and Dr. Keith Hansen. These records indicate that Mrs. Schmidt was diagnosed with breast cancer in 1989. A further review of these records documents the fact that Ms. Schmidt took prescription medication (Tamoxifen) and underwent follow-up exams for cancer within the ten years prior to the application date. Had we been aware of this information at the time of the application, an offer of coverage would not have been extended to Ms. Schmidt....
>
> After careful review of this matter, we find that our actions have been appropriate.

A second letter from Chase to the Iowa Insurance Commissioner, dated June 19, 2003, states, in part:

> Enclosed, please find copies of Ms. Karen Schmidt's medical records. The highlighted areas pertain primarily to question 18k which asks: *Within the last 10 years has any proposed insured: 18. Had any diagnosis of, received treatment for, or consulted with a physician concerning: k. "Cancer? Provide location, type of cancer and treatment received.*" The medical records indicate that Ms. Schmidt consulted with a physician and received treatment with Tamoxifen until 1995. Based on our underwriting guidelines, an offer of coverage would not have been extended.

A September 12, 2003, letter from Michael Prudlow to the Schmidts' counsel stated, in pertinent part:

> According to [Dr. Silberstein and Dr. Hansen], Ms. Schmidt was prescribed Tamoxifen as a prophylaxis to prevent the recurrence of cancer. While this is true, it should also be considered that had Ms. Schmidt not had cancer, she would not have been prescribed Tamoxifen. This medication is commonly used by breast cancer survivors due to the frequency of recurrence.
>
> While annual mammograms may be part of a routine exam, it is also true that these are more urgent for those women with a history of breast cancer. Ms. Schmidt's exam results were certainly reviewed with her history of cancer taken into consideration as her doctors were aware of this history.
>
> Please refer to the Other Provisions page of the certificate, specifically the paragraph regarding Misstatements. As the certificate indicates, "if any relevant fact about you is found to have been misstated, the true facts will be used to determine if the insurance is in force." This paragraph is applicable to question 18k regarding Ms. Schmidt's health history. Furthermore, the final paragraph on page 6 of the enrollment form states:
>
>> *"We, the undersigned Proposed Insured(s) and agent acknowledge that the Proposed Insured(s) has read the complete enrollment form. We understand and acknowledge that any fraudulent statement or material misrepresentation on the enrollment form and/or any amendments may result in claim denial or contract rescission, subject to the time limit on certain defenses or incontestability provisions of this contract.*
>
> The decision to review additional medical information via medical records is based upon the history as provided by the applicants. If an application provides a "clean" or uneventful medical history, an offer of coverage is extended

> as the applicant has attested to the fact that the information they have provided is complete and accurate.
>
> Applicants are not expected to have knowledge of what the company underwriting guidelines are. They are expected to provide a complete and accurate personal health history to be reviewed and considered for an offer of coverage. There are no guarantees of coverage as all applications for major medical insurance are fully underwritten.
>
> As stated in our prior correspondence of August 6, 2003, if the amendment agreeing to remove Ms. Schmidt is not signed and returned, the entire policy will be rescinded back to its original effective date. This deadline has been extended since May 30, 2003 and will not be extended any longer. Since the amendment has not been returned, we will proceed with the rescission of Mr. and Ms. Schmidt's policy. They will receive an entire refund of their premiums, less any claims paid.

In a September 22, 2003, letter to Daniel Schmidt, Fortis notified him of the rescission of the Schmidts' entire health insurance policy/certificate back to the effective date of September 1, 2001. A separate correspondence from Fortis to Daniel, also dated September 22, 2002, indicates that the policy was terminated effective September 1, 2001, as there had been no response to Fortis's reformation offer. Included in this second correspondence was a check in the amount of $7,365.97, which represented all premiums paid by the Schmidts minus all claims paid by Fortis.

...

B. Equitable Rescission

1. Generally

Under Iowa law, fraudulent misrepresentation in the inducement to contract gives rise to three distinct actions: (1) a cause of action at law for money damages; (2) a defense to a breach-of-contract claim; and (3) a ground for rescission of a contract in an action in equity. In this instance, the case at hand concerns whether Fortis's rescission of the policy based on an alleged fraudulent misrepresentation by the plaintiffs in filling out the enrollment form was wrongful. Therefore, at this juncture the focus is only on fraudulent misrepresentation as grounds for rescission.

Generally, in Iowa, "fraudulent misrepresentations leading to the creation of a contract give[s] rise to a right of rescission." Under Iowa law, five elements must be proven where a party seeks to rescind a contract based on a fraudulent misrepresentation: (1) a representation, (2) falsity, (3) materiality, (4) an intent to induce the other to act or refrain from acting, and (5) justifiable reliance.... As this court thoroughly discussed in *Utica Mutual Insurance Company v. Stockdale Agency,* 892 F.Supp. 1179 (N.D.Iowa 1995), lack of the element of scienter is a historical distinction between the proof required to sustain an action in equity to rescind the contract and that required to sustain an action at law for fraudulent misrepresentation.... In order to uphold the historical distinction between at law and in equity relief for fraudulent misrepresentation, the concept of scienter must never enter the equation in determining whether a party is justified in pursuing the equitable relief of rescission—therefore, the intent necessary to sustain an equity action is merely the intent to induce the complaining party to contract. In an equity action for fraudulent misrepresentation, fraud may be inferred from the circumstances, words and actions in evidence.

In this case, Fortis identifies the Schmidts "no" responses to Questions 15 and 18(k) as fraudulent misrepresentations giving rise to Fortis's right to rescind the policy back to its effective date of September 1, 2001. The Schmidts concede that the only element of equitable rescission at issue is falsity, and that all of the remaining four elements are established. Therefore, like the parties, the court will focus exclusively on the element of "falsity" in determining whether the record supports summary judgment for either party. However, before delving into the arguments of the parties and the legal analysis of the cross-motions for summary judgment, the court will first set forth the basic principles of contract construction and interpretation under Iowa law.

2. Construing and interpreting insurance contracts under Iowa law

Under Iowa law, an application for insurance becomes a part of the insurance contract by virtue of Iowa Code § 515.94 where the application "by the terms of such policy, is made a part of the policy, or of the contract of insurance, or [is] referred to in the contract of insurance, or which may in any manner affect the validity of such policy." Iowa Code § 515.94. The Fortis enrollment form specifically states that "[t]he enrollment form and any amendments shall be the basis for the contract" and that "any fraudulent statement or material misrepresentation on the enrollment form and/or any amendment may result in claim denial or contract rescission." Further, the letter accompanying the policy states that the "contract has been issued based on the statements ... made in [the] Application for Insurance," and "[a]ny incorrect statement ... could void ... coverage or cause a claim to be denied." Therefore, the question of whether any terms in the enrollment form are ambiguous must be decided under the standards for determination of the ambiguity of terms in an insurance contract. Therefore, the court will briefly review the rules and principles governing interpretation of insurance contracts under Iowa law.

The policy must be construed as a whole, giving its terms their ordinary, not technical, meaning. Words left undefined by the policy are not given their technical meaning, but rather the ordinary meaning which a reasonable person would accord them. In some cases, an objective inquiry into the meaning of the policy language reveals it is susceptible to two fair interpretations—it is in this instance that this language is deemed ambiguous. A mere disagreement between the parties as to the meaning of a policy term does not equate to ambiguity. The court must be diligent in according the policy language only its ordinary and natural interpretation, and must not "give a strained or unnatural reading to the words of a policy to create ambiguity where there is none." It is fundamental that where a term is ambiguous, the interpretation most favorable to the insured must be adopted due to the adhesive nature of insurance policies.

Construction of insurance contracts is always a matter of law for the court.... However, interpretation becomes a question of fact where the interpretation depends on "extrinsic evidence or on a choice among reasonable inferences from extrinsic evidence." Extrinsic evidence refers to evidence other than the words of the policy. The bottom line is that the court must "'ascertain from [the policy's words] the intent of the insurer and insured at the time the policy was sold.'" ...

3. Question 18(k)

a. The question

Though Question 18(k), and the Schmidts' response thereto on the application, has been discussed above, it would be most prudent to reiterate the precise question and response prior to delving into the parties' arguments for summary judgment. Question 18(k) asked:

> Within the last 10 years has any proposed insured:
>
> 18. Had any diagnosis of, received treatment for, or consulted with a physician concerning:....
>
> k) Cancer? Provide location, type of cancer and treatment received.

In response to this question the Schmidts checked "no." Further, as additional medical information was requested only as to any "yes" responses, the Schmidts did not provide additional details regarding medical details in the space so designated in the enrollment form. As Question 18(k) asked only for information for the ten years preceding the application, the pertinent time window in this case is from August 9, 1991 through August 9, 2001. The parties concede that Karen was not diagnosed with cancer during the pertinent ten-year time window. However, there is serious contention as to whether Karen received "treatment for ... cancer" or "consulted with a physician concerning ... cancer," and whether these phrases are ambiguous.

...

... Karen was concerned about answering Question 18(k) correctly, especially in light of her breast cancer history.[2] Even in the light most favorable to Fortis, a scheme to defraud Fortis *cannot* be derived from the fact that Kiel, Baumler [insurance brokers for Midwest] and the Schmidts found the language requesting health history for only the past ten years advantageous and a better opportunity for the Schmidts to secure health insurance coverage—*especially* in light of the fact that Fortis was *ultimately in control* of the language used on the application. Fortis had *every right and opportunity* to pose any question regarding the health history of a proposed insured, and it chose to only ask for health history over the previous ten years. The fact that the Schmidts, Kiel and Baumler felt that this created a better opportunity than an insurance company asking if a proposed insured "ever" had a certain condition, especially in light of the fact that Fortis was the only remaining company to which the Schmidts could apply via Midwest Benefits, does not create a genuine issue of material fact that Kiel and Karen intended to defraud Fortis through the responses to any of the enrollment form questions.

...

In sum, the court finds that the facts, circumstances and actions surrounding the application process, even when viewed in the light most favorable to Fortis, do not generate a genuine issue of material fact that Kiel and Karen intended to deceive, or perpetrate a fraud upon, Fortis in answering Question 18(k), or Question 15, on the Fortis enrollment form. Nothing in the record illustrates conduct that raises a clear presumption that Kiel and Karen were engaged in a scheme to defraud Fortis. Therefore, there is no genuine issue of material fact that Kiel and the Schmidts conspired to defraud Fortis, and whatever Kiel's knowledge as to Karen's medical history may be, it can be imputed to Fortis. The court will now move on to an analysis of the language of Question 18(k)

---

2. Despite Fortis's contentions to the contrary, the interpretation accorded Question 18(k) by Kiel, Baumler and Karen was not unreasonable as the language of the question was ambiguous-this is explored in great detail below.

to determine if it is ambiguous, and furthermore, whether the Schmidts' "no" response was false.

c. "Treatment for"

i. Arguments of the parties.

In their motion for summary judgment, the Schmidts next contend that Karen did not receive treatment between August 9, 1991 and August 9, 2001. The Schmidts assert that it is undisputed that Karen did not undergo a mastectomy, chemotherapy, or radiation during the applicable ten-year time frame. Moving on to the first contentious issue, the Schmidts turn to whether Karen's tamoxifen use until 1996 constituted treatment. First, the Schmidts point to Fortis's current underwriting guidelines—which provide that "Hormonal therapy (tamoxifen, Arimidex, Femara) should not be included when determining 'time since treatment completed'." Further, Fortis's current underwriting guidelines state that cancer treatment includes only "surgery, radiation, and/or chemotherapy." The Schmidts note that Fortis's current underwriting guidelines mirror the position stated by Dr. Silberstein in his March 24, 2003, letter, ("Tamoxifen, at that point in time, was a preventative prophylactic measure to prevent cancer from recurring"); and Dr. Hansen in his April 2, 2003, letter. ("The Tamoxifen she was on for seven years was purely as a prophylaxis."). As no doctor treated Karen using radiation, chemotherapy or surgery from August 9, 1991 through August 9, 2001, Karen therefore did not receive "treatment for" cancer and the Schmidts' "no" response to Question 18(k) was therefore not false. In closing, the Schmidts assert that the "no" answer was truthful, and that the undisputed facts reveal that "Karen Schmidt, Loren Kiel and Karla Baumler all studied [Question 18(k)] in light of Karen Schmidt's cancer history and believed that the answer was truthful."

Fortis first argues that Karen's use of the prescription drug tamoxifen during the pertinent ten year period constituted "treatment for" cancer, thereby making the Schmidts' "no" response to Question 18(k) false as a matter of law. Fortis dismisses the Schmidts' arguments for summary judgment as relying on "semantic artifice," while Fortis claims its argument is based on "a number of authoritative sources." One such "authoritative source" is the opinion of board certified oncologist Dr. Roscoe Morton. Fortis's argument reiterates many of the points Dr. Morton made in a letter he composed after reviewing Karen's breast cancer history. Dr. Morton opined that in 1989, the prevailing treatment for stage II breast cancer, to increase the ten-year-disease free rate, following mastectomy, included adjuvant therapy including cytotoxic chemotherapy, radiation, and hormonal therapy such as tamoxifen use. Dr. Morton opined that the ten-year disease-free survival rate for those patients not partaking in any of these post-mastectomy adjuvant therapies was 41–42%. Dr. Morton opined that by receiving chemotherapy followed by hormonal therapy in the form of taking tamoxifen, a patient could improve her ten-year disease free survival rate from 41–42% to 63%. Based on a review of Karen's medical records, Dr. Morton came to the following conclusions regarding Karen's tamoxifen use:

> Based on review of the supplied medical records and the state of the art of adjuvant therapy in 1989, it is my opinion that the tamoxifen was used in this case as a treatment due to its salubrious effect on reducing the chance of recurrence of breast cancer and death rather than for prevention of breast cancer. Tamoxifen was combined with the CAF chemotherapy regimen and was given after the chemotherapy was completed. Thus, tamoxifen was an active part of

> the treatment of her breast cancer. The prevention capabilities of tamoxifen were incidental to its treatment component in this case.

Fortis also points to the fact that use of tamoxifen to reduce the risk of breast cancer in women who had never had breast cancer, a "purely prophylactic" measure, was not an approved use for tamoxifen until 1996.

Fortis also points to the fact that Karen, at various points between 1989 and 1996, considered ceasing her use of tamoxifen but was counseled otherwise by Dr. Silberstein and Dr. Hansen as establishing that Karen understood that she was deriving a health benefit from staying on tamoxifen. Fortis also points to the fact that tamoxifen usage is not without risk, and that an April 9, 1994, release by the Food and Drug Administration (FDA) warned women and doctors that tamoxifen posed an increased risk of uterine cancer, but recognized that as tamoxifen could delay or prevent recurrence in patients that have undergone surgery for breast cancer that it "continue[d] to be indicated for the treatment of breast cancer." The April 9, 1994, warning also stated that outside of a clinical trial, tamoxifen should not be used prophylactically: "[T]amoxifen should not be used as a preventative agent outside of a clinical trial." Fortis points out that in spite of the risks, Karen continued to use tamoxifen. Fortis concludes its arguments that tamoxifen use constituted "treatment for" cancer by asserting that Karen continued to take tamoxifen in spite of all the risks associated with taking the drug and that Karen's regimen of tamoxifen from 1989 through 1996 was an "integral part of her treatment for breast cancer"—thus making her response to Question 18(k) false and Fortis's rescission justified.

In their resistance, the Schmidts first turn to the opposing opinions of Dr. Silberstein and Dr. Morton. The Schmidts point out that Dr. Silberstein sees a distinction between active treatment and adjuvant therapy: "Adjuvant treatment is where the patient may or may not have cancer and then you're trying to reduce the risk of cancer.... [A]djuvant therapy is reducing the risk of cancer. And I emphasize to [my patients] that some of them may not have any cancer so that we are giving this measure to reduce the risk of recurrence when they may or may not have any cancer. So we're not treating a cancer if there's no cancer there." And, under Dr. Silberstein's distinction, one cannot be actively treating something that is not *actually* present. Because Karen has had *no detectable residual cancer* since her mastectomy since March 1989, Dr. Silberstein contends that her tamoxifen usage cannot be treatment as there was nothing to treat—it was merely used as a preventative measure. The Schmidts dismiss Dr. Morton's opinions as based on statistical modeling, as employing incorrect calculations of tumor size (i.e. adding together the biopsy sample and mastectomy sample), and as irrelevant because his population models admittedly cannot predict for a specific individual's outcome. The Schmidts then argue that construing the policy giving the word "treatment" its ordinary meaning there is no other conclusion but that the use of the term "treatment" in the enrollment form is ambiguous as pertains to Karen's tamoxifen use—particularly in light of the fact that there is disagreement between two oncologists (Dr. Silberstein and Dr. Morton) having specialized knowledge of the subject matter as to the meaning of the term in this context. The Schmidts then argue that, according treatment the ordinary meaning most favorable to themselves, as the insureds, Fortis must show that there *was something to treat* in order for it to be considered treatment and that even shifting all reasonable inferences in Fortis's favor, as Karen never had cancer between 1991 and 1996, her tamoxifen use *cannot*, as a matter of law, be considered "treatment for ... cancer." Further, the Schmidts dismiss Fortis's reference, in its motion for summary judgment, to a policy document defining treatment as "the medical or surgical management of a patient ... includ[ing] any ... Prescription Drug," as irrelevant because it was not available to the Schmidts at the time they filled out the enrollment form on August 9, 2001. Finally, the Schmidts contend that the United States District Court for the District of Montana, in *Elliot v. Fortis Benefits Insurance Company*, Cause No. 01-11-BLG-GFC, already held that tamoxifen use does not constitute treatment.

In its reply brief, Fortis focuses primarily on what it claims to be a definition for "treatment" in the policy as establishing both unambiguity and ultimately justifying Fortis's rescission of the contract. Following acceptance of the Schmidts' application, Fortis delivered the policy along with a copy of the completed application to the Schmidts, as required by Iowa law. *See* Iowa Code § 515.94 (compelling insurance companies to attach a copy of the completed application to the policy). A letter accompanying the policy and certificate indicated that the policy was issued based on the representations on the enrollment form, and that the policy and the enrollment form should be reviewed by the Schmidts to ensure that the answers were accurate and complete. As quoted above, the certificate does contain language indicating that treatment includes prescription drugs—which Fortis contends is a "definition" of the term treatment. Fortis contends that it is irrelevant that the Schmidts did not have this definition of treatment while they filled out their enrollment form, as they were requested to review the enrollment form in light of all policy documents to determine if there were any misstatements or inaccuracies. Fortis contends that, as a matter of law, the term "treatment" is unambiguous as it was defined in the policy to include prescription drugs, and the Schmidts have failed to produce *any* evidence that a definition of treatment to include prescription drugs is unreasonable or oppressive. Further, Fortis discounts the Schmidts' reliance on its 2004 underwriting guidelines, which exclude tamoxifen use from the determination of when cancer treatment ends, as they were *not* in effect at the time the Schmidts applied for coverage in 2001. Finally, Fortis reiterates that during the time Karen was taking tamoxifen, the *only* approved use of the drug was for treatment and that purely prophylactic use of tamoxifen was not approved until 1996. Finally, Fortis discounts the *Elliot* case as not having any precedential value on this court, and as clearly factually distinguishable from this case—as the issue was whether tamoxifen use constituted treatment in terms of defining a "pre-existing condition," and where "pre-existing" was defined by the disability policy in question. In closing, Fortis asks that the court find "treatment" unambiguous, accord it the "definition" set forth in the policy, and grant Fortis's motion for summary judgment.

ii. Analysis.

Before embarking on a discussion of the nuances of the parties' arguments, it is important to put the policy language discussing "treatment" into context. Therefore, the court will briefly set forth some of the pertinent language in the context it actually exists in the policy—as it bears directly on the court's obligation to determine if the term "treatment" as used in Question 18(k) is ambiguous. A letter dated August 20, 2001, from Fortis to the Schmidts indicated that Fortis had accepted the Schmidts' application and was extending them health insurance coverage. In part, this letter stated as follows:

> Your contract has been issued based on the statements you made in your Application for Insurance, a copy of which is attached to your contract. *It is important that you again take a few minutes to review this form carefully to make sure it is accurate and complete. Any incorrect statement ... could void your coverage or cause a claim to be denied. If you find an error or missing information on your Application, please advise us in writing immediately.*

In addition to a copy of the Schmidts' filled-out enrollment form, the policy certificate was attached to the letter. The certificate contained a sheet entitled "Definitions" which contains the language at issue regarding treatment. [In the reproduced certificate, treatment is defined in the context of "Covered Charges":] "Treatment is the medical or surgical management of a patient. Treatment includes any prescribed service, supply, test, consultation, advice or Prescription Drug." Looking at the language from this perspective it becomes obvious that the term "treatment" was defined only in reference to "Covered Charges." Further, the header explicitly limits the definitions to *"terms used in [the] certificate,"* and not the terms as used in any other portion of the insurance policy, including the enrollment form. Therefore, while it is true that the application for insurance becomes a part of the policy under Iowa law, *see* IOWA CODE § 515.94, in this instance the document clearly reflects that it is defining only the terms in the certificate, and further that the term "treatment" is only defined *in reference to* "Covered Charges." Therefore, the court finds that this definition of "treatment" is limited to the express limitations placed on it by the document—that it is only applicable in determining "Covered Charges" as that term is used in the insurance certificate. Fortis authored all of these documents, so if Fortis wanted to include a definition solely for treatment, it could have done so. At *no place* in either the enrollment form or the policy is the term "treatment" defined independently of any other term. Therefore, the court finds that "treatment," as used in Question 18(k) is undefined.

As "treatment" is undefined by the policy, the court must now determine whether the term is objectively "susceptible to two or more meanings." In answering this question the court must look only to the language present on the enrollment form,[3] which in pertinent part asks: "Within the last 10 years has any proposed insured ... Received treatment for ... Cancer?" Question 18(k) indicates that the "treatment" inquired of must be "for cancer"—therefore, "cancer" is the purpose of the "treatment." However, even in light of this indicator, examining the language as a whole, and giving the words their ordinary meanings, the court concludes that the term "treatment" as used in this context is ambiguous. First, the term "treatment," as used in this context, is reasonably susceptible to at *least* two meanings: the process of treating, and the specific techniques used to treat. In other words, "treatment" could mean either "the act or manner ... of treating ... something" or "the techniques ... customarily applied in a specified situation." MERRIAM WEBSTER'S COLLEGIATE DICTIONARY 1258 (10th ed.1995); *see also* THE AMERICAN HERITAGE COLLEGE DICTIONARY 1440 (3d ed.1997) (breaking down treatment into two similar definitions). Looking only at these two ordinary definitions of "treatment," the term is clearly ambiguous when looked at in conjunction with the indicator "for cancer"—the first speaks to treating "something," while the second speaks to treatment applied "in a specified situation." The context of the use of "treatment" in Question 18(k) reveals nothing about which one of these common, ordinary meanings of the word apply. This ambiguity would allow an interpretation of "treatment," in the context of Question 18(k), to include the entire spectrum of means by which cancer can be managed—ranging from such drastic measures as surgical intervention to alternative therapies such as acupuncture, aromatherapy or meditation. Further, without further guidance, the term "treatment" could refer to any combination of active treatment,

3. In their arguments, the parties point to a variety of sources that they claim should be used in defining "treatment," for instance: (1) Fortis underwriting guidelines; (2) the opinions of Dr. Morton and/or Dr. Hansen; (3) the April 9, 1994, FDA release cautioning against use of tamoxifen for prophylactic treatment; and (4) the orders filed in the *Elliot* case out of the District of Montana. However, *none* of these sources can be addressed in determining *if* a term is ambiguous—that determination comes from a review of the contract language *alone*. To consider any of these sources in answering the threshold question of ambiguity would be an impermissible reliance on extrinsic evidence.

preventative/prophylactic treatment, or treatment received in an adjuvant setting. In fact, if accorded the broad definition Fortis proffers, the term could feasibly include any measure a proposed insured took which any source believed to lower the risk of cancer—even extending to a doctor's recommendation that a person with cancer history eat a diet that includes extra fruit and vegetables in combination with specific vitamin supplements. Clearly, use of the term "treatment" in Question 18(k) is the epitome of ambiguity.

This ambiguity in Question 18(k) as to the meaning of "treatment" must be construed against Fortis. Consequently, the court must employ the definition of "treatment" most favorable to the Schmidts, which is "the act or manner ... of treating ... something" as that is arguably more restrictive than "the techniques ... customarily applied in a specified situation." MERRIAM WEBSTER'S COLLEGIATE DICTIONARY at 1258. However,

> [a]lthough interpreting the meaning of an (sic) insurance policy words is most often an issue of law for the court to decide, the interpretation becomes a question of fact where the interpretation depends on "extrinsic evidence or on a choice among reasonable inferences from extrinsic evidence." Extrinsic evidence refers to evidence other than the words of the policy.

In this case, even according "treatment" the common interpretation most favorable to the insured, inferences from evidence outside of the words of the policy—for example: (1) the deposition testimony of Dr. Morton and Dr. Hansen concerning whether Karen's tamoxifen use constituted treatment, and discussing the statistical modeling results as to whether her tamoxifen use was treating "something" or improved her likelihood of survival; (2) Karen's deposition testimony; (3) Kiel and Baumler's deposition testimony; (4) the April 9, 1994, FDA release cautioning against use of tamoxifen for prophylactic treatment; (5) the Fortis underwriting guidelines; and (6) orders filed in the *Elliot* case out of the District of Montana—are necessary in order to determine if Karen's tamoxifen use falls under this definition of "treatment." This is precisely because, looking purely at the words of the policy, it remains unclear as to what "something" would be in the context of the act or manner ... of treating ... something." MERRIAM WEBSTER'S COLLEGIATE DICTIONARY at 1258. The plaintiffs urge that the "something" would be active cancer, and as it is undisputed that the last time that Karen had detectable residual cancer was March 29, 1989, her tamoxifen use during the relevant ten-year period would not constitute "treatment" as there was nothing to treat. On the other hand, Fortis would assert that "something" could include the recurrence of cancer, or undetectable residual cancer which was treated by Karen's tamoxifen use. These questions of fact cannot be resolved without turning to the extrinsic evidence noted above, therefore a genuine issue of material fact exists as to whether Karen's tamoxifen use constituted "treatment" as used in Question 18(k). As such, both the Schmidts' and Fortis's Motion for Summary Judgment are denied with respect to whether the Schmidts' "no" response was false as to the portion of Question 18(k) inquiring into whether any proposed insured had received "treatment for ... cancer" in the previous ten years.

d. "Consulted with a physician concerning"

i. Arguments of the parties.

The Schmidts vigorously argue that Karen did not "consult[] with a physician concerning ... cancer" between August 9, 1991 and August 9, 2001. In support of their argument that there is no genuine issue of material fact as to whether Karen consulted a physician concerning cancer, the Schmidts rely on Dr. Hansen's Affidavit in which he avers that he "did not consult with Karen regarding her breast cancer or her cancer treatment after 1989." ...

In regard to whether Karen consulted with a physician concerning cancer, Fortis argues that Karen's medical records detailing a host of follow-up procedures—specifically, mammograms, bone scans, blood testing and chest x-rays—during the relevant ten year period constituted consultations with a physician concerning cancer. Fortis asserts that it is of particular import that Karen's regimen of follow-up procedures mirrors the treatment protocols for post-surgery breast cancer patients in 1989. Fortis also contends that despite Karen's assertions to the contrary, her almost annual mammograms were not routine, in that the standard for thirty-five to forty year-old women required only a single baseline mammogram, whereas Karen did not turn forty years-old until 1994—therefore, the mammograms received in 1991 through 1993 could not be routine as they were outside of the standard protocol for her age group. Fortis also points to Karen's five-year survivalship visit with Dr. Hansen on March 25, 1994, and her visit with Dr. Hansen on November 19, 1991, in which Dr. Hansen's notations indicate he consulted an oncologist regarding Karen's questions around her continuing tamoxifen usage, and progress note by Nurse Krones of the Mason City Clinic on February 14, 1997 (which references Dr. Faust) as specific instances in which Karen consulted with a physician about cancer—thereby entitling Fortis to judgment as a matter of law as to the falsity of the Schmidts' response to Question 18(k).

In resistance, the Schmidts predictably argue that the series of physician-patent encounters that Karen had between August 9, 1991, and August 9, 2001, were not consultations about cancer. The Schmidts point out that at no point during this time period did Karen see her oncologist Dr. Silberstein—whose last documented visit with Karen was December 26, 1990. Further, Dr. Hansen stated that while he and Karen "discussed her history of cancer [between August 9, 1991 and August 2001], [they] never actually discussed active cancer." The Schmidts also argue that the language "consult with a physician concerning ... cancer" is *more* ambiguous than the "treatment for ... cancer" language. Citing the Webster's Collegiate Dictionary defining "consult" as "to ask the advice or opinion of," the Schmidts note that a person could ask the advice or opinion of a physician about any number of conditions they currently had, never had, or had in the past—and as such, Fortis's interpretation of this language to include the follow-up tests and five-year survivalship appointment, is unreasonable. The Schmidts argue that an ordinary reading of the language by a layperson would indicate that a person had to actually *have* the condition in order to consult with a doctor about it. Turning to Karen's five-year survivalship checkup with Dr. Hansen on March 15, 1994, the Schmidts argue that the progress note indicates that this was a consultation about the use of tamoxifen, not about cancer. Ultimately, the Schmidts contend that the ambiguity of the phrase "consult with a physician concerning" prevents a finding that the Schmidts "no" answer to Question 18(k) was false as a matter of law—thus, defeating Fortis's motion for summary judgment.

In its reply, Fortis asserts that there is no evidence that the Schmidts understood the phrase "consult with a physician concerning" in the manner in which they claim an ordinary layperson would understand it. Further, Fortis contends that the blood panels, chemical testing, bone scans, chest x-rays and mammograms were conducted to monitor for a recurrence of breast cancer due to Karen's breast cancer history, and Karen discussed the need for her to continue this regimen of testing with Dr. Hansen. Fortis takes issue with the Schmidts' categorization of the five-year survivalship visit with Dr.

Hansen, and reasserts that the purpose was to consult about cancer. Additionally, Fortis finds Karen's "efforts to feign ignorance" as to whether she consulted with physicians concerning cancer during the ten-year period in question are unsupported by the record—which paints her as a proactive and inquisitive patient, demonstrates her knowledge of an increased risk of recurrence due to being estrogen receptor positive, and recounts that she stopped taking tamoxifen of her own volition after learning from a layperson that it was only beneficial for five-years following cancer treatment. Finally, Fortis reiterates that Karen underwent these various procedures (i.e. mammograms, chest x-rays, blood panels, etc.) *only because of* her breast cancer, to monitor recurrence. Fortis points to the fact that the coding on Karen's medical records for these procedures show that they were not part of an annual physical exam, but that they were *in addition* to those normally done at a routine exam. Finally, Fortis argues that the Schmidts have failed to show that the phrase is ambiguous in the context of the enrollment form, and that the plaintiffs have generated no genuine issue of material fact as to this issue.

ii. Analysis.

As before, the court must first look to the pertinent language and determine if it is objectively susceptible to two or more meanings. In this instance, the language in question is: "consulted with a physician concerning ... cancer." In the context of the phrase, "consulted," stemming from "consult," when accorded an ordinary meaning, is defined as "to ask the advice or opinion of." MERRIAM WEBSTER'S COLLEGIATE DICTIONARY 248. This is relatively straightforward standing alone, but when paired with the term "concerning" the interpretation of this language becomes far from clear. "Concerning," when given an ordinary meaning in the context of Question 18(k), could be either "relating to" or "regarding." Which definition is accorded to these terms could significantly alter the meaning of the phrase "consulted with a physician concerning! ... cancer." For example, giving "concerning" the "relating to" interpretation would cause the inquiry to encompass discussion about anything "relating to ... cancer," which, as discussed in conjunction with the "treatment" language above, could encompass the whole spectrum of subjects relating to cancer, cancer risk, cancer prevention and cancer history. On the other hand, according "concerning" the interpretation of "regarding" appears to restrict the scope of the definition from anything even tangentially related to cancer to only those consultations revolving around cancer. Clearly, this language is susceptible to at least two different meanings, it is ambiguous and therefore must be construed against Fortis, and accorded the interpretation most favorable to insured.

In this instance, the most restrictive interpretation of the phrase "consulted with a physician concerning ... cancer" would be that most favorable to Karen. Therefore, according "concerning" the more restrictive interpretation of "regarding," the interpretation most favorable to Karen would be: "ask[ing] the advice or opinion" of a physician "regarding" cancer. MERRIAM WEBSTER'S COLLEGIATE DICTIONARY 238, 248. Though the court has found the phrase ambiguous, and accorded it the interpretation most favorable to the insured, questions of fact requiring analysis of extrinsic evidence still remain. In this case, as before in discussing "treatment," the extrinsic evidence would include the deposition testimony of Karen, Dr. Hansen, Dr. Silberstein and Dr. Morton.

First, does undergoing follow-up procedures such as mammograms, blood panels, chest x-rays, and bone scans constitute "asking the advice or opinion" of a physician merely because it requires a doctor to interpret the results? Further, are these tests "regarding" cancer even if the only purpose of these tests is for the *detection* and *prevention* of cancer? These questions cannot be resolved without turning to extrinsic evidence—

which, in addition to deposition testimony, would include the "special codes" Fortis claims are on Karen's medical records. Turning to the five-year cancer survivalship checkup with Dr. Hansen, the crux of the visit appears to have been Karen's questions regarding the effects of long-term tamoxifen use in light of medical conditions that ran in her family, whether she should continue on tamoxifen, and what other routine-follow up exams she should continue to undergo. Questions remain as to whether this visit, in which Karen and Dr. Hansen discussed her five year cancer survivalship, and the propriety of continued tamoxifen use, was "regarding" cancer. This, too, cannot be resolved without turning to extrinsic evidence. Finally, the court turns to whether the progress note by Nurse Krones of the Mason City Clinic on February 14, 1997 was "regarding" cancer. The progress note indicates that Karen was experiencing a number of gynecological problems and was concerned about these problems in light of her breast cancer history. From the context of the progress note, it appears as though Nurse Krones consulted with Dr. Faust about Karen's medical issues and concerns, and that an appointment was set up with Dr. Faust the following week. Does consultation with a nurse, who in turn consults with a physician amount to "consulting with a physician"? Further, is contact in which the proposed insured's chief complaint is not cancer related, but where the proposed insured voices concern over cancer risks in light of her cancer history "regarding" cancer? Again, these questions of fact cannot be resolved without a review of evidence outside of the words of the policy.

Therefore, although the court has held the phrase "consulted with a physician concerning ... cancer" ambiguous, as interpretation of this phrase depends on "extrinsic evidence or on a choice among reasonable inferences from extrinsic evidence," a genuine issue of material fact precluding summary judgment in favor of either party has been generated. As such, as to whether the Schmidts' "no" response to Question 18(k) was false, both the Schmidts' and Fortis's Motions for Summary Judgment are denied.

4. Question 15

a. The question

Question 15 of the Fortis enrollment form asks for a "yes" or "no" response to the following question:

> Have any of the proposed insureds ever been declined, postponed, charged an extra premium or had a portion of coverage excluded for life, disability, or medical insurance or had such coverage rescinded?

To this question the Schmidts checked "no."

b. Arguments of the parties

Rightfully predicting an argument by Fortis that their "no" response to Question 15 was false, the Schmidts, in their resistance, include an argument as to why their response was truthful. First, the Schmidts point out that it is undisputed that as of the date they filled out the Fortis enrollment form, they had not received any written response from Life Investors regarding the status of their application. In fact, the Schmidts claim that the only written correspondence they received from Life Investors was dated August 30, 2001, and that indicated that Life Investors had been informed of the Schmidts' request to withdraw their application. The only other written response was to Kiel, dated August 10, 2001, which stated that Karen *would be* denied and questioned whether they would like to continue with the application review. The Schmidts contend that there is no evidence that Kiel knew of Karen's denial prior to August 10, 2001. The Schmidts then argue that while the August 10, 2001, letter to Kiel indicates that a decision as to Karen's coverage had been made, that it did not necessarily reflect a final decision on the part of Life Investors. In support of this position, the Schmidts point to the testimony of Debbie Tinker, the Life Investors representative, that the Schmidts could have submitted a request for reconsideration of the decision in which they could have provided additional details regarding Karen's health history—though there was no formal process for doing so at the time. The Schmidts assert that they *chose* to withdraw the application, and that if they had proceeded with the appeal, it was possible that the decision as to Karen would have been reversed. Finally, the Schmidts contend that since the most that can be established from the record is that, prior to August 9, 2001, Kiel received a call from an unidentified Life Investors employee informing him that Karen *would be* denied coverage if they continued the application process, Fortis has not raised any genuine issue of material fact as to the falsity of the Schmidts' "no" response to Question 15.

In its reply, Fortis resists the Schmidts' arguments by focusing on the fact that the option of trying to obtain coverage with Fortis was *not* pursued until *after* the Schmidts and Kiel knew there were problems with the Life Investors application prior to August 10, 2001. Fortis focuses on the language of the August 10, 2001, letter from Life Investors indicating that it is a "second request," as establishing that prior contact with Kiel or Baumler was made in which it was indicated that Karen would be denied. Therefore, by the time the Schmidts completed the Fortis enrollment form on August 9, 2001, they were well aware that Karen could not secure coverage through Life Investors. Fortis discounts the Schmidts' argument that, as they could have appealed, the denial was not final on August 9, 2001, by pointing to the deposition testimony of Life Investors's representative Debbie Tinker that Life Investors considered the decision final, and that the right to appeal did not affect the finality of this decision. Finally, Fortis addresses the Schmidts' argument that the application was withdrawn—claiming that *only the application as to Daniel and daughter Kathryn* was withdrawn as at that point Karen had already been denied. Fortis contends its argument is supported by Baumler's fax to Life Investors requesting withdrawal of the application "due to Daniel's spouse Karen being denied." Therefore, Fortis argues there is no genuine issue of material fact that the Schmidts' "no" response to Question 15 was false, making the Schmidts' representation false as a matter of law and entitling Fortis to equitably rescind the policy.

c. Analysis.

In this instance, the pertinent language at issue is "[h]ave any of the proposed insureds ever been declined, postponed, charged an extra premium or had a portion of coverage excluded for ... medical insurance ... ?" There is no argument that the language of Question 15 is ambiguous, so the only question at this juncture is whether the "no" response was false. In *Rubes v. Mega Life & Health Insurance Co.*, 642 N.W.2d 263 (Iowa 2002), the court made these observations concerning the falsity, and inducement elements:

> An action to rescind a contract is regarded as less severe, and hence less demanding in its proof requirements, than an action at law for damages based on fraud. In an equitable rescission action, it is not the knowledge of falsity that is at issue, but "whether misrepresentations induced the complaining party to contract. As this court stated in Hyler, injecting an "intent to deceive" element in a rescission case would reintroduce the concept of scienter, "making the elimination of this requirement in equity cases illusory."

Therefore, it is not a question of whether Kiel, Baumler or Karen *knew* of the falsity of the response, but only whether the Life Investors application was, objectively, denied.

Rubes, 642 N.W.2d at 270. There is no genuine issue of material fact that the August 10, 2001, letter reflected a *final* decision as to Karen's application:

> Q: Directing your attention [to] ... the August 10, 2001, underwriting status/agent action report, does that document reflect Life Investors' final decision with regard to Karen Schmidt's application for individual health insurance coverage?
>
> A: It reflects the underwriting decision on Karen.
>
> Q: Well, [the August 10, 2001, letter] reflects that Karen will be denied due to health history of breast cancer.
>
> A: That's correct.
>
> Q: Which I understand your testimony to be reflects Life Investors' final decision as to Karen Schmidt. Is that correct?
>
> A: That's correct.
>
> Q: Okay. And my earlier question may have been unclear, but is it your understanding that the application was also submitted on behalf of Daniel Schmidt and their daughter Kathryn Schmidt?
>
> A: That is correct.
>
> Q: Okay. And so had Life Investors yet made a decision on Daniel and Kathryn Schmidt's application?
>
> A: No, they did not.
>
> Q: So, it was just Karen that they had made the decision on?
>
> A: That is correct.
>
> Q: And that decision was to deny her application for individual health coverage?
>
> A: That is correct.

Therefore, as of August 10, 2001, Life Investors had officially denied Karen coverage.... However, this does not answer the question of whether Life Investors's denial of Karen was in effect on August 9, 2001—the date that the Schmidts filled out, signed, and mailed the Fortis application to Midwest Benefits.

In fact, the court finds that a genuine issue of material fact is generated as to whether or not Karen's denial was final as of the date the Schmidts filled out the Fortis Application—August 9, 2001. On one hand, there are facts favoring Fortis's position—namely, the fact that the August 10, 2001, letter mentions that this is a "second request," therefore implying that initial contact regarding the underwriting status of the application had occurred prior to that date. Kiel had no recollection of how Midwest Benefits was initially contacted regarding the underwriting status—but believed it was either by telephone call or fax. Life Investors testified that its normal practice and procedure was to contact the agent via telephone and explain the specific underwriting decision. The procession of events, specifically the fact that the Schmidts prepared an application with Fortis prior to August 10, 2001, viewed in the light most favorable to Fortis, supports the inference that Life Investors did indeed contact Kiel and informed him that Karen would be denied due to her breast cancer history—which spurred the Fortis application. Karen testified that she had received a call from Kiel stating that the Life Investors application was not going to work out, and it was at that time they started pursuing other options.... And, in fact, nothing more was done to try to salvage the Life Investors application. The final fact in favor of Fortis is Baumler's fax to Life Investors on August 28, 2001, which asked Life Investors to discontinue evaluation of the Schmidts' application "due to Daniel's spouse Karen being denied." Drawing all reasonable inferences in Fortis's favor, the plaintiffs are clearly not entitled to judgment as a matter of law that their "no" response to Question 15 was not false.

On the other hand, viewing the facts most favorable to the plaintiffs, a genuine issue of material fact prevents summary judgment in favor of Fortis. While Life Investors's standard practice is to call the agent and inform them of the underwriting decision, Life Investors could not attest to whether such a call was made to Kiel, and if it was, what information was relayed to him. Further, Kiel, Baumler and Karen all testified that the Fortis application wasn't pursued until they knew there was a problem with the Life Investors application, or until they knew that Karen *would be* denied—never that she *had been* denied.... Further, it is undisputed that the Schmidts did not receive any direct correspondence from Life Investors before August 30, 2001, and that Midwest Benefits received only a single written correspondence from Life Investors—the August 10, 2001, letter. Further, though it was not argued by the parties, Baumler's potential knowledge of Karen's denial by Life Investors (as could be inferred from her faxed request to Life Investors to discontinue examining the Schmidts' application due to Karen be denied) could be imputed to Fortis on the basis that Baumler was also an agent under Iowa Code §515.125. Viewing the facts in the light most favorable to the plaintiffs, while it is clear that there was "a problem" with the Life Investors application as of August 9, 2001, there is a genuine issue of material fact as to whether it was denied as to Karen as of that date.

As a genuine issue of material fact as to Karen's denial by Life Investors as of August 9, 2001, is raised when looking at the facts in the light most favorable to either party, both the Schmidts' and Fortis's Motions for Summary Judgment are denied as to the falsity of Schmidts' response to Question 15.

III. Conclusion

For the foregoing reasons, as to Fortis's claim that Loren Kiel and Karen Schmidt acted together to perpetrate a fraud upon Fortis, the Schmidts' Motion for Summary Judgment is granted in part and Fortis's Motion for Summary Judgment is denied in part. As a genuine issue of material fact has been raised as to the falsity of the Schmidts' "no" responses to Question 18(k) and Question 15 of the Fortis enrollment form, which thereby raises a genuine issue of material fact as to whether Fortis's rescission of the policy was justified, both the Schmidts' Motion for Summary Judgment and Fortis's Motion for Summary Judgment are denied in part. Finally, as the plaintiffs' breach of contract claim is predicated on a finding that Fortis wrongfully rescinded the policy, summary judgment on that claim is likewise inappropriate and both the Schmidts' Motion for Summary Judgment and Fortis's Motion for Summary Judgment are denied in part.

Therefore, the ultimate disposition of the cross-motions for summary judgment is that the Schmidts' Motion for Summary Judgment is granted as to Fortis's claim of fraud upon the principal, and denied in all other respects. Fortis's Motion for Summary Judgment is denied in its entirety.

Notes & Questions

1. As noted in the text, the study done by Mark Hall is one of the few attempts to empirically analyze the incidence of genetic underwriting by health plans and the impact of antidiscrimination laws. Hall concludes that presymptomatic genetic test information is not accessed or sought by health plans at the present time. He comes to this

conclusion after surveying genetic counselors, insurance regulators, insurance brokers, and insurance industry sources, finding that there is virtually no genetic discrimination with respect to access to health insurance. This result is consistent with the nature of the health plan market, which can be characterized as volatile, focused on near-term medical illness and losses, and predicated on group not individualized underwriting. Although health insurance antidiscrimination statutes may be a cure for a non-existent disease, Hall posits that perhaps the value of these laws may be in their psychological impact and validation of social norms. Do you agree? If so, in a world of limited resources, are the energy and efforts expended on these positive effects justifiable, given the lack of legislative effort directed at solving the problem of the uninsured? If you were a legislative aide to a state legislator, where would you place genetic discrimination on his or her list of priority items?

In Chapter 3, you read the Rothstein/Anderlik short article defining genetic discrimination. You also read of the Burlington Northern case in which the employer surreptitiously tested blood samples for a rare genetic causation of a very common medical problem, carpal tunnel syndrome. It seems obvious that Burlington Northern did not appreciate that only one in 2500–5000 individuals with carpal tunnel will have the genetic HNPP disorder. Given the difficulties in defining genetic discrimination and the even greater difficulties in understanding genetic science, do you think that health plans and health insurers are likely to make "mistakes" similar to that made by Burlington Northern? Is antidiscrimination legislation the best way to guard against misuse or misinterpretation of genetic information? What other public policy options exist and how might you go about pursuing and implementing them?

For additional reading on genetic discrimination, its definition, and public policy implications, see Frederick Levy & Joseph F. Lawler, *The Potential Impact of Genetic Sequencing on the American Health Care System*, 6 J. HEALTH CARE L. & POL'Y 203 (2003); Jennifer S. Geetter, *Coding for Change: The Power of the Human Genome to Transform the American Health Insurance System*, 28 AM. J.L. & MED. 1 (2002); Natalie E. Zindorf, *Discrimination in the 21st Century: Protecting the Privacy of Genetic Information in Employment and Insurance*, 36 TULSA L.J. 703 (2001); Nathalie Smith, *The Right to Genetic Privacy? Are We Unlocking the Secrets of the Genome Only to Risk Insurance and Employment Discrimination?*, 2000 UTAH L. REV. 705 (2000); Deborah A. Stone, *The Implications of the Human Genome Project for Access to Health Insurance*, *in* THE HUMAN GENOME PROJECT AND THE FUTURE OF HEALTH CARE 133, 138 (Thomas H. Murray, et al., eds. 1996); Deborah Hellman, *What Makes Genetic Discrimination Exceptional?*, 29 AM. J. L. & MED. 77 (2003); Colin S. Diver & Jane Maslow Cohen, *Genophobia: What is Wrong with Genetic Discrimination?*, 149 U. Pa. L. Rev. 1439 (2001).

2. In *Schmidt v. Fortis*, the story of the Schmidt's search for coverage demonstrates the difficulty in obtaining individual coverage. Obtaining this type of health care policy will require a detailed health history, although testing and physical examinations usually are not required. Nevertheless, the process for obtaining individual coverage is in marked contrast to obtaining coverage through an employer, where health information is virtually irrelevant to coverage status. Karen Schmidt believed, with good reason, she would not qualify for health care coverage if she revealed her history of breast cancer, use of Tamoxifen, and ongoing surveillance for recurrence of her cancer. Does exclusion of patients like Karen Schmidt evidence "fair" or unfair discrimination? Is a history of breast cancer at age thirty-five a significant issue from an actuarial risk standpoint? When Fortis rescinds Karen Schmidt's coverage for a past history of breast cancer and treatment for same, are they acting on the basis of her phenotype or genotype?

In this case, once the knowledge of Karen Schmidt's health history becomes known, the insurer (Fortis) rescinds her insurance. Her health history becomes known through her choosing to pursue BRCA testing in 2002, just eleven months after she had obtained an individual health care coverage policy. She argues that they have acted in bad faith and breached their contract by rescinding her coverage. They argue that she and the insurance broker have committed fraud by concealing her history of cancer, treatment with Tamoxifen, and increased surveillance for detection of cancer recurrence.

As the court struggles through this case, it considers the language used in the application process and policy. When considering Question 18(k) in the application, the court notes that Karen Schmidt had not been diagnosed with cancer during the "window" of ten years addressed in the question. However, it is the "received treatment" part of the question that is contentious. Schmidt answered this question "no," despite that fact that she was taking prophylactic Tamoxifen during this time period. Fortis argues that this qualifies as treatment. Schmidt argues that she did not perceive it as treatment because she did not have active cancer during the time period. At issue is the meaning of the term "treatment." In this case, the court follows classic contract law with respect to "ambiguous" terms—that is, terms that a reasonable person might find to have more than one meaning. Although Fortis has defined the term in the policy itself with respect to "Covered Charges," it had not defined it elsewhere in the policy, the application, or enrollment materials. Thus, the term is essentially undefined and susceptible to two or more meanings. The court resorts to lay dictionaries in determining that "treatment" is indeed an ambiguous term. Such ambiguities are typically construed against the drafter under the theory that the drafter was in the best position to provide clarity and should bear the costs of failing to do so. *See, e.g., Kunin v. Benefit Trust Life Ins. Co.*, 910 F.2d 534, 539 (9th Cir. 1990); *see also Frendeis v. Blue Cross Blue Shield*, 873 F. Supp. 1153 (N.D. Ill. 1995) (ambiguous contracts should be construed to benefit the insured); *DiDomenico v. Employers Coop. Indus. Trust*, 676 F. Supp. 903 (N.D. Ind. 1987) (ambiguous terms in medical plans should be interpreted in favor of the policyholder). *See generally* Eileen M. Dacey, *Introduction to Insurance Law and Concepts*, 629 PLI/Lit 9 (April, 2000) (doctrine of *contra proferentem* requires ambiguities in insurance contracts to be construed against the drafter of the contract, which is normally the insurer). For an interesting public policy counterpoint to the justice issues inherent in the doctrine of *contra proferentem, see* David S. Miller, *Insurance as Contract: The Argument for Abandoning the Ambiguity Doctrine*, 88 Colum. L. Rev. 1849 (1988).

The court in *Schmidt v. Fortis* goes on to look at the phrase "consult [] with a physician concerning ... cancer" in much the same way and finds that phrase equally ambiguous. The court declines to grant summary judgment for either party on these issues, leaving them to be determined at trial.

A slightly different question arises with respect to Schmidt's veracity in answering the question as to whether she had previously been denied coverage by another carrier. Here, while there is no ambiguity about the terms, there is ambiguity about the facts. It is unclear whether Schmidt knew that Life Investors had rejected her application, when they filed their application with Fortis. It appears that Schmidt withdrew her application to Life Investors before a denial was issued. Thus the court is willing to grant summary judgment for the Schmidts with respect to the fraud claim made by Fortis. For a collection of cases and discussion of responsibility and legal consequences of false statements by an insured or an insurer's agent/broker, *see* William H. Danne, Jr., *Modern Status of Rules Regarding Materiality and Effect of False Statement by Insurance Applicant as to Previous Insurance Cancellation or Rejections*, 66 A.L.R.3d 749 (2005) (annotation of cases where an insurance applicant has denied previous rejection and role of materiality of the false statement in right of insurer to rescind); B. H. Glenn, *Insured's Responsibility for False Answers Inserted by Insurer's Agents in Application Following Correct Answers by Insured, or Incorrect Answers Suggested by Agent*, 26 A.L.R.3d 6 (2005) (discussing rule and cases holding that an insurer is responsible for a false answer which its agent inserted in the application).

3. Health Plan Coverage for Genetic Tests, Technologies, and Related Health Care Services

A separate, and perhaps more timely and realistic, concern is access to coverage and reimbursement of genetic tests, technologies, and related health care services. Such tests are likely to confront questions as to medical necessity, investigational and/or experimental nature, and clinical utility in terms of improved outcome. Some of these issues are beginning to be addressed in the recently released Draft Report from the Secretary's Advisory Committee on Genetics, Health and Society.

Coverage and Reimbursement of Genetic Tests and Services: Draft Report of the Secretary's Advisory Committee on Genetics Health and Society

Apr. 2005, 19–34

Every public program and private health insurance plans outlines the scope of services the payer will cover, the circumstances under which the payer will reimburse, and any cost sharing components (e.g., deductibles, co payments) or coverage limits. Whether a particular treatment, service, test, drug, etc., is covered under a contract is dependent on several key factors: consumer or purchaser demand; state and federal law (e.g., mandated benefits or Medicare/Medicaid laws); experimental/investigational status; whether there is sufficient evidence supporting the safety and effectiveness of the requested service; and whether such service is medically necessary given the insured's particular circumstances.

Coverage Decisions

Overview of Coverage Decision Making. Generally speaking, there are three tiers to coverage decision-making (although the term "coverage decision" generally refers to the second step). First, broad benefit categories (e.g., diagnostic testing, preventive services) are chosen to serve as an initial framework defining which services are generally covered. Second, decisions are made about which specific services will or will not be covered (e.g., BRCA1/2 testing) under these broad categories as well as the circumstances under which a service will be covered (e.g., strong family history, age). Third, during claims processing or a pre-authorization process, if the broad benefit category is included in the plan member's benefits package, and if the specific service is covered or not excluded from coverage, a determination is made about whether the individual circumstances of the plan member meet the coverage criteria. If the circumstances meet the coverage criteria, then the service is generally covered.

As new information becomes available and as new tests or services are developed, new benefit categories may be added, new policies may be issued granting or excluding coverage for a particular service, or modifications may be made to existing coverage policies. Member or employer requests, new state mandates, or fiscal considerations can prompt or influence such decisions. Benefits changes also are strongly influenced by the actions of CMS and large health plans.

Coverage decision making is also initiated when a claim, pre-authorization application, or appeal is submitted requesting coverage for a particular service for which coverage is not explicitly specified or when the criteria for coverage are not clearly defined. Private health insurance plans also may make exceptions to their policies on a case-by-case basis depending on individual circumstances.

Private Plan Coverage of Genetic Tests and Services. Since few private health insurance plans make their coverage policies publicly available, it is difficult to assess which genetic tests and services tend to be covered and which ones are not covered as well as the circumstances for and extent of coverage. Of the coverage policies that are available, most cover genetic testing for chromosomal abnormalities, prenatal and neonatal diagnosis, and, in some cases, preimplantation genetic diagnosis in situations of advanced maternal age, suspected fetal anomaly, history of multiple miscarriage or developmental problems. Diagnostic genetic testing for rare diseases is usually covered under general policies for genetic tests. Some health plans have policies for specific conditions, such as hereditary cancer testing, cystic fibrosis, Tay-Sachs disease, and hereditary hemochromatosis. Other policies specify non-coverage, such as genetic testing for Alzheimer's disease, which is considered by some health plans to be experimental.

Based on the few coverage policies that are publicly available, genetic tests and services are typically covered under the following circumstances, as appropriate:

- The patient has current signs and/or symptoms (i.e., test is being used for diagnostic purposes)
- Conventional diagnostic procedures are inconclusive
- The patient has risk factors or a particular family history that indicate a genetic cause
- The patient meets defined criteria that place them at high genetic risk for the condition
- The test is not considered experimental or investigational
- The test is performed by a CLIA-certified laboratory
- The test result will directly influence the treatment or disease management of the covered member
- In some cases, testing is accompanied by pre-and post-test counseling

Generally, genetic testing is not covered for:

- Population screening without a personal or family history, with the exception of newborn screening and preconception or prenatal carrier screening for cystic fibrosis;
- Informational purposes;
- Testing of minors for adult-onset conditions;
- A relative of a plan member who is not also a plan member unless: 1) the genetic test results are necessary for the medical care of the plan member, and 2) the relative can provide evidence of coverage denial from his/her health insurance plan.

Evidence-based Coverage Decisions. Today's health care market (e.g., need for cost containment) and legal environment (e.g., medical liability) as well as the influx of new technologies and procedures available for clinical use have required health care payers to be much more stringent about what tests and services they will cover and under what conditions they will reimburse. Health insurance plans have emphasized evidence-based coverage decision-making as a way to decide which technologies and services are appropriate to cover.

Role of Technology Assessments. Technology assessments have an important role in coverage decision making. They involve an evaluation of existing evidence to ascertain whether the test or service has been found to be safe, effective and appropriate for coverage and reimbursement. Some health insurance plans and purchasers have established formal processes for conducting these technology assessments, whereas others utilize less formal review processes performed by their medical directors or human resources staff, for instance. Still others rely on technology assessments conducted by other groups such as Blue Cross Blue Shield Association, ECRI, or Hayes Inc. These technology assessments are critical to ensuring that coverage decisions are based on sound evidence.

Blue Cross Blue Shield's Technology Evaluation Center (TEC) systematically evaluates the clinical effectiveness and appropriateness of new technologies. Their technology assessments and review criteria have been used industry-wide to make coverage decisions.

TEC uses the following criteria for assessing new technologies:

- When applicable, the technology must have final approval from the appropriate governmental regulatory bodies.
- The scientific evidence must permit conclusions concerning the effect of the technology on health outcomes. Specifically:
    - Evidence should consist of well-designed and well-conducted investigations that are published in peer-reviewed journals. The quality of the body of studies and the consistency of results are considered in evaluating the evidence.
    - The evidence should demonstrate that the technology can measure or alter the physiological changes related to disease, injury, illness or condition. In addition, there should be evidence or a convincing argument based on established medical facts that such measurement or alteration affects health outcomes.
    - Opinions and evaluations by national medical associations, expert panels, or other technology evaluation bodies are considered in the context of the quality of the supporting evidence and rationale.
- The technology must improve the net health outcome (i.e., the technology's beneficial effects on health outcomes should outweigh any harmful effects).
- The technology must be at least as beneficial as any established alternative.
- The improvement must be attainable outside the investigational setting when used under the usual conditions of medical practice.

Evidence-based Coverage of Genetic Tests. For genetic tests, evidence-based coverage decision making involves assessing existing data on a test's analytical and clinical validity and clinical utility that is relevant to the populations the health insurance plan serves (e.g., for Medicare, data on individuals age 65 and older should be available). Coverage decision making also involves consideration of other factors such as the test's safety and effectiveness, the test's benefits, risks, cost, and impact on health outcomes in relation to established alternatives, the subsequent costs involved in responding to the test results, and patient preference.

Some genetic tests that currently are available clinically are supported by little or no clinical data and, thus, may not provide accurate or interpretable results. An historically lesser focus on translational research compared to basic research has hindered the collection and analysis of clinical data to satisfy evidence standards for coverage decisions. If coverage decisions are based on insufficient data, the economic and personal costs may be high.

The novelty and predictive nature of genetic tests present additional challenges to the standards traditionally used to assess the evidence base for coverage decision making. These challenges are described below.

Informational Utility. Evidence-based coverage decision making favors technologies and services that can demonstrate improved health outcomes. Some genetic tests for conditions that lack therapeutic and preventive options have difficulty meeting this criterion. Even though there are not therapeutic options, many people may find this information to be useful for purposes of family and estate planning and preparing for long-term care needs.

Such tests raise the question of whether the information provided is significant and meaningful enough in a health care context to warrant coverage by payers as well as broader questions about the appropriateness of using finite health care resources and the extent to which health insurance coverage should extend beyond the role of health maintenance and promotion. These questions will need to be explored in any discussion of genetic testing since many presymptomatic genetic tests will become available in the absence of effective clinical interventions, either preventive or therapeutic.

Short-run Costs, Long-run Savings. For private health insurance plans, because plan members change plans at fairly frequent intervals, coverage for preventive services can be difficult to rationalize from an economic standpoint since the cost savings may not accrue to the plan that paid for the service. This challenge is of particular concern to health insurance plans when coverage for the test throughout the health insurance market is minimal. Also, this concern is more prevalent when the test is first introduced into clinical practice and the extent to which the market will cover it is uncertain. This concern lessens when coverage becomes more widespread. Health insurance plans who cover such tests and services need to calculate whether it makes economic sense to provide genetic tests and follow-up care even though they do not stand to reap future savings (in effect, they are sparing a future health insurance plan from the costs associated with treating the illness at a later date).

Amassing Sufficient Evidence for Translation of Genetic Tests into Clinical Use. Many genetic tests may be excluded from coverage due to the "experimental" nature of the technology or service and insufficient evidence. Like many tests, determining when genetic tests have moved beyond a research phase, and thus are no longer experimental, can be difficult because their transition from research to clinical use is not clear-cut. This is a particular problem for genetic tests for rare diseases. The low prevalence of rare diseases makes it particularly difficult to establish clinical validity and amass sufficient data to achieve statistically significant results that satisfy evidence standards. In addition, scientific interest in any given rare disease is also a factor affecting data collection (and access to research testing). A specific rare disease may be studied by only one investigator in the country or world. Insufficient funding for the study of rare diseases can also impede the amassing of adequate data.

Role of Cost-Effectiveness Data. Cost-effectiveness data, when available and appropriate, are one piece of information among many that health insurance plans can use in making evidence-based coverage decisions. Health insurance plans' interest in economic data is especially heightened for expensive, novel tests, when downstream follow-up or treatment costs are substantial, or when several similar products are available. Genetic tests have not yet had a significant enough impact on health plan budgets to be a priority for economic evaluations; however, as utilization of pharmacogenetic tests and genetic tests for common diseases becomes more widespread and drives consumption of more resources, interest in cost-effectiveness data for genetic tests is likely to intensify.

Cost-effectiveness data can be particularly useful in supporting coverage decisions for genetic tests and services that are used to predict increased genetic susceptibility to disease and to prevent disease occurrence. Detecting an individual's disease risk before symptoms develop or progress can be beneficial if measures can be taken to prevent or delay disease onset or to minimize the severity of symptoms. Although covering a genetic test or service will generally increase overall health care spending, from a societal standpoint, preventive services can be beneficial for their potential to offset other health care costs. Preventive services are covered by most managed care organizations because they are valued by healthy potential plan members and their per-person cost is relatively low compared to per-person disease treatment costs.

There are several characteristics that are important to consider when conducting economic evaluations of genetic tests:

- Genotype-phenotype association (clinical validity)—there should be sufficient evidence of an association between the gene variant and clinically relevant outcomes
- Prevalence of the gene variant—the prevalence of a gene variant will have a significant impact on the cost-effectiveness of a genetic test and should be described for the patient population of interest
- Outcome characteristics—the severity of the outcomes associated with the gene variant should be considered, potentially including patient quality of life, mortality, and economic costs
- Intervention for the variant group (clinical utility)—an intervention guided by the genetic test results should be specified and the risk reduction for that intervention quantified, preferably as measured by the attributable risk reduction.
- Test characteristics—the test sensitivity and specificity (analytical validity) should be considered as well as direct and indirect costs associated with the test, including induced costs such as additional provider visits

Thus far, relatively few cost-effectiveness analyses have been conducted for genetic tests. Of those that have been performed, results have been mixed. Such results have often been sensitive to the prevalence of the genetic mutation in the population, disease characteristics, severity of outcomes, treatment costs and length, and accuracy of the genetic test. The dearth of favorable cost analyses and deficiencies in the availability of data to inform such studies may be limiting health plans' willingness to consider coverage of genetic tests and services.

Considering cost-effectiveness data as part of coverage decision-making has been controversial but is currently being considered in some areas of health policy-making. For example, the U.S. Preventive Services Task Force has begun reviewing published cost-effectiveness studies as part of its development of recommendations for clinical preventive services. Appropriately incorporating cost considerations in coverage decision-making requires answering hard questions about how cost-effectiveness data ought to affect decisions and what threshold of cost-effectiveness is appropriate

Role of Consumer Demand. Despite the emphasis on evidence-based coverage decision making, consumer demand has been shown to also exert influence over coverage decisions. In instances where consumer demand is strong, health insurance plans have responded by reversing their decisions even when the evidence to support coverage was weak or non-existent. With regard to genetic tests, direct-to-consumer advertising for such tests may be having an impact on consumer demand, especially given greater patient access to health information through the internet and other media.

Evidence Base for Genetic Counseling Services. The value and effectiveness of genetic counseling services have been measured several ways in the literature. Various studies have shown increased knowledge, lower costs as a result of more appropriate use of genetic tests, and higher rates of risk identification as some of the outcomes of genetic counseling services. Genetic counseling services provided by non-physician providers also can lead to cost containment since non-physician providers typically charge 20 to 50 percent less than physicians.

Influence of Medicare on Private Plans. As the largest provider of health insurance in the U.S., Medicare's decisions are important to and monitored closely by private sector insurance plans. When Medicare decides to cover a service or test, the private market very often follows suit. It is not clear whether this reliance on Medicare's decision making is appropriate with respect to genetic tests. Genetic tests are often used for preventive purposes and can be used to inform reproductive decision-making and life planning. Many, if not most, hereditary diseases will manifest prior to age 65. For these reasons, the utility of many genetic tests and services (including predictive and predisposition genetic tests and genetic counseling) in the Medicare population is not straightforward. Since the patient population is a relevant factor in coverage decision making, it may not be optimal for the private sector to determine its coverage policies based on Medicare policy for genetic tests and services. Perhaps in realizing that Medicare policy may not be the most appropriate model, some health plans have not waited for Medicare's assessment prior to covering a genetic test or service.

Medicare Coverage

Although Medicare faces many of the same challenges as private health insurance plans, there are several that are unique to or experienced differently by the government program, including how coverage decisions are made and what services can be considered for coverage.

Role of Congress. When Medicare was established in 1965, Congress broadly outlined the scope of benefits that were covered by the program.... Congress continues to have a role in defining the scope of benefits, as evidenced by the recent addition of prescription drug benefits.

Role of the Centers for Medicare & Medicaid Services. The Centers for Medicare & Medicaid Services (CMS) is responsible for interpreting and implementing Medicare law. More specifically, the agency determines whether specific services fall within the Congressionally defined benefit categories and decides whether to add a service to the scope of benefits. CMS also has a role in establishing and implementing policies that guide coverage decisions.

Medicare Coverage Advisory Committee. When a service to be considered for coverage is the subject of significant scientific, medical or public controversy, has the potential to have a major impact on the health of beneficiaries and/or the Medicare program itself, or raises important social, legal or ethical issues, CMS will seek the assistance of the Medicare Coverage Advisory Committee for additional expertise and public input.

Local Coverage Determinations. Medicare coverage decisions are made both at the local and national level, though the majority of Medicare coverage policy decisions are made by the 36 local contractors. This approach allows Medicare to be responsive to geographic variations in clinical practice and beneficiary needs and to extend coverage to new tests and services more rapidly than the national coverage process. Local coverage determinations (LCDs) can also help manufacturers collect necessary evidence to support a national coverage determination (NCD). LCDs are primarily based on expert medical opinion and empirical evidence. They apply only to the area that the contractor serves and must adhere to national statutes and regulations.

National Coverage Determinations. NCDs are made at the federal level and apply to all beneficiaries and carriers. National coverage review processes can be initiated internally within CMS or through a formal request from a member of the public. A review process may be initiated internally for many reasons, including if:

1) There are conflicting LCDs;

2) The service represents a significant medical advance with no comparable covered service;

3) There is question about the service's medical effectiveness or about appropriate administration of the service;

4) The service is covered but widely held to be obsolete or ineffective; or

5) There are concerns about over- or underutilization.

Impact of National-Local Decisionmaking Process. Although the current combination of national and local systems used by Medicare for making coverage decisions is intended to maximize regional flexibility, this bifurcated system can create impediments to securing coverage in certain circumstances. Variations in coverage policies can cause confusion and engender a sense of inequity among Medicare beneficiaries. Also, entering into the national coverage review process is not without risk in that the process can result in a non-coverage or limited coverage decision. In such cases, the NCD pre-empts any existing LCDs for the technology or service and prevents implementation of future LCDs. Also, Medicare decisions are closely followed by private health plans, so non-coverage decisions can also affect coverage by private health plans. Furthermore, while it is possible to appeal a non-coverage decision, it is an extremely lengthy process with multiple requirements.

FDA Approval Requirement. In order to be considered for coverage, tests under the purview of the Food and Drug Administration (FDA) must be FDA-approved. In the case of laboratory-developed genetic tests, which are not subject to FDA pre-market review, this criterion is not applicable. Genetic test kits that are packaged and sold commercially, on the other hand, are subject to FDA review and must be proven to be safe and effective for clinical use before CMS will consider coverage.

Reasonable and Necessary Requirement. Tests and services also must be shown to be "reasonable and necessary" for the diagnosis and treatment of illness or injury or to improve the functioning of a malformed body member. While there is no statutory or regulatory definition of reasonable and necessary, CMS has interpreted the phrase to require that the item or service should, at a minimum, improve net health outcome for Medicare beneficiaries who would receive the item or service. To reach a conclusion, CMS uses standard principles of evidence-based medicine, which requires a thorough evaluation of relevant clinical evidence to determine whether or not the evidence is of sufficient quality to support a finding of reasonable and necessary. The assessment of clinical evidence is divided into three stages:

1) Quality of the individual studies;

2) Relevance of findings from individual studies to the Medicare population; and

3) Overarching conclusions that can be drawn from the body of the evidence on the direction and magnitude of the technology's risks and benefits.

Possible Outcomes of Coverage Decision-making Process. The following are possible outcomes of the policy decision-making process:

1) A national coverage decision is issued with limitations on coverage;

2) A national coverage decision is issued with no limits on coverage;

3) A national non-coverage decision is issued precluding local contractors from making payment; or

4) No national decision is issued, leaving coverage to the discretion of the local contractor.

Medicare Coverage of Genetic Tests. Of the approximately 274 national coverage decisions issued by CMS, only one relates to genetic tests and services—cytogenetic analyses for monitoring acute leukemia, myelodysplasia, and congenital abnormalities. A few local Medicare coverage policies have been developed for HER-2/*neu* and BRCA testing. However, for BRCA testing in the absence of signs, symptoms, or personal history of the disease, most local contractors do not cover the test because they consider it to be a screening test, which CMS has interpreted not to be a statutory benefit.

Screening Exclusion. In order for Medicare to cover a service or technology, it must fall within one of the statutorily authorized benefit categories. Items and services that do not fit within one of the benefit categories prescribed by Congress are not reimbursable.

CMS has a long-standing policy that states that "tests that are not reasonable and necessary for the diagnosis or treatment of an illness or injury are not covered" and more specifically, that "tests for screening purposes that are performed in the absence of signs, symptoms, complaints, or personal history of disease or injury are not covered *except as explicitly authorized by statute*." This policy is largely based on an interpretation of statutory language that includes coverage of expenses that are "reasonable and necessary for the diagnosis of illness or injury or to improve the functioning of a malformed body member" and that excludes coverage of expenses "for routine physical checkups, eyeglasses, or eye examination, ... hearing aids or examination." The preventive screening tests that Medicare does cover have been legislatively authorized by an act of Congress on a service-by-service basis.

Application of Screening Exclusion to Genetic Tests. Since predictive and predispositional genetic tests are considered to be screening tests performed in the absence of signs, symptoms, complaints, or personal history of disease or injury, they are not covered under Medicare statute. Diagnostic genetic tests, on the other hand, can be covered under Medicare because they are performed in the presence of signs and symptoms of disease. Pharmacogenetic tests that are performed in the presence of signs, symptoms, or a personal history of disease or adverse drug reactions could be covered under

Medicare. However, it is not clear whether pharmacogenomic testing using microarrays (e.g., Roche's CYP450 AmpliChip) to test several different drug-metabolizing genes for a large variety of single nucleotide polymorphisms (SNPs) at one time would be covered since these genes and SNPs may not all be informative with respect to the treatment of the disease at hand. Pharmacogenomic testing used as a screening tool (in the absence of signs, symptoms, personal history, or complaints of disease) to help guide drug therapy decisions probably would not be covered under Medicare.

Application of Screening Exclusion to Genetic Counseling Services. Reimbursement by Medicare for genetic counseling is also limited by the program's screening exclusion. Much of genetic counseling involves discussions with patients who have a strong family history of disease; however, family history of disease does not meet Medicare's reasonable and necessary criterion. Therefore, Medicare does not cover genetic counseling accompanying a predictive or predisposition genetic test in the absence of signs, symptoms, or personal history of disease.

Increasing Receptiveness to Coverage of Preventive Services. Recent discussions in both Congress and throughout HHS suggest that policy makers may be growing more receptive to the idea that the Medicare program should broaden its coverage of preventive services. In the past two decades, Congress has authorized Medicare coverage for several screening tests and services (e.g., mammography). The enactment of the Medicare Prescription Drug, Modernization, and Improvement Act of 2003 reflects an increasing focus on prevention. Congress also authorized several demonstration projects in disease management. Given the potential role for preventive andlor diagnostic genetic tests in disease management, there may be an opportunity to include them in these ongoing demonstration projects.

Medicaid Coverage

Medicaid Coverage of Genetic Tests and Services. The federal government mandates that certain benefits be provided to Medicaid recipients, and states have discretion to cover additional benefits that reflect its specific population's needs. With the exception of newborn screening and follow-up, which is state mandated, coverage of genetic tests and services are an optional benefit. Limited data have been gathered on the extent of state Medicaid coverage of genetic tests and services, and states' Medicaid statutes are often broadly defined, making it difficult to determine with any certainty the extent to which genetic tests and services are covered under Medicaid.

State Variation. Because states are responsible for making coverage decisions for genetic tests and services, significant heterogeneity in Medicaid coverage across states can result. Such heterogeneity may constitute a significant source of disparate access to genetic tests and services, especially since Medicaid recipients may not have other available sources of health insurance or be able to pay for care out-of-pocket.

Revenues and the political climate are two factors that can affect a state's decisions to cover genetic tests and services. The size of a state's revenue stream and tax base can affect its ability to offer coverage for new medical technologies, including genetic tests, under Medicaid. States with higher tax rates and more generous welfare benefits may be more likely to cover new genetic tests and services under Medicaid. Coverage decisions in some states also may be affected by the fact that genetic tests are used for reproductive decision-making or family planning, and thereby are seen by some as tests that can lead to pregnancy termination. As of May 2004, 23 states use their own funds to cover abortion services under Medicaid (use of federal funds for such services is prohibited). If coverage for genetic tests bearing upon reproductive decision-making follows the same pattern, access to such tests within the Medicaid population would be similarly uneven.

State Budgets. Unlike the Federal government, which can legally operate with a deficit, by state law or custom, all 50 states balance their budgets at the end of their fiscal year. States cannot create money in the way the Federal government can and as such their tax revenues primarily determine spending levels. This key distinction in fiscal management translates into major differences in how Medicare and Medicaid operate. Economic difficulties since 2001 have affected most states, and their budgets have been extremely constrained as a result. As a means-tested welfare program, Medicaid represents possibly the largest source of pressure on state budgets. Across the board, Medicaid expenditures account for approximately 21 percent of all state spending. In times of fiscal difficulty, states often reduce Medicaid expenditures by limiting coverage or payment rates in order to balance their budgets.

In contrast to Medicare, whose NCDs guarantee coverage for a service from that point forward (unless it is subsequently modified), Medicaid benefits that go beyond the federal requirements can be scaled back or dropped at any time by states, and eligibility requirements can be made more stringent. The balanced budget mandate creates instability in the level of coverage states can provide for health services and tests. Even if a state decides to add a new genetic test or service to its benefit package one year, it could be dropped the next. States' fiscal policy thus makes it extremely difficult to secure access over the long term to new tests and services for the Medicaid population.

Katskee v. Blue Cross/Blue Shield of Nebraska

515 N.W.2d 645 (Neb. 1994)

White, Justice.

...

In January 1990, upon the recommendation of her gynecologist, Dr. Larry E. Roffman, appellant consulted with Dr. Henry T. Lynch regarding her family's history of breast and ovarian cancer, and particularly her health in relation to such a history. After examining appellant and investigating her family's medical history, Dr. Lynch diagnosed her as suffering from a genetic condition known as breast-ovarian carcinoma syndrome. Dr. Lynch then recommended that appellant have a total abdominal hysterectomy and bilateral salpingo-oophorectomy, which involves the removal of the uterus, the ovaries, and the fallopian tubes. Dr. Roffman concurred in Dr. Lynch's diagnosis and agreed that the recommended surgery was the most medically appropriate treatment available.

After considering the diagnosis and recommended treatment, appellant decided to have the surgery. In preparation for the surgery, appellant filed a claim with Blue Cross/Blue Shield. Both Drs. Lynch and Roffman wrote to Blue Cross/Blue Shield and explained the diagnosis and their basis for recommending the surgery. Initially, Blue Cross/Blue Shield sent a letter to appellant and indicated that it might pay for the surgery. Two weeks before the surgery, Dr. Roger Mason, the chief medical officer for Blue Cross/Blue Shield, wrote to appellant and stated that Blue Cross/Blue Shield would not cover the cost of the surgery. Nonetheless, appellant had the surgery in November 1990.

Appellant filed this action for breach of contract, seeking to recover $6,022.57 in costs associated with the surgery. Blue Cross/Blue Shield filed a motion for summary judgment. The district court granted the motion. It found that there was no genuine issue of material fact and that the policy did not cover appellant's surgery. Specifically, the court stated that (1) appellant did not suffer from cancer, and although her high-risk condition warranted the surgery, it was not covered by the policy; (2) appellant did not have a bodily illness or disease which was covered by the policy; and (3) under the terms of the policy, Blue Cross/Blue Shield reserved the right to determine what is medically necessary. Appellant filed a notice of appeal to the Nebraska Court of Appeals, and on our motion, we removed the case to the Nebraska Supreme Court.

Appellant contends that the district court erred in finding that no genuine issue of material fact existed and granting summary judgment in favor of appellee.

...

In reviewing an order granting summary judgment, the appellate court views the evidence in a light most favorable to the nonmoving party and gives that party the benefit of all reasonable inferences deducible from the evidence.

The substantive issues raised in this appeal are governed by the rule that the interpretation and construction of an insurance contract ordinarily involve questions of law in connection with which an appellate court has an obligation to reach conclusions independent of the determinations made by the court below.

Blue Cross/Blue Shield contends that appellant's costs are not covered by the insurance policy. The policy provides coverage for services which are medically necessary. The policy defines "medically necessary" as follows:

> The services, procedures, drugs, supplies or Durable Medical Equipment provided by the Physician, Hospital or other health care provider, in the diagnosis or *treatment of the Covered Person's Illness*, Injury, or Pregnancy, which are:
>
> 1. *Appropriate for the symptoms and diagnosis of the patient's Illness*, Injury or Pregnancy; and
>
> 2. Provided in the most appropriate setting and at the most appropriate level of services[;] and
>
> 3. Consistent with the standards of good medical practice in the medical community of the State of Nebraska; and
>
> 4. Not provided primarily for the convenience of any of the following:
>
> a. the Covered Person;
>
> b. the Physician;
>
> c. the Covered Person's family;
>
> d. any other person or health care provider; and
>
> 5. Not considered to be unnecessarily repetitive when performed in combination with other diagnoses or treatment procedures.
>
> We shall determine whether services provided are Medically Necessary. Services will not automatically be considered Medically Necessary because they have been ordered or provided by a Physician.

(Emphasis supplied.) Blue Cross/Blue Shield denied coverage because it concluded that appellant's condition does not constitute an illness, and thus the treatment she received was not medically necessary. Blue Cross/Blue Shield has not raised any other basis for its denial, and we therefore will limit our consideration to whether appellant's condition constituted an illness within the meaning of the policy.

The policy broadly defines "illness" as a "bodily disorder or disease." The policy does not provide definitions for either bodily disorder or disease.

An insurance policy is to be construed as any other contract to give effect to the parties' intentions at the time the contract was made. When the terms of the contract are clear, a court may not resort to rules of construction, and the terms are to be accorded their plain and ordinary meaning as the ordinary or reasonable person would understand them. In such a case, a court shall seek to ascertain the intention of the parties from the plain language of the policy.

Whether a policy is ambiguous is a matter of law for the court to determine. If a court finds that the policy is ambiguous, then the court may employ rules of construction and look beyond the language of the policy to ascertain the intention of the parties. A general principle of construction, which we have applied to ambiguous insurance policies, holds that an ambiguous policy will be construed in favor of the insured. However, we will not read an ambiguity into policy language which is plain and unambiguous in order to construe it against the insurer.

When interpreting the plain meaning of the terms of an insurance policy, we have stated that the "'"natural and obvious meaning of the provisions in a policy is to be adopted in preference to a fanciful, curious, or hidden meaning."'" We have further stated that "'[w]hile for the purpose of judicial decision dictionary definitions often are not controlling, they are at least persuasive that meanings which they do not embrace are not common.'"

Applying these principles, our interpretation of the language of the terms employed in the policy is guided by definitions found in dictionaries, and additionally by judicial opinions rendered by other courts which have considered the meaning of these terms. Webster's Third New International Dictionary, Unabridged 648 (1981), defines disease as

> an impairment of the normal state of the living animal or plant body or of any of its components that interrupts or modifies the performance of the vital functions, being a response to environmental factors ... to specific infective agents ... to inherent defects of the organism (as various genetic anomalies), or to combinations of these factors: Sickness, Illness.

The same dictionary defines disorder as "a derangement of function: an abnormal physical or mental condition: Sickness, Ailment, Malady."

These lay definitions are consistent with the general definitions provided in Dorland's Illustrated Medical Dictionary (27th ed. 1988). Dorland's defines disease as

> any deviation from or interruption of the normal structure or function of any part, organ, or system ... of the body that is manifested by a characteristic set of symptoms and signs and whose etiology [theory of origin or cause], pathology [origin or cause], and prognosis may be known or unknown.

Dorland's defines disorder as "a derangement or abnormality of function; a morbid physical or mental state."

The Iowa Supreme Court considered the meaning of the terms "disease" and "illness" as these terms are used in insurance policies. In *Witcraft v. Sundstrand Health & Dis. Gr.*, 420 N.W.2d 785 (Iowa 1988), the Iowa Supreme Court stated that the terms "illness," "sickness," and "disease" are ordinarily synonymous in the context of an insurance policy and that these terms are defined as a "'morbid condition of the body, a deviation from the healthy or normal condition of any of the functions or tissues of the body.'" The Iowa court explained that because the insurance policy opted to define the terms regarding coverage by using broad language, the court would likewise consider and apply the broad and ordinary definition of these terms.

In *Cheney v. Bell National Life*, 556 A.2d 1135 ([Md.] 1989), the Court of Appeals for Maryland considered whether hemophilia was a disease or sickness in the context of an exclusionary clause of an accidental death insurance policy. The insurer argued that hemophilia is not a disease because it is a genetic or hereditary condition of the body which tends to make the individual susceptible to certain diseases, but the court disagreed. The court recognized that the scientific community is not unanimous in its descriptions and characterizations of hemophilia. The court, however, stated that its interpretation of the term "disease" should be controlled by its ordinary and common meaning. Relying on definitions found in several dictionaries and reference materials, the court broadly interpreted disease to encompass an abnormal condition of such a degree that in its natural progression would be expected to be a source of trouble; a condition which has impaired, or will impair if it progresses, the working of bodily functions; a significant condition which would be commonly referred to as a disease; or an inherent defect which impairs the normal state of the body. Applying the commonly accepted meaning of the term "disease," the court concluded that hemophilia is a disease as that term is used in the insurance policy

We find that the language used in the policy at issue in the present case is not reasonably susceptible of differing interpretations and thus not ambiguous. The plain and ordinary meaning of the terms "bodily disorder" and "disease," as they are used in the policy to define illness, encompasses any abnormal condition of the body or its components of such a degree that in its natural progression would be expected to be problematic; a deviation from the healthy or normal state affecting the functions or tissues of the body; an inherent defect of the body; or a morbid physical or mental state which deviates from or interrupts the normal structure or function of any part, organ, or system of the body and which is manifested by a characteristic set of symptoms and signs.

The issue then becomes whether appellant's condition—breast-ovarian carcinoma syndrome—constitutes an illness.

Blue Cross/Blue Shield argues that appellant did not suffer from an illness because she did not have cancer. Blue Cross/Blue Shield characterizes appellant's condition only as a "predisposition to an illness (cancer)" and fails to address whether the condition itself constitutes an illness. This failure is traceable to Dr. Mason's denial of appellant's claim. Despite acknowledging his inexperience and lack of knowledge about this specialized area of cancer research, Dr. Mason denied appellant's claim without consulting any medical literature or research regarding breast-ovarian carcinoma syndrome. Moreover, Dr. Mason made the decision without submitting appellant's claim for consideration to a claim review committee. The only basis for the denial was the claim filed by appellant, the letters sent by Drs. Lynch and Roffman, and the insurance policy. Despite his lack of information regarding the nature and severity of appellant's condition, Dr. Mason felt qualified to decide that appellant did not suffer from an illness.

Appellant's condition was diagnosed as breast-ovarian carcinoma syndrome. To adequately determine whether the syndrome constitutes an illness, we must first understand the nature of the syndrome.

The record on summary judgment includes the depositions of Drs. Lynch, Roffman, and Mason. In his deposition, Dr. Lynch provided a thorough discussion of this syndrome. In light of Dr. Lynch's extensive research and clinical experience in this particular area of medicine, we consider his discussion extremely helpful in our understanding of the syndrome.

According to Dr. Lynch, some forms of cancer occur on a hereditary basis. Breast and ovarian cancer are such forms of cancer which may occur on a hereditary basis. It is our understanding that the hereditary occurrence of this form of cancer is related to the genetic makeup of the woman. In this regard, the genetic deviation has conferred changes which are manifest in the individual's body and at some time become capable of being diagnosed.

At the time that he gave his deposition, Dr. Lynch explained that the state of medical research was such that detecting and diagnosing the syndrome was achieved by tracing the occurrences of hereditary cancer throughout the patient's family. Dr. Lynch stated that at the time of appellant's diagnosis, no conclusive physical test existed which would demonstrate the presence of the condition. However, Dr. Lynch stated that this area of research is progressing toward the development of a more determinative method of identifying and tracing a particular gene throughout a particular family, thus providing a physical method of diagnosing the condition.

Women diagnosed with the syndrome have at least a 50-percent chance of developing breast and/or ovarian cancer, whereas unaffected women have only a 1.4-percent risk of developing breast or ovarian cancer. In addition to the genetic deviation, the family history, and the significant risks associated with this condition, the diagnosis also may encompass symptoms of anxiety and stress, which some women experience because of their knowledge of the substantial likelihood of developing cancer.

The procedures for detecting the onset of ovarian cancer are ineffective. Generally, by the time ovarian cancer is capable of being detected, it has already developed to a very advanced stage, making treatment relatively unsuccessful. Drs. Lynch and Roffman agreed that the standard of care for treating women with breast carcinoma syndrome ordinarily involves surveillance methods. However, for women at an inordinately high risk for ovarian cancer, such as appellant, the standard of care may require radical surgery which involves the removal of the uterus, ovaries, and fallopian tubes.

Dr. Lynch explained that the surgery is labeled "prophylactic" and that the surgery is prophylactic as to the prevention of the onset of cancer. Dr. Lynch also stated that appellant's condition itself is the result of a genetic deviation from the normal, healthy state and that the recommended surgery treats that condition by eliminating or significantly reducing the presence of the condition and its likely development.

Blue Cross/Blue Shield has not proffered any evidence disputing the premise that the origin of this condition is in the genetic makeup of the individual and that in its natural development it is likely to produce devastating results. Although handicapped by his limited knowledge of the syndrome, Dr. Mason did not dispute the nature of the syndrome as explained by Dr. Lynch and supported by Dr. Roffman, nor did Dr. Mason dispute the fact that the surgery falls within the standard of care for many women afflicted with this syndrome.

In light of the plain and ordinary meaning of the terms "illness," "bodily disorder," and "disease," we find that appellant's condition constitutes an illness within the meaning of the policy. Appellant's condition is a deviation from what is considered a normal, healthy physical state or structure. The abnormality or deviation from a normal state arises, in part, from the genetic makeup of the woman. The existence of this unhealthy state results in the woman's being at substantial risk of developing cancer. The recommended surgery is intended to correct that morbid state by reducing or eliminating that risk.

Although appellant's condition was not detectable by physical evidence or a physical examination, it does not necessarily follow that appellant does not suffer from an illness. The record establishes that a woman who suffers from breast-ovarian carcinoma syndrome does have a physical state which significantly deviates from the physical state of a normal, healthy woman. Specifically, appellant suffered from a different or abnormal genetic constitution which, when combined with a particular family history of hereditary cancer, significantly increases the risk of a devastating outcome.

We are mindful that not every condition which itself constitutes a predisposition to another illness is necessarily an illness within the meaning of an insurance policy. There exists a fine distinction between such conditions, which was recognized by Chief Justice Cardozo in *Silverstein v. Metropolitan Life Ins. Co.*, 171 N.E. 914 ([N.Y.] 1930). Writing for the court, Chief Justice Cardozo explained that when a condition is such that in its probable and natural progression it may be expected to be a source of mischief, it may reasonably be described as a disease or an illness. On the other hand, he stated that if the condition is abnormal when tested by a standard of perfection, but so remote in its potential mischief that common speech would not label it a disease or infirmity, such a condition is at most a predisposing tendency. The *Silverstein* court found that a pea-size ulcer, which was located at the site of damage caused by a severe blow to the deceased's stomach, was not a disease or infirmity within the meaning of an exclusionary clause of an accident insurance policy because if left unattended, the ulcer would have been only as harmful as a tiny scratch.

Blue Cross/Blue Shield relies upon our decision in *Fuglsang v. Blue Cross*, 456 N.W.2d 281 ([Neb.] 1990), and contends that we have already supplied a definition for the terms "disease," "condition," and "illness." Although we find that reliance on *Fuglsang* is somewhat misplaced, the opinion is relevant to our determination of the meaning of "disease," "illness," and "disorder," and whether the condition from which appellant suffered constitutes an illness.

The issue raised in *Fuglsang* was whether the disease from which the plaintiff suffered constituted a preexisting condition which was excluded from coverage by the terms of the policy. Blue Cross/Blue Shield relies on the following rule from *Fuglsang* as a definition of "disease":

> A disease, condition, or illness exists within the meaning of a health insurance policy excluding preexisting conditions only at such time as the disease, condition, or illness is manifest or active or when there is a distinct symptom or condition from which one learned in medicine can with reasonable accuracy diagnose the disease.

This statement concerns *when* an illness exists, not whether the condition itself is an illness. If the condition is not a disease or illness, it would be unnecessary to apply the above rule to determine whether the condition was a preexisting illness. In the present case, Blue Cross/Blue Shield maintains that the condition is not even an illness.

Even assuming arguendo that the rule announced in *Fuglsang* is a definition of "disease," "illness," and "condition," the inherent problems with the argument put forth by Blue Cross/Blue Shield undermine its reliance on that rule. Blue Cross/Blue Shield emphasizes the fact that appellant was never diagnosed with cancer and therefore, according to Blue Cross/Blue Shield, appellant did not have an illness because cancer was not active or manifest. Appellant concedes that she did not have cancer prior to her surgery. The issue is whether the condition she did have was an illness. Blue Cross/Blue Shield further argues that "[n]o disease or illness is 'manifest or active' and there is no 'distinct symptom or condition' from which Dr. Lynch or Dr. Roffman could diagnose a disease." We stated above that lack of a physical test to detect the presence of an illness does not necessarily indicate that the person does not have an illness.

When the condition at issue—breast-ovarian carcinoma syndrome—is inserted into the formula provided by the *Fuglsang* rule, the condition would constitute an "illness" as Blue Cross/Blue Shield defines the term. The formula is whether the breast-ovarian carcinoma syndrome was manifest or active, or whether there was a distinct symptom or condition from which one learned in medicine could with reasonable accuracy diagnose the disease. The record establishes that the syndrome was manifest, at least in part, from the genetic deviation, and evident from the family medical history. The condition was such that one learned in medicine, Dr. Lynch, could with a reasonable degree of accuracy diagnose it. Blue Cross/Blue Shield does not dispute the nature of the syndrome, the method of diagnosis, or the accuracy of the diagnosis.

In the present case, the medical evidence regarding the nature of breast-ovarian carcinoma syndrome persuades us that appellant suffered from a bodily disorder or disease and, thus, suffered from an illness as defined by the insurance policy. Blue Cross/Blue Shield, therefore, is not entitled to judgment as a matter of law. Moreover, we find that appellant's condition did constitute an illness within the meaning of the policy. We reverse the decision of the district court and remand the cause for further proceedings.

Notes & Questions

1. Although much of the concern and legislative activity concentrates on preventing insurers from excluding people deemed to be genetic risks from eligibility and underwriting with respect to health insurance, the issue of what services and products are covered by plans is an equally, if not more, significant access issue. The Secretary's Advisory Committee's Draft Report provides insight into how coverage decisions are made by health plans. Generally, health plans cover illnesses that have manifested and provide only for services and products that are safe, effective, and medically authenticated. Although preventive care is increasingly covered by health plans, that preventive care usually is limited to well-recognized modalities to detect common diseases that can be definitively treated or prevented. Examples would be pap smears to detect cervical cancer, colonoscopy to detect colon cancer, mammography to find breast cancer, and blood pressure monitoring. Genetic tests typically are not covered unless they are diagnostic with respect to currently manifested signs and symptoms, or provide definitive information to allow an already identified at-risk person to avail themselves of treatment or prevention strategies to stave off their genetic destiny. As noted in the Secretary's Report, testing for informational purposes, even if that information might influence the individual's non-medical life decisions and planning, is not a covered service.

Genetic tests, as well as other innovative medical diagnostics and treatments, increasingly are scrutinized in terms of evidence-based outcome criteria, in which the analytic validity, clinical validity, and clinical utility must be proven before a health plan is willing to cover it. Genetic tests face numerous challenges in meeting these criteria. Cost-effectiveness is one of the most difficult hurdles and there are few analyses on cost-effectiveness of genetic tests. In addition, even though genetic tests may offer a look into the future, the health plan covering the cost today may not have a vested interest in that future, especially given the fact that subscribers change plans frequently.

Coverage for genetic testing and counseling cannot be viewed in isolation from the other technologies and treatments that compete for the limited health care dollars. As health care costs continue to escalate, employers and public payers are finding it increasingly difficult to pay the health care bill. They are seeking ways to contain costs and limit coverage and genetic tests are contrary to this aim. Genetic tests are costly and benefit the few; employers and public payers are likely to invest in tests and preventive care that are relatively inexpensive and have the potential to benefit many. It seems likely that health plans, both private and public, will try to avoid covering expensive genetic tests. Indeed, it is possible that even if a test has clinical utility, the cost may be so prohibitive that health plans will specifically exclude coverage to defray costs.

A very real justice concern arises in the context of access to genetic tests. This concern is exacerbated not only by the difficult resource allocation decisions faced by health plans and employers, but by society at large. Approximately 45 million people in America are uninsured. None of the uninsured have ready access to preventive or therapeutic care, much less expensive genetic tests. Many millions more are underinsured or enrolled in health plans that provide "bare bones" coverage. This segment of the population also is unlikely to have access to genetic tests and technologies. If genetic discrimination indeed violates our "cherished beliefs in justice and equality" by leading to a genetic underclass, how can we fail to address discrimination in access to the innovations of genetic science with respect to this already manifest class of underserved Americans?

2. In *Katskee v. Blue Cross/Blue Shield of Nebraska*, coverage for a specific service is at issue. The plaintiff underwent a hysterectomy and oophorectomy as a preventive measure because of a strong family history of breast and ovarian cancer. This case, which was decided in 1994, predates BRCA1/2 testing. Katskee's health plan balks at paying the cost of the surgery, given that Katskee has no diagnosis of breast or ovarian cancer and underwent the surgery as a purely preventive measure. The court ultimately decides that Katskee's family history and risk, characterized as breast-ovarian carcinoid syndrome, qualifies as a bodily disorder and disease. Thus the surgery can be construed as treatment for the disease. For a detailed discussion of the Katskee case, *see* Alexandra K. Glazier, *Genetic Predisposition, Prophylactic Treatments and Private Health Insurance: Nothing is Better than a Good Pair of Genes*, 23 Am. J.L. & Med. 45 (1997); *see also Witcraft v. Sundstrand Health & Disability Group Benefits Plan*, 420 N.W.2d 785 (Iowa 1988) (illness and disease are synonymous terms that should be given broad and ordinary meaning); *Cheney v. Bell Nat'l Life*, 556 A.2d 1135 (Md. 1989) (holding that hemophilia is a "disease" within its ordinary and common meaning); *Orman v. Prudential Ins. Co. of Am.*, 296 N.W.2d 380 (Minn. 1980) (a condition defined as "unhealthy" by the medical community meets the definition of disease or sickness in health insurance policy).

How does the court's characterization of Katskee's familial susceptibility as a "disease" square with the Rothstein/Anderlik distinction between *genotype* and *phenotype?* Recall that they argue that differential treatment based on genotype is illegitimate discrimination and should be legally prohibited. Here Katskee is seeking coverage for an elective surgery, not on the basis of phenotype, but genotype—and a presumed one at that. Shouldn't differential treatment apply in both the negative and the positive contexts especially given the cost and resource constraints in health care? If Blue Cross is prohibited from discriminating against Katskee on the basis of genotype, shouldn't it also be absolved from paying for services associated with that genotype unless they have actually manifested as pathology? Katskee's family history is not revealed in the case, but suppose it consists of two aunts who died at seventy and seventy-two of breast cancer and a mother who died of ovarian cancer at sixty-five. This pedigree is not characteristic of BRCA1/2 mutation families in which the cancers are characterized by their early onset. Does this change your view on the outcome of the case?

4. State and Federal Legislative Attempts to Deter Genetic Discrimination in Health Care

Wis. Stat. § 631.89 (2005), Restrictions on Use of Genetic Test Results

(1) In this section, "genetic test" means a test using deoxyribonucleic acid extracted from an individual's cells in order to determine the presence of a genetic disease or disorder or the individual's predisposition for a particular genetic disease or disorder.

(2) An insurer, the state with respect to a self-insured health plan, or a county, city, village or school board that provides health care services for individuals on a self-insured basis, may not do any of the following:

(a) Require or request directly or indirectly any individual or a member of the individual's family to obtain a genetic test.

(b) Require or request directly or indirectly any individual to reveal whether the individual or a member of the individual's family has obtained a genetic test or what the results of the test, if obtained by the individual or a member of the individual's family, were.

(bm) Require or request directly or indirectly a health care provider, ... who is or may be providing or who has or may have provided health care services to an individual to reveal whether the individual or a member of the individual's family has obtained a genetic test or what the results of the test, if obtained by the individual or a member of the individual's family, were.

(c) Condition the provision of insurance coverage or health care benefits on whether an individual or a member of the individual's family has obtained a genetic test or what the results of the test, if obtained by the individual or a member of the individual's family, were.

(d) Consider in the determination of rates or any other aspect of insurance coverage or health care benefits provided to an individual whether an individual or a member of the individual's family has obtained a genetic test or what the results of the test, if obtained by the individual or a member of the individual's family, were.

(3) (a) Subsection (2) does not apply to an insurer writing life insurance coverage or income continuation insurance coverage.

(b) An insurer writing life insurance coverage or income continuation insurance coverage that obtains information under sub. (2)(a) or (b) may not do any of the following:

1. Use the information contrary to sub. (2)(c) or (d) in writing a type of insurance coverage other than life or income continuation for the individual or a member of the individual's family.

2. Provide for rates or any other aspect of coverage that is not reasonably related to the risk involved.

Colo. Rev. Stat. § 10-3-1104.7 (2005), Genetic Testing—Declaration—Definitions—Limitations on Disclosure of Information—Liability—Legislative Declaration

(1) The general assembly hereby finds and determines that recent advances in genetic science have led to improvements in the diagnosis, treatment, and understanding of a significant number of human diseases. The general assembly further declares that:

(a) Genetic information is the unique property of the individual to whom the information pertains;

(b) Any information concerning an individual obtained through the use of genetic techniques may be subject to abuses if disclosed to unauthorized third parties without the willing consent of the individual to whom the information pertains;

(c) To protect individual privacy and to preserve individual autonomy with regard to the individual's genetic information, it is appropriate to limit the use and availability of genetic information;

(d) The intent of this statute is to prevent information derived from genetic testing from being used to deny access to health care insurance, group disability insurance, or long-term care insurance coverage.

(2) For the purposes of this section:

(a) "Entity" means any sickness and accident insurance company, health maintenance organization, nonprofit hospital, medical-surgical and health service corporation, or other entity that provides health care insurance, group disability insurance, or long-term care insurance coverage and is subject to the jurisdiction of the commissioner of insurance.

(b) "Genetic testing" means any laboratory test of human DNA, RNA, or chromosomes that is used to identify the presence or absence of alterations in genetic material which are associated with disease or illness. "Genetic testing" includes only such tests as are direct measures of such alterations rather than indirect manifestations thereof.

(3) (a) Information derived from genetic testing shall be confidential and privileged. Any release, for purposes other than diagnosis, treatment, or therapy, of genetic testing information that identifies the person tested with the test results released requires specific written consent by the person tested.

(b) Any entity that receives information derived from genetic testing may not seek, use, or keep the information for any nontherapeutic purpose or for any underwriting purpose connected with the provision of health care insurance, group disability insurance, or long-term care insurance coverage.

(4) Notwithstanding the provisions of subsection (3) of this section, in the course of a criminal investigation or a criminal prosecution, and to the extent allowed under the federal or state constitution, any peace officer, district attorney, or assistant attorney general, or a designee thereof, may obtain information derived from genetic testing regarding the identity of any individual who is the subject of the criminal investigation or prosecution for use exclusively in the criminal investigation or prosecution without the consent of the individual being tested.

(5) Notwithstanding the provisions of subsection (3) of this section, any research facility may use the information derived from genetic testing for scientific research purposes so long as the identity of any individual to whom the information pertains is not disclosed to any third party; except that the individual's identity may be disclosed to the individual's physician if the individual consents to such disclosure in writing.

(6) This section does not limit the authority of a court or any party to a parentage proceeding to use information obtained from genetic testing for purposes of determining parentage pursuant to section 13-25-126, C.R.S.

(7) This section does not limit the authority of a court or any party to a proceeding that is subject to the limitations of part 5 of article 64 of title 13, C.R.S., to use information obtained from genetic testing for purposes of determining the cause of damage or injury.

(8) This section does not limit the authority of the state board of parole to require any offender who is involved in a sexual assault to submit to blood tests and to retain the results of such tests on file as authorized under section 17-2-201(5)(g), C.R.S.

(9) This section does not limit the authority granted the state department of public health and environment, the state board of health, or local departments of health pursuant to section 25-1-122, C.R.S.

(10) Notwithstanding any provision of this section to the contrary, the only requirements that shall apply to an insurer in connection with life insurance or individual disability insurance are as follows:

(a) Except as otherwise specifically authorized or required by another section of state or federal law, an insurer shall not require the performance of or perform a genetic test without first receiving the specific, written, informed consent of the subject of the test who has the capacity to consent or, if the person subject to the test lacks the capacity to consent, of a person authorized by law to consent on behalf of the subject of the test. Written consent shall be in a form prescribed by the commissioner.

(b) The results of a genetic test performed pursuant to this subsection (10) are privileged and confidential and shall not be released to any person except as specifically authorized under applicable state or federal law.

(11) Any violation of this section is an "unfair practice", as defined in section 10-3-1104(1), and is subject to the provisions of sections 10-3-1106 to 10-3-1113.

(12) Any individual who is injured by an entity's violation of this section may recover in a court of competent jurisdiction the following remedies:

(a) Equitable relief, which may include a retroactive order, directing the entity to provide health insurance, group disability insurance, or long-term care insurance coverage, whichever is appropriate, to the injured individual under the same terms and conditions as would have applied had the violation not occurred; and

(b) The greater of:

(I) An amount equal to any actual damages suffered by the individual as a result of the violation; or

(II) Ten thousand dollars per violation.

(13) The prevailing party in an action under this section may recover costs and reasonable attorney fees.

Robert F. Rich & Julian Ziegler, *Genetic Discrimination in Health Insurance for a (Not So) Special Problem?*

2 Ind. Health L. Rev. 5 (2005)

...

In this Article, we argue the common legal conception of "genetic discrimination" is fundamentally flawed. Consequently, the current legal and public policy approach, based on this concept and reflected in the enactment of HIPAA and GINA, is neither sound nor fully defensible.

HIPAA [Health Insurance Portability and Accountability Act] and GINA [proposed Genetic Information Nondiscrimination Act] respond to fears of a "genetic determinism," which rely on incomplete information about the nature and invasiveness of genetic information. Furthermore, genetic information as expressed and defined in the provisions of both statutes, is a concept that evades a precise definition; it is difficult, if not impossible, to distinguish it from regular medical information. Nevertheless, both statutes provide differing definitions of genetic information and try to distinguish between medical and genetic information. Consequently, we conclude that HIPAA and GINA do not provide a clear statutory basis for legal decisions concerning discrimination based solely on the use or application of genetic information. The language of these statutes stems from a biased public policy conception of genetic information, which seems to be based on a misperception or misunderstanding of genetic testing methods and the empirical results derived from such testing. The current statutory approach also neglects the legitimate information needs of the private health insurance market. The common fear of health insurers seems to be that if genetic test kits become widely available, adverse selection resulting from an asymmetry of information could occur. In turn, this could eventually lead to an increase in the pricing of health insurance policies and consequently lead to a higher number of people without health insurance coverage.

In order to support our arguments, we will analyze the potential influence of HIPAA and GINA on genetic discrimination in private health insurance. In the first Part of this Article we analyze what is meant by the term "discrimination." We will examine the scientific basis underlying the concept of "genetic discrimination" in order to pinpoint what exactly makes "genetic discrimination" different from "normal" discrimination in health insurance. The second Part of the Article focuses on whether genetic discrimination, as described in the first Part, is likely to occur and if so, in which market segment. The third Part examines protections against genetic discrimination in health insurance offered by the ADA and Executive Order 13,145. In the fourth Part, the impact of HIPAA and GINA on "genetic discrimination" in health insurance will be analyzed. Since the idea of "genetic discrimination" is rooted in the definition of genetic information, we will examine the various meanings of the term "genetic information" provided by HIPAA, the HIPAA final interim regulations, and GINA. We will show that HIPAA and GINA do not even offer comprehensive protection against "genetic discrimination", as defined by the laws themselves. The fifth and final Parts of the Article present our overall conclusions.

I. What is Unfair "Genetic Discrimination" in Health Insurance?

In order to analyze the influence of HIPAA and GINA on unfair "genetic discrimination" in the market for health insurance, it is imperative to understand what the term "genetic discrimination" actually means. As "discrimination" is widely used to describe a behavior that is perceived in a negative fashion, it is important to emphasize the difference between this kind of "negatively connotative" discrimination on the one hand, and insurance discrimination on the other hand.

Despite the semantic difficulties in the use of the term "discrimination," the legal view of discrimination is founded in the Fourteenth Amendment to the U.S. Constitution. In Section 1, the Fourteenth Amendment provides for a general legal framework of appropriate and inappropriate differentiation. Under the Fourteenth Amendment, "[c]lass legislation, discriminating against some and favoring others, is prohibited, but legislation which, in carrying out a public purpose, is limited in its application, if within the sphere of its operation it affects alike all persons similarly situated, is not within the amendment." Thus "it is only invidious 'discrimination' which offends the Constitution." Given this foundation, the issue is, how one differentiates between permissible and invidious discrimination. The rules which are used to determine that question are summarized in Lindsley v. Natural Carbonic Gas Co., whereby a differentiation is unconstitutional if it is without any reasonable basis and therefore purely arbitrary. The court also developed another standard which stipulates that "the classification must be reasonable, not arbitrary, and must rest upon some ground of difference having a fair and substantial relation to the object of the legislation, so that all persons similarly circumstanced shall be treated alike." Therefore, the core principle of the legal definition of unlawful (e.g. unconstitutional) discrimination is that similarly circumstanced individuals have to be treated alike in the absence of a reasonable basis for a differentiated treatment.

Since insurance discrimination is legally permissible, only as long as it is based on reason and not purely arbitrary, we will at first explain the use of discrimination in health insurance. Next, we will analyze if the insurers' use of genetic testing procedures justifies a different legal treatment of genetic discrimination in insurance.

The health insurance market in the United States is divided into several market segments. According to the U.S. Census Bureau, in 2002, 84.8% of the American population had health insurance coverage. That left 15.2% of the population (43,574,000 people) without health insurance coverage. Approximately, 25.7% of the insured population was covered through government issued health insurance, such as Medicare, Medicaid and Military health care. The remaining 69.6% of the population received health care through private health insurance, either employment based or individually purchased.

Since eligibility for governmentally issued health insurance coverage is not based on the applicants' health status, this market segment is not likely to be affected by genetic discrimination. Private health insurance, in contrast to governmentally subsidized plans, is financed solely by individuals seeking coverage, such as employers, employees and private individuals. In this market segment, health insurers commonly use medical information for underwriting purposes, which is fully permissible. On the one hand, insurance companies ask for the family history of applicants in order to determine if any hereditary disease is likely to manifest itself in the person of the applicant. On the other hand, medical examinations are conducted in order to screen out already manifest diseases.

Usually health insurance is obtained as an employment benefit. In 2002, roughly 85% of the privately insured American population (175,296,000 of 198,973,000 people) received health insurance coverage through employment in policies written for large groups. This means that most medical insurance coverage is provided on a group basis and financed jointly (in some "shared arrangement") by employers and employees. The insurance industry classifies the risk of such groups based on a group's size, on its past claims experience or on data of the claims experience of similar groups in the same industry or region. The group's premium rates are also set according to these factors. Since the risk incurred in employment-based health insurance plans is spread among the whole group, premium rates can be maintained at a relatively low price level. Furthermore, employer sponsored group health plans are usually subsidized by the employer. Because of these subsidizations, the pricing of the group's policy does not increase due to high claims experiences, which may occur if many high-risk individuals are enrolled in the plan. As this subsidization practice helps to maintain stable premium rates, low-risk individuals are also attracted to enroll in the policy. Consequently, the same average number of low-risk and high-risk individuals are attracted by the stable premium rates.

As employment-based group health insurance plans are experience rated, individual insurance underwriting practices are not used in calculating the group's premium rates. The risk of individuals can be spread among the whole group. This is only different in small group health plans with less than twenty-five employees. When the group size is too small to qualify for experience rating, the individual underwriting practices are used. Given the rate-setting practices just described, health-status related information is of no actuarial value in the larger group market where underwriting practices are not used. Consequently, any attempt to obtain and use such information for underwriting in this market segment should be considered both unnecessary and unfairly discriminatory.

In contrast to employment-based large group health plans, small group health plans and individual insurance plans are underwritten in order to calculate appropriate, i.e. actuarially fair, premium rates. Risk-classification is one method utilized in the underwriting process. Risk-classification enables insurers to divide individuals into groups with similar projected claims and obtain an estimate of the projected costs associated with an individual. Thereby, insurers are able to calculate the lowest premium rates compatible with the projected costs (reasonable discrimination). Furthermore, risk-classification allows insurers to offset the impact of adverse selection.

Consumers, when faced with different insurance plans, must weigh the premium rates against the value they expect to receive. If the insurance applicant has critical information about his or her health status which is unknown to the insurer, this asymmetry of information might lead to insurance becoming less affordable. Because high-risk individuals would be more likely to buy insurance, the insurer would be forced to eventually raise the premium rates to cover the losses, which occur due to the higher claims costs. With increasing premiums, low-risk individuals would discontinue the plan, which would lead to a further increase in premium rates to keep the plan balanced. This process, which can result in cases of asymmetric information, is called adverse selection. By contrast, a situation of asymmetric information is not likely to occur if applicants disclose all relevant information to insurers. Thus, the possibility of adverse selection could be offset and premium rates could be stabilized through fair risk classification.

As mentioned above, insurers differentiate among individuals seeking health insurance coverage. The purpose of this practice is maintaining a system in which each insured person's premium is rated according to the amount of his or her risk. Implementation of this notion of actuarial fairness requires that insurers are allowed to create classifications that represent real differences between individuals. In order to stay in business, insurers must be allowed to risk-classify, which means, that they must be allowed to discriminate or distinguish among individual health insurance applicants. Because the private health insurance system covers nearly seventy percent of the American public without discrimination through risk-classification, the cornerstone of health insurance in the United States would be endangered. Although discrimination is important in the health insurance market, it is necessary to distinguish between reasonable, legally permissible discrimination, which is vital to the health insurance market, and discrimination that is not. The legal permissibility of insurance discrimination depends upon its foundation of "reason," which in this case refers to medical, clinical, or statistical data about the insurance applicant. Therefore, in the absence of this reasonable basis, insurance discrimination would be arbitrary and, thus, unlawful.

Reasonable legally permissible discrimination and unreasonable discrimination can also be described as fair and unfair discrimination. In determining unfair discrimination, it is important to analyze whether insurers' use of genetic information for underwriting purposes justifies a substantially different legal treatment than common methods of risk-classification in the process of insurance underwriting. As genetic discrimination arises from the "discriminatory" use of genetic information, we will examine the sources of this kind of information; genetic defects, gene-associated diseases, and the scientific and clinical methods used to detect them. In an effort to determine what is "reasonable," we will briefly explain genetic defects and the testing methods used to identify such defects.

A. The Nature of Diseases

From a legal perspective, in order to define "genetic information" it is essential to understand the role of genes in the development of diseases. If a person has a genetic defect, this defect can cause the development of a certain disease. While certain genetic defects translate into various diseases, others do not. In some cases, the presence of a particular genetic defect is connected to the inevitable development of a disease associated with that defect. In most cases though, this relationship is more complex.

There are three large and heterogeneous groups of gene-associated diseases: (1) Monogenic diseases, which are caused by defects affecting a single gene; (2) Polygenic-multifactorial diseases, which stem from the interaction of one or more genes and environmental factors; and (3) Chromosomal aberrations, which are due to a change in the structure or number of the chromosomes

...

Information about an individual's genotype can be derived using four different analytical approaches: (1) phenotype-analysis; (2) cytogenetic analysis; (3) protein-chemical analysis; and (4) DNA-analysis. In phenotype-analysis, the outward appearance of an individual, the phenotype, is examined in order to reach conclusions concerning certain genetic traits of an individual. In cytogenetic analysis, abnormalities in the number or structure of the chromosomes are examined by the use of microscopic techniques. The protein-chemical analysis is an examination method by which one tries to discover gene-associated diseases linked to the presence, absence, or alteration of proteins, which can lead to metabolic defects. In contrast to the three preceding methods, the DNA-analysis tries to discover genetic defects by examining the DNA itself. If a genetic defect is known to be associated with the development of a certain disease, it is possible to estimate the likelihood of the development of this disease, if the genetic defect is present. DNA-analysis, therefore, does not predict the development of a disease. It only serves as a means to discover whether a genetic defect is present or not. The "penetrance," the likelihood of the development of a certain disease due to a genetic defect, differs according to whether the disease is monogenic or polygenic-multifactorial. Except for the DNA-analysis, all these methods are commonly used in regular medical examinations and only use different strategies in uncovering genotype-related information.

C. Is Genetic Information Different?

As summarized above, the methods used to unveil genetic information are not, from a scientific perspective, fundamentally different from the methods used in gathering other medical information. One could say that all medical information has a genetic basis. As already indicated, genetic information can be derived by various methods, which are commonly used during regular medical examinations. Phenotype-analysis, for example, can provide information about an individual's genetic makeup and is part of every routine medical examination. Cytogenetic analysis and protein-chemical analysis are commonly used in the diagnosis of hereditary diseases. Thus, the only "new" form of gene-analysis is the DNA-analysis. Although the basic techniques used in DNA-analysis were developed before 1990, DNA-analysis is not widely used in medical examinations. This is primarily because of the laborious, and thus, expensive character of this technique, rather than because of its "exceptional" or "unusual" character. Therefore, even DNA-analysis cannot be labeled a truly "new" or "unusual" form of examination that has to be regarded as strictly set apart from the other methods of gene-analysis, which are already used during regular medical examinations.

Consequently, we conclude the methods used in gathering genetic information are not fundamentally different from, but rather inseparably linked, to the methods used in gathering regular medical information. Therefore, from a legal and public policy perspective, "genetic" discrimination cannot be fundamentally different from "normal" discrimination based on regular medical information. If this is true, then like commonly used underwriting criteria, genetic testing procedures have to be considered reasonable sources of data and, as such, are a reasonable basis for legally permissible insurance discrimination.

Nevertheless, critics of gene-analysis in health insurance maintain their opposing view by arguing there is a difference between regular medical information and genetic information, which consists of several factors resulting in a "genetic exceptionalism." One argument is that a person's genotype is beyond that person's control. Other arguments stipulate that only a small number of people would actually be affected by a genetic predisposition, and that genetically "unlucky" people would be stigmatized. The critics maintain the position that genetic information is different in its depth, scope and influence on the affected individual. It is argued, therefore, that the use of genetic information leads to genetic discrimination.

Although these arguments seem convincing at first, it is questionable that they can be employed to justify a different legal treatment of genetic tests as compared to regular medical.

. . .

IV. Provisions of HIPAA and GINA Concerning Genetic Tests and Genetic Information in Health Insurance

The final step in this paper is to analyze the influence of the Health Insurance Portability and Accountability Act of 1996 (HIPAA) and Genetic Information Nondiscrimination Act of 2003 (GINA) provisions on genetic discrimination in health insurance. It is notable that both laws are based on the assumption that genetic discrimination represents a new form of discrimination, based on a new form of information, i.e. genetic information. Although it is shown this assumption is not sufficiently backed by scientific reality, we will analyze HIPAA and GINA in terms of what is specified in the laws and reflected in their definitions of genetic information. However, as we will show, even based on these assumptions, both laws do not offer comprehensive protection against genetic discrimination. The analysis will deal separately with the group and individual markets.

A. Definition of "Genetic Information" Under HIPAA and GINA

In order to analyze the influence of HIPAA and GINA on genetic discrimination in health insurance, it is imperative to establish what HIPAA and GINA include under the term "genetic information." As we have concluded above in Part I, genetic information can be derived from several sources, including family histories, phenotype analysis, cytogenetic tests, and DNA-tests. Many of these sources are currently used in the diagnosis of diseases in regular medical examinations. Furthermore, as we have shown in Part I, genetic information is not distinguishable from regular medical information. However, in this context, it is important to stress to basic assumption underlying the development of HIPAA and GINA.

In contrast to the argument presented in this Article, both laws are based on the concept of genetic discrimination as being something "new," which requires special legal attention. This concept is mirrored in the definitions of "genetic information" employed by HIPAA and GINA. As these definitions are the basis for the statutory provisions, the underlying conceptual assumption is directly expressed in the scope of protection offered by each statute.

1. Definition of "Genetic Information" Under HIPAA

Although HIPAA itself does not include a definition of genetic information, the HIPAA regulations offer a definition. The HIPAA regulations define "genetic information" as information about genes, gene products, and inherited characteristics that may derive from the individual or a family member. This includes information regarding carrier status and information derived from laboratory tests that identify mutations in specific genes or chromosomes, physical medical examinations, family histories, and direct analysis of genes or chromosomes. It is interesting to note that in this definition, genetic information includes information derived from physical medical examinations and family histories. As our earlier explanation of genetic testing methods show, a distinctive differentiation between information derived from genetic tests and information derived from regular medical examinations is not justifiable. The difficulty involved with pinpointing what actually constitutes genetic information seems to be reflected in the definition of genetic information offered in the HIPAA regulations. These regulations employ a definition which effectively equals genetic information to health status information derived from physical medical examinations. Because information derived from physical medical examinations is already protected under the "health status" provision of HIPAA, genetic information automatically is included under this protection. Thus, the inclusion of genetic information under HIPAA only has clarifying value.

2. Definition of "Genetic Information" Under GINA

Under GINA, "genetic information" means information derived from an individual's genetic test, the test of a family member, and the occurrence of a defect or disease in family members of the individual, but excludes information about the sex and age of the individual. Let's quote GINA directly: "Genetic test" means "an analysis of human DNA, RNA, chromosomes, proteins, and metabolites, that detects genotypes, mutations or chromosomal changes." Nevertheless, it does not include an analysis of proteins or metabolites that does not detect genotypes, mutations, or chromosomal changes, or an analysis of proteins or metabolites that is directly related to a manifested disease, disorder, or pathological condition that could reasonably be detected by a health care professional with appropriate training and expertise in the field of medicine involved.

This means the definition of "genetic information" under GINA does not include health status information that is directly related to an already manifested disease in an individual or information concerning the sex and age of an individual. Thus, GINA clearly exempts individuals with diseases, whether gene-associated or not, from its nondiscrimination provisions.

B. The Group Market

In the group market for health insurance, both HIPAA and GINA provide protections against genetic discrimination. Both laws amend the following statutes relating to health insurance: the Employee Retirement Income Security Act of 1974 (ERISA), the Public Health Service Act (PHSA), the Internal Revenue Code of 1986 and Title XVIII Social Security Act relating to medigap.

1. HIPAA Provisions for the Group Market

The Health Insurance Portability and Accountability Act of 1996 offers nondiscrimination provisions concerning the group market, including small employers. We will divide these provisions into provisions for eligibility and provisions relating to nondiscrimination in premium contributions, and discuss them accordingly.

a. Rules for eligibility

The provisions for eligibility are entwined with the rules concerning similarly situated individuals. Insurance issuers are still allowed to treat groups of similarly situated individuals differently. However, they are prohibited from treating the similarly situated individuals inside one group of similarly situated individuals differently from one another. The groups of similarly situated individuals may not be established using health status related factors. Likewise, any differentiation among the group members may neither be based on health status related factors (including genetic information), nor be directed at a specific individual's health status.

The purpose of the statute is a provision of health insurance portability. As such a prohibition of discrimination in (or denial of) enrollment against individuals based on their health status, which includes genetic information as defined in the regulations, is part of the statute. The question relating to genetic discrimination is whether the rules concerning the eligibility have a significant effect as nondiscrimination legislation with regard to genetic information as defined by HIPAA. In relation to genetic information, the provisions of HIPAA concerning the eligibility of individuals to enroll in a group health plan can be summarized as follows:

1. The insurance issuers have to apply rules for eligibility uniformly at all the plan members. The insurance issuers are neither allowed to establish groups of high risk based on the health status of the individuals, nor can they to impose preexisting condition exclusions on genetic risks, as these are

not regarded as preexisting conditions. Thus, they may not use genetic information as a basis for the eligibility of an individual to enroll in a group health plan.

2. Nevertheless, insurance issuers are still able to restrict the amounts of benefits or cancel the coverage for certain medical conditions, if they apply these restrictions uniformly on a group of similarly situated individuals. The only exception might be that a restriction was being directed at specific individual participants in the plan; however, this would have to be established.

3. Since there is no mandatory minimum benefit or coverage package provided by the statute or the regulations, insurance issuers are free to place a cap on benefits or coverage relating to genetically identifiable diseases, as long as the benefit or coverage or coverage in question is denied to the whole group.

Although a genetic predisposition to a disease may not be excluded from coverage as a preexisting condition, this provision is open to debate. Since insurers are still allowed to exclude the coverage of certain diseases for the whole group, a preexisting condition exclusion for a specific disorder, which would only be in force for twelve months, seems less favorable for the insurers. Thus, in the context of this provision, the provision against preexisting condition exclusions based on genetic information seems irrational from a clinical or legal perspective. This is even more apparent if the insurance industry is faced with late-onset diseases, such as Alzheimer's, which is unlikely to occur during the first twelve months of coverage. Therefore, a preexisting condition exclusion concerning genetic information can be meaningless, since the insurer could exclude coverage for a specific disorder in a renewal decision, as long as it applies to the whole group. Considering the above findings, the HIPAA provisions relating to the eligibility to enroll provide no safety against genetic discrimination to insurance applicants, other than the guarantee of enrollment in a health insurance plan with uncertain coverage.

b. Nondiscrimination in premium amounts

The provisions relating to the prohibition of discrimination in setting premium rates stipulate that an individual may not be charged more than the other enrollees in the same group of similarly situated individuals based on any health status related factor of the individual or a dependent of the individual. Furthermore, the HIPAA interim final regulations clarify, that list-billing (billing with separate individual premium rates) practices are prohibited. This serves as a protection of small groups, containing less than twenty-five to fifty employees, against individual insurance underwriting, and as such against the use of genetic information in the underwriting process.

Nevertheless, HIPAA does not restrict the amount an insurance issuer may charge an employer for coverage of a group of similarly situated individuals. Consequently, insurance issuers are still able to charge employers higher premium rates based on the claims-experience of the individuals inside the group. Therefore, the insurance issuers could still use an estimate of genetic predispositions in a group based on a group's claims experience in order to adjust the price an employer has to pay for coverage of a group.

A real protection against higher premium rates based on health factors and especially genetic information is not achieved, because insurance issuers still can reflect a negative claims experience in higher premium amounts, not directed against the "cause," the actual individual requiring expensive treatment, but instead directed against the group as a whole. Thus, HIPAA only shifts the burden of high medical expenses of individuals to the whole group.

Taking the above findings into consideration, it is arguable that no comprehensive protection against discrimination based on genetic information is offered by HIPAA in the group market of health insurance. The prohibition of underwriting for small groups might be regarded as a protection against discrimination in premium amounts. However as we have explained earlier in Part I, small groups with less than twenty-five employees are usually too small to sustain a risk-spreading system and qualify for experience rating. This legal obligation to experience rate in the small group market forces insurance issuers to set premium rates according to the past claims experience of groups, which are too small to sufficiently compensate high medical expenses by the group's premium pool. In order to keep the policies profitable, insurers would either have to raise the group's premium rates, which is still allowed under HIPAA, or discontinue offering health insurance coverage for small groups. Thus, insurance for small groups would become either very expensive or unavailable. Although the prohibition of list-billing in the small group market might be regarded as being a provision against discrimination in premium amounts, it should instead be seen as what it is: a menace to the stability of the small group market of health insurance.

2. GINA Provisions for the Group Market

Following basically the same conception of genetic information as HIPAA, GINA enhances the protections given by HIPAA. GINA prohibits employer-sponsored group health plans and health insurance issuers offering health insurance in connection with a group health plan by doing the following:

(1) Imposing enrollment restrictions based on genetic information (which includes the request for or receipt of genetic services by an individual or a family member of such individual).

(2) Adjusting premiums or contribution amounts for a group on the basis of genetic information of an individual in the group or a family member of such an individual.

(3)Requesting or requiring an individual to undergo a genetic test.

In sum, GINA specifies that even the request for or receipt of genetic services by an individual, which might hint at a predisposition, is considered to be genetic information and is therefore prohibited from serving as a basis for the application of enrollment restrictions. It is safe to conclude the new provision by GINA only clarifies the comprehensiveness of protection of "genetic information," since HIPAA already restricts the eligibility of an individual for group health insurance coverage based on genetic information.

The third provision concerning the request for, or requirement, of a genetic test as a condition for enrollment, is also little more than a clarification. As the request for, or requirement, of a genetic test per definition leads to genetic information, the HIPAA-provision concerning the restriction of eligibility already applies. Although the possibility of a request for, or requirement, of a genetic test might be used by health insurance issuers for other purposes (that is other than the determination of the eligibility of an individual to enroll in a plan), this remaining interest in genetic tests or the results thereof is already covered by the second provision.

In this second provision, GINA fills a gap left by HIPAA concerning the calculation of premium rates for the groups of similarly situated individuals. Under the HIPAA provisions, the insurance issuers were still allowed to adjust the premium rates for a group as a whole, and to consider all relevant health factors in order to establish aggregate rates for coverage provided under a group health plan. This could lead to unfair discrimination against the healthy group members; consequently GINA prohibits this kind of discrimination against the group. In other words, the only new anti-discrimination provision introduced by GINA in the group market of health insurance is the prohibition of discrimination against a group as a whole based on genetic information concerning an individual in the group.

C. The Individual Market

As is true for the group market, both HIPAA and GINA offer protections against genetic discrimination in the individual health insurance market.

1. HIPAA Provisions for the Individual Market

HIPAA amends the provisions of the Public Health Service Act concerning the individual market of health insurance. We will divide the HIPAA provisions into: (1) provisions for eligible individuals, and (2) provisions for all individuals seeking health insurance coverage in the individual market of health insurance.

a. Provisions for eligible individuals

The central provision of HIPAA concerning the individual health insurance market is a provision for "eligible" individuals only. It states that insurance issuers have to offer eligible individuals coverage and enrollment in insurance policies actively marketed in the individual health insurance market.

According to the interpretation in the HIPAA regulations, a health insurance issuer meets these requirements, if it provides information about all available options, enrolls the individual in any coverage the individual selects and if it does not impose preexisting condition exclusions on the individual. Nevertheless, insurance issuers are still free to set premium rates for individual health insurance coverage for eligible individuals. Thus, the basic provision for eligible individuals consists of guaranteed health insurance issuance without the possibility of being subjected to a preexisting condition exclusion.

In the context of genetic testing and genetic information, this means that eligible individuals have to be offered individual health insurance, and be enrolled in a plan of their choice, regardless of their genetic makeup.

Still, the regulations do not restrict the amount an issuer may charge for enrollment under the policy. Furthermore, the regulations only implement a restriction on preexisting condition exclusion periods, which do not apply to genetic information, as genetic information does not constitute a preexisting condition under the statute and the regulations. Nevertheless, genetic testing as a condition for enrollment is prohibited, because that would be contrary to the main purpose of the regulations; which is to guarantee individual health insurance coverage portability through guaranteed access.

Insurance issuers still can base the premium rates for insurance coverage of eligible individuals according to their individual risk, and still are allowed to do so by demanding and using genetic information. This could offer health insurance issuers a possibility to protect themselves from adverse selection.

Because the regulations do not impose restrictions on the pricing of the policies, this could still be done by the states. There is no preemption of state legislation regarding this dimension.

However, states are allowed to evade the provisions for eligible individuals by implementing an alternative mechanism. This alternative mechanism has to provide for a guaranteed offer of health insurance coverage to all eligible individuals, and for a prohibition of preexisting condition exclusion or affiliation periods for coverage of eligible individuals. Nevertheless, the implementation of an alternative mechanism by a state actually does not limit the possibilities of the insurance issuers to set premium rates according to individual risk.

If a state does not implement such an alternative mechanism, an insurance issuer may elect to limit the coverage required under the regulations if it offers eligible individuals at least two policy forms, which must meet certain requirements. As 45 C.F.R. § 148.120(g)(4) clarifies, issuers making this election are still able to adjust premium rates according to the individual risk, and thus based on genetic information, of eligible individuals. Nevertheless, the premium adjustments have to be consistent with applicable state law.

b. Provisions for all individuals

According to 45 C.F.R. § 148.122, insurance issuers in the individual market are required to renew the health insurance coverage of all individuals at the option of the individual. Thus, a health insurance issuer may only discontinue a particular type of coverage, if it provides notice in writing ninety days prior to the termination of the coverage and offers individuals the option to purchase any other individual health insurance currently offered in the state. Furthermore, the insurance issuers have to act uniformly without regard to health status related factors of the individuals or their covered dependents.

Insurance issuers are still permitted to modify a health insurance coverage policy form at the time of renewal of coverage if it applies the modification uniformly for all individuals with that policy form. In addition, this modification has to be consistent with applicable state law.

This means that all individuals are guaranteed renewal of their individual health insurance coverage, and individual level genetic information may not be used in this decision. Furthermore a discontinuation of coverage may not be based on the individual's, or a covered dependent of the individual's, genetic information. An insurance issuer can still modify the offered coverage based on genetic information, if it acts uniformly for all individuals with that policy form, and the modification is consistent with state law.

As long as a state does not enact laws prohibiting the adjustment of premiums based on genetic information, genetic information and testing may still be used to calculate and adjust premium amounts for non-eligible individuals in that state. Furthermore, genetic testing and information derived from such tests may be used by issuers to restrict and condition enrollment of non-eligible individuals.

2. GINA Provisions for the Individual Market

The possible uses of genetic information allowable under HIPAA, as specified above, are significantly reduced by GINA. GINA stipulates that health insurance issuers offering health insurance coverage in the individual market may not require an individual to undergo a genetic test, may not establish rules for the eligibility or continued eligibility to enroll based on genetic information, and may not adjust premium or contribution amounts based on genetic information. This means eligible individuals, as defined under HIPAA, may not be charged different premiums based on their genetic information (or that of a family member), as was still permitted under HIPAA.

Noneligible individuals may not be subjected to enrollment restrictions based on their genetic information (or that of a family member), or be subjected to premium adjustments based on their genetic information (or that of a family member), and neither may be required to undergo a genetic test prior to enrollment. Therefore noneligible individuals may still be denied enrollment based on other than genetic information (as defined under GINA).

Eligible individuals, as defined under HIPAA, still have guaranteed access to health insurance coverage in the individual market. The pricing of the individuals' coverage, which was still adjustable under HIPAA, may not be adjusted on the basis of genetic information concerning that individual (or a family member of the individual).

D. Summary of the Offered Protections in Light of Unfair Genetic Discrimination

In summary, the results of the analysis of the provisions of HIPAA and GINA concerning unfair discrimination in the group market of health insurance are:

- HIPAA guarantees enrollment in group health plans with uncertain coverage;
- Under HIPAA, insurance issuers can still reflect a negative claims experience of a group in setting higher premium rates for the whole group;
- No real protection against unfair discrimination based on genetic information is offered by HIPAA for the group market, except for the prohibition of underwriting for small groups, which, as explained above, does not constitute unfair genetic discrimination as underwriting is necessary in the small group market;
- GINA prohibits the discrimination against a group as a whole based on genetic information concerning an individual in the group.

In summary, the results of the analysis of the provisions of HIPAA and GINA concerning unfair genetic discrimination in the individual market are:

- HIPAA provides that eligible individuals are guaranteed health insurance coverage, regardless of genetic information concerning them or their family members;
- Under HIPAA, all individuals are guaranteed an offer of policy renewal;
- Under HIPAA, insurance issuers are still able to calculate their premiums according to genetic information concerning eligible individuals, as long as the states do not enact contrary legislation and policies are ultimately issued;
- The implementation of an alternative mechanism through a State only restricts issuers in the premium calculation process, thereby forcing them to subsidize high-risk individuals;
- The election to limit coverage under 45 C.F.R. § 148.120(c) actually leads to adverse selection problems;
- HIPAA limits the use of genetic information and genetic testing by health insurance issuers to the determination of premium rates and to the determination of the enrollment of noneligible individuals;
- Under HIPAA, the states are left to legislate insurance issuer's use of genetic information;
- Under GINA, noneligible individuals may still be denied enrollment based on factors other than genetic information;

- The pricing of the individual's coverage, under GINA may not be adjusted on the basis of genetic information concerning that individual or a family member of the individual.

V. Conclusion

The current legal and public policy approach for dealing with "genetic discrimination" is fundamentally flawed. As we have shown there is no reason to treat genetic information derived from genetic tests different from information derived from regular medical examinations. Moreover, we have shown that the two types of information are not readily distinguishable from each other. Yet the information derived from regular medical examinations has a different legal status.

GINA, in combination with HIPAA, provides broader protection for genetic information than for information derived from regular medical examinations. This effect matches the Greely's proposal, who proposed that the possibility of an individual to sue for genetic discrimination on the ground that a manifested disease provided evidence about a genotype might be prevented. Because a probative basis for this differentiation does not exist, we have to conclude that HIPAA and GINA, as they provide for a differentiation between genetic information and regular medical information, are laws merely reacting to fears in the American public, which were fueled by a biased view of the underlying science.

Taking the above analysis into consideration, we conclude that GINA prohibits the use of genetic information in a market where the availability of such information is crucial for health insurers to offset the impact of asymmetric information. GINA fails to acknowledge the necessity of underwriting through fair discrimination in the individual and small group health insurance market. Thus, GINA endangers the stability of these markets, especially in the small group market. Furthermore, the different treatment of presymptomatic and symptomatic conditions is incomprehensible in view of gene-associated diseases. Yet, the current legal approach would allow for such differentiation.

In the individual health insurance market, HIPAA provides guaranteed enrollment for eligible individuals, regardless of their health status. Although under HIPAA, the possibilities to calculate actuarially fair premiums according to genetic information concerning all individuals, as well as to determine the eligibility of noneligible individuals to enroll in a policy according to genetic information concerning these individuals are left to health insurers, both possibilities are prohibited by GINA. Thus, the insurers' possibility to calculate actuarially fair premium rates is limited to information about the health status of individuals that is not derived from genetic information as defined by GINA. According to the definition of genetic information of GINA, this means that insurers are allowed to calculate premiums only based on information about already manifested diseases.

Furthermore, contrary to our findings concerning unfair discrimination in the small group market of health insurance, HIPAA prohibits list billing practices in this market. Thereby, HIPAA prohibits the possibility of insurers to use underwriting in a market where risk-spreading alone is insufficient to keep the group profitable, and thus, insurable. Because of the guaranteed enrollment provision, small groups do not have to fear that insurers would deny them enrollment. Nevertheless, insurers who are confronted with the mandatory enrollment of individuals in unprofitable small group plans will have an incentive to limit the coverage offered in connection with small group health plans in order to keep the plans profitable. This might ultimately lead to a decrease in the level of insurance coverage for small groups, as the extent of coverage is not guaranteed by HIPAA. As mentioned above, both HIPAA and GINA fail to resolve this problem. Instead both statutes prohibit the underwriting practices, which are necessary for this market segment.

HIPAA provides for the states and insurance companies offering health insurance coverage in the individual market the possibility to prevent the application of the requirements and provisions for eligible individuals. However, the offered methods are undesirable for the health insurers. On the one hand, the implementation of an alternative mechanism by a state forces insurers to either subsidize eligible individuals through a subsidization system between different policies or to subsidize each other in order to cover the expectable higher costs. The possibility for the insurance issuers to limit the required coverage leads to adverse selection problems and is therefore also not desirable for them.

In the group market, the gap left by HIPAA concerning the possibility of health insurance issuers to limit the level of coverage offered for a group health plan remains open. Because insurers are not allowed to react to higher claims experiences of a group by raising premium amounts, they might instead restrict the amounts of benefits offered in connection with that group health plan. GINA tries to differentiate clearly between information about genotypes and information about (gene-associated) manifested diseases. Although the former is protected from insurers use, the latter is not. Because of this differentiation, GINA does not cover the possibility that the genotypes translate into diseases. Despite the protection of genotype related information, GINA fails to prohibit the use of information about the diseases that result from these genotypes. Consequently, GINA fails to protect against the possibility of unfair discrimination because of gene-associated diseases. This documents the failure to employ an all-inclusive definition of genetic information.

Genetic information is inseparably intertwined with information derived from regular medical examinations. Since many diseases are caused by the interaction of genetic predispositions and environmental factors, this leads to difficulties in distinguishing between discrimination which is based only on genetic predispositions and discrimination that is based on diseases which are at least partly caused by such predispositions. Why discrimination based on an individual's genotype should be protected and discrimination based on an individual's (gene-associated) already manifested disease, should not be, is incomprehensible. Because the limitation of coverage for group health plans, based on higher claims for gene-associated diseases constitutes unfair genetic discrimination, this type of discrimination should be prohibited. Unfortunately neither HIPAA nor GINA provides the necessary protection.

Overall, the main flaw of both HIPAA and GINA is the assumption that genetic information and thus genetic discrimination is different from discrimination based on regular medical examinations. First, the methods used in getting the information are not fundamentally different for genetic and regular medical examinations. Second, the quality of information does not differ fundamentally because the only suggested distinguishing feature, the better predictability of gene-associated diseases, is usually unreliable. Discrimination based on the possibility of the development of a disease-as shown-is less intrusive or stigmatizing than discrimination based on already manifest diseases. Third, by prohibiting the use of genetic information, HIPAA and GINA systematically neglect the information requirements of the individual and small group health insurance market and thereby endanger the availability and affordability of these health insurance market segments.

GINA in combination with HIPAA only provides for two protections against genetic discrimination. First, GINA fills the gap left open by HIPAA concerning the calculation of premiums of the whole group based on genetic information concerning an individual inside the group. Second, in the group market of health insurance, the use of genetic information is effectively banned in enrollment and premium calculation. These two provisions correspond to the view which we adopted earlier in this paper. In the group market of health insurance genetic information serves no actuarial purpose. Therefore, any use of genetic information in this market should be considered to be unfairly discriminatory. Unfortunately, these two protections are the only parts of HIPAA and GINA that are comprehensibly directed against unfair discrimination in health insurance.

Many new technological developments encompassing the Human Genome Project, such as gene-chips and microarrays, will offer great possibilities for diagnosis and treatment of diseases. Newborn screening, somatic cell therapy, and ultimately the field of pharmacogenomics show tremendous progress towards improving health care.

As "pharmacogenomics holds the promise that drugs might one day be tailor-made for individuals and adapted to each person's own genetic makeup," genetic information about an individual will be crucial in order to reach this goal. Unfortunately, the current legal environment counteracts the achievement of this goal by blocking access to genetic information and by fueling unjust fears of genetic discrimination.

In contrast to our findings relating to the impact of HIPAA and GINA on "genetic discrimination" in health insurance, we think that public policy should welcome this technological progress and promote the offered benefits to the American public instead of focusing on the creation of a negative view of genetics throughout society. Consequently, laws should not be oriented toward blocking society from receiving the benefits these new technological developments offer.

. . .

Notes & Questions

1. The Wisconsin statute restricting use of genetic test results is typical in that it focuses on the use of genetic information in determining eligibility for health insurance. Forty-five states have similar restrictions and nearly all of these (including Wisconsin) also forbid use of genetic information for risk classification purposes. *See* National Conference of State Legislatures, Genetic and Health Insurance: State Antidiscrimination Laws, http://www.ncsl.org/programs/health/genetics/ndishlth.htm. This means that genetic tests cannot be a factor in determining the premium rate of someone enrolled in a health plan provided by "an insurer, self-insured health plan, or county, city, village, or school board" in Wisconsin. What plans would be included within this ambit? Would Karen Schmidt be subject to exclusion by an individual health plan in Wisconsin? Suppose that she has learned about BRCA testing and been tested, but has not yet developed breast cancer; would Wisconsin's law afford her easier access to an individual health plan?

Note that the Wisconsin statute defines genetic test as "a test using [DNA] extracted from an individual's cells in order to determine the presence of a genetic disease or disorder or the individual's predisposition for a particular genetic disease or disorder." Is this a narrow or a broad proscription with respect to the use of genetic information? For a discussion of narrow and broad definitions of genetic information, *see* Chapter 3.

Contrast Wisconsin's statute with that of Colorado. Does it offer greater protection against discrimination by health insurers? The Colorado statute defines "genetic testing" as "any laboratory test of human DNA, RNA or chromosomes that is used to identify the presence or absence of alterations in genetic material which are associated with disease or illness." However it limits this definition to tests which are direct measures, rather than indirect indicators. What is an indirect indicator? Suppose the genetic mutation produces a protein or absence of a protein that can be tested for in the blood or urine. Would this qualify as an "indirect indicator"? Suppose the applicant is taking Tamoxifen as prophylaxis because of a family history of breast cancer. Is that an indirect indicator? Would Karen Schmidt be able to get health insurance in Colorado because of the protection of this law?

The Colorado statute contains a provision that requires the consent of the individual before any information derived from genetic testing is released and, moreover, forbids any entity that has received information derived from genetic testing from using the information in underwriting in any type of insurance. Slightly over half of the states have enacted enhanced confidentiality provisions with respect to genetic information. *See* National Conference of State Legislatures, *supra*; *see also* National Human Genome Research Institute, Policy and Legislation Database, http://www.genome.gov/PolicyEthics/LegDatabase/PubSearchResult.cfm (maintaining a searchable database). This treats genetic information in the same way that other stigmatizing medical information, such as presence of a mental health condition, is treated under the law. Is this genetic exceptionalism warranted? Is genetic information such a special class of the medical information that it should be accorded enhanced confidentiality protections? If so, why? Wouldn't other medical conditions, such as chronic back pain or chronic fatigue syndrome, be equally or more stigmatizing? Colorado's law is particularly far-reaching in that it provides both equitable relief as well as significant monetary damages for violation. In addition, the injured party may recover attorney fees and court costs. This allows the individual who has been injured by illegitimate use of genetic testing information to receive damages independent of being able to clearly demonstrate ascertainable dollar damages.

For discussion on the pros and cons of state antidiscrimination legislation, *see* Sonia M. Suter, *The Allure and Peril of Genetics Exceptionalism: Do We Need Special Genetics Legislation?*, 79 WASH. U. L. Q. 669 (2001); Chetan Gulati, *Genetic Antidiscrimination Laws in Health Insurance: A Misguided Solution*, 4 QUINNIPIAC HEALTH L.J. 149 (2001); Trudo Lemmens, *Selective Justice, Genetic Discrimination, and Insurance: Should We Single Out Genes in Our Laws?*, 45 MCGILL L.J. 347 (2000); George J. Annas, *The Limits of State Laws to Protect Genetic Information*, 345 N. ENG. J. MED. 385 (2001); Allison Ito, *Privacy and Genetics: Protecting Genetic Test Results in Hawai'i*, 25 U. HAW. L. REV. 449 (2003); Henry T. Greely, *Genotype Discrimination: The Complex Case for Some Legislative Protection*, 149 U. PA. L. REV. 1483 (2001); Richard A. Epstein, *The Legal Regulation of Genetic Discrimination: Old Responses to New Technology*, 74 B.U. L. REV. 1 (1994).

2. In addition to state antidiscrimination laws, the United States Congress has also considered and debated the issue of genetic discrimination repeatedly over the last several years. *See* Jonathan Weems, *A Proposal for a Federal Genetic Privacy Act*, 24 J. LEGAL MED. 109 (2003); Jeremy A. Colby, *An Analysis of Genetic Discrimination Legislation Proposed by the 105th Congress*, 24 AM. J. L. & MED. 443 (1998); Sharon J. Hussong, *Medical Records and Your Privacy: Developing Federal Legislation to Protect Patient Privacy Rights*, 26 AM. J.L. & MED. 453 (2000). For an ongoing catalog of federal laws and legislative bills, *see* National Human Genome Research Institute, Policy and Legislation Database, *supra*.

To date, however, the Health Insurance Portability and Accountability Act of 1996, Pub. L. No. 104-191, §§ 701–702 (HIPAA) is the only law that specifically addresses genetic discrimination with respect to health insurance. HIPAA prohibits group health plans from discriminating in eligibility or premium cost on the basis of health-related factors, including genetic information. As detailed in the Rich and Ziegler article, the definition in the implementing regulations is broad, encompassing "information about genes, gene products, and inherited characteristics that may derive from the individual or a family member." *See also* 26 C.F.R. § 54.9801-2T (2005). This does include family history and indirect indicators of genetic disorders. Under HIPAA, genetic information is broadly construed but is simultaneously undistinguished from other health status information.

While HIPAA does indeed prohibit genetic discrimination with respect to enrollment and premium cost in group health plans, its protections are not as far reaching as it may seem on first impression. As noted by Rich and Ziegler, the nondiscrimination requirements with respect to premium cost in a group plan prohibit an insurer or health plan from charging more for an individual in such a plan. However, HIPAA does not prohibit insurers or health plans from charging higher premiums to groups that have evidenced a higher claim payout history. Moreover, the provisions in HIPAA that relate to the individual market speak only to eligibility, not to assessment of premium cost.

Unlike HIPAA, the proposed Genetic Information Nondiscrimination Act (GINA), reproduced in Chapter 3, focuses specifically on genetics. It defines genetic information more narrowly and does not lump genetic information together with other health status information. With respect to group insurance, GINA protections would be more extensive than those provided by HIPAA in that premium cost for a group could not be adjusted on the basis of genetic information known about individuals in the group. Given the dynamics of the group market and the lack of medical underwriting, this may be a distinction without a difference. Increased claims payout costs would still be a rationale for different premiums among groups. However, with respect to individual insurance, GINA prohibits discrimination in eligibility or premium cost on the basis of genetic information. GINA's protections do not extend to other health status factors and insurers would still be able to assess actuarially justifiable premium costs on the basis of other health issues. Although GINA passed unanimously in the Senate in February 2005, it remains mired in the legislative process and, at present, is stalled.

3. Below are abbreviated, slightly modified versions of the three hypothetical cases presented in Part A of Chapter 3.

> (1) Sam, a twenty-five year-old engineer, learns that his father (age sixty) has been diagnosed with Huntington Disease (HD) and subsequently decides to be tested for the mutation. His test is positive. However, at age twenty-five, he is completely unaffected, actively working as a chief engineer in a small construction firm in Colorado. Sam's employer, Joe, knows of Sam's positive test. Joe wants to purchase health insurance for his company, but is worried about the effect Sam will have on his premium. He seeks your advice on what protections will apply to his company and Sam as he seeks a health plan product. Sam is also concerned and doesn't want his situation to imperil the chance for the rest of the employees to get health insurance. Sam is currently covered by his wife's policy, but his wife's employer is dropping dependent coverage. Sam is wondering if he should seek individual coverage so that he doesn't push the company's premium up. Joe is willing to put money in a health savings account to subsidize Sam's premium if Sam wants to get individual coverage. Is individual

coverage likely to be available to Sam at an affordable price? What effect does HIPAA have on the decisions Joe and Sam are contemplating? Suppose GINA passes. Does that change the analysis? What about Colorado law? How does that affect the decision-making process?

(2) Sally is a twenty-six year-old university graduate with a Master's Degree in special education. She suffers from cystic fibrosis (CF), an autosomal recessive disorder associated with a range of respiratory and gastrointestinal problems, as well as sterility in males. Unfortunately Sally's CF significantly limits her respiratory capacity and renders her exceptionally prone to infections. In other words, Sally's disease is both symptomatic and physically limiting. Heretofore, Sally has made a good living as an illustrator for children's books. She has paid out a significant percentage of her income to pay for individual coverage. Sally now has a chance to go to work as an illustrator for Good Kid Children's Books, the largest children's book publisher in the world. Good Kid has an excellent employee insurance package. Sally wants to know if she can depend on being covered by their group health plan. She has heard that HIPAA has an antidiscrimination provision with respect to genetics and other health status factors, but wants to be certain.

(3) Ted is a forty-two year old emergency room physician who is employed by an HMO. Ted has a strong family history of heart disease and his primary care physician recommends he undergo genetic testing to see if he has inherited any of the APOE gene variants that are linked to increased risk for some cardiovascular disorders (CVD). The testing reveals that Ted has one copy of the APOE e4 variant, which, in addition to indicating increased risk for CVD, is also associated with an increased risk for late onset familial Alzheimer's disease. Ted is covered by a group health policy provided by the HMO. However, in the wake of his testing results, Ted has decided to move to Hawaii, work part-time as a locum tenems doctor, and live his life-long dream of being a surfer. His concern is that in making this change he will have to buy individual coverage once his COBRA extension is exhausted and he is worried about the effect his genetic test will have on his eligibility and the cost of his premium. What protection does he have under HIPAA? Suppose GINA passes. Does that make Ted's decision easier?

4. The ADA, while primarily an employment antidiscrimination statute (*see* full discussion of the ADA in Chapter 3), also has provisions that relate to health insurance. The ADA addresses employer-provided health insurance plans and prohibits employers from participating in health insurance and other contracts that may discriminate against employees with disabilities. *See* 42 U.S.C. § 12112(b)(2). The pertinent provision states:

> [T]his Act shall not be construed to prohibit or restrict—
>
> (1) an insurer ... from underwriting risks, classifying risks, or administering such risks that are based on ... State law; or
>
> (2) a person or organization covered by this [Act] from establishing, sponsoring, observing or administering the terms of a bona fide benefit plan that are based on underwriting risks, classifying risks, or administering such risks that are ... not inconsistent with State law; or
>
> (3) a person or organization covered by this [Act] from establishing, sponsoring, observing or administering the terms of a bona fide benefit plan that is not subject to State laws that regulate insurance.

> Paragraphs (1), (2), and (3) shall not be used as a subterfuge to evade the purposes of [the Act].

42 U.S.C. § 12201(c). To have a claim under the ADA, the aggrieved employee must show that the terms of the plan make a disability-based distinction. Even if the plan contains a disability-based distinction, the employer may be able to show that it falls within a "safe harbor" because the plan is "bona fide" and that the distinction is not a subterfuge for disability discrimination. A "bona fide" plan is one that a) exists and pays benefits and b) has terms that have been accurately communicated to eligible employees. To demonstrate that a disability-based distinction is not a subterfuge, it is necessary for an employer to provide specific and detailed evidence of a legitimate business/insurance justification. *See* Steven Eisenstat, *Capping Health Insurance Benefits for AIDS: An Analysis of Disability-Based Distinctions Under the Americans with Disabilities Act*, 10 J.L. & Pol. 1 (1993). The question of genetic information being used in the connection with employer-provided health insurance was addressed in 1995 by the EEOC. The EEOC clarified the role of genetic information as follows:

> This part of the definition of "disability" applies to individuals who are subjected to discrimination on the basis of genetic information relating to illness, disease, or other disorders. Covered entities that discriminate against individuals on the basis of such genetic information are regarding the individuals as having impairments that substantially limit a major life activity. Those individuals, therefore, are covered by the third part of the definition of "disability."

EEOC Compliance Manual § 902, at 902–45 (1995) (definition of the term "disability"); *see also* Lynda M. Fox & Sherman G. Finesilver, *Genetics and the Workplace: ADA Applicability to Genetic Information*, Colo. Law., Apr. 1997, at 75. To date, the ADA provisions addressing genetic information have not generated any litigation with respect to health insurance eligibility or coverage.

B. Genetic Discrimination in Life, Disability, and Long Term Care Insurance

Ashley Biser & Peter Shorett, *Genetics and Life, Disability, and Long-Term Care Insurance: A Report on Law in the United States*

(2004), *available at* http://www.genelaw.info/reports/ldltcc.pdf

I. Introduction

Insurance provides financial protection against unanticipated losses. In contrast to health insurance, which pays for the expected costs of routine health care and the unexpected medical costs of catastrophic events, life, disability, and long-term care insurance serve a different goal. Life insurance offers protection against unanticipated loss of income caused by a death in the family, allowing dependents to pay off a mortgage or other debts. In the case of disability insurance, offsetting an unanticipated loss of earnings caused by a disabling injury or disease is the primary aim. Long-term care insurance both supports full-time assistance for those who can no longer function on their own and protects assets from being devoured by such costs.

Advances in the life sciences are transforming the assessment of health risks in individuals and groups. As these predictive and diagnostic technologies begin to alter insurance underwriting practices, policymakers are struggling to develop appropriate safeguards to ensure fair and equitable use of genetic information. This report evaluates current legal and legislative responses to genetic discrimination in life, disability, and long-term care insurance.

Following the criteria outlined by Paul Billings et al in their seminal study of the subject, this report defines genetic discrimination as "discrimination against an individual or against members of that individual's family solely because of real or perceived differences from the 'normal' genome of that individual. Genetic discrimination is distinguished from discrimination based on disabilities caused by altered genes by excluding, from the former category, those instances of discrimination against an individual who at the time of the discriminatory act was affected by the genetic disease." Genetic information is defined as any information used to define a hereditary component of risk, including, but not limited to, the results of DNA and RNA-based tests; chemical, blood and urine analyses; physical examinations; and family history information. Genetic test is defined as any test or exam, or information about a test or an exam that produces genetic information.

Before continuing, it is also necessary to review the ways in which life, disability, and long-term care insurance function. Life insurance pays a set amount of money to the beneficiaries of a policy-holder in the event of his or her death. This money can help pay burial expenses, as well as a mortgage and other outstanding debt. While term insurance policies pay out benefits only if the insured dies within a specified period of time, permanent insurance continues as long as premiums are paid. Approximately 70% of American families owned some form of life insurance in 1998.

Disability income insurance provides payments to individuals and families in the event of an accident or illness that interferes with the ability to work. Instead of providing a set amount, disability benefits depend on the insured individual's pre-disability income and the extent of the disability. Indemnity payments partially replace the income lost due to disability and can continue either temporarily or over an extended period of time. While non-cancellable policies keep premiums at the same level throughout the life of the policy, guaranteed renewable policies can adjust premiums based on more recent information. In each case, the policies cannot be cancelled so long as premiums are paid.

Finally, long-term care insurance offers protection against medical events that interfere with the ability to care for oneself. These benefits offset the cost of care for those who can no longer perform the basic activities of daily life. Depending on the plan, the insured is reimbursed a set amount for the cost of care in a residential facility, hospice, or for in-home assistance. While currently a relatively small market, long-term care insurance is increasing in importance rapidly and is projected to continue doing so, given the advancing age of the population. Because it is purchased later in life, and it is difficult to estimate how long the insured will survive and need care, premiums for long-term care insurance are comparatively high.

II. Genetic Information and Insurance Underwriting

Insurers rely on a process of risk selection and risk classification in order to determine eligibility and premiums. For life insurance, eligibility and premiums are based on age, sex, and medical history.

For disability insurers, the insured individual's income and occupation, as well as any particularly risky behaviors, are also factored into the equation. Long-term care insurers rely on factors similar to those used by life insurers, but include an exam of an applicant's cognitive and functional abilities. Overall, life insurers offer coverage to more than 90% of applicants, with a small percentage being offered coverage at substandard rates. Disability and long-term care insurers, on the other hand, have a higher refusal rate of about 10%.

While most health insurance plans are group-based and involve only limited individual underwriting, a far greater proportion of life, disability and long-term care policies are individual in nature. Two-thirds of life insurance policies and over a quarter of all disability insurance policies are individual plans. The numbers jump even higher for long-term care, where individual underwriting is involved in over two-thirds of all policies. Given the importance of long-term risk analysis and individual underwriting in life, disability and long-term care insurance, genetic information is perceived to be a powerful tool for determining an individual's risk of mortality or morbidity.

For life insurers, early death results in fewer premiums payments (and sometimes higher benefits). So the ability of life insurers to predict who is at risk for diseases which significantly reduce life span is central to the life insurance industry. Already, significant use is made of family medical histories for just this purpose. Access to genetic information might allow for greater precision in determining risk, thus allowing premiums to more closely mirror risk.

For disability insurers, as well, the ability to predict who is more likely to develop a debilitating disease allows insurers to weed out those who are most likely to make costly claims. Or, depending on the severity of the disease, insurers might provide reduced benefits or charge certain individuals higher premiums. Again, the oft-lauded predictive ability of genetic information could be invaluable to these insurers.

For long-term care insurers, the likelihood of incapacitation is of primary interest. The ability to predict who is likely to develop a condition that will inhibit the ability to care for oneself and thus require extensive assistance gives insurance companies an incentive to predict who is at greater risk for such disorders. The ability to predict one's susceptibility to mental disorders, such as Alzheimer's disease, is of particular interest to this industry. Because mental disorders are not necessarily accompanied by swift physical deterioration, they are often difficult to clinically detect. Moreover, patients with such disorders often spend years in care facilities and account for a large percentage of long-term care costs. Alzheimer's patients require a great deal of nursing care and live for an average of eight to ten years after diagnosis. Especially given the late purchase age of those with long-term care insurance and the shorter time period during which premiums are paid before making a claim, long-term care insurers have a great interest in eliminating such high-risk persons from the insurance pool.

At present, however, the ability of genetic information to provide predictive health data is limited. Except for rare cases, such as Huntington's Disease, the predictive data on the future onset of a disease is either inaccurate, imprecise, or both. Genetic tests rarely provide insight into whether an individual will be severely afflicted by a disease, or simply exhibit mild symptoms. Precisely because of the preliminary nature of most genetic research, its use in current insurance practices has yet to be explored and there is little data on its prevalence. In a 1998 survey of insurance companies operating in Kentucky for the state legislature, researchers found no evidence of required testing on the part of life and disability insurance companies. Insurers did, however, make use of the results of genetic tests reported in an applicant's medical history. Additionally, life and disability insurers utilize the Medical Information Bureau (MIB), which also contains information about insurance applicant's medical history and genetic tests.

While data on the prevalence of genetic testing remains scarce, the usage of family history information by life, disability and long-term care insurers is well-documented. In the Kentucky survey, every single life and disability insurer reported using family history data in their underwriting procedures. In the American Council of Life Insurers' pamphlet on the "Life Insurers' Need for Medical Information," current medical information and family history are both port rayed as essential to the process of life insurance underwriting.

At the moment, available genetic tests offer little more information than that provided by detailed and accurate family histories. Indeed, actuaries suggest that accurate and well-researched family history information is sufficient for accurate risk classification. Given the adequacy of family history data relative to current tests, the prohibitive cost of such testing, and the aforementioned limits on genetic tests' applicability—not to mention the fact that few genes have been discovered for which such tests have been developed—the low prevalence of the use of genetic information in life, disability and long-term care insurance underwriting is hardly surprising.

III. The Potential for Genetic Discrimination in Life, Disability, and Long-Term Care Insurance

Despite the lack of an industry-wide standard on the use of genetic tests in life, disability and long-term care insurance, insurance companies appear to be willing to use genetic information gained from other sources. There are documented instances of discrimination in life insurance against presymptomatic individuals with Huntington's Disease and Hurler syndrome, as well as cases of discrimination against asymptomatic individuals with hemochromatosis and Charcot-Marie-Tooth (CMT) disease. Discrimination against asymptomatic individuals seeking disability insurance is also documented in these studies. Because Huntington's and Hurler syndrome are both fatal, it is arguable that discrimination against such pre-symptomatic individuals is not unfair. However, in the case of hemochromatosis and CMT, these diseases are clinically variable and pose no great threat to a long, healthy life. In the United Kingdom, additional cases of genetic discrimination in life insurance have been documented against individuals with tuberous sclerosis (TS) and cardiomyopathy. Even more troubling is discrimination against those whose genetic tests indicate merely a predisposition or susceptibility toward a disorder. While data remains scarce, discrimination against women who test positive for breast cancer susceptibility has also been documented. Regardless of whether coverage is eventually offered, it appears to be more difficult for individuals with a genetic risks [sic] to obtain coverage than average individuals. In a 1998 study of individuals belonging to genetic support groups in the United Kingdom, researchers found that 33.4% of the study group with a genetic predisposition had difficulty obtaining life insurance, as opposed to five percent of those in the general population. In the Kentucky survey, two out of five life and disability insurers reported that they had used genetic information to deny coverage.

Moreover, reliable studies have shown that the fear of genetic discrimination, regardless of whether it is practiced, has prompted individuals to resist participating in genetic research studies. Even among genetic counselors, fear of discrimination runs high. In one study, 68% of respondents would not bill their insurance companies for a genetic test for either colon or breast cancer and 26% of respondents would go so far as to use an alias in order to make sure that the results of genetic tests could not be used against them. Not only are possible cases of genetic discrimination averted when people refuse to get tested, but the interest in encouraging such research would suggest that prohibiting discriminatory use, regardless the actual incidence of genetic discrimination, might still be worthwhile.

Most observers argue that future genetic discrimination in life, disability, and long-term care insurance is much more likely relative to health insurance for several reasons. First, as mentioned earlier, individual underwriting is more important in these industries than in health insurance. Because life, disability and long-term care insurance are voluntary and employees often pay most of the premiums (even when plans are employer-sponsored), individually underwritten plans are more prevalent. Second, life, disability and long-term care contracts are generally longer in duration than are health plans. Whereas people change health plans frequently along with changes in employment, most life, disability and long-term care insurance policies are permanent and can be cancelled only upon non-payment of premiums. Indeed, some plans do not even raise premiums over this period of time. According to the insurance industry, this gives life, disability and long-term care insurers only one chance to classify an individual's risk, rather than the numerous opportunities afforded to health insurers. Third, these types of insurance protect against harms that may occur twenty to thirty years in the future, whereas health insurers are primarily worried about short-term changes in health status.

For health insurers, an individual's current medical status is a sufficient and much more accurate predictor than is genetic information. Lastly, supplemental life, disability and long-term care insurance are often available for purchase. Since there is no natural limit to benefits (as in health insurance), individuals can use life insurance as an investment option. It is this ability to purchase "extra" insurance, especially in the case of life insurance, that is of primary concern to the insurance industry. Fairness in insurance allocation requires an equality of information between providers and applicants. Adverse selection refers to the tendency of insurers to issue standard policies to sub-standard applicants because of uncontemplated risks. Such outcomes result from applicants withholding information relevant to risk selection and classification. The assumption is thus that greater accuracy provided by genetic information will reduce overall premiums by allowing insurers to weed out those who are likely to tax the insurance pool. Because genetic testing can also be used to show that individuals who are at risk for a genetic disorder do not in fact carry a specific mutation, insurance companies argue that denying access to this sort of information unfairly discriminates against those with certain family histories.

The primary players in this debate are life insurers, who suggest that blocking insurer access to genetic information would, in effect, signal an end to medical underwriting and establish a "right" to life insurance. Warnings of a fundamental restructuring of the industry are frequent. This fear of financial insolvency hinges on the assumption that individuals would alter their purchasing habits on the basis of their genetic information. Many industry advocates argue that anti-discrimination laws, especially for life insurers, will result in individual's purchasing more coverage because they are certain of making a claim. The argument suggests that this would result in more claims than the industry can financially accommodate, and necessitate higher premiums or financial collapse. While few studies have been performed to test this assumption, those that exist suggest that adverse selection is less likely than insurers have suggested. For instance, in a study of women who had tested positive for BRCA1 (one of the known genes associated with breast cancer), researchers found no evidence of a change in life insurance purchasing habits on the part of those who had tested positive. Of the women who already had life insurance, none sought additional coverage. Nor did those without insurance seek to purchase larger policies on the basis of this knowledge.

IV. State Legislation

Compared to the legislation of genetic discrimination in health insurance, the regulation of genetic information in life, disability and long-term care insurance is limited. Only nineteen states have any legislation that addresses the use of genetic information by life, disability, and long-term care insurers, and only twelve of these restrict such use. State regulation of these industries exists in a federal vacuum and is widely varied. While Arizona offers disability insurance applicants the exact same protections offered to those seeking health insurance, most states exempt life, disability and long-term care insurance from general prohibitions against genetic discrimination. At least four (AK, DE, MO, NH) states explicitly allow the use of genetic information in life, disability and long-term care insurance.

Life Insurance

Sixteen states restrict life insurance underwriting on the basis of genetic information (AZ, CA, FL, KS, ME, MD, MA, MN, MT, NM, NJ, NC, NY, OR,VT, WI).This legislation attempts to regulate, rather than prohibit, the use of genetic information. Either through exceptions to general prohibitions or through explicit regulations requiring that genetic information be used in accordance with actuarial projections and/or claims experience, each of these laws carries with it a conception of fair discrimination. Whether the law offers protection does not hinge on whether discrimination is practiced, but on whether it is performed accurately. Only discrimination that is deemed "unfair" is proscribed.

This model closely approximates the industry norm of actuarial fairness or the requirement that equal risks be treated equally. Not all insurance decisions are made on the basis of this norm, however. In some cases, societal interests in prohibiting discrimination outweigh actuarial projections; insurers are not allowed to discriminate on the basis of race, religion, zip code and other factors in setting insurance premiums and eligibility, despite the fact that African-Americans, for example, have a lower average life-expectancy than do Caucasians. At the beginning of the AIDS epidemic, California and other states prohibited discrimination on the basis of sexual orientation in life insurance, despite the high initial prevalence of the disease in the gay community. Whether a risk is actuarially significant or not, permissible use is determined socially, and not simply by insurers.

While no state outright prohibits the use of genetic information in life insurance, some state statutes are stricter than others. The primary differences between state laws hinge on the question of how to determine the fairness of discrimination. Nine states require that the use of genetic information in underwriting for life insurance be in accordance with actuarial projections, claims experience, and/or a reasonable relationship between the genetic condition and increased risk. For instance, New Jersey prohibits unfair discrimination on the basis of genetic information in the issuance, witholding, extension, or renewal of life insurance policies. Unfair discrimination includes, but is not restricted to an application of the results of a genetic test that is not reasonably related to anticipated claims experience.

Stricter statutes cover all stages of the insurance application process and also deal with differences in claims on the basis of genetic information. They also provide enforcement mechanisms to ensure that infractions can be punished. Four states (ME, NJ,

NY, VT) allow the office that oversees insurance companies in the state to penalize violators, though only Vermont provides criminal penalties and a private right of action.

Since many genetic conditions could be associated with increased costs for insurers, much legislation only covers persons who are carriers for genetic disease—but are not themselves affected. Four states make this restriction explicit by prohibiting discrimination against carriers a "genetic trait that is harmless in itself," or "a gene which may, under some circumstances, be associated with disability in that person's offspring, but which causes no adverse effects on the carrier." However, the exceptions inherent in broader legislation severely limit the applicability of such statutes. Admittedly, legislation on fair trade practices protects against gross discrepancies between risk and premium increases, but it does not provide protection for asymptomatic and pre-symptomatic individuals.

Moreover, such legislation provides little guidance on how to treat cases in which the phenotypic expression of a genetic condition varies greatly and cannot be predicted on the basis of genetic testing alone. For instance, sufferers of tuberous sclerosis (TS) all have the same genetic mutation, but the effects of this condition vary from a mild skin rash to severe mental and health problems. In its severe state, TS might qualify as a condition on the basis of which it is legal to discriminate.

Since life insurance legislation is limited, many analysts have suggested the use of privacy laws to restrict insurers' access to the results of genetic testing. Genetic and health privacy statutes in 29 states provide varying restrictions on third-party disclosure of genetic information. Yet, unlike laws regulating health insurance, which often ban both insurer access to and use of the results of genetic tests, the legislation dealing with the life, disability, and long-term care insurance industries is far less stringent. While nine states specifically require informed consent for life and disability insurers to access genetic information, some states simply require that the insurer bear the cost of any such testing. Maine's life insurance privacy protections protect individuals' right not to know their genetic information and require individuals to consent to being informed of the results of their tests. Three additional states provide specific restrictions on life and disability insurer access to genetic information, yet do not prohibit its use. Four states define genetic information as personal property, though the ramifications of these laws have yet to be tested in court. At the present moment, the overall effect of such privacy legislation in the context of life insurance is unclear.

Disability Insurance

Much of the regulation surrounding disability insurance treats the industry in the same manner as life insurance, though two states (CO and WY) that do not provide protection in life insurance offer some form of regulation in terms of disability insurance. Sixteen states restrict the use of genetic information in disability insurance underwriting. Arizona, California and Kansas offer the most extensive protection; each of these states prohibits the use of genetic information in disability insurance underwriting without exception. The remaining states prohibit "unfair" discrimination on the basis of genetic information; in other words, the use of such information to either deny coverage or raise premiums must be supported by actuarial projections or claims experience. In Colorado and Wyoming, similar protections are in place, but their applicability is restricted to group disability plans. Vermont exempts employee benefit plans from its legislation.

Long-Term Care Insurance

Regulation of long-term care insurance is even more limited than that of life and disability insurance. While several states cover long-term care insurance under regulations regarding "other types of insurance," only nine states (CA, CO, KS, MA, ME, MT, NM, OR, VT) have regulations specific to long-term care insurance. Four of these states (CO, MA, OR, VT) restrict the insurer's ability to require tests, but do not place restrictions on the use of test results. Like legislation dealing with life insurance, laws restricting the use of genetic information in long-term care insurance are framed in terms of prohibiting unfair discrimination. New Mexico prohibits use of tests unless actuarially justified. Kansas requires a reasonable relationship to risk, and Maine demands a relationship to anticipated claims experience. Overall, however, the relatively small size of the market and its comparatively small legislative weight have meant that long-term care insurance goes largely unregulated.

V. Relevant Case Law

To date, no court case addressing genetic discrimination in life, disability or long-term care insurance has been decided. However, numerous legal precedents effect both the relationship of genetic testing to definitions of disease and non-genetic discrimination in life insurance. In *Katskee v. Blue Cross/Blue Shield*, Katskee underwent prophylactic surgery to remove her uterus, ovaries and fallopian tubes on the basis of her family's history of breast and ovarian cancer. Blue Cross/Blue Shield refused to cover the cost of the surgery, arguing that a predisposition toward cancer did not qualify as an illness, and thus that the surgery was not medically necessary. However, the appellate court held that a diagnosis on the basis of family history of disease does constitute an illness as covered under Katskee's health insurance policy; in this case, an illness was defined as a "deviation from what is considered a normal, healthy physical state." The implications of this case for those concerned about genetic discrimination remain unclear. The equation of a genetic risk with a disease may result in considering all genetic susceptibilities as clinical diagnoses. Since most laws allow discrimination in life, disability and long-term care insurance on the basis of a disease that has been clinically diagnosed, this would greatly limit the applicability of such statutes.

Even if a genetic susceptibility would be considered a clinical diagnosis, the court has upheld laws requiring a reasonable relationship between increases in insurance premiums and the risk posed by such a condition. In *Chabner v. United of Omaha Life Insurance Company*, the court found that the insurance company violated California state law requiring discrimination in insurance be in accordance with sound actuarial principles. While the disease in question was not genetic and Chabner had exhibited clinical symptoms, the decrease in life expectancy was found to be incongruous with the 96.5% increase in premiums Chabner was asked to pay. Although the court decided in favor of Chabner according to California's Insurance Code, it denied his claim that the Americans with Disabilities Act accessibility requirement would demand that standard premiums be offered to all applicants. Instead, the court held that the ADA accessibility requirement applies only to the physical accessibility of the insurance office and not to the accessibility of its products.

VI. Conclusion: An Overview of Model Legislation

To provide guidance for states wishing to enact legislation dealing with genetic discrimination in life, disability and long-term care insurance, the National Conference of Insurance Legislators (NCOIL) has drafted a model act on the use of genetic information in life and disability insurance. This act requires informed consent for insurer access to genetic information and sets out the ways in which such information could be used. The act defines a genetic test as "the analysis of human DNA, RNA, chromosomes, proteins, and certain metabolites, including analysis of genotypes, mutations, or karyotypes (i.e. family history), for the purpose of predicting risk of disease in asymptomatic or undiagnosed individuals."

In order to both ensure access to insurance products for those with genetic risk factors and protect insurance companies against the risk of adverse selection, the model law sets up a two-tiered system. For all policies above a certain value ($100,000 for life insurance, $60,000 for disability insurance), the NCOIL Model Act specifically allows insurers to ask about genetic tests for catastrophic diseases and related genes, gain access to results of tests taken and use genetic information in accordance with actuarial projections of a significant increase in mortality and morbidity. Those who refuse to answer questions regarding genetic tests when applying for policies above these limits can be refused coverage. The law also allows for favorable use of genetic tests in order for individuals to prove to the company that they do not carry a certain genetic mutation. Genetic information cannot be accessed or used for policies below these limits.

In order to determine which genes qualify as indicators of catastrophic illness, the act instructs the state's Insurance Commissioner to create a list for both life and disability insurers of catastrophic diseases and related genes. Only genes and diseases included on this list would be acceptable bases for discrimination. The act also sets out the criteria for the creation of this list. A gene must have at least an 80% correlation with the eventual development of a disease and a disease must pose a probability of death or disability (respectively) of at least 50%.

In the process of drafting its suggested legislation, NCOIL solicited comments on the act from various organizations representing the interested parties. In their responses, these organizations were uniformly concerned about the logistical difficulties of such a two-tiered system and the list of catastrophic diseases and genes. Blue Cross/Blue Shield of America underscored the importance of insurer access to information for treatment, administrative and billing purposes. Also of common concern was the ambiguity surrounding the act's definitions of genetic tests and genetic information.

Those organizations representing the insurance industry saw in the act dangerous tendencies that would inhibit insurers' ability to continue the practice of medical underwriting. The American Council of Life Insurers (ACLI), specifically, saw the act as a "radical solution" to a non-existent problem, which would, in effect, end all medical underwriting for life and disability insurers because of its overly broad definitions of genetic information and tests. By allowing applicants for policies below the set limits to withhold information, ACLI suggests that the act "legitimizes fraud." The American Academy of Actuaries (AAA) also suggested that the act undermines the principle of informational symmetry that is at the heart of the insurance industry and offers protections unnecessarily to those who could already be insured at a higher rate.

Those organizations representing consumers and those applying for insurance had opposite worries. Both the National Society of Genetic Counselors (NSGC) and the Council for Responsible Genetics (CRG) worried that the policy limits set for in the law were too low to offer protection for the majority of insurance applicants. NSGC also questioned the use of genetic information in life-insurance decision-making given that all consumers have genetic dispositions toward disease, only some of which are known or testable. NSGC was also concerned by the complexity of tests and the likelihood of misunderstanding/misuse of test results by untrained personnel.

Chabner v. United of Omaha Life Insurance

225 F.3d 1042 (9th Cir. 2000)

Hug, Chief Judge:

...

Howard Chabner suffers from a progressive condition called fascioscapulohumeral muscular dystrophy (FSH MD), a rare form of muscular dystrophy. The condition has confined Chabner to a wheelchair since 1991 and has caused "marked wasting" of his extremities. Chabner takes medication to help control the condition, and his doctor administers annual electrocardiograms to detect any cardiomyopathy that may arise.

On May 3, 1993, Chabner, who was 35 years old at the time, applied to United for whole life insurance. United forwarded Chabner's application to an underwriter who had experience in underwriting insurance policies for applicants with muscular dystrophy, but not with FSH MD. United possessed no internally developed actuarial data for people with FSH MD, and so its underwriter turned to external sources to estimate Chabner's mortality risk. The underwriter, who was not a doctor, arranged to have Chabner examined by a paramedic, reviewed Chabner's medical records, and consulted two underwriting source materials: the Cologne Life Reinsurance Company's "Life Underwriting Manual" ("Cologne manual"); and "Medical Selection of Life Risks" by R.D.C. Brackenridge and W. John Elder ("Brackenridge manual"). After reviewing these materials, the underwriter authorized a policy with a "Table 6" rating, which corresponded to a mortality rate of 150 percent above standard.

United offered Chabner a $100,000 whole life policy at a cost of $1,076 per year. Of the $1,076 annual premium, $305.44 was applied to the cost of insurance, and the remainder was invested in the policy's cash accumulation and surrender values. By contrast, even though the annual premium for a standard whole life policy (without an increased mortality rating) would have been the same $1,076, only $155.44 of that annual premium would have been applied to the cost of insurance, which would result in an additional $150 being invested in the policy's cash accumulation and surrender values each year.

Chabner accepted the policy, but inquired about the reason for his nonstandard premium. United's Vice President and Senior Medical Director of Underwriting sent Chabner a letter attempting to explain the nonstandard rating. In the letter, United acknowledged that FSH MD "has only a small effect on mortality" and stated that it reduced life expectancy by four years for a non-smoking man of his age. Unsatisfied, Chabner wrote United on two more occasions to inquire why his premium was 96.5% greater than standard if his condition had only a small effect on mortality. United did not respond, and Chabner filed this action.

Chabner filed his original complaint in California Superior Court on January 3, 1995, alleging violations of California's Insurance Code, its Business and Professions Code, its Unruh Civil Rights Act, and common law fraud. After United removed the case to federal court based on diversity jurisdiction, Chabner amended his complaint to add a claim under the ADA. Chabner sought class certification and moved for summary judgment on all but his fraud claim. The district court denied class certification, but granted Chabner's motion for summary judgment. The district court held that the ADA applies to insurance underwriting, that California law provides Chabner with a private cause of action for the alleged violation of the state insurance code, and that

United's actions in this case violated the ADA, the California Insurance Code and the Business and Professions Code, and the Unruh Civil Rights Act. In subsequent orders the court denied United's motions for reconsideration and ultimately ordered United to issue Chabner a new policy that conformed to the court's order granting summary judgment. The court dismissed Chabner's remaining fraud claim, pursuant to Chabner's request, and entered final judgment on September 28, 1998. United timely filed its notice of appeal on October 23, 1998. We have jurisdiction pursuant to 28 U.S.C. § 1291.

Discussion
I. The ADA

...

Chabner alleges that the nonstandard premium that United charged him for his insurance policy violated the ADA. Recently, however, we held that although Title III of the ADA requires an insurance office to be physically accessible to the disabled, it does not address the terms of the policies the insurance companies sells. *See Weyer v. Twentieth Century Fox Film Corp.,* 198 F.3d 1104, 1115 (9th Cir.2000). We therefore hold that United did not violate the ADA by offering Chabner a nonstandard policy.

Title III of the ADA provides: "No individual shall be discriminated against on the basis of disability in the full and equal enjoyment of the goods, services, facilities, privileges, advantages, or accommodations of any place of public accommodation by any person who owns, leases (or leases to), or operates a place of public accommodation." 42 U.S.C. § 12182(a). The ADA also includes a "safe harbor" provision, which says that "[the ADA] shall not be construed to prohibit or restrict ... an insurer ... from underwriting risks, classifying risks, or administering such risks that are based on or not inconsistent with State law...." 42 U.S.C. § 12201(c).

Weyer, which was handed down after the district court's order was issued, concerned the question of whether an insurance company that administers an employer-provided disability plan was a "place of public accommodation" under Title III of the Americans with Disabilities Act. We found that the term "place of public accommodation" required a connection between the good or service complained of and an actual physical place.... In adopting this approach, we followed the Third and Sixth Circuits, each of which agreed that an insurance company that administered an employer-provided disability plan was not a "place of public accommodation" under the ADA because the employees received their benefits through employment, and not through a public accommodation. Taking these cases at face value, we are led to conclude that a similar distinction between "access" and "content" applies to this case. Here, we reiterate our observation, set forth in *Weyer*, that "an insurance office must be physically accessible to the disabled but need not provide insurance that treats the disabled equally with the non-disabled." Therefore, we do not uphold the district court's decision based upon the ADA.

II. California Law

...

A. Business and Professions Code section 17200 and Insurance Code section 10144.

In his complaint Chabner alleged violations of California Insurance Code section 10144, and California Business and Professions Code section 17200. Insurance Code Section 10144 provides, in relevant part:

> No insurer issuing [life insurance] shall refuse to insure, or refuse to continue to insure, ... or charge a different rate for the same coverage solely because of a physical or mental impairment, except where the refusal ... or rate differential is based on sound actuarial principles or is related to actual and reasonably anticipated experience....

Cal. Ins.Code § 10144. This statutory provision would have prohibited United from charging Chabner a nonstandard premium due to his FSH MD, unless the premium was based on sound actuarial principles or was related to actual and reasonably anticipated experience. However, it is unclear whether this insurance code section provides Chabner with a private cause of action. The parties did not address this issue in their briefs, and therefore we do not address it.

Chabner, however, also claimed violations of California Business and Professions Code section 17200. Section 17200 is part of the Unfair Competition Law, Cal. Bus. & Prof.Code §§ 17200–17209, and provides, in relevant part, that "unfair competition shall mean and include any unlawful, unfair or fraudulent business act or practice." Cal. Bus. & Prof.Code § 17200. Private causes of action for violations of Business and Professions Code section 17200 are authorized by Business and Professions Code section 17204. The district court held that Insurance Code section 10144 may be used to define the contours of a private cause of action under Business and Professions Code section 17200. We agree.

The California Supreme Court has held that section 17200 "defines 'unfair competition' very broadly, to include 'anything that can properly be called a business practice and that at the same time is forbidden by law.'" By proscribing 'any unlawful' business practice, section 17200 'borrows' violations of other laws and treats them as unlawful practices that the unfair competition law makes independently actionable." It does not matter whether the underlying statute also provides for a private cause of action; section 17200 can form the basis for a private cause of action even if the predicate statute does not.

There are limits on the causes of action that can be maintained under section 17200. A court may not allow a plaintiff to "plead around an absolute bar to relief simply by recasting the cause of action as one for unfair competition." This limit is rather narrow, however. "To forestall an action under [section 17200], another provision must actually 'bar' the action or clearly permit the conduct."

As applied to this case, the district court was correct in holding that Chabner could maintain a cause of action under section 17200 for United's alleged violation of section 10144. Setting the premium for a life insurance policy can quite "properly be called a business practice." Also, United's alleged misconduct (charging Chabner a discriminatory premium that is neither actuarially sound nor based on reasonably anticipated experience) would run afoul of section 10144, if proven. Accordingly, the prerequisites for "borrowing" a violation of section 10144 and treating it as a violation of section 17200 exist in this case.

Moreover, the narrow limitations on causes of action under section 17200 do not prevent this claim. First, no statutory provision permits United to charge arbitrarily discriminatory premiums, and United does not dispute this fact. Second, nothing specifically bars this cause of action.

United points to *Moradi-Shalal v. Fireman's Fund Insurance Cos.*, 758 P.2d 58 ([Cal.] 1988), and *Manufacturers Life Insurance Co. v. Superior Court*, 895 P.2d 56 ([Cal.] 1995), to argue otherwise. *Moradi-Shalal* held that Insurance Code section 790.03, which is part of the Unfair Insurance Practices Act ("UIPA"), did not create a private cause of action against an insurer that violated section 790.03(h) (regulating insurers' unfair practices in settling claims). *Manufacturers Life* then held that plaintiffs could not use section 17200 to plead a cause of action based on a violation of section 790.03(h), because to do so would undermine *Moradi-Shalal.* United argues that these two cases apply here because another subsection of the UIPA, subsection 790.03(f), defines unfair rate discrimination and therefore governs United's alleged misconduct in this case. United argues that because private plaintiffs cannot bring a direct cause of action under section 790.03(h), and because they cannot get around that bar by using section 17200, they also cannot do so for violations of section 790.03(f).

United's argument overlooks the fact that Chabner predicates his section 17200 action on a violation of section 10144, not on a violation of section 790.03(f). The two statutes, section 10144 and section 790.03(f), regulate similar types of conduct: charging different premiums for arbitrary reasons. However, even assuming that *Moradi-Shalal* and *Manufacturers Life* prevent causes of action based on section 790.03(f), it does not necessarily follow that they also prevent causes of action based on section 10144. In *Manufacturers Life,* although the court held that the plaintiff could not proceed with a section 17200 claim where the predicate statute was section 790.03(h), it allowed the plaintiff to proceed with a section 17200 claim where the predicate statute was the Cartwright Act, even though the conduct that allegedly violated the Cartwright Act was the same conduct that allegedly violated section 790.03(h). In this case, as in *Manufacturers Life,* "[t]here is no attempt to use [section 17200] to confer private standing to enforce a provision of the UIPA," because section 10144, like the Cartwright Act, is not part of the UIPA. Nor is Chabner's cause of action "based on conduct which is absolutely privileged or immunized by another statute." As the California Supreme Court has explained, the *Manufacturers Life* court, in construing the UIPA and section 17200, "expressly concluded that in adopting the UIPA the Legislature had not granted a general exemption from antitrust and unfair competition statutes." Therefore, section 790.03 and *Moradi-Shalal* do not prevent Chabner from using section 10144 to define the contours of his section 17200 action, and the district court correctly allowed him to proceed with that claim.

B. The Unruh Civil Rights Act.

Chabner also claims that United's actions violated California's Unruh Civil Rights Act. The Unruh Civil Rights Act provides, in relevant part, that "[a]ll persons within the jurisdiction of this state are free and equal, and no matter what their ... disability are entitled to the full and equal accommodations, advantages, facilities, privileges, or services in all business establishments of every kind whatsoever." Cal. Civ.Code § 51. The Act also provides that a violation of the ADA is also a violation of the Unruh Act. Cal. Civ.Code § 51. The district court held that because United had violated the ADA, it also violated the Unruh Act. In light of our decision in *Weyer v. Twentieth Century Fox Film Corp.,* 198 F.3d 1104 (9th Cir.2000), as discussed above, the district court's decision cannot be upheld on this basis.

We may, however, "affirm the district court on a ground not selected by the district judge so long as the record fairly supports such an alternative disposition." Chabner, and the State of California as amicus curiae, argue that United's actions violated the Unruh Act, regardless of whether they also violated the ADA. We agree that Chabner's allegations support an Unruh Civil Rights Act claim independently of the alleged ADA violation.

The Unruh Civil Rights Act works to ensure that all persons receive the full accommodations of any business within California, regardless of the person's disabilities. Cal.

Civ.Code § 51. The insurance business is subject to the Unruh Civil Rights Act. Cal. Ins.Code. § 1861.03(a). Unruh prevents more than discrimination in access to a business or its services; it also prevents discrimination in the form of pricing differentials. However, disparities in treatment and pricing that are reasonable do not violate the Unruh Act. The critical question, therefore, is whether the nonstandard premium United charged Chabner was "reasonable."

To determine whether the nonstandard premium was reasonable, we are again informed by Insurance Code section 10144. Section 10144 prevents an insurer from charging "a different rate for the same coverage solely because of a physical or mental impairment," unless the "rate differential is based on sound actuarial principles or is related to actual and reasonably anticipated experience." Cal. Ins.Code § 10144. If Chabner's nonstandard premium was based on "sound actuarial principles" or "actual and reasonably anticipated experience," then it would certainly be reasonable for purposes of the Unruh Act because it would have been specifically allowed by statute. By contrast, if the premium was not based on one of the section 10144 prongs, then there would be no reasonable justification for it, and in that case we may consider the nonstandard premium to be arbitrary and a violation of the Unruh Act. Therefore, we hold that if United violated Insurance Code section 10144, it also violated the Unruh Act, but if section 10144 authorized United's actions, then Chabner's Unruh Act claim necessarily fails as well.

[The court discussed and dismissed United argument that the claim should be resolved by the Insurance Commissioner because they could be construed to have primary jurisdiction.]

D. Summary Judgment.

As discussed earlier, even though Chabner's state law causes of action arose under Business and Profession Code section 17200 and the Unruh Civil Rights Act, the standards of liability for each of these claims are set by Insurance Code section 10144. Under section 10144, a nonstandard premium is lawful only if it meets one of two prongs: it must be "based on sound actuarial principles," or it must be "related to actual and reasonably anticipated experience." Cal. Ins.Code § 10144.

The parties argue at length about the proper definitions of "sound actuarial principles" or "actual and reasonably anticipated experience." For example, they dispute whether an insurance company must base its rating decisions on "hard data" that is specific to each person, or whether it may take into account more generalized estimates of mortality when it lacks specific data. We need not resolve the debate about exactly what can justify a mortality decision as actuarially sound or related to actual and reasonably anticipated experience, for in this case there is no question that United's mortality rating was arbitrarily high.

The mortality rating United assigned to Chabner was not actuarially sound. United assigned Chabner a "Table 6" rating, which corresponds with a 150% mortality rating. The 150% mortality rating, in turn, reflects an estimate that Chabner's life expectancy is nine to eleven years less than that of a standard male non-smoker. United points to the Brackenridge manual, which recommended a mortality rating of 75%–150%, and the Cologne manual, which recommended a mortality rating of 300%, to argue that the 150% mortality rating was justified. However, United's own admissions subvert its reliance on these manuals. In his letter to Chabner, Dr. Robert Quinn, the Vice President and Senior Medical Director of Underwriting at United, admitted that FSH MD "has only a small effect on mortality." Moreover, Dr. Quinn estimated Chabner's life expectancy to be only four years less than standard. Even assuming that the estimate of a four year decrease in life expectancy is correct, it does not justify a rating that estimates a nine to eleven year decrease. Accordingly, by United's own admission, the 150% mortality rating (i.e., the estimate of a nine to eleven year decrease in life expectancy) was not actuarially sound.

Nor does the second prong of section 10144, which allows rate differentials if they are based on actual and reasonably anticipated experience, provide refuge for the 150% mortality rating. United's underwriter handling Chabner's application had experience with muscular dystrophy, but not with Chabner's rare fascioscapulohumeral muscular dystrophy. She thus had no "actual experience" with underwriting applicants with FSH MD. Moreover, she was not a doctor, she did not have a doctor examine Chabner, and she did not have a doctor review Chabner's medical records. Thus, the underwriter's basis for "reasonably anticipated experience" in evaluating an applicant with FSH MD was virtually nonexistent, especially considering that Dr. Quinn, who was a medical doctor and who was familiar with FSH MD, subsequently admitted that FSH MD has little effect on mortality. Therefore, viewing the evidence in the light most favorable to United, we hold that no reasonable jury could find that the 150% mortality rating was either based on sound actuarial principles or related to actual and reasonably anticipated experience. Section 10144 did not justify the discriminatory premium, and summary judgment on Chabner's Business and Professions Code section 17200 claim, and on his Unruh Civil Rights Act claim, was therefore proper.

E. The Modification Order.

After it granted summary judgment for Chabner, the district court ordered United to modify the policy it offered Chabner such that the policy would conform with the court's order granting summary judgment. United argues that the district court erred by ordering this modification, because the court did not specify what premium United should charge Chabner. We review the district court's order to modify the insurance policy, an equitable remedy, for abuse of discretion. It was not an abuse of discretion.

The district court order merely requires United to issue Chabner a policy that conforms with its order granting summary judgment—i.e., one that is based on sound actuarial principles or actual and reasonably anticipated experience. This injunctive relief is fully authorized by California law. Cal. Bus. & Prof.Code § 17203; Cal. Civ.Code § 52(c). To comply with this order United may either issue Chabner a policy with a standard premium, or it may charge him a nonstandard premium that does conform with section 10144. In any event, giving United this choice is not an abuse of discretion in this case, and we therefore affirm the district court's order.

Protective Life Insurance v. Sullivan

682 N.E.2d 624 (Mass. 1997)

Marshall, Justice.

Protective Life Insurance Company (Protective Life) commenced the underlying action in the United States District Court for the District of Massachusetts seeking rescission of a life insurance policy issued by it to the defendant Dennis J. Sullivan, a resident of Massachusetts. Protective Life claimed that Sullivan obtained the policy through fraudulent misrepresentation. The policy form, which had been approved by the Commissioner of Insurance (commissioner), provided that Protective Life could not "bring any legal action to contest the validity of this policy after it has been in force for two years except for failure to pay the premiums *unless fraud is involved*" (emphasis supplied). The defendants moved to dismiss the action, asserting that the plaintiff's action to rescind the policy more than two years after its date of issue was prohibited by G.L. c. 175, § 132, the Massachusetts incontestability statute. The District Court denied the motion.

After a bench trial, the District Court judge found by clear and convincing evidence that Sullivan committed fraud, and on November 17, 1995, entered judgment in favor of Protective Life against Dignity Viatical Settlement Partners, L.P., and Dignity Partners, Inc. (collectively, Dignity. Dignity appealed and, on its own motion, the United States Court of Appeals for the First Circuit certified the following two questions of State law to this court pursuant to S.J.C. Rule 1:03, as appearing in 382 Mass. 700 (1981):

> "1. Does Mass. Gen. L. ch. 175, § 132, taken together with § 124, bar an insurance company from contesting the validity of a life insurance policy more than two years after its date of issue on the ground that the insured made fraudulent misrepresentations in applying for the policy, where the policy provided that it was contestable for fraud at any time and where the Massachusetts Commissioner of Insurance approved the policy form?
>
> "2. If the incontestability statute bars such an action, is the contestability period nonetheless equitably tolled under the circumstances of this case by Sullivan's failure to apply for the disability waiver to which he was entitled until two years after the policy was issued?"

We answer the first question certified in the affirmative, and the second question certified in the negative.

I

We summarize the facts relevant to the questions certified. See S.J.C. Rule 1:03, § 3(2). In November, 1990, Sullivan was first diagnosed as Human Immunodeficiency Virus (HIV) positive and began a course of treatment including use of the drug AZT. On September 24, 1991, Sullivan applied to Protective Life for a life insurance policy in the amount of $100,000, with an annual premium of $175. In his application, he falsely stated that he was not taking any medication, and he omitted the names of those doctors who knew of his diagnosis. Sullivan authorized Protective Life to conduct medical tests, including a test for HIV infection, but on November 8, 1991, Protective Life issued a policy to Sullivan without having ordered an HIV or any other medical test. The policy included an optional provision that, for an increase in the annual premium, gave Sullivan the right to waive the premium in the event he became disabled.

In 1992, Sullivan's health worsened and by June, 1992, Sullivan's HIV infection had progressed to Acquired Immune Deficiency Syndrome (AIDS), and he stopped working. In October, 1992, Sullivan applied for disability benefits from another insurance company. He did not apply to Protective Life for a waiver of his life insurance premiums due to his disability until November 8, 1993, exactly two years after Protective Life had issued its policy to Sullivan.

In October, 1993, Sullivan informed Protective Life through a broker that he wished to assign ownership of his policy to Dignity, a firm engaged in making viatical settlements, agreements under which an insured sells a life insurance policy for an immediate payment approximating the discounted face value of the policy. On December 14, 1993, Dignity delivered the assignment forms to Protective Life, which Protective Life approved on December 22, 1993. On the same day, Dignity paid Sullivan $73,000.

It is undisputed that Sullivan knew he was HIV positive when he applied for the life insurance policy, and that he failed to disclose in his application that he was receiving medical treatment and any medication for his condition, despite questions calling for this information. It is also undisputed that Protective Life would not have issued Sullivan the policy had it known his true medical condition.

II

The first question certified asks whether G.L. c. 175, § 132, taken together with G.L. c. 175, § 124, bars an insurance company from contesting the validity of a life insurance policy more than two years after its date of issue on the basis of fraud, where the policy provided that it was contestable for fraud at any time and where the policy form was approved by the commissioner.

The commissioner's approval of Protective Life's life insurance policy form (in this case with a fraud exception to incontestability) reflects the commissioner's interpretation of G.L. c. 175, § 132, as permitting an implied exception for fraud. The proper interpretation of that statute is a question of law, and we review the commissioner's interpretation de novo. In general, we grant substantial deference to an interpretation of a statute by the administrative agency charged with its administration. But this principle is one of deference, not abdication, and we have overruled an agency's interpretation when it is contrary to the plain language of the statute and its underlying purpose. "While we will not lightly second-guess the Commissioner's interpretation of a statute, his approval is 'hardly persuasive' where the [interpretation] violates the language and policy of the statute."

We have not before squarely decided the issue whether G.L. c. 175, § 132, read together with G.L. c. 175, § 124, permits an insurer to include a fraud exception to the required two-year contestability period for life insurance policies. Our analysis begins, as it must, with the language of the statute itself. General Laws c. 175, § 132, provides, in relevant part, that no life insurance policy may be issued in the Commonwealth unless it contains in substance the following:

> "2. A provision that the policy shall be incontestable after it has been in force during the lifetime of the insured for a period of two years from its date of issue except for non-payment of premiums or violation of the conditions of the policy relating to military or naval service in time of war and except, if the company so elects, for the purpose of contesting claims for total and permanent disability benefits or additional benefits specifically granted in case of death by accident."

Thus G.L. c. 175, § 132, requires all Massachusetts life insurance policies to provide that, after the policy has been in force during the lifetime of the insured for two years, the policy cannot be contested by the insurer for any but three specific reasons. There is no exception for fraud.

We have said that "[t]he fact that the Legislature specified one exception ... strengthens the inference that no other exception was intended." Although a maxim of statutory construction is not to be followed "slavishly" where to do so would undermine the legislative purpose behind a statute and case cited, we are persuaded that the Legislature's omission of an exception for fraud in G.L. c. 175, § 132(2), reflects its intent that there be no such exception.

This has particular relevance here because the Legislature has demonstrated that, when it intends to have a fraud exception to an incontestability statute, it knows how to create one. General Laws c. 175, § 108(3)(a)(2), sets forth the incontestability provision required in all health insurance policies issued in this Commonwealth. That statute specifically excepts "fraudulent misstatements": "After two years from the date of issue of this policy no misstatements, except fraudulent misstatements, made by the applicant in the application for such policy shall be used to void the policy or to deny a claim for loss incurred or disability as defined in the policy commencing after the expiration of such two-year period."

Protective Life argues that our interpretation of G.L. c. 175, § 132, is inconsistent with G.L. c. 175, § 124, which, it argues, does allow insurers to contest for fraud at any time those policies issued without a medical examination. On Protective Life's reading of G.L. c. 175, §§ 124, 132, and 186, a life insurance policy issued without a medical examination can be contested within two years of the date of issue on the ground that the insured made a material misrepresentation. After two years have passed, insurers must prove not only materiality, but also willful fraudulent intent on the part of the insured. We disagree with Protective Life's interpretation of the statutory scheme.

General Laws c. 175, § 124, first enacted in 1892 (St.1892, c. 372), fifteen years before the Legislature enacted any incontestability statute, provides:

> "In any claim arising under a policy issued in the commonwealth by any life company, without previous medical examination ... the statements made in the application as to the age, physical condition and family history of the insured shall be held to be valid and binding on the company; but the company shall not be debarred from proving as a defense to such claim that said statements were willfully false, fraudulent or misleading."

We are persuaded that the purpose of G.L. c. 175, § 124, was to raise the burden of proof that an insurer must sustain when it contests a life insurance policy issued without a medical examination. It could not have been intended to create an exception to the later-enacted incontestability statute.

We believe that the statutory history confirms this interpretation. In *Torres v. Fidelity & Guar. Life Ins. Co.*, 611 N.E.2d 733 ([Mass. App. Ct.] 1993), the Appeals Court discussed the interrelationship between G.L. c. 175, § 124 and § 186. Section 186, applicable to all insurance policies, specifies that an insured's misrepresentation is not "material" unless it is made with actual intent to deceive or unless it increases the risk of loss to the insurer. Section 124, adopted fourteen years after the adoption of G.L. c. 175, § 186 (St.1878, c. 157), imposes a heavier burden on the insurer when it contests a life insurance policy issued without a medical examination Statements in applications for life insurance policies issued without a medical examination are binding on the insurer unless it proves that the statements were willfully false, fraudulent, or misleading.

Protective Life argues that G.L. c. 175, § 124, was designed to encourage insurers to issue policies without medical examinations by permitting contests for fraud without limitation. Our reading of the statutory history is different. In its attempt to discern the legislative intent behind G.L. c. 175, § 124, the Appeals Court in *Torres* relied in part on statements made by the commissioner in annual reports submitted to the Legislature in the years preceding the enactment of G.L. c. 175, § 124. The court quoted from the Thirty-third Annual Report of the Insurance Commissioner, Pub. Doc. No. 9, at vii (1888):

> "if ... risks are taken without a medical examination, alleged misrepresentation by the applicant—who in a large number of these cases is made to understand next to nothing of the statement he is asked to sign—as to his physical condi-

> tion, ought not to be permitted as a bar when a claim arises. Misrepresentation by the agent and misunderstanding by the assured now lead, under the methods thus pursued, to almost innumerable cases of hardship and injustice."

The commissioner repeated his recommendation that insurance contracts issued without a medical examination should not be subject to a claim that misrepresentation bars payment in 1889:

> "Experience only the more strongly commends the suggestion made in this report last year; that, when any company issues [a life insurance] policy ... no matter for how small an amount,—with no medical examination, it should be forbidden by law from setting up, as a bar to an accrued claim, alleged misrepresentation by the applicant as to his physical condition. *It is the business of the company to ascertain whether lives presented for insurance are impaired;* and, if it chooses to waive any pretence of an examination to test this vital question, the responsibility should be upon itself. Existing contrary practice leads to a wilderness of misunderstanding and misrepresentation, with hardships and losses to a class of people illy able to bear it."

The commissioner made this same recommendation again in his 1891 report, submitted to the Legislature in the year immediately preceding its enactment of G.L. c. 175, § 124. The commissioner stated that he

> "would repeat and emphasize the suggestion, twice before made in these reports, that when any company effects insurance upon a life, without medical examination, it should be forbidden from setting up, as a bar to any claim, alleged misrepresentation by the insured as to his family history or his physical condition at the time the policy was issued.... Doubtless four-fifths of the misunderstanding, disappointment and loss in this class of business, now grown to vast magnitude, arise from these grave defects ... which ought to be speedily and radically remedied."

General Laws c. 175, § 186, already had been enacted when the commissioner made these recommendations in 1888, 1889 and 1891. The purpose of G.L. c. 175, § 124 (based on the commissioner's recommendation), was to curb perceived unfair practices by insurance companies, by making it even more difficult for them to contest life insurance policies issued without medical examinations than it was to contest life insurance policies issued with medical examinations. We conclude, therefore, that the effect of G.L. c. 175, § 124, when read together with the later enacted § 132 (see St.1907, c. 576, § 75), is to increase the insurers' burden of proof when it attempts to rescind, within two years, life insurance policies issued without medical examinations. Neither the purpose nor the effect of G.L. c. 175, § 124, was to create a fraud exception to the later enacted incontestability statute.

The legislative history of G.L. c. 175, § 132, such as it is, confirms our interpretation....

We conclude that the Legislature did not intend to create any fraud exception to the incontestability statute.

We are also not persuaded that our interpretation of the interplay between G.L. c. 175, § 132, and G.L. c. 175, § 124, would violate any public policy. In *Reagan v. Union Mut. Life Ins. Co.*, 76 N.E. 217[, 218] ([Mass.] 1905), decided two years before the incontestability statute was first adopted by the Legislature, we ruled that a policy provision that precluded all contests after the date of the issuance of the policy, without affording the insurer *any* reasonable time to investigate and initiate appropriate contests, was void as against public policy. We observed, however:

> "This is not like the numerous cases in which the policy provides that it shall be incontestable for fraud after the expiration of a specified time, which is not unreasonably short. It has often been held that a provision of that kind is valid because it is in the nature of a limitation of the time within which the [insurer] may avoid the policy for this cause. Such a provision is reasonable and proper, as it gives the insured a guaranty against possible expensive litigation to defeat his claim after the lapse of many years, and at the same time gives the company time and an opportunity for investigation, to ascertain whether the contract should remain in force. It is not against public policy as tending to put fraud on a par with honesty"

Our view is reflected in our later discussion of the incontestability clause, and its purposes in *Metropolitan Life Ins. Co. v. DeNicola*, 58 N.E.2d 841[, 842] ([Mass.] 1944):

> "[The incontestability clause] is designed to require the insurer to investigate and act with reasonable promptness if it wishes to deny liability on the ground of false representation or warranty by the insured. It prevents an insurer from lulling the insured, by inaction, into fancied security during the time when the facts could best be ascertained and proved, only to litigate them belatedly, possibly after the death of the insured. The insurer, within the period prescribed by the policy, must contest the policy, that is, must set up its invalidity in some judicial proceeding, by way either of attack or of defence."

There were sound policy reasons why the Legislature adopted a requirement that life insurance policies issued in Massachusetts contain incontestability provisions. The Legislature was, at the time, cognizant of the possibility that an insured might obtain a policy by fraudulent misrepresentations to the insurance company. It nevertheless declined to include—as it surely could have—an exception to incontestability for fraud. Where the Legislature has not provided for a fraud exception to the incontestability provision, and where the absence of a fraud exception does not violate public policy, we shall not imply such an exception. We recognize that Sullivan's wilful concealment of his medical condition was deplorable and deserves condemnation. We do not pass judgment favorably or unfavorably on the balance that the Legislature has struck between the competing policy interests that underlay G.L. c. 175, § 132(2). We simply conclude that the Legislature was within its province in striking such a balance in the first instance.

III

The second question certified asks whether, if the incontestability statute bars rescission on the basis of fraud after two years, the incontestability period was equitably tolled under the circumstances of this case by Sullivan's failure to apply for the disability waiver to which he was entitled until two years after the policy was issued.

Protective Life contends that the incontestability period was tolled in this case because Sullivan "concealed" his misrepresentations by delaying his application for a waiver of his premiums on account of his disability—a waiver to which he was entitled—for precisely two years, the same time period beyond which the policy was incontestable. Dignity replies that G.L. c. 175, § 132, is more in the nature of a statute of repose than a statute of limitations, and that any tolling of the two-year period is inappropriate. Dignity further contends that, even if the incontestability statute can be tolled under some circumstances, Sullivan's delay in applying for a waiver of his premium on account of his disability does not warrant a tolling of the incontestability statute. Because we conclude that Sullivan's conduct (or rather absence of conduct) did not toll the running of the incontestability period, we need not—and do not—decide whether G.L. c. 175, § 132, is subject to tolling under any other circumstances.

We begin by noting that the doctrine of equitable tolling is applicable only where the prospective plaintiff did not have, and could not have had with due diligence, the information essential to bringing suit. A party attempting to invoke that doctrine will be held to a duty of reasonable inquiry. Here, Sullivan specifically authorized Protective Life to conduct whatever medical tests it desired, including a test for HIV infection. Had Protective Life exercised reasonable diligence, and had it not chosen to waive the authorized medical tests, it presumably would have discovered Sullivan's fraud.

Under the discovery rule, a statute of limitations does not begin to run until the prospective plaintiff learns or should have learned that he has been injured. The discovery rule operates to toll a limitations period only where a misrepresentation concerns a fact that was "inherently unknowable" to the aggrieved, or where a wrongdoer concealed the existence of a cause of action through some affirmative act done with the intent to deceive, or breached some duty of disclosure. We cannot say that Protective Life's action for rescission is based on an "inherently unknowable" wrong on the part of Sullivan; through the exercise of reasonable inquiry, Protective Life could have learned of Sullivan's medical condition either before granting him the policy or within the two-year period.

Moreover, although the District Court found that Sullivan's delay in applying for a disability waiver of the premium amounted to an ongoing course of fraudulent conduct designed to conceal his fraud in the application, we do not believe that Sullivan's delay constitutes an "affirmative act" that warrants application of the discovery rule. Sullivan was under no obligation to file a claim for a disability waiver of his premium. The incontestability period cannot be tolled where, as here, the insured did not perform any affirmative acts to conceal the existence of his original fraud in the application

IV

For the reasons stated, we answer the first question certified, "Yes," and the second question certified, "No."

Parker v. Metropolitan Life Insurance Co.

121 F.3d 1006 (6th Cir. 1997)

Kennedy, Circuit Judge.

...

Plaintiff, Ouida Sue Parker, was employed by Schering-Plough Health Care Products, Inc. ("Schering-Plough") from April 20, 1981 through October 29, 1990. During her employment, Parker participated in a long-term disability plan offered by Schering-Plough to its employees; the plan was issued by Metropolitan Life Insurance Co. ("MetLife"). Under the plan, an individual who is deemed to be totally disabled due to a mental or nervous disorder may receive benefits for up to twenty-four months, unless at the termination of the twenty-four month period, the individual was hospitalized or receiving inpatient care for the disorder. For physical disorders, however, the plan provides for benefits until the individual reaches sixty-five years of age.

On October 29, 1990, Parker became disabled due to severe depression. On April 29, 1991, Parker began to receive benefit payments under the plan. Because Parker suffered from a mental disorder, Schering-Plough terminated her payments twenty-four months later, on April 28, 1993, pursuant to the terms of the plan. Following Schering-Plough's denial of two administrative appeals filed by Parker, plaintiff filed this action alleging violations of the Americans with Disabilities Act, 42 U.S.C. §§ 12101–12213, and the Employee Retirement Income Security Act, 29 U.S.C. §§ 1001–1461 ("ERISA"). The District Court granted the defendants' motion for summary judgment. The District Court first found that Parker did not have standing to sue under Title I of the ADA, 42 U.S.C. §§ 12111–12117, because only a "qualified individual with a disability" may obtain relief under Title I and Parker was not a "qualified individual with a disability" when her benefits were terminated because her disorder prevented her from performing the essential functions of her employment position. The District Court also dismissed Parker's claim against the defendants under Title III of the ADA, 42 U.S.C. §§ 12165–12189. MetLife was not a proper defendant under Title III, the court concluded, because Title III only covers discrimination in the physical access to goods and services, not discrimination in the terms of insurance policies. The Title III claim against Schering-Plough, Parker's employer, was dismissed because Title I, not Title III, governs discrimination in employment practices. Because Parker was not a qualified individual under Title I, a suit against her employer could not be maintained under the ADA. Lastly, the District Court granted summary judgment in favor of the defendants on Parker's ERISA claim because the classification of her disorder as "nervous/mental" was not arbitrary or capricious.

On appeal from the District Court's order, a panel of this Court affirmed the District Court's judgment as to Parker's ERISA claim and Title I claim under the ADA. The panel, however, reversed the District Court's judgment as to plaintiff's claim under Title III of the ADA. Disagreeing with the District Court, the panel concluded that Title III "prohibits discrimination in the contents of the goods and services offered at places of public accommodation, rather than just discrimination in terms of physical access to places of public accommodation." Accordingly, the panel found that Title III covers insurance products because "insurance products are 'goods' or 'services' provided by a 'person' who owns a 'public accommodation.'"

Because the panel concluded that the contents of insurance products are governed by Title III, it then turned to whether Title IV of the ADA, 42 U.S.C. § 12201(c), commonly referred to as the "safe harbor provision," precluded application of Title III to insurance products. The panel concluded that the safe harbor provision was ambiguous on its face as to whether it intended to exempt insurance products from ADA coverage. It, therefore, looked to legislative history for guidance. The panel concluded that the legislative history indicated that "insurance practices are protected by the 'safe harbor' provision, but only to the extent that they are consistent with 'sound actuarial principles,' 'actual reasonably anticipated experience,' and 'bona fide risk classification.'" Responding to the defendants' argument that an insurance plan violates the ADA only if it is a "subterfuge" under § 12201(c), the panel declined to adopt the Supreme Court's definition of subterfuge pronounced in *Ohio Public Employees Retirement System v. Betts*, 492 U.S. 158 (1989). In *Betts*, the Court defined the term subterfuge in the Age Discrimination in Employment Act ("ADEA") as an intent to discriminate. Declining to follow the ADEA definition of subterfuge, the panel held that an insurance plan is a subterfuge under the ADA if it is "based on speculation, and not on sound actuarial principles, actual or reasonably anticipated experience, or bona fide risk classification."

Finally, in response to Schering-Plough's contention that Title I, not Title III, governs employment practices, the panel held that "based on our affirmance of Plaintiff's Title I claim, it is not clear whether Schering remains a proper defendant to the remaining claim [Title III] of this suit." The panel did not resolve this question of law; rather, it instructed the lower court that the issue was ripe for its determination on remand.

Following the panel's decision, the defendants sought rehearing *en banc* on the panel's disposition of Parker's Title III claim. We granted their petition and vacated our prior judgment. Accordingly, the case is again before us for our determination. Upon review, we conclude that the judgment of the District Court will be AFFIRMED.

II.

Our standard of review of a grant of summary judgment is de novo; we use the same test as used by the district court....

III.

A. Title III: Places of Public Accommodation

To determine whether a benefit plan provided by an employer falls within the prohibitions of Title III, we must begin by examining the statutory text. The ADA generally prohibits discrimination against the disabled by employers, public entities, and by operators of public accommodations. *See* 42 U.S.C. §§ 12101–12213. Title III of the ADA specifically addresses discrimination by owners, lessors, and operators of public accommodations. It provides as follows:

> No individual shall be discriminated against on the basis of disability in the full and equal enjoyment of the goods, services, facilities, privileges, advantages, or accommodations of any place of public accommodation by any person who owns, leases (or leases to), or operates a place of public accommodation.

42 U.S.C. § 12182(a).

Section 12181 sets forth the following list of private entities that are considered public accommodations for purposes of Title III:

> (A) an inn, hotel, motel, or other place of lodging ...
>
> (B) a restaurant, bar, or other establishment serving food or drink;
>
> (C) a motion picture house, theater, concert hall, stadium, or other place of exhibition or entertainment;
>
> (D) an auditorium, convention center, lecture hall, or other place of public gathering;
>
> (E) a bakery, grocery store, clothing store, hardware store, shopping center, or other sales or rental establishment;
>
> (F) a laundromat, dry-cleaner, bank, barber shop, beauty shop, travel service, shoe repair service, funeral parlor, gas station, office of an accountant or

> lawyer, pharmacy, *insurance office*, professional office of a health care provider, hospital, or other service establishment;
>
> (G) a terminal, depot, or other station used for specified public transportation;
>
> (H) a museum, library, gallery, or other place of public display or collection;
>
> (I) a park, zoo, amusement park, or other place of recreation;
>
> (J) a nursery, elementary, secondary, undergraduate, or postgraduate private school, or other place of education;
>
> (K) a day care center, senior citizen center, homeless shelter, food bank, adoption agency, or other social service center establishment; and
>
> (L) a gymnasium, health spa, bowling alley, golf course, or other place of exercise or recreation.

42 U.S.C. § 12181(7) (emphasis added).

Title III specifically prohibits, inter alia, the provision of unequal or separate benefits by a place of public accommodation. See 42 U.S.C. §§ 12182(b)(1)(A)(i)–(iii). For example, 42 U.S.C. § 12182(b)(1)(A)(ii) provides that it is "discriminatory to afford an individual or class of individuals, on the basis of a disability ... with the opportunity to participate in or benefit from a good, service, facility, privilege, advantage, or accommodation that is not equal to that afforded to other individuals ..." 42 U.S.C. § 12182(b)(1)(a)(ii). To the extent that subsections (i), (ii), and (iii) do not explicitly state that they apply only to public accommodations, subsection (iv) expressly provides that "... the term 'individual or class of individuals' refers to the clients or customers of the covered public accommodation ..." 42 U.S.C. § 12182(b)(1)(a)(iv).

While we agree that an insurance office is a public accommodation as expressly set forth in § 12181(7), plaintiff did not seek the goods and services of an insurance office. Rather, Parker accessed a benefit plan provided by her private employer and issued by MetLife. A benefit plan offered by an employer is not a good offered by a place of public accommodation. As is evident by § 12187(7), a public accommodation is a physical place and this Court has previously so held. Furthermore, we held that "the prohibitions of Title III are restricted to 'places' of public accommodation ..." A "place," as defined by the applicable regulations, is "'a facility, operated by a private entity, whose operations affect commerce and fall within at least one of the' twelve 'public accommodation' categories....

Similarly, the good that plaintiff seeks is not offered by a place of public accommodation. The public cannot enter the office of MetLife or Schering-Plough and obtain the long-term disability policy that plaintiff obtained. Parker did not access her policy from MetLife's insurance office. Rather, she obtained her benefits through her employer. There is, thus, no nexus between the disparity in benefits and the services which MetLife offers to the public from its insurance office.

The Department of Justice's explanation of whether wholesale establishments are places of public accommodation supports our conclusion that MetLife's offering of a disability plan to Schering-Plough is not a service offered by a place of public accommodation.... Thus, the offering of disability policies on a discounted rate solely to a business is not a service or good offered by a place of public accommodation.

Furthermore, Title III does not govern the content of a long-term disability policy offered by an employer. The applicable regulations clearly set forth that Title III regulates the availability of the goods and services the place of public accommodation offers as opposed to the contents of goods and services offered by the public accommodation. According to the Department of Justice:

> The purpose of the ADA's public accommodations requirements is to ensure accessibility to the goods offered by a public accommodation, not to alter the nature or mix of goods that the public accommodation has typically provided. In other words, a bookstore, for example, must make its facilities and sales operations accessible to individuals with disabilities, but is not required to stock Brailled or large print books. Similarly, a video store must make its facilities and rental operations accessible, but is not required to stock closed-captioned video tapes.

While Title IV of the ADA, 42 U.S.C. § 12201(c), may address the contents of insurance policies provided by a public accommodation, Title IV does not address the contents of a long-term disability plan offered by an employer because it is not a place of public accommodation. We, therefore, disagree with the First Circuit's decision in *Carparts Distribution Center, Inc. v. Automotive Wholesaler's Association of New England, Inc.*, 37 F.3d 12 (1st Cir.1994). In *Carparts*, the health benefit plan offered by the employer contained a $25,000 cap on benefits for AIDS related illnesses while the plan provided $1,000,000 in coverage for any other illness. The executors of the estate of an employee, who suffered from AIDS, brought suit against the provider of the self-funded medical reimbursement plan under the ADA alleging that the lifetime cap on health benefits for individuals with AIDS was discriminatory The court rejected the district court's conclusion that defendants were not liable under Title III because they were not places of public accommodation. In rejecting the district court's construction, the court cited to the list of private entities considered public accommodations in § 12181(7) of Title III. The court particularly noted that the list includes a "'travel service,' a 'shoe repair service,' an 'office of an accountant, or lawyer,' an 'insurance office,' a 'professional office of a healthcare provider,' and 'other service establishment[s]'". The plain meaning of those terms, the court concluded, "does not require 'public accommodations' to have physical structures for persons to enter." Id. The court further noted that "[b]y including 'travel service' among the list of services considered 'public accommodations,' Congress clearly contemplated that 'service establishments' include providers of services which do not require a person to physically enter an actual physical structure." The court, therefore, concluded that a defendant who provides medical benefit plans could be considered a public accommodation under Title III.

In arriving at this conclusion, the First Circuit disregarded the statutory canon of construction, *noscitur a sociis*. The doctrine of *noscitur a sociis* instructs that "a ... term is interpreted within the context of the accompanying words 'to avoid the giving of unintended breadth to the Acts of Congress.'" Black's Law Dictionary defines the term as:

> It is known from its associates. The meaning of a word is or may be known for the accompanying words. Under the doctrine of "noscitur a sociis", the meaning of questionable or doubtful words or phrases in a statute may be ascertained by reference to the meaning of other words or phrases associated with it.

The clear connotation of the words in § 12181(7) is that a public accommodation is a physical place. Every term listed in § 12181(7) and subsection (F) is a physical place open to public access. The terms travel service, shoe repair service, office of an accountant or lawyer, insurance office, and professional office of a healthcare provider do not suggest otherwise. Rather than suggesting that Title III includes within its purview entities other than physical places, it is likely that Congress simply had no better term than "service" to describe an office where travel agents provide travel services and a place where shoes are repaired. Office of an accountant or lawyer, insurance office, and professional office of a healthcare provider, in the context of the other terms listed, suggest a physical place where services may be obtained and nothing more. To interpret these terms as permitting a place of accommodation to constitute something other than a physical place is to ignore the text of the statute and the principle of *noscitur a sociis.*

Accordingly, we conclude that the provision of a long-term disability plan by an employer and administered by an insurance company does not fall within the purview of Title III.

B. Title I of the ADA Governs Employment Practices

Because the statutory framework of the ADA expressly limits discrimination in employment practices to Title I of the ADA, the District Court properly dismissed Schering-Plough, Parker's employer, from this action. As set out by the statute, Title I provides:

> No covered entity shall discriminate against a qualified individual with a disability because of the disability of such individual in regard to job application procedures, the hiring, advancement, or discharge of employees, employee compensation, job training, and other terms, conditions, and privileges of employment.

42 U.S.C. § 12112(a). The regulations governing the ADA specifically provide that it is unlawful for an employer to discriminate on the basis of disability against a qualified individual with a disability in regard to "[f]ringe benefits available by virtue of employment, whether or not administered by the [employer]." 29 C.F.R. § 1630.4(f)(1996). As noted by the Equal Employment Opportunity Commission ("EEOC"), the agency charged with administering and enforcing Title I of the ADA, "[e]mployee benefit plans, including health insurance plans provided by an employer to its employees, are a fringe benefit available by virtue of employment. Generally speaking, therefore, the ADA prohibits employers from discriminating on the basis of disability in the provision of health insurance to their employees."

It is, thus, clear that Schering-Plough is not a proper defendant under Title III, except to the extent that it is alleged to be a plan fiduciary; discrimination in the provision of fringe benefits during employment is governed strictly by Title I and the provision of a long-term disability plan is a fringe benefit of employment.

Because the provision of a long-term disability plan by an employer and administered by an insurance company does not fall within the purview of Title III and because the statutory framework of the ADA expressly limits discrimination in employment practices to Title I of the ADA, the District Court properly granted summary judgment on behalf of the defendants.

C. The ADA Prohibits Only Discrimination Between the Disabled and Non-Disabled

The disparity in benefits provided in the policy at issue is also not prohibited by the ADA because the ADA does not mandate equality between individuals with different disabilities. Rather, the ADA prohibits discrimination between the disabled and the non-disabled; specifically, the ADA mandates that the owners, lessors, and operators of public accommodations provide equal access to the disabled and non-disabled. Because all employees at Schering-Plough, whether disabled or not, received the same access to the long-term disability plan, neither the defendants nor the plan discriminated between the disabled and the able bodied.

In *Traynor v. Turnage*, 485 U.S. 535 (1988), the Supreme Court considered whether a benefit given to a certain class of disabled persons and not to others violated the Rehabilitation Act, 29 U.S.C. § 794. At issue in *Traynor* was the Veterans' Readjustment Benefit Act of 1966 ("GI Bill"), 38 U.S.C. § 1661, which affords educational assistance benefits to honorably discharged veterans. The benefits ordinarily must be used within ten years following the veteran's discharge; however, if the veteran was unable to utilize his or her benefits within the ten year period due to " 'a physical or mental disability which was not the result of [their] own willful misconduct,' " the veteran may obtain an extension. The petitioners in *Traynor* sought an extension because their alcoholism rendered them disabled during the ten year period following their discharge. The Veterans' Administration denied the requested extensions because it concluded that their alcoholism constituted "willful misconduct."

The petitioners' contention that the "willful misconduct" provision of the GI Bill violated the Rehabilitation Act was rejected by the Court. In rejecting the petitioners' argument, the Court noted that the central purpose of the Rehabilitation Act is "to assure that handicapped individuals receive 'evenhanded treatment' in relation to nonhandicapped individuals." The Court clarified that "[t]his litigation does not involve a program or activity that is alleged to treat handicapped persons less favorably than nonhandicapped persons." Rather, the "willful misconduct" provision "provides a special benefit to disabled veterans who bear no responsibility for their disabilities that is not provided to other disabled veterans or to any able-bodied veterans." The benefits provided to a particular class did not violate the Act, in the Court's view, because "[t]here is nothing in the Rehabilitation Act that requires that any benefit extended to one category of handicapped persons also be extended to all other categories of handicapped persons." Thus, the Court held it is "not inconsistent with the Rehabilitation Act for only those veterans whose disabilities are not attributable to their own 'willful misconduct' to be granted extensions of the 10-year delimiting period applicable to all other veterans."

Following the Supreme Court's decision in *Traynor*, the United States Court of Appeals for the District of Columbia held in *Modderno v. King*, 82 F.3d 1059 (D.C.Cir.1996), that the Foreign Service Benefit Plan provided to foreign service officers and their spouses, which limited lifetime coverage for mental health benefits to $75,000 while placing no similar restriction on benefits for physical illnesses, did not violate the Rehabilitation Act. The D.C. Circuit found that, if across-the-board limits were permissible in *Alexander v. Choate*, then an insurance provider could cap the benefits for all illnesses. When an insurance provider, instead, places a limit on only one type of illness, such as mental illness, the disabled, as a class, benefit; if the cap were placed on all illnesses, the disabled as a class would be worse off, in the court's view. According to the court, "[i]f [the Rehabilitation Act] permits across-the-board limits on coverage, as *Alexander* holds, then it cannot forbid partial limits that leave some disabled individuals better off and the remainder no worse off." Accordingly, the court concluded that "distinctions between mental and physical care are no more vulnerable under § 504 [the Rehabilitation Act] than are completely generalized limits."

Citing to *Alexander v. Choate* and the D.C. Circuit's decision in *Modderno*, the United States Court of Appeals for the Seventh Circuit in *Equal Employment Opportunity Commission v. CNA Insurance Cos.*, 96 F.3d 1039 (7th Cir.1996), held that a limitation on mental health benefits in a long-term disability plan does not violate the ADA. In CNA Insurance, the defendant companies offered a long-term disability policy to their employees in which benefits for mental illness were paid only for a two-year period while benefits for physical illnesses were paid until the employee reached age sixty-five. The EEOC brought suit against the defendants after an employee was informed by defendants that benefits for her mental disorder would be paid only for twenty-four months.

In determining whether the former employee had standing to sue under the ADA for discrimination occurring during the employment period, the Seventh Circuit held that the employee suffered no discrimination under Title I of the ADA while she was employed. In the court's words:

> [a]ll employees—the perfectly healthy, the physically disabled, and the mentally disabled—had a plan that promised them long-term benefits from the onset of disability until age 65 if their problem was physical, and long-term benefits for two years if the problem was mental or nervous. This may or may not be an enlightened way to do things, but it was not discriminatory in the usual sense of the term.

In determining whether the plan discriminates against employees who will sometime in the future become mentally disabled because they are unknowingly purchasing only twenty-four months of benefits, the court stated:

> However this is dressed up, it is really a claim that benefit plans themselves may not treat mental health conditions less favorably than they treat physical health conditions. Without far stronger language in the ADA supporting this result, we are loath to read into it a rule that has been the subject of vigorous, sometimes contentious, national debate for the last several years. Few, if any, mental health advocates have thought that the result they would like to see has been there all along in the ADA. This is well-illustrated by the debate over a proposed amendment to the Health Insurance Portability and Accountability Act of 1996. The amendment, which was defeated before final passage of the bill, would have required parity of coverage for mental and physical conditions. This debate reinforces our conclusion based on the language of the ADA that the issue of parity among physical and mental health benefits is one that is still in the legislative arena.

On September 26, 1996, the day before the Seventh Circuit's decision in *CNA Insurance* was released, Congress enacted the Mental Health Parity Act, 42 U.S.C. § 300gg-5, as an amendment to the Health Insurance Portability Act. *See* 42 U.S.C. § 300gg. The Mental Health Parity Act mandates, *inter alia*, that where a health insurance plan contains no lifetime limit or annual limit for medical or surgical benefits, the plan may not contain a lifetime or annual limit for mental health benefits. *See* 42 U.S.C. § 300gg-5(1)-(2). Similarly, if the health insurance policy includes an annual or lifetime limit on medical or surgical benefits, the plan must apply the same limits to mental health benefits. *Id.* As several of the amici curiae argue, Congress' passage of the Mental Health Parity Act suggests Congress believed that the ADA neither governs the content of insurance policies nor requires parity between physical and mental illnesses; thus, passage of a law requiring such parity was required if Congress desired insurance carriers to cease including disparate mental and physical health benefits in insurance policies. Particularly pertinent to the instant case, however, the Health Insurance Portability Act specifically exempts from its coverage "disability income insurance." 42 U.S.C. § 300gg-91(c)(1)(A). While Congress likely realized that equality between the two types of disabilities was not covered by the ADA, it sought to remedy the absence only in the context of health insurance coverage, not long-term disability policies. Thus, it appears that Congress did not believe the necessity for parity between mental and physical disabilities in long-term disability plans was sufficiently compelling to include them within the purview of the Act.

Without discussing the Mental Health Parity Act, the United States Court of Appeals for the Eighth Circuit in *Krauel v. Iowa Methodist Medical Center,* 95 F.3d 674 (8th

Cir.1996), held that the ADA prohibits only discrimination between the disabled and non-disabled. In *Krauel*, an employee brought suit under the ADA against her employer alleging that the exclusion of infertility treatments from her employee medical benefits plan constituted discrimination because the exclusion was a disability based distinction. The Eighth Circuit, citing to EEOC guidelines interpreting the ADA, held that "[i]nsurance distinctions that apply equally to all insured employees, that is, to individuals with disabilities and to those who are not disabled, do not discriminate on the basis of disability." The court specifically cited to the language of the following EEOC guideline for support:

> ... a feature of some employer provided health insurance plans is a distinction between the benefits provided for the treatment of physical conditions on the one hand, and the benefits provided for the treatment of "mental/nervous" conditions on the other. Typically, a lower level of benefits is provided for the treatment of mental/nervous conditions than is provided for the treatment of physical conditions. Similarly, some health insurance plans provide fewer benefits for "eye care" than for other physical conditions. Such broad distinctions which apply to the treatment of a multitude of dissimilar conditions and which constrain individuals both with and without disabilities, are not distinctions based on disability. Consequently, although such distinctions may have a greater impact on certain individuals with disabilities, they do no intentionally discriminate on the basis of disability and do not violate the ADA.

In accordance with these guidelines, the court concluded that the plan's exclusion of benefits for infertility treatments did not single out a particular group of disabilities. "Rather, the Plan's infertility exclusion applies equally to all individuals, in that no one participating in the Plan receives coverage for treatment of infertility problems." Thus, the court held, the plan did not contain a disability-based distinction.

In conclusion, we agree with those circuits that have extended the Supreme Court's holdings in *Traynor v. Turnage* and *Alexander v. Choate* to the ADA. As the Court concluded regarding the Rehabilitation Act, the ADA similarly does not prohibit an insurance company from differentiating between different disabilities. The same policy is provided to all employees who, when they receive it, are not disabled but working. The fact that some may become disabled for different reasons does not amount to discrimination in providing the policy. The ADA simply does not mandate equality between individuals with different disabilities. Rather, the ADA, like the Rehabilitation Act, prohibits discrimination between the disabled and the non-disabled.

IV.

For the foregoing reasons, the judgment of the District Court is AFFIRMED.

Notes & Questions

1. The Biser and Shorett article discusses the nature of life, disability, and long-term care insurance. Unlike health insurance, access to these products is less of a human right and more of a discretionary good. In essence, the purpose of life insurance is to provide an estate for the insured's survivors. Disability and long-term care insurance seek to ensure and protect income should the insured be unable to work or care for themselves. While both estate provision and income protection are socially advantageous, it is questionable as to whether the law can, or should, shackle insurers, prevent-

ing them from fully considering actuarial risks. Vendors selling these products assess risks carefully to provide the soundest product at an affordable price. As genetic testing becomes more available, accurate, and less expensive, it is possible that it will be a risk assessment tool, just as blood tests and physical exams presently are. This has been recognized by legislatures who have been considerably less willing to extend antidiscrimination provisions to life, disability and long-term care insurance. Moreover, many of the states that have enacted laws allow use of genetic information if it can be actuarially justified. For an up-to-date list of state antidiscrimination laws, *see* National Conference of State Legislatures, Genetics and Life, Disability, and Long-term Care Insurance, http://www.ncsl.org/programs/health/genetics/ndislife.htm.

For additional articles discussing the use of genetic information in life, disability and long-term care insurance, *see* Kyle D. Logue, *The Current Life Insurance Crisis: How the Law Should Respond*, 32 Cumb. L. Rev. 1 (2002); Robyn B. Nicoll, *Long-term Care Insurance and Genetic Discrimination—Get it While You're Young and Ignorant: An Examination of Current Discriminatory Problems in Long-term Care Insurance Through the Use of Genetic Information*, 13 Alb. L. J. Sci. & Tech 751 (2003); Mark A. Rothstein, *Predictive Genetic Testing for Alzheimer's Disease in Long-Term Care Insurance*, 35 Ga. L. Rev. 707 (2001); Roberta B. Meyer, *Justification for Permitting Life Insurers to Continue to Underwrite on the Basis of Genetic Information and Genetic Test Results*, 27 Suffolk U. L. Rev. 1271 (1993); Christopher M. Keefer, *Bridging the Gap Between Life Insurer and Consumer in the Genetic Testing Era: The RF Proposal*, 74 Ind. L.J. 1375 (1999).

2. *Chabner v. United of Omaha Life Insurance* is one of the few cases alleging genetic discrimination in life insurance. Chabner has a relatively rare form of muscular dystrophy, FSH MD that has already manifested, impairing his mobility to the extent that he requires a wheelchair. However, this form of muscular dystrophy does not result in a significantly shortened life span. Despite this, when Chabner seeks to purchase a life insurance product, he is rated as high risk and, as a result, his whole life insurance product will accrue less value than others of his age. Chabner alleges that United has violated several provisions of California insurance law, committed common law fraud, and violated the ADA. Was the underwriting of Chabner's policy based on sound actuarial principles? Why must the court piggyback its decision on section 10144 of the California Insurance Code? Why does the ADA claim fail? When United complies with the modification order, is it likely that Chabner will receive the same rate as someone without illness or disability? *Chabner* is one of the few life insurance cases involving a genetic disease. It illustrates a case of sloppy underwriting with respect to an already present and manifested medical disorder, rather than underwriting of a latent, unexpressed genetic mutation. It presents the problem of lack of knowledge about the impact of a genetic disorder on health and life expectancy. In this sense, it is similar to the *Burlington Northern* case discussed in Chapter 3, where the employer clearly had little understanding of the importance—or lack of importance—of genetics in a common medical problem.

In contrast to the *Chabner* case, *Protective Life Insurance v. Sullivan* involves a life insurance applicant who misrepresented his health history when applying for life insurance. Sullivan purchases life insurance in November 1991, concealing his HIV status. Protective Life Insurance does not obtain an HIV test, although it reserved the right to do so when selling Sullivan the policy. Two years later, Sullivan seeks to assign ownership of his policy to a firm providing viatical settlements. Protective Life Insurance seeks to rescind the policy on the basis of fraud—the court recognizes that

Sullivan has willfully concealed his illness with the intent of cashing in on the policy at the first possible moment. Indeed, he has taken the precaution of continuing to pay the premium after becoming disabled, not even taking advantage of a disability premium waiver provision in the policy. Protective Life Insurance is left without remedy, because Massachusetts law dictates that policies are incontestable after 2 years, regardless of whether there has been a fraudulent misrepresentation. Moreover, the fact the Sullivan's misrepresentation was perseverated by his failure to use the disability waiver does not vitiate the incontestability. Is this result just? Has Sullivan achieved an unjust enrichment that is inconsistent with public policy aims? Is Protective Life Insurance likely to forego its right to obtain an HIV test with future applicants?

Recall our hypothetical engineer, Sam, the twenty-five year-old whose father has been diagnosed with Huntington Disease (HD) and who himself has tested positive for HD. He is completely unaffected, but is beginning to plan ahead for his life. Assume that Sam and his wife, Susie, have two children, a toddler and infant. Now knowing that his life span will be shortened and that he will likely be disabled for many years, Sam decides to purchase life insurance. He gathers up several applications and finds one that has many questions about current health status, but few about family history. It requires a blood pressure check and an HIV test, but Sam knows he can pass those tests without difficulty. Can he get life insurance? Is such adverse selection just? Suppose that while Sam has been surveying the opportunities, life insurers have added genetic testing to the application process. Review the Colorado law, *supra*; would a life insurer's request for genetic testing constitute an unfair practice under Colorado law?

3. *Parker v. Metropolitan Life* addresses the question of a differential approach being taken by a long-term disability plan on the basis of whether the individual suffers from a mental versus a physical disability. Parker is disabled due to a mental illness; as a result she is able to collect from the employer-provided long-term disability plan for a two-year period. However, had her disability been physical in nature, she would have been eligible for disability insurance income until age sixty-five. As is reflected in the text of the case, the District Court and Sixth Circuit panel have grappled with virtually every provision of the ADA in trying to address this case. What does the court conclude with respect to the applicability of Title III of the ADA in this case? How about Title IV? Why does the court conclude that Schering-Plough, Parker's employer, was rightfully dismissed as a defendant? In the final analysis, the court concludes that Title I is the only provision of the ADA that may apply. Citing the precedents of *Traynor v. Turnage*, 485 U.S. 535 (1988), *Modderno v. King*, and *Alexander v. Choate*, 469 U.S. 287 (1985), the Sixth Circuit holds that Title I prohibits discrimination between the disabled and the non-disabled, but does not prohibit discrimination among different disabilities in terms of coverage limitations.

Recall Sally, the twenty-six year-old university graduate with a Master's Degree in special education in the hypothetical, *supra*. She suffers from cystic fibrosis (CF), an autosomal recessive disorder associated with a range of respiratory and gastrointestinal problems, as well as sterility in males. Sally's CF significantly limits her respiratory capacity and renders her exceptionally prone to infections. In other words, Sally's disease is both symptomatic and physically limiting. However, Sally's new employer, Good Kids Children's Books, offers an elective long-term disability plan. If Sally elects it within 60 day of becoming employed, she can purchase the plan without underwriting. Sally figures this would be a good investment. What should she look for in determining whether the plan is a good choice for her?

Ted, the forty-two year old emergency room physician employed by an HMO, is in a similar quandary. Ted's strong family history of heart disease has become more omnipresent in his mind and psyche since he found out about his APOE e-4 genetic trait. He too is contemplating electing the HMO's disability and long-term care insurance plan. Both are offered through the HMO as an elective fringe benefit. However, because Ted has worked for the HMO for years, he will have to fill out a lengthy health information questionnaire for both policies. Is he likely to be underwritten for the policies? Can he be required to reveal his genetic testing by the insurer?

Chapter 5

Legal Issues in Genetics Research Involving Human Subjects

A. Historical Background of Human Subjects Research Regulation

At the end of World War II, as the civilized world reeled from revelations of the shocking research conducted by Nazi physicians on prisoners, the Nuremburg trial court produced one of the first codifications of ethical standards for research involving human subjects.

Nuremberg Code[1]

1. The voluntary consent of the human subject is absolutely essential.

This means that the person involved should have legal capacity to give consent; should be so situated as to be able to exercise free power of choice, without the intervention of any element of force, fraud, deceit, duress, over-reaching, or other ulterior form of constraint or coercion; and should have sufficient knowledge and comprehension of the elements of the subject matter involved as to enable him to make an understanding and enlightened decision. This latter element requires that before the acceptance of an affirmative decision by the experimental subject there should be made known to him the nature, duration, and purpose of the experiment; the method and means by which it is to be conducted; all inconveniences and hazards reasonably to be expected; and the effects upon his health or person which may possibly come from his participation in the experiment.

The duty and responsibility for ascertaining the quality of the consent rests upon each individual who initiates, directs or engages in the experiment. It is a personal duty and responsibility which may not be delegated to another with impunity.

2. The experiment should be such as to yield fruitful results for the good of society, unprocurable by other methods or means of study, and not random and unnecessary in nature.

---

1. 2 Trials of War Criminals before the Nuremberg Military Tribunals under Control Council Law No. 10, 181–182 (Washington, D.C.: U.S. Government Printing Office, 1949).

3. The experiment should be so designed and based on the results of animal experimentation and a knowledge of the natural history of the disease or other problem under study that the anticipated results will justify the performance of the experiment.

4. The experiment should be so conducted as to avoid all unnecessary physical and mental suffering and injury.

5. No experiment should be conducted where there is an *a priori* reason to believe that death or disabling injury will occur; except, perhaps, in those experiments where the experimental physicians also serve as subjects.

6. The degree of risk to be taken should never exceed that determined by the humanitarian importance of the problem to be solved by the experiment.

7. Proper preparations should be made and adequate facilities provided to protect the experimental subject against even remote possibilities of injury, disability, or death.

8. The experiment should be conducted only by scientifically qualified persons. The highest degree of skill and care should be required through all stages of the experiment of those who conduct or engage in the experiment.

9. During the course of the experiment, the human subject should be at liberty to bring the experiment to an end, if he has reached the physical or mental state, where continuation of the experiment seems to him to be impossible.

10. During the course of the experiment the scientist in charge must be prepared to terminate the experiment at any stage, if he has probable cause to believe, in the exercise of the good faith, superior skill and careful judgment required of him that a continuation of the experiment is likely to result in injury, disability, or death to the experimental subject.

* * *

Following this establishment of fundamental ethical principles in human subjects research, various professional and governmental guidelines were promulgated with varying degrees of binding import. The Clinical Center at the National Institutes of Health ("NIH") claims to have produced the first U.S. federal policy for the protection of human research subjects in 1953.[2] Despite this evidence of the apparent support for the principles in the Nuremberg Code, even research funded by federal agencies was not compliant with those principles, especially in the areas of disclosure and informed consent. Admittedly, one of the worst examples—the Tuskegee Syphilis Study administered under the authority of the U.S. Public Health Service[3]—commenced in 1932, before the horrors of Nazi human experimentation brought into stark relief the question of whether the ends of scientific and medical progress can justify inhumane means to get there. Or, in the alternative, is a strict utilitarian ethos of the needs of the many outweighing the needs of the few the proper lens through which to view scientific and medical research?

It took the thalidomide scare of the early 1960s to bring these issues to a head in the United States.[4] This drug had already been on the market in Europe, Canada, and else-

---

2. National Institutes of Health, Office of Human Subjects Research, Regulations and Ethical Guidelines, Appendix 1, http://www.nihtraining.com/ohsrsite/guidelines/graybook.html.

3. Discussed in more detail *infra*.

4. This section is summarized from Linda Bren, *Frances Oldham Kelsey: FDA Medical Reviewer Leaves Her Mark on History*, FDA CONSUMER MAGAZINE (U.S. Food and Drug Administration, March–April 2001).

where since the late 1950s when it was submitted for marketing approval to the U.S. Food and Drug Administration ("FDA") in 1960. The FDA medical reviewer, Frances Oldham Kelsey, had reservations about the drug due to the paucity of testing that its U.S. proponent, the Richardson-Merrell pharmaceutical company, had conducted to date. As she delayed the drug's formal introduction on the U.S. market by requesting more information and studies, evidence that thalidomide was contributing to horrific birth defects—extremely stunted limbs, for example, with toes growing directly out of the baby's hips or hands growing directly out of the baby's shoulders (phocomelia)—was mounting in countries such as Germany where the drug had been on the market the longest. Thus, by late 1961, most countries had pulled thalidomide from the market. In March 1962, Richardson-Merrell formally withdrew its own application from the FDA.

While Kelsey's refusal to approve the drug in the United States likely forestalled an enormous public health crisis, Richardson-Merrell was still able to distribute millions of thalidomide tablets to over 1,000 doctors, who in turn gave them to almost 20,000 patients, hundreds of whom were pregnant women. The company did so under the investigational study exemption of the Federal Food, Drug and Cosmetic Act in effect at the time.[5] That law did not require any particular disclosures or consents for clinical or other investigational studies, despite the principles set out in the Nuremberg Code. It did, however, require that sponsors have clinical evidence that a drug for which they sought approval was safe.[6] In fact, it was the inadequacy of this required information in Kelsey's opinion that caused her to delay approval of the drug for the general public.[7] But none of this was particularly helpful to those subjects who, whether they were entirely aware of it or not, were participating in these investigational safety studies. Thus, at least 17 babies were born in the U.S. with the birth defects associated with the use of thalidomide by pregnant women.

In the wake of the tremendous publicity surrounding this tragedy, and the understanding that the U.S. public had only narrowly missed a far more widespread crisis, Congress added control over investigational drug trials to the FDA through the Drug Amendments of 1962.[8] This included authorization for the FDA to require preclinical tests, such as animal studies, as well as agreements that investigators keep patients who receive the new drugs under their personal supervision.[9] It also required that manufacturers or the sponsors of investigational new drugs obtain certification from the doctors or other experts actually administering the drugs in trials that the latter have: (1) disclosed to patients that the drugs are being used for investigational purposes; and (2) obtained the consent of the patients in this use.[10] There were, however, some exceptions to the consent requirement.[11] The new amendments also added the requirement that investigators show the efficacy of their proposed new drugs, in addition to the drug's safety.[12]

---

5. Federal Food, Drug, and Cosmetic Act, § 505(i), 52 Stat. 1040, 1053 (1938) ("The Secretary shall promulgate regulations for exempting from the operation of this section drugs intended solely for investigational use by experts qualified by scientific training and experience to investigate the safety of drugs.").

6. Federal Food, Drug, and Cosmetic Act, § 505(b), 52 Stat. 1040, 1052 (1938).

7. *Id.* § 505(d).

8. 76 Stat. 780 (1962).

9. *Id.* § 103(b).

10. *Id.*

11. Investigators must obtain consent "except where they deem it not feasible or, in their professional judgment, contrary to the best interests of such human beings." *Id.*

12. *Id.* §§ 102–103.

Two years later, the World Medical Association adopted the next major international statement on human subjects research guidelines, *The Declaration of Helsinki: Recommendations Guiding Medical Doctors in Biomedical Research Involving Human Subjects.* This document has been continually in use since then, with its most recent amendment completed in 2004.

Declaration of Helsinki[13]

A. INTRODUCTION

1. The World Medical Association has developed the Declaration of Helsinki as a statement of ethical principles to provide guidance to physicians and other participants in medical research involving human subjects. Medical research involving human subjects includes research on identifiable human material or identifiable data.

2. It is the duty of the physician to promote and safeguard the health of the people. The physician's knowledge and conscience are dedicated to the fulfillment of this duty.

3. The Declaration of Geneva of the World Medical Association binds the physician with the words, "The health of my patient will be my first consideration," and the International Code of Medical Ethics declares that, "A physician shall act only in the patient's interest when providing medical care which might have the effect of weakening the physical and mental condition of the patient."

4. Medical progress is based on research which ultimately must rest in part on experimentation involving human subjects.

5. In medical research on human subjects, considerations related to the well-being of the human subject should take precedence over the interests of science and society.

6. The primary purpose of medical research involving human subjects is to improve prophylactic, diagnostic and therapeutic procedures and the understanding of the aetiology and pathogenesis of disease. Even the best proven prophylactic, diagnostic, and therapeutic methods must continuously be challenged through research for their effectiveness, efficiency, accessibility and quality.

7. In current medical practice and in medical research, most prophylactic, diagnostic and therapeutic procedures involve risks and burdens.

8. Medical research is subject to ethical standards that promote respect for all human beings and protect their health and rights. Some research populations are vulnerable and need special protection. The particular needs of the economically and medically disadvantaged must be recognized. Special attention is also required for those who cannot give or refuse consent for themselves, for those who may be subject to giving consent under duress, for those who will not benefit personally from the research and for those for whom the research is combined with care.

---

13. WORLD MEDICAL ASSOCIATION, DECLARATION OF HELSINKI: ETHICAL PRINCIPLES FOR MEDICAL RESEARCH INVOLVING HUMAN SUBJECTS (adopted by the 18th WMA General Assembly, Helsinki, Finland, June 1964, and amended by the: 29th WMA General Assembly, Tokyo, Japan, October 1975; 35th WMA General Assembly, Venice, Italy, October 1983; 41st WMA General Assembly, Hong Kong, September 1989; 48th WMA General Assembly, Somerset West, Republic of South Africa, October 1996; and the 52nd WMA General Assembly, Edinburgh, Scotland, October 2000. Note of Clarification on Paragraph 29 added by the WMA General Assembly, Washington 2002; Note of Clarification on Paragraph 30 added by the WMA General Assembly, Tokyo 2004.) *available at* http://www.wma.net/e/policy/b3.htm.

9. Research Investigators should be aware of the ethical, legal and regulatory requirements for research on human subjects in their own countries as well as applicable international requirements. No national ethical, legal or regulatory requirement should be allowed to reduce or eliminate any of the protections for human subjects set forth in this Declaration.

B. BASIC PRINCIPLES FOR ALL MEDICAL RESEARCH

10. It is the duty of the physician in medical research to protect the life, health, privacy, and dignity of the human subject.

11. Medical research involving human subjects must conform to generally accepted scientific principles, be based on a thorough knowledge of the scientific literature, other relevant sources of information, and on adequate laboratory and, where appropriate, animal experimentation.

12. Appropriate caution must be exercised in the conduct of research which may affect the environment, and the welfare of animals used for research must be respected.

13. The design and performance of each experimental procedure involving human subjects should be clearly formulated in an experimental protocol. This protocol should be submitted for consideration, comment, guidance, and where appropriate, approval to a specially appointed ethical review committee, which must be independent of the investigator, the sponsor or any other kind of undue influence. This independent committee should be in conformity with the laws and regulations of the country in which the research experiment is performed. The committee has the right to monitor ongoing trials. The researcher has the obligation to provide monitoring information to the committee, especially any serious adverse events. The researcher should also submit to the committee, for review, information regarding funding, sponsors, institutional affiliations, other potential conflicts of interest and incentives for subjects.

14. The research protocol should always contain a statement of the ethical considerations involved and should indicate that there is compliance with the principles enunciated in this Declaration.

15. Medical research involving human subjects should be conducted only by scientifically qualified persons and under the supervision of a clinically competent medical person. The responsibility for the human subject must always rest with a medically qualified person and never rest on the subject of the research, even though the subject has given consent.

16. Every medical research project involving human subjects should be preceded by careful assessment of predictable risks and burdens in comparison with foreseeable benefits to the subject or to others. This does not preclude the participation of healthy volunteers in medical research. The design of all studies should be publicly available.

17. Physicians should abstain from engaging in research projects involving human subjects unless they are confident that the risks involved have been adequately assessed and can be satisfactorily managed. Physicians should cease any investigation if the risks are found to outweigh the potential benefits or if there is conclusive proof of positive and beneficial results.

18. Medical research involving human subjects should only be conducted if the importance of the objective outweighs the inherent risks and burdens to the subject. This is especially important when the human subjects are healthy volunteers.

19. Medical research is only justified if there is a reasonable likelihood that the populations in which the research is carried out stand to benefit from the results of the research.

20. The subjects must be volunteers and informed participants in the research project.

21. The right of research subjects to safeguard their integrity must always be respected. Every precaution should be taken to respect the privacy of the subject, the confidentiality of the patient's information and to minimize the impact of the study on the subject's physical and mental integrity and on the personality of the subject.

22. In any research on human beings, each potential subject must be adequately informed of the aims, methods, sources of funding, any possible conflicts of interest, institutional affiliations of the researcher, the anticipated benefits and potential risks of the study and the discomfort it may entail. The subject should be informed of the right to abstain from participation in the study or to withdraw consent to participate at any time without reprisal. After ensuring that the subject has understood the information, the physician should then obtain the subject's freely-given informed consent, preferably in writing. If the consent cannot be obtained in writing, the non-written consent must be formally documented and witnessed.

23. When obtaining informed consent for the research project the physician should be particularly cautious if the subject is in a dependent relationship with the physician or may consent under duress. In that case the informed consent should be obtained by a well-informed physician who is not engaged in the investigation and who is completely independent of this relationship.

24. For a research subject who is legally incompetent, physically or mentally incapable of giving consent or is a legally incompetent minor, the investigator must obtain informed consent from the legally authorized representative in accordance with applicable law. These groups should not be included in research unless the research is necessary to promote the health of the population represented and this research cannot instead be performed on legally competent persons.

25. When a subject deemed legally incompetent, such as a minor child, is able to give assent to decisions about participation in research, the investigator must obtain that assent in addition to the consent of the legally authorized representative.

26. Research on individuals from whom it is not possible to obtain consent, including proxy or advance consent, should be done only if the physical/mental condition that prevents obtaining informed consent is a necessary characteristic of the research population. The specific reasons for involving research subjects with a condition that renders them unable to give informed consent should be stated in the experimental protocol for consideration and approval of the review committee. The protocol should state that consent to remain in the research should be obtained as soon as possible from the individual or a legally authorized surrogate.

27. Both authors and publishers have ethical obligations. In publication of the results of research, the investigators are obliged to preserve the accuracy of the results. Negative as well as positive results should be published or otherwise publicly available. Sources of funding, institutional affiliations and any possible conflicts of interest should be declared in the publication. Reports of experimentation not in accordance with the principles laid down in this Declaration should not be accepted for publication.

C. ADDITIONAL PRINCIPLES FOR MEDICAL RESEARCH COMBINED WITH MEDICAL CARE

28. The physician may combine medical research with medical care, only to the extent that the research is justified by its potential prophylactic, diagnostic or therapeutic

value. When medical research is combined with medical care, additional standards apply to protect the patients who are research subjects.

29. The benefits, risks, burdens and effectiveness of a new method should be tested against those of the best current prophylactic, diagnostic, and therapeutic methods. This does not exclude the use of placebo, or no treatment, in studies where no proven prophylactic, diagnostic or therapeutic method exists.[14]

30. At the conclusion of the study, every patient entered into the study should be assured of access to the best proven prophylactic, diagnostic and therapeutic methods identified by the study.[15]

31. The physician should fully inform the patient which aspects of the care are related to the research. The refusal of a patient to participate in a study must never interfere with the patient-physician relationship.

32. In the treatment of a patient, where proven prophylactic, diagnostic and therapeutic methods do not exist or have been ineffective, the physician, with informed consent from the patient, must be free to use unproven or new prophylactic, diagnostic and therapeutic measures, if in the physician's judgment it offers hope of saving life, re-establishing health or alleviating suffering. Where possible, these measures should be made the object of research, designed to evaluate their safety and efficacy. In all cases, new information should be recorded and, where appropriate, published. The other relevant guidelines of this Declaration should be followed.

* * *

Both the Drug Amendments of 1962 and The Declaration of Helsinki may have been a case of too little too late. In 1966, Henry Beecher, a well known and respected anesthesiologist and researcher, published the eye-opening article "Ethics and Clinical Research" in the New England Journal of Medicine.

> Human experimentation since World War II has created some difficult problems with the increasing employment of patients as experimental subjects when it must be apparent that they would not have been available if they had been truly aware of the uses that would be made of them. Evidence is at hand that many of the patients in the examples that follow never had the risk satisfactorily explained to them, and it seems obvious that further hundreds have not known that they were the subjects of an experiment although grave consequences have been suffered as a direct result of experiments described here.

---

14. The WMA hereby reaffirms its position that extreme care must be taken in making use of a placebo-controlled trial and that in general this methodology should only be used in the absence of existing proven therapy. However, a placebo-controlled trial may be ethically acceptable, even if proven therapy is available, under the following circumstances:

—Where for compelling and scientifically sound methodological reasons its use is necessary to determine the efficacy or safety of a prophylactic, diagnostic or therapeutic method; or

—Where a prophylactic, diagnostic or therapeutic method is being investigated for a minor condition and the patients who receive placebo will not be subject to any additional risk of serious or irreversible harm.

All other provisions of the Declaration of Helsinki must be adhered to, especially the need for appropriate ethical and scientific review.

15. The WMA hereby reaffirms its position that it is necessary during the study planning process to identify post-trial access by study participants to prophylactic, diagnostic and therapeutic procedures identified as beneficial in the study or access to other appropriate care. Post-trial access arrangements or other care must be described in the study protocol so the ethical review committee may consider such arrangements during its review.

> There is a belief prevalent in some sophisticated circles that attention to these matters would "block progress." ...
>
> Experimentation in man takes place in several areas: in self-experimentation; in patient volunteers and normal subjects; in therapy; and in the different areas of *experimentation on a patient not for his benefit but for that, at least in theory, of patients in general....*
>
> Since World War II the annual expenditure for research (in large part in man) in the Massachusetts General Hospital has increased a remarkable 17-fold. At the National Institutes of Health, the increase has been a gigantic 634-fold. This "national" rate of increase is over 36 times that of the Massachusetts General Hospital. These data, rough as they are, illustrate vast opportunities and concomitantly expanded responsibilities....
>
> [Other issues that must be considered are]: a general awakening of social conscience; greater power for good or harm in new remedies, new operations and new investigative procedures than was formerly the case; new methods of preventive treatment with their advantages and dangers that are now applied to communities as a whole as well as to individuals, with multiplications of the possibilities for injury; medical science has shown how valuable human experimentation can be in solving problems of disease and its treatment; one can therefore anticipate an increase in experimentation; and the newly developed concept of clinical research as a profession (for example, clinical pharmacology)—and this, of course, can lead to unfortunate separation between the interests of science and the interests of the patient....
>
> The Problem of Consent
>
> All so-called codes are based on the bland assumption that meaningful or informed consent is readily available for the asking. As pointed out elsewhere, this is very often not the case. Consent in any fully informed sense may not be obtainable. Nevertheless, except, possibly, in the most trivial situations, it remains a goal toward which one must strive for sociologic, ethical and clear-cut legal reasons. There is no choice in the matter.
>
> If suitably approached, patients will accede, on the basis of trust, to about any request their physician may make. At the same time, every experienced clinician investigator knows that patients will often submit to inconvenience and some discomfort, if they do not last very long, but the usual patient will never agree to jeopardize seriously his health or his life for the sake of "science."[16]

Beecher documented 50 different clinical studies where questionable practices were employed on human subjects. Of these studies, only two made any attempt at all to obtain consent. Among some of the most shocking examples were the following: (1) penicillin, a known effective treatment for the illness at issue, was withheld from some members of a study;[17] (2) various known toxic substances, including live cancer cells and hepatitis, were intentionally introduced into subjects to record effects; (3) artificial devices, such as a mercury filled resistance gauge, were introduced into subjects for research only; and (4) in perhaps the oddest experiment, healthy babies less than two

16. H.K. Beecher, *Ethics and Clinical Research*, 274 New Eng. J. of Med. 1354 (1966).

17. Although Beecher did not seem to be referring to the infamous Tuskegee study, discussed *infra*, his criticism of this particular practice occurred while that study was still underway but not yet disclosed to the public.

days old were subjected to extensive x-ray exposure in the lower abdominal region just so that researchers could try to determine whether "ureteral reflux can occur in the normal bladder."

While calling for increased efforts by researchers to obtain informed consent of human subjects—of which he was skeptical—Beecher also called for investigators to exercise their own restraint and ethics. But he further insisted that scientific and medical journals should refuse to publish results from tainted studies, arguing that the ends should never justify the means. The media latched on to the stories in his article and the public was galvanized about human "guinea pigs" unwittingly subjected to life-threatening procedures and investigational drugs and biologics. Beecher had successfully drawn the line between "practice"—procedures done for the benefit of the patient—and research—procedures done either not at all for the subject's direct benefit, or only partly for the subject's benefit—that would become a key part of the Belmont Report (discussed *infra*).

The furor generated by Beecher's article, and the subsequent media coverage, appears to have directly led both the NIH and FDA to amend their policies regarding human subjects research later that year. By the end of 1966, the NIH had issued its first Public Health Service Policy on the Protection of Human Subjects which ultimately expanded to cover all human subjects research conducted or supported by the then Department of Health, Education and Welfare (HEW). As part of this Policy, methods of obtaining informed consent would be reviewed, and such consent was required to be documented and signed by the parties.

Yet, less than a decade later the truth about the still ongoing Tuskegee study would be revealed, demonstrating the apparent failure of existing NIH policies to protect test subjects.

Report of the Tuskegee Syphilis Study Legacy Committee—Final Report[18]

May 20, 1996

In 1932, the United States Public Health Service (USPHS) initiated the Tuskegee Syphilis Study to document the natural history of syphilis. The subjects of the investigation were 399 poor black sharecroppers from Macon County, Alabama, with latent syphilis and 201 men without the disease who served as controls. The physicians conducting the Study deceived the men, telling them that they were being treated for "bad blood."[19] However, they deliberately denied treatment to the men with syphilis and they went to extreme lengths to ensure that they would not receive therapy from any other sources. In exchange for their participation, the men received free meals, free medical examinations, and burial insurance.

On 26 July 1972, a front-page headline in the *New York Times* read, "Syphilis Victims in U.S. Study Went Untreated for 40 Years." The accompanying article publicly revealed the details of the Tuskegee Syphilis Study—"the longest nontherapeutic experiment on human beings in medical history." In the almost 25 years since its disclosure,

18. The Committee was established at a meeting at Tuskegee University, January 18–19, 1996. The Final Report and related materials are available at http://hsc.virginia.edu/hs-library/historical/apology/report.html.

19. The term "bad blood" encompassed several conditions including syphilis, anemia, and fatigue.

the Study has moved from a singular historical event to a powerful metaphor. It has come to symbolize racism in medicine, ethical misconduct in human research, paternalism by physicians, and government abuse of vulnerable people.

The Tuskegee Syphilis Study continues to cast its long shadow on the contemporary relationship between African Americans and the biomedical community. Several recent articles have argued that the Tuskegee Syphilis Study has predisposed many African Americans to distrust medical and public health authorities. The authors point to the Study as a significant factor in the low participation of African Americans in clinical trials and organ donation efforts and in the reluctance of many black people in seeking routine preventive care. As one AIDS educator put it, "so many African-American people that I work with do not trust hospitals or any of the other community health care service providers because of that Tuskegee experiment. It is like ... if they did it then they will do it again."

The Tuskegee Syphilis Study Legacy Committee is dedicated to preserving the memory of the Study while moving beyond it, transforming the legacy into renewed efforts to bridge the chasm between the health conditions of black and white Americans. To this end, the Committee is pursuing two inseparable goals:

1) to persuade President Clinton to publicly apologize for past government wrongdoing to the Study's living survivors, their families, and to the Tuskegee community, and

2) to develop a strategy to redress the damages caused by the Study and to transform its damaging legacy....

1. A Presidential Apology for the Tuskegee Syphilis Study

Moral and physical harms to the community of Macon County

It is clear that the U.S. government scientists irreparably harmed hundreds of socially and economically vulnerable African-American men in Macon County, their family members, and their descendants by deliberately deceiving them and withholding from them state of the art treatment. When the Tuskegee Study began, the standard therapy for syphilis consisted of painful injections of arsenical compounds, supplemented by topical applications of mercury or bismuth ointments. Although this therapy was less effective than penicillin would prove to be, in the 1930s every major textbook on syphilis recommended it for the treatment of the disease. After penicillin became available, the researchers withheld its use as well. Published medical reports have estimated that between 28 and 100 men died as a result of their syphilis. Due to a lax study protocol, we cannot be sure that all the men had latent syphilis. It is therefore entirely possible that the infected men passed syphilis to their sexual partners and to their children in utero. Thus the physical harm may not be limited just to the men enrolled in the Study.

No public apology has ever been made

In the aftermath of a Health, Education and Welfare Task force report, a Senate hearing, and an out of court legal settlement, the U.S. government provided economic compensation and continues to give free health benefits to the surviving subjects and their families. However, no public apology has ever been offered for the moral wrongdoing that occurred in the name of government medical research. No public official has ever stated clearly to the nation that the Tuskegee Syphilis Study was morally wrong from its inception, and no public official has ever apologized to the survivors and their families. Yet, an apology is sorely needed. The Committee believes that an apology from the President could facilitate the healing of the victims and the nation.

The harmful legacy of the Study

The historical record makes plain that African American's distrust of the medical profession predates the revelations of the Tuskegee Syphilis Study and involves a myriad of other social and political factors. Nevertheless, the Study has become a powerful symbol for the fear of exploitation in research and the deprivation of adequate medical care that is widespread in the African-American community. Recent articles argue that Tuskegee has created a climate of suspicion that taints the relationship between many African Americans and the medical profession. The Tuskegee Study is offered as the reason why few blacks participate in research trials, why the need for transplant organs by African Americans widely surpasses the supply, and why African Americans often avoid medical treatment. It is also offered as an explanation as to why rumors about genocide persist in the African-American community, ranging from the notion that AIDS is a plot to exterminate black people to the idea that needle exchange programs fuel a drug epidemic that disproportionately affects black neighborhoods. For many African Americans, the fact that the Tuskegee Study occurred at all proves that black life is not valued. The Committee believes that an apology combined with a strategy for addressing the damages of the Tuskegee legacy would begin the process of regaining the trust of people of color.

The harm done to the community and the University

Because the name of the study points to Tuskegee Institute (now Tuskegee University) rather than the United States Public Health Service, it clouds the funding and responsibility for the Study. Although facilities and staff of the Tuskegee Institute were involved, primary direction came from the government under the auspices of the USPHS. The notoriety of the Study obscures the achievements of the Tuskegee Institute in improving the health care of African Americans. These achievements include initiating National Negro Health Week, building the John A. Andrew Hospital, creating the John A. Andrew Clinical Society, establishing a nurse training school, and organizing a school for midwives.

[2]. The Apology: Context and Opportunity

The Committee urges President Clinton to apologize on behalf of the American government for the harms inflicted at Tuskegee. The apology should be directed to those most directly harmed: to the elderly survivors of the Study, to their families, and to the wider community of Tuskegee and its university. Also included within the apology should be all people of color whose lives reverberate with the consequences of the Study.

As the highest elected official of the United States, the President should offer the apology for the Study which was conducted under the auspices of the United States government. The significance of a presidential apology was recognized recently when the President apologized to those harmed by Cold War radiation experiments as a way to regain confidence of the American people. In the context of President Clinton's stated desire to bridge the racial divide, this apology provides the opportunity to begin to heal the racial wounds that persist in this country.

Given the ages of the living participants and the period of time since the Study was disclosed, we believe that the apology should be offered swiftly. There are only eleven survivors; a twelfth died as recently as March 3, 1996. We recommend that the government issue the apology from Tuskegee University, perhaps linked with an early meeting of the new National Bioethics Advisory Commission (NBEAC). Because the Tuskegee study is a starting point for all modern moral reflection on research ethics, a meeting of the NBEAC at Tuskegee in conjunction with a Presidential apology would be an ideal new beginning.

[3]. Transforming the Legacy

Although a public apology is necessary to heal the wounds of Tuskegee, it alone would not be sufficient to assure the nation that research like the Tuskegee Syphilis Study will not be duplicated. Despite the significance of a Presidential apology, it must not be an isolated event. Consequently, the Committee also recommends the development of a mechanism to move beyond Tuskegee and to address the effects of its legacy. The Committee strongly urges the development of a professionally staffed center at Tuskegee University, focused on preserving the national memory of the Study and transforming its legacy.

Regret for past mistakes must be accompanied by a determination to prevent future wrongs. Until now for black Americans the legacy of the Tuskegee Syphilis Study has been a negative one—a symbol of their mistreatment within American society. The proposed Center could help transform the legacy of Tuskegee into a positive symbol for all Americans by demonstrating the importance of acknowledging past wrongs, rebuilding trust, and practicing ethical research.

The new center's mission would be to preserve the national memory of the Syphilis Study for public education and scholarly research, and to analyze and disseminate findings on effective and ethically acceptable ways to address the profound mistrust that is the tragic and enduring legacy of this Study, especially among African Americans and other persons of color....

Although the Committee sees the creation of a Center as the most valuable attempt to redress the damages of Tuskegee, we envision several possible concurrent programs. These include:

1. a Minority Health Initiative, similar in scope to the newly established Women's Health Initiative;

2. training programs for health care providers to better understand the social and cultural issues of providing health care and of conducting research in communities of color;

3. a clearinghouse to help investigators conduct ethically responsible research.

The Committee recommends that funding for the Center must combine government and private funding. The announcement of a federal challenge grant would be very useful as a catalyst for future fundraising efforts. It is undeniable that the Tuskegee Syphilis Study has adversely affected the attitudes that many African Americans hold toward the biomedical community and the United States government. But despite the long shadow that it casts, we now have an opportunity to challenge this legacy and create a more beneficial one.

* * *

President Clinton did indeed take up the challenge of the Committee and issued a formal apology on behalf of the American people for the study in a formal ceremony at the White House.[20] Back in 1972, however, no such apology was forthcoming. But Sen-

20. *See* The White House, Office of the Press Secretary, Remarks by the President in Apology for Study Done in Tuskegee, May 16, 1997, *available at* http://clinton4.nara.gov/textonly/New/Remarks/Fri/19970516-898.html.

ate hearings were convened in the aftermath of the scandal which led directly to the passage of the National Research Act of 1974.[21] This legislation established the National Commission for the Protection of Human Subjects of Biomedical and Behavioral Research. The Commission was charged with: (1) establishing the boundary between research and therapeutic practice of medicine; (2) determining the role of risk-benefit analyses in assessing the appropriateness of any particular research involving human subjects; (3) setting guidelines for the selection of human subjects to participate in research; (4) establishing the nature and definition of informed consent in different research settings; and (5) outlining mechanisms to evaluate and monitor the formal Institutional Review Boards ("IRBs") called for under a different section of the legislation.[22] The Commission would also separately consider requirements for informed consent with regard to research participation by children, prisoners, and the institutionally mentally infirm as subjects,[23] together with the need for legislation to regulate human subjects research outside HEW.[24] The Commission would further take on questions regarding research on human fetuses,[25] and the use of "psychosurgery."[26] The National Research Act also called for the Commission to "undertake a comprehensive study of the ethical, social, and legal implications of advances in biomedical and behavioral research and technology."[27]

The National Research Act also established the National Advisory Council for the Protection of Subjects of Biomedical and Behavioral Research and charged it with an ongoing role in advising, consulting, and reviewing agency policies with regard to human subjects research.[28] It further mandated that any institutions who wished to receive research funding from HEW must have established IRBs that conform with regulations to be promulgated by HEW.[29] Finally, the Act prohibited research involving human fetuses until the Commission made its final recommendations in this regard.[30]

The Commission issued its recommendations in the following landmark document.

Department of Health, Education, and Welfare, The National Commission for the Protection of Human Subjects of Biomedical and Behavioral Research, The Belmont Report: Ethical Principles & Guidelines for the Protection of Human Subjects of Research

44 Fed. Reg. 23192 (April 18, 1979)

Scientific research has produced substantial social benefits. It has also posed some troubling ethical questions. Public attention was drawn to these questions by reported abuses of human subjects in biomedical experiments, especially during the Second World War. During the Nuremberg War Crime Trials, the Nuremberg code was drafted

21. P.L. 93-348, 88 Stat. 342 (1974).
22. *Id.* § 202(a)(1)(B).
23. *Id.* § 202(a)(2).
24. *Id.* § 202(a)(3).
25. *Id.* § 202(b).
26. *Id.* § 202(c).
27. *Id.* § 203.
28. *Id.* § 211.
29. *Id.* § 212.
30. *Id.* § 213.

as a set of standards for judging physicians and scientists who had conducted biomedical experiments on concentration camp prisoners. This code became the prototype of many later codes intended to assure that research involving human subjects would be carried out in an ethical manner.

The codes consist of rules, some general, others specific, that guide the investigators or the reviewers of research in their work. Such rules often are inadequate to cover complex situations; at times they come into conflict, and they are frequently difficult to interpret or apply. Broader ethical principles will provide a basis on which specific rules may be formulated, criticized and interpreted.

Three principles, or general prescriptive judgments, that are relevant to research involving human subjects are identified in this statement. Other principles may also be relevant. These three are comprehensive, however, and are stated at a level of generalization that should assist scientists, subjects, reviewers and interested citizens to understand the ethical issues inherent in research involving human subjects. These principles cannot always be applied so as to resolve beyond dispute particular ethical problems. The objective is to provide an analytical framework that will guide the resolution of ethical problems arising from research involving human subjects.

This statement consists of a distinction between research and practice, a discussion of the three basic ethical principles, and remarks about the application of these principles.

A. Boundaries Between Practice and Research

It is important to distinguish between biomedical and behavioral research, on the one hand, and the practice of accepted therapy on the other, in order to know what activities ought to undergo review for the protection of human subjects of research. The distinction between research and practice is blurred partly because both often occur together (as in research designed to evaluate a therapy) and partly because notable departures from standard practice are often called "experimental" when the terms "experimental" and "research" are not carefully defined.

For the most part, the term "practice" refers to interventions that are designed solely to enhance the well-being of an individual patient or client and that have a reasonable expectation of success. The purpose of medical or behavioral practice is to provide diagnosis, preventive treatment or therapy to particular individuals.[31] By contrast, the term "research" designates an activity designed to test an hypothesis, permit conclusions to be drawn, and thereby to develop or contribute to generalizable knowledge (expressed, for example, in theories, principles, and statements of relationships). Research is usually described in a formal protocol that sets forth an objective and a set of procedures designed to reach that objective.

When a clinician departs in a significant way from standard or accepted practice, the innovation does not, in and of itself, constitute research. The fact that a procedure is

---

31. Although practice usually involves interventions designed solely to enhance the well-being of a particular individual, interventions are sometimes applied to one individual for the enhancement of the well-being of another (e.g., blood donation, skin grafts, organ transplants) or an intervention may have the dual purpose of enhancing the well-being of a particular individual, and, at the same time, providing some benefit to others (e.g., vaccination, which protects both the person who is vaccinated and society generally). The fact that some forms of practice have elements other than immediate benefit to the individual receiving an intervention, however, should not confuse the general distinction between research and practice. Even when a procedure applied in practice may benefit some other person, it remains an intervention designed to enhance the well-being of a particular individual or groups of individuals; thus, it is practice and need not be reviewed as research.

"experimental," in the sense of new, untested or different, does not automatically place it in the category of research. Radically new procedures of this description should, however, be made the object of formal research at an early stage in order to determine whether they are safe and effective. Thus, it is the responsibility of medical practice committees, for example, to insist that a major innovation be incorporated into a formal research project.[32]

Research and practice may be carried on together when research is designed to evaluate the safety and efficacy of a therapy. This need not cause any confusion regarding whether or not the activity requires review; the general rule is that if there is any element of research in an activity, that activity should undergo review for the protection of human subjects.

B. Basic Ethical Principles

The expression "basic ethical principles" refers to those general judgments that serve as a basic justification for the many particular ethical prescriptions and evaluations of human actions. Three basic principles, among those generally accepted in our cultural tradition, are particularly relevant to the ethics of research involving human subjects: the principles of respect of persons, beneficence and justice.

1. *Respect for Persons.* Respect for persons incorporates at least two ethical convictions: first, that individuals should be treated as autonomous agents, and second, that persons with diminished autonomy are entitled to protection. The principle of respect for persons thus divides into two separate moral requirements: the requirement to acknowledge autonomy and the requirement to protect those with diminished autonomy.

An autonomous person is an individual capable of deliberation about personal goals and of acting under the direction of such deliberation. To respect autonomy is to give weight to autonomous persons' considered opinions and choices while refraining from obstructing their actions unless they are clearly detrimental to others. To show lack of respect for an autonomous agent is to repudiate that person's considered judgments, to deny an individual the freedom to act on those considered judgments, or to withhold information necessary to make a considered judgment, when there are no compelling reasons to do so.

However, not every human being is capable of self-determination. The capacity for self-determination matures during an individual's life, and some individuals lose this capacity wholly or in part because of illness, mental disability, or circumstances that severely restrict liberty. Respect for the immature and the incapacitated may require protecting them as they mature or while they are incapacitated.

Some persons are in need of extensive protection, even to the point of excluding them from activities which may harm them; other persons require little protection beyond making sure they undertake activities freely and with awareness of possible adverse consequence. The extent of protection afforded should depend upon the risk of harm and the likelihood of benefit. The judgment that any individual lacks autonomy should be periodically reevaluated and will vary in different situations.

In most cases of research involving human subjects, respect for persons demands that subjects enter into the research voluntarily and with adequate information. In some situations, however, application of the principle is not obvious. The involvement of

32. Because the problems related to social experimentation may differ substantially from those of biomedical and behavioral research, the Commission specifically declines to make any policy determination regarding such research at this time. Rather, the Commission believes that the problem ought to be addressed by one of its successor bodies.

prisoners as subjects of research provides an instructive example. On the one hand, it would seem that the principle of respect for persons requires that prisoners not be deprived of the opportunity to volunteer for research. On the other hand, under prison conditions they may be subtly coerced or unduly influenced to engage in research activities for which they would not otherwise volunteer. Respect for persons would then dictate that prisoners be protected. Whether to allow prisoners to "volunteer" or to "protect" them presents a dilemma. Respecting persons, in most hard cases, is often a matter of balancing competing claims urged by the principle of respect itself.

2. *Beneficence.* Persons are treated in an ethical manner not only by respecting their decisions and protecting them from harm, but also by making efforts to secure their well-being. Such treatment falls under the principle of beneficence. The term "beneficence" is often understood to cover acts of kindness or charity that go beyond strict obligation. In this document, beneficence is understood in a stronger sense, as an obligation. Two general rules have been formulated as complementary expressions of beneficent actions in this sense: (1) do not harm and (2) maximize possible benefits and minimize possible harms.

The Hippocratic maxim "do no harm" has long been a fundamental principle of medical ethics. Claude Bernard extended it to the realm of research, saying that one should not injure one person regardless of the benefits that might come to others. However, even avoiding harm requires learning what is harmful; and, in the process of obtaining this information, persons may be exposed to risk of harm. Further, the Hippocratic Oath requires physicians to benefit their patients "according to their best judgment." Learning what will in fact benefit may require exposing persons to risk. The problem posed by these imperatives is to decide when it is justifiable to seek certain benefits despite the risks involved, and when the benefits should be foregone because of the risks.

The obligations of beneficence affect both individual investigators and society at large, because they extend both to particular research projects and to the entire enterprise of research. In the case of particular projects, investigators and members of their institutions are obliged to give forethought to the maximization of benefits and the reduction of risk that might occur from the research investigation. In the case of scientific research in general, members of the larger society are obliged to recognize the longer term benefits and risks that may result from the improvement of knowledge and from the development of novel medical, psychotherapeutic, and social procedures.

The principle of beneficence often occupies a well-defined justifying role in many areas of research involving human subjects. An example is found in research involving children. Effective ways of treating childhood diseases and fostering healthy development are benefits that serve to justify research involving children—even when individual research subjects are not direct beneficiaries. Research also makes it possible to avoid the harm that may result from the application of previously accepted routine practices that on closer investigation turn out to be dangerous. But the role of the principle of beneficence is no[t] always so unambiguous. A difficult ethical problem remains, for example, about research that presents more than minimal risk without immediate prospect of direct benefit to the children involved. Some have argued that such research is inadmissible, while others have pointed out that this limit would rule out much research promising great benefit to children in the future. Here again, as with all hard cases, the different claims covered by the principle of beneficence may come into conflict and force difficult choices.

3. *Justice.* Who ought to receive the benefits of research and bear its burdens? This is a question of justice, in the sense of "fairness in distribution" or "what is deserved." An

injustice occurs when some benefit to which a person is entitled is denied without good reason or when some burden is imposed unduly. Another way of conceiving the principle of justice is that equals ought to be treated equally. However, this statement requires explication. Who is equal and who is unequal? What considerations justify departure from equal distribution? Almost all commentators allow that distinctions based on experience, age, deprivation, competence, merit and position do sometimes constitute criteria justifying differential treatment for certain purposes. It is necessary, then, to explain in what respects people should be treated equally. There are several widely accepted formulations of just ways to distribute burdens and benefits. Each formulation mentions some relevant property on the basis of which burdens and benefits should be distributed. These formulations are[:] (1) to each person an equal share, (2) to each person according to individual need, (3) to each person according to individual effort, (4) to each person according to societal contribution, and (5) to each person according to merit.

Questions of justice have long been associated with social practices such as punishment, taxation and political representation. Until recently these questions have not generally been associated with scientific research. However, they are foreshadowed even in the earliest reflections on the ethics of research involving human subjects. For example, during the 19th and early 20th centuries the burdens of serving as research subjects fell largely upon poor ward patients, while the benefits of improved medical care flowed primarily to private patients. Subsequently, the exploitation of unwilling prisoners as research subjects in Nazi concentration camps was condemned as a particularly flagrant injustice. In this country, in the 1940's, the Tuskegee syphilis study used disadvantaged, rural black men to study the untreated course of a disease that is by no means confined to that population. These subjects were deprived of demonstrably effective treatment in order not to interrupt the project, long after such treatment became generally available.

Against this historical background, it can be seen how conceptions of justice are relevant to research involving human subjects. For example, the selection of research subjects needs to be scrutinized in order to determine whether some classes (e.g., welfare patients, particular racial and ethnic minorities, or persons confined to institutions) are being systematically selected simply because of their easy availability, their compromised position, or their manipulability, rather than for reasons directly related to the problem being studied. Finally, whenever research supported by public funds leads to the development of therapeutic devices and procedures, justice demands both that these not provide advantages only to those who can afford them and that such research should not unduly involve persons from groups unlikely to be among the beneficiaries of subsequent applications of the research.

C. Applications

Applications of the general principles to the conduct of research leads to consideration of the following requirements: informed consent, risk/benefit assessment, and the selection of subjects of research.

1. *Informed Consent.* Respect for persons requires that subjects, to the degree that they are capable, be given the opportunity to choose what shall or shall not happen to them. This opportunity is provided when adequate standards for informed consent are satisfied.

While the importance of informed consent is unquestioned, controversy prevails over the nature and possibility of an informed consent. Nonetheless, there is widespread agreement that the consent process can be analyzed as containing three elements: information, comprehension and voluntariness.

Information. Most codes of research establish specific items for disclosure intended to assure that subjects are given sufficient information. These items generally include: the research procedure, their purposes, risks and anticipated benefits, alternative procedures (where therapy is involved), and a statement offering the subject the opportunity to ask questions and to withdraw at any time from the research. Additional items have been proposed, including how subjects are selected, the person responsible for the research, etc.

However, a simple listing of items does not answer the question of what the standard should be for judging how much and what sort of information should be provided. One standard frequently invoked in medical practice, namely the information commonly provided by practitioners in the field or in the locale, is inadequate since research takes place precisely when a common understanding does not exist. Another standard, currently popular in malpractice law, requires the practitioner to reveal the information that reasonable persons would wish to know in order to make a decision regarding their care. This, too, seems insufficient since the research subject, being in essence a volunteer, may wish to know considerably more about risks gratuitously undertaken than do patients who deliver themselves into the hand of a clinician for needed care. It may be that a standard of "the reasonable volunteer" should be proposed: the extent and nature of information should be such that persons, knowing that the procedure is neither necessary for their care nor perhaps fully understood, can decide whether they wish to participate in the furthering of knowledge. Even when some direct benefit to them is anticipated, the subjects should understand clearly the range of risk and the voluntary nature of participation.

A special problem of consent arises where informing subjects of some pertinent aspect of the research is likely to impair the validity of the research. In many cases, it is sufficient to indicate to subjects that they are being invited to participate in research of which some features will not be revealed until the research is concluded. In all cases of research involving incomplete disclosure, such research is justified only if it is clear that (1) incomplete disclosure is truly necessary to accomplish the goals of the research, (2) there are no undisclosed risks to subjects that are more than minimal, and (3) there is an adequate plan for debriefing subjects, when appropriate, and for dissemination of research results to them. Information about risks should never be withheld for the purpose of eliciting the cooperation of subjects, and truthful answers should always be given to direct questions about the research. Care should be taken to distinguish cases in which disclosure would destroy or invalidate the research from cases in which disclosure would simply inconvenience the investigator.

Comprehension. The manner and context in which information is conveyed is as important as the information itself. For example, presenting information in a disorganized and rapid fashion, allowing too little time for consideration or curtailing opportunities for questioning, all may adversely affect a subject's ability to make an informed choice.

Because the subject's ability to understand is a function of intelligence, rationality, maturity and language, it is necessary to adapt the presentation of the information to the subject's capacities. Investigators are responsible for ascertaining that the subject has comprehended the information. While there is always an obligation to ascertain that the information about risk to subjects is complete and adequately comprehended, when the risks are more serious, that obligation increases. On occasion, it may be suitable to give some oral or written tests of comprehension.

Special provision may need to be made when comprehension is severely limited—for example, by conditions of immaturity or mental disability. Each class of subjects that one might consider as incompetent (e.g., infants and young children, mentally disable patients, the terminally ill and the comatose) should be considered on its own terms. Even for these persons, however, respect requires giving them the opportunity to choose to the extent they are able, whether or not to participate in research. The objections of these subjects to involvement should be honored, unless the research entails providing them a therapy unavailable elsewhere. Respect for persons also requires seeking the permission of other parties in order to protect the subjects from harm. Such persons are thus respected both by acknowledging their own wishes and by the use of third parties to protect them from harm.

The third parties chosen should be those who are most likely to understand the incompetent subject's situation and to act in that person's best interest. The person authorized to act on behalf of the subject should be given an opportunity to observe the research as it proceeds in order to be able to withdraw the subject from the research, if such action appears in the subject's best interest.

Voluntariness. An agreement to participate in research constitutes a valid consent only if voluntarily given. This element of informed consent requires conditions free of coercion and undue influence. Coercion occurs when an overt threat of harm is intentionally presented by one person to another in order to obtain compliance. Undue influence, by contrast, occurs through an offer of an excessive, unwarranted, inappropriate or improper reward or other overture in order to obtain compliance. Also, inducements that would ordinarily be acceptable may become undue influences if the subject is especially vulnerable.

Unjustifiable pressures usually occur when persons in positions of authority or commanding influence—especially where possible sanctions are involved—urge a course of action for a subject. A continuum of such influencing factors exists, however, and it is impossible to state precisely where justifiable persuasion ends and undue influence begins. But undue influence would include actions such as manipulating a person's choice through the controlling influence of a close relative and threatening to withdraw health services to which an individual would otherwise be entitled.

2. *Assessment of Risks and Benefits.* The assessment of risks and benefits requires a careful arrayal of relevant data, including, in some cases, alternative ways of obtaining the benefits sought in the research. Thus, the assessment presents both an opportunity and a responsibility to gather systematic and comprehensive information about proposed research. For the investigator, it is a means to examine whether the proposed research is properly designed. For a review committee, it is a method for determining whether the risks that will be presented to subjects are justified. For prospective subjects, the assessment will assist the determination whether or not to participate.

The Nature and Scope of Risks and Benefits. The requirement that research be justified on the basis of a favorable risk/benefit assessment bears a close relation to the principle of beneficence, just as the moral requirement that informed consent be obtained is derived primarily from the principle of respect for persons. The term "risk" refers to a possibility that harm may occur. However, when expressions such as "small risk" or "high risk" are used, they usually refer (often ambiguously) both to the chance (probability) of experiencing a harm and the severity (magnitude) of the envisioned harm.

The term "benefit" is used in the research context to refer to something of positive value related to health or welfare. Unlike, "risk," "benefit" is not a term that expresses probabilities. Risk is properly contrasted to probability of benefits, and benefits are properly contrasted with harms rather than risks of harm. Accordingly, so-called risk/benefit assessments are concerned with the probabilities and magnitudes of possible harm and anticipated benefits. Many kinds of possible harms and benefits need to be taken into account. There are, for example, risks of psychological harm, physical harm, legal harm, social harm and economic harm and the corresponding benefits. While the most likely types of harms to research subjects are those of psychological or physical pain or injury, other possible kinds should not be overlooked.

Risks and benefits of research may affect the individual subjects, the families of the individual subjects, and society at large (or special groups of subjects in society). Previous codes and federal regulations have required that risks to subjects be outweighed by the sum of both the anticipated benefit to the subject, if any, and the anticipated benefit to society in the form of knowledge to be gained from the research. In balancing these different elements, the risks and benefits affecting the immediate research subject will normally carry special weight. On the other hand, interests other than those of the subject may on some occasions be sufficient by themselves to justify the risks involved in the research, so long as the subjects' rights have been protected. Beneficence thus requires that we protect against risk of harm to subjects and also that we be concerned about the loss of the substantial benefits that might be gained from research.

The Systematic Assessment of Risks and Benefits. It is commonly said that benefits and risks must be "balanced" and shown to be "in a favorable ratio." The metaphorical character of these terms draws attention to the difficulty of making precise judgments. Only on rare occasions will quantitative techniques be available for the scrutiny of research protocols. However, the idea of systematic, nonarbitrary analysis of risks and benefits should be emulated insofar as possible. This ideal requires those making decisions about the justifiability of research to be thorough in the accumulation and assessment of information about all aspects of the research, and to consider alternatives systematically. This procedure renders the assessment of research more rigorous and precise, while making communication between review board members and investigators less subject to misinterpretation, misinformation and conflicting judgments. Thus, there should first be a determination of the validity of the presuppositions of the research; then the nature, probability and magnitude of risk should be distinguished with as much clarity as possible. The method of ascertaining risks should be explicit, especially where there is no alternative to the use of such vague categories as small or slight risk. It should also be determined whether an investigator's estimates of the probability of harm or benefits are reasonable, as judged by known facts or other available studies.

Finally, assessment of the justifiability of research should reflect at least the following considerations: (i) Brutal or inhumane treatment of human subjects is never morally justified. (ii) Risks should be reduced to those necessary to achieve the research objective. It should be determined whether it is in fact necessary to use human subjects at all. Risk can perhaps never be entirely eliminated, but it can often be reduced by careful attention to alternative procedures. (iii) When research involves significant risk of serious impairment, review committees should be extraordinarily insistent on the justification of the risk (looking usually to the likelihood of benefit to the subject—or, in some rare cases, to the manifest voluntariness of the participation). (iv) When vulnerable populations are involved in research, the appropriateness of involving them should itself be demonstrated. A number of variables go into such judgments, including the nature and degree of risk, the condition of the particular population involved, and the nature and level of the anticipated benefits. (v) Relevant risks and benefits must be thoroughly arrayed in documents and procedures used in the informed consent process.

3. *Selection of Subjects.* Just as the principle of respect for persons finds expression in the requirements for consent, and the principle of beneficence in risk/benefit assessment, the principle of justice gives rise to moral requirements that there be fair procedures and outcomes in the selection of research subjects.

Justice is relevant to the selection of subjects of research at two levels: the social and the individual. Individual justice in the selection of subjects would require that researchers exhibit fairness: thus, they should not offer potentially beneficial research only to some patients who are in their favor or select only "undesirable" persons for risky research. Social justice requires that distinction be drawn between classes of subjects that ought, and ought not, to participate in any particular kind of research, based on the ability of members of that class to bear burdens and on the appropriateness of placing further burdens on already burdened persons. Thus, it can be considered a matter of social justice that there is an order of preference in the selection of classes of subjects (e.g., adults before children) and that some classes of potential subjects (e.g., the institutionalized mentally infirm or prisoners) may be involved as research subjects, if at all, only on certain conditions.

Injustice may appear in the selection of subjects, even if individual subjects are selected fairly by investigators and treated fairly in the course of research. Thus injustice arises from social, racial, sexual and cultural biases institutionalized in society. Thus, even if individual researchers are treating their research subjects fairly, and even if IRBs are taking care to assure that subjects are selected fairly within a particular institution, unjust social patterns may nevertheless appear in the overall distribution of the burdens and benefits of research. Although individual institutions or investigators may not be able to resolve a problem that is pervasive in their social setting, they can consider distributive justice in selecting research subjects.

Some populations, especially institutionalized ones, are already burdened in many ways by their infirmities and environments. When research is proposed that involves risks and does not include a therapeutic component, other less burdened classes of persons should be called upon first to accept these risks of research, except where the research is directly related to the specific conditions of the class involved. Also, even though public funds for research may often flow in the same directions as public funds for health care, it seems unfair that populations dependent on public health care constitute a pool of preferred research subjects if more advantaged populations are likely to be the recipients of the benefits.

One special instance of injustice results from the involvement of vulnerable subjects. Certain groups, such as racial minorities, the economically disadvantaged, the very sick, and the institutionalized may continually be sought as research subjects, owing to their ready availability in settings where research is conducted. Given their dependent status and their frequently compromised capacity for free consent, they should be protected against the danger of being involved in research solely for administrative convenience, or because they are easy to manipulate as a result of their illness or socioeconomic condition.

Notes & Questions

1. Is it surprising that the notion of consent in medical and scientific research appears not to have been formally addressed before the Nuremberg Trials?

2. Can you draw any connections between this lack of formal requirements for consent before Nuremberg and the social, legal, and ethical attitudes that led to such con-

troversial cases as *Buck v. Bell*, 274 U.S. 200 (1927) (upholding decision to sterilize "feeble-minded" Carrie Buck against her wishes because, as Justice Holmes infamously declared, "three generations of imbeciles are enough"), and the eugenics movement in this country?

B. Current Federal Regulations Protecting Human Subjects

Following the release of The Belmont Report, the then HEW revised its earlier guidelines for human subjects research. But, even as the National Commission for the Protection of Human Subjects of Biomedical and Behavioral Research was preparing to issue The Belmont Report, Congress amended both the Public Health Service Act and the National Research Act to provide for a new President's Commission for the Study of Ethical Problems in Medicine and Biomedical and Behavioral Research that would essentially replace the existing Commission.[33] As described in the "Background" section of the Notice of Final Rulemaking excerpted below, the new President's Commission's work would lead to the adoption, by nearly all Federal agencies that conduct or support research involving human subjects, of the "Common Rule"—a set of regulations repeated throughout the Code of Federal Regulations in the relevant titles for each agency. Promulgated in 1991, the Common Rule continues to govern biomedical and behavioral research involving human subjects that is conducted or supported by Federal agencies.[34]

Federal Policy for the Protection of Human Subjects [The Common Rule]

56 Fed. Reg. 28003 (June 18, 1991)[35]

ACTION: Final rule.

SUMMARY: This document sets forth a common Federal Policy for the Protection of Human Subjects (Model Policy) accepted by the Office of Science and Technology Pol-

---

33. Act of November 9, 1978, Title III, P.L. 95-622, 92 Stat. 3412, 3437-3442.

34. The Food and Drug Administration is an exception and so its separate but similar rules are excerpted *infra*.

35. The Common Rule was promulgated by each participating agency in the relevant section of the Code of Federal Regulations as follows: Department Of Agriculture, 7 C.F.R. Part 1c; Department Of Energy, 10 C.F.R. Part 745; National Aeronautics And Space Administration, 14 C.F.R. Part 1230; Department Of Commerce, 15 C.F.R. Part 27; Consumer Product Safety Commission, 16 C.F.R. Part 1028; International Development Cooperation Agency, Agency For International Development, 22 C.F.R. Part 225; Department Of Housing And Urban Development, 24 C.F.R. Part 60; Department Of Justice, 28 C.F.R. Part 46; Department Of Defense, 32 C.F.R. Part 219; Department Of Education, 34 C.F.R. Part 97; Department Of Veterans Affairs, 38 C.F.R. Part 16; Environmental Protection Agency, 40 C.F.R. Part 26; Department Of Health And Human Services, 45 C.F.R. Part 46; National Science Foundation, 45 C.F.R. Part 690; Department Of Transportation, 49 C.F.R. Part 11. Note that section number prefixes are left blank in the Federal Register publication of the Common Rule because these prefixes would be different as finally codified in each agency's portion of the Code of Federal Regulations.

icy and promulgated in regulation by each of the listed Departments and Agencies. A Proposed Federal Policy for the Protection of Human Subjects published November 10, 1988 (53 FR 45661) has been revised in response to public comments. The Policy as revised is now set forth as a common final rule. For related documents, see other sections of this Federal Register part....

Background

This notice sets forth as a common rule requirements for the protection of human subjects involved in research conducted or funded by the following Federal Departments and Agencies: United States Department of Agriculture; Department of Energy; National Aeronautics and Space Administration; Department of Commerce; Consumer Product Safety Commission; International Development Cooperation Agency, Agency for International Development; Department of Housing and Urban Development; Department of Justice; Department of Defense; Department of Education; Department of Veterans Affairs; Environmental Protection Agency; National Science Foundation; Department of Health and Human Services and the Department of Transportation. Each of these Departments and Agencies have adopted the common rule as regulations to be codified as listed above.

The Food and Drug Administration (FDA) Final Rule to modify current regulations to conform to the Federal Policy are presented elsewhere in this issue of the Federal Register. Existing FDA regulations governing the protection of human subjects share a common core with the Federal Policy and implement the fundamental principles embodied in that policy. The agency is committed to being as consistent with the final Federal Policy as it can be, given the unique requirements of the Federal Food, Drug, and Cosmetic Act under which FDA operates; and the fact that FDA is a regulatory agency that rarely supports or conducts research under its regulations.

Adoption of the common Policy by Federal Departments and Agencies in regulatory form will implement a recommendation of the President's Commission for the Study of Ethical Problems in Medicine and Biomedical and Behavioral Research which was established on November 9, 1978, by Public Law 95-622. One of the charges to the President's Commission was to report biennially to the President, the Congress, and appropriate Federal Departments and Agencies on the protection of human subjects of biomedical and behavioral research. In carrying out that charge, the President's Commission was directed to conduct a review of the adequacy and uniformity (1) of the rules, policies, guidelines, and regulations of all Federal Departments and Agencies regarding the protection of human subjects of biomedical or behavioral research which such Departments and Agencies conduct or support, and (2) of the implementation of such rules, policies, guidelines, and regulations by such Departments and Agencies, such review to include appropriate recommendations for legislation and administrative action.

In December 1981 the President's Commission issued its First Biennial Report on the Adequacy and Uniformity of Federal Rules and Policies, and their Implementation, for the Protection of Human Subjects in Biomedical and Behavioral Research, Protecting Human Subjects.

In accord with Public Law 95-622, each Federal Department or Agency which receives recommendations from the President's Commission with respect to its rules, policies, guidelines or regulations, must publish the recommendations in the Federal Register and provide an opportunity for interested persons to submit written data, views and arguments with respect to adoption of the recommendations. On March 29,

1982 (47 FR 13262-13305), the Secretary, HHS, published the recommendation on behalf of all affected Departments and Agencies.

In May 1982 the Chairman of the Federal Coordinating Council for Science, Engineering, and Technology (FCCSET) appointed an *Ad Hoc* Committee for the Protection of Human Research Subjects under the auspices of the FCCSET. The Committee, chaired by Dr. Edward N. Brandt, Jr., Assistant Secretary for Health, Health and Human Services (HHS), was composed of representatives and ex-officio members of the affected Departments and Agencies. In consultation with the Office of Science and Technology Policy (OSTP) and the Office of Management and Budget, the *Ad Hoc* Committee, after considering all public comments, developed responses to the recommendations of the President's Commission. After further review and refinement, OSTP responded on behalf of all the affected Department and Agency Heads to the recommendations of the President's Commission, including the recommendation that:

The President should, through appropriate action, require that all federal departments and agencies adopt as a common core the regulations governing research with human subjects issued by the Department of Health and Human Services (codified at 45 CFR Part 46), as periodically amended or revised, while permitting additions needed by any department or agency that are not inconsistent with these core provisions.

The *Ad Hoc* Committee agreed that uniformity is desirable among Departments and Agencies to eliminate unnecessary regulation and to promote increased understanding and ease of compliance by institutions that conduct federally supported or regulated research involving human subjects. Therefore, the *Ad Hoc* Committee developed a Model Federal Policy, which applies to research involving human subjects conducted, supported or regulated by Federal Departments and Agencies. In accordance with the Commission's recommendation, the Model Federal Policy is based on subpart A of the regulations of HHS for the protection of human research subjects (45 CFR part 46). The Proposed Model federal Policy developed by the *Ad Hoc* Committee was modified by OSTP to enhance uniformity of implementation among the affected Federal Departments and Agencies and to provide consistency with other related policies. The revised Model Federal Policy was concurred in by all affected Federal Departments and Agencies in March 1985.

An Interagency Human Subjects Coordinating Committee was chartered in October 1983 under the auspices of FCCSET to provide continued interagency cooperation in human subject research once the *Ad Hoc* Committee had completed its assignment. It is chaired by the Director of the Office for Protection from Research Risks, HHS, and composed of representatives of all Federal Departments and Agencies that conduct, support or regulate research involving human subjects. The Committee is advisory to Department and Agency Heads and, among other responsibilities, will evaluate the implementation of the Federal Policy and recommend modification as necessary.

On June 3, 1986, OSTP published for public comment in the Federal Register (51 FR 20204) a Proposed Model Federal Policy for Protection of Human Subjects and Response to the First Biennial Report of the President's Commission. Over 200 written comments were received concerning the publication. The Interagency Human Subjects Coordinating Committee considered these comments in the revision of a common Federal Policy proposed as a common rule on November 10, 1988, for adoption by each of the Departments and Agencies listed. Response to the more than 60 public comments, discussion of revisions made to that publication and the final common rule follow....

Text of the Common Rule

The text of the Common Rule as adopted by the Department and Agencies in this document appears below:

___ CFR ___—Protection of Human Subjects ...

§__ .101 To what does this policy apply?

(a) Except as provided in paragraph (b) of this section, this policy applies to all research involving human subjects conducted, supported or otherwise subject to regulation by any federal department or agency which takes appropriate administrative action to make the policy applicable to such research. This includes research conducted by federal civilian employees or military personnel, except that each department or agency head may adopt such procedural modifications as may be appropriate from an administrative standpoint. It also includes research conducted, supported, or otherwise subject to regulation by the federal government outside the United States.

(1) Research that is conducted or supported by a federal department or agency, whether or not it is regulated as defined in §__ .102(e), must comply with all sections of this policy.

(2) Research that is neither conducted nor supported by a federal department or agency but is subject to regulation as defined in §__ .102(e) must be reviewed and approved, in compliance with §__ .101, §__ .102, and §__ .107 through §__ .117 of this policy, by an institutional review board (IRB) that operates in accordance with the pertinent requirements of this policy.

(b) Unless otherwise required by department or agency heads, research activities in which the only involvement of human subjects will be in one or more of the following categories are exempt from this policy:

(1) Research conducted in established or commonly accepted educational settings, involving normal educational practices, such as (i) research on regular and special education instructional strategies, or (ii) research on the effectiveness of or the comparison among instructional techniques, curricula, or classroom management methods.

(2) Research involving the use of educational tests (cognitive, diagnostic, aptitude, achievement), survey procedures, interview procedures or observation of public behavior, unless:

(i) Information obtained is recorded in such a manner that human subjects can be identified, directly or through identifiers linked to the subjects; and

(ii) any disclosure of the human subjects' responses outside the research could reasonably place the subjects at risk of criminal or civil liability or be damaging to the subjects' financial standing, employability, or reputation.

(3) Research involving the use of educational tests (cognitive, diagnostic, aptitude, achievement), survey procedures, interview procedures, or observation of public behavior that is not exempt under paragraph (b)(2) of this section, if:

(i) The human subjects are elected or appointed public officials or candidates for public office; or

(ii) federal statute(s) require(s) without exception that the confidentiality of the personally identifiable information will be maintained throughout the research and thereafter.

(4) Research, involving the collection or study of existing data, documents, records, pathological specimens, or diagnostic specimens, if these sources are publicly available

or if the information is recorded by the investigator in such a manner that subjects cannot be identified, directly or through identifiers linked to the subjects.

(5) Research and demonstration projects which are conducted by or subject to the approval of department of agency heads, and which are designed to study, evaluate, or otherwise examine:

(i) Public benefit or service programs;

(ii) procedures for obtaining benefits or services under those programs;

(iii) possible changes in or alternatives to those programs or procedures; or

(iv) possible changes in methods or levels of payment for benefits or services under those programs.

(6) Taste and food quality evaluation and consumer acceptance studies, (i) if wholesome foods without additives are consumed or (ii) if a food is consumed that contains a food ingredient at or below the level and for a use found to be safe, or agricultural chemical or environmental contaminant at or below the level found to be safe, by the Food and Drug Administration or approved by the Environmental Protection Agency or the Food Safety and Inspection Service of the U.S. Department of Agriculture.

(c) Department or agency heads retain final judgment as to whether a particular activity is covered by this policy.

(d) Department or agency heads may require that specific research activities or classes of research activities conducted, supported, or otherwise subject to regulation by the department or agency but not otherwise covered by this policy, comply with some or all of the requirements of this policy.

(e) Compliance with this policy requires compliance with pertinent federal laws or regulations which provide additional protections for human subjects.

(f) This policy does not affect any state or local laws or regulations which may otherwise be applicable and which provide additional protections for human subjects.

(g) This policy does not affect any foreign laws or regulations which may otherwise be applicable and which provide additional protections to human subjects of research.

(h) When research covered by this policy takes place in foreign countries, procedures normally followed in the foreign countries to protect human subjects may differ from those set forth in this policy. [An example is a foreign institution which complies with guidelines consistent with the World Medical Assembly Declaration (Declaration of Helsinki amended 1989) issued either by sovereign states or by an organization whose function for the protection of human research subjects is internationally recognized.] In these circumstances, if a department or agency head determines that the procedures prescribed by the institution afford protections that are at least equivalent to those provided in this policy, the department or agency head may approve the substitution of the foreign procedures in lieu of the procedural requirements provided in this policy. Except when otherwise required by statute, Executive Order, or the department or agency head, notices of these actions as they occur will be published in the Federal Register or will be otherwise published as provided in department or agency procedures.

(i) Unless otherwise required by law, department or agency heads may waive the applicability of some or all of the provisions of this policy to specific research activities or classes of research activities otherwise covered by this policy. Except when otherwise required by statute or Executive Order, the department or agency head shall forward advance notices of these actions to the Office for Protection from Research Risks, Department of Health and Human Services (HHS), and shall also publish them in the Federal Register or in such other manner as provided in department or agency procedures.[36]

§__ .102 Definitions.

(a) *Department or agency head* means the head of any federal department or agency and any other officer or employee of any department or agency to whom authority has been delegated.

(b) *Institution* means any public or private entity or agency (including federal, state, and other agencies).

(c) *Legally authorized representative* means an individual or judicial or other body authorized under applicable law to consent on behalf of a prospective subject to the subject's participation in the procedure(s) involved in the research.

(d) *Research* means a systematic investigation, including research development, testing and evaluation, designed to develop or contribute to generalizable knowledge. Activities which meet this definition constitute research for purposes of this policy, whether or not they are conducted or supported under a program which is considered research for other purposes. For example, some demonstration and service programs may include research activities.

(e) *Research subject to regulation*, and similar terms are intended to encompass those research activities for which a federal department or agency has specific responsibility for regulating as a research activity, (for example, Investigational New Drug requirements administered by the Food and Drug Administration). It does not include research activities which are incidentally regulated by a federal department or agency solely as part of the department's or agency's broader responsibility to regulate certain types of activities whether research or non-research in nature (for example, Wage and Hour requirements administered by the Department of Labor).

(f) *Human subject* means a living individual about whom an investigator (whether professional or student) conducting research obtains

(1) data through intervention or interaction with the individual, or

(2) identifiable private information.

Intervention includes both physical procedures by which data are gathered (for example, venipuncture) and manipulations of the subject or the subject's environment that are performed for research purposes. Interaction includes communication or interpersonal contact between investigator and subject. "Private information" includes information about behavior that occurs in a context in which an individual can reasonably expect that no observation or recording is taking place, and information which has been provided for specific purposes by an individual and which the individual can reasonably expect will not be made public (for example, a medical record). Private information must be individually identifiable (i.e., the identity of the subject is or may read-

36. Institutions with HHS-approved assurances on file will abide by provisions of title 45 CFR part 46 subparts A–D. Some of the other Departments and Agencies have incorporated all provisions of title 45 CFR part 46 into their policies and procedures as well. However, the exemptions at 45 CFR part 46.101(b) do not apply to research involving prisoners, fetuses, pregnant women, or human in vitro fertilization, subparts B and C. The exemption at 45 CFR part 46.101(b)(2), for research involving survey or interview procedures or observation of public behavior, does not apply to research with children, subpart D, except for research involving observations of public behavior when the investigator(s) do not participate in the activities being observed.

ily be ascertained by the investigator or associated with the information) in order for obtaining the information to constitute research involving human subjects.

(g) *IRB* means an institutional review board established in accord with and for the purposes expressed in this policy.

(h) *IRB approval* means the determination of the IRB that the research has been reviewed and may be conducted at an institution within the constraints set forth by the IRB and by other institutional and federal requirements.

(i) *Minimal risk* means that the probability and magnitude of harm or discomfort anticipated in the research are not greater in and of themselves than those ordinarily encountered in daily life or during the performance of routine physical or psychological examinations or tests.

(j) *Certification* means the official notification by the institution to the supporting department or agency, in accordance with the requirements of this policy, that a research project or activity involving human subjects has been reviewed and approved by an IRB in accordance with an approved assurance.

§__ .103 Assuring compliance with this policy—research conducted or supported by any federal department or agency.

(a) Each institution engaged in research which is covered by this policy and which is conducted or supported by a federal department or agency shall provide written assurance satisfactory to the department or agency head that it will comply with the requirements set forth in this policy. In lieu of requiring submission of an assurance, individual department or agency heads shall accept the existence of a current assurance, appropriate for the research in question, on file with the Office for Protection from Research Risks, HHS, and approved for federalwide use by that office. When the existence of an HHS-approved assurance is accepted in lieu of requiring submission of an assurance, reports (except certification) required by this policy to be made to department and agency heads shall also be made to the Office for Protection from Research Risks, HHS.

(b) Departments and agencies will conduct or support research covered by this policy only if the institution has an assurance approved as provided in this section, and only if the institution has certified to the department or agency head that the research has been reviewed and approved by an IRB provided for in the assurance, and will be subject to continuing review by the IRB. Assurances applicable to federally supported or conducted research shall at a minimum include:

(1) A statement of principles governing the institution in the discharge of its responsibilities for protecting the rights and welfare of human subjects of research conducted at or sponsored by the institution, regardless of whether the research is subject to federal regulation. This may include an appropriate existing code, declaration, or statement of ethical principles, or a statement formulated by the institution itself. This requirement does not preempt provisions of this policy applicable to department- or agency-supported or regulated research and need not be applicable to any research exempted or waived under §__ .101 (b) or (i).

(2) Designation of one or more IRBs established in accordance with the requirements of this policy, and for which provisions are made for meeting space and sufficient staff to support the IRB's review and recordkeeping duties.

(3) A list of IRB members identified by name; earned degrees; representative capacity; indications of experience such as board certifications, licenses, etc., sufficient to describe each member's chief anticipated contributions to IRB deliberations; and

any employment or other relationship between each member and the institution; for example: full-time employee, part-time employee, member of governing panel or board, stockholder, paid or unpaid consultant. Changes in IRB membership shall be reported to the department or agency head, unless in accord with §__ .103(a) of this policy, the existence of an HHS-approved assurance is accepted. In this case, change in IRB membership shall be reported to the Office for Protection from Research Risks, HHS.

(4) Written procedures which the IRB will follow (i) for conducting its initial and continuing review of research and for reporting its findings and actions to the investigator and the institution; (ii) for determining which projects require review more often than annually and which projects need verification from sources other than the investigators that no material changes have occurred since previous IRB review; and (iii) for ensuring prompt reporting to the IRB of proposed changes in a research activity, and for ensuring that such changes in approved research, during the period for which IRB approval has already been given, may not be initiated without IRB review and approval except when necessary to eliminate apparent immediate hazards to the subject.

(5) Written procedures for ensuring prompt reporting to the IRB, appropriate institutional officials, and the department or agency head of (i) any unanticipated problems involving risks to subjects or others or any serious or continuing noncompliance with this policy or the requirements or determinations of the IRB and (ii) any suspension or termination of IRB approval.

(c) The assurance shall be executed by an individual authorized to act for the institution and to assume on behalf of the institution the obligations imposed by this policy and shall be filed in such form and manner as the department or agency head prescribes.

(d) The department or agency head will evaluate all assurances submitted in accordance with this policy through such officers and employees of the department or agency and such experts or consultants engaged for this purpose as the department or agency head determines to be appropriate. The department or agency head's evaluation will take into consideration the adequacy of the proposed IRB in light of the anticipated scope of the institution's research activities and the types of subject populations likely to be involved, the appropriateness of the proposed initial and continuing review procedures in light of the probable risks, and the size and complexity of the institution.

(e) On the basis of this evaluation, the department or agency head may approve or disapprove the assurance, or enter into negotiations to develop an approvable one. The department or agency head may limit the period during which any particular approved assurance or class of approved assurances shall remain effective or otherwise condition or restrict approval.

(f) Certification is required when the research is supported by a federal department or agency and not otherwise exempted or waived under §__ .101 (b) or (i). An institution with an approved assurance shall certify that each application or proposal for research covered by the assurance and by §__ .03 of this Policy has been reviewed and approved by the IRB. Such certification must be submitted with the application or proposal or by such later date as may be prescribed by the department or agency to which the application or proposal is submitted. Under no condition shall research covered by §__ .103 of the Policy be supported prior to receipt of the certification that the research has been reviewed and approved by the IRB. Institutions without an approved assurance covering the research shall certify within 30 days after receipt of a request for such a certification from the department or agency, that the application or proposal has been approved by the IRB. If the certification is not submitted within these time limits, the application or proposal may be returned to the institution....

§__ .107 IRB membership.

(a) Each IRB shall have at least five members, with varying backgrounds to promote complete and adequate review of research activities commonly conducted by the institution. The IRB shall be sufficiently qualified through the experience and expertise of its members, and the diversity of the members, including consideration of race, gender, and cultural backgrounds and sensitivity to such issues as community attitudes, to promote respect for its advice and counsel in safeguarding the rights and welfare of human subjects. In addition to possessing the professional competence necessary to review specific research activities, the IRB shall be able to ascertain the acceptability of proposed research in terms of institutional commitments and regulations, applicable law, and standards of professional conduct and practice. The IRB shall therefore include persons knowledgeable in these areas. If an IRB regularly reviews research that involves a vulnerable category of subjects, such as children, prisoners, pregnant women, or handicapped or mentally disabled persons, consideration shall be given to the inclusion of one or more individuals who are knowledgeable about and experienced in working with these subjects.

(b) Every nondiscriminatory effort will be made to ensure that no IRB consists entirely of men or entirely of women, including the institution's consideration of qualified persons of both sexes, so long as no selection is made to the IRB on the basis of gender. No IRB may consist entirely of members of one profession.

(c) Each IRB shall include at least one member whose primary concerns are in scientific areas and at least one member whose primary concerns are in nonscientific areas.

(d) Each IRB shall include at least one member who is not otherwise affiliated with the institution and who is not part of the immediate family of a person who is affiliated with the institution.

(e) No IRB may have a member participate in the IRB's initial or continuing review of any project in which the member has a conflicting interest, except to provide information requested by the IRB.

(f) An IRB may, in its discretion, invite individuals with competence in special areas to assist in the review of issues which require expertise beyond or in addition to that available on the IRB. These individuals may not vote with the IRB.

§__ .108 IRB functions and operations.

In order to fulfill the requirements of this policy each IRB shall:

(a) Follow written procedures in the same detail as described in §__ .103(b)(4) and, to the extent required by, §__ .103(b)(5).

(b) Except when an expedited review procedure is used (see §__ .110), review proposed research at convened meetings at which a majority of the members of the IRB are present, including at least one member whose primary concerns are in nonscientific areas. In order for the research to be approved, it shall receive the approval of a majority of those members present at the meeting.

§__ .109 IRB Review of Research.

(a) An IRB shall review and have authority to approve, require modifications in (to secure approval), or disapprove all research activities covered by this policy.

(b) An IRB shall require that information given to subjects as part of informed consent is in accordance with §__ .116. The IRB may require that information, in addition to that specifically mentioned in §__ .116, be given to the subjects when in the IRB's judgment the information would meaningfully add to the protection of the rights and welfare of subjects.

(c) An IRB shall require documentation of informed consent or may waive documentation in accordance with §__ .117.

(d) An IRB shall notify investigators and the institution in writing of its decision to approve or disapprove the proposed research activity, or of modifications required to secure IRB approval of the research activity. If the IRB decides to disapprove a research activity, it shall include in its written notification a statement of the reasons for its decision and give the investigator an opportunity to respond in person or in writing.

(e) An IRB shall conduct continuing review of research covered by this policy at intervals appropriate to the degree of risk, but not less than once per year, and shall have authority to observe or have a third party observe the consent process and the research....

§__ .110 Expedited review procedures for certain kinds of research involving no more than minimal risk, and for minor changes in approved research.

(a) The Secretary, HHS, has established, and published as a Notice in the Federal Register, a list of categories of research that may be reviewed by the IRB through an expedited review procedure. The list will be amended, as appropriate after consultation with other departments and agencies, through periodic republication by the Secretary, HHS, in the Federal Register. A copy of the list is available from the Office for Protection from Research Risks, National Institutes of Health, HHS, Bethesda, Maryland 20892.

(b) An IRB may use the expedited review procedure to review either or both of the following:

(1) Some or all of the research appearing on the list and found by the reviewer(s) to involve no more than minimal risk,

(2) Minor changes in previously approved research during the period (of one year or less) for which approval is authorized.

Under an expedited review procedure, the review may be carried out by the IRB chairperson or by one or more experienced reviewers designated by the chairperson from among members of the IRB. In reviewing the research, the reviewers may exercise all of the authorities of the IRB except that the reviewers may not disapprove the research. A research activity may be disapproved only after review in accordance with the non-expedited procedure set forth in §__ .108(b).

(c) Each IRB which uses an expedited review procedure shall adopt a method for keeping all members advised of research proposals which have been approved under the procedure.

(d) The department or agency head may restrict, suspend, terminate, or choose not to authorize an institution's or IRB's use of the expedited review procedure.

§__ .111 Criteria for IRB approval of research.

(a) In order to approve research covered by this policy the IRB shall determine that all of the following requirements are satisfied:

(1) Risks to subjects are minimized: (i) By using procedures which are consistent with sound research design and which do not unnecessarily expose subjects to risk, and

(ii) whenever appropriate, by using procedures already being performed on the subjects for diagnostic or treatment purposes.

(2) Risks to subjects are reasonable in relation to anticipated benefits, if any, to subjects, and the importance of the knowledge that may reasonably be expected to result. In evaluating risks and benefits, the IRB should consider only those risks and benefits that may result from the research (as distinguished from risks and benefits of therapies subjects would receive even if not participating in the research). The IRB should not consider possible long-range effects of applying knowledge gained in the research (for example, the possible effects of the research on public policy) as among those research risks that fall within the purview of its responsibility.

(3) Selection of subjects is equitable. In making this assessment the IRB should take into account the purposes of the research and the setting in which the research will be conducted and should be particularly cognizant of the special problems of research involving vulnerable populations, such as children, prisoners, pregnant women, mentally disabled persons, or economically or educationally disadvantaged persons.

(4) Informed consent will be sought from each prospective subject or the subject's legally authorized representative, in accordance with, and to the extent required by §__ .116.

(5) Informed consent will be appropriately documented, in accordance with, and to the extent required by §__ .117.

(6) When appropriate, the research plan makes adequate provision for monitoring the data collected to ensure the safety of subjects.

(7) When appropriate, there are adequate provisions to protect the privacy of subjects and to maintain the confidentiality of data.

(b) When some or all of the subjects are likely to be vulnerable to coercion or undue influence, such as children, prisoners, pregnant women, mentally disabled persons, or economically or educationally disadvantaged persons, additional safeguards have been included in the study to protect the rights and welfare of these subjects.

§__ .112 Review by institution.

Research covered by this policy that has been approved by an IRB may be subject to further appropriate review and approval or disapproval by officials of the institution. However, those officials may not approve the research if it has not been approved by an IRB.

§__ .113 Suspension or termination of IRB approval of research.

An IRB shall have authority to suspend or terminate approval of research that is not being conducted in accordance with the IRB's requirements or that has been associated with unexpected serious harm to subjects. Any suspension or termination of approval shall include a statement of the reasons for the IRB's action and shall be reported promptly to the investigator, appropriate institutional officials, and the department or agency head....

§__ .114 Cooperative research.

Cooperative research projects are those projects covered by this policy which involve more than one institution. In the conduct of cooperative research projects, each institution is responsible for safeguarding the rights and welfare of human subjects and for complying with this policy. With the approval of the department or agency head, an institution participating in a cooperative project may enter into a joint review arrangement, rely upon the review of another qualified IRB, or make similar arrangements for avoiding duplication of effort.

§__ .115 IRB records.

(a) An institution, or when appropriate an IRB, shall prepare and maintain adequate documentation of IRB activities, including the following:

(1) Copies of all research proposals reviewed, scientific evaluations, if any, that accompany the proposals, approved sample consent documents, progress reports submitted by investigators, and reports of injuries to subjects.

(2) Minutes of IRB meetings which shall be in sufficient detail to show attendance at the meetings; actions taken by the IRB; the vote on these actions including the number of members voting for, against, and abstaining; the basis for requiring changes in or disapproving research; and a written summary of the discussion of controverted issues and their resolution.

(3) Records of continuing review activities.

(4) Copies of all correspondence between the IRB and the investigators.

(5) A list of IRB members in the same detail as described is §__ .103(b)(3).

(6) Written procedures for the IRB in the same detail as described in §__ .103(b)(4) and §__ .103(b)(5).

(7) Statements of significant new findings provided to subjects, as required by §__ .116(b)(5).

(b) The records required by this policy shall be retained for at least 3 years, and records relating to research which is conducted shall be retained for at least 3 years after completion of the research. All records shall be accessible for inspection and copying by authorized representatives of the department or agency at reasonable times and in a reasonable manner....

§__ .116 General requirements for informed consent

Except as provided elsewhere in this policy, no investigator may involve a human being as a subject in research covered by this policy unless the investigator has obtained the legally effective informed consent of the subject or the subject's legally authorized representative. An investigator shall seek such consent only under circumstances that provide the prospective subject or the representative sufficient opportunity to consider whether or not to participate and that minimize the possibility of coercion or undue influence. The information that is given to the subject or the representative shall be in language understandable to the subject or the representative. No informed consent, whether oral or written, may include any exculpatory language through which the subject or the representative is made to waive or appear to waive any of the subject's legal rights, or releases or appears to release the investigator, the sponsor, the institution or its agents from liability for negligence.

(a) Basic elements of informed consent. Except as provided in paragraph (c) or (d) of this section, in seeking informed consent the following information shall be provided to each subject:

(1) A statement that the study involves research, an explanation of the purposes of the research and the expected duration of the subject's participation, a description of the procedures to be followed, and identification of any procedures which are experimental;

(2) A description of any reasonably foreseeable risks or discomforts to the subject;

(3) A description of any benefits to the subject or to others which may reasonably be expected from the research;

(4) A disclosure of appropriate alternative procedures or courses of treatment, if any, that might be advantageous to the subject;

(5) A statement describing the extent, if any, to which confidentiality of records identifying the subject will be maintained;

(6) For research involving more than minimal risk, an explanation as to whether any compensation and an explanation as to whether any medical treatments are available if injury occurs and, if so, what they consist of, or where further information may be obtained;

(7) An explanation of whom to contact for answers to pertinent questions about the research and research subjects' rights, and whom to contact in the event of a research-related injury to the subject; and

(8) A statement that participation is voluntary, refusal to participate will involve no penalty or loss of benefits to which the subject is otherwise entitled, and the subject may discontinue participation at any time without penalty or loss of benefits to which the subject is otherwise entitled.

(b) Additional elements of informed consent. When appropriate, one or more of the following elements of information shall also be provided to each subject:

(1) A statement that the particular treatment or procedure may involve risks to the subject (or to the embryo or fetus, if the subject is or may become pregnant) which are currently unforeseeable;

(2) Anticipated circumstances under which the subject's participation may be terminated by the investigator without regard to the subject's consent;

(3) Any additional costs to the subject that may result from participation in the research;

(4) The consequences of a subject's decision to withdraw from the research and procedures for orderly termination of participation by the subject;

(5) A statement that significant new findings developed during the course of the research which may relate to the subject's willingness to continue participation will be provided to the subject; and

(6) The approximate number of subjects involved in the study.

(c) An IRB may approve a consent procedure which does not include, or which alters, some or all of the elements of informed consent set forth above, or waive the requirement to obtain informed consent provided the IRB finds and documents that:

(1) The research or demonstration project is to be conducted by or subject to the approval of state or local government officials and is designed to study, evaluate, or otherwise examine: (i) Public benefit of service programs; (ii) procedures for obtaining benefits or services under those programs; (iii) possible changes in or alternatives to those programs or procedures; or (iv) possible changes in methods or levels of payment for benefits or services under those programs; and

(2) The research could not practicably be carried out without the waiver or alteration.

(d) An IRB may approve a consent procedure which does not include, or which alters, some or all of the elements of informed consent set forth in this section, or waive the requirements to obtain informed consent provided the IRB finds and documents that:

(1) The research involves no more than minimal risk to the subjects;

(2) The waiver or alteration will not adversely affect the rights and welfare of the subjects;

(3) The research could not practicably be carried out without the waiver or alteration; and

(4) Whenever appropriate, the subjects will be provided with additional pertinent information after participation.

(e) The informed consent requirements in this policy are not intended to preempt any applicable federal, state, or local laws which require additional information to be disclosed in order for informed consent to be legally effective.

(f) Nothing in this policy is intended to limit the authority of a physician to provide emergency medical care, to the extent the physician is permitted to do so under applicable federal, state, or local law....

§__ .117 Documentation of informed consent.

(a) Except as provided in paragraph (c) of this section, informed consent shall be documented by the use of a written consent form approved by the IRB and signed by the subject or the subject's legally authorized representative. A copy shall be given to the person signing the form.

(b) Except as provided in paragraph (c) of this section, the consent form may be either of the following:

(1) A written consent document that embodies the elements of informed consent required by §__ .116. This form may be read to the subject or the subject's legally authorized representative, but in any event, the investigator shall give either the subject or the representative adequate opportunity to read it before it is signed; or

(2) A short form written consent document stating that the elements of informed consent required by §__ .116 have been presented orally to the subject or the subject's legally authorized representative. When this method is used, there shall be a witness to the oral presentation. Also, the IRB shall approve a written summary of what is to be said to the subject or the representative. Only the short form itself is to be signed by the subject or the representative. However, the witness shall sign both the short form and a copy of the summary, and the person actually obtaining consent shall sign a copy of the summary. A copy of the summary shall be given to the subject or the representative, in addition to a copy of the short form.

(c) An IRB may waive the requirement for the investigator to obtain a signed consent form for some or all subjects if it finds either:

(1) That the only record linking the subject and the research would be the consent document and the principal risk would be potential harm resulting from a breach of confidentiality. Each subject will be asked whether the subject wants documentation linking the subject with the research, and the subject's wishes will govern; or

(2) That the research presents no more than minimal risk of harm to subjects and involves no procedures for which written consent is normally required outside of the research context.

In cases in which the documentation requirement is waived, the IRB may require the investigator to provide subjects with a written statement regarding the research....

§__ .118 Applications and proposals lacking definite plans for involvement of human subjects.

Certain types of applications for grants, cooperative agreements, or contracts are submitted to departments or agencies with the knowledge that subjects may be involved within the period of support, but definite plans would not normally be set forth in the application or proposal. These include activities such as institutional type grants when selection of specific projects is the institution's responsibility; research training grants in which the activities involving subjects remain to be selected; and projects in which human subject's involvement will depend upon completion of instruments, prior animal studies, or purification of compounds. These applications need not be reviewed by an IRB before an award may be made. However, except for research exempted or waived under §__ .101 (b) or (i), no human subjects may be involved in any project supported by these awards until the project has been reviewed and approved by the IRB, as provided in this policy, and certification submitted, by the institution, to the department or agency.

§__ .119 Research undertaken without the intention of involving human subjects.

In the event research is undertaken without the intention of involving human subjects, but it is later proposed to involve human subjects in the research, the research shall first be reviewed and approved by an IRB, as provided in this policy, a certification submitted, by the institution, to the department or agency, and final approval given to the proposed change by the department or agency.

§__ .120 Evaluation and disposition of applications and proposals for research to be conducted or supported by a federal department or agency.

[(a)] The department or agency head will evaluate all applications and proposals involving human subjects submitted to the department or agency through such officers and employees of the department or agency and such experts and consultants as the department or agency head determines to be appropriate. This evaluation will take into consideration the risks to the subjects, the adequacy of protection against these risks, the potential benefits of the research to the subjects and others, and the importance of the knowledge gained or to be gained.

(b) On the basis of this evaluation, the department or agency head may approve or disapprove the application or proposal, or enter into negotiations to develop an approvable one....

§__ .122 Use of federal funds.

Federal funds administered by a department or agency may not be expended for research involving human subjects unless the requirements of this policy have been satisfied.

§__ .123 Early termination of research support; evaluation of applications and proposals.

(a) The department or agency head may require that department or agency support for any project be terminated or suspended in the manner prescribed in applicable program requirements, when the department or agency head finds an institution has materially failed to comply with the terms of this policy.

(b) In making decisions about supporting or approving applications or proposals covered by this policy the department or agency head may take into account, in addition to all other eligibility requirements and program criteria, factors such as whether the applicant has been subject to a termination or suspension under paragraph (a) of this section and whether the applicant or the person or persons who would direct or has have [sic] directed the scientific and technical aspects of an activity has have [sic], in the judgment of the department or agency head, materially failed to discharge responsibility for the protection of the rights and welfare of human subjects (whether or not the research was subject to federal regulation).

§__ .124 Conditions.

With respect to any research project or any class of research projects the department or agency head may impose additional conditions prior to or at the time of approval when in the judgment of the department or agency head additional conditions are necessary for the protection of human subjects.

* * *

Beyond the basic provisions of the Common Rule, some agencies have promulgated further rules, usually for specific classes of human subjects. For example, NIH has additional regulations for research involving: pregnant women, human fetuses, and neonates; prisoners; and children. As mentioned above, the FDA does not employ the Common Rule specifically—since it generally does not fund or support research—but instead has crafted regulations amenable to its authority under the Federal Food, Drug, and Cosmetics Act. These rules apply to all clinical investigations directly regulated by the FDA, as well as clinical investigations that support applications for research or marketing permits for products regulated by the FDA. Because the FDA is so central to the commercialization of genetics research, its separate regulations are also excerpted below.

FDA—Protection of Human Subjects

21 C.F.R. part 50

Subpart A—General Provisions

Sec. 50.1 Scope.

(a) This part applies to all clinical investigations regulated by the Food and Drug Administration under sections 505(i) and 520(g) of the Federal Food, Drug, and Cosmetic Act, as well as clinical investigations that support applications for research or marketing permits for products regulated by the Food and Drug Administration, including foods, including dietary supplements, that bear a nutrient content claim or a health claim, infant formulas, food and color additives, drugs for human use, medical devices for human use, biological products for human use, and electronic products. Additional specific obligations and commitments of, and standards of conduct for, persons who sponsor or monitor clinical investigations involving particular test articles may also be found in other parts (e.g., parts 312 and 812). Compliance with these parts is intended to protect the rights and safety of subjects involved in investigations filed with the Food and Drug Administration pursuant to sections 403, 406, 409, 412, 413, 502, 503, 505, 510, 513–516, 518–520, 721, and 801 of the Federal Food, Drug, and Cosmetic Act and sections 351 and 354–360F of the Public Health Service Act....

Sec. 50.3 Definitions.

As used in this part:

(a) *Act* means the Federal Food, Drug, and Cosmetic Act, as amended (secs. 201—902, 52 Stat. 1040 et seq. as amended (21 U.S.C. 321—392)).

(b) *Application for research or marketing permit* includes:

(1) A color additive petition, described in part 71.

(2) A food additive petition, described in parts 171 and 571.

(3) Data and information about a substance submitted as part of the procedures for establishing that the substance is generally recognized as safe for use that results or may reasonably be expected to result, directly or indirectly, in its becoming a component or otherwise affecting the characteristics of any food, described in §§ 170.30 and 570.30.

(4) Data and information about a food additive submitted as part of the procedures for food additives permitted to be used on an interim basis pending additional study, described in § 180.1.

(5) Data and information about a substance submitted as part of the procedures for establishing a tolerance for unavoidable contaminants in food and food-packaging materials, described in section 406 of the act.

(6) An investigational new drug application, described in part 312 of this chapter.

(7) A new drug application, described in part 314.

(8) Data and information about the bioavailability or bioequivalence of drugs for human use submitted as part of the procedures for issuing, amending, or repealing a bioequivalence requirement, described in part 320.

(9) Data and information about an over-the-counter drug for human use submitted as part of the procedures for classifying these drugs as generally recognized as safe and effective and not misbranded, described in part 330.

(10) Data and information about a prescription drug for human use submitted as part of the procedures for classifying these drugs as generally recognized as safe and effective and not misbranded, described in this chapter....

(12) An application for a biologics license, described in part 601 of this chapter.

(13) Data and information about a biological product submitted as part of the procedures for determining that licensed biological products are safe and effective and not misbranded, described in part 601.

(14) Data and information about an in vitro diagnostic product submitted as part of the procedures for establishing, amending, or repealing a standard for these products, described in part 809.

(15) An Application for an Investigational Device Exemption, described in part 812.

(16) Data and information about a medical device submitted as part of the procedures for classifying these devices, described in section 513.

(17) Data and information about a medical device submitted as part of the procedures for establishing, amending, or repealing a standard for these devices, described in section 514.

(18) An application for premarket approval of a medical device, described in section 515.

(19) A product development protocol for a medical device, described in section 515.

(20) Data and information about an electronic product submitted as part of the procedures for establishing, amending, or repealing a standard for these products, described in section 358 of the Public Health Service Act.

(21) Data and information about an electronic product submitted as part of the procedures for obtaining a variance from any electronic product performance standard, as described in § 1010.4.

(22) Data and information about an electronic product submitted as part of the procedures for granting, amending, or extending an exemption from a radiation safety performance standard, as described in § 1010.5.

(23) Data and information about a clinical study of an infant formula when submitted as part of an infant formula notification under section 412(c) of the Federal Food, Drug, and Cosmetic Act.

(24) Data and information submitted in a petition for a nutrient content claim, described in § 101.69 of this chapter, or for a health claim, described in § 101.70 of this chapter.

(25) Data and information from investigations involving children submitted in a new dietary ingredient notification, described in § 190.6 of this chapter.

(c) *Clinical investigation* means any experiment that involves a test article and one or more human subjects and that either is subject to requirements for prior submission to the Food and Drug Administration under section 505(i) or 520(g) of the act, or is not subject to requirements for prior submission to the Food and Drug Administration under these sections of the act, but the results of which are intended to be submitted later to, or held for inspection by, the Food and Drug Administration as part of an application for a research or marketing permit. The term does not include experiments that are subject to the provisions of part 58 of this chapter, regarding nonclinical laboratory studies.

(d) *Investigator* means an individual who actually conducts a clinical investigation, i.e., under whose immediate direction the test article is administered or dispensed to, or used involving, a subject, or, in the event of an investigation conducted by a team of individuals, is the responsible leader of that team.

(e) *Sponsor* means a person who initiates a clinical investigation, but who does not actually conduct the investigation, i.e., the test article is administered or dispensed to or used involving, a subject under the immediate direction of another individual. A person other than an individual (e.g., corporation or agency) that uses one or more of its own employees to conduct a clinical investigation it has initiated is considered to be a sponsor (not a sponsor-investigator), and the employees are considered to be investigators.

(f) *Sponsor-investigator* means an individual who both initiates and actually conducts, alone or with others, a clinical investigation, i.e., under whose immediate direction the test article is administered or dispensed to, or used involving, a subject. The term does not include any person other than an individual, e.g., corporation or agency.

(g) *Human subject* means an individual who is or becomes a participant in research, either as a recipient of the test article or as a control. A subject may be either a healthy human or a patient.

(h) *Institution* means any public or private entity or agency (including Federal, State, and other agencies). The word facility as used in section 520(g) of the act is deemed to be synonymous with the term institution for purposes of this part.

(i) *Institutional review board (IRB)* means any board, committee, or other group formally designated by an institution to review biomedical research involving humans as subjects, to approve the initiation of and conduct periodic review of such research. The term has the same meaning as the phrase institutional review committee as used in section 520(g) of the act.

(j) *Test article* means any drug (including a biological product for human use), medical device for human use, human food additive, color additive, electronic product, or any other article subject to regulation under the act or under sections 351 and 354–360F of the Public Health Service Act (42 U.S.C. 262 and 263b–263n)....

(m) *Family member* means any one of the following legally competent persons: Spouse; parents; children (including adopted children); brothers, sisters, and spouses of brothers and sisters; and any individual related by blood or affinity whose close association with the subject is the equivalent of a family relationship.

(n) *Assent* means a child's affirmative agreement to participate in a clinical investigation. Mere failure to object may not, absent affirmative agreement, be construed as assent.

(o) *Children* means persons who have not attained the legal age for consent to treatments or procedures involved in clinical investigations, under the applicable law of the jurisdiction in which the clinical investigation will be conducted.

(p) *Parent* means a child's biological or adoptive parent.

(q) *Ward* means a child who is placed in the legal custody of the State or other agency, institution, or entity, consistent with applicable Federal, State, or local law.

(r) *Permission* means the agreement of parent(s) or guardian to the participation of their child or ward in a clinical investigation. Permission must be obtained in compliance with subpart B of this part and must include the elements of informed consent described in § 50.25.

(s) *Guardian* means an individual who is authorized under applicable State or local law to consent on behalf of a child to general medical care when general medical care includes participation in research. For purposes of subpart D of this part, a guardian also means an individual who is authorized to consent on behalf of a child to participate in research....

Subpart B—Informed Consent of Human Subjects

Sec. 50.20 General requirements for informed consent.

Except as provided in §§ 50.23 and 50.24, no investigator may involve a human being as a subject in research covered by these regulations unless the investigator has obtained the legally effective informed consent of the subject or the subject's legally authorized representative. An investigator shall seek such consent only under circumstances that provide the prospective subject or the representative sufficient opportunity to consider whether or not to participate and that minimize the possibility of coercion or undue influence. The information that is given to the subject or the representative shall be in language understandable to the subject or the representative. No informed consent, whether oral or written, may include any exculpatory language through which the subject or the representative is made to waive or appear to waive any of the subject's legal rights, or releases or appears to release the investigator, the sponsor, the institution, or its agents from liability for negligence....

Sec. 50.23 Exception from general requirements.

(a) The obtaining of informed consent shall be deemed feasible unless, before use of the test article (except as provided in paragraph (b) of this section), both the investigator and a physician who is not otherwise participating in the clinical investigation certify in writing all of the following:

(1) The human subject is confronted by a life-threatening situation necessitating the use of the test article.

(2) Informed consent cannot be obtained from the subject because of an inability to communicate with, or obtain legally effective consent from, the subject.

(3) Time is not sufficient to obtain consent from the subject's legal representative.

(4) There is available no alternative method of approved or generally recognized therapy that provides an equal or greater likelihood of saving the life of the subject.

(b) If immediate use of the test article is, in the investigator's opinion, required to preserve the life of the subject, and time is not sufficient to obtain the independent determination required in paragraph (a) of this section in advance of using the test article, the determinations of the clinical investigator shall be made and, within 5 working days after the use of the article, be reviewed and evaluated in writing by a physician who is not participating in the clinical investigation.

(c) The documentation required in paragraph (a) or (b) of this section shall be submitted to the IRB within 5 working days after the use of the test article....

Sec. 50.24 Exception from informed consent requirements for emergency research.

(a) The IRB responsible for the review, approval, and continuing review of the clinical investigation described in this section may approve that investigation without requiring that informed consent of all research subjects be obtained if the IRB (with the concurrence of a licensed physician who is a member of or consultant to the IRB and who is not otherwise participating in the clinical investigation) finds and documents each of the following:

(1) The human subjects are in a life-threatening situation, available treatments are unproven or unsatisfactory, and the collection of valid scientific evidence, which may include evidence obtained through randomized placebo-controlled investigations, is necessary to determine the safety and effectiveness of particular interventions.

(2) Obtaining informed consent is not feasible because:

(i) The subjects will not be able to give their informed consent as a result of their medical condition;

(ii) The intervention under investigation must be administered before consent from the subjects' legally authorized representatives is feasible; and

(iii) There is no reasonable way to identify prospectively the individuals likely to become eligible for participation in the clinical investigation.

(3) Participation in the research holds out the prospect of direct benefit to the subjects because:

(i) Subjects are facing a life-threatening situation that necessitates intervention;

(ii) Appropriate animal and other preclinical studies have been conducted, and the information derived from those studies and related evidence support the potential for the intervention to provide a direct benefit to the individual subjects; and

(iii) Risks associated with the investigation are reasonable in relation to what is known about the medical condition of the potential class of subjects, the risks and benefits of standard therapy, if any, and what is known about the risks and benefits of the proposed intervention or activity.

(4) The clinical investigation could not practicably be carried out without the waiver.

(5) The proposed investigational plan defines the length of the potential therapeutic window based on scientific evidence, and the investigator has committed to attempting to contact a legally authorized representative for each subject within that window of time and, if feasible, to asking the legally authorized representative contacted for consent within that window rather than proceeding without consent. The investigator will summarize efforts made to contact legally authorized representatives and make this information available to the IRB at the time of continuing review.

(6) The IRB has reviewed and approved informed consent procedures and an informed consent document consistent with § 50.25. These procedures and the informed consent document are to be used with subjects or their legally authorized representatives in situations where use of such procedures and documents is feasible. The IRB has reviewed and approved procedures and information to be used when providing an opportunity for a family member to object to a subject's participation in the clinical investigation consistent with paragraph (a)(7)(v) of this section.

(7) Additional protections of the rights and welfare of the subjects will be provided, including, at least:

(i) Consultation (including, where appropriate, consultation carried out by the IRB) with representatives of the communities in which the clinical investigation will be conducted and from which the subjects will be drawn;

(ii) Public disclosure to the communities in which the clinical investigation will be conducted and from which the subjects will be drawn, prior to initiation of the clinical investigation, of plans for the investigation and its risks and expected benefits;

(iii) Public disclosure of sufficient information following completion of the clinical investigation to apprise the community and researchers of the study, including the demographic characteristics of the research population, and its results;

(iv) Establishment of an independent data monitoring committee to exercise oversight of the clinical investigation; and

(v) If obtaining informed consent is not feasible and a legally authorized representative is not reasonably available, the investigator has committed, if feasible, to attempting to contact within the therapeutic window the subject's family member who is not a legally authorized representative, and asking whether he or she objects to the subject's participation in the clinical investigation. The investigator will summarize efforts made to contact family members and make this information available to the IRB at the time of continuing review.

(b) The IRB is responsible for ensuring that procedures are in place to inform, at the earliest feasible opportunity, each subject, or if the subject remains incapacitated, a legally authorized representative of the subject, or if such a representative is not reasonably available, a family member, of the subject's inclusion in the clinical investigation, the details of the investigation and other information contained in the informed consent document. The IRB shall also ensure that there is a procedure to inform the subject, or if the subject remains incapacitated, a legally authorized representative of the subject, or if such a representative is not reasonably available, a family member, that he or she may discontinue the subject's participation at any time without penalty or loss of benefits to which the subject is otherwise entitled. If a legally authorized representative or family member is told about the clinical investigation and the subject's condition improves, the subject is also to be informed as soon as feasible. If a subject is entered into a clinical investigation with waived consent and the subject dies before a legally authorized representative or family member can be contacted, information about the clinical investigation is to be provided to the subject's legally authorized representative or family member, if feasible.

(c) The IRB determinations required by paragraph (a) of this section and the documentation required by paragraph (e) of this section are to be retained by the IRB for at least 3 years after completion of the clinical investigation, and the records shall be accessible for inspection and copying by FDA in accordance with § 56.115(b) of this chapter.

(d) Protocols involving an exception to the informed consent requirement under this section must be performed under a separate investigational new drug application (IND) or investigational device exemption (IDE) that clearly identifies such protocols as protocols that may include subjects who are unable to consent. The submission of those protocols in a separate IND/IDE is required even if an IND for the same drug product or an IDE for the same device already exists. Applications for investigations under this section may not be submitted as amendments under §§ 312.30 or 812.35 of this chapter.

(e) If an IRB determines that it cannot approve a clinical investigation because the investigation does not meet the criteria in the exception provided under paragraph (a) of this section or because of other relevant ethical concerns, the IRB must document its findings and provide these findings promptly in writing to the clinical investigator and to the sponsor of the clinical investigation. The sponsor of the clinical investigation must promptly disclose this information to FDA and to the sponsor's clinical investigators who are participating or are asked to participate in this or a substantially equivalent clinical investigation of the sponsor, and to other IRBs that have been, or are, asked to review this or a substantially equivalent investigation by that sponsor....

Sec. 50.25 Elements of informed consent.... [37]

Sec. 50.27 Documentation of informed consent.... [38]

Notes & Questions

1. Over time, the original benefits arising from the coordination of seventeen federal agencies in adopting the Common Rule has become a bit of a liability: Changing the Common Rule in even fairly minor respects requires the consent and action of all seventeen agencies. Thus, even as some agencies have desired to amend their human subjects research rules, they are faced with the daunting proposition of either convincing sixteen other agencies to do the same, or to break ranks and destroy the Common Rule itself (as a uniform set of rules across the agencies). Is the uniformity across the agencies worth this restriction? Do you think the Common Rule ever can, or will, be amended simultaneously by all the agencies?

2. Does the Common Rule adequately address the issues raised in Section A of this Chapter?

3. Why should the FDA regulate human subjects research that it neither funds nor directly controls?

---

37. [With minimal exceptions, this section is the same as that found in the Common Rule.]
38. [This section is also substantially similar to that found in the Common Rule.]

C. The Role of Institutional Review Boards

As is clear from the sections *supra*, Institutional Review Boards (IRBs) are intended to be a local check on research involving human subjects. Statutes and regulations require that an appropriate IRB approve all research protocols involving human subjects. The following selections describe this role and set out some of the regulations governing IRB activities. Consider whether IRBs are successful in preventing harm to human subjects as you read the following.

Protecting Human Subjects: Status of Recommendations, Statement of George Grob, U.S. Department of Health and Human Services, Testimony Before the House Committee on Government Reform, Subcommittee on Criminal Justice, Drug Policy and Human Resources

May 3, 2000[39]

Good afternoon. I am George Grob, Deputy Inspector General for Evaluation and Inspections, in the Office of Inspector General (OIG), U.S. Department of Health and Human Services. I am pleased to testify at today's hearing on the Department's responses to our June 1998 report on the Institutional Review Board system for protecting human subjects of medical research.

Mr. Chairman, the Department has taken a number of promising steps, but few of our recommended reforms have been enacted.

Our June 1998 Report on Institutional Review Boards

Background. In June 1998, we released a series of reports on the Federal system for human-subject protections centers on institutional review boards (IRBs). This broad-based review was initiated after a 1995 OIG study, requested by the Food and Drug Administration (FDA), raised significant concerns about the adequacy of subject protections and the IRB system. The report focused on medical device research and found, for example, that in one instance that an investigator had implanted 264 investigational devices when he only had approval for 75 implants. We found another investigator had not gotten informed consent from the subjects and yet other instances in which changes in the informed consent documents that IRBs had requested were not incorporated. Another investigator moved from the city of practice without informing the subjects of his clinical trial who to report to after he was gone.

Findings. In the broad 1998 report, we warned that the effectiveness of IRBs was in jeopardy. We found that the clinical research environment had changed in the 20 years since the system was first established and the changes have had significant implications for IRBs. IRBs were becoming overwhelmed by their workloads, lacking necessary resources to keep up and becoming pressured to do more in a shorter time frame and with limited information on many trials. They provided little training to investigators and Board members regarding principles and practices of human subject protection. Of

39. *Available at* http://www.oig.hhs.gov/reading/testimony/2000/00503fin.htm.

particular significance, they conducted very little oversight of clinical trials once the trials had started. In addition, Federal oversight of protections was limited, leaving Department with little sense of how well IRBs were actually doing their job.

These findings led us to present numerous recommendations to the National Institutes of Health (NIH), its Office for Protection from Research Risks (OPRR), and the Food and Drug Administration (FDA). Brief summaries of both our findings and recommendations from the June 1998 report are attached to this testimony.

A Follow-up Report

Based on the continued interest in human-subject protections and a request from this subcommittee, we recently issued a follow-up report providing an accounting of how fully our 1998 recommendations have been enacted. We drew on information obtained over the past two years from Department officials and pertinent documents, data reported to us by the NIH and FDA, and interviews with Department officials who also provided comments on a draft of this report, many of which are reflected in the final. Let me state that this report is not a further examination of the adequacy of the Federal oversight of human subject protections or of the protections themselves. Instead, we used as a starting point our prior recommendations and provide an accounting of how fully they have been carried out. Attached at the end of this testimony is a table compiling each recommendation and a brief description of what, if any, action has taken place.

The Department has taken action and initiated several promising steps.

Increased Enforcement. Since June 1998, both OPRR and FDA have significantly stepped up their on-site presence at research institutions. Between April 1997 and May 1998, OPRR had conducted an on-site investigation at only 1 institution. Between June 1998 and March 2000, it conducted on-site investigations at 10 institutions. Since June 1998, OPRR also conducted off-site investigations (document reviews) at more than 140 additional institutions. It found performance problems at a number of institutions it investigated and has required 7 of them to suspend some or all of their federally funded research. Where OPRR found weaknesses in the institutions' systems of protections, it cited institutions for substantive, broad-based deficiencies—ones that have direct consequences on the rights and safety of research subjects.

FDA's number of routine on-site investigations of IRBs increased from 213 in Fiscal Year 1997, to 253 in FY 1998, and 336 in FY 1999. The Center for Devices and Radiological Health, for example, issued eight warning letters to IRBs during FY 1999, compared to zero in FY 1998. The Center for Drug Evaluation and Research took administrative action against eight IRBs during FY 1998 and 1999.

Sentinel Effect. OPRR's oversight activities, in particular, have drawn the attention of the research community to issues of human-subject protections. The reviews at prominent medical centers, including the temporary suspension of federally funded research at 7 centers, have had a ripple effect beyond the individual institutions visited by OPRR. Many major medical journals and newspapers have given prominent attention to OPRR's enforcement actions. The adequacy of IRB oversight has been a topic at a number of national conferences and association meetings.

New Organization. In July 1999, the Secretary announced the relocation of OPRR from NIH to the Office of the Secretary and plans to establish a new advisory committee on protection from research risks to provide scientific and ethical guidance to the office. These actions, although not yet complete, have been widely publicized and are being taken to strengthen the stature and effectiveness of OPRR in its oversight role and are indicative of the Secretary's commitment to strengthening subject protections.

Other Initiatives. The Department has enacted two of our recommendations—as of October 1998, FDA now informs sponsors and IRBs associated with an investigator when FDA finds evidence of misconduct on the part of clinical investigator; and in June 1999, NIH issued a policy stating that all data and safety monitoring boards associated with NIH trials are expected to forward summary reports of adverse events to IRBs. Both actions are significant. For example, the summary information is key to an IRB's ability to ensure the continued safety of subjects. Both agencies have also increased their education outreach and resources. They have ongoing deliberations on additional proposed changes.

But overall, few of our recommended reforms have been enacted.

Despite these positive steps, there is still a need for additional reforms. What follows is a brief description of any the Department actions taken in response to our six broad recommendations. A table attached to this testimony provides a quick snapshot on the status of the Department responses.

Flexibility and Accountability

We called for the Department to lessen specific procedural requirements that add questionable of value and to require that IRBs undergo regular performance-focused evaluations. Beyond one concrete action discussed below, there have been few enacted reforms along the lines we recommended. Little has been done to grant IRBs more flexibility or to establish a Federal basis for assessing the effectiveness of IRBs.

In November 1998, FDA and NIH/OPRR jointly issued new regulation expanding the categories of research that may be reviewed by IRBs through an expedited review procedure. There are also active deliberations by an NIH Advisory Group geared towards reducing regulatory burden and streamlining processes for grantee institutions. Among its recommendations, the group proposed a change, about to be implemented, to the requirement that IRBs review all protocols before funding decisions are made, an improvement we suggested.

The most notable development around IRB performance evaluations is in the private sector. A private group devoted to the ethical conduct of research, is working to develop performance standards and apply them as part of an accreditation process. Both NIH/OPRR and FDA are participating in these discussions.

Oversight of Ongoing Research

We made several recommendations to strengthen continuing protections of clinical research subjects after the research has begun. For example, we called for more explicit policies on when and how data safety and monitoring boards could be used in certain research trials and a suggested a requirement that they share summary information with IRBs. We also called for FDA to inform IRBs when it takes action against an investigator under the IRB's purview and to establish a requirement that sponsors and investigators notify IRBs of any prior IRB review of research. Finally, we called for increased IRB awareness of on-site research practices.

As stated earlier, FDA now informs sponsors and IRBs about investigator misconduct and NIH issued a policy requiring its data and safety monitoring boards (DSMBs) to forward summary information to IRBs. But, neither NIH nor FDA has issued requirements for sponsors to notify IRBs of prior reviews, nor have they issued guidance to IRBs to increase their attention to on-site research practices. FDA has not set forth regulations regarding the appropriate use for or composition of DSMBs, which can help provide and assemble valuable information for IRBs.

FDA requires all sponsors of gene transfer research, and sponsors overseen by the Center for Devices and Radiological Health, to routinely submit monitoring plans. But both of these policies do not address a large majority of clinical trials. We urge FDA and NIH take similar initiatives directed at other research areas.

Education and Training

We called for the Department to require institutions receiving Public Health Service Act funds establish an education program for investigators and that IRBs be required to educate their members. No Federal regulations have been enacted requiring institutions to establish education programs for clinical investigators. Similarly, no Federal requirements have been enacted calling for education for IRB members.

NIH intramural researchers are required to complete a web-based tutorial in order to conduct human-subjects research on campus. We urge NIH to consider expanding this policy to all extramural researchers, who conduct the majority of research funded by NIH. Both NIH and FDA have increased their educational outreach through numerous training presentations and seminars for IRBs and professional groups. NIH has constructed a website containing bioethics resources and has launched new training grants in subject protection issues and bioethics. FDA is in the process of updating its Information Sheets, an important source of IRB guidance. NIH/OPRR hired a full-time educational staff person in January 1999, and is in the process of further expanding this staff.

Conflicts of Interest

We called for a number of steps to mitigate the potential influence of conflicts on IRB reviews such as a requirement increasing the number of nonscientific and noninstitutional members on IRBs and a prohibition on equity owners of independent IRBs from participating in the IRB review process. We did not identify any significant action in the Department to mitigate potential IRB conflicts of interest. We continue to regard this as a significant area warranting attention. In the increasingly commercialized research environment, potential for conflicts within research institutions loom larger than ever and it is ever more important that IRB reviews be sufficiently independent, both in reality and in appearance.

Workload Pressures

We called for OPRR to hold institutions accountable for the resource commitments they made in their assurances and for FDA to modify its site visit protocol to more readily identify situations in which limited resources may jeopardize subject protections. OPRR's enforcement efforts have brought attention to IRB resource shortages at individual institutions. However, no further action has been taken to develop indicators of adequate resource levels or to enable greater investments to support IRB functions.

One approach that NIH reports is under consideration, and is worthy of attention, would be to allow institutions to allocate an additional increment of grant funds to provide necessary resources for IRBs. A well-supported IRB should be considered a necessary cost of doing business.

Reengineering Federal Oversight

We called for NIH to revamp its oversight and assurance process and for FDA to revamp its on-site inspection process. We also called for the Department to require IRBs to register before being allowed to review research under the Department jurisdiction.

OPRR's and FDA's response in increasing their enforcement efforts is significant, as we have already indicated. By increasing their presence in research institutions, they have fostered compliance with Federal regulations there—and most likely at others as well. But neither body has yet enacted any significant revamping of their oversight processes as we have called for. This is unfortunate because stepped up enforcement without a more efficient, performance-oriented enforcement process will still leave us with an oversight system that falls well short of its potential.

FDA has substantially increased its IRB inspections, but it has not engineered any significant changes in its approach to these inspections. The inspections remain narrow and focused on procedural compliance, not results. NIH/OPRR reports that it has been developing plans to streamline the assurance process as we called for in our June 1998 report. But no actual change has taken place to date.

It is important to note that FDA has formed a working group to establish an IRB registration system. The working group has agreed upon specifications for this registry that reflect many of our suggestions. However, nothing has been implemented yet. We encourage the group to follow through with this effort.

The Common Rule: A Significant Barrier to Departmental Progress

The HHS core regulations concerning IRBs and human-subject protections are the basis of a common Federal policy on human-subject protections. The Federal policy, known as the Common Rule, is adhered to by the Department and 16 other Federal agencies.

Because any changes to the Rule call for the concurrence of all 17 Federal agencies, we must acknowledge that the reality of gaining concurrence among 17 Federal agencies inhibits a timely and effective the Department response to a number of our recommendations.

Several of our recommendations can be carried out through administrative changes, for example requiring education through contract and grant language or altering the assurance or inspection processes. However, other recommended changes, are subsumed in the Common Rule. A requirement, for instance, for more extensive representation on IRBs of nonscientific and noninstitutional members or stronger requirements on IRBs having sufficient independence, could be difficult to carry out without the agreement of the other 16 agencies.

The intention of having a common Federal policy on human subject protections is an important one. One set of standards fosters a level of consistency in protections of human subjects in many different areas of research and makes complying with Federal regulations easier for researchers and sponsors. However, with the clinical research environment changing rapidly, we believe it is essential for the Federal policy and regulatory actions to keep pace. Therefore, legislative change may be necessary to achieve a timely implementation of many of our recommendations.

The Need for Action on a Broad Front

Our June 1998 inquiry and continuing work in this area convinces us that IRBs alone cannot do the job; other parties in the clinical research process, including sponsors and investigators, must take responsibility for subject protections. That is why, for example, our recommendations include actions that call for investigator education. Investigators, while they are in a position to do the most harm to patients, are also in a position to do the most good. More explicit Federal guidelines on recruiting subjects and the use and composition of data safety and monitoring boards can also help. The National Bioethics

Advisory Commission is also likely to offer further guidance in the near future on the kind of changes that need to be made in the Federal regulatory system.

New Opportunity for Leadership

The Department has a significant new opportunity to exert Federal leadership in protecting human subjects with the new office in the Office of the Secretary and a new advisory committee on subject protection issues. We urge that the new office give significant attention to our prior recommendations. We also urge that it continue the *important* enforcement efforts undertaken by OPRR over the past 2 years. The NIH/OPRR efforts have served as a reminder to research institutions, sponsors, individual investigators, and IRBs that the reviews must still be substantive in order to ensure adequate protections for human subjects. In the important quest to reduce regulatory burdens, it is important not to lose sight of this underlying protection function.

Both FDA and NIH will retain significant statutory and operational responsibilities for protecting human subjects despite the impending establishment of a Departmental office for subject protections. FDA still has the most visible on-site presence and thus is in the best position to identify shortcomings and opportunities for improvement. NIH retains significant roles in ensuring human-subject protections as a major sponsor of clinical research and as a conduit to the research community.

Conclusion

We continue to support the recommendations we made in our earlier report and call for a greater sense of urgency in carrying them out. They offer actions that would strengthen human-subject protections without impeding vital clinical research. They reflect a respect for the largely collegial manner in which IRBs operate. Yet, they also recognize that verification and accountability must also be important features of a system intended to protect human subjects.

Our recommendations are not a complete blueprint for action. In the months ahead, we will be conducting further inquiry that more closely examines how the Department oversight can enhance human-subject protections.

Thank you for the opportunity to testify on this most important topic. At this time, I would be happy to answer any questions which you or the other members of the Subcommittee may have.

FINDINGS

Institutional Review Boards: A Time for Reform (OEI-01-97-00193), June 1998

The Effectiveness of IRBs Is in Jeopardy.

They Face Major Changes in the Research Environment. The current framework of IRB practices was shaped in the 1970s in an environment where research typically was carried out by a single investigator working under government funding with a small cohort of human subjects in a university teaching hospital. In recent years, that environment has been changing dramatically as a result of the expansion of managed care, the increased commercialization of research, the proliferation of multi-site trials, new types of research, the increased number of research proposals, and the rise of patient consumerism. Each of these developments has presented major disruptions and challenges for IRBs. "Never before," concluded one recent review, "has such a pressure-cooker atmosphere prevailed within the IRB system."

They Review Too Much, Too Quickly, with Too Little Expertise. This is especially apparent in many of the larger institutions. Expanded workloads, resource constraints, and extensive Federal mandates contribute to a rushed atmosphere where sufficient deliberation often is not possible. At the same time, the IRBs frequently are hard-pressed to gain access to the scientific expertise they need to reach informed judgments about the research taking place under their jurisdiction.

They Conduct Minimal Continuing Review of Approved Research. In the environment described above, continuing review often loses out. Even where there is the will, there often is not the time to go beyond the perfunctory obligations. A lack of feedback from other entities that oversee multi-site trials contributes to the problem. The result is that IRBs have all too little information about how the informed consent process really works and about how well the interests of subjects are being protected during the course of research.

They Face Conflicts That Threaten Their Independence. Clinical research provides revenue and prestige to the institutions to which many IRBs belong. The institutions expect IRBs to support these interests at the same time that they protect human subjects. The resulting tension can lessen the IRBs' focus on their basic mission. The minimal "outside" representation that typically exists on IRBs deprives them of an important counterbalance to the institutional interests. For independent IRBs, the dependence on revenue from industry sponsors exerts similar possibilities for conflict.

They Provide Little Training for Investigators and Board Members. The IRB system depends heavily on research investigators' commitment to uphold human-subject protections. But as that system now operates, it offers little educational outreach to investigators to help them become informed and sensitized about these protections. Similarly, it provides minimal orientation and continuing education for IRB members—a deficiency that is especially detrimental to nonscientific and noninstitutional members.

Neither IRBs Nor The Department Devote Much Attention to Evaluating IRB Effectiveness. IRBs rarely conduct inquiries to determine how well they are accomplishing their mission; their judgments of effectiveness rely mainly on the number of protection lapses or complaints that are brought to their attention. The Department agencies conducting oversight seldom go any further. The Office for Protection from Research Risks, in the National Institutes of Health, focuses almost entirely on up-front assurances. The Food and Drug Administration relies on compliance-focused inspections.

RECOMMENDATIONS

Institutional Review Boards: A Time for Reform (OEI-01-97-00193), June 1998

1. Recast Federal Requirements So That They Grant IRBs Greater Flexibility and Hold Them More Accountable for Results.

Eliminate or lessen specific procedural requirements that are of questionable value. Our aim was to provide overburdened IRBs with greater discretion that would enable them to develop more innovative and strategic approaches to their reviews. There are requirements, for example, that limit what IRBs can accomplish in conducting protocol reviews outside of convened board meetings. In addition, we highlighted requirements that call for IRBs to conduct full, annual reviews of approved protocols and that call for complete reviews of Federal funding applications prior to funding decisions.

Require that IRBs undergo regular performance-focused evaluations that are carried out in accordance with Federal guidelines. In our review, we were struck by how little attention Federal oversight bodies and IRBs themselves gave to evaluating how successful IRBs were in protecting human subjects. It is time, we concluded, for the Federal government to mandate self-evaluations or, better yet, evaluations conducted by independent, outside parties. We also urged that the results of such evaluations be made public.

2. Strengthen Continuing Protections for Human Subjects Participating in Research.

Require Data Safety Monitoring Boards (DSMBs) for certain high-risk and multi-site trials. DSMBs are independent assessment bodies that provide medical, scientific and other expertise that typically is not available on IRBs, thereby serving an invaluable function in protecting human subjects. We recommended that NIH and FDA take the lead in seeing that DSMBs become more firmly established as oversight mechanisms and become more clearly accountable.

Require DSMBs to provide summary information to IRBs. We urged that DSMBs provide their summary assessments of adverse event reports to IRBs. IRBs are swamped with individual adverse event reports from multi-site trials, but these reports lack the essential context to confer meaning about the relative safety of the trial. DSMBs can provide this context and thereby enhance the IRB's capacity to assess ongoing safety.

Alert IRBs to corrective actions taken against investigators under the board's purview. Although FDA provides information on its website about corrective actions that result from investigator inspections, the Agency does not routinely inform the respective IRBs of such actions. We recommended that FDA inform individual IRBs when it takes corrective action against an investigator who is conducting research reviewed by the IRB.

Require sponsors and investigators to notify IRBs of any prior IRB review of a research plan. Sometimes sponsors shop around for an IRB that will give their protocol a favorable review. We pointed out that such action can undermine the IRB review process and, accordingly, urged that this requirement be enacted.

Call for increased IRB awareness of on-site research practices involving human subjects. IRBs are rarely aware of what actually takes place between investigator and subject. We called for IRBs to move beyond their focus on the informed consent document and periodically check for themselves how the actual consent process is working. For particularly sensitive or risky projects, we suggested they might call for the participation of counselors, ombudsmen, or other third parties that could be available to make certain that the consent process functions in the interest of human subjects.

3. Enact Federal Requirements That Help Ensure That Investigators and IRB Members Are Adequately Educated About and Sensitized to Human-Subject Protections.

Require institutions to establish an education program for investigators in human-subject protections. Such a requirement exists for research involving animal subjects. We found the case for education requirements no less compelling for research involving humans. The mandatory education we called for could be provided through media such as seminars, individual instruction, videos, or on-line tutorials.

Require investigators receiving funding under the Public Health Service Act for research involving human subjects to provide a written attestation indicating that they will uphold Federal policies concerning human-subject protections. We recommended such an attestation as a way of heightening investigators' awareness of their responsibilities as investigators and interest in participating in educational programs addressing human-subject protections.

Require IRBs to educate their members about human-subject protections. In order for IRBs to adequately review research protocols to ensure human-subject protections, each board member must be educated in both applicable Federal regulations and ethical principles. We called for a specific mandate that IRBs and their parent institutions provide initial and continuing education.

4. Help Insulate IRBs from Conflicts That Can Compromise Their Mission in Protecting Human Subjects.

Require more extensive representation on IRBs of nonscientific and noninstitutional members. At present just one IRB member can wear both of these hats and satisfy the requirement. We found that to be an untenable situation, one that can deprive IRBs of a valuable counterbalance to internal, institutional pressures that can threaten their independence.

Reinforce to IRBs and their parent institutions the importance of IRBs maintaining sufficient independence. It is particularly important that IRBs not report to a part of an institution responsible for bringing in research funds.

Prohibit equity owners from participating in the IRB review process. Such a practice does not necessarily inhibit the independence of the review process, but it establishes a situation that can undermine a perception of impartiality. We recommended that it should be disallowed.

5. Recognize the Seriousness of the Workload Pressures That Many IRBs Face and Take Actions That Aim to Moderate Them.

Require that IRBs have access to sufficient resources to adequately carry out their duties. Our recommendation was directed not only to staff and board member resources, but also to space, computers, and other essential elements. We urged OPRR to hold institutions accountable for the resource commitments they made in their assurances and for FDA to modify its site visit protocol so that it could more readily identify situations where resource shortages jeopardize an IRB's ability to oversee research.

6. Reengineer the Federal Oversight Process

Revamp the NIH/OPRR assurance process. NIH/OPRR's oversight process has been concentrated on reviewing up-front assurances aimed at obtaining an institution's commitment to adhere to Federal requirements. We found that assurance process to be paperwork-laden with little effect on IRB functioning. We urged that NIH/OPRR reorient the assurance process so that it rests on an institutional attestation to conform to Federal requirements, and then devote more NIH/OPRR resources to periodic performance-based reviews of institutions and their IRBs.

Revamp the FDA on-site inspection process. We recognized that FDA has a much greater on-site presence than NIH/OPRR, but urged that FDA transform its site visit protocol from a narrow compliance orientation to one that is much more performance-based. Such an approach would pay particular attention to how individuals were actually being approached about participating as human subjects and to how IRBs were making risk-benefit trade-offs.

Require IRBs to register with the Federal government. We found that one of the major impediments to Federal oversight of human-subjects research is that there is no complete registry of the IRBs reviewing this research. Such a registry would be invaluable for FDA and NIH/OPRR as it would allow them to target their oversight and communicate more effectively with IRBs....

FDA—Regulations Regarding Institutional Review Boards

21 C.F.R. part 56[40]

...

Subpart C—IRB Functions and Operations

Sec. 56.108 IRB functions and operations.

In order to fulfill the requirements of these regulations, each IRB shall:

(a) Follow written procedures: (1) For conducting its initial and continuing review of research and for reporting its findings and actions to the investigator and the institution; (2) for determining which projects require review more often than annually and which projects need verification from sources other than the investigator that no material changes have occurred since previous IRB review; (3) for ensuring prompt reporting to the IRB of changes in research activity; and (4) for ensuring that changes in approved research, during the period for which IRB approval has already been given, may not be initiated without IRB review and approval except where necessary to eliminate apparent immediate hazards to the human subjects.

(b) Follow written procedures for ensuring prompt reporting to the IRB, appropriate institutional officials, and the Food and Drug Administration of: (1) Any unanticipated problems involving risks to human subjects or others; (2) any instance of serious or continuing noncompliance with these regulations or the requirements or determinations of the IRB; or (3) any suspension or termination of IRB approval.

(c) Except when an expedited review procedure is used (see §56.110), review proposed research at convened meetings at which a majority of the members of the IRB are present, including at least one member whose primary concerns are in nonscientific areas. In order for the research to be approved, it shall receive the approval of a majority of those members present at the meeting....

Sec. 56.109 IRB review of research.

(a) An IRB shall review and have authority to approve, require modifications in (to secure approval), or disapprove all research activities covered by these regulations.

(b) An IRB shall require that information given to subjects as part of informed consent is in accordance with §50.25. The IRB may require that information, in addition to that specifically mentioned in §50.25, be given to the subjects when in the IRB's judgment the information would meaningfully add to the protection of the rights and welfare of subjects.

(c) An IRB shall require documentation of informed consent in accordance with §50.27 of this chapter, except as follows:

(1) The IRB may, for some or all subjects, waive the requirement that the subject, or the subject's legally authorized representative, sign a written consent form if it finds that the research presents no more than minimal risk of harm to subjects and involves no procedures for which written consent is normally required outside the research context; or

(2) The IRB may, for some or all subjects, find that the requirements in §50.24 of this chapter for an exception from informed consent for emergency research are met.

---

40. [Readers should review the sections on IRBs in the Common Rule selections supra.]

(d) In cases where the documentation requirement is waived under paragraph (c)(1) of this section, the IRB may require the investigator to provide subjects with a written statement regarding the research.

(e) An IRB shall notify investigators and the institution in writing of its decision to approve or disapprove the proposed research activity, or of modifications required to secure IRB approval of the research activity. If the IRB decides to disapprove a research activity, it shall include in its written notification a statement of the reasons for its decision and give the investigator an opportunity to respond in person or in writing. For investigations involving an exception to informed consent under § 50.24 of this chapter, an IRB shall promptly notify in writing the investigator and the sponsor of the research when an IRB determines that it cannot approve the research because it does not meet the criteria in the exception provided under § 50.24(a) of this chapter or because of other relevant ethical concerns. The written notification shall include a statement of the reasons for the IRB's determination.

(f) An IRB shall conduct continuing review of research covered by these regulations at intervals appropriate to the degree of risk, but not less than once per year, and shall have authority to observe or have a third party observe the consent process and the research.

(g) An IRB shall provide in writing to the sponsor of research involving an exception to informed consent under § 50.24 of this chapter a copy of information that has been publicly disclosed under § 50.24(a)(7)(ii) and (a)(7)(iii) of this chapter. The IRB shall provide this information to the sponsor promptly so that the sponsor is aware that such disclosure has occurred. Upon receipt, the sponsor shall provide copies of the information disclosed to FDA.

(h) When some or all of the subjects in a study are children, an IRB must determine that the research study is in compliance with part 50, subpart D of this chapter, at the time of its initial review of the research. When some or all of the subjects in a study that is ongoing on April 30, 2001 are children, an IRB must conduct a review of the research to determine compliance with part 50, subpart D of this chapter, either at the time of continuing review or, at the discretion of the IRB, at an earlier date. . . .

Sec. 56.110 Expedited review procedures for certain kinds of research involving no more than minimal risk, and for minor changes in approved research.

(a) The Food and Drug Administration has established, and published in the Federal Register, a list of categories of research that may be reviewed by the IRB through an expedited review procedure. The list will be amended, as appropriate, through periodic republication in the Federal Register.

(b) An IRB may use the expedited review procedure to review either or both of the following: (1) Some or all of the research appearing on the list and found by the reviewer(s) to involve no more than minimal risk, (2) minor changes in previously approved research during the period (of 1 year or less) for which approval is authorized. Under an expedited review procedure, the review may be carried out by the IRB chairperson or by one or more experienced reviewers designated by the IRB chairperson from among the members of the IRB. In reviewing the research, the reviewers may exercise all of the authorities of the IRB except that the reviewers may not disapprove the research. A research activity may be disapproved only after review in accordance with the nonexpedited review procedure set forth in § 56.108(c).

(c) Each IRB which uses an expedited review procedure shall adopt a method for keeping all members advised of research proposals which have been approved under the procedure.

(d) The Food and Drug Administration may restrict, suspend, or terminate an institution's or IRB's use of the expedited review procedure when necessary to protect the rights or welfare of subjects....

Subpart E—Administrative Actions for Noncompliance

Sec. 56.120 Lesser administrative actions.

(a) If apparent noncompliance with these regulations in the operation of an IRB is observed by an FDA investigator during an inspection, the inspector will present an oral or written summary of observations to an appropriate representative of the IRB. The Food and Drug Administration may subsequently send a letter describing the noncompliance to the IRB and to the parent institution. The agency will require that the IRB or the parent institution respond to this letter within a time period specified by FDA and describe the corrective actions that will be taken by the IRB, the institution, or both to achieve compliance with these regulations.

(b) On the basis of the IRB's or the institution's response, FDA may schedule a reinspection to confirm the adequacy of corrective actions. In addition, until the IRB or the parent institution takes appropriate corrective action, the agency may:

(1) Withhold approval of new studies subject to the requirements of this part that are conducted at the institution or reviewed by the IRB;

(2) Direct that no new subjects be added to ongoing studies subject to this part;

(3) Terminate ongoing studies subject to this part when doing so would not endanger the subjects; or

(4) When the apparent noncompliance creates a significant threat to the rights and welfare of human subjects, notify relevant State and Federal regulatory agencies and other parties with a direct interest in the agency's action of the deficiencies in the operation of the IRB.

(c) The parent institution is presumed to be responsible for the operation of an IRB, and the Food and Drug Administration will ordinarily direct any administrative action under this subpart against the institution. However, depending on the evidence of responsibility for deficiencies, determined during the investigation, the Food and Drug Administration may restrict its administrative actions to the IRB or to a component of the parent institution determined to be responsible for formal designation of the IRB.

Sec. 56.121 Disqualification of an IRB or an institution.

(a) Whenever the IRB or the institution has failed to take adequate steps to correct the noncompliance stated in the letter sent by the agency under § 56.120(a), and the Commissioner of Food and Drugs determines that this noncompliance may justify the disqualification of the IRB or of the parent institution, the Commissioner will institute proceedings in accordance with the requirements for a regulatory hearing set forth in part 16.

(b) The Commissioner may disqualify an IRB or the parent institution if the Commissioner determines that:

(1) The IRB has refused or repeatedly failed to comply with any of the regulations set forth in this part, and

(2) The noncompliance adversely affects the rights or welfare of the human subjects in a clinical investigation.

(c) If the Commissioner determines that disqualification is appropriate, the Commissioner will issue an order that explains the basis for the determination and that prescribes any actions to be taken with regard to ongoing clinical research conducted under the review of the IRB. The Food and Drug Administration will send notice of the disqualification to the IRB and the parent institution. Other parties with a direct interest, such as sponsors and clinical investigators, may also be sent a notice of the disqualification. In addition, the agency may elect to publish a notice of its action in the Federal Register.

(d) The Food and Drug Administration will not approve an application for a research permit for a clinical investigation that is to be under the review of a disqualified IRB or that is to be conducted at a disqualified institution, and it may refuse to consider in support of a marketing permit the data from a clinical investigation that was reviewed by a disqualified IRB as conducted at a disqualified institution, unless the IRB or the parent institution is reinstated as provided in § 56.123.

Sec. 56.122 Public disclosure of information regarding revocation.

A determination that the Food and Drug Administration has disqualified an institution and the administrative record regarding that determination are disclosable to the public under part 20.

Sec. 56.123 Reinstatement of an IRB or an institution.

An IRB or an institution may be reinstated if the Commissioner determines, upon an evaluation of a written submission from the IRB or institution that explains the corrective action that the institution or IRB plans to take, that the IRB or institution has provided adequate assurance that it will operate in compliance with the standards set forth in this part. Notification of reinstatement shall be provided to all persons notified under § 56.121(c).

Sec. 56.124 Actions alternative or additional to disqualification.

Disqualification of an IRB or of an institution is independent of, and neither in lieu of nor a precondition to, other proceedings or actions authorized by the act. The Food and Drug Administration may, at any time, through the Department of Justice institute any appropriate judicial proceedings (civil or criminal) and any other appropriate regulatory action, in addition to or in lieu of, and before, at the time of, or after, disqualification. The agency may also refer pertinent matters to another Federal, State, or local government agency for any action that that agency determines to be appropriate....

Notes & Questions

1. Some claim that in practice IRBs are often composed of the researcher's faculty colleagues, who themselves will likely be seeking IRB approval for a new research project in the near future. Without necessarily alleging any intentional impropriety, these critics wonder just how objective any particular IRB can be given these circumstances.

2. Do you think that the current system of IRBs (including regulations) is properly configured to monitor human subjects research?

D. Enforcement Issues in Informed Consent, Disclosure, and Financial Conflicts of Interest

The foregoing materials suggest extensive regulation of research involving human research subjects, presumably on behalf of those subjects. Yet, courts have generally refused to find that the regulations create a private cause of action on the part of the individuals involved or their representatives. As you read the following cases, consider whether better protection for human subjects would follow from such a private cause of action. Even if it does, should such a cause of action be in addition to, or a substitute for, agency action?

One particular area of ongoing concern in human subjects research—especially acute in the area of genetic technologies—is that of financial conflicts of interest involving the researchers and investigators themselves. Increasing apparently in tandem with the rise in corporate-sponsored research at university and non-profit science research institutions, this conflict seems to pit the researchers' own financial self-interest—often tied to equity or other performance-based stakes in the sponsoring company—against his interests as an objective scientist and caretaker of the test subjects' well being. The following materials demonstrate the current interplay among the core issues of informed consent, disclosure, and financial conflicts of interest. Note that the first case below was resolved before the Common Rule became effective.

Moore v. Regents of the University of California

51 Cal.3d 120 (1990)

Panelli, J.

We granted review in this case to determine whether plaintiff has stated a cause of action against his physician and other defendants for using his cells in potentially lucrative medical research without his permission. Plaintiff alleges that his physician failed to disclose preexisting research and economic interests in the cells before obtaining consent to the medical procedures by which they were extracted. The superior court sustained all defendants' demurrers to the third amended complaint, and the Court of Appeal reversed. We hold that the complaint states a cause of action for breach of the physician's disclosure obligations, but not for conversion....

The plaintiff is John Moore (Moore), who underwent treatment for hairy-cell leukemia at the Medical Center of the University of California at Los Angeles (UCLA Medical Center). The five defendants are: (1) Dr. David W. Golde (Golde), a physician who attended Moore at UCLA Medical Center; (2) the Regents of the University of California (Regents), who own and operate the university; (3) Shirley G. Quan, a researcher employed by the Regents; (4) Genetics Institute, Inc. (Genetics Institute); and (5) Sandoz Pharmaceuticals Corporation and related entities (collectively Sandoz).

Moore first visited UCLA Medical Center on October 5, 1976, shortly after he learned that he had hairy-cell leukemia. After hospitalizing Moore and "withdr [awing] extensive amounts of blood, bone marrow aspirate, and other bodily substances," Golde confirmed that diagnosis. At this time all defendants, including Golde, were aware that "certain blood products and blood components were of great value in a number of commercial and scientific efforts" and that access to a patient whose blood contained these substances would provide "competitive, commercial, and scientific advantages."

On October 8, 1976, Golde recommended that Moore's spleen be removed. Golde informed Moore "that he had reason to fear for his life, and that the proposed splenectomy operation ... was necessary to slow down the progress of his disease." Based upon Golde's representations, Moore signed a written consent form authorizing the splenectomy.

Before the operation, Golde and Quan "formed the intent and made arrangements to obtain portions of [Moore's] spleen following its removal" and to take them to a separate research unit. Golde gave written instructions to this effect on October 18 and 19, 1976. These research activities "were not intended to have ... any relation to [Moore's] medical ... care." However, neither Golde nor Quan informed Moore of their plans to conduct this research or requested his permission. Surgeons at UCLA Medical Center, whom the complaint does not name as defendants, removed Moore's spleen on October 20, 1976.

Moore returned to the UCLA Medical Center several times between November 1976 and September 1983. He did so at Golde's direction and based upon representations "that such visits were necessary and required for his health and well-being, and based upon the trust inherent in and by virtue of the physician-patient relationship...." On each of these visits Golde withdrew additional samples of "blood, blood serum, skin, bone marrow aspirate, and sperm." On each occasion Moore traveled to the UCLA Medical Center from his home in Seattle because he had been told that the procedures were to be performed only there and only under Golde's direction.

"In fact, [however,]throughout the period of time that [Moore] was under [Golde's] care and treatment, ... the defendants were actively involved in a number of activities which they concealed from [Moore]...." Specifically, defendants were conducting research on Moore's cells and planned to "benefit financially and competitively ... [by exploiting the cells] and [their] exclusive access to [the cells] by virtue of [Golde's] ongoing physician-patient relationship...."

Sometime before August 1979, Golde established a cell line from Moore's T-lymphocytes.[41] On January 30, 1981, the Regents applied for a patent on the cell line, listing Golde and Quan as inventors. "[B]y virtue of an established policy..., [the] Regents, Golde, and Quan would share in any royalties or profits ... arising out of [the] patent."

41. A T-lymphocyte is a type of white blood cell. T-lymphocytes produce lymphokines, or proteins that regulate the immune system. Some lymphokines have potential therapeutic value. If the genetic material responsible for producing a particular lymphokine can be identified, it can sometimes be used to manufacture large quantities of the lymphokine through the techniques of recombinant DNA.

While the genetic code for lymphokines does not vary from individual to individual, it can nevertheless be quite difficult to locate the gene responsible for a particular lymphokine. Because T-lymphocytes produce many different lymphokines, the relevant gene is often like a needle in a haystack. Moore's T-lymphocytes were interesting to the defendants because they overproduced certain lymphokines, thus making the corresponding genetic material easier to identify. (In published research papers, defendants and other researchers have shown that the overproduction was caused by a virus, and that normal T-lymphocytes infected by the virus will also overproduce.)

Cells taken directly from the body (primary cells) are not very useful for these purposes. Primary cells typically reproduce a few times and then die. One can, however, sometimes continue to use cells for an extended period of time by developing them into a "cell line," a culture capable of reproducing indefinitely. This is not, however, always an easy task. "Longterm growth of human cells and tissues is difficult, often an art," and the probability of succeeding with any given cell sample is low, except for a few types of cells not involved in this case.

The patent issued on March 20, 1984, naming Golde and Quan as the inventors of the cell line and the Regents as the assignee of the patent. (U.S. Patent No. 4,438,032 (Mar. 20, 1984)).

The Regent's patent also covers various methods for using the cell line to produce lymphokines. Moore admits in his complaint that "the true clinical potential of each of the lymphokines ... [is] difficult to predict, [but] ... competing commercial firms in these relevant fields have published reports in biotechnology industry periodicals predicting a potential market of approximately $3.01 Billion Dollars by the year 1990 for a whole range of [such lymphokines]...."

With the Regents' assistance, Golde negotiated agreements for commercial development of the cell line and products to be derived from it. Under an agreement with Genetics Institute, Golde "became a paid consultant" and "acquired the rights to 75,000 shares of common stock." Genetics Institute also agreed to pay Golde and the Regents "at least $330,000 over three years, including a pro-rata share of [Golde's] salary and fringe benefits, in exchange for ... exclusive access to the materials and research performed" on the cell line and products derived from it. On June 4, 1982, Sandoz "was added to the agreement," and compensation payable to Golde and the Regents was increased by $110,000. "[T]hroughout this period, ... Quan spent as much as 70 [percent] of her time working for [the] Regents on research" related to the cell line.

Based upon these allegations, Moore attempted to state 13 causes of action.[42] [The superior court ultimately found the claim for conversion defective and declared all remaining claims insufficient, based on the defective conversion claim, while not specifically ruling on such claims. The Court of Appeal reversed, holding that a claim for conversion did exist, although not against all defendants. However, the Court of Appeal also directed the superior court to grant Moore leave to amend in order to adequately state a claim of conversion against all defendants.]

III. Discussion

A. *Breach of Fiduciary Duty and Lack of Informed Consent*

Moore repeatedly alleges that Golde failed to disclose the extent of his research and economic interests in Moore's cells before obtaining consent to the medical procedures by which the cells were extracted. These allegations, in our view, state a cause of action against Golde for invading a legally protected interest of his patient. This cause of action can properly be characterized either as the breach of a fiduciary duty to disclose facts material to the patient's consent or, alternatively, as the performance of medical procedures without first having obtained the patient's informed consent.

Our analysis begins with three well-established principles. First, "a person of adult years and in sound mind has the right, in the exercise of control over his own body, to determine whether or not to submit to lawful medical treatment." ... Second, "the patient's consent to treatment, to be effective, must be an informed consent." ... Third, in soliciting the patient's consent, a physician has a fiduciary duty to disclose all information material to the patient's decision.

42. (1) "Conversion"; (2) "lack of informed consent"; (3) "breach of fiduciary duty"; (4) "fraud and deceit"; (5) "unjust enrichment"; (6) "quasi-contract"; (7) "bad faith breach of the implied covenant of good faith and fair dealing"; (8) "intentional infliction of emotional distress"; (9) "negligent misrepresentation"; (10) "intentional interference with prospective advantageous economic relationships"; (11) "slander of title"; (12) "accounting"; and (13) "declaratory relief."

These principles lead to the following conclusions: (1) a physician must disclose personal interests unrelated to the patient's health, whether research or economic, that may affect the physician's professional judgment; and (2) a physician's failure to disclose such interests may give rise to a cause of action for performing medical procedures without informed consent or breach of fiduciary duty....

1. *Dr. Golde*

We turn now to the allegations of Moore's third amended complaint to determine whether he has stated such a cause of action....

In these allegations, Moore plainly asserts that Golde concealed an economic interest in the postoperative procedures. Therefore, applying the principles already discussed, the allegations state a cause of action for breach of fiduciary duty or lack of informed consent....

2. *The Remaining Defendants*

The Regents, Quan, Genetics Institute, and Sandoz are not physicians. In contrast to Golde, none of these defendants stood in a fiduciary relationship with Moore or had the duty to obtain Moore's informed consent to medical procedures. If any of these defendants is to be liable for breach of fiduciary duty or performing medical procedures without informed consent, it can only be on account of Golde's acts and on the basis of a recognized theory of secondary liability, such as respondeat superior....

B. *Conversion*

Moore also attempts to characterize the invasion of his rights as a conversion—a tort that protects against interference with possessory and ownership interests in personal property. He theorizes that he continued to own his cells following their removal from his body, at least for the purpose of directing their use, and that he never consented to their use in potentially lucrative medical research. Thus, to complete Moore's argument, defendants' unauthorized use of his cells constitutes a conversion. As a result of the alleged conversion, Moore claims a proprietary interest in each of the products that any of the defendants might ever create from his cells or the patented cell line.

No court, however, has ever in a reported decision imposed conversion liability for the use of human cells in medical research. While that fact does not end our inquiry, it raises a flag of caution. In effect, what Moore is asking us to do is to impose a tort duty on scientists to investigate the consensual pedigree of each human cell sample used in research. To impose such a duty, which would affect medical research of importance to all of society, implicates policy concerns far removed from the traditional, two-party ownership disputes in which the law of conversion arose. Invoking a tort theory originally used to determine whether the loser or the finder of a horse had the better title, Moore claims ownership of the results of socially important medical research, including the genetic code for chemicals that regulate the functions of every human being's immune system.[43]

We have recognized that, when the proposed application of a very general theory of liability in a new context raises important policy concerns, it is especially important to face those concerns and address them openly....

---

43. Moore alleges, for example, that "genetic sequences ... are his tangible personal property...." We are not, however, bound by that conclusion of law.... Moreover, as already mentioned, the genetic code for lymphokines does not vary from individual to individual....

Accordingly, we first consider whether the tort of conversion clearly gives Moore a cause of action under existing law. We do not believe it does. Because of the novelty of Moore's claim to own the biological materials at issue, to apply the theory of conversion in this context would frankly have to be recognized as an extension of the theory. Therefore, we consider next whether it is advisable to extend the tort to this context.

1. *Moore's Claim Under Existing Law*

"To establish a conversion, plaintiff must establish an actual interference with his *ownership* or *right of possession*.... Where plaintiff neither has title to the property alleged to have been converted, nor possession thereof, he cannot maintain an action for conversion."

Since Moore clearly did not expect to retain possession of his cells following their removal, to sue for their conversion he must have retained an ownership interest in them. But there are several reasons to doubt that he did retain any such interest. First, no reported judicial decision supports Moore's claim, either directly or by close analogy. Second, California statutory law drastically limits any continuing interest of a patient in excised cells. Third, the subject matters of the Regents' patent—the patented cell line and the products derived from it—cannot be Moore's property.

Neither the Court of Appeal's opinion, the parties' briefs, nor our research discloses a case holding that a person retains a sufficient interest in excised cells to support a cause of action for conversion. We do not find this surprising, since the laws governing such things as human tissues, transplantable organs, blood, fetuses, pituitary glands, corneal tissue, and dead bodies deal with human biological materials as objects sui generis, regulating their disposition to achieve policy goals rather than abandoning them to the general law of personal property. It is these specialized statutes, not the law of conversion, to which courts ordinarily should and do look for guidance on the disposition of human biological materials.

Lacking direct authority for importing the law of conversion into this context, Moore relies, as did the Court of Appeal, primarily on decisions addressing privacy rights.[44] One line of cases involves unwanted publicity. These opinions hold that every person has a proprietary interest in his own likeness and that unauthorized, business use of a likeness is redressible as a tort. But in neither opinion did the authoring court expressly base its holding on property law. Each court stated, following Prosser, that it was "pointless" to debate the proper characterization of the proprietary interest in a likeness. For purposes of determining whether the tort of conversion lies, however, the characterization of the right in question is far from pointless. Only property can be converted.

Not only are the wrongful-publicity cases irrelevant to the issue of conversion, but the analogy to them seriously misconceives the nature of the genetic materials and research involved in this case. Moore, adopting the analogy originally advanced by the Court of Appeal, argues that "[i]f the courts have found a sufficient proprietary interest in one's persona, how could one not have a right in one's own genetic material, something far more profoundly the essence of one's human uniqueness than a name or a face?" However, as the defendants' patent makes clear—and the complaint, too, if read with an understanding of the scientific terms which it has borrowed from the patent—

44. No party has cited a decision supporting Moore's argument that excised cells are "a species of tangible personal property capable of being converted." ...

the goal and result of defendants' efforts has been to manufacture lymphokines.[45] Lymphokines, unlike a name or a face, have the same molecular structure in every human being and the same, important functions in every human being's immune system. Moreover, the particular genetic material which is responsible for the natural production of lymphokines, and which defendants use to manufacture lymphokines in the laboratory, is also the same in every person; it is no more unique to Moore than the number of vertebrae in the spine or the chemical formula of hemoglobin.[46]

Another privacy case offered by analogy to support Moore's claim establishes only that patients have a right to refuse medical treatment. In this context the court ... wrote that "[e]very human being of adult years and sound mind has a right to determine what shall be done with his own body...." Relying on this language to support the proposition that a patient has a continuing right to control the use of excised cells, the Court of Appeal in this case concluded that "[a] patient must have the ultimate power to control what becomes of his or her tissues. To hold otherwise would open the door to a massive invasion of human privacy and dignity in the name of medical progress." Yet one may earnestly wish to protect privacy and dignity without accepting the extremely problematic conclusion that interference with those interests amounts to a conversion of personal property. Nor is it necessary to force the round pegs of "privacy" and "dignity" into the square hole of "property" in order to protect the patient, since the fiduciary-duty and informed-consent theories protect these interests directly by requiring full disclosure.

The next consideration that makes Moore's claim of ownership problematic is California statutory law, which drastically limits a patient's control over excised cells. Pursuant to Health and Safety Code section 7054.4, "[n]otwithstanding any other provision of law, recognizable anatomical parts, human tissues, anatomical human remains,

---

45. Inside the cell, a gene produces a lymphokine by attracting protein molecules, which bond to form a strand of "messenger RNA" (mRNA) in the mirror image of the gene. The mRNA strand then detaches from the gene and attracts other protein molecules, which bond to form the lymphokine that the original gene encoded....

In the laboratory, scientists sometimes use genes to manufacture lymphokines by cutting a gene from the chromosome and grafting it onto the chromosome of a bacterium. The resulting chromosome is an example of "recombinant DNA," or DNA composed of genetic material from more than one individual or species. As the bacterium lives and reproduces, the engrafted gene continues to produce the lymphokine that the gene encodes.

It can be extremely difficult to identify the gene that carries the code for a particular lymphokine. "Since the amount of DNA in a human cell is enormous compared to the amount present in an individual gene, the search for any single gene within a cell is like searching for needle in a haystack." As the Regents' patent application explains, the significance of a cell that overproduces mRNA is to make the difficult search for a particular gene unnecessary. If one has an adequate source of mRNA—the gene's mirror image—it can be used to make a copy, or clone, of the original gene. The cloned gene can then be used in recombinant DNA, as already described, for large-scale production of lymphokines.

46. By definition, a gene responsible for producing a protein found in more than one individual will be the same in each. It is precisely because everyone needs the same basic proteins that proteins produced by one person's cells may have therapeutic value for another person.... Thus, the proteins that defendants hope to manufacture—lymphokines such as interferon—are in no way a "likeness" of Moore.

Because all normal persons possess the genes responsible for production of lymphokines, it is sometimes possible to make normal cells into overproducers.... According to a research paper to which defendants contributed, Moore's cells overproduced lymphokines because they were infected by a virus, HTLV-II (human T-cell leukemia virus type II). (Chen, Quan & Golde, *Human T-cell Leukemia Virus Type II Transforms Normal Human Lymphocytes* (Nov. 1983) 80 Proceedings Nat. Acad. Sci. USA 7006.) The same virus has been shown to transform normal T-lymphocytes into overproducers like Moore's. (*Ibid.*)

or infectious waste following conclusion of scientific use shall be disposed of by interment, incineration, or any other method determined by the state department [of health services] to protect the public health and safety." ... Clearly the Legislature did not specifically intend this statute to resolve the question of whether a patient is entitled to compensation for the nonconsensual use of excised cells. A primary object of the statute is to ensure the safe handling of potentially hazardous biological waste materials. Yet one cannot escape the conclusion that the statute's practical effect is to limit, drastically, a patient's control over excised cells. By restricting how excised cells may be used and requiring their eventual destruction, the statute eliminates so many of the rights ordinarily attached to property that one cannot simply assume that what is left amounts to "property" or "ownership" for purposes of conversion law.

It may be that some limited right to control the use of excised cells does survive the operation of this statute. There is, for example, no need to read the statute to permit "scientific use" contrary to the patient's expressed wish. A fully informed patient may always withhold consent to treatment by a physician whose research plans the patient does not approve. That right, however, as already discussed, is protected by the fiduciary-duty and informed-consent theories.

Finally, the subject matter of the Regents' patent—the patented cell line and the products derived from it—cannot be Moore's property. This is because the patented cell line is both factually and legally distinct from the cells taken from Moore's body.[47] Federal law permits the patenting of organisms that represent the product of "human ingenuity," but not naturally occurring organisms.[48] Human cell lines are patentable because "[l]ong-term adaptation and growth of human tissues and cells in culture is difficult—often considered an art...," and the probability of success is low. It is this *inventive effort* that patent law rewards, not the discovery of naturally occurring raw materials. Thus, Moore's allegations that he owns the cell line and the products derived from it are inconsistent with the patent, which constitutes an authoritative determination that the cell line is the product of invention....

2. *Should Conversion Liability Be Extended?*

As we have discussed, Moore's novel claim to own the biological materials at issue in this case is problematic, at best. Accordingly, his attempt to apply the theory of conversion within this context must frankly be recognized as a request to extend that theory. While we do not purport to hold that excised cells can never be property for any purpose whatsoever, the novelty of Moore's claim demands express consideration of the policies to be served by extending liability rather than blind deference to a complaint alleging as a legal conclusion the existence of a cause of action.

---

47. The distinction between primary cells (cells taken directly from the body) and patented cell lines is not purely a legal one. Cells change while being developed into a cell line and continue to change over time. "[I]t is clear that most established cell lines ... are not completely normal. Besides [an] enhanced growth potential relative to primary cells, they frequently have highly abnormal chromosome numbers...."

The cell line in this case, for example, after many replications began to generate defective and rearranged forms of the HTLV-II virus. A published research paper to which defendants contributed suggests that "the defective forms of virus were probably generated during the passage [or replication] of the cells rather than being present in the original tumour cells of the patient." Possibly because of these changes in the virus, the cell line has developed new abilities to grow in different media. (Chen, McLaughlin, Gasson, Clark & Golde, *Molecular Characterization of Genome of a Novel Human T-cell Leukaemia Virus*, Nature (Oct. 6, 1983) vol. 305, p. 505.) ...

48. [Citing *Diamond v. Chakrabarty*, 447 U.S. 303 (1980). Discussed in Chapter 5, Part A]

There are three reasons why it is inappropriate to impose liability for conversion based upon the allegations of Moore's complaint. First, a fair balancing of the relevant policy considerations counsels against extending the tort. Second, problems in this area are better suited to legislative resolution. Third, the tort of conversion is not necessary to protect patients' rights. For these reasons, we conclude that the use of excised human cells in medical research does not amount to a conversion.

Of the relevant policy considerations, two are of overriding importance. The first is protection of a competent patient's right to make autonomous medical decisions. That right, as already discussed, is grounded in well-recognized and long-standing principles of fiduciary duty and informed consent. This policy weighs in favor of providing a remedy to patients when physicians act with undisclosed motives that may affect their professional judgment. The second important policy consideration is that we not threaten with disabling civil liability innocent parties who are engaged in socially useful activities, such as researchers who have no reason to believe that their use of a particular cell sample is, or may be, against a donor's wishes.

To reach an appropriate balance of these policy considerations is extremely important. In its report to Congress, the Office of Technology Assessment emphasized that "[u]ncertainty about how courts will resolve disputes between specimen sources and specimen users could be detrimental to both academic researchers and the infant biotechnology industry, particularly when the rights are asserted long after the specimen was obtained. The assertion of rights by sources would affect not only [] the researcher who obtained the original specimen, but perhaps other researchers as well.["]

"Biological materials are routinely distributed to other researchers for experimental purposes, and scientists who obtain cell lines or other specimen-derived products, such as gene clones, from the original researcher could also be sued under certain legal theories [such as conversion]. Furthermore, the uncertainty could affect product developments as well as research. Since inventions containing human tissues and cells may be patented and licensed for commercial use, companies are unlikely to invest heavily in developing, manufacturing, or marketing a product when uncertainty about clear title exists." ...

We need not, however, make an arbitrary choice between liability and nonliability. Instead, an examination of the relevant policy considerations suggests an appropriate balance: Liability based upon existing disclosure obligations, rather than an unprecedented extension of the conversion theory, protects patients' rights of privacy and autonomy without unnecessarily hindering research.

To be sure, the threat of liability for conversion might help to enforce patients' rights indirectly. This is because physicians might be able to avoid liability by obtaining patients' consent, in the broadest possible terms, to any conceivable subsequent research use of excised cells. Unfortunately, to extend the conversion theory would utterly sacrifice the other goal of protecting innocent parties. Since conversion is a strict liability tort, it would impose liability on all those into whose hands the cells come, whether or not the particular defendant participated in, or knew of, the inadequate disclosures that violated the patient's right to make an informed decision. In contrast to the conversion theory, the fiduciary-duty and informed-consent theories protect the patient directly, without punishing innocent parties or creating disincentives to the conduct of socially beneficial research....

The extension of conversion law into this area will hinder research by restricting access to the necessary raw materials. Thousands of human cell lines already exist in tissue repositories, such as the American Type Culture Collection and those operated by the National Institutes of Health and the American Cancer Society. These repositories respond to tens of thousands of requests for samples annually. Since the patent office requires the holders of patents on cell lines to make samples available to anyone, many patent holders place their cell lines in repositories to avoid the administrative burden of responding to requests. At present, human cell lines are routinely copied and distributed to other researchers for experimental purposes, usually free of charge. This exchange of scientific materials, which still is relatively free and efficient, will surely be compromised if each cell sample becomes the potential subject matter of a lawsuit.

To expand liability by extending conversion law into this area would have a broad impact. The House Committee on Science and Technology of the United States Congress found that "49 percent of the researchers at medical institutions surveyed used human tissues or cells in their research." Many receive grants from the National Institute of Health for this work. In addition, "there are nearly 350 commercial biotechnology firms in the United States actively engaged in biotechnology research and commercial product development and approximately 25 to 30 percent appear to be engaged in research to develop a human therapeutic or diagnostic reagent.... Most, but not all, of the human therapeutic products are derived from human tissues and cells, or human cell lines or cloned genes."

In deciding whether to create new tort duties we have in the past considered the impact that expanded liability would have on activities that are important to society, such as research. For example, in *Brown v. Superior Court*, 44 Cal.3d 1049 [(Super. Ct. 1988)], the fear that strict product liability would frustrate pharmaceutical research led us to hold that a drug manufacturer's liability should not be measured by those standards. We wrote that, "[i]f drug manufacturers were subject to strict liability, they might be reluctant to undertake research programs to develop some pharmaceuticals that would prove beneficial or to distribute others that are available to be marketed, because of the fear of large adverse monetary judgments."

As in *Brown*, the theory of liability that Moore urges us to endorse threatens to destroy the economic incentive to conduct important medical research. If the use of cells in research is a conversion, then with every cell sample a researcher purchases a ticket in a litigation lottery. Because liability for conversion is predicated on a continuing ownership interest, "companies are unlikely to invest heavily in developing, manufacturing, or marketing a product when uncertainty about clear title exists." In our view, borrowing again from *Brown*, "[i]t is not unreasonable to conclude in these circumstances that the imposition of a harsher test for liability would not further the public interest in the development and availability of these important products." ...

If the scientific users of human cells are to be held liable for failing to investigate the consensual pedigree of their raw materials, we believe the Legislature should make that decision. Complex policy choices affecting all society are involved, and "[l]egislatures, in making such policy decisions, have the ability to gather empirical evidence, solicit the advice of experts, and hold hearings at which all interested parties present evidence and express their views...." Legislative competence to act in this area is demonstrated by the existing statutes governing the use and disposition of human biological materials.... Legislative interest is demonstrated by the extensive study recently commissioned by the United States Congress.... Commentators are also recommending legislative solutions.

Finally, there is no pressing need to impose a judicially created rule of strict liability, since enforcement of physicians' disclosure obligations will protect patients against the very type of harm with which Moore was threatened. So long as a physician discloses research and economic interests that may affect his judgment, the patient is protected from conflicts of interest. Aware of any conflicts, the patient can make an informed decision to consent to treatment, or to withhold consent and look elsewhere for medical assistance. As already discussed, enforcement of physicians' disclosure obligations protects patients directly, without hindering the socially useful activities of innocent researchers.

For these reasons, we hold that the allegations of Moore's third amended complaint state a cause of action for breach of fiduciary duty or lack of informed consent, but not conversion.

Wright v. Fred Hutchinson Cancer Research Center

269 F.Supp.2d 1286 (W.D. Wash. 2002)

LASNIK, DISTRICT JUDGE.

[Plaintiffs' claims arose from the participation of their respective deceased family members in a series of clinical trials at The Fred Hutchinson Cancer Research Center in Seattle. These trials were generally designed to test the theory that depletion of T cells in donor bone marrow would reduce the risk of graft-versus-host disease following transplantation. The original protocol, Protocol 126, and its related consent form were amended a number of times between 1981 and 1993. This ultimately resulted in a series of ten trials, each of which involved slightly different procedures and/or treatment regimens.[49]]

The Fred Hutchinson Cancer Research Center ("the Hutch"), E. Donnall Thomas, John A. Hansen, Paul J. Martin, and Robert Day seek dismissal of plaintiffs' First, Second, Third, and Fourth Causes of Action. Those causes of action assert breaches of the right to be treated with dignity, violations of federal regulations, breaches of the Assurance Agreement between the Hutch and the Department of Health and Human Services, and violations of 42 U.S.C. § 1983 and § 1985 respectively. Each of these claims is considered below.

First Cause of Action: Breach of the Right to be Treated with Dignity

Although the First Cause of Action appears to set forth a distinct claim for the breach of a right created by the Nuremberg Code and the Declaration of Helsinki, plaintiffs now assert that the precepts set forth in those documents are simply evidence of this country's recognition that certain rights are fundamental under the due process clause of the Fourteenth Amendment. Plaintiffs have disavowed any private right of action under the Nuremberg Code and/or the Declaration of Helsinki making judgment on the First Cause of Action appropriate....

Second Cause of Action: 21 C.F.R. §§ 210–211, 21 C.F.R. §§ 601 and 610, and 45 C.F.R. § 46

Plaintiffs' Second Cause of Action asserts violations of federal regulations, namely 21 C.F.R. §§ 210–211, 21 C.F.R. §§ 601 and 610, and 45 C.F.R. § 46, which regulate the manufacture and control of investigational biological drugs used in clinical trials and establish certain protections for human research subjects at institutions such as the Hutch. Plaintiffs have apparently abandoned their attempt to bring a cause of action di-

---

49. Wright v. The Fred Hutchinson Cancer Research Center, 2001 WL 1782714, 1 (W.D. Wash. 2001).

rectly under the federal regulations and now assert that such regulations are enforceable through an action under § 1983 of the Civil Rights Act. Section 1983 provides a remedy for the deprivation of "rights, privileges, or immunities secured by the Constitution and laws" of the United States. "In order to seek redress through § 1983, ... a plaintiff must assert the violation of a federal *right,* not merely a violation of federal *law.*"

Only Congress can create new rights enforceable under § 1983: agency regulations cannot give rise to a private cause of action where the authorizing statute does not confer such a right. *See Gonzaga Univ. v. Doe,* 536 U.S. 273 (2002) ("if Congress wishes to create new rights enforceable under § 1983, it must do so in clear and unambiguous terms").... Because plaintiffs have not identified any statutory basis for the private rights of action they seek to assert, their claims under 21 C.F.R. §§ 210–211, 21 C.F.R. §§ 601 and 610, and 45 C.F.R. § 46 must fail.

Even if the Court were to assume that agency regulations could establish a federal right enforceable under § 1983, the regulations at issue here do not meet the *Cort v. Ash,* 422 U.S. 66, 78 (1975), criteria or the recent pronouncement of the Supreme Court in *Gonzaga Univ.* First, the regulations are not "phrased in terms of the persons benefitted." ... Rather, they require action on the part of research institutions such as the Hutch (45 C.F.R. § 46.103), investigators such as the individual defendants (45 C.F.R. § 46.116), manufacturers of biological and drug products (21 C.F.R. §§ 211.25 and 211.180, 21 C.F.R. §§ 601.2 and 610.1), and the heads of various governmental departments and agencies (21 C.F.R. § 601.5, 45 C.F.R. § 46.122). Where a statute is not focused on the individual benefitted, the courts "rarely impute to Congress an intent to create a private right of action." Second, the regulations are designed to control the aggregate behavior of research facilities, investigators, and drug manufacturers by subjecting them to overarching standards of conduct. Particularly with respect to 45 C.F.R. § 46, *de minimis* violations of the regulations appear to be of little concern to the regulating agency: only "material" failures to comply will result in sanctions. *See* 45 C.F.R. § 46.123. Such regulations are not concerned with "whether the needs of any particular person have been satisfied" and they do not, therefore, give rise to an individual right. Finally, the enforcement sections of the regulations provide for regulatory action. *See* 21 C.F.R. § 210.1(b), 45 C.F.R. § 46.122. Although such regulatory enforcement mechanisms do not explicitly preclude simultaneous enforcement through private litigation, they counsel against finding an intent to create individually enforceable private causes of action.[50]

Third Cause of Action: The Belmont Report: Breach of the Assurance Agreement

Plaintiffs assert that they are third-party beneficiaries to a contract between the Hutch and the Department of Health and Human Services in which the Hutch agreed to follow certain guidelines for the ethical conduct of research involving human subjects, to abide by all federal regulatory requirements for such research, and to present all such research to an Institutional Review Board for approval. As pointed out by defendants, however, "[p]arties that benefit from a government contract are generally assumed to be incidental beneficiaries, and may not enforce the contract absent a clear intent to the contrary." While human subjects of research conducted at the Hutch would clearly benefit from defendants' compliance with the Assurance Agreement, plaintiffs

50. This analysis is bolstered by the fact that Congress contemplated, but ultimately rejected, a statutory mechanism for the compensation of individuals and their families for injuries resulting from their participation in human subjects research. S. Rep. No 93-381, at 90 (1973).

have not identified any language in or provision of the Agreement that provides subjects with an actionable right, a fact which is sufficient to rebut the contention that plaintiffs are intended beneficiaries.

Fourth Cause of Action: Violation of 42 U.S.C. § 1983 and § 1985

As discussed above, § 1983 of the Civil Rights Act provides a remedy for the deprivation of "rights, privileges, or immunities secured by the Constitution and laws" of the United States. Plaintiffs allege deprivations of their rights to substantive and procedural due process under the Fourteenth Amendment.[51] Defendants assert that they are entitled to qualified immunity from suit because their conduct did not violate clearly established constitutional or statutory rights of which a reasonable person would have known during the period 1981 to 1993. Both plaintiffs' claims and defendants' defense require the Court to first consider whether "[t]aken in the light most favorable to the party asserting the injury, do the facts alleged show the [defendants'] conduct violated a constitutional right?"[52]

For purposes of this analysis, the Court assumes that plaintiffs' decedents were deprived of life and/or a constitutionally protected liberty interest. The relevant inquiry, therefore, is whether the procedural safeguards included in the informed consent process were constitutionally adequate. Plaintiffs do not challenge the adequacy of the statutory or regulatory protections provided for human subjects of investigational research. Nor do plaintiffs challenge the overall informed consent process established by the Hutch and its Investigational Review Board. Their claim is not that these procedures were inadequate, but that they were not followed by defendants when they intentionally withheld information and/or interfered with the IRB review process. The adequacy of the process that is due, however, is not dependant on whether defendants violated the state's established procedures. The due process clause requires that the state provide constitutionally adequate procedures: it does not guarantee their flawless implementation in every instance.

Plaintiffs' allegations that their decedents were not provided with all of the information necessary to understand the proposed treatment, the possible risks and benefits of the research protocols, or defendants' financial interests and that defendants interfered with the proper workings of the IRB do not state a § 1983 claim under the Supreme Court's decisions in *Parratt v. Taylor,* 451 U.S. 527 (1981) (*rev'd on other grounds, Daniels v. Williams,* 474 U.S. 327 (1986)), *Hudson v. Palmer,* 468 U.S. 517 (1984), and *Zinermon v. Burch,* 494 U.S. 113 (1990). The *Parratt /Hudson* doctrine provides that a random, unauthorized deprivation of a protected interest, whether negligently or intentionally done, does not violate due process as long as the state furnishes an adequate

51. In light of the procedural posture of this motion, the Court will accept as true plaintiffs' allegations that defendants were acting under the color and authority of state law for purposes of the § 1983 analysis.

52. In an effort to prevent constitutional law from stagnating, the Supreme Court insists that the trial court determine whether defendants' conduct violated a constitutional right before determining whether the constitutional right was clearly established at the time of plaintiffs' injury. Without such a two-part analysis, individual rights would be frozen in time as each reviewing court simply determined whether or not defendants' conduct had been found unconstitutional in the past. By first evaluating the constitutional claim on its merits, constitutional rights may develop over time even if the defendant in a particular case is immune from suit because the right found to have been violated was not clearly established. If similar conduct should occur in the future, the earlier finding that the conduct implicated a constitutional right would ensure that the later defendant would be held responsible and would not be entitled to qualified immunity.

post-deprivation remedy.... In such circumstances, the "meaningful post-deprivation remedy" provided by state tort law is all the process that is due....

Because the distinctions that kept the Supreme Court from applying the *Parratt/Hudson* doctrine in *Zinermon* are not present in this case, that doctrine governs plaintiffs' claims. Plaintiffs would therefore have a § 1983 claim for violation of procedural due process only if the state's post-deprivation remedies are inadequate. Washington's relevant tort claims provision, RCW 7.70.050, provides a damages remedy to persons who have suffered from the state's failure to obtain informed consent. Plaintiffs have not challenged the adequacy of that provision and have, in fact, asserted a claim thereunder. Given the existence of postdeprivation remedies that are adequate to cure what would otherwise be an unconstitutional deprivation of "life, liberty or property," plaintiffs can allege no set of facts that would entitle them to relief under a procedural due process theory.

Although the case law regarding procedural due process claims is still developing, the above analysis maintains the important distinctions between constitutional violations and state law torts. The *Parratt/Hudson* doctrine was meant to prevent the Fourteenth Amendment from becoming a "font of tort law to be superimposed upon whatever systems may already be administered by the States." Section 1983 must be preserved as a remedy for those deprivations which the state accomplishes without adequate process of law, such as when a state, through its legislature or authorized policymaker, consciously decides to ignore the protections guaranteed by the Constitution. It should not be employed to remedy deprivations which occur at the hands of state employees who are acting in direct contravention of state policies, procedures, and requirements that were designed to guarantee the rights of its citizens.

Because defendants' alleged actions in failing to obtain informed consent were random and unauthorized and because there are adequate post-deprivation remedies for their alleged conduct, plaintiffs' Fourteenth Amendment procedural due process rights were not violated and their related § 1983 claim must be dismissed.

Substantive due process protects individuals from certain arbitrary, wrongful, government actions "regardless of the fairness of the procedures used to implement them." ...

For purposes of this analysis, the Court is willing to assume that most, if not all, citizens of the United States would recoil in horror from the idea that our government could conduct the type of involuntary, non-therapeutic research on human subjects that gave rise to the Doctors Trial following World War II. As the cases cited by the parties show, however, such experimentation has occurred in this country with disturbing regularity. The judiciary has not hesitated to find that, where the human research subjects were not told that they were participating in an experiment and/or the government conducted the experiments knowing they had no therapeutic value, the subject's constitutionally protected right to life and/or liberty had been violated. *See, e.g., Heinrich v. Sweet,* 62 F.Supp.2d 282 (D. Mass. 1999) (government utilized false pretenses to lure plaintiffs into participating in radiation experiments which the government knew had no therapeutic value); *Stadt v. University of Rochester,* 921 F.Supp. 1023 (W.D.N.Y. 1996) (plaintiff, who thought she was receiving medical treatment for scleroderma, was injected with plutonium without her knowledge or consent); *In re Cincinnati Radiation Litig.,* 874 F.Supp. 796 (S.D. Ohio 1995) (plaintiffs were not informed that the radiation they were receiving was part of a military experiment rather than treatment of their cancer)....

Unlike the circumstances presented in *Stanley, Heinrich, Stadt,* and the radiation litigation, the true nature of the experiments in which plaintiffs' decedents took part was not hidden by defendants and the proposed treatment regimen, while unproven, was thought, or at least hoped, to be of benefit to the individual participants. Plaintiffs are asking this Court to find that an individual's voluntary participation in an experimental, therapeutic treatment regimen can give rise to a constitutional violation if the treating physician fails to adequately inform the patient of the risks, benefits, and alternatives to the experimental treatment and/or potential conflicts of interest unrelated to the treatment regimen itself. Plaintiffs have not alleged that the Protocol 126 series of experiments were designed to do anything other than determine whether certain treatment regimens were effective against the type of cancer from which plaintiffs' decedents suffered. At most, plaintiffs argue that defendants failed to disclose certain important facts regarding the protocol and their own pecuniary interests in the outcome of the experiments, but such failures, even if proven, would not alter the therapeutic nature of the protocol or the fact that plaintiffs' decedents knew they were participating in an experiment. Nor is the nature of the experiments disproven simply because the outcome was not what the researchers expected. Whether the therapies proved to be wildly effective or heart-breaking failures, in the absence of allegations that defendants hid the true nature of the experiments and/or conducted them for non-therapeutic reasons, there is no constitutional claim....

Keeping in mind the Supreme Court's admonition that courts should exercise judicial restraint when asked to expand the rights protected under the substantive due process clause, the Court finds that the type of wrongful conduct alleged in plaintiffs' Second Amended Complaint, namely defendants' failure to make disclosures necessary to the informed consent process in a therapeutic, experimental setting, does not implicate rights that are so rooted in the tradition and conscience of our people as to be ranked as fundamental. A doctor's tortious failure to obtain informed consent is not a threat to our citizens' enjoyment of ordered liberty, even when the doctor is employed by the state. Although the failure to obtain informed consent necessarily throws some doubt on the voluntariness of the patient's participation in a research study, such a failure does not raise the specter of the type of involuntary, non-therapeutic experimentation which shocked the nation after World War II and gave rise to the Nuremberg Code.... [T]he wrongful conduct alleged by plaintiffs does not violate a right secured under the Fourteenth Amendment due process clause.

Plaintiffs' § 1985 claim turns on the allegation that defendants conspired to deprive plaintiffs' decedents of their due process rights under the Fourteenth Amendment. Having found that the patients' due process rights were not violated and in light of the absence of any allegations of "racial, or perhaps otherwise class-based, invidiously discriminatory animus" on defendants' part, the Court finds that plaintiffs' § 1985 claim fails as a matter of law.

For all of the foregoing reasons, defendants' motion for judgment as to plaintiffs' first four causes of action is granted....

Darke v. Estate of Isner

17 Mass. L.Rptr 689, 2004 WL 1325635 (Mass. Super.)

Sanders, Justice of the Superior Court

This is a medical malpractice and wrongful death action. It stems from the death of Roger J. Darke following his participation in an experimental gene therapy program. The case is now before the Court on a Motion for Partial Summary Judgment brought by two of the five defendants, the Estate of Dr. Jeffrey Isner and Caritas St. Elizabeth's Medical Center of Boston, Inc. ("St Elizabeth's"). They contend that judgment should enter in their favor on that portion of Count III in Plaintiff's Amended Complaint which alleges that they can be held legally liable because they failed to disclose to Mr. Darke the financial interest that they had in the experimental program. For the following reasons, I conclude that the Motion must be *Denied.*[53]

BACKGROUND

... Roger Darke suffered from chronic heart disease. In November, 1993, he underwent triple bypass heart surgery. In 1998, he once again began to experience chest pains, and in January 1999, it was determined that the vein grafts in his heart had occluded. Dr[.] Lance Larsen (not named as a defendant) suggested that Mr. Darke consider an experimental gene therapy program conducted at St. Elizabeth's by Dr. Isner. After consulting with Dr. Isner, Mr. Darke and his wife agreed to his participation, and he was admitted to St. Elizabeth's on May 24, 1999 to undergo the treatment. The next morning, he underwent surgery in which the gene therapy was delivered. Less than 24 hours later, he died.

In connection with his participation in the program, Mr. Darke executed an "Informed Consent" form which disclosed the experimental nature of the procedure and listed the medical risks associated with it. The Motion before the Court does not concern the plaintiff's claim that the disclosure of medical information was inadequate. Rather, the Motion concerns the claim that both Dr. Isner and St. Elizabeth's may be held legally liable because they failed to disclose to Mr. Darke the financial stake that they held in the gene therapy program. The allegations relevant to that claim (together with the reasonable inferences which can be drawn therefrom) include the following.

Sometime prior to Mr. Darke's death, Dr. Isner, who was chief of cardiovascular research at St. Elizabeth's, developed an experimental treatment for coronary artery disease which involved the injection of a particular gene directly into the heart. In connection therewith, he formed a corporation with other individuals named Vascular Genetics, Inc. ("VGI") (also named as a defendant). Dr. Isner and St. Elizabeth's each held a 20 percent ownership interest in VGI. Because of this ownership interest, Dr. Isner and St. Elizabeth's had a financial incentive to encourage patients to participate in the program. If the gene therapy program was successful, then both Dr. Isner and St. Elizabeth's stood to profit financially in proportion to their ownership stake. Neither Dr. Isner nor anyone else from St. Elizabeth's disclosed these facts to the Darkes. If they had, then Mr. Darke would not have elected to participate. For purposes of this Motion, this Court assumes that the gene therapy was a substantial contributing factor to Mr. Darke's death.

DISCUSSION

This Motion raises a question of first impression for this Court: is the Massachusetts common law definition of informed consent broad enough to permit the imposition of tort liability on a doctor who fails to disclose to his patient that he has a financial interest in the treatment that he recommends? I conclude that it is.

The seminal Massachusetts case on the doctrine of informed consent is *Harnish v. Children's Hospital Medical Center,* 387 Mass. 152 (1982) ("*Harnish*"). In that case, the

53. The defendants also moved for summary judgment on so much of the Amended Complaint as seeks recovery for loss of consortium. For the reasons set forth in the defendants' Memorandum of Law, this Court in a margin note allowed that Motion.

Supreme Judicial Court noted that the common law has long recognized the individual's interest in being free from the nonconsensual invasion of his bodily integrity. In the medical context, that means that a patient may decline to undergo treatment even if, in the eyes of the medical professional, the treatment is in his best interest. Because of this right of the patient to decide for himself, the doctor has an obligation to disclose certain information to the patient so that he may make an informed decision. On the other hand, "there are limits to what society or an individual can reasonably expect of a physician" regarding what matters need to be disclosed. Communication of scientific information to a patient with no medical training can be difficult, and there may be no limit to those risks of a proposed treatment which are only remotely possible. Accordingly, the SJC held that the physician's duty to share information with his patient "depends upon what information he should reasonably recognize is material to the plaintiff's decision." If the physician fails to divulge sufficient information to enable the patient to make an informed judgment about whether to give or withhold consent to a medical procedure, then that constitutes medical malpractice.

The defendants argue that the rule announced in *Harnish* was limited to the disclosure of medical information, not information regarding a doctor's financial interest in the treatment itself. Certainly, the SJC in *Harnish* discussed the rule solely in medical terms. Thus, the SJC stated that a doctor must disclose "significant medical information," which includes "the nature and probability of risks involved, the benefits to be reasonably expected, the inability of the physician to predict results ... the likely result of no treatment, and the available alternatives, including their risks and benefits." This Court does not read *Harnish* to mean that *only* medical information need be disclosed, however. The touchstone to the inquiry is whether the information is material: if it is information which would be significant to a reasonable person in the patient's position, then the physician has a duty to disclose it.

Although there is no appellate decision in Massachusetts squarely addressing the issue before this Court, courts in other states have held that a physician's duty of disclosure extends to non-medical information. Thus, in *Moore v. Regents of University of California* ... the California Supreme Court reversed the trial court's dismissal of a claim for medical malpractice which predicated liability on the doctor's failure to tell his patient of his intent to use the patient's cells in potentially lucrative medical research. Acknowledging that the validity of a patient's consent typically arises from the failure to disclose medical risks, the Court noted that the real question is what is material to a patient's decision. If a doctor's judgment is influenced by a profit motive, then that is something that his patient should know. Similarly, in *D.A.B. v. Brown*, 570 N.W.2d 168, 170 (Minn.Ct.App.1997), the Minnesota Court of Appeals (relying on state professional ethical standards) held that a doctor's failure to disclose to a patient that he received payments from a drug company for prescribing a certain drug "presents a classic informed consent issue." "It is well accepted that patients deserve medical opinions about treatment plans and referrals unsullied by conflicting motives." Finally, in *Shea v. Esensten*, 107 F.3d 625 (8th Cir.1997), the court held that the plaintiff stated a claim where the allegation was that his health care provider failed to tell him about the financial incentives that it offered its employees to discourage them from making referrals. In order for the patient to make a fully informed decision about whether to trust his doctor's recommendation that a cardiology referral was not necessary, he should have been told about the doctor's financial stake.

Further support for this Court's conclusion is found in various guidelines promulgated by professional medical organizations as well as by the federal government. For example, the Association of American Medical Colleges requires that all consent forms used in connection with research by its members should disclose to any participant the existence of any significant financial interest that the researcher has in the treatment itself. And the American Medical Association's Council on Ethical and Judicial Affairs has stated that physicians working in the managed care setting should disclose to their patients financial incentives and restrictions placed on them by the HMO. See *Ethical Issues in Managed Care,* 273 J.A.M.A. 330 (Jan. 25, 1995). In an April 2000 policy statement, the American Society of Gene Therapy counseled against any clinical investigator having "equity, stock options or comparable arrangements in companies" sponsoring the research. And the Code of Federal Regulations requires clinical investigators conducting experimental treatment to disclose to the patient any benefit that might be gained by third persons as a result of the treatment. 21 C.F.R. § 50.20, § 50.25. Although these regulations are neither directly on point in the instant case nor controlling on this question of state common law, they do indicate a trend towards requiring physicians to disclose non-medical information to the patient.

Finally, the plaintiff offers the expert opinion of Dr. Cary Gross. She states that, at least in those circumstances where the procedure is highly experimental, a reasonable physician in Dr. Isner's position would have disclosed his (and St. Elizabeth's) financial interest in VGI, and that his failure to do so fell below the standard of medical care required by someone practicing his specialty. This opinion (together with the other allegations in the Plaintiff's Amended Complaint) creates a triable issue as to whether the defendants can be held liable for the failure to tell Mr. Darke about the financial interest that they had in the program which was recommended to him. As one Court stated, the question is not whether the physician must as a matter of law disclose any given fact to his patient, but rather whether the jury should be informed about a failure to make that disclosure and make up its own mind as to whether the information was material or not under the circumstances. *Arato v. Avedon,* 5 Cal.4th 1172, 1184, 858 P.2d 598, 23 Cal.Rptr.2d 131 (1993). Thus, the defendants in the instant case would be entitled to prevail on their Motion for Summary Judgment only if this Court were willing to conclude that such information cannot as a matter of law be considered material.[54] This I am not willing to do.

CONCLUSION AND ORDER

For all the foregoing reasons, the Defendants' Motion for Summary Judgment is hereby *DENIED.*

Notes & Questions

1. In *Moore,* the court refused to find a property right in the sorts of human tissue involved in the dispute, but stopped short of rejecting property rights for human tissues in all cases. In which kinds of tissue, and in what situations, should a property right lie?

2. The *Moore* court also declined to hold that Moore had intellectual property rights in his tissues, largely based on: (1) the scientific distinction between primary cells and cell lines established from them; and (2) the research goal, which was to discover the

---

54. Indeed, another way of viewing this Motion is as an attempt to foreclose the plaintiff from introducing evidence concerning Dr. Isner's and St. Elizabeth's financial interest in VGI. Because I conclude that this interest is relevant to the question of informed consent, it necessarily follows that this information should be admitted at trial (provided it meets other evidentiary requirements).

gene (shared by all humans) responsible for expressing a particular lymphokine and the process to produce relatively large quantities of that lymphokine. We will return to these intellectual property issues in the next chapter, but consider whether you agree with those who still feel that there is a compelling "but for" type argument in favor of awarding some ownership and/or compensation rights to Moore for his primary cells that gave rise to the admittedly distinct cell line. Clearly the defendants attached substantial research and commercial value to Moore's specific T-lymphocytes: not just any T-lymphocytes from any human would have worked. At the same time, Golde and Quan realized that Moore's T-lymphocytes' overproduction of lymphokine was not unique, but rather was shared by T-lymphocytes infected with the HTLV-II virus in any human. So, Moore's particular T-lymphocytes were neither unique nor generic. Query whether Golde and Quan knew this before settling on using Moore's cells for their cell line, or whether they discovered this *through* their research on Moore's cells. What import might the answer to this question have on your intuition about equitable arguments in favor of Moore's claims?

3. The *Moore* court held that proper use of informed consent procedures—including disclosure of financial interests held by the researchers—adequately protects patients/subjects in Moore's position. This seems reasonable given the general legal principle that adequate notice and disclosure go a long way towards minimizing liability for new and/or unusual activities. But it is exactly these new and unusual activities—particularly in the field of high technology life sciences research—that may prove the hardest to obtain meaningful consent from subjects. It can be argued that such subjects cannot really give informed consent because they either: (1) cannot adequately be appraised of the procedure, risks, and consequences; or (2) they are in too compromised of a position because of their need to enroll in the study or procedure at hand as a last resort therapeutic alternative when others have failed. Can subjects really give meaningful informed consent in all cases? Should the consent be limited to just the risks associated with the procedure, or should it extend to give permission to researchers open-ended further research and commercialization based on the subject's body (parts)?

4. Should a court or legislature establish legal ownership of one's body (parts)? If it did, would this be simply a personal property right, or also an intellectual property right—meaning that one would presumptively own any intellectual property rights that may attach to her body (parts)? Researchers frequently employ *material transfer agreements* ("MTAs") to transfer biological materials among themselves to document legal ownership of such materials. Should human subjects research informed consent forms contain an explicit MTA? Could this be a separate negotiation (for value), similar to those suggested in the field of data mining of personal information? Or is the value too indeterminate (in both areas)?

5. A tragic capstone to the developments in this area was the death of Jesse Gelsinger, an eighteen-year-old from Arizona who died in a gene therapy experiment at the University of Pennsylvania in 1999. *See* Sheryl Gay Stolberg, *The Biotech Death of Jesse Gelsinger*, The New York Times (November 28, 1999). At first, Jesse's father did not blame the doctors involved or the University. But after financial ties between some of the physicians and a biotechnology company set up to commercialize the gene therapy being investigated were disclosed, he changed his mind and brought suit. Even though the case settled before going to trial, the complaint and other materials can be found at the website of the law firm that brought the case on behalf of Jesse's father. *See* Sherman, Silverstein, Kohl, Rose and Podolsky Law Offices, *Gelsinger Complaint*, http://www.sskrplaw.com/gene/gelsinger.html.

6. In part because of the Gelsinger tragedy and the public outcry following it, the Association of American Medical Colleges (AAMC) convened its Task Force on Financial Conflicts of Interest in Clinical Research which issued a set of policies and guidelines for financial conflicts of interests involving member schools and their respective faculties. *See* AAMC, Task Force on Financial Conflicts of Interest in Clinical Research: Protecting Subjects, Preserving Trust, Promoting Progress—Policy and Guidelines for the Oversight of Individual Financial Interests in Human Subjects Research (December 2001), *available at* http://www.aamc.org/members/coitf/firstreport.pdf; *see also* AAMC, Protecting Subjects, Preserving Trust, Promoting Progress II: Principles and Recommendations for Oversight of an Institution's Financial Interests in Human Subjects Research (October 2002), *available at* http://www.aamc.org/members/coitf/2002coireport.pdf.

7. The Gelsinger tragedy also highlights the role of federal regulatory agencies. In particular, the NIH Recombinant DNA Advisory Committee ("RAC") held extensive hearings on the matter at its meeting and symposium held from December 8–10, 1999. *See* RAC, Minutes Of Symposium And Meeting, December 8–10, 1999, http://www4.od.nih.gov/oba/rac/minutes/1299rac.pdf. A final report was issued in January 2002. *See* NIH, *Report: Assessment of Adenoviral Vector Safety and Toxicity: Report of the National Institutes of Health Recombinant DNA Advisory Committee*, 13 HUM. GENE THERAPY 3 (Jan. 1, 2002), *available at* http://www4.od.nih.gov/oba/rac/adsat_rpt.pdf. The NIH also has amended its Guidelines for Research Involving Recombinant DNA Molecules (April 2002), http://www4.od.nih.gov/oba/rac/guidelines_02/NIH_Gdlnes_lnk_2002z.pdf. After its own investigations were completed, the FDA issued warning letters to two of the doctors involved. *See* FDA, Warning Letter to Dr. Raper (Nov. 30, 2000), http://www.fda.gov/foi/warning_letters/m4912n.pdf; FDA, Warning Letter to Dr. Batshaw (Nov. 30, 2000), http://www.fda.gov/foi/warning_letters/m4911n.pdf. Finally, note that the FDA had just amended its regulations in 1998 regarding the disclosure of financial interests by investigators (Financial Disclosure by Clinical Investigators, 21 C.F.R. part 54). *See* FDA, Financial Disclosure by Clinical Investigators, Final Rule, 63 FED. REG. 5233 (February 2, 1998). However, in response to a petition by the Pharmaceutical Research Manufacturers Association (PhRMA), the FDA amended these rules on December 31, 1998, to become effective on February 2, 1999. *See* FDA, Financial Disclosure by Clinical Investigators, Final Rule; Action on Petition for Reconsideration, 63 FED. REG. 72171 (December 31, 1998).

E. Distinct Populations and Community Consent

A third kind of genetics research is distinct from both the therapeutic medical practice and the non-therapeutic research primarily considered so far. Whereas the first two categories are still directed towards an ultimate therapeutic regime, this third category instead focuses essentially on data collection and screening techniques. While these latter outputs can lead of course to discovery or indication of specific therapies for individuals, the direct end of this category of genetic testing and screening is purely informational.

Accordingly, genetic testing and screening frequently require information and sample collection from large numbers of individuals. Often, the desirable group is a distinct population with certain recurrent traits that appear to have a genetic or hereditary basis. At the same time, a number of the populations that fit this model are minority and/or ethnic groups with a history of discriminatory treatment, including by the medical and scientific establishments. The result can be a volatile mix exacerbated by the strong contemporary trend towards commercialization in these medical and scientific communities.

Greenberg v. Miami Children's Hospital Research Institute, Inc.

264 F.Supp.2d 1064 (S.D. Fl. 2003)

Moreno, District Judge.

This case presents an unfortunate legal dilemma set against the backdrop of a historic breakthrough in the treatment of a previously intractable genetic disorder. Both parties in this case were jointly engaged in a noble and dogged pursuit to detect and find a cure for a fatal genetic disorder called Canavan disease, a rare genetic disease that occurs most frequently in Ashkenazi Jewish families.

Plaintiffs, a group of individuals and non-profit institutions, are attempting to assert legal rights against Defendant researcher and his research institution's commercialization of the fruits of their Canavan disease research. Before the Court is Defendants' Motions to Dismiss pursuant to Fed.R.Civ.P. 12(b)(6) for failure to state a claim upon which relief may be granted. Because the Court finds that Plaintiffs have failed to allege sufficient facts as to all their claims except unjust enrichment, the motions are GRANTED *in part.*

I. BACKGROUND

Plaintiffs Daniel Greenberg ("Greenberg"), Fern Kupfer ("Kupfer"), Frieda Eisen ("Eisen"), David Green ("Green"), Canavan Foundation, Dor Yeshorim, and National Tay-Sachs and Allied Diseases Association, Inc. (collectively "Plaintiffs") brought this diversity action for damages and equitable and injunctive relief to redress Defendants' alleged breach of informed consent, breach of fiduciary duty, unjust enrichment, fraudulent concealment, conversion, and misappropriation of trade secrets. The individual plaintiffs Greenberg, Kupfer, Eisen, and Green are parents of children who were afflicted with Canavan disease. The other Plaintiffs are non-profit organizations that provided funding and information to Defendants to research and discover the Canavan disease gene. Defendants are the physician-researcher, Dr. Reuben Matalon ("Matalon"), Variety Children's Hospital d/b/a Miami Children's Hospital ("MCH"), and the hospital's research affiliate, Miami Children's Hospital Research Institute ("MCHRI").

The Complaint alleges a tale of a successful research collaboration gone sour. In 1987, Canavan disease still remained a mystery—there was no way to identify who was a carrier of the disease, nor was there a way to identify a fetus with Canavan disease. Plaintiff Greenberg approached Dr. Matalon, a research physician who was then affiliated with the University of Illinois at Chicago for assistance. Greenberg requested Matalon's involvement in discovering the genes that were ostensibly responsible for this fatal disease, so that tests could be administered to determine carriers and allow for prenatal testing for the disease.

At the outset of the collaboration, Greenberg and the Chicago Chapter of the National Tay-Sachs and Allied Disease Association, Inc. ("NTSAD") located other Canavan families and convinced them to provide tissue (such as blood, urine, and autopsy samples), financial support, and aid in identifying the location of Canavan families internationally. The other individual Plaintiffs began supplying Matalon with the same types of information and samples beginning in the late 1980s. Greenberg and NTSAD also created a confidential database and compilation—the Canavan registry—with epidemiological, medical and other information about the families.

Defendant Matalon became associated in 1990 with Defendants Miami Children's Hospital Research Institute, Inc. and Variety Children's Hospital d/b/a Miami Children's Hospital. Defendant Matalon continued his relationship with the Plaintiffs after his move, accepting more tissue and blood samples as well as financial support.

The individual Plaintiffs allege that they provided Matalon with these samples and confidential information "with the understanding and expectations that such samples and information would be used for the specific purpose of researching Canavan disease and identifying mutations in the Canavan disease which could lead to carrier detection within their families and benefit the population at large." Plaintiffs further allege that it was their "understanding that any carrier and prenatal testing developed in connection with the research for which they were providing essential support would be provided on an affordable and accessible basis, and that Matalon's research would remain in the public domain to promote the discovery of more effective prevention techniques and treatments and, eventually, to effectuate a cure for Canavan disease." This understanding stemmed from their "experience in community testing for Tay-Sachs disease, another deadly genetic disease that occurs most frequently in families of Ashkenazi Jewish descent."

There was a breakthrough in the research in 1993. Using Plaintiffs' blood and tissue samples, familial pedigree information, contacts, and financial support, Matalon and his research team successfully isolated the gene responsible for Canavan disease. After this key advancement, Plaintiffs allege that they continued to provide Matalon with more tissue and blood in order to learn more about the disease and its precursor gene.

In September 1994, unbeknownst to Plaintiffs, a patent application was submitted for the genetic sequence that Defendants had identified. This application was granted in October 1997, and Dr. Matalon was listed as an inventor on the gene patent and related applications for the Canavan disease, Patent No. 5,679,635 (the "Patent"). Through patenting, Defendants acquired the ability to restrict any activity related to the Canavan disease gene, including without limitation: carrier and prenatal testing, gene therapy and other treatments for Canavan disease and research involving the gene and its mutations.

Although the Patent was issued in October 1997, Plaintiffs allege that they did not learn of it until November 1998, when MCH revealed their intention to limit Canavan disease testing through a campaign of restrictive licensing of the Patent. Specifically, on November 12, 1998, Plaintiffs allege that Defendants MCH and MCHRI began to "threaten" the centers that offered Canavan testing with possible enforcement actions regarding the recently-issued patent. Defendant MCH also began restricting public accessibility through negotiating exclusive licensing agreements and charging royalty fees.

Plaintiffs allege that at no time were they informed that Defendants intended to seek a patent on the research. Nor were they told of Defendants' intentions to commercialize the fruits of the research and to restrict access to Canavan disease testing.

Based on these facts, Plaintiffs filed a six-count complaint on October 30, 2000, against Defendants asserting the following causes of action: (1) lack of informed consent; (2) breach of fiduciary duty; (3) unjust enrichment; (4) fraudulent concealment; (5) conversion; and (6) misappropriation of trade secrets. Plaintiffs generally seek a permanent injunction restraining Defendants from enforcing their patent rights, damages in the form of all royalties Defendants have received on the Patent as well as all financial contributions Plaintiffs made to benefit Defendants' research. Plaintiffs allege that Defendants have earned significant royalties from Canavan disease testing in excess of $75,000 through enforcement of their gene patent, and that Dr. Matalon has personally profited by receiving a recent substantial federal grant to undertake further research on the gene patent....

III. ANALYSIS

...

A. Lack of Informed Consent

In Count I of the Complaint, the individual Plaintiffs, who served as research subjects, and the corporate plaintiff Dor Yeshorim claim that Defendants owed a duty of informed consent. The Complaint alleges a continuing duty of informed consent to disclose any information that might influence their decision to participate or decline to participate in his research. Defendants breached this duty, Plaintiffs claim, when they did not disclose the intent to patent and enforce for their own economic benefit the Canavan disease gene. The duty was also breached by the misrepresentation of the research purpose that Matalon had included on the written consent forms. Finally, the Plaintiffs allege that if they had known that the Defendants would "commercialize" the results of their contributions, they would not have made the contributions.

1. Duty to Obtain Informed Consent for Medical Research

Defendants first assert that the Complaint fails to state a claim because the duty of informed consent is only owed to patients receiving medical treatment. Furthermore, they claim that even if the duty extends to non-therapeutic research, it does not extend beyond the actual research to research results.

The doctrine of informed consent grew out of a treating physician's fiduciary duty to disclose to the patient all facts which might affect the patient's decision to allow medical treatment. The basic principle of informed consent has been embraced by tort law in order to guard a patient's control over decisions affecting his or her own health. *See Cruzan v. Dir., Mo. Dep't of Health,* 497 U.S. 261, 269 (1990). The state common law of informed consent is often fortified by statute. Florida's medical consent law, for example, applies to the patient/treating doctor relationship. Fla. Stat. § 766.103.

The question of informed consent in the context of medical research, however, is a relatively novel one in Florida. Medical consent law does not apply to medical researchers. *Id.; see also Cedars Med. Ctr., Inc. v. Jose R. Gomez,* 738 So.2d 362, 366 (Fla. 3d DCA 1999) (excluding Hospital from statutory duty of informed consent). Florida Statute § 760.40 does require, however, that a person's informed consent must be obtained when any genetic analysis is undertaken on his or her tissue.

Defendants argue that this statute is inapplicable to the case at bar because the statute does not apply to medical research, only test results. Moreover, none of the individual Plaintiffs have alleged that they were personally tested, just that they donated their genetic material. Furthermore, although Federal regulations do mandate that consent must be obtained from the subjects of medical research, the informed consent does not cover more than the research itself. *See, e.g.,* 21 C.F.R. §§50.1–50.27 (2000). Other courts in New York and Pennsylvania have dismissed attempts by patient plaintiffs to stretch the informed consent doctrine to cover medical research. *See Hecht v. Kaplan,* 645 N.Y.S.2d 51, 53 (N.Y.App.Div.1996) (blood test performed on unused vial of blood does not constitute human research sufficient to trigger informed consent law); *Doe v. Dyer-Goode,* 566 A.2d 889, 892–93 ([Pa. Super.] 1989) (additional test conducted on extracted sample of blood insufficient to permit action ground in battery (*i.e.* informed consent)). Plaintiffs contend these cases are distinguishable because they do not address informed consent in the research setting or the related issue of commercialization.

With Florida statutory law at best unclear on the duty of informed consent relating to medical research, Plaintiffs refer to cases in other jurisdictions where courts have found that researchers face a duty to obtain informed consent from their research subjects. *See Grimes v. Kennedy Krieger Inst.,* 782 A.2d 807 ([Md.] 2001) (medical researchers had duty to disclose that children participating in research study were subject to lead-based paint); *In re Cincinnati Radiation Litig.,* 874 F.Supp. 796 (S.D.Ohio 1995) (non-disclosure to patients about exposure to radiation).

Defendants counter that these cases are inapposite because Plaintiffs miss the crucial distinction between the use of medical research and human experimentation. Each of the cases cited by Plaintiffs as providing a duty of informed consent regarding medical research was based on some egregious practice, which Defendants argue is absent here. Additionally, there was no actual human experimentation as part of an ongoing relationship alleged in the Complaint.

Since the law regarding a duty of informed consent for research subjects is unsettled and fact-specific and further, Defendants conceded at oral argument that a duty does attach at some point in the relationship, the Court finds that in certain circumstances a medical researcher does have a duty of informed consent. Nevertheless, without clear guidance from Florida jurisprudence, the Court must consider whether this duty of informed consent in medical research can be extended to disclosure of a researcher's economic interests.

2. Extension of Duty of Informed Consent to the Researcher's Economic Interests

Defendants assert that extending a possible informed consent duty to disclosing economic interests has no support in established law, and more ominously, this requirement would have pernicious effects over medical research, as it would give each donor complete control over how medical research is used and who benefits from that research. The Court agrees and declines to extend the duty of informed consent to cover a researcher's economic interests in this case.

Plaintiffs cite a variety of authorities in support of their contention that the duty of informed consent mandates that research subjects must be informed of the financial interests of the researcher. They first rely on *Moore v. Regents of the University of California,* where the court held that a physician/researcher had a duty of informed consent to disclose that he was both undertaking research and commercializing it. Plaintiffs also reference a Florida law that requires health care providers to provide written disclosures to patients of potential financial conflicts of interest. Fla. Stat. §456.052 (precluding referrals by health care providers unless their financial interest is disclosed). Finally, in *Grimes,* the Maryland Court of Appeals found that researchers must provide "all material information" to their subjects.

These authorities do not control the outcome here, however, and the Court is not persuaded that they can be synthesized into a viable extension of the duty of informed consent. Moreover, Defendants correctly contest Plaintiffs' interpretation of *Moore*, the case that is most analogous to the situation at hand. *Moore* involved a physician breaching his duty when he asked his patient to return for follow-up tests after the removal of the patient's spleen because he had research and economic interests. The doctors did not inform their patient that they were using his blood and tissue for medical research. The allegations in the Complaint are clearly distinguishable as Defendants here are solely medical researchers and there was no therapeutic relationship as in *Moore*.

In declining to extend the duty of informed consent to cover economic interests, the Court takes note of the practical implications of retroactively imposing a duty of this nature. First, imposing a duty of the character that Plaintiffs seek would be unworkable and would chill medical research as it would mandate that researchers constantly evaluate whether a discloseable event has occurred.[55] Second, this extra duty would give rise to a type of dead-hand control that research subjects could hold because they would be able to dictate how medical research progresses. Finally, these Plaintiffs are more accurately portrayed as donors rather than objects of human experimentation, and thus the voluntary nature of their submissions warrants different treatment. Accordingly, the Court finds that Plaintiffs have failed to state a claim upon which relief may be granted, and this count is DISMISSED.

B. Breach of Fiduciary Duty

The individual Plaintiffs allege in Count II of the Complaint that all the Defendants were in a fiduciary relationship with them, and as such, they should have disclosed all material information relating to the Canavan disease research they were conducting, including any economic interests of the Defendants relating to that research.

As a threshold issue, Defendants argue that if the Court finds that there is no claim for informed consent, then the claim for breach of fiduciary duty evaporates as both claims have the same elements. Courts routinely hold that where a patient's claim that the doctor breached his fiduciary duty arises from the same operative facts and results in the same injury as another claim asserted against the doctor, then the breach of fiduciary claim is duplicative and should be dismissed. Defendants argue that the two claims are virtually identical, because the damages and liability allegations are very similar, and are both premised on the same duty of disclosure. The Court finds, nevertheless, that a full treatment of this claim is still appropriate as the two claims are not fully congruent.

1. Fiduciary Relationship

Defendants have moved to dismiss this count because Plaintiffs did not plead the elements of a fiduciary relationship. Fiduciary relations are either expressly or impliedly created. A fiduciary duty implied in law is premised upon the specific factual set of circumstances surrounding the transaction and the relationship of the parties.... Florida courts have found fiduciary relationships in this context when "confidence is reposed by one party and a trust accepted by the other." This is a two-way relationship, and a fiduciary relationship will only be found when the plaintiff separately alleges that the plain-

55. Plaintiffs claim that disclosure of a commercial interest is already mandated by the American Medical Association's Code of Ethics professional guidelines for physicians/researchers. It provides that "[p]otential commercial applications must be disclosed to the patient before a profit is realized on products developed from biological materials" and "[h]uman tissue and its products may not be used for commercial purposes without the informed consent of the patient who provided the original cellular material." AMA Code of Ethics, E-208. Yet these regulations were only promulgated in 1994 and there is no evidence that they bind the parties in this case.

tiff placed trust in the defendant and the defendant accepted that trust. In Florida, once a fiduciary relationship is established, a fiduciary has a legal duty to "disclose all essential or material facts pertinent or material to the transaction in hand."

Defendants assert that the Complaint does not allege any facts that show that the trust was recognized and accepted. Plaintiffs allege, however, that Defendants accepted the trust by undertaking research that they represented as being for the benefit of the Plaintiffs. Plaintiffs rely on other state courts which have held that researchers and research institutions are fiduciaries for their research subjects. For example, in *Grimes,* the Maryland Supreme Court held that "the very nature of nontherapuetic scientific research on human subjects can, and normally will, create special relationships out of which duties arise."

Taking all the facts alleged as true, the Court finds that Plaintiffs have not sufficiently alleged the second element of acceptance of trust by Defendants and therefore have failed to state a claim. There is no automatic fiduciary relationship that attaches when a researcher accepts medical donations and the acceptance of trust, the second constitutive element of finding a fiduciary duty, cannot be assumed once a donation is given. Accordingly, this claim is DISMISSED.

C. Unjust Enrichment

In Count III of the Complaint, Plaintiffs allege that MCH is being unjustly enriched by collecting license fees under the Patent. Under Florida law, the elements of a claim for unjust enrichment are (1) the plaintiff conferred a benefit on the defendant, who had knowledge of the benefit; (2) the defendant voluntarily accepted and retained the benefit; and (3) under the circumstances it would be inequitable for the defendant to retain the benefit without paying for it. The Court finds that Plaintiffs have sufficiently alleged the elements of a claim for unjust enrichment to survive Defendants' motion to dismiss.

While the parties do not contest that Plaintiffs have conferred a benefit to Defendants, including, among other things, blood and tissue samples and soliciting financial contributions, Defendants contend that Plaintiffs have not suffered any detriment, and note that no Plaintiff has been denied access to Canavan testing. Furthermore, the Plaintiffs received what they sought—the successful isolation of the Canavan gene and the development of a screening test. Plaintiffs argue, however, that when Defendants applied the benefits for unauthorized purposes, they suffered a detriment. Had Plaintiffs known that Defendants intended to commercialize their genetic material through patenting and restrictive licensing, Plaintiffs would not have provided these benefits to Defendants under those terms.

Naturally, Plaintiffs allege that the retention of benefits violates the fundamental principles of justice, equity, and good conscience. While Defendants claim that they have invested significant amounts of time and money in research, with no guarantee of success and are thus entitled to seek reimbursement, the same can be said of Plaintiffs. Moreover, Defendants' attempt to seek refuge in the endorsement of the U.S. Patent system, which gives an inventor rights to prosecute patents and negotiate licenses for their intellectual property fails, as obtaining a patent does not preclude the Defendants from being unjustly enriched. *See Chou v. Univ. of Chicago,* 254 F.3d 1347, 1363 (Fed.Cir.2001) (recognizing claim for unjust enrichment in context of gene patent dispute).[56] The Complaint has alleged more than just a donor-donee relationship for the purposes of an un-

56. [This case is excerpted in Chapter 5.]

just enrichment claim. Rather, the facts paint a picture of a continuing research collaboration that involved Plaintiffs also investing time and significant resources in the race to isolate the Canavan gene. Therefore, given the facts as alleged, the Court finds that Plaintiffs have sufficiently pled the requisite elements of an unjust enrichment claim and the motion to dismiss for failure to state a claim is DENIED as to this count.

D. Fraudulent Concealment

Count IV of the Complaint alleges that MCH fraudulently concealed from the Plaintiffs that (1) the Hospital would economically benefit from Canavan research; (2) it would patent the Canavan gene mutation; and (3) it would license the testing under the Patent.

The elements of a claim for fraudulent concealment under Florida law are: (1) a misrepresentation of material fact or suppression of the truth; (2)[a] knowledge of the representor of the misrepresentation, or [b] representations made by the representor without knowledge as to either the truth or falsity, or [c] representations made under circumstances in which the representor ought to have known, if he did not know, of the falsity thereof; (3) an intention that the representor induce another to act on it; and (4) resulting injury to the party acting in justifiable reliance on the representation. A fraudulent concealment claim is subject to Fed.R.Civ.P. 9(b)'s requirement that the circumstances constituting fraud shall be stated with particularity. Under Rule 9(b), the circumstances of the fraud must be alleged with specificity, *i.e.* the "who, what, when, where, and how" of the alleged fraud.

As a threshold matter, the Court finds that Plaintiffs have not satisfied this heightened pleading standard. None of the elements constituting fraudulent concealment are sufficiently pled in the Complaint. First, Plaintiffs claim that Florida law allows for a cause of action for fraudulent concealment of not disclosing one's intentions. Yet, their bare contention that the intent to patent was fraudulently concealed is not sufficient, because this intent was not accompanied by any time and place details. The Plaintiffs have failed to provide more specificity as the Defendants' concealment of intent to patent and the timing of Plaintiffs' donations.

Second, there was no duty of disclosure to the Plaintiffs. Allegations of fraudulent concealment by silence must be accompanied by allegations of a special relationship that gives rise to a duty to speak. Plaintiffs have not sufficiently alleged that they had a fiduciary relationship with Defendants, as noted in Section B, *supra.*

Third, the facts asserted as fraudulently concealed were accessible to the Plaintiffs. A patent becomes public knowledge when issued and Plaintiffs could have undertaken due diligence to uncover the facts surrounding the patent application. *In re Ford Motor Co. Bronco II Product Liability Litig.* 982 F.Supp. 388, 396–97 (E.D.La.1997) ("Claims of fraudulent concealment generally require that plaintiff allege and prove that defendant wrongfully concealed information and that plaintiff did not have actual or constructive knowledge of the information, and *could not have learned of the information through the exercise of due diligence*") (emphasis added). Plaintiffs' allegations that they were prevented from making reasonable inquiries because they had no reason to believe that patenting would occur is unavailing because if they were so concerned about a possible intent to patent then a simple phone inquiry to the Defendants would have uncovered this fact.

Finally, as to the damages element, Plaintiffs point to the specific injury that they have suffered; namely, the denial of their prolonged efforts in contributing time and resources to research that they thought was designed for non-commercial purposes. This is not any sort of cognizable injury, however, since the Complaint does not allege any individualized denial of testing nor does it claim any other economic injury.

Plaintiffs contend that, but for the fraudulent non-disclosure, they would have acted differently. Nevertheless, fraud must be specially pled, and the Complaint does not adequately allege a claim based on a special relationship or of injury nor does it allege more specifics about efforts at concealment or about any representations made by Matalon as to what he would do with the test results. Therefore, the Court finds that the Complaint lacks the specificity required by Fed.R.Civ.P. 9(b). Accordingly, the fraudulent concealment claim is DISMISSED.

E. Conversion

The Plaintiffs allege in Count V of their Complaint that they had a property interest in their body tissue and genetic information, and that they owned the Canavan registry in Illinois which contained contact information, pedigree information and family information for Canavan families worldwide. They claim that MCH and Matalon converted the names on the register and the genetic information by utilizing them for the hospitals' "exclusive economic benefit." The Court disagrees and declines to find a property interest for the body tissue and genetic information voluntarily given to Defendants. These were donations to research without any contemporaneous expectations of return of the body tissue and genetic samples, and thus conversion does not lie as a cause of action.

In Florida, the tort of "conversion is an unauthorized act which deprives another of his property permanently or for an indefinite time." ...

First, Plaintiffs have no cognizable property interest in body tissue and genetic matter donated for research under a theory of conversion. This case is similar to *Moore v. Regents of the University of California*, where the Court declined to extend liability under a theory of conversion to misuse of a person's excised biological materials. The plaintiff in *Moore* alleged that he had retained a property right in excised bodily material used in research, and therefore retained some control over the results of that research. The California Supreme Court, however, disagreed and held that the use of the results of medical research inconsistent with the wishes of the donor was not conversion, because the donor had no property interest at stake after the donation was made. The Court also recognized that the patented result of research is "both factually and legally distinct" from excised material used in the research.

Second, limits to the property rights that attach to body tissue have been recognized in Florida state courts. For example, in *State v. Powell*, 497 So.2d 1188, 1192 (Fla.1986), the Florida Supreme Court refused to recognize a property right in the body of another after death. Similarly, the property right in blood and tissue samples also evaporates once the sample is voluntarily given to a third party.

Plaintiffs rely on *Pioneer Hi-Bred v. Holden Foundation*, 1987 WL 341211 (S.D. Iowa, Oct.30, 1987), *aff'd*, 35 F.3d 1226 (8th Cir.1994), for their assertion that genetic information itself can constitute property for the purposes of the tort of conversion. In that case, the Court held that a corn seed[company?]'s property interest in the genetic message contained in a corn seed variety is property protected by the laws of conversion. Plaintiffs argue that giving permission for one purpose (gene discovery) does not mean they agreed to other uses (gene patenting and commercialization). Yet, the *Pioneer* court recognized that, "where information is gathered and arranged at some cost and sold as a commodity on the market, it is properly protected as property." This seemingly provides more support for property rights inherent in Defendants' research rather than the donations of Plaintiffs' DNA. Finally, Plaintiffs cite a litany of cases in other jurisdictions that have recognized that body tissue can be property in some circumstances. *See, e.g., Brotherton v. Cleveland,* 923 F.2d 477, 482 (6th Cir.1991) (aggregate of rights existing in body tissue is similar to property rights); *York v. Jones,* 717 F.Supp. 421, 425 (E.D.Va.1989) (couple granted property rights in their frozen embryos). These cases, however, do not involve voluntary donations to medical research.

Additionally, the Florida statute on genetic testing is cited by Plaintiffs in support of their contention that persons who contribute body tissue for researchers to use in genetic analysis do not relinquish ownership of the results of the analysis. Fla. Stat. §760.40 (2002). This statute, however, is inapplicable under a common law theory of conversion, because by its plain meaning, it only provides penalties for disclosure or lack of informed consent if a person is being genetically analyzed. Fla. Stat. §760.040(2). Plaintiffs have not cited any case that interprets the statute as applying to an analogous factual situation, and this Court's investigation did not find any relevant case either. Moreover, even assuming, *arguendo,* that the statute does create a property right in genetic material donated for medical research purposes, it is unclear whether this confers a property right for conversion, a common law cause of action.

Finally, although the Complaint sets out that Plaintiff Greenberg owned the Canavan Registry, the facts alleged do not sufficiently allege the elements of a *prima facie* case of conversion, as the Plaintiffs have not alleged how the Defendants' use of the Registry in their research was an expressly unauthorized act. The Complaint only alleges that the Defendants "utilized the information and contacts for their exclusive economic benefit." There is no further allegations of the circumstances or conditions that were attached to the Defendants' use of the Canavan Registry. Nor are there any allegations about any of the Plaintiffs' entitlement to possess the Registry.

The Court finds that Florida statutory and common law do not provide a remedy for Plaintiffs' donations of body tissue and blood samples under a theory of conversion liability. Indeed, the Complaint does not allege that the Defendants used the genetic material for any purpose *but* medical research. Plaintiffs claim that the *fruits* of the research, namely the patented material, was commercialized. This is an important distinction and another step in the chain of attenuation that renders conversion liability inapplicable to the facts as alleged. If adopted, the expansive theory championed by Plaintiffs would cripple medical research as it would bestow a continuing right for donors to possess the results of any research conducted by the hospital. At the core, these were donations to research without any contemporaneous expectations of return. Consequently, the Plaintiffs have failed to state a claim upon which relief may be granted on this issue. Accordingly, this claim is DISMISSED.

F. Misappropriation of Trade Secrets

The Plaintiffs' final claim is that MCH misappropriated a trade secret—the registry of people who had Canavan disease. Florida's Trade Secrets Act[57] defines a trade secret as:

> information, including a formula, pattern, compilation, program, device, method, technique, or process, that: (a) Derive(s) independent economic value, actual, or potential, from not being generally known to, and not being readily ascertainable by proper means by, other persons who can obtain eco-

57. Although the Complaint ostensibly claims that Defendants violated the Illinois Trade Secrets Act, the Court, following traditional choice of law precepts, applies the law of the forum.

nomic value from its disclosure or use; and (b) Is the subject of efforts that are reasonable under the circumstances to maintain its secrecy.

Fla. Stat. § 688.002(4). Whether a particular type of information constitutes a trade secret is a question of fact and cannot be resolved on a motion to dismiss.

Florida courts have repeatedly held that lists comprising information, such as names of patients, blood donors, and customers can qualify as trade secrets. However, to qualify as a trade secret, information that the Plaintiff seeks to protect must derive economic value from not being readily ascertainable by others and must be the subject of reasonable efforts to protects its secrecy.

At the outset, Defendants dismiss Plaintiffs' characterization of the Canavan registry as a trade secret. First, Defendants assert that Plaintiffs have not alleged that the registry belonged to any Plaintiff. Second, Defendants argue that the registry itself was not alleged to have any independent "economic value" for the purposes of Florida law since the Complaint does not allege the registry had any economic value derived from the confidentiality. Fla. Stat. § 688.002. Finally, a trade secret must be the subject of efforts "reasonable under the circumstances to maintain it[s] secrecy." Defendants claim that there is nothing in the Complaint which indicates that any efforts were made to keep secret the Registry.

Plaintiffs counter Defendants' assertion that the Canavan registry is not a trade secret because it had value, in that it streamlined Matalon's research and was treated as confidential because it contained confidential information such as contact details, pedigree, and familial information for families world wide.

While it is clear that the Complaint does allege that the Plaintiffs Greenberg and NTSAD created the list, "expend[ing] time, money, and other efforts," other key indicia of a trade secret are missing. Plaintiffs do not allege that the list derived economic value from not being generally know to others. The Complaint merely states that it had "substantial economic value" in streamlining Matalon's research. Second, there is no allegation that the Plaintiffs undertook measures to keep the list confidential. Plaintiffs only allege that there was an "expectation that it would remain confidential."

Even assuming, *arguendo,* that the Court finds that the Canavan Registry is a trade secret, Plaintiffs have not sufficiently alleged how the trade secret was misappropriated. To establish a claim for misappropriation of trade secrets under Florida law, Plaintiffs must show that (1) they possessed valuable confidential information and took reasonable steps to protect it and (2) the information was "misappropriated," either by one who knew or had reason to know that secret was improperly obtained or by one who used improper means to obtain it. Misappropriation includes "disclosure or use of a trade secret of another without express or implied consent by a person who ... at the time of the disclosure or use, knew or had reason to know that knowledge of the trade secret was ... acquired under circumstances giving rise to a duty to maintain its secrecy or limit its use." Fla. Stat. § 688.002(2).

The Canavan Registry was not misappropriated by MCH because there is no allegation that MCH knew or should have known that the Canavan Registry was a confidential trade secret guarded by Plaintiffs, and furthermore, that Matalon had acquired through improper means. Plaintiffs' theory that Defendants misappropriated the Registry once Matalon and MCH chose to use the Registry beyond the use for which it was authorized does not pass muster, since there was no explicit authorization that the Registry be used for a certain purpose in the first place. Plaintiffs cannot donate information that they prepared for fighting a disease and then retroactively claim that it was a protected secret.

Accordingly, the Court finds that Plaintiffs have failed to state a claim regarding misappropriation of trade secret as the they have not sufficiently alleged the requisite elements to convert the Registry into an actionable trade secret. This claim is therefore DISMISSED.

IV. Conclusion

... ADJUDGED that the motions are GRANTED *in part.* Accordingly, Count I (lack of informed consent), Count II (breach of fiduciary duty), Count IV (fraudulent concealment), Count V (conversion) and Count VI (misappropriation of trade secrets) are DISMISSED *with prejudice.*

ADJUDGED that the motions to dismiss are DENIED as to Count III (unjust enrichment)....

Notes & Questions

1. Indigenous groups, including Native Americans in this country, have also begun to express concern over the collection and use of their genetic information. One such group, the Havasupai tribe in Arizona, recently sued researchers at Arizona State University and the University of Arizona regarding what they believe to be unauthorized additional uses of information and biological samples that they had voluntarily provided for one limited purpose—research on the troubling incidence of diabetes in their community. *See* Anne Minard, *UA Scientist Named In Two Suits By Havasupai Tribe, Members*, ARIZONA DAILY STAR (March 24, 2005).

Chapter 6

Commercialization of Genetic Tests and Products

All the research and insights developed in genetics labs will remain as purely scientific enlightenment without a means to translate them into practical, commercially available applications. At the same time, there are ongoing debates as to how such commercialization should take place, who should control and profit from it, and whether certain innovations should be placed into the public domain instead. Some of these issues were raised in Chapter 5; others will be addressed in this Chapter. A subset of these issues focused on developments in agricultural biotechnology will be further discussed in Chapter 8. This Chapter follows the commercialization chain beginning with identifying patentable inventions, including allocation of ownership and other rights. Next it turns to the technology transfer system by which research that primarily occurs in university or other non-profit labs is packaged and made available for commercial development. It then considers the issues facing biotech start-ups and spin-off companies as they perform the actual commercialization activities that will lead to a saleable genetic diagnostic or therapeutic product or service. Finally, the chapter concludes with an overview of the procedure for obtaining regulatory approval for the marketing and sale of these products and services.

A. Identifying Patents in the Research Environment

Patents are not the only way to assert ownership over scientific or technological innovation, but they are perhaps the most potent and concrete means of protecting such assets. While there is some controversy over whether the USPTO should issue "gene patents"—patents on DNA fragments identified by researchers as constituting a gene—the final "kit" version of a genetic diagnostic or therapeutic product should be less objectionable. This Part considers the general elements of patentability under the U.S. patent laws by focusing on the particular issues genetic products and services raise for each element.

In the U.S., inventors have a right to have a patent issued by the USPTO, so long as their inventions meet a statutory set of criteria including: subject matter, utility, novelty, and nonobviousness. Thus, these criteria can guide anyone who is trying to determine whether they have a patentable invention. If an inventor believes that her invention meets these criteria she can file a patent application with the USPTO. This application must contain a written description of the invention that makes it clear the inventor actually is in possession of the invention *and* enables one of ordinary skill in the relevant art to "practice" or use the invention without undue experimentation. The following sections consider each of these requirements as they apply broadly in the life sciences and biotechnology and narrowly, where guidance is available, in the specialty area of genetic diagnostic or therapeutic inventions.

1. Subject Matter

The case of *Diamond v. Chakrabarty* effectively illustrates both the general issues of defining patentable subject matter as well as the specific issues of including living things in that definition.

Diamond v. Chakrabarty

447 U.S. 303 (1980)

C.J. BURGER delivered the opinion of the Court

We granted certiorari to determine whether a live, human-made micro-organism is patentable subject matter under 35 U.S.C. § 101.

I

In 1972, respondent Chakrabarty, a microbiologist, filed a patent application assigned to the General Electric Co. The application asserted 36 claims related to Chakrabarty's invention of "a bacterium from the genus *Pseudomonas* containing therein at least two stable energy-generating plasmids, each of said plasmids providing a separate hydrocarbon degradative pathway."[1] This human-made, genetically engineered bacterium is capable of breaking down multiple components of crude oil. Because of this property, which is possessed by no naturally occurring bacteria, Chakrabarty's invention is believed to have significant value for the treatment of oil spills.[2]

Chakrabarty's patent claims were of three types: first, process claims for the method of producing the bacteria; second, claims for an inoculum comprised of a carrier material floating on water, such as straw, and the new bacteria; and third, claims to the bacteria themselves. The patent examiner allowed the claims falling into the first two categories, but rejected claims for the bacteria. His decision rested on two grounds: (1) that micro-organisms are "products of nature," and (2) that as living things they are not patentable subject matter under 35 U.S.C. § 101.

---

1. Plasmids are hereditary units physically separate from the chromosomes of the cell. In prior research, Chakrabarty and an associate discovered that plasmids control the oil degradation abilities of certain bacteria. In particular, the two researchers discovered plasmids capable of degrading camphor and octane, two components of crude oil. In the work represented by the patent application at issue here, Chakrabarty discovered a process by which four different plasmids, capable of degrading four different oil components, could be transferred to and maintained stably in a single *Pseudomonas* bacterium, which itself has no capacity for degrading oil.

2. At present, biological control of oil spills requires the use of a mixture of naturally occurring bacteria, each capable of degrading one component of the oil complex. In this way, oil is decomposed into simpler substances which can serve as food for aquatic life. However, for various reasons, only a portion of any such mixed culture survives to attack the oil spill. By breaking down multiple components of oil, Chakrabarty's micro-organism promises more efficient and rapid oil-spill control.

Chakrabarty appealed the rejection of these claims to the Patent Office Board of Appeals, and the Board affirmed the examiner on the second ground.[3] Relying on the legislative history of the 1930 Plant Patent Act, in which Congress extended patent protection to certain asexually reproduced plants, the Board concluded that § 101 was not intended to cover living things such as these laboratory created micro-organisms.

The Court of Customs and Patent Appeals, by a divided vote, reversed.... The Commissioner of Patents and Trademarks ... sought certiorari....

II

The Constitution grants Congress broad power to legislate to "promote the Progress of Science and useful Arts, by securing for limited Times to Authors and Inventors the exclusive Right to their respective Writings and Discoveries." Art. I, § 8, cl. 8. The patent laws promote this progress by offering inventors exclusive rights for a limited period as an incentive for their inventiveness and research efforts. The authority of Congress is exercised in the hope that "[t]he productive effort thereby fostered will have a positive effect on society through the introduction of new products and processes of manufacture into the economy, and the emanations by way of increased employment and better lives for our citizens."

The question before us in this case is a narrow one of statutory interpretation requiring us to construe 35 U.S.C. § 101, which provides:

> "Whoever invents or discovers any new and useful process, machine, manufacture, or composition of matter, or any new and useful improvement thereof, may obtain a patent therefor, subject to the conditions and requirements of this title."

Specifically, we must determine whether respondent's micro-organism constitutes a "manufacture" or "composition of matter" within the meaning of the statute.

III

In cases of statutory construction we begin, of course, with the language of the statute. And "unless otherwise defined, words will be interpreted as taking their ordinary, contemporary, common meaning." We have also cautioned that courts "should not read into the patent laws limitations and conditions which the legislature has not expressed."

Guided by these canons of construction, this Court has read the term "manufacture" in § 101 in accordance with its dictionary definition to mean "the production of articles for use from raw or prepared materials by giving to these materials new forms, qualities, properties, or combinations, whether by hand-labor or by machinery." Similarly, "composition of matter" has been construed consistent with its common usage to include "all compositions of two or more substances and ... all composite articles, whether they be the results of chemical union, or of mechanical mixture, or whether they be gases, fluids, powders or solids." In choosing such expansive terms as "manufacture" and "composition of matter," modified by the comprehensive "any," Congress plainly contemplated that the patent laws would be given wide scope.

---

3. The Board concluded that the new bacteria were not "products of nature," because *Pseudomonas* bacteria containing two or more different energy-generating plasmids are not naturally occurring.

The relevant legislative history also supports a broad construction. The Patent Act of 1793, authored by Thomas Jefferson, defined statutory subject matter as "any new and useful art, machine, manufacture, or composition of matter, or any new or useful improvement [thereof]." Act of Feb. 21, 1793, § 1, 1 Stat. 319. The Act embodied Jefferson's philosophy that "ingenuity should receive a liberal encouragement." Subsequent patent statutes in 1836, 1870 and 1874 employed this same broad language. In 1952, when the patent laws were recodified, Congress replaced the word "art" with "process," but otherwise left Jefferson's language intact. The Committee Reports accompanying the 1952 Act inform us that Congress intended statutory subject matter to "include anything under the sun that is made by man." S. Rep. No. 1979, 82d Cong., 2d Sess., 5 (1952); H. R. Rep. No. 1923, 82d Cong., 2d Sess., 6 (1952).

This is not to suggest that § 101 has no limits or that it embraces every discovery. The laws of nature, physical phenomena, and abstract ideas have been held not patentable. Thus, a new mineral discovered in the earth or a new plant found in the wild is not patentable subject matter. Likewise, Einstein could not patent his celebrated law that E=mc2.; nor could Newton have patented the law of gravity. Such discoveries are "manifestations of ... nature, free to all men and reserved exclusively to none."

Judged in this light, respondent's micro-organism plainly qualifies as patentable subject matter. His claim is not to a hitherto unknown natural phenomenon, but to a nonnaturally occurring manufacture or composition of matter—a product of human ingenuity "having a distinctive name, character [and] use." The point is underscored dramatically by comparison of the invention here with that in [*Funk Brothers Seed Co. v. Kalo Inoculant Co.*, 333 U.S. 127 (1948)]. There, the patentee had discovered that there existed in nature certain species of root-nodule bacteria which did not exert a mutually inhibitive effect on each other. He used that discovery to produce a mixed culture capable of inoculating the seeds of leguminous plants. Concluding that the patentee had discovered "only some of the handiwork of nature," the Court ruled the product nonpatentable:

> Each of the species of root-nodule bacteria contained in the package infects the same group of leguminous plants which it always infected. No species acquires a different use. The combination of species produces no new bacteria, no change in the six species of bacteria, and no enlargement of the range of their utility. Each species has the same effect it always had. The bacteria perform in their natural way. Their use in combination does not improve in any way their natural functioning. They serve the ends nature originally provided and act quite independently of any effort of the patentee.

Here, by contrast, the patentee has produced a new bacterium with markedly different characteristics from any found in nature and one having the potential for significant utility. His discovery is not nature's handiwork, but his own; accordingly it is patentable subject matter under § 101.

IV

Two contrary arguments are advanced, neither of which we find persuasive.

(A)

The petitioner's first argument rests on the enactment of the 1930 Plant Patent Act, which afforded patent protection to certain asexually reproduced plants, and the 1970 Plant Variety Protection Act, which authorized protection for certain sexually reproduced plants but excluded bacteria from its protection.[4] In the petitioner's view, the passage of these Acts evidences congressional understanding that the terms "manufacture" or "composition of matter" do not include living things; if they did, the petitioner argues, neither Act would have been necessary.

We reject this argument. Prior to 1930, two factors were thought to remove plants from patent protection. The first was the belief that plants, even those artificially bred, were products of nature for purposes of the patent law.... The second obstacle to patent protection for plants was the fact that plants were thought not amenable to the "written description" requirement of the patent law. See 35 U.S.C. § 112. Because new plants may differ from old only in color or perfume, differentiation by written description was often impossible.

In enacting the Plant Patent Act, Congress addressed both of these concerns. It explained at length its belief that the work of the plant breeder "in aid of nature" was patentable invention. And it relaxed the written description requirement in favor of "a description ... as complete as is reasonably possible." 35 U.S.C. § 162. No Committee or Member of Congress, however, expressed the broader view, now urged by the petitioner, that the terms "manufacture" or "composition of matter" exclude living things.... Congress thus recognized that the relevant distinction was not between living and inanimate things, but between products of nature, whether living or not, and human-made inventions. Here, respondent's micro-organism is the result of human ingenuity and research. Hence, the passage of the Plant Patent Act affords the Government no support.

Nor does the passage of the 1970 Plant Variety Protection Act support the Government's position. As the Government acknowledges, sexually reproduced plants were not included under the 1930 Act because new varieties could not be reproduced true-to-type through seedlings. By 1970, however, it was generally recognized that true-to-type reproduction was possible and that plant patent protection was therefore appropriate. The 1970 Act extended that protection. There is nothing in its language or history to suggest that it was enacted because § 101 did not include living things.

In particular, we find nothing in the exclusion of bacteria from plant variety protection to support the petitioner's position. The legislative history gives no reason for this exclusion. As the Court of Customs and Patent Appeals suggested, it may simply reflect congressional agreement with the result reached by that court in deciding *In re Arzberger*, 112 F.2d 834 ([C.C.P.A.]1940), which held that bacteria were not plants for the purposes of the 1930 Act. Or it may reflect the fact that prior to 1970 the Patent Office had issued patents for bacteria under § 101.[5] In any event, absent some clear indica-

---

4. The Plant Patent Act of 1930, 35 U.S.C. § 161, provides in relevant part:

> Whoever invents or discovers and asexually reproduces any distinct and new variety of plant, including cultivated sports, mutants, hybrids, and newly found seedlings, other than a tuber propagated plant or a plant found in an uncultivated state, may obtain a patent therefor....

The Plant Variety Protection Act of 1970, provides in relevant part:

> The breeder of any novel variety of sexually reproduced plant (other than fungi, bacteria, or first generation hybrids) who has so reproduced the variety, or his successor in interest, shall be entitled to plant variety protection therefor....

5. In 1873, the Patent Office granted Louis Pasteur a patent on "yeast, free from organic germs of disease, as an article of manufacture." And in 1967 and 1968, immediately prior to the passage of the Plant Variety Protection Act, that Office granted two patents which, as the petitioner concedes, state claims for living micro-organisms.

tion that Congress "focused on [the] issues ... directly related to the one presently before the Court," there is no basis for reading into its actions an intent to modify the plain meaning of the words found in § 101.

(B)

The petitioner's second argument is that micro-organisms cannot qualify as patentable subject matter until Congress expressly authorizes such protection. His position rests on the fact that genetic technology was unforeseen when Congress enacted § 101. From this it is argued that resolution of the patentability of inventions such as respondent's should be left to Congress. The legislative process, the petitioner argues, is best equipped to weigh the competing economic, social, and scientific considerations involved, and to determine whether living organisms produced by genetic engineering should receive patent protection. In support of this position, the petitioner relies on our recent holding in *Parker v. Flook*, 437 U.S. 584 (1978), and the statement that the judiciary "must proceed cautiously when ... asked to extend patent rights into areas wholly unforeseen by Congress."

It is, of course, correct that Congress, not the courts, must define the limits of patentability; but it is equally true that once Congress has spoken it is "the province and duty of the judicial department to say what the law is." Congress has performed its constitutional role in defining patentable subject matter in § 101; we perform ours in construing the language Congress has employed. In so doing, our obligation is to take statutes as we find them, guided, if ambiguity appears, by the legislative history and statutory purpose. Here, we perceive no ambiguity. The subject-matter provisions of the patent law have been cast in broad terms to fulfill the constitutional and statutory goal of promoting "the Progress of Science and the useful Arts" with all that means for the social and economic benefits envisioned by Jefferson. Broad general language is not necessarily ambiguous when congressional objectives require broad terms.

Nothing in *Flook* is to the contrary. That case applied our prior precedents to determine that a "claim for an improved method of calculation, even when tied to a specific end use, is unpatentable subject matter under § 101." The Court carefully scrutinized the claim at issue to determine whether it was precluded from patent protection under "the principles underlying the prohibition against patents for 'ideas' or phenomena of nature." We have done that here. *Flook* did not announce a new principle that inventions in areas not contemplated by Congress when the patent laws were enacted are unpatentable *per se*.

To read that concept into *Flook* would frustrate the purposes of the patent law. This Court frequently has observed that a statute is not to be confined to the "particular application[s] ... contemplated by the legislators." This is especially true in the field of patent law. A rule that unanticipated inventions are without protection would conflict with the core concept of the patent law that anticipation undermines patentability. Mr. Justice Douglas reminded [us] that the inventions most benefiting mankind are those that "push back the frontiers of chemistry, physics, and the like." Congress employed broad general language in drafting § 101 precisely because such inventions are often unforeseeable.[6]

---

6. Even an abbreviated list of patented inventions underscores the point: telegraph (Morse, No. 1,647); telephone (Bell, No. 174,465); electric lamp (Edison, No. 223,898); airplane (the Wrights, No. 821,393); transistor (Bardeen & Brattain, No. 2,524,035); neutronic reactor (Fermi & Szilard, No. 2,708,656); laser (Schawlow & Townes, No. 2,929,922).

To buttress his argument, the petitioner, with the support of *amicus*, points to grave risks that may be generated by research endeavors such as respondent's. The briefs present a gruesome parade of horribles. Scientists, among them Nobel laureates, are quoted suggesting that genetic research may pose a serious threat to the human race, or, at the very least, that the dangers are far too substantial to permit such research to proceed apace at this time. We are told that genetic research and related technological developments may spread pollution and disease, that it may result in a loss of genetic diversity, and that its practice may tend to depreciate the value of human life. These arguments are forcefully, even passionately, presented; they remind us that, at times, human ingenuity seems unable to control fully the forces it creates—that, with Hamlet, it is sometimes better "to bear those ills we have than fly to others that we know not of."

It is argued that this Court should weigh these potential hazards in considering whether respondent's invention is patentable subject matter under § 101. We disagree. The grant or denial of patents on micro-organisms is not likely to put an end to genetic research or to its attendant risks. The large amount of research that has already occurred when no researcher had sure knowledge that patent protection would be available suggests that legislative or judicial fiat as to patentability will not deter the scientific mind from probing into the unknown any more than Canute could command the tides. Whether respondent's claims are patentable may determine whether research efforts are accelerated by the hope of reward or slowed by want of incentives, but that is all.

What is more important is that we are without competence to entertain these arguments—either to brush them aside as fantasies generated by fear of the unknown, or to act on them. The choice we are urged to make is a matter of high policy for resolution within the legislative process after the kind of investigation, examination, and study that legislative bodies can provide and courts cannot. That process involves the balancing of competing values and interests, which in our democratic system is the business of elected representatives. Whatever their validity, the contentions now pressed on us should be addressed to the political branches of the Government, the Congress and the Executive, and not to the courts.

We have emphasized in the recent past that "[o]ur individual appraisal of the wisdom or unwisdom of a particular [legislative] course ... is to be put aside in the process of interpreting a statute." Our task, rather, is the narrow one of determining what Congress meant by the words it used in the statute; once that is done our powers are exhausted. Congress is free to amend § 101 so as to exclude from patent protection organisms produced by genetic engineering. Or it may choose to craft a statute specifically designed for such living things. But, until Congress takes such action, this Court must construe the language of § 101 as it is. The language of that section fairly embraces respondent's invention.

Accordingly, the judgment of the Court of Customs and Patent Appeals is

Affirmed.

J. Brennan dissenting.

I agree with the Court that the question before us is a narrow one. Neither the future of scientific research, nor even the ability of respondent Chakrabarty to reap some monopoly profits from his pioneering work, is at stake. Patents on the processes by which he has produced and employed the new living organism are not contested. The only question we need decide is whether Congress, exercising its authority under Art. I, § 8, of the Constitution, intended that he be able to secure a monopoly on the living organism itself, no matter how produced or how used. Because I believe the Court has misread the applicable legislation, I dissent.

The patent laws attempt to reconcile this Nation's deep-seated antipathy to monopolies with the need to encourage progress. Given the complexity and legislative nature of this delicate task, we must be careful to extend patent protection no further than Congress has provided. In particular, were there an absence of legislative direction, the courts should leave to Congress the decisions whether and how far to extend the patent privilege into areas where the common understanding has been that patents are not available.

In this case, however, we do not confront a complete legislative vacuum. The sweeping language of the Patent Act of 1793, as re-enacted in 1952, is not the last pronouncement Congress has made in this area. In 1930 Congress enacted the Plant Patent Act affording patent protection to developers of certain asexually reproduced plants. In 1970 Congress enacted the Plant Variety Protection Act to extend protection to certain new plant varieties capable of sexual reproduction. Thus, we are not dealing—as the Court would have it—with the routine problem of "unanticipated inventions." In these two Acts Congress has addressed the general problem of patenting animate inventions and has chosen carefully limited language granting protection to some kinds of discoveries, but specifically excluding others. These Acts strongly evidence a congressional limitation that excludes bacteria from patentability.[7]

First, the Acts evidence Congress' understanding, at least since 1930, that § 101 does not include living organisms. If newly developed living organisms not naturally occurring had been patentable under § 101, the plants included in the scope of the 1930 and 1970 Acts could have been patented without new legislation. Those plants, like the bacteria involved in this case, were new varieties not naturally occurring. Although the Court rejects this line of argument, it does not explain why the Acts were necessary unless to correct a pre-existing situation.[8] I cannot share the Court's implicit assumption that Congress was engaged in either idle exercises or mere correction of the public record when it enacted the 1930 and 1970 Acts. And Congress certainly thought it was doing something significant. The Committee Reports contain expansive prose about the previously unavailable benefits to be derived from extending patent protection to plants. Because Congress thought it had to legislate in order to make agricultural "human-made inventions" patentable and because the legislation Congress enacted is limited, it follows that Congress never meant to make items outside the scope of the legislation patentable.

Second, the 1970 Act clearly indicates that Congress has included bacteria within the focus of its legislative concern, but not within the scope of patent protection. Congress specifically excluded bacteria from the coverage of the 1970 Act. 7 U.S.C. § 2402(a). The Court's attempts to supply explanations for this explicit exclusion ring hollow. It is true that there is not mention in the legislative history of the exclusion, but that does not

7. But even if I agreed with the Court that the 1930 and 1970 Acts were not dispositive, I would dissent. This case presents even more cogent reasons than [other cases] not to extend the patent monopoly in the face of uncertainty. At the very least, these Acts are signs of legislative attention to the problems of patenting living organisms, but they give no affirmative indication of congressional intent that bacteria be patentable. The caveat of [*Flook*], an admonition to "proceed cautiously when we are asked to extend patent rights into areas wholly unforeseen by Congress," therefore becomes pertinent. I should think the necessity for caution is that much greater when we are asked to extend patent rights into areas Congress has foreseen and considered but has not resolved.

8. If the 1930 Act's only purpose were to solve the technical problem of description referred to by the Court most of the Act, and in particular its limitation to asexually reproduced plants, would have been totally unnecessary.

give us license to invent reasons. The fact is that Congress, assuming that animate objects as to which it had not specifically legislated could not be patented, excluded bacteria from the set of patentable organisms.

The Court protests that its holding today is dictated by the broad language of § 101, which cannot "be confined to the 'particular application[s] ... contemplated by the legislators.'" But as I have shown, the Court's decision does not follow the unavoidable implications of the statute. Rather, it extends the patent system to cover living material even though Congress plainly has legislated in the belief that § 101 does not encompass living organisms. It is the role of Congress, not this Court, to broaden or narrow the reach of the patent laws. This is especially true where, as here, the composition sought to be patented uniquely implicates matters of public concern.

2. Utility

As we saw in *Chakrabarty*, 35 U.S.C. § 101 stipulates that a patent may issue to an inventor who invents "any new and useful process, machine, manufacture, or composition of matter, or any new and useful improvement thereof...." The requirement that the invention be "useful" has been translated into the so-called "utility requirement". Inventions in the mechanical arts are generally fairly straightforward as to whether they meet this requirement or not, and thus the utility requirement has been described as a fairly low bar to patentability. If the mechanical device does almost anything it will usually be deemed useful. But inventions in the life sciences, particularly those falling into the subject matter categories of manufacture or composition of matter, may face more utility challenges as the following case demonstrates.

In re Fisher

421 F.3d 1365 (Fed. Cir. 2005)

Michel, Chief Judge.

Dane K. Fisher and Raghunath Lalgudi (collectively "Fisher")[9] appeal from the decision of the U.S. Patent and Trademark Office ("PTO") Board of Patent Appeals and Interferences ("Board") affirming the examiner's final rejection of the only pending claim of application Serial No. 09/619,643 (the "'643 application"), entitled "Nucleic Acid Molecules and Other Molecules Associated with Plants," as unpatentable for lack of utility under 35 U.S.C. § 101 and lack of enablement under 35 U.S.C. § 112, first paragraph. This appeal was submitted after oral argument on May 3, 2005. Because we conclude that substantial evidence supports the Board's findings that the claimed invention lacks a specific and substantial utility and that the '643 application does not enable one of ordinary skill in the art to use the invention, we affirm.

I. Background

A. Molecular Genetics and ESTs

The claimed invention relates to five purified nucleic acid sequences that encode proteins and protein fragments in maize plants. The claimed sequences are commonly re-

9. The real party in interest is Monsanto Technology LLC, which is owned by the Monsanto Company.

ferred to as "expressed sequence tags" or "ESTs." Before delving into the specifics of this case, it is important to understand more about the basic principles of molecular genetics and the role of ESTs.

Genes are located on chromosomes in the nucleus of a cell and are made of deoxyribonucleic acid ("DNA"). DNA is composed of two strands of nucleotides in double helix formation. The nucleotides contain one of four bases, adenine ("A"), guanine ("G"), cytosine ("C"), and thymine ("T"), that are linked by hydrogen bonds to form complementary base pairs (*i.e.*, A-T and G-C).

When a gene is expressed in a cell, the relevant double-stranded DNA sequence is transcribed into a single strand of messenger ribonucleic acid ("mRNA"). Messenger RNA contains three of the same bases as DNA (A, G, and C), but contains uracil ("U") instead of thymine. mRNA is released from the nucleus of a cell and used by ribosomes found in the cytoplasm to produce proteins.

Complementary DNA ("cDNA") is produced synthetically by reverse transcribing mRNA. cDNA, like naturally occurring DNA, is composed of nucleotides containing the four nitrogenous bases, A, T, G, and C. Scientists routinely compile cDNA into libraries to study the kinds of genes expressed in a certain tissue at a particular point in time. One of the goals of this research is to learn what genes and downstream proteins are expressed in a cell so as to regulate gene expression and control protein synthesis.[10]

An EST is a short nucleotide sequence that represents a fragment of a cDNA clone. It is typically generated by isolating a cDNA clone and sequencing a small number of nucleotides located at the end of one of the two cDNA strands. When an EST is introduced into a sample containing a mixture of DNA, the EST may hybridize with a portion of DNA. Such binding shows that the gene corresponding to the EST was being expressed at the time of mRNA extraction.

Claim 1 of the '643 application recites:

> A substantially purified nucleic acid molecule that encodes a maize protein or fragment thereof comprising a nucleic acid sequence selected from the group consisting of SEQ ID NO: 1 through SEQ ID NO: 5.

The ESTs set forth in SEQ ID NO: 1 through SEQ ID NO: 5 are obtained from cDNA library LIB3115, which was generated from pooled leaf tissue harvested from maize plants (RX601, Asgrow Seed Company, Des Moines, Iowa, U.S.A.) grown in the fields at Asgrow research stations. SEQ ID NO:1 through SEQ ID NO:5 consist of 429, 423, 365, 411, and 331 nucleotides, respectively. When Fisher filed the '643 application, he claimed ESTs corresponding to genes expressed from the maize pooled leaf tissue at the time of anthesis. Nevertheless, Fisher did not know the precise structure or function of either the genes or the proteins encoded for by those genes.

The '643 application generally discloses that the five claimed ESTs may be used in a variety of ways, including: (1) serving as a molecular marker for mapping the entire maize genome, which consists of ten chromosomes that collectively encompass roughly 50,000 genes; (2) measuring the level of mRNA in a tissue sample via microarray technology to provide information about gene expression; (3) providing a source for primers for use in the polymerase chain reaction ("PCR") process to enable rapid and

10. We have discussed the basic principles of molecular genetics more extensively in prior cases. *See, e.g.*, *In re Deuel*, 51 F.3d 1552, 1554–56 (Fed. Cir. 1995); *Amgen, Inc. v. Chugai Pharm. Co., Ltd.*, 927 F.2d 1200, 1207–08 (Fed. Cir. 1991); *In re O'Farrell*, 853 F.2d 894, 895–99 (Fed. Cir. 1988).

inexpensive duplication of specific genes; (4) identifying the presence or absence of a polymorphism; (5) isolating promoters via chromosome walking; (6) controlling protein expression; and (7) locating genetic molecules of other plants and organisms.

B. Final Rejection

In a final rejection, dated September 6, 2001, the examiner rejected claim 1 for lack of utility under § 101. The examiner found that the claimed ESTs were not supported by a specific and substantial utility. She concluded that the disclosed uses were not specific to the claimed ESTs, but instead were generally applicable to any EST. For example, the examiner noted that any EST may serve as a molecular tag to isolate genetic regions. She also concluded that the claimed ESTs lacked a substantial utility because there was no known use for the proteins produced as final products resulting from processes involving the claimed ESTs. The examiner stated: "Utilities that require or constitute carrying out further research to identify or reasonably confirm a 'real world' context of use are not substantial utilities."

The examiner also rejected the claimed application for lack of enablement under § 112, first paragraph. She reasoned that one skilled in the art would not know how to use the claimed ESTs because the '643 application did not disclose a specific and substantial utility for them.

On July 19, 2000, Fisher filed a notice of appeal with the Board.

C. Board Proceedings

The Board considered each of Fisher's seven potential uses but noted that Fisher focused its appeal on only two: (1) use for the identification of polymorphisms; and (2) use as probes or as a source for primers. As to the first, the Board found that the application failed to explain why the claimed ESTs would be useful in detecting polymorphisms in maize plants. The Board reasoned that "[w]ithout knowing any further information in regard to the gene represented by an EST, as here, detection of the presence or absence of a polymorphism provides the barest information in regard to genetic heritage." Thus, the Board concluded that Fisher's asserted uses for the claimed ESTs tended to the "insubstantial use" end of the spectrum between a substantial and an insubstantial utility.

The Board also concluded that using the claimed ESTs to isolate nucleic acid molecules of other plants and organisms, which themselves had no known utility, is not a substantial utility. Specifically, the Board noted that Fisher argued that the "claimed ESTs may be useful in searching for promoters that are only active in leaves at the time of anthesis." The Board found, however, that the application failed to show that the claimed ESTs would be expressed only during anthesis or that they would be capable of isolating a promoter active in maize leaves at the time of anthesis.

Additionally, the Board addressed the remaining asserted utilities, highlighting in particular the use of the claimed ESTs to monitor gene expression by measuring the level of mRNA through microarray technology and to serve as molecular markers. The Board found that using the claimed ESTs in screens does not provide a specific benefit because the application fails to provide any teaching regarding how to use the data relating to gene expression. The Board analogized the facts to those in *Brenner v. Manson*, 383 U.S. 519 (1966), in which an applicant claimed a process of making a compound having no known use. In that case, the Supreme Court affirmed the rejection of the application on § 101 grounds. Here, the Board reasoned: "Just as the process in *Brenner* lacked utility because the specification did not disclose how to use the end-product, the products claimed here lack utility, because even if used in gene expression assays, the specification does not disclose how to use SEQ ID NO: 1-5 specific gene expression data." The Board offered a similar rationale for the use of the claimed ESTs as molecular markers. Accordingly, the Board affirmed the examiner's rejection of the '643 application for lack of utility under § 101. The Board also affirmed the examiner's rejection of the '643 application for lack of enablement under § 112, first paragraph, since the enablement rejection was made as a corollary to the utility rejection....

II. Discussion

Whether an application discloses a utility for a claimed invention is a question of fact.... We consequently review the Board's determination that the '643 application failed to satisfy the utility requirement of § 101 for substantial evidence.

A. Utility

1.

Fisher asserts that the Board unilaterally applied a heightened standard for utility in the case of ESTs, conditioning patentability upon "some undefined 'spectrum' of knowledge concerning the corresponding gene function." Fisher contends that the standard is not so high and that Congress intended the language of § 101 to be given broad construction. In particular, Fisher contends that § 101 requires only that the claimed invention "not be frivolous, or injurious to the well-being, good policy, or good morals of society," essentially adopting Justice Story's view of a useful invention from *Lowell v. Lewis*, 15 F. Cas. 1018, 1019 (No. 8568) (C.C. Mass. 1817). Under the correct application of the law, Fisher argues, the record shows that the claimed ESTs provide seven specific and substantial uses, regardless whether the functions of the genes corresponding to the claimed ESTs are known. Fisher claims that the Board's attempt to equate the claimed ESTs with the chemical compositions in *Brenner* was misplaced and that several decisions in the field of pharmaceuticals, namely, *Cross v. Iizuka*, 753 F.2d 1040 (Fed. Cir. 1985), *Nelson v. Bowler*, 626 F.2d 853 (C.C.P.A. 1980), and *In re Jolles*, 628 F.2d 1322 (C.C.P.A. 1980), are analogous and support finding utility of the claimed ESTs. Fisher likewise argues that the general commercial success of ESTs in the marketplace confirms the utility of the claimed ESTs. Hence, Fisher avers that the Board's decision was not supported by substantial evidence and should be reversed.

The government agrees with Fisher that the utility threshold is not high, but disagrees with Fisher's allegation that the Board applied a heightened utility standard. The government contends that a patent applicant need disclose only a single specific and substantial utility pursuant to *Brenner*, the very standard articulated in the PTO's "Utility Examination Guidelines" ("Utility Guidelines") and followed here when examining the '643 application. It argues that Fisher failed to meet that standard because Fisher's alleged uses are so general as to be meaningless. What is more, the government asserts that the same generic uses could apply not only to the five claimed ESTs but also to any EST derived from any organism. It thus argues that the seven utilities alleged by Fisher are merely starting points for further research, not the end point of any research effort. It further disputes the importance of the commercial success of ESTs in the marketplace, pointing out that Fisher's evidence involved only databases, clone sets, and microarrays, not the five claimed ESTs. Therefore, the government contends that we should affirm the Board's decision.

Several academic institutions and biotechnology and pharmaceutical companies[11] write as amici curiae in support of the government. Like the government, they assert that Fisher's claimed uses are nothing more than a "laundry list" of research plans, each general and speculative, none providing a specific and substantial benefit in currently available form. The amici also advocate that the claimed ESTs are the objects of further research aimed at identifying what genes of unknown function are expressed during anthesis and what proteins of unknown function are encoded for by those genes. Until the corresponding genes and proteins have a known function, the amici argue, the claimed ESTs lack utility under § 101 and are not patentable.

We agree with both the government and the amici that none of Fisher's seven asserted uses meets the utility requirement of § 101. Section 101 provides: "Whoever invents ... any new and *useful* ... composition of matter ... may obtain a patent therefor...." (emphasis added). In *Brenner*, the Supreme Court explained what is required to establish the usefulness of a new invention, noting at the outset that "a simple, everyday word ["useful," as found in § 101] can be pregnant with ambiguity when applied to the facts of life." Contrary to Fisher's argument that § 101 only requires an invention that is not "frivolous, injurious to the well-being, good policy, or good morals of society," the Supreme Court appeared to reject Justice Story's de minimis view of utility. The Supreme Court observed that Justice Story's definition "sheds little light on our subject," on the one hand framing the relevant inquiry as "whether the invention in question is 'frivolous and insignificant'" if narrowly read, while on the other hand "allowing the patenting of any invention not positively harmful to society" if more broadly read. In its place, the Supreme Court announced a more rigorous test, stating:

> The basic *quid pro quo* contemplated by the Constitution and the Congress for granting a patent monopoly is the benefit derived by the public from an invention with *substantial utility*. Unless and until a process is refined and developed to this point—where *specific benefit exists in currently available form*—there is insufficient justification for permitting an applicant to engross what may prove to be a broad field.

Following *Brenner*, our predecessor court, the Court of Customs and Patent Appeals, and this court have required a claimed invention to have a specific and substantial utility to satisfy § 101.

The Supreme Court has not defined what the terms "specific" and "substantial" mean per se. Nevertheless, together with the Court of Customs and Patent Appeals, we have offered guidance as to the uses which would meet the utility standard of § 101. From this, we can discern the kind of disclosure an application must contain to establish a specific and substantial utility for the claimed invention.

Courts have used the labels "practical utility" and "real world" utility interchangeably in determining whether an invention offers a "substantial" utility. Indeed, the Court of Customs and Patent Appeals stated that "'[p]ractical utility' is a shorthand way of attributing 'real-world' value to claimed subject matter. In other words, one skilled in the art can use a claimed discovery in a manner which provides some *immediate benefit to the public*." It thus is clear that an application must show that an invention

---

11. Amici in support of the government include Affymetrix, Inc., American College of Medical Genetics, Association of American Medical Colleges, Baxter Healthcare Corporation, Dow AgroSciences LLC, Eli Lilly and Company, Genentech, Inc., National Academy of Sciences, and the University of North Carolina School of Law.

is useful to the public as disclosed in its current form, not that it may prove useful at some future date after further research. Simply put, to satisfy the "substantial" utility requirement, an asserted use must show that that claimed invention has a significant and presently available benefit to the public.

Turning to the "specific" utility requirement, an application must disclose a use which is not so vague as to be meaningless. Indeed, one of our predecessor courts has observed "that the nebulous expressions 'biological activity' or 'biological properties' appearing in the specification convey no more explicit indication of the usefulness of the compounds and how to use them than did the equally obscure expression 'useful for technical and pharmaceutical purposes' unsuccessfully relied upon by the appellant in *In re Diedrich*." Thus, in addition to providing a "substantial" utility, an asserted use must also show that that claimed invention can be used to provide a well-defined and particular benefit to the public.

In 2001, partially in response to questions about the patentability of ESTs, the PTO issued Utility Guidelines governing its internal practice for determining whether a claimed invention satisfies § 101. *See* Utility Examination Guidelines, 66 Fed. Reg. 1092 (Jan. 5, 2001). The PTO incorporated these guidelines into the Manual of Patent Examining Procedure ("MPEP"). *See* U.S. Pat. & Trademark Off., Manual of Patent Examining Procedure § 2107 (8th ed. 2001, rev. May 2004). The MPEP and Guidelines "are not binding on this court, but may be given judicial notice to the extent they do not conflict with the statute." According to the Utility Guidelines, a specific utility is particular to the subject matter claimed and would not be applicable to a broad class of invention. The Utility Guidelines also explain that a substantial utility defines a "real world" use. In particular, "[u]tilities that require or constitute carrying out further research to identify or reasonably confirm a 'real world' context of use are not substantial utilities." Further, the Utility Guidelines discuss "research tools," a term often given to inventions used to conduct research. The PTO particularly cautions that

> [a]n assessment that focuses on whether an invention is useful only in a research setting thus does not address whether the invention is in fact "useful" in a patent sense. [The PTO] must distinguish between inventions that have a specifically identified substantial utility and inventions whose asserted utility requires further research to identify or reasonably confirm.

The PTO's standards for assessing whether a claimed invention has a specific and substantial utility comport with this court's interpretation of the utility requirement of § 101.

Turning to the parties' arguments, Fisher first raises a legal issue, charging that the Board applied a heightened standard for utility in the case of ESTs. Fisher apparently bases this argument on statements made by the Board in connection with its discussion of whether the claimed ESTs can be used to identify a polymorphism. In that context, the Board stated:

> Somewhere between having no knowledge (the present circumstances) and having complete knowledge of the gene and its role in the plant's development lies the line between 'utility' and 'substantial utility.' We need not draw the line or further define it in this case because the facts in this case represent the lowest end of the *spectrum*, *i.e.*, an insubstantial use.

(emphasis added). Fisher reads the word "spectrum" out of context, claiming that the word somehow implies the application of a higher standard for utility than required by § 101. We conclude, however, that the Board did not apply an incorrect legal standard. In its decision, the Board made reference to a "spectrum" to differentiate between a substantial utility, which satisfies the utility requirement of § 101, and an insubstantial utility, which fails to satisfy § 101. The Board plainly did not announce or apply a new test for assessing the utility of ESTs. It simply followed the Utility Guidelines and MPEP, which mandate the specific and substantial utility test set forth in *Brenner*. Indeed, we note that Example 9 of the PTO's "Revised Interim Utility Guidelines Training Materials" is applicable to the facts here. *See* U.S. Pat. & Trademark Off., Revised Interim Utility Guidelines Training Materials 50–53 (1999), *available at* www.uspto.gov/web/menu/utility.pdf. In that example, a cDNA fragment disclosed as being useful as a probe to obtain the full length gene corresponding to a cDNA fragment was deemed to lack a specific and substantial utility. Additionally, the MPEP particularly explains that a claim directed to a polynucleotide disclosed to be useful as a "gene probe" or "chromosome marker," as is the case here, fails to satisfy the specific utility requirement unless a specific DNA target is also disclosed.

Regarding the seven uses asserted by Fisher, we observe that each claimed EST uniquely corresponds to the single gene from which it was transcribed ("underlying gene"). As of the filing date of the '643 application, Fisher admits that the underlying genes have no known functions. Fisher, nevertheless, claims that this fact is irrelevant because the seven asserted uses are not related to the functions of the underlying genes. We are not convinced by this contention. Essentially, the claimed ESTs act as no more than research intermediates that may help scientists to isolate the particular underlying protein-encoding genes and conduct further experimentation on those genes. The overall goal of such experimentation is presumably to understand the maize genome—the functions of the underlying genes, the identity of the encoded proteins, the role those proteins play during anthesis, whether polymorphisms exist, the identity of promoters that trigger protein expression, whether protein expression may be controlled, etc. Accordingly, the claimed ESTs are, in words of the Supreme Court, mere "object[s] of use-testing," to wit, objects upon which scientific research could be performed with no assurance that anything useful will be discovered in the end....

Fisher compares the claimed ESTs to certain other patentable research tools, such as a microscope. Although this comparison may, on first blush, be appealing in that both a microscope and one of the claimed ESTs can be used to generate scientific data about a sample having unknown properties, Fisher's analogy is flawed. As the government points out, a microscope has the specific benefit of optically magnifying an object to immediately reveal its structure. One of the claimed ESTs, by contrast, can only be used to detect the presence of genetic material having the same structure as the EST itself. It is unable to provide any information about the overall structure let alone the function of the underlying gene. Accordingly, while a microscope can offer an immediate, real world benefit in a variety of applications, the same cannot be said for the claimed ESTs. Fisher's proposed analogy is thus inapt. Hence, we conclude that Fisher's asserted uses are insufficient to meet the standard for a "substantial" utility under § 101.

Moreover, all of Fisher's asserted uses represent merely hypothetical possibilities, objectives which the claimed ESTs, or any EST for that matter, *could* possibly achieve, but none for which they have been used in the real world. Focusing on the two uses emphasized by Fisher at oral argument, Fisher maintains that the claimed ESTs could be used to identify polymorphisms or to isolate promoters. Nevertheless, in the face of a utility rejection, Fisher has not presented any evidence, as the Board well noted, showing that the claimed ESTs have been used in either way. That is, Fisher does not present either a single polymorphism or a single promoter, assuming at least one of each exists, actually identified by using the claimed ESTs. Further, Fisher has not shown that a polymorphism or promoter so identified would have a "specific and substantial" use. The Board, in fact, correctly recognized this very deficiency and cited it as one of the reasons for upholding the examiner's final rejection.

With respect to the remaining asserted uses, there is no disclosure in the specification showing that any of the claimed ESTs were used as a molecular marker on a map of the maize genome. There also is no disclosure establishing that any of the claimed ESTs were used or, for that matter, could be used to control or provide information about gene expression. Significantly, despite the fact that maize leaves produce over two thousand different proteins during anthesis, Fisher failed to show that one of the claimed ESTs translates into a portion of one of those proteins. Fisher likewise did not provide any evidence showing that the claimed ESTs were used to locate genetic molecules in other plants and organisms. What is more, Fisher has not proffered any evidence showing that any such generic molecules would themselves have a specific and substantial utility. Consequently, because Fisher failed to prove that its claimed ESTs can be successfully used in the seven ways disclosed in the '643 application, we have no choice but to conclude that the claimed ESTs do not have a "substantial" utility under § 101.

Furthermore, Fisher's seven asserted uses are plainly not "specific." Any EST transcribed from any gene in the maize genome has the potential to perform any one of the alleged uses. That is, any EST transcribed from any gene in the maize genome may be a molecular marker or a source for primers. Likewise, any EST transcribed from any gene in the maize genome may be used to measure the level of mRNA in a tissue sample, identify the presence or absence of a polymorphism, isolate promoters, control protein expression, or locate genetic molecules of other plants and organisms. Nothing about Fisher's seven alleged uses set the five claimed ESTs apart from the more than 32,000 ESTs disclosed in the '643 application or indeed from any EST derived from any organism. Accordingly, we conclude that Fisher has only disclosed general uses for its claimed ESTs, not specific ones that satisfy § 101.

We agree with the Board that the facts here are similar to those in *Brenner*. There, as noted above, the applicant claimed a process for preparing compounds of unknown use. Similarly, Fisher filed an application claiming five particular ESTs which are capable of hybridizing with underlying genes of unknown function found in the maize genome. The *Brenner* court held that the claimed process lacked a utility because it could be used only to produce a compound of unknown use. The *Brenner* court stated: "We find absolutely no warrant for the proposition that although Congress intended that no patent be granted on a chemical compound whose sole 'utility' consists of its potential role as an object of use-testing, a different set of rules was meant to apply to the process which yielded the unpatentable product." Applying that same logic here, we conclude that the claimed ESTs, which do not correlate to an underlying gene of known function, fail to meet the standard for utility intended by Congress.

In addition to approving of the Board's reliance on *Brenner*, we observe that the facts here are even more analogous to those presented in [*In re*] *Kirk*, 376 F.2d 936 [(C.C.P.A. 1967)], and *In re Joly*, 376 F.2d 906 (C.C.P.A. 1967), two cases decided by our predecessor court shortly after *Brenner*. In *Kirk*, the applicant sought to patent new steroidal compounds disclosed as having two possible utilities. First, the applicant alleged that the claimed compounds were useful for their "biological activity" because "one skilled in the art would know how to use the compounds ... to take advantage of their presently-existing biological activity." The court rejected this claimed utility on the ground that it was not sufficiently "specific," but was instead "nebulous."

Second, the applicant asserted that the claimed compounds could be used by skilled chemists as intermediates in the preparation of final steroidal compounds of unknown use. Relying on *Brenner*, the court reasoned:

> It seems clear that, if a process for producing a product of only conjectural use is not itself "useful" within § 101, it cannot be said that the starting materials for such a process—*i.e.*, the presently claimed intermediates—are "useful." It is not enough that the specification disclose that the intermediate exists and that it "works," reacts, or can be used to produce some intended product of no known use. Nor is it enough that the product disclosed to be obtained from the intermediate belongs to some class of compounds which now is, or in the future might be, the subject of research to determine some *specific use. Cf. Reiners v. Mehltretter*, 236 F.2d 418, 421 [(C.C.P.A. 1956)] where compounds employed as intermediates to produce other directly useful compounds were found to be themselves useful.

(emphasis added). Therefore, the court affirmed the Board's rejection of the claimed compounds for lack of utility.

The facts in *Joly* are nearly identical to the facts in *Kirk*. The *Joly* applicant filed an application claiming compounds useful as intermediates in preparing steroids that were themselves not shown or known to be useful, but that were similar in chemical structure to steroids of known pharmacological usefulness. The court adopted the reasoning of the *Kirk* court in its entirety and affirmed the Board's decision rejecting the claimed intermediates for failing to comply with § 101.

Just as the claimed compounds in *Kirk* and *Joly* were useful only as intermediates in the synthesis of other compounds of unknown use, the claimed ESTs can only be used as research intermediates in the identification of underlying protein-encoding genes of unknown function. The rationale of *Kirk* and *Joly* thus applies here. In the words of the *Kirk* court:

> We do not believe that it was the intention of the statutes to require the Patent Office, the courts, or the public to play the sort of guessing game that might be involved if an applicant could satisfy the requirements of the statutes by indicating the usefulness of a claimed compound *in terms of possible use so general as to be meaningless* and then, after his research or that of his competitors has definitely ascertained an actual use for the compound, adducing evidence intended to show that a particular specific use would have been obvious to men skilled in the particular art to which this use relates.

(emphasis added).... That the *Kirk* and *Joly* decisions involved chemical compounds, while the present case involves biological entities, does not distinguish these decisions. The rationale presented therein, having been drawn from principles set forth by the Supreme Court in *Brenner*, applies with equal force in the fields of chemistry and biology as well as in any scientific discipline. In *Brenner*, the Supreme Court was primarily concerned with creating an unwarranted monopoly to the detriment of the public:

> Whatever weight is attached to the value of encouraging disclosure and of inhibiting secrecy, we believe a more compelling consideration is that a process patent in the chemical field, which has not been developed and pointed to the degree of specific utility, creates a monopoly of knowledge which should be granted only if clearly commanded by the statute. Until the process claim has been reduced to production of a product shown to be useful, the metes and bounds of that monopoly are not capable of precise delineation. It may engross

> a vast, unknown, and perhaps unknowable area. Such a patent may confer power to block off whole areas of scientific development, without compensating benefit to the public.... This is not to say that we mean to disparage the importance of contributions to the fund of scientific information short of the invention of something "useful," or that we are blind to the prospect that what now seems without "use" may tomorrow command the grateful attention of the public. But a patent is not a hunting license. It is not a reward for the search, but compensation for its successful conclusion. [A] patent system must be related to the world of commerce rather than to the realm of philosophy.

Here, granting a patent to Fisher for its five claimed ESTs would amount to a hunting license because the claimed ESTs can be used only to gain further information about the underlying genes and the proteins encoded for by those genes. The claimed ESTs themselves are not an end of Fisher's research effort, but only tools to be used along the way in the search for a practical utility. Thus, while Fisher's claimed ESTs may add a noteworthy contribution to biotechnology research, our precedent dictates that the '643 application does not meet the utility requirement of § 101 because Fisher does not identify the function for the underlying protein-encoding genes. Absent such identification, we hold that the claimed ESTs have not been researched and understood to the point of providing an immediate, well-defined, real world benefit to the public meriting the grant of a patent.

2.

Fisher's reliance on *Jolles*, *Nelson*, and *Cross*, cases which found utility in certain claimed pharmaceutical compounds, is misplaced. In *Jolles*, the applicant filed an application claiming naphthacene compounds useful in treating acute myloblastic leukemia. To support the asserted utility, the applicant presented *in vivo* data showing eight of the claimed compounds effectively treated tumors in a mouse model. Our predecessor court reversed the Board's affirmance of the final rejection for lack of utility, finding that the structural similarity between the compounds tested *in vivo* and the remaining claimed compounds was sufficient to establish utility for the remaining claimed compounds.

In *Nelson*, decided by the Court of Customs and Patent Appeals in the same year as *Jolles*, Nelson claimed prostaglandin compounds. The PTO declared an interference with an application filed by Bowler claiming the same compounds. The issue before the Board was whether Nelson had established utility for the claimed prostaglandins as smooth muscle stimulants and blood pressure modulators via *in vivo* and *in vitro* data, specifically, an *in vivo* rat blood pressure test and an *in vitro* gerbil colon smooth muscle stimulation test. The Board declined to award priority to Nelson, characterizing Nelson's tests as "rough screens, uncorrelated with actual utility [in humans]." Our predecessor court reversed, concluding that "tests evidencing pharmacological activity may manifest a practical utility even though they may not establish a specific therapeutic use."

In *Cross*, decided by the Federal Circuit five years after *Jolles* and *Nelson*, Iizuka filed an application claiming thromboxane synthetase inhibitors, alleged to be useful in treating inflammation, asthma, hypertension, and other ailments. When Cross filed an application claiming the same compounds two months after Iizuka, the PTO declared an interference. The dispositive issue concerned whether Iizuka's Japanese priority application disclosed utility for the claimed inhibitors. The Board concluded that it offered a sufficient disclosure based upon *in vitro* data showing strong inhibitory action for thromboxane synthetase for structurally-similar compounds in human or bovine platelet microsomes. We affirmed, reasoning:

> Opinions of our predecessor court have recognized the fact that pharmacological testing of animals is a screening procedure for testing new drugs for practical utility. This *in vivo* testing is but an intermediate link in a screening chain which may eventually lead to the use of the drug as a therapeutic agent in humans. We perceive no insurmountable difficulty, under appropriate circumstances, in finding that the first link in the screening chain, *in vitro* testing, may establish a practical utility for the compound in question. Successful *in vitro* testing will marshal resources and direct the expenditure of effort to further *in vivo* testing of the most potent compounds, thereby providing an immediate benefit to the public, analogous to the benefit provided by the showing of an *in vivo* utility.

The facts in these three cases are readily distinguishable from the facts here. In *Jolles*, *Nelson*, and *Cross*, the applicants disclosed specific pharmaceutical uses in humans for the claimed compounds and supported those uses with specific animal test data, *in vitro*, *in vivo*, or both. In contrast, Fisher disclosed a variety of asserted uses for the claimed ESTs, but failed to present any evidence-test data, declaration, deposition testimony, or otherwise-to support those uses as presently beneficial and hence practical. Fisher did not show that even one of the claimed ESTs had been tested and successfully aided in identifying a polymorphism in the maize genome or in isolating a single promoter that could give clues about protein expression. Adopting the language of the *Cross* court, the alleged uses in *Jolles*, *Nelson*, and *Cross* were not "nebulous expressions, such as 'biological activity' or 'biological properties' [alleged in the application in *Kirk*]," that "convey little explicit indication regarding the utility of a compound." Instead, the alleged uses in those cases gave a firm indication of the precise uses to which the claimed compounds could be put. For example, in *Nelson*, the claimed prostaglandins could be used to stimulate smooth muscle or modulate blood pressure in humans as shown by both *in vivo* and *in vitro* animal data. Hence, the *Jolles*, *Nelson*, and *Cross* courts concluded that the claimed pharmaceutical compounds satisfied the specific and substantial utility requirements of § 101. We cannot reach that same conclusion here. Fisher's laundry list of uses, like the terms "biological activity" or "biological properties" alleged in *Kirk*, are nebulous, especially in the absence of any data demonstrating that the claimed ESTs were actually put to the alleged uses.

Fisher's reliance on the commercial success of general EST databases is also misplaced because such general reliance does not relate to the ESTs at issue in this case. Fisher did not present any evidence showing that agricultural companies have purchased or even expressed any interest in the claimed ESTs. And, it is entirely unclear from the record whether such business entities ever will. Accordingly, while commercial success may support the utility of an invention, it does not do so in this case.

3.

As a final matter, we observe that the government and its amici express concern that allowing EST patents without proof of utility would discourage research, delay scientific discovery, and thwart progress in the "useful Arts" and "Science." *See* U.S. Const. art. I, § 8, cl. 8. The government and its amici point out that allowing EST claims like Fisher's would give rise to multiple patents, likely owned by several different companies, relating to the same underlying gene and expressed protein. Such a situation, the government and amici predict, would result in an unnecessarily convoluted licensing environment for those interested in researching that gene and/or protein.

The concerns of the government and amici, which may or may not be valid, are not ones that should be considered in deciding whether the application for the claimed ESTs meets the utility requirement of § 101. The same may be said for the resource and managerial problems that the PTO potentially would face if applicants present the PTO with an onslaught of patent applications directed to particular ESTs. Congress did not intend for these practical implications to affect the determination of whether an invention satisfies the requirements set forth in 35 U.S.C. §§ 101, 102, 103, and 112. They are public policy considerations which are more appropriately directed to Congress as the legislative branch of government, rather than this court as a judicial body responsible simply for interpreting and applying statutory law. Under Title 35, an applicant is entitled to a patent if his invention is new, useful, nonobvious, and his application adequately describes the claimed invention, teaches others how to make and use the claimed invention, and discloses the best mode for practicing the claimed invention. What is more, when Congress enacted § 101, it indicated that "anything under the sun that is made by man" constitutes potential subject matter for a patent. S. Rep. No. 82-1979, at 7 (1952). Policy reasons aside, because we conclude that the utility requirement of § 101 is not met, we hold that Fisher is not entitled to a patent for the five claimed ESTs....

III. Conclusion

We conclude that substantial evidence supports the Board's findings that each of the five claimed ESTs lacks a specific and substantial utility and that they are not enabled. Accordingly, the Board's decision affirming the final rejection of claim 1 of the '643 patent for lack of utility under § 101 and lack of enablement under § 112, first paragraph, is affirmed....

Circuit Judge Rader, dissenting.

This court today determines that ... ESTs[] do not satisfy 35 U.S.C. § 101 unless there is a known use for the genes from which each EST is transcribed. While I agree that an invention must demonstrate utility to satisfy § 101, these claimed ESTs have such a utility, at least as research tools in isolating and studying other molecules. Therefore, I respectfully dissent.

Several, if not all, of Fisher's asserted utilities claim that ESTs function to study other molecules. In simple terms, ESTs are research tools. Admittedly ESTs have use only in a research setting. However, the value and utility of research tools generally is beyond question, even though limited to a laboratory setting. *See* U.S. Pat. & Trademark Off., Manual of Patent Examining Procedure (MPEP) § 2107.01 at 2100–33 (8th ed. 2001, rev. Feb. 2003) ("Many research tools such as gas chromatographs, screening assays, and nucleotide sequencing techniques have a clear, specific and unquestionable utility (e.g., they are useful in analyzing compounds)."). Thus, if the claimed ESTs qualify as research tools, then they have a "specific" and "substantial" utility sufficient for § 101. If these ESTs do not enhance research, then *Brenner* controls and erects a § 101 bar for lack of utility. For the following reasons, these claimed ESTs are more akin to patentable research tools than to the unpatentable methods in *Brenner*.

In *Brenner*, the Court confronted a growing conflict between this court's predecessor, the Court of Customs and Patent Appeals (CCPA), and the Patent Office over the patentability of methods of producing compounds with no known use. This conflict began with *Nelson*, the first in a series of cases wherein the CCPA reversed several Patent Office utility rejections. *Brenner* put an end to these cases because, in the 1960s, the Court could not distinguish between denying patents to compounds with no known use and denying patents to methods of producing those useless compounds. The Court commented:

> We find absolutely no warrant for the proposition that although Congress intended that no patent be granted on a chemical compound whose sole 'utility' consists of its potential role as an object of use-testing, a different set of rules was meant to apply to the process which yielded the unpatentable product. That proposition seems to us little more than an attempt to evade the impact of the rules which concededly govern patentability of the product itself.

This court's predecessor later extended *Brenner* to bar patents on compounds as intermediates in the preparation of other compounds having no known use. These cases, however, share a common underpinning—a method of producing a compound with no known use has no more benefit to society than the useless compound itself.

This case is very different. Unlike the methods and compounds in *Brenner* and *Kirk*, Fisher's claimed EST's *are* beneficial to society. As an example, these research tools "may help scientists to isolate the particular underlying protein-encoding genes ... [with the] overall goal of such experimentation ... presumably [being] to understand the maize genome[.]" They also can serve as a probe introduced into a sample tissue to confirm "that the gene corresponding to the EST was being expressed in the sample tissue at the time of mRNA extraction."

These research tools are similar to a microscope; both take a researcher one step closer to identifying and understanding a previously unknown and invisible structure. Both supply information about a molecular structure. Both advance research and bring scientists closer to unlocking the secrets of the corn genome to provide better food production for the hungry world. If a microscope has § 101 utility, so too do these ESTs.

The Board and this court acknowledge that the ESTs perform a function, that they have a utility, but proceed quickly to a value judgment that the utility would not produce enough valuable information. The Board instead complains that the information these ESTs supply is too "insubstantial" to merit protection. Yet this conclusion denies the very nature of scientific advance. Science always advances in small incremental steps. While acknowledging the patentability of research tools generally (and microscopes as one example thereof), this court concludes with little scientific foundation that these ESTs do not qualify as research tools because they do not "offer an immediate, real world benefit" because further research is required to understand the underlying gene. This court further faults the EST research for lacking any "assurance that anything useful will be discovered in the end." These criticisms would foreclose much scientific research and many vital research tools. Often scientists embark on research with no assurance of success and knowing that even success will demand "significant additional research."

Nonetheless, this court, oblivious to the challenges of complex research, discounts these ESTs because it concludes (without scientific evidence) that they do not supply enough information. This court reasons that a research tool has a "specific" and "substantial" utility *only* if the studied object is readily understandable using the claimed tool—that no further research is required. Surely this cannot be the law. Otherwise, only the final step of a lengthy incremental research inquiry gets protection.

Even with a microscope, significant additional research is often required to ascertain the particular function of a "revealed" structure. To illustrate, a cancerous growth, magnified with a patented microscope, can be identified and distinguished from other healthy cells by a properly trained doctor or researcher. But even today, the scientific community still does not fully grasp the reasons that cancerous growths increase in mass and spread throughout the body,[12] or the nature of compounds that interact with them, or the interactions of environmental or genetic conditions that contribute to developing cancer. Significant additional research is required to answer these questions. Even with answers to these questions, the cure for cancer will remain in the distance. Yet the microscope still has "utility" under § 101. Why? Because it takes the researcher one step closer to answering these questions. Each step, even if small in isolation, is nonetheless a benefit to society sufficient to give a viable research tool "utility" under § 101. In fact, experiments that fail still serve to eliminate some possibilities and provide information to the research process.

The United States Patent Office, above all, should recognize the incremental nature of scientific endeavor. Yet, in the interest of easing its administrative load, the Patent Office will eliminate some research tools as providing "insubstantial" advances. How does the Patent Office know which "insubstantial" research step will contribute to a substantial breakthrough in genomic study? Quite simply, it does not.

In addition, this court faults Fisher for not presenting evidence of utility showing that the claimed ESTs "have been used in the real world." To the contrary, this court misapprehended the proper procedure. Fisher asserted seven different utilities. The Board rejected two of these assertions outright as "insubstantial." This summary dismissal deprived Fisher of any chance to proffer evidence. Rather than fault Fisher for not presenting evidence it was prevented from offering, this court should instead observe that the Board did not satisfy its burden of challenging Fisher's presumptively correct assertion that the ESTs were *capable* of performing those functions. *See* MPEP § 2107.02(IV) at 2100–40 (noting that the initial burden is on the office to establish a prima facie case as to lack of utility and to provide evidentiary support thereof); *In re Brana*, 51 F.3d 1560, 1566 (Fed. Cir. 1995) (where an applicant has asserted utility in the disclosure, the Patent Office has the initial burden of challenging this presumptively correct assertion of utility).

Abandoning the proper legal procedure, the Board reasoned that the molecules studied with these ESTs showed no particular use, therefore the ESTs themselves also lacked a utility. In so ruling, the Board did not reject Fisher's utilities on the basis that the ESTs were *unable to perform* the purported utilities. Thus, the Board did not establish a prima facie challenge to the ESTs' ability to perform these two utilities. Without anything to rebut, Fisher had no obligation or opportunity to provide evidence in rebuttal. Thus, I respectfully disagree with this court's conclusion that the Board's decision can be affirmed on the basis that Fisher did not supply evidence of the ESTs' ability to perform the asserted utilities.

In truth, I have some sympathy with the Patent Office's dilemma. The Office needs some tool to reject inventions that may advance the "useful arts" but not sufficiently to warrant the valuable exclusive right of a patent. The Patent Office has seized upon this utility requirement to reject these research tools as contributing "insubstantially" to the advance of the useful arts. The utility requirement is ill suited to that task, however, because it lacks any standard for assessing the state of the prior art and the contributions of the claimed advance. The proper tool for assessing sufficient contribution to the use-

---

12. ESTs have already been used to advance cancer research well beyond what is achievable using microscopes alone. *See* Andy J. Minn, *Genes That Mediate Breast Cancer Metastisis To Lung*, Nature, July 28, 2005 at 518–24 (discussing research to identify genes that mark and mediate breast cancer metastisis to the lung).

ful arts is the obviousness requirement of 35 U.S.C. § 103. Unfortunately this court has deprived the Patent Office of the obviousness requirement for genomic inventions. *See In re Deuel*, 51 F.3d 1552 (Fed. Cir. 1995); Martin J. Adelman et al., *Patent Law*, 517 (West Group 1998) (commenting that scholars have been critical of *Deuel*, which "overly favored patent applicants in biotech by adopting an overly lax nonobviousness standard." (*citing* Anita Varma & David Abraham, *DNA Is Different: Legal Obviousness and the Balance Between Biotech Inventors and the Market*, 9 Harv. J. L. & Tech. 53 (1996))); Philippe Ducor, *The Federal Circuit and In re Deuel: Does §103 apply to Naturally Occurring DNA?*, 77 J. Pat. & Trademark Off. Soc'y 871, 883 (Nov. 1995) ("The Court of Appeals for the Federal Circuit could have formulated its opinion in only one sentence: '35 U.S.C. § 103 does not apply to newly retrieved natural DNA sequences.'"); Philippe Ducor, *Recombinant Products and Nonobviousness: A Typology*, 13 Santa Clara Computer and High Tech. L.J. 1, 44–45 (Feb. 1997) ("This amounts to a practical elimination of the requirement for nonobviousness for these products, even when all the information necessary to discover them is previously available."); *see also* over fifty additional articles critical of *Deuel* in the "Citing References" tab for *Deuel* on Westlaw. Nonetheless, rather than distort the utility test, the Patent Office should seek ways to apply the correct test, the test used world wide for such assessments (other than in the United States), namely inventive step or obviousness.

Thus, for the foregoing reasons, I would find that Fisher's asserted utilities qualify the claimed ESTs as research tools useful in the study of other molecules. Because research tools provide a cognizable benefit to society, much like a microscope, the ESTs claimed here have "utility" under § 101. In addition, the enablement rejection should also be reversed because it was a consequence of the finding of lack of utility.

3. Novelty

The requirement that an invention be "new" to deserve a patent reaches far back into the antecedents of U.S. patent law. To many minds, "novelty" probably seems to be *the* fundamental criterion. If an invention is already publicly known, then why should an individual be able to obtain the exclusive rights to it? But what does it mean for an invention to be "new"? Section 102 of the Patent Act defines the requirement for "novelty" of inventions:

§ 102. Conditions for Patentability; Novelty and Loss of Right to Patent

35 U.S.C. § 102

A person shall be entitled to a patent unless—

(a) the invention was known or used by others in this country, or patented or described in a printed publication in this or a foreign country, before the invention thereof by the applicant for patent, or

(b) the invention was patented or described in a printed publication in this or a foreign country or in public use or on sale in this country, more than one year prior to the date of the application for patent in the United States, or

(c) he has abandoned the invention, or

(d) the invention was first patented or caused to be patented, or was the subject of an inventor's certificate, by the applicant or his legal representatives or assigns in a foreign country prior to the date of the application for patent in this country on an application for patent or inventor's certificate filed more than twelve months before the filing of the application in the United States, or

(e) The invention was described in—

> (1) an application for patent, published under section 122(b), by another filed in the United States before the invention by the applicant for patent, except that an international application filed under the treaty defined in section 351(a) shall have the effect under this subsection of a national application published under section 122(b) only if the international application designating the United States was published under Article 21(2)(a) of such treaty in the English language; or
>
> (2) a patent granted on an application for patent by another filed in the United States before the invention by the applicant for patent, except that a patent shall not be deemed filed in the United States for the purposes of this subsection based on the filing of an international application filed under the treaty defined in section 351(a); or

(f) he did not himself invent the subject matter sought to be patented, or

(g)(1) during the course of an interference conducted under section 135 or section 291, another inventor involved therein establishes, to the extent permitted in section 104, that before such person's invention thereof the invention was made by such other inventor and not abandoned, suppressed, or concealed, or (2) before such person's invention thereof, the invention was made in this country by another inventor who had not abandoned, suppressed, or concealed it. In determining priority of invention under this subsection, there shall be considered not only the respective dates of conception and reduction to practice of the invention, but also the reasonable diligence of one who was first to conceive and last to reduce to practice, from a time prior to conception by the other.

* * *

As is readily apparent, § 102 contains a complicated set of definitions and criteria for determining whether an invention is truly novel. The following case analyzes some of the most salient requirements of § 102 for purposes of patenting genetic technologies.

Chiron Corp. v. Genentech, Inc.

363 F.3d 1247 (Fed. Cir. 2004)

Circuit Judge Rader.

After a jury trial, the United States District Court for the Eastern District of California entered judgment in favor of Genentech that all claims of U.S. Patent No. 6,054,561 are invalid under 35 U.S.C. § 102 because none of the asserted claims is entitled to priority to a series of applications filed in 1984, 1985, and 1986. Because Chiron did not adequately disclose or support the subject matter of its '561 patent in its 1984, 1985, or 1986 applications, this court affirms the district court's denial of a motion for judgment as a matter of law (JMOL) and motion for a new trial.

I.

The '561 patent claims particular monoclonal antibodies. Specifically, independent claim 19 states:[13] "A monoclonal antibody that binds to human c-erbB-2 antigen."

According to modern understanding, a monoclonal antibody is a composition with a homogeneous antibody population. An antibody is a protein generated by the immune system that is capable of recognizing and binding to a specific antigen. Described in terms of its structure, an antibody is a Y-shaped protein consisting of four amino acid chains, two heavy and two light. In a simplified model sufficient for this appeal, each antibody has primarily two regions: a variable region and a constant region. The variable region, located on the ends of the arms of the Y, binds to and interacts with the target antigen. This variable region includes a complementary determining region (CDR) that recognizes and binds to a specific binding site on a particular antigen. The constant region, located on the tail of the Y, is recognized by and interacts with the immune system.

A target antigen generally has numerous binding sites, also called epitopes, recognized by CDRs on multiple antibodies. Each antibody that specifically binds to a different epitope has a different structure. Thus, one antigen may have more than one corresponding antibody. In this case, claim 19 of the '561 patent reads on monoclonal antibodies that bind to human c-erbB-2 antigen (also named HER2)—an antigen associated with breast cancer cells.

There are various methods of producing monoclonal antibodies. One method uses hybridoma technology, which refers to a cloned cell line that produces a single type of antibody. The hybridoma method uses the cells of various species, including mice, hamsters, rats, and humans. Murine antibodies—derived from mouse cells—are particularly important for this invention.

Another method uses genetic engineering including recombinant DNA techniques. Monoclonal antibodies made from these techniques include, among others, chimeric antibodies and humanized antibodies. A chimeric antibody combines DNA encoding regions from more than one type of species. For example, a chimeric antibody may derive the variable region from a mouse and the constant region from a human. A humanized antibody comes predominantly from a human, even though it contains nonhuman portions. Like a chimeric antibody, a humanized antibody may contain a completely human constant region. But unlike a chimeric antibody, the variable region may be partially derived from a human. The nonhuman, synthetic portions of a humanized antibody often come from CDRs in murine antibodies. In any event, these regions are crucial to allow the antibody to recognize and bind to a specific antigen.

As noted, murine antibodies play an important role in these technologies. While useful for diagnostics and short-term therapies, murine antibodies cannot be administered to people long-term without increasing the risk of a deleterious immunogenic response. This response, called Human Anti-Mouse Antibody (HAMA), occurs when a human

---

13. Chiron also relies upon independent claims 1 and 9.

Claim 1 recites:

> A monoclonal antibody that binds to a human breast cancer antigen that is also bound by monoclonal antibody 454C11 which is produced by the hybridoma deposited with the American Type Culture Collection having Accession No. HB 8484.

Claim 9 recites:

> A monoclonal antibody that binds to a human breast cancer antigen that is also bound by monoclonal antibody 520C9 which is produced by the hybridoma deposited with the American Type Culture Collection having Accession No. HB 8696.

immune system recognizes the murine antibody as foreign and attacks it. A HAMA response can cause toxic shock or even death.

Chimeric and humanized antibodies reduce the likelihood of a HAMA response by minimizing the nonhuman portions of administered antibodies. Furthermore, chimeric and humanized antibodies have the additional benefit of activating secondary human immune responses, such as antibody dependent cellular cytoxicity.

In the early 1980s, scientists at Chiron's predecessor corporation, Cetus Corp., (collectively, Chiron) began investigating monoclonal antibodies that target human breast cancer antigens. As noted above, the antigen that facilitates diagnosis and treatment of breast cancer was eventually named HER2. This investigational work led to a series of patent applications. The inventors filed their first application on February 8, 1984. Within a year, on January 11, 1985, they filed a continuation-in-part (CIP) application claiming priority based on that first 1984 application. The inventors filed another CIP application on May 21, 1986. Eventually, the application that led to the '561 patent was filed as another CIP on June 7, 1995. This appeal focuses on the '561 patent's claims to priority based on the applications filed in 1984, 1985, and 1986.

The 1984 application discloses one monoclonal antibody (454C11) that binds to HER2. The 454C11 is a murine antibody produced by the hybridoma method. While the application discloses the deposit of the hybridoma that produced the monoclonal antibody, the application does not identify the structure, function, or molecular weight of the antigen. Because the first publication that disclosed chimeric antibody technology did not appear until four months after this filing, it is not surprising that the 1984 application does not disclose any chimeric antibodies. Similarly, the first publication to disclose humanized antibodies appeared in May 1986. Thus, for good reason, this 1984 application also does not mention any humanized antibodies.

The 1985 application discloses six additional monoclonal antibodies that bind to HER2, all of which are murine antibodies. The disclosure also refers to the deposit of an additional hybridoma for one of these monoclonal antibodies, 520C9. While the application provides an approximate antigen molecular weight of 210 kilodaltons,[14] the application does not describe the identity, structure, or function of the antigen. The application does, however, note that six of the seven antibodies likely bind to the same epitope. By the time of this application, chimeric antibody technology was known in this art field. Although the application does not specifically disclose chimeric or humanized antibodies, it adds the following disclosure:

> As used herein the term "monoclonal antibody" means an antibody composition having a homogeneous antibody population. It is not intended to be limited as regards the source of the antibody or the manner in which it is made.

The 1986 application discloses six additional murine antibodies that bind to HER2 and the deposit for three additional hybridomas. Thus, this application discloses a total of thirteen murine antibodies and deposits for five of their corresponding hybridomas, including those corresponding to 454C11 and 520C9. The application discloses that these antibodies likely bind to at least three different epitopes on HER2. Although still not identifying the antigen by name, the application discloses that its molecular weight is approximately 200 kilodaltons. Although the 1986 application makes no specific mention of chimeric or humanized antibodies, it quotes again the statement that the

14. The HER2 antigen is now known to have a molecular weight of 185 kilodaltons.

term monoclonal antibody "is not intended to be limited as regards the source of the antibody or the manner in which it is made."

When the '561 patent issued, Chiron sued Genentech over sales of Herceptin(r), a humanized antibody useful for the long-term treatment of breast cancer. Herceptin binds to the HER2 antigen and thus inhibits the growth of cancerous cells. Because Herceptin is a humanized antibody, it minimizes any HAMA response in patients.

Before trial, the district court broadly construed the claims of the '561 patent to embrace chimeric and humanized antibodies in addition to the murine antibodies that bind to HER2. Accordingly, the district court subsequently granted Chiron's motion for partial summary judgment of infringement. Also before trial, the parties stipulated that the '561 patent would be invalid under § 102 based on intervening prior art if the patent were not entitled to claim priority to the filing date of any one of the 1984, 1985, and 1986 applications. Thus, the thirteen-day jury trial adjudicated only whether any of the priority applications satisfy the written description and enablement requirements of 35 U.S.C. § 112, first paragraph. Specifically the trial determined whether the 1980s applications adequately disclosed, and thus supported, the claim to chimeric and humanized antibodies claimed in the '561 patent (with its filing date in 1995). The jury determined that Genentech proved by clear and convincing evidence that none of the applications satisfy both the written description and the enablement requirement for the subject matter in the '561 patent's claims. The verdict form, however, did not require the jury to specify the particular requirement of § 112 left unfulfilled by each disclosure of the priority applications. After trial, the district court denied Chiron's motions for JMOL and a new trial.

Chiron appeals the denial of its post-trial motions, and Genentech conditionally "cross-appeals" the district court's claim construction. Although styled as a cross-appeal, this court treats this claim construction issue as an alternative ground for affirming the judgment. A cross-appeal is only proper if "a party seeks to enlarge its own rights under the judgment or to lessen the rights of its adversary under the judgment." ...

II.

...

Section 120 of title 35 provides: "An application for patent for an invention disclosed in the manner provided by the first paragraph of section 112 of this title in an application previously filed in the United States ... shall have the same effect, as to such invention, as though filed on the date of the prior application." Accordingly, the '561 patent may only claim priority to an earlier application if the earlier application fulfills the requirements of § 112, first paragraph. In turn, that paragraph requires, in part, that the application "shall contain a written description of the invention, and of the manner and process of making and using it, in such full, clear, concise, and exact terms as to enable any person skilled in the art to which it pertains, or with which it is most nearly connected, to make and use the same." 35 U.S.C. § 112, ¶ 1.

This court has interpreted this passage as setting forth two requirements: written description and enablement. As explained further below, this court affirms because neither the 1985 nor the 1986 application enables the claims of the '561 patent. The 1984 application does not support the new matter added to the '561 patent and thus does not satisfy the written description requirement.

Whether the earlier applications enable the claims of the '561 patent is a question of law based on underlying facts. This court reviews the underlying factual findings for clear error and the legal component of enablement without deference. Because the '561 patent is presumed valid, clear and convincing evidence must support a conclusion of invalidity....

Whether the earlier applications enable the claims of the '561 patent is determined as of the filing date of each application. As noted above, a patent disclosure need not enable information within the knowledge of an ordinarily skilled artisan. Thus, a patentee preferably omits from the disclosure any routine technology that is well known at the time of application. At the other end of the knowledge continuum, a patent document cannot enable technology that arises after the date of application....

"Because a patent specification must enable the full scope of a claimed invention, an enablement inquiry typically begins with a construction of the claims." In this case, neither party challenges the district court's claim construction in the first instance.... The district court's claim construction reads the claims of the '561 patent to embrace not only murine antibodies but also chimeric and humanized antibodies that bind to HER2.

At the outset, this court focuses primarily on chimeric antibodies. If the applications in this case do not enable or provide new matter support for chimeric antibodies, this court need not proceed to examine humanized antibodies. The trial record shows that genetically engineered antibodies, specifically chimeric antibodies, first appeared as a successful technology in the literature of this art field in May 1984, four months after the February filing date of the first application. Because the first publication documenting the successful creation of chimeric antibodies occurred after the filing of the 1984 application, this sequence of events shows that this new technology arose after the filing date and thus was, by definition, outside the bounds of the enablement requirement.

The district court in this case attempted to justify the jury's enablement verdict on the basis that the 1984 applicants might have known about chimeric antibodies before the initial publication on that subject. The trial court cited speculative testimony in the trial about the hypothetical possibility that information may leak out in advance of an initial publication on an important academic topic. At no point did the record show that Chiron scientists actually knew of chimeric antibodies before their filing, only that it was hypothetically possible for them to have acquired some advance knowledge. Even if the record shows that scientists routinely discuss their work with others in the same art field before publication, ethics would suggest impropriety in publishing that information in advance of the actual originator of the ideas. In any event, as noted, the enablement requirement does not extend to technology that arises after the time of filing. In sum, the district court erred to the extent that it attempted to create an obligation for Chiron scientists to enable nonexistent technology in the 1984 filing.

In the context of the 1984 application, the trial court and this court need not rely on enablement to support the jury's verdict. The jury may have found that the 1984 application does not provide any support for the new matter, chimeric antibodies, claimed in the '561 patent. Because chimeric antibody technology did not even exist at the time of the 1984 filing, the record conclusively supports that the Chiron scientists did not possess and disclose this technology in the February 1984 filing. Thus, the '561 patent cannot claim priority based on the 1984 application because it fails to comply with the written description requirement.

The written description requirement prevents applicants from using the amendment process to update their disclosures (claims or specifications) during their pendency before the patent office. Otherwise applicants could add new matter to their disclosures and date them back to their original filing date, thus defeating an accurate accounting of the priority of invention. *See* 35 U.S.C. § 132. Priority is always a vital issue in patent prosecution procedures—often determining entitlement to an invention. In 1967, this court's predecessor began to enforce priority as a component of the 35 U.S.C. § 112, first paragraph, written description requirement.... As later explained, "[t]he function of the description requirement is to ensure that the inventor had possession, as of the filing date of the application relied on, of the specific subject matter later claimed by him." In this case, the Chiron scientists, by definition, could not have possession of, and disclose, the subject matter of chimeric antibodies that did not even exist at the time of the 1984 application. Thus, axiomatically, Chiron cannot satisfy the written description requirement for the new matter appearing in the '561 patent, namely chimeric antibodies.

Turning next to the 1985 and 1986 applications, this court examines compliance with the enablement requirement. For these applications, the jury was entitled to determine as a matter of fact that chimeric antibodies were not future technology, but were nascent technology requiring a "specific and useful teaching." This question, in turn, depends on evidence that undue experimentation would be required to make and use the chimeric antibodies claimed by the '561 patent....

Evidence presented to the jury showed that creation of genetically engineered antibodies, such as chimeric antibodies, required significant experimentation in 1985 and 1986 because those antibodies were unpredictable at that early stage of development. The record also shows that only a few laboratories contained the necessary equipment to make these new antibodies—another indication of the excessive experimentation necessary to make and use that technology at that time. The 1985 and 1986 applications provide no disclosure of either how to make and use chimeric antibodies or working examples of chimeric antibodies within the scope of the '561 patent's claims.

Moreover, as mentioned above, "[t]he enabling disclosure of the specification [must] be commensurate in scope with the claim under consideration." Here, the scope of the claim includes not only murine but also chimeric antibodies. While Chiron's applications certainly enable murine antibodies, they do not enable chimeric antibodies. Although an aspect of the claimed invention included the binding of an antibody to a breast cancer antigen, Chiron's disclosure fell short of providing a "specific and useful teaching," of all antibodies within the scope of the claim.

By the filing date of the 1986 application, Chiron contends that chimeric antibodies were so well known that they had become routine technology. Chiron particularly highlights a number of publications before the 1986 application that disclosed methods of making chimeric antibodies. Accordingly, Chiron argues that the 1986 application need not specifically enable chimeric antibodies, because technicians of ordinary skill in this art could make and use them by that time without undue experimentation. Substantial evidence, however, supports the jury's implicit finding that the technology was still nascent at the time of the 1986 application (as well as, of course, at the time of the 1985 application) and thus would have still required undue experimentation.

In particular, Genentech's expert, Dr. French, testified that making chimeric antibodies was not routine technology in 1985 or 1986. Dr. French also testified that, by 1986, only a few laboratories had the capacity and expertise necessary to make genetically engineered antibodies. Dr. Larrick, another one of Genentech's experts, testified that polymerase chain reaction (PCR), a technique that facilitated the manufacture of genetically engineered antibodies including chimeric antibodies, did not become widespread until sometime between 1986 and 1988. Although PCR is not necessary to make chimeric antibodies, PCR diminishes the difficulties associated with manufacturing genetically engineered antibodies. Furthermore, by 1989, an article authored by a pioneer in the field described techniques of chimeric antibodies as "obviously those of a very young and very ambitious field." Sherie L. Morrison, *Genetically Engineered (Chimeric) Antibodies*, 24 Hosp. Practice (No. 10) 65, 75 (Oct. 15, 1989). The article further noted: "We are all new to the game." Thus, substantial evidence supports the finding that chimeric antibodies were still a nascent technology at the time the 1985 and 1986 applications were filed. Accordingly, the record amply supports the jury's conclusion that the 1985 and 1986 applications do not enable the claims of the '561 patent without undue experimentation....

Because the '561 patent is invalid for the reasons noted above, this court need not reach the question of claim construction. This case poses a particular challenge for accurate assessment of the meaning of the claim terms. In this case, the meaning of "monoclonal antibody" may not have been stagnant between the earlier applications and the '561 patent. The ordinary usage of "monoclonal antibody" in the early 1980s was narrow. For example, one treatise defines "monoclonal antibody" in these narrow terms: "Antibody secreted by a hybridoma clone. Because each such clone is derived from a single B cell, all of the antibody molecules it makes are identical." Bruce Alberts et al., Molecular Biology of the Cell G-15 (3d ed. 1994); accord Bruce Alberts et al., Molecular Biology of the Cell 182–84 (1983). Indeed, another textbook expressly equated "monoclonal antibody" with "hybridoma antibody." Leroy E. Hood et al., Immunology 20 (1984). Thus, the term "monoclonal antibody" in 1984 apparently referred to antibodies made with hybridoma and was not broad enough to encompass chimeric antibodies. *See* Alan Munro, *Uses of Chimaeric Antibodies*, 312 Nature 597 (1984) (differentiating monoclonal antibodies from chimeric antibodies). Accordingly, when the earliest priority application was filed, "monoclonal antibody" apparently referred only to a hybridoma-derived antibody. The 1984 application did not expressly redefine the term.[15]

The '561 patent, however, included a definition for "monoclonal antibody":

> The term "antibody" encompasses polyclonal and monoclonal antibody preparations, as well as preparations including hybrid antibodies, altered antibodies, chimeric antibodies and, [sic] humanized antibodies.
>
> As used herein, the term "monoclonal antibody" refers to an antibody composition having a homogeneous antibody population. The term is not limited regarding the species or source of the antibody, nor is it intended to be limited by the manner in which it is made. The term encompasses whole immunoglobulins.

Thus, the '561 patent defined "monoclonal antibody" to include chimeric and humanized antibodies. Still only a portion of this updated meaning of "monoclonal antibody" can claim priority to the earliest application. If required to engage in claim construction, therefore, this court would face a dilemma: Either construe the term according to the meaning of the earliest application but contrary to the explicit definition in the '561 patent or construe the term according to the explicit definition in the '561 patent but broader than the disclosure of the earliest application. Again, the latter alternative would run afoul of the prohibition against importing new matter into later

15. The additional disclosure of the 1985 and 1986 applications, which stated that "monoclonal antibody" "is not intended to be limited as regards the source of the antibody or the manner in which it is made," may have had some broadening effect on the ordinary meaning of the term. This court, however, need not decide that issue. In any event, the 1984 application did not exercise the lexicographer's option of expressly defining the disputed term.

patent documents. As noted, however, the record amply supports the jury's verdict of invalidity without reaching this complex claim construction question....

IV.

Because substantial evidence supported the jury's verdict that the '561 patent cannot claim priority to any of the 1984, 1985, and 1986 applications and because the district court did not err in denying Chiron's motion for a new trial, this court affirms the judgment of the district court....

4. Nonobviousness

One of the most challenging areas of patentability—and the source of most patent claim rejections from the USPTO—is the requirement that an invention must not be obvious, even if it is novel. Section 103 of the Patent Act defines nonobviousness. Note that § 103(b) is directed exclusively to patentable biotechnological processes.

§ 103 Conditions for Patentability; Non-Obvious Subject Matter

35 U.S.C. § 103

(a) A patent may not be obtained though the invention is not identically disclosed or described as set forth in section 102 of this title, if the differences between the subject matter sought to be patented and the prior art are such that the subject matter as a whole would have been obvious at the time the invention was made to a person having ordinary skill in the art to which said subject matter pertains. Patentability shall not be negatived by the manner in which the invention was made.

(b)(1) Notwithstanding subsection (a), and upon timely election by the applicant for patent to proceed under this subsection, a biotechnological process using or resulting in a composition of matter that is novel under section 102 and nonobvious under subsection (a) of this section shall be considered nonobvious if—

(A) claims to the process and the composition of matter are contained in either the same application for patent or in separate applications having the same effective filing date; and

(B) the composition of matter, and the process at the time it was invented, were owned by the same person or subject to an obligation of assignment to the same person.

(2) A patent issued on a process under paragraph (1)—

(A) shall also contain the claims to the composition of matter used in or made by that process, or

(B) shall, if such composition of matter is claimed in another patent, be set to expire on the same date as such other patent, notwithstanding section 154.

(3) For purposes of paragraph (1), the term "biotechnological process" means—

(A) a process of genetically altering or otherwise inducing a single- or multi-celled organism to—

(i) express an exogenous nucleotide sequence,

(ii) inhibit, eliminate, augment, or alter expression of an endogenous nucleotide sequence, or

(iii) express a specific physiological characteristic not naturally associated with said organism;

(B) cell fusion procedures yielding a cell line that expresses a specific protein, such as monoclonal antibody; and

(C) a method of using a product produced by a process defined by subparagraph (A) or (B), or a combination of subparagraphs (A) and (B).

(c) Subject matter developed by another person, which qualifies as prior art only under one or more of subsections (e), (f), and (g) of section 102 of this title, shall not preclude patentability under this section where the subject matter and the claimed invention were, at the time the invention was made, owned by the same person or subject to an obligation of assignment to the same person.

In re Deuel

51 F.3d 1552 (Fed. Cir. 1995)

Circuit Judge Lourie.

Thomas F. Deuel, Yue-Sheng Li, Ned R. Siegel, and Peter G. Milner (collectively "Deuel") appeal from the November 30, 1993 decision of the U.S. Patent and Trademark Office Board of Patent Appeals and Interferences affirming the examiner's final rejection of claims 4–7 of application Serial No. 07/542,232, entitled "Heparin-Binding Growth Factor," as unpatentable on the ground of obviousness under 35 U.S.C. § 103 (1988). Because the Board erred in concluding that Deuel's claims 5 and 7 directed to specific cDNA molecules would have been obvious in light of the applied references, and no other basis exists in the record to support the rejection with respect to claims 4 and 6 generically covering all possible DNA molecules coding for the disclosed proteins, we reverse.

Background

The claimed invention relates to isolated and purified DNA and cDNA molecules encoding heparin-binding growth factors ("HBGFs"). HBGFs are proteins that stimulate mitogenic activity (cell division) and thus facilitate the repair or replacement of damaged or diseased tissue. DNA (deoxyribonucleic acid) is a generic term which encompasses an enormous number of complex macromolecules made up of nucleotide units. DNAs consist of four different nucleotides containing the nitrogenous bases adenine, guanine, cytosine, and thymine. A sequential grouping of three such nucleotides (a "codon") codes for one amino acid. A DNA's sequence of codons thus determines the sequence of amino acids assembled during protein synthesis. Since there are 64 possible codons, but only 20 natural amino acids, most amino acids are coded for by more than one codon. This is referred to as the "redundancy" or "degeneracy" of the genetic code.

DNA functions as a blueprint of an organism's genetic information. It is the major component of genes, which are located on chromosomes in the cell nucleus. Only a small part of chromosomal DNA encodes functional proteins.

Messenger ribonucleic acid ("mRNA") is a similar molecule that is made or transcribed from DNA as part of the process of protein synthesis. Complementary DNA ("cDNA") is a complementary copy ("clone") of mRNA, made in the laboratory by reverse transcription of mRNA. Like mRNA, cDNA contains only the protein-encoding regions of DNA. Thus, once a cDNA's nucleotide sequence is known, the amino acid sequence of the protein for which it codes may be predicted using the genetic code relationship between codons and amino acids. The reverse is not true, however, due to the degeneracy of the code. Many other DNAs may code for a particular protein. The functional relationships between DNA, mRNA, cDNA, and a protein may conveniently be expressed as follows:

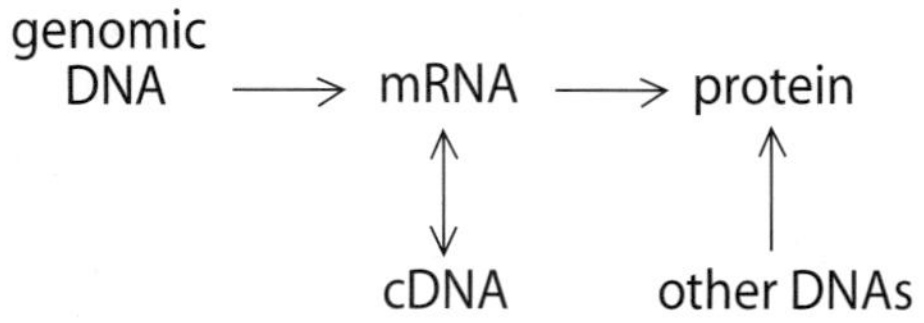

Collections ("libraries") of DNA and cDNA molecules derived from various species may be constructed in the laboratory or obtained from commercial sources. Complementary DNA libraries contain a mixture of cDNA clones reverse-transcribed from the mRNAs found in a specific tissue source. Complementary DNA libraries are tissue-specific because proteins and their corresponding mRNAs are only made ("expressed") in specific tissues, depending upon the protein. Genomic DNA ("gDNA") libraries, by contrast, theoretically contain all of a species' chromosomal DNA. The molecules present in cDNA and DNA libraries may be of unknown function and chemical structure, and the proteins which they encode may be unknown. However, one may attempt to retrieve molecules of interest from cDNA or gDNA libraries by screening such libraries with a gene probe, which is a synthetic radiolabelled nucleic acid sequence designed to bond ("hybridize") with a target complementary base sequence. Such "gene cloning" techniques thus exploit the fact that the bases in DNA always hybridize in complementary pairs: adenine bonds with thymine and guanine bonds with cytosine. A gene probe for potentially isolating DNA or cDNA encoding a protein may be designed once the protein's amino acid sequence, or a portion thereof, is known.

As disclosed in Deuel's patent application, Deuel isolated and purified HBGF from bovine uterine tissue, found that it exhibited mitogenic activity, and determined the first 25 amino acids of the protein's N-terminal sequence.[16] Deuel then isolated a cDNA molecule encoding bovine uterine HBGF by screening a bovine uterine cDNA library with an oligonucleotide probe designed using the experimentally determined N-terminal sequence of the HBGF. Deuel purified and sequenced the cDNA molecule, which was found to consist of a sequence of 1196 nucleotide base pairs. From the cDNA's nucleotide sequence, Deuel then predicted the complete amino acid sequence of bovine uterine HBGF disclosed in Deuel's application.

Deuel also isolated a cDNA molecule encoding human placental HBGF by screening a human placental cDNA library using the isolated bovine uterine cDNA clone as a probe. Deuel purified and sequenced the human placental cDNA clone, which was

16. Deuel determined that the N-terminal sequence of bovine uterus HBGF is Gly-Lys-Lys-Glu-Lys-Pro-Glu-Lys-Lys-Val-Lys-Lys-Ser-Asp-Cys-Gly-Glu-Trp-Gln-Trp-Ser-Val-Cys-Val-Pro.

found to consist of a sequence of 961 nucleotide base pairs. From the nucleotide sequence of the cDNA molecule encoding human placental HBGF, Deuel predicted the complete amino acid sequence of human placental HBGF disclosed in Deuel's application. The predicted human placental and bovine uterine HBGFs each have 168 amino acids and calculated molecular weights of 18.9 kD. Of the 168 amino acids present in the two HBGFs discovered by Deuel, 163 are identical. Deuel's application does not describe the chemical structure of, or state how to isolate and purify, any DNA or cDNA molecule except the disclosed human placental and bovine uterine cDNAs, which are the subject of claims 5 and 7.

Claims 4–7 on appeal are all independent claims and read, in relevant part, as follows:

> 4. A purified and isolated DNA sequence consisting of a sequence encoding human heparin binding growth factor of 168 amino acids having the following amino acid sequence: Met Gln Ala ... [remainder of 168 amino acid sequence].
>
> 5. The purified and isolated cDNA of human heparin-binding growth factor having the following nucleotide sequence: GTCAAAGGCA ... [remainder of 961 nucleotide sequence].
>
> 6. A purified and isolated DNA sequence consisting of a sequence encoding bovine heparin binding growth factor of 168 amino acids having the following amino acid sequence: Met Gln Thr ... [remainder of 168 amino acid sequence].
>
> 7. The purified and isolated cDNA of bovine heparin-binding growth factor having the following nucleotide sequence: GAGTGGAGAG ... [remainder of 1196 nucleotide sequence].

Claims 4 and 6 generically encompass *all* isolated/purified DNA sequences (natural and synthetic) encoding human and bovine HBGFs, despite the fact that Deuel's application does not describe the chemical structure of, or tell how to obtain, any DNA or cDNA except the two disclosed cDNA molecules. Because of the redundancy of the genetic code, claims 4 and 6 each encompass an enormous number of DNA molecules, including the isolated/purified chromosomal DNAs encoding the human and bovine proteins. Claims 5 and 7, on the other hand, are directed to the specifically disclosed cDNA molecules encoding human and bovine HBGFs, respectively.

During prosecution, the examiner rejected claims 4–7 under 35 U.S.C. § 103 as unpatentable over the combined teachings of Bohlen[17] and Maniatis.[18] The Bohlen reference discloses a group of protein growth factors designated as heparin-binding brain mitogens ("HBBMs") useful in treating burns and promoting the formation, maintenance, and repair of tissue, particularly neural tissue. Bohlen isolated three such HBBMs from human and bovine brain tissue. These proteins have respective molecular weights of 15 kD, 16 kD, and 18 kD. Bohlen determined the first 19 amino acids of the proteins' N-terminal sequences, which were found to be identical for human and bovine HBBMs.[19] Bohlen teaches that HBBMs are brain-specific, and suggests that the

17. European Patent Application No. 0326075, naming Peter Bohlen as inventor, published August 2, 1989.

18. Maniatis et al., *Molecular Cloning: A Laboratory Manual,* "Screening Bacteriophage [lambda] Libraries for Specific DNA Sequences by Recombination in *Escherichia coli,*" Cold Spring Harbor Laboratory, New York, 1982, pp. 353–361.

19. Bohlen's disclosed N-terminal sequence for human and bovine HBBMs is Gly-Lys-Lys-Glu-Lys-Pro-Glu-Lys-Lys-Val-Lys-Lys-Ser-Asp-Cys-Gly-Glu-Trp-Gln. This sequence matches the first 19 amino acids of Deuel's disclosed N-terminal sequence.

proteins may be homologous between species. The reference provides no teachings concerning DNA or cDNA coding for HBBMs.

Maniatis describes a method of isolating DNAs or cDNAs by screening a DNA or cDNA library with a gene probe. The reference outlines a general technique for cloning a gene; it does not describe how to isolate a particular DNA or cDNA molecule. Maniatis does not discuss certain steps necessary to isolate a target cDNA, *e.g.*, selecting a tissue-specific cDNA library containing a target cDNA and designing an oligonucleotide probe that will hybridize with the target cDNA.

The examiner asserted that, given Bohlen's disclosure of a heparin-binding protein and its N-terminal sequence and Maniatis's gene cloning method, it would have been *prima facie* obvious to one of ordinary skill in the art at the time of the invention to clone a gene for HBGF.[20] According to the examiner, Bohlen's published N-terminal sequence would have motivated a person of ordinary skill in the art to clone such a gene because cloning the gene would allow recombinant production of HBGF, a useful protein. The examiner reasoned that a person of ordinary skill in the art could have designed a gene probe based on Bohlen's disclosed N-terminal sequence, then screened a DNA library in accordance with Maniatis's gene cloning method to isolate a gene encoding an HBGF. The examiner did not distinguish between claims 4 and 6 generically directed to all DNA sequences encoding human and bovine HBGFs and claims 5 and 7 reciting particular cDNAs.

In reply, Deuel argued, *inter alia*, that Bohlen teaches away from the claimed cDNA molecules because Bohlen suggests that HBBMs are brain-specific and, thus, a person of ordinary skill in the art would not have tried to isolate corresponding cDNA clones from human placental and bovine uterine cDNA libraries. The examiner made the rejection final, however, asserting that

> [t]he starting materials are not relevant in this case, because it was well known in the art at the time the invention was made that proteins, especially the general class of heparin binding proteins, are highly homologous between species and tissue type. It would have been entirely obvious to attempt to isolate a known protein from different tissue types and even different species.

No prior art was cited to support the proposition that it would have been obvious to screen human placental and bovine uterine cDNA libraries for the claimed cDNA clones. Presumably, the examiner was relying on Bohlen's suggestion that HBBMs may be homologous between species, although the examiner did not explain how homology between species suggests homology between tissue types.

The Board affirmed the examiner's final rejection. In its opening remarks, the Board noted that it is "constantly advised by the patent examiners, who are highly skilled in this art, that cloning procedures are routine in the art." According to the Board, "the examiners urge that when the sequence of a protein is placed into the public domain, the gene is also placed into the public domain because of the routine nature of cloning techniques." Addressing the rejection at issue, the Board determined that Bohlen's disclosure of the existence and isolation of HBBM, a functional protein, would also advise a person of ordinary skill in the art that a gene exists encoding HBBM. The Board found that a person of ordinary skill in the art would have been motivated to isolate such a gene because the protein has useful mitogenic prop-

---

20. The examiner and the Board apparently used the term "gene" to refer both to natural (chromosomal) DNA and synthetic cDNA. We will use the several terms as appropriate.

erties, and isolating the gene for HBBM would permit large quantities of the protein to be produced for study and possible commercial use. Like the examiner, the Board asserted, without explanation, that HBBMs are the same as HBGFs and that the genes encoding these proteins are identical. The Board concluded that "the Bohlen reference would have suggested to those of ordinary skill in this art that they should make the gene, and the Maniatis reference would have taught a technique for 'making' the gene with a reasonable expectation of success." Responding to Deuel's argument that the claimed cDNA clones were isolated from human placental and bovine uterine cDNA libraries, whereas the combined teachings of Bohlen and Maniatis would only have suggested screening a brain tissue cDNA library, the Board stated that "the claims before us are directed to the product and not the method of isolation. Appellants have not shown that the claimed DNA was not present in and could not have been readily isolated from the brain tissue utilized by Bohlen." Deuel now appeals.[21]

Discussion

Obviousness is a question of law, which we review *de novo,* though factual findings underlying the Board's obviousness determination are reviewed for clear error. The examiner bears the burden of establishing a *prima facie* case of obviousness. Only if this burden is met does the burden of coming forward with rebuttal argument or evidence shift to the applicant. When the references cited by the examiner fail to establish a *prima facie* case of obviousness, the rejection is improper and will be overturned.

On appeal, Deuel challenges the Board's determination that the applied references establish a *prima facie* case of obviousness. In response, the PTO maintains that the claimed invention would have been *prima facie* obvious over the combined teachings of Bohlen and Maniatis. Thus, the appeal raises the important question whether the combination of a prior art reference teaching a method of gene cloning, together with a reference disclosing a partial amino acid sequence of a protein, may render DNA and cDNA molecules encoding the protein *prima facie* obvious under § 103.

Deuel argues that the PTO failed to follow the proper legal standard in determining that the claimed cDNA molecules would have been *prima facie* obvious despite the lack of structurally similar compounds in the prior art. Deuel argues that the PTO has not cited a reference teaching cDNA molecules, but instead has improperly rejected the claims based on the alleged obviousness of a method of making the molecules. We agree.

Because Deuel claims new chemical entities in structural terms, a *prima facie* case of unpatentability requires that the teachings of the prior art suggest *the claimed compounds* to a person of ordinary skill in the art. Normally a *prima facie* case of obviousness is based upon structural similarity, *i.e.,* an established structural relationship between a prior art compound and the claimed compound. Structural relationships may provide the requisite motivation or suggestion to modify known compounds to obtain new compounds. For example, a prior art compound may suggest its homologs because homologs often have similar properties and therefore chemists of ordinary skill would

---

21. Deuel is supported in its appeal by an *amicus curiae* brief submitted by the Biotechnology Industry Organization and the Bay Area Science Center. Amici urge that, contrary to controlling precedent, the PTO has unlawfully adopted a *per se* rule that a gene is *prima facie* obvious when at least part of the amino acid sequence of the protein encoded by the gene is known in the prior art.

ordinarily contemplate making them to try to obtain compounds with improved properties. Similarly, a known compound may suggest its analogs or isomers, either geometric isomers (cis v. trans) or position isomers (*e.g.*, ortho v. para).

In all of these cases, however, the prior art teaches a specific, structurally-definable compound and the question becomes whether the prior art would have suggested making the specific molecular modifications necessary to achieve the claimed invention.

Here, the prior art does not disclose any relevant cDNA molecules, let alone close relatives of the specific, structurally-defined cDNA molecules of claims 5 and 7 that might render them obvious. Maniatis suggests an allegedly obvious process for trying to isolate cDNA molecules, but that, as we will indicate below, does not fill the gap regarding the subject matter of claims 5 and 7. Further, while the general idea of the claimed molecules, their function, and their general chemical nature may have been obvious from Bohlen's teachings, and the knowledge that some gene existed may have been clear, the precise cDNA molecules of claims 5 and 7 would not have been obvious over the Bohlen reference because Bohlen teaches proteins, not the claimed or closely related cDNA molecules. The redundancy of the genetic code precluded contemplation of or focus on the specific cDNA molecules of claims 5 and 7. Thus, one could not have conceived the subject matter of claims 5 and 7 based on the teachings in the cited prior art because, until the claimed molecules were actually isolated and purified, it would have been highly unlikely for one of ordinary skill in the art to contemplate what was ultimately obtained. What cannot be contemplated or conceived cannot be obvious.

The PTO's theory that one might have been motivated to try to do what Deuel in fact accomplished amounts to speculation and an impermissible hindsight reconstruction of the claimed invention. It also ignores the fact that claims 5 and 7 are limited to specific compounds, and any motivation that existed was a general one, to try to obtain a gene that was yet undefined and may have constituted many forms. A general motivation to search for some gene that exists does not necessarily make obvious a specifically-defined gene that is subsequently obtained as a result of that search. More is needed and it is not found here.

The genetic code relationship between proteins and nucleic acids does not overcome the deficiencies of the cited references. A prior art disclosure of the amino acid sequence of a protein does not necessarily render particular DNA molecules encoding the protein obvious because the redundancy of the genetic code permits one to hypothesize an enormous number of DNA sequences coding for the protein. No particular one of these DNAs can be obvious unless there is something in the prior art to lead to the particular DNA and indicate that it should be prepared. We recently held that a broad genus does not necessarily render obvious each compound within its scope. Similarly, knowledge of a protein does not give one a conception of a particular DNA encoding it. Thus, *a fortiori,* Bohlen's disclosure of the N-terminal portion of a protein, which the PTO urges is the same as HBGF, would not have suggested the particular cDNA molecules defined by claims 5 and 7. This is so even though one skilled in the art knew that some DNA, albeit not in purified and isolated form, did exist. The compounds of claims 5 and 7 are specific compounds not suggested by the prior art. A different result might pertain, however, if there were prior art, *e.g.*, a protein of sufficiently small size and simplicity, so that lacking redundancy, each possible DNA would be obvious over the protein. That is not the case here.

The PTO's focus on known methods for potentially isolating the claimed DNA molecules is also misplaced because the claims at issue define compounds, not methods. In

[*In re Bell*], the PTO asserted a rejection based upon the combination of a primary reference disclosing a protein (*and its complete amino acid sequence*) with a secondary reference describing a general method of gene cloning. We reversed the rejection, holding in part that "[t]he PTO's focus on Bell's method is misplaced. Bell does not claim a method. Bell claims compositions, and the issue is the obviousness of the claimed compositions, not of the method by which they are made."

We today reaffirm the principle, stated in *Bell,* that the existence of a general method of isolating cDNA or DNA molecules is essentially irrelevant to the question whether the specific molecules themselves would have been obvious, in the absence of other prior art that suggests the claimed DNAs. A prior art disclosure of a process *reciting a particular compound* or obvious variant thereof as a product of the process is, of course, another matter, raising issues of anticipation under 35 U.S.C. § 102 as well as obviousness under § 103. Moreover, where there is prior art that suggests a claimed compound, the existence, or lack thereof, of an enabling process for making that compound is surely a factor in any patentability determination. There must, however, still be prior art that suggests the claimed compound in order for a *prima facie* case of obviousness to be made out; as we have already indicated, that prior art was lacking here with respect to claims 5 and 7. Thus, even if, as the examiner stated, the existence of general cloning techniques, coupled with knowledge of a protein's structure, might have provided motivation to prepare *a* cDNA or made it obvious to prepare *a* cDNA, that does not necessarily make obvious a particular claimed cDNA. "Obvious to try" has long been held not to constitute obviousness. A general incentive does not make obvious a particular result, nor does the existence of techniques by which those efforts can be carried out. Thus, Maniatis's teachings, even in combination with Bohlen, fail to suggest the claimed invention.

The PTO argues that a compound may be defined by its process of preparation and therefore that a conceived process for making or isolating it provides a definition for it and can render it obvious. It cites *Amgen Inc. v. Chugai Pharmaceutical Co.* for that proposition. We disagree. The fact that one can conceive a general process in advance for preparing an *undefined* compound does not mean that a claimed *specific* compound was precisely envisioned and therefore obvious. A substance may indeed be defined by its process of preparation. That occurs, however, when it has already been prepared by that process and one therefore knows that the result of that process is the stated compound. The process is part of the definition of the compound. But that is not possible in advance, especially when the hypothetical process is only a general one. Thus, a conceived method of preparing some undefined DNA does not define it with the precision necessary to render it obvious over the protein it encodes. We did not state otherwise in *Amgen.*

We conclude that, because the applied references do not teach or suggest the claimed cDNA molecules, the final rejection of claims 5 and 7 must be reversed.

Claims 4 and 6 are of a different scope than claims 5 and 7. As is conceded by Deuel, they generically encompass all DNA sequences encoding human and bovine HBGFs. Written in such a result-oriented form, claims 4 and 6 are thus tantamount to the general idea of all genes encoding the protein, all solutions to the problem. Such an idea might have been obvious from the *complete* amino acid sequence of the protein, coupled with knowledge of the genetic code, because this information may have enabled a person of ordinary skill in the art to envision the idea of, and, perhaps with the aid of a computer, even identify all members of the claimed genus. The Bohlen reference, however, only discloses a partial amino acid sequence, and thus it appears that, based on the above analysis, the claimed genus would not have been obvious over this prior art disclosure. We will therefore also reverse the final rejection of claims 4 and 6 because neither the Board nor the patent examiner articulated any separate reasons for holding these claims unpatentable apart from the grounds discussed above....

We have considered the PTO's remaining arguments and find them not persuasive.

Conclusion

The Board's decision affirming the final rejection of claims 4–7 is reversed.

5. Written Description, Enablement, and Best Mode

The final main set of requirements for patentability, with special import for biotechnology products and processes, is that of written description, enablement, and best mode within the patent application itself. Set forth in § 112 of the Patent Act, which defines the "specification" or substantive section of the patent application, these criteria seek to help examiners and others determine whether the applicant is truly in possession of the claimed invention as well as to help assure that the public is able to practice the technology of the invention from the patent application disclosure alone, without the need for extra disclosure or "undue experimentation." Some of the issues in the cases that follow were already raised along the way in cases excerpted above.

35 U.S.C. § 112. Specification

The specification shall contain a written description of the invention, and of the manner and process of making and using it, in such full, clear, concise, and exact terms as to enable any person skilled in the art to which it pertains, or with which it is most nearly connected, to make and use the same, and shall set forth the best mode contemplated by the inventor of carrying out his invention.

The specification shall conclude with one or more claims particularly pointing out and distinctly claiming the subject matter which the applicant regards as his invention.

A claim may be written in independent or, if the nature of the case admits, in dependent or multiple dependent form.

Subject to the following paragraph, a claim in dependent form shall contain a reference to a claim previously set forth and then specify a further limitation of the subject matter claimed. A claim in dependent form shall be construed to incorporate by reference all the limitations of the claim to which it refers.

A claim in multiple dependent form shall contain a reference, in the alternative only, to more than one claim previously set forth and then specify a further limitation of the subject matter claimed. A multiple dependent claim shall not serve as a basis for any other multiple dependent claim. A multiple dependent claim shall be construed to incorporate by reference all the limitations of the particular claim in relation to which it is being considered.

An element in a claim for a combination may be expressed as a means or step for performing a specified function without the recital of structure, material, or acts in support thereof, and such claim shall be construed to cover the corresponding structure, material, or acts described in the specification and equivalents thereof.

Enzo Biochem, Inc. v. Gen-Probe Inc.

323 F.3d 956 (Fed. Cir. 2002)

Circuit Judge Lourie.

Enzo Biochem, Inc. petitions for rehearing of this appeal following our prior decision ... in which we affirmed the decision of the United States District Court for the Southern District of New York. The district court had granted Gen-Probe Incorporated, Chugai Pharma U.S.A., Inc., Chugai Pharmaceutical Co., Ltd., Biomerieux, Inc., Biomerieux SA, and Becton Dickinson and Company's (collectively, "the defendants") motion for summary judgment that claims 1–6 of U.S. Patent 4,900,659 are invalid for failure to meet the written description requirement of 35 U.S.C. § 112, ¶ 1. Having considered Enzo's petition for rehearing and the defendants' response, we have determined that our prior decision that a deposit may not satisfy the written description requirement was incorrect. We therefore grant Enzo's petition for rehearing, vacate the prior decision, and reverse the district court's grant of summary judgment that Enzo's claims are invalid for failure to meet the written description requirement. Because genuine issues of material fact exist regarding satisfaction of the written description requirement, we remand.

Background

Enzo is the assignee of the '659 patent, which is directed to nucleic acid probes that selectively hybridize to the genetic material of the bacteria that cause gonorrhea, *Neisseria gonorrhoeae. N. gonorrhoeae* reportedly has between eighty and ninety-three percent homology with *Neisseria meningitidis.* Such a high degree of homology has made detection of *N. gonorrhoeae* difficult, as any probe capable of detecting *N. gonorrhoeae* may also show a positive result when only *N. meningitidis* is present. Enzo recognized the need for a chromosomal DNA probe specific for *N. gonorrhoeae,* and it derived three such sequences that preferentially hybridized to six common strains of *N. gonorrhoeae* over six common strains of *N. meningitidis.* The inventors believed that if the preferential hybridization ratio of *N. gonorrhoeae* to *N. meningitidis* were greater than about five to one, then the "discrete nucleotide sequence [would] hybridize to virtually all strains of *Neisseria gonorrhoeae* and to no strain of *Neisseria meningitidis.*". The three sequences that the inventors actually derived had a selective hybridization ratio of greater than fifty. Enzo deposited those sequences in the form of a recombinant DNA molecule within an *E. coli* bacterial host at the American Type Culture Collection.

Claim 1 is as follows:

> 1. A composition of matter that is specific for *Neisseria gonorrhoeae* comprising at least one nucleotide sequence *for which the ratio of the amount of said sequence which hybridizes to chromosomal DNA of Neisseria gonorrhoeae to the amount of said sequence which hybridizes to chromosomal DNA of Neisseria meningitidis is greater than about five,* said ratio being obtained by a method comprising the following steps;
>
> > (a) providing a radioactively labeled form of said nucleotide sequence;
> >
> > (b) providing a serial dilution series of purified chromosomal DNA from each of the *N. gonorrhoeae* strains; (1) ATCC 53420, (2) ATCC 53421, (3) ATCC 53422, (4) ATCC 53423, (5) ATCC 53424, (6) ATCC 53425, and forming test dots from each of said dilution series on a matrix;

(c) providing a serial dilution series of purified nucleotide sequences from each of the *N. meningitidis* strains: (1) ATCC 53414, (2) ATCC 53415, (3) ATCC 53416, (4) ATCC 53417, (5) ATCC 53418, (6) ATCC 53419, and forming test dots from each of said dilution series on a matrix;

(d) hybridizing equal portions of the labeled nucleotide sequences to the matrix provided in step (b) and (c), respectively; wherein the hybridization is conducted in a solution having a salt concentration of 2X SSC at (i) 65° C. in cases in which the sequence has greater than 50 base pairs or (ii) at Tm (° C.) minus 30° C. in cases in which the sequence has less than 50 base pairs, wherein Tm is the denaturation temperature of the sequence;

(e) quantifying the labeled nucleotide sequence hybridized in step (d) to each test dot;

(f) subtracting from the data of step

(e) an averaged amount of radioactivity attributable to background to obtain a corrected amount of hybridized radioactivity at each test dot;

(g) normalizing the data of step (f) by multiplying the amount of corrected radioactivity at each test dot by a factor which adjusts the amount of radioactivity to equal amounts of chromosomal DNA at each test dot;

(h) selecting two normalized values that are most nearly the same and that correspond to adjacent members of the dilution series for each of the above strains of *N. gonorrhoeae* and obtaining the average of the selected values;

(i) selecting two normalized values that are most nearly the same and that correspond to adjacent members of the dilution series for each of the above strains of *N. meningitidis* and obtaining the average of the selected values;

(j) dividing the lowest average obtained in step (h) by the highest average obtained in step (i) to obtain said ratio.

(emphasis added). Claims 2 and 3 depend from claim 1 and further limit the hybridization ratio to greater than about twenty-five and fifty, respectively. Claim 4 is directed to the three deposited sequences (referenced by their accession numbers) and variants thereof as follows:

4. The composition of claim 1 wherein said nucleotide sequences are selected from the group consisting of:

a. the *Neisseria gonorroheae* [sic] DNA insert of ATCC 53409, ATCC 53410 and ATCC 53411, and discrete nucleotide subsequences thereof,

b. mutated discrete nucleotide sequences of any of the foregoing inserts that are within said hybridization ratio and subsequences thereof; and

c. mixtures thereof.

Claim 5 is directed to an assay for detection of *N. gonorrhoeae* using the composition of claim 1. Claim 6 further limits the method of claim 5 to the nucleotide sequences that Enzo deposited (*i.e.*, those in claim 4) and variants thereof.

Enzo sued the defendants for infringement of the '659 patent, and the defendants moved for summary judgment that the claims were invalid for failure to meet the written description requirement of 35 U.S.C. § 112, ¶ 1. The district court, in oral remarks from the bench, granted that motion. It concluded that the claimed composition of matter was defined only by its biological activity or function, *viz.*, the ability to hybridize to *N. gonorrhoeae* in a ratio of better than about five with respect to *N. meningitidis*, which it was held was insufficient to satisfy the § 112, ¶ 1 requirement.... The court rejected Enzo's argument that the reference in the specification to the deposits of biological materials in a public depository inherently disclosed that the inventors were in possession of the claimed sequences. It distinguished this court's precedents concerning deposits as relating to the enablement requirement of § 112, ¶ 1. Enzo appealed to this court....

Discussion

Summary judgment is appropriate when there is no genuine issue of material fact and the moving party is entitled to judgment as a matter of law. On motion for summary judgment, the court views the evidence and any disputed factual issues in the light most favorable to the party opposing the motion. A patent is presumed to be valid, 35 U.S.C. § 282 (1994), and this presumption can be overcome only by facts supported by clear and convincing evidence to the contrary. Compliance with the written description requirement is a question of fact.

Enzo argues that the testimony of its expert, Dr. Wetmer, raised a genuine factual issue whether the reference to the deposits inherently described the claimed nucleotide sequences. Enzo also argues that its description of the binding affinity of the claimed nucleotide sequences satisfies the requirement set forth in the Guidelines for Examination of Patent Applications Under the 35 U.S.C. 112, ¶ 1 "Written Description" Requirement, 66 Fed. Reg. 1099 (Jan. 5, 2001) ("*Guidelines*"). Enzo asserts that the court erred in not evaluating the patentability of the claims separately, pointing out that claims 4 and 6 are directed to the three deposited sequences and variations and mixtures thereof. Enzo further asserts that the claims *per se* meet the written description requirement because they appear *in ipsis verbis* in the written description. Enzo also argues that this court's articulation of the written description requirement for genetic material in *Eli Lilly* should not apply to this case because Enzo reduced the invention to practice and deposited the derived biological materials, thereby demonstrating its "possession" of the invention.

The defendants respond that the district court properly granted summary judgment because the patent described the claimed nucleotide sequences only by their function, which they state is insufficient to meet the requirements of § 112, ¶ 1 as a matter of law, even as to the narrower claims directed to the deposited materials. The defendants also assert that Dr. Wetmur's opinion that the deposited genetic materials could have been sequenced did not cure the actual failure of the inventors to identify them by some distinguishing characteristic, such as their structure. Moreover, the defendants point out that claims 4 and 6, which are directed to the deposited materials, each cover a broad genus of nucleic acids. The defendants also urge that *in ipsis verbis* support for the claims in the specification does not *per se* establish compliance with the written description requirement. Finally, the defendants assert that the district court did not err in its determination that Enzo's "possession" of three nucleotide sequences that it reduced to practice and deposited nevertheless did not satisfy the written description requirement of § 112, ¶ 1.

The written description requirement of § 112, ¶ 1 is set forth as follows:

> *The specification shall contain a written description of the invention,* and of the manner and process of making and using it, in such full, clear, concise, and exact terms as to enable any person skilled in the art to which it pertains or with which it is most nearly connected, to make and use the same, and shall set forth the best mode contemplated by the inventor of carrying out his invention.

(emphasis added). We have interpreted that section as requiring a "written description" of an invention separate from enablement. Compliance with the written description requirement is essentially a fact-based inquiry that will "necessarily vary depending on the nature of the invention claimed." We have also previously considered the written description requirement as applied to certain biotechnology patents, in which a gene material has been defined only by a statement of function or result, and have held that such a statement alone did not adequately describe the claimed invention. In *Eli Lilly,* we concluded that a claim to a microorganism containing a human insulin cDNA was not adequately described by a statement that the invention included human insulin cDNA. The recitation of the term human insulin cDNA conveyed no distinguishing information about the identity of the claimed DNA sequence, such as its relevant structural or physical characteristics. We stated that an adequate written description of genetic material "'requires a precise definition, such as by structure, formula, chemical name, or physical properties,' not a mere wish or plan for obtaining the claimed chemical invention," and that none of those descriptions appeared in that patent. The specification in the *Eli Lilly* case thus did not show that the inventors had possession of human insulin cDNA.

It is not correct, however, that all functional descriptions of genetic material fail to meet the written description requirement. The PTO has issued Guidelines governing its internal practice for addressing that issue. The Guidelines, like the Manual of Patent Examining Procedure ("MPEP"), are not binding on this court, but may be given judicial notice to the extent they do not conflict with the statute. In its Guidelines, the PTO has determined that the written description requirement can be met by "show[ing] that an invention is complete by disclosure of sufficiently detailed, relevant identifying characteristics ... *i.e.,* complete or partial structure, other physical and/or chemical properties, *functional characteristics when coupled with a known or disclosed correlation between function and structure,* or some combination of such characteristics." (emphasis added). For example, the PTO would find compliance with 112, 1, for a claim to an isolated antibody capable of binding to antigen X, notwithstanding the functional definition of the antibody, in light of the well defined structural characteristics for the five classes of antibody, the functional characteristics of antibody binding, and the fact that the antibody technology is well developed and mature. Synopsis of Application of Written Description Guidelines, at 60, *available at* http:// www.uspto.gov/web/patents/guides.htm (*Application of Guidelines*). Thus, under the Guidelines, the written description requirement would be met for all of the claims of the '659 patent if the functional characteristic of preferential binding to *N. gonorrhoeae* over *N. meningitidis* were coupled with a disclosed correlation between that function and a structure that is sufficiently known or disclosed. We are persuaded by the Guidelines on this point and adopt the PTO's applicable standard for determining compliance with the written description requirement.

Applying those principles, we first inquire whether Enzo's deposits of the claimed nucleotide sequences of claims 4 and 6 may constitute an adequate description of those sequences. Secondly, we will consider whether the description requirement is met for all of the claims on the basis of the functional ability of the claimed nucleotide sequences to hybridize to strains of *N. gonorrhoeae* that are accessible by deposit.

As to the first question, Enzo asserts that the claimed sequences are inherently described by reference to deposits of three sequences that are within the scope of its claims. Whether reference to a deposit of a nucleotide sequence may adequately describe that sequence is an issue of first impression in this court. In light of the history of biological deposits for patent purposes, the goals of the patent law, and the practical difficulties of describing unique biological materials in a written description, we hold that reference in the specification to a deposit in a public depository, which makes its contents accessible to the public when it is not otherwise available in written form, constitutes an adequate description of the deposited material sufficient to comply with the written description requirement of § 112, ¶ 1.

The practice of depositing biological material arose primarily to satisfy the enablement requirement of § 112, ¶ 1. For example, in *In re Argoudelis*, the patent application claimed antibiotic compounds that were produced by a microorganism. 434 F2d 1390 ([C.C.P.A.]1970). The applicants deposited the microorganism because they could not "sufficiently disclose by written word how to obtain the microorganism starting material from nature." By making the biological material accessible to the public, they enabled the public to make and use the claimed antibiotics. In *Amgen*, we noted the relevance of deposit practice to satisfaction of the enablement requirement but rejected the defendants' argument that a deposit was necessary in that case to satisfy the best mode requirement of § 112, ¶ 1.

Recognizing the importance of biological deposits to patent practice, the PTO has promulgated rules to address the procedural requirements relating to such deposits, but it has declined to expressly correlate substantive requirements relating to deposits with particular statutory requirements. *See* Deposit of Biological Materials for Patent Purposes, 53 Fed. Reg. 39,420, 39,425 (Oct. 6, 1988) (notice of proposed rules) (codified at 37 C.F.R. Part 1) ("The rules are not intended to address which requirements of 35 U.S.C. 112 may be met by the making of deposits."). The Office does offer guidance, however, in determining when a deposit may be necessary, such as "[w]here the invention involves a biological material and words alone cannot sufficiently describe how to make and use the invention in a reproducible manner." MPEP § 2402 (8th ed. Aug. 2001). The PTO has also issued a regulation stating when a deposit is not necessary, *i.e.*, "if it is known and readily available to the public or can be made or isolated without undue experimentation." 37 C.F.R. § 1.802(b) (2001). Inventions that cannot reasonably be enabled by a description in written form in the specification, but that otherwise meet the requirements for patent protection, may be described in surrogate form by a deposit that is incorporated by reference into the specification. While deposit in a public depository most often has pertained to satisfaction of the enablement requirement, we have concluded that reference in the specification to a deposit may also satisfy the written description requirement with respect to a claimed material.

In this case, Enzo's deposits were incorporated by reference in the specification. A person of skill in the art, reading the accession numbers in the patent specification, can obtain the claimed sequences from the ATCC depository by following the appropriate techniques to excise the nucleotide sequences from the deposited organisms containing those sequences. The sequences are thus accessible from the disclosure in the specification. Although the structures of those sequences, *i.e.*, the exact nucleotide base pairs, are not expressly set forth in the specification, those structures may not have been reasonably obtainable and in any event were not known to Enzo when it filed its application in 1986. We therefore agree with Enzo that reference in the specification to deposits of nucleotide sequences describe those sequences sufficiently to the public for purposes of meeting the written description requirement.

As the defendants point out, however, Enzo's claims 4 and 6 are not limited to the deposited sequences. Claim 4 is directed to nucleotide sequences that are selected from the group consisting of the three deposited sequences, "discrete nucleotide subsequences thereof ... mutated discrete nucleotide sequences of any of the foregoing inserts that are within said hybridization ratio and subsequences thereof[,] and ... mixtures thereof."' Claim 6 is also similarly directed to the three deposited sequences and subsequences and mutated variations thereof. The specification defines a subsequence non-specifically as a nucleotide sequence "greater than about 12 nucleotides."' As the deposited sequences are about 850, 850, and 1300 nucleotides long there are at least hundreds of subsequences of the deposited sequences, an unknown number of which might also meet the claimed hybridization ratio. Moreover, Enzo's expert, Dr. Wetmur, stated that "astronomical" numbers of mutated variations of the deposited sequences also fall within the scope of those claims, and that such broad claim scope is necessary to adequately protect Enzo's invention from copyists who could otherwise make a minor change to the sequence and thereby avoid infringement while still exploiting the benefits of Enzo's invention. The defendants assert that such breadth is fatal to the adequacy of the written description. On the other hand, because the deposited sequences are described by virtue of a reference to their having been deposited, it may well be that various subsequences, mutations, and mixtures of those sequences are also described to one of skill in the art. We regard that question as an issue of fact that is best resolved on remand.[22] Because the district court's grant of summary judgment was based on its conclusion that Enzo's deposits could not satisfy the written description requirement as a matter of law, we reverse the district court's grant of summary judgment that claims 4 and 6 are invalid for failure to meet the written description requirement. On remand, the court should determine whether a person of skill in the art would glean from the written description, including information obtainable from the deposits of the claimed sequences, subsequences, mutated variants, and mixtures sufficient to demonstrate possession of the generic scope of the claims.

We next address the question whether the compositions of the broader genus claims 1–3 and 5 are sufficiently described to meet the requirements of § 112, ¶ 1, on the basis of Enzo's deposits of three sequences. If those sequences are representative of the scope of the genus claims, *i.e.*, if they indicate that the patentee has invented species sufficient to constitute the genera, they may be representative of the scope of those claims. Because the district court concluded that the deposited sequences were not themselves described, it did not determine whether that description was representative of the genera in those claims. Such determination should be made on remand.

When we addressed a similar issue in *Eli Lilly*, we determined that a disclosure of the sequence of rat cDNA was not descriptive of the broader invention consisting of mammalian and vertebrate cDNA, although it was a species falling within the scope of those claims. In *Eli Lilly*, the specification and generic claims to all cDNAs encoding for vertebrate or mammalian insulin did not describe the claimed genus because they did not set forth any common features possessed by members of the genus that distinguished them from others. Nor did the specification describe a sufficient number of species within the very broad genus to indicate that the inventors had made a generic invention, *i.e.*, that they had possession of the breadth of the genus, as opposed to merely one or two such species. The PTO has included a hypothetical example based on the facts of *Eli Lilly* in its Synopsis of Application of Written Description Guidelines in which the description

22. We do not address the issue whether the breadth of the claim may implicate other validity issues, such as enablement. Only written description is before us.

requirement is not met. The PTO has also provided a contrasting example of genus claims to nucleic acids based on their hybridization properties, and has determined that such claims may be adequately described if they hybridize under highly stringent conditions to known sequences because such conditions dictate that all species within the genus will be structurally similar. Whether the disclosure provided by the three deposits in this case, coupled with the skill of the art, describes the genera of claims 1–3 and 5 is a fact question the district court did not address. On remand, the district court should determine, consistently with the precedent of this court and the PTO's Guidelines, whether one skilled in the art would consider the subject matter of claims 1–3 and 5 to be adequately described, recognizing the significance of the deposits and the scope of the claims.

Enzo argues that all of the claims are adequately described on another basis, *viz.*, by means of the disclosed correlation of the function of hybridization with the bacterial DNA. In its petition for rehearing, Enzo states as attorney argument that "[t]he description and claiming of biological materials by their affinity to other materials that are clearly identified in the specification and claims (the particular deposited strains of *N. gonorrhoeae* and *N. meningitidis*) inherently specifies structure, and is routine in this field." Claim 1 sets forth the deposit numbers of six strains of *N. gonorrhoeae* to which the claimed nucleotide sequences preferentially hybridize, as well as the deposit numbers of six strains of *N. meningitidis* that are thereby distinguished. Again, as with the claimed nucleotide sequences, the sequences of the genomic DNA of those bacteria are not disclosed, perhaps because such sequencing would have been unduly burdensome at the time of Enzo's invention. However, as those bacteria were deposited, their bacterial genome is accessible and, under our holding today, they are adequately described in the specification by their accession numbers. Because the claimed nucleotide sequences preferentially bind to the genomic DNA of the deposited strains of *N. gonorrhoeae* and have a complementary structural relationship with that DNA, those sequences, under the PTO Guidelines, may also be adequately described. Although the patent specification lacks description of the location along the bacterial DNA to which the claimed sequences bind, Enzo has at least raised a genuine issue of material fact as to whether a reasonable fact-finder could conclude that the claimed sequences are described by their ability to hybridize to structures that, while not explicitly sequenced, are accessible to the public. Such hybridization to disclosed organisms may meet the PTO's Guidelines stating that functional claiming is permissible when the claimed material hybridizes to a disclosed substrate. That is a fact question. We therefore conclude that the district court erred in granting summary judgment that the claims are invalid for failure to meet the written description requirement. On remand, the court should consider whether one of skill in the art would find the generically claimed sequences described on the basis of Enzo's disclosure of the hybridization function and an accessible structure, consistent with the PTO Guidelines. If so, the written description requirement would be met.

We next address Enzo's additional argument that the written description requirement for the generic claims is necessarily met as a matter of law because the claim language appears *in ipsis verbis* in the specification. We do not agree. Even if a claim is supported by the specification, the language of the specification, to the extent possible, must describe the claimed invention so that one skilled in the art can recognize what is claimed. The appearance of mere indistinct words in a specification or a claim, even an original claim, does not necessarily satisfy that requirement. One may consider examples from the chemical arts. A description of an anti-inflammatory steroid, *i.e.*, a steroid (a generic structural term) described even in terms of its function of lessening inflammation of tissues fails to distinguish any steroid from others having the same activity or function. Similarly, the expression an antibiotic penicillin fails to distinguish a particular penicillin molecule from others possessing the same activity. A description of what a material does, rather than of what it is, usually does not suffice. The disclosure must allow one skilled in the art to visualize or recognize the identity of the subject matter purportedly described.

In *Eli Lilly,* we were faced with a set of facts in which the words of the claim alone did not convey an adequate description of the invention. In such a situation, regardless whether the claim appears in the original specification and is thus supported by the specification as of the filing date, § 112, ¶ 1 is not necessarily met. If a purported description of an invention does not meet the requirements of the statute, the fact that it appears as an original claim or in the specification does not save it. A claim does not become more descriptive by its repetition, or its longevity.

Inasmuch as § 112, ¶ 1 requires such description, we are not persuaded by Enzo's argument that, because the specification indicated that Enzo possessed the claimed invention by reducing three sequences within the scope of the claims to practice, Enzo necessarily described the invention. It is true that in *Vas-Cath,* we stated: "The purpose of the 'written description' requirement is broader than to merely explain how to 'make and use'; the applicant must also convey with reasonable clarity to those skilled in the art that, as of the filing date sought, he or she was in possession of the invention." That portion of the opinion in *Vas-Cath,* however, merely states a *purpose* of the written description requirement, *viz.*, to ensure that the applicant had possession of the invention as of the desired filing date. It does not state that possession alone is always sufficient to meet that requirement. Furthermore, in *Lockwood v. American Airlines, Inc.*, we rejected Lockwood's argument that "all that is necessary to satisfy the description requirement is to show that one is 'in possession' of the invention.". Rather, we clarified that the written description requirement is satisfied by the patentee's disclosure of "such descriptive means as words, structures, figures, diagrams, formulas, etc., that fully set forth the claimed invention."

The articulation of the written description requirement in terms of "possession" is especially meaningful when a patentee is claiming entitlement to an earlier filing date under 35 U.S.C. §§ 119 or 120, in interferences in which the issue is whether a count is supported by the specification of one or more of the parties, and in *ex parte* applications in which a claim at issue was filed subsequent to the application. Application of the written description requirement, however, is not subsumed by the "possession" inquiry. A showing of "possession" is ancillary to the *statutory* mandate that "[t]he specification shall contain a written description of the invention," and that requirement is not met if, despite a showing of possession, the specification does not adequately describe the claimed invention. After all, as indicated above, one can show possession of an invention by means of an affidavit or declaration during prosecution, as one does in an interference or when one files an affidavit under 37 C.F.R. § 1.131 to antedate a reference. However, such a showing of possession alone does not cure the lack of a written description in the specification, as required by statute.

Similarly, we conclude that proof of a reduction to practice, absent an adequate description in the specification of what is reduced to practice, does not serve to describe or identify the invention for purposes of § 112, ¶ 1. As with "possession," proof of a reduction to practice may show priority of invention or allow one to antedate a reference, but it does not by itself provide a written description *in the patent specification.* We are thus not persuaded by Enzo's argument, relying on the PTO's Guidelines, that its disclosure of an actual reduction to practice is an important "safe haven" by which it has demonstrated compliance with the description requirement. The Guidelines state:

> Actual reduction to practice may be crucial in the relatively rare instances where the level of knowledge and level of skill are such that those of skill in the art cannot describe a composition structurally, or specify a process of making a composition by naming components and combining steps, in such a way as to distinguish the composition with particularity from all others.

For biological inventions, for which providing a description in written form is not practicable, one may nevertheless comply with the written description requirement by publicly depositing the biological material, as we have held today. That compliance is grounded on the fact of the deposit and the accession number in the specification, not because a reduction to practice has occurred. Such description is the *quid pro quo* of the patent system; the public must receive meaningful disclosure in exchange for being excluded from practicing the invention for a limited period of time.

Conclusion

For the foregoing reasons, we conclude that the district court erred in granting summary judgment that the claims of the 659 patent are invalid for failure to meet the written description requirement of 112, 1. While the district judge clearly understood and correctly applied this courts existing precedent, we nevertheless reverse because this case has taken us into new territory and we have held, as a matter of first impression, that reference in a patent specification to a deposit of genetic material may suffice to describe that material. We therefore remand for further resolution consistent with this opinion.

Reversed and Remanded

Order
July 15, 2002.

A petition for rehearing was filed by the plaintiff-appellant, and a response thereto was invited by the court and filed by the defendants-appellees. The United States Patent and Trademark Office and Fish & Richardson P.C. filed briefs as amici curiae. This matter was referred first to the merits panel that heard this appeal, which vacated its earlier decision and prepared a revised decision for issuance. Thereafter, at the request of a non-panel judge, an en banc poll was conducted concerning whether the appeal ought to be heard en banc. The poll failed. Circuit Judges Rader, Gajarsa, and Linn would have heard the appeal en banc.

Upon consideration thereof,

It is ordered that:

The petition for rehearing is granted as set forth in the panel opinion issued concurrently with this order.

ON DENIAL OF PETITION FOR REHEARING EN BANC

Circuit Judge Lourie with whom Circuit Judge Pauline Newman joins, concurring in the court's decision not to hear the case en banc.

I agree that the court correctly declined to hear this case *en banc.*

First, it is important to note that the earlier panel majority, in response to the petition for rehearing, has reversed its earlier decision. Taking the case *en banc* would therefore delay and hence frustrate the remand of the case solely for the purpose of revising written description law. That law is sound and does not need revision, at least as proposed by the dissents.

The dissenters believe that the written description requirement is simply a requirement for enablement. With all due respect, that is incorrect. The *complete* statutory provision is as follows:

> *The specification shall contain a written description of the invention,* and of the manner and process of making and using it, in such full, clear, concise, and exact terms as to enable any person skilled in the art to which it pertains or with which it is most nearly connected, to make and use the same, and shall set forth the best mode contemplated by the inventor of carrying out his invention.

(emphasis added). I read the statute so as to give effect to its language. The statute states that the invention must be described. That is basic patent law, the *quid pro quo* for the grant of a patent. Judge Rader notes that historically the written description requirement served a purpose when claims were not required. While that may be correct, when the statute began requiring claims, it was not amended to delete the requirement; note the comma between the description requirement and the enablement provision, and the "and" that follows the comma. Judge Rich, whom Judge Rader cites, was in fact one of the earliest interpreters of the statute as having separate enablement and written description requirements. The basic requirement to describe one's invention was recently emphasized as an independent patentability requirement by the Supreme Court in *Festo:*

> In addition, the patent application must *describe,* enable, and set forth the best mode of carrying out the invention. § 112 (1994 ed.). These latter requirements must be satisfied before issuance of the patent, for exclusive patent rights are given in exchange for *disclosing* the invention to the public. *See Bonito Boats,* 489 U.S. [141,] 150–151 [(1999)]. *What is claimed by the patent application must be the same as what is disclosed in the specification; otherwise the patent should not issue.*

Festo Corp. v. Shoketsu Kinzoku Kogyo Kabushiki Co., 535 U.S. 722 (2002) (emphases added).

It is said that applying the written description requirement outside of the priority context was novel until several years ago. Maybe so, maybe not; certainly such a holding was not precluded by statute or precedent. New interpretations of old statutes in light of new fact situations occur all the time. I believe these issues have arisen in recent years for the same reason that more doctrine of equivalents issues are in the courts, *viz.,* because perceptions that patents are stronger tempt patent owners to try to assert their patents beyond the original intentions of the inventors and their attorney. That is why the issues are being raised and that is why we have to decide them. Claims are now being asserted to cover what was not reasonably described in the patent.

Moreover, the dissenters would limit the requirement, to the extent that they credit the written description portion of the statute as being a separate requirement at all, to priority issues. The statute does not say "a written description of the invention for purposes of policing priority." While it has arisen primarily in cases involving priority issues, Congress has not so limited the statute, and we have failed to so limit it as well. As for the lack of earlier cases on this issue, it regularly happens in adjudication that issues do not arise until counsel raise them, and, when that occurs, courts are then required to decide them. Even now, a written description issue should not arise unless a patentee seeks to have his claims interpreted to include subject matter that he has not adequately disclosed in his patent. Although it is true that the written description requirement has been applied rigorously in some recent cases, I do not believe that any of those cases were decided wrongly. The losing patents (or applications) involved did not adequately disclose what was claimed: a particular ratio of variables; a sofa with controls other than on the console; a cup other than a conical cup; human insulin cDNA; or beta-interferon. Interpretation of written description as this court has done furthers the goal of the law to have claims commensurate in scope with what has been disclosed to the public.

I believe that the dissenters miss the point in seeing this case as involving an original claim or *in ipsis verbis* issue. There is no question that an original claim is part of the specification. That was the question answered in the affirmative by *In re Gardner,* 480 F.2d 879 (C.C.P.A. 1973) in which the CCPA found compliance with the written description requirement over the objection of the PTO Commissioner, who argued that an original claim should not be considered part of the written description unless the specification was amended to contain the subject matter of the original claim. However, the question here is whether the disclosure, as an original claim, or in the specification,[23] adequately describes the invention. It is incorrect that the mere appearance of vague claim language in an original claim or as part of the specification necessarily satisfies the written description requirement or shows possession of a generic invention.

Not only are we not entitled to ignore the statutory written description requirement, but our court has not. Earlier cases also upheld a separate written description requirement, and the fact that they may have pertained to priority disputes does not vitiate their basic requirement to disclose one's invention. Section 112, paragraph 1, does not limit itself to priority disputes. I thus believe it is incorrect, as Judge Rader states, that our cases have limited the written description/new matter doctrine to priority protection. Opinions explain the decisions on the issues that come before them on the facts presented; those cases have not expressly limited the written description requirement to priority issues, and in fact they emphasize that the requirement arises in a "variety of situations." Any language seemingly appearing to limit the language to priority issues does so because it addresses a priority issue that was before it. Other broad language is not binding holding on different facts and raising different issues. Courts do not, or should not, purport to write treatises on the law, outlining all aspects of a statute that comes before them. They decide issues raised in light of the decision being reviewed.

Moreover, even if written description is related to and overlaps with "new matter," so what? One can fail to meet the requirements of the statute in more than one manner, and in any event the case cited as equating those two requirements in fact distinguishes §§ 112 and 132 as concerning: (1) claims not supported by the disclosure; and (2) the prohibition of new matter to the disclosure, respectively. *In re Rasmussen,* 650 F.2d 1212, 1214–15 (C.C.P.A. 1981). *Rasmussen* states that "[t]he proper basis for rejection of a claim amended to recite elements thought to be without support in the original disclosure, therefore, is § 112, first paragraph, not § 132." *Id.*

---

23. Enzo's claim 1 is actually not an original claim. It was amended to include language appearing in the original specification and it thus appears *in ipsis verbis* in the specification.

In addition, we do not "elevate 'possession' to the posture of a statutory test of patentability." Rather, the opinion refines the "possession" test for circumstances such as these in which the inventors showed possession of a species of the invention by reference to a deposit, but may not have described what else within the scope of the claims they had possession of. While "possession" is a relevant factor in determining whether an invention is described, it is only a criterion for satisfying the statutory written description requirement. Showing possession is not necessarily equivalent to providing a written description.

Judge Rader's dissenting opinion cites authors who disapprove of our decisions. While views of knowledgeable and objective commentators are surely of interest to this court, we should not interpret the law based on taking polls of discontented writers. Our commission is to apply the law to the facts and attempt to explain the reasons for our decisions. Critical articles may be written by those who have lost a case, or those who are skilled in a particular technology or not, or those who have little practical experience or who are seasoned experts. While Judge Rader cites articles critical of *Lilly,* others are favorable. Not surprisingly, an author from Eli Lilly took a positive view of the case. *See* Mark J. Stewart (patent associate at Eli Lilly), Note, *The Written Description Requirement of 35 U.S.C. § 112(1): The Standard After Regents of the University of California v. Eli Lilly & Co.,* 32 Ind. L.Rev. 537, 563 (1999) ("[T]he holding in *Lilly* actually avoided a disaster that would have crippled the biotechnology industry. The enormous amount of time and money companies spend to study DNA and protein variants, to clone homologous genes and protein family members, and to mine databases would no longer be justified had the court found the written description in '525 adequate.").

Other authors support a robust written description requirement and point out the benefits of such a requirement to the public. *See, e.g.,* Scott A. Chambers, *"Written Description" and Patent Examination Under the U.S. Patent and Trademark Office Guidelines,* IP Litigator, Sept.–Oct.2000, at 9, 10 ("Thus, the Federal Circuit's present interpretation of the written description requirement maintains the vitality of the U.S. patent system and provides disclosures that others can build on. By suggesting that disclosure of the structure or actual sequence of complex chemical entities may sometimes be required, the Federal Circuit may have advanced the goal of the patent system to actually put the claimed invention into the hands of the public."); Margaret Sampson, *The Evolution of the Enablement and Written Description Requirements under 35 U.S.C. § 112 in the Area of Biotechnology,* 15 Berkeley Tech. L.J. 1233, 1260–61 (2000) ("Without a heightened written description requirement, inventors could receive patent rights to sequences of which they have no knowledge, in organisms with which they have never worked.... Therefore, the Federal Circuit's approach to the written description requirement in the area of biotechnology has prevented nucleotide sequence claims from becoming a Pandora's box that the patent law is unable to control."). In any event, we decide cases as they come to us, based on the arguments raised, the decisions below, the law, the facts, and our best efforts, not based on occasional journal articles.

Since some of the cases implicated by this issue are in the biotech field, I should point out that, among the problems in comprehension of the issues in a biotech context is that a functional description of DNA does not indicate which DNA has been invented. And simply acknowledging the presence of a DNA that serves a particular function, whose existence has been postulated since, perhaps, Mendel, plus a general process for finding it, is not a description of the DNA. It is a research plan at best, and does not show "possession" of any invention.

Still, in terms of the more practical aspects of complying with the statute, meeting the description requirement is the first task in drafting a patent application. Enabling one of skill in the art to make and use the invention is a separate requirement. To interpret the written description requirement only as an enablement provision is to let the tail wag the dog. Perhaps there is little difference in electrical and mechanical inventions between describing an invention and enabling one to make and use it, but that is not true of chemical and chemical-like inventions.

Enzo's patent claimed a genus of chemical-like materials (a sequence of nucleic acids is of a chemical nature—note the claims begin with "a composition"). Although one may envision a general concept, what one usually does first in making or isolating a chemical or chemical-related invention is to obtain a specific material or materials. One then broadens the concept to extend it as far as one envisions that other materials will have the same utility and can be similarly made. That broadened concept becomes the genus in a patent application that is both the broadest statement constituting a written description and usually claim 1. One then elaborates to fill in the genus with representative examples of compounds or substances that fall within the genus. That is part of the written description needed to support the generic claim. *Then,* one tells how to make the materials, and then how to use them. That is enablement, separate in concept from describing *what* the invention is. The idea that there is no requirement in the statute to describe one's new invention (aside from the fact that the language of the statute contains one) separate from the requirement to enable one to make and use it is not correct. Disclosure is the first role of a patent. One must first state what one's invention is. That is quite different from telling how to make and use it.

Some commentators have had difficulty in understanding how one may have enabled an invention, but not described it. They believe they must coincide. As an example of how the written description and enablement provisions differ in chemistry, however, one may readily have enabled the making of an invention, but still not have described it. For example, a propyl or butyl compound may be made by a process analogous to a disclosed methyl compound, but, in the absence of a statement that the propyl and butyl compounds are part of the invention, they have not been described and they are not entitled to a patent (I make no implication here about coverage under the doctrine of equivalents). This is surely part of the recent history of some biotechnology patents.

In sum, we have evolved a consistent body of law over a number of years, based on the statute and basic principles of patent law. I see no reason to hear this case *en banc* and rewrite the statute.

Circuit Judge Pauline Newman concurring in the denial of rehearing en banc.

I join Judge Lourie's statement, and write separately to emphasize my concern with the position of the dissent concerning the law of written description. The description of the invention has always been the foundation of the patent specification. It sets forth what has been invented, and sets boundaries of what can be claimed. The theory of the dissent that a description of the invention is not needed in order to support the claims, but serves only to antedate prior art or establish priority in an interference, is a dramatic innovation in the theory and practice of patents. It has never been the sole purpose of the description requirement, and negates not only the logic but also the history of patent practice. The dissent's citation of cases in which the description of the invention has been relied on to antedate references and in interference contests reinforces, not reduces, the role of the description of the invention in establishing what has been invented.

The dissent argues that the subject matter that is intended to be patented need not be described, as long as it is enabled. Undoubtedly, in many patents these requirements are met by the same information content. And the special case of the biological deposit is a method of complying with the statutory requirements, as the panel now confirms; this expedient implements the statute for this special subject matter, but does not change it. It is not the law that the description of the invention serves only to establish priority, to be invoked only when priority is at issue. The invention that is covered by the claims must be described as well as enabled, as the statute has always required.

Circuit Judge Dyk concurring in the court's decision not to hear the case en banc.

The opinions of Judges Newman, Lourie, Rader, and Linn concerning the denial of *en banc* rehearing raise important and interesting questions, including questions concerning the correctness of our earlier decision in [*Eli Lilly*] that may someday warrant the court's *en banc* attention. Given the panel's decision on rehearing, remanding for further consideration by the district court, this is not the appropriate occasion for *en banc* review. The court will also benefit from further percolation of these issues before they are addressed by the full court.

Circuit Judge Rader with whom Circuit Judges Gajarsa and Linn join, dissenting from the court's decision not to hear the case en banc.

The tortuous path of this case shows the perils of ignoring the statute and over thirty years of consistent written description case law.[24] The first version of this opinion, *Enzo Biochem, Inc. v. Gen-Probe, Inc.*, 285 F.3d 1013 (Fed. Cir. 2002), purported to invalidate a patent because the inventor had not shown "possession of the invention" for written description. As this court now acknowledges, an inventor can hardly show possession of an invention better than by depositing the invention in an internationally recognized repository. This court corrects part of the mistake of *Enzo I*. Yet the court still remands to the district court to reexamine the written description requirement. Because the written description requirement as created and applied for thirty years does not apply to this case, I would grant *en banc* review and correct the rest of this court's misapplication of the description requirement.

Statute

Because the greater mistake in this case is misapplication of this court's written description case law, this opinion devotes only a few paragraphs to the statutory interpretation question. The United States' brief as *amicus curiae* in support of rehearing *en banc* states concisely this *Enzo* opinion's disregard for the statute:

A straightforward reading of the text of section 112 suggests that the test for an adequate written description is whether it provides enough written information for others to make and use the invention. The statute provides that the "specification shall contain a written description of the invention ... in such full, clear, concise, and exact terms as to enable any person skilled in the art ... to make and use the same." Thus, an adequate written description assures that others can "make and use" the invention.[25]

---

24. An appendix at the close of this opinion will briefly explicate all written description cases from its creation in 1967 in the Court of Customs and Patent Appeals to the present. This appendix shows that only two cases, this ENZO case and the 1997 LILLY case have purported to apply the doctrine outside its purpose and function.

25. This court rejected the "straightforward reading" of the statute in *Vas-Cath* because the written description (WD) doctrine was a priority control, not the general disclosure doctrine of enablement. Within the proper purpose of WD, *Vas-Cath* makes sense. When applied outside the priority context as a general disclosure doctrine, however, WD cannot depart from the enablement test

If it is possible to characterize disregard of statutory text as a secondary mistake, this case fits that classification. The more important problem is disregard for the case law that originated the written description requirement and applied it for over thirty years.

Origin and History of the Written Description Requirement

The words "written description" first appeared in the Patent Act of 1793. At that time, of course, patents did not require claims but only a written description sufficient "to distinguish [the invention] from all other things before known or used." In *Evans v. Eaton,* 20 U.S. (7 Wheat) 356 (1822), the Supreme Court construed the description language to require applicants to enable their inventions and to provide the notice function of claims:

> [After enablement,] [t]he other object of the specification is to put the public in possession of what the party claims as his own invention, so as to ascertain if he claims any thing that is in common use, or is already known....

In later enactments, this notice function was assigned to claims, leaving enablement as the only purpose of the "written description" language. As noted in the United States' brief, the modern descendant of the 1793 phrase still requires only a written description "in such ... terms as to enable [the invention]." In *J.E.M. AG Supply,* the Supreme Court acknowledged only enablement as the disclosure *quid pro quo* of the Patent Act: "In addition [to novelty, utility, and nonobviousness], to obtain a utility patent, a breeder must describe the plant with sufficient specificity to enable others to 'make and use' the invention after the patent term expires." Reading the statute, the Supreme Court correctly found no general disclosure requirement in title 35 other than enablement.[26]

Before 1967, this court's predecessor, the United States Court of Customs and Patent Appeals also did not differentiate written description from enablement. In 1966, that predecessor court wrote in detail about section 112, paragraph 1, and found only two requirements—enablement (the A requirement under Judge Rich's terminology) and best mode (the B requirement).

In 1967, the Court of Customs and Patent Appeals first separated a new written description (WD) requirement from the enablement requirement of § 112. The reason for this new judge-made doctrine needs some explanation. Every patent system must have some provision to prevent applicants from using the amendment process to update their disclosures (claims or specifications) during their pendency before the patent office. Otherwise applicants could add new matter to their disclosures and date them back to their original filing date, thus defeating an accurate accounting of the priority of invention. Priority always a vital issue in patent prosecution procedures—often determines entitlement to an invention. Before 1967, the United States Patent Office and the Court of Customs and Patent Appeals used a "new matter" rejection to ensure that applicants did not update their disclosures after the original filing date of the application. This "new matter" rejection had a statutory basis: "No amendment shall introduce new matter into the disclosure of the invention." 35 U.S.C. § 132.

In 1967, in *In re Ruschig,* 379 F.2d 990 ([C.C.P.A]1967), this court's predecessor created for the first time a new WD doctrine to enforce priority. In the context of a new

---

without replacing it. Thus, the United States advocates application of the statutory standard of enablement.

26. In *Festo,* the Supreme Court mentions a description requirement separate from enablement. *Festo Corp. v. Shoketsu Kogyo Kabushiki Co.,* 535 U.S. 722 (2002). This listing of doctrines, however, did not endorse any departure from this court's case law for more than thirty years.

claim added "[a]bout a year after the present application was filed," the *Ruschig* court sought to determine "whether [the new] claim 13 is supported by the disclosure of appellants' application." Rather than use § 132, however, *Ruschig* assigned the role of policing priority to § 112. As a technical matter, the Court of Customs and Patent Appeals distinguished between adding new matter to the specification and adding new matter to the claims. Under PTO practice, new matter in the claims would draw a § 132 *rejection* of the claims; new matter in the specification would draw a § 132 *objection* to the addition. The *Ruschig* court, for the first time, decided to treat the objection alone as a § 132 matter. To deal with new matter in the claims, the court calved a new WD doctrine out of the § 112 enablement requirement.[27] As long as the new WD doctrine applied according to its original purpose as an identical twin of the § 132 new matter doctrine, these technical distinctions were of little practical consequence.

In any event, the WD doctrine, at its inception had a very clear function preventing new matter from creeping into claim amendments. Judge Rich, the author of *Ruschig,* often reiterated the purpose of WD. For instance in the case of *In re Wertheim,* 541 F.2d 257 (CCPA 1976), the Court of Customs and Patent Appeals confronted a priority issue:

> The dispositive issue under this heading is whether appellants' parent and Swiss applications comply with 35 U.S.C. § 112, first paragraph, including the description requirement, as to the subject matter of these claims. If they do, these claims are entitled to the filing dates of the *parent* application.... [A] right of foreign *priority* in appellants' Swiss application will antedate Pfluger 1966 and remove it as prior art against the claims.

(emphasis added). In resolving this question, Judge Rich stated again the purpose of WD: "The function of the description requirement is to ensure that the inventor had possession, as of the filing date of the application relied on, of the specific subject matter *later* claimed by him." ... (emphasis added). In sum, WD was a new matter doctrine, a priority policeman.

Returning to the history of WD, after 1967, the PTO continued to use new matter rejections under § 132, but also embraced the coterminous written description analysis. Thus, for many years, the PTO rejected priority errors in claims under both § 132 and § 112.

In 1981, the Court of Customs and Patent Appeals noted that the two rejections were interchangeable: "This court, ha[s] said that a rejection of an amended claim under § 132 is *equivalent to* a rejection under § 112, first paragraph." ... (emphasis added). To avoid confusion between new matter rejections and objections, the court chose to eliminate the § 132/§ 112 rejections and to use § 112 for new matter rejections (claims): "The proper basis for rejection of a claim amended to recite elements thought to be without support in the original disclosure, therefore, is § 112, first paragraph, not § 132." The purpose of the doctrine did not change. As the sentence above states explicitly, the § 112 doctrine, like its corollary § 132, policed priority, nothing more. At no time did either the CCPA or the Federal Circuit purport to apply the equivalent new matter/written description rejections to original claims or other claims without priority

---

27. As a matter of integrity to the statute, the *Ruschig* distinction has a major problem, namely the language of § 132 embraces both new matter rejections of amended claims and new matter objections to amended specifications. Both claims and the rest of the specification are part of the patent "disclosure" within the terms of § 132. Moreover implicit in the judicial creation of a new WD requirement is the incorrect assumption that the Patent Act had no remedy for new matter in claims before 1967. In fact, § 132 embraces both new matter rejections and objections.

problems. WD, the equivalent of the statutory new matter doctrine, simply has no application to claims without priority problems.

The Federal Circuit continued to follow this binding precedent. In fact, this Circuit's test for written description required assessment of the specification to check "later claimed subject matter." In fact, this standard emphasizes that WD does not examine the specification for "literal support" of the claim language unless priority is in question. In any event, this Circuit did not apply WD to claims without priority problems because the doctrine had no purpose beyond policing priority.[28]

The deviation from thirty years of precedent

In 1997, for the first time, this court purported to apply WD as a general disclosure doctrine in place of enablement, rather than as a priority doctrine. In *Eli Lilly,* this court found that the '525 patent specification does not provide a WD of human insulin cDNA despite the disclosure of a general method of producing human insulin cDNA and a description of the human insulin A and B chain amino acid sequences that cDNA encodes. In the words of the court, "a description that does not render a claimed invention obvious does not sufficiently describe that invention for purposes of § 112, ¶ 1." At another point, the court stated: "An adequate written description of a DNA ... 'requires a precise definition, such as by structure, formula, chemical name, or physical properties....'" In sum, the *Eli Lilly* opinion does not test a later claim amendment against the specification for priority, but asserts a new free-standing disclosure requirement in place of the statutory standard of enablement. Based on the absence of a nucleotide-by-nucleotide recitation in the specification of the human insulin cDNA, the court determined that the applicant had not adequately described the invention. For the first time, this court purported to apply WD without any priority question. Even accepting that WD can be isolated as a separate requirement from enablement in § 112, ¶ 1, the words "written description" hardly prescribe a standard that requires nucleotide-by-nucleotide disclosure.

Under the correct written description test, one of skill in the art would have recognized that the '525 patent in *Lilly* had no new matter or priority problems. In terms of the statutory test for adequacy of disclosure, the patent disclosure undoubtedly warranted rejection for lack of enablement. Under the *In re Wands* test for enablement, 858 F.2d 731 (Fed. Cir.1988), the inventor certainly did not show one of skill in the art how to make human insulin cDNA.[29] Moreover the patent claimed vertebrate insulin cDNA a category ranging from fish to humans again claims whose scope far exceeds the patent's enabling disclosures. In fact, the patent disclosure only revealed that the inventor had enabled cloning of rat insulin. Instead of invalidating under the statutory test for adequacy of disclosure, i.e., enablement, the *Lilly* court purported to create a new doctrine for adequacy of disclosure that it labeled incorrectly "written description." As noted, from its creation through thirty years of application, WD had never been a free-standing substitute for enablement.

---

28. Again, the appendix at the close of this opinion shows that the Federal Circuit uniformly applies WD to police priority. Only the LILLY and this ENZO opinion purport to apply it as a general disclosure requirement in place of enablement.

29. U.S. Pat. No. 4,652,525, the patent at issue in *Lilly,* was filed in 1983, but claimed priority to a parent filed in 1977. In 1977, biotechnology was still in its infancy. In fact, the Maxam and Gilbert method of sequencing DNA was just published in 1977. Cloning in that era was, at a minimum, unpredictable and would have required vast amounts of experimentation to accomplish. Therefore, the patent's prophetic disclosure of human insulin cDNA hardly enabled its production as claimed. Instead of pursuing this obvious avenue of rejection, the Federal Circuit reached out beyond the statute and the case law to create a new general disclosure test.

Although it should not be necessary, a brief defense of the statutory standard for adequate disclosure shows the flaws of the new form of WD. Enablement already requires inventors to disclose how to *make* (reproduce, replicate, manufacture) and how to *use* the invention (by definition rendering it a "useful art"). Therefore, because the competitor can make the invention, it can then acquire the DNA sequence or any other characteristic whenever it desires. Meantime the competitor can use, exploit, commercialize (outside the patent term) or improve upon and design around (within the patent term) as much of the invention as it cares to make. In other words, the statutory standard for sufficiency of disclosure serves masterfully the values of the patent system.

Even after *Lilly,* the Federal Circuit—in all other WD cases before this *Enzo* case—applied priority principles, declining to assert the doctrine as a general test for adequacy of disclosure. One of those opinions analyzes WD with particular care:

> The written description requirement and its corollary, the new matter prohibition of 35 U.S.C. § 132, both serve to ensure that the patent applicant was in full possession of the claimed subject matter on the application filing date. When the applicant adds a claim or otherwise amends his specification after the original filing date, as Brandon did in this case, the new claims or other added material must find support in the original specification.

TurboCare Div. Of Demag Delaval Turbomachinery Corp. v. General Elec. Co., 264 F.3d 1111, 1118 (Fed. Cir. 2001).

In sum, the written description language has been in the statute since 1870, yet only since 1967 has case law separated it from enablement. The separation itself is not disruptive of the patent system, however, because the doctrine operated solely to police priority. Indeed, with the exception of *Lilly* and this *Enzo* case, this court and its predecessor have only applied the doctrine within the limits of its origin as an "equivalent" or "corollary" of 35 U.S.C. § 132, the new matter section.

Enzo and written description

The record in this case shows that no priority issues remain to invoke WD. The inventor in this case amended the original claims in response to the examiner's request to place the selective hybridization steps in the claims. Thus, the amendments were all narrowing meaning the applicant added no new matter to the claims by amendment. Instead, the applicant copied material from the original specification into the original claims. By definition, this case presents no new matter or priority issues requiring application of the original WD doctrine. The original specification contained all of the subject matter included in the inventor's claims. For this reason, the panel misapplies § 112, ¶ 1 by remanding on the question of WD. If any § 112, ¶ 1 questions remain, they are questions of the sufficiency of disclosure, an enablement question. Instead, the panel, relying on *Lilly,* advocates applying WD "regardless whether the claim appears in the original specification and is thus supported by the specification as of the filing date." To the contrary, WD has no such application consistent with the statute and the case law.

Why does this matter?

As both *Lilly* and this case show, the aberrant form of WD requires far more specific disclosure than enablement.[30] Because the *Lilly* application of § 112, ¶ 1 requires a far

30. "Conflicts in Federal Circuit Patent Law Decisions," *The Federal Circuit Bar Journal,* Vol. 11, no. 3, p. 723, chronicles this circuit's primary conflicts. Listed first as the leading conflict is "I. The Written Description Requirement of § 112, First Paragraph." The article notes: "[T]he Federal Circuit has not provided clear and consistent rules for determining precisely what type of disclosure is

more demanding disclosure, defendants will have no need to invoke enablement, but will proceed directly to the more demanding *Lilly* § 112, ¶ 1 requirements. Thus, the new breed of WD evident in *Lilly* and this case threatens to further disrupt the patent system by replacing enablement the statutory test for adequate disclosure. *See,* Rai, Arti, "Intellectual Property Rights in Biotechnology: Addressing New Technology" 34 *Wake Forest L.Rev.* 827, 834–35 (Fall, 1999) ("Thus in [*Lilly*] ... the CAFC broke new ground by applying the written description requirement not only to later-filed claims but also to claims filed in the original patent.... [T]he *Lilly* court used the written description requirement as a type of elevated enablement requirement."); Mueller, Janice M., "The Evolving Application of the Written Description Requirement to Biotechnological Inventions" 13 *Berkeley Tech. L.J.* 615, 617 (Spring 1998) ("The *Lilly* decision establishes uniquely rigorous rules for the description of biotechnological subject matter that significantly contort written description doctrine away from its historic origins and policy grounding. The *Lilly* court elevate[s] written description to an effective 'super enablement' standard....").

Furthermore, the Supreme Court repeatedly cautioned against the disruption of the settled expectations of the inventing community. *Lilly* and now this case change the application of the WD test and "up the ante" for disclosure a situation inventors might have addressed if they could have foreseen that this court would disrupt settled disclosure principles. At this point, however, those inventors have no way to change patents that comply with enablement disclosure, but not the stiffer demands of *Lilly.*

Replacement of enablement doctrines with an ill-defined general disclosure doctrine of WD imperils the integrity of the patent system. Enablement, arguably the most important patent doctrine after obviousness, has many important applications. Beyond mere adequacy of disclosure, it serves as the line of demarcation between the visionary theorist (adds nothing to the useful arts) and the visionary pioneer (contributes to the useful arts) ... and also serves to limit claim scope thus demarking the boundary between pioneer inventions and patentable improvements. The WD possession test cannot perform these functions. Professor Janis explains that WD provides a blunt tool to measure the sufficiency of disclosure:

> Today, however the written description requirement enjoys a prominence wholly out of proportion to its humble origins.
>
> ...
>
> Recent efforts to elaborate the 'possession' standard both confirm the substantial redundancy of the enablement and written description requirements....
>
> ...
>
> [T]he written description requirement is a threat to the coherence of disclosure doctrines....

Janis, Mark D., "On Courts Herding Cats: Contending with the 'Written Description' Requirement (and Other Unruly Patent Disclosure Doctrines)" 2 *Wash. U.J.L. & Pol'y* 55, 60, 70, 83 (2000).

Professors Rai, Mueller, and Wegner, among others, agree with Professor Janis's assessment. Rai, Mueller, *supra;* Wegner, Harold C., "An Enzo White Paper: A New Judi-

sufficient to comply with the § 112 written description requirement." The article then notes three separate tests for measuring compliance with § 112, ¶ 1. For instance, "[t]he strictest approach requires the written description to delineate all of the claimed elements."

cial Standard for a Biotechnology 'Written Description' Under 35 U.S.C. § 112, ¶ 1" 1 *J. Marshall Rev. Intell. Prop. L.* 254, 263 (2002) (recognizing "there may very well be problems with the scope of enablement in the facts of the *Enzo* case," but written description would not apply to "original claims.").

For biotech inventions, according to the *Lilly* standard, § 112, ¶ 1 requires a precise listing of the DNA sequence nucleotide-by-nucleotide. Enablement, on the other hand, requires that the specification show one of skill in the art how to acquire that sequence on their own. As a test for biotech claims without priority issues, WD may well jeopardize a sizeable percentage of claims filed before the *Lilly* departure in 1997. These patents had no notice of a change in the statutory standard for disclosure. Moreover the *Lilly/Enzo* rule prejudices university or small inventors who do not have the expensive and time-consuming resources to process every new biotechnological invention to extract its nucleotide sequence. *See,* Mueller, *supra* at 617 ("*Lilly* ... will likely chill development."); Sampson, Margaret, "The Evolution of the Enablement and Written Description Requirements Under 35 U.S.C. § 112 in the Area of Biotechnology." *15 Berkeley Tech. L.J.* 1233, 1262 (Fall 2000) ("The primary argument against the Federal Circuit's heightened written description requirement for biotechnological invention is that ... it also 'reduces incentives to invest in innovation by depriving potential patentees of the opportunity to fully benefit from their research.'").

Saving the obvious for last, *Lilly* and this case really cannot depart from decades of established case law on § 112, ¶ 1. Even the court's decision to issue this improved version of *Enzo* without correcting all the problems does not indicate any acceptance of written description as a general disclosure doctrine for all claims regardless of priority issues. *Lilly* and this case are panel cases and cannot override the statute that makes enablement the general disclosure doctrine and the vast body of prior case law limiting WD to its original purpose. Sadly, however, this case will perpetuate the confusion.

Conclusion

Written description a part of the Patent Act since 1870 has taken on a life separate from its statutory context only since 1967. As long as WD applied only for the reasons that occasioned its judicial creation, it did not disrupt the rest of the Patent Act. Two recent cases, however, this case and the 1997 *Lilly* case, have purported to create a new disclosure doctrine that supplants enablement. Although this court declines to take this occasion to correct those dalliances, the origin and purpose of both § 112, ¶ 1 doctrines serve notice that neither *Lilly* nor this case properly applies the otherwise orderly disclosure doctrines....

Circuit Judge Linn with whom Circuit Judges Rader and Gajarsa join, dissenting from the court's decision not to the hear the case en banc.

I am in agreement with much of the panel's reasoning in the revised opinion, but part company with the panel's treatment of written description and enablement issues, most notably in the text dealing with the *in ipsis verbis* issue.

With all due respect, the panel opinion in my view conflates and perpetuates the confusion our precedent has engendered between written description as a separate requirement ("possession of the invention")—an issue relevant to priority—and enablement—an issue relevant to the sufficiency of the disclosure. The notion of having to show "possession of the invention" was discussed in *Vas-Cath Inc. v. Mahurkar,* 935 F.2d 1555, (Fed. Cir. 1991) and other cases from our court as a convenient way to measure or test entitlement of later filed claims to an earlier priority date. It was not and should not be a test for sufficiency of disclosure, per se. It should have no place in and does not aid in the disposition of cases where the claims in question are part of the original disclosure. In those cases, entitlement to the filing date is inherent in that the claims themselves—having been filed as part of the original application—provide their own written description.

35 U.S.C. § 112 requires a written description of the invention, but the measure of the sufficiency of that written description in meeting the conditions of patentability in paragraph 1 of that statute, either by reference to a microorganism deposit or in terms *in ipsis verbis* with the language of the claims, should depend solely on whether it enables any person skilled in the art to which the invention pertains to make and use the claimed invention. Where priority is not an issue, as in the present case, the focus once a written description has been found should be on whether the description meets the enablement requirement. Satisfaction of the "possession of the invention" test simply is not relevant.

The question presented by 35 U.S.C. § 112, paragraph 1, is not, "Does the written description disclose what the invention is, or does it merely describe what it does?" The question is, "Does the written description describe the invention recited and described in the claims—themselves part of the specification—in terms that are sufficient to enable one of skill in the art to make and use the claimed invention?" That is the mandate of the statute and is all our precedent, prior to [*Eli Lilly*] and the present case, demand. For original claims, where priority is not an issue, the notion of possession of the invention is not germane, the claim itself evidencing possession of the invention as of the filing date. In the panel opinion, the discussion of the *in ipsis verbis* issue properly addresses enablement issues but does so in words not of enablement but of "possession of the invention." This conflates the two unrelated issues, elevates "possession" to the posture of a statutory test of patentability—which it is not—and fosters further confusion in what is already a confusing area of our precedent.

The U.S. Patent and Trademark Office ("PTO") aptly states the reason why this case should be taken en banc: "[a]lthough this Court has addressed the 'written description' requirement of section 112 on a number of occasions, its decisions have not taken a clear and uniform position regarding the purpose and meaning of the requirement."

This is an area of law that is of significant importance to the biotech industry and affects how patent applications are drafted, prosecuted and will be enforced in this and other areas of emerging technology. When patent attorneys set out to write patent applications, they do so for an educated audience—those skilled in the art—and attempt to describe the invention in a way that enables those of ordinary skill to make and use the invention as claimed. Before the decision in *Lilly*, the practicing bar had accepted and found workable the notion elucidated in our precedent that § 112 requires a written description sufficient to enable one of ordinary skill in the art to make and use the claimed invention—i.e., enablement. *Lilly* changed the landscape and engendered the debate the panel opinion in this case perpetuates.

Some have praised *Lilly* for maintaining the integrity of patent disclosures and for curbing patent filings for inventions that have not yet been made but are just nascent ideas. Others have been sharply critical of *Lilly*. The debate is well framed by the panel opinion and the contemporaneous dissent of Judge Rader. Those opinions highlight the uncertainty this issue raises in how inventions are protected, in how the PTO discharges its responsibilities, and in how business is conducted in emerging fields of law. These uncertainties will be left unresolved until we clarify this en banc. The issue is important, is ripe for us to consider, and deserves to be clarified, one way or the other. For these reasons, I respectfully dissent from the court's declining to consider this case en banc.

Notes & Questions

1. *Chakrabarty* is often described as the beginning of the biotech industry in the U.S., although of course there were other factors involved as well. It certainly spawned a number of new cases and controversies on patenting life, some of which are reproduced in Chapter 8.

2. An early seminal case for determining the novelty of biotechnological/genomic inventions is *Fiers v. Revel*, 984 F.2d 1164 (Fed. Cir. 1993). The excerpt below shows the impact that the highly technical rules regarding *inter alia* priority based on foreign filings have on interference proceedings.

> Walter C. Fiers, Michel Revel, and Pierre Tiollais appeal from the June 5, 1991 decision of the Patent and Trademark Office Board of Patent Appeals and Interferences, awarding priority of invention in a three-way interference proceeding, No. 101,096, to Haruo Sugano, Masami Muramatsu, and Tadatsugu Taniguchi (Sugano). We affirm.
>
> Background
>
> This interference among three foreign inventive entities relates to the DNA which codes for human fibroblast beta-interferon (β-IF), a protein that promotes viral resistance in human tissue. It involves a single count which reads:
>
> A DNA which consists essentially of a DNA which codes for a human fibroblast interferon-beta polypeptide.
>
> The parties filed U.S. patent applications as follows: Sugano on October 27, 1980, Fiers on April 3, 1981, and Revel and Tiollais (Revel) on September 28, 1982. Sugano claimed the benefit of his March 19, 1980 Japanese filing date, Revel claimed the benefit of his November 21, 1979 Israeli filing date, and Fiers sought to establish priority under 35 U.S.C. § 102(g) based on prior conception coupled with diligence up to his British filing
>
> Sugano's Japanese application disclosed the complete nucleotide sequence of a DNA coding for β-IF and a method for isolating that DNA.[31] Revel's Israeli application disclosed a method for isolating a fragment of the DNA coding for β-IF as well as a method for isolating messenger RNA (mRNA) coding for β-IF, but did not disclose a complete DNA sequence coding for β-IF.[32] Fiers, who was working abroad, based his case for priority on an alleged conception either in September 1979 or in January 1980, when his ideas were brought into the United States, coupled with diligence toward a constructive reduction to prac-

---

31. Sugano's method involved the preparation of two populations of radioactivity-labelled cDNA probes prepared from the mRNA of fibroblast cells. One population of probes was prepared from the mRNA of induced fibroblast cells and the other population from the mRNA of non-induced cells. These probes were then exposed to a cDNA library prepared from induced cells, and the clones that only hybridized with the first probe were selected. The selected clones were then used as probes to select the full-length DNA sequence encoding β-IF, which was then sequenced.

32. Revel's method involved preparing a cDNA library of clones from the mRNA of cells induced to produce β-IF, screening each clone for hybridization to mRNA from induced cells, eluting the hybridized mRNA, and assaying the eluted mRNAs for β-IF activity.

tice on April 3, 1980, when he filed a British application disclosing the complete nucleotide sequence of a DNA coding for β-IF. According to Fiers, his conception of the DNA of the count occurred when two American scientists, Walter Gilbert and Phillip Sharp, to whom he revealed outside of the United States a proposed method for isolating DNA coding for β-IF brought the protocol back to the United States.[33] Fiers submitted affidavits from Gilbert and Sharp averring that, based on Fiers' proposed protocol, one of ordinary skill in the art would have been able to isolate β-IF DNA without undue experimentation.[34] On February 26, 1980, Fiers' patent attorney brought into the United States a draft patent application disclosing Fiers' method, but not the nucleotide sequence for the DNA.

The Board awarded priority of invention to Sugano, concluding that (1) Sugano was entitled to the benefit of his March 19, 1980 Japanese filing date, (2) Fiers was entitled to the benefit of his April 3, 1980 British filing date, but did not prove conception of the DNA of the count prior to that date, and (3) Revel was not entitled to the benefit of his November 21, 1979 Israeli filing date. The Board based its conclusions on the disclosure or failure to disclose the complete nucleotide sequence of a DNA coding for β-IF.

3. The nonobviousness requirement (§ 103) as applied to biotechnological/genomic inventions was heavily litigated before Congress amended the provision in 1995 to add what is now § 103(b). Representative cases before § 103(b) was added include: *Amgen, Inc. v. Chugai Pharmaceutical Co. Ltd.*, 927 F.2d 1200 (Fed. Cir. 1991) (affirming the validity of Amgen's patent for artificially producing erythropoietin (a protein which stimulates the production of red blood cells) against claims of obviousness); *In re Bell*, 991 F.2d 781 (Fed. Cir. 1993) (reversing patent examiner's obviousness rejection of inventors' patent application claims directed to nucleic acid molecules (DNA and RNA) containing human sequences or genes which code for human insulin-like growth factors I and II (IGF), single chain serum proteins that play a role in the mediation of somatic cell growth following the administration of growth hormones); and *In re Deuel*, 51 F.3d 1552 (Fed. Cir. 1995) (reversing patent examiner's obviousness rejection of inventors' patent application claims directed to certain cDNA molecules).

4. Section 112, concerning written description, enablement, and best mode, also has a rich litigation history. Well-known cases besides those excerpted above include: *Amgen, Inc. v. Chugai Pharmaceutical Co. Ltd.*, 927 F.2d 1200 (Fed. Cir. 1991) (reversing lower court holding that erythropoietin patent was enabled) (this case is referenced for its nonobviousness holdings in the preceding Note as well); and *Regents of the Univ. of*

---

33. Fiers presented his protocols and progress to date toward isolating DNA coding for β-IF at a September 21, 1979 meeting in Paris at which Sharp and Gilbert were present. Sharp and Gilbert returned to the United States on September 23 and 24, respectively. Fiers made a second presentation in Martinique on January 12, 1980. Gilbert and Sharp were both present and returned to the United States on January 15 and 17, respectively. On March 25, 1980, Fiers disclosed by telephone to his patent attorney that he had determined the entire nucleotide sequence of a DNA coding for β-IF. Fiers presented that nucleotide sequence along with a protocol for preparing the complete DNA in Switzerland on March 28, 1980. Fiers and his attorney worked from March 31 until April 2 in Ghent drafting the final portion and claims of the British application that Fiers filed on April 3, 1980.

34. Fiers' proposed protocol involved preparing a cDNA library from the mRNA of cells induced to produce β-IF mRNA, and screening the cDNA library for a cDNA that, when introduced into a cell, would cause it to display β-IF activity.

Cal. v. Eli Lilly and Co., 119 F.3d 1559 (Fed. Cir. 1997) (affirming lower court's ruling that patent claims directed to cDNA related to production of insulin were invalid because the underlying sequence of nucleotides was not included).

B. Determining Ownership and Rights

Discovering that a patentable invention has arisen in a research laboratory is just the beginning of a long commercialization process; and only the first step in actually securing intellectual property (IP) rights in the invention. Further, patents are not the only kind of IP available to protect innovation and invention in the life sciences. Accordingly, this Part first addresses the question of inventorship under U.S. patent law, before turning to the separate issues of ownership, assignment, and licensing of patent rights. The latter are particularly considered in light of funding arrangements that often determine the ownership—but not necessarily inventorship—of later arising patents, as well as the conditions under which those patents may or must be assigned or licensed out for commercialization. The Section then considers limitations on patent owners' rights regarding the ongoing research environment, before concluding with a brief overview of trade secret law.

1. Inventorship

Under U.S. patent law, the true and original inventor must be listed on patent applications. However, inventors may *assign* their ownership of the patentable invention, patent application, or issued patent to other interested parties either before or after the invention is made or the patent is issued. In the alternative, they can *license*—on an exclusive or non-exclusive basis—any of the foregoing rights to interested parties. Absent an explicit agreement to the contrary, employees who happen to invent, either on their employer's time or with the employer's resources, must grant the employer a "shop right" or non-exclusive license to practice the invention (whether or not it is ultimately patented). However, if an employee was specifically hired to invent the thing invented—regardless of whether there is a written agreement or assignment of the invention—then the employee must assign the invention to the employer, who then becomes the sole *owner* of the invention/application/patent (even as the employer must list the employee as the *inventor* in any patent applications). Express written employment agreements can modify these default common law rules; however, some states limit the extent of invention assignments that employees can be required to give as a condition of employment: *e.g.*, California and Washington State prohibit agreements that purport to require employees to assign inventions made *without* employer resources and outside of employer's time.

Because most genetics research and inventions occur within company or university laboratories, the truly independent inventor is rare. However, one must consider not just employer-employee relationships to determine ownership of inventions, but also ownership conditions that may come along with funding arrangements. In particular, federal funding will trigger the provisions of the Bayh-Dole Act of 1980—codified as part of the patent law at 35 U.S.C. § 200 *et seq.* The case below explores these competing threads of ownership issues for a university lab invention.

Chou v. University of Chicago

254 F.3d 1347 (Fed. Cir. 2001)

Circuit Judge Lourie.

Joany Chou appeals from the decision of the United States District Court for the Northern District of Illinois granting Bernard Roizman and Aviron Company's motions to dismiss her claims for correction of inventorship, declaratory judgment of inventorship, fraud, breach of fiduciary duty, unjust enrichment, breach of express contract, and breach of implied contract. Chou also seeks reinstatement of those same claims against the University of Chicago ("University"). Because the district court erred in its determination that Chou did not have standing to sue for correction of inventorship under 35 U.S.C. § 256, we reverse its judgment as to that claim. We also reverse the court's dismissal of most of her state law claims against Roizman and direct the court to reinstate certain of her state law claims against the University. However, we affirm that court's dismissal of her breach of express contract claim against Roizman and of all her remaining claims against Aviron. We also affirm the court's grant of Roizman's motion to strike her allegations of academic theft and fraud. Finally, we reject Chou's attempt to have her case reassigned to another district court judge. We therefore affirm-in-part, reverse-in-part, and remand.

Background

Dr. Chou was a graduate student and subsequently a post-doctoral research assistant for Dr. Roizman at the University of Chicago's Department of Molecular Genetics and Cell Biology from 1983 to 1996. Roizman is named as the sole inventor on U.S. Patent 5,328,688 and a co-inventor on U.S. Patents 5,795,713 and 5,922,328, all of which relate to herpes simplex virus and its use in an avirulent vaccine. Roizman is also listed as an inventor on three foreign applications: WO 9204050 (based on the subject matter of the '688 patent), WO 9833933 (based on the subject matter of the '713 patent), and PCT/US96/14292 (based on the subject matter of the '328 patent) (collectively, "the foreign applications"). The inventorship of those patents and applications is disputed.

Under University policy, inventors receive 25% of the gross royalties and up-front payments from licensing of the patents, as well as 25% of the stock of new companies that are based on their inventions. Chou allegedly told Roizman in February of 1991 that her discoveries should be patented, and he allegedly disagreed. At that time, however, Roizman had already filed the '688 patent application,[35] which was allegedly directed to the same disputed invention, and had named himself as the sole inventor of that subject matter. During prosecution of that application, the United States Patent and Trademark Office ("PTO") cited two joint Chou-Roizman publications as prior art. In response, Roizman submitted a declaration stating that those publications were not available as prior art because he was the sole inventor of the work described therein and that she merely worked under his direction and supervision.

On July 14, 1992, Roizman assigned the '688 patent application to Institut Merieux, a French company that had supported the research. Just before that assignment, however, on July 1, 1992, it appears that Aviron had received an exclusive license to the herpes simplex virus technology from ARCH Development Corporation, a wholly owned

35. We refer to the patent application leading to the '688 patent as the '688 patent application in order to avoid using a separate application number and for ease of expression.

affiliate of the University established to license and commercialize the University's technology and intellectual property. Institut Merieux later assigned the patent application to ARCH, which in turn licensed Aviron. Aviron also obtained rights to the '713 and '328 patents and the foreign applications by license and assignment from ARCH. ARCH and Roizman each own Aviron stock and have received licensing revenue from NeuroVir, the sublicensee of Aviron's rights.

Later, in 1993, Roizman and Chou signed an agreement to share royalties from "the pending patent application to exploit the properties of the herpes simplex virus 34.5 gene." At the time the agreement was signed, Chou and Roizman were named inventors on a patent application relating to the subject matter of that agreement, which is not in dispute in this appeal. The '688 patent application was also pending when that agreement was signed, although Chou was not then aware of its existence. In 1996, Roizman asked Chou to resign, failing which he told her that he would fire her, allegedly because she would be in a stronger position to contest his inventorship if she were still conducting research at the University.

In 1999, Chou sued Roizman, the University/ARCH, and Aviron (collectively, "the defendants") for correction of inventorship under 35 U.S.C. § 256, seeking to be named as the sole inventor on the '688 patent, or, in the alternative, as a co-inventor along with Roizman. She additionally sought to be listed as a co-inventor on the '713 and '328 patents. Chou also sued for a declaratory judgment that she was an inventor on the U.S. patents and their corresponding foreign applications. In addition, Chou asserted claims of fraudulent concealment, breach of fiduciary duty, unjust enrichment, breach of express and implied contract, and academic theft and fraud.

The district court determined that Chou lacked standing to seek correction of inventorship under § 256 because she could claim no ownership of the patents, having surrendered all her rights to the University under an employment agreement. The court also dismissed her claim for a declaratory judgment of inventorship, finding that she had no reasonable grounds to believe that Roizman intended to file suit to settle the inventorship question.

The district court also dismissed under Fed. R. Civ. P. 12(b)(6) all of her state law claims except her count for conversion. It determined that Roizman had no duty as Chou's advisor and department chairman to inform Chou of the status of the patent applications, and that his opinion that some of Chou's work should not be patented, although perhaps an affirmative misrepresentation, was not fraudulent. The district court dismissed her unjust enrichment claim based on Roizman's alleged arrangement of the assignment of the '688 patent application to ARCH and then to Aviron, finding instead that Roizman assigned the application to Institut Merieux, which exercised its own "free will" to assign it to ARCH, which then licensed it to Aviron. The district court also dismissed her claim for breach of an express contract, finding that the contract signed by Chou and Roizman to split royalties related to a different patent application on which both were listed as inventors and was therefore not relevant to the dispute. The court similarly dismissed her claim for breach of an implied contract because Chou did not allege that Roizman and Chou had established a practice of sharing royalties for all joint inventions. The court also granted Roizman's motion to strike Chou's allegations of academic theft and fraud under Fed. R. Civ. P. 12(f).

The court dismissed all claims against Aviron because Chou did not allege that Roizman's actions came within the scope of his authority as Aviron's agent, and because "so much of what Dr. Roizman did was done before there was an Aviron that Aviron authorized none of it; it simply benefited from the acts after it was brought into existence." The court dismissed all her counts against Roizman except the conversion count. Chou then voluntarily dismissed the conversion count and stipulated to the dismissal with prejudice of all counts of her complaint against the University/ARCH to obtain a final, appealable judgment because she agreed that the reasoning of the district court's order applied with equal force to the University/ARCH.

Discussion

Whether a putative inventor who lacks a potential ownership interest in a patent has standing to sue is a question of law that we decide *de novo*....

On appeal, Chou presents three reasons why the district court erred in its conclusion that she did not have standing to bring an action under §256 to correct inventorship: (1) she did not assign her interest in her inventions to the University; (2) she would be entitled to receive 25% of the gross royalties and up-front payments from licensing, as well as 25% of the stock of new companies based on the invention, if she were a named inventor; or (3) she has standing solely by virtue of being a true inventor under our decision in *University of Colorado Foundation v. American Cyanamid Co.*, 196 F.3d 1366, 1374, (Fed. Cir. 1999). Chou also argues that the court erred in dismissing her declaratory judgment claim because she had a reasonable apprehension that the defendants would file a §256 action to seek reassurance of their position that Chou was correctly excluded as an inventor from the patents.

With respect to her state law claims, Chou contends that the district court erred in dismissing her claim for fraudulent concealment because such a claim lies for fraudulent non-disclosure of a patent application under *University of Colorado*, 196 F.3d at 1371–72. She also contends that she adequately pleaded a claim for breach of fiduciary duty, which she argues is construed broadly under Illinois law. She further asserts that the court erred in dismissing her unjust enrichment claim because it did not consider her allegation that Roizman arranged the assignment of the application for the '688 patent from ARCH to Aviron even before he assigned it to Institut Merieux. She also argues that her breach of contract claim should not have been dismissed because she and Roizman expressly agreed to split any royalties resulting from the patents. Alternatively, she argues that she adequately stated a claim for breach of an implied contract because she pleaded that she and Roizman established a course of dealing to share royalties, and that Roizman unjustly retained the benefits of sole inventorship to her detriment. Finally, Chou argues that the court erred in striking her allegations of academic theft and fraud and requests that we remand the case to the Executive Committee of the United States District Court for the Northern District of Illinois for reassignment to a different judge.

The defendants respond that Chou lacks standing to sue for correction of inventorship under §256 because she was obligated to assign her inventions to the University by virtue of accepting employment under the University's administrative policies. The University/ARCH also argues that it is not properly included as a defendant in her §256 action because Chou stipulated that the district court's reasoning applied to the University/ARCH to the same extent that it applied to Roizman, and that Chou has no standing to sue Roizman under §256 because she has no ownership interest in the patents at issue. The defendants also contend that Chou lacks standing to sue for a declaratory judgment because she had no reasonable ground to believe that the defendants would file suit to correct inventorship under §256.

With regard to Chou's state law claims, the defendants argue that the fraud count was properly dismissed because Roizman owed her no duty to disclose information about the filing of the patent applications, and that her breach of fiduciary duty claim is similarly deficient because the University does not impose a fiduciary duty upon its professors to disclose to their research assistants the filing of patent applications. The defendants also contend that Chou has no unjust enrichment claim because she assigned her rights to the University and has suffered no financial detriment as a result of Roizman's alleged actions. The defendants further argue that the district court did not err in dismissing her breach of contract claim because the agreement Chou relies upon for this claim refers only to an unrelated patent application upon which both Chou and Roizman were listed as joint inventors, and that her implied contract claim fails because Chou did not allege a course of dealing with Roizman to share royalties from all of the patent applications. Finally, the defendants assert that the court did not abuse its discretion in striking Chou's allegations of academic theft and fraud, and that the case should not be remanded to a different judge because Chou has not shown the threshold of bias or partiality in the trial judge that warrants such a reassignment.

A. *Standing to Sue for Correction of Inventorship under 35 U.S.C. § 256*

As a preliminary matter, we agree with the defendants that Chou was obligated to assign her inventions to the University. Although it is true that Chou never signed a contract with the University specifically obligating her to assign her inventions to the University, she accepted her academic appointment subject to the administrative policies of the University. We are not persuaded by Chou's argument that the University's administrative policies do not include its patent statutes. The Faculty Handbook refers to the patent statutes as patent policies within a section entitled "Academic Policies." The University's Patent Statute section 20 provides as follows:

> Every patentable invention or discovery that results from research or other activities carried out at the University, or with the aid of its facilities or funds administered by it, shall be the property of the University, and shall be assigned, as determined by the University, to the University, to an organization sponsoring the activities, or to an outside organization deemed capable of administering patents.

It is true that the Faculty Handbook contains the following statement: "The contents of this handbook do not create a contract or agreement between an individual and the University." That statement, however, must be read in light of the statement immediately following it: "The basic terms and conditions of the employment agreement are set out in the letter of appointment received from the Provost's Office." Chou's letter of appointment stated that the appointment was subject to "the administrative policies of the University," which include the obligation to assign inventions to the University. Illinois law, which governs our determination of Chou's assignment obligations, thus obligated Chou to assign her inventions to the University even though she never specifically agreed to do so. Chou accepted her appointment, thereby assuming the obligations set out in the University's policies. Moreover, she did not dispute her obligation when she assigned to the University other inventions for which she was a recognized inventor. We therefore conclude that if Chou is indeed an inventor of the contested subject matter, she would be obligated to assign those inventions to the University.

That conclusion, however, does not defeat Chou's standing to sue for correction of inventorship under § 256. Section 256 of title 35 provides a cause of action for judicial correction of inventorship:

> The error of omitting inventors or naming persons who are not inventors shall not invalidate the patent in which such error occurred if it can be corrected as provided in this section. The court before which such matter is called in question may order correction of the patent *on notice and hearing of all parties concerned* and the Director shall issue a certificate accordingly.

(emphasis added);.... The district court is indeed a court before which the matter was called into question, and notice and an opportunity for a hearing were provided. Chou, as a party "concerned," is clearly within the purview of the statute, but she must meet constitutional standing requirements in order to invoke it. That is, she must show that she has suffered an injury-in-fact, that the injury is traceable to the conduct complained of, and that the injury is redressable by a favorable decision. U.S. Const. art. III, § 2.

The district court determined that Chou did not have standing to sue for correction of inventorship on the basis of "[t]he principle that one who claims no ownership of the patent has no standing to seek relief under § 256." The question whether a putative inventor who is obligated to assign her invention to another is entitled to sue for correction of inventorship under § 256 action is one of first impression for this court, notwithstanding the parties' arguments to the contrary. Chou argues that *University of Colorado* holds that a true inventor has the right to bring a § 256 action even absent an ownership interest. Although that case involved a § 256 action, we did not decide whether alleged inventors had an independent right to bring suit even though they had assigned their interest to the University.

Similarly, the cases cited by the defendants do not establish a rule of law that only a party with a potential ownership interest in a patent may sue under § 256. In *Fina,* we required a declaratory plaintiff to establish that it had a reasonable apprehension that another party with a right to bring an action under § 256 would do so, but we did not explain what circumstances would give a putative inventor lacking a potential ownership interest the right to bring such an action. *Fina Oil & Chem. Co. v. Ewen,* 123 F.3d 1466, 1471 (Fed. Cir. 1997). In *Gaia Technologies., Inc. v. Reconversion Technologies, Inc.,* 93 F.3d 774, 777, (Fed. Cir. 1996), we required—as has always been required, *see Waterman v. Mackenzie,* 138 U.S. 252, 255 (1891)—joinder of the patent owner in an infringement suit where the licensee had not been assigned all substantial rights in the patent. Correction of inventorship was not at issue.

The defendants argue that *Kucharczyk* supports their position. In that case, the district court held that plaintiffs relinquished their right to sue to correct inventorship to delete an inventor when they executed an assignment of their ownership interest. *Kucharczyk*[*v. Regents of the Univ. of Cal.,* 48 F.Supp.2d 964, 974–975 (N.D. Cal. 1999)]. An Ohio district court has taken a similar position. *See E.I. Du Pont de Nemours & Co. v. Okuley,* No. C2-97-1205, 2000 WL 1911430, at *12 (S.D. Ohio Dec. 21, 2000) (stating that only an assignee has standing to challenge inventorship, citing *Kucharczyk* and *Chou*). We are not bound by the decisions of district courts; respectfully, we do not agree with them.

We conclude that an expectation of ownership of a patent is not a prerequisite for a putative inventor to possess standing to sue to correct inventorship under § 256.[36] The statute imposes no requirement of potential ownership in the patent on those seeking to invoke it. We have previously interpreted § 256 broadly as a "savings provision" to pre-

36. One other means for a putative inventor to assert her inventorship right is for her to file her own patent application and seek to have the PTO declare an interference in order to establish inventorship. However, such a procedure is not at issue here.

vent patent rights from being extinguished simply because the inventors are not correctly listed. The same considerations apply here. Chou should have the right to assert her interest, both for her own benefit and in the public interest of assuring correct inventorship designations on patents. The interest of both inventors and the public are thus served by a broad interpretation of the statute.

Chou argues that a reputational interest alone is enough to satisfy the requirements of Article III standing. That assertion is not implausible. After all, being considered an inventor of important subject matter is a mark of success in one's field, comparable to being an author of an important scientific paper. Pecuniary consequences may well flow from being designated as an inventor. However, we need not decide that issue because Chou has alleged a concrete financial interest in the patent, albeit an interest less than ownership. Chou claims that the University is obligated to provide "[f]aculty, student and staff inventors ... 25% of the gross royalties and up-front payments from licensing activities." She also claims the right to receive rights to 25% of the stock of new companies based on their inventions. If Chou has indeed been deprived of an interest in proceeds from licensing the invention and in stock ownership by the conduct that she alleges, then she will have suffered an injury-in-fact, *i.e.*, the loss of those benefits. That loss would be directly traceable to Roizman's alleged conduct in naming himself as the sole inventor of discoveries that she at least partly made, and it would be redressable by an order from the district court to the Director of the PTO to issue a certificate naming Chou as an inventor, which would entitle her under the University's policy to a share of the licensing proceeds and stock already received by Roizman. We therefore determine that Chou is entitled to sue for correction of inventorship under § 256.

We next address the question of which defendants Chou may sue under § 256. The validity of a patent requires that the inventors be correctly named. It follows that parties with an economic stake in a patent's validity are entitled to be heard on inventorship issues once a putative inventor has sued to correct inventorship. Moreover, we have cited with approval authority in which such parties have been subject to § 256 actions, even over their objection. We therefore conclude that parties with an economic stake in a patent's validity may be subject to a § 256 suit.

Each of the defendants in this case has an economic stake in the validity of the patents involved and hence in the correct inventorship designations on the patents. The University/ARCH owns the '688 and '713 patents and derives royalty income therefrom. Aviron owns the '328 patent and possesses exclusive licenses under the '688 and '713 patents; it derives royalties from its sublicense of those patents to NeuroVir. Roizman similarly receives a portion of the royalty income and stock benefits from those patents based on the University's policy to reward inventors. All of those benefits would be jeopardized by a determination that the patents are invalid for improper inventorship. Roizman's share of the profits would also be affected by joinder of Chou. Thus, each of the defendants has an economic stake in a correct inventorship designation on the patents at issue and each may properly be named as a defendant in this § 256 action.

Aviron argues that it is not properly a defendant because it is not named as a defendant in Count I, which asserts Chou's § 256 claim. Although the district court stated that Aviron was not named as a defendant in Count I, we are unaware of the basis for that statement. Chou did not specifically name any defendant in her amended § 256 count. Rather, it appears that she asserted her § 256 claim against all of the defendants. On appeal, she requests that we remand her correction of inventorship claim to clearly include Aviron. As we have already concluded that Aviron is a proper defendant in

Chou's § 256 action because it has an economic stake in the validity of the patents-in-suit, on remand the district court should grant Chou leave to amend the complaint, if necessary, to add Aviron as a defendant.

Furthermore, our conclusion that Roizman is a proper defendant in Chou's § 256 action also negates the University's argument that Chou cannot maintain her § 256 action against the University based on her stipulation that the district court's order applies with equal force and effect to the University and ARCH as it does to Roizman. Chou's § 256 claim against the University and ARCH should be reinstated.

Accordingly, we reverse the district court's conclusion that Chou has no standing to sue Roizman under 35 U.S.C. § 256, and instruct that court to reinstate her § 256 claim against the University and ARCH, and, if necessary, allow Chou leave to amend her § 256 claim to add Aviron as a defendant. The district court will determine whether Chou should be named as the sole inventor or a co-inventor on the '688 patent or a co-inventor on the '713 and '328 patents.

B. *Declaratory Judgment to Correct Inventorship*

Chou also sought a declaratory judgment under 28 U.S.C. §§ 2201 and 2202 that she is the sole inventor or, in the alternative, a joint inventor on the '688 patent and the WO '050 application, and that she is a joint inventor on the '713 and '328 patents, WO '933 application, and PCT '292 application. In view of our determination that Chou has standing to sue to correct inventorship of the U.S. patents under § 256, we need not determine if she is a proper declaratory plaintiff in an action to correct inventorship on those patents under the Declaratory Judgment Act; such a decision would not afford her any relief that is not also available through the § 256 action.

Chou claims entitlement to be named as an inventor on the foreign patent applications as well. Since inventorship on such applications normally follows the inventorship designation in the originating country, the district court, if it concludes on remand that Chou is properly an inventor of the disputed subject matter, can instruct the University to take appropriate action to change the inventorship designation on the foreign patent applications. *See, e.g.,* PCT Receiving Office Guidelines, PCT Gazette Ch. XVI, ¶¶ 309–311 (World Intellectual Property Organization Aug. 28, 1998) (setting forth the procedures for recording a change in the applicant or inventor of PCT applications).

C. *State Law Claims*

1. Fraudulent Concealment

We agree with Chou that the district court erred in dismissing her complaint for failure to state a claim for fraudulent concealment of the '688 patent application.... In Illinois, a plaintiff must allege that a defendant concealed a material fact when he was under a duty to disclose that fact to the plaintiff. The duty to disclose a material fact may arise if the plaintiff and defendant are in a fiduciary or confidential relationship, or if the plaintiff places trust and confidence in the defendant, thereby placing the defendant in a position of influence and superiority over the plaintiff. That position of superiority may arise out of friendship, agency, or experience.

Chou alleged that Roizman had a responsibility under University policies and by virtue of their advisor-advisee relationship to not misappropriate her inventions. Chou has also alleged that Roizman specifically told her that he would take care to properly protect her research, inventions and co-inventions. The University's patent policy requires the University to endeavor to "provide a return to the inventor or creator." Similarly, under the policy, "[t]he inventor or creator and his or her Dean or other administrative head shall be consulted and kept informed of the [patenting] arrangements." The University's patent policy also requires that the disposition of patent rights be consistent with the requirements of law and professional ethics. As a member of the University's faculty, Roizman had a duty to abide by those policies, and Chou alleged that she trusted that he would do so. Thus, we conclude that Chou alleged with particularity that Roizman had a duty to disclose material facts relating to the patenting of her discoveries.

With respect to his failure to disclose such facts, Chou alleged that she told Roizman in February 1991 that her discoveries should be patented, and that he disagreed with her but did not tell her that he had already filed an application on those discoveries. Thus, Chou alleges all of the elements of a claim of fraudulent concealment by Roizman, *viz.*, that Roizman concealed the material fact of a patent application of which she may have been a true inventor when he was under a duty to disclose that fact because he held a position of superiority with respect to her and was obligated by University patent policies to give her proper inventorship credit.

In *University of Colorado,* we stated that a claim for fraudulent nondisclosure turned on the status of the unnamed inventors as true inventors. Chou's claim for fraudulent concealment similarly depends on her status as a true inventor of the patents, a determination we have decided that the district court has jurisdiction to make. We therefore conclude that the district court erred in dismissing Chou's claim against Roizman for fraudulent concealment.

Chou has also alleged that Roizman is an agent of the University/ARCH and Aviron, and that those entities are liable for his fraudulent nondisclosure under agency principles. We agree that Chou has adequately stated a claim that the University is liable under the doctrine of respondeat superior for Roizman's alleged concealment of his misappropriation of Chou's inventions. In Illinois, employers may be liable for the actions of their employees if they are within the scope of employment, *i.e.,* if those actions are the kind the employee was hired to perform, the actions occur substantially within the authorized time and space limits, and they are actuated, at least in part, by a purpose to serve the master. While university faculty are not agents of the university with respect to the selection and conduct of their research projects, they may well be agents with respect to implementing policies of the university, including ownership of inventions and compensation therefor. The University's Faculty Handbook recognizes such an agency with respect to its patent policies, stating that "[t]he University, acting directly or through its designee, shall endeavor to license or assign such products in such a manner as to assure the greatest benefits to the University and the public, and provide a return to the inventor or creator." Roizman allegedly named himself as the sole inventor of Chou's discoveries and applied for a patent on those discoveries under the auspices of his authority as a department chairman of the University to recommend and direct patent prosecution on inventions made in his research lab. We therefore conclude that Chou has adequately stated a claim for fraudulent nondisclosure by the University/ARCH under principles of respondeat superior.

We do not agree, however, that Chou's allegations concerning Aviron's liability under agency principles for Roizman's alleged fraudulent nondisclosure meet the requirement of Fed. R. Civ. P. 9(b) to plead fraud with particularity. Those allegations of Roizman's being an agent of Aviron are based on his status as an Aviron director, co-founder, and scientific advisory board member. She does not allege that his acts of misappropriating her inventions were within the scope of his authority conferred by those positions. Chou alleged that Roizman had a duty to disclose the patenting of her discoveries based upon Roizman's relationship to her as a University professor and laboratory advisor, not his relationship to her as a corporate director of Aviron. Moreover, Aviron was founded in 1992, after Roizman claimed inventorship credit for the '688 patent application. We therefore conclude that the court did not err in dismissing Chou's claim for fraudulent nondisclosure against Aviron.

2. Breach of Fiduciary Duty

We also agree with Chou that the district court erred in dismissing her claim against Roizman for breach of fiduciary duty. A fiduciary duty in Illinois may arise in one of two ways. A fiduciary relationship automatically arises from particular relationships, such as attorney-client and principal-agent, as a matter of law. A fiduciary relationship may also arise from the special circumstances of the parties' relationship, such as when one party justifiably places trust in another so that the latter gains superiority and influence over the former. The relevant factors in determining whether the latter fiduciary relationship exists include the disparity in age, education, and business experience between the parties, and the extent to which the "servient" party entrusted the handling of its affairs to the "dominant" party and placed its trust and confidence in that party. The existence of a fiduciary relationship prohibits the dominant party with the duty from seeking or obtaining any selfish benefit for himself at the expense of the servient party while the fiduciary duty exists.

Chou alleged that Roizman held a position of superiority over her as her department chairman, and that he had specifically represented to her that he would protect and give her proper credit for her research and inventions. Given the disparity of their experience and roles, and Roizman's responsibility to make patenting decisions regarding Chou's inventions, Chou has adequately pleaded the existence of circumstances that place on Roizman a fiduciary duty with respect to her inventions. Furthermore, Chou pleaded that Roizman breached that duty by naming himself as an inventor of her discoveries. Resolving all inferences in favor of Chou, as we must at this stage of the proceedings, we conclude that she has sufficiently stated a claim of breach of fiduciary duty and that the district court erred in dismissing that claim.

Chou alleges a breach of fiduciary duty with respect to the foreign applications. Since, as we have indicated, the inventorship of the foreign applications is in effect determined by the inventorship of the U.S. patents, we need not dwell on that claim.

We also agree with Chou that she has stated a claim against the University for breach of fiduciary duty under the theory of respondeat superior for the same reasons as for her fraudulent concealment claim. The district court did not err, however, in dismissing Chou's claim for breach of fiduciary duty against Aviron because Chou did not adequately allege its liability under agency principles.

3. Unjust Enrichment

We also agree with Chou that the district court erred in dismissing her claim for unjust enrichment.[37] To state a cause of action based on a theory of unjust enrichment under Illinois law, a plaintiff must allege that the defendant has unjustly retained a benefit to the plaintiff's detriment, and that the defendant's retention of that benefit violates fundamental principles of justice, equity, and good conscience.

Chou has alleged that Roizman arranged a license of the '688 patent application from ARCH to Aviron on July 1, 1992, before he assigned his rights in the invention to

37. Chou alleges unjust enrichment with regard to both the U.S. patents and the foreign applications. Our resolution of the inventorship of foreign applications in addressing her breach of fiduciary duty claim applies equally to her claim for unjust enrichment.

Institut Merieux on July 14, 1992. The district court did not address this allegation. However, whatever the arrangements concerning the assignment and ownership of the patents, those decisions belonged to the University, and Roizman was acting as the University's agent when he arranged the business transactions. Chou's interest was in the financial consequences of those decisions. Roizman's possible unjust enrichment occurred not in his involvement in the business arrangements, but to the extent that he received royalties and stock that might properly have been Chou's.

Chou has alleged that Roizman's retention of those benefits is unjust, both under University policy and equity principles. If Chou is correct that she invented the subject matter of the patents, then under University policy she should have shared (if a co-inventor) or received entirely (if the sole inventor) 25% of the gross royalties and up-front payments from licensing activities that Roizman received from the University, as well as 25% of the stock of new companies based on the patents. Moreover, if Chou is correct that Roizman wrongfully usurped her proper inventorship status, equity dictates that he should not benefit from that transgression at her expense. The district court therefore erred in dismissing her claim against Roizman for unjust enrichment.

We conclude, however, that Chou failed to state a claim for unjust enrichment against the University and Aviron. Chou alleged that the University and Aviron enriched themselves from Chou's research. Because we have decided that Chou was obligated to assign her inventions to the University, both the University and Aviron would have had the same rights to the inventions and thus the same enrichment from them even if Chou had been named as an inventor. The district court did not err, therefore, in dismissing her claim for unjust enrichment against Aviron, and Chou is not entitled to have the district court reinstate that claim against the University.

4. Breach of Express Contract

We agree with Roizman that Chou has not sufficiently alleged an alternative claim against him for breach of an express contract. The basis for her claim against him is a written agreement dated June 14, 1993, in which they agreed to equally split "the royalties resulting from the pending patent application." As the district court found, however, and as Chou does not dispute, that letter referred to a different application on which both Chou and Roizman were listed as named inventors. Chou could not have expressly agreed to split the royalties resulting from the '688 patent application, which she did not know existed at the time. There was no meeting of the minds as to that application. Chou did not sufficiently plead a claim of breach of an express contract by Roizman.

We agree with Chou, however, that she has sufficiently stated a claim against the University for breach of express contract.[38] Chou has alleged that counsel for the University and Roizman reviewed her laboratory notebooks on April 20, 1999 and informed her counsel on May 13, 1999 that the University had decided that Chou was an inventor of the subject matter disclosed and claimed in the '688 patent and that paperwork would be sent to Chou to correct inventorship, but that such paperwork was never sent. Moreover, the University represents that its practice is to reward inventors with 25% of the gross royalties, as well as 25% of the stock of new companies based on their inventions. When asked at oral argument what claim Chou could have brought, assum-

38. Chou alleges breach of express contract with regard to both the U.S. patents and the foreign applications. Our resolution of the inventorship of foreign applications in addressing her breach of fiduciary duty claim applies equally to her claim for breach of express contract.

ing all that she alleged is true, University counsel suggested that her appropriate cause of action would have been for breach of contract against the University.[39]

Chou has thus alleged that the University recognized her as an inventor but did not compensate her according to its policy.[40] We therefore conclude that her breach of express contract claim against the University should be reinstated.[41]

5. Breach of Implied Contract

We also agree with Chou that the district court erred in dismissing Chou's claim for breach of an implied contract.[42] Although Chou does not distinguish between implied-in-fact and implied-in-law contracts in her complaint, her allegations involve both types of implied contracts and we evaluate them separately.

a. Implied-in-fact Contract

Under Illinois law, a contract implied-in-fact, like an express contract, arises from acts or circumstances indicating the parties' mutual intention. It generally arises from an established course of dealing between parties. The district court found that Chou did not allege a relevant course of dealing between herself and Roizman sufficient to allow an inference that they would share royalties resulting from their joint inventions and dismissed the claim. We agree with that decision. Although Chou did allege a course of dealing with Roizman to split the benefits of their joint inventions, Chou and Roizman in fact expressly agreed in writing to share the royalties on another invention not on appeal. An express writing with respect to one invention undercuts her claim that there was an established course of dealing regarding all their joint inventions. We therefore affirm the court's dismissal of Chou's implied-in-fact contract claim against Roizman.

Nor did Chou adequately allege breach of such a contract by the University. The course of dealing she alleges with the University appears to be the University's express policy to reward its inventors with a portion of the licensing and stock proceeds of their inventions. Under Illinois law, courts do not imply contracts when express agreements govern parties. We therefore conclude that Chou has not adequately stated claims against the University for breach of an implied-in-fact contract.

b. Implied-in-law Contract

Our decision that Chou did not adequately plead breach of an implied-in-fact contract does not defeat her claim for breach of implied contract if she adequately pleaded breach of an implied-in-law contract. A contract implied-in-law (quasi-con-

---

39. University counsel, however, maintained that such a contract claim would have required resolution of the inventorship issue, which it argued was not available to Chou under § 256 for lack of standing.

40. While the University's policy appears to be contained in a report of a committee of ARCH, the University's licensing arm, and it speaks of a "practice" that inventors "should continue ... to receive" compensation, the University does not question the existence or enforceability of such a policy. Thus, her claim is sufficient to meet the minimal requirements to state a claim under Fed. R. Civ. P. 8(a).

41. Although Chou stipulated that the reasoning of the district court's order dismissing all of the claims against Roizman also applied to the University and ARCH, that stipulation does not preclude reinstatement of her breach of express contract claim against the University even though we have determined that she did not adequately state such a claim against Roizman. Her contract claim depends on her status as an inventor, a determination that was precluded under the district court's reasoning but that we have decided she is entitled to under § 256.

42. Chou alleges breach of implied contract with regard to both the U.S. patents and the foreign applications. Our resolution of the inventorship of foreign applications in addressing her breach of fiduciary duty claim applies equally to her claim for breach of implied contract.

tract) results, regardless of the parties' intentions, from a duty imposed by law and is a contract only in the sense that it is created and governed by equity principles. Such a claim is related to unjust enrichment. The district court dismissed this theory solely on the basis that she did not adequately plead unjust enrichment. As we have already decided that Chou adequately pleaded unjust enrichment by Roizman, she may also pursue against him the related theory of breach of an implied agreement. However, Chou would be well advised on remand to avoid redundant claims. Our determination that she has adequately stated claims based on these theories does not entitle her to recover separate damages for each of these claims if she were to prevail at trial; we merely decide that she has sufficiently stated claims based on these theories. Chou, however, did not adequately plead unjust enrichment by the University, and therefore her claim against it for breach of an implied-in-law agreement similarly fails.

D. *Miscellaneous*

1. Academic Theft and Fraud

The district court struck Chou's allegations of academic theft and fraud under Fed. R. Civ. P. 12(f). We conclude that the court did not abuse its discretion in striking those allegations from the complaint because they are redundant and immaterial to her complaint. Rule 12(f) allows the court to strike "from any pleading any ... redundant, immaterial, impertinent, or scandalous matter." Chou's recourse for violation of the University's academic fraud policy is in the first instance through the University's systems of governance, not through litigation. If her allegations are true, Chou may obtain relief through her other state law claims. We therefore affirm the court's decision to strike these allegations under Rule 12(f)....

Conclusion

Because the district court erred in holding that Chou did not have standing to sue for correction of inventorship under § 256, we reverse and remand for adjudication of that claim against all of the defendants. We also reverse the court's determination that Chou failed to state claims for fraudulent concealment, breach of fiduciary duty, unjust enrichment, and breach of implied contract against Roizman, and we direct the court to reinstate Chou's claims for fraudulent concealment, breach of fiduciary duty, and breach of an express contract against the University/ARCH. We affirm, however, its decision dismissing all other claims against Aviron, and its decision to strike Chou's allegations of academic theft and fraud pursuant to Fed. R. Civ. P. 12(f). We do not address the court's dismissal of her declaratory judgment claim for correction of inventorship because that issue is moot. Finally, we decline to remand the case to the Executive Committee for reassignment to a different judge. Accordingly, we

AFFIRM-IN-PART, REVERSE-IN-PART, and REMAND.

2. Bayh-Dole and the Technology Transfer System

While *Chou* focuses primarily on inventorship issues, it also sets out the basic parameters of ownership claims to inventions, including direct and indirect assignment mechanisms. But a major source of ownership rights is funding arrangements, especially when federal agencies such as the NIH funnel federal dollars into university, non-profit, or even corporate research. The following article excerpt outlines the origins and mandates of the Bayh-Dole Act of 1980, as amended and codified at 35 U.S.C. § 200 *et. seq.*

Sean M. O'Connor, *Intellectual Property Rights and Stem Cell Research: Who Owns the Medical Breakthroughs?*

39 New Eng. L. Rev. 665 (2005)

... As mentioned above, federal funding has supported an enormous amount of basic scientific research in this country throughout the twentieth century.[43] Private money is not as interested in basic research because such research is almost by definition at the very early stage of exploration and is not yet directed towards a commercializable technology. This means that any calculation of a return on investment—both in amount and timeframe—is so speculative as to be nearly useless. Accordingly, private funding of basic research is often more of an altruistic gesture than an investment venture. At the same time, many educated citizens and leaders buy into the view that basic research is important because it leads, serendipitously and indirectly, to the most revolutionary breakthroughs. Stories of the accidental discovery of penicillin, for example, resound in many of these individuals' thinking and makes the rationale for the funding of basic research nearly an axiomatic principle. But, with private money largely out of the picture, the only other solution is public funding.

Accordingly, following in the path of the noble civic investment that led to the great state land grant universities of the late 1800s, the 1900s became the century of unprecedented public investment in basic scientific research. In particular, World War II and the race for the atomic bomb showed the essential nature of scientific and technological primacy for national security in the modern world, as well as the link between the most advanced theoretical science—physics in this case—and the very survival of the nation. As World War II gave way to the Cold War, the need for accelerated scientific and technological progress did not diminish as it had in the wake of previous wars. Cementing the permanent status of the science and technology race, the Soviet launch of the Sputnik satellite in the 1950s was perhaps the final push that opened the floodgates of federal spending on all sorts of R&D, basic and applied, in public institutions and even in private contractor labs.

But the growing wealth of government funded research also led to questions of its ownership and use. Private contractors wanted to retain any resulting patent rights, especially where they might cover commercial, civilian applications, but certain factions in the federal government did not want research funding to turn into a windfall for private corporations. At the same time, the mounting inventory of patentable inventions developed in government and university or non-profit institution labs was not benefiting anyone, as the private commercial sector that was needed to turn these inventions into saleable products distributed to retail outlets was often unwilling to do so on anything less than exclusive license rights. Thus a long-simmering debate commenced shortly after World War II over whether the government funding agency should grant the title or merely a license to patentable inventions arising from funded research. In time, this would be largely resolved by first the Statement of Government Patent Policy

---

43. *See, e.g.*, Organisation For Economic Co-Operation & Development, Reviews Of National Science Policy: United States (1968) (showing an annual growth rate for federal government spending on R&D of 24.9% between 1940 and 1965, culminating in the federal government's financing of 64% of all U.S. R&D at the end of that period).

issued by President John F. Kennedy in 1963 (Kennedy Patent Policy),[44] and then later by the passage of Bayh-Dole itself in 1980.[45]

In many important ways, Bayh-Dole simply codified the Kennedy Patent Policy, particularly in its definitions of key terms and focus on balancing the competing values of free public access to federally funded inventions, on the one hand, and the need for exclusive rights as an incentive for private sector commercialization of otherwise unused patented inventions.[46] Further, Bayh-Dole adopted nearly wholesale the crucial concept, mechanisms, and language of the "march-in rights," as discussed in more detail below, set out first in the Kennedy Patent Policy.[47] But in one equally critical way, the two sets of rules were very different: Whereas the Kennedy Patent Policy explicitly rejected a "one-size fits all" approach to the title vs. license question,[48] Bayh-Dole comes down firmly on the side of granting title to the patentable invention to the researcher/contractor, provided that the contractor reports the invention in a timely fashion and then affirmatively elects to retain such title.[49]

But even while Bayh-Dole appears to side with the contractor—at least insofar as the contractor is a non-profit or small business because Bayh-Dole does not speak to situations where larger businesses are the contractor[50]—it does retain and expand many of the encumbrances on the title grant, where the contractor elects to retain title in the subject invention, that were first established by the Kennedy Patent Policy. First, the federal funding agency must have "a nonexclusive, nontransferrable, irrevocable, paid-up license to practice or have practiced for or on behalf of the United States any subject invention throughout the world...."[51] Second, the contractor must give notice of the federal funding, and the concomitant rights of the federal funding agency in the subject invention, in both the patent application and any resultant issued patent.[52] Third, non-profit contractors may not assign their rights to the subject invention to any other party without the approval of the funding agency, unless the assignment is to an external technology transfer or patent portfolio management entity, in which case that entity is

44. The Kennedy order is actually set out in two parts. The first part, the Memorandum for the Heads of Executive Departments and Agencies, 3 C.F.R. 861 (1959–1963), sets out the policy and objectives and directs the agencies to follow the rules and guidelines, set out in the second part, which contains the actual "Statement of Government Patent Policy," 3 C.F.R. 862 (1959–1963).

45. *See* 35 U.S.C. §§ 200–211. The history of U.S. government patent policy is an extensive and fascinating topic, but outside the scope of this Symposium article. The cursory version presented here is based on another manuscript I am currently drafting. *See* Sean M. O'Connor, *The Evolution of Government Research Patent Policy: Putting Bayh-Dole Into the Proper Context* (working paper on file with author). A somewhat different version can be found in Rebecca S. Eisenberg, *Public Research and Private Development: Patents and Technology Transfer in Government-Sponsored Research*, 82 VA. L. REV. 1663 (1996).

46. Compare the "Policy and objective" section of Bayh-Dole, 35 U.S.C. § 200 (2000), to the policy objective set out in the Memorandum for the Heads of Executive Departments and Agencies part of the Kennedy Patent Policy, *supra* note 67.

47. *Compare* 35 U.S.C. § 203 (1988) *with* 28 Fed. Reg. 10,943 (1963).

48. *See* 3 C.F.R. 861.

49. *See* 35 U.S.C. § 202 (1988).

50. However, a subsequent order by President Ronald Reagan in 1983 adopted the rules of Bayh-Dole as the official executive branch policy across all funding agencies for large businesses as well. *See* Memorandum to the Heads of Executive Departments and Agencies: Government Patent Policy, PUB. PAPERS 248 (Feb. 18, 1983).

51. 35 U.S.C. § 202(c)(4). The funding agency is authorized to request even further license grants over this statutory minimum license grant.

52. *Id.* § 202(c)(6).

prohibited from any further assignments of the subject invention without the approval of the funding agency.[53]

The fourth title encumbrance, march-in rights, is actually a set of conditions for when the funding agency can exercise a type of compulsory license. The set of conditions that constitute march-in rights is also a continuation from the Kennedy Patent Policy, and is perhaps the most well-known—and most contested—of the provisions. The march-in rights provide the funding agency with the authority to:

> [R]equire the contractor, an assignee or exclusive licensee of a subject invention to grant a nonexclusive, partially exclusive, or exclusive license in any field of use to a responsible applicant or applicants, upon terms that are reasonable under the circumstances, and if the contractor, assignee, or exclusive licensee refuses such request, to grant such a license itself, if the Federal agency determines that such—
>
> > (a) action is necessary because the contractor or assignee has not taken, or is not expected to take within a reasonable time, effective steps to achieve practical application of the subject invention in such field of use;
> >
> > (b) action is necessary to alleviate health or safety needs which are not reasonably satisfied by the contractor, assignee, or their licensees;
> >
> > (c) action is necessary to meet requirements for public use specified by Federal regulations and such requirements are not reasonably satisfied by the contractor, assignee, or licensees; or
> >
> > (d) action is necessary because the agreement required by section 204 [that any exclusive licensee must substantially manufacture the products embodying the subject invention in the United States] has not been obtained or waived or because a licensee of the exclusive right to use or sell any subject invention in the United States is in breach of its agreement obtained pursuant to section 204 [and therefore no exclusive license is permitted or valid].[54]

As will be seen below, the proper scope of march-in rights has been hotly contested, even as they apparently have never been formally exercised by the government. This is true despite at least two formal proceedings involving petitions requesting that the relevant funding agency exercise its march-in rights.[55] One important dimension of this debate centers on the question of whether march-in rights impart a pricing control or regulation authority on the funding agency or only a more limited authority to ensure that the subject invention is actually commercialized and brought to market.

The technology transfer system codified by Bayh-Dole is also subject to two further criticisms. One is based on a claim that the law as implemented effectively forces the public to "pay twice" for products arising out of federally funded inventions.[56] We pay first through our tax dollars that are used to fund the federal agency grants to contrac-

---

53. *Id.* § 202(c)(7)(A).

54. *Id.* § 203(1).

55. [Excerpts from these two proceedings follow this article excerpt.]

56. *See* Eisenberg, *supra* note [69], at 1666; Peter S. Arno & Michael H. Davis, *Why Don't We Enforce Existing Drug Price Controls? The Unrecognized and Unenforced Reasonable Pricing Requirements Imposed Upon Patents Deriving in Whole or in Part From Federally Funded Research*, 75 TUL. L. REV. 631, 658 (2001).

tors for their research. Then we pay again through the high retail prices enabled by the allowance of exclusive control of the patents ensuing from that research. But this argument is more persuasive in situations where the patent arising from the federal funding effectively covers the eventual product that will be brought to market. Even then, the costs associated with ramping up a manufacturing, distribution, marketing, and sales operation for the product means that the final retail price may be quite expensive. Further, it is not as if the commercializing entity gets the exclusive license for free—universities and non-profits are increasingly striking savvy bargains requiring substantial upfront payments, patent prosecution and maintenance fees, and minimum royalties. Thus, one might equally question what is happening with the money that universities are making from patenting and licensing federally funded inventions.

The real test would be whether a comparably situated product that was developed from a patent arising from privately financed research was placed on the market at a far higher price. This would effectively demonstrate the discount the public receives because the first company did not incur the same patent R&D expenses. Of course, the first company would then be foolish not to raise its prices to capture the extra profit margin since the public may be willing to pay the higher price, assuming that its product is in fact a viable market substitute for the other company's product. But at the same time, the second company may not be able to enter the market at such a higher price, as it would be unable to capture market shares as against the first company's (federally subsidized) lower price. In this way, the Bayh-Dole system could theoretically work to keep prices down overall in markets with products that embody federally funded research results. This seems to fly in the face of an economic reality in which prices seem to spiral ever higher—especially in the science and technology-heavy markets—and few would believe that the grant of exclusive patent rights leads anywhere but to higher retail prices.

The problem with all of this armchair theorizing is that quite a number of largely untestable scenarios can be spun out: What if the company with the federally funded patent tries to enter the market after the company with a self-funded patent? Will it deploy a cut rate to steal market share quickly from its competitor, or will it come in just under the competitor's price so as to maximize the profit margin on each unit sold? Yet, precisely because patented technologies are at the core of these scenarios the reality check of comparing acceptable market substitutes is particularly difficult. In fact, relatively few products embody only the patent that arises from federally funded university or non-profit research. In no small part this is because much of the research that is funded is early stage, basic science that often has no commercial product in sight, or that at least will require substantial translational R&D to bring it to the level of commercialization. This translational R&D, combined with the standard commercialization costs of scaling a production and sales operation, lends some support to industry arguments that it is not improperly leveraging off of or profiting from its exclusive, albeit paid, licenses, but rather simply charging fair market value for what it has invested to bring the product to market—which may, again, include upfront payments, patent fees, and royalties to one or more universities/non-profits.

But as the U.S. Patent and Trademark Office (USPTO) has shown an increasing willingness to issue patents on early stage, pre-commercializable research results, a more trenchant concern has been raised: this second main criticism of the technology transfer system created by Bayh-Dole focuses on the USPTO's current "easy patenting" stance in combination with Bayh-Dole's strong incentives for universities and non-profits to patent research results, and argues that too many patents are being issued, particularly on so-called "up-stream" research results and research tools/platforms.[57] This, in turn, leads to "patent thickets," especially in the life sciences, that make it prohibitively difficult and/or expensive to either conduct new R&D or to commercialize important new technologies. It is prohibitively difficult because the researcher and her company must carefully set a course of R&D through a dense maze of sometimes overlapping patent claims to avoid infringement. And it is prohibitively expensive because ultimately the researcher and her company wind up paying multiple royalties to different patent holders—sometimes called "royalty stacking"—just to engage in the necessary R&D and bring a product to market.

Despite the pros and cons of federal research funding under the Bayh-Dole technology transfer system, at least this system is reasonably well fleshed out in the statute and the rules promulgated under it. Further, a fair bit of received wisdom has accumulated within the segments of the technology transfer system—universities, non-profits, start-ups, established technology companies, and venture capitalists—that arguably has achieved the level of settled expectations around things like the allocation and use of IP rights when federal funding is involved. This is all in marked contrast to the status of IP rights under state, local, or private funding. But, because federal funding is at least partly behind so much university and non-profit patentable research, the Bayh-Dole system's set of rules and settled expectations tends to be the standard....

NIH, Determination in the Case of Petition of CellPro, Inc.

August 1, 1997

The National Institutes of Health (NIH) has determined that the initiation of march-in procedures, as requested under the petition outlined below, is not warranted at this time. NIH retains jurisdiction over the instant proceedings until such time as a comparable alternative product becomes available for sale in the United States.

The CellPro Petition

On March 3, 1997, CellPro, Incorporated (CellPro) filed a petition with the Secretary of Health and Human Services (Secretary) requesting that the Government exercise march-in rights under the Bayh Dole Act (Act), 35 U.S.C. §§ 202–212, in connection with certain patents owned by The Johns Hopkins University (Hopkins) and licensed first to Becton-Dickinson and then to Baxter Healthcare Corporation (Baxter).[58] As discussed in greater detail below, the march-in provision of the Act authorizes the Government, in certain circumstances, to require the contractor (or grantee) or its exclusive licensee to license a Federally-funded invention to a responsible applicant on reasonable terms, or to grant such a license itself. CellPro asserts that such action is necessary to alleviate health or safety needs that have arisen because the United States District Court for the District of Delaware (Court) has found the stem cell separation device developed by CellPro, the Ceprate SC, to infringe two of the patents in question and has en-

57. *See* Arti K. Rai & Rebecca S. Eisenberg, *Bayh-Dole Reform and the Progress of Biomedicine*, 66 Law & Contemp. Probs. 289, 290 (2003).

58. These patents are: U.S. Patent No. 4,965,680; U.S. Patent No. 5,130,144; US. Patent No. 5,035,994 and U.S. Patent No. 4,965,204.

joined its sale.[59] Alternatively, CellPro asserts that march-in is warranted because Hopkins and Baxter have failed to take reasonable steps to commercialize the technology. At the present time, CellPro is the only company that has an FDA-approved device commercially available.

The Department of Commerce regulations implementing the Act are set forth at 37 CFR § 401.6. According to § 401.6(b):

> [w]henever an agency receives information that it believes might warrant the exercise of march-in rights, before initiating any march-in proceedings, it shall notify the contractor in writing of the information and request informal written or oral comments from the contractor, as well as information relevant to the matter.

The regulations provide that "the agency shall, within 60 days after it receives the comment, either initiate the procedures below or notify the contractor, in writing, that it will not pursue march-in rights on the basis of the available information." *Id.* Pursuant to § 401.6, the NIH, which has the delegated authority to make the march-in determination in this case, notified Hopkins of the petition and requested comment. Hopkins made its initial response on May 7, but in the interim, CellPro had made an additional submission to which Hopkins sought to respond. In sum, CellPro made supplemental filings on April 24, May 8, May 28 and July 2. After its initial response on May 7, Hopkins made supplemental filings on May 19, June 2 and July 2. Because the parties continued to make submissions and insist on the right to comment on the submissions of the other party, the NIH informed the parties that the 60 days set forth in the regulations for a determination by the agency would be calculated from June 2nd, but agreed to review and consider any submissions made by the parties through July 2.[60]

The administrative record in this matter consists of the submissions of the parties, letters from universities, corporations, members of Congress, and other members of the public on this issue, as well as other pertinent materials obtained by the NIH.

Statutory Background and Criteria

The stated policy and objective of the Bayh-Dole Act is:

> to use the patent system to promote the utilization of inventions arising from federally supported research or development; to encourage maximum participation of small business firms in federally supported research and development efforts; to promote collaboration between commercial concerns and nonprofit organizations, including universities; to ensure that inventions made by nonprofit organizations and small business firms are used in a manner to promote free competition and enterprise; to promote the commercialization and public availability of inventions made in the United States by United States industry and labor; to ensure that the Government obtains sufficient rights in federally supported inventions to meet the needs of the Government and protect the public against nonuse or unreasonable use of inventions; and to minimize the costs of administering policies in this area.

---

59. The Order for Permanent Injunction and Partial Stay of Injunction (Order), entered July 24, 1997, includes a partial stay allowing CellPro to continue selling its device under certain restrictions. CellPro has indicated that it intends to appeal the Court's ruling.

60. Hopkins made an additional submission July 29, which was not considered by NIH.

Act at §200. Toward this goal, the Act addresses not only rules governing the licensing of Government-owned inventions, but also addresses Federal contractors'[61] rights to elect title to inventions made with Federal funding. In giving Federal contractors the right to elect title to inventions, Congress altered the preexisting scheme under which the funding agency generally owned patentable inventions made with Federal support unless the contractor obtained a waiver. Congress believed that this change would promote the utilization and commercialization of inventions and would harmonize Federal patent policies. *See* Senate Rep. No. 96-480 at p.3.

In giving contractors the right to elect title to inventions made with Federal funding, the Act also includes various safeguards on the public investment in the research. For example, the Federal agency retains a nonexclusive, nontransferable, irrevocable, paid-up license to practice or have practiced for or on behalf of the United States any subject invention throughout the world. *See* 35 U.S.C. §202(c)(4). In addition, the Act includes march-in rights, which provide a Federal agency with the authority in certain, very limited circumstances, to make sure that a federally funded invention is available to the public. Section 203(1) states:

> With respect to any subject invention in which a small business firm or nonprofit organization has acquired title under this chapter, the Federal agency under whose funding agreement the subject invention was made shall have the right, in accordance with such procedures as are provided in regulations promulgated hereunder to require the contractor, an assignee or exclusive licensee of a subject invention to grant a nonexclusive, partially exclusive, or exclusive license in any field of use to a responsible applicant or applicants, upon terms that are reasonable under the circumstances, and if the contractor, assignee or exclusive licensee refuses such request, to grant such a license itself, if the Federal agency determines that such—
>
> (a) action is necessary because the contractor or assignee has not taken, or is not expected to take within a reasonable time, effective steps to achieve practical application of the subject invention in such field of use;
>
> (b) action is necessary to alleviate health or safety needs which are not reasonably satisfied by the contractor, assignee, or their licensees;
>
> (c) action is necessary to meet requirements for public use specified by Federal regulations and such requirements are not reasonably satisfied by the contractor, assignee, or licensees; or
>
> (d) action is necessary because the agreement required by section 204 has not been obtained or waived or because a licensee of the exclusive right to use or sell any subject invention in the United States is in breach of its agreement obtained pursuant to section 204.[62]

---

61. Defined in the Act as "any person, small business firm or nonprofit organization that is a party to a funding agreement," Act at §201(c). In 1983, President Reagan issued a memorandum instructing all Federal agencies, to the extent not prohibited by law, to grant all recipients the same right to their inventions as the Bayh-Dole Act provided small businesses and nonprofit institutions.

62. The legislative history to the Act indicates that Congress anticipated that third parties, such as CellPro in this case, would be likely to inform the Government of the possible need for march-in. However, it is clear that march-in remains a purely government authority. Senate Report No. 96-480 states that:

> "[m]arch-in" is intended as a remedy to be invoked by the Government and a private cause of action is not created in competitors or other outside parties, although it is ex-

Jurisdiction

In its submissions, Hopkins suggested that NIH did not have jurisdiction in this matter. CellPro disagreed. It is our conclusion that NIH has jurisdiction to determine whether to exercise march-in with respect to the patents in question. The patents which were found by the Court to be valid and infringed are U.S. Patent Nos. 4,714,680 ('680 patent) and 4,965,204 ('204 patent). Documentation submitted by Hopkins clearly establishes that the inventions claimed in these patents were funded by the NIH. For instance, with regard to the '680 patent, Hopkins submitted to the NIH a letter dated October 4, 1984, notifying the NIH that Hopkins had elected title to the invention. In addition, Hopkins provided annual utilization reports filed during the 1980's and early 1990's, and a license from Hopkins to the U.S. Government, which expressly acknowledges that "the invention was made in the course of research supported by the DHHS."[63] Since the inventions were funded by the NIH, as acknowledged by Hopkins well before the patent dispute with CellPro arose, there is a clear presumption of jurisdiction by the NIH, and Hopkins has not submitted sufficient evidence to rebut that presumption.

Decision

The NIH has evaluated the administrative record with regard to two prongs of the statutory criteria, 35 U.S.C. § 203(1)(a) and (b). The NIH has examined whether, (1) Baxter has failed to take, or is not expected to take within a reasonable time, effective steps to achieve practical application of the subject inventions; and, (2) there exists a health or safety need which is not reasonably satisfied by Hopkins or Baxter.[64] Based on these criteria and the available information, march-in is not warranted at this time.

Practical Application of the Subject Inventions

Practical application is defined under 37 C.F.R § 404.3(d) as "to manufacture in the case of a composition or product, to practice in the case of a process or method, or to operate in the case of a machine or system; and, in each case, under such conditions as to establish that the invention is being utilized and that its benefits are to the extent permitted by law or Government regulations available to the public on reasonable terms." The administrative record demonstrates that Hopkins and Baxter have clearly met this standard.

This technology was originally developed in the laboratory of Dr. Curt Civin at Hopkins and first published in 1984. Hopkins filed for patent protection and was awarded four patents, the first of which issued in 1987. The technology was first exclusively li-

---

pected that in most cases complaints from third-parties will be the basis for the initiation of agency action.

63. Although these documents relate specifically to the '680 patent, the '204 patent states that it is a divisional application of the application, serial number 670,740 (the '740 application), from which the '680 patent issued. The claims in the '204 patent are, therefore, based on the original disclosure that was contained in the '740 application, as to which Hopkins had elected title. The other two patents also involved in the patent litigation, U.S. Patent Nos. 5,035,994, and 5,130,144, also issued from divisional applications of the '740 application.

64. The two other prongs are clearly not relevant. Subparagraph (c) narrowly applies to "public use" required by particular laws. CellPro has not claimed any such law to be applicable in the present case, nor does NIH believe any to be applicable. Subparagraph (d) authorizes march-in when an exclusive licensee of a subject invention has failed to agree (or obtain a waiver of such requirement) that any products embodying the invention or produced through the use of the invention will be manufactured substantially in the United States. Baxter has agreed to manufacture substantially in the United States.

censed to Becton-Dickinson & Co. (BD). BD began marketing the first anti-CD34 antibody in 1985 and has sold anti-CD34 antibodies worldwide ever since. Since BD was only interested in the diagnostic applications, the company exclusively sublicensed therapeutic rights to Baxter. Baxter began development of a therapeutic system and sublicensed rights to Applied Immune Sciences (now part of RPR Gencell) and Systemix (now part of Novartis). Baxter also held licensing discussions with CellPro, but no license agreement was signed.

By late 1991, Baxter had developed a prototype stem cell selection device. In 1992, Dr. Civin began clinical trials with the device, and Baxter started its own clinical trials in 1993. In January 1995, Baxter's Isolex 300 System received regulatory approval in Europe (CE Mark of Conformity for Medical Devices). In the United States, Baxter's systems have been installed in numerous transplant centers over the past three years; the Baxter device has been used in clinical trials to process peripheral blood and bone marrow for hematopoietic reconstitution in patients. On February 24, 1997, Baxter filed for Pre-market Approval (PMA) of its Isolex 300SA System.[65] In addition to effectively licensing and developing the technology, Hopkins, BD and Baxter have aggressively defended the patents in court. In 1994, the three parties joined in a suit against CellPro for infringement of the Civin patents.

Accordingly, NIH concludes that Hopkins and Baxter have taken effective steps to achieve practical application, as demonstrated by Hopkins' licensing, Baxter's manufacture, practice, and operation of the Isolex 300, and the device's availability to and use by the public to the extent permitted at this time under applicable law (i.e., foreign sales as well as widespread clinical research use in the U.S.). With regard to FDA approval and commercial sale of the Baxter Isolex 300 in the United States, the administrative record indicates that Baxter is vigorously pursuing an active application. Based on these facts, we conclude that Hopkins and Baxter have met the statutory and regulatory standard for practical application.

Health or Safety Needs

The question of whether the CellPro Ceprate SC fulfills health or safety needs not reasonably satisfied by the Baxter Isolex 300 has been the central inquiry and priority of the NIH in evaluating CellPro's petition for march-in. In this regard, we note the considerable debate among scientists and clinicians as to whether immunoselection of stem cells with selection devices prior to transplantation provides a clinically significant benefit to patients over standard hematopoietic transplantation techniques. The clinical benefit upon which the CellPro Ceprate SC device was approved by FDA consisted of a reduction of infusional toxicity associated with the administration of bone marrow prepared with standard techniques.[66] To date, neither party has presented to the Biological Response Modifiers Advisory Committee any studies documenting that cell separation

65. CellPro has argued that the NIH should distinguish between the Isolex SA, an earlier, less automated device, and the Isolex 300i, Baxter's current fully-automated device. The current PMA application to FDA relates to the Isolex SA device. As is customary, the FDA recently discussed the Baxter PMA application for the 300SA device with the Biological Response Modifiers Advisory Committee (July 24, 1997). The majority of the committee members (13 out of 16) voted that the SA device yields an enriched cell population that produces successful engraftments. Thus, NIH finds that the Isolex SA and the 300i have comparable functions for the purpose of this determination.

66. *See*, Transcript, FDA Biological Response Modifiers Advisory Committee meeting, February 28, 1996; Package Description, Ceprate SC Stem Cell Concentration System (December 6, 1996).

devices improve stem cell engraftment, disease-free survival, or overall survival.[67] Thus, it is premature for either Baxter or CellPro to claim patient benefits (other than a decrease in infusional toxicities) from stem cell isolation and purification, T-cell, lymphocyte, and tumor cell purging, or other claimed uses.

It is equally premature, and inappropriate, for NIH to substitute its judgment for that of clinicians and patients seeking to avail themselves of an FDA-approved medical device. The FDA has determined that the Ceprate SC is safe and effective for selecting stem cells from autologous bone marrow for hematopoietic reconstitution. Thus, to the extent that the Ceprate SC is the only device that is available for sale in the United States for this purpose, it fulfills a health need for those who wish to use it, until such time as a comparable alternative product becomes available for sale.[68]

As explained more fully below, the administrative record demonstrates that Hopkins and Baxter have taken appropriate steps to reasonably satisfy this need. First, they have refrained from enforcing patent rights to the full extent of the law in order to allow the continuing sale of the Ceprate SC until the Baxter product is approved for sale by the FDA. Second, they have pledged to ensure that the Baxter product is as widely available as possible through clinical trials, and to ensure patient access to the fullest extent possible.

(1) Continuing Sale of CellPro Device

In deference to the health need fulfilled by the CellPro device in the absence of an FDA-approved alternative, Hopkins and Baxter have refrained from enforcing their patent rights to the full extent of the law. Specifically, they modified a proposed order of injunction filed for consideration in the patent litigation in Federal District Court. The Order issued by the Court on July 24, 1997 states, in pertinent part:

> CellPro may continue to make, have made, use and sell SC Systems and disposable products (including the 12.8 antibody) for use with SC Systems, within the United States, until such time as an alternative stem cell concentration device, manufactured under a license under the '204 and '680 patents, is approved for therapeutic use in the United States by the United States Food and Drug Administration ... and for a period of three months thereafter.

Order at p 5. In addition, certain price and volume restrictions contained in the Court's Order specifically do not apply to the provision of products solely for use in clinical trials. Order at pp. 5, 7.

CellPro argues vigorously, however, in documents filed prior to the entry of the Court's Order, that the terms of the proposed order, most specifically the requirement

---

67. Transcript, FDA Biological Response Modifiers Advisory Committee meeting, February 28, 1996. At that public meeting, Dr. Richard Champlin, MD Anderson Cancer Center, introducing the CellPro device on behalf of CellPro, stated to the Committee, "[a]gain, one has to remember this is not a treatment for cancer. This is a means to enrich stem cells for a variety of purposes. It has again been shown to be reproducible, safe, and effective for that purpose. And this technology is really critical to allow us to develop the field in a number of other very important applications." Transcript at pp. 21–22.

68. The Baxter Isolex 300 constitutes such a comparable alternative product. Both the Isolex 300 and the Ceprate SC devices are used in clinical research to isolate and purify stem cells from either bone marrow or peripheral blood, in preparation for stem cell transplantation. Both are under investigation for either autologous (patient's own) or allogeneic (donor) transplantations. We find that performance differences alleged by both parties primarily affect convenience of use, and do not alter the public health impact at issue here.

of payments to Baxter for sales of CellPro product, would force CellPro out of business and result in the loss of availability of the CellPro device.

First, we rely on the Court's finding that it is unlikely that the terms of the Order will result in the loss of availability of the CellPro product.[69] This issue was specifically before the Court, supported by an exhaustive factual record resulting from years of litigation. Although NIH is determining whether to open a fact-finding proceeding, as opposed to conducting one, we also found no convincing evidence that CellPro will be unable to supply patients with its product under the terms of the Court Order. The terms of the Order may be unpalatable to CellPro, but CellPro need only operate under those constraints pending a decision on its appeal of the Court's adverse verdict on infringement. The Court specifically found that CellPro "possesses adequate cash reserves to allow it to continue operations during the pendency of its appeal," Memorandum Opinion at p. 24, and determined that it would most likely be in CellPro's interest to continue operations pending the outcome of the appeal. Moreover, the Court has retained jurisdiction and invited the parties to apply to the Court for modification of the terms of the injunction, specifically, the payment of incremental profits to Baxter, if the amount determined by the Court "either provides inadequate relief or works an injustice inconsistent with equitable principles." *Id.*

Second, the loss of availability of the CellPro product is relevant to the "health need" criteria only during the period prior to FDA approval and availability for sale of a comparable alternative product. In petitioning NIH to open a separate proceeding on this matter, CellPro argues that its continuing viability and success, even beyond FDA approval of a comparable alternative, should be a matter of concern to the NIH because CellPro has developed and is marketing an important health care product. Invoking our prior caveat as to the investigational nature of these devices, we concur that, as a general matter, NIH supports the development and success of the biotechnology industry. It is indeed very important to the NIH that biotechnology and pharmaceutical companies thrive and compete in order to bring new health care products to the public. Developing and commercializing such products out of federally-funded research is the foundation and essence of the Bayh-Dole Act.

We are wary, however, of forced attempts to influence the marketplace for the benefit of a single company, particularly when such actions may have far-reaching repercussions on many companies' and investors' future willingness to invest in federally funded medical technologies. The patent system, with its resultant predictability for investment and commercial development, is the means chosen by Congress for ensuring the development and dissemination of new and useful technologies. It has proven to be an effective means for the development of health care technologies. In exercising its authorities under the Bayh-Dole Act, NIH is mindful of the broader public health implications of a

---

69. According to the Court in its Memorandum Opinion at p. 23, "[a]fter evaluating the parties' arguments, and their accompanying declarations, the court finds that in the absence of a conclusive statement from CellPro executives that it will discontinue operations, it has failed to establish that a highly speculative risk of shutdown during the pendency of its appeal to the Federal Circuit outweighs the harm suffered by plaintiffs as the result of CellPro's willful infringement. "Nonetheless, the Court modified one of the terms of the injunction, as proposed by Hopkins and Baxter, to require CellPro to pay 60 percent of its incremental profit from infringing sales, as opposed to the 100 percent proposed by Hopkins and Baxter.

march-in proceeding, including the potential loss of new health care products yet to be developed from federally funded research.

On balance, we believe it is inappropriate for the NIH to intercede in this matter to ensure CellPro's commercial future. Viability and success in the private sector is appropriately governed by the marketplace, and significantly influenced by management practices and decisions. CellPro had the opportunity to license the invention from Baxter but decided against doing so, and instead risked patent infringement litigation. It would be inappropriate for the NIH, a public health agency, to exercise its authorities under the Bayh-Dole Act to procure for CellPro more favorable commercial terms than it can otherwise obtain from the Court or from the patent owners. CellPro's commercial viability is best left to CellPro's management and the marketplace.

(2) Reasonable Steps to Ensure Widespread Availability of Baxter's Product

Hopkins and Baxter have also pledged to reasonably satisfy any health need created by the loss of the CellPro product in the unlikely event that patient access to this technology is restricted before a comparable alternative product is approved by the FDA and becomes available for sale.

In several of its submissions to NIH, and in a letter from Baxter CEO Vernon Loucks to Secretary Donna Shalala, Baxter committed to ensuring there would be no gap in patient access to stem cell separation technology. Baxter committed to installing its device free of charge at any site from which CellPro might withdraw, and to provide that site with the same level of support on the same terms as CellPro. Baxter also committed to obtaining all clinical and regulatory approvals necessary to place the Isolex system into operation as soon as possible.

CellPro asserted that Baxter is unable to fulfill this pledge; however, neither party submitted evidence sufficient for a definitive determination, and it would be premature for the NIH to act based on Baxter's failure to accomplish what events have not yet required it to do. In any event, we believe the likelihood of Baxter having to substitute devices in order to ensure patient access is remote, as discussed above. Nevertheless, pending FDA approval and availability for sale of a comparable alternative product, NIH will continue to monitor the situation and will retain jurisdiction to initiate march-in without the filing of a new request, in the event that health needs are not being reasonably satisfied.

Conclusion

The NIH has determined not to initiate proceedings to pursue march-in rights on the basis of the available information. NIH has examined the criteria of 35 U.S.C. §203(1)(a) and (b) and found that march-in is not warranted under either criteria. Specifically, the NIH has determined that Hopkins and Baxter have taken, or are expected to take within a reasonable time, effective steps to achieve practical application of the applicable patents, as demonstrated by Hopkins' licensing activities and Baxter's manufacture, practice, and operation of the Isolex 300, as well as the pending applications for FDA approval. NIH also finds that the available information fails to demonstrate an unmet health need that is not reasonably satisfied by Hopkins and Baxter.

The NIH will continue to monitor issues related to patient access to the CellPro or Baxter devices during the period prior to FDA approval and availability for sale of a comparable alternative device.

/s/ Harold Varmus, M.D.

Director, NIH

NIH, In the Case of Norvir(r) Manufactured by Abbott Laboratories, Inc.

July 29, 2004

Introduction

The NIH received letters from members of Congress and the public requesting that the Government exercise its march-in rights under the Bayh Dole Act (Act), 35 U.S.C. §§200–212, in connection with one or more patents owned by Abbott Laboratories, Inc. (Abbott). The letters expressed concern over the price of Norvir(r), which is covered by the patents and marketed by Abbott for the treatment of patients with HIV/AIDS....

After careful analysis of the Bayh-Dole Act and considering all the facts in this case as well as comments received, the National Institutes of Health (NIH) has determined that it will not initiate a march-in proceeding as it does not believe that such a proceeding is warranted based on the available information and the statutory and regulatory framework.

Background on the Invention

From 1988 through 1993, ritonavir was developed at Abbott Laboratories partly through the use of Federal funds and falls within the claims of a number of patents owned by Abbott.[70] In 1996, ritonavir (sold under the tradename "Norvir(r)") was approved by the FDA for marketing.

Other U.S. and foreign patents may exist which cover certain aspects of the marketed compound including specific formulations or delivery techniques, and may not be subject inventions within the meaning of the term as defined in 35 U.S.C. §201(e).[71] These inventions would not be subject to the Government's march-in authority....

Public Comments

The NIH held a public meeting on May 25, 2004 at which comments were presented by advocates for and against the use of the Government's march-in authority in connection with Norvir(r). The speakers presented differing perspectives regarding the interpretation and intention of the march-in provisions, the reasons for the increase in the price of ritonavir, and the anti-competitive effect of that price increase.

The NIH also has received written comments from a variety of groups and individuals representing universities, the AIDS community, pharmaceutical interests, drafters of the Bayh-Dole Act, and other interested parties. These comments along with those submitted at the public meeting are available on the NIH Office of Technology Transfer website at http://ott.od.nih.eov/Meeting/Mav25.htm.

The NIH is aware that members of Congress and the public have asked the Federal Trade Commission (FTC) to investigate the potential anti-competitive effects of the increase in the price of Norvir(r). The NIH agrees that the FTC is the appropriate agency to address this issue.

After carefully considering all the information provided and otherwise made available, the NIH does not believe the initiation of a march-in proceeding is warranted.

---

70. These patents are: U.S. Patent Nos. 5,541,206, 5,635,523, 5,648,497, 5,674,882, 5,846,987, and 5,886,036.

71. The term "subject invention" means any invention of the funding recipient conceived or first actually reduced to practice in the performance of work under a funding agreement.

Discussion

The NIH is the steward of medical and behavioral research for the nation. Its mission is science in pursuit of fundamental knowledge about the nature and behavior of living systems and the application of that knowledge to extend healthy life and reduce the burdens of illness and disability. Each year, a wealth of scientific discoveries emanates from the NIH intramural laboratories and from extramural activities under grants and contracts. Bringing these discoveries from "the bench to the bedside" requires drug and product development, scale-up, clinical testing, and finally marketing and distribution. Success in accomplishing this colossal task and fulfilling our primary mission of improving public health requires the participation of industry partners.

The NIH supports fundamental research that may lead to the development of pharmaceutical products. Occasionally, the NIH funds a technology that ultimately is incorporated into a commercial product or process for making a commercial product. It is important to the NIH that pharmaceutical companies commercialize new health care products and processes incorporating NIH-funded technology thereby making the technology available to the public. A central purpose of the Bayh-Dole Act involves the development and commercialization of such products out of federally-funded research.

Section 203(a) of the Act provides in part that march-in rights maybe exercised by the funding Federal agency based on any of four conditions: (1) when "practical application" of the subject invention has not been achieved or is not expected to be achieved in a reasonable time, (2) when the action is necessary to alleviate health or safety needs, (3) when action is necessary to meet requirements for public use specified by Federal regulation that the contractor has failed to meet or (4) when the U.S. industry preference of Section 204 of the Act has not been met. The third and fourth conditions are not relevant to this discussion.[72]

Practical Application of the Subject Inventions

A composition or product, such as Norvir(r), that has achieved practical application is defined in Section 201 (f) to mean that it is manufactured "under such conditions as to establish that the invention is being utilized and that its benefits are to the extent permitted by law or Government regulations available to the public on reasonable terms."

In 1997, the NIH reviewed a march-in request from CellPro, Inc. that asserted Baxter Healthcare Corporation (Baxter) had failed to take effective steps to achieve practical application of the subject inventions. NIH determined that Baxter "met the statutory and regulatory standard for practical application" as evidenced by its "manufacture, practice, and operation" of the invention and the invention's "availability to and use by the public." Accordingly, the NIH determined not to initiate march-in proceedings.[73]

Similarly, the record in this instance demonstrates that Abbott has met the standard for achieving practical application of the applicable patents by its manufacture, practice, and operation of ritonavir and the drug's availability and use by the public.

---

72. The last two conditions are clearly not relevant. Subparagraph (3) narrowly applies to "public use" specified by Federal regulations, but there are no regulations that apply in this case. Subparagraph (4) is not relevant because Abbott manufactures Norvir(r) in the United States.

73. The determination also evaluated the health or safety need prong and found that Baxter had "taken appropriate steps to reasonably satisfy this need." The other two prongs were held to be "clearly not relevant."

Ritonavir has been on the market and available to patients with HIV/AIDS since 1996, when it was introduced and sold under the trade name Norvir(r) as both a standalone protease inhibitor and a booster to increase the effectiveness of protease inhibitors marketed by other companies. Thus, the invention has reached practical application because it is being utilized and has been made widely available for use by patients with HIV/AIDS for at least eight years.

Health or Safety Needs

Norvir(r) has been approved by the Food and Drug Administration as safe and effective and is being widely prescribed by physicians for its approved indications. No evidence has been presented that march-in could alleviate any health or safety needs that are not reasonably satisfied by Abbott. Rather, the argument advanced is that the product should be available at a lower price, which is addressed below. Thus, the NIH concludes that Abbott has met the statutory and regulatory standard for health or safety needs.

Drug Pricing

Finally, the issue of the cost or pricing of drugs that include inventive technologies made using Federal funds is one which has attracted the attention of Congress in several contexts that are much broader than the one at hand.[74] In addition, because the market dynamics for all products developed pursuant to licensing rights under the Bayh-Dole Act could be altered if prices on such products were directed in any way by NIH, the NIH agrees with the public testimony that suggested that the extraordinary remedy of march-in is not an appropriate means of controlling prices. The issue of drug pricing has global implications and, thus, is appropriately left for Congress to address legislatively.

Conclusion

Norvir(r) has been available for use by patients with HIV/AIDS since 1996 and is being actively marketed by Abbott and prescribed by physicians primarily as a booster drug. Accordingly, this drug has reached practical application and met health or safety needs as required by the Bayh-Dole Act. The NIH believes that the issue of drug pricing is one that would be more appropriately addressed by Congress, as it considers these matters in a larger context. The NIH also maintains that the FTC is the appropriate agency to address the question of whether Abbott has engaged in anti-competitive behavior.

The NIH is cognizant of the care with which Congress crafted the march-in language and understands that it has the responsibility to exercise its march-in authority deliberately and with great care. As such, the NIH has determined that it does not have information that leads it to believe that the exercise of march-in rights might be warranted in this case within the meaning of 35 U.S.C. §203.

/s/ Elias A. Zerhouni, M.D.

Director, NIH

3. Experimental Use Exception/Defense

While the foregoing sections focused primarily on identifying and securing patent rights, the successful patent applicant also faces some limitations on her ability to en-

74. In addition, NIH addressed "The NIH 'Reasonable Pricing' Clause Experience" in its report to Congress, "A Plan to Ensure Taxpayers' Interests are Protected," July 2001, available at http://www.nih.gov/news/070101wyden.htm.

force that patent against infringers. In the research environment, the primary limitations are two different doctrines that, unfortunately, often are referred to by the same term (or its variants): "experimental use exception".[75] The critical difference, however, is between the two doctrines themselves. The first may also be referred to as the "common law research use defense" and is discussed in *Madey v. Duke* excerpted below. It originates from case law in the 1800s and has never been statutorily codified. As discussed in *Merck v. Integra* below, the second may alternately be referred to as the "271(e)(1) exemption" because that is the section of the Patent Act where the rule was codified after Congress passed the Drug Price Competition and Patent Term Restoration Act of 1984.[76] The 271(e)(1) exemption was primarily created to allow generic drug manufacturers to begin clinical studies of a new generic version of a pioneer patented drug, so that the FDA approval process could be started even before the pioneer drug went "off patent." Without such an exemption, these clinical studies would amount to actionable patent infringement. Accordingly, prior to passage of the exemption, many argued that pioneer drug patent holders received a *de facto* extension on their patent because generic drug companies had to wait until the patent expired before they could even commence the FDA approval process—meaning that the generic company could not market or sell the generic version during the period of post-patent expiration, pre-FDA market approval and thus the pioneer company retained its monopoly position in the marketplace.

The first case, which considers the scope of the experimental use defense, does not involve life sciences research. However, it fundamentally altered the perception of the scope of the defense and stands as the current definitive interpretation of that defense in the university and non-profit research environment.

Madey v. Duke

307 F.3d 1351 (Fed. Cir. 2002)

Circuit Judge Gajarsa.

Dr. John M.J. Madey ("Madey") appeals from a judgment of the United States District Court for the Middle District of North Carolina. Madey sued Duke University ("Duke"), bringing claims of patent infringement and various other federal and state law claims. Pursuant to a motion filed by Duke under Federal Rule of Civil Procedure ("FRCP") 12(b)(1), the district court dismissed-in-part certain patent infringement claims and dismissed certain other claims. After discovery, the district court granted summary judgment in favor of Duke on the remaining claims. For a first set of alleged infringing acts, it held that the experimental use defense applied to Duke's use of Madey's patented laser technology. For a second set of alleged infringing acts, it held that Duke was not the infringing party because a third-party owned and controlled the allegedly infringing laser equipment. The district court erred in its partial dismissal, erred in applying the experimental use defense, but, for the second set of alleged in-

75. Variants are "experimental use defense"; "experimental use exemption"; "research use exception"; "research use exemption"; and "research use defense". To the extent that there is any real difference among these terms, it may be based on the speaker's belief that the doctrine means either a) that there is no infringement in the first place, or b) that there is infringement but it is excused and/or not actionable.

76. Pub. L. No. 98-417, 98 Stat. 1585 (September 24, 1984) (also popularly referred to as the "Hatch-Waxman Act"). The new § 271(e)(1) is contained in § 202 of the Act. *See* 98 Stat. 1603.

fringing acts, correctly determined that Duke did not infringe because it did not own or control the equipment. Accordingly, we reverse-in-part, affirm-in-part, and remand.

I. Background

In the mid-1980s Madey was a tenured research professor at Stanford University. At Stanford, he had an innovative laser research program, which was highly regarded in the scientific community. An opportunity arose for Madey to consider leaving Stanford and take a tenured position at Duke. Duke recruited Madey, and in 1988 he left Stanford for a position in Duke's physics department. In 1989 Madey moved his free electron laser ("FEL") research lab from Stanford to Duke. The FEL lab contained substantial equipment, requiring Duke to build an addition to its physics building to house the lab. In addition, during his time at Stanford, Madey had obtained sole ownership of two patents practiced by some of the equipment in the FEL lab.

At Duke, Madey served for almost a decade as director of the FEL lab. During that time the lab continued to achieve success in both research funding and scientific breakthroughs. However, a dispute arose between Madey and Duke. Duke contends that, despite his scientific prowess, Madey ineffectively managed the lab. Madey contends that Duke sought to use the lab's equipment for research areas outside the allocated scope of certain government funding, and that when he objected, Duke sought to remove him as lab director. Duke eventually did remove Madey as director of the lab in 1997. The removal is not at issue in this appeal, however, it is the genesis of this unique patent infringement case. As a result of the removal, Madey resigned from Duke in 1998. Duke, however, continued to operate some of the equipment in the lab. Madey then sued Duke for patent infringement of his two patents, and brought a variety of other claims.

A. The Patents and Infringing Equipment

One of Madey's patents, U.S. Patent No. 4,641,103 ("the '103 patent"), covers a "Microwave Electron Gun" used in connection with free electron lasers. The other patent, U.S. Patent No. 5,130,994 ("the '994 patent"), is titled "Free-Electron Laser Oscillator For Simultaneous Narrow Spectral Resolution And Fast Time Resolution Spectroscopy." The details of these two patents are not material to the issues on appeal. Their use in the lab, however, as embodied in certain equipment, is central to this appeal.

The equipment at the Duke FEL lab that practices the subject matter disclosed and claimed in the patents is set forth in the list below, which first lists the equipment and then the patent(s) it embodies.

• An infrared FEL called the "Mark III FEL," embodying the '994 patent and the '103 patent (by incorporating the microwave electron gun in the infrared FEL).

• A "Storage Ring FEL," embodying the same patents as the Mark III FEL because it incorporates a Mark III FEL.

• A "Microwave Gun Test Stand," embodying the '103 patent (by incorporating the microwave electron gun).

The three alleged infringing devices are the Mark III FEL, the Storage Ring FEL, and the Microwave Gun Test Stand. Although it is not clear from the record, perhaps because Duke defended by asserting experimental use and government license defenses, Duke seems to concede that the alleged infringing devices and methods read on the claims of the patents. Although the three devices were housed in Duke's physics facilities, the Microwave Gun Test Stand was not Duke's asset, but rather belonged to North Carolina Central University ("NCCU")....

D. The District Court's Summary Judgment Opinion

Among Duke's motions for summary judgment, two are relevant on appeal, entitled by the district court as: (i) the "Patent Motion;" and (ii) the "Test Stand Gun Motion."

The Patent Motion and the Experimental Use Defense

The district court acknowledged a common law "exception" for patent infringement liability for uses that, in the district court's words, are "solely for research, academic or experimental purposes." The district court recognized the debate over the scope of the experimental use defense, but cited this court's opinion in *Embrex, Inc. v. Service Engineering Corp.,* 216 F.3d 1343, 1349 (Fed. Cir. 2000), to hold that the defense was viable for experimental, non-profit purposes.

After having recognized the experimental use defense, the district court then fashioned the defense for application to Madey in the passage set forth below.

> Given this standard [for experimental use], for [Madey] to overcome his burden of establishing actionable infringement in this case, he must establish that [Duke] has not used the equipment at issue "solely for an experimental or other non-profit purpose." More specifically, [Madey] must sufficiently establish that [Duke's] use of the patent had "definite, cognizable, and not insubstantial commercial purposes."

On appeal, Madey attacks this passage as improperly shifting the burden to the plaintiff to allege and prove that the defendant's use was not experimental.

Before the district court, Madey argued that Duke's research in its FEL lab was commercial in character and intent. Madey relied on *Pitcairn v. United States,* 212 Ct.Cl. 168 (1976), where the government used patented rotor structures and control systems for a helicopter to test the "lifting ability" and other attributes of the patented technology. The *Pitcairn* court held that the helicopters were not built solely for experimental purposes because they were also built to benefit the government in its legitimate business. Based on language in Duke's patent policy, Madey argues that Duke is in the business of "obtaining grants and developing possible commercial applications for the fruits of its 'academic research.'"

The district court rejected Madey's argument, relying on another statement in the preamble of the Duke patent policy which stated that Duke was "dedicated to teaching, research, and the expansion of knowledge ... [and] does not undertake research or development work principally for the purpose of developing patents and commercial applications." The district court reasoned that these statements from the patent policy refute any contention that Duke is "in the business" of developing technology for commercial applications. According to the district court, Madey's "evidence" was mere speculation,[77] and thus Madey did not meet his burden of proof to create a genuine issue of material fact.[78] The court went on to state that "[w]ithout more concrete evidence to rebut [Duke's] stated purpose with respect to its research in the FEL lab, Plain-

---

77. Madey also argued that Duke's acceptance of funding from the government and private foundations was evidence of developing patented devices with commercial intent. The district court also rejected this proposition.

78. The district court discussed and dismissed in a footnote other evidence suggested by Madey, including the fact that Duke had established (but not yet applied) an hourly fee for industrial users wishing to use the FEL lab's resources, and statements from Duke's website for the FEL lab indicating an interest in corporate partnerships.

tiff has failed to meet its burden of establishing patent infringement by a preponderance of the evidence." ...

The Test Stand Gun Motion

Under the Test Stand Gun Motion, Duke argued that any use of the patented equipment before June 1997 is not infringement because Madey consented to the manufacture and use of the Microwave Gun Test Stand by Duke and NCCU before this date. The district court agreed, concluding that there was no infringement before such date because Madey approved of such use via his direct involvement. Madey does not appeal this issue.

After June 1997, however, Duke's defense is that no one affiliated with Duke used the Microwave Gun Test Stand. Duke relied on attestations by Dr. Jones, the NCCU professor who was the principal investigator for the AFOSR contract. The district court determined that Dr. Jones was not an agent of Duke. It also determined that Dr. Jones controlled physical access to the Microwave Gun Test Stand because he had the key switch to operate the device. The district court held any contrary assertions by Madey to be "bald allegations and mere speculation."

Given Dr. Jones' attestation that he was unaware of any Duke faculty members or employees using the Microwave Gun Test Stand after June 1997, the district court determined that there was no genuine issue of material fact and awarded summary judgment of no infringement to Duke on this issue....

II. Discussion

...

C. The District Court's Application of Experimental Use

On appeal, Madey asserts three primary errors related to experimental use. First, Madey claims that the district court improperly shifted the burden to Madey to prove that Duke's use was not experimental. Second, Madey argues that the district court applied an overly broad version of the very narrow experimental use defense inconsistent with our precedent. Third, Madey attacks the supporting evidence relied on by the district court as overly general and not indicative of the specific propositions and findings required by the experimental use defense, and further argues that there is no support in the record before us to allow any court to apply the very narrow experimental use defense to Duke's ongoing FEL lab operation. We substantially agree with Madey on all three points. In addition, Madey makes a threshold argument concerning the continued existence of the experimental use doctrine in any form, which we turn to first. Our precedent, to which we are bound, continues to recognize the judicially created experimental use defense, however, in a very limited form.

The Experimental Use Defense

Citing the concurring opinion in *Embrex*, Madey contends that the Supreme Court's opinion in *Warner-Jenkinson Co. v. Hilton Davis Chem. Co.*, 520 U.S. 17 (1997) eliminates the experimental use defense. The Supreme Court held in *Warner-Jenkinson* that intent plays no role in the application of the doctrine of equivalents. Madey implicitly argues that the experimental use defense necessarily incorporates an intent inquiry, and thus is inconsistent with *Warner-Jenkinson*. Like the majority in *Embrex*, we do not view such an inconsistency as inescapable, and conclude the experimental use defense persists albeit in the very narrow form articulated by this court in *Embrex* and in *Roche*.

The District Court Improperly Shifted the Burden to Madey

As a precursor to the burden-shifting issue, Madey argues that the experimental use defense is an affirmative defense that Duke must plead or lose. We disagree. Madey points to no source of authority for its assertion that experimental use is an affirmative defense. Indeed, we have referred to the defense in a variety of ways. Given this lack of precise treatment in the precedent, Madey has no basis to support its affirmative defense argument. The district court and the parties in the present case joined the issue during the summary judgment briefing. We see no mandate from our precedent, nor any compelling reason from other considerations, why the opportunity to raise the defense if not raised in the responsive pleading should not also be available at the later stages of a case, within the procedural discretion typically afforded the trial court judge.

The district court held that in order for Madey to overcome his burden to establish actionable infringement, he must establish that Duke did not use the patent-covered free electron laser equipment solely for experimental or other non-profit purposes. Madey argues that this improperly shifts the burden to the patentee and conflates the experimental use defense with the initial infringement inquiry.

We agree with Madey that the district court improperly shifted the burden to him. The district court folded the experimental use defense into the baseline assessment as to whether Duke infringed the patents. Duke characterizes the district court's holding as expressing the following sequence: first, the court recognized that Madey carried his burden of proof on infringement; second, the court held that Duke carried its burden of proof on the experimental use defense; and third, the court held that Madey was unable to marshal sufficient evidence to rebut Duke's shifting of the burden. We disagree with Duke's reading of the district court's opinion. The district court explicitly contradicts Duke's argument by stating that Madey failed to "meet its burden to establish patent infringement by a preponderance of the evidence." This statement is an assessment of whether Madey supported his initial infringement claim. It is not an assessment of which party carried or shifted the burden of evidence related to the experimental use defense. Thus, the district court did not conclude that Madey failed to rebut Duke's assertion of the experimental use defense. Instead, it erroneously required Madey to show as a part of his initial claim that Duke's use was not experimental. The defense, if available at all, must be established by Duke.

The District Court's Overly Broad Conception of Experimental Use

Madey argues, and we agree, that the district court had an overly broad conception of the very narrow and strictly limited experimental use defense. The district court stated that the experimental use defense inoculated uses that "were solely for research, academic, or experimental purposes," and that the defense covered use that "is made for experimental, non-profit purposes only." Both formulations are too broad and stand in sharp contrast to our admonitions in *Embrex* and *Roche* that the experimental use defense is very narrow and strictly limited. In *Embrex*, we followed the teachings of *Roche* and *Pitcairn* to hold that the defense was very narrow and limited to actions performed "for amusement, to satisfy idle curiosity, or for strictly philosophical inquiry." Further, use does not qualify for the experimental use defense when it is undertaken in the "guise of scientific inquiry" but has "definite, cognizable, and not insubstantial commercial purposes." The concurring opinion in *Embrex* expresses a similar view: use is disqualified from the defense if it has the "slightest commercial implication." Moreover, use in keeping with the legitimate business of the alleged infringer does not qualify for the experimental use defense. The district court supported its conclusion with a citation to *Ruth v. Stearns-Roger Mfg. Co.,* 13 F.Supp. 697, 713 (D. Colo. 1935), a case that is not binding precedent for this court.

The *Ruth* case represents the conceptual dilemma that may have led the district court astray. Cases evaluating the experimental use defense are few, and those involving non-profit, educational alleged infringers are even fewer. In *Ruth,* the court concluded that a manufacturer of equipment covered by patents was not liable for contributory infringement because the end-user purchaser was the Colorado School of Mines, which used the equipment in furtherance of its educational purpose. Thus, the combination of apparent lack of commerciality, with the non-profit status of an educational institution, prompted the court in *Ruth,* without any detailed analysis of the character, nature and effect of the use, to hold that the experimental use defense applied. This is not consistent with the binding precedent of our case law postulated by *Embrex, Roche* and *Pitcairn.*

Our precedent clearly does not immunize use that is in any way commercial in nature. Similarly, our precedent does not immunize any conduct that is in keeping with the alleged infringer's legitimate business, regardless of commercial implications. For example, major research universities, such as Duke, often sanction and fund research projects with arguably no commercial application whatsoever. However, these projects unmistakably further the institution's legitimate business objectives, including educating and enlightening students and faculty participating in these projects. These projects also serve, for example, to increase the status of the institution and lure lucrative research grants, students and faculty.

In short, regardless of whether a particular institution or entity is engaged in an endeavor for commercial gain, so long as the act is in furtherance of the alleged infringer's legitimate business and is not solely for amusement, to satisfy idle curiosity, or for strictly philosophical inquiry, the act does not qualify for the very narrow and strictly limited experimental use defense. Moreover, the profit or non-profit status of the user is not determinative.

In the present case, the district court attached too great a weight to the non-profit, educational status of Duke, effectively suppressing the fact that Duke's acts appear to be in accordance with any reasonable interpretation of Duke's legitimate business objectives.[79] On remand, the district court will have to significantly narrow and limit its conception of the experimental use defense. The correct focus should not be on the non-profit status of Duke but on the legitimate business Duke is involved in and whether or not the use was solely for amusement, to satisfy idle curiosity, or for strictly philosophical inquiry.

D. The District Court's Analysis of the Test Stand Gun Motion

In contrast to our conclusion that the district court erred in its dismissal-in-part of the alleged '103 patent infringement and its application of the experimental use defense, we find no error in the court's summary judgment conclusion that there is no genuine issue of material fact concerning Duke's non-use of the NCCU Microwave Gun Test Stand during the relevant time period.

Specifically, the district court found that NCCU, through the subcontractor agreement it had with Duke, owned the Microwave Gun Test Stand, and that Dr. Jones of

79. Duke's patent and licensing policy may support its primary function as an educational institution. *See Duke University Policy on Inventions, Patents, and Technology Transfer* (1996), *available at* http://www.ors.duke.edu/policies/patpol.htm (last visited Oct. 3, 2002). Duke, however, like other major research institutions of higher learning, is not shy in pursuing an aggressive patent licensing program from which it derives a not insubstantial revenue stream.

NCCU controlled the gun with a key switch. Even though the gun was located on Duke's premises, Dr. Jones stated that no Duke faculty member or employee had used the gun during the relevant time period. This evidence of ownership, control, and no known Duke use, is sufficient to shift the summary judgment burden to Madey, who, in the district court's words, offers in response only bare allegations and speculation. Most of the response is testimony by Madey himself.

Madey contends that Duke and Dr. Jones have tacitly admitted to disputed questions of fact concerning whether Duke had any control or benefit over the Microwave Gun Test Stand. In addition, Madey contends that joint publications by Dr. Jones and Duke faculty, as well as research interests held by Duke faculty in areas potentially implicated by the Microwave Gun Test Stand, demonstrate disputed material facts about Duke's benefit and influence over the gun. Like the district court, we do not find that the record supports Madey's contentions, nor do we concur in the inferences in which Madey would have us draw.

In addition, we note that the record does not indicate that Madey plead any vicarious liability claims, such as alleging that Duke induced NCCU's infringement, or contributory infringement claims. To the extent that this was a strategic decision or tactical choice on Madey's part, he should not be allowed to overcome this choice now by acceptance of allegations and speculation as genuine issues of material fact....

III. Conclusion

The district court erred in its application of the common law experimental use defense, and, consequently, incorrectly found that there was no genuine issue of material fact upon which Madey could prevail. In addition, the court's dismissal-in-part of Duke's use of the '103 patent embodiments under the government ONR grant was in error. Due to these errors, further proceedings are necessary. This includes the opportunity for the district court to reevaluate the issues we remand in light of this opinion, for the parties to litigate Duke's asserted government license defense, and for the court to potentially consider the state law claims in accordance with the case's progression. Accordingly, we affirm-in-part and reverse-in-part the district court's decision and remand for additional proceedings consistent with this opinion.

* * *

The next case addresses the scope of the 271(e)(1) exemption that was created under the Hatch-Waxman Act. It also provides an introduction to the FDA drug approval process covered in more detail in Section D, *infra*.

Merck v. Integra

545 U.S. 193 (2005)

Justice Scalia delivered the opinion for a unanimous Court.

This case presents the question whether uses of patented inventions in preclinical research, the results of which are not ultimately included in a submission to the Food and Drug Administration (FDA), are exempted from infringement by 35 U.S.C. §271(e)(1).

I

It is generally an act of patent infringement to "mak[e], us[e], offe[r] to sell, or sel[l] any patented invention ... during the term of the patent therefor." §271(a). In 1984,

Congress enacted an exemption to this general rule, *see* Drug Price Competition and Patent Term Restoration Act of 1984, § 202, 98 Stat. 1585, as amended, 35 U.S.C. § 271(e)(1), which provides:

> "It shall not be an act of infringement to make, use, offer to sell, or sell within the United States or import into the United States a patented invention (other than a new animal drug or veterinary biological product (as those terms are used in the Federal Food, Drug, and Cosmetic Act and the Act of March 4, 1913) ...) solely for uses reasonably related to the development and submission of information under a Federal law which regulates the manufacture, use, or sale of drugs...."

The Federal Food, Drug, and Cosmetic Act (FDCA), ch. 675, 52 Stat. 1040, as amended, 21 U.S.C. § 301 *et seq.*, is "a Federal law which regulates the manufacture, use, or sale of drugs." Under the FDCA, a drugmaker must submit research data to the FDA at two general stages of new-drug development.[80] First, a drugmaker must gain authorization to conduct clinical trials (tests on humans) by submitting an investigational new drug application (IND). *See* 21 U.S.C. § 355(i); 21 CFR § 312.1 *et seq.* (2005). The IND must describe "preclinical tests (including tests on animals) of [the] drug adequate to justify the proposed clinical testing." 21 U.S.C. § 355(i)(1)(A); *see* 21 CFR §§ 312.23(a)(5) and (a)(8) (specifying necessary information from preclinical tests). Second, to obtain authorization to market a new drug, a drugmaker must submit a new drug application (NDA), containing "full reports of investigations which have been made to show whether or not [the] drug is safe for use and whether [the] drug is effective in use." 21 U.S.C. § 355(b)(1). Pursuant to FDA regulations, the NDA must include all clinical studies, as well as preclinical studies related to a drug's efficacy, toxicity, and pharmacological properties. *See* 21 CFR §§ 314.50(d)(2) (preclinical studies) and (d)(5) (clinical studies).

II

A

Respondents Integra Lifesciences I, Ltd., and the Burnham Institute, own five patents related to the tripeptide sequence Arg-Gly-Asp, known in single-letter notation as the "RGD peptide." U.S. Patent Nos. 4,988,621, 4,792,525, 5,695,997, 4,879,237, and 4,789,734. The RGD peptide promotes cell adhesion by attaching to $\alpha_V \beta_3$ integrins, receptors commonly located on the outer surface of certain endothelial cells.

Beginning in 1988, petitioner Merck KGaA provided funding for angiogenesis research conducted by Dr. David Cheresh at the Scripps Research Institute (Scripps). Angiogenesis is the process by which new blood vessels sprout from existing vessels; it plays a critical role in many diseases, including solid tumor cancers, diabetic retinopathy, and rheumatoid arthritis. In the course of his research, Dr. Cheresh discovered that it was possible to inhibit angiogenesis by blocking the $\alpha_V \beta_3$ integrins on proliferating endothelial cells. In 1994, Dr. Cheresh succeeded in reversing tumor growth in chicken embryos, first using a monoclonal antibody (LM609) he developed himself and later

80. Drugmakers that desire to market a generic drug (a drug containing the same active ingredients as a drug already approved for the market) may file an abbreviated new drug application (ANDA) with the FDA. *See* 21 U.S.C. § 355(j). The sponsor of a generic drug does not have to make an independent showing that the drug is safe and effective, either in preclinical or clinical studies. *See* § 355(j)(2)(A). It need only show that the drug includes the same active ingredients as, and is bioequivalent to, the drug that it is mimicking. *See* §§ 355(j)(2)(A)(ii) and (iv); § 355(j)(8)(B).

using a cyclic RGD peptide (EMD 66203) provided by petitioner.[81] Dr. Cheresh's discoveries were announced in leading medical journals and received attention in the general media.

With petitioner's agreement to fund research at Scripps due to expire in July 1995, Dr. Cheresh submitted a detailed proposal for expanded collaboration between Scripps and petitioner on February 1, 1995. The proposal set forth a 3-year timetable in which to develop "integrin antagonists as angiogenesis inhibitors" beginning with *in vitro* and *in vivo* testing of RGD peptides at Scripps in year one and culminating with the submission of an IND to the FDA in year three. Petitioner agreed to the material terms of the proposal on February 20, 1995 and on April 13, 1995, pledged $6 million over three years to fund research at Scripps. Petitioner's April 13 letter specified that Scripps would be responsible for testing RGD peptides produced by petitioner as potential drug candidates but that, once a primary candidate for clinical testing was in "the pipeline," petitioner would perform the toxicology tests necessary for FDA approval to proceed to clinical trials, *see* 21 CFR § 312.23(a)(8)(iii) (2005) (requirement that "nonclinical laboratory study" include a certification that it was performed under good laboratory practices); *see also* § 58.3(d) (2004) (defining "[n]onclinical laboratory study"). Scripps and petitioner concluded an agreement of continued collaboration in September 1995.

Pursuant to the agreement, Dr. Cheresh directed *in vitro* and *in vivo* experiments on RGD peptides provided by petitioner from 1995 to 1998. These experiments focused on EMD 66203 and two closely related derivatives, EMD 85189 and EMD 121974, and were designed to evaluate the suitability of each of the peptides as potential drug candidates. Accordingly, the tests measured the efficacy, specificity, and toxicity of the particular peptides as angiogenesis inhibitors, and evaluated their mechanism of action and pharmacokinetics in animals. Based on the test results, Scripps decided in 1997 that EMD 121974 was the most promising candidate for testing in humans. Over the same period, Scripps performed similar tests on LM609, a monoclonal antibody developed by Dr. Cheresh.[82] Scripps also conducted more basic research on organic mimetics designed to block α_V β_3 integrins in a manner similar to the RGD peptides; it appears that Scripps used the RGD peptides in these tests as "positive controls" against which to measure the efficacy of the mimetics.

In November 1996, petitioner initiated a formal project to guide one of its RGD peptides through the regulatory approval process in the United States and Europe. Petitioner originally directed its efforts at EMD 85189, but switched focus in April 1997 to EMD 121974. Petitioner subsequently discussed EMD 121974 with officials at the FDA. In October 1998, petitioner shared its research on RGD peptides with the National Cancer Institute (NCI), which agreed to sponsor clinical trials. Although the fact was excluded from evidence at trial, the lower court's opinion reflects that NCI filed an IND for EMD 121974 in 1998.

---

81. In the proceedings below, the Court of Appeals held that respondents' patents covered the cyclic RGD peptides developed by petitioner. Petitioner does not contest that ruling here.

82. Scripps licensed the patent for the monoclonal antibody to Ixsys, a California biotechnology company. Based on research conducted at Scripps and at Ixsys in consultation with Dr. Cheresh, an IND application for a humanized version of the antibody called Vitaxin was filed with the FDA on December 30, 1996. In addition to toxicology tests, the application included information from Dr. Cheresh's *in vitro* and *in vivo* experiments related to the antibody's mechanism of action and efficacy as an inhibitor of angiogenesis. Ixsys began clinical testing of the antibody as an angiogenesis inhibitor in February 1997.

B

On July 18, 1996, respondents filed a patent-infringement suit against petitioner, Scripps, and Dr. Cheresh in the District Court for the Southern District of California. Respondents' complaint alleged that petitioner willfully infringed and induced others to infringe respondents' patents by supplying the RGD peptide to Scripps, and that Dr. Cheresh and Scripps infringed the same patents by using the RGD peptide in experiments related to angiogenesis. Respondents sought damages from petitioner and a declaratory judgment against Dr. Cheresh and Scripps. Petitioner answered that its actions involving the RGD peptides did not infringe respondents' patents, and that in any event they were protected by the common-law research exemption and 35 U.S.C. § 271(e)(1).

At the conclusion of trial, the District Court held that, with one exception, petitioner's pre-1995 actions related to the RGD peptides were protected by the common-law research exemption, but that a question of fact remained as to whether petitioner's use of the RGD peptides after 1995 fell within the § 271(e)(1) safe harbor. With the consent of the parties, the District Court gave the following instruction regarding the § 271(e)(1) exemption:

> "To prevail on this defense, [petitioner] must prove by a preponderance of the evidence that it would be objectively reasonable for a party in [petitioner's] and Scripps' situation to believe that there was a decent prospect that the accused activities would contribute, relatively directly, to the generation of the kinds of information that are likely to be relevant in the processes by which the FDA would decide whether to approve the product in question.
>
> "Each of the accused activities must be evaluated separately to determine whether the exemption applies.
>
> "[Petitioner] does not need to show that the information gathered from a particular activity was actually submitted to the FDA."

The jury found that petitioner, Dr. Cheresh, and Scripps infringed respondents' patents and that petitioner had failed to show that its activities were protected by § 271(e)(1). It awarded damages of $15 million.

In response to post-trial motions, the District Court dismissed respondents' suit against Dr. Cheresh and Scripps, but affirmed the jury's damage award as supported by substantial evidence and denied petitioner's motion for judgment as a matter of law With respect to the last, the District Court explained that the evidence was sufficient to show that "any connection between the infringing Scripps experiments and FDA review was insufficiently direct to qualify for the [§ 271(e)(1) exemption]."

A divided panel of the Court of Appeals for the Federal Circuit affirmed in part, and reversed in part. The panel majority affirmed the denial of judgment as a matter of law to petitioner, on the ground that § 271(e)(1)'s safe harbor did not apply because "the Scripps work sponsored by [petitioner] was not clinical testing to supply information to the FDA, but only general biomedical research to identify new pharmaceutical compounds." It reversed the District Court's refusal to modify the damages award, and remanded for further proceedings.[83] Judge Newman dissented on both points. The panel unanimously affirmed the District Court's ruling that respondents' patents covered the cyclic RGD peptides developed by petitioner. We granted certiorari to review the Court of Appeals' construction of § 271(e)(1).

83. On remand, the District Court reduced the damages award to $6.375 million.

III

As described earlier, 35 U.S.C. § 271(e)(1) provides that "[i]t shall not be an act of infringement to ... use ... or import into the United States a patented invention ... solely for uses reasonably related to the development and submission of information under a Federal law which regulates the ... use ... of drugs." Though the contours of this provision are not exact in every respect, the statutory text makes clear that it provides a wide berth for the use of patented drugs in activities related to the federal regulatory process.

As an initial matter, we think it apparent from the statutory text that § 271(e)(1)'s exemption from infringement extends to all uses of patented inventions that are reasonably related to the development and submission of *any* information under the FDCA. This necessarily includes preclinical studies of patented compounds that are appropriate for submission to the FDA in the regulatory process. There is simply no room in the statute for excluding certain information from the exemption on the basis of the phase of research in which it is developed or the particular submission in which it could be included.[84]

Respondents concede the breadth of § 271(e)(1) in this regard, but argue that the only preclinical data of interest to the FDA is that which pertains to the safety of the drug in humans. In respondents' view, preclinical studies related to a drug's efficacy, mechanism of action, pharmacokinetics, and pharmacology are not reasonably included in an IND or an NDA, and are therefore outside the scope of the exemption. We do not understand the FDA's interest in information gathered in preclinical studies to be so constrained. To be sure, its regulations provide that the agency's "primary objectives in reviewing an IND are ... to assure the safety and rights of subjects," 21 CFR 312.22(a) (2005), but it does not follow that the FDA is not interested in reviewing information related to other characteristics of a drug. To the contrary, the FDA requires that applicants include in an IND summaries of the pharmacological, toxicological, pharmacokinetic, and biological qualities of the drug in animals. *See* § 312.23(a)(5); Department of Health and Human Services, Guidance for Industry, Good Clinical Practice: Consolidated Guidance 45 (Apr.1996) ("The results of all relevant nonclinical pharmacology, toxicology, pharmacokinetic, and investigational product metabolism studies should be provided in summary form. This summary should address the methodology used, the results, and a discussion of the relevance of the findings to the investigated therapeutic and the possible unfavorable and unintended effects in humans"). The primary (and, in some cases, only) way in which a drugmaker may obtain such information is through preclinical *in vitro* and *in vivo* studies.

Moreover, the FDA does not evaluate the safety of proposed clinical experiments in a vacuum; rather, as the statute and regulations reflect, it asks whether the proposed clinical trial poses an "unreasonable risk." 21 U.S.C. § 355(i)(3)(B)(i); see also 21 CFR § 312.23(a)(8) (2005) (requiring applicants to include pharmacological and toxicological studies that serve as the basis of their conclusion that clinical testing would be "reasonably safe"); § 56.111(a)(2) (2004) (providing that the Institutional Review Boards that oversee clinical trials must consider whether the "[r]isks to subjects are reasonable

84. Although the Court of Appeals' opinion suggests in places that § 271(e)(1)'s exemption from infringement is limited to research conducted in *clinical* trials we do not understand it to have adopted that position. The Court of Appeals recognized that information included in an IND would come within § 271(e)(1)'s safe harbor. Because an IND must be filed *before* clinical trials may begin, such information would necessarily be developed in preclinical studies.

in relation to anticipated benefits"). This assessment involves a comparison of the risks and the benefits associated with the proposed clinical trials. As the Government's brief, filed on behalf of the FDA, explains, the "FDA might allow clinical testing of a drug that posed significant safety concerns if the drug had a sufficiently positive potential to address a serious disease, although the agency would not accept similar risks for a drug that was less likely to succeed or that would treat a less serious medical condition." Accordingly, the FDA directs that an IND must provide sufficient information for the investigator to "make his/her own unbiased risk-benefit assessment of the appropriateness of the proposed trial." Such information necessarily includes preclinical studies of a drug's efficacy in achieving particular results.

Respondents contend that, even accepting that the FDA is interested in preclinical research concerning drug characteristics other than safety, the experiments in question here are necessarily disqualified because they were not conducted in conformity with the FDA's good laboratory practices regulations. This argument fails for at least two reasons. First, the FDA's requirement that preclinical studies be conducted under "good laboratory practices" applies only to experiments on drugs "to determine their safety," 21 CFR §58.3(d). *See* 21 CFR §58.1(a); §312.23(a)(8)(iii) (2005) (only "nonclinical laboratory study subject to the good laboratory practice regulations under part 58" must certify compliance with good laboratory practice regulations). The good laboratory practice regulations do not apply to preclinical studies of a drug's efficacy, mechanism of action, pharmacology, or pharmacokinetics. Second, FDA regulations do not provide that even safety-related experiments not conducted in compliance with good laboratory practices regulations are not suitable for submission in an IND. Rather, such studies must include "a brief statement of the reason for the noncompliance."

The Court of Appeals' conclusion that §271(e)(1) did not protect petitioner's provision of the patented RGD peptides for research at Scripps appeared to rest on two somewhat related propositions. First, the court credited the fact that the "Scripps-Merck experiments did not supply information for submission to the [FDA], but instead identified the best drug candidate to subject to future clinical testing under the FDA processes." The court explained:

> "The FDA has no interest in the hunt for drugs that may or may not later undergo clinical testing for FDA approval. For instance, the FDA does not require information about drugs other than the compound featured in an [IND] application. Thus, the Scripps work sponsored by [petitioner] was not 'solely for uses reasonably related to' clinical testing for FDA."

Second, the court concluded that the exemption "does not globally embrace all experimental activity that at some point, however attenuated, may lead to an FDA approval process."[85]

We do not quibble with the latter statement. Basic scientific research on a particular compound, performed without the intent to develop a particular drug or a reasonable belief that the compound will cause the sort of physiological effect the researcher in-

85. The Court of Appeals also suggested that a limited construction of §271(e)(1) is necessary to avoid depriving so-called "research tools" of the complete value of their patents. Respondents have never argued the RGD peptides were used at Scripps as research tools, and it is apparent from the record that they were not. 331 F.3d, at 878 (Newman, J., dissenting) ("Use of an existing tool in one's research is quite different from study of the tool itself"). We therefore need not—and do not—express a view about whether, or to what extent, §271(e)(1) exempts from infringement the use of "research tools" in the development of information for the regulatory process.

tends to induce, is surely not "reasonably related to the development and submission of information" to the FDA. It does not follow from this, however, that § 271(e)(1)'s exemption from infringement categorically excludes either (1) experimentation on drugs that are not ultimately the subject of an FDA submission or (2) use of patented compounds in experiments that are not ultimately submitted to the FDA. Under certain conditions, we think the exemption is sufficiently broad to protect the use of patented compounds in both situations.

As to the first proposition, it disregards the reality that, even at late stages in the development of a new drug, scientific testing is a process of trial and error. In the vast majority of cases, neither the drugmaker nor its scientists have any way of knowing whether an initially promising candidate will prove successful over a battery of experiments. That is the reason they conduct the experiments. Thus, to construe § 271(e)(1), as the Court of Appeals did, not to protect research conducted on patented compounds for which an IND is not ultimately filed is effectively to limit assurance of exemption to the activities necessary to seek approval of a generic drug. One can know at the outset that a particular compound will be the subject of an eventual application to the FDA only if the active ingredient in the drug being tested is identical to that in a drug that has already been approved.

The statutory text does not require such a result. Congress did not limit § 271(e)(1)'s safe harbor to the development of information for inclusion in a submission to the FDA; nor did it create an exemption applicable only to the research relevant to filing an ANDA for approval of a generic drug. Rather, it exempted from infringement *all* uses of patented compounds "reasonably related" to the process of developing information for submission under *any* federal law regulating the manufacture, use, or distribution of drugs. We decline to read the "reasonable relation" requirement so narrowly as to render § 271(e)(1)'s stated protection of activities leading to FDA approval for all drugs illusory. Properly construed, § 271(e)(1) leaves adequate space for experimentation and failure on the road to regulatory approval. At least where a drugmaker has a reasonable basis for believing that a patented compound may work, through a particular biological process, to produce a particular physiological effect, and uses the compound in research that, if successful, would be appropriate to include in a submission to the FDA, that use is "reasonably related" to the "development and submission of information under ... Federal law." § 271(e)(1).

For similar reasons, the use of a patented compound in experiments that are not themselves included in a "submission of information" to the FDA does not, standing alone, render the use infringing. The relationship of the use of a patented compound in a particular experiment to the "development and submission of information" to the FDA does not become more attenuated (or less reasonable) simply because the data from that experiment are left out of the submission that is ultimately passed along to the FDA. Moreover, many of the uncertainties that exist with respect to the selection of a specific drug exist as well with respect to the decision of what research to include in an IND or NDA. As a District Court has observed, "[I]t will not always be clear to parties setting out to seek FDA approval for their new product exactly which kinds of information, and in what quantities, it will take to win that agency's approval." This is especially true at the preclinical stage of drug approval. FDA regulations provide only that "[t]he amount of information on a particular drug that must be submitted in an IND ... depends upon such factors as the novelty of the drug, the extent to which it has been studied previously, the known or suspected risks, and the developmental phase of the drug." 21 CFR § 312.22(b). We thus agree with the Government that the use of patented compounds in preclinical studies is protected under § 271(e)(1) as long as there is a reasonable basis for believing that the experiments will produce "the types of information that are relevant to an IND or NDA."

...

Before the Court of Appeals, petitioner challenged the sufficiency of the evidence supporting the jury's finding that it failed to show that "all of the accused activities are covered by [§ 271(e)(1)]." That court rejected the challenge on the basis of a construction of § 271(e)(1) that was not consistent with the text of that provision or the relevant jury instruction.[86] Thus, the evidence presented at trial has yet to be reviewed under the standards set forth in the jury instruction, which we believe to be consistent with, if less detailed than, the construction of § 271(e)(1) that we adopt today. We decline to undertake a review of the sufficiency of the evidence under a proper construction of § 271(e)(1) for the first time here. Accordingly, we vacate the judgment of the Court of Appeals and remand the case for proceedings consistent with this opinion.

4. Know-How and Trade Secret Law

Although patent protection is often deemed the best way to secure rights to core life sciences inventions, trade secret protection is used quite frequently as well. In cases where a patent is granted for a core invention, there is still a substantial amount of both "positive" and "negative" know-how. The former are practical tips on how to use the full technology developed, which is often broader than the patented invention. The latter are practical tips on what *does not* work in exploiting the full technology. This know-how is frequently not patentable itself, and so trade secret protection is really the only other IP category that might afford some exclusivity. At the same time, in some cases the core invention will fail to receive a patent, or it will be clear that it is not patentable from the beginning. For these inventions, trade secret protection will again provide the only viable IP rights. In limited cases, an inventor or research entity might opt not to patent a patentable invention, instead wagering that the invention is a good candidate for trade secret protection. In these cases, the inventor/research entity is banking on the potentially greater value of the indefinite term of trade secret protection—the owner retains exclusivity for as long as it can maintain and practice the invention as a secret—over the fixed twenty-year term of patent protection.

Trade secret law operates for the most part as state law and most states have adopted the Uniform Trade Secrets Act, excerpted below.

---

86. The relevant jury instruction provided only that there must be a "decent prospect that the accused activities would contribute, relatively directly, to the generation of the kinds of information that are likely to be relevant in the processes by which the FDA would decide whether to approve the product in question." It did not say that, to fall within § 271(e)(1)'s exemption from infringement, the patented compound used in experimentation must be the subject of an eventual application to the FDA. And it expressly rejected the notion that the exemption only included experiments that produced information included in an IND or NDA.

Uniform Trade Secret Act

National Conference of Commissioners on Uniform State Laws (NCCUSL) (1985)

SECTION 1. DEFINITIONS. As used in this [Act], unless the context requires otherwise:

(1) "Improper means" includes theft, bribery, misrepresentation, breach or inducement of a breach of a duty to maintain secrecy, or espionage through electronic or other means;

(2) "Misappropriation" means:

(i) acquisition of a trade secret of another by a person who knows or has reason to know that the trade secret was acquired by improper means; or

(ii) disclosure or use of a trade secret of another without express or implied consent by a person who

(A) used improper means to acquire knowledge of the trade secret; or

(B) at the time of disclosure or use, knew or had reason to know that his knowledge of the trade secret was

(I) derived from or through a person who had utilized improper means to acquire it;

(II) acquired under circumstances giving rise to a duty to maintain its secrecy or limit its use; or

(III) derived from or through a person who owed a duty to the person seeking relief to maintain its secrecy or limit its use; or

(C) before a material change of his [or her] position, knew or had reason to know that it was a trade secret and that knowledge of it had been acquired by accident or mistake.

...

(4) "Trade secret" means information, including a formula, pattern, compilation, program, device, method, technique, or process, that:

(i) derives independent economic value, actual or potential, from not being generally known to, and not being readily ascertainable by proper means by, other persons who can obtain economic value from its disclosure or use, and

(ii) is the subject of efforts that are reasonable under the circumstances to maintain its secrecy.

SECTION 2. INJUNCTIVE RELIEF.

(a) Actual or threatened misappropriation may be enjoined. Upon application to the court, an injunction shall be terminated when the trade secret has ceased to exist, but the injunction may be continued for an additional reasonable period of time in order to eliminate commercial advantage that otherwise would be derived from the misappropriation.

(b) In exceptional circumstances, an injunction may condition future use upon payment of a reasonable royalty for no longer than the period of time for which use could have been prohibited. Exceptional circumstances include, but are not limited to, a material and prejudicial change of position prior to acquiring knowledge or reason to know of misappropriation that renders a prohibitive injunction inequitable.

(c) In appropriate circumstances, affirmative acts to protect a trade secret may be compelled by court order.

SECTION 3. DAMAGES.

(a) Except to the extent that a material and prejudicial change of position prior to acquiring knowledge or reason to know of misappropriation renders a monetary recovery inequitable, a complainant is entitled to recover damages for misappropriation. Damages can include both the actual loss caused by misappropriation and the unjust enrichment caused by misappropriation that is not taken into account in computing actual loss. In lieu of damages measured by any other methods, the damages caused by misappropriation may be measured by imposition of liability for a reasonable royalty for a misappropriator's unauthorized disclosure or use of a trade secret.

(b) If willful and malicious misappropriation exists, the court may award exemplary damages in an amount not exceeding twice any award made under subsection (a).

SECTION 4. ATTORNEY'S FEES. If (i) a claim of misappropriation is made in bad faith, (ii) a motion to terminate an injunction is made or resisted in bad faith, or (iii) willful and malicious misappropriation exists, the court may award reasonable attorney's fees to the prevailing party.

SECTION 5. PRESERVATION OF SECRECY. In an action under this [Act], a court shall preserve the secrecy of an alleged trade secret by reasonable means, which may include granting protective orders in connection with discovery proceedings, holding in-camera hearings, sealing the records of the action, and ordering any person involved in the litigation not to disclose an alleged trade secret without prior court approval.

SECTION 6. STATUTE OF LIMITATIONS. An action for misappropriation must be brought within 3 years after the misappropriation is discovered or by the exercise of reasonable diligence should have been discovered. For the purposes of this section, a continuing misappropriation constitutes a single claim....

Syntron Bioresearch, Inc. v. Fan

2002 WL 660446 (Cal. App. 4 Dist.) (unpublished and nonprecedential)

Justice Huffman.

Joe Fan appeals a judgment for Syntron Bioresearch, Inc. (Syntron) entered after a bench trial on its complaint for conspiracy, misappropriation of trade secrets and several other related causes of action against Genix Biotek, Inc. (Genix), Fan and several other defendants. Fan was found liable for $5,217,601 in exemplary damages, jointly and severally liable for $3,820,317 in compensatory damages plus prejudgment interest at 7 percent per annum, and jointly and severally liable for reasonable attorney fees and costs. He contends the trial court lacked subject matter jurisdiction because the case was subject to exclusive federal jurisdiction given Syntron's right to relief necessarily rested on substantial federal questions of law regarding patent infringement. Fan also asserts Syntron failed to demonstrate the elements required to establish a trade secret; the trial court erred in granting Syntron's motion in limine precluding evidence about Leeco cell lines; and Genix did not use any Syntron cell line. Continuing his multifaceted challenge, he argues the court failed to apply the correct theory of damages; the award of unjust enrichment damages and injunctive relief constituted impermissible double recovery; prejudgment interest was improper as a matter of law; the statement of decision was reversibly deficient; the court failed to offset certain good faith settlements; the punitive damages award was unwarranted; and the failure to issue an interlocutory judgment amounted to reversible error.

As we shall explain, we conclude Fan's contentions challenging jurisdiction, sufficiency of the evidence, liability, unjust enrichment damages, no offset for the consideration paid by the settling defendants to Syntron on the good-faith settlements, the statement of decision and other procedural matters are not well taken. However, his remaining damages contentions challenging the awards for prejudgment interest and punitive damages have merit. More specifically, the $508,468.49 prejudgment interest award is improper to the extent it awards interest on research and development costs and the $5,217,601 punitive damages award is excessive as a matter of law. Accordingly, we reverse those portions of the judgment with directions the trial court on remand recalculate the prejudgment interest award and reduce the punitive damages award to $2,331,812. In all other respects, the judgment is affirmed.

Factual and Procedural Background

In 1986, Joe Fan and Ted Chen founded Syntron, a small biotechnology research development and manufacturing company specializing in making diagnostic test kits. They also established an affiliated company in China called Tianjin Syntron (Tianjin). The two entities entered into a mutual nondisclosure agreement to protect the secrecy of each other's trade secrets. Six years later, Dr. James Lee joined Syntron as president. Before doing so, he had developed several useful hybridomas that produced antibodies that worked particularly well in pregnancy test kits. Upon joining Syntron, Dr. Lee sold it the hybridomas for $100,000. Syntron has since significantly grown, employing approximately 300 employees and occupying two large industrial buildings in Carlsbad, California. All employees are required to execute confidentiality agreements. Syntron manufactures more than 100 types of diagnostic test kits for detecting such things as pregnancy, ovulation, the presence of illegal drugs, and various diseases, such as hepatitis and cancer.

The vast majority of Syntron's test kits utilize monoclonal antibodies to detect minute amounts of targeted substances. For example, its pregnancy test targets the hormone known as human chorionic gonadotropin (hCG), which is produced by a pregnant woman. This technique for creating monoclonal antibodies was discovered in 1975 by two scientists at Cambridge University. The antibodies are produced by the B lymphocyte cells of the immune system. That is, by fusing a B cell with an immortal cancer cell results in a "hybridoma" that if properly cared for can secrete identical monoclonal antibodies forever. A monoclonal antibody will bind to a certain epitope, occurring only on certain proteins. Because different monoclonal antibodies will bind to different epitopes, they can be used to detect specific proteins. Syntron and Dr. Lee created hybridomas that secrete monoclonal antibodies that bind to precise regions of the targeted molecules. These hybridomas were then copied into lines of identical cells. Syntron has more than 80 such hybridoma cell lines, each producing an antibody that binds to a particular epitope. They are stored in liquid nitrogen tanks at Syntron's research and development department until needed.

Of relevance here, four different antibodies are used in Syntron's pregnancy test. Through an outside supplier, Syntron purchased batches of the 5008 antibody, but not the hybridoma that secretes it, that binds to hCG. However, the 5008 antibody cross-reacts with the luteinizing hormone (LH), which is almost identical to hCG but indicates only ovulation and not pregnancy. Dr. Lee resolved this problem by creating the 1102 "scavenger" antibody that blocks the 5008 antibody from binding to LH. He also created the 1004 antibody, which avoids the "hook effect," a paradox in which the 5008 antibody actually binds less effectively as the concentration of hCG increases, potentially giving a false negative. Finally, before Dr. Lee arrived, Syntron created the 1001 hybridoma cell line, that produces the capture antibody used on the test line of the pregnancy and ovulation test kits. Consequently, Syntron asserts these latter three cell lines are its property.

The manufacturing processes for each of Syntron's tests are set out in its proprietary Good Manufacturing Practices (GMP) manuals. Each manual contains essentially a recipe for the particular test covered, whether it is pregnancy, drug, hepatitis, etc. Each production process is designed to work solely with Syntron's particular antibodies. The recipe describes the steps to be followed in preparing and manufacturing the test kits and in mixing and applying the many chemicals and components that make them up. The GMP manuals include detailed lists of the necessary raw materials, specialty chemicals and approved suppliers for each test, the result of years of experimentation.

Similarly, Syntron has refined and customized its manufacturing equipment. Over the years, it has developed an extensive list of customers from all over the world.

Fan was Syntron's treasurer and quality control manager, as well as a member of its board of directors and a 17.5 percent shareholder. He decided to misappropriate Syntron's trade secrets and establish his own company in August 1995, first calling it Taigene Biotech and then later Genix. Genix recruited key Syntron managers to help. The Genix facility resembled Syntron's.

After a former Syntron employee discovered Genix and reported its activities to Dr. Lee confirming his suspicions and a supplier apologized to him for providing its packaging to Genix, Syntron investigated. It hired private investigators who found numerous incriminating documents in Genix's trash. Although many of them had been shredded, the investigators were able to reassemble them. They found partial copies of Syntron's production process, with pink highlighting showing how to renumber the steps to disguise the process as that belonging to Genix. That renumbering corresponded exactly with Genix's printed production process, as these modifications had no effect on the end product. Moreover, in the beginning of 1997, Dr. Lee discovered all 80 different cell lines had been taken from the spare nitrogen tank.

On June 10, 1997, Syntron filed a complaint for conspiracy, misappropriation of trade secrets, breach of fiduciary duty, breach of contract, and several other related causes of action against six individual defendants, including Fan and Genix. In September, the trial court issued a preliminary injunction barring Genix and its employees from using any trade secrets, trademark or tradename belonging to Syntron or manufacturing diagnostic test kits relating to pregnancy or drugs of abuse.[87] Before trial, Syntron dismissed with prejudice all claims against Dr. Vladimir Cherepakhin and Dr. Louis Liu in exchange for their promises to testify truthfully at trial, to provide consulting services, to keep Syntron secrets confidential and not to compete with Syntron. On November 23, 1998, a bench trial began during which the court would hear testimony from 40 witnesses and admit 744 exhibits.

87. The defendants evaded the injunction by forming another company, called Nobel Biotek, and making former Genix employee, Emily Hwang, the president. Upon being caught, they moved their equipment to a new location and established another company called Nobel Bioscience. Fan was videotaped helping unload Genix's equipment at the new location and visiting the site regularly.

At trial, Dr. Liu, Syntron's head of research and development, acknowledged he worked for Syntron by day and Genix by night, helping the latter with the misappropriated hybridomas. He also acknowledged he gave Genix a list of the exact models of equipment Syntron used in its production process. He also admitted that the president of Genix, Frank Lin, advised him to invest in Genix using a false name. He used the name of his father, who resided in China. Dr. Cherepakhin, Syntron's production manager, admitted that while he was still employed by Syntron, he sold Genix's products to Syntron's customers in Russia. In addition, Michael Rainey of Waterfront Packaging, which manufactured Syntron's packaging, admitted that Genix persuaded him to print Syntron packaging for Genix. The packages were duplicates of Syntron's packaging, complete with its trademarked name and logo. Thus, Genix, using Syntron's employees and production processes, put its own tests in the counterfeit Syntron packaging and marketed them to Syntron's customers.

Genix's production process was essentially identical to Syntron's. Dr. Joel Ehrenkranz so testified, explaining that the order of steps had been changed and that the lot size had been reduced so that the volume of each ingredient could be reduced pro rata, but that it was otherwise identical. He noted that Genix had copied Syntron's process so slavishly, that it contained the same typographical errors. Genix employee Hwang admitted that she used Syntron's production process documents as a reference guide, making modifications as required by the procedure followed by Genix. Wen Young, a former Syntron production department employee, admitted he physically took Syntron's production manuals.

Examination of samples of Genix's antibodies revealed that the odds against the Genix and Syntron antibodies being derived independently was more than 1000 to one. This conclusion was the result of analyzing the antibodies using mass spectrometry, which breaks down the antibodies into individual amino acids, and gives the amino acid sequence of each (antibodies are proteins which are made up of amino acids). The trial court found the defense story of the hybridoma cell lines having been unexpectedly dropped off free of charge at Genix by an unknown man named Dr. Su, thus refocusing Genix's original business from that of a rabbit farm to producing hospital-quality test kits, as "patently incredible."[88] Indeed, one Genix director was so enamored with the Dr. Su story that he testified the latter had also dropped off completed drug test kits. The next witness, another Genix director, testified the other director had admitted during the break that the story was false and that he had made it up on the stand.

Fan was inextricably involved in Genix. Its corporate secretary, Dr. Long Lee, wrote in the company's minutes that a person named Yen Chueh Hsu attended a shareholders' meeting. According to Genix records, Hsu was the largest shareholder, owning 33 percent of the stock, and had paid only a penny per share ($3,135), while others paid a dollar per share (or later ten dollars per share). The penny per share price was offered to those who had made additional, non-monetary contributions such as contribution of technology. Hsu turned out to be the sister-in-law of Fan's wife, a relative who lived and worked in Taiwan. Bank records showed that the Hsu investment in Genix came from an account that Fan's wife, Su-Jen Fan, alone controlled, which she utilized as an appar-

88. Casting aside [sic] the defendants changed their business plan and began to manufacture pregnancy tests without employing any scientists, Genix was selling five types of test kits (pregnancy, morphine, methamphetamine, cocaine and marijuana) within two months. These sales were of doubtful legality, because the defendants never obtained the required approval from the Federal Drug Administration (FDA) or the California Department of Health Services.

ent conduit for Genix and for various other purposes including the payment of her husband's personal expenses. A handwritten note by Lin in Genix's bank records, next to the $3,135 deposit, read "Joe Fan." Genix's accountant also wrote next to that deposit amount "Joe Fan."

On May 4, 1999, the trial court found the defendants jointly and severally liable on all causes of action. It awarded compensatory damages of $4,328,789.49 and punitive damages against Fan of $5,217,601, plus attorney fees and costs of $2,442,853. The court noted that the evidence was so massive that on many of the causes of action Syntron had proved liability beyond a reasonable doubt. The court also concluded that the defendants' testimony was uniformly incredible as much of it was completely unbelievable. Fan timely appealed.

The Trial Court Had Subject Matter Jurisdiction

Fan contends the trial court erred in denying his motion to dismiss the case for lack of subject matter jurisdiction,[89] asserting that to the extent Syntron's alleged trade secrets mirror the claims set forth in the United States patents the subject matter jurisdiction is federal. He argues that Syntron's right to relief necessarily depends on substantial questions of federal law, giving rise to exclusive federal jurisdiction. He explains that under state law Syntron must prove as part of its prima facie case that its alleged "trade secrets" derived independent economic value, actual or potential, from not being generally known to the public or to other persons who can obtain economic value from its disclosure or use. However, to the extent the alleged "trade secrets" mirrored patent claims, he asserts the information was easily acquired through the patents and thus did not amount to trade secrets that could be misappropriated. Moreover, to the extent Syntron's "trade secrets" within its misappropriation claim duplicated patent claims, he suggests they form in reality a patent infringement action, disguised as a trade secret action that gives rise to exclusive federal jurisdiction. As we shall explain, the trial court had subject matter jurisdiction.

Federal courts have exclusive jurisdiction over "any civil action arising under any Act of Congress relating to patents." However, not every matter that incidentally involves United States patents are governed exclusively by federal law. A case arises under federal patent law where "the plaintiff ... set[s] up some right, title or interest under the patent laws, or, at least, make[s] it appear that some right or privilege will be defeated by one construction, or sustained by the opposite construction of these laws." "'Arising under' jurisdiction is measured by the 'well-pleaded complaint' rule. Under this rule, '7F'... federal jurisdiction exists only when a federal question is presented on the face of the plaintiff's properly pleaded complaint." In other words, only in those cases where a well-pleaded complaint establishes either that federal patent law creates the cause of action or that the plaintiff's right to relief necessarily depends on resolution of a substantial question of federal patent law that as pleaded constitutes a necessary element of one of the plaintiff's claims. The determination of whether a claim arises under federal patent law must be made from what necessarily appears in the plaintiff's statement of

---

89. More precisely, in his reply to Syntron's opposition to his motion to dismiss, Fan redrafted the motion in the alternative, requesting the court to dismiss the case or recess it and reopen the case in chief to conduct an evidentiary hearing on the issues of subject matter jurisdiction. In his opening brief, Fan also asserts for the first time the trial court abused its discretion in failing to retain its own expert pursuant to Evidence Code section 730 to compare Syntron's alleged trade secrets with the information disclosed in the various United States patents.

his or her claim, unaided by anything alleged in anticipation or avoidance of defenses which defendant may interpose. Consequently, a case that raises a federal patent-law defense does not, for that reason alone, arise under federal patent law, even where it is anticipated in the plaintiff's complaint and both parties acknowledge it is the only true question at issue in the case. Moreover, "a claim supported by alternative theories in the complaint may not form the basis for [exclusive federal] jurisdiction unless patent law is essential to each of those theories."

"Thus, there is broad state jurisdiction over matters affecting patents, the 'Supreme Court has clearly blessed such state power,' and the federal courts have shown a clear lack of concern with state adjudication of such matters. The federal courts have exclusive jurisdiction only over cases arising under the federal patent laws and not over patent questions. The state courts are said to be fully competent to adjudicate patent questions that come before them in contract, property and tort cases so long as the case itself does not arise under the patent laws."

For example, regarding trade secrets, a complaint seeking to enjoin former employees from using to their advantage information obtained in course of employment concerning secret plans and designs for a patented amusement device manufactured and distributed by plaintiffs, and plaintiffs' customer lists, stated a cause of action for some equitable relief of which state court had jurisdiction and was not a matter arising under federal patent laws within the exclusive jurisdiction of the federal courts. Similarly, a complaint setting forth a series of causes of action based upon misappropriation of plaintiff's technology by defendants who utilized it in their patent application was appropriate for state court jurisdiction. However, where under state law a business disparagement claim requires plaintiff to prove as part of its prima facie case the falsity of defendant's allegedly disparaging statement which accused plaintiff of infringing a patent, then in order to establish the falsity, plaintiff must show that its product does not infringe the patent. Consequently, under such circumstances, plaintiff's right to relief necessarily depended upon resolution of a substantial question of patent law, in that proof relating to patent infringement constituted a necessary element of plaintiff's business disparagement claim.

Here, Fan and the other defendants contended in their motion the court lacked subject matter jurisdiction because the claims within Syntron's Patent No. 5,384,264 mirror its designation of trade secrets and thus to the extent they are duplicative the misappropriation actions are in reality patent infringement claims giving rise to exclusive federal jurisdiction.[90] In its opposition, Syntron argued the trial court had jurisdiction to resolve a patent question asserted as a defense (e.g. whether the patent discloses Syntron's trade secrets). It explained that patent rights and trade secret rights can coexist in the same technology, as pertinently here where the inventor combines various patented elements into a process or devise. Syntron further asserted that its trade secrets are separate and distinct from the test kit design concept set forth in the patent. It argued that its trade secret designation of "formulae, processes, methods and techniques" used by it in the manufacturing and evaluation of its diagnostic test kits, as well as its hybridoma cell lines, includes its manufacturing and quality testing procedures and cell lines used

---

90. In their motion, the defendants compared the language of Syntron's first trade secret claim within its designation of "[t]he structure and internal construction, make-up and components of Syntron diagnostic tests, including, without limitation ..." with the language of Syntron's first claim under the patent stating "[a]n apparatus for use in assays of fluid samples to detect the presence of one or more ligands of interest therein, comprising...."

to produce its proprietary antibodies, antigens, proteins and reagents, that are not discussed within the patents. Moreover, Syntron's marketing software and customer lists, supplier or material lists, sales and business plans or other business related information are not included within any patent. Fan and the defendants replied by modifying its motion to alternatively request the court to permit them to re-open their case to introduce new evidence pertaining to other patents, including Leeco Patent No. 5,026,653 allegedly disclosing the immunological principles necessary to construct a pregnancy kit using Syntron's monoclonal antibodies. In denying defendants' motion, the trial court explained:

> "Contrary to most questions involving jurisdiction, this Court had the opportunity of hearing all of the evidence in the case prior to being presented with the jurisdictional question. Having reviewed the evidence, it is crystal clear that this Court need not decide any patent law issue for the plaintiff to prevail on its allegations of theft of proprietary information."

Later, in its statement of decision, the trial court declared:

> "A review of the patent material presented after trial was utilized only to determine any jurisdictional questions involved. Patents played no part of plaintiff's case, were never referenced by plaintiff, nor was the court required to review any portion of any patent in the case in chief to determine liability. While there may be a 'patent question' involved, the Court finds that it has jurisdiction to resolve those issues that were before it."

The trial court correctly denied the motion, as Fan and the other defendants simply and belatedly posed an incidental "patent question" fully within the court's jurisdiction. The patent question they belatedly posed after trial was in the nature of a defense regarding whether Syntron had disclosed within its patents its alleged trade secrets rendering them unactionable as such. Syntron correctly asserts that it bears the burden of proving the trade secret element, as the disclosure of technological know-how is not an issue of patent law, but rather a question of fact. Expert testimony can compare the information disclosed in a patent to the information claimed by Syntron to be a trade secret and determine whether there has been disclosure without applying any federal patent law. State courts thus have jurisdiction to determine whether a plaintiff's trade secrets have been disclosed in a patent.[91] In contrast, issues of federal patent law which give rise to exclusive federal jurisdiction include infringement, inventor-

---

91. Fan's suggestion the trial court, by granting Syntron's motion in limine prohibiting the defense from introducing evidence that Syntron's technology allegedly infringed on patents owned by Becton Dickinson, precluded it from presenting evidence that Syntron's trade secrets were disclosed in various patents, is simply inaccurate. The defense was free throughout the trial to present evidence that Syntron's trade secrets were disclosed by patents held by Syntron or anyone else.

Additionally, the trial court did not abuse its discretion by not reopening the evidence to determine whether Syntron's trade secrets were disclosed by technology described in eight patents. "A motion to reopen a case for further evidence can be granted only on a showing of good cause. Reopening is not a matter of a right but rests upon the sound discretion of the trial court. That discretion should not be overturned on appeal absent a clear showing of abuse." Here, mindful that issued patents give constructive notice of their content to all Fan failed to establish good cause because five of the patents were issued at least seven years before the close of his case (Leeco Patent No. 5,026,653 (6/25/91); Leeco Patent No. 4,722,889 (2/2/88); Becton Dickinson Patent No. 4,703,017 (10/27/87); Abbott Patent No. 5,073,484 (12/17/91); Akzona Patent No. 4,313,734 (2/2/82)), one he acknowledged having notice of that predated the filing of the complaint (Syntron Patent No. 5,384,264 (1/24/95)), another that likewise predated the filing of the complaint (Becton Dickinson Patent No. 5,591,645 (1/7/97)) and the remaining two were issued after the complaint was filed but

ship, abandonment and revival, the right to file an application, validity and enforceability. Syntron's misappropriation of trade secret claims do not depend on who invented the patents, whether they are valid or enforceable, or whether any person or entity is infringing them. Contrary to Fan's assertion otherwise, where alleged trade secrets prove to be duplicative of patent claims, it does not necessarily follow that a patent infringement action has been disguised as a trade secret claim giving rise to exclusive federal jurisdiction.

Fan next incorrectly contends Syntron's trademark infringement claims under the federal Lanham Act (15 U.S.C. § 1121), set forth in its 15th, 16th and 17th causes of action, fall within the exclusive jurisdiction of the federal courts. However, unlike the exclusive jurisdiction the federal courts have over patent and copyright claims (28 USC § 1338(a)), the federal and state courts have concurrent jurisdiction over cases arising under the Lanham Act.[92]

Trade Secrets Were Misappropriated

Fan contends Syntron failed to establish the elements required for a trade secret.[93] Specifically, he asserts there was no evidence of "competitive advantage," there was no evidence of an alleged "trade secret" that was not "generally known," and there was insufficient evidence to show that Syntron had consistent security measures in place to protect the secrecy of its alleged trade secrets. Substantial evidence in the record establishes otherwise.

Upon its enactment of the Uniform Trade Secrets Act in 1994 (Civ. Code,[94] § 3426 et seq. (UTSA)), California effectively abandoned the broad approach of the Restatement of Torts in defining a trade secret and adopted the common-law definition. Section 3426.1, subdivision (d) defines "trade secret" as meaning:

> "information, including a formula, pattern, compilation, program, device, method, technique, or process, that:

---

before the trial started (Abbott Patent No. 5,654,162 (8/5/97); Syntron Patent No. 5,821,073 (10/13/98)).

92. Fan contends the trial court in finding infringement of Syntron's trademark under the Lanham Act failed to consider the fact that the only alleged use of the trademark was from one sale in Russia. He further argues that no testimony was taken regarding the ownership of the mark in Russia and whether United States trademarks or trade names in Russia are recognized. However, the record shows that Genix used Syntron's trademarks to sell counterfeit Syntron pregnancy test kits to Farmaplus, an American company, that then sold the test kits overseas. Even if Genix had sold the test kits directly to a purchaser in Russia, the Lanham Act confers extraterritorial jurisdiction over trademark infringement in foreign countries by American companies.

93. Although we address Fan's contention here and find it meritless, we note Syntron accurately points out that whether its technology constituted a trade secret does not necessarily relieve Fan from liability here because he was found liable for breach of fiduciary duty as an officer, manager, director and substantial shareholder of Syntron. The only cause of action requiring proof that Syntron possessed a trade secret was for misappropriation of trade secrets. The cause of action for breach of fiduciary duty does not require such proof. "In order to plead a cause of action for breach of fiduciary duty, there must be shown the existence of a fiduciary relationship, its breach, and damage proximately caused by the breach." Given his various capacities with Syntron, Fan had a fiduciary duty of loyalty to it, the breach of which under the factual circumstances presented here resulted in the same aggregate damages award the trial court made for the misappropriation of trade secrets, state trade name infringement, and punitive damages for the trade secret misappropriation. Consequently, dismissal of the misappropriation of trade secrets cause of action against Fan would have no effect on his total liability to Syntron if the breach of fiduciary duty cause of action were sustained.

94. All statutory references are to the Civil Code unless otherwise specified.

(1) Derives independent economic value, actual or potential, from not being generally known to the public or to other persons who can obtain economic value from its disclosure or use; and

(2) Is the subject of efforts that are reasonable under the circumstances to maintain its secrecy."

A reviewing court must accept the trial court's finding of a trade secret unless the record reveals no substantial evidence to support it....

The trial court concluded that Syntron "possessed multiple trade secrets, including monoclonal antibodies, hybridoma cell lines, processes for manufacturing pregnancy test kits, and GMP production documents including raw material specifications and customer lists deriving independent economic value both actual and potential from not being generally known to the public or other persons which secrets Syntron made reasonable efforts to maintain." Substantial evidence supports the trial court's determination. Syntron's expert, Dr. Joel Ehrenkranz, testified that he had reviewed and even audited many other companies' pregnancy test kit production processes and that Syntron's process included numerous unique elements. He testified as to four examples where Syntron's process was distinctly different from any other he had seen, involving the use of particular nitrocellulose membranes, a specific stabilizing chemical, a specific protein for blocking nonspecific binding and freeze drying or lyophilization. Moreover, Syntron's hybridoma cell lines,[95] each with a unique DNA sequence, and customer list were also trade secrets entitled to protection. These trade secrets had actual or potential economic value from not being generally known. The facts that the science of producing hybridomas is well known throughout the science community and the antibodies, elements or relevant information necessary for manufacturing pregnancy test kits can be acquired through various public sources, do not necessarily render the information found by the trial court to constitute trade secrets to be not so. Rather, the unique methodology of Syntron's processes, the discovery of certain antibodies and the formulistic combination and integration of these components, utilized to overcome problems with inaccurate results, shelf life and manufacturing efficiency amply warrants the determinations such information were trade secrets. Fan's further attempt to sidestep this issue by arguing that the only possible value in pregnancy test kits is accuracy, similarly ignores this uniqueness of Syntron's methodology. Granted, regarding the general availability of customer information, courts are reluctant to protect customer lists to the extent they reflect information which is readily ascertainable through public sources, such as business directories. However, "where the employer has expended time and effort identifying customers with particular needs or characteristics, courts will prohibit former employees from using this information to capture a share of the market. Such lists are to be distinguished from mere identities and locations of customers where anyone could easily identify the entities as potential customers. As a general principle, the more difficult information is to obtain, and more time and re-

95. Fan unpersuasively contends the trial court erred in granting Syntron's motion in limine precluding evidence regarding Leeco cell lines. He sought to introduce evidence that Dr. Lee allegedly stole technology from the company he formerly owned. The trial court ordered in limine that such evidence would not be admitted because the defendants had no standing to assert the misappropriation, concluding that any potential property dispute between Syntron and a third party was irrelevant as a matter of law regarding the question of whether the defendants misappropriated Syntron's trade secrets. The decision in *Germo Mfg. Co. v. McClellan*, 107 Cal.App. 532, 545–546, 290 P. 534 (1930), confirms the correctness of that ruling.

sources expended by an employer in gathering it, the more likely the court will find such information constitutes a trade secret." Such is the case here, as Syntron's customer list is thus entitled to protection.

Fan asserts a trade secret plaintiff like Syntron should have been required to prove what other competitors were doing, citing *National Tile Board Corp. v. Panelboard Mfg. Co.*, 99 A.2d 440, 444 (N.J. [Super. Ct. Ch. Div.]1953). Casting aside [sic] Fan waived this argument by not making it below, Syntron's expert, Dr. Ehrenkranz, testified that Syntron's production process and equipment are different from those of the many other competitors he had reviewed. It is ironic to note that Fan attempted to counter this testimony through a former Syntron employee who now works for Mizuho Diagnostics. However, when the witness was asked a detail regarding the process utilized by his company in making its pregnancy tests, he refused to answer, declaring that its process was a trade secret. He acknowledged that many companies utilize the same basic process, but vary considerably in their individual process details.

Fan challenges the trial court's finding Syntron took reasonable steps under the circumstances to maintain the secrecy of its information. However, he specifically addresses only the adequacy of the measures taken to protect the cell lines, thus waiving any such argument as to the remaining trade secrets. As we shall explain, substantial evidence supports the trial court's conclusion that Syntron took reasonable steps to protect the secrecy of its information. Its employees are required to sign confidentiality agreements; its personnel manuals emphasize the strictly confidential nature of their work for Syntron; confidential material was stamped as such; and, the facility itself is reasonably secure. Fan argues that the storage of the cell lines in unsecured locations in unlocked nitrogen tanks with no inventory system was unreasonable. Specifically, he contends that storing cell lines at Jung Wei Wu's home was unreasonable.[96] When Syntron occupied only one building, it needed to store a spare set of cell lines off-site in case of fire and did so at Fan's house. To avoid refilling the liquid nitrogen every month, Fan transferred the cell lines to the home of another Syntron employee, Wu. Dr. Lee discovered this only after Syntron opened its second building and the cell lines were returned. Wu and his wife testified that Dr. Lee told them that the cell lines they stored were those that he had stolen from Leeco. The Wus acknowledged they were founding shareholders in Genix. Fan also asserts that the storing of spare cell lines in liquid nitrogen tanks in an unlocked manner in Syntron's main building and in a similar manner in its adjacent building was unreasonable, because an employee could break in and steal them. As noted above, Syntron's employees, including Fan, were bound by their confidentiality agreements and the law not to steal their employer's property. Fan and the top managers and researchers had the only keys to that room. Fan also argues that it is unreasonable to send some of the cell lines to a company in China. That company, however, was Tianjin Syntron, a Syntron affiliate bound by a confidentiality agreement to protect Syntron's trade secrets. It was not an entity unknown to Syntron with which it had had no prior dealings.

Regarding misappropriation,[97] Fan does not challenge the trial court's finding that he and his co-conspirators stole Syntron's production process, customer lists and in-

96. Fan's reliance on the testimony of Dr. Trowbridge, Director of the Cancer Biology Laboratory of the Salk Institute, is misplaced. He testified only that if you wanted to protect a cell line you would not put it in the home of an *individual you neither knew nor trusted.* He also noted that the real problem with cell line theft is that it can be easily accomplished by simply taking a sample from a live culture, rendering the theft undetectable.

97. Under the UTSA, a trade secret is misappropriated where a person (1) acquires it knowing or having reason to know that it has been acquired by "improper means," or (2) discloses or uses a

ventory. He again addresses only the theft of the cell lines, asserting Genix did not "use any Syntron cell line." Substantial evidence supports the trial court finding Genix stole those cell lines. Syntron's expert, Dr. Weigel, compared Genix's antibodies to those of Syntron using mass spectrometry, which can readily detect a difference as small as an amino acid. She concluded that this test alone showed that it is highly improbable that Genix's cells were derived independently of those of Syntron. She specifically testified that she could find no convincing evidence the Syntron and Genix antibodies were different. She further broke down the antibodies to determine their amino-acid sequences, which are analogous to a DNA sequence. Genix's antibodies matched those of Syntron identically. The sequences were then run through a database of known proteins and found to match none. In fact, one Genix antibody and its Syntron counterpart were found to have a very rare type of mutation at exactly the same point. Dr. Weigel concluded that the likelihood these antibodies were independently derived was less than one in 1000, a "very small possibility." Fan's reliance on the testimony of his expert, Dr. Kym Faull, to the effect that any difference in the mass spectrometry results means that the antibodies are different, is misplaced. Dr. Faull abandoned that position when he was shown that even when the same antibody was run through the test twice, there were slight variations in the results. He conceded that only repeatable and consistent differences would mean that the antibodies were different. He then changed his mind about each of the four differences he had observed earlier, declaring that they either were not repeatable or were so insignificant that he would have to study them further to determine whether they were meaningful.

The Validity Of The Compensatory Damages Award And Injunction

Fan challenges the validity of the trial court's compensatory damages award to Syntron. The court awarded $3,820,317, plus prejudgment interest at the rate of 7 percent per year ($508,468.49), consisting of 75 percent of Syntron's research and development cost of $3,600,000 ($2,700,000); $760,679 for lost profits arising out of the sale of pregnancy test kits; $193,732 for lost profits for sales of stolen drugs-of-abuse tests; and $165,906 for sales of pregnancy test kits bearing Syntron trademarks. Fan contends this aggregate award that exceeds its gross sales ($837,859.87) by more than $3,400,000 is facially excessive. Noting Syntron had 80 other products besides the pregnancy test kits and drugs-of-abuse tests, he asserts the research and development cost attributable to the cited tests is excessive—a matter of conjecture given its uncertainty, which should have invoked the doctrine of reasonable royalty damages under section 3426.3, subdivision (b). He further contends that the court's award of unjust enrichment damages and injunctive relief constitutes an impermissible double recovery under section 3426.3. As we shall explain, we conclude that substantial evidence supports the trial court's award of research and development costs as a reasonable approximation of all misappropri-

---

trade secret of another without express or implied consent by a person who acquired it by "improper means" or, at the time of disclosure or to use, knew or had reason to know that his or her knowledge of the trade secret was derived by "improper means," under circumstances giving rise to the duty to maintain its secrecy he or limit its use, or in violation of a nondisclosure obligation, or (3) discloses or uses a trade secret after learning that it is a trade secret but before a material change of position. (§ 3426.1, subd. (b).) "'Improper means'" includes theft, bribery, misrepresentation, breach or inducement of a breach of a duty to maintain secrecy, or espionage through electronic or other means. Reverse engineering or independent derivation alone should not be considered improper means." (§ 3426.1, subd. (a).)

ated trade secrets relating to the pregnancy test kits and that the court's award of unjust enrichment damages and injunctive relief did not amount to double recovery.

Remedies under the UTSA for the misappropriation of trade secrets include injunctive relief, damages, royalties, punitive damages and attorney fees. (§§ 3426.2–3426.4) Section 3426.2, subdivision (a) authorizes the enjoining of actual or threatened misappropriation. Section 3426.3 provides several measures of damages upon proof of misappropriation of trade secrets. Under subdivision (a), a complainant may recover damages for the actual loss caused by misappropriation, as well as for any unjust enrichment not taken into account in computing actual loss damages. Subdivision (b) provides for an alternate remedy of the payment of royalties from future profits where "neither damages nor unjust enrichment caused by misappropriation are provable." The law is well settled that "the imposition of a reasonable royalty is reserved for those instances where the court finds that neither actual damages to the holder of the trade secret nor unjust enrichment to the user is provable." That is, royalties can neither be awarded as damages if actual damages or unjust enrichment are provable, nor combined with any other damage valuation method such as the cost of creating the trade secret. Such is the case here, as explained below. Finally, subdivision (c) and section 3426.4 respectively provide for the awarding of exemplary damages and attorney fees for willful and malicious misappropriation.

In challenging the compensatory damages award as being excessive and inferentially unsupported by the evidentiary record, Fan does not contend the trial court's assessments of lost profits attributable to the pregnancy test kits, drugs-of-abuse tests and pregnancy test kits bearing its trademark were arbitrary or unsupported by substantial evidence.[98] Rather, Fan focuses on the unjust enrichment award predicated upon 75 percent of Syntron's research and development costs incurred from 1990 through 1997. He asserts the award is excessive and the apportionment is arbitrary. He argues the evidence concerning the research and development costs for the trade secrets misappropriated is insufficient to justify the trial court's award of such a large amount. In reviewing this claim, we consider the whole record, view the evidence in light most favorable to the judgment, presume every fact the trier of fact could reasonably deduce from the evidence and indeed defer to the trier of fact's determination of the weight and credibility of the evidence. However, in order for the evidence to be substantial, it must be of ponderable legal significance. It must be reasonable in nature, credible and of solid value, substantial proof of the essentials that the law requires in a particular matter. "Although the plaintiff must prove damages, complete precision is not required. Evidence of speculative profits, speculative lost profits, or speculation as to the existence of damages are improper, but once the *existence* of damages or lost profits has been established, the

---

98. Indeed, the record amply supports the court's reasonable calculation of these amounts. As to the pregnancy test kits, Syntron provided audited financial records establishing its sales prices and profit margins. Genix made sales to Syntron's existing customers, customers that were contacts of Fan and unrelated customers. The court found that all of Genix's sales to Syntron's customers and Fan's contacts would have been made by Syntron but for Genix's wrongful conduct. Five percent of its sales to the unrelated customers would have been made by Syntron because it held a five percent share of the pregnancy test market. Multiplying Syntron's lost sales of 1,226,901 units by its profit margin of 62 cents per unit, the court arrived at $760,679 for Syntron's lost profits on pregnancy tests. As to the pregnancy test kits sold bearing Syntron's trademarks, the court reasonably awarded $165,906 in lost profits based on Genix's sales of 638,100 counterfeit Syntron pregnancy tests multiplied by its average profit margin of 26 cents per unit. Finally, as to the drugs-of-abuse tests, a different calculation was required because Genix actually stole the finished tests out of Syntron's warehouse. The court obtained its $193,732 award by multiplying the 149,025 tests sold by Genix by Syntron's sales price of $1.30 per unit.

courts are much more lenient in determining the *amount* of damages." Thus, plaintiff bears the burden of establishing with reasonable certainty the *existence* of damages, not its *amount*, as recovery will not be denied because of difficulty in ascertainment.

Preliminarily, *without considering the impact of the injunctive relief granted*, the record convincingly establishes that Syntron is entitled to damages for *any* unjust enrichment to Genix and Fan, savings attributable to the latter's not having to independently develop the misappropriated trade secrets and which was not taken into account in computing damages for actual loss. Syntron's damages theory was globally based on Genix's misappropriation of all 80 cell lines encased in the stolen nitrogen tank, not just the two pregnancy test antibodies that were allegedly produced by Genix and subject to detailed comparative analysis and testimony at trial, and the vast amount of proprietary information set forth in its trade secret designation. Consistent with this theory that the defendants misappropriated Syntron's comprehensive GMP manuals and all of their contents, its customized manufacturing equipment, and its extensive customer lists as well, the statement of decision does not limit the scope of its finding that the defendants misappropriated Syntron's trade secrets to only those two cell lines as Fan would like. The record amply supports Syntron's expert's opinion as to all research and development costs incurred by Syntron as to all its products. In fact, Fan acknowledged research and development costs were incurred by Syntron up until he left in 1997 and that the record supports $411,000 in such costs for all of Syntron's products. Misappropriated secrets need not be actually used or commercially implemented by defendants to form the basis for assessing actual damages under a research and development costs theory. Syntron's expert, Michael Samson, testified that Syntron spent $3.6 million to develop its trade secrets as to *all* its products during the time period of 1990 through 1997. Relying on Syntron's financial statements, Samson's $3.6 million figure included $1.3 million for fixed assets (property and equipment), $2.0 million in research and development expenses, and $300,000 for procuring cell lines. Consequently, Samson's *foundational* figure encompassing all of Syntron's research and development costs for all products was amply supported by the record and reasonable.

Although the trial court relied on Samson's $3.6 million figure in making its compensatory damages award, it reduced the sum by 25 percent, declaring in its statement of decision the resulting amount of $2.7 million reflects "the value of the development of the pregnancy tests." In other words, the trial court awarded unjust enrichment damages *only* for the value of research and development costs incurred in developing those misappropriated trade secrets related to the pregnancy tests. Fan asserts this "apportionment" does not reasonably reflect the unjust enrichment for those trade secrets actually misappropriated. He notes that during cross-examination, Samson acknowledged he did not know how much of either the $2 million in research and development expenses or the $300,000 in procurement expenses was spent on the pregnancy test kits. Moreover, Samson testified that he did not know how much money was spent individually on research and development for each Syntron product. When asked if he had an opinion as to how much money Syntron spent on developing products allegedly taken, he responded in the negative. He later testified that it would be difficult to segregate research and development costs on a product-by-product basis because Syntron simply did not do so in its accounting.

Preliminarily, as explained below, the court correctly did not award unjust enrichment damages here for costs incurred in developing misappropriated trade secrets that were neither used nor commercially implemented. Moreover, the court could have reasonably reduced Samson's figure for research and development costs because Syntron had benefited and continues to benefit from the time and costs expended developing the misappropriated trade secrets....

Upon reviewing this record and gleaning the extent of the defendants' misappropriation, we cannot say the court's approximation was arbitrary, unreasonable or unsupported by the record. Syntron dedicated six years to extensively researching and developing its in-home pregnancy test kits. They played the dominant role in generating income for both Syntron and Genix. The defendants misappropriated not only the monoclonal antibodies and hybridoma cell lines, but also the processes for manufacturing the various pregnancy test kits and the GMP production documents containing raw material specifications and suppliers as well as developed customer lists. Simply stated, through this massive misappropriation of trade secrets, Genix was able to clone Syntron and become instantaneously commercially active, avoiding the substantial costs and years of independently developing the stolen trade secrets and essentially the boutique biodiagnostic systems manufacturing business. No point is more pervasive in restitutionary recoveries than although apportionment is largely a question of evidence, all doubts are resolved against the intentional wrongdoers.... Granted, the court's $2.7 million unjust enrichment award may not have been established with mathematical precision. Nevertheless, it is reasonable in light of the whole record, as the difficulty in ascertaining damages "should not militate in favor of the wrongdoer." ...

Fan further contends the court's award of unjust enrichment damages and injunctive relief constitutes an impermissible double recovery under section 3426.3. Although he is unclear in his argument and prayer which remedy he deems inappropriate under the circumstances, he primarily focuses on the unjust enrichment award. He emphasizes that where the actual damages award exceeds Genix's gross sales, coupled with the injunctive relief summarized below, Syntron has been fully compensated—relief that necessarily includes any unjust enrichment to Genix. In addition to the compensatory damages award, the court enjoined the defendants from using Syntron's trade secrets and "from directly or indirectly manufacturing or selling diagnostic pregnancy or drugs-of-abuse test kits for a period of six years from date of judgment." Syntron asserts this was entirely proper, because it was entitled to recover damages for its lost profits and defendants' unjust enrichment (§ 3426.3, subd. (a)) and to enjoin defendants from using its trade secrets for a duration equivalent to the amount of time it would take for them to independently develop the technology necessary to manufacture and sell the diagnostic test kits (§ 3426.2, subd. (a)).

Upon proving actual misappropriation, Syntron was entitled to injunctive relief under section 3426.2, subdivision (a).[99] ... Moreover, the duration of the injunction is reasonable, representing the amount of time it would take the defendants to independently develop the technology necessary to manufacture and sell the specific diagnostic test kits.... For, "[a]n injunction in a trade secret case seeks to protect the secrecy of misappropriated information and to eliminate any unfair head start the defendant may have gained." ... However, the issue posed in context is not so singularly presented, but rather whether the two remedies were duplicative—amounting to double recovery—given Syntron's recovery of all its losses—an award that exceeded Genix's gross sales. In other words, did the trial court err when it awarded damages of $2.7 million based on savings Genix unjustly received from lower research and development costs because it had already made Syntron whole by awarding all lost profits and issuing a permanent

99. Section 3426.2, subdivision (a) provides: "Actual or threatened misappropriation may be enjoined. Upon application to the court, an injunction shall be terminated when the trade secret has ceased to exist, but the injunction may be continued for an additional period of time in order to eliminate commercial advantage that otherwise would be derived from the misappropriation."

injunction prohibiting any further misappropriation and thus preventing any possibility of further damages? As we shall explain, we conclude the unjust enrichment award of $2.7 million was not excessive for the trial court did not intend to cover research and development costs attributable to misappropriated trade secrets that have not been actually used and commercially implemented by Genix.

Under appropriate circumstances, the UTSA authorizes the court to award unjust enrichment damages as well as grant injunctive relief. With regard to the trade secrets associated with the pregnancy and drugs-of-abuse test kits that Genix misappropriated, used and commercially implemented, the injunctive relief does not amount to double recovery in light of the compensatory damages award, because the latter was based on actual losses sustained by Syntron and research and development costs avoided by Genix and did not include damages based on future gains realized by Genix related to the misappropriated information. However, as to those misappropriated trade secrets that were neither used nor commercially implemented, the injunctive relief granted by the court prohibiting defendants from using these misappropriated trade secrets provided Syntron with complete relief. Because they had not been used and commercially implemented by Genix, Syntron suffered no actual losses as a result of their misappropriation and there existed no Genix profits to disgorge. Indeed, the possibility of derivative future profits is at best speculative. Regarding restitution for unjust enrichment within this context, the retention, but nonuse, of Syntron's proprietary information did not quantitatively enrich Genix. Accordingly, the injunction deprives Genix of any benefit (unjust enrichment) it might gain from avoiding the research and development costs incurred by Syntron, both financially and temporally, while shielding Syntron from any potential harm from Genix's competition which these advantages may have rendered unfair. Here, the trial court correctly excluded from its $2.7 million unjust enrichment award the research and development costs incurred by Syntron as to misappropriated trade secrets that were neither used nor commercially implemented by Genix. Consequently, the relief it granted did not amount to duplicative recovery....

Notes & Questions

1. Considering the *Chou* case, *supra*, do you think that a researcher's non-pecuniary interest in a patent—for example, as a mark of prestige, or a factor in one's promotion within the workplace—should be sufficient to grant standing in a suit regarding the correct listing of inventorship on a patent application?

2. Regarding the march-in rights under Bayh-Dole, do you think they should be exercised as a form of market price control, or only for failure to commercialize the patented technology?

3. To date, there appear to have been a total of three formal proceedings regarding a march-in rights petition: *CellPro*; *Norvir/Abbott Laboratories*; and one not excerpted above involving Pfizer and Xalatan glaucoma treatment. *See* NIH, Office of the Director, In the Case of Xalatan Manufactured by Pfizer, Inc. (September 17, 2004) (declining to exercise march-in rights because Xalatan has been available for use by glaucoma patients since 1996 and is being actively marketed by Pfizer and prescribed by physicians).

4. In *CellPro, o*ne of the arguments against exercising march-in rights was that other actions/venues would be more appropriate for the types of harms alleged. In particular, an investigation by the Federal Trade Commission or an antitrust lawsuit brought by interested parties have been suggested as the proper legal avenues. However, in *Schor v. Abbott Laboratories*, 378 F.Supp.2d 850 (N.D. Ill. 2005), the court dismissed a group of

AIDS patients' antitrust claims under § 2 of the Sherman Act against Abbott Laboratories. The judge reasoned that because Abbott's patents covered Norvir as both a stand-alone protease inhibitor and a "booster" to be used in conjunction with other protease inhibitors, there could be no antitrust violations in either setting where Abbott raised its prices on Norvir. The court also chose to follow case law from the Federal Circuit, rather than developing case law in the Ninth Circuit that might lead to a different result. In fact, in two similar (now consolidated) antitrust lawsuits against Abbott brought in the Northern District of California, the judge denied Abbott's similar motion to dismiss the Sherman Act claims, relying on Ninth Circuit case law, and, in particular, its acceptance of the "monopoly leveraging theory." *See Doe v. Abbott Laboratories*, C 04-1511 CW, unpub. order (N.D. Cal. Oct. 21, 2004); *Service Employees International Union Health and Welfare Fund v. Abbott Laboratories*, 2005 WL 528323 (N.D. Cal. Mar. 2, 2005); *In re Abbott Laboratories Norvir Antitrust Litigation*, 2005 WL 2206700 (N.D. Cal. Sept. 12, 2005). If Abbott prevails in the antitrust proceedings in California as well, will this change your perception of whether NIH should have further considered march-in rights? Or does it just mean that this was neither a good march-in rights case nor an antitrust violation? If the latter, then what recourse, if any, do the aggrieved AIDS patients have? Perhaps, instead, Abbott has acted immorally and/or against the public interest, but not illegally. Consider the court's statement in *Schor*: "The court is not unsympathetic to plaintiff's seemingly legitimate concerns that the drastic price increase will prevent him and other AIDS patients from receiving the best drug treatments for their disease, but antitrust laws do not impose liability for a business entity's failure to act morally or in the public interest." *Schor*, 378 F.Supp.2d at 860.

5. Some other nations have a broad research use exemption that allows even for-profit, commercial firms to pursue R&D with others' patented inventions without being held liable for infringement. The limit is that when the firm seeks to actually commercialize the results of this R&D, then appropriate licenses must be obtained so that the firm is not liable for patent infringement. Should the U.S. adopt this model as well?

6. Does the Supreme Court's holding in *Merck v. Integra* essentially destroy the value of research tool patents in the life sciences (despite the Court's statement in a footnote that it is *not* addressing research tools in the opinion)? It may help to review the materials regarding the FDA approval process in Section D, *infra*.

7. Taking into account the increasingly collaborative nature of life sciences research and development (R&D)—including its cross-border, cross-firm, and cross-institution dimensions—is trade secret protection, which is based on state law, becoming proportionately risky for investors/owners? In particular, given the critical role of bioinformatics in biotechnological/genomic research, where are key data and results "located", and hence where does misappropriation occur for purposes of jurisdiction and choice of law issues? Does the existence of the USTA, as a uniform law adopted by many states, reduce some of these concerns?

C. Commercialization through Start-Up Companies

Once a patentable genetic technology has been identified in the lab and inventorship/ownership has been established, the patent owner will consider how best to "commercialize" it. "Commercialization" is the process of translating the technology prototype created in the original research lab into a mass producible product or service that can be marketed, distributed, and sold, at commercially viable price points, to the public. Technology that is invented in a government, university, or nonprofit research lab must be assigned or licensed to a commercial entity to undertake this process, because these other types of organizations do not really operate in the commercial sphere. In some limited cases, government agencies could consider having a genetic technology manufactured and/or distributed by a private contractor on behalf of the government to be provided as a government public service.

In most instances, however, genetic technologies will be assigned or licensed to small start-up or spin-off companies to engage in the high-risk R&D process that will hopefully lead from a raw lab technology to a viable "proof of concept" stage. At this point, the company must be able to demonstrate how the developed technology can be placed into a manufacturing scale-up program either at an established "big pharma" company or a private contract manufacturer. This scale-up may well occur under a strategic alliance or joint venture project with a big pharma company. The small start-up or spin-off company may also begin the animal studies that will lay the groundwork for the formal FDA approval process covered in the last section of this Chapter.

The extremely high-risk nature of this process—not necessarily in terms of injury and tort liability, but rather the reality that most of these commercialization R&D projects will fail—leads to the biotech industry's reliance on specialized risk capital as the primary financing tool. Generally, an "angel" investor—a wealthy individual who can afford to invest a few hundred thousand dollars—will get things rolling in tandem with some more modest investment by the company's founders and their friends and family members. The company may also try to take advantage of the SBIR (Small Business Innovation Research) and STTR (Small Business Technology Transfer) financing programs sponsored by the Small Business Administration (SBA).[100] Once the company has shown some success with its commercialization R&D program, it can approach venture capitalists (VCs) who may invest anywhere from millions to hundreds of millions of dollars in the company, over a series of investment rounds tied to different issued series of the company's stock (*e.g.*, "Series A Convertible Preferred Stock"). VCs, however, will demand special rights and privileges, including seats on the company's board of directors, to enable them to exercise a degree of control over the company to better monitor their investment.

The process for forming and governing corporations and limited liability companies—the two primary legal entity forms used for start-up and spin-off companies—is governed primarily by state law. However, the offering and sale of "securities" (stock or other investment contracts established by a company to raise capital) is governed primarily by federal securities laws, in conjunction with state securities laws. The following excerpted Congressional testimony by a Securities and Exchange Commission ("SEC") representative summarizes the process of capital formation by small businesses, including the federal laws and regulations that govern it.

---

100. *See* SBA, SBIR and STTR Programs and Awards *available at* http://www.sba.gov/sbir/indexsbir-sttr.html.

Alan L. Beller, Director, Division of Corporation Finance, U.S. Securities and Exchange Commission, Testimony Concerning Small Business Capital Formation

September 23, 2004

Regulation for Small Businesses

A number of SEC rules and regulations are specifically tailored to provide accommodations for small businesses that seek to raise capital in the U.S. markets. Some of the accommodations come in the form of exemptions from the general requirement to register public offerings of securities under the Securities Act of 1933. Other rules and exemptions are available to all types of companies that fulfill certain criteria, but their nature makes them especially useful for many small businesses.

One of the exemptions is Regulation A,[101] which provides an exemption from registration requirements for non-reporting U.S. and Canadian companies issuing up to $5 million in any 12-month period. Offerings under Regulation A share many characteristics with registered offerings, but have certain advantages for issuers over full registration. Principal among these advantages are: (1) the financial statements are simpler and do not need to be audited; (2) there are no continuing reporting obligations after the offering unless the company has more than $10 million in total assets and more than 500 shareholders; (3) companies may choose among three formats to prepare the offering circular, one of which is a simplified question-and-answer document; and (4) companies may "test the waters" to determine if there is adequate interest in their securities before going through the expense of filing with the SEC. We have received suggestions, including from the 2003 Government-Business Forum, to increase the amount of capital a company could raise under Regulation A. The staff is considering whether it should recommend that the Commission raise this cap consistent with its investor protection mandate, as well as whether larger offerings should trigger additional conditions to the exemption.

The Commission's Regulation D[102] exempts certain transactions from registration under three separate rules, each of which reflects a Commission determination that registration and prospectus delivery should not be required for offers and sales that meet certain criteria. The exemptions in Regulation D most often used by small businesses are in Rules 504 and 506.

Rule 504 exempts offerings of up to $1 million per 12-month period; this exemption allows for the issuance of freely traded securities only if the company files an offering document with a state having review and prospectus delivery requirements or sells under a state law exemption that limits sales to "accredited investors."[103] In 1999, the

---

101. 17 C.F.R. § 230.251-263.

102. 17 C.F.R. § 230.501-508.

103. An "accredited investor" is: (1) a bank, insurance company, registered investment company, business development company, or small business investment company; (2) an employee benefit plan, within the meaning of the Employee Retirement Income Security Act, if a bank, insurance company, or registered investment adviser makes the investment decisions, or if the plan has total assets in excess of $5 million; (3) a charitable organization, corporation or partnership with assets exceeding $5 million; (4) a director, executive officer, or general partner of the company selling the securities; (5) a business in which all the equity owners are accredited investors; (6) a natural person with a net worth of at least $1 million; (7) a natural person with income exceeding $200,000 in each

Commission revised Rule 504, which had allowed all securities issued under Rule 504 to be freely traded, in order to curb fraudulent secondary transactions in the over-the-counter markets of "microcap" companies. As I described, the current version of Rule 504 provides that only securities that are issued in accordance with state law can be freely traded after issuance. All other issuances under Rule 504 result in restricted securities that may not be freely offered or sold to the public. During this Subcommittee's June 2001 hearing on the SEC's role in capital formation, some witnesses suggested that we could better facilitate capital formation for small businesses if we reverted to the pre-1999 version of Rule 504. The Commission determined in 1999 that significant fraud was occurring following the use of Rule 504, and I believe it would have to be convinced that those abuses would not be repeated before rolling back those changes.

Rule 506 is a "safe harbor" and is available to all companies. It permits sales to accredited investors and to a limited number of non-accredited investors. All non-accredited investors to whom a Rule 506 offering is sold must be sophisticated—that is, they must have sufficient knowledge and experience in financial and business matters to make them capable of evaluating the merits and risks of the prospective investment. We have received suggestions, again including from the 2003 Government-Business Forum, to eliminate or loosen the restrictions on the use of general solicitation of investors, over the Internet or otherwise, using Rule 506. The staff is considering these recommendations in the overall context of the Commission's investor protection mandate.

The SEC's Rule 701 exempts from registration sales of securities made by companies that are not subject to Exchange Act reporting requirements to compensate their employees. Such companies can issue up to $1 million under this exemption, and that amount may increase if a company satisfies certain formulas based on assets or on the number of its outstanding securities. If a company sells more than $5 million in securities in a 12-month period, it must provide limited disclosure to employees. Employees receive restricted securities in offerings made under Rule 701.

In addition to the exemptions in Regulation A, Regulation D and Rule 701, there are other rules, regulations and forms for small business issuers that do register and report with us. For example, small business issuers offering up to $10 million worth of securities in a 12-month period may use Form SB-1 to register its securities, if they have not registered more than $10 million in any previous 12-month period. This form allows small issuers to provide information in a question and answer format, similar to that used in Regulation A offerings. Unlike offerings under Regulation A, however, Form SB-1 requires audited financial statements.

A small business issuer may register an unlimited dollar amount of securities using Form SB-2, and may use this form for registering securities so long as it satisfies the "small business issuer"[104] definition. One advantage of Form SB-2 is that all its disclosure requirements are in Regulation S-B, a set of rules written specifically for small businesses. Form SB-2 also permits small companies: (1) to provide audited financial

---

of the two most recent years or joint income with a spouse exceeding $300,000 for those years and a reasonable expectation of the same income level in the current year; or (8) a trust with assets of at least $5 million, not formed to acquire the securities offered, and whose purchases are directed by a sophisticated person. See 17 C.F.R. § 230.501.

104. "Small Business Issuers" are U.S. or Canadian companies, other than investment companies, with less than $25 million in revenues and less than $25 million in market capitalization. If the company is a majority owned subsidiary, the parent corporation must also be a small business issuer. See 17 C.F.R. § 228.10(a)(1).

statements, prepared according to generally accepted accounting principles, for two fiscal years, rather the three years required of larger companies, and (2) to include less extensive narrative disclosure than larger companies are required to include, particularly regarding the description of business, and executive compensation.

Qualifying small business issuers can also use specially tailored forms for their annual and quarterly reports, the content of which is governed by Regulation S-B.

Sarbanes-Oxley Act of 2002

One issue that small businesses consistently raise with us is compliance costs for the requirements put in place by the Sarbanes-Oxley Act of 2002. While the Act did not make any distinctions based on company size, in implementing our rules under the Act, we tried very hard to be sensitive to the concerns of small business issuers, and we made a number of accommodations for them. For example:

- We gave small business issuers extra time to comply with the rule requiring disclosure of whether they have a financial expert on their audit committees.
- We gave public companies with less than $75 million in market capitalization additional time to comply with the rules requiring a report on internal control over financial reporting. As a result, this requirement will apply for the first time to most small business issuers for filings they make in 2006.
- In the adopting release for the internal control rules, and again in recent staff guidance on Frequently Asked Questions (or FAQs) about the rules published on our Web site, the Commission and the staff have encouraged the Committee of Sponsoring Organizations (COSO) of the Treadway Commission, or a similar group, to develop guidance that can help address the special concerns of small businesses by providing a more tailored framework for internal controls.
- Small auditing firms with fewer than five public-company audit clients and ten partners are exempt from the audit partner rotation requirements and the prohibitions on compensation based on providing non-audit services to public company clients.

Despite these accommodations, the cost of Sarbanes-Oxley compliance continues to be a source of concern for small companies. We also have heard anecdotal evidence that some smaller public companies may forego their public reporting status rather than comply with the new Sarbanes-Oxley governance requirements. Although our rulemaking under Sarbanes-Oxley has been completed, we continue to consider the impact of recent rules on small businesses, while recognizing that good corporate governance and financial reporting are important for all companies, regardless of size.

Notes & Questions

1. Bayh-Dole and the tech transfer system established under it have resulted in a decent mechanism for transferring (by assignment or license) the necessary IP rights from universities and research institutions to private commercializing entities. However, many commercializing entities consider it an imperative to have access to the consulting services of the faculty researchers who actually invented the technology. Materials in Chapter 5 considered the risks of financial conflicts of interest that can arise when researchers have a financial stake in the private commercializing entities outside of their research institution. Are there ways to structure consulting relationships that would minimize the risks of these conflicts—without overly stifling the commercialization

process itself? Finally, keep this question in mind while reviewing the materials in Section E involving Sam Waksal, Martha Stewart, and the ImClone saga.

D. Obtaining Regulatory Approval for Sales and Marketing

Before a genetic technological product or service can be distributed in interstate commerce, it must satisfy the approval process mandated under the Federal Food, Drug and Cosmetic Act (FFDCA)[105] as administered by the U.S. Food and Drug Administration (FDA). As an overview, the FDA is comprised of a number of centers corresponding to the different categories of items that it regulates: Center for Food Safety and Applied Nutrition (CFSAN); Center for Drug Evaluation and Research (CDER); Center for Devices and Radiological Health (CDRH); Center for Biologics Evaluation and Research (CBER); and the Center for Veterinary Medicine (CVM). Because of the increase in products that include components that fit into separate categories, the FDA also has the Office of Combination Products to facilitate regulation of such products.

The first step in seeking regulatory approval of a new genetic technology is to determine which categories it falls into: food, drug, biologic, device, or veterinary product. This will determine which center within the FDA should be approached to begin the review process. Because this Chapter focuses on human therapeutic and diagnostic genetic technologies, the following subsections outline the approval process, first for drugs and biologics (similar processes for each), and second for devices. The approval processes for biotechnological foods and veterinary products are outlined in Chapter 8.

Definitions of each of the categories are included in the relevant subsection. Finally, note that the human subjects research issues raised in Chapter 5 fully apply to the clinical trials discussed below—in fact, a number of the cases in that Chapter arose from clinical studies of genetic products for marketing approval.

1. The Approval Process for Drugs and Biologics

The definition of a drug is set out in the FFDCA:

> The term "drug" means (A) articles recognized in the official United States Pharmacopoeia, official Homoeopathic Pharmacopoeia of the United States, or official National Formulary, or any supplement to any of them; and (B) articles intended for use in the diagnosis, cure, mitigation, treatment, or prevention of disease in man or other animals; and (C) articles (other than food) intended to affect the structure or any function of the body of man or other animals; and (D) articles intended for use as a component of any article specified in clause (A), (B), or (C). A food or dietary supplement for which a claim, subject to sections 343(r)(1)(B) and 343(r)(3) of this title or sections 343(r)(1)(B) and 343(r)(5)(D) of this title, is made in accordance with the requirements of section 343(r) of this title is not a drug solely because the label

105. P.L. 75-717, 52 Stat. 1040 (June 25, 1938).

> or the labeling contains such a claim. A food, dietary ingredient, or dietary supplement for which a truthful and not misleading statement is made in accordance with section 343(r)(6) of this title is not a drug under clause (C) solely because the label or the labeling contains such a statement.[106]

Biologics are defined in the Public Health Service Act:

> the term "biological product" means a virus, therapeutic serum, toxin, antitoxin, vaccine, blood, blood component or derivative, allergenic product, or analogous product, or arsphenamine or derivative of arsphenamine (or any other trivalent organic arsenic compound), applicable to the prevention, treatment, or cure of a disease or condition of human beings.[107]

The power to regulate drugs and biologics in interstate commerce is established in the FFDCA and the Public Health Service Act[108] and delegated to the FDA. The primary vehicle for drug and biologic approval is the New Drug Application (NDA). However, because this document requires substantial clinical data on the safety and efficacy of the submitted drug/biologic, the drug/biologic's sponsors must have already conducted significant human subject clinical studies before the NDA is approved. At the same time, the nature of contemporary clinical studies means that the tested matter must often be transported across state lines just to undergo such testing. Accordingly, the FFDCA was amended to enable the FDA to establish an Investigational New Drug Application (IND) process that can authorize a new drug/biologic's sponsors to begin human subject clinical studies, including transportation of the new drug across state lines, before the NDA process commences. As documented below, a crucial component of the IND is toxicological and other data to be collected through animal studies before the IND is compiled and submitted.

FDA, CDER, Investigational New Drug Application (IND) Process

October 26, 2004

Introduction

Current Federal law requires that a drug be the subject of an approved marketing application before it is transported or distributed across state lines. Because a sponsor will probably want to ship the investigational drug to clinical investigators in many states, it must seek an exemption from that legal requirement. The IND is the means through which the sponsor technically obtains this exemption from the FDA.

During a new drug's early preclinical development, the sponsor's primary goal is to determine if the product is reasonably safe for initial use in humans, and if the compound exhibits pharmacological activity that justifies commercial development. When a product is identified as a viable candidate for further development, the sponsor then focuses on collecting the data and information necessary to establish that the product will not expose humans to unreasonable risks when used in limited, early-stage clinical studies.

FDA's role in the development of a new drug begins when the drug's sponsor (usually the manufacturer or potential marketer) having screened the new molecule for pharma-

106. 21 U.S.C. §321(g)(1).
107. 42 U.S.C. §262(I).
108. P.L. 78-184, 57 Stat. 587 (November 11, 1943).

cological activity and acute toxicity potential in animals, wants to test its diagnostic or therapeutic potential in humans. At that point, the molecule changes in legal status under the Federal Food, Drug, and Cosmetic Act and becomes a new drug subject to specific requirements of the drug regulatory system.

There are three IND types:

- An Investigator IND is submitted by a physician who both initiates and conducts an investigation, and under whose immediate direction the investigational drug is administered or dispensed. A physician might submit a research IND to propose studying an unapproved drug, or an approved product for a new indication or in a new patient population.
- Emergency Use IND allows the FDA to authorize use of an experimental drug in an emergency situation that does not allow time for submission of an IND in accordance with 21 CFR, Sec. 312.23 or Sec. 312.34. It is also used for patients who do not meet the criteria of an existing study protocol, or if an approved study protocol does not exist.
- Treatment IND is submitted for experimental drugs showing promise in clinical testing for serious or immediately life-threatening conditions while the final clinical work is conducted and the FDA review takes place.

There are two IND categories:

- Commercial
- Research (non-commercial)

The IND application must contain information in three broad areas:

- Animal Pharmacology and Toxicology Studies—Preclinical data to permit an assessment as to whether the product is reasonably safe for initial testing in humans. Also included are any previous experience with the drug in humans (often foreign use).
- Manufacturing Information—Information pertaining to the composition, manufacturer, stability, and controls used for manufacturing the drug substance and the drug product. This information is assessed to ensure that the company can adequately produce and supply consistent batches of the drug.
- Clinical Protocols and Investigator Information—Detailed protocols for proposed clinical studies to assess whether the initial-phase trials will expose subjects to unnecessary risks. Also, information on the qualifications of clinical investigators—professionals (generally physicians) who oversee the administration of the experimental compound—to assess whether they are qualified to fulfill their clinical trial duties. Finally, commitments to obtain informed consent from the research subjects, to obtain review of the study by an institutional review board (IRB), and to adhere to the investigational new drug regulations.

Once the IND is submitted, the sponsor must wait 30 calendar days before initiating any clinical trials. During this time, FDA has an opportunity to review the IND for safety to assure that research subjects will not be subjected to unreasonable risk.

* * *

Upon the successful submission of the IND, the sponsor may then begin the human clinical trials required for the NDA. Human trials are broken into three types: Phase I, Phase II, and Phase III, as defined in the following FDA regulations.

FDA, Phases of an Investigation

21 C.F.R. § 312.21

An IND may be submitted for one or more phases of an investigation. The clinical investigation of a previously untested drug is generally divided into three phases. Although in general the phases are conducted sequentially, they may overlap. These three phases of an investigation are a follows:

(a) Phase 1. (1) Phase 1 includes the initial introduction of an investigational new drug into humans. Phase 1 studies are typically closely monitored and may be conducted in patients or normal volunteer subjects. These studies are designed to determine the metabolism and pharmacologic actions of the drug in humans, the side effects associated with increasing doses, and, if possible, to gain early evidence on effectiveness. During Phase 1, sufficient information about the drug's pharmacokinetics and pharmacological effects should be obtained to permit the design of well-controlled, scientifically valid, Phase 2 studies. The total number of subjects and patients included in Phase 1 studies varies with the drug, but is generally in the range of 20 to 80.

(2) Phase 1 studies also include studies of drug metabolism, structure-activity relationships, and mechanism of action in humans, as well as studies in which investigational drugs are used as research tools to explore biological phenomena or disease processes.

(b) Phase 2. Phase 2 includes the controlled clinical studies conducted to evaluate the effectiveness of the drug for a particular indication or indications in patients with the disease or condition under study and to determine the common short-term side effects and risks associated with the drug. Phase 2 studies are typically well controlled, closely monitored, and conducted in a relatively small number of patients, usually involving no more than several hundred subjects.

(c) Phase 3. Phase 3 studies are expanded controlled and uncontrolled trials. They are performed after preliminary evidence suggesting effectiveness of the drug has been obtained, and are intended to gather the additional information about effectiveness and safety that is needed to evaluate the overall benefit-risk relationship of the drug and to provide an adequate basis for physician labeling. Phase 3 studies usually include from several hundred to several thousand subjects.

* * *

For biologics, there is also a biologics licensing application (BLA) process administered by CBER in conformance with the following regulations:

FDA, Biologics Licensing

21 C.F.R. Part 601

§ 601.2 Applications for biologics licenses; procedures for filing.

(a) *General.* To obtain a biologics license under section 351 of the Public Health Service Act for any biological product, the manufacturer shall submit an application to the Director, Center for Biologics Evaluation and Research or the Director, Center for Drug Evaluation and Research..., on forms prescribed for such purposes, and shall submit data derived from nonclinical laboratory and clinical studies which demonstrate that the manufactured product meets prescribed requirements of safety, purity, and potency; with respect to each nonclinical laboratory study, either a statement that the study was conducted in compliance with the requirements set forth in part 58 of this chapter, or, if the study was not conducted in compliance with such regulations, a brief statement of the reason for the noncompliance; statements regarding each clinical investigation involving human subjects contained in the application, that it either was conducted in compliance with the requirements for institutional review set forth in part 56 of this chapter; or was not subject to such requirements in accordance with § 56.104 or § 56.105, and was conducted in compliance with requirements for informed consent set forth in part 50 of this chapter. A full description of manufacturing methods; data establishing stability of the product through the dating period; sample(s) representative of the product for introduction or delivery for introduction into interstate commerce; summaries of results of tests performed on the lot(s) represented by the submitted sample(s); specimens of the labels, enclosures, and containers, and if applicable, any Medication Guide required under part 208 of this chapter proposed to be used for the product; and the address of each location involved in the manufacture of the biological product shall be listed in the biologics license application. The applicant shall also include a financial certification or disclosure statement(s) or both for clinical investigators as required by part 54 of this chapter. An application for a biologics license shall not be considered as filed until all pertinent information and data have been received by the Food and Drug Administration. The applicant shall also include either a claim for categorical exclusion under § 25.30 or § 25.31 of this chapter or an environmental assessment under § 25.40 of this chapter. The applicant, or the applicant's attorney, agent, or other authorized official shall sign the application. An application for any of the following specified categories of biological products subject to licensure shall be handled as set forth in paragraph (c) of this section:

(1) Therapeutic DNA plasmid products;

(2) Therapeutic synthetic peptide products of 40 or fewer amino acids;

(3) Monoclonal antibody products for in vivo use; and

(4) Therapeutic recombinant DNA-derived products....

(c)(1) To obtain marketing approval for a biological product subject to licensure which is a therapeutic DNA plasmid product, therapeutic synthetic peptide product of 40 or fewer amino acids, monoclonal antibody product for in vivo use, or therapeutic recombinant DNA-derived product, an applicant shall submit a biologics license application in accordance with paragraph (a) of this section except that the following sections in parts 600 through 680 of this chapter shall not be applicable to such products: §§ 600.10(b) and (c), 600.11, 600.12, 600.13, 610.11, 610.53, and 610.62 of this chapter....

(d) Approval of a biologics license application or issuance of a biologics license shall constitute a determination that the establishment(s) and the product meet applicable requirements to ensure the continued safety, purity, and potency of such products. Applicable requirements for the maintenance of establishments for the manufacture of a product subject to this section shall include but not be limited to the good manufacturing practice requirements set forth in parts 210, 211, 600, 606, and 820 of this chapter.

(e) Any establishment and product license for a biological product issued under section 351 of the Public Health Service Act (42 U.S.C. 201 et seq.) that has not been revoked or suspended as of December 20, 1999, shall constitute an approved biologics license application in effect under the same terms and conditions set forth in such product license and such portions of the establishment license relating to such product.

§ 601.4 Issuance and denial of license.

(a) A biologics license shall be issued upon a determination by the Director, Center for Biologics Evaluation and Research or the Director, Center for Drug Evaluation and Research that the establishment(s) and the product meet the applicable requirements established in this chapter. A biologics license shall be valid until suspended or revoked.

(b) If the Commissioner determines that the establishment or product does not meet the requirements established in this chapter, the biologics license application shall be denied and the applicant shall be informed of the grounds for, and of an opportunity for a hearing on, the decision. If the applicant so requests, the Commissioner shall issue a notice of opportunity for hearing on the matter pursuant to § 12.21(b) of this chapter.

2. The Device Approval Process

The approval process for medical devices follows a somewhat different procedure—as outlined in the documents below—but certain devices still require an investigational phase clearance process similar to the IND before testing can be done to support the final marketing approval application.

FDA, CDRH, Getting to Market with a Medical Device

June 10, 2003

Introduction

One of the most difficult aspects of getting a medical device to market is *knowing where to begin* i.e., what are the steps for marketing and in what order they are to be taken. Essentially, medical devices are subject to the general controls of the Federal Food Drug & Cosmetic (FD&C) Act which are contained in the final procedural regulations in Title 21 Code of Federal Regulations Part 800–1200 (21 CFR Parts 800–1299). These controls are the baseline requirements that apply to all medical devices necessary for marketing, proper labeling and monitoring its performance once the device is on the market.

Three Steps to Obtaining Marketing Clearance from CDRH

STEP ONE in the marketing process is to make absolutely sure that the product that you wish to market is a medical device, that is, does it meet the definition of a medical device in section 201(h) of the FD&C Act. For example, the product may be a drug or biological product that is regulated by a component in the FDA other than the Center for Devices and Radiological Health (CDRH) and for which there are different provisions in the FD&C Act. Or your product may be a medical device and is also an electronic radiation emitting product with additional requirements.

Classify Your Device

STEP TWO is to determine how FDA may classify your device—which one of the three classes the device may fall into. Unless exempt, FDA will classify your device. Classification identifies the level of regulatory control that is necessary to assure the safety and effectiveness of a medical device. Most importantly, the classification of the device will identify, unless exempt, the marketing process (either premarket notification [510(k)] or premarket approval (PMA)) the manufacturer must complete in order to obtain FDA clearance/approval for marketing.

Selecting the Appropriate Marketing Application

STEP THREE is the development of data and/or information necessary to submit a marketing application, and to obtain FDA clearance to market. For some [510(k)] submissions and most PMA applications, clinical performance data is required to obtain clearance to market. In these cases, conduct of the trial must be done in accord with FDA's Investigational Device Exemption (IDE) regulation, in addition to marketing clearance....

Other Requirements Besides Marketing Clearance

Premarket Requirements: Labeling, Registration, Listing

Before marketing clearance is obtained the manufacturer must assure that the device is properly labeled in accordance with FDA's labeling regulations. Once clearance for marketing is obtained, the manufacturer must register their establishment and list the type of device they plan to market with the FDA. This registration and listing process is accomplished by the submission of FDA Form 2891 and 2892.

Postmarket Requirements: Quality System, Medical Device Reporting

Once on the market, there are postmarket surveillance controls with which a manufacturer must comply. These requirements include the Quality Systems (QS) (also known as Good Manufacturing Practices, GMPs) and Medical Device Reporting (MDR) regulations. The QS regulation is a quality assurance requirement that covers the design, packaging, labeling and manufacturing of a medical device. The MDR regulation is an adverse event reporting program.

In Vitro Diagnostic Devices

In vitro diagnostics (IVD)

IVDs are medical devices that analyze human body fluids, such as blood or urine, to provide information for the diagnosis, prevention, or treatment of a disease. The device classification for these devices can be found under 21 CFR § 862, 21 CFR § 864, and 21 CFR § 866.

Clinical Laboratory Improvement Act (CLIA) of 1988

In addition to FDA regulation under the Food, Drug, and Cosmetic Act, in vitro diagnostic (IVD) devices are also subject to the Clinical Laboratory Improvement Amendments (CLIA) of 1988. This law established quality standards for laboratory testing and an accreditation program for clinical laboratories.

The requirements that apply vary according to the technical complexity in the testing process and risk of harm in reporting erroneous results. The regulations established three categories of testing on the basis of the complexity of the testing methodology: a) waived tests, b) tests of moderate complexity, and c) tests of high complexity. Laboratories performing moderate- or high-complexity testing or both must meet requirements for proficiency testing, patient test management, quality control, quality assurance, and personnel. These specific requirements do not apply to tests in the waived category.

In January 2000 the categorization of commercially marketed in vitro diagnostic tests under CLIA was transferred from the Center for Disease Control (CDC) to FDA. CDRH's Office of Device Evaluation/Division of Clinical Laboratory Devices (DCLD) will determine the appropriate complexity categories for clinical laboratory devices as they evaluate premarket submissions. Waived products, devices exempt from premarket notification, and devices under premarket review by other FDA centers also will be processed by DCLD. Responsibilities currently assigned to CDC, including review of test systems, assays, or examinations not commercially marketed as IVD products, will remain with CDC....

Labeling

Specific labeling requirements for IVDs can be found under 21 CFR §809. Additional guidance can be found under "Device Advice Labeling Requirements for In Vitro Diagnostic Devices."

FDA, CDRH, Clinical Trials and Investigational Device Exemption

July 8, 2003

IDE Overview

An investigational device exemption (IDE) allows the investigational device to be used in a clinical study in order to collect safety and effectiveness data required to support a Premarket Approval (PMA) application or a Premarket Notification [510(k)] submission to FDA. Clinical studies are most often conducted to support a PMA. Only a small percentage of 510(k)'s require clinical data to support the application. Investigational use also includes clinical evaluation of certain modifications or new intended uses of legally marketed devices. All clinical evaluations of investigational devices, unless exempt, must have an approved IDE before the study is initiated.

Clinical evaluation of devices that have not been cleared for marketing requires:

- an IDE approved by an institutional review board (IRB). If the study involves a significant risk device, the IDE must also be approved by FDA;
- informed consent from all patients;
- labeling for investigational use only
- monitoring of the study and;
- required records and reports.

An approved IDE permits a device to be shipped lawfully for the purpose of conducting investigations of the device without complying with other requirements of the Food, Drug, and Cosmetic Act (Act) that would apply to devices in commercial distribution. Sponsors need not submit a PMA or Premarket Notification 510(k), register their establishment, or list the device while the device is under investigation. Sponsors of IDE's are also exempt from the Quality System (QS) Regulation except for the requirements for design control.

Good Clinical Practices (GCP)

Good Clinical Practices (GCP) refers to the regulations and requirements that must be complied with while conducting a clinical study. These regulations that apply to the manufacturers, sponsors, clinical investigators, institutional review boards, and the medical device. The primary regulations that govern the conduct of clinical studies are included in the Code of Federal Regulations, Title 21 (21 CFR):

- 21 CFR 812, *Investigational Device Exemptions*, covers the procedures for the conduct of clinical studies with medical devices including application, responsibilities of sponsors and investigators, labeling, records, and reports.
- 21 CFR 50, *Protection of Human Subjects*, provides the requirements and general elements of informed consent;

- 21 CFR 56, *Institutional Review Boards*, covers the procedures and responsibilities for institutional review boards (IRBs) that approve clinical investigations protocols;
- 21 CFR 54, *Financial Disclosure by Clinical Investigators*, covers the disclosure of financial compensation to clinical investigators which is part of FDA's assessment of the reliability of the clinical data.
- 21 CFR 820 Subpart C, *Design Controls of the Quality System Regulation*, provides the requirement for procedures to control the design of the device in order to ensure that the specified design requirements are met.

FDA, CDRH, Premarket Approval (PMA)

November 1, 2002

Overview

Introduction

Premarket approval (PMA) is the FDA process of scientific and regulatory review to evaluate the safety and effectiveness of Class III medical devices. Class III devices are those that support or sustain human life, are of substantial importance in preventing impairment of human health, or which present a potential, unreasonable risk of illness or injury. Due to the level of risk associated with Class III devices, FDA has determined that general and special controls alone are insufficient to assure the safety and effectiveness of class III devices. Therefore, these devices require a premarket approval (PMA) application under section 515 of the FD&C Act in order to obtain marketing clearance. Please note that some Class III preamendment devices may require a Class III 510(k). *See* "Historical Background" below for additional information.

PMA is the most stringent type of device marketing application required by FDA. The applicant must receive FDA approval of its PMA application prior to marketing the device. PMA approval is based on a determination by FDA that the PMA contains sufficient valid scientific evidence to assure that the device is safe and effective for its intended use(s). An approved PMA is, in effect, a private license granting the applicant (or owner) permission to market the device. The PMA owner, however, can authorize use of its data by another.

The PMA applicant is usually the person who owns the rights, or otherwise has authorized access, to the data and other information to be submitted in support of FDA approval. This person may be an individual, partnership, corporation, association, scientific or academic establishment, government agency or organizational unit, or other legal entity. The applicant is often the inventor/developer and ultimately the manufacturer.

FDA regulations provide 180 days to review the PMA and make a determination. In reality, the review time is normally longer. Before approving or denying a PMA, the appropriate FDA advisory committee may review the PMA at a public meeting and provide FDA with the committee's recommendation on whether FDA should approve the submission. After FDA notifies the applicant that the PMA has been approved or denied, a notice is published on the Internet (1) announcing the data on which the decision is based, and (2) providing interested persons an opportunity to petition FDA within 30 days for reconsideration of the decision.

The regulation governing premarket approval is located in Title 21 Code of Federal Regulations (CFR) Part 814, Premarket Approval. A class III device that fails to meet

PMA requirements is considered to be adulterated under section 501(f) of the FD&C Act and cannot be marketed....

When a PMA is Required

PMA requirements apply to Class III devices, the most stringent regulatory category for medical devices. Device product classifications can be found by searching the Product Classification Database, http://www.accessdata.fda.gov/scripts/cdrh/cfdocs/cfPCD/classification.cfm. The database search provides the name of the device, classification, and a link to the Code of Federal Regulations (CFR), if any. The CFR provides the device type name, identification of the device, and classification information.

A regulation number for Class III devices marketed prior to the 1976 Medical Device Amendments is provided in the CFR. The CFR for these Class III devices that require a PMA states that the device is Class III and will provide an effective date of the requirement for PMA. If the regulation in the CFR states that "No effective date has been established of the requirement for premarket approval," a Class III 510(k) should be submitted.

Please note that PMA devices often involve new concepts and many are not of a type marketed prior to the Medical Device Amendments. Therefore, they do not have a classification regulation in the CFR. In this case, the product classification database will only cite the device type name and product code.

If it is unclear whether the unclassified device requires a PMA, use the three letter product code to search the PMA database and the Premarket Notification 510(k) database. These databases can be found by clicking on the hypertext links at the top of the product classification database web page. Enter only the three letter product code in the product code box. If there are 510(k)'s cleared by FDA and the new device is substantially equivalent to any of these cleared devices, then the applicant should submit a 510(k).

Furthermore, a new type of device may not be found in the product classification database. If the device is a high risk device (supports or sustains human life, is of substantial importance in preventing impairment of human health, or presents a potential, unreasonable risk of illness or injury) and has been found to be not substantially equivalent (NSE) to a Class I, II, or III [Class III requiring 510(k)] device, then the device must have an approved PMA before marketing in the U.S. Some devices that are found to be not substantially equivalent to a cleared Class I, II, or III (not requiring PMA) device, may be eligible for the de novo process as a Class I or Class II device. For additional information on the de novo process, see "New section 513(f)(2)—Evaluation of Automatic Class III Designation: Guidance for Industry and CDRH Staff" http://www.fda.gov/cdrh/modact/classiii.html or http://www.fda.gov/cdrh/modact/clasiii.pdf .

Historical Background

PMA requirements apply to Class III preamendment devices, transitional devices, and postamendment devices.

<u>Preamendment Devices</u>

A preamendments device is one that was in commercial distribution before May 28, 1976, the date the Medical Device Amendments were signed into law. After the Medical Device Amendments became law, the classification of devices was determined by FDA classification panels. Eventually all Class III devices will require a PMA. However, preamendment Class III devices require a PMA only after FDA publishes a regulation calling for PMA submissions. The preamendment devices must have a PMA filed for the device by the effective date published in the regulation in order to continue marketing the device. The CFR will state the date that a PMA is required. Prior to the

PMA effective date, the devices must have a cleared Premarket Notification 510(k) prior to marketing. Class III Preamendment devices that require a 510(k) are identified in the CFR as Class III and include the statement "Date premarket approval application (PMA) or notice of completion of product development protocol (PDP) is required. No effective date has been established of the requirement for premarket approval." Examples include intra-aortic balloon and control system (21 CFR 870.3535), ventricular bypass (assist) device (21 CFR 870.3545), cardiovascular permanent pacemaker electrode (21 CFR 870.3680), and topical oxygen chamber for extremities (21 CFR 878.5650).

Postamendment Devices

A postamendment device is one that was first distributed commercially on or after May 28, 1976. Postamendment devices equivalent to preamendment Class III devices are subject to the same requirements as the preamendment devices.

Transitional Devices

Transitional devices are devices that were regulated by FDA as new drugs before May 28, 1976. Any Class III device that was approved by a New Drug Application (NDA) is now governed by the PMA regulations. The approval numbers for these devices begin with the letter N. These devices are identified in the CFR as Class III devices and state that an approval under section 515 of the Act (PMA) is required as of May 28, 1976 before this device may be commercially distributed. An example of such device is intraocular lenses (21 CFR 886.3600). Please note that some of the transitional devices have been subsequently downclassified to Class II....

Devices Used in Blood Establishments

The Center for Biologic, Evaluation, Research (CBER) has expertise in blood, blood products, and cellular therapies as well as the integral association of certain medical devices with these biological products. To utilize this expertise marketing and investigational device submissions (Premarket Notification, Premarket Approval, and Investigational Device Exemption) for medical devices associated with the blood collection and processing procedures as well as those associated with cellular therapies are reviewed by CBER. Although these products are reviewed by CBER, the medical device laws and regulations still apply. The list of medical devices reviewed by CBER are available on the Internet http://www.fda.gov/cber/dap/devlst.htm

In addition to CDRH guidance on Premarket Approval, specific medical device guidance for devices reviewed by CBER is available at http://www.fda.gov/cber/devices.htm or by contacting [CBER]....

Data Requirements

A Premarket Approval (PMA) application is a scientific, regulatory documentation to FDA to demonstrate the safety and effectiveness of the class III device. There are administrative elements of a PMA application, but good science and scientific writing is a key to the approval of PMA application. If a PMA application lacks elements listed in the administrative checklist, FDA will refuse to file a PMA application and will not proceed with the in-depth review of scientific and clinical data. If a PMA application lacks valid clinical information and scientific analysis on sound scientific reasoning, it will delay FDA's review and approval. PMA applications that are incomplete, inaccurate, inconsist, omit critical information, and poorly organized have resulted in delays in approval or denial of PMA applications. Manufacturers should perform a quality control audit of a PMA application before sending it to FDA to assure that it is scientifically sound and presented in a well organized format.

Technical Sections: The technical sections containing data and information should allow FDA to determine whether to approve or disapprove the application. These sections are usually divided into non-clinical laboratory studies and clinical investigations.

Non-clinical Laboratory Studies' Section: Non-clinical laboratory studies' section includes information on microbiology, toxicology, immunology, biocompatibility, stress, wear, shelf life, and other laboratory or animal tests. Non-clinical studies for safety evaluation must be conducted in compliance with 21 CFR Part 58 (Good Laboratory Practice for Nonclinical Laboratory Studies).

Clinical Investigations' Section: Clinical investigations' section includes study protocols, safety and effectiveness data, adverse reactions and complications, device failures and replacements, patient information, patient complaints, tabulations of data from all individual subjects, results of statistical analyses, and any other information from the clinical investigations. Any investigation conducted under an Investigational Device Exemption (IDE) must be identified as such.

Like other scientific reports, FDA has observed problems with study designs, study conduct, data analyses, presentations, and conclusions. Investigators should always consult all applicable FDA guidance documents, industry standards, and recommended practices. Numerous device-specific FDA guidance documents that describe data requirements are available. The guidance document database on the Internet can be found at http://www.accessdata.fda.gov/scripts/cdrh/cfdocs/cfGGP/Search.cfm. Study protocols should include all applicable elements described in the device-specific guidance documents.

FDA, CDRH, Premarket Notification [510(k)]

January 14, 2004

What is Premarket Notification [510(k)]

Each person who wants to market Class I, II and some III devices intended for human use in the U.S. must submit a 510(k) to FDA at least 90 days before marketing unless the device is exempt from 510(k) requirements. There is no 510(k) form but instead a format for the submission described in 21 CFR 807 and in the pages that follow.

A 510(k) is a premarketing submission made to FDA to demonstrate that the device to be marketed is as safe and effective, that is, substantially equivalent (SE), to a legally marketed device that is not subject to premarket approval (PMA). Applicants must compare their 510(k) device to one or more similar devices currently on the U.S. market and make and support their substantial equivalency claims. A legally marketed device is a device that was legally marketed prior to May 28, 1976 (preamendments device), or a device which has been reclassified from Class III to Class II or I, a device which has been found to be substantially equivalent to such a device through the 510(k) process, or one established through Evaluation of Automatic Class III Definition. The legally marketed device(s) to which equivalence is drawn is known as the "predicate" device(s).

Applicants must submit descriptive data and, when necessary, performance data to establish that their device is SE to a predicate device. Again, the data in a 510(k) is to show comparability, that is, substantial equivalency (SE) of a new device to a predicate device.

What is Substantial Equivalence

Unlike PMA, which requires demonstration of reasonable safety and effectiveness, 510(k) requires demonstration of substantial equivalence. SE means that the new device is as safe and effective as the predicate device(s).

A device is SE if, in comparison to a predicate device it:

- has the same intended use as the predicate device; *and*
- has the same technological characteristics as the predicate device; *or*
- has different technological characteristics, that do not raise new questions of safety and effectiveness, and the sponsor demonstrates that the device is as safe and effective as the legally marketed device.

A claim of substantial equivalence does not mean the new and predicate devices must be identical. Substantial equivalence is established with respect to intended use, design, energy used or delivered, materials, performance, safety, effectiveness, labeling, biocompatibility, standards, and other applicable characteristics. Detailed information on how FDA determines substantial equivalence can be found in the Premarket Notification Review Program 6/30/86 (K86-3) blue book memorandum.

Until the applicant receives an order declaring a device SE, they may not proceed to market the device. Once the device is determined to be SE, it can then be marketed in the U.S. If FDA determines that a device is *not* SE, the applicant may resubmit another 510(k) with new data, file a reclassification petition, or submit a premarket approval application (PMA). The SE determination is usually made within 90 days and is made based on the information submitted by the applicant.

Who is Required to Submit a 510(k)

The Food, Drug and Cosmetic (FD&C) Act and 510(k) regulations in 21 CFR 807 do not specify who must apply for a 510(k)—anyone may do so. Instead, they specify which actions, such as introducing a device to the U.S. market, require a 510(k) submission.

Based on the specified actions, the following four categories of parties must submit a 510(k) to the FDA:

1. Domestic manufacturers introducing a device to the U.S. market;

   Finished device manufacturers have to submit a 510(k) if they assemble a device according to their own specifications and market it in the U.S. However, manufacturers of device components are not required to submit a 510(k) unless such components are promoted for sale to an end user as replacement parts. Also, contract manufacturers, those firms assembling devices on contract according to someone else's specifications, are not required to submit a 510(k).

2. Specification developers introducing a device to the U.S. market;

   FDA views specification developers almost the same as manufacturers. These are persons who develop specifications for a finished device, but have it manufactured under contract by another firm or entity. The specification developer submits the 510(k), not the contract manufacturer.

3. Repackers or relabelers who make labeling changes, or whose operations significantly affect the device.

Repackagers or relabelers may be required to submit a premarket notification if they significantly change the labeling or otherwise affect any condition of the device. Here you must ascertain if you are significantly changing labeling, by modifying manuals, deleting or adding warnings, contraindications, etc., and if your packaging operation could alter the condition of the device. However, most repackagers or relabelers are not required to submit a 510(k).

4. Foreign manufacturers/exporters or U.S. representatives of foreign manufacturers/exporters introducing a device to the U.S. market.

When a 510(k) is Required

A 510(k) is required when:

1. Introducing a device into commercial distribution (marketing) for the first time. After May 28, 1976 (effective date of the Medical Device Amendments to the FD&C Act), anyone who wants to sell a device in the U.S. has been required to make a 510(k) submission at least 90 days prior to offering the device for sale, even though it may have been under development or clinical investigation before that date. If your device was not marketed by your firm before May 28, 1976 a 510(k) is required. Refer to the guidance entitled Deciding When to Submit a 510(k) for a Change to an Existing Device
2. You propose a different intended use for a device which you already have in commercial distribution. The 510(k) regulation (21 CFR § 807) specifically requires a premarket notification submission for *major* changes in intended use. Intended use is indicated by claims made for a device in labeling or advertising. However, most, if not all changes in intended use will require a 510(k).
3. There is a change or modification of a device you already market, if that change could significantly affect its safety or effectiveness.

The burden is on you to decide whether or not a modification could significantly affect safety or effectiveness. Whatever your conclusion, make a record which should be reflected in your device master record and change control records, required under the medical device good manufacturing practices. Then, if you're challenged, you will be able to document that in good faith you evaluated the change.

A new, complete 510(k) application is required for changes or modifications to an existing device, where the modifications could significantly affect the safety or effectiveness of the device, or the device is to be marketed for a new or different indication.

When a 510(k) is Not Required

The following are 7 examples of when a 510(k) is not required.

1. If you sell unfinished devices to another firm for further processing, including components to be used in the assembling of devices by other firms. However, if your components are to be sold directly to end users as replacement parts, a 510(k) is required
2. If your device is not being marketed or commercially distributed. You do not need a 510(k) to develop, evaluate, or test a device. This includes clinical evaluation. It is important to mention that if you do perform clinical trials with your device, you may be subject to the Investigational Device Exemption (IDE) Regulation.

3. If you distribute other firm's domestically manufactured devices you need not submit a 510(k). You may place a label on the device "Distributed by ABC Firm", and sell it to end users without submission of a 510(k).
4. In most cases if you are a repackager or a relabeler you are not required to submit a 510(k) if the existing labeling or condition of the device is not significantly changed.
5. If your device was legally in commercial distribution before May 28, 1976, you do not have to submit a 510(k) unless it has been modified or there has been a change in its intended use. These devices are "grandfathered".
6. If you are an importer of a foreign made medical device, a 510(k) is not required if:
   a. 510(k) has been submitted by the foreign manufacturer and received marketing clearance, or
   b. 510(k) has been submitted by an importer on behalf of the foreign manufacturer and has received marketing clearance. If one importer submits a 510(k) on behalf of the foreign manufacturer, all other importers of that device, imported from the same foreign manufacturer (the 510(k) Holder) are not required to submit a 510(k) for that device.
7. If your device is exempted from this requirement by final classification regulation subject to the limitations on exemptions. That means certain Class I or II devices can be marketed for the first time without having to submit a 510(k). A compilation of the Class I and II exempted devices can be found in the MEDICAL DEVICE EXEMPTIONS page.

For more information go Deciding When to Submit a 510(k) for a Change to an Existing Device page especially for numbers 3 and 4.

The Modernization Act and the 510(k) Submission Process—Different Types of Submissions for Differing Situations

To streamline the evaluation of premarket notifications for the reserved Class I devices, Class II devices subject to premarket notification, and preamendments Class III devices for which FDA has not yet called for PMAs, the Agency has developed The New 510(k) Paradigm which in certain instances presents device manufacturers with two new optional approaches for obtaining marketing clearance for devices subject to 510(k) requirements. The document contains the following reference chart for use in determining which type of 510(k) is suitable for a given set of circumstances.

The New 510(k) Paradigm

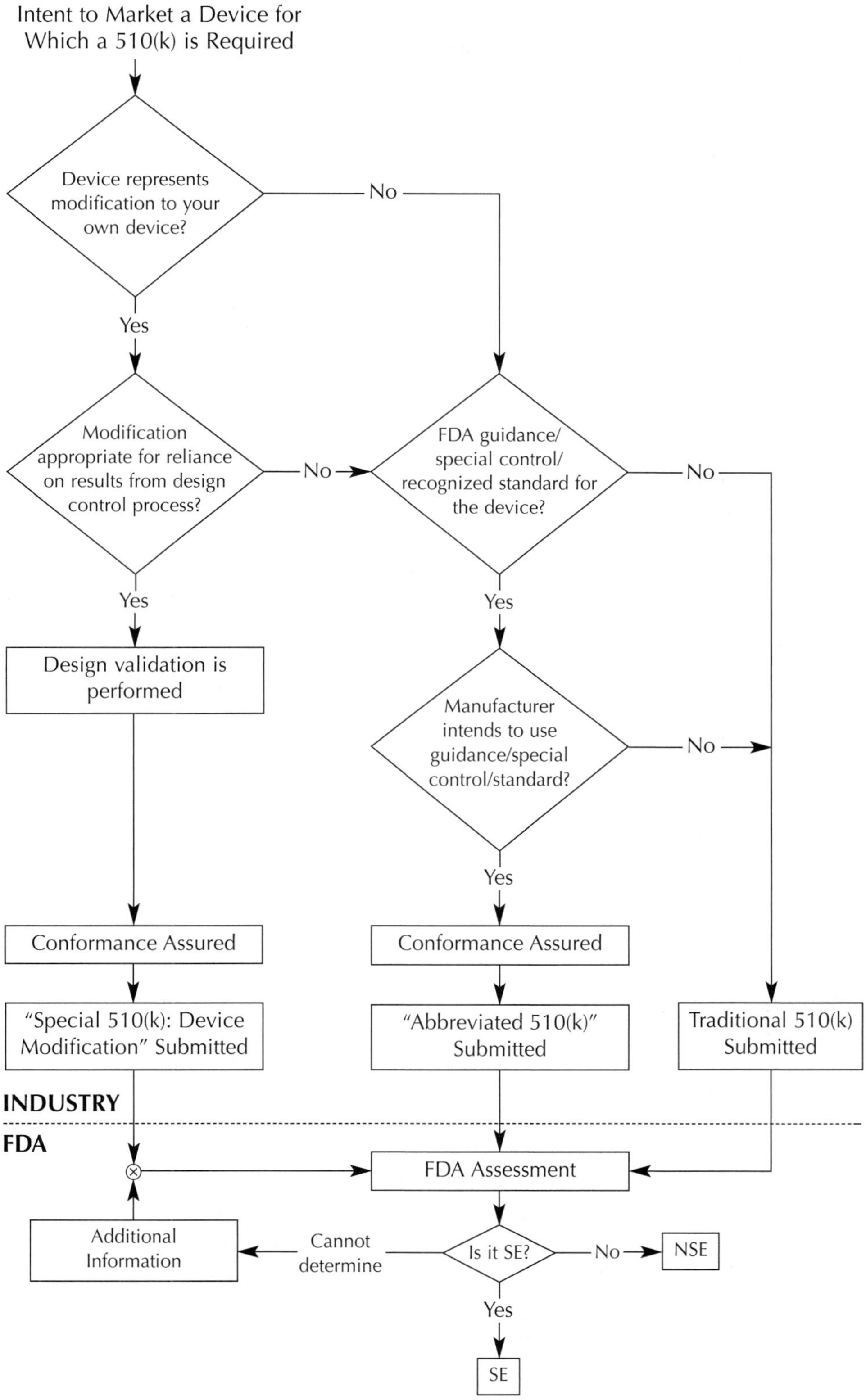

Notes & Questions

1. Does your understanding of the FDA approval process change your opinion about the correctness or implications of the holding in *Merck v. Integra* from Section B *supra*?

2. Acknowledging the sometimes blurred distinction between drugs and biologics in the biotech field, CDER and CBER have worked together to jointly produce a set of guidelines for IND's submitted on biotechnology-derived products. *See* FDA, CDER & CBER, Guidance for Industry: Content and Format of Investigational New Drug Applications (INDs) for Phase I Studies of Drugs, Including Well-Characterized, Therapeutic, Biotechnology-Derived Products (Nov. 1995), http://www.fda.gov/cder/guidance/clin2.pdf.

E. Special Disclosure Issues at the Intersection of the FDA Approval Process and the Securities Laws

Because of the critical role that FDA approval plays in the viability of biotechnology companies, investors are keenly sensitive to any information or developments in this process. Forward progress often is the key to the next round of crucial financing that will keep the company operating, while any setback may effectively end future financing and force the company into bankruptcy. Even larger, publicly traded corporations are not immune to the impact of adverse FDA actions. These companies also have the added pressure of heightened responsibility and scrutiny under the securities laws—including the Sarbanes-Oxley Act of 2002—for both information disclosures and the trading activities of directors, officers, and regular employees.

The following materials document the travails of ImClone Systems, Inc., and its co-founder, Samuel Waksal, in an escalating series of events starting from a BLA filed with CBER and leading, oddly enough, to the imprisonment of home fashion guru, Martha Stewart.

SEC, Second Amended Complaint against Samuel D. Waksal, et al.

02 Civ. 4407, S.D. NY (2003)

Plaintiff, Securities and Exchange Commission ("Commission"), for its Second Amended Complaint against defendants Samuel D. Waksal ("Sam Waksal") and Jack Waksal (collectively the "Defendants"), and Relief Defendant Patti Waksal alleges as follows:

1. The Commission charges Sam Waksal, co-founder and former chief executive officer of ImClone Systems, Inc. ("ImClone"), with violating the federal securities laws in late December 2001 by actual and attempted insider trading in ImClone stock, and by illegally tipping his father Jack Waksal about disappointing, confidential developments at ImClone. Additionally, the Commission charges Jack Waksal with illegal insider trading in ImClone stock after receiving Sam Waksal's illegal tip. On December 26, 2001, Sam Waksal privately learned that the United States Food and Drug Administration ("FDA") was expected to reject consideration of ImClone's application to approve Im-

Clone's primary product, a cancer treatment called "Erbitux." On December 27 and 28, 2001, while in possession of that non-public information, Sam Waksal attempted to sell over $5 million worth of shares of ImClone stock from one of his brokerage accounts; caused his daughter, Aliza Waksal ("Aliza"), to sell more than $2 million worth of ImClone stock from her brokerage account; and purchased ImClone put option contracts in a Swiss brokerage account. In addition, Sam Waksal told Jack Waksal of the impending FDA decision, and on December 27 and December 28, 2001, with that non-public information in hand, Jack Waksal sold over $8 million worth of his own ImClone stock. In addition, Jack Waksal sold approximately $83,000 worth of ImClone stock out of the brokerage account of his daughter, Patti Waksal. ImClone received written notification of the FDA's decision at approximately 4:00 p.m. on December 28, 2001 and publicly announced the FDA's decision in a press release at about 6:00 p.m. that day. This news prompted ImClone's stock price to drop 16% from $55.25 to $46.46 by the close of the next trading day, December 31. By engaging in insider trading before the public disclosure of ImClone's disappointing news, the Defendants and Relief Defendant illegally avoided trading losses and Sam Waksal received illegal options trading profits.

2. By the conduct alleged herein, the Defendants have engaged, directly or indirectly, in transactions, acts, practices, or courses of business that constitute violations of Section 17(a) of the Securities Act of 1933 ("Securities Act"), 15 U.S.C. §77q(a), Section 10(b) of the Securities Exchange Act of 1934 ("Exchange Act"), 15 U.S.C. §78j(b), and Rule 10b-5,17 C.F.R. §240.10b-5, thereunder. Sam Waksal has also engaged, directly or indirectly, in transactions, acts, practices, or courses of business that constitute violations of Section 16(a) of the Exchange Act, 15 U.S.C. §78p(a), and Rule 16a-3,17 C.F.R. §240.16a-3. Absent permanent injunctions by this Court, the Defendants will continue to engage in the transactions, acts, practices and courses of business set forth in this Complaint and in transactions, acts, practices and courses of business of similar type and object....

<u>RELEVANT PERSONS</u>

5. The Defendants and Relief Defendant are:

a. Sam Waksal is 56 years old and resides in Minersville, Pennsylvania at the Schuylkill Federal Correctional Institution. He is the co-founder of ImClone and was its CEO until he resigned on or about May 22, 2002. On June 12, 2002, he was arrested for securities fraud and perjury. On August 7, 2002, Sam Waksal was indicted for bank fraud, securities fraud, and perjury, based on the same facts giving rise to this action. On October 15, 2002, Sam Waksal pleaded guilty to all of the counts in the indictment except those counts based on allegations that he passed material, nonpublic information to Jack Waksal. On March 3, 2003, Sam Waksal also pleaded guilty to tax evasion charges for failing to pay New York State sales tax on certain art purchases. On June 10, Sam Waksal was sentenced to 87 months in prison and was ordered to pay a $3 million fine and $1.2 million in restitution to the New York State Tax Commission. Sam Waksal began serving his prison sentence on July 23, 2003. On or about March 17, 2003, the Court entered a Partial Judgment and Order on Consent against Samuel D. Waksal ("Consent Judgment") in this action in which, as more fully set forth therein, the Court, *inter alia* (a) permanently enjoined Sam Waksal from violating Section 17(a) of the Securities Act, 15 U.S.C. §77q(a), Section 10(b) of the Exchange Act, 15 U.S.C. §78j(b), and Rule 10b-5,17 C.F.R. §240.10b-5, Section16(a) of the Exchange Act, 15 U.S.C. §78p(a), and Rule 16a-3,17 C.F.R. §240.16a-3; (b) directed Sam Waksal to disgorge $804,367; (c) barred Sam Waksal from acting as an officer or director of any issuer that has a class of securities registered pursuant to Section 12 of the Exchange Act,

15 U.S.C.§78l, or that is required to file reports pursuant to Section 15(d) of the Exchange Act, 15 U.S.C.§78o(d); (d) entered partial judgment on the First, Second, Third and Fourth Claims for Relief in the Amended Complaint dated March 11, 2003 ("Amended Complaint"); and (e) stayed resolution of the Fifth Claim for Relief of the Amended Complaint and all issues concerning civil penalties arising out of the totality of the allegations in the Amended Complaint pending resolution of criminal charges against Sam Waksal. As more fully set forth in the Consent of Defendant Samuel D. Waksal dated March 4, 2003 accompanying the Consent Judgment, Waksal neither admitted nor denied the allegations of the Amended Complaint (except as to personal and subject matter jurisdiction, which he admitted) to the extent not inconsistent with the Consent Judgment.

b. Jack Waksal is 82 years old and resides in East Hampton, New York and Hallandale, Florida. He is Sam Waksal's and Patti Waksal's father.

c. Patti Waksal is 47 years old and resides in Bethesda, Maryland. She is Jack Waksal's daughter and Sam Waksal's sister.

6. ImClone is a Delaware corporation headquartered in New York, New York. ImClone securities are registered with the Commission pursuant to Section 12(g) of the Exchange Act, 15 U.S.C. §§78l(g), and are traded on The Nasdaq Stock Market. The company is a biopharmaceutical corporation, which is currently developing several cancer treatments including its lead product, Erbitux.

<u>THE ILLEGAL CONDUCT</u>

<u>Sam Waksal's Fiduciary Duty</u>

7. At the time of the transactions and events alleged in this Complaint, Sam Waksal was ImClone's CEO, and therefore owed a fiduciary duty to ImClone and its shareholders. As a result, Sam Waksal had a fiduciary duty, among other things, not to trade while in possession of material non-public information and to keep material non-public information confidential.

<u>ImClone's Erbitux Application</u>

8. Over the past several years, ImClone has devoted significant resources to developing a cancer treatment called "Erbitux," with the objective of obtaining FDA approval to market the product. ImClone's Form 10-K Annual Report for the fiscal year ended December 31, 2001 described Erbitux as ImClone's "lead product candidate" and said that Erbitux "has been shown in several early stage clinical trials ... when administered with either radiation therapy or chemotherapy, to cause tumor reduction in certain cases." ImClone intends to market Erbitux in the United States and Canada with its development, promotional and distribution partner, Bristol-Myers Squibb Company ("Bristol-Myers"). On September 19, 2001, ImClone announced that Bristol-Myers would invest a total of $1 billion in Erbitux and also buy $1 billion in outstanding ImClone stock and would co-develop and co-promote Erbitux with ImClone. Sam Waksal played a direct role in coordinating and publicizing ImClone's efforts to develop, and obtain FDA approval for, Erbitux.

9. On June 28, 2001, ImClone began the process of submitting a rolling application for FDA approval for Erbitux, called a Biologics License Application ("BLA"). On October 31, 2001, ImClone submitted to the FDA the final substantial portion of its BLA.

10. ImClone's October 31, 2001 submission of its BLA gave the FDA 60 days, until Monday, December 31, to decide whether to accept ImClone's BLA for filing. By the end of December 2001, the FDA had three options. It could (1) accept ImClone's BLA for filing; (2) accept the BLA for filing, but simultaneously issue a disciplinary review

letter notifying ImClone that the BLA still had serious deficiencies that it would need to correct before the BLA could be approved; or (3) refuse to file the BLA by issuing a Refusal to File ("RTF") letter. The issuance of an RTF letter is a disappointing development for an applicant because it means that the applicant must file a new BLA to begin the process again.

Sam Waksal Learns of the FDA Decision And Attempts to Trade ImClone Securities

11. On December 25, 2001, Bristol-Myers learned from a source at the FDA, that the FDA would issue an RTF letter to ImClone on December 28, 2001. On the evening of Wednesday, December 26, 2001, Sam Waksal learned about the FDA's decision to issue an RTF letter on December 28, 2001. When Sam Waksal returned to the office the following morning, December 27, among other things, he learned that the company was preparing draft press releases focusing entirely on disclosing the FDA's issuance of an RTF letter.

12. The information Sam Waksal received on December 26 and 27, 2001, as set forth in Paragraph 11, above, was material and non-public. This information was not disclosed to the public until approximately 6:00 p.m. on Friday, December 28, 2001, when, after the close of trading, ImClone issued a press release stating, in pertinent part, that the FDA "has advised the Company that at this time it is not accepting for filing in its current form the Company's rolling ... BLA for ERBITUX TM."

13. Beginning on the evening of Wednesday, December 26, when Sam Waksal became aware that ImClone would receive an RTF letter that Friday, Sam Waksal, in breach of a fiduciary duty to ImClone and its shareholders, attempted to dispose of 79,797 shares of ImClone stock that originated in his brokerage account at Merrill Lynch, Pierce, Fenner & Smith, Incorporated ("Merrill Lynch"). Initially, in the evening of December 26, Sam Waksal instructed his agent to transfer those shares to his daughter's account at Merrill Lynch. The following morning, Sam Waksal instructed his agent to sell those shares. When Sam Waksal's agent contacted Merrill Lynch to accomplish this, a representative of Merrill Lynch told him that the shares were restricted and could not be sold without ImClone's counsel's approval. When Merrill Lynch refused to execute the trades, Sam Waksal instructed his agent to transfer the shares from Merrill Lynch to Bank of America ("B of A") and then to sell them. After B of A informed Sam Waksal's agent that they would not sell the shares, the transfer never occurred and the shares were never sold.

Sam Waksal Causes Aliza to Sell ImClone Stock

14. In the morning of December 27, before the market opened, Sam Waksal knowingly or recklessly, for his direct or indirect benefit and in breach of a fiduciary duty to ImClone and its shareholders, had a telephone conversation with his daughter, Aliza, while in possession of material, non-public information that the FDA had decided to issue an RTF letter to ImClone on December 28.

15. At that time, Sam Waksal was Aliza's sole means of support and controlled her bank and brokerage accounts.

16. During the conversation referred to in Paragraph 14, Sam Waksal directed Aliza to sell all of her ImClone shares. By causing Aliza to sell ImClone stock, Sam Waksal benefited because he was her entire means of financial support.

17. Immediately after speaking with Sam Waksal, Aliza placed an order at 9 a.m. to sell 39,472 shares of ImClone stock. That order was executed on December 27 in four blocks between 9:35 a.m. and 9:48 a.m., at prices between $62.28 and $63.20 per share.

18. By selling the 39,472 shares of ImClone stock on December 27, instead of waiting until news of the RTF letter became public, Aliza avoided $630,295 in trading losses.

Sam Waksal Purchases ImClone Option Contracts

19. On December 28, 2001, while in possession of the material non-public information that ImClone would receive an RTF letter that day, Sam Waksal, in breach of a fiduciary duty to ImClone and its shareholders, purchased 200 ImClone Jan 02 50 put option contracts and 10 ImClone Jan 02 55 put option contracts. Sam Waksal made these purchases through an account at Discount Bank and Trust AG in Switzerland. Sam Waksal sold all 210 put option contracts on January 4, 2002 and profited in the amount of $130,130.

20. Sam Waksal failed to file a statement disclosing a change of ownership of his ImClone securities as required by Section 16(a) of the Exchange Act and Rule 16a-3.

Sam Waksal Tips Jack Waksal, Who Sells

21. On December 26, 2001, the night Sam Waksal learned of the impending RTF letter, Sam Waksal, knowingly or recklessly, for his direct or indirect benefit and in breach of a fiduciary duty to ImClone and its shareholders, communicated to Jack Waksal, in words or in substance, material, non-public information that the FDA had decided to issue an RTF letter to ImClone on or about December 28.

22. Sam Waksal, intending to bestow upon Jack Waksal a gift of illegal profits or illegal loss avoidance, communicated the information described in Paragraph 21 to Jack Waksal, knowing or having reason to know that Jack Waksal would sell ImClone stock.

23. On December 27, 2001, while aware of the information described in Paragraph 21, Jack Waksal placed orders to sell a total of 110,000 shares of ImClone stock. Jack Waksal placed these orders with three different broker-dealers between 9:18 a.m. and 9:45 a.m. The orders were executed between 9:45 a.m. and 10:02 a.m., at prices between $61.25 and $62.16 per share.

24. Additionally, that same morning, December 27, while aware of the information described in Paragraph 21, Jack Waksal called Prudential Securities before 9:30 a.m. and placed an order to sell 1,336 shares of ImClone stock from the account of Patti Waksal. That order was executed at 9:30 a.m. at about $62.20 per share. Jack Waksal had exercised control over Patti Waksal's investments in this Prudential Securities account since Jack Waksal arranged for the opening of that account in August 2000.

25. On the following morning, December 28, while aware of the information described in Paragraph 21, Jack Waksal sold another 25,000 shares of ImClone stock. This order was placed at 9:29 a.m. and executed at 10:09 a.m. at $57.19 per share.

26. On December 27 and December 28, when Jack Waksal sold his and Patti Waksal's ImClone stock, he knew or acted in reckless disregard of the fact that (1) he possessed confidential, non-public information that ImClone would receive an RTF letter from the FDA; and (2) Sam Waksal breached a fiduciary duty he owed to ImClone and its shareholders when he gave Jack Waksal that information.

27. Jack Waksal provided false and misleading explanations for his trades, and falsely testified about the events of December 26 through 28, 2001 when questioned about them by the Commission staff.

28. By selling 135,000 shares of his ImClone stock on December 27 and December 28, instead of waiting until the news of the RTF letter became public, Jack Waksal avoided losses in an amount to be determined at trial.

29. By selling 1,336 shares of Patti Waksal's ImClone stock on December 27, Jack Waksal avoided losses for Patti Waksal in an amount to be determined at trial....

Irvine v. ImClone Systems, Inc.

2003 WL 21297285 (S.D.N.Y.)

JUDGE OWEN.

Defendants ImClone Systems, Inc. ("ImClone"), Harlan Waksal, Ronald Martell, John Landes and the outside director defendants[109] have moved to dismiss the Irvine action as to them, and defendants ImClone and Harlan Waksal have moved to dismiss the Flynn action as to them.[110] For the following reasons the motion in the Irvine action is denied as to defendants ImClone and Harlan Waksal and granted as to defendants Martell, Landes, and the outside directors and the motion in the Flynn action is denied.

ImClone, a biotechnology company, developed a drug called Erbitux which, in combination with standard forms of chemotherapy, was purported to inhibit the growth of cancerous tumors, particularly colorectal tumors. ImClone announced on February 1, 2001 that the FDA had granted "Fast Track" status to Erbitux, which essentially meant that the FDA would expedite the review of the drug. In the following months, during the class period, ImClone advised the market that they intended to initiate the filing of a Biologics License Application ("BLA") by June 2001 and that they reasonably expected approval by the FDA in early 2002. The Complaint alleges a number of misrepresentations and fraudulent statements, some oral by the Waksals, and others published, made to the market while it is alleged to have been known that there were a number of deficiencies with the study and that it was not reasonably foreseeable that the FDA would approve Erbitux on that time line. As a result of these alleged misrepresentations, the Complaint further alleges that ImClone's stock was artificially inflated and that the individual defendants sold large amounts of their stock during this period.

Defendants argue that some of the statements are covered by the "safe harbor" provision of the Private Securities Litigation Reform Act ("PSLRA"). This provides that a forward-looking statement, which is identified as being such, may be protected if it is accompanied by "meaningful cautionary statements identifying important factors that could cause actual results to differ materially from those in the forward-looking statement." 15 U.S.C. § 78u-5(c). The majority of alleged misrepresentations here are not forward-looking, and those that can be characterized as such, do not include sufficient cautionary language. While it is argued that investors were repeatedly warned that ImClone's business was "subject to regulation primarily by the FDA," that "[n]oncompliance with applicable requirements can result in refusal to approve product licenses or other applications," that there are "risks and uncertainties associated with completing pre-clinical and clinical trials ... [and] obtaining and maintaining regulatory approval for such compounds," and that "actual results may differ materially" from those predicted, this language is not sufficient to place these statements under the "safe harbor" provisions of the PSLRA. *See In re Amylin Pharmaceuticals, Inc. Securities Litigation,* 2002 WL 31520051, at *9 (S.D.Cal.2002) (In considering similar cautionary language to that present here, the court noted that "[i]ndividuals commonly ignore such boilerplate warnings. Even if investors read them, merely warning investors that FDA may not approve the drug does not warn investors about some of the specific shortcomings of the ... trials....").

---

109. The outside director defendants in the Irvine action are Richard Barth, Robert Goldhammer, David Kies, Paul Kopperl, John Mendelsohn, and William Miller.

110. Samuel Waksal is also a defendant in both of these actions but is not a party to these motions.

Having concluded that the statements are not covered by the "safe harbor" provision, the Complaint adequately alleges with sufficient particularity all the elements of a 10(b) and 10b-5 claim against defendants ImClone and Harlan Waksal, as he had personally made a number of the statements and was then Chief Operating Officer of ImClone.

Plaintiff argues that the group pleading doctrine allows liability to attach to the other individual defendants even though the Complaint does not allege any misrepresentations or fraudulent statements as having been made by them. The group pleading doctrine is "an exception to the requirement that the fraudulent acts of each defendant be identified separately in the complaint." This doctrine "is extremely limited in scope. [And c]ourts in the Second Circuit and elsewhere have construed the doctrine as applying only to clearly cognizable corporate insiders with active daily roles in the relevant companies or transactions." None of the oral statements made by either of the Waksals can be attributed to the other individual defendants under this doctrine, as the doctrine "allows plaintiffs to rely on a presumption that statements in prospectuses, registration statements, annual reports, press releases, or other group-published information, are the collective work of those individuals with direct involvement in the everyday business of the company." But here, the Complaint makes no allegations regarding the outside directors which would support the conclusion that they were anything more than typical *outside* directors or that they played any daily role with regard to the statements at issue. With regard to Landes, as General Counsel, and Martell, as Vice President of Marketing and Sales, the Complaint does not allege that either, even assuming they had any role in preparing the published statements, had any reason to know that the technical and scientific information included was anything other than true at the time they were made. Accordingly, the motion to dismiss count one of the Irvine complaint is granted as to the outside director defendants, and Martell, and Landes.

Next I turn to whether the Complaint satisfies the scienter requirement of the PSLRA. "In order to plead scienter, plaintiffs must state with particularity facts giving rise to a strong inference that the defendant acted with the requisite state of mind." This standard is met by pleading facts showing either "motive and opportunity to commit fraud, or ... that constitute strong circumstantial evidence of conscious misbehavior or recklessness." Plaintiffs have adequately alleged facts to satisfy either prong of this test. For these reasons, the motion to dismiss count one of the Irvine action as to defendants ImClone and Harlan Waksal is denied.

Count two of the Complaint charges the individual defendants with control person liability. The motion to dismiss this count is denied as to Harlan Waksal, as the Complaint sufficiently alleges the required elements: (1) that there was a primary violation; (2) control of the primary violator by the defendant; (3) and that the "controlling person was in some meaningful sense a culpable participant" in the primary violation. Harlan Waksal was the COO of ImClone and one of the company's founders. In addition, he personally made a number of the alleged misrepresentations, which were substantially similar to those alleged to have been made by his brother Sam Waksal. As to Martell, Landes, and the outside directors, however, this count is dismissed as well. "[M]uch more than a bare allegation of "control status" is required." The Complaint here alleges that "each of the Individual Defendants, by virtue of his office and/or directorship at ImClone and his specific acts, and by virtue of his significant holdings of ImClone securities, was a controlling person of ImClone within the meaning of Section 20(a) of the Exchange Act." It does not allege anything substantially further that would support a finding of control person liability. This is not sufficient to maintain control person liability against the outside directors, Landes, or Martell and the second cause of action is dismissed as to them.

The Complaint in the Flynn action also charges defendants ImClone and Harlan Waksal with violations of 10(b) and 10b-5 and charges Harlan Waksal with control person liability. The Flynn Complaint adequately alleges all elements of these claims, for many of the reasons discussed above with regard to the Irvine action, and as such, this motion is also denied.

United States v. Stewart

323 F.Supp.2d 606 (S.D.N.Y. 2004)

District Judge Cedarbaum.

Defendants Martha Stewart and Peter Bacanovic have moved for a new trial pursuant to Fed. R. Cr. P. 33 on the ground that an expert witness for the Government has been charged with committing perjury in his testimony. Because there is no reasonable likelihood that this perjury could have affected the jury's verdict, and because overwhelming independent evidence supports the verdict, the motions are denied.

Background

Stewart and Bacanovic were indicted on criminal charges arising from Martha Stewart's December 27, 2001 sale of 3,928 shares of stock in ImClone Systems, Inc. ("ImClone"). ImClone is a biotechnology company whose then-chief executive officer, Samuel Waksal, was a friend of Stewart's and a client of Stewart's stockbroker at Merrill Lynch, defendant Bacanovic. On December 25, 2001, ImClone learned that the Food and Drug Administration had rejected the company's application for approval of Erbitux, a cancer-fighting drug. On December 28, the day after Stewart sold her shares, ImClone publicly announced that the Erbitux application had been rejected. Shortly after ImClone's announcement, the Securities and Exchange Commission ("SEC") and the United States Attorney's Office for the Southern District of New York launched investigations into trading in ImClone stock in advance of the announcement to the public of the news about Erbitux.

Each defendant was questioned twice in the course of these investigations. Stewart was interviewed at the office of the United States Attorney on February 4, 2002 and by telephone on April 10, 2002. Among those present during Stewart's interviews were Special Agent Catherine Farmer of the FBI and Helene Glotzer, a lawyer with the SEC's Enforcement Division. Bacanovic was interviewed by telephone on January 7, 2002. Present at that interview were Glotzer and another SEC attorney, Jill Slansky, as well as David Marcus, a Merrill Lynch attorney. On February 13, 2002, Bacanovic testified under oath before the SEC. He was questioned by three SEC attorneys: Glotzer, Slansky, and Laurent Sacharoff. His testimony was tape recorded.

The jury convicted Stewart of making false statements to investigators during her February 4 interview, in violation of 18 U.S.C. § 1001. The jury found Stewart guilty of making the following false statements, each of which was a specification in Count Three of the Indictment. Stewart told the Government investigators that she spoke to Bacanovic on December 27 and instructed him to sell her ImClone shares after he informed her that ImClone was trading below $60 per share. Stewart also stated that during the same telephone call, she and Bacanovic discussed the performance of the stock of her own company, Martha Stewart Living Omnimedia ("MSLO"), and discussed K-Mart. She told investigators that she had decided to sell her ImClone shares at that time because she did not want to be bothered during her vacation. Stewart stated that she did not know if there was any record of a telephone message left by Bacanovic on December 27 in her assistant's message log. She also said that since December 28, she had only spoken with Bacanovic once regarding ImClone, and they had only discussed matters in the public arena. Finally, Stewart told investigators that since December 28, Bacanovic had told her that Merrill Lynch had been questioned by the SEC regarding ImClone, but that he did not tell her that he had been questioned by the SEC or that he had been questioned about her account.

The jury acquitted Stewart of one specification charged in Count Three: her statement that she and Bacanovic had agreed, at a time when ImClone was trading at $74 per share, that she would sell her shares when ImClone started trading at $60 per share.

The jury found Stewart guilty of making the following false statements to investigators during her April 10 interview. Each of these statements was a specification in Count Four of the Indictment. Stewart said that she did not recall if she and Bacanovic had spoken about Waksal on December 27 and that she did not recall being informed that any of the Waksals were selling their ImClone stock. Stewart also reiterated that she spoke to Bacanovic on December 27, that he told her the price of ImClone shares, and that he suggested that she sell her holdings.

The jury did not find Stewart guilty of one false statement specification charged in Count Four: her statement that sometime in November or December of 2001, after she sold ImClone shares held in the Martha Stewart Defined Pension Trust, she and Bacanovic decided she would sell her remaining ImClone shares when they started trading at $60 per share.

The jury found Bacanovic guilty of making one false statement during his January 7 interview with the SEC, in violation of 18 U.S.C. § 1001. This was a specification in Count Two of the Indictment, which charged Bacanovic with falsely stating that he had spoken to Stewart on December 27, that he told Stewart during that conversation that ImClone's share price had dropped, and that Stewart had instructed him to sell her shares.

The jury found Bacanovic not guilty of the other false statement charged in Count Two: his statement that on December 20, 2001, he had a conversation with Stewart in which she decided to sell her ImClone stock at $60 per share.

The jury also convicted Bacanovic of perjury in violation of 18 U.S.C. § 1621, for one statement he made during his February 13 testimony before the SEC. Perjury was the charge in Count Six of the Indictment. Bacanovic stated that on the morning of December 27, he had left a message for Stewart with her assistant, Ann Armstrong. He said that the message requested that Stewart return his call, and advised her of the price at which ImClone was then trading.

The jury acquitted Bacanovic of five other perjury specifications charged in Count Six. These specifications related to conversations Bacanovic had had with Stewart subsequent to her December 27 trade, the circumstances of her decision on December 20 to sell ImClone at $60 per share, and a worksheet he had used during their December 20 conversation.

The jury acquitted Bacanovic of a charge of making and using a false document, which was charged as a violation of 18 U.S.C. § 1001 in Count Five of the Indictment. This count was based on a worksheet that Bacanovic gave the SEC in the course of their investigation. Bacanovic claimed that he had used the worksheet during his December

20 conversation with Stewart. The worksheet listed Stewart's holdings and contained numerous handwritten notations in blue ink. The bullet point before ImClone's entry on the worksheet was circled in blue ink, as were the bullet points preceding several other entries on the page. Beside ImClone's name was a notation, "*@60,*" also in blue ink. The "*@60*" notation was the basis of the charge.

The jury also convicted defendants of conspiracy and obstruction of an agency proceeding in violation of 18 U.S.C. § 1505. With respect to the conspiracy charge, the jury found that the defendants conspired to carry out all three objects of the conspiracy: making false statements, perjury, and obstruction of an agency proceeding.

The prosecution's key witness against both defendants was Bacanovic's former assistant, Douglas Faneuil, who testified pursuant to a cooperation agreement with the Government. Faneuil testified that on the morning of December 27, 2001, he learned that Sam Waksal and several members of Waksal's family were attempting to sell their ImClone holdings. Bacanovic, who was on vacation and out of the office that day, learned of the Waksals' trading activity when he telephoned Faneuil. Faneuil testified that when he told Bacanovic that Sam Waksal and his daughters wanted to sell their ImClone stock, Bacanovic said: "Oh, my God, get Martha on the phone." Faneuil dialed the telephone number of Stewart's New York office and transferred Bacanovic to Stewart's assistant, Ann Armstrong. Faneuil testified that he did not listen to their ensuing conversation. Later that morning, Bacanovic called Faneuil again. Bacanovic told Faneuil that Stewart would be calling and instructed Faneuil to "tell her what's going on." When Faneuil asked whether that meant that he should tell Stewart "about Sam," Bacanovic replied, "Of course. You must. You've got to. That's the whole point." Faneuil testified that when Stewart called that afternoon, she immediately said: "Hi, this is Martha, what's going on with Sam?" Faneuil responded: "well, we have no news on the company, but Peter thought you might like to act on the information that Sam Waksal was trying to sell all of his shares." Stewart said: "all his shares?" When Faneuil responded that Waksal was attempting to sell all of the shares he held at Merrill Lynch, Stewart asked Faneuil the price of the stock and then instructed him to sell all of her shares. She also asked him whether she held any additional shares of ImClone in her pension accounts, and he told her that she did not. Faneuil offered to e-mail Stewart's assistant, Ann Armstrong, to confirm the sale, which caused Stewart to become angry and inform him that he had no right to tell her assistant about her personal transactions. They then agreed that Faneuil would send an e-mail to Stewart's private e-mail address when her stock was sold. He subsequently placed the order for the sale and e-mailed Stewart when it was completed. Faneuil testified that Bacanovic called later that day, eager to know whether Martha had called and what Faneuil had told her. Faneuil informed Bacanovic that he had told Stewart that Waksal was trying to sell all his shares, and that Stewart had sold hers. Documents in evidence demonstrated that Stewart's ImClone stock had been sold shortly before 2 p.m. on December 27, 2001.

Faneuil also testified that within a few days after the Erbitux announcement, one of his supervisors at Merrill Lynch approached him with questions about the events on December 27. Faneuil called Bacanovic, who was still on vacation at that time. Bacanovic told him that Stewart sold her ImClone shares pursuant to a tax-loss selling plan which Bacanovic and Stewart had developed earlier in December. When Faneuil later learned that the sale actually disrupted Stewart's tax-loss selling because Stewart sold the shares at a significant profit, Faneuil again turned to Bacanovic, who informed him that Stewart sold her ImClone stock pursuant to an agreement they had reached that she would sell if the share price fell to $60. Faneuil testified that this was the first time that he had heard of such a $60 agreement.

Faneuil admitted that he initially lied to investigators about his conversation with Stewart. He testified that in the months following the sale, he felt increasing pressure from Bacanovic not to reveal the truth about the events of December 27. In mid-January, Bacanovic told him: "I've spoken to Martha. I've met with her. And everyone's telling the same story. Everyone's telling the same story. This was a $60 stop-loss order. That was the reason for her sale. We're all on the same page, and it's the truth. It's the true story. Everyone's telling the same story." Faneuil testified that he had similar conversations with Bacanovic at least five times before June 2002, when he decided to correct the statements he had made to investigators and cooperate with the Government.

Faneuil's direct examination lasted approximately four hours. Defense counsel cross-examined him for more than nine hours over a period of three days, and sought to impeach his credibility through evidence of his prior experiences with Stewart, former drug use, and his cooperation agreement with the Government.

The Government's evidence also included the testimony of Emily Perret, Sam Waksal's assistant. Perret testified that Stewart called ImClone's New York office on December 27. According to Perret, Stewart immediately said "get Sam, or where is Sam. This is Martha. There is something going on with ImClone. Do you know what it is? I need you to go find him." Perret informed Stewart that she did not know Waksal's whereabouts and had no information about ImClone. Perret recorded the following message in her telephone log: "1:43 Martha Stewart, something is going on with ImClone and she wants to know what She is on her way to Mexico and is staying at Los Ventanos [sic]." Telephone records admitted at trial showed that Stewart placed this call after speaking with Faneuil.

Stewart's assistant, Ann Armstrong, also testified during the Government's case. Armstrong testified that Bacanovic called on the morning of December 27 and asked to speak to Stewart. Armstrong informed him that Stewart was on an airplane en route to Mexico, and typed the following message into her computer message log: "Peter Bacanovic thinks ImClone is going to start trading downward." Armstrong testified that Bacanovic did not say what the price of ImClone was. When Stewart called later that day, Armstrong relayed the message to her, and then transferred her call to Peter Bacanovic's office.

Telephone records corroborated the testimony of Faneuil and Armstrong with respect to the timing and sequence of the telephone conversations which occurred on December 27.

Armstrong also testified that on January 31, 2002, Stewart spoke with her attorney on the telephone, then approached Armstrong and asked to see the message log for December 26 through January 7. After Armstrong opened the document on her computer screen, Stewart seated herself at Armstrong's desk and began scrolling through the messages. When she came to the messages listed for December 27, Stewart deleted the message from Bacanovic, changing it to: "Peter Bacanovic re imclone." Armstrong testified that Stewart then stood up and told Armstrong to "put it back the way it was." This occurred five days before Stewart's interview at the United States Attorney's Office. The Government introduced into evidence the original message log as well as a copy of the altered version which Armstrong had kept.

The Government also presented the testimony of Mariana Pasternak, Stewart's best friend. Pasternak traveled with Stewart to Mexico on December 27, 2001, and testified about a conversation she had with Stewart in Mexico. The two were talking about mutual friends, and the conversation turned to Sam Waksal. Pasternak testified that Stewart said Waksal "was selling or trying to sell his stock, that his daughter was selling or trying to sell her stock, and Merrill Lynch didn't sell." Stewart also stated: "His stock is going down, or went down, and I sold mine." Pasternak also testified that at some point while she and Stewart were still in Mexico, Stewart said: "Isn't it nice to have brokers who tell you those things." On cross-examination, Pasternak stated that she could not recall whether Stewart said this or whether Pasternak herself had merely thought it. On redirect examination, Pasternak testified that it was her best belief that Stewart had made the statement. Pasternak's testimony was admitted only against Stewart.

The Government also presented the testimony of Lawrence F. Stewart (hereinafter "Lawrence"), Director of the Forensic Services Division of the United States Secret Service. Lawrence's specialty is ink analysis—he testified that he has been designated the "National Expert for Ink Analysis." At trial, Lawrence introduced the jury to the forensic tests which were performed on the worksheet to determine whether there was any variation in the pens used to make the handwritten notations. His laboratory tested the document twice: in July and August 2002 and January 2004. Lawrence stated that the tests revealed that all but one of the tested notations on the document—including the circle around the ImClone bullet point—were made with an inexpensive type of Paper Mate pen. The exception was the "@*60*" notation, which was made with a pen Lawrence could not identify. Lawrence testified that while there are scientific tests which can measure the age of ink on a document, they could not be used on the "@*60*" notation because they require multiple samples of the same ink placed on a document over a span of time. The Government argued, on the basis of the use of different pens, that Bacanovic did not make the "@*60*" notation at the same time that he made the other notation on the same line.

Lawrence was extensively cross-examined regarding the wording of his laboratory's reports on the worksheet and regarding a mark that his laboratory did not fully test: a small dash beside an entry for "Apple Computer Inc." Lawrence testified that he had not tested this mark because the process of testing necessarily destroys the sample, and he was concerned that by testing the dash he would not leave enough of the sample for the defense to analyze. However, Lawrence did conclude that the dash was not made with a Paper Mate pen, and that it was possible that it was made by the same pen that made the "@*60*" notation.

Throughout his testimony, Lawrence indicated that he had performed much of the work involved in testing the ink on the worksheet. Lawrence also testified that although another ink examiner, Susan Fortunato, had written the laboratory report on the July 2002 tests, he had participated in those tests, reviewed her work and assisted in the creation of the exhibits prepared for the trial. He also stated that he had participated in the January 2004 testing.

In his defense case, Bacanovic presented the expert testimony of another ink examiner, Dr. Albert Lyter. Lyter used one of the same forensic tests the Secret Service laboratory had used to analyze the worksheet, and agreed with Lawrence's conclusion that the ink used to create the "@*60*" notation was different from the ink used to create all of the other notations tested by the Government, including the circle around the bullet point preceding the ImClone entry. Lyter did not dispute Lawrence's statement that the comparative age of the entries could not be scientifically determined. Lyter's analysis for the worksheet varied from Lawrence's in only two respects. First, Lyter analyzed the dash beside the Apple Computer entry, and concluded that it was made with the same pen that had made the "@*60*" entry. Second, Lyter testified that densitometry, a method of statistical analysis based on measurements of ink density, demonstrated that Bacanovic used at least two different Paper Mate pens to make all of the remaining marks on the page. That is, while the pens used to make those notations contained ink of the same recipe, minor variations in the composition of the inks revealed that they were from different batches, and therefore must have been contained in different pens. This testimony was offered to support the defense's contention that Bacanovic used multiple pens during his conversation with Stewart.

Lawrence returned to the stand during the Government's rebuttal case to explain that densitometry lacks scientific validity. During cross-examination, he was asked whether he was familiar with a proposal for a forensic science textbook by several of his colleagues at the Forensic Services Division, which includes a chapter about the use of densitometry to detect batch variations in inks of the same recipe. Lawrence stated that he had seen the textbook proposal.

Bacanovic's lawyer spent the majority of his time during summation attacking Faneuil's credibility and pointing out inconsistencies in his testimony. With respect to the worksheet, Bacanovic's lawyer stated, among other things: "We had a lot of expert testimony about this document. But our expert and their expert really agreed on almost everything about the main important points." Stewart's lawyer conceded during his closing argument that Faneuil's testimony concerning what he told Stewart on December 27 was accurate: "Nobody is disputing whether or not Ms. Stewart was told that the Waksals were selling on December 27th. What we are disputing is that it made a difference to her."

After a five-week trial, the jury returned the verdict described above. Two conclusions relevant to the current motions can be drawn from the jury's verdict: first, that the jury found that the Government had not proved beyond a reasonable doubt that defendants had fabricated the $60 agreement; and second, that the jury found beyond a reasonable doubt that Stewart and Bacanovic agreed to lie and did lie to Government investigators to conceal the fact that when Stewart sold her ImClone stock on December 27, 2001, she had been tipped by Bacanovic's assistant that the CEO of ImClone was trying to sell his ImClone shares held at Merrill Lynch....

B. *The Effect of Lawrence Stewart's Perjury on the Jury's Judgment*

Defendants have failed to demonstrate that the prosecution knew or should have known of Lawrence's perjury. However, even under the stricter prejudice standard applicable when the Government is aware of a witness's perjury, defendants' motions fail. There is no reasonable likelihood that knowledge by the jury that Lawrence lied about his participation in the ink tests and whether he was aware of a book proposal could have affected the verdict.

1. *The Jury Did Not Rely on Lawrence Stewart's Testimony To Convict Defendants*

The verdict, the nature of Lawrence's perjury, and the corroboration that Lawrence's substantive testimony received from the defense's expert demonstrate that Lawrence's misrepresentations could have had no effect on defendants' convictions.

First, the jury found that the Government did not satisfy its burden of proof on the charges to which Lawrence's testimony was relevant. Defendants do not dispute that Bacanovic was acquitted of the charge of making and using a false document, and that none of the false statement and perjury specifications concerning the existence of the $60 agreement were found by the jury to have been proved beyond a reasonable doubt. Instead, the jury found that Stewart lied when she told investigators that she spoke to Bacanovic on December 27 and instructed him to sell her shares after he informed her that ImClone was trading below $60 per share, that she could not remember whether she had been told about Waksal's attempted sale, that she sold her stock because she did not want to be bothered during her vacation, that she discussed MSLO and K-Mart with Bacanovic on December 27, and that she did not discuss the ImClone investigations with Bacanovic. The jury found that Bacanovic lied when he said he spoke to Stewart on December 27 and when he said that the message he left with Armstrong only quoted the market price of ImClone shares. In other words, the jury convicted defendants of lies that had nothing to do with the $60 agreement. The outcome would have been no different had Lawrence's entire testimony been rejected by the jury, or had Lawrence not testified at all....

Defendants argue that acquittal on some charges does not establish that the jury completely disregarded Lawrence's testimony. They contend that the $60 agreement constituted Stewart and Bacanovic's core defense and that the "*@60*" notation was evidence which supported that defense; thus, to the extent that awareness of Lawrence's perjury could have caused the jury to discredit his testimony and have greater confidence in the existence of the agreement and the validity of the notation, the jury would have been more willing to believe defendants' version of the events.

This argument is wholly speculative and logically flawed. The existence of the $60 agreement would not have exonerated defendants. It would not have been inconsistent for the jury to find that defendants did make the $60 agreement, but that the agreement was not the *reason* for the sale. Defendants do not persuasively explain how knowledge of Lawrence's lies could have made the jury more likely to believe that the agreement was the reason for the sale.

Second, Lawrence's false statements were entirely collateral to the substance of his testimony and to defendants' culpability for the crimes charged....

Defendants attempt to characterize Lawrence as central to the prosecution's case and his misrepresentations as critical to the Government's "core theory" that the $60 agreement was a fabrication. As an initial matter, defendants overstate the importance of the $60 agreement to this prosecution. That a $60 agreement was the reason for Stewart's sale was only one of many lies defendants were charged with telling investigators to conceal that Stewart sold her stock because of Bacanovic's tip. The evidence against defendants, defendants' own closing arguments, and the jury's verdict reveal that before Lawrence's perjury was disclosed, no one considered him the "centerpiece" of the Government's case. Moreover, the appropriate analysis is not the importance of the witness to the prosecution's theory of the case, but "the materiality of the perjury *to the jury's verdict.*" Lawrence's testimony concerning who performed the forensic tests and his knowledge of a textbook proposal circulated by his colleagues have nothing to do with the validity of the ink tests his laboratory performed or the crimes of which defendants were convicted. While it is true that new impeachment evidence may satisfy the reasonable likelihood standard, as when "a conviction depends on the testimony of ... a witness whose credibility was not attacked on cross-examination," this is not such a case. Bacanovic's lawyer sought to impeach Lawrence's credibility and the quality of the Government's scientific analysis, by, among other things, questioning Lawrence repeatedly concerning the Government's decision not to test the dash beside the Apple Computer entry.

Third, in the words of Bacanovic's lawyer, the prosecution and defense experts "really agreed on almost everything about the main important points." Lyter agreed that the "*@60*" notation was made with ink which was different from the rest of the ink the Government had tested and that it was not possible to tell whether the "*@60*" notation was made at the same time as the other notations. Accordingly, even putting aside indications that the jury did not give credence to Lawrence's testimony, it is clear that the impeachment value of Lawrence's perjury would be severely limited since the most critical aspects of his scientific analysis were corroborated by the defense.

2. *Evidence Unrelated to Lawrence Stewart's Testimony Supports Defendants' Convictions*

In addition to the substantial basis for concluding that the jury's decision could not have been affected by the revelation of Lawrence's misrepresentations, ample evidence unrelated to the $60 agreement or to Lawrence's testimony supports defendants' convictions. Faneuil's testimony supports the jury's determination that defendants lied when they claimed that Stewart spoke to Bacanovic on December 27 and sold her ImClone stock after he informed her that it was trading below $60 per share. Telephone records support Faneuil's version of events.

Armstrong's testimony concerning the wording of Bacanovic's December 27 message supports the jury's finding that Bacanovic lied about the substance of the message. Armstrong's testimony concerning Stewart's attempt to alter her telephone message log on January 31 gave powerful support to the jury's finding that Stewart lied five days later when she said she was not sure whether there was a December 27 message from Bacanovic in Armstrong's log. Armstrong's testimony was corroborated by the telephone log as well as by her record of Stewart's attempt to alter it.

The testimony of Faneuil, Perret, and Pasternak support the jury's determinations that Stewart lied when she told investigators that she did not recall being informed of Waksal's trading on December 27, that she sold her stock because she did not want to be bothered over her vacation, and that she and Bacanovic discussed MSLO and K-Mart during their conversation. Faneuil testified that he informed Stewart of Waksal's trade and that they did not talk about other stocks. Perret testified that Stewart called that afternoon looking for Waksal and asking questions about ImClone, which supports an inference that she was given information about Waksal and ImClone, not merely a market price. And Pasternak testified that only a few days after December 27, Stewart informed her that Waksal had sold his ImClone stock and that Stewart had sold hers.

Finally, Faneuil's testimony supports the jury's determination that Stewart lied when she claimed not to have spoken with Bacanovic about the Government investigation into ImClone trading or Stewart's ImClone trade. Faneuil stated that Bacanovic repeatedly told him in January 2002 and afterward that Bacanovic had spoken to Stewart and that everyone was "on the same page."

The ample evidence of defendants' false statements and Bacanovic's perjury also supports defendants' convictions for conspiracy and obstruction of an agency proceeding. It is clear from the trial record that the worksheet and evidence concerning the $60 agreement were only part of the substantial evidence that defendants conspired, obstructed an SEC investigation, and lied in order to conceal what Stewart learned right before her sale of ImClone stock....

Conclusion

For the foregoing reasons, defendants' motions for a new trial are denied. Defendants have not demonstrated how additional discovery or a hearing would assist in the determination of these motions. Accordingly, their requests for additional discovery and an evidentiary hearing are also denied.

* * *

In an ironic postscript to the entire affair, the FDA ultimately *did* approve the Erbitux BLA.

FDA, FDA Approves Erbitux for Colorectal Cancer

(February 12, 2004)
http://www.fda.gov/bbs/topics/NEWS/2004/NEW01024.html

FDA today approved Erbitux (cetuximab) to treat patients with advanced colorectal cancer that has spread to other parts of the body. Erbitux is the first monoclonal antibody approved to treat this type of cancer and is indicated as a combination treatment to be given intravenously with irinotecan, another drug approved to fight colorectal cancer, or alone if patients cannot tolerate irinotecan.

Erbitux was approved under FDA's accelerated approval program, which allows FDA to approve products for cancer and other serious or life-threatening diseases based on early evidence of a product's effectiveness. Although treatment with Erbitux has not been shown to extend patients' lives, it was shown to shrink tumors in some patients and delay tumor growth, especially when used as a combination treatment.

Erbitux is a genetically engineered version of a mouse antibody that contains both human and mouse components. (Antibodies in the body are substances produced by the immune system to fight foreign substances.) It can be produced in large quantities in the laboratory. This new monoclonal antibody is believed to work by targeting a natural protein called "epidermal growth factor receptor" (EGFR) on the surface of cancer cells, interfering with their growth.

For patients with tumors that express EGFR and who no longer responded to treatment with irinotecan alone or in combination with other chemotherapy drugs, the combination treatment of Erbitux and irinotecan shrank tumors in 22.9% of patients and delayed tumor growth by approximately 4.1 months. For patients who received Erbitux alone, the tumor response rate was 10.8% and tumor growth was delayed by 1.5 months.

Colorectal cancer—cancer of the colon or rectum—is the third most common cancer affecting men and women in the U.S. and, according to the Centers for Disease Control and Prevention (CDC), and is the second leading cause of cancer-related death. Colorectal cancer is also one of the most commonly diagnosed cancers in the U.S.; approximately 147,500 new cases were diagnosed in 2003.

"In their review activities, FDA staff work hard to ensure doctors and patients can have confidence in the safety and effectiveness of new therapies such as Erbitux," said Mark B. McClellan, M.D., Ph.D. "FDA believes it is crucial for cancer patients to have many proven treatment options in their battle against this disease."

The efficacy and safety of Erbitux alone or in combination with irinotecan were studied in a randomized, controlled trial with 329 patients and also in combination with irinotecan in 138 patients in which all patients received both drugs. Erbitux was further evaluated as a single agent in a third clinical trial with 57 patients. Safety data from an additional 111 patients treated only with Erbitux was also evaluated. All of the trials included patients with EGFR-expressing metastatic colorectal cancer, whose disease had progressed after receiving irinotecan.

The manufacturer of Erbitux, ImClone Systems Incorporated, Branchburg, N.J., submitted their original request for approval in several sections between June 28 and October 31, 2001. Subsequent to ImClone's original submissions, FDA determined that their application could not be reviewed because approximately half of the patients (94) studied had not failed the approved treatments for colon cancer; and important information about the safety and effectiveness of Erbitux in a portion of the remaining patients (102) was missing. In their new request for approval on August 14, 2003, ImClone submitted the results of a large, well-run trial that included 329 patients as well as the results of the earlier two studies. For the studies submitted in their original 2001 request for approval, ImClone successfully collected substantial amounts of missing information from hospital records and other sources.

Two studies involving approximately 2000 patients are currently underway to assess the clinical benefits of Erbitux. These studies are specifically examining the ability of Erbitux to stop the progression of colorectal cancer and to extend the amount of time patients survive with the disease.

Erbitux can cause serious side-effects, usually during the administration of the first treatment, which may include difficulty breathing and low blood pressure. Infrequent interstitial lung disease (ILD) has been reported; however, it is difficult to determine if Erbitux caused ILD. ILD occurs when the lung becomes stiff due to scarring of the tissue between the air sacs of the lungs.

Other more common side-effects of Erbitux treatment include acne-like rash, dry skin, tiredness or weakness, fever, constipation, and abdominal pain.

Erbitux will be distributed and marketed by Bristol-Myers Squibb Company, Princeton, N.J.

FDA also today approved a test kit, manufactured by DakoCytomation California, Inc., that is used by doctors to analyze a colon tissue sample. The kit detects a protein in the body (HER-1) that stimulates cancerous tissue cell growth. Presence of this protein indicates that a patient is eligible for colon cancer treatment with Erbitux.

* * *

In part because of the perceived increase in insider trading and/or market manipulation by biotech companies and their insiders regarding material non-public information arising from FDA approval processes, the SEC and FDA agreed in 2004 to cooperate and share information to better police such improper activities.

SEC, SEC and FDA Take Steps to Enhance Inter-Agency Cooperation

February 5, 2004

Washington, D.C., Feb. 5, 2004—The Securities and Exchange Commission announced today that members of its senior staff and senior personnel of the Food and Drug Administration (FDA) are continuing and enhancing their cooperative efforts in support of the Commission's activities. An exchange of letters memorializes the initiatives to be taken by the FDA to support the Commission in carrying out its mission to protect investors and maintain the integrity of the nation's securities markets.

The FDA generally assists the Commission by: (1) providing technical assistance, when appropriate, to the Division of Corporation Finance in its review of Commission filings, and (2) providing documents and information to the Division of Enforcement. These forms of assistance to the staff will continue, but with certain enhancements.

Among the initiatives described in the letters exchanged by the SEC and FDA staff are:

- A centralized procedure adopted by the FDA for referring to the SEC staff possible instances of securities laws violations by public companies regulated by the FDA.
- Identification of contacts in each of the FDA's main organizational components (known as Centers) to serve as points of contact for the SEC and its staff to use in requesting information from FDA. These individuals would be responsible for assuring that such requests are handled promptly and thoroughly.
- The continued sharing of non-public information by the FDA with the SEC, consistent with FDA's current practice, and a commitment to endeavor to take steps to further expedite this process.

Stephen M. Cutler, Director of the Commission's Division of Enforcement, and a signatory of the SEC's letter, said, "The Commission staff appreciates FDA's strong interest in coordinating our agencies' activities in a cooperative manner. When companies misrepresent the status of the FDA's review of their products, investors can be harmed. We are eager to continue working with the FDA to aggressively address such situations and to enhance our already-productive relationship."

Notes & Questions

1. In an interesting additional lawsuit against Sam Waksal, Samuelson Trading Corp sued him for the "improper purchase of ImClone put options" from that company. *See Samuelson Trading Corp. v. Waksal*, 2004 WL 813534 (N.D. Ill.).

2. After reviewing the materials in this Chapter, you will notice that the commercialization of biotechnological and genomic technologies involve issues cutting across a perhaps surprisingly wide swath of legal areas, including IP, corporate law, securities law, health law, and administrative agency law. Traditionally, lawyers have specialized in areas defined by categories of law, such as IP law. But increasingly, lawyers are carving out industry-focused niches, because clients in a particular industry want to have at least one lawyer representing them who can act as "quarterback" and see the whole picture. Thus, many "biotech lawyers" must be able to have expertise across an unconventional mix of traditional legal disciplines. This kind of cross-discipline competency can also help lawyers guide their clients away from some of the perhaps unexpected legal risks posed by industries such as biotech, as exemplified by the ImClone saga. Do you think it is possible to achieve this kind of cross-disciplinary competence, or will the lawyer who seeks to do this forever be a "jack of all trades, master of none"?

Chapter 7

Clinical Applications of Genetics: Genetic Testing and Legal Liability

This chapter concentrates on legal issues arising in the context of clinical applications of genetics and their ramifications for patients and health care providers. Presently, the primary clinical application of genetics is genetic testing. Genetic therapy remains in the experimental stages, but has already generated research liability, as discussed in Chapter 5. Genetic testing, however, has moved beyond the research stage and is available in the medical marketplace. Genetics tests fall into three major categories: diagnostic testing, susceptibility testing, and predictability testing. Of these, diagnostic testing has generated the most robust body of case law, most of which is in the context of preconception, prenatal, and newborn testing.

Part A of this chapter focuses on reproductive medicine, prenatal genetic diagnosis and newborn testing. Part B considers the downstream implications of assisted reproductive technology and genetics on legal concepts of parenthood. Part C discusses susceptibility and predictive testing, reviewing some of the medical, social, and policy issues that have arisen to date, despite the dearth of case law. As genetic testing becomes more available in the marketplace, there are profound questions as to what the standard of care is from a medical perspective, and how it translates into legal standards for informed consent and medical negligence. This chapter will provide a foundation for further consideration of these questions.

A. Genetics and Reproductive Medicine

Genetic testing has generated a significant body of case law related to alleged negligence in preconception, prenatal, and newborn testing. Case law has been further enriched as additional assisted reproductive technologies have become available to prospective parents.

1. Assisted Reproductive Technologies

Beginning with the birth of the first "test tube" baby in the 1970s, reproduction increasingly became possible for those who could not supply gametes, become pregnant, or carry a pregnancy to term. With assisted reproductive technologies (ART), parenthood can be achieved using donor gametes, microtechnologies, and donor or leased wombs for gestation. Typically, prospective parents having difficulty becoming pregnant first undergo a medical workup to assess fertility of both the woman and the man. Medical therapy for the woman may include administration of drugs to induce ovulation and egg production. In the case of the man, the goal will be to determine whether sperm are present and capable of fertilizing an egg. If there is a dearth of vigorous gametes in either partner, the couple may seek to increase their odds of conception by using donor eggs and/or donor sperm, coupled with one or more assisted reproductive technologies:

In Vitro Fertilization (IVF)—*In vitro* fertilization involves the fertilization of a woman's eggs outside the body and the subsequent replacement of the embryos into the uterus. The woman may be either the intended mother or merely the egg donor. The woman is given fertility drugs to stimulate egg production. The eggs are then extracted from the ovary and placed with sperm for approximately eighteen hours. The sperm may be provided either by the woman's partner or by a donor. The embryos created *in vitro* are then placed into the gestational mother's uterus and she is given daily hormone injections to optimize implantation. The success rate of this procedure ranges from 20% to 35%. 2002 data published by the CDC found a clinical pregnancy success rate of 34.3%, with 19.9% resulting in a single fetus, and 12.4% in multiple fetuses. Multiple embryos are inserted into the woman's uterus because implantation is uncertain; thus when implantation is more successful than anticipated, three or more fetuses may result. This will increase the risk of premature birth or miscarriage. Frozen embryos may also be implanted; however, this reduces the success rate by about a third.

Gamete Intrafallopian Transfer (GIFT)—Gamete intrafallopian transfer is very similar to IVF, except that the egg and sperm are not fertilized in the laboratory. Instead, the egg and sperm are placed directly into the gestational mother's fallopian tube, where it is hoped that fertilization will occur. The success rate of this procedure is 25.4% according to 2002 CDC data.

Zygote Intrafallopian Transfer (ZIFT)—Zygote intrafallopian transfer is similar to both IVF and GIFT, except that the egg is fertilized in the laboratory. Unlike IVF (where the fertilized egg is allowed to develop into an embryo before it is placed into the uterus) and GIFT (where the egg is not fertilized before injection into the fallopian tubes), the egg and sperm become a zygote in the laboratory, but are not allowed to develop into a multi-celled embryo. The zygotes are then placed into the gestational mother's fallopian tube. The success rate for this procedure is 26.3% according to 2002 CDC data.

Intracytoplasmic Sperm Injection (ICSI)—Intracytoplasmic sperm injection involves the injection of sperm directly into a woman's harvested eggs. Then, using standard IVF, the embryos are placed into the uterus. Currently, slightly over half (53.8%) of the ART procedures performed use ICSI. ICSI technology has evolved over the last several years. Initially, attempts were made to open the wall of the egg cell to allow the sperm easier access. With better technology, it has become possible to microinject a single sperm into the egg, thus ensuring penetration. Typically ICSI is used when the sperm are scarce or lack motility. This allows men who might otherwise not be able to be genetic fathers to do so. Unfortunately, male infertility may also signal chromosomal aberrations or genetic risks. IVF with ICSI results in a slightly lower clinical pregnancy rate than IVF in the absence of ICSI.

Use of ART increased steadily over the last decade with a 78% increase in ART procedures between 1996 and 2002 and a 120% increase in live births. IVF, with or without ICSI, comprises 99% of the ART procedures performed in the United States. IVF success rates are better when fresh, not frozen, embryos, are used. ART success is heavily dependent on maternal age, with a 43% live birth rate for women under age thirty-five. This decreases to only 6.6% when mothers are older than forty-two. Cost is a significant issue for couples and individuals seeking to avail themselves of ART. These procedures typically cost as much as $25,000 per attempt. Because health plans typically do not cover these procedures, cost forecloses many would-be parents from accessing these technologies.

2. Preconception and Prenatal Genetic Testing

IVF frequently is coupled with prenatal genetic testing, especially when the parents have, or perceive, a genetic risk. Once an embryo has been created inside or outside of the womb, prenatal testing is done to check for chromosomal, morphologic, and genetic disorders.

Many parents seek diagnostic testing before conception to determine if they are carriers of a genetic mutation that may affect their progeny. This approach has been used with great success in the context of Tay-Sachs disease, a hereditary neurogenetic disorder fatal within the first few months of life. Tay-Sachs disease is a recessive disorder; for the disease to manifest in a child, both parents must contribute the affected recessive gene. The net result is that 25% of children born to carrier couples will be affected with the disorder. Cystic Fibrosis (CF) is another genetic disorder that is mediated by recessive genes. However, unlike Tay-Sachs, CF does not result in death. Children with CF have variable levels of pulmonary and gastrointestinal dysfunction, ranging from minimal to severe. Because of improved medical care, CF patients are now living well into adulthood. That said, care of these children can be heart-wrenching and expensive for a family, and many prospective parents seek preconception, prenatal, and newborn testing to determine the risk of CF.

Some prospective parents at risk for a genetic disorder choose not to pass it on to their children. This may be the case in a disorder that is passed on in autosomal dominant fashion, or on the basis of linkage to a sex chromosome. For example, Factor 8 hemophilia is the result of a mutation on the X chromosome. A woman may carry this mutation, not have the disease, but pass the mutation on to 50% of her children. The female children will have another X chromosome that will prevent expression of the mutation, although 50% of the female children will be carriers of the gene. Fifty percent of the male children will inherit the affected X chromosome, not have a second X chromosome, and the mutation will be expressed as hemophilia. Many parents with a family history of hemophilia choose to either select for only female children or to do direct genetic testing on the male embryos to determine if they have hemophilia.

Other parents may know, or suspect, that they harbor a disease for a late-onset disorder that will affect them and their progeny. They may seek to test their embryos to ensure that their children will not be burdened with an unfortunate genetic destiny. Several programs offer prenatal testing of embryos for highly penetrant, autosomal dominant disorders like Huntington Disease (HD). Note, however, that diagnosis of such a disorder in the embryo also implicitly diagnoses the parent. Some of the prenatal testing programs that provide such testing have reporting mechanisms that protect the parents from the inflicted insight that one of them is destined to develop the disease.

As the number of genetic tests available in the marketplace increase, there are an ever-increasing number of disorders or genetic anomalies that can be tested for using the DNA obtained from mother, fetus, or *in vitro* embryo. Prenatal testing modalities available to prospective parents include the following:

> Maternal AFP—The AFP test, also called the maternal serum alpha-fetoprotein (MSAFP), tests blood drawn from the pregnant woman at sixteen weeks. It measures the amount of alpha-fetoprotein (AFP), which is found in the fetal circulation; estriol, the dominant estrogen in pregnancy; human chorionic gonadotropin (hCG), produced by the developing embryo; and one or more additional metabolites. The test can reliably indicate 95% of fetuses with anencephaly, a condition in which all or part of the brain is missing, and 80% of cases of spina bifida, in which the tissue over the spinal cord fails to close completely. It can also indicate an increased risk for Down Syndrome or other chromosomal disorders. It is not a diagnostic tool for disorders, like CF and HD, that result from genetic mutations.
>
> Ultrasound—Developed in 1958 and first widely used in the early to mid-1970s, ultrasound technology employs sound waves to create a visual image of the fetus by moving an instrument across the abdomen or placing a small device in the vagina. It can be performed as early as ten weeks, although it is not used to predict sex until sixteen to eighteen weeks. It poses no risk of miscarriage. Targeted ultrasound studies may be performed which look for abnormalities in the head and neck anatomy, spine, heart, chest and diaphragm, stomach, kidneys and bladder, abdominal wall and umbilical cord, upper and lower extremities, the placenta, and amniotic fluid volume. Targeted ultrasounds are usually performed at about eighteen to twenty weeks. Further ultrasound studies may be recommended later in the pregnancy. This would be the case if there are risks that could affect the growth and development of the fetus, or possible difficulties affecting amniotic fluid volume or the function of the umbilical cord and its blood flow. Ultrasound is of limited utility in prenatal diagnosis of disorders resulting from genetic mutations.
>
> Amniocentesis—First used in the 1960s, this test involves extracting amniotic fluid (the liquid around the fetus inside the uterus) through a thin needle that is inserted through the abdomen into the uterus. The test is usually reserved for high-risk pregnancies and for women who will be thirty-five or older on their due date. Amniocentesis is done at fourteen to twenty weeks gestation; results are available in about two weeks. The amniotic fluid will yield a large number of shed fetal skin cells that can be cultured, and then subjected to chromosomal analysis or direct genetic testing. The DNA retrieved through amniocentesis is as "testable" as DNA recovered from other sources. Amniocentesis carries a one half of one percent risk of miscarriage. If done earlier than twelve weeks, it can increase the risk of a foot deformity as well as slightly increase the chance of a miscarriage or stillbirth. Amniocentesis has only 25 to 50% as many serious complications as CVS.
>
> Chorionic Villus Sampling (CVS)—Developed in the 1980s, CVS is also typically reserved for high-risk pregnancies. The test involves taking a sample of the chorionic villi (small cells) from the placenta. These cells are fetal

cells and can be tested for chromosomal abnormalities and genetic mutations. As in the case of amniocentesis, the DNA retrieved from CVS can be used for the whole realm of genetic testing. The sampling is usually performed at ten to twelve weeks and results are available in about two weeks. CVS has a .8% risk of miscarriage and has been associated with limb defects in the fetus.

Maternal Blood Fetal Cell Recovery—Fetal cells in maternal blood can be examined in an experimental test performed at only a few medical centers. We now know that a few fetal cells are liberated into the maternal blood supply. Using high-tech cell sorting technology, these cells are distinguished, and separated, from other cells in the maternal blood sample. The fetal cell may then be subjected to chromosomal and DNA analysis. Maternal blood fetal cell recovery is performed at the end of the first trimester and yields results in three days. Because it presents virtually no risk to either mother or fetus, it may eventually become the prenatal testing modality of choice.

Preimplantation Genetic Diagnosis (PGD)—In this procedure, which can be used only with *in vitro* fertilization, a woman uses fertility drugs so that she releases several eggs in one cycle. The eggs are removed from her body, and sperm and eggs are mixed in a petri dish. The embryo is allowed to divide to approximately the eight cell stage, and then a single cell can be cleaved off and separated from the embryo mass. Polymerase chain reaction (PCR) makes it possible to take very small amounts of DNA, and, by making copies of it, quickly produce enough for direct DNA analysis and testing. Rates of a successful pregnancy are similar to IVF without PGD. PGD costs anywhere from $6,000 to $10,000 depending on the types of genetic tests performed.

3. Regulation of ART and Genetic Testing

ART and genetic testing are subject to limited, obliquely aimed, regulation in the United States. With respect to ART procedures, the Fertility Clinic Success Rate and Certification Act of 1992, Pub. L. No. 102-493, 106 Stat. 3146 (codified at 42 U.S.C. 263a-1 to -7), is the primary source of regulation. This Act authorizes the CDC to compile and publish annual data on success rates at fertility clinics in the United States on an annual basis. See CDC, 2002 ASSISTED REPRODUCTIVE TECHNOLOGY SUCCESS RATES (2004), http://www.cdc.gov/ART/ART02/index.htm, for the most the most recent CDC report. Although the Act requires fertility clinics to report their ART success rates, it does not set forth any additional mandatory regulatory requirements. Indeed, the reporting is via the American Society for Reproductive Medicine (ASRM) and the Society for Assisted Reproductive Technology, the two major professional societies associated with ART. The reporting requirement requires clinics to submit age-specific, procedure-specific, and result-specific data. The CDC also requires, under the aegis of other authority, reporting of complications. In addition, clinics must identify the embryology laboratories they are using and document their status. Although the Act authorized the CDC to "develop a model program for the certification of embryo laboratories," it does not require, or mandate, certification of ART or any laboratories associated with it. *See* Pub. L. 102-493, § 3a. As such, the Fertility Clinic Success Rate and Certification Act generates voluntary reporting and does not affirmatively regulate the ART industry in terms of safety, effectiveness, or practice standards.

Deborah Spar, *Reproductive Tourism and the Regulatory Map*

352 New Eng. J. Med. 531 (2005)

... [There is a] quiet but burgeoning market in reproductive tourism, one that stretches around the globe and already encompasses thousands of people. These people are not ill in the usual sense, and they generally don't view themselves as engaged in commercial activity. What binds them together are three shared characteristics: the desire for a child who is genetically "theirs," the inability to produce this child through natural means, and a willingness to do whatever is necessary to produce one.... Americans travel to Mexico for an immunologic treatment banned in the United States; Germans acquire donor eggs in Spain; Australian lesbians secure sperm abroad.

At a personal level, such stories are tragic and touching. They reveal a longing so intense that people will do anything to fulfill it. They speak as well to several decades of remarkable scientific progress—from artificial insemination to *in vitro* fertilization (IVF) and egg donation—that has enabled once-infertile couples to produce children. In the United States, roughly 40,000 babies are born each year as a result of assisted reproduction. Surely, this is a desirable outcome—a fine example of medical science enhancing life. At the same time, though, the explosive growth of high-tech reproduction has led to a lopsided market in baby making and to critical public policy questions: Do parents have the right to procure children by any available means? Should society treat reproductive medicine as a luxury good (like Botox) or a fundamental right (like emergency health care)? And who, most critically, gets to decide?

To understand these issues, we must understand the role governments play in regulating reproduction. Historically, reproduction has been largely a private affair-occurring out of view of any authority and beyond government's reach. Yet time and again, governments have extended their power into the reproductive realm, determining, for example, the illegitimacy of certain births or the illegality of certain modes of birth control. Even in the United States, where privacy ostensibly reigns supreme, state governments have traditionally wielded authority over such intimate issues as marriage, contraception, and abortion. Meanwhile, state and federal governments have played a steadily expanding role in allocating and providing health care services. Reproductive medicine, therefore, attracts government in two different guises: as an arbiter of reproduction and as a regulator of health care.

This two-pronged approach has subjected assisted reproduction to a patchwork of competing and conflicting regulations. Even at the most fundamental level, governments disagree about what constitutes "disease" in this field and what defines health. They disagree about the distinction between medical necessity and elective choice and about the permissible bounds of medical intervention. They also split distinctly in the ways in which they permit commerce to come into play and in terms of the portions of the reproductive process that they allow to be bartered, traded, or sold. Take, for example, IVF, a procedure that has produced more than a million babies since its debut in 1978. In Denmark, IVF is regarded as a medical necessity, a pro forma treatment for couples who cannot conceive otherwise. In the United States, by contrast, IVF is generally treated as a medical or personal choice; there are no limits on who can use the treatment, but payment is subject to a baffling array of state-specific insurance provisions. Some states require insurance companies to cover the costs of infertility treatment; some provide for voluntary coverage; and some say nothing at all.

When techniques are newer and less well proven, this patchwork of regulation is even more complex. The acceptability of egg "donation," for instance, varies sharply across national boundaries. In the United Kingdom, eggs are regulated as a commodity: women may donate oocytes, but may not sell them. The German government, by contrast, bans any transfer of eggs, while the U.S. government imposes no rules whatsoever, leaving individual states to preside over widely divergent regimes for selling eggs and disparate egg markets. The liveliest market prevails in California, where a series of court cases have established both the legality of egg transfer and the enforceability of surrogate-mother contracts. As a result, would-be parents who want to acquire eggs from one woman and implant them in another (an option for both severely infertile women and homosexual men) often travel to California in pursuit of a child. Indeed, one leading provider of these services estimates that one third of her firm's business now comes from outside the country.

This "California syndrome" is hardly confined to that state or to the market for eggs. Instead, prospective parents are increasingly traveling all over the world, searching for particular fertility treatments and providers. Preimplantation genetic diagnosis (PGD), for example, is a sophisticated technique that enables doctors to detect—at the eight-cell stage—whether an embryo is carrying a specific genetic mutation. Parents who suspect that their children are at risk for diseases such as Tay-Sachs or cystic fibrosis now regularly travel to Detroit or Chicago, where leading practitioners of PGD can perform the analyses they need. Other clinics—in Brazil, Spain, and Italy—offer similar types of early-stage analysis, even in controversial cases in which the parents are seeking to produce a second child in hopes of saving a first who already has an otherwise fatal disease. A growing number of clinics are also using PGD to allow preselection of a baby's sex. Because such sex selection is illegal in some locales, the clinics are flocking to more permissive spots (Saudia Arabia [*sic*], for example, and the United States)—followed by a growing legion of international customers.

One might argue that this market for reproductive services is not so remarkable. We trade all kinds of services internationally—why not babies, or the components thereof? One might also argue that the current regulatory patchwork makes political and commercial sense: if Germany wants to ban egg transfer, it should. And if German couples want to avoid this regulation, they should procure their eggs abroad. The problem with this approach, however, is that it turns assisted reproduction into a for-profit business, a lucrative marketplace in which rich couples scour the world in pursuit of high-tech offspring, while poorer would-be parents are consigned to fate. A cross-border market for reproduction also means that societies that oppose assisted reproduction may nevertheless pay its costs. For who can prove that premature quintuplets born in Bremen were conceived in Istanbul?

Currently, there is no easy way of addressing this international imbalance. But as the market for reproductive medicine expands, policymakers in the United States will have to grapple with issues that they have thus far avoided, crafting policies to deal with the burgeoning business of reproductive tourism.

In theory, the ideal policy might be to follow the United Kingdom's example, establishing a central regulatory agency for the reproductive field. In the United Kingdom, the Human Fertilisation and Embryology Authority licenses fertility clinics and approves procedures for assisted reproduction; it considers controversial techniques on an individual basis and oversees a system in which infertile couples are eligible for one free cycle of IVF. In the United States, however, such a system is politically unfeasible. Americans, with their distrust of bureaucratic authority, would never condone the extension of federal power into the intimate affairs of reproduction. In the current political climate, moreover, any federal foray into this area would probably fall prey to the politics of abortion, squeezing science in the process and limiting options for fertility treatment.

A second approach would be to embrace the laissez-faire policies now in place, leaving U.S. fertility specialists to venture along the technological edge and allowing reproductive tourism to flourish. The implications of such an open market, however, are harsh. Many Americans would not be able to afford reproductive treatments, and society would have no opportunity to debate the broader effects of high-tech reproduction. Do we really want to create children with three sets of DNA or children genetically altered for particular physical characteristics? As science continues to expand our menu of reproductive options, it will be increasingly important to engage in some kind of political debate and to ensure that some consideration stretches beyond the desires of individual parents.

Which leaves us with a final option—a messy one, but one that offers the best chance for bringing public policy and order into the realm of assisted reproduction. This path would involve a combination of minimal federal guidelines and increased oversight by individual states. It would mean encouraging the federal government to periodically release guidelines for assisted reproduction, outlawing procedures that Americans deem abhorrent (reproductive cloning, for example, or human-nonhuman chimeras) and imposing the kind of safety standards that prevail in other areas of medicine. Presumably, some of these regulations could subsequently be agreed upon at the international level, curtailing the most egregious prospects for reproductive tourism. Meanwhile, state legislatures would more actively review the fertility procedures practiced in their states. Rather than leaving these decisions to the courts or the vagaries of the open market, they would tackle the complex process of making public policy—determining, for example, whether sex selection is acceptable, whether insurance companies should cover IVF as a medical necessity, and when procedures for assisted reproduction go too far. If states were to make the "wrong" decision, the combined weight of local lobbying and intrastate competition would most likely force a reversal before too long.

A state-based model would not eliminate reproductive tourism. In fact, it could well expand it, increasing the variation even among neighboring states. But it would also bring such tourism into the open, subjecting novel procedures ... to the scrutiny of public debate. In the process, it might well create a safer and more certain market for reproductive medicine—one that would force fewer ... to test their luck abroad.

* * *

Although the ART industry is largely unregulated, some aspects of it are susceptible to regulations governing clinical laboratories. Under the Clinical Laboratories Improvement Amendments of 1988 ("CLIA"), laboratories examining biological materials (including human embryos) for diagnostic or other purposes must comply with CLIA regulations. *See* 42 U.S.C. §263a (a)-(b) (2000). With respect to the ART procedures themselves, CLIA does not apply; however some of the genetic testing done in the preconception and prenatal time frame will fall under CLIA. CLIA sets forth quality standards for laboratory testing designed to ensure accuracy, reliability and timeliness in laboratory testing. A laboratory is defined as any facility that performs laboratory testing on specimens derived from humans for the purpose of providing information for the diagnosis, prevention, treatment of disease, or impairment of, or assessment of health. CLIA is enforced by the Centers for Medicare & Medicaid Services (CMS) and funded through a user fee system.

Under CLIA, *in vitro* laboratory tests are categorized into one of three regulatory categories: (1) waived tests; (2) tests of moderate complexity; and (3) tests of high complexity. The level of regulatory requirements and oversight increases with test complexity and potential risk to public health. CLIA regulations set standards of laboratory proficiency, laboratory staff education and qualifications, and test accuracy and reliability. CLIA's regulations are policed through on-site inspection, disclosure requirements, and proficiency testing. CLIA monitoring is a massive undertaking and much of it has been delegated to professional societies, such as the College of American Pathologists (CAP) and the Joint Commission on the Accreditation of Healthcare Organizations (JCAHO).

CLIA regulations do not address the clinical utility or medical efficacy of laboratory tests. Moreover, CLIA is foreclosed from regulating laboratories that are engaged in research and or providing "home brew" genetic tests. Such tests frequently use analyte-specific reagents (ASRs), raw materials, and components in performing genetic tests. Such "home brew" tests are widely used in genetic testing, both in the research and commercial context. Although ASRs that are sold commercially as reagents are subject to regulation under CLIA, ASRs and other components developed, and used, within a given lab are not. As a result of all of these factors, many genetic tests fall through the cracks in that they are quite different from other high complexity tests, may not be susceptible to FDA device regulation as kits, and many are "home brews" proffered by research laboratories.

4. Prenatal Testing and Legal Liability: Wrongful Birth, Wrongful Life, and Wrongful Conception

With the panoply of assisted reproductive technologies and the ever-increasing variety of genetic tests, it is not surprising that case law addressing negligent testing has already begun to evolve. These cases struggle with an unclear medical standard of care coupled with the novelty of genetic testing. This struggle is made more complicated by the fact that there is no backdrop of regulatory review to establish the validity and indications for a given test. In addition, genetic counseling is primarily conducted using a non-directive approach, in which the counselor discusses the various possibilities and options, but refrains from advising one course of action over another. The goal is laudable: It allows people making major life decisions to do so with full, but not extraneous information, unaccompanied by the biases of the counselor. However, the non-directive approach may increase the confusion—both for the patient and the courts—when an adverse outcome occurs.

Munro v. Regents of the University of California

263 Cal.Rptr. 878 (Cal. Ct. App. 1989)

Lillie, Presiding Justice

...

Plaintiffs Pamela and Allen Munro are a married couple. In September 1984 Mrs. Munro saw Dr. William Growdon, an obstetrician-gynecologist. Dr. Growdon confirmed that Mrs. Munro, then 37 years old, was pregnant with her second child. Because of the increased risk of Down Syndrome in children born to women over the age of 35, Dr. Growdon referred Mrs. Munro to defendant Barbara Crandall, a physician, for genetic counseling.

In October 1984 Mrs. Munro met with Dr. Crandall at the UCLA Neuropsychiatric Institute. At this meeting Dr. Crandall took a family history of Mr. and Mrs. Munro. Mrs. Munro told Dr. Crandall her father's background was "primarily German" and her mother's background was English and Canadian. She said that her husband's father's father was Scottish and his father's mother was either Scottish or Irish. Mrs. Munro also told Dr. Crandall that Mr. Munro's mother's father was Norwegian and his "mother's father's [*sic*] family was some peculiar type of French." The information Dr. Crandall obtained from Mrs. Munro indicated that neither she nor Mr. Munro is of Jewish heritage. Because of the extremely low incidence of non-Jewish carriers of Tay-Sachs disease, Dr. Crandall does not recommend genetic testing for Tay-Sachs disease unless one or both parents indicate they are of Ashkenazic (eastern European) Jewish background. Accordingly, when Mrs. Munro underwent genetic testing at UCLA Medical Center in November 1984, no test was given to determine whether she or her husband had the genetic makeup for transmission of Tay-Sachs disease to their unborn child. About three weeks later an employee of the UCLA Medical Center telephoned Mrs. Munro and told her she was carrying a healthy baby boy.

On May 11, 1985, Pamela Munro gave birth to plaintiff Alexander Munro. In March 1986 Alexander was diagnosed as suffering from Tay-Sachs disease. When Mrs. Munro came to her for genetic counseling in 1984, Dr. Crandall knew that in addition to Ashkenazic Jews, there is a small-inbred community in French Canada which is said to have a slightly higher prevalence of Tay-Sachs disease than the general population. Not until after the counseling session did the Munros learn that Mr. Munro's maternal grandfather's parents were French Canadian.

Plaintiffs sued defendants for medical malpractice and intentional and negligent infliction of emotional distress. The complaint's first cause of action ("negligence"), on behalf of all plaintiffs, alleged that plaintiff Alexander Munro, by his guardians ad litem plaintiffs Pamela and Allen Munro, engaged the services of defendants to care for and treat "a problem pertaining to the health and well-being" of Alexander Munro and Pamela Munro. Defendants undertook to provide genetic counseling for Pamela Munro, and consequently for Alexander Munro. In providing such counseling defendants negligently failed to possess and exercise the degree of knowledge and skill ordinarily possessed and exercised by other physicians and hospitals in the same locality as defendants. As a direct result of said negligence plaintiffs Pamela Munro and Allen Munro suffered severe, serious and permanent physical and emotional injuries. Plaintiff Alexander Munro, by and through his guardians ad litem, incurred hospital and medical expenses and will continue to incur such expenses for an indefinite period of time in the future.

The second cause of action (intentional infliction of emotional distress), on behalf of plaintiffs Pamela and Allen Munro, incorporated the allegations of the first cause of action and further alleged: When she received genetic counseling from defendants, Pamela Munro was pregnant with Alexander and sought the services of defendants for the purpose of diagnosis and treatment of any genetic fetal abnormality. Defendants held themselves out to the general public, including plaintiffs, as experts in the field of genetic counseling and diagnosis; plaintiffs had no education or training in that field and relied upon defendants to undertake all necessary and proper testing so as to render a professional opinion regarding potential genetic disorders in Alexander. Defendants represented to plaintiffs that all such testing would be done. Plaintiffs believed that tests to rule out Tay-Sachs disease were performed by defendants and that said tests were negative. In fact, defendants intentionally and maliciously either omitted said tests or if said tests were performed, recklessly disregarded their results and failed to inform plaintiffs Pamela and Allen Munro that Alexander, in utero, was afflicted with Tay-Sachs disease. As a result of defendants' conduct plaintiffs suffered severe emotional distress.

...

II

Plaintiffs' first cause of action alleged medical malpractice. The standard of care in a medical malpractice case requires that physicians exercise in diagnosis and treatment that reasonable degree of skill, knowledge and care ordinarily possessed and exercised by members of the medical profession under similar circumstances. "'The standard of care against which the acts of a physician are to be measured is a matter peculiarly within the knowledge of experts; it presents the basic issue in a malpractice action and can only be proved by their testimony, unless the conduct required by the particular circumstances is within the common knowledge of the layman.'" The circumstances under which genetic testing for Tay-Sachs disease is indicated, are beyond a layman's knowledge. Accordingly, expert testimony was required in order to determine whether defendants' alleged failure to administer such genetic testing to plaintiffs met the standard of care imposed on physicians.

Recognizing this, defendants submitted expert evidence in the form of Dr. Kaback's declaration wherein he stated: Since it is medically impossible to screen all patients for all known genetic abnormalities, the standard of care requires that specific screening tests be performed only on those patients who meet specific profile characteristics that warrant such tests. Because individuals of Jewish heritage have a much higher incidence of carrying the gene which causes Tay-Sachs disease than is found in the general population, they have been targeted for screening for Tay-Sachs disease; on the other hand, since the incidence of Tay-Sachs in the non-Jewish population is statistically so low, screening of that population for Tay-Sachs never has been advocated. The information which defendants obtained from plaintiffs disclosed that neither Pamela Munro nor Allen Munro is of Jewish heritage. While it was known that certain rare and isolated groups other than those of Ashkenazic Jewish heritage did have a statistically increased chance of Tay-Sachs over the general population, review of the depositions of plaintiffs and Dr. Crandall shows that, at the time plaintiffs received genetic counseling from defendants, plaintiffs were unaware of any information concerning their genetic background which would have placed them in one of those groups. Based on the foregoing facts it was Dr. Kaback's opinion that plaintiffs did not meet the profile characteristics necessary to warrant performing a Tay-Sachs carrier screening test and therefore it was within the standard of care for defendants not to perform such testing on plaintiffs.

...

III

Plaintiffs contend that defendants had a duty to disclose material information to enable plaintiffs to make an informed decision whether to take the Tay-Sachs test. Plaintiffs further argue that because such duty of disclosure is not governed by the standard practice of the physicians' community, but is instead a duty imposed by law, expert evidence is not required to establish the existence of the duty and a triable issue of fact was presented as to whether defendants complied with that duty.

...

Plaintiffs' second cause of action, while labeled "intentional infliction of emotional distress," appears to allege fraud on the part of defendants by falsely representing to plaintiffs that testing for all "potential genetic disorders" would be done. In her declaration in opposition to the motion for summary judgment plaintiff Pamela Munro stated: During genetic counseling by defendants, plaintiff was not told why she was asked questions about her family history and that of her husband. If defendants' exclusion of Tay-Sachs testing was based on the fact that plaintiffs are not Jewish, defendants should have so informed plaintiff. They also should have told her of the easy availability of Tay-Sachs screening. If plaintiffs had known this, they would have availed themselves of such screening regardless of the rarity of the Tay-Sachs trait in non-Jewish people.

...

In *Scalere v. Stenson* (1989) 211 Cal. App.3d 1446, 260 Cal.Rptr. 152, we recently held that ... a physician has no duty to disclose where no diagnostic testing or treatment is recommended.

" ... Though a doctor proposes neither surgery nor medical procedure, though he recommends no therapy and is unaware of any other school of doctors who would recommend therapy, the dissent would require such a doctor to disclose 'the risks and benefits of non-treatment.' Such a line, like one drawn with a finger in the air, is without precision and predictability. It would impose significant new burdens on already harried doctors without awarding demonstrable benefits to their patients. 'It seems obviously prohibitive and unrealistic to expect physicians to discuss with their patients every risk of proposed treatment [[l]et alone *non* treatment—no matter how small or remote—and generally unnecessary from the patient's viewpoint as well.'" (*Scalere v. Stenson, supra,* 211 Cal. App. 3d at p. 1453, 260 Cal. Rptr. 152.)

The passage quoted in *Scalere* is a complete answer to plaintiffs' argument that even though defendants did not recommend plaintiffs undergo a Tay-Sachs screening test, defendants were under a duty to inform plaintiffs of the incidence of Tay-Sachs disease in the general population, the higher incidence of the disease among French Canadians, and that the Tay-Sachs test is simply a blood test which, together with the amniocentetic culture test therefor, costs $500. As is natural in view of their son's tragic affliction, plaintiffs focus on defendants' failure to give them any information which would have enabled them to decide whether or not to undergo testing for Tay-Sachs disease. However, when Pamela Munro received genetic counseling she provided defendants with no facts which should have alerted them to the possibility that one or both of the plaintiffs might be carriers of Tay-Sachs disease, which is but one of approximately 70 genetic disorders that can be detected by testing. This is truly a case in which it can be said that the information plaintiffs now claim defendants were under a duty to divulge related to a "'small or remote'" risk and was "'generally unnecessary from the patient's viewpoint'" in light of what plaintiffs knew of their respective ethnic backgrounds at the time of genetic counseling.

Plaintiffs would have us impose on defendants a duty to give plaintiffs information regarding a genetic test defendants did not recommend because it was not indicated by any facts which plaintiffs told to defendants, or even any facts of which plaintiffs were aware. Reason, as well as precedent, compels our refusal to impose such a duty.

...

The judgment is affirmed.

Gallagher v. Duke University

852 F.2d 773 (4th Cir. 1988)

BUTZNER, SENIOR CIRCUIT JUDGE:

Mrs. Gallagher gave birth to a daughter, Jennifer, who suffered severe, multiple birth defects. She was transferred from a hospital in Jacksonville, North Carolina, to Duke for treatment, and died less than three weeks later. Dr. Mickey, a cytogeneticist at Duke, performed a chromosome analysis on a sample of Jennifer's blood and concluded that she had no genetic abnormalities.

The Gallaghers met with Duke staff members after Jennifer's death and were informed that based on Dr. Mickey's tests their chances of having a normal child were the same as the general population. The staff also informed the Gallaghers that there was no reason for either of them to be tested for any abnormal genetic traits because of the negative results of Jennifer's tests. Relying on this advice, the Gallaghers conceived a second child. They were referred to the University of North Carolina Genetic Counseling Department, where the staff concluded after examining Dr. Mickey's test results that an amniocentesis was unnecessary.

Lisa Gallagher was born on March 21, 1983, suffering severe birth defects similar to those that afflicted Jennifer. Lisa was transferred to Duke, where Dr. Mickey conducted a chromosome analysis on a sample of her blood. This time, Dr. Mickey discovered a genetic abnormality. He then re-examined the slides he had taken of Jennifer Gallagher and discovered that she possessed the same or a similar abnormality. Tests later conducted at the University of North Carolina revealed that Mr. Gallagher carried a genetic abnormality which he passed on to both Jennifer and Lisa and would likely pass on to some or all of his future children.

The Gallaghers sued Duke and Dr. Mickey, claiming that they would not have conceived and given birth to Lisa if they knew about Mr. Gallagher's genetic defect. The Gallaghers' complaint sought damages for the extraordinary expenses of caring for Lisa for the rest of her life, the loss of Lisa's future earnings, and for their own emotional distress. The court ruled that even if Duke and Dr. Mickey were liable, the Gallaghers could only recover damages for the extraordinary medical expenses that they would incur for Lisa's care during their lifetimes, despite the fact that Lisa was expected to outlive them and would continue to require medical attention and care. The jury returned a verdict in favor of the Gallaghers and awarded them $1,031,000 in damages, and the court entered judgment on the verdict. The court held that North Carolina law did not permit under the circumstances recovery for emotional distress, and the Gallaghers assign cross error to this ruling. The court dismissed a claim filed on behalf of Lisa for her "wrongful life" holding that it was not cognizable under North Carolina law. The Gallaghers do not appeal this dismissal. The jury exonerated another defendant, the Private Diagnostic Clinic, and the Gallaghers do not appeal the judgment in its favor.

II

Dr. Mickey and Duke state that the sole issue for which they seek review is: "Did the district court err in concluding that a claim for relief for the wrongful birth of a genetically defective child is cognizable under North Carolina law?" They rely primarily on *Jackson v. Bumgardner*, 347 S.E.2d 743 (N.C. 1986), and *Azzolino v. Dingfelder*, 337 S.E.2d 528 (N.C. 1985).

In *Jackson*, the Supreme Court of North Carolina held that a complaint alleging that a physician's failure to replace an intrauterine device resulting in the plaintiff's pregnancy and the consequent birth of a healthy child states a claim for medical malpractice based on wrongful conception.... The court noted that it followed the majority rule, saying:

> Our survey shows that the vast majority of courts which have considered wrongful conception cases have viewed the case as being indistinguishable from an ordinary medical malpractice action where the plaintiff alleges a breach of duty on the part of a physician and resulting injury for failure to perform that duty.

Tested by Jackson, the Gallaghers have proved a cause of action for medical malpractice based on wrongful conception that is recognized in North Carolina. They consulted Dr. Mickey to determine whether they should attempt to have a second child after their first child was born with severe defects. The doctor had a duty to exercise reasonable care in responding to their requests. *See Jackson,* 347 S.E.2d at 747. The evidence disclosed that Dr. Mickey and Duke deviated from an acceptable standard of care in analyzing the cause of the defects to the Gallaghers' first child. Relying on this faulty analysis, the defendants misinformed the Gallaghers that they could have a normal child. Consequently, the defendants' negligence was the proximate cause of the birth of a profoundly defective child, Lisa. *Jackson* establishes that the Gallaghers' evidence is sufficient to show "the existence of a duty, breach of that duty, and damages resulting from the breach." 347 S.E.2d at 747. Because the North Carolina Supreme Court recognizes a cause of action for medical malpractice based on wrongful conception when a normal child is born, we are confident that the Court would recognize a cause of action based on the same malpractice when a genetically defective child is born.

III

The next question is the proper measure of damages. The North Carolina Supreme Court cited with approval the reasoning of *Miller v. Johnson*, 343 S.E.2d 301 (Va. 1986), a wrongful conception case, which held that the parents could recover medical expenses and damages for pain and emotional distress suffered by the mother. *Jackson*, 347 S.E.2d at 750.

The North Carolina Court, however, held (with one justice dissenting) that the Jacksons could not recover the cost of rearing their healthy baby....

The Gallaghers' claim, unlike the Jacksons', does not present the difficulty of offsetting the costs of care with the benefits of parenthood. No evidence of benefits was introduced. Lisa is profoundly impaired. Her learning and cognitive skills will never develop past those of a one and one-half year old child....

The court's charge did not require the jury to attempt to offset the extraordinary costs of caring for Lisa by any benefits. The instruction on the calculation of damages followed traditional tort principles and resulted in a verdict that was neither speculative nor conjectural. Dr. Mickey and Duke do not assign error to the size of the verdict. In view of Lisa's impairments we are confident that North Carolina courts would not attempt to offset the expense of caring for her by the benefits that a normal daughter affords her parents....

We also are persuaded that the district court correctly decided that the North Carolina Supreme Court would not hold that *Azzolino* bars the Gallaghers' cause of action and recovery of damages. *Azzolino* dealt with a claim of wrongful birth brought by parents of an impaired child. The complaint alleged that after Mrs. Azzolino became pregnant, employees of a clinic failed to advise her about the availability of amniocentesis and genetic counseling. As a result, she gave birth to a defective child. She alleged that if she had been properly advised, she would have terminated her pregnancy by abortion. The court described Mrs. Azzolino's claim as one for "wrongful birth." It defined this term as follows: "'Wrongful birth' refers to the claim for relief of parents who allege that the negligent treatment or advice deprived them of the choice of terminating pregnancy by abortion and preventing the birth of the defective child."

The Court held (with three justices dissenting) that "claims for relief for wrongful birth of defective children shall not be recognized in this jurisdiction...." Explaining its reasons, the court first observed that when Mrs. Azzolino consulted the doctor the defective fetus was in existence and assumed for the purpose of argument that birth was the proximate result of the defendants' negligence. The court then reasoned that traditional tort analysis could go no further because the next step required holding that the existence of human life, because it was defective, was an injury cognizable at law. The court declined to take this step. In *Jackson*, the defendant urged the Court to dismiss the Jacksons' claim on the basis of Azzolino. The Supreme Court, however, rejected this argument by explaining the difference between a claim for wrongful birth and a claim for wrongful conception as follows:

> Defendant has failed to make a critical distinction between the types of claims involved in *Azzolino* and in the instant case. Mrs. Azzolino did not complain about becoming pregnant; she complained about having a child with certain defects. In reaching its result in *Azzolino*, the Court stressed the fact that defendant Dingfelder was not responsible for the existence of either little Michael Azzolino or his defects. ("It should be reemphasized here that the plaintiffs only allege that the defendants negligently caused or permitted an already conceived and defective fetus not to be aborted. The plaintiffs do not allege that the defendants in any way directly caused the genetic defect. Therefore, the only damages the plaintiffs allege they have suffered arise, if at all, from the failure of the defendants to take steps which would have led to abortion of the already existing and defective fetus.")

Here, what plaintiff sought was a means to avoid pregnancy itself. The injury she alleges is that she became pregnant. She also alleges that defendant's negligence contributed to her pregnancy. In arguing that plaintiff has alleged no cognizable damages under *Azzolino*, defendant is equating the condition of the pregnant plaintiff with the life of her child. Rather, it is the fact of the pregnancy *as a medical condition* that gives rise to compensable damages and completes the elements for a claim of negligence. (emphasis in original).

Although the parties and the district court sometimes referred to the Gallaghers' action as a claim for wrongful birth, it is evident that, like the claim of Mrs. Jackson, it was for wrongful conception. The differences the court emphasized between Mrs. Azzolino's claim for wrongful birth and Mrs. Jackson's claim for wrongful conception apply to Mrs. Gallagher's claim for wrongful conception. Therefore, just as *Azzolino* did not bar Mrs. Jackson's cause of action for wrongful conception, *Azzolino* does not bar Mrs. Gallagher's cause of action for wrongful conception.

Also, neither *Azzolino* standing alone nor read in conjunction with *Jackson* bars the Gallaghers' claim for the extraordinary expenses of Lisa's care. *Azzolino* pointed out the difficulty in a wrongful birth case of measuring the damages resulting from life as compared to the termination of life through abortion. *Jackson* perceived the same difficulty in a somewhat different context. In Jackson it was the difficulty of offsetting the costs of care with the incalculable benefits of having a healthy child. The result would be speculative and conjectural. Hence under traditional tort principles, the result was unacceptable.

The Gallaghers' claim, in contrast, presents no occasion for attempting to value a life that were it not for the defendants' negligence would have been terminated by abortion. Nor is there any need to attempt an offset of the costs of care with the incalculable benefits of having a healthy child. *Jackson* establishes that the Gallaghers' claim for medical malpractice based on wrongful conception is cognizable under North Carolina law. Unlike the damages sought in *Jackson* and *Azzolino*, the Gallaghers' damages can be ascertained by the application of traditional tort principles that apply in medical malpractice cases. We conclude that the district court properly entered judgment on the verdict of the jury.

IV

The district court refused to allow Mr. and Mrs. Gallagher to recover damages for any of the extraordinary medical expenses that Lisa will incur after her parents' deaths. It rejected the Gallaghers' argument that, because they will have to put money aside during their lives in order to insure that Lisa is properly cared for after their deaths, they are bearing all of Lisa's medical expenses for the rest of her life and should be compensated for all of them.

We too must reject this argument. As the Gallaghers' own brief makes clear, the injury for which they seek compensation is to them, not to their child. While it is certainly understandable that the Gallaghers wish to insure that Lisa receives proper care after their deaths, we cannot ignore the North Carolina law that terminates their obligation to support Lisa at their deaths. Any decision to put money aside for her care after their deaths, as far as North Carolina law is concerned, is voluntary.

V

The Gallaghers also urge us to reverse the district court's order denying them recovery for the emotional distress that they alleged they suffered and continue to suffer as a result of the defendants' negligence. After the district court denied recovery, the North Carolina Court of Appeals decided two cases which we believe afford precedent for allowing the Gallaghers' claim to proceed to trial.

...

Mrs. Gallagher has suffered physical injuries similar to those suffered by the plaintiff in *Ledford*. She suffered the abdominal pains associated with the labor and delivery of Lisa. She would not have suffered those pains had the defendants' negligence not induced her to conceive....

Mrs. Gallagher's emotional distress as a result of giving birth to and raising a handicapped child is certainly ... foreseeable ... Mrs. Gallagher specifically informed Dr. Mickey that she did not wish to conceive unless she had a normal chance of giving birth to a healthy child. Thus, any claim that it was not reasonably foreseeable that she would suffer emotional distress if the defendants' negligence induced her to conceive a handicapped child is groundless.

In *Johnson v. Ruark Obstetrics and Gynecology Associates, P.A.*, 365 S.E.2d 909 ([N.C. Ct. App.] 1988), the North Carolina Court of Appeals allowed both parents to assert claims for emotional distress arising out of the death of a fetus allegedly caused by the defendants' negligent failure to treat Mrs. Johnson's diabetes.... Accordingly, we hold that Mr. and Mrs. Gallaghers' claims for emotional distress should not have been denied as a matter of law.

We affirm the district court's entry of judgment on the verdict returned in favor of the Gallaghers. We vacate the district court's ruling denying recovery for emotional distress as a matter of law and remand the case for further proceedings on this issue....

Afffirmed in part; Vacated in part; and Remanded.

Turpin v. Sortini

643 P.2d 954 (Cal. 1982)

KAUS, JUSTICE.

This case presents the question of whether a child born with an hereditary affliction may maintain a tort action against a medical care provider who—before the child's conception—negligently failed to advise the child's parents of the possibility of the hereditary condition, depriving them of the opportunity to choose not to conceive the child. Although the overwhelming majority of decisions in other jurisdictions recognize the right of the parents to maintain an action under these circumstances, the out-of-state cases have uniformly denied the child's right to bring what has been commonly termed a "wrongful life" action....

I

The allegations of the complaint disclose the following facts. On September 24, 1976, James and Donna Turpin, acting on the advice of their pediatrician, brought their first—and at that time their only—daughter, Hope, to the Leon S. Peters Rehabilitation Center at the Fresno Community Hospital for evaluation of a possible hearing defect. Hope was examined and tested by Adam J. Sortini, a licensed professional specializing in the diagnosis and treatment of speech and hearing defects.

The complaint alleges that Sortini and other persons at the hospital negligently examined, tested and evaluated Hope and incorrectly advised her pediatrician that her hearing was within normal limits when, in reality, she was "stone deaf" as a result of an hereditary ailment. Hope's parents did not learn of her condition until October 15, 1977 when it was diagnosed by other specialists. According to the complaint, the nature of the condition is such that there is a "reasonable degree of medical probability" that the hearing defect would be inherited by any offspring of James and Donna.

The complaint further alleges that in December 1976, before learning of Hope's true condition and relying on defendants' diagnosis, James and Donna conceived a second child, Joy. The complaint avers that had the Turpins known of Hope's hereditary deafness they would not have conceived Joy. Joy was born August 23, 1977, and suffers from the same total deafness as Hope.

On the basis of these facts, James, Donna, Hope and Joy filed a complaint setting forth four causes of action against defendants Sortini, the hospital, the rehabilitation center and various Does. The first cause of action, brought on behalf of Hope, seeks damages for the harm Hope has allegedly suffered as a result of the delay in the diagnosis of her condition. The second cause of action—the only cause before us on this appeal—was brought on behalf of Joy and seeks (1) general damages for being "deprived of the fundamental right of a child to be born as a whole, functional human being without total deafness" and (2) special damages for the "extraordinary expenses for specialized teaching, training and hearing equipment" which she will incur during her lifetime as a result of her hearing impairment. The third and fourth causes of action, brought on behalf of James and Donna, seek, respectively, special damages relating to the support and medical care of Joy to the age of majority, and general damages for emotional distress sustained by James and Donna "attendant to the raising and caring of a totally deaf child."

...

II

Although this is the first case in which we have faced the question of potential tort liability in a "wrongful life" or "wrongful birth" context, there is no dearth of authority in this area. In recent years, many courts in other jurisdictions have confronted similar claims brought by both parents and children against medical professionals whose negligence had allegedly proximately caused the birth of hereditarily afflicted children. The overwhelming majority of the recent cases have permitted parents to recover at least some elements of damage in such actions. At the same time, the out-of-state authorities have uniformly rejected the children's own claims for general damages.

The explanation for the divergent results is that while courts have been willing to permit parents to recover for medical costs or—in some cases—other harms which the parents would not have incurred "but for" the defendants' negligence, they have been reluctant to permit the child to complain when, but for the defendant's negligence, he or she would not have been born at all. In this context the recent decisions have either concluded that the child has sustained no "legally cognizable injury" or that appropriate damages are impossible to ascertain.

...

The third and most recent Court of Appeal decision in this area is *Curlender v. Bio-Science Laboratories*, *supra*, 106 Cal. App.3d 811, 165 Cal.Rptr. 477, an action brought solely on behalf of a child, not her parents. Unlike *Custodio* and *Stills*, in which the defendants' negligence had led to the births of healthy, albeit unplanned, children, in *Curlender* the child-plaintiff was afflicted with Tay-Sachs disease, a fatal illness " 'characterized by partial or complete loss of vision, mental underdevelopment, softness of the muscles, convulsions, etc.' " in which the child has a very reduced life span. (*Id.*, at p. 815, fn. 4, 165 Cal. Rptr. 477, quoting Schmidt's Attorneys' Dict. of Medicine (1980).) The principal defendant in *Curlender* was a medical laboratory which allegedly had been negligent in performing blood tests which the child's parents had undergone for the specific purpose of determining if their offspring were likely to suffer from Tay-Sachs disease.

In *Curlender*, the court reviewed the out-of-state and California precedents in this area at some length.... Disagreeing with the out-of-state decisions which had found that a child who has been born with serious hereditary defects as opposed to not being born at all has suffered no legally cognizable injury, the Curlender court stated: "The reality of the 'wrongful life' concept is that such a plaintiff exists and suffers, due to the negligence of others. It is neither necessary nor just to retreat into meditation on the mysteries of life. We need not be concerned with the fact that had defendants not been negligent, the plaintiff might not have come into existence at all. The certainty of genetic impairment is no longer a mystery. In addition, a reverent appreciation of life compels recognition that plaintiff, however impaired she may be, has come into existence as a living person with certain rights."

Taking up the issue of damages, the Curlender court rejected the plaintiff's request for damages "based upon an actuarial life expectancy ... of more than 70 years—the life expectancy if plaintiff had been born without Tay-Sachs disease" but, at the same time, also rejected "the notion that a 'wrongful life' cause of action involves any attempted evaluation of a claimed right not to be born." Instead, the court held that in such an action a child may "recover damages for the pain and suffering to be endured during the limited life span available to such a child and any special pecuniary loss resulting from the impaired condition." The court also made it clear that, to the extent that the costs of care were not recovered by the child's parents in a separate or consolidated action, the child should be permitted to recover such costs in her own suit. Plaintiff, of course, relies heavily—indeed exclusively—on the *Curlender* decision in support of her action in this case. Before analyzing *Curlender* and the out-of-state wrongful life decisions, however, we briefly consider the effect of a new statute enacted in the wake of *Curlender.*

III

As noted, the defendant in *Curlender* was a medical laboratory which allegedly had been negligent in conducting blood tests. In the course of its opinion, however, the Curlender court indicated in dictum that in an appropriate case parents of a seriously impaired infant, who, with full knowledge of the child's likely condition, "made a conscious choice to proceed with a pregnancy" could be held liable "for the pain, suffering and misery which they have wrought upon their offspring."

In evident response to this suggestion of possible parental liability for deciding to conceive or failing to abort a potentially defective child, the Legislature enacted section 43.6 of the Civil Code, effective January 1, 1982. Section 43.6 relieves the parents of any liability in this situation and also provides that the parents' decision shall neither be "a defense in any action against a third party" nor "be considered in awarding damages in any such action."

We conclude that section 43.6 has no significant effect on the issue before us. In this case, of course, the child is suing allegedly negligent providers of medical services, not her parents, and thus the statute clearly poses no explicit bar to the action. Although subdivision (b) of the provision implicitly recognizes that, under Curlender, a wrongful life action may lie against a "third party," we do not think that the statute can properly be viewed as a legislative codification of the *Curlender* holding, transforming the common law tort perceived in *Curlender* into a statutory cause of action. Both the Legislative Counsel's Digest accompanying the bill, and the adjacent sections in the Civil Code suggest that the purpose of the legislation was simply to eliminate any liability or other similar economic pressure which might induce potential parents to abort or decline to conceive a potentially defective child. Nothing in the statutory language or legislative history suggests that the new provision was intended to impose liability on any party. Under these circumstances, the section cannot properly be read as creating a statutory wrongful life cause of action against third parties. In sum, the new statute does not change the fact that the issue before our court is whether, and to what extent, such a cause of action should be recognized as a matter of California common law.

IV

In analyzing *Curlender,* ... and the numerous out-of-state cases, it may be helpful to recognize that although the cause of action at issue has attracted a special name—"wrongful life"—plaintiff's basic contention is that her action is simply one form of the familiar medical or professional malpractice action. The gist of plaintiff's claim is that she has suffered harm or damage as a result of defendants' negligent performance of their professional tasks, and that, as a consequence, she is entitled to recover under generally applicable common law tort principles.

...

In this case, although the Turpins' older daughter Hope, and not Joy, was defendants' immediate patient, it was reasonably foreseeable that Hope's parents and their potential offspring would be directly affected by defendants' negligent failure to discover that Hope suffered from an hereditary ailment and defendants do not contend that they owed no duty of care either to James and Donna or to Joy. Nor do defendants assert that the complaint fails to allege adequately either a breach of their duty of care or that Joy's birth was a proximate result of the breach.

Instead, defendants' basic position—supported by the numerous out-of-state authorities—is that Joy has suffered no legally cognizable injury or rationally ascertainable damages as a result of their alleged negligence. Although the issues of "legally cognizable injury" and "damages" are intimately related and in some sense inseparable, past cases have generally treated the two as distinct matters and, for purposes of analysis, it seems useful to follow that approach.

With respect to the issue of legally cognizable injury, the parties agree that the difficult question here does not stem from the fact that defendants' allegedly negligent act and plaintiff's asserted injury occurred before plaintiff's birth. Although at one time the common law denied recovery for injuries inflicted before birth, California—in tune with other American jurisdictions—has long abandoned that arbitrary limitation. Thus, if Joy's deafness was caused by negligent treatment of her mother during pregnancy, or if it resulted from a tort committed upon her mother before conception, it is clear that she would be entitled to recover against the negligent party.

Joy's complaint attempts, in effect, to bring her action within the scope of the foregoing line of cases, asserting that as a result of defendants' negligence she was "deprived of the fundamental right of a child to be born as a whole, functional human being without total deafness...." While the *Curlender* decision did not embrace this approach to "injury" completely—refusing to permit the plaintiff to recover for a reduced lifespan—it too maintained that the proper point of reference for measuring defendant's liability was simply plaintiff's condition after birth, insisting that "[w]e need not be concerned with the fact that had defendants not been negligent, the plaintiff might not have come into existence at all" and rejecting "the notion that a 'wrongful life' cause of action involves any attempted evaluation of a claimed right not to be born."

The basic fallacy of the *Curlender* analysis is that it ignores the essential nature of the defendants' alleged wrong and obscures a critical difference between wrongful life actions and the ordinary prenatal injury cases noted above. In an ordinary prenatal injury case, if the defendant had not been negligent, the child would have been born healthy; thus, as in a typical personal injury case, the defendant in such a case has interfered with the child's basic right to be free from physical injury caused by the negligence of others. In this case, by contrast, the obvious tragic fact is that plaintiff never had a chance "to be born as a whole, functional human being without total deafness"; if defendants had performed their jobs properly, she would not have been born with hearing intact, but—according to the complaint—would not have been born at all.

...

Although it is easy to understand and to endorse these decisions' desire to affirm the worth and sanctity of less-than-perfect life, we question whether these considerations alone provide a sound basis for rejecting the child's tort action. To begin with, it is hard to see how an award of damages to a severely handicapped or suffering child would "disavow" the value of life or in any way suggest that the child is not entitled to the full measure of legal and nonlegal rights and privileges accorded to all members of society.

Moreover, while our society and our legal system unquestionably place the highest value on all human life, we do not think that it is accurate to suggest that this state's public policy establishes—as a matter of law—that under all circumstances "impaired life" is "preferable" to "nonlife." ...

Of course, in the wrongful life context, the unborn child cannot personally make any choice as to the relative value of life or death. At that stage, however, just as in the case of an infant after birth, the law generally accords the parents the right to act to protect the child's interests. As the wrongful birth decisions recognize, when a doctor or other medical care provider negligently fails to diagnose an hereditary problem, parents are deprived of the opportunity to make an informed and meaningful decision whether to conceive and bear a handicapped child. Although in deciding whether or not to bear such a child parents may properly, and undoubtedly do, take into account their own interests, parents also presumptively consider the interests of their future child. Thus, when a defendant negligently fails to diagnose an hereditary ailment, he harms the potential child as well as the parents by depriving the parents of information which may be necessary to determine whether it is in the child's own interest to be born with defects or not to be born at all.

In this case, in which the plaintiff's only affliction is deafness, it seems quite unlikely that a jury would ever conclude that life with such a condition is worse than not being born at all. Other wrongful life cases, however, have involved children with much more serious, debilitating and painful conditions, and the academic literature refers to still other, extremely severe hereditary diseases. Considering the short life span of many of these children and their frequently very limited ability to perceive or enjoy the benefits of life, we cannot assert with confidence that in every situation there would be a societal consensus that life is preferable to never having been born at all.

While it thus seems doubtful that a child's claim for general damages should properly be denied on the rationale that the value of impaired life, as a matter of law, always exceeds the value of nonlife, we believe that the out-of-state decisions are on sounder grounds in holding that—with respect to the child's claim for pain and suffering or other general damages—recovery should be denied because (1) it is simply impossible to determine in any rational or reasoned fashion whether the plaintiff has in fact suffered an injury in being born impaired rather than not being born, and (2) even if it were possible to overcome the first hurdle, it would be impossible to assess general damages in any fair, nonspeculative manner.

...

V

Although we have determined that the trial court properly rejected plaintiff's claim for general damages, we conclude that her claim for the "extraordinary expenses for specialized teaching, training and hearing equipment" that she will incur during her lifetime because of her deafness stands on a different footing.

As we have already noted, in the corresponding "wrongful birth" actions parents have regularly been permitted to recover the medical expenses incurred on behalf of such a child. In authorizing this recovery by the parents, courts have recognized (1) that these are expenses that would not have been incurred "but for" the defendants' negligence and (2) that they are the kind of pecuniary losses which are readily ascertainable and regularly awarded as damages in professional malpractice actions.

Although the parents and child cannot, of course, both recover for the same medical expenses, we believe it would be illogical and anomalous to permit only parents, and not the child, to recover for the cost of the child's own medical care. If such a distinction were established, the afflicted child's receipt of necessary medical expenses might well depend on the wholly fortuitous circumstance of whether the parents are available to sue and recover such damages or whether the medical expenses are incurred at a time when the parents remain legally responsible for providing such care.

Realistically, a defendant's negligence in failing to diagnose an hereditary ailment places a significant medical and financial burden on the whole family unit. Unlike the child's claim for general damages, the damage here is both certain and readily measurable. Furthermore, in many instances these expenses will be vital not only to the child's well-being but to his or her very survival. If, as alleged, defendants' negligence was in fact a proximate cause of the child's present and continuing need for such special, extraordinary medical care and training, we believe that it is consistent with the basic liability principles of Civil Code section 1714 to hold defendants liable for the cost of such care, whether the expense is to be borne by the parents or by the child. As Justice Jacobs of the New Jersey Supreme Court observed ... "While the law cannot remove the heartache or undo the harm, it can afford some reasonable measure of compensation toward alleviating the financial burdens."

Moreover, permitting plaintiff to recover the extraordinary, additional medical expenses that are occasioned by the hereditary ailment is also consistent with the established parameters of the general tort "benefit" doctrine discussed above. As we have seen, under that doctrine an offset is appropriate only insofar as the defendant's conduct has conferred a special benefit "to the interest of the plaintiff that was harmed." Here, the harm for which plaintiff seeks recompense is an economic loss, the extraordinary, out-of-pocket expenses that she will have to bear because of her hereditary ailment. Unlike the claim for general damages, defendants' negligence has conferred no incidental, offsetting benefit to this interest of plaintiff. Accordingly, assessment of these special damages should pose no unusual or insoluble problems.

VI

In sum, we conclude that while a plaintiff-child in a wrongful life action may not recover general damages for being born impaired as opposed to not being born at all, the child—like his or her parents—may recover special damages for the extraordinary expenses necessary to treat the hereditary ailment.

The judgment is reversed and the case is remanded to the trial court for further proceedings consistent with this opinion.

Mosk, Justice, dissenting.

...

An order is internally inconsistent which permits a child to recover special damages for a so-called wrongful life action, but denies all general damages for the very same tort. While the modest compassion of the majority may be commendable, they suggest no principle of law that justifies so neatly circumscribing the nature of damages suffered as a result of a defendant's negligence.

As recently as 1980, the Court of Appeal unanimously decided in *Curlender v. Bio-Science Laboratories,* (1980) 106 Cal.App.3d 811, 165 Cal.Rptr. 477, that a cause of action exists for a wrongful-life tort. This court subsequently denied a petition for hearing. Thus *Curlender* was, and remains, the prevailing law of California. I see no persuasive reason to either abandon its doctrine, or to dilute its effectiveness by limiting recovery to special damages.

Curlender found a breach of duty by the medical laboratory there involved, not only to the parents but to the child yet to be born. It then proceeded to carefully analyze the applicable law, in part, as follows:

"The circumstance that the birth and injury have come hand in hand has caused other courts to deal with the problem by barring recovery. The reality of the 'wrongful-life' concept is that such a plaintiff both exists and suffers, due to the negligence of others. It is neither necessary nor just to retreat into meditation on the mysteries of life. We need not be concerned with the fact that had defendants not been negligent, the plaintiff might not have come into existence at all. The certainty of genetic impairment is no longer a mystery. In addition, a reverent appreciation of life compels recognition that plaintiff, however impaired she may be, has come into existence as a living person with certain rights.

"In our consideration of whether the child plaintiff has stated a cause of action, we find it instructive to look first to the statutory law of this state. Our Civil Code section 3281 provides that '[e]very person who suffers detriment from the unlawful act or omission of another, may recover from the person in fault a compensation therefor in money, which is called damages.' Civil Code section 3282 defines detriment as 'a loss or harm suffered in person or property.' Civil Code section 3333 provides: 'For the breach of an obligation not arising from contract, the measure of damages, except where otherwise expressly provided by this Code, is the amount which will compensate for all the detriment proximately caused thereby, whether it could have been anticipated or not.'

"In addition, we have long adhered to the principle that there should be a remedy for every wrong committed. 'Fundamental in our jurisprudence is the principle that for every wrong there is a remedy and that an injured party should be compensated for all damage proximately caused by the wrongdoer. Although we recognize exceptions from these fundamental principles, no departure should be sanctioned unless there is a strong necessity therefor. The general rule of damages in tort is that the injured party may recover for all detriment caused whether it could have been anticipated or not."

"We have concluded that it is clearly consistent with the applicable principles of statutory and decisional tort law in this state to recognize a cause of action stated by plaintiff against the defendants. To do otherwise would negate and run counter to the course of tort law so nobly chartered and enunciated in the landmark cases such as *Dillon v. Legg* [(1968) 68 Cal.2d 728, 69 Cal.Rptr. 72, 441 P.2d 912], *Rowland v. Christian* [(1968) 69 Cal.2d 108, 70 Cal.Rptr. 97, 443 P.2d 561], *Crisci v. Security Ins. Co.*, and *Rodriguez v. Bethlehem Steel Corp.* [(1974) 12 Cal.3d 382, 115 Cal.Rptr. 765, 525 P.2d 669].

" ... Plaintiff's right to damages must be considered on the basis of plaintiff's mental and physical condition at birth and her expected condition during the ... life span ... anticipated for one with her impaired condition. In similar fashion, we reject the notion that a 'wrongful-life' cause of action involves any attempted evaluation of a claimed right not to be born. In essence, we construe the 'wrongful-life' cause of action by the defective child as the right of such child to recover damages for the pain and suffering to be endured during the ... life span available to such a child and any special pecuniary loss resulting from the impaired condition.

"In California, infants are presumed to experience pain and suffering when injury has been established, even if the infant is unable to testify and describe such pain and suffering. In *Capelouto v. Kaiser Foundation Hospitals* (1972) 7 Cal. 3d 889 [103 Cal. Rptr. 856, 500 P.2d 880], the trial court had failed to instruct the jury on the infant plaintiff's pain and suffering; our high court reversed the jury verdict that awarded only plaintiff's medical expenses. It was observed, with respect to pain and suffering, that '[a]dmittedly these terms refer to subjective states, representing a detriment which can be translated into monetary loss only with great difficulty. But the detriment, nevertheless, is a genuine one that requires compensation, and the issue generally must be resolved by the "impartial conscience and judgment of jurors who may be expected to act reasonably, intelligently and in harmony with the evidence."'"

I conclude, as did the Court of Appeal in Curlender, that a cause of action can be stated and that this handicapped child is entitled to her day in court.

Notes & Questions

1. Although there is some debate as to the appropriate measures of success in the ART industry, three optimal parameters of excellence have been suggested. They include: the number of oocytes retrieved from the egg donor; the rate of implantation per embryo transfer; and the number of deliveries achieved per embryo transferred. *See* Anja Pinborg, et al., *What is the Most Relevant Standard of Success in Assisted Reproduction?*, 19 HUM. REPRODUCTION 1052 (2004). The success of IVF has resulted in its being the primary type of ART, far eclipsing GIFT and ZIFT procedures. The growing expertise with ICSI has led to an increasing use of ICSI in combination with IVF. *See* DEPARTMENT OF HEALTH AND HUMAN SERVICES, CDC, 2002 ASSISTED REPRODUCTIVE TECHNOLOGY (ART) REPORT, http://www.cdc.gov/ART/ART02/PDF/ART2002.pdf.

Typically, multiple embryos are transferred in each cycle of IVF, with fewer embryos (2.7) transferred when the mother is under thirty-five, as opposed to more (3.5) when the mother is over forty. The larger number of transferred embryos is an attempt to enhance overall IVF pregnancy rates, which decrease markedly with maternal age (43.5% in mothers under thirty-five and only 17.3% in mothers over forty). *Id.* The mean number of embryos transferred per IVF cycle has decreased over the last several years. This decrease is associated with a decline in the number of pregnancies with multiple fetuses. In 1999, the national rate of triplet and higher-order multiple birth numbers began to stabilize after many years of steady increase. *See* Jain Tarun, et al., *Trends in Embryo-Transfer Practice and in Outcomes of the Use of Assisted Reproductive Technology in the United States*, 350 NEW ENG. J. MED. 1639 (2004). This may be at least partially attributable to the publication of the American Society of Reproductive Medicine's (ASRM) embryo-transfer guidelines in 1998. *Id.* ASRM recently revised its guideline on embryo transfer, again emphasizing prudence, with respect to the number of embryos transferred per IVF cycle. For example, ASRM currently states that, absent extraordinary circumstances, only two embryos should be implanted in patients under thirty-five, and that in most cases, two is the appropriate number in the thirty-five to thirty-seven age group as well. ASRM guidelines provide for four or more embryos to be implanted when the mother is older than thirty-eight and/or has a history of failed IVF attempts. *See*

ASRM, *Guidelines on the Number of Embryos Transferred*, 82 FERTILITY AND STERILITY 773 (2004).

Assisted reproductive technologies are in a constant state of flux because improvements on existing methods and new technologies are continually emerging. For example, cytoplasmic (ooplasmic) transfer seeks to "rejuvenate" the aging mother's egg while maintaining the nuclear genetic material. On the theory that the egg's cytoplasm has become devitalized with age, and thus, is less able to be successfully fertilized, an egg is removed from the mother and injected with cytoplasm from a donor. Then the egg is inseminated by the father's sperm, with or without ICSI, and implanted in the mother. *See* J. Cohen, et al., *Ooplasmic Transfer in Mature Human Oocytes*, MOLECULAR HUM. REPROD., Mar. 4,1998, at 269–80. Although this technique is actively being used in other countries, it has been curtailed in the U.S. as a result of a 2001 FDA determination that it constitutes a form of gene transfer research. The FDA's rationale is that mitochondrial DNA will be transferred with the cytoplasm, thus altering the genetics of the egg cell. *See* J.A. Barritt, et al., *Mitochondria in Human Offspring Derived from Ooplasmic Transplantation*, 16 HUM. REPROD. 513 (2001).

There are recent reports of a new technology that will allow artificial insemination to be more successful, thus obviating the need for the more expensive and arduous IVF procedure. An Israeli company, Fertiligent, has developed a disposable pump connected to a catheter that controls the flow of sperm into the uterine cavity. The catheter is inserted into the uterus with a small balloon at the tip, which holds it in place. The catheter is then connected to a syringe pump that gradually releases the sperm over four hours. The theory is that this more closely mimics the natural process and facilitates successful fertilization. *See* Nicky Blackburn, *Mimicking Mother Nature*, THE JERUSALEM POST, Apr. 8, 2005, at 15, *available at* 2005 WLNR 5636007. In another recent report, Japanese scientists have discovered a sperm-related protein that plays a key role in the fusion of a sperm and an egg and may offer future products and technology to assist reproduction. *See Key Protein for Sperm-Egg Marriage Found*, JIJI PRESS ENG. NEWS SERV., Mar. 25, 2005 *available at* 2005 WLNR 4716879.

2. Professional Societies such as American Society for Reproductive Medicine (ASRM) play a significant role in establishing the standard of care with respect to ART. In addition to the aforementioned guideline published by the ASRM Practice Committee, ASRM's Ethics Committee has also published a number of pertinent reports including:

> *Fertility Treatment When the Prognosis Is Very Poor or Futile*, 82 FERTILITY & STERILITY 806 (2004): This report addresses the ethical stance of the physician when the patient seeks infertility services despite a very poor prognosis. It states that clinicians may refuse to provide infertility services when they regard it as a futile endeavor. However, the report cautions the clinician to fully inform the patient of the futility. Moreover, the guideline states that treatment even in the face of a poor prognosis may be undertaken if the patient understands the low odds of success but still seeks treatment.
>
> *Informing Offspring of Their Conception by Gamete Donation*, 81 FERTILITY & STERILITY 527 (2004): Noting the parallel to identity disclosure in adoption, the ASRM Ethics Committee encourages parents to disclose the use of donor gametes to their children in a carefully planned manner. They cite the value of

> open and honest communication in the parent-child relationship and the risk of harm from an accidental, inadvertent disclosure.
>
> *Family Members as Gamete Donors and Surrogates*, 80 FERTILITY & STERILITY 1124 (2003): ASRM encourages all ART programs to develop policies and procedures for dealing with requests that family members provide donor gametes. While the ASRM finds that use of family members as donors is ethically and medically acceptable, especially in the context of brothers donating sperm to brothers, and sisters donating eggs to sisters, consanguineous gamete donations from first-degree relatives are deemed unacceptable. All such family member donations need to be accompanied by counseling prior to the donation.

The Society for Assisted Reproductive Technology (SART), the other professional society involved in ART reporting, has over 370 members, representing over ninety-five percent of the ART clinics in the nation. It defines itself as:

> The governmental watchdog for ART-prospectively preventing governmental intrusion. SART's Public Affairs committee in conjunction with the ASRM Public Affairs office in Washington, DC and legal counsel as appropriate interact with many governmental agencies. An example is the detailed and referenced response produced by SART, ASRM, and SREI to the FDA's proposal to quarantine frozen donor egg IVF embryos. SART's action alert fax spurred many of you to write to the FDA to object to this unwarranted action. SART keeps its members apprised about relevant publications in the Federal Register through informational alerts via fax and email. Past examples include the CDC publications regarding "proposed model program for certification of embryo laboratories" and the "reporting of success rates in IVF."

See Society for Assisted Reproductive Technology, What does SART [Society for Assisted Reproductive Technology] Do Anyway? (2000), http://www.sart.org/whatis.html. It also actively engages in patient education, publishing materials designed to inform patients about options for treatment of infertility. *See, e.g.*, Society for Assisted Reproductive Technology, A Patient's Guide to Assisted Reproductive Technologies, http://www.sart.org/PDFs/TextPatients.pdf.

3. As noted in the text, there is a relative dearth of regulation with respect to ART and genetic testing. In the United States, regulation is limited to oversight by professional societies and reporting of procedure success rates and demographics. Moreover, this oversight and reporting regime was established well after ART and prenatal testing became widely available—at least to those who could afford to pay for them. *See* Don P. Wolf, et al., *An Opinion on Regulating Assisted Reproductive Technologies*, 20 ASSISTED REPROD. & GENETICS 290 (July 2003). Other countries exhibit a range of legislative approaches, from a permissive approach with administrative oversight to a restrictive approach with legislated prohibition. For example, Austria, France, India, Germany, Israel, The Netherlands, Switzerland, and the United Kingdom have all enacted laws setting conditions on accessibility to prenatal diagnosis, taking a public ordering approach. Some of these (Austria, Switzerland, Germany, and the State of Western Australia) prohibit preimplantation genetic diagnosis. Japan, Israel, and Australia use a self-regulatory private ordering approach heavily dependent upon professional society guidelines. Bartha M. Knoppers & Rosario M. Isasi, *Regulatory Approaches to Reproductive Testing*, 18 HUM. REPROD. 2695 (2004); *see also* Naoki Takeshita, et al., *Regulating Assisted Reproductive Technologies in Japan*, 20 ASSISTED REPROD. & GENETICS 260 (2003); Trees A. M. te Braake, *Regulation of Assisted Reproductive Technology in the*

Netherlands, 35 TEX. INT'L L.J. 93 (2000); Ichiro Matsuda & Kaoru Suzumori, *Prenatal Genetic Testing in Japan*, 3 CMTY GENETICS 12 (2000).

4. As indicated in the article by Deborah Spar, there is a vigorous global market in ART that has given rise to "reproductive tourism." The Spar article details the willingness of prospective parents to circumvent the barriers presented in the U.S. when certain procedures are banned or the parents believe that they will not be viable recipients of infertility services. This reproductive tourism has developed even in the face of the vibrant, relatively uncontrolled marketing of ART services here in the U.S. A Scandinavian company, Cryobank, actively markets sperm to infertility providers and patients through its New York office. Its marketing materials include the following slogans: "Congratulations, it's a Viking" and "You'd Better Build a Strong Crib." Cryobank's advertisements feature a blond, blue-eyed baby, noting that his ancestors beat Columbus to North America. *See* Jamie Talin, *Cultural Ideals and Commodities: For Prospective Parents in the Market for a Blonde-haired Blue-eyed Tot, Danish Sperm Makes the Sale*, NEWSDAY, June 5, 2005 at A7; *see also* Scandinavian Cryobank, Welcome to Scandinavian Cyrobank, http://www.scandinaviancryobank.com. Online donor catalogs actively sell eggs and sperm replete with donor information detailing height, weight, appearance, personal and family medical history, occupation, educational background, personality traits, interests, etc. *See* Don Oldenburg, *Infertile Couples Can Be Choosy*, TORONTO STATE, Nov. 26, 1999 at 1. One alleged entrepreneur proposed to auction off the eggs of young models to the highest bidder in 1999. *Id.* Most recently, embryo "adoption" has been proposed by a Christian organization that seeks to have infertile couples "adopt" the unused embryos of other couples. *See* Nightlight Christian Adoptions, Snowflakes Embryo Adoptions, http://www.nightlight.org/snowflakes_description.asp. Such "Snowflake" adoptions have been widely covered by the media and embraced by right-to-life politicians.

The increasing number of adoptees seeking the identity and information about their genetic "parents" may chill donor participation in the future. In some cases, there is a desire to learn information to address medical risks faced by the child. For example, in *Johnson v. Superior Court of Los Angeles County*, 177 Cal. Rptr. 63 (1981), a couple sought access to the identity and medical history of the sperm donor when their daughter developed polycystic kidney disease, an autosomal dominant disorder that results in kidney failure. The couple sought disclosure of the donor identity to inform their negligence suit against the sperm bank. The Court ultimately allowed the couple access to the donor's medical information, but required his identity to remain anonymous. *Id.* In other cases, there is growing belief that children should be able to access their genetic parent, either with respect to information or personal contact. In 2002, the U.K.'s Human Fertilisation and Embryology Authority announced its plan to change existing regulations applying to the anonymity of those donating sperm, eggs, or embryos. *See* Human Fertilisation and Embryology Authority, Response to the Department of Health's Consultation on 'Donor Information: Providing Information About Sperm, Egg and Embryo Donors' (2002), http://www.hfea.gov.uk/AboutHFEA/Consultations/Donor%20Info%20response.pdf. Under the new regulations, children born as a result of sperm, eggs, or embryos donated after April 2005 will be able to access the identity of their donor when they reach the age of eighteen. The earliest eighteen-year-olds will be able to do this will be in 2023. *Id.*; *see also* Claire Ainsworth, *Making Babies*, NEW SCIENTIST, Dec. 22, 2001, *available at* 2005 WLNR 3681062.

Ironically, a recent study of adolescent adoptees indicates that most are nonplussed with respect to information about their genetic parents. In a study published in 2004, researchers at the University of California studied adolescents who had been conceived through 'open-identity' sperm donors and found that all but one of the twenty-nine subjects had a neutral or positive response to their origins. Although most of them said they were likely to ask for the donor's identity and try to contact him, few saw him as being an important person in their lives and not one reported wanting any money from him. *See* J.E. Scheib, et al., *Adolescents with Open-identity Sperm Donors: Reports from 12 to 17 year olds*, 20 HUM. REPROD. 239 (2005) *available at* http://www3.oup.co.uk/eshre/press-release/freepdf/id_donors.pdf .

A recent twist on the stored gamete business is the freezing and storage of eggs for women seeking to "beat the biological clock" and preserve their options for parenthood. Although cryopreservation of eggs is more technically challenging than freezing sperm and relatively few babies (approximately 100) have been born using frozen eggs, many believe that technology will likely improve the outcome in the future. Extend Fertility, a company that offers egg freezing services to women wanting to preserve their ability to have children later in life, now has clinics in Los Angeles, San Francisco, Dallas and New York. Extend's clinics charge $10,000 for the egg retrieval process, forty dollars a month for storage, and women can expect to pay an additional $3,000 to $4,000 for the necessary fertility drugs. Such "fertility savings accounts" resonate with women who are actively engaged in careers at present, but who want to preserve their reproductive options. *See* Sally Wadyka, *For Women Worried About Fertility, Egg Bank is New Option*, N.Y. TIMES, Sept. 21, 2004, at F5.

5. In *Munro v. Regents of the University of California*, the plaintiffs alleged negligence in genetic counseling. At issue was the standard of care that applied to the genetic counselor. It is now known that several discrete population groups, besides the Ashkenazi Jews, are carriers of the Tay-Sachs mutation. However, this fact was little known information at the time the *Munro* case occurred, a fact which was instrumental in determining whether the counselor had been negligent in failing to consider this possibility. Moreover, because the Munros were vague in describing their French Canadian origins, if indeed they even knew of them, at the time of counseling, the Court ultimately found that Dr. Crandall had not breached the standard of care. Do you think that the standard of care has become more rigorous as a result of genetic knowledge accrued through the Human Genome Project? Would Munro be decided the same way today? Would the genetic counselor's duty require her to delve more deeply into the family origins when the patient reported an ancestor that was some "peculiar kind of French"? Suppose delving more deeply did not yield more detailed information? How much investigation of the family history should the counselor do in such a case?

The genetic counselor in *Munro* was a physician. Although physicians, especially physician/geneticists do provide counseling, many genetic counselors are trained in Masters' programs to provide dedicated counseling services. The National Society of Genetic Counselors (NSGC) describes genetic counselors as follows:

> Genetic counselors are health professionals with specialized graduate degrees and experience in the areas of medical genetics and counseling. Most enter the field from a variety of disciplines, including biology, genetics, nursing, psychology, public health and social work.
>
> Genetic counselors work as members of a health care team, providing information and support to families who have members with birth defects or genetic disorders and to families who may be at risk for a variety of inherited conditions. They identify families at risk, investigate the problem present in the fam-

ily, interpret information about the disorder, analyze inheritance patterns and risks of recurrence and review available options with the family.

National Society of Genetic Counselors, Genetic Counseling as a Profession (1983), http://www.nsgc.org/about/definition.asp. The NSGC Code of Ethics emphasizes values of care and respect for the client's autonomy, individuality, welfare, and freedom. It urges genetic counselors to strive to "enable their clients to make informed independent decisions, free of coercion, by providing or illuminating the necessary facts and clarifying the alternatives and anticipated consequences." National Society of Genetic Counselors, Code of Ethics, http://www.nsgc.org/about/code_of_ethics.asp.

Key to the genetic counseling practice ethic is the concept of nondirective counseling. Nondirective counseling requires the counselor to refrain from imposing his or her personal view and values upon the information they share with the patient. The goal of nondirective communication is that it be "value neutral." Such nondirective counseling seeks to maximize patient autonomy, while simultaneously providing information, clarifying options and their consequences, and assisting, but not leading, patients to their decisions. *See* Gwen Anderson, *Nondirectiveness in Prenatal Genetics: Patients Read Between the Lines*, 6 Nursing Ethics 126 (1999). However, the nondirective goal of genetic counseling may be difficult to achieve, even assuming the patient is fully able to assimilate the complexity of the increasing genetic testing options. For example, can someone really be value neutral when talking about abortion? What if a client wants a treatment that the counselor believes is not medically indicated, is futile, or immoral?

One study surveying members of the National Society of Genetic Counselors assessed how they defined "nondirectiveness," its importance to their practice, and when, and how, they take a more directive stance. Nearly ninety-six percent of 383 respondents reported viewing nondirectiveness as very important, but seventy-two percent stated they are sometimes directive. The most common reasons for directiveness include: (1) difficulties ensuring that verbal and nonverbal cues remain nondirective; (2) to recommend testing; (3) the client is unable to understand; (4) a better choice is clear; (5) to recommend medical care or counseling; or (6) the client has difficulty making an informed decision. *See* D.M. Bartels, *Nondirectiveness in Genetic Counseling: A Survey of Practitioners*, 72 Am J. Med. Genetics 172 (2000).

6. *Gallagher v. Duke University* is one of many cases in which the plaintiffs allege that negligent counseling resulted in the birth of a defective child. Unlike the *Munro* case, where the child faced certain death, the Gallagher infant, although severely disabled, potentially could outlive her parents. The Gallaghers argued that, had they known that there first child had died as a result of the genetic mutation she inherited from her father, they would not have chosen to conceive another child. The court found that the Gallaghers could recover the damages flowing from the wrongful conception, including the costs of the pregnancy, extraordinary costs of caring for their disabled daughter during her minority, and pain and suffering. The court cited the precedent of *Azzolino v. Dingfelder*, 337 S.E.2d 528 (N.C. 1985). In that case, the plaintiffs alleged that had they been properly advised, they would have had amniocentesis performed, and would have discovered that their child would suffer from Down Syndrome. The plaintiffs alleged that had they been aware of this outcome, they would have chosen to terminate the pregnancy via abortion. In *Azzolino,* the North Carolina Supreme Court observed that "[t]he jurisdictions which have reached the merits of claims for wrongful birth currently appear to be almost unanimous in their recognition of them when, but for the defendants' negligence, the parents would have terminated the defective fetus by abor-

tion." *Id.* at 533. The Court noted, however, that in order to allow recovery for such claims, courts must hold "that the existence of a human life can constitute an injury cognizable at law." *Id.* at 534. The Court concluded, "[w]e are unwilling to take any such step because we are unwilling to say that life, even life with severe defects, may ever amount to a legal injury." *Id.* Although the terms "wrongful conception" and "wrongful birth" are distinguished in a way that will still allow the *Gallagher* plaintiffs to recover despite *Azzolino*, most other courts have distinguished between wrongful conception and wrongful birth more concretely.

Wrongful conception, or wrongful pregnancy, cases arise in three major scenarios. First, when a physician performs a sterilization procedure, such as a vasectomy or tubal ligation, and an unwanted, unplanned pregnancy results. Second, when the physician negligently fails to diagnose the pregnancy and the mother is deprived of her chanced to terminate an unwanted, unplanned pregnancy. Finally, when the woman has sought a termination and the physician's negligent performance of the abortion has resulted in the maintenance of the pregnancy and an unplanned child is born. *See, e.g., Taylor v. Kurapati*, 600 N.W.2d 670 (Mich. Ct. App. 1999). Key to the distinction between wrongful pregnancy and wrongful birth is that the former results in the birth of an unplanned, unwanted, albeit healthy child. In such cases, the damages will typically be limited to the costs, pain and suffering of the pregnancy and delivery and the costs of a successful sterilization procedure, if a failed sterilization procedure is at issue. Courts are generally unwilling to consider the birth and responsibility of a normal, healthy child as damage with an ascertainable dollar value. In most cases, the court will offset such alleged damages with the love, affection and benefits of having a normal healthy child and find that the benefits outweigh the harms. *But see Thomas C. v. Physicians Ins. Co.*, 509 N.W. 2d 81 (Wis. 1993) (parents can recover costs of raising a normal healthy child conceived following a negligent sterilization operation.)

In contrast, wrongful birth cases arise when the parents engage in the pregnancy with the aim of having a child. In most wrongful birth cases, the allegation is that the parents wanted a child, but would not have chosen to continue a pregnancy had they known that the child would have a congenital defect or be encumbered with a genetic disease. Like *Gallagher*, most of these cases involve a discoverable risk of fetal harm or defect where the physician negligently failed to discover the defect or inform the parents of a genetic risk. As a result, the parents are foreclosed from the opportunity to terminate the pregnancy at an early stage or avoid the risk by foregoing pregnancy in the first place. Courts recognizing wrongful births do not consider the award of damages to cover the extraordinary costs of the disabled child as either a windfall, or a denigration, of the value of the child. For example, in *Shroeder v. Perkel*, 432 A.2d 834 (N.J. 1981), a couple was awarded wrongful birth damages when their physician failed to warn them of their risk of a second child afflicted with cystic fibrosis

> By limiting damages to those expenses that are actually attributable to the affliction, we are not conferring a windfall on Mr. and Mrs. Schroeder. Although they may derive pleasure from Thomas, that pleasure will be derived in spite of, rather than because of, his affliction. Mr. and Mrs. Schroeder will receive no compensating pleasure from incurring extraordinary medical expenses on behalf of Thomas. There is no joy in watching a child suffer and die from cystic fibrosis.

Id. at 852. A growing number of jurisdictions recognize such wrongful birth claims when there has been negligent genetic counseling, negligent prenatal testing, or other failure to diagnose fetal abnormality. See, e.g., *Robak v. United States,* 658 F.2d 471 (7th Cir. 1981) (interpreting Alabama law); *Daniels v. Delaware,* 120 F. Supp. 2d 411 (D. Del.

2000) (interpreting Pennsylvania law); *Phillips v. United States,* 508 F. Supp. 544 (D.S.C. 1981) (interpreting South Carolina law); *Gildiner v. Thomas Jefferson Univ. Hosp.,* 451 F. Supp. 692 (E.D. Pa. 1978); *Moores v. Lucas,* 405 So. 2d 1022 (Fla. Dist. Ct. App. 1981) (disapproved of by *Kush v. Lloyd,* 616 So. 2d 415 (Fla. 1992)); *Blake v. Cruz,* 698 P.2d 315 (Idaho 1984); *Goldberg v. Ruskin,* 499 N.E.2d 406 (Ill. 1986); *Arche v. U.S. Dep't of Army,* 798 P.2d 477 (Kan. 1990); *Reed v. Campagnolo,* 630 A.2d 1145 (Md. 1993); *Viccaro v. Milunsky,* 551 N.E.2d 8 (Mass. 1990); *Shelton v. St. Anthony's Med. Ctr.,* 781 S.W.2d 48 (Mo. 1989); *Smith v. Cote,* 513 A.2d 341 (N.H. 1986); *Berman v. Allan,* 404 A.2d 8 (N.J. 1979); *Becker v. Schwartz,* 386 N.E.2d 807 (N.Y. 1978); *Nelson v. Krusen,* 678 S.W.2d 918 (Tex. 1984); *Naccash v. Burger,* 290 S.E.2d 825 (Va. 1982); *Harbeson v. Parke-Davis, Inc.,* 656 P.2d 483 (Wash. 1983); *James G. v. Caserta,* 332 S.E.2d 872 (W. Va. 1985); *see also* Katherine Say, *Wrongful Birth-Preserving Justice for Women and Their Families,* 28 OKLA. CITY U. L. REV. 251 (2003); Jennifer R. Granchi, *The Wrongful Birth Tort: A Policy Analysis and the Right to Sue for an Inconvenient Child,* 43 S. TEX. L. REV. 1261 (2002); Monique Ann-Marie Croon, *Case Note: Taylor v. Kurapati, The Court of Appeals of Michigan's Decision of Refusing to Recognize the Tort of Wrongful Birth,* 5 DEPAUL J. HEALTH CARE L. 317 (2002); Paula Bernstein, *Fitting a Square Peg in a Round Hole: Why Traditional Tort Principles Do Not Apply to Wrongful Birth Actions,* 18 J. CONTEMP. HEALTH L. & POL'Y 297 (2001); Mary B. Sullivan, *Wrongful Birth and Wrongful Conception: A Parent's Need for a Cause of Action,* 15 J.L. & HEALTH 105 (2000–2001).

7. *Turpin v. Sortini* illustrates a case in which wrongful life damages are at issue. Wrongful life cases are brought on behalf of the child, whereas wrongful birth actions are brought on behalf of the parent. In wrongful life actions, the child typically seeks compensation for the ongoing medical and extraordinary expenses they will suffer as a result of their disability. Because, in most cases, the parents are simultaneously bringing a wrongful birth action, the child's economic damages will be those that will accrue after the child reaches majority age and is no longer accorded the care and support of the parents. Although wrongful birth actions and damages are available in most jurisdictions, only three jurisdictions recognize wrongful life actions. California, New Jersey, and Washington currently recognize a cause of action for wrongful life. *See, e.g., Curlender v. Bio-Science Labs.,* 165 Cal. Rptr. 477, 489–90 (Cal. Ct. App. 1980); *Procanik v. Cillo,* 478 A.2d 755, 764 (N.J. 1984); *Harbeson v. Parke-Davis, Inc.,* 656 P.2d 483, 496 (Wash. 1983).

By far, the most expansive of these wrongful life decisions is the *Curlender* case, the earlier California case cited in *Turpin*. The plaintiff in *Curlender,* a child born with Tay-Sachs disease, sued for wrongful life on the ground that the defendant laboratory negligently performed tests and thus failed to detect that her parents were both carriers of the genes known to cause the disorder. The *Curlender* court was the first to recognize a wrongful life action brought the afflicted child. The court even indicated, in dicta, that theoretically wrongful life liability could extend to the parents who might negligently inflict harm by choosing to give birth, knowing that they were conferring injury upon their unborn child. This language stimulated legislative action to protect parents from being sued by their children on the ground that the child should not have been born. See Cal. Civ. Code § 43.6.

Turpin, decided two years later, reaffirms the legitimacy of wrongful life actions in California, noting that "it is hard to see how an award of damages to a severely handicapped or suffering child would 'disavow' the value of life or in any way suggest that the child is not entitled to the full measure of legal and nonlegal rights and privileges accorded to all members of society." 643 P.2d 954, 961 (Cal. 1982) (*en banc*). The few jurisdictions that do recognize wrongful life are reluctant, as is the court in *Turpin*, to award the child general damages. Such damages are considered too speculative to be ascertained, given that they relate to the pain and suffering the child will suffer after reaching majority. Pain and suffering of the child during minority is usually encompassed in the damages awarded the parents through the wrongful birth cause of action.

Most jurisdictions do not recognize wrongful life cases. *See, e.g.*, *Berman v. Allan*, 404 A.2d 8, 11–13 (N.J. 1979); *Becker v. Schwartz*, 386 N.E.2d 807 (N.Y. 1978); *Speck v. Finegold*, 439 A.2d 110, 112 (Pa. 1981); *Dumer v. St. Michael's Hospital*, 233 N.W.2d 372, 374–376 (Wis. 1975); *Elliot v. Brown*, 361 So. 2d 546 (Ala.1978). The majority view is that it is impossible to determine whether, if the "child-to-be" had been informed of the risks, he or she would have preferred not to be born. "Who then can say, as it was essential to the parents' cause of action that they say for themselves, that, had it been possible to make the risk known to the children-to-be—in their cellular or fetal state or, let us say, in the mind's eye of their future parents—that the children too would have preferred not to be born at all?" *Becker v. Schwartz*, 386 N.E. 2d 807, 815 (N.Y. 1979); *see also* Philip J. VanDerhoef, *Washington Recognizes Wrongful Birth and Wrongful Life—A Critical Analysis—Harbeson v. Parke-Davis, Inc.*, 58 WASH. L. REV. 649 (1983); Thomas A. Burns, *When Life is an Injury: An Economic Approach to Wrongful Life Lawsuits*, 52 DUKE L.J. 807 (2003); Kurtis J. Kearl, *Turpin v. Sortini: Recognizing the Unsupportable Cause of Action for Wrongful Life*, 71 CAL. L. REV. 1278 (1983); Anne Morris & Severin Saintier, *To Be or Not To Be: Is That the Question? Wrongful Life and Misconceptions*, 11 MED. L. REV. 167 (2003); Suzann M. Weber, *Pay Me Now or Pay Me Later? The Question of Prospective Damage Claims for Genetic Injury in Wrongful Life Cases*, 23 IND. L. REV. 753 (1990). There is also a growing body of scholarship considering wrongful life actions from a disability rights perspective. *See, e.g.*, Wendy F. Hensel, *The Disabling Impact of Wrongful Birth and Wrongful Life Actions*, 40 HARV. C.R.-C.L. L. REV. 141 (2005); Christy Hetherington, *Rhode Island Facing the Wrongful Birth/Wrongful Life Debate: Pro-Disabled Sentiment Given Life*, 6 ROGER WILLIAMS U. L. REV. 565 (2001); Lara Butler, *Cowe by Cowe c. Forum Group Inc.: Wrongful Life and the Dilemma of Comparing Impaired Existence with Non-Existence*, 22 MEM. ST. U. L.REV. 881 (1992).

B. Assisted Reproduction, Genetics, and the Changing Concepts of Legal Parenthood

Traditionally, parenthood meant that the child, born to a married couple, would have its birth/genetic/gestational mother as its legal mother and the mother's husband, presumably the genetic father, as the legal father. Indeed, even when there was a dispute or a question about the actual genetic father, the law was disposed to find the husband the father of children born or conceived during the marriage. This predisposition conformed to traditional social norms and the concept of a "unitary family" composed of a married couple and their children.

Law has begun to cope with a variety of different models of parenthood. Much of this has resulted from the new ability to sever the ties between genetics and gestation, and further, between gestation and parenthood. As discussed in Part A, with the magic of assisted reproductive technology, the genetic parents can engage in prenatal, and even preconception, genetic testing to better ensure that their child will be free of certain disorders. Moreover, the 21st century parent need not be involved in the medical transaction of pregnancy and birth. Would-be parents can act on their intent using assisted reproductive technologies and contracts with others to create their child. The ever-increasing reproductive opportunities are changing the concept of the "unitary family" and leading to a reformulation of what constitutes parenthood.

As we consider parenthood in the age of genetic testing and assisted reproductive technologies, we are presented with several constructs for parenthood. This part of the chapter considers various approaches to determine legal parenthood. First, of course, there are the traditional "unitary family" and genetic definitions of parenthood. Easy accessibility to paternity testing, and determination of misattributed paternity, presents challenges to the concept of the unitary family. Genetics, long considered the definitive "proof" of parenthood, is now being questioned as to its validity as a determinant of parenthood. What about the rights of the gestational or surrogate mother, the woman who nurtures and sustains the child, from embryo to viability to birth? The "birth mother" is viewed as the legal mother in most states. How do the rights of the gestational mother and/or the genetic mother square with the rights of the "intended" parents, who may well have funded the reproductive venture? These issues have already generated compelling and challenging case law.

1. Genetics and the "Unitary Family"

Michael H. v. Gerald D.

491 U.S. 110 (1989)

Justice Scalia, joined by The Chief Justice, and in part by Justice O'Connor and Justice Kennedy:

...

The facts of this case are, we must hope, extraordinary. On May 9, 1976, in Las Vegas, Nevada, Carole D., an international model, and Gerald D., a top executive in a French oil company, were married. The couple established a home in Playa del Rey, California, in which they resided as husband and wife when one or the other was not out of the country on business. In the summer of 1978, Carole became involved in an adulterous affair with a neighbor, Michael H. In September 1980, she conceived a child, Victoria D., who was born on May 11, 1981. Gerald was listed as father on the birth certificate and has always held Victoria out to the world as his daughter. Soon after delivery of the child, however, Carole informed Michael that she believed he might be the father.

In the first three years of her life, Victoria remained always with Carole, but found herself within a variety of quasi-family units. In October 1981, Gerald moved to New York City to pursue his business interests, but Carole chose to remain in California. At the end of that month, Carole and Michael had blood tests of themselves and Victoria, which showed a 98.07% probability that Michael was Victoria's father. In January 1982, Carole visited Michael in St. Thomas, where his primary business interests were based. There Michael held Victoria out as his child. In March, however, Carole left Michael and returned to California, where she took up residence with yet another man, Scott K. Later that spring, and again in the summer, Carole and Victoria spent time with Gerald in New York City, as well as on vacation in Europe. In the fall, they returned to Scott in California.

In November 1982, rebuffed in his attempts to visit Victoria, Michael filed a filiation action in California Superior Court to establish his paternity and right to visitation. In March 1983, the court appointed an attorney and guardian ad litem to represent Victoria's interests. Victoria then filed a cross-complaint asserting that if she had more than one psychological or de facto father, she was entitled to maintain her filial relationship, with all of the attendant rights, duties, and obligations, with both. In May 1983, Carole filed a motion for summary judgment. During this period, from March through July 1983, Carole was again living with Gerald in New York. In August, however, she returned to California, became involved once again with Michael, and instructed her attorneys to remove the summary judgment motion from the calendar.

For the ensuing eight months, when Michael was not in St. Thomas he lived with Carole and Victoria in Carole's apartment in Los Angeles and held Victoria out as his daughter. In April 1984, Carole and Michael signed a stipulation that Michael was Victoria's natural father. Carole left Michael the next month, however, and instructed her attorneys not to file the stipulation. In June 1984, Carole reconciled with Gerald and joined him in New York, where they now live with Victoria and two other children since born into the marriage.

In May 1984, Michael and Victoria, through her guardian ad litem, sought visitation rights for Michael pendente lite. To assist in determining whether visitation would be in Victoria's best interests, the Superior Court appointed a psychologist to evaluate Victoria, Gerald, Michael, and Carole. The psychologist recommended that Carole retain sole custody, but that Michael be allowed continued contact with Victoria pursuant to a restricted visitation schedule. The court concurred and ordered that Michael be provided with limited visitation privileges pendente lite.

On October 19, 1984, Gerald, who had intervened in the action, moved for summary judgment on the ground that under Cal. Evid. Code §621 there were no triable issues of fact as to Victoria's paternity. This law provides that "the issue of a wife cohabiting with her husband, who is not impotent or sterile, is conclusively presumed to be a child of the marriage." Cal. Evid. Code Ann. §621(a) (West Supp.1989). The presumption may be rebutted by blood tests, but only if a motion for such tests is made, within two years from the date of the child's birth, either by the husband or, if the natural father has filed an affidavit acknowledging paternity, by the wife. §§621(c) and (d).

On January 28, 1985, having found that affidavits submitted by Carole and Gerald sufficed to demonstrate that the two were cohabiting at conception and birth and that Gerald was neither sterile nor impotent, the Superior Court granted Gerald's motion for summary judgment, rejecting Michael's and Victoria's challenges to the constitutionality of §621. The court also denied their motions for continued visitation pending the appeal under Cal. Civ. Code §4601, which provides that a court may, in its discretion, grant "reasonable visitation rights ... to any ... person having an interest in the welfare of the child." Cal. Civ. Code Ann. §4601 (West Supp. 1989). It found that allowing such visitation would "violat[e] the intention of the Legislature by impugning the integrity of the family unit." Supp. App. to Juris. Statement A-91.

...

II

The California statute that is the subject of this litigation is, in substance, more than a century old. California Code of Civ. Proc. §1962(5), enacted in 1872, provided that "[t]he issue of a wife cohabiting with her husband, who is not impotent, is indisputably presumed to be legitimate." ... In their present form, the substantive provisions of the statute are as follows:

§621. Child of the marriage; notice of motion for blood tests

(a) Except as provided in subdivision (b), the issue of a wife cohabiting with her husband, who is not impotent or sterile, is conclusively presumed to be a child of the marriage.

(b) Notwithstanding the provisions of subdivision (a), if the court finds that the conclusions of all the experts, as disclosed by the evidence based upon blood tests performed pursuant to Chapter 2 (commencing with Section 890) of Division 7 are that the husband is not the father of the child, the question of paternity of the husband shall be resolved accordingly.

(c) The notice of motion for blood tests under subdivision (b) may be raised by the husband not later than two years from the child's date of birth.

(d) The notice of motion for blood tests under subdivision (b) may be raised by the mother of the child not later than two years from the child's date of birth if the child's biological father has filed an affidavit with the court acknowledging paternity of the child.

(e) The provisions of subdivision (b) shall not apply to any case coming within the provisions of Section 7005 of the Civil Code [dealing with artificial insemination] or to any case in which the wife, with the consent of the husband, conceived by means of a surgical procedure.

III

We address first the claims of Michael. At the outset, it is necessary to clarify what he sought and what he was denied. California law, like nature itself, makes no provision for dual fatherhood. Michael was seeking to be declared the father of Victoria. The immediate benefit he evidently sought to obtain from that status was visitation rights. See Cal. Civ. Code Ann. § 4601 (West 1983) (parent has statutory right to visitation "unless it is shown that such visitation would be detrimental to the best interests of the child"). But if Michael were successful in being declared the father, other rights would follow—most importantly, the right to be considered as the parent who should have custody, Cal. Civ. Code Ann. § 4600 (West 1983), a status which "embrace[s] the sum of parental rights with respect to the rearing of a child, including the child's care; the right to the child's services and earnings; the right to direct the child's activities; the right to make decisions regarding the control, education, and health of the child; and the right, as well as the duty, to prepare the child for additional obligations, which includes the teaching of moral standards, religious beliefs, and elements of good citizenship." 4 California Family Law § 60.02[1][b] (C. Markey ed. 1987). All parental rights, including visitation, were automatically denied by denying Michael status as the father. While Cal. Civ. Code Ann. § 4601 places it within the discretionary power of a court to award visitation rights to a nonparent, the Superior Court here, affirmed by the Court of Appeal, held that California law denies visitation, against the wishes of the mother, to a putative father who has been prevented by § 621 from establishing his paternity. *See* 191 Cal.App.3d, at 1013, 236 Cal.Rptr., at 821, citing Vincent B. v. Joan R., 126 Cal.App.3d, at 627–628 179 Cal.Rptr., at 13.

Michael raises two related challenges to the constitutionality of § 621. First, he asserts that requirements of procedural due process prevent the State from terminating his liberty interest in his relationship with his child without affording him an opportunity to demonstrate his paternity in an evidentiary hearing. We believe this claim derives from a fundamental misconception of the nature of the California statute. While § 621 is phrased in terms of a presumption, that rule of evidence is the implementation of a substantive rule of law. California declares it to be, except in limited circumstances, irrelevant for paternity purposes whether a child conceived during, and born into, an existing marriage was begotten by someone other than the husband and had a prior relationship with him.

...

Michael contends as a matter of substantive due process that, because he has established a parental relationship with Victoria, protection of Gerald's and Carole's marital union is an insufficient state interest to support termination of that relationship. This argument is, of course, predicated on the assertion that Michael has a constitutionally protected liberty interest in his relationship with Victoria.

...

In an attempt to limit and guide interpretation of the Clause, we have insisted not merely that the interest denominated as a "liberty" be "fundamental" (a concept that, in isolation, is hard to objectify), but also that it be an interest traditionally protected by our society....

This insistence that the asserted liberty interest be rooted in history and tradition is evident, as elsewhere, in our cases according constitutional protection to certain parental rights. Michael reads the landmark case of *Stanley v. Illinois,* 405 U.S. 645 (1972), and the subsequent cases of *Quilloin v. Walcott,* 434 U.S. 246 (1978), *Caban v. Mohammed,* 441 U.S. 380 (1979), and *Lehr v. Robertson,* 463 U.S. 248 (1983), as establishing that a liberty interest is created by biological fatherhood plus an established parental relationship—factors that exist in the present case as well. We think that distorts the rationale of those cases. As we view them, they rest not upon such isolated factors but upon the historic respect—indeed, sanctity would not be too strong a term—traditionally accorded to the relationships that develop within the unitary family....

Thus, the legal issue in the present case reduces to whether the relationship between persons in the situation of Michael and Victoria has been treated as a protected family unit under the historic practices of our society, or whether on any other basis it has been accorded special protection. We think it impossible to find that it has. In fact, quite to the contrary, our traditions have protected the marital family (Gerald, Carole, and the child they acknowledge to be theirs) against the sort of claim Michael asserts.

The presumption of legitimacy was a fundamental principle of the common law. Traditionally, that presumption could be rebutted only by proof that a husband was incapable of procreation or had had no access to his wife during the relevant period.... The primary policy rationale underlying the common law's severe restrictions on rebuttal of the presumption appears to have been an aversion to declaring children illegitimate, ... thereby depriving them of rights of inheritance and succession, ... and likely making them wards of the state. A secondary policy concern was the interest in promoting the "peace and tranquility of States and families," ... a goal that is obviously impaired by facilitating suits against husband and wife asserting that their children are illegitimate. Even though, as bastardy laws became less harsh, "[j]udges in both [England and the United States] gradually widened the acceptable range of evidence that could be offered by spouses, and placed restraints on the 'four seas rule'... [,] the law retained a strong bias against ruling the children of married women illegitimate."

We have found nothing in the older sources, nor in the older cases, addressing specifically the power of the natural father to assert parental rights over a child born into a woman's existing marriage with another man. Since it is Michael's burden to establish that such a power (at least where the natural father has established a relationship with the child) is so deeply embedded within our traditions as to be a fundamental right, the lack of evidence alone might defeat his case. But the evidence shows that even in modern times—when, as we have noted, the rigid protection of the marital family has in other respects been relaxed—the ability of a person in Michael's position to claim paternity has not been generally acknowledged.... Not a single decision is set forth specifically according standing to the natural father, and "express indications of the nonexistence of any ... limitation" upon standing were found only "in a few jurisdictions." Moreover, even if it were clear that one in Michael's position generally possesses, and has generally always possessed, standing to challenge the marital child's legitimacy, that would still not establish Michael's case. As noted earlier, what is at issue here is not entitlement to a state pronouncement that Victoria was begotten by Michael. It is no conceivable denial of constitutional right for a State to decline to declare facts unless some legal consequence hinges upon the requested declaration. What Michael asserts here is a right to have himself declared the natural father and thereby to obtain parental prerogatives. What he must establish, therefore, is not that our society has traditionally allowed a natural father in his circumstances to establish paternity, but that it has traditionally accorded such a father parental rights, or at least has not traditionally denied them. Even if the law in all States had always been that the entire world could challenge the marital presumption and obtain a declaration as to who was the natural father, that would not advance Michael's claim. Thus, it is ultimately irrelevant, even for purposes of determining current social attitudes towards the alleged substantive right Michael asserts, that the present law in a number of States appears to allow the natural father—including the natural father who has not established a relationship with the child—the theoretical power to rebut the marital presumption, *see Note, Rebutting the Marital Presumption: A Developed Relationship Test,* 88 COLUM.L.REV. 369, 373 (1988). What counts is whether the States in fact award substantive parental rights to the natural father of a child conceived within, and born into, an extant marital union that wishes to embrace the child. We are not aware of a single case, old or new, that has done so. This is not the stuff of which fundamental rights qualifying as liberty interests are made.

In *Lehr v. Robertson*, a case involving a natural father's attempt to block his child's adoption by the unwed mother's new husband, we observed that "[t]he significance of the biological connection is that it offers the natural father an opportunity that no other male possesses to develop a relationship with his offspring," 463 U.S., at 262 and we assumed that the Constitution might require some protection of that opportunity, *id.*, at 262–265. Where, however, the child is born into an extant marital family, the natural father's unique opportunity conflicts with the similarly unique opportunity of the husband of the marriage; and it is not unconstitutional for the State to give categorical preference to the latter. In *Lehr* we quoted approvingly from Justice Stewart's dissent in *Caban v. Mohammed,* 441 U.S., at 397, to the effect that although "'[i]n some circumstances the actual relationship between father and child may suffice to create in the unwed father parental interests comparable to those of the married father,'" "'the absence of a legal tie with the mother may in such circumstances appropriately place a limit on whatever substantive constitutional claims might otherwise exist.'" 463 U.S., at 260, n. 16. In accord with our traditions, a limit is also imposed by the circumstance that the mother is, at the time of the child's conception and birth, married to, and cohabitating with, another man, both of whom wish to raise the child as the offspring of their union. It is a question of legislative policy and not constitutional law whether California will allow the presumed parenthood of a couple desiring to retain a child conceived within and born into their marriage to be rebutted.

... Here, to provide protection to an adulterous natural father is to deny protection to a marital father, and vice versa. If Michael has a "freedom not to conform" (whatever that means), Gerald must equivalently have a "freedom to conform." One of them will pay a price for asserting that "freedom"—Michael by being unable to act as father of the child he has adulterously begotten, or Gerald by being unable to preserve the integrity of the traditional family unit he and Victoria have established. Our disposition does not choose between these two "freedoms," but leaves that to the people of California....

IV

We have never had occasion to decide whether a child has a liberty interest, symmetrical with that of her parent, in maintaining her filial relationship. We need not do so here because, even assuming that such a right exists, Victoria's claim must fail. Victoria's due process challenge is, if anything, weaker than Michael's. Her basic claim is not that California has erred in preventing her from establishing that Michael, not Gerald, should stand as her legal father. Rather, she claims a due process right to maintain filial relationships with both Michael and Gerald. This assertion merits little discussion, for, whatever the merits of the guardian ad litem's belief that such an arrangement can be of great psychological benefit to a child, the claim that a State must recognize multiple fatherhood has no support in the history or traditions of this country. Moreover, even if we were to construe Victoria's argument as forwarding the lesser proposition that, whatever her status vis-à-vis Gerald, she has a liberty interest in maintaining a filial relationship with her natural father, Michael, we find that, at best, her claim is the obverse of Michael's and fails for the same reasons.

Victoria claims in addition that her equal protection rights have been violated because, unlike her mother and presumed father, she had no opportunity to rebut the presumption of her legitimacy. We find this argument wholly without merit. We reject, at the outset, Victoria's suggestion that her equal protection challenge must be assessed under a standard of strict scrutiny because, in denying her the right to maintain a filial relationship with Michael, the State is discriminating against her on the basis of her illegitimacy. *See Gomez v. Perez,* 409 U.S. 535, 538 (1973). Illegitimacy is a legal construct, not a natural trait. Under California law, Victoria is not illegitimate, and she is treated in the same manner as all other legitimate children: she is entitled to maintain a filial relationship with her legal parents.

We apply, therefore, the ordinary "rational relationship" test to Victoria's equal protection challenge. The primary rationale underlying §621's limitation on those who may rebut the presumption of legitimacy is a concern that allowing persons other than the husband or wife to do so may undermine the integrity of the marital union. When the husband or wife contests the legitimacy of their child, the stability of the marriage has already been shaken. In contrast, allowing a claim of illegitimacy to be pressed by the child—or, more accurately, by a court-appointed guardian ad litem—may well disrupt an otherwise peaceful union. Since it pursues a legitimate end by rational means, California's decision to treat Victoria differently from her parents is not a denial of equal protection.

The judgment of the California Court of Appeal is

Affirmed.

Justice Brennan, with whom Justice Marshall and Justice Blackmun join, dissenting.

In a case that has yielded so many opinions as has this one, it is fruitful to begin by emphasizing the common ground shared by a majority of this Court. Five Members of the Court refuse to foreclose "the possibility that a natural father might ever have a constitutionally protected interest in his relationship with a child whose mother was married to, and cohabiting with, another man at the time of the child's conception and birth." Five Justices agree that the flaw inhering in a conclusive presumption that terminates a constitutionally protected interest without any hearing whatsoever is a procedural one. Four Members of the Court agree that Michael H. has a liberty interest in his relationship with Victoria, ... and one assumes for purposes of this case that he does, ...

In contrast, only one other Member of the Court fully endorses Justice Scalia's view of the proper method of analyzing questions arising under the Due Process Clause. Nevertheless, because the plurality opinion's exclusively historical analysis portends a significant and unfortunate departure from our prior cases and from sound constitutional decision-making, I devote a substantial portion of my discussion to it.

I

Once we recognized that the "liberty" protected by the Due Process Clause of the Fourteenth Amendment encompasses more than freedom from bodily restraint, today's plurality opinion emphasizes, the concept was cut loose from one natural limitation on its meaning. This innovation paved the way, so the plurality hints, for judges to substitute their own preferences for those of elected officials. Dissatisfied with this supposedly unbridled and uncertain state of affairs, the plurality casts about for another limitation on the concept of liberty.

It finds this limitation in "tradition." Apparently oblivious to the fact that this concept can be as malleable and as elusive as "liberty" itself, the plurality pretends that tradition places a discernible border around the Constitution. The pretense is seductive; it would be comforting to believe that a search for "tradition" involves nothing more idiosyncratic or complicated than poring through dusty volumes on American history....

Even if we could agree, moreover, on the content and significance of particular traditions, we still would be forced to identify the point at which a tradition becomes firm enough to be relevant to our definition of liberty and the moment at which it becomes too obsolete to be relevant any longer. The plurality supplies no objective means by which we might make these determinations. Indeed, as soon as the plurality sees signs that the tradition upon which it bases its decision (the laws denying putative fathers like Michael standing to assert paternity) is crumbling, it shifts ground and says that the case has nothing to do with that tradition, after all. "[W]hat is at issue here," the plurality asserts after canvassing the law on paternity suits, "is not entitlement to a state pronouncement that Victoria was begotten by Michael." But that is precisely what is at issue here, and the plurality's last-minute denial of this fact dramatically illustrates the subjectivity of its own analysis.

...

It is not that tradition has been irrelevant to our prior decisions. Throughout our decision making in this important area runs the theme that certain interests and practices—freedom from physical restraint, marriage, childbearing, childrearing, and others—form the core of our definition of "liberty." Our solicitude for these interests is partly the result of the fact that the Due Process Clause would seem an empty promise if it did not protect them, and partly the result of the historical and traditional importance of these interests in our society. In deciding cases arising under the Due Process Clause, therefore, we have considered whether the concrete limitation under consideration impermissibly impinges upon one of these more generalized interests.

Today's plurality, however, does not ask whether parenthood is an interest that historically has received our attention and protection; the answer to that question is too clear for dispute. Instead, the plurality asks whether the specific variety of parenthood under consideration—a natural father's relationship with a child whose mother is married to another man—has enjoyed such protection.

If we had looked to tradition with such specificity in past cases, many a decision would have reached a different result.... The plurality's interpretive method is more than novel; it is misguided. It ignores the good reasons for limiting the role of "tradition" in interpreting the Constitution's deliberately capacious language. In the plurality's constitutional universe, we may not take notice of the fact that the original reasons for the conclusive presumption of paternity are out of place in a world in which blood tests can prove virtually beyond a shadow of a doubt who sired a particular child and in which the fact of illegitimacy no longer plays the burdensome and stigmatizing role it once did. Nor, in the plurality's world, may we deny "tradition" its full scope by pointing out that the rationale for the conventional rule has changed over the years, as has the rationale for Cal. Evid. Code Ann. § 621 (West Supp.1989); instead, our task is simply to identify a rule denying the asserted interest and not to ask whether the basis for that rule—which is the true reflection of the values undergirding it—has changed too often or too recently to call the rule embodying that rationale a "tradition." Moreover, by describing the decisive question as whether Michael's and Victoria's interest is one that has been "traditionally protected by our society," ... rather than one that society traditionally has thought important (with or without protecting it), and by suggesting that our sole function is to "discern the society's views," ... the plurality acts as if the only purpose of the Due Process Clause is to confirm the importance of interests already protected by a majority of the States. Transforming the protection afforded by the Due Process Clause into a redundancy mocks those who, with care and purpose, wrote the Fourteenth Amendment.

In construing the Fourteenth Amendment to offer shelter only to those interests specifically protected by historical practice, moreover, the plurality ignores the kind of society in which our Constitution exists. We are not an assimilative, homogeneous society, but a facilitative, pluralistic one, in which we must be willing to abide someone else's unfamiliar or even repellent practice because the same tolerant impulse protects our own idiosyncracies. Even if we can agree, therefore, that "family" and "parenthood" are part of the good life, it is absurd to assume that we can agree on the content of those terms and destructive to pretend that we do. In a community such as ours, "liberty" must include the freedom not to conform. The plurality today squashes this freedom by requiring specific approval from history before protecting anything in the name of liberty.

...

II

The plurality's reworking of our interpretive approach is all the more troubling because it is unnecessary. This is not a case in which we face a "new" kind of interest, one that requires us to consider for the first time whether the Constitution protects it. On the contrary, we confront an interest—that of a parent and child in their relationship with each other—that was among the first that this Court acknowledged in its cases defining the "liberty" protected by the Constitution, and I think I am safe in saying that no one doubts the wisdom or validity of those decisions. Where the interest under consideration is a parent-child relationship, we need not ask, over and over again, whether that interest is one that society traditionally protects.

Thus, to describe the issue in this case as whether the relationship existing between Michael and Victoria "has been treated as a protected family unit under the historic practices of our society, or whether on any other basis it has been accorded special protection," ... is to reinvent the wheel. The better approach—indeed, the one commanded by our prior cases and by common sense—is to ask whether the specific parent-child relationship under consideration is close enough to the interests that we already have protected to be deemed an aspect of "liberty" as well. On the facts before us, therefore, the question is not what "level of generality" should be used to describe the relationship between Michael and Victoria, ... but whether the relationship under consideration is sufficiently substantial to qualify as a liberty interest under our prior cases.

On four prior occasions, we have considered whether unwed fathers have a constitutionally protected interest in their relationships with their children. Though different in factual and legal circumstances, these cases have produced a unifying theme: although an unwed father's biological link to his child does not, in and of itself, guarantee him a constitutional stake in his relationship with that child, such a link combined with a substantial parent-child relationship will do so. "When an unwed father demonstrates a full commitment to the responsibilities of parenthood by 'com [ing] forward to participate in the rearing of his child,'... his interest in personal contact with his child acquires substantial protection under the Due Process Clause. At that point it may be said that he 'act[s] as a father toward his children.'" Michael H. is almost certainly Victoria D.'s natural father, has lived with her as her father, has contributed to her support, and has from the beginning sought to strengthen and maintain his relationship with her.

...

The evidence is undisputed that Michael, Victoria, and Carole did live together as a family; that is, they shared the same household, Victoria called Michael "Daddy," Michael contributed to Victoria's support, and he is eager to continue his relationship with her. Yet they are not, in the plurality's view, a "unitary family," whereas Gerald, Carole, and Victoria do compose such a family. The only difference between these two sets of relationships, however, is the fact of marriage. The plurality, indeed, expressly recognizes that marriage is the critical fact in denying Michael a constitutionally protected stake in his relationship with Victoria: no fewer than six times, the plurality refers to Michael as the "adulterous natural father" (emphasis added) or the like....

The plurality's exclusive rather than inclusive definition of the "unitary family" is out of step with other decisions as well. This pinched conception of "the family," crucial as it is in rejecting Michael's and Victoria's claims of a liberty interest, is jarring in light of our many cases preventing the States from denying important interests or statuses to those whose situations do not fit the government's narrow view of the family.... Today's rhapsody on the "unitary family" is out of tune with such decisions.

...

The plurality has wedged itself between a rock and a hard place. If it limits its holding to those situations in which a wife and husband wish to raise the child together, then it necessarily takes the State's interest into account in defining "liberty"; yet if it extends that approach to circumstances in which the marital union already has been dissolved, then it may no longer rely on the State's asserted interest in protecting the "unitary family" in denying that Michael and Victoria have been deprived of liberty.

A

We must first understand the nature of the challenged statute: it is a law that stubbornly insists that Gerald is Victoria's father, in the face of evidence showing a 98 percent probability that her father is Michael. What Michael wants is a chance to show that he is Victoria's father. By depriving him of this opportunity, California prevents Michael from taking advantage of the best-interest standard embodied in § 4601 of California's Civil Code, which directs that parents be given visitation rights unless "the visitation would be detrimental to the best interests of the child." Cal. Civ. Code Ann. § 4601 (West Supp.1989).

As interpreted by the California courts, however, § 621 not only deprives Michael of the benefits of the best-interest standard; it also deprives him of any chance of maintaining his relationship with the child he claims to be his own. When, as a result of § 621, a putative father may not establish his paternity, neither may he obtain discretionary visitation rights as a "nonparent" under § 4601....

...

Section 621 as construed by the California courts thus cuts off the relationship between Michael and Victoria—a liberty interest protected by the Due Process Clause—without affording the least bit of process. This case, in other words, involves a conclusive presumption that is used to terminate a constitutionally protected interest—the kind of rule that our preoccupation with procedural fairness has caused us to condemn.

...

The question before us, therefore, is whether California has an interest so powerful that it justifies granting Michael no hearing before terminating his parental rights.

...

The purported state interests here, however, stem primarily from the State's antagonism to Michael's and Victoria's constitutionally protected interest in their relationship with each other and not from any desire to streamline procedures. Gerald D. explains that § 621 promotes marriage, maintains the relationship between the child and presumed father, and protects the integrity and privacy of the matrimonial family. It is not, however, § 621, but the best-interest principle, that protects a stable marital relationship and maintains the relationship between the child and presumed father. These interests are implicated by the determination of who gets parental rights, not by the determination of who is the father; in the hearing that Michael seeks, parental rights are not the issue. Of the objectives that Gerald stresses, therefore, only the preservation of family privacy is promoted by the refusal to hold a hearing itself. Yet § 621 furthers even this objective only partially.

Gerald D. gives generous proportions to the privacy protected by § 621, asserting that this provision protects a couple like Gerald and Carole from answering questions on such matters as "their sexual habits and practices with each other and outside their marriage, their finances, and their thoughts, beliefs, and opinions concerning their relationship with each other and with Victoria." Yet invalidation of § 621 would not, as Gerald suggests, subject Gerald and Carole to public scrutiny of all of these private matters. Family finances and family dynamics are relevant, not to paternity, but to the best interests of the child—and the child's best interests are not, as I have stressed, in issue at the hearing that Michael seeks. The only private matter touching on the paternity presumed by § 621 is the married couple's sex life. Even there, § 621 as interpreted by California's intermediate appellate courts pre-empts inquiry into a couple's sexual relations, since "cohabitation" consists simply of living under the same roof together; the wife and husband need not even share the same bed. *See, e.g., Vincent B. v. Joan R.*, 179 Cal.Rptr. 9 ([Cal. Ct. App.] 1981). Admittedly, §621 does not foreclose inquiry into the husband's fertility or virility—matters that are ordinarily thought of as the couple's private business. In this day and age, however, proving paternity by asking intimate and detailed questions about a couple's relationship would be decidedly anachronistic. Who on earth would choose this method of establishing fatherhood when blood tests prove it with far more certainty and far less fuss? The State's purported interest in protecting matrimonial privacy thus does not measure up to Michael's and Victoria's interest in maintaining their relationship with each other.

Make no mistake: to say that the State must provide Michael with a hearing to prove his paternity is not to express any opinion of the ultimate state of affairs between Michael and Victoria and Carole and Gerald. In order to change the current situation among these people, Michael first must convince a court that he is Victoria's father, and even if he is able to do this, he will be denied visitation rights if that would be in Victoria's best interests. See Cal. Civ. Code Ann. §4601 (West Supp.1989). It is elementary that a determination that a State must afford procedures before it terminates a given right is not a prediction about the end result of those procedures.

IV

The atmosphere surrounding today's decision is one of make-believe. Beginning with the suggestion that the situation confronting us here does not repeat itself every day in every corner of the country, ... moving on to the claim that it is tradition alone that supplies the details of the liberty that the Constitution protects, and passing finally to the notion that the Court always has recognized a cramped vision of "the family," today's decision lets stand California's pronouncement that Michael—whom blood tests show to a 98 percent probability to be Victoria's father—is not Victoria's father. When and if the Court awakes to reality, it will find a world very different from the one it expects.

2. Genetic Parenthood

In re the Parentage of J.M.K.

119 P.3d 840 (Wash. 2005)

MADSEN, JUSTICE.

Michael Kepl, the respondent, had a long-term romantic relationship with Teresa Brock, the petitioner, while he was married to another woman. Brock was not married during her relationship with Kepl. The parties met in the late 1980s at work and shortly thereafter began a sexual relationship that continued for approximately one year, ending in 1990 or 1991. Kepl's wife gave birth to his daughter, AK, in 1991. The parties renewed their sexual relationship in the early-to mid-1990s (1992–1994) which lasted nearly 10 years. The parties dispute whether their sexual relationship ended by January or March 2001.

In 1995, the parties began to try actively to conceive a child. The parties first had unprotected sexual intercourse. Brock then sought help from doctors and fertility clinics in Tacoma and Seattle. Brock used fertility drugs and the parties timed intercourse.

These processes were unsuccessful. Brock then asked Kepl to donate sperm which he did multiple times. Brock then underwent multiple artificial insemination procedures using Kepl's sperm when the parties were not able to time intercourse. Although the parties at times inaccurately refer to the fertility process as "artificial insemination," the record indicates that Brock eventually conceived her children using in vitro fertilization, a type of assisted reproduction involving the implantation of preembryos in Brock created with Kepl's sperm.

Brock gave birth to her first son, JMK, on December 30, 1998. Apparently, Brock was induced a week earlier at Kepl's request so that he could attend the birth given his other commitments. When the first inducement was not successful, Brock was induced again and gave birth approximately one week later. Kepl was present at the hospital the day she gave birth and Kepl was the first person other than hospital staff to hold JMK.

Photographs in the record show Kepl at the hospital holding JMK and with Brock. Kepl gave Brock flowers and cards, including messages of "It's a Boy—Finally!" and "Bunches of love to you [Brock] and our bundle of joy" with Kepl signing with both his first name and as "Dad." At the hospital, Kepl completed and signed a paternity affidavit with Brock and Kepl's name was placed on JMK's birth certificate. A number of Brock's friends were present in the hospital room when Kepl and Brock completed and signed the paternity affidavit.

Kepl visited JMK weekly. Kepl took Brock and JMK on vacation and participated in holiday events with Brock and JMK. The record contains numerous photographs of Kepl holding and playing with JMK including Kepl and JMK at Woodland Park Zoo in 2000, at Mount Rainer Park in 2001, and at his home and at Brock's home. Photographs also show Kepl attending JMK's first and second birthday parties. The record also contains professional photographs of Kepl, Brock and JMK posed as a traditional family taken in April 1999.

In April 1999, when JMK was four months old, Kepl applied for a $100,000 life insurance policy identifying JMK as his son and primary beneficiary and identifying Brock as his significant other and contingent beneficiary. Kepl had a separate life insurance policy in effect for his daughter, AK, for $500,000. Kepl's insurance policy application was approved in May 1999 for $100,000 coverage requiring annual payments of $749 for 20 years.

In February 2001, Brock conceived a second child, again using *in vitro* fertilization. Brock claims that having a second child, a sibling for JMK, was Kepl's idea and that Kepl paid Brock $700 to help pay for the medical procedure. Kepl claims that he had no input into the decision to conceive a second child. Brock gave birth to a second son, DRK, on October 27, 2001. Kepl visited the hospital while Brock was in labor and the day after DRK was born. However, Kepl did not sign a paternity affidavit for DRK.

Prior to the first child's birth, Kepl and Brock set up a joint savings account for JMK. Kepl paid approximately $400–600 a month, which was briefly increased to $1,000 after the second child was born. The record contains bank records indicating that Kepl made child support payments until January 2002, when JMK was three years old and DRK was three months old. According to both parties, Kepl stopped making the payments after Kepl's wife found out about his extramarital affair in January 2002.

Kepl claims he paid child support payments in order to continue his sexual relationship with Brock and due to blackmail, to keep Brock from telling his wife about their relationship. Kepl also claims that he was under a lot of stress during the time Brock gave birth to her first child and signed the paternity affidavit under blackmail, duress and/or fraud. Additionally, Kepl claimed he donated sperm only as a friend, and did not intend to be a parent. In contrast, Brock claims that Kepl voluntarily made child support payments and purchased the life insurance policy for JMK, consistent with his involvement and visitation with her first son, and voluntarily signed the paternity affidavit.

PROCEDURAL HISTORY

On February 20, 2002, Brock filed a petition to establish JMK's and DRK's parentage in the Superior Court of Pierce County. In the petition, Brock requested the court enter an order and judgment that (1) Kepl be declared the natural father of JMK and DRK, (2) the birth certificate of DRK be amended to identify Kepl as the father, (3) child support be determined pursuant to the Washington State Support Schedule, (4) Kepl pay past support (being credited for earlier payments), (5) a parenting plan be adopted, and (6) court costs, blood tests, guardian ad litem and attorney fees be awarded by the court. Brock also moved the court for an order appointing a guardian ad litem for the two boys, which the court granted that same day, appointing John Brooks as guardian ad litem for JMK and DRK.

Kepl responded to Brock's parentage petition by requesting paternity blood testing, claiming he was not necessarily the biological father of the two boys. Kepl urged the court not to enter child support or a parenting plan until paternity was established using blood tests.

Kepl's counsel sent letters and subpoena duces tecum to two fertility clinics and three doctors, requesting all medical records and documentation from 1990 to 2002 relating to Kepl and Brock. Brock moved for a protective order protecting her medical records. On April 12, 2002, Judge Larkin granted the protective order and urged Kepl and the boys to complete the blood testing promptly as suggested by the guardian ad litem.

On May 3, 2002, Brock filed a motion to require Kepl to submit to paternity blood testing. Kepl opposed the motion, arguing that under former RCW 26.26.050(2) (1976), he cannot be the natural father of either child because he did not sign a written agreement in advance of impregnation as provided under the artificial insemination statute. Additionally, Kepl argued that the court lacked authority to require blood testing because under former RCW 26.26.100(1) (1997) a court may order blood testing only when there is a reasonable possibility that the "requisite sexual contact" occurred. Kepl asserted that because these children were conceived using artificial reproduction, the "requisite sexual contact" could not have occurred. Thus, even though Kepl and Brock were in a sexual relationship, the children were not conceived from natural sexual contact.

On May 21, 2001, Commissioner Johnson ordered that Kepl and the two boys submit to blood testing. Judge Larkin denied Kepl's order seeking revision of the order requiring blood tests. The blood tests indicate that Kepl is the biological father of JMK with a combined probability index of 99.997 percent and of DRK with a combined probability index of 99.97 percent.

On June 21, 2002, Brock filed a motion for summary judgment on parentage of JMK under former RCW 26.26.040 and former RCW 70.58.080 (1997) due to the signed paternity affidavit. Brock argued that Kepl is "presumed to be the father based on RCW 26.26.040" and there is no "clear, cogent, and convincing evidence" to rebut the presumption. On July 23, 2002, after the blood tests conclusively determined that Kepl was the biological father to both boys, Brock filed a second summary judgment motion to establish Kepl as the legal father to both JMK and DRK.

Commissioner Fleury granted Brock's summary judgment motion, concluding that Kepl was the legal (natural) father of both JMK and DRK. A subsequent hearing was held to determine child support. There, Commissioner Haarmann granted Brock's temporary order, directing child support be paid, and ordering Kepl to pay Brock's attorney fees. Kepl sought revision of the summary judgment decision on parentage, the orders on child support and attorney fees and of the protective order regarding Brock's medical records.

The Court of Appeals reversed stating, "Because former RCW 26.26.050(2) protected semen donors and because Kepl donated semen, the proper inquiry for the parentage of J.M.K. and D.R.K. begins with the artificial insemination statute. Brock and Kepl did not agree in writing that Kepl, by donating semen, would become the children's legal father. Nor is there any evidence in the record from which we could infer such a writing. Thus, Brock's arguments fail." *In re Parentage of J.M.K. and D.R.K.*, 121 Wash.App. 578, 583, 89 P.3d 309 (2004).

ANALYSIS

...

As the trial court did, given the factual differences in this case, we address each child separately. Brock moved for summary judgment on the parentage of JMK under the theory that, under former RCW 26.26.040(1)(e) and former RCW 70.58.080(4), Kepl became the legal (natural) father 60 days after Kepl signed the paternity affidavit. Alternatively, Brock argued that Brock and Kepl's completion of the paternity affidavit establishes Kepl's written consent to paternity under former RCW 26.26.050(2).

Kepl argues that his signature on the paternity affidavit had no legal effect because of the statutory protections granted by former RCW 26.26.050(2) for semen donors who do not sign written consents in advance of insemination of a woman to whom the man is not married. Kepl argues that Brock invites the court to ignore former RCW 26.26.050(2) in favor of former RCW 26.26.040(1)(e) and former RCW 70.58.080(4). Kepl asserts that Brock's approach must be rejected because "it is neither the function nor the prerogative of the Court to ignore legislative enactments" and instead, the proper approach is to "harmonize statutes" pertaining to the subject matter and maintain the integrity of the statutes within the overall statutory scheme, quoting *Philippides v. Bernard*, 151 Wash.2d 376, 385, 88 P.3d 939 (2004).

The meaning of a statute is inherently a question of law and our review is de novo. The primary goal of statutory interpretation is to ascertain and give effect to the legislature's intent and purpose. This is done by considering the statute as a whole, giving effect to all that the legislature has said, and by using related statutes to help identify the legislative intent embodied in the provision in question. *Dep't of Ecology v. Campbell & Gwinn*, 146 Wash.2d at 11, 43 P.3d 4. If, after this inquiry, the statute can reasonably be interpreted in more than one way, then it is ambiguous and it is appropriate to resort to principles of statutory construction to assist in interpretation. Strained, unlikely or absurd consequences resulting from a literal reading are to be avoided. If, among alternative constructions, one or more would involve serious constitutional difficulties, the court will reject those interpretations in favor of a construction that will sustain the constitutionality of the statute.

Former RCW 26.26.040(1)(e) provides that a man is presumed to be the natural father of a child for all intents and purposes if he acknowledges his paternity of the child pursuant to former RCW 70.58.080. Former RCW 70.58.080(4) contains the rules regarding how an unmarried mother and the father complete an affidavit acknowledging paternity of the father. The affidavit must contain (i) a sworn statement by the mother consenting to the assertion of paternity and stating that he is the natural father of the child, (ii) a statement by the father that he is the natural father of the child, (iii) a sworn statement by the mother and the putative father that each has been given notice, both orally and in writing, of the alternatives to, the legal consequences of, and the rights and responsibilities that arise from signing the affidavit acknowledging paternity and the social security numbers of both parents. Former RCW 70.58.080(4)(a). It is undisputed that the paternity affidavit completed by Brock and Kepl in 1998 for JMK meets all of the above requirements.

The law then provides that an acknowledgment of paternity under former RCW 70.58.080 "shall be a legal finding of paternity of the child sixty days after the acknowledgment is filed with the center for health statistics unless the acknowledgment is sooner rescinded or challenged." Former RCW 26.26.040(1)(e). It is undisputed that in this case the paternity affidavit was filed with the center for health statistics and that Kepl did not rescind or challenge the paternity affidavit within 60 days after filing. Accordingly, we hold that, as a matter of law, Kepl became the natural father of JMK in 1999, 60 days after the paternity affidavit was filed. The law provides further that "[j]udicial and administrative proceedings are neither required nor permitted to ratify an unchallenged acknowledgment of paternity filed after July 27, 1997." Former RCW 26.26.040(1)(e). Therefore, as this paternity affidavit was filed after July 27, 1997, there is no further legal action necessary, required or permitted by this court (or any court) regarding the legal determination that Kepl is the father of JMK.

Assuming former RCW 26.26.050(2) applies, Kepl contends that the former RCW 70.58.080(4) allows only a "natural" father to sign an affidavit of paternity and that he cannot be a natural father because former RCW 26.26.050(2) provides that unless a donor of semen signs a consent to paternity, such a donor is not the "natural" father of the child conceived using artificial insemination. Kepl's argument is not persuasive. As discussed above, under former RCW 26.26.040(1)(e), Kepl became the natural father of JMK 60 days after the signed paternity affidavit was filed with the center for health statistics. Thus, through his actions and operation of law Kepl has waived any rights to possible statutory protection under former RCW 26.26.050(2) regarding his paternity of JMK. Moreover, contrary to Kepl's claim, this interpretation is consistent with the overall statutory scheme of encouraging parental responsibility for married and unmarried parents. *See, e.g.*, former RCW 26.26.020 (the parent and child relationship extends equally to every child and to every parent, regardless of the marital status of the parents); former RCW 70.58.080 (requiring all attending physicians and midwives to provide an opportunity for a child's mother and father to complete an affidavit acknowledging paternity, formally accepting their statutory and common law duty to provide support for their child); former RCW 26.26.180 (1983) (a promise to render support by a supposed or alleged father does not require consideration and is enforceable according to its terms).

Former RCW 26.26.050 is an exception to the long-standing rule that a parent is the biological mother or father of his or her child and has a duty to support that child. 19 Kenneth W. Weber, Washington Practice: Family and Community Property Law ch. 21 (1997). The duty to support children exists regardless of marital status.

Furthermore, Kepl's contention raises serious constitutional concerns. Under Kepl's theory, a written agreement for paternity and legal responsibility including financial support between an unmarried couple, the mother and biological father, evidenced by a signed paternity acknowledgment, would not be sufficient to establish fatherhood responsibilities. Commentators have noted that serious constitutional concerns regarding the treatment of illegitimate children and their fathers led to the creation of the Uniform Parentage Act. Accordingly, we hold that Kepl became the legal (natural) father of JMK 60 days after the paternity affidavit, signed by Brock, the mother, and Kepl, the biological father, was filed.

Lastly, Kepl argues that summary judgment was not appropriate as to his paternity of JMK because there are unresolved issues regarding credibility as to whether Kepl signed the paternity affidavit under blackmail, duress and/or fraud. Under former RCW 26.26.040(1)(e), Kepl has the burden of proof. Based on overwhelming evidence, including the numerous photographs, letters and cards submitted and the undisputed fact of the long-term romantic relationship between the parties, we affirm the trial court's summary judgment determination of paternity of JMK because reasonable minds would not conclude that Kepl signed the paternity affidavit for JMK under fraud, duress and/or blackmail.

We now turn to DRK. Because Kepl did not sign a paternity affidavit for DRK, the legal argument above is not available regarding the paternity of DRK. Kepl maintains that he cannot be the legal (natural) father of DRK because former RCW 26.26.050(2), the artificial insemination statute, shields him from legal fatherhood status.

A threshold question is whether former RCW 26.26.050 is applicable given that Brock conceived DRK using *in vitro* fertilization and not through artificial insemination. Brock argues that under former RCW 26.26.050(2), the legislature enacted a provision designed to prevent an unintended paternity through "artificial insemination." Brock asserts that, "by its terms, the statute is limited to the process of 'artificial insemination.'

Brock correctly notes that the process of artificial insemination is completely different from the process *in vitro* fertilization. Because Brock conceived her children through the creation of embryos that were later implanted into Brock's uterus, Brock concludes that under a plain reading of the unambiguous statutory language former RCW 26.26.050(2) does not apply to this case. Brock also cites the commentary to the Uniform Parentage Act, on which the statutory provision is based, which provides in part that the Act "'does not deal with many complex and serious legal problems raised by the practice of artificial insemination'" and deals only with one fact situation that occurs frequently—the artificial insemination with sperm from donors who have no intention of being the father.

Kepl provides two arguments as to why the former artificial insemination statute should apply in this case. First, Kepl claims that former RCW 26.26.050(2) should be read by focusing on the "purpose" of the donor, and not on the actual method used by the woman to become pregnant. Kepl claims that since "artificial insemination" is not defined in the statute, a donor, such a Kepl, who donates semen to a licensed physician with a purpose of "for use" in a woman is entitled to the protection of the statute, regardless of the method actually employed to achieve pregnancy.

Alternatively, Kepl argues that if a definition of "artificial insemination" is required, it is appropriate to consider the current statutory provision of RCW 26.26.011(4). RCW

26.26.011(4) defines "Assisted reproduction" to mean "a method of causing pregnancy other than sexual intercourse." The term includes "(a) intrauterine insemination; (b) donation of eggs; (c) donation of embryos; (d) *in vitro* fertilization and transfer of embryos; and (e) intracytoplsmic sperm injection." *Id.* Kepl claims that RCW 26.26.011(4) is both curative and remedial and it is thus appropriate to apply the statute retroactively.

Neither of Kepl's arguments is persuasive. The first argument requires this court to effectively ignore the terms "artificial insemination." Courts are not permitted to simply ignore terms in a statute. *Arborwood Idaho, L.L.C. v. City of Kennewick*, 151 Wash.2d 359, 367, 89 P.3d 217 (2004) (if the statute's meaning is plain on its face, then the court must give effect to that plain meaning as an expression of legislative intent). While Kepl correctly explains the holding in *Barstad,* his second argument overlooks the legislature's clear intent in this case to apply the revised parentage provisions in chapter 26.26 RCW prospectively. RCW 26.26.904, a transitional provision, provides, "[a] proceeding to adjudicate parentage which was commenced before June 13, 2002, is governed by the law in effect at the time the proceeding was commenced." Thus, the legislature did not intend the new parentage provisions to apply retroactively. Accordingly, we hold that former RCW 26.26.050(2) is not applicable.

Next, Kepl contends that the trial court lacked authority to order blood tests. Former RCW 26.26.100(1) (1997) provides, in relevant part, that the court may, and upon the request of a party shall, require any alleged or presumed father who has been made a party to submit to blood tests. If a party objects to a proposed court order for blood or genetic tests, the party requesting blood tests must provide testimony stating the facts and the court is then required to order blood tests if it appears that a reasonable possibility exists that the requisite sexual contact occurred. Former RCW 26.26.100. Kepl claims that the court had no authority because former RCW 26.26.050(2) shields him from legal paternity for JMK and DRK.

As discussed above, with regards to both JMK and DRK, Kepl does not have recourse to any statutory defenses under former RCW 26.26.050(2). Furthermore, in response to Brock's parentage petition, Kepl initially claimed that he was not necessarily the biological father of the two boys because Brock may have been "impregnated by another donor's sperm" and Kepl himself requested blood testing for paternity of both boys. Given Kepl's shifting legal position, combined with the intimate, sexual relationship between the parties and the inapplicability of former RCW 26.26.050, we hold that the trial court did not abuse its discretion in ordering Kepl to submit to blood tests.

As noted earlier, genetic testing here indicates a 98 percent or greater probability that Kepl is DRK's biological father. There is no dispute as to the procedures or accuracy of the genetic testing. Thus, under former RCW 26.26.040(1)(g), Kepl is presumed to be the natural father of DRK. Accordingly, we affirm the trial court's summary judgment determination that Kepl is the legal (natural) father of DRK.

Kepl also claims that the trial court erred in requiring Kepl to pay child support and to provide tax returns because he is not the natural father under former RCW 26.26.050(2). Because we hold that Kepl is the natural father for both boys, Kepl's claims are without merit. Orders setting forth child support obligations in paternity actions are reviewed for abuse of discretion. *State ex rel. Partlow v. Law*, 39 Wash.App. 173, 178, 692 P.2d 863 (1984). RCW 26.26.130(2) provides that the judgment and order regarding parentage shall contain provisions concerning the duty of future and current child support. Kepl makes no claim that the amount of support determined by the court was not reasonable or that the court failed to consider relevant factors. RCW 26.26.130(6) (after considering all relevant factors, the court shall order either or both parents to pay an amount determined pursuant to the schedule and standards contained in chapter 26.19 RCW). The record contains the Washington State Child Support Schedule Worksheets used to determine the support payments. We hold that the trial court did not abuse its discretion in determining child support.

Robert B. v. Susan B.

135 Cal.Rptr.2d 785 (Cal. Ct. App. 2003)

Elia, J.

...

In May 2000 respondents Robert and Denise B. contracted with an anonymous ovum donor to obtain the donor's eggs for fertilization with Robert's sperm. The contract reflected the intent of the contracting parties that Robert and Denise would be the parents of any children produced from the resulting embryos.

Meanwhile, Susan went to the same fertility clinic with the intent of purchasing genetic material from "two strangers who would contractually sign away their rights" so that "there would be no paternity case against her, ever." She therefore contracted with the clinic for an embryo created from anonymously donated ova and sperm.

About 13 embryos were produced for Robert and Denise. In June 2000 some of them were implanted in Denise's uterus. Through an apparent clinic error, Susan received three of these embryos. When she became pregnant, Susan believed that the child she was carrying was the result of the anonymous donation procedure for which she had contracted. In February 2001, ten days apart, Susan gave birth to Daniel and Denise gave birth to Daniel's genetic sister, Madeline.

In December 2001 the fertility physician informed Robert and Denise that "a mistake had occurred," in that the clinic had "inadvertently" implanted some of Robert and Denise's embryos in Susan's uterus, resulting in Daniel's birth. Robert and Denise promptly sought contact with Daniel. Susan was initially receptive, but after the three adults and two children met, she refused to relinquish custody, and Robert and Denise brought this parentage action.

Over Susan's opposition the trial court determined that Robert had standing to bring a paternity action under section 7630, subdivision (c), and it ordered genetic testing. After receiving the test results, the court declared Robert to be the father of Daniel.

The court next took up the question of Denise's standing, an issue it had deferred. Denise argued that while she was not biologically related to Daniel, she "st[ood] in the shoes of a genetic mother" because the ovum donor had "assigned whatever [parental] rights she had" to Denise. Denise further sought to preserve the question of whether Susan had acted criminally to obtain Robert and Denise's embryos. In order to determine whether any improper conduct had occurred, Denise argued, she needed to complete discovery. Consequently, she asked that the court withhold a determination of standing, or at least dismiss her from the action without prejudice.

The court, however, dismissed Denise with prejudice. The court noted that Susan was the gestational mother and that Denise had no genetic connection with Daniel, and it concluded that "there really is only one mother in this case at this point." Any contractual rights Denise had were to embryos, "but now what we're talking about is a live person, not an embryo." The court then proceeded to hear the issues regarding custody and visitation. Temporary custody was awarded to Susan, with temporary visitation to Robert.

Discussion

1. Susan's Appeal

On appeal, Susan challenges the court's paternity order. Seeking a liberal construction of section 7613, subdivision (b) (section 7613(b)), Susan contends that Robert must be deemed a sperm donor in order to protect "the integrity of [her] single parent family unit." Any other result, she argues, would contravene the Legislature's intent to preserve the "procreative rights of unmarried women," unfairly burden her with a situation she had done her best to prevent, and impair "Daniel's established constitutional right to maintain a stable, permanent placement." Susan does not question the court's resort to section 7630, subdivision (c), as the authority for Robert's paternity action, nor does she contend it was improper to order genetic testing to determine Robert's biological relationship to Daniel. (§ 7551.)

We need not go beyond the language of section 7613(b) to resolve Susan's claim. This provision states: "The donor of semen provided to a licensed physician and surgeon for use in artificial insemination of a woman other than the donor's wife is treated in law as if he were not the natural father of a child thereby conceived." As the trial court recognized, the plain meaning of the statutory language does not permit the application Susan urges. A "donor" is simply a person who gives, presents, or contributes. In order to be a donor under section 7613(b) a man must provide semen to a physician for the purpose of artificially inseminating "a woman other than the donor's wife." It is uncontested that Robert did not provide his semen for the purpose of inseminating anyone other than Denise. On the contrary, the consent form he signed indicated that the unused embryos were to be frozen and stored "for the exclusive use" of him and Denise. Consequently, section 7613(b) is inapplicable in these circumstances.

Because the language of section 7613(b) is clear, we will not engage in statutory construction to determine the intended purpose and scope of this provision. Susan's appeal to the "clear social policy supporting single parenthood" would more appropriately be directed to the Legislature.

Susan does not assert equal protection or any other constitutional ground for her assertion of the right to an intact single-parent family. The only constitutional claims she alludes to are Robert's assertion of a constitutional right to be recognized as Daniel's legal father and her argument that Daniel has a constitutional right to a stable and permanent placement. We need not address Robert's argument because his statutory right to establish paternity under section 7630 is uncontested. And Daniel's "constitutional right to ... a stable, permanent placement" is not at issue in this appeal. Indeed, much of Susan's appellate argument is a misdirected attack on any future effort Robert and Denise might make to obtain custody of Daniel.

2. Denise's Appeal

Denise contends that she should be accorded standing as an "interested person" within the meaning of Family Code section 7650. She seeks an opportunity to show that Susan colluded with the fertility clinic to obtain the embryo and/or that she herself is the "intended" mother of Daniel.

Section 7650 permits "[a]ny interested person [to] bring an action to determine the existence or nonexistence of a mother and child relationship. Insofar as practicable, the provisions of this part [the Uniform Parentage Act] applicable to the father and child relationship apply." On its face, this provision does not restrict the standing of alleged mothers to those who are genetically or gestationally related to the child.

Two appellate courts, however, have refused to recognize a biologically unrelated woman as an "interested person" under section 7650. Addressing a former lesbian partner's attempt to obtain recognition of her parental status for purposes of custody or visitation, the Third District stated: "Here, there is no ... statutory standing. As a person unrelated to [the child], [the partner] is not an 'interested person' and, therefore, may not drag West [the genetic and gestational mother] into the courts, under the Uniform Parentage Act, on the issue of visitation with West's daughter." (*West v. Superior Court,* (1997) 59 Cal.App.4th 302, 306, 69 Cal.Rptr.2d 160.) This holding was consistent with the court's previous decision in which it had stated that section 7650 (then Civil Code section 7015) "has no application where, as here, it is undisputed [that the gestational and genetic mother] is the natural mother of the child." (*Curiale v. Reagan* (1990) 222 Cal.App.3d 1597, 1600, 272 Cal.Rptr. 520.) In October 2002 the Second District, Division 1, reached the same result. In *Prato-Morrison v. Doe* (2002) 103 Cal.App.4th 222, 126 Cal.Rptr.2d 509 (Prato-Morrison), a husband and wife suspected unauthorized use of their genetic material for another couple, who had used the same clinic and thus became the parents of twins. Responding to the plaintiff wife's assertion of standing, the appellate court quoted the "interested person" language of section 7650 and then added, "but an unrelated person who is not a genetic parent is not an 'interested person' within the meaning of section 7650." (*Id.* at p. 229, 126 Cal.Rptr.2d 509.) Because the wife was unable to offer admissible evidence of a genetic relationship to the twins (who were by then almost 14 years old), she had no standing to pursue a parentage action. (*But see Rubano v. DiCenzo* (2000) 759 A.2d 959, 967 ["any interested party" may be person alleging a "parent-like relationship"].)

Denise disputes the holding of *Prato-Morrison,* arguing that it is inconsistent with *Johnson v. Calvert* (1993) 5 Cal.4th 84, 19 Cal.Rptr.2d 494, 851 P.2d 776 and *Marriage of Buzzanca* (1998) 61 Cal.App.4th 1410, 72 Cal.Rptr.2d 280 (*Buzzanca*), on which she relies. Neither of these cases, however, provides support for Denise's claim. In *Johnson v. Calvert, supra*, the Supreme Court made it clear that "California law recognizes only one natural mother." (5 Cal.4th at p. 92, 19 Cal.Rptr.2d 494, 851 P.2d 776.) A mother-child relationship may be established by proof of having given birth to the child, or by another provision of the Uniform Parentage Act. (§ 7610.) Susan clearly established a mother-child relationship by the undisputed fact that she gave birth to Daniel.

Denise's attempt to show that she was entitled to assert her own parental status as Daniel's intended mother must fail. The concept of "intended mother" is employed only as a tie-breaker when two women have equal claims by "genetic consanguinity" and childbirth.... There is no tie here, however, because Denise has neither a gestational nor a genetic relationship to Daniel, whereas Susan does.

Nor does *Buzzanca* help Denise establish her claim to maternity. There, ... a husband and wife had entered into a surrogacy arrangement that resulted in the birth of a child.... We need only observe that the case before us is completely distinguishable. Susan did not agree to be a surrogate under a contract with Denise; she has instead asserted an independent, competing claim to the child, and she has in fact been declared Daniel's mother....

We decline Denise's implied invitation to extend *Buzzanca* to a situation in which (1) a woman has no genetic or gestational relationship to the child, (2) she has no status comparable to that of a presumed father under section 7611, subdivision (d), and (3) another woman does assert a legally recognized claim. It is undisputed that Denise had no factual basis on which to claim the status of a presumed mother.

We further reject Denise's comparison of Daniel to a plot of land or the timber growing on it. (*Wetherbee v. Green* (1871) 22 Mich. 311, 1871 WL 2990) This is a parentage action, not a replevin proceeding. Denise provides no other basis for either challenging Susan's maternity status or establishing her own.

We must conclude, therefore, that the trial court properly declared Robert to be Daniel's father and Susan to be Daniel's mother under sections 7630 and 7610 respectively. The court's ruling comported with this state's interest "in establishing paternity for all children" (§7570), recognized the valid claims of gestational mothers, and adhered to the Supreme Court's determination that there can be only one natural mother under California law.

In re Paternity of Cheryl

746 N.E.2d 488 (Mass. 2001)

MARSHALL, C.J.

...

The mother gave birth to the child (Cheryl) on August 29, 1993....

...

On December 16, 1993, the mother and the father executed an acknowledgment of parentage in which the father acknowledged that he was the father of Cheryl, that he understood his acknowledgment would have the effect of a judgment against him, and that the acknowledgment would obligate him to support Cheryl. He acknowledged that his execution of the agreement was his free act and deed. The father also executed a support agreement whereby he agreed to pay child support in the amount of $56.50 each week for Cheryl's benefit. The mother, in turn, acknowledged and affirmed that he was the father of Cheryl. That same day, a judge in the Probate and Family Court entered a judgment of paternity. The father, who was not represented by counsel at the time, did not submit to genetic marker testing prior to the entry of the paternity judgment. Nothing in the record explains why.

The mother and the father apparently were never married. In the years following the entry of the paternity judgment, the father behaved as though he were Cheryl's father. He and his family visited and bonded with Cheryl. In 1995 and again in 1996, the father, acting pro se, sought successfully to expand and enforce his visitation rights with his daughter. According to the mother, Cheryl, now seven years old, has always called the father "Daddy" and "is bonded to and loves [him] as her father." Cheryl also has a relationship with the father's parents and siblings, whom she knows as her grandparents, aunt, and uncles. The judge also noted that the father has fostered "a substantial relationship" with Cheryl. From December, 1993, the father has regularly paid child support to the mother on Cheryl's behalf.

In April, 1999, the department filed a complaint seeking to increase the father's child support obligation, and on May 27, 1999, a Probate Court judge ordered the father to pay $90 per week, an increase of $33.50 each week. Five days later, on June 1, 1999, the father filed for the first time a motion requesting an order for genetic marker testing, and an amendment to the 1993 paternity judgment should the test results warrant it. The motion contained a number of unsworn statements, tending to suggest that he believed he was not Cheryl's biological father. More particularly, and of relevance to this appeal, the father's motion suggested that, as early as Cheryl's birth, he may have had reason to suspect that he might not be Cheryl's biological father. By no later than 1995, when Cheryl was two years old, he had information confirming that fact: He said that, in 1995, two friends of the mother informed him on separate occasions that he was not the father of the child, and that subsequently the mother had said "unequivocally," and in circumstances "indicating sincerity," that he was not Cheryl's father. The motion stated that Cheryl does not resemble the father "in features or skin color," because she is "very light skinned," while he, his parents, Cheryl's mother, and her parents are not light skinned. With his 1999 motion, the father submitted a doctor's letter stating that laboratory testing of the father's semen conducted in June, 1996, had revealed that he has a low sperm count, with his physician noting that "[t]his finding may explain your problem with infertility...." The motion also stated that, in 1993, the father had acknowledged his paternity "based on misleading information and without the benefit of a paternity test of any kind."

On July 21, 1999, a judge, "after careful review," denied the father's motion for genetic marker testing. Three days later, the father filed a complaint seeking reduction of the increased child support judgment, which was dismissed.

On November 12, 1999, following these unsuccessful attempts to obtain genetic marker testing and a reduction of child support, the father took Cheryl for genetic testing, without the knowledge of the mother. The test report, contained in the record, concluded that he was not the biological father of Cheryl. Relying on the report, on January 27, 2000, the father moved for a second time to amend or to vacate the paternity judgment. He also requested reimbursement for all of the child support that he had paid since the 1993 judgment of paternity. The department and the mother opposed the motion.

On May 30, 2000, following a nonevidentiary hearing, a judge in the Probate & Family Court filed a memorandum and order in which he ordered the mother, the father, and Cheryl to participate forthwith in blood or genetic marker testing, with a status conference to be scheduled after the results were obtained.... [T]he judge said that if the tests established that the father was not the biological parent of Cheryl, he would be entitled to relief from the prospective application of the 1993 paternity judgment, ... but that he was not entitled to retroactive relief. The judge explained that the father's "interests in no longer being obligated to support a child not his own" outweighed Cheryl's interests "in maintaining a relationship with someone she believed to be her biological father." He said that a contrary conclusion would prolong "an apparent fraud and falsehood."

II

The mother argues that the father's generalized attack on the paternity judgment is actually a claim based on fraud, mistake, or newly discovered evidence and, properly construed, should be seen as a claim under Mass. R. Dom. Rel. P. 60(b)(1)-(3), and not as a claim under Mass. R. Dom. Rel. P. 60(b)(5). As such, she argues, the claim is time-barred because the father did not make his motion within one year of the entry of the paternity judgment as required by the rule. She also maintains that, even if relief under rule 60(b)(5) is available, the father's motions were not timely filed because he did not seek relief "within a reasonable time," as required by rule 60(b), or within one year of the execution of the paternity agreement as now required by G.L. c. 209C, § 11.

The father ... argues that, because he now knows with "scientific certainty" that he is not Cheryl's biological father, the prospective application of the 1993 paternity judgment is no longer equitable. His motion is timely, he says, because he did not discover the mother's "deceit" until he received the results of the genetic marker tests in late 1999.

A

. . .

There is a compelling public interest in the finality of paternity judgments. Where a father challenges a paternity judgment, courts have pointed to the special needs of children that must be protected, noting that consideration of what is in a child's best interests will often weigh more heavily than the genetic link between parent and child. See, e.g., Ex parte *State ex rel. J.Z.*, 668 So.2d 566, 569 (Ala.1995) ("policy in favor of finality [of paternity judgments] means that a prior adjudication should not be subject to relitigation in the absence of truly compelling circumstances"); *Richard B. v. Sandra B.B.*, 625 N.Y.S.2d 127 (1995), quoting *Ettore I. v. Angela D.*, 513 N.Y.S.2d 733 (1987) ("unequivocal trend" has been to "zealously safeguard the welfare, stability, and best interests of the child by rejecting untimely challenges affecting his or her legitimacy"); *Godin v. Godin*, 725 A.2d 904 ([Vt.] 1998), and cases cited (noting that many courts have rejected attempts to reopen paternity judgments based on postjudgment blood tests "absent clear and convincing evidence that it serves the best interests of the child"). Like those courts, we have recognized that stability and continuity of support, both emotional and financial, are essential to a child's welfare.

Where a father and child have a substantial parent-child relationship, as the father and Cheryl apparently have, and the father has provided the child with consistent emotional and financial support, an attempt to undo a determination of paternity "is potentially devastating to a child who ha[s] considered the man to be the father." It was in part for these reasons that we concluded that a man who has comported himself as a child's father "may be obliged to continue to support the child when he, for the first time, renounces his apparent paternity in an attempt to avoid court-imposed support obligations."

We assess the reasonableness of the five and one-half year interval between the entry of the paternity judgment in 1993, and the father's first motion for relief filed in 1999, in light of this jurisprudence. In 1993, the father had an opportunity to, but did not seek, genetic testing, and it avails him little to attempt to obviate that fact. He never claimed, and the record, such as it is, does not establish that his decision to acknowledge paternity voluntarily at that time was conditioned solely on his understanding that he was Cheryl's biological father. A man may acknowledge paternity for a variety of reasons, and we cannot assume that biology is the sole impetus in every case.

Moreover, the father failed to challenge the paternity judgment at the earliest reasonable opportunity, in the face of what he acknowledges was mounting evidence that he might not be Cheryl's biological father. He took no action in 1995 after he was informed, he says, by friends of the mother that he was not Cheryl's biological father. He took no action after the mother "unequivocally" confirmed, he says, that he was not Cheryl's biological father. He took no action after he observed that Cheryl did not share his, his parents', the mother's, or the mothers' parents' physical attributes. He took no action in 1996 when he discovered that his low sperm count could explain his and his wife's fertility problems. During all those years, Cheryl knew and relied on him as her father, and he enjoyed her love and companionship.

It is illuminating that the judge in the Probate and Family Court reached the same decision as do we when first asked to rule on the father's challenge. In 1999, the judge initially denied the father's request for genetic testing, even though the father's motion made clear his belief that he was not Cheryl's biological father. The judge granted the father relief only when confronted with the results of genetic testing the father had obtained privately. He did so relying on Department of Revenue v. W.Z., *supra* at 721, 592 N.E.2d 1297, where we said we "assume[d]" that a father could obtain prospective relief from a paternity judgment pursuant to rule 60(b)(5).

We differ with the judge because we conclude that, as a consequence of the father's long delay before he challenged the paternity judgment, Cheryl's interests now outweigh any interest of his. Our conclusion is consistent with our prior jurisprudence, and the decisions of numerous other courts, that a father's challenge to a paternity judgment may be untimely even though he may establish conclusively that he is not a child's genetic parent....

B

We next consider the father's motion for relief under Mass. R. Dom. Rel. P. 60(b)(6), the catchall provision of that rule. The judge acted well within his discretion in denying the father relief pursuant to that subsection. A motion under subsection (6) must, like subsection (5), be brought within a reasonable time: for all the reasons just discussed, the father's motion was not....

C

The father argues that his claim is not subject to any time limit under rule 60(b) because it also provides that "[t]his rule does not limit the power of a court ... to set aside a judgment for fraud upon the court." The mother committed "fraud on the court," he says, by failing to disclose that he was not the father of Cheryl. We disagree. Even if the mother knew in December, 1993, that the father was not Cheryl's biological father (a proposition not established by this record), her failure to disclose that information to the court would not amount to "fraud on the court."

D

We harbor no illusion that our decision will protect Cheryl from the consequences of her father's decision to seek genetic testing and to challenge his paternity. We cannot protect Cheryl from learning about her genetic parentage: If Cheryl does not yet know of her father's challenge, he (or others) may disclose it to her. No judgment can force him to continue to nurture his relationship with Cheryl, or to protect her from whatever assumptions she may have about her father. But we can protect her financial security and other legal rights. It appears that the father first challenged his paternity because of the increase of child support ordered in 1999. Relieving him of child support obligations might itself unravel the parental ties, as the payment of child support "is a strand tightly interwoven with other forms of connection between father and child," and often forms a critical bond between them. *Bowen v. Gilliard,* 483 U.S. 587, (1987) (Brennan, J., dissenting). We can ensure that Cheryl, who may be deprived of her father's affection and long-held assumptions about her paternity, is not also deprived of the legal rights and financial benefits of a parental relationship.

The law places on men the burden to consider carefully the permanent consequences that flow from an acknowledgment of paternity. The judge in this case properly noted that the father has significant interests at stake in the outcome of this litigation, financial and otherwise. We also recognize the anomaly of enforcing the parental obligations of a man who was identified as a parent only (it seems) because the State insisted that the mother name Cheryl's biological father, where he has now established that he is not that man. The State intervened when the mother, in her efforts to obtain public assistance for her child, was required to name her child's biological father. So far as we can discern from this sparse record, there was not, and has not been since, any ongoing intimate relationship between the mother and the father. A different result might be mandated if a man named by a mother in these circumstances had no opportunity to undergo genetic testing before he acknowledged paternity. A different result might be mandated if a man named by a mother in these circumstances promptly challenged the paternity judgment on obtaining information that he might not be the child's biological father. In this case, even if the father's acknowledgment of paternity were triggered by State intervention (withholding public assistance unless the mother named the father of her child) or misleading information from the mother (assuming she did not name the father in good faith), he had the opportunity to undergo genetic testing, and he waited too long to challenge his paternity.

3. Gestation and Surrogacy: The Legal Standing of the "Birth" Mother

R.R. v. M.H.

689 N.E.2d 790 (Mass. 1998)

Wilkins, Chief Justice:

...

The baby girl who is the subject of this action was born on August 15, 1997, in Leominster. The defendant mother and the plaintiff father are her biological parents. The father and his wife, who live in Rhode Island, were married in June, 1989. The wife is infertile. Sometime in 1994, she and the father learned of an egg donor program but did not pursue it because the procedure was not covered by insurance and had a relatively low success rate. Because of their ages (they were both in their forties), they concluded that pursuing adoption was not feasible. In April, 1996, responding to a newspaper advertisement for surrogacy services, they consulted a Rhode Island attorney who had drafted surrogacy contracts for both surrogates and couples seeking surrogacy services. On the attorney's advice, the father and his wife consulted the New England Surrogate Parenting Advisors (NESPA), a for-profit corporation that helps infertile couples find women willing to act as surrogate mothers. They entered into a contract with NESPA in September, 1996, and paid a fee of $6,000.

Meanwhile, in the spring of 1996, the mother, who was married and had two children, responded to a NESPA advertisement. She reported to NESPA that her family was complete and that she desired to allow others less fortunate than herself to have children. The mother submitted a surrogacy application to NESPA. The judge found that the mother was motivated to apply to NESPA by a desire to be pregnant, in order to earn money, and to help an infertile couple.

In October, Dr. Angela Figueroa of NESPA brought the mother together with the father and his wife. They had a seemingly informative exchange of information and views. The mother was advised to seek an attorney's advice concerning the surrogacy agreement. Shortly thereafter, the mother, the father, and his wife met again to discuss the surrogacy and other matters. The mother also met with a clinical psychologist as part of NESPA's evaluation of her suitability to act as a surrogate. The psychologist, who also evaluated the father and his wife, advised the mother to consult legal counsel, to give her husband a chance to air his concerns, to discuss arrangements for contact with the child, to consider and discuss her expectations concerning termination of the pregnancy, and to arrange a meeting between her husband and the father and his wife. The psychologist concluded that the mother was solid, thoughtful, and well grounded, that she would have no problem giving the child to the father, and that she was happy to act as a surrogate. The mother told the psychologist that she was not motivated by money, although she did plan to use the funds received for her children's education. The mother's husband told the psychologist by telephone that he supported his wife's decision.

The mother signed the surrogate parenting agreement and her signature was notarized on November 1. The father signed on November 18. The agreement stated that the parties intended that the "Surrogate shall be inseminated with the semen of Natural Father" and "that, on the birth of the child or children so conceived, Natural Father, as the Natural Father, will have the full legal parental rights of a father, and surrogate will permit Natural Father to take the child or children home from the hospital to live with he [sic] and his wife." The agreement acknowledged that the mother's parental rights would not terminate if she permitted the father to take the child home and have custody, that the mother could at any time seek to enforce her parental rights by court order, but that, if she attempted to obtain custody or visitation rights, she would forfeit her rights under the agreement and would be obligated to reimburse the father for all fees and expenses paid to her under it. The agreement provided that its interpretation would be governed by Rhode Island law.

The agreement provided for compensation to the mother in the amount of $10,000 "for services rendered in conceiving, carrying and giving birth to the Child." Payment of the $10,000 was to be made as follows: $500 on verification of the pregnancy; $2,500 at the end of the third month; $3,500 at the end of the sixth month; and $3,500 at the time of birth "and when delivery of child occurs." The agreement stated that no payment was made in connection with adoption of the child, the termination of parental rights, or consent to surrender the child for adoption. The father acknowledged the mother's right to determine whether to carry the pregnancy to term, but the mother agreed to refund all payments if, without the father's consent, she had an abortion that was not necessary for her physical health. The father assumed various expenses of the pregnancy, including tests, and had the right to name the child. The mother would be obliged, however, to repay all expenses and fees for services if tests showed that the father was not the biological father of the child, or if the mother refused to permit the father to take the child home from the hospital. The agreement also provided that the mother would maintain some contact with the child after the birth.

The judge found that the mother entered into the agreement on her own volition after consulting legal counsel. There was no evidence of undue influence, coercion, or duress. The mother fully understood that she was contracting to give custody of the baby to the father. She sought to inseminate herself on November 30 and December 1, 1996. The attempt at conception was successful.

The lawyer for the father sent the mother a check for $500 in December, 1996, and another for $2,500 in February. In May, the father's lawyer sent the mother a check for $3,500. She told the lawyer that she had changed her mind and wanted to keep the child. She returned the check uncashed in the middle of June. The mother has made no attempt to refund the amounts that the father paid her, including $550 that he paid for pregnancy-related expenses.

Procedure

Approximately two weeks after the mother changed her mind and returned the check for $3,500, and before the child was born, the father commenced this action against the mother seeking to establish his paternity, alleging breach of contract, and requesting a declaration of his rights under the surrogacy agreement. Subsequently, the wife's husband was added as a defendant. The judge appointed a guardian ad litem to represent the interests of the unborn child. Proceedings were held on aspects of the preliminary injunction request (now resolved) and on the mother's motion to determine whether surrogacy contracts are enforceable in Massachusetts.

On August 4, 1997, the judge entered an order directing the mother to give the child to the father when it was discharged from the hospital and granting the father temporary physical custody of the child. She did so based on her determination that the father's custody claim was likely to prevail on the merits of the contract claim, and, if not on that claim, then on the basis of the best interests of the child. The mother was granted the right to frequent visits.

...

Other Jurisdictions

A significant minority of States have legislation addressing surrogacy agreements. Some simply deny enforcement of all such agreements. *See* Ariz. Rev. Stat. Ann. § 25-218(A) (West 1991); D.C. Code Ann. § 16-402(a) (1997); Ind. Code Ann. §§ 31-20-1-1, 31-20-1-2 (Michie 1997); Mich. Comp. Laws Ann. § 722.855 (West 1993); N.Y. Dom. Rel. Law § 122 (McKinney Supp.1997); N.D. Cent. Code § 14-18-05 (1991); Utah Code Ann. § 76-7-204 (1995). Others expressly deny enforcement only if the surrogate is to be compensated. *See* Ky. Rev. Stat. Ann. § 199.590(4) (Michie 1995); La. Rev. Stat. Ann. § 9:2713 (West 1991); Neb. Rev. Stat. § 25-21, 200 (1995); Wash. Rev. Code §§ 26.26.230, 26.26.240 (1996). Some States have simply exempted surrogacy agreements from provisions making it a crime to sell babies. *See* Ala. Code § 26-10A-34 (1992); Iowa Code § 710.11 (1997); W. Va. Code § 48-4-16(e)(3) (1996). A few States have explicitly made unpaid surrogacy agreements lawful. *See* Fla. Stat. ch. 742.15 (1995); Nev. Rev. Stat. § 126.045 (1995); N.H. Rev. Stat. Ann. § 168-B:16 (1994 & Supp.1996); Va. Code Ann. §§ 20-159, 20-160(B)(4) (Michie 1995). Florida, New Hampshire, and Virginia require that the intended mother be infertile. *See* Fla. Stat. ch. 742.15(2)(a); N.H. Rev. Stat. Ann. § 168-B:17(II) (1994); Va. Code Ann. § 20-160(B)(8). New Hampshire and Virginia place restrictions on who may act as a surrogate and require advance judicial approval of the agreement. *See* N.H. Rev. Stat. Ann. §§ 168-B:16(I)(b), 168-B:17; Va. Code Ann. §§ 20-159(B), 20-160(B)(6). Last, Arkansas raises a presumption that a child born to a surrogate mother is the child of the intended parents and not the surrogate. Ark. Code Ann. § 9-10-201(b), (c) (Michie 1993).

There are few appellate court opinions on the enforceability of traditional surrogacy agreements. The Kentucky Legislature, ... has provided that a compensated surrogacy agreement is unenforceable (Ky. Rev. Stat. Ann. § 199.590[4]), thus changing the rule that the Supreme Court of Kentucky announced in *Surrogate Parenting Assocs., Inc. v. Commonwealth ex rel. Armstrong,* 704 S.W.2d 209 (Ky.1986). In *In re Marriage of Moschetta,* 25 Cal. App. 4th 1218, 30 Cal. Rptr. 2d 893 (1994), the court declined to enforce a traditional surrogacy agreement because it was incompatible with California parentage and adoption statutes. *Id.* at 1222, 30 Cal. Rptr. 2d 893. The surrogate, who was to be paid $10,000, had agreed that (a) the father could obtain sole custody of any resulting child, (b) she would agree to terminate her parental rights, and (c) she would aid the father's wife in adopting the child. *Id.* at 1223, 30 Cal. Rptr. 2d 893. The court sent the case back to the trial court for a determination whether the father should be awarded primary physical custody. *Id.* at 1234, 30 Cal. Rptr. 2d 893.

The best known opinion is that of the Supreme Court of New Jersey *in Matter of Baby M.*, 537 A.2d 1227 ([N.J.] 1988), where the court invalidated a compensated surrogacy contract because it conflicted with the law and public policy of the State. The Baby M surrogacy agreement involved broader concessions from the mother than the agreement before us because it provided that the mother would surrender her parental rights and would allow the father's wife to adopt the child. The agreement, therefore, directly conflicted with a statute prohibiting the payment of money to obtain an adoption and a statute barring enforcement of an agreement to adoption made prior to the birth of the child. The court acknowledged that an award of custody to the father was in the best interests of the child, but struck down orders terminating the mother's parental rights and authorizing the adoption of the child by the husband's wife. The court added that it found no "legal prohibition against surrogacy when the surrogate mother volunteers, without any payment, to act as a surrogate and is given the right to change her mind and to assert her parental rights."

Discussion

1. The governing law. The agreement before us provided that "Rhode Island Law shall govern the interpretation of this agreement." No party has argued that Rhode Island law has any application to the issues before us. We are, in any event, not concerned with "the interpretation of this agreement," but rather with the legal significance, if any, of its provisions. The child was conceived and born in Massachusetts, and the mother is a Massachusetts resident, all as contemplated in the surrogacy arrangement. The significance, if any, of the surrogacy agreement on the relationship of the parties and on the child is appropriately determined by Massachusetts law.

2. General Laws c. 46, §4B. The case before us concerns traditional surrogacy, in which the fertile member of an infertile couple is one of the child's biological parents. Surrogate fatherhood, the insemination of the fertile wife with sperm of a donor, often an anonymous donor, is a recognized and accepted procedure. If the mother's husband consents to the procedure, the resulting child is considered the legitimate child of the mother and her husband. Section 4B does not comment on the rights and obligations, if any, of the biological father, although inferentially he has none. In the case before us, the infertile spouse is the wife. No statute decrees the consequences of the artificial insemination of a surrogate with the sperm of a fertile husband. This situation presents different considerations from surrogate fatherhood because surrogate motherhood is never anonymous and her commitment and contribution is unavoidably much greater than that of a sperm donor.

We must face the possible application of G.L. c. 46, §4B, to this case. Section 4B tells us that a husband who consents to the artificial insemination of his wife with the sperm of another is considered to be the father of any resulting child. In the case before us, the birth mother was married at the time of her artificial insemination. Despite what he told the psychologist, her husband was not supportive of her desire to become a surrogate parent but acknowledged that it was her decision and her body. The husband, who filed a complaint for divorce on August 8, 1997, may have simply been indifferent because he knew that the marriage was falling apart. The judge found that he was not the biological father of the child. His interest might have been vastly greater if he had been informed that §4B literally says that any child produced by the artificial insemination of his wife with his consent would be his legitimate child whom he would have a duty to support. It is doubtful, however, that the Legislature intended §4B to apply to the child of a married surrogate mother. Section 4B seems to concern the status of a child born to a fertile mother whose husband, presumably infertile, consented to her artificial insemination with the sperm of another man so that the couple could have a child biologically related to the mother.

3. Adoption statutes. Policies underlying our adoption legislation suggest that a surrogate parenting agreement should be given no effect if the mother's agreement was obtained prior to a reasonable time after the child's birth or if her agreement was induced by the payment of money. Adoption legislation is, of course, not applicable to child custody, but it does provide us with some guidance. Although the agreement makes no reference to adoption and does not concern the termination of parental rights or the adoption of the child by the father's wife, the normal expectation in the case of a surrogacy agreement seems to be that the father's wife will adopt the child with the consent of the mother (and the father). Under G.L. c. 210, § 2, adoption requires the written consent of the father and the mother but, in these circumstances, not the mother's husband. Any such consent, written, witnessed, and notarized, is not to be executed "sooner than the fourth calendar day after the date of birth of the child to be adopted." *Id.* That statutory standard should be interpreted as providing that no mother may effectively agree to surrender her child for adoption earlier than the fourth day after its birth, by which time she better knows the strength of her bond with her child. Although a consent to surrender custody has less permanency than a consent to adoption, the legislative judgment that a mother should have time after a child's birth to reflect on her wishes concerning the child weighs heavily in our consideration whether to give effect to a prenatal custody agreement. No private agreement concerning adoption or custody can be conclusive in any event because a judge, passing on custody of a child, must decide what is in the best interests of the child.

Adoptive parents may pay expenses of a birth parent but may make no direct payment to her. *See* G.L. c. 210, § 11A; 102 Code Mass. Regs. § 5.09 (1997). Even though the agreement seeks to attribute that payment of $10,000, not to custody or adoption, but solely to the mother's services in carrying the child, the father ostensibly was promised more than those services because, as a practical matter, the mother agreed to surrender custody of the child. She could assert custody rights, according to the agreement, only if she repaid the father all amounts that she had received and also reimbursed him for all expenses he had incurred. The statutory prohibition of payment for receiving a child through adoption suggests that, as a matter of policy, a mother's agreement to surrender custody in exchange for money (beyond pregnancy-related expenses) should be given no effect in deciding the custody of the child.

4. Conclusion. The mother's purported consent to custody in the agreement is ineffective because no such consent should be recognized unless given on or after the fourth day following the child's birth. In reaching this conclusion, we apply to consent to custody the same principle which underlies the statutory restriction on when a mother's consent to adoption may be effectively given. Moreover, the payment of money to influence the mother's custody decision makes the agreement as to custody void. Eliminating any financial reward to a surrogate mother is the only way to assure that no economic pressure will cause a woman, who may well be a member of an economically vulnerable class, to act as a surrogate. It is true that a surrogate enters into the agreement before she becomes pregnant and thus is not presented with the desperation that a poor unwed pregnant woman may confront. However, compensated surrogacy arrangements raise the concern that, under financial pressure, a woman will permit her body to be used and her child to be given away.

There is no doubt that compensation was a factor in inducing the mother to enter into the surrogacy agreement and to cede custody to the father. If the payment of $10,000 was really only compensation for the mother's services in carrying the child and giving birth and was unrelated to custody of the child, the agreement would not have provided that the mother must refund all compensation paid (and expenses paid) if she should challenge the father's right to custody. Nor would the agreement have provided that final payment be made only when the child is delivered to the father. We simply decline, on public policy grounds, to apply to a surrogacy agreement of the type involved here the general principle that an agreement between informed, mature adults should be enforced absent proof of duress, fraud, or undue influence.

We recognize that there is nothing inherently unlawful in an arrangement by which an informed woman agrees to attempt to conceive artificially and give birth to a child whose father would be the husband of an infertile wife. We suspect that many such arrangements are made and carried out without disagreement.

If no compensation is paid beyond pregnancy-related expenses and if the mother is not bound by her consent to the father's custody of the child unless she consents after a suitable period has passed following the child's birth, the objections we have identified in this opinion to the enforceability of a surrogate's consent to custody would be overcome. Other conditions might be important in deciding the enforceability of a surrogacy agreement, such as a requirement that (a) the mother's husband give his informed consent to the agreement in advance; (b) the mother be an adult and have had at least one successful pregnancy; (c) the mother, her husband, and the intended parents have been evaluated for the soundness of their judgment and for their capacity to carry out the agreement; (d) the father's wife be incapable of bearing a child without endangering her health; (e) the intended parents be suitable persons to assume custody of the child; and (f) all parties have the advice of counsel. The mother and father may not, however, make a binding best-interests-of-the-child determination by private agreement. Any custody agreement is subject to a judicial determination of custody based on the best interests of the child.

The conditions that we describe are not likely to be satisfactory to an intended father because, following the birth of the child, the mother can refuse to consent to the father's custody even though the father has incurred substantial pregnancy-related expenses. A surrogacy agreement judicially approved before conception may be a better procedure, as is permitted by statutes in Virginia and New Hampshire. A Massachusetts statute concerning surrogacy agreements, pro or con, would provide guidance to judges, lawyers, infertile couples interested in surrogate parenthood, and prospective surrogate mothers.

We do not reach but comment briefly on the mother's argument that the agreement was unconscionable. She actively sought to become a surrogate and entered into the surrogacy agreement voluntarily, advised by counsel, not under duress, and fully informed. Unconscionability is not apparent on this record.

A declaration shall be entered that the surrogacy agreement is not enforceable. Such further orders as may be appropriate, consistent with this opinion, may be entered in the Probate and Family Court.

Johnson v. Calvert

851 P.2d 776 (Cal. 1993)

PANELLI, JUSTICE.

... Mark and Crispina Calvert are a married couple who desired to have a child. Crispina was forced to undergo a hysterectomy in 1984. Her ovaries remained capable of producing eggs, however, and the couple eventually considered surrogacy. In 1989,

Anna Johnson heard about Crispina's plight from a coworker and offered to serve as a surrogate for the Calverts.

On January 15, 1990, Mark, Crispina, and Anna signed a contract providing that an embryo created by the sperm of Mark and the egg of Crispina would be implanted in Anna and the child born would be taken into Mark and Crispina's home "as their child." Anna agreed she would relinquish "all parental rights" to the child in favor of Mark and Crispina. In return, Mark and Crispina would pay Anna $10,000 in a series of installments, the last to be paid six weeks after the child's birth. Mark and Crispina were also to pay for a $200,000 life insurance policy on Anna's life.

The zygote was implanted on January 19, 1990. Less than a month later, an ultrasound test confirmed Anna was pregnant.

Unfortunately, relations deteriorated between the two sides. Mark learned that Anna had not disclosed she had suffered several stillbirths and miscarriages. Anna felt Mark and Crispina did not do enough to obtain the required insurance policy. She also felt abandoned during an onset of premature labor in June.

In July 1990, Anna sent Mark and Crispina a letter demanding the balance of the payments due her or else she would refuse to give up the child. The following month, Mark and Crispina responded with a lawsuit, seeking a declaration they were the legal parents of the unborn child. Anna filed her own action to be declared the mother of the child, and the two cases were eventually consolidated. The parties agreed to an independent guardian ad litem for the purposes of the suit.

The child was born on September 19, 1990, and blood samples were obtained from both Anna and the child for analysis. The blood test results excluded Anna as the genetic mother. The parties agreed to a court order providing that the child would remain with Mark and Crispina on a temporary basis with visits by Anna.

At trial in October 1990, the parties stipulated that Mark and Crispina were the child's genetic parents. After hearing evidence and arguments, the trial court ruled that Mark and Crispina were the child's "genetic, biological and natural" father and mother, that Anna had no "parental" rights to the child, and that the surrogacy contract was legal and enforceable against Anna's claims. The court also terminated the order allowing visitation. Anna appealed from the trial court's judgment. The Court of Appeal for the Fourth District, Division Three, affirmed. We granted review.

Discussion

...

Anna, of course, predicates her claim of maternity on the fact that she gave birth to the child. The Calverts contend that Crispina's genetic relationship to the child establishes that she is his mother. Counsel for the minor joins in that contention and argues, in addition, that several of the presumptions created by the Act dictate the same result. As will appear, we conclude that presentation of blood test evidence is one means of establishing maternity, as is proof of having given birth, but that the presumptions cited by minor's counsel do not apply to this case.

We turn to those few provisions of the [Uniform Parentage] Act directly addressing the determination of maternity. "Any interested party," presumably including a genetic mother, "may bring an action to determine the existence ... of a mother and child relationship." (Civ. Code, § 7015.) Civil Code section 7003 provides, in relevant part, that between a child and the natural mother a parent and child relationship "may be established by proof of her having given birth to the child, or under [the Act]." (Civ. Code, §7003, subd. (1),emphasis added.) Apart from Civil Code section 7003, the Act sets forth no specific means by which a natural mother can establish a parent and child relationship. However, it declares that, insofar as practicable, provisions applicable to the father and child relationship apply in an action to determine the existence or nonexistence of a mother and child relationship. (Civ. Code, §7015.) Thus, it is appropriate to examine those provisions as well.

A man can establish a father and child relationship by the means set forth in Civil Code section 7004. (Civ. Code, §§7006, 7004.) Paternity is presumed under that section if the man meets the conditions set forth in section 621 of the Evidence Code. (Civ. Code, §7004, subd. (a).) The latter statute applies, by its terms, when determining the questioned paternity of a child born to a married woman, and contemplates reliance on evidence derived from blood testing. (Evid. Code, §621, subds. (a), (b); *see* Evid. Code, §§890–897 [Uniform Act on Blood Tests to Determine Paternity].) Alternatively, Civil Code section 7004 creates a presumption of paternity based on the man's conduct toward the child (e.g., receiving the child into his home and openly holding the child out as his natural child) or his marriage or attempted marriage to the child's natural mother under specified conditions.

In our view, the presumptions contained in Civil Code section 7004 do not apply here. They describe situations in which substantial evidence points to a particular man as the natural father of the child. (9B West's U.Laws Ann. (1987) Unif. Parentage Act, com. foll. §4, p. 299.) In this case, there is no question as to who is claiming the mother and child relationship, and the factual basis of each woman's claim is obvious. Thus, there is no need to resort to an evidentiary presumption to ascertain the identity of the natural mother. Instead, we must make the purely legal determination as between the two claimants.

...

Disregarding the presumptions of paternity that have no application to this case, then, we are left with the undisputed evidence that Anna, not Crispina, gave birth to the child and that Crispina, not Anna, is genetically related to him. Both women thus have adduced evidence of a mother and child relationship as contemplated by the Act. (Civ. Code, §§7003, subd. (1), 7004, subd. (a), 7015; Evid.Code, §§621, 892.) Yet for any child California law recognizes only one natural mother, despite advances in reproductive technology rendering a different outcome biologically possible....

Because two women each have presented acceptable proof of maternity, we do not believe this case can be decided without enquiring into the parties' intentions as manifested in the surrogacy agreement. Mark and Crispina are a couple who desired to have a child of their own genetic stock but are physically unable to do so without the help of reproductive technology. They affirmatively intended the birth of the child, and took the steps necessary to effect *in vitro* fertilization. But for their acted-on intention, the child would not exist. Anna agreed to facilitate the procreation of Mark's and Crispina's child. The parties' aim was to bring Mark's and Crispina's child into the world, not for Mark and Crispina to donate a zygote to Anna. Crispina from the outset intended to be the child's mother. Although the gestative function Anna performed was necessary to bring about the child's birth, it is safe to say that Anna would not have been given the opportunity to gestate or deliver the child had she, prior to implantation of the zygote, manifested her own intent to be the child's mother. No reason appears why Anna's later change of heart should vitiate the determination that Crispina is the child's natural mother.

We conclude that although the Act recognizes both genetic consanguinity and giving birth as means of establishing a mother and child relationship, when the two means do not coincide in one woman, she who intended to procreate the child—that is, she who intended to bring about the birth of a child that she intended to raise as her own—is the natural mother under California law.

...

In deciding the issue of maternity under the Act we have felt free to take into account the parties' intentions, as expressed in the surrogacy contract, because in our view the agreement is not, on its face, inconsistent with public policy.

Preliminarily, Mark and Crispina urge us to interpret the Legislature's 1992 passage of a bill that would have regulated surrogacy as an expression of this state's public policy despite the fact that Governor Wilson's veto prevented the bill from becoming law. Senate Bill No. 937 contained a finding that surrogate contracts are not against sound public and social policy. (Sen. Bill No. 937 (1991–1992 Reg.Sess.).) Had Senate Bill No. 937 become law, there would be no room for argument to the contrary. The veto, however, raises a question whether the legislative declaration truly expresses California's public policy.

In the Governor's veto message we find, not unequivocal agreement with the Legislature's public policy assessment, but rather reservations about the practice of surrogate parenting. Surrogacy is a relatively recent phenomenon. The full moral and psychological dimensions of this practice are not yet clear. In fact, they are just beginning to emerge. Only two published court opinions in California have treated this nettlesome subject.... Comprehensive regulation of this difficult moral issue is premature....

Anna urges that surrogacy contracts violate several social policies. Relying on her contention that she is the child's legal, natural mother, she cites the public policy embodied in Penal Code section 273, prohibiting the payment for consent to adoption of a child. She argues further that the policies underlying the adoption laws of this state are violated by the surrogacy contract because it in effect constitutes a prebirth waiver of her parental rights.

We disagree. Gestational surrogacy differs in crucial respects from adoption and so is not subject to the adoption statutes. The parties voluntarily agreed to participate in *in vitro* fertilization and related medical procedures before the child was conceived; at the time when Anna entered into the contract, therefore, she was not vulnerable to financial inducements to part with her own expected offspring. As discussed above, Anna was not the genetic mother of the child. The payments to Anna under the contract were meant to compensate her for her services in gestating the fetus and undergoing labor, rather than for giving up "parental" rights to the child. Payments were due both during the pregnancy and after the child's birth. We are, accordingly, unpersuaded that the contract used in this case violates the public policies embodied in Penal Code section 273 and the adoption statutes. For the same reasons, we conclude these contracts do not implicate the policies underlying the statutes governing termination of parental rights. (*See* Welf. & Inst. Code, § 202.)

It has been suggested that gestational surrogacy may run afoul of prohibitions on involuntary servitude. (*See* U.S. Const., Amend. XIII; Cal. Const., art. I, § 6; Pen.Code, § 181.) Involuntary servitude has been recognized in cases of criminal punishment for refusal to work. We see no potential for that evil in the contract at issue here, and extrinsic evidence of coercion or duress is utterly lacking. We note that although at one point the contract purports to give Mark and Crispina the sole right to determine whether to abort the pregnancy, at another point it acknowledges: "All parties understand that a pregnant woman has the absolute right to abort or not abort any fetus she is carrying. Any promise to the contrary is unenforceable." We therefore need not determine the validity of a surrogacy contract purporting to deprive the gestator of her freedom to terminate the pregnancy.

Finally, Anna and some commentators have expressed concern that surrogacy contracts tend to exploit or dehumanize women, especially women of lower economic status. Anna's objections center around the psychological harm she asserts may result from the gestator's relinquishing the child to whom she has given birth. Some have also cautioned that the practice of surrogacy may encourage society to view children as commodities, subject to trade at their parents' will.

We are all too aware that the proper forum for resolution of this issue is the Legislature, where empirical data, largely lacking from this record, can be studied and rules of general applicability developed. However, in light of our responsibility to decide this case, we have considered as best we can its possible consequences.

We are unpersuaded that gestational surrogacy arrangements are so likely to cause the untoward results Anna cites as to demand their invalidation on public policy grounds. Although common sense suggests that women of lesser means serve as surrogate mothers more often than do wealthy women, there has been no proof that surrogacy contracts exploit poor women to any greater degree than economic necessity in general exploits them by inducing them to accept lower-paid or otherwise undesirable employment. We are likewise unpersuaded by the claim that surrogacy will foster the attitude that children are mere commodities; no evidence is offered to support it. The limited data available seem to reflect an absence of significant adverse effects of surrogacy on all participants.

The argument that a woman cannot knowingly and intelligently agree to gestate and deliver a baby for intending parents carries overtones of the reasoning that for centuries prevented women from attaining equal economic rights and professional status under the law. To resurrect this view is both to foreclose a personal and economic choice on the part of the surrogate mother, and to deny intending parents what may be their only means of procreating a child of their own genetic stock. Certainly in the present case it cannot seriously be argued that Anna, a licensed vocational nurse who had done well in school and who had previously borne a child, lacked the intellectual wherewithal or life experience necessary to make an informed decision to enter into the surrogacy contract.

Constitutionality of the Determination That Anna Johnson Is Not the Natural Mother

Anna argues at length that her right to the continued companionship of the child is protected under the federal Constitution.

First, we note the constitutional rights that are not implicated here.

There is no issue of procedural due process: although Anna broadly contends that the procedures prescribed for adoptions should be followed in the situation of a gestational surrogate's relinquishment to the genetic parents of the child she has carried and delivered, she cites no specific deficiency in the notice or hearing this matter received.

Furthermore, neither Anna nor amicus curiae ACLU articulates a claim under the equal protection clause, and we are unable to discern in these facts the necessary predicate to its operation. This is because a woman who voluntarily agrees to gestate and deliver for a married couple a child who is their genetic offspring is situated differently from the wife who provides the ovum for fertilization, intending to mother the resulting child.

Anna relies mainly on theories of substantive due process, privacy, and procreative freedom, citing a number of decisions recognizing the fundamental liberty interest of natural parents in the custody and care of their children. Most of the cases Anna cites deal with the rights of unwed fathers in the face of attempts to terminate their parental relationship to their children. These cases do not support recognition of parental rights for a gestational surrogate. Although Anna quotes language stressing the primacy of a developed parent-child relationship in assessing unwed fathers' rights..., certain language in the cases reinforces the importance of genetic parents' rights.

Anna's argument depends on a prior determination that she is indeed the child's mother. Since Crispina is the child's mother under California law because she, not Anna, provided the ovum for the *in vitro* fertilization procedure, intending to raise the child as her own, it follows that any constitutional interests Anna possesses in this situation are something less than those of a mother. As counsel for the minor points out, the issue in this case is not whether Anna's asserted rights as a natural mother were unconstitutionally violated, but rather whether the determination that she is not the legal natural mother at all is constitutional.

Anna relies principally on the decision of the United States Supreme Court in *Michael H. v. Gerald D.*, (1989) 491 U.S. 110, to support her claim to a constitutionally protected liberty interest in the companionship of the child, based on her status as "birth mother." In that case, a plurality of the court held that a state may constitutionally deny a man parental rights with respect to a child he fathered during a liaison with the wife of another man, since it is the marital family that traditionally has been accorded a protected liberty interest, as reflected in the historic presumption of legitimacy of a child born into such a family. (491 U.S. at pp. 124–125, (plur. opn. by Scalia, J.).) The reasoning of the plurality in Michael H. does not assist Anna. Society has not traditionally protected the right of a woman who gestates and delivers a baby pursuant to an agreement with a couple who supply the zygote from which the baby develops and who intend to raise the child as their own; such arrangements are of too recent an origin to claim the protection of tradition. To the extent that tradition has a bearing on the present case, we believe it supports the claim of the couple who exercise their right to procreate in order to form a family of their own, albeit through novel medical procedures.

Moreover, if we were to conclude that Anna enjoys some sort of liberty interest in the companionship of the child, then the liberty interests of Mark and Crispina, the child's natural parents, in their procreative choices and their relationship with the child would perforce be infringed. Any parental rights Anna might successfully assert could come only at Crispina's expense. As we have seen, Anna has no parental rights to the child under California law, and she fails to persuade us that sufficiently strong policy reasons exist to accord her a protected liberty interest in the companionship of the child when such an interest would necessarily detract from or impair the parental bond enjoyed by Mark and Crispina.

Amicus curiae ACLU urges that Anna's right of privacy, embodied in the California Constitution (Cal. Const., art. I, § 1), requires recognition and protection of her status as "birth mother." We cannot agree. Certainly it is true that our state Constitution has been construed to provide California citizens with privacy protections encompassing procreative decisionmaking—broader, indeed, than those recognized by the federal

Constitution. However, amicus curiae fails to articulate persuasively how Anna's claim falls within even the broad parameters of the state right of privacy. Amicus curiae appears to assume that the choice to gestate and deliver a baby for its genetic parents pursuant to a surrogacy agreement is the equivalent, in constitutional weight, of the decision whether to bear a child of one's own. We disagree. A woman who enters into a gestational surrogacy arrangement is not exercising her own right to make procreative choices; she is agreeing to provide a necessary and profoundly important service without (by definition) any expectation that she will raise the resulting child as her own.

Drawing an analogy to artificial insemination, Anna argues that Mark and Crispina were mere genetic donors who are entitled to no constitutional protection. That characterization of the facts is, however, inaccurate. Mark and Crispina never intended to "donate" genetic material to anyone. Rather, they intended to procreate a child genetically related to them by the only available means. Civil Code section 7005, governing artificial insemination, has no application here.

Finally, Anna argues that the Act's failure to address novel reproductive techniques such as *in vitro* fertilization indicates legislative disapproval of such practices. Given that the Act was drafted long before such techniques were developed, we cannot agree. Moreover, we may not arrogate to ourselves the power to disapprove them. It is not the role of the judiciary to inhibit the use of reproductive technology when the Legislature has not seen fit to do so; any such effort would raise serious questions in light of the fundamental nature of the rights of procreation and privacy. Rather, our task has been to resolve the dispute before us, interpreting the Act's use of the term "natural mother" (Civ. Code, § 7003, subd. (1)) when the biological functions essential to bringing a child into the world have been allocated between two women.

4. Intention: The Twenty-First Century Construct of Parenthood?

In re Marriage of Buzzanca

72 Cal.Rptr.2d 280 (Cal. Ct. App. 1998)

SILLS, PRESIDING JUSTICE.

...

John filed his petition for dissolution of marriage on March 30, 1995, alleging there were no children of the marriage. Luanne filed her response on April 20, alleging that the parties were expecting a child by way of surrogate contract. Jaycee was born six days later. In September 1996 Luanne filed a separate petition to establish herself as Jaycee's mother. Her action was consolidated into the dissolution case. In February 1997, the court accepted a stipulation that the woman who agreed to carry the child, and her husband, were not the "biological parents" of the child. At a hearing held in March, based entirely on oral argument and offers of proof, the trial court determined that Luanne was not the lawful mother of the child and therefore John could not be the lawful father or owe any support.

The trial judge said: "So I think what evidence there is, is stipulated to. And I don't think there would be any more. One, there's no genetic tie between Luanne and the child. Two, she is not the gestational mother. Three, she has not adopted the child. That, folks, to me, respectfully, is clear and convincing evidence that she's not the legal mother."

After another hearing on May 7, regarding attorney fees, a judgment on reserved issues in the dissolution was filed, terminating John's obligation to pay child support, declaring that Luanne was not the legal mother of Jaycee, and declining "to apply any estoppel proposition to the issue of John's responsibility for child support." Luanne then filed a petition for a writ of supersedeas to stay the judgment; she also filed an appeal from it. This court then granted a stay which had the effect of keeping the support order alive for Jaycee. We also consolidated the writ proceeding with the appeal.

...

Discussion

The Statute Governing Artificial Insemination Which Makes a Husband the Lawful Father of a Child Unrelated to Him Applies to Both Intended Parents In This Case

Perhaps recognizing the inherent lack of appeal for any result which makes Jaycee a legal orphan, John now contends that the surrogate is Jaycee's legal mother; and further, by virtue of that fact, the surrogate's husband is the legal father. His reasoning goes like this: Under the Uniform Parentage Act (the Act), and particularly as set forth in section 7610 of California's Family Code, there are only two ways by which a woman can establish legal motherhood, i.e., giving birth or contributing genetically. Because the genetic contributors are not known to the court, the only candidate left is the surrogate who must therefore be deemed the lawful mother. And, as John's counsel commented at oral argument, if the surrogate and her husband cannot support Jaycee, the burden should fall on the taxpayers.

The statute ... contains no direct reference to genetics (i.e., blood tests) at all. The Johnson decision teaches us that genetics is simply subsumed in the words "under this part." In that case, the court held that genetic consanguinity was equally "acceptable" as "proof of maternity" as evidence of giving birth.

It is important to realize, however, that in construing the words "under this part" to include genetic testing, the high court in Johnson relied on several statutes in the Evidence Code (former Evid. Code, §§ 892, 895, and 895.5) all of which, by their terms, only applied to paternity. It was only by a "parity of reasoning" that our high court concluded those statutes which, on their face applied only to men, were also "dispositive of the question of maternity." (5 Cal. 4th at p. 92)

The point bears reiterating: It was only by a parity of reasoning from statutes which, on their face, referred only to paternity that the court in *Johnson v. Calvert* reached the result it did on the question of maternity. Had the Johnson court reasoned as John now urges us to reason—by narrowly confining the means under the Uniform Parentage Act by which a woman could establish that she was the lawful mother of a child to texts which on their face applied only to motherhood (as distinct from fatherhood)—the court would have reached the opposite result.

In addition to blood tests there are several other ways the Act allows paternity to be established. Those ways are not necessarily related at all to any biological tie. Thus, under the Act, paternity may be established by:

> marrying, remaining married to, or attempting to marry the child's mother when she gives birth (see § 7611, subds. (a) & (b));
>
> marrying the child's mother after the child's birth and either consenting to being named as the father on the birth certificate (§ 7611, subd. (c) (1)) or making a written promise to support the child (*see* § 7611, subd. (c)(2)).

A man may also be deemed a father under the Act in the case of artificial insemination of his wife, as provided by section 7613 of the Family Code. To track the words of the statute: "If, under the supervision of a licensed physician and surgeon and with the consent of her husband, a wife is inseminated artificially with semen donated by a man not her husband, the husband is treated in law as if he were the natural father of a child thereby conceived."

As noted in Johnson, "courts must construe statutes in factual settings not contemplated by the enacting legislature." So it is, of course, true that application of the artificial insemination statute to a gestational surrogacy case where the genetic donors are unknown to the court may not have been contemplated by the legislature. Even so, the two kinds of artificial reproduction are exactly analogous in this crucial respect: Both contemplate the procreation of a child by the consent to a medical procedure of someone who intends to raise the child but who otherwise does not have any biological tie.

If a husband who consents to artificial insemination under section 7613 is "treated in law" as the father of the child by virtue of his consent, there is no reason the result should be any different in the case of a married couple who consent to *in vitro* fertilization by unknown donors and subsequent implantation into a woman who is, as a surrogate, willing to carry the embryo to term for them. The statute is, after all, the clearest expression of past legislative intent when the legislature did contemplate a situation where a person who caused a child to come into being had no biological relationship to the child.

Indeed, the establishment of fatherhood and the consequent duty to support when a husband consents to the artificial insemination of his wife is one of the well-established rules in family law.... [I]n the one case we are aware of where the court did not hold that the husband had a support obligation, the reason was not the absence of a biological relationship as such, but because of actual lack of consent to the insemination procedure. (*See In re Marriage of Witbeck-Wildhagen* (1996) 667 N.E.2d 122, 125–126 [(Ill.)] [it would be "unjust" to impose support obligation on husband who never consented to the artificial insemination].)

It must also be noted that in applying the artificial insemination statute to a case where a party has caused a child to be brought into the world, the statutory policy is really echoing a more fundamental idea—a sort of grundnorm to borrow Hans Kelsen's famous jurisprudential word—already established in the case law. That idea is often summed up in the legal term "estoppel." Estoppel is an ungainly word from the Middle French (from the word meaning "bung" or "stopper") expressing the law's distaste for inconsistent actions and positions—like consenting to an act which brings a child into existence and then turning around and disclaiming any responsibility.

While the *Johnson v. Calvert* court was able to predicate its decision on the Uniform Parentage Act rather than making up the result out of whole cloth, it is also true that California courts, prior to the enactment of the Act, had based certain decisions establishing paternity merely on the common law doctrine of estoppel....

There is no need in the present case to predicate our decision on common law estoppel alone, though the doctrine certainly applies. The estoppel concept, after all, is already inherent in the artificial insemination statute. In essence, Family Code section 7613 is nothing more than the codification of the common law rule ...

John argues that the artificial insemination statute should not be applied because, after all, his wife did not give birth. But for purposes of the statute with its core idea of estoppel, the fact that Luanne did not give birth is irrelevant. The statute contemplates the establishment of lawful fatherhood in a situation where an intended father has no biological relationship to a child who is procreated as a result of the father's (as well as the mother's) consent to a medical procedure.

Luanne is the Lawful Mother of Jaycee, Not the Surrogate, and Not the Unknown Donor of the Egg

In the present case Luanne is situated like a husband in an artificial insemination case whose consent triggers a medical procedure which results in a pregnancy and eventual birth of a child. Her motherhood may therefore be established "under this part," by virtue of that consent. In light of our conclusion, John's argument that the surrogate should be declared the lawful mother disintegrates. The case is now postured like the *Johnson v. Calvert* case, where motherhood could have been "established" in either of two women under the Act, and the tie broken by noting the intent to parent as expressed in the surrogacy contract. The only difference is that this case is not even close as between Luanne and the surrogate. Not only was Luanne the clearly intended mother, no bona fide attempt has been made to establish the surrogate as the lawful mother.

We should also add that neither could the woman whose egg was used in the fertilization or implantation make any claim to motherhood, even if she were to come forward at this late date. Again, as between two women who would both be able to establish motherhood under the Act, the *Johnson* decision would mandate that the tie be broken in favor of the intended parent, in this case, Luanne.

Our decision in *In re Marriage of Moschetta, supra*, 25 Cal.App.4th 1218, relied on by John, is inapposite and distinguishable. In *Moschetta*, this court held that a contract giving rise to a "traditional" surrogacy arrangement where a surrogate was simply inseminated with the husband's sperm could not be enforced against the surrogate by the intended father. (*Id.* at p. 1231) In order for the surrogate not to be the lawful mother she would have to give the child up for adoption. (*See id.* at pp. 1231) In *Moschetta*, the surrogate was the mother both by birth and genes; the woman contemplated as the intended mother in the surrogacy contract gave up any claim to the child. (*Id.* at pp. 1223–1225) In fact, at the appellate level, she went so far as to file a brief in favor of the birth mother's claim. (*See id.* at p. 1224)

Moschetta is inapposite because this court never had occasion to consider or discuss whether the original intended mother's participation in the surrogacy arrangement, which brought about the child's birth, might have formed the basis for holding her responsible as a parent. She had given up her claim; the issue was not before the court. Unlike the Johnson case there was no tie to break between two women both of whom could be held to be mothers under the Act....

In the case before us, we are not concerned, as John would have us believe, with a question of the enforceability of the oral and written surrogacy contracts into which he entered with Luanne. This case is not about "transferring" parenthood pursuant to those agreements. We are, rather, concerned with the consequences of those agreements as acts which caused the birth of a child.

The legal paradigm adopted by the trial court, and now urged upon us by John, is one where all forms of artificial reproduction in which intended parents have no biological relationship with the child result in legal parentlessness. It means that, absent adoption, such children will be dependents of the state. One might describe this paradigm as the "adoption default" model: The idea is that by not specifically addressing some permutation of artificial reproduction, the Legislature has, in effect, set the default switch on adoption. The underlying theory seems to be that when intended parents resort to artificial reproduction without biological tie the Legislature wanted them to be screened first through the adoption system. (Thus John, in his brief, argues that a surrogacy contract must be "subject to state oversight.")

The "adoption default" model is, however, inconsistent with both statutory law and the Supreme Court's Johnson decision. As to the statutory law, the Legislature has already made it perfectly clear that public policy (and, we might add, common sense) favors, whenever possible, the establishment of legal parenthood with the concomitant responsibility. Family Code section 7570, subdivision (a) states that "There is a compelling state interest in establishing paternity for all children." The statute then goes on to elaborate why establishing paternity is a good thing: It means someone besides the taxpayers will be responsible for the child: "Establishing paternity is the first step toward a child support award, which, in turn, provides children with equal rights and access to benefits...." (Ibid.) In light of this strong public policy, the statutes which follow section 7570, subdivision (a) seek to provide a "simple system allowing for the establishment of voluntary paternity." (*See* Fam. Code, § 7570, subd. (b).)

Section 7570 necessarily expresses a legislative policy applicable to maternity as well. It would be lunatic for the Legislature to declare that establishing paternity is a compelling state interest yet conclude that establishing maternity is not. The obvious reason the Legislature did not include an explicit parallel statement on "maternity" is that the issue almost never arises except for extraordinary cases involving artificial reproduction.

Very plainly, the Legislature has declared its preference for assigning individual responsibility for the care and maintenance of children; not leaving the task to the taxpayers. That is why it has gone to considerable lengths to insure that parents will live up to their support obligations. (Cf. *Moss v. Superior Court* (1998) 17 Cal.4th 396,[noting legislative priority put on child support obligations].) The adoption default theory flies in the face of that legislative value judgment.

As this court noted in *Jaycee B. v. Superior Court* (1996) 42 Cal.App.4th 718, 731, the Johnson court had occasion, albeit in dicta, to address "pretty much the exact situation before us." The language bears quoting again: "In what we must hope will be the extremely rare situation in which neither the gestator nor the woman who provided the ovum for fertilization is willing to assume custody of the child after birth, a rule recognizing the intending parents as the child's legal, natural parents should best promote certainty and stability." (*Johnson v. Calvert*, *supra*, 5 Cal.4th at pp. 94–95) This language quite literally describes precisely the case before us now: Neither the woman whose ovum was used nor the woman who gave birth have come forward to assume custody of the child after birth.

John now argues that the Supreme Court's statement should be applied only in situations, such as that in the *Johnson* case, where the intended parents have a genetic tie to the child. The context of the *Johnson* language, however, reveals a broader purpose, namely, to emphasize the intelligence and utility of a rule that looks to intentions.

...

In context, then, the high court's considered dicta is directly applicable to the case at hand. The context was not limited to just *Johnson*-style contests between women who gave birth and women who contributed ova, but to any situation where a child would not have been born " 'but for the efforts of the intended parents.' " (*Id.* at p. 94, quoting Hill, op. cit., *supra*, 66 N.Y.U.L. Rev. at p. 415.)

Finally, in addition to its contravention of statutorily enunciated public policy and the pronouncement of our high court in Johnson, the adoption default model ignores the role of our dependency statutes in protecting children. Parents are not screened for the procreation of their own children; they are screened for the adoption of other people's children. It is the role of the dependency laws to protect children from neglect and abuse from their own parents. The adoption default model is essentially an exercise in circular reasoning, because it assumes the idea that it seeks to prove; namely, that a child who is born as the result of artificial reproduction is somebody else's child from the beginning.

In the case before us, there is absolutely no dispute that Luanne caused Jaycee's conception and birth by initiating the surrogacy arrangement whereby an embryo was implanted into a woman who agreed to carry the baby to term on Luanne's behalf. In applying the artificial insemination statute to a gestational surrogacy case where the genetic donors are unknown, there is, as we have indicated above, no reason to distinguish between husbands and wives. Both are equally situated from the point of view of consenting to an act which brings a child into being. Accordingly, Luanne should have been declared the lawful mother of Jaycee.

John is the Lawful Father of Jaycee Even If Luanne Did Promise to Assume All Responsibility for Jaycee's Care

The same reasons which impel us to conclude that Luanne is Jaycee's lawful mother also require that John be declared Jaycee's lawful father. Even if the written surrogacy contract had not yet been signed at the time of conception and implantation, those occurrences were nonetheless the direct result of actions taken pursuant to an oral agreement which envisioned that the fertilization, implantation and ensuing pregnancy would go forward. Thus, it is still accurate to say, as we did the first time this case came before us, that for all practical purposes John caused Jaycee's conception every bit as much as if things had been done the old-fashioned way. (*Jaycee B.*, *supra*, 42 Cal.App.4th at p. 730.)

When pressed at oral argument to make an offer of proof as to the "best facts" which John might be able to show if this case were tried, John's attorney raised the point that Luanne had (allegedly, we must add) promised to assume all responsibility for the child and would not hold him responsible for the child's upbringing. However, even if this case were returned for a trial on this point (we assume that Luanne would dispute the allegation) it could make no difference as to John's lawful paternity. It is well established that parents cannot, by agreement, limit or abrogate a child's right to support. The rule is nicely illustrated by the case of *In re Marriage of Ayo* (1987) 190 Cal.App.3d 442. There, a husband adopted his wife's son from a previous marriage, then the couple were divorced. (*Id.* at p. 445) A year after the dissolution, the son's natural father (despite the fact he had already been adopted) started visiting him. (Ibid.) In light of the natural father's renewed interest, and in settlement of some arrearages in the division of community property and child support by a lump sum payment, the parties entered into a written agreement in which the wife promised, as Luanne has allegedly promised in this case, to hold the husband "harmless from any claims of any kind regarding her minor child." (*See id.* at pp. 447–448.) The agreement was filed as a written stipulation with the court and was even signed by the trial judge after the words, "it is so ordered." (*Id.* at p. 448, 235 Cal.Rptr. 458.)

More than five years later the wife reneged on the agreement and sought to renew the husband's child support obligation. (*Id.* at p. 445.) The appellate court held that the agreement was invalid, reasoning that the "rights of the contracting parties under agreements such as this one affecting children must yield to the welfare of the children." (*Id.* at p. 451.)

The rule against enforcing agreements obviating a parent's child support responsibilities is also illustrated by *Stephen K. v. Roni L.* (1980) 105 Cal.App.3d 640, a case which is virtually on point about Luanne's alleged promise. In *Stephen K.*, a woman was alleged to have falsely told a man that she was taking birth control pills. In "reliance" upon that statement the man had sexual intercourse with her. (*Id.* at p. 642) The woman became pregnant and brought a paternity action. While the man did not attempt to use the woman's false statement as grounds to avoid paternity, he did seek to achieve the same result by cross-complaining against the woman for damages based on her fraud.

There is no meaningful difference between the rule articulated in *Stephen K.* and the situation here—indeed, the result applies a fortiori to the present case: If the man who engaged in an act which merely opened the possibility of the procreation of a child was held responsible for the consequences in *Stephen K.,* how much more so should a man be held responsible for giving his express consent to a medical procedure that was intended to result in the procreation of a child. Thus, it makes no difference that John's wife Luanne did not become pregnant. John still engaged in "procreative conduct." In plainer language, a deliberate procreator is as responsible as a casual inseminator

Conclusion

Even though neither Luanne nor John are biologically related to Jaycee, they are still her lawful parents given their initiating role as the intended parents in her conception and birth. And, while the absence of a biological connection is what makes this case extraordinary, this court is hardly without statutory basis and legal precedent in so deciding.... [I]n our Supreme Court's *Johnson v. Calvert* decision, the court looked to intent to parent as the ultimate basis of its decision. Fortunately, as the Johnson court also noted, intent to parent "'correlate[s] significantly'" with a child's best interests. That is far more than can be said for a model of the law that renders a child a legal orphan.

5. Intent, Collaborative Reproduction and Unconventional Family Contexts

With increasing availability of assisted reproductive technologies, the class of intended parents is far broader and more diverse than that provided through nature—yet another construct for parenthood. Single parents, elderly parents, parents in gay/lesbian relationships, and other alternative family structures may now evidence and act upon their intent to become parents.

Kristine Renee H. v. Lisa Ann R.

16 Cal.Rptr.3d 123 (Cal. Ct. App. 2004)

Croskey, J.

...

In 1992, Kristine, the natural mother, and Lisa, her former partner, began a relationship that lasted for a decade. Shortly after meeting each other, Kristine quit her job, relocated to Southern California, and moved into Lisa's house. Later, the couple purchased a home together. While living together, the couple paid for expenses through a joint checking account. They also prepared durable powers of attorney for healthcare decisions in which they named each other as their healthcare agent.

In approximately 1998, Lisa and Kristine began to take the necessary steps to have and raise a child together. Kristine wanted to have a child of her own, and the couple decided to conceive the child through artificial insemination. The couple obtained sperm from a sperm bank and jointly selected the donor. For one year, Kristine went through several insemination procedures, became pregnant once, but suffered a miscarriage.

Because the couple could not afford to continue using the sperm bank, Kristine and Lisa turned to a friend who agreed to donate sperm. Kristine and Lisa prepared a donor agreement, which Kristine and the donor signed. Lisa worked with the donor to arrange the time and place to pick up the sperm. Kristine was inseminated at home and after one failed pregnancy, became pregnant with Lauren in February 2000. During Kristine's pregnancy, Lisa went with Kristine to every doctor visit and attended parenting classes.

2. *Entry of Judgment Establishing Lisa as a Second Parent*

When Kristine was eight months pregnant, Kristine and Lisa commenced an action in Los Angeles Superior Court to obtain a judgment establishing their parental rights to the unborn child. In a verified complaint to establish parental rights, filed on or about September 1, 2000, Kristine, as plaintiff, and Lisa, as defendant, alleged that Kristine is the legal mother of the unborn child and that Lisa is the "legal second mother/parent" of the unborn child. The parties based their complaint to establish their rights as legal parents on *Johnson, supra,* 5 Cal.4th 84, and *In re Marriage of Buzzanca* (1998) 61 Cal.App.4th 1410, (*Buzzanca*). They sought a judgment stating that they would be the parents of the unborn child, that they would be awarded joint custody after birth, that they would both be responsible for the payment of postnatal care, and that the hospital would be instructed to list Kristine as "mother" and Lisa as "father" on the original birth certificate.

Thereafter, Kristine and Lisa entered into a "stipulation for entry of judgment" establishing parentage in which they agreed to be the "joint intended legal parents" of the unborn child. On September 8, 2000, the family court entered the judgment establishing parental rights in both Kristine and Lisa. The judgment provides that Kristine is the "biological, genetic and legal mother/parent" of the unborn child and shall have joint custody with Lisa, who "is the legal second mother/parent" of the unborn child; that on the original birth certificate Kristine "shall be listed as mother"; and Lisa "shall be listed in the space provided for 'father'"; and that Kristine and Lisa are "the only legally recognized parents" of the unborn child and "take full and complete legal, custodial and financial responsibility of said child."

3. *The Parties Raised the Child Together for Almost Two Years*

On October 3, 2000, the child was born. Lisa was present during delivery and took one month off work to bond with the child. Kristine and Lisa named the child Lauren. Lauren's middle name is a combination of Kristine's and Lisa's middle names, and Lauren's surname combines their last names. Lisa was named as Lauren's "father" on her birth certificate. After Lauren's birth, she became a dependent on Lisa's medical insurance. Both Kristine and Lisa provide financial support for Lauren and share in childcare responsibilities. For almost two years, Kristine, Lisa, and Lauren lived together as a family in the home they shared. Lauren refers to Lisa as "momma," and Kristine as "mommy."

Before Lauren's birth, statutory provisions authorizing domestic partnership registration and its attendant rights became effective. Kristine and Lisa registered as domestic partners about a year after Lauren's birth. In January 2002, statutory provisions authorizing stepparent adoption for domestic partners became effective. (§ 9000, subds.(b), (f).) Lisa, however, never took the steps to adopt Lauren, presumably under the belief that the previously obtained judgment was sufficient to establish her parental rights. In September 2002, the couple's relationship ended, and Lisa moved out of the family home. Lauren was 23 months old.

4. *Kristine Unsuccessfully Moves to Vacate the Judgment and Lisa Seeks Custody and Visitation*

After their separation and termination of their domestic partnership, Kristine sought to sever Lisa's status as a legal parent by filing a motion to vacate the judgment. Kristine originally contended (but has since abandoned this theory) that the family court could not determine their respective legal parental rights before Lauren's birth.

On April 28, 2003, the family court denied the motion....

On May 5, 2003, Lisa filed an order to show cause for modification of child custody and visitation. The hearing was originally set for June 16, 2003.

Kristine then filed a writ of supersedeas, or in the alternative, a petition for writ of mandate (1) challenging the family court's order denying her motion to vacate the judgment, and (2) seeking to stay the custody and visitation proceedings. This court granted a stay in the custody and visitation proceedings. On June 19, 2003, however, we lifted the stay (and thus effectively denied the petition for a writ of supersedeas) and directed the family court to make appropriate temporary visitation orders pending the resolution of this appeal. We have consolidated the appellate proceedings to be decided in a single opinion.

The Parties Contentions

Kristine collaterally attacks the judgment on the ground that it is void. Kristine contends that the family court could not enter the judgment establishing Lisa as a second parent based on the parties' stipulation because the Act is the sole means upon which to determine parentage, and Lisa is not a parent under any provision of the Act. According to Kristine, the only lawful way Lisa could become a second parent was through adoption.

Lisa contends that the judgment establishing her status as a second parent cannot be collaterally attacked by Kristine as void for lack of jurisdiction because the parties could stipulate to parentage, and even if they could not, Lisa is a legal parent based on a gender-neutral application of two provisions of the Act—the presumed father statute (section 7611, subdivision (d)), and/or the artificial insemination statute (section 7613, subdivision (a)).

...

The parties (and the family court) mistakenly believed that based on *Buzzanca, supra*, 61 Cal.App.4th 1410, the parties' intention to become the legal parents of the unborn child was sufficient to establish their parental rights. This judgment is apparently not the only one entered based on what we believe is a misreading of *Buzzanca*. To our knowledge, this case presents the first appellate challenge to such a judgment. We therefore must dispel any notion that *Buzzanca* can be read to support a prebirth parentage judgment based on a mere contractual expression of the parties' intentions.

In *Buzzanca, supra*, 61 Cal.App.4th 1410, a married couple agreed to have a fertilized embryo—genetically unrelated to either one of them—implanted in a surrogate. (*Id.*

at p. 1412.) The court held that the husband and wife were the child's mother and father by construing the artificial insemination statute in the Act (§ 7613, subd. (a)), in a gender-neutral manner, to apply to both the husband and to the wife, and by looking to the parties' intent to create a child. (*Id.* at pp. 1421–1428.) Had the court not done so, the child would have been a legal orphan.

... The focus on the parties' intent was based on *Johnson, supra*, 5 Cal.4th 84. In that case, our Supreme Court had to resolve a parentage dispute between two mothers, a genetic mother and surrogate mother. Because two women qualified as a natural mother under the Act, the court looked at the parties' intention as manifested in the surrogacy agreement. (*Id.* at pp. 93–95.) The "tie" was broken in favor of the genetic mother because she who intended to bring about the birth of a child that "she intended to raise as her own—is the natural mother under California law." (*Id.* at p. 93.) The Buzzanca court concluded that this intent-based analysis "was not limited to just *Johnson*-style contests between a woman who gave birth and a woman who contributed ova, but to any situation where a child would not have been born but for the efforts of the intended parents." (61 Cal.App.4th at p. 1425.)

Neither *Buzzanca* nor *Johnson*, however, endorse contractual stipulations of parentage based on the parties' intentions without regard to the Act. In those cases the court looked at the parties' intent as a part of the interpretation and application of the Act. Only when the Act was unclear or yielded an ambiguous result did the courts consider intent to determine parentage. (*In re Marriage of Moschetta* (1994) 25 Cal.App.4th 1218, 1231.)

We therefore conclude that the judgment based on the parties' intent to become parents exceeded the family court's jurisdiction and is void and of no legal effect. Nevertheless, for reasons discussed below, this does not mean that the Lisa cannot successfully assert a claim of parentage.

4. *Lisa is Entitled to Assert Parentage under a Gender-Neutral Interpretation of the Act*

Though we have concluded that the family court could not enter the judgment establishing Lisa as a second parent based on the parties' stipulation, we must now address the second question, that is, whether Lisa can establish her parental rights under the Act.

As section 7610 states: "The parent and child relationship may be established as follows: (a) Between a child and the natural mother, it may be established by proof of her having given birth to the child, or under this part. (b) Between a child and the natural father, it may be established under this part. (c) Between a child and an adoptive parent, it may be established by proof of adoption." Because Lisa is not the natural mother and did not adopt Lauren, Lisa must rely on a gender-neutral application of the provisions that apply to establish a father-child relationship.

a. *The Act Permits Establishing a Parent-Child Relationship in Two Unmarried Parents of the Same Sex*

As a starting point, under the Act, the parent-child relationship extends equally to every child and to every parent regardless of the marital status of the parent. Therefore, the marital status of Kristine and Lisa is irrelevant for purposes of determining whether Lisa is Lauren's second parent.

Moreover, though the Act is predicated on determining legal "motherhood" and "fatherhood," contrary to Kristine's position, the statutory language does not restrict the parent-child relationship based on gender to a mother and father. The Act requires that we read it in a gender-neutral manner and declares that "insofar as practicable," provisions applicable to the father and child relationship apply in an action to determine the existence or nonexistence of a mother and child relationship. (§ 7650.)

Kristine's position that a child may have only one mother is based on *Johnson*, *supra*, in which our Supreme Court stated that "California law recognizes only one natural mother." (5 Cal. 4th at p. 92.) That statement, however, was made in a case involving competing claims for motherhood, one asserted by the surrogate mother and the other by the genetic mother. (*Id.* at pp. 89–93) In that case, amicus curiae, the American Civil Liberties Union (ACLU), encouraged the Supreme Court to find the child had two mothers. The Johnson court, however, refused and found that "[t]o recognize parental rights in a third party with whom the Calvert family has had little contact since shortly after the child's birth would diminish Crispina's [the genetic mother's] role as mother." (*Id.* at p. 92, fn. 8.) The court's comment, however, was based on its belief that interjecting a third party would upset the child's stable, intact, and nurturing home. The Johnson court did not foreclose the possibility, in an appropriate case, of finding two parents of the same sex where only two parties are attempting to establish legal parentage.

Kristine also cites prior decisions in which the courts of appeal have determined that a lesbian partner who is not a biological or adoptive parent is not entitled to custody or visitation of children conceived during the relationship. (*See West*, *supra*, 59 Cal. App.4th at pp. 305–306, 309; Nancy S., *supra*, 228 Cal. App.3d at pp. 835–836; *Curiale*, *supra*, 222 Cal. App. 3d at pp. 1599–1600.) None of these cases, however, analyzed the Act in a gender-neutral manner to determine whether a second parent of the same sex could establish parentage under the provisions of the Act that applied to establishing a father-child relationship. Moreover, these cases were decided before our Supreme Court and Legislature recognized that a child may have two legal parents of the same sex, with equal status in terms of their relationship with the child. (*Sharon S. v. Superior Court*, *supra*, 31 Cal. 4th at pp. 430–435; § 9000, subds. (b), (f).)

... As we now discuss, the presumed father statute, when read in a gender-neutral manner, enables Lisa to assert her parental rights as a second parent.

b. *Section 7611, Subdivision (d), the Presumed Father Statute*

As stated, it is undisputed that Lisa is neither a natural mother nor an adoptive mother. (§ 7610, subds.(a), (c).) Under a gender-neutral application of the Act, however, we may consider the provisions applicable to the father and child relationship to determine whether Lisa can establish parentage. (§ 7650.)

The Act sets forth the methods for a father to establish a parent-child relationship. Although there are a number of provisions to establish paternity, we are concerned here with section 7611. Because Lisa and Kristine are not married, the only provision of section 7611 that could apply here is subdivision (d). Subdivision (d) provides that a man may be a presumed father if he receives the child into his home and openly holds out the child as his natural child. The proponent has the burden of proving the foundational facts by a preponderance of the evidence, that is, that he received the child into his home and openly and publicly acknowledged the child as his own. This presumption, however is rebuttable.

...

The Act distinguishes between a presumed father and one who is a natural father, evidencing the Legislature's clear intent "to provide natural fathers with far less rights than ... presumed fathers...." (*Adoption of Kelsey S.* (1992) 1 Cal.4th 816.) Only a presumed father is entitled to custody of a child and, in a dependency proceeding, only a presumed father is entitled to reunification services. (*In re Zacharia D.* (1993) 6 Cal.4th 435, 451; In re Jerry P. (2002) 95 Cal.App.4th 793, 801 (*Jerry P.*).) "A 'natural father' can be, but is not necessarily, a 'presumed father' and a 'presumed father' can be, but is not necessarily, a 'natural father.'" (*Jerry P., supra*, at p. 801.)

c. *The Presumed Father Statute has been Applied in a Gender-Neutral Manner to Establish Parentage in an Adult not Biologically Related to the Child*

Under the Act, by receiving a child into his or her home and holding the child out as his own or her own, a man or woman can achieve presumed parent status without a biological connection to the child. (*In re Nicholas H.* (2002) 28 Cal.4th 56, 70 (*Nicholas H.*); *Karen C., supra*, 101 Cal.App.4th 932, 936–939.) Moreover, when there are competing presumptions under section 7611, subdivision (d), biology is not dispositive. (*In re Jesusa V.* (2004) 32 Cal.4th 588, 604–607 (*Jesusa V.*).)

In *Nicholas H., supra*, 28 Cal.4th 56, the man seeking to establish paternity under section 7611, subdivision (d), admitted that he was not the biological father. (*Id.* at pp. 58–59.) The Nicholas H. court considered whether a presumption of fatherhood arising under section 7611 is necessarily rebutted under section 7612, subdivision (a), when the presumed father admitted that he is not the biological father of the child. The Supreme Court concluded that a presumption arising under section 7611, subdivision (d), is not, under section 7612, subdivision (a), necessarily rebutted by clear and convincing evidence that the presumed father is not the biological father of the child. (*Id.* at p. 70.)

...

While *Nicholas H.*, did not involve competing presumptive father claims, it relied on two Court of Appeal cases that addressed competing paternity claims. (28 Cal.4th at pp. 64–66 .) Those cases upheld the finding that the nonbiological father was the presumed father under the Act. (*In re Kiana A.* (2001) 93 Cal. App. 4th 1109, 1118–1121 (*Kiana A.); Steven W. v. Matthew S.* (1995) 33 Cal. App. 4th 1108, 1116–1117 (*Steven W.*).) Following the Supreme Court's decision in *Nicholas H., supra*, 28 Cal. 4th 56, the Court of Appeal in *Karen C., supra*, 101 Cal.App.4th 932, expanded that decision to apply with "equal force to a woman, as a presumed mother." (*Id.* at p. 934.) In *Karen C.*, the court held that a woman who was not the biological mother but had raised Karen C. as though she were her natural child could attempt to establish her legal rights as a parent based on a gender-neutral application of the presumed father statute. (*Id.* at pp. 938–939.)

The Karen C. court noted that "one of the key holdings of *Nicholas H.* is 'that a man does not lose his status as a presumed father by admitting he is not the biological father.'" (*Karen C., supra*, at p. 938, 124 Cal. Rptr.2d 677.) The court reasoned the same analysis would apply to a woman based on a gender-neutral application of the statute. (*Id.* at p. 939; see *also In re Salvador M., supra*, 111 Cal. App. 4th at pp. 1357–1359.) In reaching this conclusion, the Karen C. court rejected the argument, advanced by Kristine here, that section 7611, subdivision (d), does not apply to women because the statutory presumption was intended to erase the stigma of illegitimacy. (101 Cal. App. 4th at p. 939.)

Kristine argues that *Nicholas H.* and *Karen C.* are inapposite because in those cases there was no biologically related adult who wanted to assume the role of parent. That argument, however, actually supports the application here of section 7611, subdivision (d), because there are no other competing claims to become Lauren's second parent. Moreover, Kristine's argument incorrectly assumes that Lauren may not have two parents of the same sex absent adoption.

We also reject Kristine's argument that by applying section 7611, subdivision (d), to determine whether Lisa is a parent, we are endorsing a rule of law pursuant to which a third, or fourth person not biologically related to a child might also establish legal parentage. That argument appears to assume, however, that Lauren's second legal parent must be the sperm donor. This argument is without merit. The sperm donor has not asserted any claim of parental rights. More to the point, this case only involves a person seeking to become a second parent, so we have no occasion to address this issue. Our focus here is not on competing interests by several persons but on whether Lisa is a second parent. Just like in *Karen C.* and *Nicholas H.*, no one else but Lisa is attempting to fill that position.

d. *Courts Have Previously Limited the Application of Section 7611, Subdivision (d), to Determine Parentage*

... Up until now, no appellate decision has applied section 7611, subdivision (d), to determine parental rights in a same-sex partner with no biological connection to the child.

...

Here, we are not determining who is the natural mother. Kristine is the natural mother. Our inquiry is whether a presumption of parentage may apply to determine "second parent" status. For that inquiry, the lack of a biological connection to a child does not automatically defeat a presumption of parentage under subdivision (d) of section 7611....

In sum, we conclude that when read in a gender-neutral manner, section 7611, subdivision (d), may be applied to establish legal parentage in a partner of the same sex with no biological connection to the child. Our construction of this statute would not be any different if, instead of affirming her parental obligations, Lisa was seeking to deny her parental obligations of support. Our conclusion also is consistent with the recent amendments to the Family Code that, although not directly applicable here, recognize that domestic partners who create children have the same rights and responsibilities as spouses for children conceived during the domestic partnership.

6. *Lisa May Be Able to Establish Legal Parental Status if She Can Satisfy the Requirements of Section 7611, Subdivision (d)*

To qualify as a presumed parent under section 7611, subdivision (d), Lisa must (1) receive the child into her home, and (2) hold out the child as her own.

a. *The "Holding Out" Requirement May Be Established by Lisa's Course of Conduct*

Addressing the latter point first, on the record before us, Lisa's declaration indicates that she might be able to prove that she satisfies the statutory requirement of holding Lauren out as her own. She has presented evidence of her course of conduct, which began with the child's conception, from which the family court might be able to conclude that she has fulfilled the role of a presumed parent.

Though these facts must be established on remand by the family court, Lisa has stated that she and Kristine took the necessary steps to create Lauren, and both of them participated in the artificial insemination process. When Kristine became pregnant, Lisa and Kristine lived together in their shared home and prepared for Lauren's birth. Lisa economically and emotionally supported Kristine during the pregnancy, attended doctor's appointments and parenting classes, and was present during the child's delivery.

One month before the child was born, Lisa and Kristine invoked the jurisdiction of the family court to declare Lisa as the child's parent. While the judgment is not itself enforceable, it provides an undisputed evidentiary basis from which the family court might be able to assess Lisa's conduct in holding out the child as her own. Lisa and Kristine signed and presented to the court a stipulation in which Lisa declared her intent to be "the joint intended legal parent" of the unborn child, sought joint custody as soon as the child was born, and agreed to financially support the unborn child. She further agreed to be listed in the space provided for "father" on the unborn child's birth certificate. Lisa, along with Kristine, asked the court to acknowledge that they "are the only legally recognized parents of the unborn child" and "take full and complete legal, custodial and financial responsibility for said child."

In addition, Lisa has presented evidence of her conduct following Lauren's birth. In her declaration, Lisa stated that she is listed as a parent on Lauren's birth certificate, that Lauren's middle name and surname are a combination of Lisa's and Kristine's names, and that after Lauren was born she took time off work to bond with the child. Moreover, Lauren is a dependent on Lisa's medical insurance. Lisa further stated in her declaration that she and Kristine share childcare responsibilities, and Lauren calls Lisa "momma." The family court must look to this evidence, and the additional evidence presented by the parties on remand, to determine whether Lisa's course of conduct demonstrates a full commitment to Lauren's welfare—emotional, financial, and otherwise—to satisfy the holding out requirements of section 7611, subdivision (d).

b. *The "Receiving Into One's Home" Requirement May Be Established by Lisa's Conduct Following the Child's Birth*

Though these facts must be established by the family court on remand, Lisa has stated in her declaration that she, Kristine, and Lauren lived together as a family in their shared home until the break up of the adults' relationship. Lisa, however, did more than just live with Kristine and Lauren. One month before her birth, she agreed to become her joint legal parent, and to financially support Lauren. Upon birth, Lisa was listed on Lauren's birth certificate, gave Lauren her family name, and provided financial and emotional support for Lauren. According to Lisa, she acted in every way as Lauren's second parent and believes that she demonstrated the level of diligent commitment the law requires in order to satisfy the statutory requirement of receiving Lauren into her home.

We reject Kristine's argument that even if Lisa could establish the statutory requirements of a presumed parent, Lisa's claim to parentage has been rebutted as a matter of law by Kristine, the biological and gestational mother. Such a conclusion erroneously assumes that a child may not have a natural mother and another parent of the same sex unless that parent adopts the child. Moreover, we do not agree with Kristine's characterization that should the family court determine that Lisa is a legal parent, such a ruling would be an "imposition of a presumed mother on an intact family." The record before us indicates that when Lauren was conceived, born, and up until she was almost two-years old, the family consisted of Kristine, Lisa, and Lauren. Whether this is an appropriate action to rebut the section 7611, subdivision (d), presumption is a factual determination left to the family court on remand.

We therefore will remand the case to the family court to determine whether Lisa has satisfied the statutory requirements to become a presumed parent under a gender-neutral application of section 7611, subdivision (d), and whether this would be an appropriate action in which to conclude that the presumption has been rebutted. If Lisa is found to be Lauren's parent, then the family court must proceed to determine Lisa's rights, if any, to custody and visitation of Lauren. In making that determination, the family court should consider and apply all of the factors and criteria set out in the applicable provisions of the Family Code.

7. *Impact of the "Intended Parent Doctrine"*

Although it is clear that the issue of parentage must be established under provisions of the Act, the result we reach is also fully supported by an application of the so-called "intended-parent doctrine."

...

This intent-based standard for recognizing parental rights clearly buttresses the conclusion that we reach. Keeping the focus of the Johnson test in mind, based on this record, at the time Lauren was conceived, Kristine and Lisa were in a committed relationship, and they acted together to cause the birth of their child. Their plans to raise the child together led them to enter into a stipulation to establish them as the legal parents of the unborn child and obtain a judgment establishing their parental rights. Upon Lauren's birth, Kristine and Lisa raised the child in the family home until they separated. Now, because Kristine no longer wants to be Lisa's partner, she disputes Lisa's claim to parental rights. As we have stated, the parties cannot make up the rules to establish a parental relationship, nor can they make up the rules to sever one. The same rules that apply to all other parents should apply to Kristine and Lisa. Determining that Kristine and Lisa are both Lauren's parents (assuming the family court so concludes), no matter what happens to their adult relationship, would be consistent with their own intentions when they took the steps to create Lauren and is based on an application of the Act—the same rules that apply to other parents in their situation who must deal with the legal consequences of their procreative actions long after they have separated.

6. Genetics and Adoption

Meracle v. Children's Service Society of Wisconsin

437 N.W.2d 532 (Wis. 1989)

CALLOW, JUSTICE ...

In 1977, the Meracles contacted Children's Service Society of Wisconsin (CSS), an adoption agency, about adopting a child. They told CSS they wanted a "normal, healthy child," which they defined as a child without a "disabilitating" or terminal disease, who is not deformed and who is of average or above average intelligence.

On October 10, 1979, the Meracles met with Josephine Braden (Braden), a social worker at CSS, to discuss the foster placement and adoption of Erin, a twenty-three month-old child. According to the Meracles' deposition testimony, Braden told them the following at the meeting: that Erin's paternal grandmother had died of Huntington's Disease; that Huntington's was a degenerative brain disease which is genetically transmitted between generations; that if one generation was free of the disease, the next generation would be free of it; that each child of a Huntington's Disease victim had a fifty-fifty chance of developing the disease; and that the disease was always fatal. According to the Meracles, Braden also told them that Erin's father had tested negative for the disease and that, therefore, Erin had no more chance of developing the disease than did any other child.

In her deposition, Braden recalled discussing Huntington's Disease with the Meracles at this meeting. However, she did not recall telling the Meracles there was no chance of Erin developing the disease, and could not believe she had done so.

On October 18, 1979, CSS placed Erin with the Meracles, and on November 12, 1980, the adoption was completed.

On February 8, 1981, Nancy Meracle saw a segment of the television program 60 Minutes which dealt with Huntington's Disease. The show stated that a child of a Huntington's Disease victim has a fifty percent chance of developing the disease. It also stated that there was no reliable test for someone at risk to determine whether he or she had inherited the disease.

"Alarmed" and "frightened," Nancy told her husband about the program. The Meracles obtained a pamphlet about Huntington's Disease from a library the next day which confirmed there was no test for the disease. They took no further action at this time.

On September 27, 1984, a neurologist diagnosed Erin as having Huntington's Disease. On September 25, 1985, the Meracles filed a complaint against CSS in the Milwaukee County Circuit Court. They subsequently amended the complaint twice to include two insurance companies as co-defendants: American Home Assurance Company (American Home) and St. Paul Fire & Marine Insurance Company.

The second amended complaint contained two claims for relief. First, the Meracles contended that CSS negligently placed Erin with them. Second, they contended that CSS negligently misrepresented to them that Erin's father was free of Huntington's Disease. The Meracles demanded judgment of ten million dollars for each of the claims. They sought to recover damages for loss of society and companionship of Erin, emotional pain and suffering, interference with their enjoyment of life, lost wages and medical expenses.

[Summary judgment for the defendant was granted on September 8, 1986 on ground that claim was not brought within the three-year statute of limitations. A subsequent request for reconsideration was denied.]

The Meracles appealed from both the judgment and order [denying reconsideratrion] on March 17, 1987. The court of appeals reversed. It held that the Meracles' complaint is actually composed of two separate claims. The first claim is for emotional distress based upon the Meracles' fear that Erin might contract Huntington's Disease. *Meracle*, 143 Wis.2d at 481. The second claim is for future medical expenses and emotional distress the Meracles suffered by adopting a child who had actually developed the disease. *Id.* The court found that the first claim accrued in 1981 and thus was barred by the statute of limitations. *Id.* at 482. However, it held that the second claim did not accrue until Erin was diagnosed as having the disease in September of 1984. *Id.* at 483. It held that this claim was not time-barred and that it did not violate public policy. *Id.* at 483–84.

We first turn to CSS's contention that the Meracles' claim is barred by the three-year statute of limitations for negligence.... We find that in 1981, while the Meracles had learned of CSS's negligence, they had suffered no injury which would support a cause of action...."[A] cause of action accrues where there exists a claim capable of present enforcement, a suable party against whom it may be enforced, and a party who has a present right to enforce it.".... In 1981, the Meracles did not have a claim which they could have enforced in court either for pecuniary damages or for emotional distress.

We first consider the Meracles' ability to recover pecuniary damages. CSS contends that the Meracles could have stated a claim for the $1000 adoption fee and for the cost of raising Erin between the time of her adoption and the discovery of the disease in 1981. This is incorrect. These are costs which would have been incurred in any case during the adoption of a child. The Meracles wanted to adopt a child. These were ordinary expenses pursuant to that end. It is only the extraordinary expenses, the unexpected expenses resulting from Erin's special needs, which are actionable.

CSS also contends that the Meracles could have stated a claim for Erin's future medical expenses in 1981. This also is incorrect. In order to sue for future medical expenses in 1981, while Erin had not yet contracted the disease, the Meracles would have had to base their claim on the mere possibility that Erin would develop the disease. To recover for future expenses due to an injury, a plaintiff must demonstrate that the anticipated expenses are reasonably certain to occur....

There was no reasonable medical certainty in 1981 that the Meracles would incur any future medical expenses because Erin had not developed Huntington's Disease. At the time, the Meracles only knew that Erin's paternal grandmother had developed the disease. They did not know whether her father would develop it. While Erin's father was not known to have developed the disease, there is a fifty percent chance that a Huntington's victim will genetically transmit the disease to his or her off-spring. The Meracles only knew that Erin's grandmother had the disease and her father had a fifty percent of developing Huntington's, and therefore Erin had only a twenty-five percent chance of developing the disease.

Further, Erin's chances of developing the disease within her first eighteen years, when the Meracles would have been responsible for medical payments, was even smaller. Deposition testimony revealed that only four to five percent of the people who develop Huntington disease do so while they are juveniles. In sum, even assuming that Erin would develop the disease at some point in her life, in 1981 there was only a four to five percent chance that the Meracles would incur future medical expenses for Erin. This risk constitutes a "mere possibility" and it was not an injury for which the Meracles could have recovered in 1981. They could not have shown with a reasonable medical certainty in 1981 that they would incur any future medical expenses. Thus, they did not suffer a pecuniary injury which would support a cause of action.

The Meracles likewise did not have a compensable claim for emotional distress in 1981. The general rule in Wisconsin is that, to recover for the negligent infliction of emotional distress, the "plaintiff's emotional distress must be manifested by physical injury." ... This rule exists because of the "fear of flooding the courts with fraudulent claims and exposing defendants to potentially unlimited liability for every type of mental disturbance." The existence of physical injury makes the genuineness of the claim much more likely.

CSS correctly points out that an exception to this rule exists.... [We] allowed a fourteen-year-old girl to recover damages for emotional distress when she was negligently confined in a police department cell for thirteen hours with no food, water or blankets. We stated that, "under the unique facts presented in this case," the nature of the confinement itself guaranteed the genuineness of the claim. We emphasized the fact that the tort involved "a substantial and unwarranted deprivation of liberty," which itself was "a sufficient guarantee that the claim is not frivolous."

CSS contends that the Meracles' claim in 1981 was such that we should make another exception to the requirement that a claim for the negligent infliction of emotional distress be accompanied by physical injury. We disagree. The Meracles were not deprived of liberty or any other constitutional right in 1981 nor does the nature of their claim present a similar guarantee of the genuineness and severity of the injury.

We find, therefore, that the Meracles suffered no injury, pecuniary or emotional, which would support a compensable claim in 1981.

The Meracles did suffer an injury which could form the basis for a cause of action in 1984 when they learned that Erin had developed Huntington's Disease. The Meracles had a cause of action for pecuniary damages at this time. They could then demonstrate with reasonable medical certainty that Erin would need extensive future medical care. They were now certain to incur future expenses because of the adoption which they allege was induced by the affirmative misrepresentation that Erin's father had tested negative for the disease and therefore that Erin would not contract it. In 1984, the Meracles had "a claim capable of present enforcement." As in 1981, however, the Meracles could not maintain a claim for emotional distress in 1984. They still did not demonstrate the existence of any physical injury accompanying their claim. The distress that is usually experienced by close relatives when illness strikes a family member is normal and is not compensable. The rule that a claim for the negligent infliction of emotional distress must be accompanied by physical injury is important and strikes "the appropriate balance between the rights of injured parties to obtain a remedy for a wrong, and the rights of defendants to be free from potentially unlimited liability and the meritless claims." The claim for emotional distress must be dismissed.

Under the discovery rule of *Borello*, 388 N.W.2d 140 [(Wis.)], the Meracles' cause of action for medical expenses accrued on September 27, 1984, when Erin was diagnosed with the disease. They filed their first complaint on September 25, 1985, well within the three-year limitations period. Therefore, their claim for future medical expenses is not time-barred and should be remanded for trial.

CSS also contends that, even if the Meracles' suit is not barred by the statute of limitations, it should be barred because it violates public policy.... In support of its position CSS cites two California decisions which discuss the policy implications of wrongful adoption actions. In *Richard P. v. Vista Del Mar Child Care Service*, 106 Cal.App.3d 860 (1980), the California Court of Appeals held that it would violate public policy to allow the adoptive parents of a child to sue an adoption agency which stated that the child, who later developed severe neurological damage, was healthy. The court feared that allowing such a suit to proceed would make adoption agencies the guarantors of the health of the children they place. In *Michael J. v. Los Angeles County Department of Adoptions*, 247 Cal.Rptr. 504 (1988), the California Court of Appeals held that public policy did not bar a suit based on intentional misrepresentation by an adoption agency. However, the court reaffirmed its decision in Richard P. that adoption agencies were not liable for negligence in placing adoptive children. *Michael J.*, 247 Cal.Rptr. at 513. CSS likewise contends that allowing this suit to proceed would place an unreasonable burden on adoption agencies, exposing them to potentially unlimited liability and making them guarantors of the health of the children they place.

Before determining whether we should bar this cause of action on public policy grounds, we feel it necessary to emphasize the uniqueness of this case. This is not a case in which an adoption agency placed a child without discovering and informing the prospective parents about the child's health problems. Therefore we need not and do not address the question of whether adoption agencies have a duty to discover and disclose health information about children they place for adoption. In this case, accepting the alleged facts as true for purposes of this summary judgment motion, CSS affirmatively misrepresented Erin's risk of developing Huntington's Disease. The agency assumed the duty of informing the Meracles about Huntington's Disease and about Erin's chances of developing the disease. Having voluntarily assumed this duty, the complaint alleges, CSS negligently breached it.

Given these unique circumstances, we hold that the Meracles' claim is not barred by public policy. Such a conclusion does not expose adoption agencies to potentially unlimited liability nor does it make such agencies guarantors of the health of adopted children. To avoid liability, agencies simply must refrain from making affirmative misrepresentations about a child's health. We do not hold that agencies have any duty to disclose health information. Further, our decision will not inhibit adoption. Indeed, it will give potential parents more confidence in the adoption process and in the accuracy of the information they receive. Such confidence would be eroded if we were to immunize agencies from liability for false statements made during the adoption process.

We also emphasize that we do not create liability which is remote from or out of proportion to the negligence because, as we discussed above, we only allow recovery for the extraordinary medical expenses which will be incurred by the Meracles as a result of the negligent misrepresentation. This case is very different from *Rieck*, in which we determined based upon public policy that parents could not maintain a wrongful birth action to recover ordinary expenses of raising a normal child against a doctor who failed to diagnosis a pregnancy. *Rieck*, 64 Wis.2d at 518–19. Finally, this decision does not open the way for fraudulent claims to be brought. There is no greater chance of fraud in a case like this than in any case in which the dispute centers over what words were spoken during a particular conversation. Based upon the unique factors in this case we conclude this suit is not barred by public policy.

Notes & Questions

1. In *Michael H. v. Gerald D.*, 491 U.S. 110 (1989), the Court held that, even though a child ultimately was proven to not be genetically related to the husband, the fact that she had been born during the marriage was sufficient to establish legal parenthood. The Court chose to decide the case in terms of traditional norms, and affirm the concept of a "unitary family" composed of a married couple and their children. In this case, there are two fathers laying claim to a child. Gerald D. is the husband of the birth/gestational mother and has held out and treated the child as his, both at the time of birth and during times thereafter, when he and his wife were together. Gerald D.'s claim is based on the California's statute that provided that the child of a "wife cohabiting with her husband, who is neither impotent nor sterile, is conclusively presumed to be a child of the marriage." Although statute does allow a biological father to seek legal designation as the father, he may only do so in concert with the mother or her husband—and then only within two years of the birth of the child. The biological father is foreclosed from seeking parenthood on his own. *See* California Family Code §§ 7540–41 (West 2004) (formerly California Evidence Code § 621).

Michael H., on the other hand, argued that, not only was he the biological father of the child, he had a parental relationship with her and had held her out as his child. He argued that he had a constitutionally protected liberty interest that trumped the interests of the non-biological parent. In essence, the conundrum was that both Michael H. and Gerald D. had held out the child as theirs and had lived with her in a father/child relationship. Gerald D. had marriage to the mother on his side of the parental equation; Michael H. had genetics on his side of the equation. Ultimately, the Supreme Court found that the liberty interest asserted by Michael H. was not his to assert in the absence of a traditional family relationship:

> [T]he legal issue in the present case reduces to whether the relationship between persons in the situation of Michael and Victoria has been treated as a protected family unit under the historic practices of our society, or whether on any other basis it has been accorded special protection. We think it impossible to find that it has. In fact, quite to the contrary, our traditions have protected the marital family (Gerald, Carole, and the child they acknowledge to be theirs) against the sort of claim Michael asserts.

504 U.S. 905. Would Michael H.'s liberty interest be stronger had Gerald D. been divorced from Carole? Suppose Gerald D. had repudiated his interest in the child. Would Michael H. then have had a stronger claim? In *Heidbreder v. Carton*, 645 N.W.2d 355 (Minn. 2002), cert. denied 537 U.S. 1046, the Minnesota Supreme Court held that the putative father and birth mother of a child born out of wedlock were not similarly situated, for purposes of equal protection analysis, with respect to their relationship to the child. There, the birth mother's interests and opinion as to the child's best interests was more highly credited than that of the putative father. However, in that case, unlike Michael H., the father had not established a relationship with the child.

The Uniform Parentage Act, adopted in about twenty jurisdictions, addresses the issue of competing fatherhood claim in § 607, which is the basis for the pertinent provision of California law in *Michael H. v. Gerald D.* However, as noted in the commentary to the 2000 version of the UPA, "the right of an 'outsider' to claim paternity of a child born to a married woman varies considerably among the States. Thirty-three States allow a man alleging himself to be the father of a child to rebut the marital presumption. Some States have granted this right through legislation. In other States, courts have recognized the alleged father's right to rebut the presumption and establish his paternity. Further, in some States, there is both statutory and common law support for the standing of a man alleging himself to be the father to assert his paternity of a child born to a married woman." See comments to § 607, *available at* http://www.law.upenn.edu/bll/ulc/upa/final2002.htm.

For additional reading on this case and the concept of the unitary family, see Lynne Marie Kohm, *Marriage and the Intact Family: The Significance of* Michael H. v. Gerald D., 22 Whittier L. Rev. 327 (2000); Michael L. Oddenino, *The Good, the Bad, and the Ugly: A Critical Analysis of the U.S. Supreme Court Decision in* Michael H. v. Gerald D., 25 Fam. L.Q. 125 (1991); Stanley H. Friedman, *Reassessing Family Relations Law: Issues and Inquiries in the State Courts*, 68 Alb. L. Rev. 225 (2005); Mary Kay Kisthardt, *Of Fatherhood, Families and Fantasy: The Legacy of* Michael H. v. Gerald D., 65 Tul. L. Rev. 585 (1991); Robin L. West, *The Ideal of Liberty: A Comment on* Michael H. v. Gerald D., 139 U. Pa. L. Rev. 1373 (1991); Elizabeth A. Hadad, *Tradition and the Liberty Interest: Circumscribing the Rights of the Natural Father*, 56 Brook. L. Rev. 291 (1990); Mindy S. Halpern, *Father Knows Best—But Which Father? California's Presumption of Legitimacy Loses Its Conclusiveness:* Michael H. v. Gerald D. *and Its Aftermath*, 25 Loy. L.A. L. Rev. 275 (1991); Gail A. Secor, Michael H. v. Gerald D.: *Due Process and Equal Protection Rights of Unwed Fathers*, 17 Hastings Const. L.Q. 759 (1990).

2. *In the Matter of the Parentage of J.M.K.*, the mother is attempting to get the genetic father to support the two children conceived, albeit by *in vitro* fertilization, but arguably within a long-term romantic relationship. Washington is one of the nineteen states that have enacted the Uniform Parentage Act (UPA). In § 202 of the UPA, echoed

in RCW 26.26.106, the Act seeks to provide substantive legal equality for all children regardless of the marital status of their parents and to protect the rights and ensure the obligations of parents of children born out of wedlock. *See, e.g., Doe v. Doe*, 52 P.3d 255 (Haw. 2002). Thus, one could argue that the genetic father, Kepl, has an inherent responsibility, recognized by the UPA, to support the child.

However, in tension with that provision is RCW 26.26.705, which unambiguously states that a "donor is not a parent of a child conceived by means of assisted reproduction." This section is further bolstered by RCW 26.26.715, which addresses consent to assisted reproduction entirely within the context of marriage:

> (1) A consent to assisted reproduction by a married woman must be in a record signed by the woman and her husband. This requirement does not apply to the donation of eggs for assisted reproduction by another woman.
>
> (2) Failure of the husband to sign a consent required by subsection (1) of this section, before or after birth of the child, does not preclude a finding that the husband is the father of a child born to his wife if the wife and husband openly treated the child as their own.

In contrast, the UPA addresses the paternity in the context of assisted reproduction as follows:

> A man who provides sperm for, or consents to, assisted reproduction by a woman as provided in Section 704 with the intent to be the parent of her child, is a parent of the resulting child.

See UPA, § 703. In commentary to this section, the commission notes:

> The father-child relationship is created between a man and the resulting child if the man provides sperm for, or consents to, assisted reproduction by a woman with the intent to be the parent of her child, see § 704, infra. This provision reflects the concern for the best interests of nonmarital as well as marital children of assisted reproduction demonstrated throughout the Act. Given the dramatic increase in the use of ART in the United States during the past decade, it is crucial to clarify the parentage of all of the children born as a result of modern science.

In the *JMK* case, Kepl consented to the use of his sperm for the birth of the first child. Should his obligation to this child be lessened merely because the child was conceived by artificial insemination? Kepl and Brock had an on-going romantic relationship. Had that child been conceived naturally, it seems likely that Kepl would have been legally responsible for the support of the child. In the case of the second child, the relationship had devolved and Kepl's consent is doubtful. On the other hand, if Kepl had fathered a child with an estranged spouse with a similar lack of commitment and consent to the pregnancy, he would be required to support the child. From the perspective of the child's best interests, who should have responsibility?

The Washington Court of Appeals held that the artificial insemination statute protected Kepl and he could not be deemed to be the legal parent or be responsible for child support. *See In the Matter of the Parentage of J.M.K,* 89 P.3d 309 (Wash. Ct. App. 2004). However, the Washington Supreme Court reversed the appellate court and held that Kepl was the legal father of both boys, and that the donor protection statute relevant to sperm donors did not apply to *in vitro* fertilization, especially when donor had previously waived his rights and affirmed paternity in an affidavit. *In the Matter of the Parentage of J.M.K,* 119 P.3d 840 (Wash. 2005).

3. *Robert B. v. Susan B.* exemplifies a case of switched embryos. In this case, Robert and Denise have contracted with a fertility clinic to create embryos composed of Robert's sperm and donor eggs. Their goal is to implant the resulting embryos into Denise and thus become parents. Susan, a single woman, has contracted with the same fertility clinic. She too wishes to become a parent and has specifically sought an anonymous donor embryo to use in becoming pregnant. Because of a fertility clinic error, the embryo Susan gets is not an anonymous donor embryo, but one of those created at the behest of Robert and Denise. Should Robert have a claim to Susan's child? Isn't he in the position of an anonymous donor with respect to her and her intent? Isn't it an intrusion on Susan and her child for the court to allow Robert designation as a legal parent? Susan's life is now inextricably linked to Robert, a man with whom she has had no relationship. What about Susan's rights to privacy in this case? How are the child's best interests served in this case? Even if Robert is required to contribute to the support of the child, is this contribution outweighed by the confusion and emotional stress of being torn between the Robert/Denise family and Susan?

In another case of switched embryos, two couples seeking infertility treatment both had created embryos for implantation. In each case, the embryos were composed of sperm from the husband and eggs retrieved from the wife. Several embryos were implanted in one of the wives, Mrs. Fasano. She became pregnant with twins. Shortly thereafter the clinic realized that it had mistakenly included an embryo from another couple, the Perry-Rogers, among the embryos implanted in Mrs. Fasano. The clinic informed all of the parties and genetic testing, both before and after the birth of the twins, revealed that one of the twins was from a Fasano embryo, and the other, from a Perry-Rogers embryo. However, by the time the testing was concluded, the Fasanos had gone through the pregnancy and birth and had bonded to both of the twins. After a long custody battle, the Perry-Rogers were awarded custody of "their" child, due to their intent and genetic connection to the child. *See Perry-Rogers v. Fasano*, 715 N.Y.S.2d 19 (N.Y. App. Div. 2000). What about the concept of the traditional "unitary" family? The twins were born in the context of a marriage and the Fasanos had held both twins out as their children. Shouldn't these facts, accompanied by the gestation bond, have been compelling to the court? In this case, the Perry-Rogers were African-American and the Fasanos were white. Should that affect the calculus in determining parenthood? Contrast this case with that of *Robert B. v. Susan B.* Should genetics trump, no matter what the emotional cost to the child and gestational mother? Contrast with *In re the Parentage of J.M.K.*; if indeed genetics is preeminent, why should Kepl be able to repudiate responsibility for his genetic child?

For additional commentary on switched embryos and gametes, see John A. Robertson, *The Case of the Switched Embryos*, 25 Hastings Center Rep. 13 (1995); Leslie Bender, *Genes, Parents and Assisted Reproductive Technologies: ARTs, Mistakes, Sex, Race and Law*, 12 Colum. J. Gender & L. 1 (2003); *After Embryo Mix-up, Genetic Parents Get Baby*, N.Y. Times, May 27, 1999, at B10; Jeremy Manier, *Parents Seeking Defense Against Switched Babies*, Chi. Trib., Aug. 7, 1998; Tina Nguyen, *Mistakes Conceded in Newborn Mix-Up*, L.A. Times, Feb. 16, 1999.

4. *In re Paternity of Cheryl* is one of a raft of cases alleging misattributed paternity. As in this case, once a father has functioned as father with respect to his relationship with the child, courts are reluctant to disrupt the child's attachment, even if the now-disillusioned father seeks to sever his relationship with the child. Cheryl's "father" had voluntarily acknowledged paternity, but later sought DNA testing of the child to prove misat-

tributed fatherhood. This is increasingly easy to obtain. Billboards and popular press advertisements offer men innumerable opportunities to verify that they are truly fathers. For example, a recent news article reported on a laboratory offering a "Father's Day Special" for discounted paternity testing. *See* Tom Hundley, *DNA Paternity Test: Father's Day Special*, SEATTLE TIMES, May 15, 2005, at A2.

The issue of misattributed paternity, usually unintentional, is increasing prone to inadvertent discovery. There is anywhere from a ten percent to a thirty percent rate of unanticipated misattributed paternity. Such situations are often inadvertently discovered by a health care provider engaged in caring for a child. What options are available to a health care provider who discovers misattributed paternity? Should he disclose this fact to one or both of the parents? Should he disclose the issue to only the mother, leaving her to decide whether to further disclose? Or should the health care provider simply avoid discussing this issue unless there is a compelling medical reason to do so? For a discussion of the various approaches, see Jean McEwen, *Genetic Information, Ethics, and Information Relating to Biological Parenthood, in* 1 ENCYCLOPEDIA OF ETHICAL, LEGAL, AND POLICY ISSUES IN BIOTECHNOLOGY 359–62 (Thomas H. Murray & Maxwell J. Mehlman, eds. 2000). For additional discussion of issues flowing from misattributed paternity, *see* Melanie B. Jacobs, *When Daddy Doesn't Want to Be Daddy Anymore: An Argument Against Paternity Fraud Claims*, 16 YALE J.L. & FEMINISM 193 (2004); Cynthia R. Mabry, *Who is the Baby's Daddy (And Why is it Important For the Child to Know)*, 34 U. BALT. L. REV. 211 (2004); Steven N. Peskind, *Who's Your Daddy? An Analysis of Illinois' Law of Parentage and the Meaning of Parenthood*, 35 LOY. U. CHI. L.J. 811 (2004).

5. *R.R. v. M.H., Johnson v. Calvert,* and *In re Marriage of Buzzanca* illustrate some of the legal complexities of gestation, surrogacy, and intent in determining parenthood. *R.R. v. M.H.* is one of the many cases involving surrogate mothers. Surrogate motherhood became widely debated in the wake of the celebrated *Baby M.* case. In *Baby M.*, a couple, the Sterns, wanted to have a child, but Mrs. Stern was unable to become pregnant. Mr. Stern was committed to having a biological child, so the couple entered into a contract with a surrogate. Under the contract, the surrogate agreed to become pregnant using Mr. Stern's sperm through artificial insemination, carry the child and then turn it over to the Sterns, whereupon the Sterns would adopt the child. The surrogate's husband was also a party to the contract and his role was to agree to terminate any parental rights he had to the child. In return for the surrogacy, the surrogate mother was to be paid $10,000 plus medical expenses after the child was delivered to the Sterns. However, after the child was born, the surrogate changed her mind and sought to keep the child, absconding to Florida with the child. After a protracted custody battle, the New Jersey Supreme Court held that surrogate mother contracts conflicted with existing laws regarding termination of parental rights, prohibiting use of money in adoption, and legal constraint on legality of adoption. Although the Court ultimately awarded custody of the Baby M. to the Sterns, the surrogate mother retained parental rights and was allowed visitation with the child. *See In the Matter of Baby M.*, 537 A.2d 1227 (N.J. 1988).

The *R.R. v. M.H.* case, like the *Baby M.* case, finds the surrogacy contract unenforceable. The opinion highlights some of the features necessary in finding such an agreement enforceable:

(1) the mother's husband gave his informed consent to the agreement in advance;

(2) the mother is an adult and had had at least one successful pregnancy;

(3) the mother, her husband, and the intended parents have been evaluated for the soundness of their judgment and for their capacity to carry out the agreement;

(4) the father's wife is incapable of bearing a child without endangering her health;

(5) the intended parents are suitable persons to assume custody of the child; and

(6) all parties have the advice of counsel.

Moreover, the Court emphasized that the "mother and father may not, however, make a binding best-interests-of-the-child determination by private agreement. Any custody agreement is subject to a judicial determination of custody based on the best interests of the child." *See also In re the Marriage of Moschetta*, 30 Cal. Rptr. 2d 893 (Cal. Ct. App. 1994).

In most of the surrogate mother cases, the court analogizes the role of the intended mother to that of an adopting mother. This is particularly true, when, as in *Baby M.* and *R.H v. M.H.*, the surrogate is both the genetic and the gestational mother while the husband of the intended mother contributes his sperm. In all of these cases, the surrogate mother is viewed as the legal mother, who must terminate her parental rights in order for the surrogacy contract to be fulfilled. *See generally* Amy M. Larkey, *Redefining Motherhood: Determining Legal Maternity in Gestational Surrogacy Arrangements*, 88 DRAKE L. REV. 605 (2001); Ryiah Lilith, *The G.I.F.T. of Two Biological and Legal Mothers*, 139 AM. U.J. GENDER SOC. POL'Y & L. 207 (2001); Ilana Hurwitz, *Collaborative Reproduction: Finding the Child in the Maze of Legal Motherhood*, 33 CONN. L. REV. 127 (2000).

The analogy breaks down however, as the genetic links become more tenuous either by virtue of the surrogate being a gestational, but not genetic mother and/or the intended father not being the genetic father. Such is the case in *Johnson v. Calvert*. There, the embryo, composed of the gametes of a married couple, was implanted in a surrogate. During the course of the pregnancy, relations between the surrogate and the genetic parents deteriorated, and after the birth, the surrogate was unwilling to terminate her parental rights to the child. *Johnson v. Calvert* is a watershed case in that it is one of the first cases to articulate and give legal validation to intent. Although intent played a major role in the *Johnson v. Calvert* case, intention was bolstered by the genetic connection between the intended parents and the child. Indeed, intent was the tie-breaker between the rights of the genetic versus the gestational parents.

The concept of intended parenthood has been increasingly dispositive in determining legal parenthood. In the *Buzzanca* case, intent is the only determinant of parenthood. In this case, neither of the Buzzancas is genetically related to the embryo. By the time the child, Jaycee, is born, the Buzzancas have divorced. Jaycee is not genetically related to the surrogate and the surrogate exerts no claim over the child. The now ex-husband denies all rights and responsibilities with respect to the child. The Court notes that under traditional constructions of parenthood, the child could be in the position of having no parents; it determines that such a construction would clearly be contrary to public policy. It holds that the divorcing couple, who set the reproductive ball rolling during their marriage, are the legal parents of Jaycee on the basis of their intent and Mr. Buzzanca is forestalled from disclaiming his responsibilities. For other cases deciding legal parenthood on intent, see, for example, *McDonald v. McDonald*, 608 N.Y.S.2d 477 (App. Div. 1994); *L.M.S. v. S.L.S.*, 312 N.W.2d 853 (Wis. Ct. App. 1981). *See also*

Richard F. Storrow, *Parenthood by Pure Intention: Assisted Reproduction and the Functional Approach to Parentage*, 53 Hastings L.J. 597 (2002).

6. Reproductive technology has also opened the doors to parenthood for gay and lesbian couples. These parents are subject to the same difficulties heterosexual couples face as couples and parents. However in the case of gay/lesbian couples, there are substantially more parental complications if the couple splits up after the children are born. *See, e.g., Sharon S. v. Superior Court*, 73 P.3d 554 (Cal. 2003); *Maria B. v. Superior Court*, 13 Cal. Rptr. 3d 494 (Cal. Ct. App. 2004). For example, in *K.M. v. E.G.*, 13 Cal. Rptr. 3d 136 (Cal. Ct. App. 2004), K.M. donated eggs to her partner, E.G., so that they could have a shared child through *in vitro* fertilization. Twin girls are born and both women take on parenting responsibilities. Later K.M. seeks to adopt the twins, but E.G. is unwilling to agree. Shortly thereafter, the couple separates. The Court finds that despite her genetic connection to the twins, K.M. essentially waived her parental rights when donating her eggs, did not evidence clear intent to be a parent at the time the children were conceived, and is not a "natural" mother with parental rights. *See id.*

In an even more convoluted case, a lesbian couple, Carvin and Britain, seek to become parents. Britain becomes pregnant by artificial insemination, using the sperm of a gay male friend, Auseth, who initially had no interest in retaining parental involvement. Britain and Carvin care for L.B. with Carvin assuming most of the care-taking of the child. Carvin and Britain become estranged. Carvin seeks a co-parenting arrangement with respect to L.B. Soon afterwards, Britain re-establishes contact with Auseth and subsequently marries him. Auseth acknowledges paternity and becomes the legal parent along with Britian. Carvin seeks recognition of her parental status citing her long-term and substantial parental relationship with L.B. The Court of Appeals held that the Washington Uniform Parentage Act did not provide Carvin with parental rights. *See in re the Parentage of L.B.*, 89 P.3d 271 (Wash. Ct. App. 2004). The Washington Supreme Court reversed the Appeals Court, holding that the common law grants Carvin standing as a *de facto* parent, and that she stands in parity with an otherwise legal parent. *See in re the Parentage of L.B.*, No. 75626-1 (Wa. Nov. 3, 2005) *available at* http://www.courts.wa.gov/opinions. *De facto* parenthood results when: the natural or legal parent consented to and fostered the parent-like relationship; the petitioner and the child lived together in the same household; the petitioner assumed obligations of parenthood without expectation of financial compensation; and the petitioner has been in a parental role for a length of time sufficient to have established with the child a bonded, dependent relationship, parental in nature. In addition, a *de facto* parent must be one who has fully and completely undertaken a permanent, unequivocal, committed, and responsible parental role in the child's life. *See id.*

Kristine Renee H. v. Lisa Ann R. introduces the rationality of intended parenthood into the custody dispute of a lesbian couple and simultaneously furthers a gender-neutral approach to parenthood. In this case, Kristine is the gestational and genetic mother, but her partner, Lisa, demonstrates her intent by caring for the child, financially supporting the child, and holding out the child as her daughter. The Court holds that, using a gender-neutral interpretation of the California's UPA, Lisa can be construed to be a parent using the Act in the same way that a non-genetically related father has been deemed to be a parent. Lisa has "held out" the child as hers, and received her into her home as her child. To support its holding, the Court cites the case of *In re Nicholas H.*, 46 P.3d 932 (Cal. 2002), in which a man who has cared for the child of a former girlfriend for several years, seeks to be declared the child's legal parent. The child's mother, a drug addict, has become a street person, and the child's biological father is unknown. The California Supreme Court, in reversing the Appeals Court, held that when there is no competing claim by the biological father, a man who has fathered and held out the child as his can be found to be the legal parent, especially in a case like this when the mother is unfit. *See also in re Karen C.*, 124 Cal. Rptr. 2d 677 (Cal. Ct. App. 2002) (a similar case involving a child abandoned by her genetic parents into the care of a friend.)

For additional reading on the complex parenthood issues presented by gay, lesbian and other unconventional couples, see generally Deborah L. Forman, *Married with Kid and Moving: Achieving Recognition for Same-Sex Parents Under the Uniform Parentage Act*, 4 Whittier J. Child & Fam. Advoc. 241 (2005); Alona R. Croteau, *Voices in the Dark: Second Parent Adoptions When the Law is Silent*, 50 Loy. L. Rev. 675 (2004); Lynn D. Wardie, *Considering the Impact on Children and Society of "Lesbigay" Parenting*, 23 Quinnipiac L. Rev. 541 (2004); Stacy A. Werman, *There's Nothing Psychological About It: Defining a New Role for the Other Mother in a State that Treats her as Legally Invisible*, 24 Nova L. Rev. 907 (2000).

7. ART has also expanded reproductive opportunities in terms of time and age horizons. With the aid of donor ovum and pharmaceutical/hormonal treatment of the post-menopausal uterus, post-menopausal women can become "natural" mothers. In 2000, the CDC attempted to collect data on births by women between fifty and fifty-four and found that there were approximately 250. Although pregnancy at later ages may increase risk for complications like gestational diabetes, technology does make it possible for women to give birth well past menopause. This, of course, raises questions about who will parent the children if the elderly parents die before the children reach majority. One recent news report considered this issue as it reported the death of a sixty-four year old man who left a fifty-eight year old widow with twins, who had been born five months before with the help of assisted reproductive technology.

Even more challenging is posthumous reproduction. Technology allows couples or individuals to freeze their sperm, ovum, or embryos. This offers people who are ill with cancer or other diseases to preserve their reproductive options when treatment might otherwise obliterate their capacity to become parents. It offers couples facing medical crises an opportunity to concentrate their efforts on recovery from the critical illness, knowing that they are not sacrificing their hope of becoming parents. This is particularly useful for men, because sperm freeze well and have an almost infinite "shelf life," if properly stored. But what are the legal ramifications when the critically ill parent does not recover and the survivor embarks on parenthood alone with the aid of the deceased partner's gametes? Several cases have begun to consider some of the ramifications. In *In re Estate of William J. Kolacy*, 753 A.2d 1257 (N.J. Super. Ct. Ch. Div. 2000), a young man was diagnosed with testicular cancer and deposited sperm for future procreation. Unfortunately, he did not survive his cancer. After his death, his widow became pregnant using the deposited sperm and twin daughters were born. A court found the twins to be the legal heirs of William under the intestacy laws of New Jersey. In a similar case, a Massachusetts court used a three-part test to address inheritance by children posthumously conceived: Is there a genetic relationship between the deceased parent and the child? Did the deceased parent consent to becoming a posthumous parent? Did the deceased parent affirmatively express an intention to support any child resulting from the posthumous use of his/her gametes? *See Woodward v. Comm'r of Soc. Sec.*, 760 N.E.2d 257 (Mass. 2002). The Court determined that the posthumously conceived child was indeed a legal heir and thus was entitled to social security benefits from the deceased father. *See also Hart v. Shalala*, No. 94-3944 (E.D. La. 1994) (holding that child conceived posthumously entitled to social security benefits); Kristine S. Knaplund, *Postmortem Conception and a Father's Last Will*, 46 Ariz. L. Rev. 91 (2004); Brianne M. Star, *A Mat-*

ter of Life and Death: Posthumous Conception, 64 La. L. Rev. 613 (2004); Michael K. Elliott, *Tales of Parenthood From the Crypt: The Predicament of the Posthumously Conceived Child*, 39 Real Prop. Prob. & Tr. J. 47 (2004); Sharona Hoffman, *Birth After Death: Perpetuities and the New Reproductive Technologies*, 38 Ga. L. Rev. 575 (2004); Susan C. Stevenson-Popp, Comment, *"I Have Loved You In My Dreams": Posthumous Reproduction and the Need for Change in the Uniform Parentage Act*, 52 Cath. U.L. Rev. 727 (2003); Susan M. Kerr, et al., *Postmortem Sperm Procurement*, 157(6) J. Urology 2154 (1997); John A. Robertson, *Posthumous Reproduction*, 69 Ind. L.J. 1027 (1994). But see *Gillette-Netting v. Barnhart*, 231 F. Supp. 2d 961 (D. Ariz. 2002) (holding that Arizona's intestacy laws do not provide for posthumously conceived heirs and therefore children are not considered heirs under Arizona law and thus are not eligible for Social Security benefits.)

8. Yet another reproductive barrier that has begun to be questioned is the issue of prisoner reproductive rights. Courts thus far seem to be reluctant to find a right to assisted reproductive technology for prisoners. In *Goodwin v. Turner*, 908 F.2d 1395 (8th Cir. 1990), an inmate sought to be able to procreate by providing sperm via artificial insemination to his wife, while she was still young and the pregnancy would not be imperiled by maternal age. While the court found that Goodwin's right to procreate was not inconsistent with his status as a prisoner, they also held that the restrictions placed upon Goodwin were not inconsistent with the legitimate prison policy interest in treating all inmates—male and female—equally. Similarly in *Gerber v. Hickman*, 291 F.3d 617 (9th Cir. 2002), the Ninth Circuit, rehearing *en banc*, held that the right to procreate while in prison is not a protected Constitutional right, reversing the lower court and earlier Ninth Circuit decision. For additional comment on these cases, see Joseph J. Bozzuti, *Judicial Birth Control?: The Ninth Circuit's Examination of the Fundamental Right to Procreate in Gerber v. Hickman*, 77 St. John's L. Rev. 625 (2003); H.B. Hodge, *Prisoner of Love: Incarceration as a Contraceptive or Should Lifers Beget Life?*; Gerber v. Hickman, 22 Quinnipiac L. Rev. 947 (2004); Rachel Michael Kirkley, *Prisoners and Procreation: What Happened Between Goodwin and Gerber?*, 30 Pepp. L. Rev. 95 (2002). For articles focusing on the rights of female prisoners to procreate using ART, see Sarah L. Dunn, *The "ART" of Procreation: Why Assisted Reproduction Technology Allows for the Preservation of Female Prisoners' Right to Procreate*, 70 Fordham L. Rev. 2561 (2002); Lisa Walgenbach, *Artificial Insemination Behind Bars: the Boundaries of Due Process*, 36 Loy. L.A. L. Rev. 1357 (2003).

9. *Meracle v. Children's Services Society* is one of the earliest and well-known cases of "wrongful adoption". This tort, once considered an anomaly, now boasts a significant body of case law. Plaintiffs usually seek damages for pain, suffering and the excess costs related to the needs of the adopted child, rather than seeking to nullify the adoption. Typically, plaintiffs bring these cases on the basis of negligent and material misrepresentation on the part of the adoption agency. In order to succeed in such an action, the adoptive parents must show that they inquired about future risks of illness, and that their inquiry was rational and relevant with respect to the child's risks. Second, the plaintiffs must prove that the adoption agency falsely reassured the adoptive parents, knowing of the child's risks. And finally, the plaintiffs must allege that, but for the adoption agency's false reassurance, they would not have adopted the child. *See Roe v. Jewish Children's Bureau of Chicago*, 790 N.E.2d 882 (Ill. App. Ct. 2003) (parents allege that the agency made false statements regarding the mental health of their son's biological mother and that the son later developed a mental illness.); *Wolford v. Children's Home Soc. of W. Va.*, 17 F. Supp. 2d 577 (S.D. W. Va. 1998) (prospective adoptive parents inquire whether the child's unusual facial feature were the result of fetal alcohol syn-

drome and adoption agency conceals fact the child's birth mother was an alcoholic.) Generally emotional distress damages are limited to cases in which there has been extreme and outrageous misconduct or misrepresentation.

At the present time, every state has disclosure statutes that allow adoptive parents access to known medical and relevant family medical history. In order to be liable for wrongful adoption, the adoption agency must have misrepresented known medical facts about the adoptee. For example, in another case involving a genetic disorder, *Foster by Foster v. Bass*, 575 So. 2d 967 (Miss. 1990), the Court held that an adoption agency could not be held liable for negligent misrepresentation when the adopted child's mental retardation was due to undiagnosed phenylketonuria (PKU), a potentially disabling genetic metabolic disorder. The failure to obtain the PKU screen was a result of failure on the part of the neonatal physician. The court held that the agency could not reasonably have anticipated such a failure and thus could not be negligent for failing to disclose unknown information. *See also Mallette v. Children's Friend and Service,* 661 A.2d 67 (R.I. 1995) (adoption agency does not have duty to investigate genetic background of child.); *Gibbs v. Ernst,* 647 A.2d 882 (Pa. 1994) (agency had no duty to investigate child's mental and physical health).

The tort of wrongful adoption is grounded within the constraints of tort law. Although an agency has to be certain that what it reveals to the prospective parents is true, they are not required to conduct *de novo* investigations into the child's medical and family history. For additional reading on the nuances of wrongful adoption tort actions, see Harriet Dinegar Milks, Annotation, *"Wrongful Adoption" Causes of Action Against Adoption Agencies Where Children Have or Develop Mental or Physical Problems that are Misrepresented or Not Disclosed to Adoptive Parents,* 74 A.L.R.5th 1 (2005); Jennifer Emmaneel, *Beyond Wrongful Adoption: Expanding Adoption Agency Liability to Include a Duty to Investigate and a Duty to Warn,* 29 Golden Gate U. L. Rev. 181 (1999); Michelle A. Bernstein, *Extending Tort of Negligent Misrepresentation to Adoption Context*—Mallette v. Children's Friend & Service, 661 A.2d 67 (R.I. 1995), 30 Suffolk U. L. Rev. 615 (1997); Amanda Trefethen, *The Emerging Tort of Wrongful Adoption,* 11 J. Contemp. Legal Issues 620 (2000).

The American Society of Human Genetics (ASHG) and the American College of Medical Genetics (ACMG) have issued two policy statements related to genetic testing in the context of adoption. The latest, published in 2000, recommends the following:

> All genetic testing of newborns and children in the adoption process should be consistent with the tests performed on all children of a similar age for the purposes of diagnosis or of identifying appropriate prevention strategies.
>
> Because the primary justification for genetic testing of any child is a timely medical benefit to the child, genetic testing of newborns and children in the adoption process should be limited to testing for conditions which manifest themselves during childhood or for which preventive measures or therapies may be undertaken during childhood.
>
> In the adoption process, it is not appropriate to test newborns and children for the purpose of detecting genetic variations of or predispositions to physical, mental, or behavioral traits within the normal range.

See American College of Medical Genetics/American Society of Human Genetics, *Genetic Testing in Adoption,* 66 Am. J. Hum. Genet. 761 (2000). In formulating its recommendation, ACMG/ASHG used an interest analysis weighing the best interests of the child as preeminent and secondarily considering the interests of the adoptive parents, the birth parents, the adoption agency, and the public at large. *See id.* Would the ASHG/ACMG recommendations provide for the testing of a child with a family history of Huntington disease, a late-onset fatal neurodegenerative disease? Do adoptive parents deserve a greater guarantee than natural parents get? *See also* A. Lorandos, *Secrecy and Genetics in Adoption Law and Practice*, 27 Loy. U. Chi. L.J. 277 (1996).

C. Genetic Screening and Diagnosis

As we have seen in the prenatal context, prenatal or preconception genetic diagnosis of genetic risks can allow parents the opportunity to forego parenthood or terminate a pregnancy. This capacity, however, has placed prenatal genetic testing squarely in the crosshairs of societal controversy over selective abortion. Prenatal testing has also raised ire in the disability rights community; is a child with a disability less valuable in our society? In addition, there is concern that the ever-increasing prenatal testing opportunities have resulted in parents who enter pregnancy more tentatively than in the past, and may cause parents to delay their attachment and emotional investment in their fetus.

Genetic testing is now available in several different contexts. Diagnostic testing can reveal if an individual has inherited a genetic mutation in one or both of a pair of alleles. In the case of the recessive trait, the individual may be a carrier of a disorder, but not experience the illness themselves. Cystic Fibrosis (CF) and Tay-Sachs are such disorders. Only if two carriers parent a child will the child be at risk for inheriting two copies of the mutation and have the disease. However, while Tay-Sachs is a genetic disorder resulting in a distinctive phenotypic disease and early death, CF patients may experience a variety of symptom complexes of variable severity.

Other genetic mutations are dominant in nature. Huntington disease, Achondroplasia, and several incurable, neurodegenerative diseases are transmitted in an autosomal dominant fashion. A parent with the mutation will develop the disease and will transmit it to fifty percent of their progeny. In these aforementioned autosomal dominant disorders, there is a high positive predictive value resulting in expression of the disease. In contrast, the breast cancer susceptibility mutations (BRCA1/2) and colon cancer susceptibility genes are also inherited in an autosomal dominant manner. These mutations, however, result in a greater susceptibility, but not a certainty, of cancer.

As genetic tests enter the marketplace, they challenge physicians, medical policy analysts and patients. Although genetic tests provide a new level of knowledge about human physiology and pathology, they also raise profound questions about when a test is indicated. When is a test sufficiently well developed to be used as a diagnostic tool in medical practice? What does the test tell the patient and the doctor? If the test reveals information only, but offers no opportunity to mitigate illness, should the test be covered by health care payers? What are the downsides of knowledge revealed by a genetic test? Is there stigma attached to a positive test that is harmful to the individual? When does a test merit widespread use as a screening modality? These are just some of the questions that have come to the forefront as genetic testing has moved from the laboratory to the market. Virtually all genetic testing modalities require careful analysis of their clinical validity, clinical utility, risks and benefits. The following article summarizes the state of genetic medicine and highlights the challenges faced by providers and patients.

Wylie Burke, *Genomic Medicine: Genetic Testing*

347 New Eng. J. Med. 1867 (2002)

Introduction

Genetic testing can provide dramatic clinical benefits. A child known to have Multiple Endocrine Neoplasia Type 2 (MEN2) can be spared medullary carcinoma by a prophylactic thyroidectomy and an adult with hereditary hemochromatosis can be spared cirrhosis by the early initiation of phlebotomy treatment. Genetic testing can also provide diagnostic and prognostic information that aids in difficult decision-making. For example, a test for a deletion in the dystrophin gene, the cause of Duchenne Muscular Dystrophy, can be used to identify women who are carriers for this condition. A carrier may avoid having an affected child by avoiding pregnancy or, alternatively, by undergoing prenatal testing for Duchenne Muscular Dystrophy, with possible pregnancy termination if the fetus is found to be affected.

As these examples illustrate, most genetic tests now available address questions related to rare or uncommon diseases. Even hemochromatosis, often described as a common genetic disease, has a prevalence of 0.5 percent or less. However, the scope of genetic testing is expanding to include tests that assess genetic risk for common diseases like cancer and cardiovascular disease.

Definition of genetic testing

A genetic test is "the analysis of human DNA, RNA, chromosomes, proteins and certain metabolites in order to detect heritable disease-related genotypes, mutations, phenotypes, or karyotypes for clinical purposes." This definition reflects the broad range of technologies that can be used in the testing process. Genetic tests also have diverse purposes, including the diagnosis of genetic disease in newborns, children, and adults; the identification of future health risks; the prediction of drug responses; and the assessment of risks to future children.... [A] comprehensive listing of available tests can be found at the GeneTests-GeneClinics web site.

Genetic diagnosis

Genetic testing is often the best way to confirm a diagnosis in a patient with signs or symptoms suggestive of genetic disease. The technology chosen depends on both the clinical question and the predictive value of the available tests. For a young patient with medullary cancer of the thyroid, for example, the identification of a mutation in the RET oncogene confirms that the cancer is a manifestation of MEN2. This rare disorder accounts for approximately one quarter of medullary thyroid cancer cases, with implications for the patient and family members; the RET mutation test can identify 85 percent to 95 percent of affected people.

Similarly, testing for the presence of dystrophin gene deletions using DNA-based technology is now the preferred diagnostic test for Duchenne Muscular Dystrophy, when clinical signs and symptoms suggest the diagnosis. A positive test confirms the diagnosis. A muscle biopsy is needed if the DNA-based test is negative, because a negative test occurs in about 30 percent of patients with Duchenne Muscular Dystrophy, as a result of mutations in the dystrophin gene that are not detected by current testing.

This genetic complexity is termed allelic heterogeneity—the occurrence of multiple different mutations (or alleles) in the same gene, all of which may lead to disease—and is a common phenomenon. For example, hundreds of different disease-causing mutations have been found for the cystic fibrosis gene and for the BRCA1 and BRCA2 genes associated with susceptibility to breast and ovarian cancer.

In contrast, the most common form of sickle cell anemia, a disease occurring in one in 700 African-Americans, is caused by a single specific mutation in the beta-globin gene, resulting in a modified hemoglobin termed Hemoglobin S (HbS). Both hematological and DNA-based tests are available. Diagnostic testing can be done reliably by hemoglobin electrophoresis, but the DNA-based test for the HbS mutation is an important additional option because it makes prenatal diagnosis possible.

Chromosomal disorders represent a different category of genetic diseases, in which chromosomal segments containing multiple genes are duplicated, deleted or translocated to different chromosomes; these are diagnosed by cytogenetic tests. Starting in the 1950s, methods for preparing human chromosomes made it possible to identify the chromosomal basis of conditions like Down syndrome, which is caused by the presence of an extra chromosome 21. Subsequent technical refinements allowed the identification of more subtle abnormalities in chromosomal structure. Recently, the technique of fluorescence in situ hybridization (FISH), in which specific chromosomal regions are identified by fluorescent DNA probes, has identified small chromosomal duplications and deletions missed by previous methods. For example, 22q11 deletion syndrome, a genetic condition caused by small deletions of chromosome 22 results in a syndrome characterized by a varying mix of learning disabilities, palatal abnormalities and congenital heart disease. Using FISH, it has been possible to show that six previously described clinical syndromes, each with an overlapping cluster of physical and cognitive deficits; all represent manifestations of the 22q11 deletion syndrome.

Family risk

A genetic diagnosis often indicates that other family members are at risk for the same condition. Genetic testing can help in evaluating this risk. For example, when the causative mutation for a genetic condition is known, presymptomatic diagnosis of family members is often possible, and may offer an important opportunity for disease prevention. Thus, after a person is diagnosed with MEN2 and the causative RET mutation identified, testing of all first-degree relatives is recommended so that prophylactic thyroidectomy can be offered to those who inherited the mutation. A small number of other inherited cancer syndromes, such as familial adenomatous polyposis, offer a similar opportunity.

Identification of future risk does not necessarily lead to treatment options, however. Genetic testing for Huntington disease, an autosomal dominant condition causing progressive motor and cognitive dysfunction starting in mid-life, allows people with an affected parent to determine whether they have inherited the mutation that confers disease. If the mutation is present, the risk to develop Huntington disease is virtually 100 percent, given a normal life span. Yet, no effective intervention or preventive treatment is available. The choice to be tested is thus highly personal, and test results have the potential to be stigmatizing or psychologically harmful. For this reason, careful pre-test counseling is recommended. A 10-year experience in the UK suggests that only about 20 percent of those at risk for Huntington disease pursue such testing.

For X-linked and autosomal recessive conditions, genetic testing often has the purpose of identifying family members who are carriers—that is, individuals who are themselves unaffected but who are at risk to have affected children. As with decisions about Huntington disease testing, tests for carrier status are done primarily for personal, rather than medical, reasons: in this case to facilitate reproductive decision-making. For women who are carriers of an X-linked recessive disease, each male child has a 50 percent risk of inheriting the disease. With autosomal recessive diseases, such as sickle cell anemia or cystic fibrosis, the risk to have an affected child occurs only if both parents are carriers, and is then 25 percent for each pregnancy. If carrier status is confirmed, prenatal testing can be offered for pregnancies at risk, to provide an opportunity to inform parents about the genetic diagnosis prior to birth, so that they can decide what course of action is best for them.

...

Genetic testing is also sometimes used to identify mildly affected individuals within the family. For example, mild cases of 22q11 deletion syndrome have been documented among parents and siblings of people diagnosed with the condition. Identifying these affected relatives may explain otherwise unexpected clinical findings, and also provides information about recurrence risks within the family: if a parent is affected, the condition can be passed on to future children.

Clinical validity of genetic tests

These different examples help to illustrate the importance of a test's clinical validity, defined as the accuracy with which a test predicts a clinical outcome. Clinical validity reflects both the sensitivity of the test—the proportion of affected people with a positive test—and the penetrance of the mutations identified by the test. Penetrance refers to the proportion of mutation carriers who will manifest the disease; in the case of genetic diseases like Duchenne Muscular Dystrophy, the proportion is virtually 100 percent in a normal life span.

Many DNA-based tests have reduced sensitivity because they identify only a subset of causative mutations. This limitation is due to the state of scientific knowledge—some causative mutations may not yet be known—and also to the properties of clinically available tests. For some conditions, a test for all known mutations would be prohibitively expensive, leading to a pragmatic trade-off between cost and sensitivity. Because scientific knowledge and costs change over time, so will the sensitivity and predictive value of available tests.

Reduced sensitivity has important implications for testing of family members. For example, when a child with Duchenne Muscular Dystrophy is found to have a dystrophin deletion, the carrier status of female relatives can be determined by the same test. However, if the affected child does not have an identifiable mutation, the test cannot be used effectively for either carrier status or prenatal diagnosis. An alternative approach—linkage analysis—is possible if two or more family members are affected and available for testing; this approach identifies patterns of DNA markers associated with the disease in a particular family. But if the affected child is the only known member of the family with Duchenne Muscular Dystrophy, linkage cannot be established, and this testing approach will not work.

When a genetic test has high sensitivity, people can be tested for carrier status without reference to the test results of an affected family member. This is the case for sickle cell anemia, which is caused by a specific mutation in the beta-globin gene. In contrast, cystic fibrosis testing can identify many (but not all) carriers in the general population; tests currently available utilize the most common CF mutations and usually detect 85 percent of carriers. (Use of genetic testing in population screening is discussed in another article in this series.)

Most well-defined genetic diseases are caused by mutations with high penetrance and, as a result, have high positive predictive value (PPV)—that is, the likelihood of disease is high when the test is positive. This observation may contribute to the expectation that current genetic tests are always highly predictive. However, even when mutations are highly penetrant, the negative predictive value (NPV) of a test—the likelihood that disease is absent if the test is negative—can be low, if the test fails to identify all causative mutations.

In the future, many genetic tests will be based on genetic contributions to common disease risk. As described below, such tests will have lower positive and negative predictive value than most currently available genetic tests, but will have potential implications for a larger number of people.

Genetic testing to improve preventive care

The use of genetic testing to guide preventive care is likely to be an important byproduct of the Human Genome Project. This use is demonstrated by testing for MEN2, to identify people at high risk for medullary thyroid cancer. Additional testing opportunities are emerging. For example, testing for BRCA1 and BRCA2 mutations provides an opportunity to identify people who may benefit from tailored screening and prevention protocols based on their genetic susceptibility to breast and ovarian cancer. Penetrance for BRCA1 and BRCA2 mutations is, however, lower than for MEN2. Estimates of the lifetime risk of breast cancer associated with these mutations range from 26 percent to 85 percent; risk for ovarian cancer is also elevated, but to a lesser extent than for breast cancer, and risk estimates also vary.

In conditions with low penetrance, more evidence is needed to establish the efficacy of interventions to reduce risk. In the case of MEN2, the evidence favoring prophylactic thyroidectomy derives from the observation of a low medullary thyroid cancer rate in patients who had the surgery. The power of such studies derives from historical data demonstrating a lifetime risk of cancer of close to 100 percent in untreated MEN2, with associated high premature mortality. When a genetic test predicts an increased risk, rather than a certainty of future disease, the efficacy of interventions to reduce risk is more difficult to measure, particularly when the level of risk is uncertain, as with BRCA1 and BRCA2. If risk is initially over-estimated—a common bias when mutations conferring risk are identified in families selected for high risk—the efficacy of an intervention may be greatly over-estimated in the absence of controlled observations.

This issue will take on greater importance as genetic factors conferring smaller risks are identified. Mutations associated with high risk account for only a small percentage of common diseases: BRCA1/2 mutations are a rare cause of breast cancer, for example. The largest genetic contribution to health is in the form of common variants that increase or decrease risk to a moderate degree. Two examples offer insights into the implications of genetic tests of this kind: hemochromatosis and factor V Leiden.

Hemochromatosis is a condition involving excess accumulation of iron. Over time, iron overload can occur in body tissues, resulting in complications such as cirrhosis, diabetes, cardiomyopathy, and arthritis. Two mutations in the HFE gene, C282Y and H63D, promote excess iron accumulation. C282Y is the more severe mutation, and the C282Y/C282Y genotype accounts for a majority of clinically penetrant cases. But current data suggest that a substantial proportion of people with this genotype do not develop clinical disease. A pooled analysis found that patients with the HFE genotypes C282Y/H63D and H63D/H63D are also at increased risk of iron overload, yet overall, fewer than 1 percent of people with these genotypes are likely to develop disease. Thus, DNA-based tests for hemochromatosis identify a genetic risk, rather than the disease itself. Environmental factors such as diet and exposure to alcohol or other hepatotoxins may modify clinical outcome in hemochromatosis, and variation in other genes affecting iron metabolism may also be a factor. As a result, the clinical condition of iron overload is most reliably diagnosed by biochemical evidence of excess body iron. Whether it is beneficial to screen asymptomatic people for genetic risk of iron overload is a matter of debate.

Factor V Leiden offers another example. This factor V gene mutation is relatively common, ranging in prevalence from 1 percent to 5 percent in different American ethnic groups, and results in up to an 8-fold increased risk of venous thrombosis. Estimates of the annual incidence of venous thrombosis in people heterozygous with factor V Leiden range from 0.19 percent to 0.58 percent, suggesting a lifetime risk of 12 percent to 30 percent. However, more than half of the thromboembolic events associated with factor V Leiden occur when other risk factors—such as surgery, oral contraceptives and bed rest—are also present. Both gene-gene and gene-environment interactions are known to contribute to overall risk of venous thrombosis. Thus factor V Leiden, like mutations in the HFE gene, is a risk factor rather than a diagnostic test.

As with predictive testing for hemochromatosis, the clinical utility of factor V Leiden testing is not established. Although a positive test identifies people with increased risk of venous thrombosis, the implications for management are unclear. Interventions such as prophylactic anti-coagulation therapy or avoidance of risk factors might be of considered, but evidence of clinical benefit from such interventions in this genetic risk group is so far lacking.

The issue of specificity of treatment is an important one. New genetic tests to assess risk for common disease risks are likely to have properties similar to factor V Leiden. They will identify relatively common genetic traits that interact with other genetic and environmental factors to increase risk. Their clinical utility will depend on the availability of effective interventions to reduce risk that are specific to the genetic risk state. In the absence of genotype-specific interventions, knowledge about genetic susceptibility could cause stigma without compensating health benefits, or even harm health by reducing motivation to pursue risk-reducing measures.

Informed consent and genetic counseling

Detailed counseling is usually provided prior to genetic testing, to ensure informed decisions about the use of tests with complex personal implications. Genetic counseling is traditionally "non-directive" that is, counseling provides sufficient information to allow families or individuals to determine the best course of action for themselves but avoids making testing recommendations. This approach was developed in the context of genetic tests for reproductive decision-making and untreatable conditions such as Huntington disease, where the value of testing is determined by personal preference.

When tests are done to improve clinical management, pre-test counseling needs differ. A testing recommendation is appropriate, for example, when a test offers an opportunity to prevent disease—e.g., in the case of MEN2 testing. In the future, some tests for genetic risk factors may become a routine part of clinical practice, potentially falling under a general informed consent for clinical care. In approaching the question of informed consent for any specific genetic test, however, the potential social and family implications need to be acknowledged, including the potential for discrimination on the basis of genetic risk status, and the potential that the predictive value of genetic information may be over-estimated. These considerations suggest that clinicians should err on the side of careful informed consent procedures for genetic testing, unless outcome studies suggest otherwise.

Conclusions

Genetic testing already offers important opportunities for diagnosis and assessment of genetic risk. The sensitivity of tests for rare conditions will continue to improve as new causative mutations are identified and better tests developed. Increasingly, tests will be available to determine genetic risk for common diseases, but these will often have limited predictive value. Evaluating the clinical utility of these tests will require careful assessment of the risks and benefits of testing; the availability of specific measures to reduce risk in genetically susceptible people will be a major consideration.

One of the difficult challenges in the use of genetic tests is a constantly changing knowledge base. Fortunately, a growing number of internet sites are available to provide clinicians with up-to-date information. Research to evaluate interventions based on genetic risk will take on increasing importance as new tests become available. Because tests to assess risk are likely to precede knowledge about risk reduction, an on-going dialogue involving clinicians and policy makers will be needed, to develop consensus about their appropriate clinical use.

* * *

At the present time, testing is available in three major contexts. First is newborn genetic screening, in which all infants are tested to rule out certain genetic diseases. Second is diagnostic testing to confirm present or future genetic disease or carrier status. Third is susceptibility and predictability testing to determine increased propensity for development of disease in the future.

1. Newborn Screening and Genetic Testing of Children

Newborn screening historically sought to identify infants born with inborn errors of metabolism as early as possible so that timely intervention could mitigate the harm and improve the overall outcome. One of the earliest victories in newborn screening was testing for phenylketonuria (PKU), a genetic disorder that makes it impossible for the individual to break down phenylalanine, an amino acid found in many foodstuffs. In 1960, Dr. Richard Guthrie developed a screening test that could determine PKU from a small sample of infant blood by testing for presence of PKU disease metabolites. Although not a direct genetic test, the PKU metabolite test accurately reveals the genetic disorder. Patients diagnosed in infancy with PKU can forestall the mental retardation and other effects of the disease by consuming a phenylalanine-free diet.

This testing originated as a medical practice modality and eventually evolved into the standard of care, ultimately becoming public health law as a result of legislative advocacy on the part of parent and patient support groups. By 1973, forty-three states had mandatory testing and public health authorities became the prime movers for newborn screening programs. In 1976, federal legislation was passed to support state genetic service programs that would develop screening programs for genetic disease. The newborn screening and testing movement has increased in volume and vitality over the last three decades providing testing for a growing number of metabolic conditions, hemoglobinopathies (blood cell disorders), endocrine disorders, and other congenital medical problems. Moreover, there has been substantial improvement in the testing technologies, notably through multiplex technology (laboratory techniques that test for several disorders on one test "platform") and the improved predictive values of the tests themselves.

By 2005, all fifty states had substantial newborn screening programs. All fifty states require newborns to be screened for PKU, congenital thyroid disease, and benign hyperphenylalanemia. All but one state requires all newborns to be tested for sickle cell trait, sickle cell disease and thalassemia (hemoglobinopathies). In addition to those that are required, virtually all of the states have a list of newborn screening tests offered but not yet required, offered to select populations, or in the pipeline for the immediate future. Over eighty newborn screening tests are now available. *See* National Newborn Screening and Genetics Resource Center, National Newborn Screening Status Report, http://genes-r-us.uthscsa.edu/nbsdisorders.pdf (2005). Most recently, the American College of Medical Genetics (ACMG), in collaboration with the U.S. Health Resources Services Administration (HRSA) has outlined a process by which to rationalize state newborn screening programs to better evaluate outcome data. The role of this report with respect to public health screening programs is fully discussed in Chapter 10. The ACMG/HRSA Panel concluded that twenty-nine conditions are appropriate for newborn screening and met criteria for availability of a screening test, opportunities for efficacious treatment, and sufficient knowledge of the natural history of the disorder. The ACMG/HRSA Panel's recommendations represent a substantial increase in the number of "standard" newborn screening tests, far outpacing the number provided in the past. It remains to be seen whether the ASCMG/HRSA recommendations become the new standard for medical care of the newborn. Assuming that such expansive newborn screening becomes the standard of medical care, it will likely add to the body of case law related to newborn screening, which, at present, is largely limited to negligent failure to screen for congenital hypothyroidism and PKU.

Humana of Kentucky v. McGee

834 S.W.2d 711 (Ky. Ct. App. 1992)

JUDGE GUDGEL

...

Brian was born on May 1, 1977, at Humana Hospital. On that date KRS 214.155 required hospitals to cause the performance of a PKU test on each newborn infant no sooner than 24 hours after birth. The test requires blood to be drawn from the infant's heel and to be placed directly on filter paper which is part of a form provided by and returned to the state laboratory in Frankfort. The blood specimen is analyzed and the results then are returned to the hospital. The blood of an infant who suffers from PKU will show an elevated level of phenylalanine, which is an amino acid formed from protein. As PKU is a metabolic disorder which causes the body to be unable to process phenylalanine, the ingestion of protein causes abnormal levels of phenylalanine to accumulate in the affected child's body and to damage the developing central nervous system, especially the brain, resulting in mental retardation and a likelihood of major seizures. Untreated PKU children are totally dependent as adults and require lifelong medical care from families or institutions. The harmful accumulation of phenylalanine, however, can easily be prevented if the diagnosis of PKU is made at or near birth, as the treatment is a simple case of restricting a child's dietary intake of proteins. With timely treatment, a PKU child can be expected to lead a normal, healthy and productive life.

Brian's hospital record indicates that on May 19, 1977, when he was eighteen days old, hospital personnel noted in his record that the state laboratory reported that Brian's PKU test result was negative. Although developmental problems were subsequently noted during Brian's infancy and early childhood, Brian's parents and doctors assumed that he was progressing slowly or that he was suffering from some vague psychological difficulties. Upon his entering first grade, however, it became apparent that Brian had suffered significant developmental delays. He then was referred to the University of Kentucky Child Evaluation Center, and in 1983 he was diagnosed as having classic PKU.

The evidence established that, barring "biologic variation," a PKU test of Brian's blood soon after birth should have been positive. There was no entry in Brian's hospital record by either a nurse or a lab technician, however, to show that a blood specimen was actually taken from him. His hospital chart reflected only that upon Brian's birth, the doctor routinely ordered that a PKU test be performed "on the day of discharge," and a notation of "009" following that order indicated that the McKees were charged for the test when the order was transmitted from the nursery to Humana's laboratory. The record also shows that the night nursery staff forwarded the test order to the laboratory, and that the nurse made an entry in the nursery log book indicating that a PKU test would be performed. Although Brian's mother testified that he had a small bandage on his heel while hospitalized as a newborn infant, she could not recall whether she observed the bandage during his hospitalization immediately after birth or during a subsequent hospitalization a few days later. It was undisputed that a blood specimen was drawn from Brian during the second hospitalization.

Sally New, one of Humana's corporate representatives and the Director of Nursing Administration, testified that the fact of taking a blood specimen for a PKU sample was a significant piece of clinical information. She also affirmed the existence of standards by which Humana was required to ensure that recorded entries of all significant pieces of clinical information were made in patients' hospital charts.

The McKees introduced into evidence Humana's written "PKU Procedures" which provide a step-by-step outline of the actions which Humana personnel are required to take in obtaining PKU samples. Brian's chart reflects that in his case, requisite procedures were not met as follows:

1. The spaces for date and time on the requisition slip were left blank, as was the space for the initials of the person who drew the blood, and the lab technician did not stamp the requisition slip with the laboratory timer clock;

2. The lab technician did not date or initial the state laboratory 228 form (Lab 228 form) for PKU screening; and

3. According to the records of Brian's physician, the latter received no letter from Humana regarding the test results.

The record shows that the morning of the alleged test, May 4, 1977, was an unusually busy one, and that apparently one laboratory technician drew blood from seven infants for PKU testing and placed that blood on the filter paper portions of Lab 228 forms. This unidentified technician failed to record his or her initials on the requisition slips or the screening cards, however, or to stamp the slips in any of the seven cases. Moreover, although each Lab 228 form is supposed to be marked with the infant's name and patient number, in Brian's case the night nurse mistakenly entered on the form the patient number of Brian's mother (60804-2) rather than that of Brian (60051-0). Brian's Lab 228 form does include a correction as to his patient number, as well as a handwritten notation as to the McKees' home telephone number, both of which were shown by the evidence to have been entered on the form after Brian's blood specimen allegedly was placed on the Lab 228 form and returned to the hospital laboratory.

Ordinarily, after conducting a PKU test, hospital laboratory personnel enter the child's name, patient number and other data into a PKU log book. The log book entry for Brian, however, erroneously included his mother's patient number rather than Brian's. The evidence also showed that although it was not customary for night nursery personnel to write telephone numbers on the Lab 228 forms, the May 4 Lab 228 forms for both Brian and a McCullah baby did contain telephone numbers. Moreover, the evidence showed that the Lab 228 forms identified Brian and the McCullah baby by nearly identical patient numbers (60804-2 and 60805-9), although Brian's actual patient number was 60051-0. Further, the evidence showed that the patient number of yet another baby boy in the nursery on May 4, the Ping baby, was 60408-2, which also was very similar to the patient number of 60804-2 erroneously listed on Brian's Lab 228 form.

Dr. Strand, Humana's Director of Pathology, testified that hospital procedures provide for a laboratory technician to obtain the Lab 228 forms from the nursery staff, and to then locate and identify the babies whose blood will be drawn. The foot of each baby's bassinet contains the baby's patient number, which the technician matches to the baby's patient number as shown on the Lab 228 form. The technician does not rely upon either the baby's name or the patient number shown on the requisition slip. The testimony adduced on behalf of the McKees therefore showed that on May 4, 1977, the unidentified technician who was attempting to find a baby boy with the erroneous patient number of 60804-2 would not have found Brian, as he was in a bassinet with his correct patient number of 60051-0.

Bernice Brown, a laboratory employee, testified that she noticed when Brian's Lab 228 form was brought to the laboratory that it was marked with the wrong patient number. She called the nursery to point out this mistake, but apparently nothing more was done to follow up this call.

In January 1984, which was several months after Brian's PKU was diagnosed, a Cabinet for Human Resources, Division of Maternal and Child Health employee in Frankfort, Beth Harp, received a telephone call from Humana's Medical Records Director, Judy Owens. Ms. Harp testified that Ms. Owens asked whether a positive PKU test had ever been obtained on Brian, and stated that Ms. Owens said "she had the chart in front of her and there was nothing written in the baby's chart about a PKU test; there was nothing in the chart ... there was not a positive; there was not a negative. There was nothing written in the chart." Ms. Harp further testified that Ms. Owens told her that normally Humana would have placed a copy of the PKU test result in the chart, and that the clinic where Brian's doctor worked also "had nothing in the chart." However, evidence was also adduced to show that although Brian's specialist for his PKU treatment, Dr. Mabry, apparently received no answer to two routine requests for Brian's birth chart after he began to treat Brian in 1983 and did not finally receive the chart until after this litigation began, at that time Brian's chart did contain a written notation which showed that a negative PKU test result had been received. Bernice Brown, the laboratory technician who earlier had attempted to look into the suspected mistake as to Brian's hospital number, only reluctantly conceded that she had no actual memory of receiving and transcribing a negative test result.

Affirmative evidence was adduced by the McKees negating the probability that the state laboratory was negligent in testing the PKU blood specimen submitted by Humana. Further, Humana conceded in an interrogatory read to the jury that it knew of no facts which would indicate any faulty action by the state. The McKees also offered testimony through Suzanne Black and Dr. B.F. Brown regarding the procedures followed by the state laboratory.

Ms. Black, a microbiologist who was employed in 1977 as a state laboratory technician, testified regarding the state laboratory's written procedures for performing the Guthrie assay for PKU screening, and regarding the quality control procedures which "assured the consistency from test to test." She indicated that the screening test was designed to be "overly sensitive" so as to identify all babies who might possibly have the PKU disorder. Moreover, if there was any doubt as to the integrity of the testing procedure, such as if a testing tray of filter paper blood specimens was accidentally knocked over, the tests were repeated on additional samples of blood-impregnated filter paper from the infants' Lab 228 forms. Finally, Ms. Black indicated that the state laboratory was adequately staffed and managed.

Dr. Brown, Director of the State Division of Laboratory Services in 1977, testified regarding the quality control of the PKU test. He testified that the Guthrie assay method is "one of the best controlled tests that I know of." Whenever a positive result occurred on one of the specimens being tested, the technician would repeat the tests on new filter paper samples from each of the subjects included in the first tray of specimens in order to verify both the positive result and the correct identity of the positive specimen so as to "make sure that there are no possibilities of clerical error in reporting." In regard to the Guthrie assay method, which includes twelve known controls on each tray of one hundred and one specimens, Dr. Brown testified in conclusion that "I don't know of any other procedure that has that many safeguards in it. There's a very high number of known specimens to each known control to each batch."

Further, both Dr. Mabry and Dr. Guthrie, the inventor of the Guthrie assay method, testified that any blood specimen which might have been taken from Brian four days after birth would have tested positive for PKU. Although they recognized that the literature reports several instances of a so-called "biologic variation," both physicians rejected its application here.

Humana attempted to show that due to "biologic variations" which may cause the measurable levels of blood phenylalanine to rise unusually slowly, some PKU children do not test positive for PKU within their first few days of life. Humana's expert witness in this vein, Dr. Larry Cook, based his opinion on a 1983 article which, based upon letters, reported that there had been two Polish babies and one Australian baby who suffered from PKU but yet failed to test positive on days 1, 5 and 7 of life. However, Dr. Cook admitted that other unspecified conditions might have accounted for those "false negatives" and that the statistical occurrence of such "biologic variations," when the baby is tested on day 4 of life as was Brian, is .05%, or 1 out of 20,000, of all PKU babies. Since PKU babies constitute only 1 out of 15,000 babies screened in the United States it follows that only 1 out of 300,000,000 four-day-old screened babies might be a "biologic variant." Moreover, Dr. Cook admitted that in twenty-five years of PKU screening, there has not been one reported incident of a "biologic variation" in the United States or one documented case report of a "biologic variation" worldwide.

The trial was bifurcated into two phases upon Humana's motion. The jury first returned a unanimous verdict as to liability. After the damage phase was submitted, the same jury returned an 11–1 combined verdict for Brian and his father in the total amount of $5,504,271.68. These appeals followed.

II.

First, Humana contends that the court erred by failing to grant its motions for a directed verdict. Humana argues that three possibilities exist to explain Brian's negative test result. It states that those possibilities are that the hospital negligently failed to collect a blood specimen from Brian as was contended at trial, that the state lab was negligent in its duties, or that Brian is the first documented case in the United States involving a "biologic variation." According to Humana, the McKees failed to meet their burden of both showing by their proof that the hospital was probably rather than merely possibly negligent in failing to collect a blood specimen from Brian, and eliminating all reasonable possibilities for this negative PKU test result other than the hospital's negligence. Humana urges that the evidence adduced at trial required the jury to speculate as to who, if anyone, was negligent in this case and therefore that the evidence was not sufficient to support a verdict.

Specifically, Humana cites to the testimony by the McKees' expert and the inventor of the Guthrie assay method, Dr. Robert Guthrie, that it is impossible to scientifically know whether the error in Brian's case resulted from a clerical mistake of some kind at the hospital or from a mistake at the state laboratory. Further, Dr. Guthrie stated that it usually cannot be determined why missed cases such as Brian's occur, but that Brian could have been a case of "biologic variation." According to Humana, since Dr. Guthrie could not determine which of the possibilities explained Brian's negative test result, a jury should not have been allowed to speculate in this vein.

Moreover, Humana argues that the evidence adduced shows that the hospital exercised ordinary care in collecting Brian's blood specimen. Humana bases its argument upon evidence which was summarized in its brief as follows:

> 1) It was established at trial that Brian's hospital records contained an order from the physician for a PKU test to be performed and that the doctor's order had a routine notation on it by a nurse that the order was carried out;
>
> 2) Brian's medical record contained a laboratory requisition slip, generated by the nursery at 4:57 a.m. on May 4, 1977, indicating that the laboratory was directed to draw blood for the PKU test that morning; the hospital's nursery log book also shows that Brian's test for PKU was ordered on May 4, 1977;
>
> 3) The hospital's pathology department's log book shows that Brian's blood was transmitted to the state laboratory on May 4, 1977 and that a negative result was received back from the state laboratory on May 19, 1977; and
>
> 4) The laboratory requisition slip, signed by Bernice Brown, the laboratory clerk, shows that the state laboratory reported the test result for the PKU test as negative, and that the result was received from the state laboratory on May 19, 1977. (Omitting Humana's supportive references to the record.)

In addition, Humana relies upon the evidence that the original PKU test results for Brian and six other infants who had blood drawn on May 4 were in the possession of a Somerset pediatric clinic, and upon Mrs. McKee's prior inconsistent testimony on two occasions to the effect that Brian had a bandage on his heel during his birth admission which indicated that blood had been drawn from him for a PKU test. The latter evidence tended to impeach her testimony on direct examination at trial that she could not remember during which of his two separate admissions in May

1977 he had a bandage on his heel. Finally, Humana relies upon testimony by a state laboratory employee that errors could and did occur at that facility and testimony by several expert doctors concerning the concept of Brian being a "biologic variant." Based upon the evidence summarized above, Humana argues that there was not enough proof to show that the hospital was probably negligent, or to eliminate the other reasonable possibilities for the negative PKU test result. Citing numerous authorities, it therefore argues that it was entitled to a directed verdict. We are constrained to disagree.

In recent years, the standard for our review of cases in order to determine whether a trial court has erred by failing to grant a motion for a directed verdict has undergone significant change. The rule to which we presently are bound to adhere is set forth in *Lewis v. Bledsoe Surface Mining Company,* Ky., 798 S.W.2d 459, 461–462 (1990), as follows:

> Upon review of the evidence supporting a judgment entered upon a jury verdict, the role of an appellate court is limited to determining whether the trial court erred in failing to grant the motion for directed verdict. All evidence which favors the prevailing party must be taken as true and the reviewing court is not at liberty to determine credibility or the weight which should be given to the evidence, these being functions reserved to the trier of fact. *Kentucky & Indiana Terminal R. Co. v. Cantrell,* 184 S.W.2d 111 ([Ky.]1944), and *Cochran v. Downing,* Ky., 247 S.W.2d 228 (1952). The prevailing party is entitled to all reasonable inferences which may be drawn from the evidence. Upon completion of such an evidentiary review, the appellate court must determine whether the verdict rendered is "'palpably or flagrantly' against the evidence so as 'to indicate that it was reached as a result of passion or prejudice.'" *NCAA v. Hornung,* Ky., 754 S.W.2d 855, 860 (1988). If the reviewing court concludes that such is the case, it is at liberty to reverse the judgment on the grounds that the trial court erred in failing to sustain the motion for directed verdict. Otherwise, the judgment must be affirmed. (Emphasis added.)

As we view this directive, we are no longer free to analyze cases, as Humana suggests, in terms of the weight and value of the evidence. Indeed, *Lewis* specifically directs that we should ignore all issues of credibility and weight of the evidence, and that we should instead treat all evidence in favor of the prevailing party as true and give that party all reasonable inferences which may be drawn from the evidence. Once having done that, our inquiry is then limited to the issue of whether the verdict is so palpably or flagrantly against the evidence as to indicate that it was reached as a result of passion or prejudice. Obviously, the *Lewis* test is a much more liberal standard than that which was followed by the court in earlier cases. In fact, as we view the matter, except in the most extreme circumstances the present test in effect prevents this court from reversing a judgment on the ground that the trial court erred by failing to grant a motion for a directed verdict.

As noted by the McKees, the evidence adduced below which was favorable to them must be taken as true, and they must be given the benefit of all reasonable inferences which might legitimately be drawn from that evidence. *Lewis, supra.* The McKees assert in their brief that substantive evidence established and supported the following facts and reasonable inferences in their favor:

> 1. There is not one record entry that a PKU blood specimen was taken from Brian, nor is there a record of the technician who would have taken it, nor the time taken.

2. The lab technician taking any blood specimens had had only the Lab 228 form. Brian's Lab 228 form incorrectly listed his hospital number. Any lab technician looking for a baby in the nursery with a hospital number of "60804-2" would not have found Brian's. Instead, there were three babies with numbers similar to that listed, 60408-2, 60805-9 60384-5.

3. The laboratory technician did not discover the error in the hospital number, and must have thought he took a blood specimen from a baby with a hospital number of 60804-2 on the specimen card titled Brian McKee. That blood specimen would not have been from Brian McKee.

4. To assure the accuracy of the blood specimens, and to assure that they are taken from the correct patient, Humana's protocol required five steps which were not performed: no initials, time or timer clock on the laboratory requisition slip, and no initials or date on the lab 228 form.

5. When the specimen card bearing Brian's name—but not his blood—was delivered to Humana's pathology lab, the mistake in the source of the specimen was noted but never corrected.

6. In 1984, Humana's Director of Medical Records, well familiar with reading charts, advised an independent witness that Brian McKee's hospital chart did not indicate any result whatsoever of a PKU test.

7. Humana stonewalled Dr. Mabry when he twice requested Brian's complete birth record in 1983.

8. Mrs. McKee testified that she did not remember whether the band-aid she once saw on Brian's heel was from Brian's birth admission or his admission two weeks later, when the chart indicated that Brian had a CBC test performed, which also would have required a heel stick and a band-aid.

9. The State Laboratory had extensive quality control procedures assuring accurate administration of the PKU test. The State Laboratory had extensive procedures to ensure the absence of testing errors.

10. Humana admitted it knew of no evidence indicating neglect on the part of the State Laboratory.

11. There is no basis for concluding that Brian McKee might have been a "biologic variant," (a 1 out of 300,000,000 chance).

Our reading of the transcript of the trial convinces us that based upon the evidence adduced at trial, a jury could reasonably have made the inferences enumerated above. Although we might have reached a different conclusion than that of the jury, we are unable to conclude that the verdict is so palpably or flagrantly against the evidence as to indicate that it was reached as a result of passion or prejudice. Consistent with Lewis, therefore, we hold that the court did not err by denying Humana's motion for a directed verdict.

Moreover, we note that the line of cases cited and relied upon by Humana, such as *Huffman v. SS. Mary and Elizabeth Hospital*, Ky., 475 S.W.2d 631 (1972), and *Briner v. General Motors Corp.*, Ky., 461 S.W.2d 99 (1970), simply has no application to the instant action. In each of those cases the court was concerned with the issue of causation and whether the proof was sufficient to establish the probability that the alleged negligence of the defendant caused the damages and injuries sustained by the plaintiff. Here, by contrast, the principal issue was whether Humana was negligent by breaching its duty to administer a PKU test to Brian. There was no significant dispute that, if Humana was negligent and failed to send a specimen of Brian's blood to the state laboratory for testing, this was the cause of the failure to diagnose him as suffering from PKU. This is particularly true since Humana admitted it had no proof that the state laboratory erred in conducting a test on the specimen it received, and the evidence as to Brian being a "biologic variant" was so extremely speculative as to make it questionable as to whether that evidence was sufficient to create even so much as a possible explanation for Brian's negative test result. In short, unlike the situations in the cases cited by Humana, the evidence as a whole was clearly sufficient to establish that if Humana was negligent, its negligence was a probable cause of the failure to diagnose Brian as suffering from PKU.

[The Court goes on to itemize the errors in instruction and procedure alleged by Humana and refute them.]

In summary, we are of the opinion that the errors, if any, assigned by Humana in ... its brief were neither singularly nor collectively egregious enough to warrant the reversal of the trial court's judgment.

f. Excessive Damages

Finally, Humana argues that the jury awarded excessive damages, particularly in regard to the award of $1,000,000 for Brian's pain and suffering. Again, we disagree.

This issue is governed by the supreme court's decisions in *Cooper v. Fultz,* Ky., 812 S.W.2d 497 (1991), and *Davis v. Graviss,* Ky., 672 S.W.2d 928 (1984). As explained in *Hazelwood v. Beauchamp,* Ky. App., 766 S.W.2d 439 (1989), the Davis standard on appeal for determining whether the trial court abused its discretion by not awarding a new trial on the ground that the award of damages was excessive is as follows:

> The amount of damages is a dispute left to the sound discretion of the jury, and its determination should not be set aside merely because we would have reached a different conclusion. If the verdict bears any reasonable relationship to the evidence of loss suffered, it is the duty of the trial court and this Court not to disturb the jury's assessment of damages. It therefore follows that this court may reverse the trial court's order only if the latter was clearly erroneous.

Here, the jury's verdict clearly bears a reasonable relationship to the evidence adduced below regarding the losses sustained by Brian. Indeed, Humana's argument is limited to a general allegation that the jury's verdict was excessive and the result of passion or prejudice, and the cases cited in support of its contention are outmoded and impliedly overruled by *Davis, supra.* More importantly, we find no merit in Humana's argument that the damages awarded by the jury were excessively disproportionate to the actual damages suffered. On the contrary, as we view the matter, just the opposite is true. Finally, we also reject Humana's argument that the award of $1,000,000 for pain and suffering amounted to an impermissible award of hedonic damages. The jury was instructed to make an award for the mental and physical pain and suffering which Brian has incurred and will continue to incur in the future. Given the evidence adduced as to Brian's physical and mental limitations, and as to his awareness of them, the award for past and future pain and suffering is clearly not excessive.

...

American Academy of Pediatrics, Committee on Bioethics, *Ethical Issues with Genetic Testing in Pediatrics*

107 Pediatrics 1451 (2001) (Reaffirmed May 1, 2005)

...

Medical testing is familiar to physicians in the routine practice of medicine. A legitimate question may be raised whether genetic testing is sufficiently different from other forms of testing to justify additional scrutiny. Several aspects of genetic testing should be considered in this regard. First, genetic information is familial. Thus, the test results of one person have direct health implications for others who are genetically related. Second, the risks of genetic testing may not be obvious because the primary risks are psychological, social, and financial. The psychosocial risks include guilt, anxiety, impaired self-esteem, social stigma, and insurance and employment discrimination. Third, genetic information often has limited predictive power. Our genes interact with our environments in complex ways, often making predictions impossible about whether disease will develop or the severity of its manifestations. Finally, many genetic conditions remain difficult to treat or prevent, meaning the value of genetic information may be limited for altering the clinical care of the person. Genetic testing is not unique in any of these respects, but the cumulative complexity of these issues requires that genetic testing receive careful consideration. Given these concerns, detailed counseling, informed consent, and confidentiality should be key aspects of the genetic testing process, particularly when the benefits are uncertain. Because young children are unable to discern the value of genetic information for their own lives, particular care must be exercised by parents and pediatricians when making decisions about genetic testing for children.

The American Academy of Pediatrics (AAP) believes pediatricians can best help children and parents by working to promote child and parent understanding of relevant information, ensure privacy and confidentiality for test results to the extent permissible by law, and provide or refer children for counseling and testing only when it is in the best interest of the child or when the legitimate interests of the parents or family can be promoted without anticipated harm to the child. This statement addresses 3 potentially problematic applications of genetic testing and screening: newborn screening, carrier testing and screening, and predictive testing for late-onset disorders.

Newborn Screening

The purpose of newborn screening for genetic disorders is to limit the morbidity and mortality attributable to selected inherited diseases. Because newborn screening programs are organized through state governments, substantial variability in testing exists between states. As new genetic tests become available, extensive consideration will be given to the introduction of these tests into newborn screening programs. Consistent with earlier guidelines on the issue, the IOM report recommends that 3 principles govern the introduction of new tests and the maintenance of established tests: 1) identification of the genetic condition must provide a clear benefit to the child; 2) a system must be in place to confirm the diagnosis; and 3) treatment and follow-up must be available for affected newborns.

The challenges of introducing new tests have been brought into focus by discussions about the appropriateness of newborn screening for cystic fibrosis (CF). In 1983, the Task Force on Neonatal Screening of the AAP advised against the introduction of state programs until the validity of screening tests and the relative benefits and risks of newborn screening for CF had been evaluated. A key question has been whether detection of CF in the neonatal period improves the long-term pulmonary or nutritional status of affected children. The effects of false-positive results on parental anxiety also are a serious concern. In addition, a small percentage of parents may have a persistent misunderstanding of their child's risk for developing CF after a false-positive newborn screen, and false-positive results may influence parental reproductive decisions. Thus, the justification for newborn screening for CF has been a subject for debate, although several states, including Wyoming and Colorado, have initiated programs. A long-term study in Wisconsin demonstrated nutritional benefits to early detection of CF, and reports on the effects of screening for pulmonary function are anticipated. Similarly, 19 states have introduced newborn screening for congenital adrenal hyperplasia, and a number of studies are under way to evaluate the sensitivity and specificity of different approaches used by these programs and their impact on the health of affected children.

The AAP recommends that new newborn screening tests be introduced in a carefully designed manner that facilitates evaluation of the risks and benefits of screening, including the efficacy of follow-up and treatment protocols. The Wisconsin program for evaluating CF screening was a model in this regard. Furthermore, the AAP concurs with the IOM recommendation that established programs be reviewed periodically to consider the addition, elimination, or modification of current screening modalities.

A persistent ethical issue in newborn screening is whether screening should be voluntary or mandatory. Whether programs are voluntary or mandatory has significant implications for informed responses to test results and for the integration of new tests into established programs. A *voluntary* approach in this context entails an informed decision by parents about newborn screening. Wyoming and Maryland are the only 2 states that require informed consent for newborn screening, although 13 other states require that parents be informed about newborn screening before testing. A *mandatory* approach in this context requires an explicit refusal of screening by parents who object to this intervention. All states except South Dakota permit parental refusal of newborn screening for religious or personal reasons.

The principal ethical justification offered for mandatory screening is the claim that society's obligation to promote child welfare through early detection and treatment of selected conditions supersedes parental prerogatives to refuse this simple medical intervention. An opposing argument maintains that parents traditionally have broad discretion for making health care decisions for their children. Although parents do not have the prerogative to forgo effective treatments for life-threatening conditions, they generally have the prerogative to pursue a variety of options in less threatening circumstances, including options that some medical professionals would consider unwise. Furthermore, it is argued that the great majority of parents will continue to be supportive of newborn screening when they are informed adequately of the risks and benefits. With continued broad public support, approaches involving informed consent (that is, parental permission) may fulfill the important goals of the programs and enhance program quality while respecting traditional parental prerogatives to be informed participants in health care decisions for their children. In a study of newborn screening in Maryland involving informed consent, the majority of women preferred that permission be asked before screening, and the informed refusal rate was only 5 per 1000 infants. In the Maryland study, the consent process typically took 5 minutes or less of staff time. Additional research to develop and evaluate models of parental education and consent will be valuable.

Two potential advantages of obtaining informed consent for newborn screening include more prompt and efficient responses to positive results and an ability to incorporate experimental tests into established screening programs. Under current programs, the information provided to parents about newborn screening is often minimal. A significant source of problems in newborn screening programs is slow or uninformed responses to test results by parents and physicians. If an informed consent process promotes more thorough understanding of the implications of the tests, slow or inappropriate responses to positive results may decrease. Second, advances in genetic research will offer many additional tests for consideration by newborn screening programs. The relative risks and benefits of new tests will be uncertain until adequate clinical research has been conducted. In these circumstances, experimental tests should be offered on a voluntary basis with informed consent. Experimental tests could be integrated more easily in screening programs that routinely sought informed consent for newborn screening tests.

The IOM report suggests that it is appropriate for states to mandate the *offering* of "established tests (e.g. phenylketonuria, hypothyroidism) where early diagnosis leads to improved treatable outcomes." The AAP Committee on Genetics concurred that state governments should mandate the *offering* of tests (although some members of the Committee expressed the opinion that testing should be mandated). Consistent with the recent report of the Newborn Screening Task Force, the AAP recommends that states evaluate an informed consent process for newborn screening tests to foster parental education and promote informed responses to test results. Given the established efficacy of newborn screening programs, it will be essential to demonstrate that expanded education and consent function to enhance the quality of these programs. Carefully conducted pilot programs to document benefits and costs of newborn screening and the frequency and consequences of informed refusal of newborn screening tests will be important. In addition, research to develop an efficient and effective informed consent process for newborn screening is necessary. Attention should be given to the education of women and couples about newborn screening before the immediate postpartum period. Publication and peer review of this research will be appropriate before substantial changes in state health policy on this issue to ensure that efficacy of screening programs is not impaired. Informed consent in this context need not involve a signed consent form for tests of established value, but must include basic information on the purpose of screening and the importance of prompt responses to abnormal results.

Carrier Screening

Medical technology permits the identification of persons who are carriers for mutations in genes responsible for a variety of conditions, including Tay-Sachs disease, muscular dystrophy, sickle cell anemia, CF, and thalassemia major. Carrier testing and counseling of prospective parents can permit informed reproductive choices. A significant concern raised by carrier screening programs is the possibility for individual and community misunderstanding of the carrier state. Confusion about the difference between being an asymptomatic carrier for a genetic condition and being affected with the condition may lead to stigma and discrimination, as well as to adverse psychological reactions in those being screened. An historical example is provided by the carrier screening programs for sickle cell disease in the 1970s in the United States that were not preceded by adequate broad-based education. The subsequent misunderstanding of the benign nature of being a sickle cell carrier by employers, insurance companies, government agencies, and the community being screened led to many cases of discrimination and stigmatization.

To date, carrier testing or screening has not been applied extensively to children or adolescents in the United States. Theoretically, carrier testing or screening before the initiation of sexual activity would increase the reproductive choices of those found to be carriers in comparison with carrier testing during pregnancy. However, children and adolescents may be more psychologically vulnerable than adults to knowledge of carrier status, and it remains uncertain whether testing at younger ages would result in changes in future reproductive behavior. Of note, however, a report of 2 decades of carrier screening in high school students in Montreal, Quebec, suggests that many persons can effectively use the genetic information in later reproductive decisions. Additional research is necessary to thoroughly evaluate these issues in the US health care system and in a variety of different cultures and ethnic communities. The AAP does not support the broad use of carrier testing or screening in children or adolescents. Carrier testing for the pregnant adolescent or for the adolescent who is planning a pregnancy and who has been fully informed of the benefits and risks of carrier testing may be appropriate.

In some circumstances, carriers will be identified through newborn screening programs. For example, newborn screening for sickle cell disease will identify infants who are carriers (in addition to those who are homozygous for the disease). Reporting the infant's carrier status to parents has the theoretical advantages of informing parents that they may be at risk for bearing an affected child (if both parents are carriers) and of enabling the family to be aware of the child's future reproductive risk. However, identification of infants as carriers may lead to misinterpretation by parents and others, resulting in changes in the parent-child relationship and social discrimination. Furthermore, parents should have the opportunity to obtain or refuse their own testing for carrier status (newborn screening should not be used as a surrogate for parental testing). Finally, it remains to be determined whether newborn screening results can be used effectively years later when the person is making reproductive decisions. The AAP concurs with the IOM recommendations that newborns not be screened for the purpose of determining carrier status. Carrier status results that are obtained incidentally should be conveyed to parents who have undergone previous counseling and have given consent. Newborn screening tests should be conducted with adequate parental education, including information about implications for genetically related persons.

Predictive testing for Late Onset Disorders

Genetic technology provides the means to diagnose disorders that develop beyond infancy, including some that become manifest only in adulthood. Examples of late-onset diseases with a high degree of predictability based on genetic tests include myotonic dystrophy, hemochromatosis, polycystic kidney disease, Huntington disease, and some cancers. Furthermore, it soon may be possible to identify genetic factors that increase the probability that common disorders, such as coronary artery disease, diabetes, stroke, hypertension, Alzheimer disease, forms of colon and breast cancer, several psychiatric conditions, and some rheumatoid diseases, will develop.

For some of these conditions, knowledge of risk status may help persons reduce morbidity or risk of mortality. In addition, members of at-risk families may benefit psychologically from learning that they are not mutation carriers or from a reduction in uncertainty if they are found to be mutation carriers. However, a reduction in morbidity or mortality as a result of genetic testing has not been demonstrated for many conditions for which predispositional testing is available. Whether current recommendations for prevention or early detection will be effective in this high-risk population remains unclear. Furthermore, the knowledge of increased risk status may trigger adverse psychological responses and, potentially, discrimination by insurers, employers, or others. For these reasons, the rapid introduction of BRCA1/BRCA2 (which confer increased risk for breast and ovarian cancer) and HNPCC (or hereditary nonpolyposis colon cancer, which confers increased risk for colon cancer) mutation testing into clinical medicine for adults has been discouraged. The complexities of genetic testing and the uncertain risks and benefits of the results support the use of detailed genetic counseling for predictive testing for late-onset disorders. Many adults choose not to be tested for late-onset conditions, indicating that we cannot presume that children would want or will benefit from such testing. Further, testing in childhood inappropriately eliminates the possibility of future autonomous choice by the person and risks stigma and discrimination. Unless there is anticipated benefit to the child, pediatricians should decline requests from parents or guardians to obtain predispositional genetic testing until the child has the capacity to make the choice.

...

Recommendations

1. Established newborn screening tests should be reviewed and evaluated periodically to permit modification of the program or elimination of ineffective components. The introduction of new newborn screening tests should be conducted through carefully monitored research protocols.
2. Genetic tests, like most diagnostic or therapeutic endeavors for children, require a process of informed parental consent and the older child's assent. Newborn screening programs are encouraged to evaluate protocols in which informed consent from parents is obtained. The frequency of informed refusals should be monitored. Research to improve the efficiency and effectiveness of informed consent for newborn screening is warranted.
3. The AAP does not support the broad use of carrier testing or screening in children or adolescents. Additional research needs to be conducted on carrier screening in children and adolescents. The risks and benefits of carrier screening in the pediatric population should be evaluated in carefully monitored clinical trials before it is offered on a broad scale. Carrier screening for pregnant adolescents or for some adolescents considering pregnancy may be appropriate.
4. Genetic testing for adult-onset conditions generally should be deferred until adulthood or until an adolescent interested in testing has developed mature decision-making capacities. The AAP believes that genetic testing of children and adolescents to predict late-onset disorders is inappropriate when the genetic information has not been shown to reduce morbidity and mortality through interventions initiated in childhood.
5. Because genetic screening and testing may not be well understood, pediatricians need to provide parents the necessary information and counseling about the limits of genetic knowledge and treatment capabilities, the potential harm that may be done by gaining certain genetic information, including the possibilities for psychological harm, stigmatization, and discrimination, and medical conditions and disability and potential treatments and services for children with genetic conditions. Pediatricians can be assisted in managing many of the complex issues involved in genetic testing by collaboration with geneticists, genetic counselors, and prenatal care providers.

6. The AAP supports the expansion of educational opportunities in human genetics for medical students, residents, and practicing physicians and the expansion of training programs for genetic professionals.

American Society of Human Genetics/American College of Medical Genetics, *Points to Consider: Ethical, Legal, and Psychosocial Implications of Genetic Testing in Children and Adolescents*

57 AM. J. HUM. GENET. 1233 (1995)

Rapid developments in genetic knowledge and technologies increase the ability to test asymptomatic children for late-onset diseases, disease susceptibilities, and carrier status. These developments raise ethical and legal issues that focus on the interests of children and their parents. Although parents are presumed to promote the well-being of their children, a request for a genetic test may have negative implications for children, and the health-care provider must be prepared to acknowledge and discuss such issues with families.

This report is grounded in several social concepts: First, the primary goal of genetic testing should be to promote the well-being of the child. Second, the recognition that children are part of a network of family relationships supports an approach to potential conflicts that is not adversarial but, rather, emphasizes a deliberative process that seeks to promote the child's well-being within this context. Third, as children grow through successive stages of cognitive and moral development, parents and professionals should be attentive to the child's increasing interest and ability to participate in decisions about his or her own welfare.

Counseling and communication with the child and family about genetic testing should include the following components: (1) assessment of the significance of the potential benefits and harms of the test, (2) determination of the decision-making capacity of the child, and (3) advocacy on behalf of the interests of the child. The following points should be considered:

I. Points to Consider

A. The Impact of Potential Benefits and Harms on Decisions about Testing

1. Timely medical benefit to the child should be the primary justification for genetic testing in children and adolescents. Under this condition, genetic testing is similar to other medical diagnostic evaluations. Medical benefits include preventive measures and therapies, as well as diagnostic information about symptomatic children. If the medical benefits are uncertain or will be deferred to a later time, this justification for testing is less compelling.

2. Substantial psychosocial benefits to the competent adolescent also may be a justification for genetic testing. The benefits and harms of many genetic tests are psychosocial rather than physical. Relevant issues include anxiety, self-image, uncertainty, and the impact on decisions relating to reproduction, education, career, insurance, and lifestyle.

3. If the medical or psychosocial benefits of a genetic test will not accrue until adulthood, as in the case of carrier status or adult-onset diseases, genetic testing generally should be deferred. Exceptions to this principle might occur

when the adolescent meets conditions of competence, voluntariness, and adequate understanding of information. Further consultation with other genetic services providers, pediatricians, psychologists, and ethics committees may be appropriate to evaluate these conditions.

4. If the balance of benefits and harms is uncertain, the provider should respect the decision of competent adolescents and their families. These decisions should be based on the unique circumstances of each family. The provider should enter into a thorough discussion about the potential benefits and harms and should assess the family's understanding of these issues.
5. Testing should be discouraged when the provider determines that potential harms of genetic testing in children and adolescents outweigh the potential benefits. A health-care provider has no obligation to provide a medical service for a child or adolescent that is not in the best interest of the child or adolescent.

B. The Family's Involvement in Decision Making

1. Education and counseling for parents and the child, commensurate on maturity, should precede genetic testing. Follow-up genetic counseling and psychological counseling also should be readily available. Providers of genetic testing should be prepared to educate, counsel, and refer, as appropriate.
2. The provider should obtain the permission of the parents and, as appropriate, the assent of the child or consent of the adolescent. Decisions about competence should not depend arbitrarily on the child's age but should be based on an evaluation of the child's cognitive and moral development. The provider should also attempt to establish that the child's decision is voluntary.
3. The provider is obligated to advocate on behalf of the child when he or she considers a genetic test to be—or not to be—in the best interest of the child. Continued discussion about the potential benefits and harms—and about the interests of the child—may be helpful in reaching a consensus.
4. A request by a competent adolescent for the results of a genetic test should be given priority over parents' requests to conceal information. When possible, these issues should be explored prior to testing. When a younger child is tested and the parents request that the provider not reveal results, the provider should engage the parents in an ongoing discussion about the benefits and harms of the nondisclosure, the child's interest in the information, and when and in what manner the results should be disclosed.

C. Considerations for Future Research

As genetic testing for children and adolescents becomes increasingly feasible, research should focus on the effectiveness of proposed preventive and therapeutic interventions and on the psychosocial impact of tests. Such data are necessary to define the empirical benefits and harms of testing before judgments about the advisability of testing are formulated.

II. Discussion

Benefits and Harms of Genetic Testing in Children

Parents sometimes request that their children be tested for adult-onset problems, so that they can address psychosocial issues. Such nonmedical uses by parents are one of the most controversial issues in testing children (Working Party of the Clinical Genetics Society 1994). While some providers argue that parents should be able to obtain such information (Pelias 1991), other providers suggest that access to such information should be restricted or prohibited if the children will realize little or no immediate medical benefit (Harper and Clarke 1990). Some geneticists already limit testing for adult-onset diseases to individuals who are >18 years of age, e.g., in some protocols for Huntington disease (Bloch and Hayden 1990) and breast cancer (Biesecker et al. 1993). One justification has been that, since such testing requires informed consent, and since children are not competent to give consent, therefore children should not be tested. However, this argument is so broad that it would preclude all pediatric care.

As with any other medical intervention, when children do not have the capacity to provide voluntary, informed consent, the decisive consideration in genetic testing in children should be the welfare of the child. Decisions about genetic testing in children should be based on an assessment of the possible benefits and harms that may be associated with the tests (see Table 1). The putative benefits and harms include medical, psychosocial, and reproductive issues that have implications for the child, the immediate family, and more distant relatives.

Table 1
Potential Benefits and Harms of Genetic Testing of Children

Category	Benefits	Harms
Medical issues	Early and effective preventive or therapeutic interventions	Ineffective or harmful preventive or therapeutic interventions
		Increased surveillance
		Avoiding unnecessary surveillance
		Refinement of prognosis
		Clarification of diagnosis
Psychosocial issues	Reduction of uncertainty	Alteration of self image
	Reduction of anxiety	Distortion of parents' perception of child
	Opportunity for psychological adjustment	Increased anxiety and guilt
	Ability to make realistic plans for education, employment, insurance, and personal relationships	Altered expectations by self or others for education, employment, and personal relationships identifying other family members with late-onset diseases
	Alerting other family members to genetic risk	Discrimination in employment and in obtaining insurance
		Detection of misattributed paternity or adoption
Reproductive issues	Avoiding birth of child with genetic disease	Coerced decisions
	Preparing for birth of child with genetic disease	
	Informed family-planning decisions by parents	

Medical issues.

Medical issues include the possibilities of treatment and prevention, decisions about surveillance, and the resolution of questions about prognosis and diagnosis.

1. Treatment and prevention. Tests that offer children the potential for therapeutic benefit are most likely to be supported by the public and by medical professionals. For example, testing for familial hypertrophic cardiomyopathy, a disease associated with increased risk for sudden death, allows drug therapy to prevent arrhythmias (Maron et al. 1987). Individuals identified as having genetic diseases or disease susceptibility may also benefit from preventive advice about lifestyle changes. For example, children with familial hyperlipidemia may benefit from dietary restrictions (Cortner et al. 1993).

   Although some medical benefits from diagnosis in childhood are established, others remain unconfirmed—and may even be associated with the possibility of harm. One possible harm to a child determined to have a deleterious gene is increased medical tests and treatment regimens that may not have proved benefits. For example, presymptomatic diagnosis of cystic fibrosis has not yet demonstrated any medical benefit and may be associated with increased costs, unnecessary treatments, and familial distress (Farrell and Mischler 1992). Thus, the potential for benefit of unestablished treatment and/or prevention regimens is a questionable justification for testing. Empirical verification of the benefits and harms of prevention and treatment should precede recommendations for routine testing (Wilfond and Nolan 1993; Marteau 1994).

2. Surveillance. Genetic testing can identify patients with an increased susceptibility to disease. The identification of genes associated with cancer might prompt surveillance to detect presymptomatic cancer. For some disorders, such as retinoblastoma, monitoring is associated with effective treatment (Gallie et al. 1991), although the medical benefit of surveillance is less certain in other syndromes with cancer predispositions (Li et al. 1992; Garber and Diller 1994). The benefits of tests depend on the accuracy of additional diagnostic tools and protocols and diminish when early detection fails to improve the patient's prognosis.

3. Reduction of surveillance. When genetic testing excludes a child from risk for a disease, the child may benefit from discontinued medical surveillance. Thus, a child with a prior risk for Von Hippel-Lindau disease may avoid further surveillance procedures when test results are normal (Glenn et al. 1992).

4. Refinement of prognosis. Genetic testing can be helpful in refining prognosis, either when it leads to a precise diagnosis or when the genotype is well correlated with phenotype. The severity of phenotypic expression in diseases associated with trinucleotide repeats is often correlated with the number of repeats (Sutherland and Richards 1993).

5. Clarification of diagnosis. Genetic testing may provide clarification of an uncertain diagnosis if diagnostic data from other sources are inconclusive, or if interpretations of diagnostic data are limited by the sensitivity of other evaluations. DNA studies are now especially useful in confirming a diagnosis of fragile X, because conventional cytogenetic studies may yield equivocal results (Tarleton and Saul 1993), or in confirming a diagnosis of neurofibromatosis in patients whose physical exams are inconclusive (Hofman and Boehm 1992).

Testing children may also benefit other family members when it is necessary to improve the reliability of linkage analysis and mutation analysis desired by other family members. However, participants in such studies should understand that unexpected information about paternity or adoption could be revealed.

Psychosocial issues.

Psychosocial issues associated with medical problems or preexisting issues may be either exacerbated or alleviated by testing. The provider should discuss these issues with children and parents. The presence of severe anxiety or other psychopathology should be an indication for further psychological intervention-and not necessarily an indication for genetic testing.

1. Reduction of uncertainty. A significant psychological benefit of genetic testing is resolution of uncertainty. Data from adults at risk for Huntington disease confirmed a reduction of anxiety, both in persons determined by linkage analysis not to be at risk and in those found to be at increased risk, while the least reduction of anxiety occurred in those who had indeterminate test results (Wiggins et al. 1992). Even for individuals identified as having a life-shortening disease, testing may lead to appropriate adjustment and preparation.

   Both parents and children may be anxious about their uncertain future. Genetic testing, even if confirming the presence of disease, may remove the uncertainty and allow parents the opportunity to confront the issues directly. When test results are favorable, psychological benefits may accrue to both parents and children.

2. Alteration of self-image. Children with genetic diseases may suffer a loss of self-esteem during a critical period when children's self-identity is developing (Koocher 1986). Children's understanding of illness and disease is often limited and may foster self-blame for their disease (Perrin and Gerrity 1981). If a child's genetic information is disclosed outside the family, the ensuing loss of privacy may exacerbate poor self-esteem. Alternatively, in some instances, an affected child may view the disease state as being normal and may even develop positive attitudes of identification with the affected family member (Petersen and Boyd, in press).

   Those individuals whose tests reveal that they are not at genetic risk may develop "survivor guilt," based on the knowledge that one or more of their siblings will develop—and perhaps die from—a serious genetic disease (Wexler 1985). For a child who is at risk of carrying recessive genes, the status of "not knowing" may allow the child to assume that he or she is a carrier and to share some of the burden (Fangs and Johnson 1993). For some children, whose assumption of carrier status provides an important source of self-identity, the knowledge of being a noncarrier could generate a shift in such identity. Further, the fact that siblings may make unfounded assumptions about their genetic status emphasizes the need for thorough age-appropriate genetic counseling, regardless of a decision to provide a genetic test during childhood.

3. Impact on family relationships. Presymptomatic diagnosis in children also has the potential to alter the relationships that exist between parents and their offspring and among siblings (Fangs and Johnson 1993). A child known to have a deleterious gene may be overindulged, rejected, or treated as a scapegoat (Gardiner 1969). The "vulnerable child" syndrome occurs when the perception of serious illness causes parents to become overprotective and to restrict a child's participation in childhood activities (Green and Solnit 1964), responses that can occur even when test results reveal a normal genotype. Unaffected siblings may also experience altered relationships with their parents, particularly in the case

of children who feel disenfranchised if they see that an affected sibling is receiving a disproportionate amount of care and attention (Carandang et al. 1979).

Testing a child for an adult-onset disease may inadvertently provide predictive information to other family members, who may not be interested in this information. However, identifying a child with a genetic disease or a gene predisposing to disease could benefit relatives who may wish to consider testing for themselves. Although the provider might presume an obligation to inform other family members at risk, some patients may prefer not to inform other family members. Current recommendations (President's Commission for the Study of Ethical Problems in Medicine and Biomedical and Behavioral Research 1983) and practices (Wertz and Fletcher 1988) suggest that the patient's wishes for confidentiality should be respected as long as the failure to disclose genetic information is not likely to result in immediate serious physical harm to the relative.

4. Impact on life planning. Information about future health can have implications for planning one's life. The possibility of serious disease or early death may influence an individual's educational goals, occupational choices, and specific career plans. This information also may influence choice of domicile, perhaps to live closer to family, to other support systems, or to adequate medical facilities. Genetic test results may have financial implications for retirement planning and for obtaining life, disability, and health insurance (McEwen et al. 1993).

   Individuals at risk for developing a disease or for transmitting a deleterious gene to their children may be stigmatized and subject to inappropriate discrimination (Billings et al. 1992). Expectations of others for education, social relationships, and/or employment may be significantly altered when a child is found to carry a gene associated with a late-onset disease or susceptibility. Such individuals may not be encouraged to reach their full potential, or they may have difficulty obtaining education or employment if their risk for early death or disability is revealed. Presymptomatic diagnosis may preclude insurance coverage (Ostrer et al. 1993) or may thwart long-term goals such as advanced education or home ownership (Billings et al. 1992; Alper and Natowicz 1993). Finally, this information could be used to assess the suitability of both parents and children in questions of adoption (Wertz et al. 1994). At present, the extent of protection under the Americans with Disabilities Act of 1990 is unclear and untested (Natowicz et al. 1992).

Reproductive issues.

Reproductive issues continue to be a major source of concern when genetic testing is contemplated. Genetic information often influences the reproductive choices of individuals at risk for transmitting a genetic disorder, although genetics-service providers strive to offer nondirective counseling. Individuals who want to avoid having a child with a certain genetic disorder have several options, including adoption, artificial insemination by donor, *in vitro* fertilization with preimplantation diagnosis, prenatal diagnosis, and termination of pregnancy. Prenatal diagnosis, when feasible, offers benefits independent of abortion, including improved perinatal management and the opportunity to prepare psychologically for the birth of an affected child or by changing employment, obtaining insurance, or moving closer to social support services or medical facilities.

Reproductive benefits may be of minimal value to children—and even to sexually active adolescents who are not likely to make family—planning decisions primarily on the basis of their genetic status. Additionally, children may not receive genetic information in an understandable or usable form—or at the appropriate time for the benefit to accrue. However, the knowledge of presymptomatic disease in a young child could have some impact on the reproductive decisions of parents, who may use this information for prenatal diagnosis in future pregnancies or to make decisions about the number or spacing of future children.

Promoting the Interests of Children and Their Families

Parents generally have the authority to make medical decisions for their children. This authority may be limited if a decision is likely to cause a child serious harm without the prospect of compensating benefit. What further complicates these issues in genetic testing is the uncertainty about the putative benefits and harms. Additionally, as children grow, their ability to participate in decisions increases, and, at times, their choices may be at odds with the wishes of their parents. These issues emphasize the provider's obligations to explore both the interests of children and the interests of their parents.

Presumption of parental authority.

Presumption of parental authority is a fundamental principle for families and professionals who are discussing genetic testing for children.

1. Roots of parental authority. Prior to the 20th century, the law viewed children as chattel, or property, of their fathers (Melton 1983). Although children were certainly valued, parents had full authority to make decisions about raising their offspring. Although children today are viewed as individuals rather than as property, the law still recognizes parental authority over decisions relating to a child's education, nourishment, medical care, and general well-being (Pelias 1991).

   The most compelling justification for parental authority focuses on the well-being of the child and acknowledges that parents are usually in the best position to make such a determination and have the greatest interest in making decisions to promote the well-being of the child (Melton 1983). A second justification for parental authority rests on the interests of parents in their own self-determination, including the authority to make decisions on behalf of their children (Holder 1988). This justification derives in part from the moral principle of autonomy, a concept that supports the personal choices of individuals, without interference from third parties such as health-care providers or the government. This principle is the basis of the doctrine of informed consent, the precept that competent adults must receive appropriate information and give consent for diagnostic tests or therapeutic interventions. Because most children lack the capacity to make appropriate decisions, this role generally falls to the parents or guardians, who, by extension of their own autonomy, are entitled to make decisions on behalf of their children (Buchanan and Brock 1989).

2. Limits of parental authority. In spite of the presumption of parental prerogative, parental authority can be limited if there are objective reasons to believe that a decision or action has significant potential for an adverse impact on the health or well-being of the child (Wadlington 1983). Such limitations are best exemplified by child-abuse and -neglect laws, which prohibit parents from acts of omission or commission that could or do result in serious harm to the child.

   The law also requires parents to provide certain medical benefits for their children, even if those benefits are contrary to the beliefs of the parents. Newborn screening for phenylketonuria (PKU) may be justified because of the child's interest in dietary treatment to avoid mental retardation (Laberge and Knoppers 1990). Similarly, immunizations may be required both in the interest of the child and in the interest of the public health. Further, specific life-saving treatments, such as blood transfusions and treatment for bacterial meningitis, may be administered over the objections of a child's parents, because these treatments have a high probability of restoring the child to health (American Academy of Pediatrics Committee on Bioethics 1988).

Parents also may be legally constrained in choosing medical interventions for their children. Parents may not, for example, generally authorize the involuntary sterilization of their minor children, without approval of a court of law (Reilly 1991). Nor are parents at complete liberty to consent to having their children used as research subjects. Although competent adults may consent to participate in nontherapeutic research, federal regulations stipulate that parents may give permission for their child's participation in nontherapeutic research only if the research meets more stringent requirements of benefit and safety (45 CFR 46.408, 1994).

In the clinical setting, providers may refuse to provide requested diagnostic or therapeutic interventions that offer no or few benefits but that incur more than minimal risk or cost. Although respect for personal autonomy reinforces the principle of noninterference by third parties, patients are not at liberty to assert entitlements to services by third parties (Brett and McCullough 1986; Youngner 1988). For example, providers are not obligated to acquiesce to parental requests for antibiotics for viral infections or for a computed-tomography scan for evaluation of a simple headache. The provider does, however, have a responsibility to explain why he or she will not provide the requested intervention and, if feasible, to identify other providers who may be willing to provide the requested services.

3. Legal trend to recognize the authority of minors. Although the law protects the autonomy of adults, on the presumption that adults are competent to make their own decisions, the law presumes that minors are not competent in this respect. Many states, however, permit adolescents to consent to medical treatment in the absence of parental consent (Wadlington 1983; Holder 1988). These states recognize a "mature minor rule," which views some adolescents as capable of understanding the consequences of some medical decisions. Mature-minor rules are circumstance specific and generally address situations in which the state has an interest in the adolescent's seeking medical attention that might not be sought if the problem were disclosed to the parents. These circumstances typically include reproductive issues, such as contraception, as well as sexually transmitted diseases. Other sensitive areas, such as treatment for drug and alcohol abuse and psychotherapy, are protected as well. The "emancipated minor" status also acknowledges an adolescent as competent to make decisions, by virtue of adult status under the law. For example, adolescents who are living on their own or who are married, pregnant, or have children are generally permitted to make medical and other decisions usually reserved for adults.

The decision-making capacity of the child.

Although 18 years of age is the general legal standard for decision making, the concepts of the mature minor and the emancipated minor derive, in part, from empirical observations about the gradual development of a child's cognitive skills and moral reasoning. These capacities mature over time and at different rates in different children (Weithorn 1983; Buchanan and Brock 1989). As children progress through successive stages of development, they become capable of greater participation in decisions about their own welfare. The child's maximal participation, commensurate with his or her best capacity, may even contribute to the further development of these very skills. Thus, there are strong psychological and philosophical justifications for a more nuanced understanding that grants some level of decision-making authority to children <18 years of age.

Competence to make decisions depends on three broad capacities: the capacity for understanding and communication, the capacity for reasoning and deliberation, and the capacity to develop and sustain a set of moral values (Buchanan and Brock 1989). By the age of 7 years, children can usually begin to participate in decisions, since they have sufficient cognitive and language skills to understand some information. Thus, in the United States, a 7-year-old is generally entitled to give "assent" to participation in research involving human subjects (45 CFR 46.408, 1994). Although consent requires competence to make an independent choice, assent only requires a rudimentary understanding of risk and benefit—and a decision to participate or not (Grodin 1994).

During adolescence, children begin to develop concepts of mortality, cause and effect, and right and wrong, as well as a sense of connection to the future (Buchanan and Brock 1989). As adolescents' decision-making capacity increases, additional consideration should be given to their wishes, even when these wishes differ from those of their parents or when these wishes are not clearly in the child's best interest. Adolescents may have a genuine interest in information about career and child-bearing choices, although they may still be vulnerable to coercion by family or peers, to stigmatization, or to altered self-image. By the age of 12 or 14 years, some children, though, will have sufficient decision-making capacity to evaluate the specific risks and benefits of tests or treatments (Wadlington 1983; Weithorn 1983).

The provider as a fiduciary for the child.

The provider, as fiduciary for the child, must be conscientious about considering requests for testing, as well as requests for nondisclosure.

1. Assessing requests for tests. Providers of genetics services emphasize the importance of a nondirective approach in the counseling of patients about reproductive issues. However, health-care providers also have a fiduciary relationship with patients and often make specific recommendations about medical services. Providers caring for children may discourage actions that may be adverse to the interests or the well-being of the child. Although providers generally should respect parents' wishes, the provider ultimately must balance the responsibilities to the health and well-being of the child and to the wishes of the parents. Thus, a provider must sometimes evaluate whether a request by parents is appropriate in view of the relative benefits and harms to a child. In situations where these factors are primarily psychosocial rather than medical, such an assessment may be difficult.

   Until more information is available regarding the risks and benefits of genetic testing, the provider's guiding principle continues to be primum non nocere—first do no harm. Thus, when faced with uncertainty, the provider may be obligated to avoid the possibility of harm, rather than to provide unclear benefits. There may be rebuttable presumption to defer testing unless the risk/ benefit ratio is favorable. On the other hand, in specific cases where the benefits and harms of genetic testing are more uncertain, more weight should be given to the wishes of the competent adolescent and the parents. These issues are not always straightforward, and, at the very least, the provider has a responsibility to engage in detailed conversations with the family. Parents may overestimate the power of genetic testing or be unaware of potential risks. It also may be advisable to obtain consultation from other genetic-service providers, pediatricians, psychologists, and ethics committee, to evaluate benefits/harms, decision-making capacity, and voluntariness. Sometimes a dialogue with parents about the nature of testing will lead to a consensus about its value to the child and the family. If a consensus is not attainable, the provider may decline to conduct the test or might suggest other providers, who may be willing to provide the testing.

The practice of medical genetics provides some examples of tests that may not be in the best interest of the child. For example, parents may request a determination of their young daughter's Tay-Sachs carrier status, for the purpose of encouraging her to be sexually responsible when she is older. The possibility of stigmatization without any clear immediate benefit is a serious concern. On the other hand, different issues may arise when, to help the parents make their own family-planning and socioeconomic decisions, parents request that young children be tested for adult-onset diseases. For example, the parents choice about future children might be dependent on the genetic status of the child, or parents may wish to know about adult-onset diseases prior to deciding how much to save for a college education. In such cases, the balance swings between benefit to the family and benefit to the child. The unique potential of presymptomatic genetic testing to predict a child's future should be approached with great caution.

Adolescents who request tests prompt additional considerations. For example, if an adolescent requests testing for Huntington disease, it may be important to ascertain whether the request originates from the adolescent or from the parent. In the face of uncertain benefits and harms, an adolescent's request for a test necessitates an individual assessment of competence and voluntariness.

2. Assessing requests for nondisclosure. Parents occasionally may request that a test result not be disclosed to the child. This may pose a conflict between the interest of the parents in making decisions that they believe are for the well-being of the child and the interest of the child in self-determination. As the child matures, justifying such a request may become more difficult, even if the provider agrees that disclosure might not promote the well-being of the child.

   A request for nondisclosure may indicate some ambivalence on the part of the parent regarding the significance of the test results-and thus a potential for harm either from the parent's interpretation of the test results or from the child's eventual discovery of the concealment. The provider should consider deferring testing pending a detailed discussion of these issues.

   If genetic testing occurs prior to the request for nondisclosure to the child, the provider may wish to defer a decision about disclosure. until after the issues have been explored fully. Factors such as the age of the child, the need for medical interventions, and the need for the child to participate in therapeutic plans must be explored in comprehensive genetic counseling. It is recommended that, on reaching adulthood, the individual should be informed of the existence of the test results and should be given the option to know the results.

Conclusion

Providers who receive requests for genetic testing in children must weigh the interests of children and those of their parents and families. The provider and the family both should consider the medical, psychosocial, and reproductive issues that bear on providing the best care for children. This will require the provider to engage individual families in comprehensive discussions of these issues and to provide them with specific information and recommendations about genetic testing. Because such testing has potential for both great benefit and great harm, and because the availability of tests continues to expand, providers of genetic services will play increasingly important roles in counseling families about the suitability of genetic testing for their children.

Notes & Questions

1. Professor Burke's article provides an overview of genetic testing and some of the issues that are important with respect to clinical application of genetic testing. In considering testing, one of the first issues of import is the status of the test in terms of analytic validity, clinical validity, and clinical utility. Analytic validity refers to how well the genetic assessment performs in measuring the property or characteristic it is intended to measure. With respect to a genetic mutation, analytic validity refers to the accuracy of the test in testing for the specific mutation. Once analytic validity is established, it is necessary to assess clinical validity. Clinical validity refers to the predictive value of a test for a given clinical outcome—that is the likelihood that a disease will develop in someone with a positive test for the gene related to that disease. Clinical validity is primarily determined by the sensitivity and specificity with which a test identifies people with a defined clinical condition. Sensitivity of a test refers to the proportion of persons who test positive from among those with a clinical condition; specificity refers to the proportion of persons who test negative from among those without the clinical condition. The clinical validity of a genetic test is the likelihood that the disease associated with that genetic mutation will develop in someone with a positive test result. This likelihood is affected not only by the presence of the gene itself, but also by any modifying factors that affect penetrance of the mutation, such as the environment, nutrition, and interaction with other genes. Finally, and perhaps most important, is the clinical utility of a genetic test. Will the test, and the interventions that flow from it, produce an improved health outcome? Will the doctor and patient be able to prevent the disease now that they know about a genetic proclivity? Is there a treatment for the disease that can cure, improve the outcome, or better the quality of life? The question of clinical utility is the ultimate determinant of whether a genetic test has merit for clinical application.

Thus, in the case of testing for a disorder that cannot be prevented, ameliorated or cured, the clinical utility of the test is questionable. Such would be the case with genetic tests for incurable diseases that cannot be prevented. It may be, as in the case of hemochromatosis or Factor V Leiden, that the genetic mutation is but one of many factors disposing an individual to the disease and clinical utility is questionable at best. Only if identification of the mutation results in a change in medical management *and* an improved qualitative and/or quantitative outcome is the aim of clinical utility realized. Analysis of analytic validity, clinical validity, and clinical utility are critical to the risk/benefit analysis of each genetic test. It is essential that this analysis be performed before the test is adopted in practice or by a legislatively sanctioned screening program. For additional reading on the role of clinical utility and cost-benefit issues in genetic testing, see Ezra C. Holston & Debra L. Schutte, *The Clinical*

Utility of Genetic Information in the Care of Persons with Alzheimer's Disease, 13 MED-SURG. NURSING 415 (2004); Richard C. Press, et al., *Clinical Utility of Factor V Leiden* (R506Q) *Testing for the Diagnosis and Management of Thromboembolic Disorders*, 126 ARCH. PATHOLOGY LAB. Med. 1304 (2002); Ryan A. Harris, et al., *Cost Utility of Prenatal Diagnosis and the Risk Bases Threshold*, 363 LANCET 9405 (2004); Scott D. Ramsey, et al., *Attitudes Towards Genetic Screening for Predisposition to Colon Cancer Among Cancer Patients, Their Relatives and Members of the Community*, 6 COMMUNITY GENETICS 1 (2003); Melissa A. Austin, et al., *Genetic Causes of Monogenic Heterozygous Familial Hypercholesterolemia: A Huge Prevalence Review*, 160 AM. J. EPIDEMIOL. 407 (2004).

2. Newborn screening programs evolved as a result of patient and provider advocacy during the 1970s. Now, as noted in the text, all fifty states have substantial newborn screening programs. Alas, there is significant variation from state to state. *See* U.S. GEN. ACCOUNTING OFFICE, NEWBORN SCREENING: CHARACTERISTICS OF STATE PROGRAMS (2003), *available at* http://www.gao.gov/new.items/d03449.pdf. *Humana of Kentucky v. McGee* involves the failure of providers administering a newborn screening program to detect PKU. Brian McKee appears to have been the victim of multiple clerical errors that led to having a "normal" blood test attributed to him. It is not until the child is six year old that he is finally diagnosed as having PKU and by then, much damage has been done. Humana's appeal is unsuccessful and the appeals court upholds the verdict and damages ($5,504,271.68), including $1,000,000 for Brian's pain and suffering, awarded by the lower court. Note that, in *Humana of Kentucky v. McGee*, there was no evidence of negligence on the part of the state or its public health program. It seems clear that they received a blood sample allegedly associated with Brian and it tested negative. An argument that Brian's PKU is of an unusual biologic variant is deemed to be without basis. Rather, it seems clear that the state lab never received any sample drawn from Brian and that somehow, the hospital neglected to draw a sample from him. In failing to draw a sample and/or failing to attribute the correct sample to Brian, the Hospital and its personnel breached the standard of care with respect to newborn testing.

3. Newborn screening leads to questions about the ethical, legal, and psychosocial implications of genetic testing in children. As more tests become available, these questions are likely to become ever more pressing. For example, when should newborn screening or diagnostic tests that are beyond those recommended be done? Should parents have unfettered rights to obtain genetic testing on their infant or child? Suppose the test is for a disease that will not manifest until later in life? Is testing justified if there is no treatment for the disease? In 1997, a Task Force created by the National Institutes of Health-Department of Energy Working Group on Ethical, Legal, and Social Implications of Human Genome Research concluded that genetic testing of children for adult onset diseases should not be undertaken unless direct medical benefit will accrue to the child and this benefit would be lost by waiting until the child has reached adulthood. See NATIONAL HUMAN GENOME RESEARCH INSTITUTE, NIH, PROMOTING SAFE AND EFFECTIVE GENETIC SCREENING IN THE UNITED STATES (1997), *available at* http://www.genome.gov/10001733. In so doing, the Task Force agreed with the positions taken by the American Society of Human Genetics, the American College of Medical Genetics, and the American Academy of Pediatrics (AAP). The AAP recommends the following:

> 1. Established newborn screening tests should be reviewed and evaluated periodically to permit modification of the program or elimination of ineffective components. The introduction of new newborn screening tests should be conducted through carefully monitored research protocols.

> 2. Genetic tests, like most diagnostic or therapeutic endeavors for children, require a process of informed parental consent and the older child's assent. Newborn screening programs are encouraged to evaluate protocols in which informed consent from parents is obtained. The frequency of informed refusals should be monitored. Research to improve the efficiency and effectiveness of informed consent for newborn screening is warranted.
>
> 3. The AAP does not support the broad use of carrier testing or screening in children or adolescents. Additional research needs to be conducted on carrier screening in children and adolescents. The risks and benefits of carrier screening in the pediatric population should be evaluated in carefully monitored clinical trials before it is offered on a broad scale. Carrier screening for pregnant adolescents or for some adolescents considering pregnancy may be appropriate.
>
> 4. Genetic testing for adult-onset conditions generally should be deferred until adulthood or until an adolescent interested in testing has developed mature decision-making capacities. The AAP believes that genetic testing of children and adolescents to predict late-onset disorders is inappropriate when the genetic information has not been shown to reduce morbidity and mortality through interventions initiated in childhood.

Robert M. Nelson, et al., *Ethical issues with Genetic Testing in Pediatrics*, 107 PEDIATRICS 1451, 1455 (2001).

As the AAP recommendations note, informed consent in genetic testing of children is crucial. But the question arises as to who is qualified to provide informed consent on behalf of the child. Classically, for infants and young children, parents have been assumed to be in the best position to provide consent. A recent study of parental attitudes indicates that parents believe that their decisional authority should trump professional policy statements. *See* Elizabeth Campbell & Lainie Friedman Ross, *Parental Attitudes and Beliefs Regarding the Genetic Testing of Children,* 8 COMMUNITY GENETICS 94 (2005). The Task Force cited *supra* argues that even taking into account the difficulty in living with uncertainty about the health status of the child, the child has an inherent right to make an independent decision with respect to testing after he is an adult, unless there is some treatment that needs to be undertaken before then. NATIONAL HUMAN GENOME RESEARCH INSTITUTE, NIH, PROMOTING SAFE AND EFFECTIVE GENETIC SCREENING IN THE UNITED STATES (1997), *available at* http://www.genome.gov/10001733. Scholars agree, promoting the child's right to an "open future." *See* Marcia Sue DeWolf Bosek, *Commentary on Genetic Testing of Children: Maintaining an Open Future,* 25 PEDIATRIC NURSING 66 (1999).

The consent and ethical issues become even more muddled as the child ages into adolescence. At what point should the child have the right to seek testing, with or without parental consent. We allow many mature minors to access medical services without parental knowledge and consent. Is genetic testing so different? Suppose the adolescent is contemplating parenthood, perhaps early parenthood, given his or her knowledge of a familial late-onset disease? Suppose the same adolescent wishes to permanently foreclose reproduction for the same reason? The few scholars studying this issue agree that the primary justification for undergoing testing should be timely medical intervention and benefit. In the absence of a benefit, there must be careful consideration of the psychosocial risks, which may be significant for both the adolescent and other family members. *See* David A. Stevenson & Victor C. Strasberger, *Advise or Consent: Issues in Genetic Testing of Adolescents,* 13 ADOLESCENT MEDICINE 213 (2002).

2. Carrier Testing

Hilary Vallance & *Jason Ford, Carrier Testing for Autosomal-Recessive Disorders*

40 Critical Rev. Clinical Lab. Science 473 (2003)

I. Introduction

Carrier testing for serious autosomal recessive genetic disorders began in the early 1970s for Tay-Sachs disease (TSD), a lethal lysosomal storage disorder with a high carrier frequency (3%) in Ashkenazi Jewish individuals (Eastern European origin). Community-based screening programs have identified thousands of carrier couples who have been offered genetic counselling and a variety of reproductive options, including prenatal testing. As a result of this screening program, the incidence of TSD has dramatically declined, and this has served as a model for subsequent carrier screening programs.

Several other autosomal-recessive disorders occur with increased incidence in the Ashkenazi Jewish population, but, unlike TSD, enzymatic carrier testing has not been possible. In the last decade, the genes responsible for most of these disorders have been identified, and mutation analysis has revealed common alleles in the Ashkenazi Jewish population. Both commercial and academic centers in the U.S. and Israel have begun offering screening 'panels' that include testing for many of these disorders. Some of these disorders are similar to TSD in that they involve deterioration of the nervous system and may be lethal in infancy or childhood (Canavan Disease, Familial Dysautonomia, Niemann-Pick disease [NPD]), while others are serious and may lead to death in early or mid-adulthood (Cystic fibrosis [CF], Fanconi anemia [FA], Bloom syndrome [BS]).

The cloning of genes and the identification of disease-causing mutations have provided new opportunities to reduce the incidence of other genetic disorders in a variety of ethnic groups. Well-defined ethnic groups are of particular interest because some have a higher incidence of specific genetic disorders, and because the mutations in a given gene are often limited to one or a few so that molecular testing is sensitive and relatively cost effective.

Approximately 4.5% of the world's population (Mediterranean, Indian, Middle Eastern, and Southeast Asian) are carriers for a mutation affecting one of the globin chains of the hemoglobin molecule. Among the most common disorders of hemoglobin are [alpha] and [beta] thalassemia, severe forms of which may be lethal or result in greatly reduced lifespan. Carrier testing for the thalassemias, through a variety of methods, can detect most carriers. As described above for TSD, carrier couples are offered genetic consultation when their reproductive options, including prenatal diagnosis, are explained.

This review discusses a range of disorders for which carrier testing is now possible. Section II reviews carrier testing in the Ashkenazi Jewish population. Section III reviews [alpha] and [beta] thalassemia carrier testing and Section IV is a review of resource and planning issues that are relevant to those clinical and laboratory-based professionals involved in the delivery of carrier screening programs.

II. Carrier Screening in the Ashkenazi Jewish Population

A. Tay-Sachs Disease

Infantile TSD is a lethal autosomal-recessive lysosomal storage disorder caused by a deficiency of the alpha subunit of beta-hexosaminidase A (Hex A). Although TSD is rare in the general population, the incidence is much higher in some ethnic groups, particularly Jews of Ashkenazi descent.

Hex A is required to cleave the terminal N-acetylgalactosamine from GM2 ganglioside. In TSD, failure to degrade GM2 ganglioside leads to neuronal lysosomal storage and neuronal degeneration. TSD becomes evident in the first year of life and causes irreversible deterioration of the nervous system, resulting in immobility, difficulty with feeding, blindness, seizures, and eventually death between 3 to 5 years of age.

In 1970, Kaback introduced carrier testing for TSD by measuring the activity of the hexosaminidase isoenzymes, Hex A and Hex B. Hex A consists of one alpha subunit and one beta subunit, while Hex B is made up of two beta subunits. The alpha and beta subunits are encoded by the HEXA and HEXB genes, respectively. Individuals heterozygous for TSD have a reduced level of the Hex A isoenzyme (alpha-beta heterodimer) relative to the Hex B isoenzyme (beta-beta homodimer).

Approximately 1 in 30 Ashkenazi Jewish individuals is a carrier for TSD. Therefore, the overall risk of an Ashkenazi Jewish couple having a child with TSD is approximately 1 in 3600. Since the start of TSD carrier screening and prenatal testing in the 1970s, the incidence of TSD among Ashkenazi Jewish people has dramatically declined. In North America since 1983, there have been 3 to 5 TSD-affected children born per year compared with approximately 60 new cases per year prior to screening.

Possibly less well known is that the frequency of TSD is increased in other ethnic groups, particularly the French-Canadian population in eastern Canada, a French-Acadian (Cajun) population, the Pennsylvania Dutch, and Moroccan Jews. Unique mutations have been identified that account for most disease-causing alleles. Targeted screening programs have been successful in reducing the incidence of disease in these groups as well.

As it is now common for Jewish individuals to marry non-Jewish partners, there is a growing experience with carrier testing in the non-Jewish population. Based on enzymatic analysis, the carrier frequency appears to be 1 in 70, but this is far greater than estimates (1 in 300) based on incidence of the disease in the non-Jewish population. There are two specific mutations that account for 35 and 3%, respectively, of all mutant alleles in non-Jewish Caucasians and for 2 to 3% of enzyme-defined Ashkenazi Jewish carriers. These mutations are associated with biochemical deficiency of Hex A activity when synthetic substrates are used but are not associated with disease manifestations. These are known as pseudodeficiency alleles. The routine enzyme test does not distinguish between the one-third of non-Jews who have a pseudodeficiency mutation from those who carry a disease-causing mutation. Therefore, molecular testing is required in enzymatically identified non-Jewish carriers to rule out pseudodeficiency.

B. Canavan Disease

Canavan disease is another severe neurodegenerative autosomal-recessive disorder more common in the Ashkenazi Jewish population that leads to death in the first or second decade of life. The clinical features usually become apparent in the first few months of life with hypotonia, head lag, and macrocephaly. As the infant gets older spasticity, seizures and visual loss develop. The first pathological description of this disorder was reported in 1931 by Dr. M.M. Canavan, who described the characteristic histologic finding of spongy degeneration of the white matter (leukodystrophy). Until the enzyme defect was delineated in 1988, brain biopsy was usually required for diagnosis. Canavan disease is caused by a deficiency of the enzyme, aspartoacylase, which leads to accumulation of N-acetylaspartic acid (NAA) in the brain and body fluids. The diagnosis of Canavan disease can now be made with urine or blood analysis for NAA.

The aspartoacylase gene was cloned in 1993,and molecular studies revealed that two specific mutations account for 98% of the disease-causing alleles in Ashkenazi Jewish Canavan disease patients. A missense mutation (A854C) results in the substitution of glutamic acid for an alanine residue and accounts for 83.6% of alleles. A nonsense mutation (C693A) alters a tyrosine residue to a stop codon and is found in 13.4% of the alleles from Jewish patients. In non-Jewish patients a missense mutation, substituting alanine for glutamic acid in codon 305, accounts for 35.7% of the 70 alleles from 35 unrelated non-Jewish patients. The common Jewish mutations are not prevalent in the non-Jewish population.

The identification of two common disease-causing mutations in the Ashkenazi Jewish population has allowed the determination of the carrier frequency of Canavan disease. Matalon et al. screened 4000 Ashkenazi Jewish individuals for both the codon 285 and 231 mutations and found a carrier frequency of 1 in 38. A study of the Ashkenazi Jewish population in New York found 1 in 40 carriers. Based on these carrier frequency studies, the risk of an affected offspring would be approximately 1 in 5000 births. Prenatal diagnosis can be performed by quantifying NAA in amniotic fluid or by molecular analysis.

C. Familial Dysautonomia

Familial Dysautonomia (FD) is an autosomal-recessive disorder affecting the sensory and autonomic nervous system. Features are lack of tearing, paroxysmal hypertension, increased sweating, cold hands and feet, corneal anesthesia, and the absence of the fungi form papillae of the tongue.

The autonomic crises can be life-threatening. Life expectancy is variable, with approximately 50% mortality in childhood. Adults suffer progressive peripheral sensory dysfunction with poor balance, unsteady gait, and psychiatric disturbance. Sympathovagal balance becomes increasingly unstable with worsening orthostatic hypotension, supine hypertension, and bradyarrhythmias.

FD is almost exclusively a disorder of Ashkenazi Jewish individuals with a carrier frequency of 1 in 32. A single mutation (IVS2507+6T>C) in the IKBKAP gene accounts for > 95% of mutant alleles. Along with a second mutation R696P, the carrier detection rate is > 99%.

D. Niemann-Pick Disease

Niemann-Pick disease (NPD) is caused by a deficiency of the lysosomal enzyme, sphingomyelinase (ASM; E.C.3.1.2.12), which is involved in the catabolism of sphingomyelin. There are mild and severe forms of the disease, and both types occur more frequently among individuals of Ashkenazi Jewish descent (1 in 30,000). The severe form (type A) is a neurodegenerative disorder of infancy characterized by progressive neurodegeneration, failure to thrive, hepatosplenomegaly, and death by about 3 years of age. The other form (type B) has little or no neurological involvement and is characterized by hepatosplenomegaly, respiratory involvement, and survival into adulthood. The onset of type B disease is variable. Some patients present early with massive hepatosplenomegaly and severe respiratory insufficiency that can lead to death in childhood or early adolescence. Other type B NPD patients remain asymptomatic until adulthood.

The sphingomyelinase gene (ASM) was cloned and expressed in 1991. Three common ASM mutations have been identified in type A NPD patients and account for 92% of mutant alleles.

Li studied 1000 randomly-selected Ashkenazi Jewish individuals and identified 11 carriers (carrier frequency 1 in 90), with an estimated disease incidence of 1 in

30,000. The L302P and fsP330 mutations have not been identified in any non-Jewish NPD patients.

In type B NPD, several patients have been reported to carry the deltaR608 mutation, and this mutation appears to protect against neurological involvement. So far, this mutation has only been reported in type B NPD patients. Yet even among type B NPD patients who are homozygous for this mutation, there is a wide range of phenotypic involvement with respect to age of onset and degree of hepatosplenomegaly.

This mutation is a 3-base deletion that results in the loss of a single arginine residue at position 608. Interestingly, this mutation has also been reported in North African NPD patients and accounts for 87% of mutant ASM alleles in a series of 15 unrelated North African type B patients.

E. Fanconi Anemia

Fanconi anemia (FA) is an autosomal-recessive DNA instability disorder characterized by progressive pancytopenia, congenital abnormalities, and a predisposition to cancer, particularly acute myelogenous leukemia (AML). FA affects all ethnic groups, but it is more common in the Ashkenazi Jewish population. The diagnosis of FA is confirmed by study of chromosomal breakage induced by diepoxybutane or other crosslinking agents. FA includes at least five complementation groups, and the gene FAC corresponding to complementation group C has been cloned. The most common mutation in the FAC gene is the IVS4+4A>T, a splice site mutation that has been found only in patients with Jewish ancestry.

Clinical features of FA have been well documented through the International Fanconi Anemia Registry. Hematologic abnormalities are usually detected in childhood (range birth to 31 years). Virtually all patients develop hematologic abnormalities by 40 years of age, and the risk of death from hematologic causes is 81% by 40 years of age. Congenital malformations are variable and include short stature, skeletal malformations, microphthalmia, elfin-like facies and renal anomalies. The common Ashkenazi mutation (IVS+4A>T) has been shown to be associated with a severe FA phenotype characterized by multiple major congenital malformations, early onset of hematologic disease, and shorter lifespan. The median age at diagnosis of leukemia was 15.9 years.

Verlander et al. screened for the IVS4 +4 A-to-T mutation in an Ashkenazi Jewish population (n = 3,104) and found a carrier frequency of 1 in 89 (1.1 %; 95% confidence interval 0.79 to 1.56%). At the present time, only a few U.S. centers offer carrier testing for FA.

F. Bloom Syndrome

Bloom syndrome (BS) is an autosomal-recessive disorder characterized by small stature, sun-sensitive erythema, immunodeficiency, and a predisposition to different types of cancer. Cytogenetically there is increased chromosome breakage and sister chromatid exchange. German and Ellis reported on 132 cases of BS; 39 patients were deceased, and of those 31 had died of cancer at a mean age of 28 years.

BS is most prevalent in the Ashkenazi Jewish population, with an incidence of about 1 in 48,000. A common mutation has been identified that involves the deletion of six bases and insertion of seven bases (2281 delATCTGAinsTAGATTC, abbreviated blm^sup ASH^). This frame-shift mutation leads to an early termination of the BLM gene product and accounts for 97% of BS alleles in Ashkenazi Jewish patients. Roa et al.screened 1016 American Ashkenazi Jews for the blm^sup ASH^ mutation and found 10 carriers (1 in 102). A second American study of 1491 Ashkenazi Jewish persons in

New York found a carrier frequency of 1 in 107. Similar results were obtained by Shahrabani-Gargir et al. in an Israeli Ashkenazi Jewish population. Sixteen blm^sup ASH^ carriers were detected among a group of 1613 Ashkenazi Jews (1 in 101) and among those individuals who were specifically of Polish descent the carrier frequency was 1 in 37.

Like FA, carrier testing for BS is limited to a few centers at present. On the one hand, the detection rate is high with just a single mutation accounting for 97% of alleles. On the other hand the carrier frequency is relatively low, and there is little experience with the action a carrier couple would take with regard to an at-risk pregnancy.

G. Cystic Fibrosis

Cystic fibrosis (CF) is a recessive disorder characterized by progressive lung disease, pancreatic dysfunction, and male infertility. Age of onset is variable (median age 6 to 8 months), and nearly two-thirds are diagnosed before 1 year of age. Median survival has increased from 18 years in 1976 to 30.1 years in 1995. There was little increase in life span extension between 1990 to 1995. The most common cause of death is from complications of lung disease.

CF is one of the most common genetic diseases in Caucasians, with a carrier frequency of 1 in 25 and an incidence of about 1 in 3300. The gene responsible for CF, discovered in 1989, is a chloride channel named CF transmembrane conductance regulator (CFTR). There are hundreds of mutations that have been described in the CFTR gene. The delta F508 mutation is the most common and accounts for approximately 70% of CF alleles. A panel of 25 mutations accounts for approximately 90% of disease-causing alleles in the Caucasian population. The incidence of CF is similar in the Ashkenazi Jewish population, with five mutations accounting for 97% of alleles.

The American Society of Human Genetics (ASHG) recommended that CF carrier screening, with appropriate counselling regarding the nature of the disease and its current management, be offered to all couples contemplating or involved in a pregnancy. Although now commonplace in the U.S. it has been more difficult to obtain funding in Canada within the framework of our public health care system to provide such screening.

H. Gaucher Disease

Gaucher disease is the most common lysosomal storage disease and is caused by a deficiency of the enzyme beta-glucocerebrosidase (EC3.2.1.45). Three clinical phenotypes have been described. The nonneuropathic (type I) form is by far the most common and is more prevalent in the Ashkenazi Jewish population compared with other ethnic groups. In type I disease, the enzyme deficiency results in storage of lipid-laden material in the macrophages of bone marrow, spleen, and liver. This leads to progressive hepatosplenomegaly, pancytopenia, and bone disesase. The involvement of bone may manifest as aseptic necrosis of the femoral heads, bone infarcts, and pathologic fractures of the long bones. Bone crises (episodes of pain and swelling) may also occur. There is tremendous variability in age of onset and severity of disease, ranging from asymptomatic individuals, to adult onset mild thrombocytopenia and splenomegaly, to early childhood onset, with significant bone disease and organ involvement. As seen below, this phenotypic spectrum is seen within the same genotype.

The gene for Gaucher disease was cloned in 1989. The most common mutation identified in the gene is a missense mutation (A1226G) that results in an asparagine (Asn) residue being substituted for a serine (Ser) residue at amino acid 370 (N370S).54,55 Zimran et al. found a carrier frequency of the N370S mutation in the Ashkenazi Jewish population of 1 in 16. In a larger series of 1208 Israeli Ashkenazi individuals, the carrier frequency of the N370S mutation was 1 in 17.5. The prevalence of the N370S mutation implies that 1 in 1225 Ashkenazi Jews will be homozygous for the N370S mutation. The actual number of known Ashkenazi Jewish Gaucher patients with this genotype is much lower than that expected according to the frequency of the N370S mutation, suggesting low penetrance of this mutation. Further support for reduced penetrance of this mutation (in the homozygous state) comes from the frequency of disease-causing alleles among patients with Gaucher disease. The second most common disease-causing allele is a single base insertion frameshift mutation, 84GG. This mutation was found in only 10 of 2305 (1 in 230) normal Ashkenazi Jewish subjects, but it is represented in an unexpectedly large number of patients with Gaucher disease. The allele frequency ratio of the N370S mutation to the 84GG mutation in Gaucher patients is 6.4 in 1. Yet in the Ashkenazi Jewish population the relative frequency of the N370S mutation is almost 15 times as great as that of the 84GG mutation (14.8 in 1). The most likely explanation is that most N370S/N370S individuals are asymptomatic or have mild disease, and that only about one-third of the N370S/ N370S homozygotes come to medical attention. Yet, at the present time, there is no way to predict the phenotype from the N370S/N370S genotype, except that it is known not to cause neuropathic disease.

The tremendous phenotypic variability of the N370S/N370S genotype has created controversy in carrier testing for Gaucher disease. Some N370S homozygotes can present in childhood with debilitating hepatosplenomegaly, bone pain, and anemia, although the majority do not come to medical attention. In a study at NYU Medical Center, the acceptance rate of screening for Gaucher disease was quite high. All carrier couples detected elected to have prenatal diagnosis (amniocentesis). The two main reasons for choosing testing were the desire to avoid potential problems in offspring and the expense of enzyme replacement therapy. Should carrier testing and subsequent prenatal testing be offered at all if it cannot predict the outcome of a fetus? One argument is that this should be left up to the carrier couple to decide, bearing in mind that the way information is presented (description of the illness, potential response to therapy) significantly influences the decision-making process. Although carrier testing is "offered", patients are often looking for "advice" from the health care professional providing the genetic information. At this time, there does not appear to be strong support among health care professionals for Gaucher carrier testing in the Ashkenazi Jewish population.

III. [alpha] AND [beta] Thalassemia Carrier Screening

Normal adult hemoglobin is a globin heterotetramer composed of two [alpha] chains and two [beta] chains, with a heme prosthetic group linked non-covalently to each globin chain. Approximately 4.5% of the world's population carries a mutation affecting the globin chains of the hemoglobin molecule. Worldwide, the most commonly encountered disorders of hemoglobin are the thalassemias, which as a general rule are diseases of inadequate globin chain quantity; in most cases of thalassemia, the globin chains are qualitatively normal. Mutations in the genes encoding the globin chains lead to reduced or absent globin expression, which in turn leads to reduced or absent production of normal hemoglobin molecules. Thalassemia is subdivided into [several different classifications] This classification centers on the globin chain whose production is reduced or ablated, [alpha] and [beta] thalassemia are by far the most common thalassemias: indeed, mild [beta] thalassemia is thought to be the most common genetic trait in the world.

The clinical severity of thalassemia depends on the number and type of mutations inherited. Mild thalassemia cases (thalassemia trait) are clinically benign, although patients may be mildly anemic. In contrast, children with severe thalassemia present at a young age with failure to thrive, severe anemia, splenomegaly, and recurrent infections. Interestingly, it is not reduced hemoglobin production that directly causes the anemia and other problems facing thalassemics. In [beta] thalassemia, the reduced production of [beta] chains leads to a relative excess of [alpha] chains. These excess [alpha] chains precipitate in red blood cell (RBC) precursors in the bone marrow, leading to markedly ineffective erythropoiesis and decreased RBC survival; this in turn leads to anemia as well as compensatory marrow hyperplasia. In [alpha] thalassemia, the excess [beta] chains do not precipitate in the same fashion, but they aggregate into [beta]^sub 4^ homotetramers, an unstable hemoglobin molecule (hemoglobin H) that causes decreased RBC survival. The most severely affected [beta] thalassemics are transfusion-dependent children and adolescents who may develop iron overload syndromes as a result of both their repeated transfusions and their disregulated iron metabolism. The most severe type of [alpha] thalassemia (Hemoglobin Bart's Hydrops Fetalis) is generally not compatible with life, usually leading to death in utero or early in the neonatal period. In fact, Hemoglobin Bart's Hydrops Fetalis is the single greatest cause of late fetal loss in Southern Chinese, Filipino, and other Southeast Asian populations. There have been only rare case reports of patients surviving with this condition. Pregnant women whose fetuses suffer from this disease are also prone to severe complications, including preeclampsia, ante- or post-partum hemorrhage, and congestive heart failure.

Both [alpha] and [beta] thalassemia traits are considered to provide some selective advantage against malaria, which partially explains their geographic distribution. These disorders occur most commonly in people whose ethnic origin is Mediterranean, Middle Eastern, Indian, and Southeast Asian, with a gene frequency in some groups exceeding 80%. Low-risk groups include Northern Europeans, Japanese, Inuit, and Native Americans (First Nations). Normal individuals carry four [alpha] genes, two copies on each chromosome 16, and two [beta] genes, one on each chromosome 11. [alpha] thalassemia generally results from loss or inactivation of entire genes. Nondeletional [alpha] thalassemia, including [alpha] chain mutants such as Hemoglobin Constant Spring, are less common. In contrast, [beta] thalassemia usually arises as a consequence of point mutations or small deletions/insertions.

...

As suggested by the variety of screening programs listed previously, there are many options relating to which populations and age groups should be offered screening. Indaratna133 lists five potential situations in which an individual may be screened for thalassemia: members of a couple prior to marriage; members of a married couple prior to the first pregnancy; pregnant women; members of the general population (i.e., no particular period targeted); and school-age children. From the list of other alternatives, Indaratna and others support screening pregnant women during their first pregnancy, for reasons of convenience, cost, compliance, and the high likelihood of testing the partner if necessary. The populations that carry the highest gene frequencies for thalassemia, that is, the ethnic groups that a screening program could most efficiently target, are for double gene deletion [alpha] thalassemia, Thai, Filipino, Vietnamese, Chinese, Cambodian, Laotian, Italian, Greek, and Sardinian; and for [beta] thalassemia, Mediterranean (particularly Italian and Cypriot), Middle Eastern, Indian, Southeast Asian, and African. Some authors argue that it is simpler and safer to treat all groups not of Northern European origin as being at risk for thalassemia.

One reasonable screening approach therefore would be to examine all pregnant women who are not of Northern European ethnic origin. Although this approach clearly could not be used to avoid the initial pregnancy, it offers greater convenience, lower cost, and a higher likelihood of compliance (for both patient and partner) than targeting other patient groups. Such women should be screened during a first pregnancy for microcytosis and/or hypochromia. If positive, further phenotypic assays such as iron studies, hemoglobin A^sub 2^ quantification, and H-body staining would be triggered. The patient's partner must also be assessed if iron deficiency has been excluded. Molecular studies could be limited to borderline cases, or to cases where urgent genetic counselling is required. Naturally a broader use of molecular testing is also possible, depending on the resources of individual laboratories. The results of these screening analyses could be used to guide prenatal diagnosis of the current pregnancy, as well as to assist in genetic counselling prior to subsequent gestations.

IV. Guidelines and Requirements for Screening Programs

The purpose of carrier screening is to identify carrier couples who are at high risk of having offspring with a serious genetic disorder. Carrier couples are referred for genetic counselling and offered reproductive options, including prenatal diagnosis.

The following issues need to be considered in the development of a carrier screening program:

A. A simple, accurate, and relatively inexpensive test is available to identify most carriers (generally accepted to be > 95% sensitivity) with few false positives. The test should be cost effective. The expense of testing is likely to drop in the next few years as molecular technological advances lead to more automation. At the present time, the cost of testing remains one of the major obstacles, especially in a solely publicly funded health care system. Resource issues: As molecular testing becomes more routine and automated, the costs associated with the test itself will likely drop precipitously. There are other costs associated with expanding test menus, such as the cost of genetic counselling by genetic counsellors and/or physicians involved in prenatal care.

B. The disorder has significant clinical severity. TSD, Canavan disease, FD, and NPD are serious and lethal in childhood. No curative treatment is available at present. BS, FA, CF, and the severe thalassemias are serious disorders with significant morbidity and reduced lifespan.

   In contrast, Gaucher disease is clinically highly variable and the phenotype cannot be predicted from the most common genotype. For these reasons, most centers do not advocate carrier testing for Gaucher disease.

C. There is a clearly defined target population to offer screening. Physicians will need to consider ethnic background in referring patients for carrier testing as these tests become more routine. It should be clear which tests can be offered to Jewish-non-Jewish couples. Testing is often offered sequentially, to the Ashkenazi Jewish partner first, unless the couple is pregnant. In TSD/CF/Canavan disease the Jewish partner first is recommended. Information concerning the sensitivity of the carrier test (allele frequencies) in the non-Jewish population is important. If the genotype is poorly defined in non-Jewish patients, it may not be appropriate to offer testing to Jewish-non-Jewish couples (NPD/BS/FA). In thalassemia, patients of Northern European ethnicity will be less likely to benefit from carrier screening than, for example, Mediterranean or Southeast Asian patients.

D. The test predicts the clinical course of the disease. As described in this review, the N370S mutation in the Gaucher gene does not predict severity of disease. Therefore, most health professionals do not recommend Gaucher carrier testing despite the fact that the N370S allele is so prevalent (1 in 17).

E. A public and professional education program is in place. Reaching out to target communities is particularly challenging for thalassemia carrier testing. The development of sufficient educational materials and genetic counselling resources is required. Not only are there language barriers but also differences in cultural and/or religious beliefs. As in all communities, there is diversity of literacy and education levels. It is crucial before embarking on any carrier testing program to understand the history and make-up of the target audience. Educational materials need to be translated into all relevant languages. Involving community leaders, establishing trust and maintaining a community presence are the most important aspects of a successful carrier testing program. Some screening programs in Canada focus on community-wide mass screening efforts sponsored by community organizations (e.g., TSD) or target certain groups (e.g., high school students).

F. Informed consent for screening. Clear and current information should be available to the public and to health professionals involved in genetic counselling. Decisions about genetic testing are made in keeping with the values of the individual. Professional groups that should not be overlooked in the dissemination of information are religious and community leaders. They often play an important role in the delivery of information (for example, as part of premarital counselling). Religious leaders may be called on to help couples make difficult reproductive decisions, such as whether to seek prenatal testing or to continue a pregnancy after an abnormal prenatal diagnosis. In a survey by Steiner-Grossman and David, only 24% of rabbis knew that 1 in 25 Ashkenazi Jews carried the Tay-Sachs gene. Over half the rabbis thought that the correct number was somewhere between 1 in 100 and 1 in 250. In this survey, rabbis expressed a willingness to learn more and recognized their role in disseminating information to congregants.

   Although experience has shown that most individuals will choose carrier testing for serious autosomal recessive conditions, it must be possible to consent to each carrier test rather than to a group or panel of tests. Carrier testing should not be offered as an all-or-none package. As new carrier tests become available the impact on the time required for genetic counselling must be considered. This includes the time required for education and the informed consent process. With DNA-based testing, there is a need for signed, informed consent to address the issues of testing to be pursued, DNA banking, and access to DNA once the test or battery of tests has been completed.

G. Awareness of community needs. In our center most Jewish individuals come for carrier testing when they get married or when they are pregnant with their first child. However, in some orthodox Jewish communities, programs have been designed to detect individual carriers in young adults with the purpose of avoiding marriages in which both partners are carriers for the same genetic disorder. This avoids the risk of affected offspring in a community where prenatal diagnosis and abortion are generally not acceptable. Again, early involvement of the target community is essential to achieve the intended outcome of the genetic screening program being offered.

* * *

As the Vallance & Ford article notes, the primary purpose for carrier testing is in the reproductive context. There are a number of recessive and sex-linked disorders. Typically, a couple will seek carrier testing when one or both of them have a family history of a disorder, or when they are a member of a high risk group with respect to incidence of a known mutation. Much of the case law with respect to carrier testing occurs in the context of wrongful birth suits, brought by parents alleging negligence with respect to carrier testing done on one of the parents prior to the pregnancy.

Jorge v. New York City Health and Hospitals Corp.

563 N.Y.S.2d 411 (N.Y. App. Div. 1991)

Kassal, Justice.

...

In January 1985, plaintiff Lillian Jorge, then 29 years of age, began to receive prenatal care at Bellevue Hospital, which is owned and operated by defendant, the New York City Health and Hospitals Corporation. Ms. Jorge, an employee of Bellevue Hospital, is black and a carrier of the genetic trait of sickle cell anemia. Aware that a child of parents who both have the sickle cell trait has a one-in-four chance of being born with the fatal disease, Ms. Jorge sought and obtained genetic counseling as a part of her prenatal care at Bellevue, and arrangements were made for the father, plaintiff Emory White, to be tested for sickle cell trait on January 16, 1985. Having been erroneously advised by Bellevue Hospital that Mr. White's test result was negative, Ms. Jorge, who would otherwise have terminated the pregnancy, carried to term, and on August 30, 1985, the infant plaintiff, Emory Elijah White, was born with sickle cell anemia.

On November 27, 1985, a notice of claim was filed against the defendant, and on or about September 11, 1986, this lawsuit was commenced. Plaintiffs do not assert a "wrongful life" claim, which is not recognized in this state but, rather, seek damages for the pecuniary expenses to be incurred in the care and treatment of the infant during his lifetime.

The disease of sickle cell anemia, largely suffered by blacks, is characterized by the presence of blood cells shaped in a crescent, or "sickle" shape, instead of the normal round shape, which impede blood circulation and thus interfere with the function of a number of the body's organs. It generally requires many hospitalizations during the patient's lifetime, and results in death in early adulthood. Consistent with this pattern, the infant plaintiff has had nine hospitalizations for pneumonia, and one for heart failure, in the first three years of his life.

In granting defendant's motion to dismiss the complaint as time-barred, the IAS part determined the date on which the causes of action accrued to be January 16, 1985, when the plaintiff father's test result was incorrectly read as negative for sickle cell trait, and ruled that no toll for continuing treatment was available in these circumstances.

A medical malpractice claim generally accrues on the date of the alleged wrongful act or omission, which, in the instant case, was correctly determined by the IAS part to be January 16, 1985. Under the continuous treatment doctrine, established in *Borgia v. City of New York*, 187 N.E.2d 777, and subsequently codified in CPLR § 214-a, the time in which to institute such an action is stayed when the course of treatment which includes the wrongful acts or omissions has run continuously and is related to the same original condition or complaint. This rule applies to both the two years and six months statute of limitations for medical malpractice, CPLR § 214-a, and the one year and ninety days statute of limitations applicable to the municipal defendant.

In the facts presented, the statute of limitations, absent a toll, would render plaintiffs' notice of claim, filed November 27, 1985, and lawsuit commenced September 11, 1986, time-barred (General Municipal Law §§ 50-e, 50-i). Defendant argues that the ruling in *Delaney v. Muscillo*, 525 N.Y.S.2d 221, precludes application of the continuous treatment doctrine in this case, which would provide such a toll. There, the erroneous reading of an Rh factor test given during the plaintiff mother's first pregnancy resulted in the birth of an impaired child in her fourth pregnancy. In denying the applicability of the continuous treatment doctrine, this Court reasoned that "there was neither continuity of treatment nor identity of condition" in the four pregnancies but, rather, "discrete" and unrelated obstetric care given for each pregnancy. *Id.*, 138 A.D.2d at 260, 261, 525 N.Y.S.2d 221.

The case before us is distinguishable, inasmuch as it involves a single pregnancy, for which, significantly, plaintiff sought and received genetic counseling regarding a specific condition, requested and obtained the testing of the baby's father in connection therewith, and continued to make inquiry, during subsequent consultations with her physician, about the possibility that the child would be born with sickle cell anemia. Because the testing of plaintiff father was sought and conducted solely in connection with Ms. Jorge's pregnancy, and was an integral part of her treatment, we hold that the act of medical malpractice, consisting of an erroneous negative reading of the test results, was committed in the context of her care, treatment, and genetic counseling. This medical care began in January 1985 and continued until the birth of the plaintiff infant on August 30, 1985. Of particular significance is that, despite Ms. Jorge's repeated inquiries during the course of her pregnancy, no further tests were administered, or other action taken, to allay her fears and confirm the absence of the sickle cell trait in the baby's father.

Nelson v. Krusen

678 S.W.2d 918 (Tex. 1984)

SPEARS, JUSTICE.

...

Tom and Gloria Nelson brought a wrongful birth suit in their own behalf and a wrongful life suit as next friends of Mark Nelson, their minor son, against Dr. Edward Krusen and Baylor University Medical Center. The Nelsons' suits alleged that Dr. Krusen negligently advised them that Mrs. Nelson was not a genetic carrier of Duchenne muscular dystrophy and was no more likely than any other woman to have a child afflicted by the disease. The Nelsons further alleged that, had they known of the risk that their child would be born with the disease, they would have terminated the pregnancy. The Nelsons alternatively claimed that Baylor negligently conducted or reported certain tests thereby causing Dr. Krusen to misinform them.

The trial court rendered summary judgment for Dr. Krusen and Baylor on the grounds that the statute of limitations had run on the wrongful birth claim and that no cause of action for wrongful life exists in Texas. The court of appeals affirmed....

The summary judgment evidence showed that the Nelsons already had one child with Duchenne muscular dystrophy when they learned in 1976 that Mrs. Nelson was again pregnant. The Nelsons consulted Dr. Krusen to determine whether Mrs. Nelson was a genetic carrier of the disease. Dr. Krusen examined Mrs. Nelson on three separate occasions between April and June of 1976, and based on test results, assured Mrs. Nelson that she was not a carrier. In light of Dr. Krusen's opinion, the Nelsons chose not to terminate the pregnancy, and Mark Nelson was born November 24, 1976. On November 12, 1979, a nursery school examination revealed that Mark had tight heel cords bilaterally. As a result, Mark was referred to a pediatric neurologist, who determined from an examination on February 20, 1980, that Mark had Duchenne muscular dystrophy. Mark was three years and three months old at this time.

The neurologist based his diagnosis in part on Mark's "lordotic and clumsy gait." Although this clumsiness may have been evident during Mark's first two years, during that time these symptoms could be discounted as simply the result of being two years old and learning to walk. Only as the child grew older and continued to exhibit this clumsiness, however, did the possibility of a neuromuscular defect become detectable to the trained eye.

I. Statute of Limitations

Dr. Krusen and Baylor moved for summary judgment, claiming that the Nelsons' actions were barred because they were not brought within two years of the last examination by Dr. Krusen. The defendants relied on the limitations period prescribed by article 5.82, section 4 of the Insurance Code, which provides:

> Notwithstanding any other law, no claim ... for compensation for a medical treatment or hospitalization may be commenced unless the action is filed within two years of the breach or the tort complained of or from the date the medical treatment that is the subject of the claim or the hospitalization for which the claim is made is completed....

The limitations period of article 5.82, by its terms, arguably began running on the date of the last examination by Dr. Krusen or on the date of Mark's birth and barred the Nelsons' claims two years later. Under our holding in *Sax v. Votteler,* 648 S.W.2d 661 (Tex. 1983), the statute cannot cut off Mark's cause of action before he reaches the age of legal capacity. If applied literally, the statute would, however, operate to bar the parents' cause of action before they knew it existed, even though they did not discover, and could not reasonably have discovered, their injury within two years. The Nelsons contend that applying the statute in this manner is unconstitutional.

In *Gaddis v. Smith,* 417 S.W.2d 577 (Tex. 1967), a medical malpractice case, this court adopted the "discovery rule," providing that the statute of limitations did not begin to run until the patient learned of, or, in the exercise of reasonable care and diligence, should have learned of, the alleged malpractice. *Id.* at 580. The rule in *Gaddis* was adopted as a matter of statutory construction, because the limitations provision, article 5526, Tex. Rev. Civ. Stat. Ann., provided that the suit must be brought within two years of the date the cause of action *accrued.* We held that a cause of action does not accrue until the plaintiff knows, or has reason to know, of his injury. In contrast, article 5.82, section 4 contains no accrual language and thus imposes an absolute two-year statute of limitations, regardless of when the injury was discovered.

The Nelsons challenge the statute on several constitutional grounds. They claim that the statute denies them equal protection and due process under the fourteenth amendment to the United States Constitution. Under the Texas Constitution, they claim that the statute violates the article I, section 3 prohibition against public emoluments, the section 19 due process guarantee, and the section 13 "open courts" provision. Article I, section 13 provides in part:

> ... All courts shall be open, and every person for an injury done him, in his lands, goods, person or reputation, shall have remedy by due course of law.

The Nelsons argue that this guarantee of a remedy by due course of law makes any legislative attempt to bar their cause of action prior to its discovery unconstitutional. Our disposition of the Nelsons' open courts argument makes consideration of the other constitutional claims unnecessary.

The numerous decisions of this court construing article I, section 13 establish that the guarantee of a remedy by due course of law is a substantial right, independent of other constitutional provisions. Although sections 13 and 19 of article I both guarantee due process, *Sax v. Votteler*, 648 S.W.2d 661, 664 (Tex. 1983), the two Texas due course of law provisions are not coterminous. Separate due process and open courts guarantees were included in the seventh and eleventh declarations of rights in the first constitution of Texas as a sovereign republic. These separate rights have been preserved in every constitution since. *See* Tex. Const. (1836); *see also* 1 G. Braden, *The Constitution of the State of Texas: An Annotated and Comparative Analysis* 47 (1977).

The common thread of this court's decisions construing the open courts provision is that the legislature has no power to make a remedy by due course of law contingent on an impossible condition. In *H. Runge & Co. v. Wyatt*, 25 Tex. (Supp.) 291 (1860), the court was faced with the issue of whether a defendant had the right to be sued in his home county when that county was newly severed from an existing county and did not yet have courts. Relying on the open courts provision, the court concluded that the legislature could not have intended to force plaintiffs to sue in a county where there were no tribunals to provide a remedy by due course of law. *Id.* at 294; *accord Clark v. Goss*, 12 Tex. 395 (1854); *O'Shea v. Twohig*, 9 Tex. 336 (1852).

In *Dillingham v. Putnam*, 14 S.W. 303 ([Tex.]1890), this court stated, "A law which practically takes away from either party to litigation the right to a fair and impartial trial in the courts provided by the constitution for the determination of a given controversy, denies a remedy by due course of law." 14 S.W. at 304. The court went on to hold that a legislative act making the right of appeal depend on the giving of a supersedeas bond, without reference to the appellant's ability to pay, was unconstitutional. *Id.*, 14 S.W. at 305. Of course, for those unable to pay, the bond was an impossible condition.

This principle was best illustrated in the case of *Hanks v. City of Port Arthur*, 48 S.W.2d 944 ([Tex.]1932). The city charter exempted the city from liability for injuries caused by street defects, unless the city had written notice of the defect at least twenty-four hours prior to the injury. In other words, the plaintiff, Mrs. Hanks, was required to give the city notice of the defect before she was injured.... The court declared the notice provision unconstitutional,....

The court in *McCrary v. City of Odessa*, 482 S.W.2d 151 (Tex. 1972), applied similar reasoning. A city charter provision requiring notice within sixty days of an accident was challenged as violating article I, section 13, to the extent the notice requirement applied to minors. The court reasoned that the notice provision presupposed the existence of a person capable of complying. In the case of minors, this presupposition was false, because minors were legally incapacitated from bringing suit and, hence, powerless to comply with the notice requirement. For this reason, they, like those unable to comply because of physical or mental incapacity, were excused from compliance until their disabilities were removed.

The reasoning of these decisions was reaffirmed in *Sax v. Votteler*, 648 S.W.2d 661 (Tex. 1983), a medical malpractice case specifically addressing the constitutionality of article 5.82, section 4 of the Insurance Code as applied to minors. We recognized that article I, section 13 of the Texas Constitution guarantees that Texas citizens bringing common law causes of action will not unreasonably be denied access to the courts. 648 S.W.2d at 664. Based on *Hanks v. City of Port Arthur* and *McCrary v. City of Odessa,* we held that "the right to bring a well-established common law cause of action cannot be effectively abrogated by the legislature absent a showing that the legislative basis for the statute outweighs the denial of the constitutionally-guaranteed right of redress." 648 S.W.2d at 665–66. We concluded that the legislative basis for article 5.82 was legitimate and adopted a two-step analysis for weighing the litigant's constitutional right to redress against the purpose of the statute.

The minor plaintiff, Lori Beth Sax, satisfied the first criterion, because she was denied an established common law cause of action for malpractice. *See, e.g., Texas & P. Ry. Co. v. Morin,* 18 S.W. 503 ([Tex.]1886). We held that Lori Beth Sax also satisfied the second criterion, which required that she show the restriction was unreasonable and arbitrary. Because article 5.82 cut off forever her cause of action before she was legally able to sue, without providing a reasonable substitute, we held that the limitations provision unconstitutionally abrogated her right to redress. 648 S.W.2d at 667 (citing *Middleton v. Texas Power & Light Co.*, 185 S.W. 556 ([Tex.]1916), *aff'd* 249 U.S. 152 (1919)).

These decisions lead to the conclusion that article 5.82 as applied here violates the open courts provision by cutting off a cause of action before the party knows, or reasonably should know, that he is injured. How is the impossible condition placed on the Nelsons any less onerous than requiring a party to sue where there are no courts? *See H. Runge & Co. v. Wyatt,* 25 Tex. (Supp.) 291 (1860). How is the condition less arbitrary than requiring a bond from one unable to pay? *See Dillingham v. Putnam,* 14 S.W. 303 ([Tex.]1890). Is the Nelsons' position any different from Mrs. Hanks, and others incapacitated for any reason, who likewise could not meet the impossible requirement of giving notice of that of which they were not aware? *See Hanks v. City of Port Arthur,* 48 S.W.2d 944 ([Tex.]1932). Is a person whose injuries are not immediately discoverable any more able to sue during the period of undiscoverability than are children during their period of legal disability? *See Sax v. Votteler,* 648 S.W.2d 661 (Tex.1983); *McCrary v. City of Odessa,* 482 S.W.2d 151 (Tex.1972).

There is no qualitative difference between the unreasonable condition imposed on the Nelsons and those previously struck down by this court. In one respect, the circumstances in the present case are even more compelling than in *Sax* and *McCrary*. In those cases, it was possible for the parents to bring their children's suits in time, even if limitations were allowed to run. In the present case, if the Nelsons' assertions are true, the nature of the injury made it unreasonable to expect that anyone, parent or child, would be able to bring suit within two years.

The limitation period of article 5.82, section 4, if applied as written, would require the Nelsons to do the impossible—to sue before they had any reason to know they should sue. Such a result is rightly described as "shocking" and is so absurd and so unjust that it ought not be possible. *Hays v. Hall,* 488 S.W.2d 412, 414 (Tex.1972); *Gaddis v. Smith,* 417 S.W.2d 577, 580, 581 (Tex.1967). Deferring to the legislative imposition of such an unreasonable condition would amount to an abdication of our judicial duty to protect the rights guaranteed by the Texas Constitution, the source and limit of legislative as well as judicial power. This, we cannot do. We hold that article 5.82, section 4 of the Insurance Code is unconstitutional, under the open courts provision, to the extent it purports to cut off an injured person's right to sue before the person has a reasonable opportunity to discover the wrong and bring suit.

Neither *Sax v. Votteler,* 648 S.W.2d 661 (Tex.1983), nor *Robinson v. Weaver,* 550 S.W.2d 18 (Tex.1977), is to the contrary. In both cases, the adult litigants discovered their injuries while there was still a reasonable time to sue. In both cases the parties had over one year from the date the injuries were discovered, even if the two year limitations period was not tolled. The statutes of limitation were not unconstitutional as applied to the parties in *Sax* and *Robinson*; hence, there was no reason to strike down the statutes merely because they might operate in an unconstitutional manner in another case. *See City of Waco v. Landingham*, S.W.2d 631 (Tex. 1941); *see also Kentucky Union Co. v. Kentucky,* 219 U.S. 140 (1910). In stark contrast, the Nelsons were cut off well before they discovered Mark's condition. There was no time within two years of the last examination or of Mark's birth when they could have sued.

We hold that article 5.82, section 4 of the Insurance Code as applied in this case violates the open courts provision of article I, section 13 of the Texas Constitution. Therefore, the parents' cause of action for "wrongful birth" is not barred by limitations. In *Jacobs v. Theimer*, 519 S.W.2d 846 (Tex. 1975), we approved a cause of action for "wrongful birth," under which parents may recover the expenses reasonably necessary for the care and treatment of their child's impairment from a physician who has negligently failed to inform the parents of the risk of that impairment.

[The Court went on to affirm the Appeal Court's decision that there is no cause of action for wrongful life in Texas]

3. Susceptibility and Predictability Testing

James P. Evans, et al., *The Complexities of Predictive Genetic Testing*

322 British Med. J. 1052 (2001)

Predictive genetic testing is the use of a genetic test in an asymptomatic person to predict future risk of disease. These tests represent a new and growing class of medical tests, differing in fundamental ways from conventional medical diagnostic tests. The hope underlying such testing is that early identification of individuals at risk of a specific condition will lead to reduced morbidity and mortality through targeted screening, surveillance, and prevention. Yet the clinical utility of predictive genetic testing for different diseases varies considerably. We explore here the factors that contribute to this variation and which will dictate the utility of any of these new tests now or in the future.

Methods and definition of terms

The observations in this paper derive from our experience in clinical medicine, medical genetics, genetic counselling, and molecular biology and from participation in educational programmes for generalists on medical genetics. The definition of utility used here encompasses all aspects of a test (individual and societal) that render it more or less useful in the clinical arena.

Difference from conventional medical testing: Current and future use

A conventional medical diagnostic test, such as a blood count or an imaging study, defines something about the patient's current condition. Although such information may have implications for the future, its overwhelming utility lies in the information it provides about the patient's current state.

A predictive genetic test, in contrast, informs us only about a future condition that may (or may not) develop. The identified risk is sometimes high-for example, in a positive test for Huntington disease—but always contains a substantial component of uncertainty, not only about whether a specific condition will develop, but also about when it may appear and how severe it will be. Predictive genetic tests often carry a further element of uncertainty: the interventions available for individuals at risk are often untested, and recommendations may be based on presumed benefit rather than observations of outcomes.

These uncertainties contrast with the presentation of predictive genetic testing in the popular media, which often fosters an illusion that genetic risk is highly predictable and determinative. 'A New York Times article, for example, recently described a "genetic report card" that would predict a baby's health history at birth.' In fact, uncertainties inherent in most genetic tests represent a major limitation to their clinical utility.

Individual versus family

Whereas conventional diagnostic testing rarely has medical importance for anyone other than the person tested (except in the case of communicable diseases) predictive genetic testing typically has direct implications for family members. Concern for relatives may be an important motivating factor for a patient wanting to undergo such testing; some family members, however, may resist participating in the testing because they prefer not to have information about their genetic risk. The-utility of a predictive genetic test will therefore depend on whose point of view is considered.

Utility of predictive genetic testing for different diseases

An examination of predictive genetic testing in various diseases helps to identify factors that determine utility.... These diseases are discussed below, from those for which testing is most useful through to those for which testing is least useful or even harmful.

Multiple endocrine neoplasia type 2

The rare disorder multiple endocrine neoplasia type 2 results from mutations in the RET proto-oncogene. People with the disorder are almost certain to develop medullary thyroid carcinoma unless they undergo prophylactic thyroidectomy. Studies comparing children with multiple endocrine neoplasia type 2 who underwent thyroidectomy with those who did not, offer compelling evidence that such surgery reduces the likelihood of dying from cancer. Predictive genetic testing makes it possible to identify those who will benefit from surgery.

This example illustrates that when predictive genetic testing strongly predicts a deleterious clinical outcome and an efficacious early intervention exists, it is of high utility. Indeed, such testing for multiple endocrine neoplasia type 2 is the accepted standard of care for individuals at risk.

Haemochromatosis

Haemochromatosis is an uncommon (but not rare) condition of tissue iron deposition, leading to diabetes, cirrhosis, heart disease, arthritis, and gonadal dysfunction. Phlebotomy is a simple and effective preventive treatment, and predictive genetic testing is therefore useful to raise suspicion of this often elusive diagnosis. Testing is less useful for haemochromatosis than for multiple endocrine neoplasia type 2, however, because of low predictive value.

Although excess iron accumulation results from a genetic predisposition, other factors contribute to the development of clinically important iron overload, including sex, diet, and exposure to liver toxins such as alcohol. Thus the penetrance of the haemochromatosis genotype (the proportion of individuals with genetic susceptibility who will develop the associated clinical condition) is low. The resultant uncertainty limits the utility of predictive genetic testing because preventive action based only on the results of such testing would subject many individuals who would never develop clinical sequelae to unnecessary phlebotomy.

Colorectal cancer

About 5–10% of colorectal cancer results from inheritance of a few highly penetrant gene mutations that confer a high lifetime risk of the disease. "Predictive genetic testing can be useful when family history suggests increased risk—for example, three or more affected relatives, with one in whom the disease was diagnosed before age 50—and is compatible with a diagnosis of hereditary non-polyposis colon cancer. Affected individuals have about a 70% lifetime risk of colorectal cancer. Periodic colonoscopic surveillance of these individuals reduces the development of colorectal cancer by 62% when compared with unscreened controls," showing the utility of predictive genetic testing in this circumstance.

However, hereditary non-polyposis colon cancer involves other cancer risks as well. Affected women have a high risk of endometrial cancer, as well as increased risks of ovarian cancer, other gastrointestinal cancers, and cancers of the ureteral tract. No established surveillance strategies are available for these other cancers. Thus predictive genetic testing provides an established outcome benefit for only one of the risks identified, and therefore although useful, it provides less clear cut benefit than in a condition such as multiple endocrine neoplasia type 2.

Breast and ovarian cancer

About 5–10% of breast and ovarian cancers result from the inheritance of mutations in the BRCAI or BRCA2 gene. Predictive genetic testing for breast and ovarian cancer, as for hereditary non-polyposis colon cancer, can be useful to identify those at increased risk. In both breast and ovarian cancer, however, utility is limited because of considerable uncertainty about the predictive value of the test.

A woman carrying a mutation in the BRCAI or BRCA2 gene may develop breast cancer, ovarian cancer, both cancers, or neither. Penetrance estimates range from 36–85% for breast cancer and 10–44% for ovarian cancer. Moreover, the age at which cancer occurs is widely variable. These uncertainties probably reflect a combination of factors, including the environment, modifying genes, the nature of a woman's specific mutation, and purely stochastic processes.

The utility of predictive genetic testing for breast and ovarian cancer is further limited by the nature of available surveillance and prevention strategies. Starting mammography at age 25 to 35 is recommended for carriers of the BRCAl or BRCA2 gene, but the efficacy of this early surveillance is unknown. Because mammography is already widely encouraged for women aged over 40 (in the United States) or 50 (in the United Kingdom), information on genetic susceptibility is less relevant at later ages. Finally, adequate surveillance for ovarian cancer is not available.

Chemoprevention with tamoxifen shows promise for reducing risk of breast cancer, but conflicting data exist. Moreover, chemoprevention increases risk of endometrial cancer and venous thromboembolic disease. Oral contraceptives may reduce risk of ovarian cancer but may also increase risk of breast cancer. Prophylactic oophorectomy and mastectomy are reasonable options for some women and seem to be effective in reducing cancer risk. Such measures carry substantial burdens, however, and mastectomy in particular is not widely accepted by women at risk.

In short, knowledge of an inherited predisposition to breast or ovarian cancer does not lead to simple, straightforward measures to reduce risk, thus limiting the utility of predictive genetic testing.

Alzheimer's disease

Alzheimer's disease illustrates the potential for predictive genetic testing to cause harm. Measurement of the apolipoprotein E genotype can predict risk of developing Alzheimer's disease in people of European descent. Two copies of the apolipoprotein E4 gene (present in 2% of the general population) are associated with a 10-fold increased risk of Alzheimer's disease; one copy is associated with a twofold increased risk, and the inheritance of an apolipoprotein e2 allele is protective. Thus a positive test is an imprecise measure of risk and could result in anxiety, stigmatisation, or discrimination. The principle of avoiding harm suggests that currently such testing would generally be unethical because no effective prevention is available.

Factors affecting utility

The ideal context, therefore, is a highly predictive test for a disease that is serious and incurable but preventable by means that are imperfect or expensive....

Severity of disease and availability of effective treatment

The utility of predictive genetic testing declines when a disease is curable. Testing for tuberculosis, for example, makes little sense, even though genetics contributes to susceptibility to the disease. Similarly, as scientific advances make breast or colon cancer curable by increasingly innocuous means, the utility of predictive genetic testing will decline.

Screening and prevention

Effective and inexpensive screening methods also make predictive genetic testing less useful because these measures can be readily applied to the entire population. Testing for hypertension makes little sense—despite evidence of strong genetic contributors to this condition—because universal screening and treatment are the rule. As the expense of screening rises, predictive genetic testing becomes more appealing. Thus, if magnetic resonance imaging (which is expensive) were shown to be superior to mammography (less expensive) in screening for breast cancer, testing could target those who would benefit most

Available preventive measures must be either imperfect or expensive for predictive genetic testing to be of high utility. Testing makes sense in women at high risk of breast or ovarian cancer if they are considering oophorectomy or mastectomy: a positive test would confirm risk and support the use of invasive, imperfect interventions. When prevention is simple, however, the value of testing decreases. Vaccination is so cheap, safe, and effective that universal administration is rational. Thus testing has no utility in measles, mumps, or rubella despite evidence of genetic differences in susceptibility to infectious disease. The same would be true if an effective, safe, and inexpensive vaccination existed for breast cancer.

Perceptions of utility

Family history and experience are important factors in determining how an individual perceives the utility of predictive genetic testing. [For example] a woman's perception of the utility of testing for risk of breast cancer, can vary depending on whether other close relatives have died of the disease or on her own family structure.

Conclusion

Predictive genetic testing has great potential for accurate risk assessment and for guiding the use of an expanding armamentarium of screening and prevention methods. The utility of testing varies widely, however, depending on the magnitude of risk, the accuracy of risk prediction, options available to reduce risk, an individual's previous experience, and the needs and experience of family members. In addition, the utility of a given predictive genetic test is likely to change over time as knowledge grows, new strategies for prevention are developed, and costs change. The complexity of these factors calls for discussions about testing that are highly tailored to the testing context and the individual's needs and preferences.

Susan Sobel & C. Brookes Cowan, *Ambiguous Loss and Disenfranchised Grief: The Impact of DNA Testing on the Family as a System*

Family Process, Spring 2003

DNA predictive testing identifies the presence of hereditary diseases in asymptomatic individuals. It provides genetic information that has implications not only for the individual tested but also for relatives. When hereditary disease that is serious and/or fatal is revealed, as is the case for predictive testing for Huntington disease (HD), it has profound psychosocial consequences.

Many illnesses thought to be idiosyncratic in origin have recently been identified as hereditary. Because DNA testing will be progressively used, we need to know about the psychosocial impact of this procedure on the individual and the family. In this article, we specifically address the families' loss and grief as precipitated by predictive testing for HD.

In a recently published exploratory study, we examined the impact on the family as a system of DNA predictive testing of asymptomatic people at risk for HD. Although loss was an implicit feature in families' narratives, we did not initially focus on it. Subsequently, we decided it deserved attention because healthcare professionals are uniquely qualified to help families cope with disease in the family. The description of these losses is presented in the context of several perspectives, each of which suggests clinical interventions. We drew on ambiguous loss as defined by Boss (1999; Boss, Caron, & Horbal, 1988; Kaplan & Boss, 1999), disenfranchised grief as described by Doka (1989), and anticipatory loss and unresolved grief as described by Rolland (1990, 1994a).

"Ambiguous loss" has been defined by Boss as "an incomplete or uncertain loss". Ambiguous loss occurs either when a family member is physically absent but psychologically present to the family, as is the case for families with MIAs, or when a member is physically present but psychologically absent, as is the situation for families with a member with Alzheimer disease. Such loss affects family boundaries. There is confusion about who is in the family and who is out. Families' belief systems are challenged. It is a loss that defies meaning because ambiguity interferes with making meaning. Without meaning, a loss is one without resolution.

Asymptomatic individuals who have tested positive for HD, i.e., they have the gene, but are currently physically and psychologically present. However, because our social norms define people as either sick or well, these individuals are in an ambiguous situation. Generally, the definition of any loss and its impact is socially and culturally influenced. Rituals for mourning, says Boss, are "reserved for the clearly dead. There are few ceremonies to comfort us when our loved ones are partially gone."

Families whose members have undergone predictive testing have no social sanction for their grief. It is "disenfranchised." Doka defines disenfranchised grief as, "grief that persons experience when they incur a loss that is not or cannot be openly acknowledged, publicly mourned, or socially supported", e.g., the loss precipitated by knowledge of infertility.

Until recently, the loss and bereavement literature focused on an individual's experience in the terminal phases of a loved one's illness. There is little information about how families cope with loss or anticipatory grief. However, "in the context of a family's loss of one of its members—be it nuclear, family of origin or extended family—all the bereaved continue to relate to one another, and, in so doing, their experiences of grief inevitably are influenced, and in turn influence the experiences of the relatives."

Understandably, families with a long history of loss because of inherited diseases that were misdiagnosed or unexplained, as was the case for HD, are predisposed to particular difficulty. Whatever their prior explanations for the death of relatives, their fates are now intertwined.

Background

Our Initial HD Study

HD is an inherited disease caused by a mutated, autosomal dominant gene that has nearly 100% penetrance. Each offspring of an affected adult has a 50% chance of inheriting the gene that produces the disease. HD causes changes in the brain and central nervous system that affect movement, mood, and cognition. It is terminal. There are few palliative measures. In 1993 a predictive blood test became available that identified the presence or absence of the gene in asymptomatic people with 99% accuracy.

Background for our research included studies that explored the psychological impact of the test on individuals. Also relevant was literature that described the effects of chronic and/or terminal illness on family functioning. Other recent and pertinent articles devoted specifically to the subject of genetic testing and families' psychosocial responses include Davidson, Weingarten, Pollin, et al., (2000), Kaplan and Boss (1999), and Street and Soldan, (1998). The theoretical framework for the study was family systems.

Methods

Eighteen families, comprised of 55 individuals, were interviewed in their homes during a 12 hour, semi-structured interview. These were individuals who had been tested at least one year prior to the beginning of the study and had been asymptomatic at the time. Geographical breakdown of study families includes three from Canada, seven from Vermont, one from Massachusetts, one from Rhode Island, two from Pennsylvania, three from Maryland, and one from Arizona. It is possible that because of the nature of the recruitment that was done, i.e., through a few large testing centers, and the nature of the population who chose to be tested, the families were ethnically homogeneous. All were Caucasian, most of northern European descent, and college educated. The choice of family members to include in the interview was determined by the subjects who had been tested. Interviews were arranged to coincide with visits from extended family members. Half of the recruited individuals had tested normal. Half had tested positive. Usually, more than one individual in each family had been tested.

The data obtained were the families' perceptions. The rationale for our approach was consistent with the tenets of qualitative research. In a field in which little is known, such as clinical genetics, the subjects need to be the ones to identify areas of significance. It was expected that issues would emerge that we had not yet considered.... Every interview was tape recorded and transcribed verbatim. The principle investigator and her collaborator, who was not present in the interview and who was not part of the development of the study's design, read and reread each transcript many times. [We] developed a list of themes contained in each transcript and marked their occurrence in the text (open coding). We then grouped the themes into more abstract categories (axial coding). Finally, we focused on categories that appeared to have the most relevance for theory development from a systems perspective (selective coding). Inter-rater reliability was high.

Results from the Initial Study

In the initial examination of the data, three areas of family functioning emerged as significant. They were (a) family membership (81%), (b) members' role changes (61%), and (c) family patterns of communication (56%). The analysis suggested that families should be more involved in the decision for testing. It was surmised that greater family involvement would reduce the ruptures in family cohesion, the conflict around communication, and the premature role changes for asymptomatic family members who tested positive.

Loss and Grief: Results

The Nature of the Losses

We first present the kinds of losses families identified. Some of these losses were unique to the process of testing. Others were similar to those that accompany any crisis or change. Second, we present how families coped with their losses. In this section, we seek to understand families' coping in the context of ambiguous loss and disenfranchised grief. Third, we discuss the impact of the larger social context on their grieving and their consequent adjustment. Although the numbers of families experiencing each of the following types of losses is presented, the study involves too few families to identify trends.

In all cases, given the nature of the test, the primary loss was the loss of uncertainty with respect to carrying the HD gene. Families' initial responses to test results varied. "If we hadn't been tested, we wouldn't be in this mess now," was one family's response. Others appeared to have responses that were more positive. Families' responses were not only based on the results of the test for an individual member. They were also influenced by the test results of other family members and by the presence of already symptomatic members. When all offspring tested normal (four families), knowledge of the results produced relief and closure in the immediate family. Family members "lost" the preoccupation with impending illness. They lost the need to search for symptoms in themselves and each other. However, these families reported that normal test results of members did not free them from a sense of loss. Their concern for other relatives dampened their good news.

It is noteworthy that four subjects in the study who experienced the most severe depression were those who tested normal. These individuals, prior to testing, assumed they carried the HD gene and planned their lives accordingly. Upon learning they were normal, they mourned for opportunities they had not taken because of their assumption that they had the HD gene. When their siblings tested positive or were already symptomatic, their bond with siblings, forged by the common threat of disease, was broken. Consequently, they lost their membership in the family. One subject had said to her parents, "I don't want to be left out of the family because I'm not sick." Her sisters who tested positive were now "special people." In addition, this subject lost her rescue fantasy, a fantasy common among people who assume they have the HD gene. Before testing, she had assumed that she carried the HD gene. This would somehow protect others in the family from harboring it.

When a member tested positive, families experienced the loss of a future predicated on the normal life cycle. "Whenever my husband and I look at an older couple, we go, 'that's not going to be us.'"

The life cycle was topsy-turvy for a woman whose sisters tested positive. "At some point, you as the child will probably have to take care of your parents. You will give them back some of what they've given you. That's been taken away. My sisters will never have that chance." It was "unnatural" that her mother would have to watch her children die.

The universal hope that one's children will grow up to lead healthy lives was dampened for parents who tested positive. They now knew that their offspring were at risk. Although they understood that each offspring had a 50% chance of having the disease, they also realized that the uncertainty that accompanies the recognition that one is at risk could lead to severe psychological difficulties. The uncertainty of one's genetic status may cause the individual at risk to feel that his or her life choices, e.g., marriage, children, profession, are limited.

Because of the uncertain status conferred on asymptomatic members who tested positive, families sometimes tended to see those members as "already in the grave." This was the case in four families. Members testing positive lost not only the uncertainty of their genetic status, but their role in the family as well. "I used to be the one everyone would come to and talk to about problems, and now people would take that role away from me." Such loss of roles is referred to by sociologists as "psychosocial death." Unlike people with Alzheimer disease who lose their roles, asymptomatic individuals who tested positive and experienced this psychosocial death were keenly aware of their loss.

Surprisingly some individuals who tested normal also lost their roles. "Our daughter, who erroneously assumed she was positive, was going to be basically the tragic queen who would wave to us all and say, 'I'm doing fine. Don't worry about me. You get on with your lives.' She can no longer play that part."

Families with members who tested positive lost a sense of meaning. "You hear all these percentages and I've always thought, 'big deal for the one that gets it—with anything—heart disease, whatever.' You're the loser, and that's the one thing we have to prepare ourselves for. We can be the losers in the game."

Coping with Loss and Ambiguity

How the families dealt with their losses is the focus of the following analysis. The nature of their attempts to cope with loss are explicable in the context of the ambiguity of their loss, the disenfranchisement of their grief, and their inability to resolve their anticipatory grief in the absence of finding meaning for the situation. There are many dimensions to coping with grief: behavioral, cognitive, and emotional. We present how families responded in each of these ways.

Behavioral responses. In three families, there was an attempt to deal with the anticipatory loss and grief by replacing family members. One of three adult daughters, the only one to have tested normal, longed to have a baby for her affected sisters. A child would be "something that was untainted, that would be okay to love and it would be all right." However, in a pact to not perpetuate the illness, she and her sisters had their tubes tied. Her current need to have a child changed her perspective on the tubal ligation. It was now one more loss for her. Another woman who tested normal felt that starting her own family would enable her to forget her family of origin and the pain of HD for its members. "I am the mother root. My family begins with me."

Other behavioral ways in which families dealt with grief were either to increase connections between members or to distance from them. An example of the former was a son whose mother tested positive. He said, "I feel a lot more need to stay in connection with my mother so that I have good memories of her." The opposite was the case for the partner of a man who tested positive. "It smothered me. I found myself treating him as if he were already dead." One woman who tested normal divorced her husband in an effort to put the past behind her. She later considered this a mistake. Another who tested positive left a relationship that had already been strained by issues unrelated to HD.

In order to cope with the uncertainty of the status of at-risk family members, six families put pressure on untested members to be tested. The oldest offspring and the first one tested in a family known to have HD said, "I could not rest until I knew everyone was safe." Untested members spoke of coercion. "When my sister tested positive, my family said I owed it to them to be tested so they might know that there was at least one who was okay."

In an effort to protect members who tested positive, families evaluated their rituals. Ambiguous loss may make rituals seem hollow. Families may attempt to find new ones or to abandon their rituals all together. In two families, greater attention was given to holidays and family gatherings, with mixed results. "This was the most loving Christmas. But then it was designed to be."

Suicide attempts by those who learned they had the HD gene (3) and those who learned did not (2), were reported by five families. The risk of suicide in families with HD is high. Feelings of helplessness, guilt, and lack of control result when there is no meaning. Families in which genetic knowledge had been kept secret are at enormous risk. It is not yet clear whether or not some suicide attempts made by people who received a positive test result were caused by incipient depression, a symptom of HD. A father affected with HD who had not disclosed this to his daughter before she had two small children made numerous suicide attempts when he learned she had tested positive. A young woman attempted suicide because her normal test result disconnected her from her siblings, whom she knew were affected. One family's behavioral response to a positive test was to use the internet to be socially and psychologically connected to others who understood the nature of the loss and grief and who could validate it.

Emotional responses. Doka (1989) describes how feelings ordinarily experienced in grief such as anger, guilt, sadness, and depression are magnified many-fold when the grief is not socially recognized and validated. When their grief is disenfranchised, families become isolated. Isolation and lack of social support may intensify conflict. Three families in which a member tested positive experienced severe emotional turmoil. "There were some wicked fights because all of our emotions were too close to the surface. It wasn't very pretty. It was harsh. Nobody knew what to do with what they were feeling." Three families experienced increased conflict in matters unrelated to HD. "My brothers and sisters find it easier to fight about mom's care for her heart problems than to face the HD."

Family members who tested normal, as well as those who did not, experienced guilt. The guilt was sometimes in response to wishes that another member would be "the one to have it." In others, their guilt related to a previous decision to have children in spite of their knowledge that HD was in the family. The mother of a 21-year-old daughter who tested positive described the father's response. Both mother and father had known of HD in his family when they married. "He [the father] was extremely upset because he felt he had done this to his daughter. He started to hate himself. I think he loathes himself and wants an excuse not to live anymore." For families who keep secrets, "the members with genetic knowledge live with a unique extended form of anticipatory loss they may not have considered. The burden of future blame, shame, and guilt are real risks should unsuspecting family members contract the disease without preparation." Offspring who learned they had the HD gene felt guilty because their unaffected parent would have to witness their deaths. "My sisters feel like they're doing something to my mom. They feel guilty that she has to go through this again."

A woman who tested positive related her anger to the lack of knowledge and support in the community. "People at church brushed it off with, 'God will provide a miracle,' and they weren't allowing me to face the reality." There was anger in families when members were "in denial," and not emotionally available for support. Anger in the person tested frequently rendered other family members helpless and consequently increased everyone's isolation. "There were a lot of times when I didn't know what to say to her. I was even afraid because I saw how angry she was. It was hard for me to be happy around her but not hard to be happy around other people. I went out a lot." Inconceivable as it seems, one family dealt with the bad news with humor, telling the investigator "funny stories."

The reactions of both anticipatory loss and grief were influenced by the ambiguous status of the healthy person who tested positive. Although the loss had not yet occurred, a positive result made it seem imminent. One woman described her reaction to the news of her sister's test. "You look at my sister. She's no different than five minutes before and all of a sudden, she's dying. I guess we all started grieving immediately. It was like we lived the next fifteen years in those five minutes."

Of course, not all members in the same family had the same responses. Said one son of a mother who tested positive, "We're all leading happy lives now. Let's not worry about it until it's here." Their father, for whom news of his wife's impending illness prompted his own concerns about dying, remonstrated his sons. "My life's running out, but you're still shying away from it."

The greater the diversity of responses in a given family, the greater was the potential for conflict. Diverse responses led to distancing and to silence. "We are all thinking before we speak and that is generally a good thing, but in our case it is not natural." The families in the study were vulnerable to silence because of a history of silence. Their HD-affected relatives had frequently been misdiagnosed with labels that were felt to be shameful, such as alcoholism or "mental illness." The subject of HD and predictive testing easily became one more of the unspeakable topics for them.

A salient finding was that test results for those who were normal, as well as for those who carried the HD gene, sometimes facilitated delayed grief reactions. A 38 year-old man who had been his father's caretaker in the advanced stages of the disease explained his reactions upon learning he was normal. "I was more sad and concerned that my father had it. I felt bad by him. I'm thinking, 'Great for me. I'm negative.' But I'm thinking about him more. He was not so lucky." It was, however, not only deaths that were mourned but also births. A woman who was pregnant at the time of her testing and learned she carried the HD gene grieved at her daughter's birth because she could not be a mother for her children.

Cognitive responses. For the 15 families who experienced considerable changes in their family relationships as a consequence of testing, finding meaning was crucial. Families needed to understand the nature of their loss to combat feelings of helplessness and despair. This goal was complicated by unanticipated information, which the test provided. Sometimes families learned that each sibling could expect a different future. The test results also challenged the family's predetermination of which offspring were affected. "Preselection" has been described as a collective, unconscious coping mechanism whereby families attempt to ward off the anxiety of dealing with uncertainty by designating a particular member to be the one to have HD.

In many families, currently healthy members were revealed to be only "apparently healthy." This category, so recently created by predictive testing, defied proscribed responses. One family, after finding that a member was positive, concluded that the meaning of this situation was that there was, in fact, no meaning. The 16-year-old brother of a sister who tested positive told his mother, "God doesn't have a plan. He just sets up a guideline and away we all go." His mother's response was, "Yes. Your sister lost the lottery." Another family, in response to positive test results, had taken up the study of various philosophies. Its members attempted to convince themselves that these results "made us a better, closer family." "Live for the moment," was the expressed goal of many families. They viewed this perspective as an enlightened one because they felt it changed their priorities. "I think it just made us realize that our family is more important than anything else. Slow down. Take time to be more with your kids. Call each other every day." Families' attempts to identify a good outcome from the testing were not always convincing for them. New information from testing challenged long held beliefs. Without finding meaning, their grief remained unresolved and disenfranchised. They had lost their direction and control.

Normal test results also led to a loss of meaning. When one woman found she was normal, she felt adrift. "Nothing will ever have that much importance to me [as HD]." Most families in this study with members who had been tested 1 to 5 years before our study began were still struggling to reconcile their past belief systems and their sense of their family identity with the facts revealed by the testing.

Discussion

The families' responses of loss and grief as a consequence of predictive testing were consistent with responses of families suffering from ambiguous loss as described by Boss (1999). The testing produced a sense of loss that was "incomplete and uncertain." Those asymptomatic individuals who tested positive had become "the apparently well." The genetic status of offspring and other relatives was thrown into doubt. The families' confusion about the nature of the loss challenged their family identity. Boundaries that had defined family membership were called into question or redrawn. Some members who tested normal were excluded. Some who tested positive lost their roles and were seen as "already in the grave." Previous family rituals seemed inadequate or hollow. The families' grief was not validated by the larger social community.

The families' grief was cumulative and frequently complicated. Some families were caught off guard by the resurgence of complicated grief reactions for the many members whose deaths from HD had been previously unmourned. Although one loss may naturally trigger the memories of other losses, the sense of ambiguous loss for the families with members tested for HD was not a consequence of only one kind of uncertain loss. These families, for generations, had experienced the kind of ambiguous loss described by Boss in which affected relatives, in the terminal phases of HD, were physically present but psychologically absent. Their family history and its cumulative affects on family dynamics that often resulted in conflict, alcoholism, physical abuse, and suicide poorly prepared them to cope with the information revealed by the test.

In order to prepare families adequately to cope with the emotional aftermath, people in the healthcare system need to be aware of the many and varied grief responses among family members. Families need to be prepared for the lack of social support and the isolation they may encounter. We surmised in a previous article that one of the reasons families chose to participate in our study was that the interview provided them with a unique and potentially therapeutic opportunity to mourn their losses publicly and receive social validation.

The losses described by families with members tested for an inherited disease differ from those losses described by families with a member who suffers from a chronic or terminal illness of a nonhereditary nature such as AIDS. For families tested for HD, when a member tests positive, it is a loss without a foreseeable end. Positive test results for asymptomatic individuals produce an ambiguous situation that promotes multiple perspectives among family members. Multiple perspectives may increase the potential for conflict. The systemic patterns of the varied perceptions about loss are intricate. Losses are multiple, cumulative, and circular.

Our findings may be pertinent to other autosomal dominant diseases for which predictive testing is available. They would not necessarily apply to families' responses to testing for other types of inherited diseases that are multifactorial, and/or not life threatening.

Limitations of the Present Analysis

Relevant to any research on the subject of loss and grief are factors of gender, ethnicity, and spirituality. In our study, gender did not appear to influence the management of loss and grief. The cultural and ethnic background of our subjects probably influenced their responses but it was beyond the scope of this study to explore that dimension. Finally, we expected to find connections between subjects' faith and spirituality and their response to loss. We did not. Matters of faith and spirituality were not part of the families' narratives. One possible explanation is that those families who chose to participate in the study did not have a spiritual or religious conviction that sustained them.

Families are a work in progress. The data obtained in our study are examinations of frozen sections—slices of families adapting to the impact of hereditary testing at a particular moment in their development. The data raise questions that we hope to address in future research that follows families over time. How will people who have lost a sense of the future that is guided by the social conceptions of the normal life cycle respond to the developmental milestones and the rituals that our culture provides? Those are the norms that give the rest of us a sense of predictability and continuity.

...

Notes & Questions

1. The article by Vallance and Ford details some of the more common disorders that are transmitted by mutations in recessive genes. In these disorders, heterozygotes will be a carrier of the disorder, but will be unaffected themselves. Only if an individual inherits two copies of the mutation is the individual afflicted with the disease—and even then, the expression of the genetic mutation may be variable. As the article notes, several of the more well-known disorders of this type are associated with the Ashkenazi Jewish population, including Tay-Sachs Disease, Canavan Dis-

ease, Familial Dysautonomia, Niemann-Pick Disease, Fanconi Anemia, Bloom Disease, and Gaucher Disease. Carrier testing for many of these disorders is relatively inexpensive and accurate. Moreover, the at-risk population is identifiable. For example, in addition to persons of Ashkenazi Jewish descent, there are a number of other discrete populations at risk for Tay-Sachs. A subgroup of French-Canadians and the Cajun community of Louisiana have the same carrier rate as Ashkenazi Jews, one in twenty-seven. Irish Americans also have an increased carrier rate of about one in fifty.

Carrier testing programs have been dramatically successful with respect to several of these disorders, notably Tay-Sachs disease. Jewish communities promote testing for Tay-Sachs and similarly devastating genetic disorders among people of marriageable age, so that carriers of a given genetic disease can have this information before contemplating marriage and a family. When two carriers do marry, prenatal diagnosis is encouraged so that the couple may proceed with full knowledge, or elect to terminate the pregnancy if the fetus is affected. *See* Nat'l Tay-Sachs & Allied Diseases Ass'n of Delaware Valley, What Is Tay-Sachs Disease?, http://www.tay-sachs.org/taysachs.php.

As opposed to the Tay-Sachs screening program successes, the screening program for sickle cell trait was less successful. During the 1970s, widespread testing for sickle cell trait and carrier status was undertaken in the African-American population. However as Professor Vernellia Randall describes, the screening was more harmful than helpful:

> Although sickle-cell disease has been described since 1910, it did not become a priority for federal or private funding until the 1970s. In the 1970s, large scale screening was undertaken with the goal of changing African American mating behavior. Unfortunately, the initiative promoted confusion regarding the difference between carriers and those with the disease. This confusion resulted in widespread discrimination against African Americans. Some states passed legislation requiring all African American children entering school to be screened for the sickle-cell trait, even though there was no treatment or cure for the sickle-cell disease. Some states required prisoners to be tested, even though there would be no opportunity for them to pass on the trait. Job and insurance discrimination were both real and attempted. The military considered banning all African Americans from the armed services. African American airline stewardesses were fired. Insurance rates went up for carriers. Some companies refused to insure carriers. During that period, many African Americans came to believe that the sickle-cell screening initiative was merely a disguised genocide attempt, since often the only advice given to African Americans with the trait was, "Don't have kids."

Vernellia R. Randall, *Slavery, Segregation and Racism: Trusting the Health Care System Ain't Always Easy! An African American Perspective on Bioethics*, 15 St. Louis U. Pub. L. Rev. 191, 201 (1996). For additional background on the sickle cell screening program of the 1970s, see James Bowman & Robert F. Murray, Jr., Genetic Variation and Disorders in Peoples of African Origin 365–66 (1990); Patricia A. King, The Past as Prologue: Race, Class, and Gene Discrimination in Gene Mapping: Using Law and Ethics as Guides 94 (George J. Annas & Sherman Elias eds., 1992).

Even under the best of circumstances, carrier testing may have an adverse impact on the individual, the couple, or child. Both the ASHG and ACMG recommend that carrier testing of children be discouraged until the child reaches majority age. The World Health Organization's position is that testing should be deferred until adulthood to preserve the autonomy of the minor. That said, especially during the 1980s, carrier testing of children was undertaken in several scenarios. One study, that considered the impact of carrier testing on young females in families with a history of hemophilia or Duchenne's muscular dystrophy (both X-linked recessive genetic disorders), found that, although childhood testing did not cause serious harm, it also conferred no discernable benefits. The study also noted that genetic counseling was markedly deficient in many of these situations. *See* Outi Jarvinen, et al., *Carrier Testing of Children for Two X-linked Diseases: A Retrospective Study of Comprehension of the Test Results and Social and Psychological Significance of the Testing, 106* PEDIATRICS 1460 (2000). Do you think that testing of young females for these diseases could leave them susceptible to stigmatization within the family or damage to their self-esteem? Can you identify any benefit to the testing?

2. The two cases in the text, *Jorge v. New York City Health and Hospitals Corp.* and *Nelson v. Krusen*, involve failure to identify carriers, negligent advice to prospective parents, and birth of children with genetic disorders. In *Jorge v. New York City Health and Hospital Corp.*, the plaintiffs knew they were at risk for having a child with sickle cell disease. The mother knew she was a carrier and the couple sought testing as to the father's status, which was erroneously reported as negative. Believing that the father was not a carrier, the couple proceeded to have a child ultimately diagnosed as having sickle cell anemia. At issue in the case is when the malpractice action accrued, given the fact that the testing was sought on the father and it is the mother who is the named plaintiff. Here, the Court determines that the negligent testing of the father was committed in the context of the mother's care. As the court notes in this case, the plaintiff is seeking "wrongful birth" damages for the excess costs of caring for the child during his lifetime. What limitations are likely to be placed on the damages awarded to the Jorges? Why is the court careful to not characterize the damages as "wrongful life" damages?

In *Nelson v. Krusen*, the misdiagnosis involves a young woman who likely is a carrier of the X-linked Duchenne's muscular dystrophy (DMD) mutation. With this disorder, half of the female children of a carrier will be carriers themselves, but all of the male children will be afflicted with the disease. The Nelsons already have a child with DMD and the mother seeks testing and counseling when they become pregnant a second time. Assured that the mother is not a carrier, the couple maintains the pregnancy. Their second child is diagnosed with DMD when he is three and one-half years old. At issue in this case is the statute of limitations. Defendants allege that the action is time-barred. However, because the Nelsons do not know that they have a cause of action until their child is diagnosed, they have been foreclosed from bringing their malpractice action earlier. Because the Nelsons can't be expected to sue before they know they have an action, the Court holds that their "wrongful birth" action is not time-barred.

3. Susceptibility and predictive testing raises a host of ethical and social issues. First, the testing seeks to reveal an increased risk, or certainty, of a future disease, not a disease that is presently bedeviling the patient. The clinical utility of the information is highly variable. As the excerpted article from the British Medical Journal notes, some genetic mutations, such as those associated with multiple endocrine neoplasia type 2 (MEN2), are strongly predictive of future disease, and there is an effective intervention that will improve outcome. Others disorders, like hemochromatosis, manifest only when the genetic predisposition is combined with other factors contributing to increased risk. This same situation applies with respect to beryllium sensitivity, where the individual develops permanent lung damage when exposed to this workplace toxin.

Chapter 3 discusses the issue of genetic susceptibility coupled with workplace factors, and the pros and cons of workplace testing.

In contrast, predictive testing for Huntington disease and several other incurable single mutation disorders determines, with certainty, that an individual will develop the disease in later life. However, there is no treatment or preventive measures available to ameliorate this disease. Not all predictive testing is clearly dispositive of future disease. For example, testing for apolipoprotein E4 is noteworthy for its lack of precision and high risk of stigma. Is the "inflicted insight" of knowing that you will develop a disease more harmful than beneficial? Does testing alter family dynamics in a negative way? Does knowledge of future disease, or risk of disease, impair an individual's ability to compete in jobs, educational opportunities, and the "marriage game?" Even if there is no externally applied stigmatization, will the individual's self esteem be irrevocably diminished? The Sobel and Cohen article in the text addresses some of these issues under the rubric of ambiguous loss and disenfranchised grief. In their article, the authors document the breadth and scope of responses by family members, regardless of their status as positive or negative for the HD mutation. Virtually no family member is untouched psychologically and there are profound effects on the concepts of family membership, the role of the family members vis-à-vis each other before and after testing, and family communication patterns. For additional reading on the impact of HD testing, see Bettina Meiser & Stewart Dunn, *Psychological Effect of Genetic Testing for Huntington's Disease: An Update of the Literature*, 174 WESTERN. J. MED. 336 (2001); A. Christine Bourwer-DudokdeWit, et al., *A Hereditary Disorder in the Family and the Family Life Cycle; Huntingon Disease as a Paradigm*, 41 FAMILY PROCESS 677 (2002); Benno Bonke, et al., *Favourable Mutation test Outcomes for Individuals at Risk for Huntington Disease Change the Perspectives of First Degree Relatives*, 111 HUMAN GENETICS 297 (2002); A Maat-Klevit, et al., *Paradox of a Better Test for Huntington's Disease*, 69 J. NEUROLOGY, NEUROSURGERY AND PSYCHIATRY 579 (2000); Michael R. Hayden, *Predictive Testing for Huntington's Disease: The Calm After the Storm*, 356 LANCET 9246 (2000); Abbyann Lynch, *The Price of Silence*, 20 HASTINGS CENTER RPT. 3 (1990). *See also* Corrine O Smith, et al., *Impact of Presymptomatic Genetic Testing for Hereditary Ataxia and Neuromuscular Disorders*, 61 ARCH. NEUROLOGY 875 (2004) (documenting similar impact of testing for other neurogenetic disorders).

In addition to the impact on family members when one member is diagnosed with a highly penetrant, devastating, genetic disorder like HD, there is the question of the rights of the other family members. What if some family members would rather not partake of this genetic revelation? What if some family members don't want awareness of the family disease to taint their children's childhoods and self-image? Do they have a right not to know? Alternatively, how about the rights of those who do want to know—should they be held back from attaining knowledge they feel would be valuable by a relative who is reluctant to confront reality? For cases and discussion of third-party rights and the duty to warn of genetic danger, see Chapter 2.

It is perhaps not surprising that the test uptake for HD is relatively low. One study documented a 16 % uptake among persons registered in a genetic register of HD families; this rate was actually significantly higher than several other studies on uptake of HD testing. *See* David Craufurd, et al., *Uptake of Presymptomatic Predictive Testing for Huntington's Disease*, 334 LANCET 603 (1989).

A recent area of controversy is prenatal and preimplantation testing for late onset diseases like HD. One author documents requests made by women who, knowing that their spouses are at risk for HD, want to verify that the fetus or embryo does not have the mutation. Questions about the rights of the prospective mother, the at-risk father, and the fetus abound with no clear consensus as yet emerging. *See, e.g.*, Ros Tassiker, *Prenatal Requests for Huntington's Disease When the Father Is at Risk and Does Not Want to Know His Genetic Status: Clinical, Legal and Ethical Viewpoints*, 326 British Med. J. 7384 (2003); M. Spriggs, *Genetically Selected Baby Free of Inherited Predisposition to Early-onset Alzheimer's*, 28 J. Med. Ethics 290 (2002).

Yet another cascade of issues accompanies susceptibility testing for breast cancer and colon cancer. Such susceptibility testing is only useful for the five to 10% of persons with such a gene and then only indicates an increased susceptibility, rather than a certainty of disease. For a detailed summary of role of BRCA1 and BRCA2 mutations in breast cancer, see Wylie Burke & Melissa A. Austin, *Genetic Risk in Context: Calculating the Penetrance of BRCA1 and BRCA2 Mutations*, 94 J. Nat'l Cancer Institute 1185 (2002); *see also* Lawrence C. Brody & Barbara Bowles Bieseker, *Breast Cancer Susceptibility Genes*, 77 Medicine 208 (1998). Preventive and surveillance measures can be increased, but many of the cancers related to these genetic susceptibilities are not prone to early detection, even with enhanced surveillance. In the case of colon cancer, a genetically at-risk individual can optimize their diet, have frequent colonoscopies to detect polyps and precancerous changes, and undergo removal of the colon at the extreme. Similar choices flow from breast cancer screening. Clinical utility of susceptibility in these contexts is heavily dependent on the individual's willingness to engage in arduous, often uncomfortable and even disfiguring measures to address increased risk. Like testing for late-onset disease, testing for cancer susceptibility may provoke anxiety, depression, guilt and psychological stress for both the patient and family. *See, e.g.*, Barbara A, Pockaj, *Impact of BRCA1/BRCA2 Counseling and Testing on Newly Diagnosed Breast Cancer Patients*, 4 Women's Oncology Review 237 (2004); Caryn Lerman & Robert Croyle, *Emotional and Behavioral Responses to Genetic Testing for Susceptibility to Cancer*, 10 Oncology 191 (1996); Jean E. Wylie, et al., *Effects of Spouses on Distress Experienced by BRCA1 Mutation Carriers Over Time*, 119C American J. Med. Genetics 35 (2003).

Uptake for breast and colon cancer testing is just beginning to be studied. One early study has documented that African-American women with a strong family history of breast and ovarian cancer are significantly less likely to undergo genetic counseling for or engage in breast cancer testing. This racial disparity cannot be justified on the basis of probability of mutation, socioeconomic status, knowledge and attitudes about the specific test, or cancer risk perceptions. *See* Katrina Armstrong, et al., *Racial Differences in the Use of BRCA1/2 Testing Among Women With a Family History of Breast or Ovarian Cancer*, 293 J. Am. Med. Ass'n 1729 (2005).

Complicating the uptake scenario is the aggressive direct-to-consumer marketing that has been undertaken by vendors of BRCA1/2 and colon cancer testing. *See* J. Jacobellis, et al., *Genetic Testing for Breast and Ovarian Cancer Susceptibility: Evaluating Direct-to-Consumer Marketing—Atlanta, Denver, Raleigh-Durham and Seattle*, 2003, 292 J. Am. Med. Ass'n 796 (2004); Bryn Williams-Jones, *Where There's A Web, There's A Way: Commercial Genetic Testing and the Internet*, 6 Community Genetics 46 (2003). In the United States, there is virtually no regulatory oversight of genetic testing and even less with respect to direct-to-consumer marketing. What dangers might result from direct-to-consumer marketing? How might such marketing mislead women? Given that overall risk of lifetime breast cancer risk is one in nine for the women in the absence of BRCA1/2 mutation, might women falsely believe that a negative test ensures that they will not get breast cancer? In a resource-poor health care system, how does the clinical utility of breast cancer testing for a few fare against mammography for the general population?

Chapter 8

Agricultural Biotechnology: Genetics and Food

While the application of genetic research and technology to animals and plants is really just a subset of genetic research and technology generally, it is often treated as a categorically different area in the public discourse. Accordingly, the issues raised by such agricultural biotechnology (defined here to include genetic technologies applied to both plants and animals), or "ag-biotech," are separated out into their own chapter in this casebook. This Chapter first considers intellectual property issues specific to ag-biotech, and then concludes with the complicated ag-biotech regulatory environment based on overlapping federal agency oversight.

A. Intellectual Property Issues

In 1980, the Supreme Court decided the seminal case of *Diamond v. Chakrabarty*[1] which established that living things could be the subject of a utility patent. Following this case, a host of patents on living organisms—both plant and animal—as well as their constituent components have been granted. Some of these, focused on human genetic products and processes, were excerpted in Chapter 6 above. However, a substantial number of the patents flowing from the *Chakrabarty* decision are directed towards non-human animals or plants. At the same time, running alongside utility patents for plants, the plant patent system has been actively used to afford IP protection for new plant types. The following subsection considers these animal and plant patents. It is important to keep in mind that some animal/plant patents are directed to modifications of living organisms to create bio-active therapeutic products for humans, while others are directed to modifications that either increase the yield of the organisms as foodstuffs or increase the nutritive value of the resultant food.

1. Patents on Transgenic Animals

Shortly after *Chakrabarty* was decided, Standish K. Allen, Jonathan A. Chaiton, and Sandra L. Downing submitted a patent application with process claims directed to producing sterile Pacific oysters and product claims for the resulting oysters. The patent ex-

1. Excerpted in Chapter 5 above. Readers are encouraged to review *Chakrabarty* again before proceeding with this Chapter.

aminer rejected the product claims (while allowing the process claims) based on both § 101 rejections (unpatentable subject matter) and § 103 rejections (obviousness).[2] The PTO Board of Patent Appeals overturned the § 101 rejections but affirmed the § 103 rejections. On appeal, the Federal Circuit upheld the Board on all counts. Both opinions are excerpted below. While the process claimed was merely that of "hydrostatic pressure" and not one of genetic modification, the case was one of the first to explore the reach of *Chakrabarty* for multicellular organisms.

Ex parte Allen

2 U.S.P.Q.2d (BNA) 1425 (B.P.A.I. 1987)

R. Smith, Examiner-in-Chief.

This is an appeal from the rejection of claims 8, 12, 13 and 14. Claims 1 through 7 and 9 through 11 have been allowed....

The subject matter on appeal relates to polyploid oysters. The four rejected claims are product-by-process claims. They read as follows:

8. Polyploid Pacific oysters produced by the method of claim 1.

12. Polyploid Pacific oysters produced by the method of claim 9.

13. The Pacific oysters of claim 8 belonging to the species *Crassostrea gigas.*

14. The Pacific oysters of claim 12 belonging to the species *Crassostrea gigas.*

The rejected claims are dependent on allowed claims drawn to a method of inducing polyploidy in oysters utilizing hydrostatic pressure which read as follows:

1. A method of inducing polyploidy in oysters, comprising:

separating oysters from one another such that male oysters are isolated from female oysters;

inducing said oysters to spawn;

controlling the temperature of eggs from said oysters;

fertilizing said eggs with sperm to form zygotes;

applying hydrostatic pressure to said zygotes at a predetermined intensity for a predetermined duration after a predetermined time following formation of said zygotes to induce polyploidy; and

cultivating said polyploid zygotes.

9. A method of inducing polyploidy in oysters, comprising:

separating oysters from one another such that male oysters are isolated from female oysters;

inducing said oysters to spawn;

controlling the temperature of eggs from said oysters at approximately 25°C;

fertilizing said eggs with sperm to form zygotes;

2. The reader is encouraged to review the patent materials in Chapter 5 *supra*.

applying hydrostatic pressure of approximately 6000 to 10,000 psi for a predetermined duration approximately 15 minutes after fertilization to said zygotes to induce polyploidy; and

cultivating said polyploid zygotes.

The reference of record relied on by the examiner is:

Stanley et al., "Growth of American Oysters Increased by Polyploidy Induced by Blocking Meiosis I But Not Meiosis II," *Aquaculture*, 37 (1984), pages 147–155.

Claims 8 and 12 through 14 are rejected for obviousness under 35 USC 103 in view of Stanley et al. and are also rejected under 35 USC 101 on the ground that the claimed invention is directed to nonstatutory subject matter.

In support of his rejection under 35 USC 101, the examiner states that polyploid oysters are held to be living entities and do not fall within the statutory subject matter of 35 USC 101. The examiner adds that the animal produced by the method claimed is "controlled by laws of nature and not a manufacture by man that is patentable." The examiner also relies on *In re Merat*, 519 F.2d 1390 (CCPA 1975) and *In re Bergy*, 563 F.2d 1031 (CCPA 1977) in support of his position. In its 1975 decision in *Merat* the Court affirmed a rejection under 35 USC 112 and did not reach the 35 USC 101 rejection made by the examiner and affirmed by the Board of Appeals. Although the Court reversed a 35 USC 101 rejection in *Bergy* and held that living microorganisms were within the terms "manufacture" and "composition of matter" in § 101, the examiner notes that the Court in its opinion categorized the claimed microorganisms as "more akin to inanimate chemical compositions such as reactants, reagents, and catalysts than they are to horses and honeybees or raspberries and roses."

We shall not sustain this rejection. As we have previously noted in our decision in *Ex parte Hibberd*, 227 USPQ 443 (BPAI 1985), the Supreme Court has interpreted the scope of 35 USC 101 in the recent case of *Diamond v. Chakrabarty*. The Court noted that the use of the expansive terms "manufacture" and "composition of matter" modified by the comprehensive "any" indicated that Congress "plainly contemplated that the patent laws would be given wide scope." The Supreme Court also noted that the legislative history of Section 101 supports a broad construction and concluded from the Committee Reports accompanying the 1952 Act that Congress intended statutory subject matter to "include anything under the sun that is made by man." Thus, the Court held that the involved microorganism plainly qualified as patentable subject matter.

The examiner's position that the claimed polyploid oysters are "held to be living entities" is not controlling on the question of whether the claims are drawn to patentable subject matter under 35 USC 101 because the Supreme Court made it clear in its decision in *Diamond v. Chakrabarty* that Section 101 includes man-made life forms. The issue, in our view, in determining whether the claimed subject matter is patentable under Section 101 is simply whether that subject matter is made by man. If the claimed subject matter occurs naturally, it is not patentable subject matter under Section 101. The fact, as urged by the examiner, that the oysters produced by the claimed method are "controlled by the laws of nature" does not address the issue of whether the subject matter is a non-naturally occurring manufacture or composition of matter. The examiner has presented no evidence that the claimed polyploid oysters occur naturally without the intervention of man, nor has the examiner urged that polyploid oysters occur naturally. The record before us leads to no conclusion other than that the claimed polyploid oysters are non-naturally occurring manufactures or compositions of matter within the confines of patentable subject matter under 35 USC 101. Accordingly, the rejection under Section 101 must be reversed.

The examiner's reliance on the 35 USC 101 rejection affirmed by the Board of Appeals, which the Court did not address in *In re Merat*, supra, is misplaced because *Merat* was decided before the decision by the Supreme Court in *Chakrabarty*. The Board in *Merat* did not have the benefit of the Supreme Court's analysis of the scope of Section 101 as set forth in *Chakrabarty*. The Board of Patent Appeals and Interferences is now obliged to interpret Section 101 in accordance with *Chakrabarty*.

Nor does the examiner's position find any support in the *Bergy* decision. The holding in *Bergy* that the fact that the claimed culture was alive did not remove it from the categories of invention enumerated in § 101 is consistent with *Chakrabarty*. The Court in *Bergy* made clear that it was only deciding the case before it and was not "deciding whether living things in general, or, at most, whether any living things other than microorganisms, are within § 101." Moreover, the decision by the Supreme Court in *Chakrabarty* is controlling authority that Congress intended statutory subject matter to "include anything under the sun that is made by man."

With respect to the rejection under 35 USC 103 we have carefully considered the respective positions of the examiner and the appellants and the declaration of co-inventor Allen, who is also a co-author of the Stanley et al. reference relied on by the examiner in support of the rejection. We have decided that we will affirm this rejection.

Stanley et al. disclose a method of inducing polyploidy in oysters involving the use of cytochalasin B. Stanley et al. report that they successfully induced polyploidy in the American oyster, *Crassostrea virginica*, by treating the fertilized eggs with cytochalasin B. The treatment resulted in polyploidy of over half the individuals. Stanley et al. recommend the induction of polyploidy in oysters as a way to increase growth as follows:

> We have shown a clear growth advantage in triploid American oysters produced by blocking the first meiosis division. We recommend induction of polyploidy as a way to increase growth in cultured oysters.

We agree with the examiner that in view of the express recommendation by Stanley et al., experts in the art who have successfully induced polyploidy in one species of oysters, it would have been obvious to one of ordinary skill in the art to induce polyploidy in Pacific *Crassostrea gigas* oysters. Moreover, one of ordinary skill in the art would have a reasonable expectation that the Stanley et al. method would be successful in inducing polyploidy in *Crassostrea gigas* oysters based on the success by Stanley et al. with *Crassostrea virginica* oysters and the recommendation by Stanley et al. to utilize the method with cultured oysters. Although appellants utilize a different process than Stanley et al. to induce polyploidy in oysters, involving the use of hydrostatic pressure rather than chemical treatment, the patentability of a product does not depend on its method of production. If the product in a product-by-process claim is the same as or obvious from a product of the prior art, the claim is unpatentable even though the prior product was made by a different process. Thus, the examiner has correctly adduced a prima facie case of obviousness for the claimed polyploid oysters, and the burden shifted to appellants to rebut the prima facie obviousness. In our view appellants have not done so.

In an attempt to rebut the examiner's prima facie case of obviousness, appellants rely on the declaration of co-inventor Allen. Allen declares in paragraph 6 of his declaration that:

> ... there are distinctive phenotypic differences between *c. gigas* and *c. virginica*, and that it would not have been obvious to apply the prior art techniques to *c. gigas*, because the techniques disclosed by Stanley et al. do not work on *c. gigas*.

Appellants argue that, based on the Allen declaration, the claimed Pacific *c. gigas* oysters would not have been obvious from the disclosure of Stanley et al. because the Stanley et al. techniques do not work on *c. gigas* oysters. Allen urges further that a modification of a prior art process which renders the process inoperable cannot serve as a basis for a § 103 rejection.

We agree with the Examiner that the Allen declaration is not persuasive of nonobviousness. Preliminarily, we note that mere conclusory statements, such as the one quoted, supra, are entitled to little weight when the Patent and Trademark Office questions the efficacy of the statements.... Here, the examiner challenged the noted conclusion of inoperability, as do we, and pointed out that the declaration as a whole supports the examiner's position of obviousness. Thus, as noted by the examiner, the declaration indicates in paragraphs 12–15 that low yields are obtained and near total mortality is experienced when treating *c. gigas* oysters at the precise temperature and duration of chemical treatment utilized by Stanley et al. Such facts do not establish inoperability of the reference. Quite clearly, inoperativeness is not established merely by showing that the particular disclosed embodiment for carrying out the principles of the invention is lacking in perfection. Cf. *Bennett v. Halahan*, 48 CCPA 782 (1961), where the Court said:

> It is well settled that the apparatus disclosed in an application need not necessarily be operative in the exact form in which it is shown and described.
>
> It is sufficient if it can be rendered operative by adjustments and corrections which would naturally occur to a skilled worker in the art attempting to construct the apparatus on the basis of the application disclosure.

We agree with the examiner that it is well within the skill of the art to optimize the parameters such as temperature and time of chemical treatment when applying the Stanley et al. process to a different species of oyster in order to obtain the optimum yield of polyploid oysters. The fact that such optimization may be required when utilizing the Stanley et al. recommended method to induce polyploidy in *c. gigas* oysters does not in our view render polyploid *c. gigas* oysters unobvious. The Allen declaration indicates in paragraph 20 that an "acceptable" treatment was developed for including polyploidy in *c. gigas* utilizing cytochalasin B as recommended by Stanley et al. as follows:

> 20. That extensive experimentation was in fact done to develop an acceptable cytochalasin B treatment for induction of polyploidy in *c. gigas*, involving 3 years ... of effort by trained scientists.

We attach no significance to the fact that appellants may have experimented for three years to develop an "acceptable" treatment in the absence of any indication of what experimentation was undertaken and what constitutes an "acceptable" treatment. The fact remains that Stanley et al. recommended the cytochalasin B treatment for the induction of polyploidy in cultured oysters generally, and that appellants followed that recommendation by using the cytochalasin B treatment to induce polyploidy in *c. gigas* oysters. After some modifications in process parameters, such as temperature and time of treatment, the process was "acceptable."

Appellants urge that the examiner misconstrued what the declarant was saying, and appellants explain in their supplemental reply brief what the declarant intended. However, we find the examiner's construction of the declaration to be entirely consistent therewith. Nonobviousness cannot be based on lawyer's arguments in the brief, but rather must find clear, unequivocal support in the evidence relied on. We find it significant that, although appellants rely on the alleged inoperability of the Stanley et al. process, there is no clear indication in the declaration that the Stanley et al. process was carried out using the precise conditions utilized by Stanley et al. Rather, appellants rely on a conclusory statement by the declarant based on conditions other than those utilized by Stanley et al.

We disagree with appellants' characterization of the examiner's rejection as "obvious to try." In the circumstances here where experts in the art have successfully utilized the process with one species of oyster and have specifically recommended that the process be utilized with cultured oysters generally, we agree with the examiner that it would have been obvious to one skilled in the art to apply the process to Pacific *c. gigas* oysters, and that he would have had a reasonable expectation, indeed a strong expectation, of success in producing a polyploid oyster. In our view the successful utilization of the Stanley et al. process to produce an "acceptable" cytochalasin B treatment for induction of polyploidy in *c. gigas* oysters, albeit with some optimization of process parameters, substantiates the reasonableness of the expectation of success.

Appellants' argument that the claimed polyploid *c. gigas* oysters are unobvious because they are sterile and do not devote significant portions of their body weight to reproduction, thereby remaining edible year around, is not persuasive. It was known in the art that polyploids exhibit sterility. Thus, it is not unexpected that sterile, polyploid *c. gigas* oysters do not devote significant portions of their body weight to reproductive gamete formation.

The decision of the examiner is affirmed.

In re Allen (unpublished and non precedential)

846 F.2d 77 (Fed. Cir. 1988)

FRIEDMAN, CIRCUIT JUDGE.

Decision

The decision of the Board of Patent Appeals and Interferences rejecting four claims of a patent application for a type of oyster, *Ex parte Allen,* 2 USPQ2d 1425 (1987), is *affirmed.*

Opinion

I

Oysters reproduce by discharging their gametes (sperm or eggs) into the water, where the eggs are fertilized (at which time they are called "zygotes"). The zygotes develop into larvae and then grow to become oysters.

Two of the most important species of edible oysters in the United States are the Atlantic (or American) oyster found generally in the Atlantic Ocean and the Pacific oyster (*Crassostrea gigas*) found in the cooler waters of the Pacific Ocean. The main difference between the two species is the percentage of body weight that is involved in producing gametes during the breeding season. The Atlantic oyster devotes up to 40 percent of its body weight to gamete production; the Pacific oyster expends up to twice that amount. The Atlantic oyster is edible throughout the year whereas the Pacific oyster is soft and unsuitable for human consumption during its reproductive phase.

The appellants' application discloses (1) a method of producing sterile Pacific oysters, which are edible year round, by inducing polyploidy in the oysters, and (2) the oysters produced by that method. Most cells are "diploid" or have two sets of chromosomes. "Polyploid" cells have three or more sets of chromosomes. Appellants induce polyploidy by fertilizing oyster eggs under controlled temperatures and applying hydrostatic pressure to the zygotes. The zygotes are then cultivated using known techniques until they develop into adult oysters. The claimed process is used only on Pacific oysters. The product claims, 8 and 12 and dependent claims 13 and 14, cover polyploid Pacific oysters produced by the process.

The examiner allowed the process claims but rejected the product claims as not disclosing patentable subject matter under 35 U.S.C. § 101 (1982) and as obvious under 35 U.S.C. § 103 (1982). The Board reversed the section 101 rejection because "the Supreme Court made it clear in its decision in *Diamond v. Chakrabarty* ... that Section 101 includes man-made life forms." ... The Board affirmed the section 103 rejection in light of a prior art publication by Stanley et al., which discloses a method of chemically inducing polyploidy in more than half of the Atlantic oysters so treated. The Board stated:

> Stanley et al. recommend the induction of polyploidy in oysters as a way to increase growth as follows: "We have shown a clear growth advantage in triploid American oysters produced by blocking the first meiosis division. We recommend induction of polyploidy as a way to increase growth in cultured oysters."

The Board concluded that

> in view of the express recommendation by Stanley et al., experts in the art who have successfully induced polyploidy in one species of oysters, it would have been obvious to one of ordinary skill in the art to induce polyploidy in Pacific *Crassostrea gigas* oysters.
>
> ...
>
> Appellants' argument that the claimed polyploid *c. gigas* oysters are unobvious because they are sterile and do not devote significant portions of their body weight to reproduction, thereby remaining edible year around, is not persuasive. It was known in the art that polyploids exhibit sterility.... Thus, it is not unexpected that sterile, polyploid *c. gigas* oysters do not devote significant portions of their body weight to reproductive gamete formation.

II

The appellants contend (A) that the Board erred in concluding that a prima facie case of obviousness had been established and, (B) that if a prima facie case was established, the Board applied an improper standard in reviewing and rejecting the appellants' rebuttal evidence.

A.

The burden initially is upon the Patent Office to show prima facie obviousness.... The appellants challenge the Board's ruling that the polyploid Pacific oysters produced by their process would have been obvious. Whether a product defined as made by a process would have been prima facie obvious is determined without regard to the process that produced it.

> If the product in a product-by-process claim is the same as or obvious from a product of the prior art, the claim is unpatentable even though the prior product was made by a different process.

To overcome an obviousness rejection, therefore, the appellants' polyploid Pacific oyster must be different from, and unobvious in light of, a polyploid Atlantic oyster made by the Stanley process.

As the Board noted, Stanley successfully produced polyploid Atlantic oysters and "'recommend[ed] induction of polyploidy as a way to increase growth in cultured oysters.'" It was known that polyploid oysters were sterile. It therefore would have been obvious that polyploid (and therefore sterile) Pacific oysters would have "increase[d] growth" by not devoting substantial portions of their body weight to reproduction. The Patent Office established prima facie obviousness.

The appellants assert, however, that prima facie obviousness was not shown because in determining that question for life forms the inherent unpredictability of biological systems has to be considered. The appellants cite *In re Grabiak*, 769 F.2d 729 (Fed. Cir. 1985) and *Ex parte Old*, 229 U.S.P.Q. 196 (B.P.A.I. 1985). *Grabiak* held that although a chemical homologue may be prima facie obvious, in that case it was not obvious because, at least in part, of the unpredictable activity of chemical substitutions. *Old* held that although the method there involved would have been obvious, the results it produced were unpredictable. "[The] technology is an empirical art in which the routineer is unable to foresee what ... will be produced.... Only by actually carrying out the requisite steps can the nature of the ... [product] be determined and ascertained; no 'expected' results can thus be said to be present."

The *Grabiak* court acknowledged the unpredictable properties that chemical substitution produces. Here, however, polyploid oysters have very predictable properties: they are sterile and, therefore, larger. *Old*, while not binding precedent, notes that until the process was performed, the properties of the resultant product were unknown and therefore would not be obvious. A polyploid oyster produced by any process has known properties and is prima facie obvious.

B.

Once a prima facie case is established, the burden shifts to the applicant to rebut the prima facie case "with objective evidence of unobviousness." The appellants argue that the declaration of co-inventor Allen carried that burden.

The Allen declaration states that the Stanley techniques are not effective in producing polyploidy in the Pacific oyster, which it asserts has distinctly different characteristics from the Atlantic oyster. Allen describes the applicants' experiments and uses general terms to describe the results (*e.g.*, "near total mortality," "extremely low yields," "very low survival rates"). The declaration concludes that "extensive experimentation with all possible variables would be required in order to develop a process that would work with *C. gigas.*"

The Board considered the Allen declaration and "agree[d] with the Examiner that the Allen declaration is not persuasive of nonobviousness." The Board noted that the Allen declaration contained "mere conclusory statements ... entitled to little weight when the Patent and Trademark Office questions the efficacy of the statements." The fact that the Stanley process may require "extensive experimentation ... in order to develop a process that would work with [Pacific oysters]" does not render polyploid Pacific oysters themselves unobvious. To state that the Pacific oyster is genetically and phenotypically distinct from the Atlantic oyster does not rebut the prima facie case. Both are a species of oyster which are sterile and, therefore, larger when polyploid. The Board found that the Allen declaration did not rebut the prima facie obviousness determination. We have no reason to disagree with that conclusion.

* * *

Also in 1988, the PTO granted the landmark patent, reproduced below, for the so-called "Harvard Oncomouse," a mouse genetically engineered for a predisposition to developing cancer.

United States Patent [19]
Leder et al.

[11] **Patent Number: 4,736,866**
[45] **Date of Patent: Apr. 12, 1988**

[54] **TRANSGENIC NON-HUMAN MAMMALS**

[75] Inventors: **Philip Leder, Chestnut Hill, Mass.; Timothy A. Stewart, San Francisco, Calif.**

[73] Assignee: **President and Fellows of Harvard College, Cambridge, Mass.**

[21] Appl. No.: **623,774**

[22] Filed: **Jun. 22, 1984**

[51] Int. Cl.[4] C12N 1/00; C12Q 1/68; C12N 15/00; C12N 5/00

[52] U.S. Cl. 800/1; 435/6; 435/172.3; 435/240.1; 435/240.2; 435/320; 435/317.1; 935/32; 935/59; 935/70; 935/76; 935/111

[58] Field of Search 435/6, 172.3, 240, 317, 435/320, 240.1, 240.2; 935/70, 76, 59, 111, 32; 800/1

[56] **References Cited**

U.S. PATENT DOCUMENTS

4,535,058 8/1985 Weinberg et al. 435/91
4,579,821 4/1986 Palmiter et al. 435/240

OTHER PUBLICATIONS

Ucker et al, Cell 27:257–266, Dec. 1981.
Ellis et al, Nature 292:506–511, Aug. 1981.
Goldfarb et al, Nature 296:404–409, Apr. 1981.
Huang et al, Cell 27:245–255, Dec. 1981.
Blair et al, Science 212:941–943, 1981.
Der et al, Proc. Natl. Acad. Sci. USA 79:3637–3640, Jun. 1982.
Shih et al, Cell 29:161–169, 1982.
Gorman et al, Proc. Natl. Acad. Sci. USA 79:6777–6781, Nov. 1982.
Schwab et al, EPA-600/9-82-013, Sym: Carcinogen, Polynucl. Aromat. Hydrocarbons Mar. Environ., 212–32 (1982).
Wagner et al. (1981) Proc. Natl. Acad. Sci USA 78, 5016–5020.
Stewart et al. (1982) Science 217, 1046–8.
Costantini et al. (1981) Nature 294, 92–94.
Lacy et al. (1983) Cell 34, 343–358.
McKnight et al. (1983) Cell 34, 335.
Binster et al. (1983) Nature 306, 332–336.
Palmiter et al. (1982) Nature 300, 611–615.
Palmiter et al. (1983) Science 222, 814.
Palmiter et al. (1982) Cell 29, 701–710.

Primary Examiner—Alvin E. Tanenholtz
Attorney, Agent, or Firm—Paul T. Clark

[57] **ABSTRACT**

A transgenic non-human eukaryotic animal whose germ cells and somatic cells contain an activated oncogene sequence introduced into the animal, or an ancestor of the animal, at an embryonic stage.

12 Claims, 2 Drawing Sheets

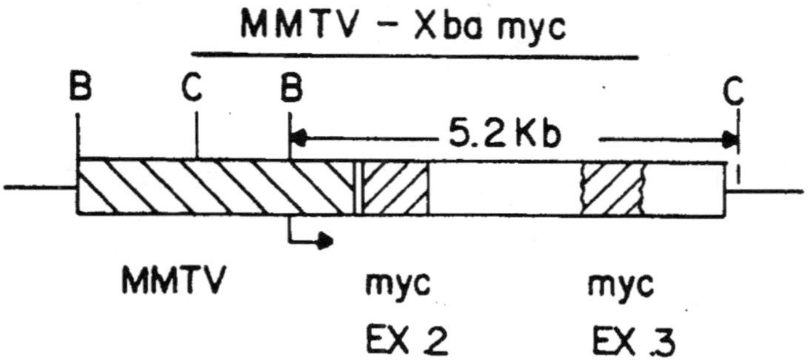

U.S. Patent **Apr. 12, 1988** **Sheet 1 of 2** **4,736,866**

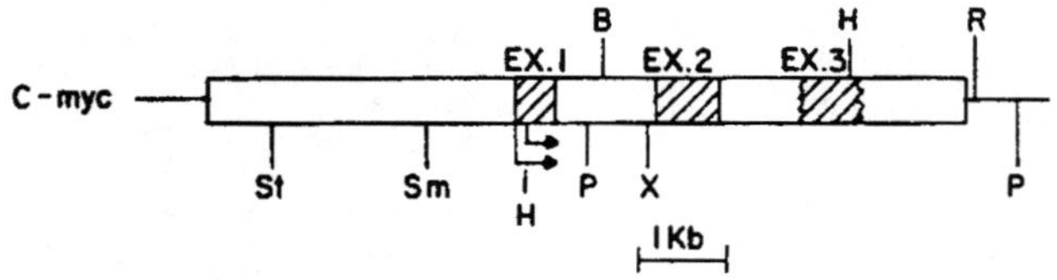

FIG 1

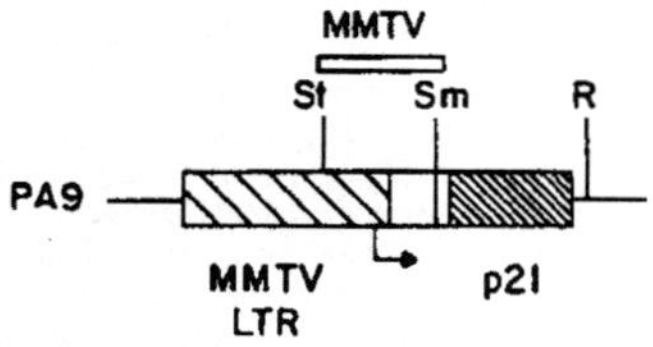

FIG 2

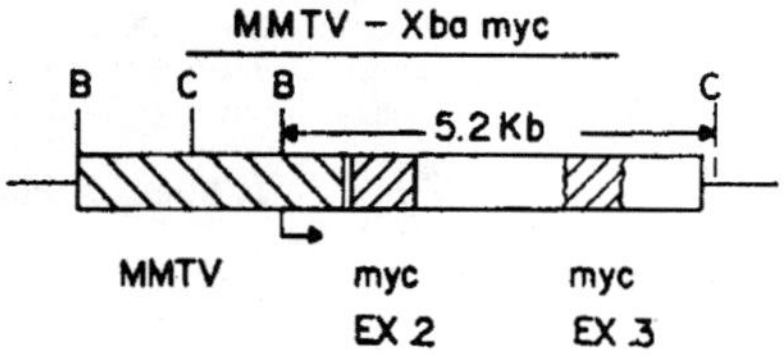

FIG 3

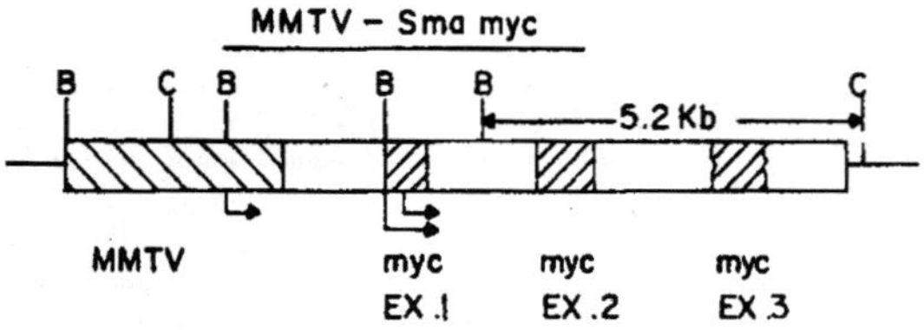

FIG 4

U.S. Patent Apr. 12, 1988 Sheet 2 of 2 **4,736,866**

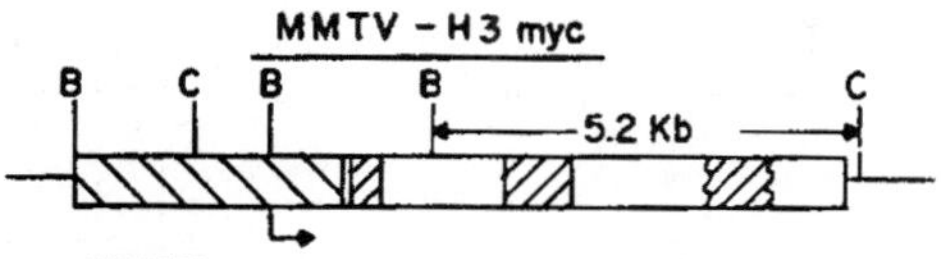

FIG 5

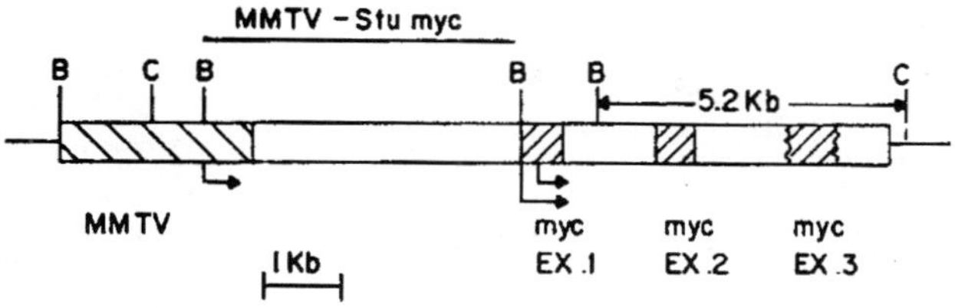

FIG 6

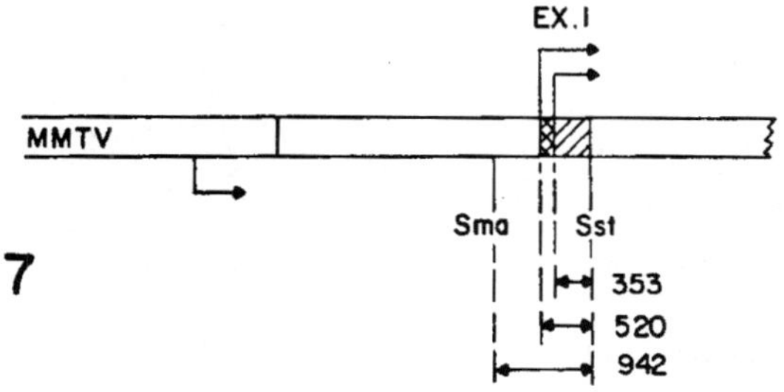

FIG 7

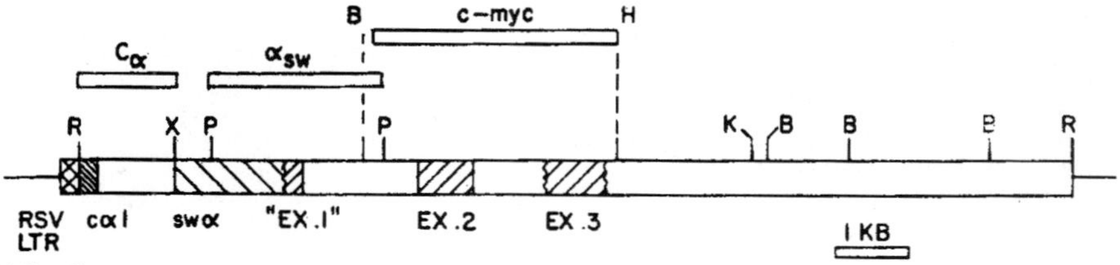

FIG 8

4,736,866

1

TRANSGENIC NON-HUMAN MAMMALS

BACKGROUND OF THE INVENTION

This invention relates to transgenic animals.

Transgenic animals carry a gene which has been introduced into the germline of the animal, or an ancestor of the animal, at an early (usually one-cell) developmental stage. Wagner et al. (1981) *P.N.A.S. U.S.A.* 78, 5016; and Stewart et al. (1982) *Science* 217, 1046 describe transgenic mice containing human globin genes. Constantini et al. (1981) *Nature* 294, 92; and Lacy et al. (1983) *Cell* 34, 343 describe transgenic mice containing rabbit globin genes. McKnight et al. (1983) *Cell* 34, 335 describes transgenic mice containing the chicken transferrin gene. Brinster et al. (1983) *Nature* 306, 332 describes transgenic mice containing a functionally rearranged immunoglobulin gene. Palmiter et al. (1982) *Nature* 300, 611 describes transgenic mice containing the rat growth hormone gene fused to a heavy metal-inducible metalothionein promoter sequence. Palmiter et al. (1982) *Cell* 29, 701 describes transgenic mice containing a thymidine kinase gene fused to a metallothionein promoter sequence. Palmiter et al. (1983) *Science* 222, 809 describes transgenic mice containing the human growth hormone gene fused to a metalothionein promoter sequence.

SUMMARY OF THE INVENTION

In general, the invention features a transgenic non-human eukaryotic animal (preferably a rodent such as a mouse) whose germ cells and somatic cells contain an activated oncogene sequence introduced into the animal, or an ancestor of the animal, at an embryonic stage (preferably the one-cell, or fertilized oocyte, stage, and generally not later than about the 8-cell stage). An activated oncogene sequence, as the term is used herein, means an oncogene which, when incorporated into the genome of the animal, increases the probability of the development of neoplasms (particularly malignant tumors) in the animal. There are several means by which an oncogene can be introduced into an animal embryo so as to be chromosomally incorporated in an activated state. One method is to transfect the embryo with the gene as it occurs naturally, and select transgenic animals in which the gene has integrated into the chromosome at a locus which results in activation. Other activation methods involve modifying the oncogene or its control sequences prior to introduction into the embryo. One such method is to transfect the embryo using a vector containing an already translocated oncogene. Other methods are to use an oncogene whose transcription is under the control of a synthetic or viral activating promoter, or to use an oncogene activated by one or more base pair substitutions, deletions, or additions.

In a preferred embodiment, the chromosome of the transgenic animal includes an endogenous coding sequence (most preferably the c-myc gene, hereinafter the myc gene), which is substantially the same as the oncogene sequence, and transcription of the oncogene sequence is under the control of a promoter sequence different from the promoter sequence controlling transcription of the endogenous coding sequence. The oncogene sequence can also be under the control of a synthetic promoter sequence. Preferably, the promoter sequence controlling transcription of the oncogene sequence is inducible.

2

Introduction of the oncogene sequence at the fertilized oocyte stage ensures that the oncogene sequence will be present in all of the germ cells and somatic cells of the transgenic animal. The presence of the onocogene sequence in the germ cells of the transgenic "founder" animal in turn means that all of the founder animal's descendants will carry the activated oncogene sequence in all of their germ cells and somatic cells. Introduction of the oncogene sequence at a later embryonic stage might result in the oncogene's absence from some somatic cells of the founder animal, but the descendants of such an animal that inherit the gene will carry the activated oncogene in all of their germ cells and somatic cells.

Any oncogene or effective sequence thereof can be used to produce the transgenic mice of the invention. Table 1, below, lists some known viral and cellular oncogenes, many of which are homologous to DNA sequences endogenous to mice and/or humans, as indicated. The term "oncogene" encompasses both the viral sequences and the homologous endogenous sequences.

TABLE 1

Abbreviation	Virus
src	Rous Sarcoma Virus (Chicken)
yes	Y73 Sarcoma Virus (Chicken)
fps	Fujinami (St Feline) Sarcoma Virus (Chicken, Cat)
abl	Abelson Murine Leukemia Virus (Mouse)
ros	Rochester-2 Sarcoma Virus (Chicken)
fgr	Gardner-Rasheed Feline Sarcoma Virus (Cat)
erbB	Avian Erythroblastosis Virus (Chicken)
fms	McDonough Feline Sarcoma Virus (Cat)
mos	Moloney Murine Sarcoma Virus (Mouse)
raf	3611 Murine Sarcoma+ Virus (Mouse)
Ha-ras-1	Harvey Murine Sarcoma Virus (Rat) (Balb/c mouse; 2 loci)
Ki-ras 2	Kirsten Murine Sarcoma Virus (Rat)
Ki-ras 1	Kirsten Murine Sarcoma Virus (Rat)
myc	Avian MC29 Myelocytomatosis Virus (Chicken)
myt	Avian Myelo Blastomas (Chicken)
fos	FBJ Osteosarcoma Virus (Mouse)
ski	Avian SKV T10 Virus (Chicken)
rel	Reticuloendotheliosis Virus (Turkey)
sis	Simian Sarcoma Virus (Woolly Monkey)
N-myc	Neuroblastomas (Human)
N-ras	Neuroblastoma, Leukemia Sarcoma Virus (Human)
Blym	Bursal Lymphomas (Chicken)
mam	Mammary Carcionoma (Human)
neu	Neuro, Glioblastoma (Rat)
ertAl	Chicken AEV (Chicken)
ra-ras	Rasheed Sarcoma Virus

TABLE 1-continued

Abbreviation	Virus
	(Rat)
mnt-myc	Carcinoma Virus MH2 (Chicken)
myc	Myelocytomatosis OK10 (Chicken)
myb-ets	Avian myeloblastosis/ erythroblastosis Virus E26 (Chicken)
raf-2	3611-MSV (Mouse)
raf-1	3611-MSV (Mouse)
Ha-ras-2	Ki-MSV (Rat)
erbB	Erythroblastosis virus (Chicken)

The animals of the invention can be used to test a material suspected of being a carcinogen, by exposing the animal to the material and determining neoplastic growth as an indicator of carcinogenicity. This test can be extremely sensitive because of the propensity of the transgenic animals to develop tumors. This sensitivity will permit suspect materials to be tested in much smaller amounts than the amounts used in current animal carcinogenicity studies, and thus will minimize one source of criticism of current methods, that their validity is questionable because the amounts of the tested material used is greatly in excess of amounts to which humans are likley to be exposed. Furthermore, the animals will be expected to develop tumors much sooner because they already contain an activated oncogene. The animals are also preferable, as a test system, to bacteria (used, e.g., in the Ames test) because they, like humans, are vertebrates, and because carcinogenicity, rather than mutogenicity, is measured.

The animals of the invention can also be used as tester animals for materials, e.g. antioxidants such as beta-carotine or Vitamin E, thought to confer protection against the development of neoplasms. An animal is treated with the material, and a reduced incidence of neoplasm development, compared to untreated animals, is detected as an indication of protection. The method can further include exposing treated and untreated animals to a carcinogen prior to, after, or simultaneously with treatment with the protective material.

The animals of the invention can also be used as a source of cells for cell culture. Cells from the animals may advantageously exhibit desirable properties of both normal and transformed cultured cells; i.e., they will be normal or nearly normal morphologically and physiologically, but can, like cells such as NIH 3T3 cells, be cultured for long, and perhaps indefinite, periods of time. Further, where the promoter sequence controlling transcription of the oncogene sequence is inducible, cell growth rate and other culture characteristics can be controlled by adding or eliminating the inducing factor.

Other features and advantages of the invention will be apparent from the description of the preferred embodiments, and from the claims.

DESCRIPTION OF THE PREFERRED EMBODIMENTS

The drawings will first briefly be described.

DRAWINGS

FIG. 1 is a diagrammatic representation of a region of a plasmid bearing the mouse myc gene and flanking regions.

FIG. 2 is a diagrammatic represenation of a region of a plasmid, pA9, bearing the mouse mammary tumor virus long terminal repeat (MMTV LTR) sequences.

FIGS. 3–6 and 8 are diagrammatic representations of activated oncogene fusions.

FIG. 7 is a diagrammatic representation of a probe useful for detecting activated myc fusions.

MMTV-MYC FUSED GENES

Gene fusions were made using the mouse myc gene and the MMTV LTR. The myc gene is known to be an activatable oncogene. (For example, Leder et al. (1983) *Science* 222, 765 explains how chromosomal translocations that characterize Burkitt's Lymphoma and mouse plasmacytomas result in a juxtaposition of the myc gene and one of the immunoglobulin constant regions; amplification of the myc gene has also been observed in transformed cell lines.) FIG. 1 illustrates the subclone of the mouse myc gene which provided the myc regions.

The required MMTV functions were provided by the pA9 plasmid (FIG. 2) that demonstrated hormone inducibility of the p21 protein; this plasmid is described in Huang et al. (1981) *Cell* 27, 245. The MMTV functions on pA9 include the region required for glucocorticoid control, the MMTV promoter, and the cap site.

The above plasmids were used to construct the four fusion gene contructions illustrated in FIGS. 3–6. The constructions were made by deleting from pA9 the Sma-EcoRI region that included the p21 protein coding sequences, and replacing it with the four myc regions shown in the Figures. Procedures were the conventional techniques described in Maniatis et al. (1982) *Molecular Cloning: A Laboratory Manual* (Cold Spring Harbor Laboratory). The restriction sites shown in FIG. 1 are StuI (St), SmaI (Sm), EcoRI (R), HindIII (H), PvuI (P), BamHI (B), XbaI (X), and ClaI (C). The solid arrows below the constructions represent the promoter in the MMTV LTR and in the myc gene. The size (in Kb) of the major fragment, produced by digestion with BamHI and ClaI, that will hybridize to the myc probe, is shown for each construction.

MMTV-H3 myc (FIG. 5) was constructed in two steps: Firstly, the 4.7 Kb Hind III myc fragment which contains most of the myc sequences was made blunt with Klenow polymerase and ligated to the pA9 SmaI-EcoRI vector that had been similarly treated. This construction is missing the normal 3' end of the myc gene. In order to introduce the 3' end of the myc gene, the PvuI-PvuI fragment extending from the middle of the first myc intron to the pBR322 PvuI site in the truncated MMTV-H3 myc was replaced by the related PvuI-PvuI fragment from the mouse myc subclone.

The MMTV-Xba myc construction (FIG. 3) was produced by first digesting the MMTV-Sma myc plasmid with SmaI and XbaI. The XbaI end was then made blunt with Klenow polymerase and the linear molecule recircularized with T4 DNA ligase. The MMTV-Stu myc (FIG. 6) and the MMTV-Sma myc (FIG. 4) constructions were formed by replacing the p21 protein coding sequences with, respectively, the StuI-EcoRI or SmaI-EcoRI myc fragments (the EcoRI site is within the pBR322 sequences of the myc subclone). As shown in FIG. 1, there is only one StuI site within the myc gene. As there is more than one SmaI site within the myc gene (FIG. 4), a partial SmaI digestion was carried out to generate a number of MMTV-Sma myc plasmids; the plasmid illustrated in FIG. 4 was selected as not showing rearrangements and also including a sufficiently long region 5' of the myc promoter (approximately 1 Kb) to include myc proximal controlling regions.

The constructions of FIGS. 4 and 6 contain the two promoters naturally preceding the unactivated myc gene. The contruction of FIG. 5 has lost both myc promoters but retains the cap site of the shorter transcript. The construction of FIG. 3 does not include the first myc exon but does include the entire protein coding sequence. The 3' end of the myc sequence in all of the illustrated constructions is located at the HindIII site approximately 1 Kb 3' to the myc polyA addition site.

These constructions were all checked by multiple restriction enzyme digestions and were free of detectable rearrangements.

PRODUCTION OF TRANSGENIC MICE CONTAINING MMTV-MYC FUSIONS

The above MMTV-myc plasmids were digested with SalI and EcoRI (each of which cleaves once within the pBR322 sequence) and separately injected into the male pronuclei of fertilized one-cell mouse eggs; this resulted in about 500 copies of linearized plasmid per pronucleus. The injected eggs were then transferred to pseudo-pregnant foster females as described in Wagner et al. (1981) *P.N.A.S. U.S.A.* 78, 5016. The eggs were derived from a CD-1 X C57Bl/6J mating. Mice were obtained from the Charles River Laboratories (CD^R-1-Ha/Icr (CD-1), an albino outbred mouse) and Jackson Laboratories (C57Bl/6J), and were housed in an environmentally controlled facility maintained on a 10 hour dark: 14 hour light cycle. The eggs in the foster females were allowed to develop to term.

ANALYSIS OF TRANSGENIC MICE

At four weeks of age, each pup born was analyzed using DNA taken from the tail in a Southern hybridization, using a ^{32}P DNA probe (labeled by nick-translation). In each case, DNA from the tail was digested with BamHI and ClaI and probed with the ^{32}P-labeled BamHI/HindIII probe from the normal myc gene (FIG. 1).

The DNA for analysis was extracted from 0.1–1.5 cm sections of tail, by the method described in Davis et al. (1980) in Methods in Enzymology, Grossman et al., eds., 65, 404, except that one chloroform extraction was performed prior to ethanol precipitation. The resulting nucleic acid pellet was washed once in 80% ethanol, dried, and resuspended in 300 μl of 1.0 mM Tris, pH 7.4, 0.1 mM EDTA.

Ten μl of the tail DNA preparation (approximately 10 μg DNA) were digested to completion, electrophoresed through 0.8% agarose gels, and transferred to nitrocellulose, as described in Southern (1975) *J. Mol. Biol.* 98, 503. Filters were hybridized overnight to probes in the presence of 10% dextran sulfate and washed twice in 2 X SSC, 0.1% SDS at room temperature and four times in 0.1 X SSC, 0.1% SDS at 64° C.

The Southern hybridizations indicated that ten founder mice had retained an injected MMTV-myc fusion. Two founder animals had integrated the myc gene at two different loci, yielding two genetically distinct lines of transgenic mice. Another mouse yielded two polymorphic forms of the integrated myc gene and thus yielded two genetically distinct offspring, each of which carried a different polymorphic form of the gene.

Thus, the 10 founder animals yielded 13 lines of transgenic offspring.

The founder animals were mated to uninjected animals and DNA of the resulting thirteen lines of transgenic offspring analyzed; this analysis indicated that in every case the injected genes were transmitted through the germline. Eleven of the thirteen lines also expressed the newly acquired MMTV-myc genes in at least one somatic tissue; the tissue in which expression was most prevelant was salivary gland.

Transcription of the newly acquired genes in tissues was determined by extracting RNA from the tissues and assaying the RNA in an SI nuclease protection procedure, as follows. The excised tissue was rinsed in 5.0 ml cold Hank's buffered saline and total RNA was isolated by the method of Chrigwin et al. (1979) *Biochemistry* 18, 5294, using the CsCl gradient modification. RNA pellets were washed twice by reprecipitation in ethanol and quantitated by absorbance at 260 nm. An appropriate single stranded, uniformly labeled DNA probe was prepared as described by Ley et al. (1982) *PNAS USA* 79, 4775. To test for transcription of the MMTV-Stu myc fusion of FIG. 6, for example, the probe illustrated in FIG. 7 was used. This probe extends from a SmaI site 5' to the first myc exon to an SstI site at the 3' end of the first myc exon. Transcription from the endogenous myc promoters will produce RNA that will protect fragments of the probe 353 and 520 base pairs long; transcription from the MMTV promoter will completely protect the probe and be revealed as a band 942 base pairs long, in the following hybridization procedure.

Labelled, single-stranded probe fragments were isolated on 8M urea 5% acrylamide gels, electroeluted, and hybridized to total RNA in a modification of the procedure of Berk et al. (1977) *Cell* 12, 721. The hybridization mixture contained 50,000 cpm to 100,000 cpm of probe (SA=10^8 cpm/μg), 10 μg total cellular RNA, 75% formamide, 500 mM NaCl, 20 mM Tris pH 7.5, 1 mM EDTA, as described in Battey et al. (1983) *Cell* 34, 779. Hybridization temperatures were varied according to the GC content in the region of the probe expected to hybridize to mRNA. The hybridizations were terminated by the addition of 1500 units of SI nuclease (Boehringer Mannheim). SI nuclease digestions were carried out at 37° C. for 1 hour. The samples were then ethanol-precipitated and electrophoresed on thin 8M urea 5% acrylamide gels.

Northern hybridization analysis was also carried out, as follows. Total RNA was electrophoresed through 1% formaldehyde 0.8% agarose gels, blotted to nitrocellulose filters (Lehrach et al. (1979) *Biochemistry* 16, 4743), and hybridized to nick-translated probes as described in Taub et al. (1982) *PNAS USA* 79, 7837. The tissues analyzed were thymus, pancreas, spleen, kidney, testes, liver, heart, lung, skeletal muscle, brain, salivary gland, and preputial gland.

Both lines of mice which had integrated and were transmitting to the next generation the MMTV-Stu myc fusion (FIG. 6) exhibited transcription of the fusion in salivary gland, but in no other tissue.

One of two lines of mice found to carry the MMTV-Sma myc fusion (FIG. 4) expressed the gene fusion in all tissues examined, with the level of expression being particularly high in salivary gland. The other line expressed the gene fusion only in salivary gland, spleen, testes, lung, brain, and preputial gland.

Four lines of mice carried the MMTV-H3 myc fusion (FIG. 5). In one, the fusion was transcribed in testes, lung, salivary gland, and brain; in a second, the fusion was transcribed only in salivary gland; in a third, the fusion was transcribed in none of the somatic tissues tested; and in a fourth, the fusion was transcribed in salivary gland and intestinal tissue.

In two mouses lines found to carry the MMTV-Xba myc fusion, the fusion was transcribed in testes and salivary gland.

RSV-MYC FUSED GENES

Referring to FIG. 8, the plasmid designated RSV-S107 was generated by inserting the EcoRI fragment of the S107 plasmacytoma myc gene, (Kirsch et al. (1981) *Nature* 293, 585) into a derivative of the Rous Sarcoma Virus (RSV) enhancer-containing plasmid (pRSVcat) described in Gorman et al. (1982) *PNAS USA* 79, 6777, at the EcoRI site 3' to the RSV enhancer sequence, using standard recombinant DNA techniques. All chloramphenicol acetyl transferase and SV40 sequences are replaced in this vector by the myc gene; the RSV promoter sequence is deleted when the EcoRI fragments are replaced, leaving the RSV enhancer otherwise intact. The original translocation of the myc gene in the S107 plasmacytoma deleted the two normal myc promoters as well as a major portion of the untranslated first myc exon, and juxtaposed, 5' to 5', the truncated myc gene next to the α immunoglobulin heavy chain switch sequence.

The illustrated (FIG. 8) regions of plasmid RSV-S107 are: crosshatched, RSV sequences; fine-hatched, alpha 1 coding sequences; left-hatched, immunoglobulin alpha switch sequences; right-hatched, myc exons. The thin lines flanking the RSV-S107 myc exon represent pBR322 sequences. The marked restriction enzyme sites are: R, EcoRI; X, XbaI; P, Pst 1; K, Kpn 1; H, HindIII; B, BamHI. The sequences used for three probes used in assays described herein (C-α, α-sw and c-myc) are marked.

PRODUCTION OF TRANSGENIC MICE

Approximately 500 copies of the RSV-S107 myc plasmid (linearized at the unique Kpn-1 site 3' to the myc gene) were injected into the male pronucleus of eggs derived from a C57BL/6J x CD-1 mating. Mice were obtained from Charles River Laboratories (CD-1, an albino outbred mouse) and from Jackson Laboratories (C57BL/6J). These injected eggs were transferred into pseudopregnant foster females, allowed to develop to term, and at four weeks of age the animals born were tested for retention of the injected sequences by Southern blot analysis of DNA extracted from the tail, as described above. Of 28 mice analyzed, two males were found to have retained the new genes and both subsequently transmitted these sequences through the germline in a ratio consistent with Mendelian inheritance of single locus.

First generation transgenic offspring of each of these founder males were analyzed for expression of the rearranged myc genes by assaying RNA extracted from the major internal tissues and organs in an Sl nuclease protection assay, as described above. The hearts of the offspring of one line showed aberrant myc expression; the other 13 tissues did not.

Backcrossing (to C57Bl/6J) and in-breeding matings produced some transgenic mice which did not demonstrate the same restriction site patterns on Southern blot analysis as either their transgenic siblings or their parents. In the first generation progeny derived from a mating between the founder male and C57BL/6J females, 34 F1 animals were analyzed and of these, 19 inherited the newly introduced gene, a result consistent with the founder being a heterozygote at one locus. However, of the 19 transgenic mice analyzed, there were three qualitatively different patterns with respect to the more minor myc hybridizing fragments.

In order to test the possibility that these heterogenous genotypes arose as a consequence of multiple insertions and/or germline mosaicism in the founder, two F1 mice (one carrying the 7.8 and 12 Kb BamHI bands, and the other carrying only the 7.8 Kb BamHI band) were mated and the F2 animals analyzed. One male born to the mating of these two appeared to have sufficient copies of the RSV-S107 myc gene to be considered as a candidate for having inherited the two alleles; this male was backcrossed with a wild-type female. All 23 of 23 backcross offspring analyzed inherited the RSV-S107 myc genes, strongly suggesting that the F2 male mouse had inherited two alleles at one locus. Further, as expected, the high molecular weight fragment (12 Kb) segregated as a single allele.

To determine whether, in addition to the polymorphisms arising at the DNA level, the level of aberrant myc expression was also altered, heart mRNA was analyzed in eight animals derived from the mating of the above double heterozygote to a wild-type female. All eight exhibited elevated myc mRNA, with the amount appearing to vary between animals; the lower levels of expression segregated with the presence of the 12 Kb myc hybridizing band. The level of myc mRNA in the hearts of transgenic mice in a second backcross generation also varied. An F1 female was backcrossed to a C57Bl/6J male to produce a litter of seven pups, six of which inherited the RSV-S107 myc genes. All seven of these mice were analyzed for expression. Three of the six transgenic mice had elevated levels of myc mRNA in the hearts whereas in the other three the level of myc mRNA in the hearts was indistinguishable from the one mouse that did not carry the RSV-S107 myc gene. This result suggests that in addition to the one polymorphic RSV-S107 myc locus from which high levels of heart-restricted myc mRNA were transcribed, there may have been another segregating RSV-S107 myc locus that was transcriptionally silent.

CARCINOGENICITY TESTING

The animals of the invention can be used to test a material suspected of being a carcinogen, as follows. If the animals are to be used to test materials thought to be only weakly carcinogenic, the transgenic mice most susceptible of developing tumors are selected, by exposing the mice to a low dosage of a known carcinogen and selecting those which first develop tumors. The selected animals and their descendants are used as test animals by exposing them to the material suspected of being a carcinogen and determining neoplastic growth as an indicator of carcinogenicity. Less sensitive animals are used to test more strongly carcinogenic materials. Animals of the desired sensitivity can be selected by varying the type and concentration of known carcinogen used in the selection process. When extreme sensitivity is desired, the selected test mice can consist of those which spontaneously develop tumors.

TESTING FOR CANCER PROTECTION

The animals of the invention can be used to test materials for the ability to confer protection against the development of neoplasms. An animal is treated with the material, in parallel with an untreated control transgenic animal. A comparatively lower incidence of neoplasm development in the treated animal is detected as an indication of protection.

TISSUE CULTURE

The transgenic animals of the invention can be used as a source of cells for cell culture. Tissues of transgenic mice are analyzed for the presence of the activated oncogene, either by directly analyzing DNA or RNA, or by assaying the tissue for the protein expressed by the gene. Cells of tissues carrying the gene can be cultured, using standard tissue culture techniques, and used, e.g., to study the functioning of cells from normally difficult to culture tissues such as heart tissue.

DEPOSITS

Plasmids bearing the fusion genes shown in FIGS. 3, 4, 5, 6, and 8 have been deposited in the American Type Culture Collection, Rockville, Md., and given, respectively, ATCC Accession Nos. 39745, 39746, 39747, 39748, and 39749.

OTHER EMBODIMENTS

Other embodiments are within the following claims. For example, any species of transgenic animal can be employed. In some circumstances, for instance, it may be desirable to use a species, e.g., a primate such as the rhesus monkey, which is evolutionarily closer to humans than mice.

We claim:

1. A transgenic non-human mammal all of whose germ cells and somatic cells contain a recombinant activated oncogene sequence introduced into said mammal, or an ancestor of said mammal, at an embryonic stage.

2. The mammal of claim 1, a chromosome of said mammal including an endogenous coding sequence substantially the same as a coding sequence of said oncogene sequence.

3. The mammal of claim 2, said oncogene sequence being integrated into a chromosome of said mammal at a site different from the location of said endogenous coding sequence.

4. The mammal of claim 2 wherein transcription of said oncogene sequence is under the control of a promoter sequence different from the promoter sequence controlling the transcription of said endogenous coding sequence.

5. The mammal of claim 4 wherein said promoter sequence controlling transcription of said oncogene sequence is inducible.

6. The mammal of claim 1 wherein said oncogene sequence comprises a coding sequence of a c-myc gene.

7. The mammal of claim 1 wherein transcription of said oncogene sequence is under the control of a viral promoter sequence.

8. The mammal of claim 7 wherein said viral promoter sequence comprises a sequence of an MMTV promoter.

9. The mammal of claim 7 wherein said viral promoter sequence comprises a sequence of an RSV promoter.

10. The mammal of claim 1 wherein transcription of said oncogene sequence is under the control of a synthetic promoter sequence.

11. The mammal of claim 1, said mammal being a rodent.

12. The mammal of claim 11, said rodent being a mouse.

* * * * *

* * *

In response to the emergence of animal patents—particularly transgenic ones—some activist groups launched an unsuccessful challenge to the PTO patent guidelines issued in the wake of *Ex parte Allen*. In the case below, these groups assert both procedural and substantive challenges to PTO policy regarding animal patents. The court's discussion of the substantive challenges provides a good overview of the criticisms of both GMOs and IP protection thereof.

Animal Legal Defense Fund v. Quigg

932 F.2d 920 (Fed. Cir. 1991)

NIES, CHIEF JUDGE.

This is an appeal from the order of the District Court for the Northern District of California (Smith, J.) granting defendants' motion to dismiss the complaint in *Animal Legal Defense Fund v. Quigg*, 710 F.Supp. 728, 9 USPQ2d 1816 (N.D.Cal.1989), for failure to state a claim under the Administrative Procedure Act, Pub.L. No. 89-554, 80 Stat. 383 (1966) (APA). Various plaintiffs, individual farmers and groups of animal husbanders or non-profit organizations whose goal is the protection of animals, filed suit in district court under the APA challenging, on procedural and substantive grounds, a Notice issued by the Department of Commerce Patent and Trademark Office (PTO) which stated, *inter alia*, that the PTO "now considers non-naturally occurring, non-human multicellular organisms, including animals, to be patentable subject matter within the scope of 35 U.S.C. § 101 [the patent statute]." Plaintiffs seek to impede, indeed, stop issuance of patents for animals. The defendants, Donald Quigg, then Commissioner of Patent & Trademarks, and C. William Verity, then Secretary of Commerce, countered with a motion to dismiss the complaint under Fed.R.Civ.P. 12(b)(6) for failure to state a claim. The district court granted defendants' motion on the grounds that the challenged Notice fell within an exception to the public notice and comment requirements of the APA and that the Commissioner did not exceed his statutory authority in issuing the Notice. The court further held that whether any "animal" patents which might be issued by the PTO would exceed its authority under section 101 was not raised by the suit. We affirm but on the alternative ground that the plaintiffs lack standing. Because of the nature of the injury alleged by some of the parties, however, our ruling on standing subsumes the ground relied on by the district court.

I

... On April 7, 1987, within days of the Board's decision in [*Ex parte*] *Allen*, the PTO issued the following notice:

> A decision by the Board of Patent Appeals and Interferences in *Ex parte Allen* held that claimed polyploid oysters are nonnaturally occurring manufactures or compositions of matter within the meaning of 35 U.S.C. 101. The Board relied upon the opinion of the Supreme Court in *Diamond v. Chakrabarty*, as it had done in *Ex parte Hibberd*, as controlling authority that Congress intended statutory subject matter to "include anything under the sun that is made by man." The Patent and Trademark Office now considers nonnaturally occurring non-human multicellular living organisms, including animals, to be patentable subject matter within the scope of 35 U.S.C. 101.
>
> The Board's decision does not affect the principle and practice that products found in nature will not be considered to be patentable subject matter under

> 35 U.S.C. 101 and/or 102. An article of manufacture or composition of matter occurring in nature will not be considered patentable unless given a new form, quality, properties or combination not present in the original article existing in nature in accordance with existing law.
>
> A claim directed to or including within its scope a human being will not be considered to be patentable subject matter under 35 U.S.C. 101. The grant of a limited, but exclusive property right in a human being is prohibited by the Constitution. Accordingly, it is suggested that any claim directed to a non-plant multicellular organism which would include a human being within its scope include the limitation "non-human" to avoid this ground of rejection. The use of a negative limitation to define the metes and bounds of the claimed subject matter is a permissible form of expression.
>
> Accordingly, the Patent and Trademark Office is now examining claims directed to multicellular living organisms, including animals. To the extent that the claimed subject matter is directed to a non-human "nonnaturally occurring manufacture or composition of matter—a product of human ingenuity," such claims will not be rejected under 35 U.S.C. 101 as being directed to non-statutory subject matter. [Hereinafter "Notice" or "Rule".]

1077 Official Gazette 24 (April 21, 1987).

More than a year after this Notice was published, the various plaintiffs[3] filed suit in district court alleging in Count I that the Commissioner of Patents and Trademarks had violated the APA in issuing this Rule without complying with the public notice and comment period of the APA, 5 U.S.C. § 553 (1988). Plaintiffs sought to enjoin the PTO from approving or issuing any patents on multicellular living organisms, including animals,[4] or taking any action to effectuate the Rule, until it complied with the APA procedural requirements. In Count II plaintiffs alleged that the Commissioner violated section 706(2)(C) of the APA, 5 U.S.C. § 706(2)(C) (1988), by acting in excess of statutory authority under the Patent Act, 35 U.S.C. § 1, *et seq.* As relief under Count II, plaintiffs sought a declaration that the Commissioner acted in excess of his statutory jurisdiction or authority by including animals as patentable subject matter and an injunction against his issuance of any patents on multicellular living organisms, including animals, until authorized and mandated to do so by Congress. Defendants filed a motion to dismiss the complaint for failure to state a claim, and this motion was granted by the district court.

The district court expressly assumed without deciding that the various plaintiffs had standing and based the order of dismissal of Count I solely on its conclusion that the Rule fell outside the public notice and comment provisions of the APA, 5 U.S.C. § 553(b), (c) (1988). Per the district court, the Rule was "interpretative" of prior decisional precedent and thus was expressly exempt from notice and comment under section 553(b)(A). The court held further that because the Rule itself, which did no

3. The various plaintiffs in this case are nine:
Animal Legal Defense Fund (ALDF), The American Society for the Prevention of Cruelty to Animals (ASPCA), The Marin Humane Society (MHS), Wisconsin Family Farm Defense Fund (WFFDF), John Kinsman, Michael Cannell, Humane Farming Association (HFA), Association of Veterinarians for Animal Rights (AVAR), and People for the Ethical Treatment of Animals (PETA).

4. The Rule covers only non-naturally occurring animals; plaintiffs erroneously speak of the Rule as covering all "animals."

more than interpret decisional law, neither abridged nor enlarged the rights of anyone, it was clearly within the Commissioner's authority to promulgate. Finally, the court concluded that the question whether the precedent was correct and whether any "animal" patents actually issued were invalid was not raised by the subject action....

III

Count I

A.

Count I of the complaint alleges that the putative illegal conduct lies in the Commissioner's failure to publish a notice of his proposed action in the Federal Register as required by 5 U.S.C. § 553(b); his failure to allow interested persons an opportunity to submit data and arguments per section 553(c); and his failure to state the basis and purpose of the Notice following consideration of public comment.

Every organizational plaintiff in this case alleges that it was injured as a result of its having been denied participation in the PTO's rulemaking process....

Whether there is any viability in such allegation of injury by reason of the alleged procedural defect,[5] namely, the Commissioner's failure to provide public notice and comment procedures in adopting the rule, depends on the resolution of an issue of law: Was the Commissioner required to comply with section 553 before issuing the Rule? For reasons which follow, we conclude he was not. Thus, appellants' allegations of injury also fail as a matter of law.

B.

...

The genesis and effect of the Notice demonstrates that it represents no change in the law effected by the Commissioner and that, in reality, it is merely "interpretative" of prior decisional precedent. As acknowledged by appellants, in 1981 the Supreme Court decided, in [*Chakrabarty*], that live, non-naturally occurring microorganisms fell within the patentable subject matter covered by section 101. Following the Supreme Court's ruling on the scope of section 101, the Board of Patent Appeals decided *Ex Parte Hibberd*, wherein the Board, relying on the Supreme Court's decision in *Chakrabarty*, held that non-naturally occurring, multicellular living plants were patentable subject matter under section 101. Thereafter, the Board decided *Ex Parte Allen* where it reversed an examiner's rejection that claims drawn to a particular non-naturally occurring polyploid oyster were directed to nonpatentable subject matter, although ultimately upholding the examiner's rejection that the oysters would have been obvious in view of prior art under section 103. In this decision, the Board stated that "the Supreme Court made it clear in its decision in *Diamond v. Chakrabarty*, ... that Section 101 includes man-made life forms. The issue, in our view, in determining whether the claimed subject matter is patentable under Section 101 is simply whether that subject matter is made by man." This court affirmed that decision on appeal, although the panel did not expressly endorse or even mention the section 101 issue.[6]

5. In light of our disposition of the legal question whether the Notice is "substantive" or "interpretative" under section 553, we do not address appellees' argument that actual injury cannot rest solely on allegations of denial of input into the rulemaking process.

6. It is interesting to note that the first patent on a non-naturally occurring animal issued within a month after this court affirmed the *Allen* decision. *See* U.S. Patent No. 4,736,866 (issued April 12, 1988) (The "Harvard mouse").

Four days after the Board's decision in *Allen,* the Commissioner issued the Notice in issue here. The language used by the Commissioner in the Notice largely tracks the above history and the language of *Allen.* In the first paragraph, the Commissioner summarizes the foregoing decisional law of *Allen, Hibberd,* and *Chakrabarty* and, based on the conclusions of the Supreme Court and the Board as to the scope of section 101, states that the PTO "*now* considers nonnaturally occurring non-human multicellular living organisms, including animals, to be patentable subject matter within the scope of 35 U.S.C. 101." 1077 Official Gazette 24 (emphasis added). In the next paragraph, the Commissioner reiterates, as the Board recognized in *Allen,* that the scope of the "Board's decision does not affect the principle that products found in nature will not be considered to be patentable subject matter...." Finally, in the last paragraph, the Commissioner quotes language from the Supreme Court decision in *Chakrabarty* that a claim to a "nonnaturally occurring manufacture or composition of matter—a product of human ingenuity" will not be subject to a section 101 rejection. The Notice clearly corresponds with the interpretations of section 101 set out by the Board in *Allen* and *Hibberd,* in reliance on *Chakrabarty,* with the only caveat being the statement that section 101 does not extend to humans. Thus, the Notice falls within the class of agency action which is merely interpretative of previous valid administrative action, and, as a result, represents no "change" in the law *by the Commissioner....*

Here appellants assert no adverse effect on any individual's rights to benefits under the patent statute. Rather, they assert that the general public has an interest in the statutory limitations to patentability. Essentially, appellants assert a right, as members of the public particularly interested in animals, to sue for what they perceive to be an unwarranted interference with the discretionary judgment of an examiner. However, it must be noted that whether patents are allowable for animal life forms is not a matter of discretion but of law. Thus, if we assume examiners must follow the Notice—which the Commissioner denies—such action has no effect on the ultimate validity of any patent. Either the subject matter falls within section 101 or it does not, and that question does not turn on any discretion residing in examiners.

Moreover, we find nothing in the law which gives rise to a right in nonapplicants to object to the way in which patent applications of others are prosecuted. A third party has no right to intervene in the prosecution of a particular patent application to prevent issuance of an allegedly invalid patent. Appellants are in effect attempting to intervene as third parties in the prosecution of *all* animal patent applications. By analogy, merely because appellants make a broadside attack gives no greater right of intervention against all than against one....

Having reviewed all of appellants' arguments, we are persuaded that the Commissioner's Notice falls within the "interpretative" exception to the section 553 public notice and comment procedures. Appellants thus have no standing to assert Count I of the Complaint by reason of "procedural harm." ...

IV
Count II

Count II alleges that the Commissioner's rule declaring the patentability of animals exceeds the authority delegated to the Commissioner under the patent statute.... As relief for this alleged violation, appellants seek a declaration that "animals" are not patentable subject matter under section 101 and an injunction against the issuance of any "animal" patents.

A.

Injury-in-Fact to Farmers and Farm Groups

As personal injury, various appellants, namely WFFDF, HFA, and the individual farmers, assert economic injury from the Commissioner's allegedly erroneous interpretation of section 101. The individual farmers, John Kinsman and Michael Cannell, allege in the complaint that:

> Defendants' rule will increase Kinsman and Cannell's costs of operation, by forcing them to pay royalties to purchase patented, genetically altered animals, and, alternatively, will render Kinsman and Cannell less able to compete in the production of uniform and predictable traits and products, thereby lowering their annual net profits, all to their economic harm....

Similarly, WFFDF alleges on behalf of its members that economic injury will result from defendant's rule because:

> Said rule will: increase such members' costs of operation by forcing them to purchase high priced "patented" animals, or lose profits producing genetically inferior "unpatented" animals; substantially increase livestock productivity and decrease herd size, causing a significant reduction in the number of small farms and negatively impacting their communities; substantially increase the economic competition that said members presently encounter, render these members unable or less able to compete in producing uniform and predictable traits or products; accelerate farm consolidation; and drive many of these members out of the farming business altogether.

As these appellants point out, the Commissioner concedes that the above allegations of economic injury, which must be assumed to be true, suffice to establish a judicially cognizable personal injury to them. However, the Commissioner challenges causation; that is, whether these parties could possibly prove that these identified economic injuries can be attributed to the Commissioner's allegedly unlawful issuance of patents.

The element of causation requires a party to show that "the injury must be fairly traceable to the challenged action." ... We conclude that the alleged economic injuries of the farmers and farm groups are not "fairly traceable" to the Commissioner's action.

It is readily apparent that because the alleged injuries depend upon issuance of a patent, such injuries are speculatively dependent at a minimum on the acts of potential inventors who must develop novel transgenic non-naturally occurring animals, specifically farm animals; who must decide to file an application for patent on those animals rather than, for example, maintaining their discoveries as trade secrets; and who must ultimately successfully prosecute such applications to issuance as a patent. Appellants would, nevertheless, link such third party action to the government because inventors have been "encouraged" to seek patent protection by the Notice....

As previously indicated, the farmers' alleged injuries are (1) having to pay increased costs in the form of royalties on patented animals and (2) suffering decreased profits because of competition from more productive non-naturally occurring animals. With respect to the alleged "royalties" injury, farmers cannot be forced to purchase improved animals and pay the premium (*i.e.*, "royalty") which the farmers say is likely to be asked. Indeed, their allegation that their costs of operation will *increase* by reason of "royalties" is at best speculative. The motivation to purchase normally arises from the prospect of an economic advantage. Further, the ability of a market participant to affect price, *i.e.*, exert market power, depends on whether competitive patented or non-patented animals are available. This in turn depends on the speculative activities of third party competitors whose market actions would determine the existence and extent of acceptable, non-infringing substitutes in the relevant product market. Such speculation as to market actors and their activities further beclouds the issue of causation as it concerns the farmers' alleged economic injury.

Similarly, the farmers' alleged injury from increased competition can only result from the development and commercialization of genetically improved animals—not from the grant of a patent. We do not denigrate the stimulation of invention that the possibility of patent protection provides. However, were we to enjoin issuance of patents for non-naturally occurring animals, the requested relief would not prevent the development of such animals. It should hardly need saying that the issuance of a patent gives no right to make, use or sell a patented invention,[7] or that the absence of a patent creates no legal prohibition against continued research or development....

... Here ... we conclude that the alleged economic injuries of individual farmers and farm organizations are not "fairly traceable" to the allegedly erroneous interpretation of the statute by the Commissioner.

B.

Injury-in-Fact to Animal Protection Associations

The standing allegations of the animal protection associations are patently insufficient under controlling precedent. As the various appellants correctly point out, the alleged injury need not be economic in nature to constitute "injury" for purposes of standing.

> [T]he interests alleged to have been injured "may reflect 'aesthetic, conservational, and recreational' as well as economic values." But broadening the categories of injury that may be alleged in support of standing is a different matter from abandoning the requirement that the party seeking review must himself have suffered an injury.

Sierra Club [*v. Morton*], 405 U.S. [727,] 738. However, as the Supreme Court held in *Sierra Club*, the APA does not "authorize judicial review at the behest of organizations or individuals who seek to do no more than vindicate their own value preferences through the judicial process." HFA and AVAR assert only a general interest in preventing cruelty to animals. That these appellants allege they will expend more dollars on organizational activities and expenses as a result of the Notice does not serve to distinguish them from any member of the public with a particularized conviction about protecting animals. As the court stated in *Sierra Club*:

> If any group with a bona fide "special interest" could initiate such litigation, it is difficult to perceive why any individual citizen with the same bona fide special interest would not also be entitled to do so.

Thus, HFA and AVAR have failed to allege *any* legally cognizable injury.

ASPCA and MHS attempt to escape from the mere "value preference" category by reason of state statutes that delegate to these organizations certain police power to protect and care for animals. They allege they will need to increase their budgets and enforcement staffs by reason of the increased experimentation on animals fostered by the

---

7. A patent provides only a right to exclude others from practicing the invention for a limited time.

potential for patent protection. The government counters this point first by uncontroverted assertions that the state statutes impose no duties on the organizations so that any action they might take would be purely voluntary, and thus, no different from the action of anyone interested in protecting animals. Nevertheless, we recognize that courts have found the type of allegations made by ASPCA and MHS here sufficient for showing personal injury. We will presume these allegations of personal injury are sufficient to meet the initial requirement.

Turning to causation, however, we conclude that the injury alleged by these groups cannot be attributed to the Commissioner's interpretation of section 101.... With respect to these associations, not only does the need for action by independent third parties, who must successfully invent and prosecute to issuance patent applications for "animals," sever any link between the injury and governmental action, but also additional acts by third parties are required. The potential for patent protection leading to increased experimentation must lead to increased cruelty. Yet for increased experimentation to lead to increased cruelty, appellants would have to allege that the existing animal cruelty laws are insufficient or that the issuance of "animal" patents would "encourage" researchers to disobey these laws. We cannot baldly speculate by favorable inference that researchers would likely disregard applicable animal protection laws because of the Notice. Without such allegations, ASPCA and MHS have also failed to allege an injury "fairly traceable" to the Commissioner's interpretation of section 101....

VI

Accepting the allegations of the complaint as true and drawing all inferences favorable to appellants, we conclude that appellants have failed to allege facts sufficient to meet the standing requirements of Article III § 2 of the Constitution.

Affirmed on other grounds.

2. Plant Patents

Flowing simultaneously with the new animal patents from the Supreme Court's decision in *Chakrabarty*, a new set of utility patents on plants began being issued by the PTO. However, because plants may also be protected by "plant patents" or certificates—as opposed to *utility* patents—under either the Plant Patent Act ("PPA"), 35 U.S.C. §§ 161–164, or the Plant Variety Protection Act ("PVPA"), 7 U.S.C. § 2321 *et seq.*, any reference to a "plant patent" should be scrutinized to determine whether it was issued under the PPA, PVPA, or the standard utility patent provisions of the Patent Act. Technically, a "plant patent" issues only for asexually reproduced plants under the provisions of the PPA; utility patents on plants issue only under the utility patent sections of the Patent Act; and "certificates," which grant patent-like protection for sexually reproduced plants, are issued by the Department of Agriculture under the PVPA.

J.E.M. AG Supply, Inc. v. Pioneer Hi-Bred Int'l, Inc.

534 U.S. 124 (2001)

Justice Thomas delivered the opinion of the Court.

This case presents the question whether utility patents may be issued for plants under 35 U.S.C. § 101 (1994 ed.), or whether the Plant Variety Protection Act, 84 Stat.

1542, as amended, 7 U.S.C. § 2321 *et seq.*, and the Plant Patent Act of 1930, 35 U.S.C. §§ 161–164 (1994 ed. and Supp. V), are the exclusive means of obtaining a federal statutory right to exclude others from reproducing, selling, or using plants or plant varieties. We hold that utility patents may be issued for plants.

I

The United States Patent and Trademark Office (PTO) has issued some 1,800 utility patents for plants, plant parts, and seeds pursuant to 35 U.S.C. § 101. Seventeen of these patents are held by respondent Pioneer Hi-Bred International, Inc. (Pioneer). Pioneer's patents cover the manufacture, use, sale, and offer for sale of the company's inbred and hybrid corn seed products. A patent for an inbred corn line protects both the seeds and plants of the inbred line and the hybrids produced by crossing the protected inbred line with another corn line. See, *e.g.*, U.S. Patent No. 5,506,367, col. 3, App. 42. A hybrid plant patent protects the plant, its seeds, variants, mutants, and trivial modifications of the hybrid. See U.S. Patent No. 5,491,295, cols. 2–3.

Pedigree inbred corn plants are developed by crossing corn plants with desirable characteristics and then inbreeding the resulting plants for several generations until the resulting plant line is homogenous. Inbreds are often weak and have a low yield; their value lies primarily in their use for making hybrids. See, *e.g.*, U.S. Patent No. 5,506,367, col. 6 (describing the traits and applications of the inbred corn line PHP38 by reference to the qualities exhibited in hybrid plants created with PHP38).

Hybrid seeds are produced by crossing two inbred corn plants and are especially valuable because they produce strong and vibrant hybrid plants with selected highly desirable characteristics. For instance, Pioneer's hybrid corn plant 3394 is "characterized by superior yield for maturity, excellent seedling vigor, very good roots and stalks, and exceptional stay green." Hybrid plants, however, generally do not reproduce true-to-type, *i.e.*, seeds produced by a hybrid plant do not reliably yield plants with the same hybrid characteristics. Thus, a farmer who wishes to continue growing hybrid plants generally needs to buy more hybrid seed.

Pioneer sells its patented hybrid seeds under a limited label license that provides: "License is granted solely to produce grain and/or forage." The license "does not extend to the use of seed from such crop or the progeny thereof for propagation or seed multiplication." It strictly prohibits "the use of such seed or the progeny thereof for propagation or seed multiplication or for production or development of a hybrid or different variety of seed."

Petitioner J.E.M. Ag Supply, Inc., doing business as Farm Advantage, Inc., purchased patented hybrid seeds from Pioneer in bags bearing this license agreement. Although not a licensed sales representative of Pioneer, Farm Advantage resold these bags. Pioneer subsequently brought a complaint for patent infringement against Farm Advantage and several other corporations and residents of the State of Iowa who are distributors and customers for Farm Advantage (referred to collectively as Farm Advantage or petitioners). Pioneer alleged that Farm Advantage has "for a long-time past been and still [is] infringing one or more [Pioneer patents] by making, using, selling, or offering for sale corn seed of the ... hybrids in infringement of these patents-in-suit."

Farm Advantage answered with a general denial of patent infringement and entered a counterclaim of patent invalidity, arguing that patents that purport to confer protection for corn plants are invalid because sexually reproducing plants are not patentable subject matter within the scope of 35 U.S.C. § 101 (1994 ed.). Farm Advantage maintained that the Plant Patent Act of 1930 (PPA) and the Plant Variety Protection Act (PVPA) set forth the exclusive statutory means for the protection of plant life because these statutes are more specific than § 101, and thus each carves out subject matter from § 101 for special treatment.[8]

The District Court granted summary judgment to Pioneer. Relying on this Court's broad construction of § 101 in [*Chakrabarty*], the District Court held that the subject matter covered by § 101 clearly includes plant life. It further concluded that in enacting the PPA and the PVPA Congress neither expressly nor implicitly removed plants from § 101's subject matter. In particular, the District Court noted that Congress did not implicitly repeal § 101 by passing the more specific PVPA because there was no irreconcilable conflict between the PVPA and § 101.

The United States Court of Appeals for the Federal Circuit affirmed the judgment and reasoning of the District Court. We granted certiorari and now affirm.

II

The question before us is whether utility patents may be issued for plants pursuant to 35 U.S.C. § 101 (1994 ed.). The text of § 101 provides:

> "Whoever invents or discovers any new and useful process, machine, manufacture, or composition of matter, or any new and useful improvement thereof, may obtain a patent therefor, subject to the conditions and requirements of this title."

As this Court recognized over 20 years ago in *Chakrabarty,* the language of § 101 is extremely broad. "In choosing such expansive terms as 'manufacture' and 'composition of matter,' modified by the comprehensive 'any,' Congress plainly contemplated that the patent laws would be given wide scope." This Court thus concluded in *Chakrabarty* that living things were patentable under § 101, and held that a manmade micro-organism fell within the scope of the statute. As Congress recognized, "the relevant distinction was not between living and inanimate things, but between products of nature, whether living or not, and human-made inventions."

In *Chakrabarty,* the Court also rejected the argument that Congress must expressly authorize protection for new patentable subject matter:

> "It is, of course, correct that Congress, not the courts, must define the limits of patentability; but it is equally true that once Congress has spoken it is 'the province and duty of the judicial department to say what the law is.' ... Congress has performed its constitutional role in defining patentable subject matter in § 101; we perform ours in construing the language Congress has employed.... The subject-matter provisions of the patent law have been cast in broad terms to fulfill the constitutional and statutory goal of promoting 'the Progress of Science and the useful Arts' with all that means for the social and economic benefits envisioned by Jefferson." ...

8. Petitioners favor a holding that the PVPA is the only means of protecting these corn plants primarily because the PVPA's coverage is generally less extensive and the hybrid seeds at issue do not have PVPA protection. Most notably, the PVPA provides exemptions for research and for farmers to save seed from their crops for replanting. Utility patents issued for plants do not contain such exemptions.

Thus, in approaching the question presented by this case, we are mindful that this Court has already spoken clearly concerning the broad scope and applicability of § 101.[9]

Several years after *Chakrabarty,* the PTO Board of Patent Appeals and Interferences held that plants were within the understood meaning of "manufacture" or "composition of matter" and therefore were within the subject matter of § 101. *In re Hibberd,* 227 USPQ 443, 444 (1985). It has been the unbroken practice of the PTO since that time to confer utility patents for plants. To obtain utility patent protection, a plant breeder must show that the plant he has developed is new, useful, and non-obvious. 35 U.S.C. §§ 101–103. In addition, the plant must meet the specifications of § 112, which require a written description of the plant and a deposit of seed that is publicly accessible. *See* 37 CFR §§ 1.801–1.809 (2001).

Petitioners do not allege that Pioneer's patents are invalid for failure to meet the requirements for a utility patent. Nor do they dispute that plants otherwise fall within the terms of § 101's broad language that includes "manufacture" or "composition of matter." Rather, petitioners argue that the PPA and the PVPA provide the exclusive means of protecting new varieties of plants, and so awarding utility patents for plants upsets the scheme contemplated by Congress. We disagree. Considering the two plant specific statutes in turn, we find that neither forecloses utility patent coverage for plants.

A

The 1930 PPA conferred patent protection to asexually reproduced plants. Significantly, nothing within either the original 1930 text of the statute or its recodified version in 1952 indicates that the PPA's protection for asexually reproduced plants was intended to be exclusive.

Plants were first explicitly brought within the scope of patent protection in 1930 when the PPA included "plants" among the useful things subject to patents. Thus the 1930 PPA amended the general utility patent provision, Rev. Stat. § 4886, to provide:

> "Any person who has invented or discovered any new and useful art, machine, manufacture, or composition of matter, or any new and useful improvements thereof, or who has invented or discovered and asexually reproduced any distinct and new variety of plant, other than a tuber-propagated plant, not known or used by others in this country, before his invention or discovery thereof, ... may ... obtain a patent therefor."

Act of May 23, 1930, § 1, 46 Stat. 376. This provision limited protection to the asexual reproduction of the plant. Asexual reproduction occurs by grafting, budding, or the like, and produces an offspring with a genetic combination identical to that of the single parent—essentially a clone.[10] The PPA also amended Revised Statutes § 4888 by adding: "No plant patent shall be declared invalid on the ground of noncompliance with this section if the description is made as complete as is reasonably possible."

---

9. Justice Breyer argues that [*Chakrabarty*] cannot determine the outcome of this case because it did not answer the precise question presented. *See post,* at 607–608 (dissenting opinion). But this simply misses the mark. *Chakrabarty* broadly interpreted the reach of § 101. This interpretation is surely germane to the question whether sexually reproduced plants fall within the subject matter of § 101. In addition, *Chakrabarty's* discussion of the PPA and the PVPA is relevant to petitioners' primary arguments against utility patent protection for sexually reproduced plants.

10. By contrast, sexual reproduction occurs by seed and sometimes involves two different plants.

In 1952, Congress revised the patent statute and placed the plant patents into a separate chapter 15 of Title 35 entitled, "Patents for plants." 35 U.S.C. §§ 161–164.[11] This was merely a housekeeping measure that did nothing to change the substantive rights or requirements for a plant patent. A "plant patent"[12] continued to provide only the exclusive right to asexually reproduce a protected plant, § 163, and the description requirement remained relaxed, § 162.[13] Plant patents under the PPA thus have very limited coverage and less stringent requirements than § 101 utility patents.

Importantly, chapter 15 nowhere states that plant patents are the exclusive means of granting intellectual property protection to plants. Although unable to point to any language that requires, or even suggests, that Congress intended the PPA's protections to be exclusive, petitioners advance three reasons why the PPA should preclude assigning utility patents for plants. We find none of these arguments to be persuasive.

First, petitioners argue that plants were not covered by the general utility patent statute prior to 1930. In advancing this argument, petitioners overlook the state of patent law and plant breeding at the time of the PPA's enactment. The Court in *Chakrabarty* explained the realities of patent law and plant breeding at the time the PPA was enacted: "Prior to 1930, two factors were thought to remove plants from patent protection. The first was the belief that plants, even those artificially bred, were products of nature for purposes of the patent law.... The second obstacle to patent protection for plants was the fact that plants were thought not amenable to the 'written description' requirement of the patent law." Congress addressed these concerns with the 1930 PPA, which recognized that the work of a plant breeder was a patentable invention and relaxed the written description requirement. The PPA thus gave patent protection to breeders who were previously unable to overcome the obstacles described in *Chakrabarty.*

This does not mean, however, that prior to 1930 plants could not have fallen within the subject matter of § 101. Rather, it illustrates only that in 1930 Congress *believed* that plants were not patentable under § 101, both because they were living things and because in practice they could not meet the stringent description requirement. Yet these premises were disproved over time. As this Court held in *Chakrabarty,* "the relevant distinction" for purposes of § 101 is not "between living and inanimate things, but between products of nature, whether living or not, and human-made inventions." In addition, advances in biological knowledge and breeding expertise have allowed plant breeders to satisfy § 101's demanding description requirement.

Whatever Congress may have believed about the state of patent law and the science of plant breeding in 1930, plants have always had the *potential* to fall within the general subject matter of § 101, which is a dynamic provision designed to encompass new and

---

11. The PPA, as amended, provides:

> Whoever invents or discovers and asexually reproduces any distinct and new variety of plant, including cultivated sports, mutants, hybrids, and newly found seedlings, other than a tuber propagated plant or a plant found in an uncultivated state, may obtain a patent therefor, subject to the conditions and requirements of this title.

35 U.S.C. § 161.

12. Patents issued under § 161 are referred to as "plant patents," which are distinguished from § 101 utility patents and § 171 design patents.

13. To obtain a plant patent under § 161 a breeder must meet all of the requirements for § 101, except for the description requirement. *See* § 162 ("No plant patent shall be declared invalid for noncompliance with section 112 [providing for written description] of this title if the description is as complete as is reasonably possible").

unforeseen inventions. "A rule that unanticipated inventions are without protection would conflict with the core concept of the patent law that anticipation undermines patentability."

Petitioners essentially ask us to deny utility patent protection for sexually reproduced plants because it was unforeseen in 1930 that such plants could receive protection under § 101. Denying patent protection under § 101 simply because such coverage was thought technologically infeasible in 1930, however, would be inconsistent with the forward-looking perspective of the utility patent statute. As we noted in *Chakrabarty,* "Congress employed broad general language in drafting § 101 precisely because [new types of] inventions are often unforeseeable."

Second, petitioners maintain that the PPA's limitation to asexually reproduced plants would make no sense if Congress intended § 101 to authorize patents on plant varieties that were sexually reproduced. But this limitation once again merely reflects the reality of plant breeding in 1930. At that time, the primary means of reproducing bred plants true-to-type was through asexual reproduction. Congress thought that sexual reproduction through seeds was not a stable way to maintain desirable bred characteristics.[14] Thus, it is hardly surprising that plant patents would protect only asexual reproduction, since this was the most reliable type of reproduction for preserving the desirable characteristics of breeding. *See generally* E. Sinnott, Botany Principles and Problems 266–267 (1935); J. Priestley & L. Scott, Introduction to Botany 530 (1938).

Furthermore, like other laws protecting intellectual property, the plant patent provision must be understood in its proper context. Until 1924, farmers received seed from the Government's extensive free seed program that distributed millions of packages of seed annually. *See* Fowler, The Plant Patent Act of 1930: A Sociological History of its Creation, 82 J. Pat. & Tm. Off. Soc. 621, 623, 632 (2000).[15] In 1930, seed companies were not primarily concerned with varietal protection, but were still trying to successfully commodify seeds. There was no need to protect seed breeding because there were few markets for seeds. *See* Kloppenburg 71 ("Seed companies' first priority was simply to establish a market, and they continued to view the congressional distribution as a principal constraint").

By contrast, nurseries at the time had successfully commercialized asexually reproduced fruit trees and flowers. These plants were regularly copied, draining profits from

14. The Senate Report accompanying the bill notes: "All such plants must be asexually reproduced in order to have their identity preserved. This is necessary since seedlings either of chance or self-pollenization from any of these would not preserve the character of the individual." S. Rep. No. 315, 71st Cong., 2d Sess., 3 (1930).

This Report, like the text, indicates Congress' intent to limit plant patent coverage to asexual reproduction, but explains that this limitation "recognizes a practical situation"—*i.e.,* that propagation by seeds does not preserve the character of the original. *See id.* at 4 ("[T]he patent right granted is a right to propagate the new variety by asexual reproduction. It does not include the right to propagate by seeds. This limitation in the right granted recognizes a practical situation and greatly narrows the scope of the bill"). The limitation to asexual reproduction was a recognition of the "practical situation" that seedlings did not reproduce true-to-type. An exclusive right to asexual reproduction was the only type of coverage needed and thought possible given the state of plant breeding at the time.

15. At its high point in 1897, over 20 million packages of seed were distributed to farmers. *See* N. Klose, America's Crop Heritage 98 (1950). Even at the time the program was eliminated in 1924, it was the third largest line item in the Department of Agriculture's budget. *See* J. Kloppenburg, First the Seed: The Political Economy of Plant Biotechnology 1492–2000, at 71 (1988) (hereinafter Kloppenburg).

those who discovered or bred new varieties. Nurseries were the primary subjects of agricultural marketing and so it is not surprising that they were the specific focus of the PPA. *See* Fowler, *supra,* at 634–635; Kneen, Patent Plants Enrich Our World, National Geographic 357, 363 (1948).

Moreover, seed companies at the time could not point to genuinely new varieties and lacked the scientific knowledge to engage in formal breeding that would increase agricultural productivity. *See* Kloppenburg 77; Fowler, *supra,* at 633 ("Absent significant numbers of distinct new varieties being produced by seed companies, variety protection through something like a patent law would hardly have been considered a business necessity"). In short, there is simply no evidence, let alone the overwhelming evidence needed to establish repeal by implication that Congress, by specifically protecting asexually reproduced plants through the PPA, intended to preclude utility patent protection for sexually reproduced plants.[16]

Third, petitioners argue that in 1952 Congress would not have moved plants out of the utility patent provision and into § 161 if it had intended § 101 to allow for protection of plants. Petitioners again rely on negative inference because they cannot point to any express indication that Congress intended § 161 to be the exclusive means of patenting plants. But this negative inference simply does not support carving out subject matter that otherwise fits comfortably within the expansive language of § 101, especially when § 101 can protect different attributes and has more stringent requirements than does § 161.

This is especially true given that Congress in 1952 did nothing to change the substantive rights or requirements for obtaining a plant patent. Absent a clear intent to the contrary, we are loath to interpret what was essentially a housekeeping measure as an affirmative decision by Congress to deny sexually reproduced plants patent protection under § 101.

B

By passing the PVPA in 1970, Congress specifically authorized limited patent-like protection for certain sexually reproduced plants. Petitioners therefore argue that this legislation evidences Congress' intent to deny broader § 101 utility patent protection for such plants. Petitioners' argument, however, is unavailing for two reasons. First, nowhere does the PVPA purport to provide the exclusive statutory means of protecting sexually reproduced plants. Second, the PVPA and § 101 can easily be reconciled. Because it is harder to qualify for a utility patent than for a Plant Variety Protection (PVP) certificate, it only makes sense that utility patents would confer a greater scope of protection.

1

The PVPA provides plant variety protection for:

> The breeder of any sexually reproduced or tuber propagated plant variety (other than fungi or bacteria) who has so reproduced the variety....

---

16. The dissent relies on *United States v. Estate of Romani*, 523 U.S. 517 (1998), for the proposition that "a later, more specific statute trumps an earlier, more general one." *See post*, at 611. Yet in *Estate of Romani* this purported rule was applied because the meaning of the earlier statute was "unresolved." The Court noted that "despite the age of the statute, and despite the fact that it has been the subject of a great deal of litigation," its meaning had not been definitively established. By contrast, the statutory terms "manufacture or composition of matter" were not similarly unresolved at the time the PPA was passed. In addition, these subject-matter terms have been interpreted broadly to evolve with developments in science and technology. Moreover, even in *Estate of Romani*, the Court considered that there was no "plain inconsistency" between the earlier and later statutes.

7 U.S.C. § 2402(a).

Infringement of plant variety protection occurs, *inter alia,* if someone sells or markets the protected variety, sexually multiplies the variety as a step in marketing, uses the variety in producing a hybrid, or dispenses the variety without notice that the variety is protected.[17]

Since the 1994 amendments, the PVPA also protects "any variety that is essentially derived from a protected variety," § 2541(c)(1), and "any variety whose production requires the repeated use of a protected variety," § 2541(c)(3). Practically, this means that hybrids created from protected plant varieties are also protected; however, it is not infringement to use a protected variety for the development of a hybrid. *See* 7 U.S.C. § 2541(a)(4).[18]

The PVPA also contains exemptions for saving seed and for research. A farmer who legally purchases and plants a protected variety can save the seed from these plants for replanting on his own farm. *See* § 2543 ("[I]t shall not infringe any right hereunder for a person to save seed produced by the person from seed obtained, or descended from seed obtained, by authority of the owner of the variety for seeding purposes and use such saved seed in the production of a crop for use on the farm of the person...."). In addition, a protected variety may be used for research. *See* 7 U.S.C. § 2544 ("The use and reproduction of a protected variety for plant breeding or other bona fide research shall not constitute an infringement of the protection provided under this chapter"). The utility patent statute does not contain similar exemptions.[19]

---

17. Title 7 U.S.C. § 2541(a) provides in full:

(a) Acts constituting infringement

Except as otherwise provided in this subchapter, it shall be an infringement of the rights of the owner of a protected variety to perform without authority, any of the following acts in the United States, or in commerce which can be regulated by Congress or affecting such commerce, prior to expiration of the right to plant variety protection but after either the issue of the certificate or the distribution of a protected plant variety with the notice under section 2567 of this title:

(1) sell or market the protected variety, or offer it or expose it for sale, deliver it, ship it, consign it, exchange it, or solicit an offer to buy it, or any other transfer of title or possession of it;

(2) import the variety into, or export it from, the United States;

(3) sexually multiply, or propagate by a tuber or part of a tuber, the variety as a step in marketing (for growing purposes) the variety;

(4) use the variety in producing (as distinguished from developing) a hybrid or different variety therefrom;

(5) use seed which had been marked 'Unauthorized Propagation Prohibited' or 'Unauthorized Seed Multiplication Prohibited' or progeny thereof to propagate the variety;

(6) dispense the variety to another, in a form which can be propagated, without notice as to being a protected variety under which it was received;

(7) condition the variety for the purpose of propagation, except to the extent that the conditioning is related to the activities permitted under section 2543 of this title;

(8) stock the variety for any of the purposes referred to in paragraphs (1) through (7);

(9) perform any of the foregoing acts even in instances in which the variety is multiplied other than sexually, except in pursuance of a valid United States plant patent; or

(10) instigate or actively induce performance of any of the foregoing acts.

18. It is, however, infringement of a utility patent to use a protected plant in the development of another variety. *See infra*, at 604–605.

19. The dissent argues that our "reading would destroy" the PVPA's exemptions. *Post*, at 611. Yet such bold predictions are belied by the facts. According to the Government, over 5,000 PVP certificates have been issued, as compared to about 1,800 utility patents for plants. Since 1985 the PTO has interpreted § 101 to include utility patents for plants, and there is no evidence that the availability of such patents has rendered the PVPA and its specific exemptions obsolete.

Thus, while the PVPA creates a statutory scheme that is comprehensive with respect to its particular protections and subject matter, giving limited protection to plant varieties that are new, distinct, uniform, and stable, § 2402(a), nowhere does it restrict the scope of patentable subject matter under § 101. With nothing in the statute to bolster their view that the PVPA provides the exclusive means for protecting sexually reproducing plants, petitioners rely on the legislative history of the PVPA. They argue that this history shows the PVPA was enacted because sexually reproducing plant varieties and their seeds were not and had never been intended by Congress to be included within the classes of things patentable under Title 35.[20]

The PVPA itself, however, contains no statement that PVP certificates were to be the exclusive means of protecting sexually reproducing plants. The relevant statements in the legislative history reveal nothing more than the limited view of plant breeding taken by some Members of Congress who believed that patent protection was unavailable for sexually reproduced plants. This view stems from a lack of awareness concerning scientific possibilities.

Furthermore, at the time the PVPA was enacted, the PTO had already issued numerous utility patents for hybrid plant processes. Many of these patents, especially since the 1950's, included claims on the products of the patented process, *i.e.*, the hybrid plant itself. *See* Kloppenburg 264. Such plants were protected as part of a hybrid process and not on their own. Nonetheless, these hybrids still enjoyed protection under § 101, which reaffirms that such material was within the scope of § 101.

2

Petitioners next argue that the PVPA altered the subject-matter coverage of § 101 by implication. Yet "the only permissible justification for a repeal by implication is when the earlier and later statutes are irreconcilable." "The rarity with which [the Court has] discovered implied repeals is due to the relatively stringent standard for such findings, namely, that there be an irreconcilable conflict between the two federal statutes at issue."

To be sure, there are differences in the requirements for, and coverage of, utility patents and PVP certificates issued pursuant to the PVPA. These differences, however, do not present irreconcilable conflicts because the requirements for obtaining a utility patent under § 101 are more stringent than those for obtaining a PVP certificate, and the protections afforded by a utility patent are greater than those afforded by a PVP certificate. Thus, there is a parallel relationship between the obligations and the level of protection under each statute.

It is much more difficult to obtain a utility patent for a plant than to obtain a PVP certificate because a utility patentable plant must be new, useful, and nonobvious, 35 U.S.C. §§ 101–103. In addition, to obtain a utility patent, a breeder must describe the plant with sufficient specificity to enable others to "make and use" the invention after the patent term expires. § 112. The disclosure required by the Patent Act is "the *quid pro quo* of the right to exclude." The description requirement for plants includes a deposit

20. Petitioners point to a House Report that concluded: "Under patent law, protection is presently limited to those varieties of plants which reproduce asexually, that is, by such methods as grafting or budding. No protection is available to those varieties of plants which reproduce sexually, that is, generally by seeds." H.R. Rep. No. 91-1605, at 1 (1970), U.S. Code Cong. & Admin. News 1970, pp. 5082, 5083.

of biological material, for example, seeds, and mandates that such material be accessible to the public. *See* 37 CFR §§ 1.801–1.809 (2001).

By contrast, a plant variety may receive a PVP certificate without a showing of usefulness or nonobviousness. *See* 7 U.S.C. § 2402(a) (requiring that the variety be only new, distinct, uniform, and stable). Nor does the PVPA require a description and disclosure as extensive as those required under § 101. The PVPA requires a "description of the variety setting forth its distinctiveness, uniformity and stability and a description of the genealogy and breeding procedure, when known." 7 U.S.C. § 2422(2). It also requires a deposit of seed in a public depository, § 2422(4), but neither the statute nor the applicable regulation mandates that such material be accessible to the general public during the term of the PVP certificate. *See* 7 CFR § 97.6 (2001).

Because of the more stringent requirements, utility patent holders receive greater rights of exclusion than holders of a PVP certificate. Most notably, there are no exemptions for research or saving seed under a utility patent. Additionally, although Congress increased the level of protection under the PVPA in 1994, a PVP certificate still does not grant the full range of protections afforded by a utility patent. For instance, a utility patent on an inbred plant line protects that line as well as all hybrids produced by crossing that inbred with another plant line. Similarly, the PVPA now protects "any variety whose production requires the repeated use of a protected variety." 7 U.S.C. § 2541(c)(3). Thus, one cannot use a protected plant variety to produce a hybrid for commercial sale. PVPA protection still falls short of a utility patent, however, because a breeder can use a plant that is protected by a PVP certificate to "develop" a new inbred line while he cannot use a plant patented under § 101 for such a purpose. See 7 U.S.C. § 2541(a)(4) (infringement includes "use [of] the variety in producing (as distinguished from developing) a hybrid or different variety therefrom").

For all of these reasons, it is clear that there is no "positive repugnancy" between the issuance of utility patents for plants and PVP coverage for plants. Nor can it be said that the two statutes "cannot mutually coexist." Indeed, "when two statutes are capable of coexistence, it is the duty of the courts, absent a clearly expressed congressional intention to the contrary, to regard each as effective." Here we can plainly regard each statute as effective because of its different requirements and protections. The plain meaning of § 101, as interpreted by this Court in *Chakrabarty,* clearly includes plants within its subject matter. The PPA and the PVPA are not to the contrary and can be read alongside § 101 in protecting plants.

3

Petitioners also suggest that even when statutes overlap and purport to protect the same commercially valuable attribute of a thing, such "dual protection" cannot exist. Yet this Court has not hesitated to give effect to two statutes that overlap, so long as each reaches some distinct cases. Here, while utility patents and PVP certificates do contain some similar protections, as discussed above, the overlap is only partial.

Moreover, this Court has allowed dual protection in other intellectual property cases. "Certainly the patent policy of encouraging invention is not disturbed by the existence of another form of incentive to invention. In this respect the two systems [trade secret protection and patents] are not and never would be in conflict." In this case, many plant varieties that are unable to satisfy the stringent requirements of § 101 might still qualify for the lesser protections afforded by the PVPA.

III

We also note that the PTO has assigned utility patents for plants for at least 16 years and there has been no indication from either Congress or agencies with expertise that such coverage is inconsistent with the PVPA or the PPA. The Board of Patent Appeals and Interferences, which has specific expertise in issues of patent law, relied heavily on this Court's decision in *Chakrabarty* when it interpreted the subject matter of § 101 to include plants. *In re Hibberd,* 227 USPQ 443 (1985). This highly visible decision has led to the issuance of some 1,800 utility patents for plants. Moreover, the PTO, which administers § 101 as well as the PPA, recognizes and regularly issues utility patents for plants. In addition, the Department of Agriculture's Plant Variety Protection Office acknowledges the existence of utility patents for plants.

In the face of these developments, Congress has not only failed to pass legislation indicating that it disagrees with the PTO's interpretation of § 101; it has even recognized the availability of utility patents for plants. In a 1999 amendment to 35 U.S.C. § 119, which concerns the right of priority for patent rights, Congress provided: "Applications for plant breeder's rights filed in a WTO [World Trade Organization] member country ... shall have the same effect for the purpose of the right of priority ... as applications for patents, subject to the same conditions and requirements of this section as apply to applications for patents." 35 U.S.C. § 119(f). Crucially, § 119(f) is part of the general provisions of Title 35, not the specific chapter of the PPA, which suggests a recognition on the part of Congress that plants are patentable under § 101.

IV

For these reasons, we hold that newly developed plant breeds fall within the terms of § 101, and that neither the PPA nor the PVPA limits the scope of § 101's coverage. As in *Chakrabarty,* we decline to narrow the reach of § 101 where Congress has given us no indication that it intends this result. Accordingly, we affirm the judgment of the Court of Appeals.

It is so ordered.

...

JUSTICE SCALIA, concurring.

This case presents an interesting and difficult point of statutory construction, seemingly pitting against each other two perfectly valid canons of interpretation: (1) that statutes must be construed in their entirety, so that the meaning of one provision sheds light upon the meaning of another; and (2) that repeals by implication are not favored. I think these sensible canons are reconcilable only if the first of them is limited by the second. That is to say, the power of a provision of law to give meaning to a previously enacted ambiguity comes to an end once the ambiguity has been authoritatively resolved. At that point, use of the later enactment produces not clarification (governed by the first canon) but amendment (governed by the second).

In the present case, the only ambiguity that could have been clarified by the words added to the utility patent statute by the Plant Patent Act of 1930 (PPA) is whether the term "composition of matter" included living things. The newly enacted provision for plants invited the conclusion that this term which preceded it did not include living things. (The term "matter," after all, is sometimes used in a sense that excludes living things. See Webster's New International Dictionary 1515 (2d ed. 1950): "Physical substance as made up of chemical elements and distinguished from incorporeal substance, action, qualities, etc.... '*Matter* is inert, senseless, and lifeless.' *Johnson*.") It is important to note that this is *the only way* in which the new PPA language could have clarified the ambiguity: There was no way in which "composition of matter" could be regarded as a category separate from plants, but not separate from other living things.

Stare decisis, however, prevents us from any longer regarding as an open question—as ambiguous—whether "composition of matter" includes living things. [*Chakrabarty*] holds that it does. As the case comes before us, therefore, the language of the PPA—if it is to have any effect on the outcome—must do so by way of *amending* what we have held to be a statute that covers living things (and hence covers plants). At this point the canon against repeal by implication comes into play, and I agree with the Court that it determines the outcome. I therefore join the opinion of the Court.

JUSTICE BREYER, with whom JUSTICE STEVENS joins, dissenting.

The question before us is whether the words "manufacture" or "composition of matter" contained in the utility patent statute, 35 U.S.C. § 101 (Utility Patent Statute), cover plants that also fall within the scope of two more specific statutes, the Plant Patent Act of 1930 (PPA), 35 U.S.C. § 161 *et seq.*, and the Plant Variety Protection Act (PVPA), 7 U.S.C. § 2321 *et seq.* I believe that the words "manufacture" or "composition of matter" do *not* cover these plants. That is because Congress intended the two more specific statutes to exclude patent protection under the Utility Patent Statute for the plants to which the more specific Acts directly refer. And, as the Court implicitly recognizes, this Court neither considered nor decided this question in [*Chakrabarty*]. Consequently, I dissent.

I

Respondent and the Government claim that *Chakrabarty* controls the outcome in this case. This is incorrect, for *Chakrabarty* said nothing about the specific issue before us. *Chakrabarty,* in considering the scope of the Utility Patent Statute's language "manufacture, or composition of matter," 35 U.S.C. § 101, asked whether those words included such living things as bacteria—a substance to which neither of the two specific plant Acts refers. The Court held that the Utility Patent Statute language included a "new" bacterium because it was "a nonnaturally occurring manufacture or composition of matter" that was "not nature's handiwork." It quoted language from a congressional Committee Report indicating that "Congress intended statutory subject matter to 'include anything under the sun that is made by man.'" But it nowhere said or implied that this Utility Patent Statute language also includes the very subject matter with which the two specific statutes deal, namely, plants. Whether a bacterium technically speaking is, or is not, a plant, the Court considered it a "life form," and not the kind of "plant" that the two specific statutes had in mind.

The Court did consider a complicated argument that sought indirectly to relate the two specific plant statutes to the issue before it. That argument went roughly as follows: (1) Congress enacted two special statutes related to plants. (2) Even though those two statutes do not cover bacteria, the fact that Congress enacted them shows that Congress thought the Utility Patent Statute's language ("manufacture, or composition of matter") did not cover any living thing, including bacteria. (3) Congress consequently must have intended the two special Acts to provide exclusive protection for all forms of "life" whether they do, or do not, count as the kinds of "plants" to which the specific statutes refer.

The Court, in reply, wrote that Congress, when enacting the specific statutes, might have (wrongly) believed that the Utility Patent Statute did not apply to plants, probably because Congress thought that plants were "natural products," not human products. It added that Congress also might have believed that it was too difficult for plant inventors to meet patent law's ordinary "written description" requirement. In addition, the Court pointed out that the relevant distinction between unpatentable and patentable subject matter was not between living and inanimate things, but rather between products of nature and human-made inventions. As such, the bacteria at issue were patentable because they were products of human invention. And the Court concluded that "nothing" in Congress' decision to *exclude* bacteria from the PVPA supported "petitioner's position," namely, that Congress intended no utility patent protection for any living thing.

Neither this refutation nor the argument itself decides the question here. That question is *not* about general coverage for matters that the special statutes *do not* mention (namely, nonplant life forms such as bacteria). It *is* about general coverage for matters to which the special plant statutes do refer (namely, plants). *Chakrabarty* neither asked, nor answered, this latter question, the question now before us. And nothing in the Court's opinion indicates the contrary.

II

The critical question, as I have said, is whether the two specific plant statutes embody a legislative intent to deny coverage under the Utility Patent Statute *to those plants to which the specific plant statutes refer.* In my view, the first of these statutes, the PPA, reveals precisely that intent. And nothing in the later history of either the Utility Patent Statute or the PVPA suggests the contrary.

As initially enacted in 1930, the PPA began by amending the Utility Patent Statute to read as follows:

> Any person who has invented or discovered any new and useful art, machine, manufacture, or composition of matter, or any new and useful improvements thereof, *or who has invented or discovered and asexually reproduced any distinct and new variety of plant, other than a tuber-propagated plant* ... may ... obtain a patent therefor[e].

Rev. Stat. §4886, as amended by Act of May 23, 1930, §1, 46 Stat. 376 (language added by the PPA italicized). This language refers to *all* plants. It says that an inventor—in principle—can obtain a patent on *any* plant (the subject matter of the patent) that meets three requirements. It must be distinct; it must be new; and on one or more occasions it must have been "asexually reproduced," *e.g.*, reproduced by means of a graft.

This last-mentioned "graft" requirement does not separate (1) those plants that can reproduce through grafting from (2) those plants that can reproduce by seed. The two categories are not mutually exclusive. P. Raven, R. Evert, & S. Eichhorn, Biology of Plants 179–180, 255 (6th ed.1999). Many plants—perhaps virtually any plant—can be reproduced "asexually" as well as by seed. S.Rep. No. 315, 71st Cong., 2d Sess., 5 (1930). Rather, the "asexual reproduction" requirement sought to ensure that the inventor was capable of reproducing the new variety "asexually" (through a graft) because that fact would guarantee that the variety's new characteristics had genetic (rather than, say, environmental) causes and would prove genetically stable over time. *See ibid.* ("A plant patent covers only the exclusive right of asexual reproduction, and obviously it would be futile to grant a patent for a new and distinct variety unless the variety had been demonstrated to be susceptible to asexual reproduction"); *cf. Dunn v. Ragin*, 50 USPQ 472, 474, 1941 WL 9724 (1941) (noting that asexual reproduction "determine[s] that the progeny in fact possess the characteristic or characteristics which distinguish it as a new variety").

Although the section defining the PPA's coverage does not limit its scope to plants that reproduce primarily through grafting, a later section does so limit the protection that it offers. That section specifies that the patent holder will receive "the exclusive right to asexually reproduce the plant," *e.g.*, the right to reproduce it through grafting, but he will not receive an exclusive right to reproduce the plant sexually, *i.e.*, the right to reproduce it through seeds. And this is true *regardless* of whether the patent holder could reproduce true to type offspring through seeds. *See* S.Rep. No. 315, at 4 ("On the other hand, [the PPA] does not give any patent protection to the right of propagation of the new variety by seed, irrespective of the degree to which the seedlings come true to type"). This was a significant limitation because, the Court's contrary claim notwithstanding, *ante,* at 600, and n. 7, it was readily apparent in 1930 that a plant's desirable characteristics *could* be preserved through reproduction by seed. *See* Fowler, The Plant Patent Act of 1930: A Sociological History of its Creation, 82 J. Pat. & Tm. Off. Soc. 621, 635, 644 (2000).

In sum, the PPA permits patenting of new and distinct varieties of (1) plants that breeders primarily reproduce through grafts (say, apple trees), (2) plants that breeders primarily reproduce through seeds (say, corn), and (3) plants that reproduce both ways (say, violets). *See* C. Chong, Plant Propagation, *reprinted in* 1 CRC Handbook of Plant Science in Agriculture 91–92, 94, 104 (B. Christie & A. Hanson eds., 1987); Raven, Evert, & Eichhorn, *supra,* at 179. But, because that statute left plant buyers free to keep, to reproduce, and to sell seeds, the statute likely proved helpful *only* to those in the first category. Both the PPA's legislative history and the earliest patents granted under the Act fully support this interpretation. See S.Rep. No. 315, at 3 (explaining that varieties that "resul[t] from seedlings of cross pollenization of two species" were patentable under the Act); Plant Patent Nos. 1–2, 5–6, 8–11 (roses); Plant Patent Nos. 7, 15 (peach trees).

Given these characteristics, the PPA is incompatible with the claim that the Utility Patent Statute's language ("manufacture, or composition of matter") also covers plants. To see why that is so, simply imagine a plant breeder who, in 1931, sought to patent a new, distinct variety of plant that he invented but which he has *never been able to reproduce through grafting, i.e., asexually.* Because he could not reproduce it through grafting, he could not patent it under the more specific terms of the PPA. Could he nonetheless patent it under the more general Utility Patent Statute language "manufacture, or composition of matter?"

Assume the court that tried to answer that question was prescient, *i.e.,* that it knew that this Court, in *Chakrabarty*, would say that the Utility Patent Statute language ("manufacture," or "composition of matter") in principle might cover "anything under the sun," including bacteria. Such a prescient court would have said that the Utility Patent Statute did cover plants had the case reached it in 1929, before Congress enacted the more specific 1930 law. But how could any court decide the case similarly in 1931 after enactment of the 1930 amendment? To do so would virtually nullify the PPA's primary condition—that the breeder have reproduced the new characteristic through a graft—reading it out of the Act. Moreover, since the Utility Patent Statute would cover, and thereby forbid, reproduction by seed, such a holding would also have read out of the statute the PPA's more limited list of exclusive rights. Consequently, even a prescient court would have had to say, as of 1931, that the 1930 Plant Patent Act had, in amending the Utility Patent Statute, placed the subject matter of the PPA—namely, plants—outside the scope of the words "manufacture, or composition of matter."

Nothing that occurred after 1930 changes this conclusion. In 1952, the Utility Patent Statute was recodified, and the PPA language I have quoted was given its own separate place in the Code. See 35 U.S.C. § 161 *et seq.* As Pioneer itself concedes, that change was not "substantive." Indeed, as recodified the PPA still allows a breeder to obtain a patent when he "invents or discovers and asexually reproduces *any* distinct and new variety of plant," 35 U.S.C. § 161 (emphasis added), but it only allows the patent holder to "exclude others from *asexually* reproducing the plant or selling or using the plant so reproduced," § 163 (emphasis added).

Nor does the enactment of the Plant Variety Protection Act of 1970 change the conclusion. The PVPA proved necessary because plant breeders became capable of creating new and distinct varieties of certain crops, corn, for example, that were valuable only when reproduced through seeds—a form of reproduction that the earlier Act freely permitted. See S.Rep. No. 91-1246, pp. 2–3 (1970). Just prior to its enactment a special Presidential Commission, noting the special problems that plant protection raised and favoring the development of a totally new plant protection scheme, had recommended that "[a]ll provisions in the patent statute for plant patents be deleted...." President's Commission on the Patent System, To Promote the Progress of Useful Arts, S. Doc. No. 5, 90th Cong., 1st Sess., 20–21 (1967) (hereinafter S. Doc.). Instead Congress kept the PPA while adding the PVPA. The PVPA gave patent-like protection (for 20 years) to plants reproduced by seed, and it excluded the PPA's requirement that a breeder have "asexually reproduced" the plant. 7 U.S.C. §§ 2402, 2483. It imposed certain specific requirements. § 2402 (variety must be new, distinct, uniform, and stable). And it provided the breeder with an exclusive right to sell, offer to sell, reproduce, import, or export the variety, including the seeds. § 2483.

At the same time, the PVPA created two important exceptions. The first provided that a farmer who plants his fields with a protected plant "shall not infringe any right hereunder" by saving the seeds and planting them in future years. § 2543. The second permitted "use and reproduction of a protected variety for plant breeding or other bona fide research." § 2544.

Nothing in the history, language, or purpose of the 1970 statute suggests an intent to reintroduce into the scope of the general words "manufacture, or composition of matter" the subject matter that the PPA had removed, namely, plants. To the contrary, any such reintroduction would make meaningless the two exceptions—for planting and for research—that Congress wrote into that Act. It is not surprising that no party argues that passage of the PVPA somehow enlarged the scope of the Utility Patent Statute.

III

The Court replies as follows to the claim that its reading of the Utility Patent Statute nullifies the PPA's limitation of protection to plants produced by graft and the PVPA's exemptions for seeds and research: (1) The Utility Patent Statute applies only to plants that are useful, novel, nonobvious, and for which the inventor provides an enabling written description of the invention. 35 U.S.C. §§ 101, 102, 103, 112. (2) The PVPA applies to plants that are novel, distinct, uniform, and stable. 7 U.S.C. § 2402. (3) The second set of criteria seem slightly easier to meet, as they do not include nonobviousness and a written description (Pioneer does not argue that the "useful" requirement is significant). (4) And Congress could reasonably have intended the planting and research exceptions to apply only to the set of plants that can meet the easier, but not the tougher, criteria.

I do not find this argument convincing. For one thing, it is not clear that the general patent law requirements are significantly tougher. Counsel for Pioneer stated at oral argument that there are many more PVP certificates than there are plant patents. But he added that the major difference in criteria is the difference between the utility patent law's "nonobviousness" requirement and the specific Acts' requirement of "newness"—a difference that may reflect the Patent Office's more "rigorous" examination process.

In any case, there is no relationship between the criteria differences and the exemptions. Why would anyone want to limit the exemptions—related to seed-planting and research—only to those new plant varieties that are slightly less original? Indeed, the research exemption would seem more useful in respect to more original, not less original, innovation. The Court has advanced no sound reason why Congress would want to destroy the exemptions in the PVPA that Congress created. And the Court's reading would destroy those exemptions.

The Court and Justice Scalia's concurrence also rely upon the interpretive canon that disfavors repeal by implication. The Court says that "there is simply no evidence" that the PPA was meant to preclude § 101 protection for sexually reproduced plants. *Ante,* at 601. But reliance on the canon of "implied repeal" is misplaced. The canon has traditionally been embraced when a party claims that a later statute—*that does not actually modify an earlier statute*—implicitly repeals the earlier legislation. That canon has *no* relevance to the PPA—which *explicitly* amended the Utility Patent Statute by limiting protection to plants produced by graft. Even were that not so, the Court has noted that a later, more specific statute will ordinarily trump the earlier, more general one.

Regardless, canons are not mandatory rules. They are guides to help courts determine likely legislative intent. And that intent is critical. Those who write statutes seek to solve human problems. Fidelity to their aims requires us to approach an interpretive problem not as if it were a purely logical game, like a Rubik's Cube, but as an effort to divine the human intent that underlies the statute. Here that effort calls not for an appeal to canons, but for an analysis of language, structure, history, and purpose. Those factors make clear that the Utility Patent Statute does not apply to plants. Nothing in *Chakrabarty* holds to the contrary.

For these reasons, I dissent.

Monsanto Company v. McFarling

363 F.3d 1336 (2004)

Clevenger, Circuit Judge.

The United States District Court for the Eastern District of Missouri entered summary judgment against defendant Homan McFarling and in favor of the Monsanto Company ("Monsanto") under Federal Rule of Civil Procedure 54(b) on some, but not all, of the claims being litigated. The district court held that, when McFarling replanted some of Monsanto's patented ROUNDUP READY(r) soybeans that he had saved from his prior year's crop, McFarling breached the Technology Agreement that he had signed as a condition of his purchase of the patented seeds. The district court also held that McFarling had failed to demonstrate a genuine issue of material fact that prevented entry of summary judgment on any of his counterclaims or his defenses to Monsanto's breach-of-contract claim. Finally, the district court held that a liquidated damages provision in the Technology Agreement was valid and enforceable under Missouri law and entered a judgment in the amount of $780,000.00. McFarling appeals the district court's rulings on several of his counterclaims and defenses, as well as its ruling on the contractual damages provision. We affirm the district court on the counterclaims and defenses, but we vacate the district court's judgment as it relates to the damages provision and remand for a determination of Monsanto's actual damages.

I

Monsanto manufactures ROUNDUP(r) herbicide. ROUNDUP(r) contains glyphosate, a chemical that indiscriminately kills vegetation by inhibiting the metabolic activity of a particular enzyme, 5-enolpyruvyl-shikimate-3 phosphate synthase ("EPSPS"). EPSPS is necessary for the conversion of sugars into amino acids—and thus for growth—in many plants and weeds.

Monsanto also markets ROUNDUP READY(r) genetic-modification technology. In soybean seeds, the ROUNDUP READY(r) technology operates by inserting the gene sequence for a variant of EPSPS that is not affected by the presence of glyphosate but that still performs the sugar-conversion function required for cell growth. Thus, ROUNDUP READY(r) soybean seeds produce both a "natural" version of EPSPS that is rendered ineffective in the presence of the glyphosate in ROUNDUP(r) herbicide, and a genetically modified version of EPSPS that permits the soybean seeds to grow nonetheless. ROUNDUP(r), or other glyphosate-based herbicides, can thus be sprayed over the top of an entire field, killing the weeds without harming the ROUNDUP READY(r) soybeans.

The Monsanto Technology Agreement in dispute in this case lists six patents related to the various seeds that are licensed by the agreement, but Monsanto has asserted infringement in this case only under two patents that read on aspects of the use of the ROUNDUP READY(r) technology in soybeans. United States Patent No. 5,633,435 ("the '435 patent") relates to the gene encoding the modified EPSPS enzyme, and sweepingly claims, *inter alia,* the "isolated DNA molecule" encoding it, '435 patent, claim 1; "[a] glyphosate-tolerant plant cell comprising" that DNA molecule, *id.,* claim 24; "[a] glyphosate-tolerane [sic] plant comprising" that plant cell, *id.,* claim 28; "[a] seed of a glyphosate-tolerant plant," *id.,* claim 79; a particular "transgenic soybean plant," *id.,* claim 86; and "[a] method of producing genetically transformed plants which are tolerant toward glyphosate herbicide," *id.,* claim 15. United States Patent No. 5,352,605 ("the '605 patent") relates to the use of a particular promoter in genetically modified plant cells. The '605 patent claims, *inter alia,* DNA sequences and plant cells containing the promoter. A promoter sequence is a DNA sequence located in proximity to the DNA sequence that encodes a protein and that, in part, tells the cellular machinery how much of the protein to make.

Monsanto licenses its proprietary ROUNDUP READY(r) technology through two interrelated licensing schemes. First, it licenses the patented gene to seed companies that manufacture the glyphosate-tolerant seeds that are sold to farmers. Under this license, seed companies gain the right to insert the genetic trait into the germplasm of their own seeds (which can differ from seed company to seed company), and Monsanto receives the right to a royalty or "technology fee" of $6.50 for every 50-pound bag of seed containing the ROUNDUP READY(r) technology sold by the seed company. Monsanto also owns several subsidiary seed companies that comprise approximately 20 percent of the market for ROUNDUP READY(r) soybeans.

Second, Monsanto requires that seed companies execute licenses, rather than conduct unconditional sales, with their farmer customers. The 1998 version of this "Monsanto Technology Agreement" (the "Technology Agreement") between Monsanto and the soybean farmers using ROUNDUP READY(r) soybeans places several conditions on the soybean farmers' use of the licensed soybeans. In exchange for the "[o]pportunity to purchase and plant seed containing" the ROUNDUP READY(r) technology, soybean farmers agree, *inter alia:*

> To use the seed containing Monsanto gene technologies for planting a commercial crop only in a single season.
>
> To not supply any of this seed to any other person or entity for planting, and to not save any crop produced from this seed for replanting, or supply saved seed to anyone for replanting.
>
> To not use this seed or provide it to anyone for crop breeding, research, generation of herbicide registration data or seed production.

The Technology Agreement also contains a clause specifying damages in the event of breach by the farmer:

> In the event that the Grower saves, supplies, sells or acquires seed for replant in violation of this Agreement and license restriction, in addition to other remedies available to the technology provider(s), the Grower agrees that damages will include a claim for liquidated damages, which will be based on 120 times the applicable Technology Fee.

II

Homan McFarling operates a 5000-acre farm in Pontotoc County, Mississippi. In 1998, McFarling executed the Technology Agreement in connection with the license of 1000 bags of ROUNDUP READY(r) soybean seed. McFarling concedes that he saved 1500 bushels of seed from his 1998 crop, enough to plant approximately 1500 acres, and that he replanted them in 1999. He subsequently saved 3075 bags of soybeans from his 1999 crop, replanting them in 2000.

Soybeans destined for replanting are apparently cleaned after harvest. When McFarling sent his seeds saved from the 1998 season to a third party for cleaning, Monsanto had some samples taken, had the genetic makeup of the seeds tested at Mississippi State University, and thus learned that McFarling was saving ROUNDUP READY(r) seeds.

III

In January 2000, Monsanto filed suit against McFarling, alleging, *inter alia*, infringement of the '435 and '605 patents and breach of the Technology Agreement, and seeking a preliminary injunction prohibiting McFarling from "planting, transferring or selling the infringing articles to a third party." In his answer, McFarling raised affirmative defenses (styled alternatively as counterclaims when possible) both to liability—including, *inter alia*, violations of the Plant Variety Protection Act ("PVPA"), 84 Stat. 1542, as amended, 7 U.S.C. § 2321 et seq., the federal antitrust laws, the patent misuse doctrine, and the patent exhaustion and first sale doctrines—and to damages as calculated under the 120 multiplier in the Technology Agreement. He did not, however, challenge the validity of Monsanto's patents....

... [I]n the district court, Monsanto moved for summary judgment on the infringement claim under the '605 patent, the breach of the Technology Agreement claim, and all of McFarling's affirmative defenses. The district court granted summary judgment in favor of Monsanto on all of McFarling's defenses as well as on liability with respect to Monsanto's '605 patent infringement claim and the Technology Agreement claim. On damages, however, the district court denied Monsanto's summary judgment motion. It left the damages issue regarding infringement of the '605 patent for trial. Additionally, although it held the liquidated damages clause in the Technology Agreement to be valid and enforceable (provided the 120 multiplier was applied to the number of bags of seed purchased rather than the number replanted), it concluded that there was insufficient evidence of the number of bags purchased by McFarling in 1998 to enter judgment on damages on the breach-of-contract claim. After McFarling stipulated that he purchased 1000 bags of ROUNDUP READY(r) soybean seed in 1998, the district court entered final judgment pursuant to Federal Rule of Civil Procedure 54(b) on Monsanto's breach-of-contract claim only in the amount of $780,000.00 (120 x $6.50 x 1000), and against McFarling on his counterclaims.

In the district court, Monsanto had argued that the 120 multiplier in the liquidated damages clause should be interpreted to produce damages of 120 times the technology fee times the number of bags of seed replanted by McFarling. The district court rejected that formula, reasoning that it would constitute an unlawful penalty because it simply imposes a multiple of 120 times Monsanto's actual damages. To avoid that result and sustain the lawfulness of the liquidated damages clause, the district court fashioned a formula that multiplies 120 times the licensing fee times the number of bags of seed purchased.

IV

[On appeal,] McFarling argues that the district court's grant of summary judgment on the breach-of-contract claim was erroneous on the following issues: (1) his patent-misuse defense, (2) his antitrust counterclaim, (3) his defense under the PVPA, and (4) his defense that the 120 multiplier in the liquidated damages provision of the Technology Agreement is a penalty clause that is unenforceable under Missouri law. We address each in turn below.

...

V

McFarling argues that Monsanto has committed patent misuse because Monsanto has impermissibly tied an unpatented product to a patented product. In McFarling's words, "[b]y prohibiting seed-saving, Monsanto has extended its patent on the gene technology to include an unpatented product—the germplasm—or God-made soybean seed which is not within the terms of the patent."

The policy of the patent misuse doctrine is "to prevent a patentee from using the patent to obtain market benefit beyond that which inures in the statutory patent right." Therefore, in evaluating a patent-misuse defense, "[t]he key inquiry is whether, by imposing conditions that derive their force from the patent, the patentee has impermissibly broadened the scope of the patent grant with anticompetitive effect." In the cases in which the restriction is reasonably within the patent grant, the patent misuse defense can never succeed. In cases in which a condition controlling the use of a patented invention extends beyond the patentee's statutory right to exclude, however, either a per se rule of patent misuse or a rule of reason analysis must be applied.

Tying can constitute patent misuse: A patent licensor who conditions the license on a patent licensee's purchase of an unpatented material for use in the invention may, under certain conditions, be impermissibly extending the scope of the subject matter encompassed by the patent grant.

We need not plumb the complexities of tying as misuse of a patent, however, to determine that the district court correctly granted summary judgment for Monsanto. Mc-

Farling does not raise a typical tying allegation, and the mere recitation of the word "tying" is not sufficient to state a patent misuse defense. McFarling does not argue that he cannot purchase soybean germplasm without the genetic trait that brings the soybean within the ambit of Monsanto's patent. In fact, a market for such unmodified soybeans exists. Neither does McFarling argue that he sought (or is capable of performing under) the type of license granted to the seed companies to purchase, make or use the patented gene sequence prior to its insertion into the seed.

McFarling's "tying" argument instead centers on his desire to replant the entire seed, including the genetic modifications, and on Monsanto's refusal to grant him permission to do so. McFarling proposes that Monsanto could "untie" the seed and the trait by permitting the farmer to save and replant ROUNDUP READY(r) seed each year, provided the farmer still pays directly to Monsanto the required technology fee, rather than requiring a farmer to purchase both the seed and the genetic technology together at the beginning of each growing season. By suggesting that he should be allowed to pay the technology fee in conjunction with replanting of the second-generation soybeans, the closest McFarling comes to alleging a tying argument is a suggestion that Monsanto has tied together the legal right to exclude granted by a patent and the entire, physical patented product (or combination of germplasm and trait). At its simplest, McFarling effectively argues in different words that he should be granted a compulsory license to use the patent rights in conjunction with the second-generation ROUNDUP READY(r) soybeans in his possession after harvest. We decline to hold that Monsanto's raw exercise of its right to exclude from the patented invention by itself is a "tying" arrangement that exceeds the scope of the patent grant.

What perhaps truly irks McFarling is that the license controls what McFarling can do with second-generation seeds—the seeds that McFarling "made" using the seeds that he acquired under a strict license. McFarling argues that the prohibition in the Technology Agreement on "sav[ing] any crop produced from this seed for replanting" constitutes patent misuse; he does not suggest that the prohibitions on "supply[ing] any of this seed to any other person or entity for planting" and on "supply[ing] saved seed to anyone for replanting" should render the patent unenforceable. Nonetheless, Monsanto tries rather unconvincingly to paint its restrictions in the Technology Agreement as permissible field-of-use restrictions on the first-generation seeds. Monsanto argues that it "may license a grower to 'use' its patented ROUNDUP READY(r) biotechnology to grow a commercial crop, but decline to license a grower to 'make' patented seed for use or sale as a crop seed." Based on the record before us, McFarling plants and grows the first-generation seed in an identical fashion whether he intends to sell the second-generation seed as a commercial crop for consumption or whether he intends to replant it. Thus, the Technology Agreement does not impose a restriction on the use of the product purchased under license but rather imposes a restriction on the use of the goods made by the licensed product.

Our case law has not addressed in general terms the status of such restrictions placed on goods made by, yet not incorporating, the licensed good under the patent misuse doctrine. However, the Technology Agreement presents a unique set of facts in which licensing restrictions on the use of goods produced by the licensed product are not beyond the scope of the patent grant at issue: The licensed and patented product (the first-generation seeds) and the good made by the licensed product (the second-generation seeds) are nearly identical copies. Thus, given that we must presume that Monsanto's '435 patent reads on the first-generation seeds,[21] it also reads on the second-generation seeds. *See* '435 patent, col. 165, l. 12 (claiming "[a] seed of a glyphosate-tolerant plant"). Because the '435 patent would read on all generations of soybeans produced, we hold that the restrictions in the Technology Agreement prohibiting the replanting of the second generation of ROUNDUP READY(r) soybeans do not extend Monsanto's rights under the patent statute.

VI

McFarling next repackages his tying patent-misuse defense as a tying antitrust counterclaim. However, because we have found McFarling's allegations insufficient to present a genuine issue of material fact concerning whether Monsanto's licensing restrictions went beyond the boundaries of its patent grant, McFarling's antitrust counterclaim also fails. In this instance, the anticompetitive effect of which McFarling complains is part and parcel of the patent system's role in creating incentives for potential inventors.

McFarling also argues that "the district court improperly assumed the role of the fact finder and decided that the patented technology (the patented 'trait') and the seed are not two separate markets" without examining consumer demand for either. We agree with McFarling that, for antitrust purposes, whether there are two distinct products for tying purposes is a question of fact usually determined by examining consumer demand. Furthermore, we agree that the district court failed to consider consumer demand. However, the district court's finding concerning the unified nature of the market for the trait and the seed is not relevant to our holding, so we expressly decline to reach or review it. McFarling is not alleging that he is unable to, or even that he desires to, purchase a "natural" soybean seed and the ROUNDUP READY(r) genetic trait as distinct items; he alleges only that Monsanto refuses to grant him a license to use the second-generation genetically modified seeds in his possession after harvest in his preferred manner.

VII

McFarling asks that we reconsider our ruling in *McFarling I* that the Plant Variety Protection Act does not demonstrate a congressional intent to preempt and invalidate all prohibitions on seed saving contained in utility-patent licenses. We remain unpersuaded by McFarling's arguments.

In *J.E.M. AG Supply, Inc. v. Pioneer Hi-Bred International, Inc.*, the Supreme Court held that plants were subject matter eligible for utility-patent protection under 35 U.S.C. § 101, and that hybrid seeds also eligible for protection under the PVPA were not an exception to that general rule. In considering whether Congress's enactment of the PVPA implicitly altered the scope of patentable subject matter under section 101, the Court recognized that "there are no exemptions for ... saving seed under a utility

21. In a post-argument letter, McFarling notes that Monsanto included a count of infringement under the '435 patent in its complaint but that it did not move for summary judgment on this count. McFarling argues that because the validity of the '435 patent will be subject to attack if and when the claim of infringement under the '435 patent is addressed in the district court, it is improper for this court to presume the patent's validity at this juncture. We disagree. We can review only the claims considered final by the district court under Federal Rule of Civil Procedure 54(b). McFarling failed to raise or argue the alleged invalidity of the '435 patent as a defense to the breach of the Technology Agreement claim or as an element of its patent misuse defense, and at this stage of the proceedings we deem the argument to have been waived for purposes of deciding this appeal.

patent," as there is in the PVPA, *see* 7 U.S.C. §2543 (2000), yet it held nonetheless that the two statutory schemes could "mutually coexist." In light of the Supreme Court's interpretation of Congress's intent, we conclude that Congress did not intend to prohibit owners of utility patents from enforcing seed-saving prohibitions in their licenses.

VIII

Finally, McFarling argues that the district court erred in holding that the 120 multiplier on the technology fee in the Technology Agreement was a valid and enforceable liquidated damages clause under Missouri law. Upon independent review, we agree with McFarling that the liquidated damages clause in the Technology Agreement is invalid and unenforceable under Missouri law as it applies to McFarling's breach of replanting of saved seed....

B

We conclude that the 120 multiplier in the Technology Agreement is not valid under Missouri law. It was not, at the time of contracting, a reasonable estimate of the harm that Monsanto would likely suffer in the event that McFarling breached the contractual prohibition on saving ROUNDUP READY(r) soybeans.

Monsanto's principal argument to the contrary is that ROUNDUP READY(r) soybeans can self-replicate at an exponential rate. One bag of soybean seed can yield 36 bags of soybean seed to save for the following season, although this figure may vary with different types of crops, seed varieties, geographic growing locations, planting rates, cultural practices, and growing conditions, among other factors. Based on this figure together with assumptions of infinite acreage on which to plant and no commercial sale of any soybeans, a farmer planting one bag of soybeans in year one would reap 36 bags to replant in year two, 1296 bags to replant in year three, and 46,656 bags to replant in year four. This simple narrative is forceful insofar it illustrates the potential magnitude of the harm that Monsanto could suffer from losing control of its proprietary technology. However, an illustration that breach of the Technology Agreement under particular conditions may be reasonably expected to lead to harm of a great magnitude is not sufficient to uphold the validity of the damages clause in its entirety. The damages clause is not valid as applied to the provision of the Technology Agreement that prohibits saving soybean seed and that was breached by McFarling....

1

The 120 multiplier in the Technology Agreement violates [Missouri law] because the identical Technology Agreement is used to govern a grower's rights with respect to several different crops that would be expected to replicate at different rates. If the anticipated harm flows from the self-replicating capacity of genetically modified seeds, then a reasonable estimate of compensation upon breach must logically be adjusted to incorporate the different rates of self-replication. The Technology Agreement makes no such adjustment.

The Technology Agreement signed by McFarling is used with Monsanto's proprietary strains of genetically modified cotton, soybeans, and corn: "This Monsanto Technology Agreement covers Roundup Ready(r) cotton, Bollgard(r) cotton, Bollgard(r) with Roundup Ready(r) cotton, Roundup Ready(r) soybeans, YieldGard(r) corn and Roundup Ready(r) corn." The report of Monsanto's damages expert and Monsanto's brief on appeal assume "a ratio of 36 to 1 for seed produced from seed planted" to calculate the harm from the self-replication of soybeans from one growing season to the next. This same report, however, quotes Monsanto's 1997 Technology Agreement applicable to cotton only as stating that "[t]he average ratio of cotton seed produced from cotton seed planted is 120 to 1." (Based on the information presented in this report, the 120 figure first appeared in this cotton-only license and was only subsequently used in the cotton-soybean-corn license.) Because the rates of self-replication of cotton and soybeans differ by over a factor of three,[22] it is difficult to understand how the same 120 multiplier as applied to the technology fee could be a reasonable forecast of harm in the event of a breach by both a cotton farmer and a soybean farmer.

2

The 120 multiplier in the Technology Agreement also violates [Missouri law] because it specifies the same measure of damages in the event of breach of several different restrictive provisions of the contract that lead to different types of damage. The licensee can trigger the 120 multiplier in the Technology Agreement by violating any one of several distinct provisions: "In the event that the Grower *saves, supplies, sells* or *acquires seed for replant* in violation of this Agreement and license restriction ... the Grower agrees that damages will include a claim for liquidated damages ..." (emphases added). We conclude that the nature of the harm to Monsanto flowing from breach of the provision prohibiting seed saving is fundamentally different from the nature of the harm to Monsanto flowing from breach of the provision prohibiting seed supplying and seed selling.

In fact, Monsanto repeatedly acknowledged the importance of the distinction between seed saving by the farmer for replant on his own farm and seed transfer to third parties for replant. Monsanto argued in its brief that "[w]hether an infringer saves seed for himself only or transfers saved seed to other growers ... significantly impacts the multiplier effect and the harm to Monsanto." ...

Proof of loss is of course substantially more difficult when the breaching farmer supplies or sells the seed to another farmer in violation of the agreement. If a farmer transfers seed to a third-party for replant, Monsanto not only has no privity of contract with the purchasers, but it also faces difficulty tracing the seed, locating and deposing the individuals who purchased it, and thus determining the amount of harm caused by the breach. In this situation, the difficulty of proof of loss would be considerable. However, if a farmer saves seed for replant in a future growing season, the number of bags planted is more readily ascertainable from a single defendant who is in privity with Monsanto.

Monsanto's expectation of the compensable loss flowing from the breach should also be lower when the breaching farmer replants on his own farm. The testimony of Monsanto's own damages expert suggests that a distinction between replanting and transferring is in part due to different rates of seed-replication in each scenario. The acreage of an individual grower for replanting is finite, placing a brake on the replication rate, whereas the geographical area available to plant resold seed is practically unlimited. Monsanto's damages expert assumed that soybeans self-replicated at a linear rather than an exponential rate in his only example demonstrating the harm to Monsanto that could flow from a farmer breaching by replanting seed rather than by transferring seed. The damages expert presumed that the farmer would save the same amount of seed each year, likely just enough to plant the farm's acreage.

---

22. The record does not contain information concerning the self-replication rate of corn.

Additionally, the harm flowing from a farmer's decision to replant soybeans on his own farm can be arrested through injunctive relief such as the preliminary injunction Monsanto received in this case. Because of the difficulty of tracing seed once it has left the purchaser's farm, however, injunctive relief may never fully arrest the harm that would flow from the transfer of seed to a third party for replant. Thus, when the contractual damages clause is applied to calculate the damages arising from the replanting of seed on the purchaser's farm, the reasonableness of the 120 multiplier as a forecast of compensation must be measured vis-à-vis the harm that would occur between the date on which breach by replanting occurred and the date on which some form of injunctive relief could be obtained.[23] When the contractual damages clause is applied to calculate the damages arising from the transfer of seed to third parties, however, the 120 multiplier as a reasonable forecast of compensation may be measured by the possibility of long-term, unenjoined use of the seed by unidentified purchasers.

Because Monsanto could not have known at the time of contracting whether McFarling would breach the no-seed-transfer provisions or the no-seed-saving provision of the Technology Agreement, Monsanto argues that the harm is of a kind that is difficult to estimate, and that this difficulty of estimating harm should forgive the breadth of breaches of different magnitudes covered by the same damages formula. This argument fails for two reasons.

First, as explained above, the contracting parties must expect at the time of contracting that the actual harm will be difficult to measure at the time of breach. In other words, actual harm must be difficult to calculate when one traditionally calculates harm in a contract cause of action; uncertainty only at the time of contracting is insufficient. Second, a violation of [Missouri's] anti-one-size [liquidated damages] rule cannot be explained away merely by stating that one is unsure, at the time of contracting, which provision of the contract will be breached. Monsanto asserted in its post-argument letter that the damages provision did not violate the anti-one-size rule because "[a]t the time of contracting, Monsanto cannot know whether a grower bent upon breach will do so by transferring or replanting saved seed, or both." Monsanto, however, misunderstands the rule. Were Monsanto's formulation of the anti-one-size rule correct, the rule could never be enforced because the parties can never know, at the time of contracting, whether one or another of the contractual provisions, the breach of which is covered by a damages clause, will in fact be breached.

In summary, we hold that the 120 multiplier in the Technology Agreement is an unenforceable penalty clause ... : While we express no opinion on whether the clause would be a reasonable forecast of the compensation required to make Monsanto whole

---

23. If we were to reference future harm in our determination of whether the 120 multiplier is a reasonable forecast, McFarling's payment of the liquidated damages clause would amount to a license to practice the licensed technology in perpetuity. Monsanto would already have been compensated for all future use of the seed, and Missouri law does not permit double recovery via liquidated and actual damages for the same injury.

Because it sought to reserve the possibility of permanent injunctive relief, Monsanto at oral argument stated that it did not believe that the 120 damages multiplier was intended to compensate it completely for all the harm that could ensue from a breach, extending from the time of the breach into the indefinite future. Instead, Monsanto reserved the right to seek a permanent injunction against McFarling, arguing that the 120 multiplier could be a reasonable forecast "of the amount of past harm ... that could have occurred as of the time that Monsanto obtained a contract judgment." That is, the 120 multiplier was "a reasonable estimate of the range of injury that would have already occurred by the time that Monsanto could (a) discover a violation, (b) bring a lawsuit, and (c) obtain a judgment" enabling an injunction, preliminary or permanent.

upon breach of the contractual provision prohibiting supplying or selling seed to third parties, we conclude that it is not a reasonable estimate of the harm that would be anticipated to flow from breach of the provision prohibiting replanting seed.

3

As interpreted by the district court, the 120 multiplier in the Technology agreement also fixes an unreasonable forecast of compensation because it is measured by the number of bags purchased, a number which does not necessarily relate to the number of bags replanted, supplied or sold.

The damages specified in the Technology Agreement are measured by multiplying the number 120 by the "applicable technology fee." As an issue of contract interpretation, the district court held that the "applicable technology fee" is measured by multiplying the $6.50 per-bag technology fee by the number of bags *purchased* in connection with the execution of the technology agreement. However, the number of bags *replanted or transferred* is the more accurate departure point for measuring harm. The harm caused by McFarling to Monsanto in the next year's growing season would be ten times greater to Monsanto if McFarling saved or transferred ten times more seed with the intent that it be replanted. There is no necessary relation, however, between the number of bags purchased and the number of bags replanted or transferred. McFarling would cause Monsanto a specific amount of harm if he saved a thousand bags of seed and replanted it for only one year, but he would be obligated to pay a vastly different amount of damages under the district court's interpretation of the Technology Agreement if he had purchased a hundred or a thousand bags. It is therefore difficult to understand how any figure based on the number of bags purchased, rather than replanted or transferred, is a reasonable forecast of compensation....

C

Monsanto also argues that the 120 multiplier was justified based on types of harm other than the harm from the self-replicating nature of the soybean seeds. We disagree.

Monsanto argues that the 120 multiplier is a reasonable forecast because it includes harm to Monsanto's ROUNDUP READY(r) brand. As Monsanto's expert testified, "[t]he loss of quality control may result in reduced yields, improper seed segregation and lower quality crops, causing a reduction in the value of Monsanto's brand" to purchasing farmers. We are skeptical of the magnitude of harm to Monsanto's ROUNDUP READY(r) brand that would flow from violations of the licensing agreement. Damage to a brand occurs when a consumer, here the farmer, receives a substandard product believing that the product is genuine. The farmer who saves and replants seeds, however, is well aware that he is not using the seeds in accordance with the terms required by Monsanto, and he is able to attribute any alleged reduction in quality of the second- or third-generation seeds to his own decision to replant rather than to Monsanto's initial product. Without denying that some minimal harm to the ROUNDUP READY(r) brand may result from a decision to save and replant seed, we do not believe that this harm contributes significantly to justifying a 120 multiplier as a reasonable forecast of the damages for breach of the Technology Agreement. Were McFarling to sell the saved seeds to other farmers and pass them off as first-generation seeds rather than as the second-generation seeds that they are, however, the potential for harm to the brand would increase.

Monsanto next argues that the 120 multiplier is necessary because if McFarling's breach in the form of saving and replanting seed were to pass undetected, then McFarling would gain a competitive advantage in the marketplace. "[O]therwise law abiding growers" would then be encouraged "also to use saved soybean seed containing Monsanto's patented ROUNDUP READY(r) biotechnology" in order to compete. This argument, however, is inimical to the compensatory nature of contract remedies: it sounds in deterrence, not compensation, and therefore suggests that the multiplier is in the nature of a penalty clause rather than a liquidated damages clause.

Finally, Monsanto argues that it loses the revenue from its technology fee each time a saved bag of ROUNDUP READY(r) soybeans is replanted. We agree that Monsanto suffers this harm, and we have no reason to suspect that the technology fee does not "reflect[] a reasonable return on Monsanto's significant research and development expenditures" as Monsanto argues. Yet, this argument standing by itself suggests that the technology fee alone, rather than 120 times the technology fee, is a reasonable forecast of harm.

D

When a damages clause is a penalty clause, the clause is unenforceable under Missouri law and only actual damages are available. We therefore remand to the district court to compute actual damages based on the number of bags of seed saved and replanted.

IX

In conclusion, we affirm the district court's entry of summary judgment against McFarling on Monsanto's breach-of-contract claim on liability only. McFarling does not contest the prima facie case made by Monsanto that he breached the Technology Agreement, and he has not presented a genuine issue of material fact concerning his defenses as argued in the court below. We also affirm the district court's dismissal of McFarling's antitrust counterclaim. However, we vacate the district court's damages award because we hold that under Missouri law the provision in the Technology Agreement applying a 120 multiplier to the technology fee is an unenforceable and invalid penalty clause. We therefore remand to the district court for determination of actual damages, and for any other proceedings not inconsistent with this opinion....

Affirmed in part, vacated in part and remanded.

Notes & Questions

1. Do you see any distinction between patents on animals versus plants? Does one present more concerns or problems than the other? Why has no analogy to plant patents arisen for new breeds of animals produced by traditional breeding techniques? Can private organizations that control registration or certification of individual animals for pedigree and breeding—for example, American Kennel Club (www.akc.org)—create and effectively enforce a sort of shadow IP system for new breeds? These organizations could rely on "certification marks," a type of trademark that is exclusive but open to all whose wares meet the mark owner's criteria, or "collective marks," a different type of trademark that is exclusive to all the members of a group whose admission policies are controlled by the mark owner. But would these organizations then essentially monopolize the shadow IP system itself as against the actual breed innovators?

2. Why should the PTO refuse to issue patents on or directed to humans? What rights or control would a patent on a whole, perhaps genetically engineered, human grant to the patent owner? Even if the PTO were to grant such a patent, would it be enforceable in any of the ways that really concern most people—for example, the patented human is enslaved by the patent owner? Clearly this would violate the constitutional civil rights of the patented human. So what patent rights could be enforced by the patent owner? Reproductive rights (as implicating "copies")? But many reproductive rights have been interpreted to be protected under the Constitution as well.

Further, what exactly constitutes a patent claim "directed to or including within its scope a human being"? Does this include so-called "meat puppets"—human-like organisms created and grown for organ harvesting or even prurient interests? What about chimeras—organisms that contain genetic material from multiple distinct species, in this case some combination of human and non-human genetic material? Chimeras have already been created, for example cows and pigs with some human genes. How much human genetic content in such a chimera would trigger a finding that it is "human" and not susceptible to patenting under the PTO policy? Finally, what about human embryos? In a 2004 appropriations bill, Congressman Dave Weldon (R-Fl) successfully inserted the so-called Weldon Amendment that directs that "[n]one of the funds appropriated or otherwise made available under this Act may be used to issue patents on claims directed to or encompassing a human organism." Consolidated Appropriations Act of 2004, Pub. L. No. 108-199, §634, 118 Stat. 3. Weldon himself has this to say about his eponymous amendment:

> What I want to point out is that the U.S. Patent Office has already issued patents on genes, stem cells, animals with human genes, and a host of non-biologic products used by humans, but it has not issued patents on claims directed to human organisms, including human embryos and fetuses. My amendment would not affect the former, but would simply affirm the latter.

149 Cong. Rec. E2417 (daily ed. Nov. 22, 2003) (statement of Rep. Weldon). Congress has used its "power of the purse" in the past to effect social policy that it might not be able to set directly—*i.e.*, an attitude of "we can't ban it, but we don't have to pay for it with tax dollars." But should important social policy issues involving patenting be decided by Congress through the indirect appropriations mechanism? For that matter, should the PTO or even individual examiners be allowed to make these policy decisions?

B. Regulatory Environment

Ag-biotech innovations also clearly have implications for the food supply and environment. In fact, the concerns over releasing GMOs that may proliferate out of control, displace wild type pre-existing versions of the organism, or, at the most extreme, destroy ecosystems, have arguably generated more of the public debate than the IP issues discussed above. Accordingly, federal regulatory agencies within the Department of Health and Human Services (*e.g.*, NIH and FDA), Department of Agriculture (*e.g.*, APHIS), and Department of Labor (*e.g.*, OSHA), together with the Environmental Protection Agency, have been compelled to take actions regarding the release and use of GMOs. But questions quickly arise as to the coordination of these actions and the structure of the regulatory framework.

Executive Office of the President, Office of Science and Technology Policy, Coordinated Framework for Regulation of Biotechnology

51 Fed. Reg. 23302 (June 26, 1986)

I. Preamble

A. Introduction

This notice describes the comprehensive federal regulatory policy for ensuring the safety of biotechnology research and products. Specifically addressed are agency policies that formed part of the previously proposed Coordinated Framework for the Regulation of Biotechnology, published in the Federal Register December 31, 1984 (49 FR 50856, hereinafter "the December 84 Notice"). These agency policies build upon experience with agricultural, pharmaceutical, and other commercial products developed by traditional genetic modification techniques.

Existing statutes provide a basic network of agency jurisdiction over both research and products; this network forms the basis of this coordinated framework and helps assure reasonable safeguards for the public. This framework is expected to evolve in accord with the experiences of the industry and the agencies, and, thus, modifications may need to be made through administrative or legislative actions.

The application of traditional genetic modification techniques is relied upon broadly for enhanced characteristics of food (e.g., hybrid corn, selective breeding), manufactured food (e.g., bread, cheese, yogurt), waste disposal (e.g., bacterial sewage treatment), medicine (e.g., vaccines, hormones), pesticides (e.g. *Bacillus thuringiensis*) and other uses. Federal agencies implement an array of laws which seek to ensure the safety of these products. A concise index of these U.S. laws was published in the Federal Register November 14, 1985 (50 FR 47174, hereinafter "the November 85 Notice"). These laws are product-specific because they regulate certain product uses, such as foods or pesticides. This approach provides the opportunity for similar products to be treated similarly by particular regulatory agencies.

Biotechnology also includes recently developed and newly emerging genetic manipulation technologies, such as recombinant DNA (rDNA), recombinant RNA (rRNA) and cell fusion, that are sometimes referred to as genetic engineering. While the recently developed methods are an extension of traditional manipulations that can produce similar or identical products, they enable more precise genetic modifications, and therefore hold the promise for exciting innovation and new areas of commercial opportunity.

Concerns were raised as to whether products resulting from the recently developed techniques would pose greater risks than those achieved through traditional manipulation techniques. For example, what might be the possible environmental consequences of the many anticipated agricultural and environmental applications that will take place outside the physical constraints of a contained facility? In particular, the environmental application of genetically engineered microorganisms may elicit concern because they are of microscopic size, and some may be able to reproduce, proliferate, and become established.

The underlying policy question was whether the regulatory framework that pertained to products developed by traditional genetic manipulation techniques was adequate for products obtained with the new techniques. A similar question arose regarding the sufficiency of the review process for research conducted for agricultural and environmental applications.

The Administration, recognizing its responsibility to confront these concerns, formed an interagency working group under the former White House Cabinet Council on Natural Resources and the Environment in the spring of 1984. The working group sought to achieve a balance between regulation adequate to ensure health and environmental safety while maintaining sufficient regulatory flexibility to avoid impeding the growth of an infant industry.

Upon examination of the existing laws available for the regulation of products developed by traditional genetic manipulation techniques, the working group concluded that, for the most part, these laws as currently implemented would address regulatory needs adequately. For certain microbial products, however, additional regulatory requirements, available under existing statutory authority, needed to be established.

The existing health and safety laws had the advantage that they could provide more immediate regulatory protection and certainty for the industry than possible with the implementation of new legislation. Moreover, there did not appear to be an alternative, unitary, statutory approach since the very broad spectrum of products obtained with genetic engineering cut across many product uses regulated by different agencies.

Because of the rapid growth in the scientific knowledge base, the working group felt strongly that the federal agencies needed to have an interagency mechanism for sharing scientific information related to biotechnology, particularly information on research and product applications submitted to the agencies.

The December 1984 Notice described the regulatory framework envisioned by the working group, and recognizing the evolutionary nature of its development, asked for comments. In summary, the Notice stated that the Food and Drug Administration (FDA) would regulate genetic engineering products no differently that those achieved through traditional techniques. The Environmental Protection Agency (EPA) described existing and proposed new policies for regulating pesticidal and nonpesticidal microorganisms. The Department of Agriculture (USDA) stated that under its different legislative authorities it could broadly regulate genetically engineered plants and animals, and plant and animal pathogens. The Notice also proposed an interagency science coordinating mechanism.

Many comments were received in response to the Notice. These contributed to the refinement of both the regulatory requirements and the interagency science coordination mechanism.

The interagency coordination mechanism, the Biotechnology Science Coordinating Committee (BSCC), discussed in more detail in section C, of this Preamble, came into being while the agencies were still in process of refining their regulatory proposals. Consequently, the BSCC was able to play a helpful role in the formulation of two basic principles: (1) Agencies should seek to adopt consistent definitions of those genetically engineered organisms subject to review to the extent permitted by their respective statutory authorities; and, (2) agencies should utilize scientific reviews of comparable rigor.

The regulatory framework anticipates that future scientific developments will lead to further refinements. Experience with earlier basic scientific research has shown that as the science progressed and became better understood by the public, regulatory regimens could be modified to reflect more complete understanding of the potential risks involved. Similar evolution is anticipated in the regulation of commercial products as scientists and regulators learn to predict more precisely particular product use that require greater or lesser controls or even exemption from any federal review.

This framework has sought to distinguish between those organisms that require a certain level of federal review and those that do not. This follows a traditional approach to regulation. Within agriculture, for example, introductions of new plants, animals and microorganisms have long occurred routinely with only some of those that are not native or are pathogenic requiring regulatory approval. It should be noted that microorganisms play many essential and varied roles in agriculture and the environment and that for decades agricultural scientists have endeavored to exploit their advantages through routine experimentation and introduction into the environment; and as a rule these agricultural and environmental introductions have taken place without harm to the environment.

B. The Coordinated Framework for the Regulation of Biotechnology

[1.] General Comments

This notice includes separate descriptions of the regulatory policies of FDA, EPA, OSHA and USDA and the research policies of the National Institutes of Health (NIH), NSF, EPA and USDA. The agencies will seek to operate their programs in an integrated and coordinated fashion and together should cover the full range of plants, animals and microorganisms derived by the new genetic engineering techniques. To the extent possible, responsibility for a product use will lie with a single agency. Where regulatory oversight or review for a particular product is to be performed by more than one agency, the policy establishes a lead agency, and consolidated or coordinated reviews. While this preamble seeks to convey an overview of the coordinated framework, it must be noted that the regulatory requirements are highly technical; reliance only on the simplified summary statements herein could be misleading and, thus, the agency policy statements must be consulted for specific details. In the event that questions arise regarding which federal agency has jurisdiction, an information contact is provided at the beginning of this notice.

While in part certain USDA and EPA requirements are new, the underlying regulatory regimens are not new. Members of the agricultural and industrial communities are familiar with the general requirements under these laws which include the Federal Plant Pest Act, The Plant Quarantine Act, the Toxic Substances Control Act (TSCA), and the Federal insecticide, Fungicide, and Rodenticide Act (FIFRA).

Because this comprehensive regulatory framework uses a mosaic of existing federal law, some of the statutory nomenclature for certain actions may seem inconsistent. Certain laws, such as USDA's Federal Plant Pest Act, require a "permit" before a microorganism pathogenic to plants may be transported or imported. Under other laws such as FIFRA, the agencies "license" or "approve" the use of particular products. TSCA requires a "premanufacturing notification (PMN)". There are also some variations among the agencies in the use of the phrase "genetic engineering." Regardless of the nomenclature, the public should be aware that the reviews conducted by each of the regulatory agencies are intended to be of comparable rigor. Agencies have agreed to have scientists from each other's staff participate in reviews. Each regulatory review will require that the safety, or safety and efficacy, of a particular agricultural or industrial product be satisfactorily demonstrated to the regulatory agency prior to commercialization.

The National Environmental Policy Act (NEPA) imposes procedural requirements on all federal agencies to prepare an analysis prior to making a decision to take any action that may significantly affect the environment. Depending on the characteristics of a proposal, an environmental assessment, or a broader environmental impact statement may need to be prepared in connection with the release of genetically manipulated organisms. EPA's actions under most of its environmental statutes have been considered to be the functional equivalent of NEPA compliance.

For the handling of microorganisms, agencies of the Department of Health and Human Services have established recommendations for the safe use of infectious agents. The CDC/NIH publication, *Biosafety in Microbiological and Biomedical Laboratories*, describes combinations of standard and special microbiological practices, safety equipment and facilities which are recommended for working with a variety of infectious agents in research laboratories, academic and industrial. The USDA also has issued guidance on other infectious agents.

The NIH has published guidelines for the contained use of DNA organisms in the *NIH Guidelines for Research Involving Recombinant DNA Molecules*, Federal Register, May 7, 1986 (51 FR 16958, NIH guidelines). The guidelines recommend physical containment at specific levels for different experiments, and exempt other experiments from containment requirements. However, they recommend Biosafety Level 1, the least stringent level of physical containment, for some "exempt" experiments. For large-scale exempt experiments, the NIH guidelines recommended "Biosafety Level 1-Large-Scale" although following review by the Institutional Biosafety Committee, "some latitude" in the application of these requirements is permitted.

The appropriate large-scale containment requirements for many low risk DNA derived industrial microorganisms will be no greater than those appropriate for the unmodified parental organisms. This concept is discussed further in the Organization for Economic Cooperation and Development (OECD) document, described in the International Aspects section below.

OSHA in its Federal Register Notice of April 12, 1984 (50 FR 14468) stated that its authority under the Occupational Safety and Health Act of 1970 (29 U.S.C. et seq.) provides an adequate and enforceable basis for protecting the safety and health of employees in the field of biotechnology and that no additional regulation is necessary. After consideration of comments in the April 1984 notice, OSHA is publishing this policy statement in final form without change.

[2.] Product Regulation

Agencies involved with regulating agriculture, foods, medical devices, drugs, biologics and pesticides have had extensive experience with products that involve living organisms in their manufacture and/or ultimate use including releases into the environment for these purposes. By the time a genetically engineered product is ready for commercialization, it will have undergone substantial review and testing during the research phase, and thus, information regarding its safety should be available. The manufacture by the newer technologies of food, the development of new drugs, medical devices, biologics for humans and animals, and pesticides, will be reviewed by FDA, USDA and EPA in essentially the same manner for safety and efficacy as products obtained by other techniques. The new products that will be brought to market will generally fit within these agencies' review and approval regimens.

The regulatory scheme for products is described in Chart I *Coordinated Framework—Marketing Approval of Biotechnology Products.*

CHART I.—COORDINATED FRAMEWORK—
APPROVAL OF COMMERCIAL BIOTECHNOLOGY PRODUCTS

Subject	Responsible agency(ies)
Foods/Food Additives	FDA,* FSIS[24]
Human Drugs, Medical Devices and Biologics	FDA
Animal Drugs FDA	
Animal Biologics APHIS	
Other Contained Uses	EPA
Plants and Animals	APHIS,* FSIS, FDA.[25]
Pesticide Microorganisms Released in the Environment	EPA,* APHIS
Other Uses (Microorganisms):	
Intergeneric Combination	EPA,* APHIS
Intrageneric Combination:	
Pathogenic Source Organism:	
1. Agricultural Use	APHIS
2. Non-Agricultural use	EPA,*[26] APHIS[27]
No Pathogenic Source Organisms	EPA Report
Nonengineered Pathogens:	
1. Agricultural Use	APHIS
2. Non-agricultural Use	EPA,[28] APHIS[29]
Nonengineered Nonpathogens	EPA Report

* Lead agency.

Jurisdiction over the varied biotechnology products is determined by their use, as has been the case for traditional products. The detailed description of the products and their review are found in the individual agency policy statements contained in this Federal Register Notice. The following is a brief summary of jurisdiction as described in Chart I.

Foods, food additives, human drugs, biologics and devices, and animal drugs are reviewed or licensed by the FDA. Food products prepared from domestic livestock and poultry are under the jurisdiction of the USDA's Food Safety Inspection Service (FSIS).

Animal biologics are reviewed by the Animal and Plant Health Inspection Service, (APHIS). APHIS, also reviews plants, seeds, animal biologics, plant pests, animal pathogens and "regulated articles", i.e., certain genetically engineered organisms containing genetic material from a plant pest. An APHIS permit is required prior to the shipment (movement) or release into the environmental of regulated articles, or the shipment of a plant pest or animal pathogen.

---

24. FSIS, Food Safety and Inspection Service, under the Assistant Secretary of Agriculture for Marketing and Inspection Services is responsible for food use.

25. FDA is involved when in relation to a food use.

26. EPA requirements will only apply to environmental release under a "significant new use rule" that EPA intends to propose.

27. APHIS, Animal and Plant Health Inspection Service, is involved when the microorganism is plant pest, animal pathogen or regulated article requiring a permit.

28. EPA requirements will only apply to environmental release under a "significant new use rule" that EPA intends to propose.

29. APHIS . . . is involved when the microorganism is plant pest, animal pathogen or regulated article requiring a permit.

"Other contained uses" refers to the closed system uses of those microorganisms, subject the TSCA, that are intergeneric combinations, i.e., deliberately formed microorganisms which contain genetic material from dissimilar source organisms. These are subject to EPA's PMN requirement. EPA is considering promulgating a rule to exempt certain classes of microorganisms from this requirement.

Microbial pesticides will be reviewed by EPA, with APHIS involvement in cases where the pesticide is also a plant pest, animal pathogen, or regulated article requiring a permit. (FDA may become involved in implementing pesticide tolerances for foods.)

"Other uses (microorganisms)" include uses involving release into the environment. For these, jurisdiction depends on the characteristics of the organism as well as its use. "Intergeneric combination"[30] microorganisms will be reported to EPA under PMN requirements, with APHIS Involvement in cases where the microorganism is also a regulated article requiring a permit.

"Intrageneric combinations" are those microorganisms formed by genetic engineering other than intergeneric combinations. For these, when there is a pathogenic source organism, and the microorganism is used for agricultural purposes, APHIS has jurisdiction. If the microorganism is used for nonagricultural purposes, then EPA has jurisdiction, with APHIS involvement in cases where the microorganism is also a regulated article requiring a permit. Intrageneric combinations with no pathogenic source organisms are under EPA jurisdiction although EPA will only require an informational report.

"Nonengineered pathogens" that are used for an agricultural use will fall under APHIS jurisdiction. Those that are for a nonagricultural use come under EPA jurisdiction, with APHIS involvement in cases where the microorganism is also a plant pest or animal pathogen requiring a permit. Nonengineered nonpathogenic microorganisms are under EPA jurisdiction which will require only an informational report.

[3.] Research

The coordinated framework for the regulation of biotechnology establishes requirements for the conduct of research.

Approximately ten years ago the NIH issued the NIH guidelines describing the manner in which research with organisms derived by rDNA techniques should be conducted. Since then the guidelines have been modified many times with gradual relaxation of these requirements. The guidelines prescribe the conditions under which institutions which receive NIH funds must conduct experiments. For a very small category of NIH funded experiments including environmental release, the guidelines require that the Director, NIH, approve each experiment on an individual basis. For each of these experiments, the RAC conducts a scientific review with an opportunity for public comment, and makes a recommendation to the NIH Director. As research experiments have expended out of the biomedical area to environmental applications both agricultural and nonagricultural, other agencies have become involved, with shifting of responsibility for research approval to NSF (described in the November 85 Notice), USDA's S&E, and EPA. These other agencies' policies build, in part, on the NIH guidelines and NIH experience.

The S&E guidelines for agricultural research published separately for comment in this issue of the Federal Register have adopted the NIH guidelines with certain modifi-

30. "Intergeneric organisms (new organisms)" and "pathogen" are defined in section D. of the preamble.

cations including expansion of the scope to manipulation techniques other than rDNA; the table included with the S&E guidelines shows where particular elements of the NIH guidelines are used.

It should be noted that not all experiments involving the environmental release of genetically engineered organisms require prior federal approval. In plant applications there is a substantial body of research indicating that such experiments are of low risk. For certain categories of microorganisms modified by traditional genetic modification techniques, there is also a substantial body of research indicating low risk for environmental experiments.

Chart II—*Coordinated Framework—Biotechnology Research Jurisdiction* shows which agency has responsibility for a particular experiment. If more than one agency has potential jurisdiction, one agency has been designated as the lead agency and it is marked with an asterisk on Chart II. The lead agency designation depends on which research agency is funding the research (e.g., NIH, S&E, or NSF) or which regulatory agency reviews specific purpose research (e.g. pesticides). In the chart and in this discussion, the authority refers to approval of the actual execution of experiments and not to their funding.

CHART II.—COORDINATED FRAMEWORK—
BIOTECHNOLOGY RESEARCH JURISDICTION

Subject	Responsible agency(ies)
Contained Research, No Release in Environment:	
1. Federally Funded	Funding agency[31]
2. Non-Federally Funded	NIH or S&E voluntary review APHIS[32]
Foods/Food Additives, Human Drugs, Medical Devices, Biologics, Animal Drugs:	
1. Federally Funded	FDA,* NIH guidelines & review
2. Non-Federally Funded	FDA,* NIH voluntary review
Plants, Animals and Animal Biologics:	
1. Federally Funded	Funding agency,*[33] APHIS[34]
2. Non-Federally Funded	APHIS,* S&E voluntary review
Pesticide Microorganisms:	
Genetically Engineered:	
Intergeneric	EPA,* APHIS[35]
Pathogenic Intergeneric	EPA,* APHIS,[36] S&E voluntary review

31. Review and approval of research protocols conducted by NIH, S&E, or NSF.

32. APHIS issues permits for the importation and domestic shipment of certain plants and animals, plant pests and animal pathogens, and for the shipment or release in the environment of regulated articles.

33. Review and approval of research protocols conducted by NIH, S&E, or NSF.

34. APHIS issues permits for the importation and domestic shipment of certain plants and animals, plant pests and animal pathogens, and for the shipment or release in the environment of regulated articles.

35. *[Id.]*

36. *[Id.]*

Intrageneric Nonpathogen	EPA,* S&E voluntary review
Nonengineered:	
Nonindigenous Pathogens	EPA,* APHIS
Indigenous Pathogens	EPA,*[37] APHIS
Nonindigenous Nonpathogen	EPA*
Other Uses (Microorganisms) Released in the Environment:	
Genetically Engineered:	
Intergeneric Organisms:	
1. Federally Funded	Funding agency,*[38] APHIS,[39] EPA[40]
2. Commercially Funded	EPA, APHIS, S&E voluntary review
Intrageneric Organisms:	
Pathogenic Source Organism:	
1. Federally Funded	Funding agency,*[41] APHIS,[42] EPA[43]
2. Commercially Funding	APHIS,[44] EPA (* if non-agricultural use)
Intrageneric Combination:	
No Pathogenic Source Organisms	EPA Report
Nonengineered	EPA Report,* APHIS[45]

* Lead Agency.

For contained federally funded research for biomedical and agricultural purposes, research approval will be granted by the funding agency. The NIH guidelines relate primarily to biomedical experiments and only to those using rDNA techniques. Research on foods/food additives, human drugs, medical devices and biologics will continue to rely on the NIH guidelines, with NIH approval required for certain experiments such as human gene therapy, and FDA permission for clinical trials.

Fashioned after the NIH guidelines, the S&E guidelines apply to agricultural research on plants, animals, and microorganisms and provide guidance for laboratory and field testing of organisms derived using rDNA manipulation and other technologies. Adher-

---

37. EPA jurisdiction for research on a plot greater than 10 acres.

38. Review and approval of research protocols conducted by NIH, S&E, or NSF.

39. APHIS issues permits for the importation and domestic shipment of certain plants and animals, plant pests and animal pathogens, and for the shipment or release in the environment of regulated articles.

40. EPA reviews federally funded environmental research only when it is for commercial purposes.

41. Review and approval of research protocols conducted by NIH, S&E, or NSF.

42. APHIS issues permits for the importation and domestic shipment of certain plants and animals, plant pests and animal pathogens, and for the shipment or release in the environment of regulated articles.

43. EPA reviews federally funded environmental research only when it is for commercial purposes.

44. APHIS issues permits for the importation and domestic shipment of certain plants and animals, plant pests and animal pathogens, and for the shipment or release in the environment of regulated articles.

45. *[Id.]*

ence to the appropriate set of guidelines is required for institutions receiving financial support from NIH, S&E, or NSF. These guidelines specify what type of review procedures are required for specific categories of experiments. Some experiments require individual approval by the respective agency providing institutional support. For those experiments that require agency approval, advisory committees at NIH, S&E, and NSF, composed primarily of nongovernment scientists, may be asked to provide expert review. In addition, research on plants, animals, and animal biologics will come under APHIS permit requirements if a regulated article, plant pest, animal pathogen is involved. An APHIS permit is required prior to the shipment (movement) or release of a regulated article, or the importation or shipment of a plant pest or regulated article used in any research experiment.

EPA has authority for all environmental research on microbial pesticides regardless of whether research is federally funded or not. EPA will regulate research under a two level review system based upon its evaluation of the potential risks posed by various types of microorganisms with lesser notification required for level reporting and full review for level II.

For the "the uses" category from Chart II (research involving nonpesticide microorganisms released into the environment), jurisdiction for release may be under S&E, NSF, APHIS, or EPA depending primarily upon the source of the funding, but also upon the purpose of the research and the characteristics of the genetically engineered microorganism. Thus, federally funded research conducted for an agricultural use will require adherence to S&E guidelines and approval of certain experiments by S&E or NIH depending on which is the funding agency. EPA will review commercial research. APHIS's jurisdiction applies to issuing permits for regulated articles, plant pests, or animal pathogens. EPA will require an informational report for nonengineered microorganisms released into the environment, with APHIS involvement for the review of plant pests or animal pathogens.

There may be situations where one agency may choose to defer to, or ask advice from, another agency. If experiments requiring NIH, NSF or S&E review/approval are submitted for review to another agency, then NIH, NSF, or S&E may determine that such review serves the same purpose, and based upon that determination, notify the submitter that no NIH, NSF, or S&E review will take place, and the experiment may proceed upon approval from the other agency.

C. Interagency Coordination Mechanisms

[1.] The Domestic Policy Council Working Group on Biotechnology

The Domestic Policy Council Working Group on Biotechnology has been responsible for this coordinated framework for the regulation of biotechnology; it also considers policy matters related to agency jurisdiction, commercialization, and international biotechnology matters. The Working Group monitors developments in biotechnology and is ready to identify problems and make appropriate recommendations for their solution. The Domestic Policy Council Working Group on Biotechnology is a continuation of a similar group established under the former Cabinet Council on Natural Resources and the Environment.

Although at the present time existing statutes seem adequate to deal with the emerging processes and products of modern biotechnology, there always can be potential problems and deficiencies in the regulatory apparatus in a fast moving field. The Working Group will be alert to the implications these changes will have on regulation, and in a timely fashion will make appropriate recommendations for administrative or legislative action.

[2.] The Biotechnology Science Coordinating Committee (BSCC)

The BSCC is responsible for coordination and consistency of scientific policy and scientific reviews. The BSCC, established October 31, 1985 as part of the Federal Coordinating Council for Science, Engineering and Technology (FCCSET), consists of senior policy officials of agencies involved in the oversight of biotechnology research and products. FCCSET is a statutory interagency coordinating mechanism managed by the Office of Science and Technology Policy, Executive Office of the President, with a mission to coordinate federal science activities among federal agencies. The November 85 Notice described the structure and activities of the BSCC.

One of the primary activities of the BSCC has been the development of definitions because a common scientific approach is essential to a coordinated federal regulatory framework. The underlying scientific issue, therefore, was defining those organisms subject to certain types of agency review.

The definitions are included in the following section of this preamble and have been incorporated, with modification, into the individual policy notices of the involved agencies. Explanatory material is also included in the agency policy statements. As mentioned elsewhere, the BSCC is seeking comments on these definitions

Research to develop genetically modified organisms for environmental and agricultural applications (as for research on traditionally modified organisms) generally proceeds in a stepwise manner from highly contained facilities to progressively lesser degrees of containment as the investigator determines the safety and efficacy of experimental applications; there are conducted sequentially under controlled laboratory conditions, greenhouse testing, small field trials, and full field trials. The BSCC recognizes the need for further work to define the nature and extent of physical and biological barriers that limit or manage environmental release of modified organisms during greenhouse testing and field research.

The BSCC is authorized to hold public meetings in order to discuss public concerns about scientific and other issues. Accordingly, the BSCC will hold its first public meeting shortly after publication of this notice for discussion of the scientific aspects of this notice and the receipt of comments from the public. The public meeting will be held in July 1986. Details regarding time and location will be separately announced in the Federal Register.

D. BSCC Definitions

Any proposal to regulate the research and products of genetic manipulation techniques quickly confronts the issue of what organisms should be considered appropriate for certain types of review. The BSCC formulated definitions are effective immediately but are open to comment; the text following the definition of "pathogen" contains details of the request for comments.

Organisms meeting two different sets of criteria are proposed. First are organisms formed by deliberate combination of genetic material from sources in different genera. It was recognized, however, that in certain precisely constructed "intergeneric organisms" the genetic material is not considered to pose an increased risk to human health or the environment; thus, such combinations are excluded from the definition. A detailed explanation of the scientific basis for these exclusions is found in the footnote after the definition of pathogen. The BSCC specifically requests comments on whether also to consider for exclusion those organisms that exchange DNA by known physiological processes, as explained in the text immediately following the definition of "intergeneric organism (new organism)."

The second definition is "pathogen." This includes microorganisms that belong to a pathogenic species or that contain genetic material from source organisms that are pathogenic. In certain precisely constructed modified organisms, the genetic material from a pathogenic donor is not considered to pose an increased risk to human health or the environment; and, therefore, such combinations are excluded from the definition.

The BSCC definitions of "intergeneric organism (new organism)" and "pathogen" describe the combinations genetic material that would cause a modified organism to come under review. This does not mean to suggest that the behavior of a genetically manipulated organism exempted from these definitions is wholly predictable (since any biological organism is never 100% predictable), but that the probability of any incremental hazard compared to the unmodified organism host is low. Also, this does not mean that any product manufacture or research experiment using an organism exempted from the definition should be conducted without adherence to proper manufacturing standards or research guidelines.

Given the statutory differences in the laws that they administer, the agencies adopted the principles underlying the definitions in ways consistent with their legislation. EPA, APHIS, and S&E are using the definitions to identify levels of review for microbial products within their jurisdiction. EPA, APHIS, FDA, S&E, and NSF are using the definitions as factors to consider in the review of products or experiments.

The BSCC is attempting to define what constitutes "release into the environment." The BSCC is establishing a working group on greenhouse containment and small field trials in order to develop scientific recommendations. The concept of "containment" has traditionally been used to describe physical conditions which severely limit release (for example, a contained laboratory fermentation facility). Containment can also be "biologic" because the ability of an organism to reproduce, exchange genetic information, or become established can be effectively limited biologically. Thus, the BSCC's exploration of the conditions that constitute release into the environment will consider circumstances of both physical and biological containment for particular organisms and the circumstances of their release. While the concept of physical containment may imply the high containment conditions found in certain laboratories and greenhouses, in agricultural practice many simpler effective barriers are routinely used; these include microplots for soil bacteria and fungi, paddocks for noninfective animals, and removing or covering the reproductive parts of plants and animals.

Release into the environment, for the time being, will have somewhat varying definitions for the regulatory and research review of the different agencies. There may be minor differences between agricultural and nonagricultural approaches and between macro- and microorganisms.

[1.] Intergeneric Organism (New Organism)

Those organisms deliberately formed to contain an intergeneric combination of genetic material; excluded are organisms that have resulted from the addition of intergeneric materials that is well-characterized and contains only non-coding regulatory regions such as operators, promoters, origins of replication, terminators and ribosome binding regions.

"Well-characterized and contains only non-coding regulatory regions" means that the producer of the microorganism can document the following:

a. The exact nucleotide base sequence of the regulatory region and any inserted flanking nucleotides;

b. The regulatory region and any inserted flanking nucleotides do not code independently for a protein, peptide of functional RNA molecules;

c. The regulatory region solely controls the activity of other sequences that code for protein or petide molecules or act as recognition sites for the initiation of nucleic acid or protein synthesis.

[2.] Pathogen

A pathogen is a virus or microorganism (including its viruses and plasmids, if any) that has the ability to cause disease in other living organisms (i.e., humans, animals, plants, microorganisms).

A microorganism (including viruses) will be subject to regulatory policies regarding pathogens if;

a. the microorganism belongs to a pathogenic species, according to sources identified by the agency, or from information known to the producer that the organism is a pathogen; excepted are organisms belonging to a strain used for laboratory research or commercial purposes and generally recognized as non-pathogenic according to sources identified by a federal agency, or information known to the producer and the appropriate federal agency (an example of a nonpathogenic strain of a species which contains pathogenic strains is *Escherichia coli* K-12; examples of nonpathogenic species are *Bacillus subtilis*, *Lactobacillus acidophilus*, and *Saccharomyces* species); or

b. The microorganism has been derived form a pathogen or has been deliberately engineered such that it contains genetic material from a pathogenic organism as defined in item a. above. Excepted are genetically engineered organisms developed by transferring a well-characterized, non-coding regulatory region from a pathogenic donor to a non-pathogenic recipient.

"Well-characterized, non-coding regulatory region" means the producer of the microorganism can document the following:

a. The exact nucleotide base sequence of the regulatory region and any inserted flanking nucleotides;

b. The regulatory region and any inserted flanking nucleotides do not code independently for a protein, peptide, or functional RNA molecules; and,

c. The regulatory region solely controls the activity of other sequences that code for protein or peptide molecules or act as recognition sites for the initiation of nucleic acid or protein synthesis.

This definition excludes organisms such as competitors or colonizers of the same substrates, commensal or mutualistic microorganisms, or opportunistic pathogens.

The footnote contains the scientific basis for exempting non-coding regulatory regions from the definitions of intergeneric organisms and pathogen.[46]

---

46. The BSCC has based the exemption of intergeneric transfers of regulatory regions on their lack of coding capacity for the production of proteins, peptides or functional RNA molecules. It has been recommended by other members of the scientific community that there should be additional exemptions such as ribosomal proteins, ribosomal RNAs and transfer RNAs. The BSCC has chosen to examine these suggestions in more detail during the next few months. At the present the BSCC has excluded:

1. Origins of replications;
2. Ribosome binding sites;
3. Promoters;
4. Operators; and,

The BSCC is requesting comments on these definitions during the period of sixty days following the date of this notice and specifically seeks comments addressing the following:

1. The suitability and applicability of these definitions to applications involving release into the environment, contained industrial large-scale applications, foods/food additives, drugs, medical devices, and other possible products.

2. Whether combinations of genetic material from organisms that exchange DNA by known physiological processes should be excluded from the definition of intergeneric organisms: i.e., should organisms be excluded which contain intergeneric combinations of certain specified rDNA molecules that consist entirely of DNA segments from different genera that exchange DNA by known physiological processes? As certain rDNA organisms are exempted under section III-D-4 of the NIH guidelines, the question was raised whether these organisms when used in the environment should be similarly exempted from federal product review. This exemption would not, however, exclude from review such "natural exchangers" that are also pathogens or plant pests. In the event that the exclusion of such different species that exchange DNA by known physiological processes is accepted as appropriate, a list of such species combinations that has been maintained and updated by the Office of Recombinant DNA Activities of the National Institutes of Health will be updated, in light of environmental use.

3. What are the most appropriate definitions of "release into the environment" for macro- and microorganisms.

E. International Aspects

The United States seeks to promote international scientific cooperation and understanding of scientific considerations in biotechnology on a range of technical matters. These activities add to scientific knowledge and ultimately contribute to protection of health and the environment.

---

5. Terminators.

The basis for these exemptions is as follows. Each of these regulatory elements has no coding capacity for the production of any gene product and therefore does not promote the production of any new material. What these elements are responsible for is the initiation and modulation of nucleic acid synthesis at the specific region where they appear in the chromosome.

Bacterial genes are precisely regulated and this regulation is based on a series of regulatory elements. The principal regulatory unit is the *operon.* Operons are controlled primarily, but not exclusively, through the regulation of the rate of initiation of messenger RNA synthesis. This regulation is based on the interaction of two short nucleotide sequences in the DNA, the *promoter,* which is the site of RNA polymerase binding and the *operator,* which follows closely and acts as an off-on switch for the movement of the polymerase into the structural gene which follows. The function of the operator is to *bind* a cellular repressor protein which is synthesized in response to changing nutritional stimuli. *Terminator* regions are short nucleotide sequences which signal the termination of mRNA synthesis by the polymerase. They act as a signal for the dissociation of the polymerase from the DNA.

Replication of DNA in every biological system that has been examined is initiated at a specific site or group of sites in the chromosome. Those sites have broad specificity and a DNA molecule without the appropriate site will not be replicated. The sites which are critical to the initiation of replication are known as *origins of replication.* These regions are short nucleotide sequences which serve as initiation sites for specific enzyme action during the DNA replication process. For example, in order for mammalian DNA to replicate in bacteria, it must be associated with a bacterial origin of replication and vice versa.

Ribosome binding sites are short nucleotide segments at the beginning of messenger RNA molecules which signal the attachment of ribosomes for the initiation of protein synthesis. Functioning in this role they are not translated into the protein or peptide being processed.

The United States also seeks to reduce barriers to international trade. U.S. agencies apply the same regulation and approval procedures on domestic and foreign biotechnological products. We are seeking recognition among nations of the need to harmonize, to the maximum extent possible, national regulatory oversight activities concerning biotechnology. Barriers to trade in biotechnological products should be avoided as nations join together in working toward this mutual goal.

The U.S. agencies that have published separate policy statements as part of this notice are committed to the policy described in this section on international harmonization and have incorporated by reference the language in this International Aspects section as part of their respective agency policy statements.

Organization for Economic Cooperation and Development (OECD)

The approach of the comprehensive framework contained in this notice takes into account, *inter alia*, the broad goals described by an Ad Hoc Group of Government Experts convened by OECD in their recent report entitled, "*Recombinant DNA Safety Considerations, Safety Considerations for Industrial, Agricultural and Environmental Applications of Organisms Derived by Recombinant DNA Techniques*." The United States is pleased to have had the opportunity for its experts to work with those of other governments in the preparation of this report. The report includes the following concepts:

[1.] Summary of Major Points

Recombinant DNA techniques have opened up new and promising possibilities in a wide range of applications and can be expected to bring considerable benefits to mankind. They contribute in several ways to the improvement of human health and the extent of this contribution is expected to increase significantly in the near future.

The vast majority of industrial rDNA large-scale applications will use organisms of intrinsically low risk which warrant only minimal containment, Good Industrial Large-Scale Practice (GILSP).

When it is necessary to use rDNA organisms of higher risk, additional criteria for risk assessment can be identified and furthermore, the technology of physical containment is well known to industry and has successfully been used to contain pathogenic organisms for years. Therefore, rDNA microorganisms of higher risks can also be handled safely under appropriate physical and/or biological containment.

Assessment of potential risks of organisms for environmental or agricultural applications is less developed than the assessment of potential risks for industrial applications. However, the means for assessing rDNA organisms can be approached by analogy with the existing data base gained from the extensive use of traditionally modified organisms in agriculture and the environment generally. With step-by-step assessment during the research and development process, the potential risk to the environment of the applications of rDNA organisms should be minimized.

[2.] General Recommendations

1. Harmonization of approaches to rDNA technology can be facilitated by exchanging: Principles or guidelines for national regulations; developments in risk analysis; and practical experience in risk management. Therefore, information should be shared as freely as possible.

2. There is no scientific basis for specific legislation for the implementation of rDNA technology and applications. Member countries should examine their existing oversight and review mechanisms to ensure that adequate review and control may be applied

while avoiding any undue burdens that may hamper technological developments in this field.

3. Any approach to implementing guidelines should not impede future developments in rDNA technology. International harmonization should recognize this need.

4. To facilitate data exchange and minimize trade barriers between countries, further developments such as testing methods, equipment design, and knowledge of microbial taxonomy should be considered by both national and international levels. Due account should be taken of ongoing work on standards within international organizations such as: World Health Organization; Commission of the European Communities; International Standards Organization; Food and Agricultural Organization; and, Microbial Strains Data Network.

5. Special efforts should be made to improve public understanding of various aspects of rDNA technology.

6. For rDNA applications in industry, agriculture and the environment, it will be important for OECD Member countries to watch the development of these techniques. For certain industrial applications and for environmental and agricultural applications of rDNA organisms, some countries may wish to have a notification scheme.

7. Recognizing the need for innovation, it is important to consider appropriate means to protect intellectual property and confidentiality interests while assuring safety.

[3.] Recommendations Specific for Industry

1. The large-scale industrial application of rDNA technology should wherever possible utilize microorganisms that are intrinsically of low risk. Such microorganisms can be handled under conditions of Good Industrial Large-Scale Practice (GILSP).

2. If, following assessment using the criteria outlined in the document, a rDNA microorganism cannot be handled merely by GILSP, measures of containment corresponding to the risk assessment should be used in addition to GILSP.

3. Further research to improve techniques for monitoring and controlling non-intentional release of rDNA organisms should be encouraged in large-scale industrial applications requiring physical containment.

[4.] Recommendations Specific for Environmental and Agricultural Applications

1. Considerable data on the environmental and human health effects of living organisms exist and should be used to guide risk assessments.

2. It is important to evaluate rDNA modified organisms for potential risk, prior to applications in agricultural and the environment. However, the development of general international guidelines governing such applications is premature at this time. An independent review of potential risks should be conducted on a case-by-case basis prior to application. Case-by-case means an individual review of a proposal against assessment criteria which are relevant to the particular proposal; this is not intended to imply that every case will require review by a national or other authority since various classes of proposals may be excluded.

3. Development of organisms for agricultural or environmental applications should be conducted in a stepwise fashion, moving, where appropriate, from the laboratory to the growth chamber and greenhouse, to limited field testing and finally, to large-scale field testing.

4. Further research to improve the prediction, evaluation, and monitoring of the outcome of applications of rDNA organisms should be encouraged.

II. Statements of Policy

Department of Health and Human Services, Food and Drug Administration, Statement of Policy for Regulating Biotechnology Products

Summary: In the Federal Register of December 31, 1984 (43 FR 50878), the Food and Drug Administration (FDA) published a policy statement for regulating biotechnology products.... The current action constitutes FDA's final policy statement which has been revised in response to the comments....

[A.] Introduction

A small but important and expanding fraction of the products the Food and Drug Administration (FDA) regulates represents the fruits of new technological achievements. These achievements are in areas as diverse as polymer chemistry, molecular biology, and micro-miniaturization. It is also noteworthy that technological advancement in a given area may give rise to very diverse product classes, some or all of which may be under FDA's regulatory jurisdiction. For example, new developments in recombinant DNA research can yield products as diverse as food additives, drugs, biologics, and medical devices.

Although there are no statutory provisions or regulations that address biotechnology specifically, the laws and regulations under which the agency approves products place the burden of proof of safety as well as effectiveness of products on the manufacturer. The agency possesses extensive experience with these regulatory mechanisms and applies them to the products of biotechnological processes. In this notice, FDA proposes no new procedures or requirements for regulated industry or individuals. Rather, the administrative review of products using biotechnology is based on the intended use of each product on a case-by-case basis.

The marketing of new drugs and biologics for human use, and new animal drugs, requires prior approval of an appropriate new drug application (NDA), biological product license, or new animal drug application (NADA). For new medical devices, including diagnostic devices for human use, either a premarket approval application (PMA) or reclassification petition is required. If the device is determined to be substantially equivalent to an already marketed device, a premarket notification under section 510(k) of the Federal Food, Drug, and Cosmetic Act (the act) is required. For food products, section 409 of the act requires preclearance of food additives including those prepared using biotechnology. Section 706 of the act requires preclearance of color additives. The implementing regulations for food and color additive petitions and for affirming generally recognized as safe (GRAS) food substances are sufficiently comprehensive to apply to those involving new biotechnology.

Genetic manipulations of plants or animals may enter FDA's jurisdiction in other ways; for example, the introduction into a plant of a gene coding for a pesticide or growth factor may constitute adulteration of foodstuff derived from the plant, or the use of a new microorganism found in a food such as yogurt could be considered a food additive. Such situations will be evaluated case-by-case and in cooperation with the U.S. Department of Agriculture (USDA), where appropriate.

[B.] The Regulatory Process

Congress has provided FDA authority under the act and the Public Health Service (PHS) Act to regulate products regardless of how they are manufactured. Each request for product approval will be considered using the appropriate statutory and regulatory criteria. The following sections summarize general requirements for various kinds of products and address specific comments concerning particular product categories. Individual regulations should be consulted for additional details.

...

[D.] General Requirements for Animal Food Additives and Drugs

Animal food additives and drugs are subject to similar mandatory requirements of the act as the like products for use in humans. Animal biologics, however, are licensed by the U.S. Department of Agriculture (USDA) under the authority of the Virus-Serum-Toxin Act of 1913. Questions as to whether a product is an animal biological subject to USDA licensure, or a new animal drug to be regulated by FDA are referred to a standing committee of representatives from USDA and FDA.

New animal drugs must go through the Investigational New animal Drug (INAD) and New Animal Drug Application (NADA) process, a procedure similar to that required for human drugs, as discussed earlier. However, INAD regulations do not require advance agency approval for clinical investigations for the drug, although authorization is required for use of edible products derived from food-producing animals in which the drug has been used. The data must be specific for each animal species for which the drug is intended. For NADA approval, it must be shown that the product is safe and effective when used in accordance with approved label directions. Also, it must be shown that those drugs which are intended for use in food-producing animals and used in accordance with approved label directions, do not accumulate as unsafe residues in the edible tissues of the animal at the time of slaughter. Moreover, the manufacturer must submit acceptable methods for measurement of any drug residue in edible tissues. Further, animal drugs, including premixes for use in medicated feeds and medicated feeds, must be manufactured in conformance with CGMPs. Substances that are used in animal feeds, other than drugs, and that are produced by recombinant DNA technology, are considered to be food additives and require approval of a separate food additive petition (FAP), even though a similar substance is currently approved as a food additive.

There have been questions about the requirement of an original application for a biotechnology product, even when the product is identical to a currently approved animal drug held by the same applicant. FDA's Center for Veterinary Medicine (CVM) has determined that, when the new substance produced by biotechnology is identical or virtually identical to an approved substance produced by conventional technology, only a supplemental application is necessary. Of course, in this instance the sponsor of the biotechnology product must also be the sponsor of the conventionally produced product. If, on the other hand, the new substance produced by biotechnology is significantly different from that produced by conventional means, an original application will be needed.

Two examples, each involving the adoption of rDNA technology as an alternative means of producing a substance that is currently the subject of an approved NADA, will illustrate. In the first example, the drug is (or appears to be) unchanged by the new production method. Under the current regulations, such a departure in manufacturing procedure requires a supplemental application which requires approval before implementation. The supplement would be a Category II supplement under CVM's supplemental policy in that it involves a revised method of synthesis or fermentation for the new drug substance. However, in accordance with the CVM's supplemental policy the underlying safety and effectiveness data supporting the original NADA usually would not be reviewed (for compliance with contemporary standards) since there is likely no increased risk of human exposure to the drug. Data may be required to demonstrate the new animal drug product is essentially biologically equivalent to the drug product for which approval has already been granted. Approval of such a supplemental NADA is not required to be published in the Federal Register.

In the second example, a new method of manufacture changes the molecular structure or chemical composition of the active ingredient. Such a change in the identity of the new animal drug normally will require an original new animal drug application and subsequent publication of a notice of approval in the Federal Register. Ordinarily, an original NADA requires complete safety and effectiveness studies, meeting contemporary standards. However, reference to data in another NADA sometimes suffices to support a separate NADA approval, where the existing NADA is owned by the applicant of the new NADA, or where the new applicant obtains authorization to reference might be made to data contained in the NADA supporting approval of the drug as produced by conventional means.

It may be possible to regard the new application as if it were a Category II supplement. This finding would be dependent upon data showing the new substance to be sufficiently similar to the original in terms of its pharmacology, toxicology, bioequivalence, and metabolism.

Thus, regardless of the type of application required, there is no legal requirement for the generation of new safety and effectiveness data if the applicant has access to previously submitted data, and there is no scientific need.

...

[F.] General Requirements for Foods

Several sections of the Food, Drug and Cosmetic Act apply to the Agency's regulation of food. No particular statutory provision or regulation deals expressly with food produced by new biotechnology. Accordingly, when confronted by an issue concerning the regulation of food produced by new biotechnology, the Agency will apply the relevant statutory or regulatory provisions. Most issues concerning the safety of a food will involve the application of either section 402(a)(1) or section 409 of the Act.

Section 402(a)(1) of the Act provides, in part, that a food is adulterated if it bears or contains any poisonous or deleterious "added substance" which may render it injurious to health." Courts have agreed with the agency's interpretation of this section that any substance that is not an inherent constituent of food may be regulated as an "added substance." *See*, for example, *United States* v. *Cartons of Swordfish*, 395 F. Supp. 1194 (S.D.N.Y. 1975). Furthermore, if the quantity of the constituent exceeds the amount that would normally be present because of some technological adjustment to the product, that excess quantity may also be viewed as "added substance" within the meaning of the section. *See United States* v. *Anderson Sea Foods, Inc.*, 622 F.2d 157 (5th Cir. 1980). Thus, section 401(a)(1) applies to most of the harmful substances that may occur in human food. For example, is a food produced by new biotechnology contains a higher level of a substance than it might ordinarily have, then that level "may be injurious to health" and the agency could regulate the product under section 402(a)(1). Similarly, if a food produced by new biotechnology contains, as a result of the production process, a harmful or deleterious substances not contained ordinarily in the food, the food could be in violation of the section.

The other primary statutory provisions that FDA relies upon in determining the safety of food and food constituents are sections 201(s) and 409, the food additive provisions of the Act. The definition of food additive appears in section 201(s) of the Act and includes both artificial and natural substances. The definition provides that:

> the term food additive means any substance the intended use of which results or may reasonably be expected to result, directly or indirectly, in its becoming a component or otherwise affecting the characteristics of any food (including any substance intended for use in producing, manufacturing, packing, processing, preparing, treating, packaging, transporting, or holding food; and including any source of radiation intended for any such use), if such substance is not generally recognized as safe by qualified experts.

If the substance is generally recognized as safe (GRAS) for a given food use, the product is not a food additive.

Comments questioned whether a substance (including microbes) that is GRAS could lose its GRAS status solely because it was produced or modified by new biotechnology. The answer is yes, if the substance (and its contaminants) has been altered in such a way that it can no longer be generally recognized by qualified experts to be safe. In this instance, the substance would be a food additive and the provisions of section 409 would apply. Section 409 provides that in order to be lawfully used in food, a food additive must be the subject of an approved food additive regulation, published upon approval of a food additive petition. The FDA may not approve a food additive regulation until certain basic evidentiary criteria are met. Most important of these is that the additive must be shown to be safe under the conditions that it will be used. This requires a demonstration to a reasonable certainty that the additive will not adversely affect the health of consumers.

FDA anticipates that the techniques of new biotechnology used in producing food will, for the most part, involve rDNA and microbial isolation. The agency applies certain general principles that it will follow in determining the safety of foods produced by such techniques.

When determining the safety of food produced by rDNA techniques, the agency takes into consideration, but is not restricted to, whether:

1. The cloned DNA as well as the vector used are properly identified;

2. The details of the construction of the production organism are available;

3. There is information documenting that the inserted DNA is well-characterized and free from sequences that code for harmful products, and

4. The food produced is purified, characterized, and standardized.

When determining the safety of food produced by microbial isolation, the agency will take into consideration, but is not restricted to, whether:

1. The microbial isolate used for production is identified taxonomically, and if the strain of the isolate has been genetically manipulated, whether each strain contributing genetic information to the production strain is identified;

2. The cultural purity and genetic stability of isolate has been maintained;

3. Fermentation has been performed with a pure culture and monitored for purity;

4. The microbial isolate used for production also produces antibiotics or toxins;

5. The isolates are pathogenic; and

6. Viable cells of the production strain are present in the final product.

. . .

[G.] Obligations Under the National Environmental Policy Act

All premarketing approvals of FDA-regulated products are subject to the requirements of the National Environmental Policy Act (NEPA) as defined by the Council on Environmental Quality's regulations (40 CFR Parts 1500–1508) and as further described by FDA's NEPA-implementing procedures (21 CFR Part 25, final rule published April 26, 1985; 50 FR 16636). For new products or major new uses for existing products, these procedures ordinarily require the preparation of an environmental assessment. An environmental impact statement is required if the manufacture, use, or disposal of the product is anticipated to cause significant environmental impacts.

. . .

Environmental Protection Agency (EPA), Statement of Policy; Microbial Products Subject to the Federal Insecticide, Fungicide, and Rodenticide Act and the Toxic Substances Control Act

. . .

A. Purpose

For centuries, humans have used organisms to generate commercial products or to perform useful functions. During the last decade, advances in the biological sciences have increased the ability of humans to change or combine the inherited characteristics of microorganisms, plants, and animals. These advances, along with more traditional genetic engineering and biological techniques, are expected to lead to a wide variety of useful products. Among these are microorganisms that will be used to degrade toxic pollutants, leach minerals, enhance oil recovery, produce industrial chemicals, and act as pesticides. As with chemicals used for the same types of purposes, many of these microorganisms will be reviewed by EPA for potential health and environmental risks.

Specifically, EPA reviews and may register pesticide products under the Federal Insecticide, Fungicide, and Rodenticide Act (FIFRA), and reviews chemical substances (except those used as pesticides, foods, food additives, cosmetics, drugs, and medical devices) under the Toxic Substances Control Act (TSCA). EPA's Office of Pesticides and Toxic Substances (OPTS) is responsible for implementing both FIFRA and TSCA.

This notice describes how EPA plans to address microbial products that are subject to FIFRA and TSCA, and explains the scope of coverage and procedures for review of these products under both statutes. The following questions are addressed in this notice:

1. What microbial products are subject to review under FIFRA and how will they be reviewed? (Unit II)

2. What microbial products are subject to review under TSCA and how will they be reviewed? (Unit III)

3. What definitions will be used to identify the products that will be addressed by the appropriate statute? (Unit IV)

In reviewing products, the Agency is required under both FIFRA and TSCA to consider the potential benefits to society as well as any potential risks. EPA will take both risks and benefits into account in its regulatory decisions concerning these products, and will implement the two statutes in as consistent a fashion as possible within statutory constraints.

...

C. Summary of EPA Policy

This notice focuses on oversight and review procedures for microorganisms that are subject to FIFRA or TSCA. Microorganisms intended for use as pesticides are subject to FIFRA, and many microorganisms intended for general commercial and environmental applications (e.g., metal leaching, pollutant degradation, enhanced nitrogen fixation) are subject to TSCA. This notice addresses the rationale for various requirements and provides guidelines for compliance.

Specifically, EPA's policies that apply to microbial products subject to FIFRA or TSCA jurisdiction will include the following specific requirements:

1. Microorganisms deliberately formed to contain genetic material from dissimilar source organisms (inter-generic) will be subject to review before any environmental releases, including small-scale field testing and other environmental research and development (R&D). Under the statute, those that are subject to TSCA and used in closed systems (i.e., never intentionally released to the environment) must be reported before they are manufactured for non-R&D commercial purposes. However, EPA is considering promulgating a rule to exempt certain contained uses from this requirement.

2. Microorganisms formed by genetic engineering other than inter-generic combinations will be subject to the following provisions: (a) if any source organism is a pathogen, the resulting microbial products are subject to review under FIFRA or TSCA prior to any environmental release, except if used solely for non-pesticidal agricultural uses, in which case they are subject only to U.S. Department of Agriculture (USDA) review (see the USDA notice in this Federal Register) (b) if source organisms are not pathogens, the resulting microbial products are subject to abbreviated review under FIFRA (if they are pesticides) before any small-scale environmental release, or will be subject to the reporting requirements of sections 8 (a) and (e) of TSCA.

3. Nonengineered microorganisms: (a) indigenous pathogens will be reviewed under FIFRA or TSCA prior to use on greater than 10 acres of land and greater than 1 acre of water, except those that are solely for non-pesticidal agricultural purposes, which will be subject only to USDA authority; (b) nonindigenous pathogens will be reviewed under FIFRA prior to any environmental release, and under TSCA prior to release at greater than 10 acres, unless they are pathogens used solely for non-pesticidal agricultural purposes in which case they will be reviewed by USDA (see USDA notice in this Federal Register); (c) nonindigenous microbial pesticides that are not pathogens will be subject to abbreviated review under FIFRA before any small scale environmental release; (d) indigenous microbial pesticides that are not pathogens will be reviewed under FIFRA prior to use on greater than 10 acres.

4. All other microorganisms used or intended for use as pesticides and not covered in Unit I.C. 1 through 3, regardless of source, mode of action, or method of manufacture will be reviewed under FIFRA prior to use on greater than 10 acres unless exempted by regulation.

5. Manufacturers and importers of microorganisms under TSCA, if they are not otherwise subject to review, will be required to submit general information, before environmental release, that the Agency can use to monitor environmental uses and to determine if additional requirements are necessary in the future. EPA will gather such information by means of a TSCA section 8(a) reporting rule.

6. Manufacturers and importers of all microorganisms subject to TSCA must report any information on substantial risks under TSCA section 8(e). Registrants of microbial pesticides must report any information regarding unreasonable adverse effects of the pesticide on the environment under FIFRA section 6(a)(2).

A table at the end of Unit I summarizes the policies for prior notification and review of microorganisms applied in the environment.

This policy is immediately effective for microbial pesticides under FIFRA and for "new" microorganisms subject to premanufacture notification under TSCA. Implementing other aspects of the policy for TSCA substances, however, will require rulemaking. Until final rules are effective, EPA expects manufacturers to comply with most aspects of the policy voluntarily. The one exception is that manufacturers of microorganisms, described in Unit I.C.5, that are excluded from other TSCA notification requirements are not expected to report until a final section 8(a) rule is promulgated.

This notice also describes the types of information EPA expects to receive from persons subject to these policies to permit an evaluation of possible risks. EPA will determine specific information needs on a case-by-case basis, and will frequently use non-Agency experts with specific knowledge of the relevant microorganisms and uses to assist in reviews. In addition, EPA is establishing a biotechnology Science Advisory Committee (SAC) to provide peer review of specific cases and advice on technical issues. The SAC will be composed of non-Agency scientists and members of the lay public. More information on the SAC may be found in Unit I.F.

Although many of the policies described in this notice are immediately effective, the Agency recognizes that biotechnology is a rapidly developing field and that newly available information may affect the judgments underlying these policies. Accordingly, EPA recognizes that modifications of these policies may be necessary in the future, and it is willing to make such modifications as may be appropriate. Therefore, EPA encourages all interested persons to provide comments on the policies described in this notice. Comments should be submitted to the address provided at the beginning of this EPA notice. The public will have additional opportunities for comment when the Agency proposes rules for those parts of its policy that require rulemaking procedures. These parts are specifically indicated in Units II and III.

D. Rationale for Approach

This unit provides a discussion of EPA's rationale for giving special focus to environmental release, pathogens, and microorganisms with new characteristics (e.g., containing genetic material from dissimilar source organisms or nonindigenous organisms).

1. Environmental releases. Physical containment can be used to mitigate undesirable or unexpected characteristics of a microorganism by providing the means to control a microorganism's growth, reproduction, and exposure to other organisms. However, microorganisms meant to be released in the environment are not subject to this control mechanism. Although many microorganisms will be biologically contained, that is, they will have existing and inherent limitations on their growth and survival, some of them may reproduce and thereby increase in number in the environment beyond the amounts originally released. Some will also have independent mobility, or may be spread beyond the area in which they are used. Thus, to ensure that environmental releases of microorganisms do not pose unreasonable adverse effects, the Agency has determined that it should review and evaluate proposals for certain environmental releases before they are allowed to proceed. The microorganisms to be subject to review before any environmental release are described in the following paragraphs, and in Units II and III of this notice.

The Agency acknowledges the difficulty of defining environmental release. For now, the Agency's approach will focus on when an organism is considered to be contained rather than when it is released. Guidance is provided in Unit IV on how to determine whether a microorganism is considered to be contained. The definition of environmental release will be refined in subsequent rulemaking activities.

2. *Pathogenic microorganisms.* Given their ability to cause disease in plants, animals, humans, and microbes, EPA generally believes pathogenic microorganisms should be reviewed before they are released in the environment.

As used in this notice, a "pathogen" is a microorganism that has the ability to cause disease in living organisms. This includes previously documented pathogens, and microorganisms deliberately formed to contain genetic material from pathogens (e.g., through genetic engineering techniques). A complete discussion of the definition of pathogenicity is included in Unit IV, as well as guidance to aid in the determination of whether a particular microorganism falls within the scope of the EPA policies that address pathogens.

Pathogens are a clearly defined category of organisms known to cause adverse effects. In addition, because of the increased uncertainty about behavioral changes that may be associated with genetically engineered pathogens, the Agency has decided to review genetically engineered pathogens prior to any environmental release (including small-scale field testing). However, the Agency will defer review of nonengineered indigenous pathogens until they are used in larger scale applications (greater than 10 acres), because ample experience indicates that nonengineered, indigenous pathogens are sufficiently well controlled by natural mechanisms in small-scale environmental applications. Further, the Agency will not review pathogens used solely for non-pesticidal agricultural purposes (except those formed through inter-generic combinations, which are "new") because these are adequately reviewed by the USDA (see the USDA notice in this Federal Register).

The Agency's decision to focus on pathogens does not mean that EPA has concluded that nonpathogens are necessarily safe or that all pathogens present unreasonable risks. In fact, the Agency expects to identify widely varying degrees of risk among different uses of pathogens. It should be clear that other considerations besides pathogenicity will affect the evaluation of risk, e.g., functions of the recombined genes, possibilities for genetic transfer, environmental fate, and potential competition with other organisms. When other considerations indicate that it is appropriate, the Agency will consider excluding specific categories of pathogens from review, or may provide guidance that would limit the information requirements associated with its reviews of pathogens. As explained in Unit IV, the Agency has already exempted from review as pathogens organisms that incorporate only certain genetic material from pathogens.

3. *Microorganisms with new characteristics.* A third factor that makes potential adverse effects of microorganisms less predictable is the existence of new traits or characteristics. These traits may be new to the organism, or new to the environment in which the organism is released.

a. *Microorganisms having significant potential to exhibit new traits.* Modern genetic engineering techniques permit genetic material to be intentionally combined in organisms that would not normally share that genetic material. Some of these genetically engineered microorganisms may exhibit new or altered traits affecting, for example, their survivability, host range, substrate utilization, competition with other organisms, or protein or polysaccharide production. In some cases such microorganisms may be able to evade or overcome natural controls on their growth, or controls on their ability to cause adverse effects. In many other cases, their natural hardiness will be reduced.

In addition to the possibility that certain engineered organisms may exhibit new traits, if they are released they may be transported through natural dispersal mechanisms to other areas in the environment that have not previously contained organisms having these new combinations of traits.

Because of these considerations, EPA's policies will give particular regulatory attention to organisms that have a significant probability of exhibiting a new trait or combination of traits (standards for this are explained below). This approach accomplishes two important objectives. First, it identifies a group of microorganisms whose behavior in the environment poses significant uncertainty and thus warrants regulatory review. Simultaneously, it provides a way of defining "new" microorganisms that are subject to PMN requirements under TSCA (see Unit III.C.1).

EPA's policy, specifically, focuses on microorganisms that have been deliberately altered to contain genetic material from dissimilar source organisms, because such organisms are more likely to exhibit new combinations of traits and their behavior is therefore less predictable. Given this conceptual basis, the question then becomes how dissimilar two organisms must be before combinations of genetic material between them are likely to produce "new combinations of traits."

Based on the following considerations, EPA has decided that inter-generic combinations (combinations from source organisms of different genera) but not intra-generic combinations (source organisms from the same genus) are sufficiently likely to result in new combinations of traits that they should be given special attention. First, combinations of genetic material from microorganisms from different genera are more likely to result in new traits than combinations of genes from microorganisms within the same genus. Also, while genetic exchange occurs naturally and somewhat commonly among many microorganisms, it is more likely to occur in nature within a single genus than across many different genera (Refs. 2, 12, 13). Finally, genus designations provide a practical criterion for administrative and regulatory purposes.

The Agency has decided to exclude certain combinations from special consideration as inter-generic organisms. Excluded are inter-generic combinations in which the genetic material added to the recipient microorganism consists only of well-characterized, non-coding regulatory regions. The resulting organisms do not possess new combinations of traits; rather, they exhibit quantitative changes in preexisting traits. In addition, if experience or data indicate that certain other inter-generic combinations warrant exclusion, the Agency will use the appropriate statutory or policy mechanisms under FIFRA and TSCA to waive certain requirements for reviewing them. For example, EPA is considering exempting from PMN review under TSCA those inter-generic combinations used only in physically contained systems.

Although EPA considers intra-generic combinations to be less likely to produce new combinations of traits than inter-generic combinations, the Agency realizes that science provides no absolute standard for such distinctions. Nevertheless, EPA believes the approach it has adopted is practical and facilitates the identification of those microorganisms that should be subject to special attention and also that should be considered "new" under TSCA. If experience reveals that intra-generic combinations that could cause adverse effects will be developed, the Agency will modify its policies to require review of these products.

Unit IV contains more detailed guidance for determining if a given microorganism is the result of an inter-generic combination. The determinations are based on taxonomic designations of organisms. The Agency is aware that microbial taxonomy is a dynamic and often controversial science (Refs. 4, 18) and that new information concerning microorganisms' properties and interrelationships will alter taxonomic designations. However, the Agency believes that its procedures can be sufficiently flexible to accommodate the developments that will occur, and that there are many significant advantages to using taxonomic standards. These advantages are discussed in more detail in Unit IV.

b. *Nonindigenous microorganisms.* Another category of organisms that are likely to exhibit traits new to an environment is nonindigenous microorganisms. Applications of nonindigenous microorganisms in the environment could pose a high degree of uncertainty with respect to their behavior. Experience shows that scientists cannot always accurately predict how such organisms will behave in their new environment (Ref. 15, 16). It can be difficult to predict whether a nonindigenous microorganism will be subject to the physical and biological control factors present in the environment where it is to be introduced. In a small number of cases, nonindigenous pathogens such as the chestnut blight fungus and the Dutch elm disease fungus have caused significant adverse effects. As a result, there exist today regulations that govern the intentional movement of some, but not all, nonindigenous species (e.g., the Plant Pest Act administered by USDA). EPA believes that nonindigenous microorganisms whose uses are covered by FIFRA should be subject to Agency review and evaluation before they are released in the environment, to minimize the uncertainties with respect to their behavior. However, EPA does recognize that small-scale use of certain nonindigenous microbial pesticides (i.e., pathogens) may pose greater potential risk than others, and has accordingly adopted abbreviated review procedures for small-scale use of nonpathogenic nonindigenous microbial pesticides. Unit II addresses these issues, and Unit IV provides guidance on determining whether a microorganism is nonindigenous.

. . .

F. EPA Biotechnology Science Advisory Committee

EPA is establishing a Science Advisory Committee for biotechnology. The formation of this committee is consistent with intentions stated in two Federal Register notices issued by the Office of Science and Technology Policy (49 FR 50904, December 31, 1984 and 50 FR 47174, November 14, 1985). The committee's primary functions will be to provide peer review of specific product submissions under TSCA, FIFRA, and other EPA statutes and scientific oversight of the Agency's biotechnology programs.

The committee will consist of independent scientists and members of the lay public. It will be of sufficient size and diversity to provide the range of expertise required to assess the scientific and technical issues pertinent to its responsibilities. The committee will be supplemented by consultants when they are needed to extend the range of expertise of the standing committee, and will be authorized to form subcommittees or panels for any purpose consistent with its charter.

Scientific members of the committee will be selected on the basis of their professional qualifications to examine the questions of hazard, exposure, and risk to humans, other non-target organisms, and ecosystems. Some committee members will serve as liaisons (holding joint membership) with the FIFRA Scientific Advisory Panel (SAP) and with the EPA Science Advisory Board (SAB). The SAC will also include nonvoting representatives from other Federal agencies that are involved in regulating products of biotechnology.

The Agency intends for meetings of the SAC to be open to the public. Meetings may be closed by the Chairperson when necessary, such as during discussion of issues subject to statutory confidentiality requirements, but EPA will encourage open public discussion of issues to the greatest extent possible (see unit I.G).

G. Confidential Business Information

Both FIFRA and TSCA generally prohibit the Agency from releasing certain confidential business information (CBI). These prohibitions apply to information on products of biotechnology, and the Agency will meet its obligations to protect information claimed confidential by applicants and other data submitters. However, the Agency also recognizes that there is strong public interest in many aspects of biotechnology, particularly in the possibility of adverse effects resulting from the environmental release of genetically engineered organisms. Accordingly, if is the Agency's policy to carry out as much of its review as possible in the open, in order to provide an opportunity for public participation and to increase public confidence in the review process. The Agency is encouraged by the extent to which industry and other submitters have been willing to authorize the release of relevant information to date and urges future data submitters to limit confidentiality claims as much as possible in order to foster an open review process.

. . .

SUMMARY TABLE.—PRIOR NOTIFICATION AND REVIEW MICROORGANISMS APPLIED IN THE ENVIRONMENT

[Coverage by notification and review policy[47]]

	FIFRA		TSCA	
Type of microbial product	≤ 10 acres	≥ 10 acres	≤ 10 acres	≥ 10 acres
1. Genetically engineered microorganisms				
a. Formed by deliberate combinations of genetic material from dissimilar source organisms (inter-generic combinations)	X	X	X	X
b. Formed by genetic engineering other than inter-generic combinations				
i. pathogenic source organisms[48]	X	X	X	X
ii. nonpathogenic source organisms	O	X	O	O
2. Nonengineered microorganisms				
a. Nonindigenous pathogens[49]	X	X	O	X

47. "X" designates that the microorganism will be subject to EPA review prior to small-scale (10 acres or less) or large scale (greater than 10 acres) environmental application, as indicated. Under TSCA, submitters would only notify the Agency once (at the first appropriate time), unless during the original review EPA specifies that further reporting is required.

"O" designates that the microorganism will be subject to abbreviated review prior to small-scale (10 acres or less) or large scale (greater than 10 acres) environmental applications, as indicated. Under FIFRA, this provision is effective immediately. Under TSCA, the abbreviated notification will be implemented through rulemaking.

48. Pathogens in this category used solely for non-pesticidal agricultural purposes will not be subject to EPA notification requirements. They will be subject only to USDA review. See Unit IV for a definition of "agricultural uses" and "pathogens."

49. *[Id.]*

b. Nonindigenous nonpathogens	O	X	O	O
c. Indigenous pathogens[50]		X	O	X
d. Indigenous nonpathogens		X	O	O

Department of Agriculture, Final Policy Statement for Research and Regulation of Biotechnology Processes and Products

I. Introduction

The USDA portion of the "Proposal for a Coordinated Framework for Regulation of Biotechnology" (hereafter referred to as the December 31, 1984 Notice) appeared at 49 FR 50897-50904. As a part of its policy perspective, USDA stated that agriculture and forestry products developed by biotechnology will not differ fundamentally from conventional products and that the existing regulatory framework is adequate to regulate biotechnology.

USDA has both research and regulatory responsibilities for biotechnology activities. This document provides significant new information in both areas. Section II describes 1985 Federal Register notices concerning USDA policies and responsibilities for biotechnology. Included in this discussion is an explanation of the assignment of responsibilities within USDA for the oversight of USDA funded research and for the regulation of the products of biotechnology. An understanding of the way in which USDA has divided these responsibilities should prove helpful to those in the private sector seeking review and/or approval of biotechnology applications.

A new section III has been added describing USDA's policy for agricultural biotechnology research. USDA is publishing as a companion document, USDA Guidelines for Biotechnology Research that will closely parallel the NIH Guidelines. The USDA guidelines will be issued under the authority of the Food Security Act of 1985 (Pub. L. 99-198). This Act amended section 1404(2) of the National Agriculture Research, Extension, and Teaching Policy Act (NARETPA). The Amendment gave the Secretary of Agriculture responsibility for establishing "appropriate controls with respect to the development and use of the application of biotechnology to agriculture." All USDA funded agriculture biotechnology research or research conducted at an entity receiving USDA funds would be subject to the USDA Guidelines for Biotechnology Research unless the specific research project is supported by and subject to the guidelines or regulations of another Federal agency. These Guidelines would encompass all phases of agricultural biotechnology research, i.e. (1) Contained laboratory experiments; (2) specialized isolation research (e.g., greenhouse, biotron); and (3) environmental research release (e.g., controlled and segregated field plots). USDA hopes that entities not required to comply with the Guidelines would voluntarily adhere to the requirements. To encourage compliance, USDA proposes to adopt the NIH policy of providing the researchers not required to comply with these Guidelines the opportunity to have their new biotechnology research proposals reviewed by USDA.

Those entities covered by the USDA Guidelines for Biotechnology Research would also be required to comply with any applicable statutes such as those set forth in section IV of this document, and any regulatory issues thereunder.

The Secretary of Agriculture has established an Office of Agriculture Biotechnology (OAB), which will have primary responsibility for implementing and coordinating the Department's policies and procedures pertaining to all facets of biotechnology. This in-

50. *[Id.]*

cludes the conduct of laboratory and field research, experimentation on biotechnology products prior to their commercialization, and all matters of oversight of biotechnology in agriculture. The new office will report to the Assistant Secretary for Science and Education through the authority provided in the amendment to the Food Security Act of 1985. The Assistant Secretary for Science and Education will seek to establish an Agriculture Biotechnology Recombinant DNA Advisory Committee (ABRAC) and shall continue the responsibilities for agriculture formerly handled by the NIH-RAC during the last 10 years. The OAB shall operate in a close parallel manner to the Office of Recombinant DNA Activities (ORDA) of the National Institutes of Health. This includes the responsibility of the ABRAC and the implementation of the USDA Guidelines for Biotechnology Research. The NIH system is well respected both domestically and worldwide, and has achieved a high degree of efficiency in achieving broad confidence in the safety of new biological research conducted under its requirements.

The OAB also will serve as a focal point for coordinating a National Biological Impact Assessment Program, which is to evaluate and monitor the potential impacts of biotechnological processes and products on safety and the environment.

Section IV contains USDA's regulatory policy statements for veterinary biological products, plants and plant products, meat and poultry products, and seeds. USDA stated in the December 31, 1984 Notice that while its existing regulatory framework is adequate, it would constantly reevaluate its regulatory position and should additional regulatory measures become necessary, amend its regulations (49 FR 50904). For veterinary biologicals regulated under the Virus-Serum-Toxin Act (VSTA), USDA has identified three categories which may be derived by recombinant DNA techniques or developed from hybridomas. The categories are based on biological characteristics and safety concerns, and are described fully in section IV(A). The first category consists of inactivated recombinant DNA-derived vaccines, bacterins, bacterin-toxoids, virus subunits, or bacterial subunits, as well as monoclonal products. This category presents no new or unusual safety or environmental concerns. The second category includes those products containing live microorganisms that have been modified by the addition or deletion of one or more genes. Such products will be evaluated under current regulatory policies and procedures to assure that the addition or deletion of specific genetic information does not impart increased virulence, pathogenicity, or survival advantages. The third category included products using live vectors to carry recombinant derived foreign genes for immunizing antigens and/or other immune stimulants. Characteristics of safety and transmission must be established fully before questions and concerns dealing with safety to humans, animals, and release into the environment can be answered and before such products can be considered for licensing. Section IV(A) also includes new information about revised USDA review procedures for the importation of cell cultures and hybridomas. A brief discussion is included about the proposed regulations implementing the provisions of the amendments to the VSTA contained in the Food Security Act of 1985.

For organisms and products derived by the techniques of genetic engineering, USDA is proposing new rules to regulate organisms which are plant pests or which there is reason to believe are plant pests. It is USDA's policy to regulate certain genetically engineered organisms if the donor, vector/vector agent, or recipient organism is a member of a group of organisms that are known to contain plant pests, or if based on experience, USDA determines that a genetically engineered organism or product is a plant pest or if USDA has reason to believe that a genetically engineered organism or product is a plant pest. The proposed regulations are summarized in section IV(B).

The USDA policy for regulating meat and poultry products and seeds derived through biotechnology remains substantially as stated in the December 31, 1984 Notice, and appears in section IV (C) and (D).

A new section (V) has been added describing the scientific review mechanisms to be established by USDA to assist USDA Agencies in biotechnology research and regulatory decision-making. USDA has established a Committee on Biotechnology in Agriculture (CBA) chaired by the Assistant Secretary for Science and Education and the Assistant Secretary for Marketing and Inspection Services.

...

III. USDA Research Policy Statement

USDA supports research to promote and protect the general health and welfare of the people of the United States. Research program include: Studies on production of food and agricultural processing and marketing; identity and development of new crop and animal sources of food, fiber, and energy; increased agricultural efficiency and reduction of dependence on petroleum-based products; development of improved management and conservation of soil, water, forest, and range resources. The programs are fulfilled through State, Federal, and private industry cooperative efforts.

In the areas of agricultural research relevant to biotechnology, many plant, animal, and microbial alterations have been developed for release through traditional genetic approaches such as mutagenesis and hybridization. In a complementary vein, beneficial introduction of organisms from abroad have established a sound base for research and regulatory oversight. The experience with these bases provide a substantial knowledge base for conducting evaluations of the safety and efficacy of biotechnology processes and products.

USDA will evaluate the environmental impacts in the context of individual experiments that encompass the entire range of experimentation from contained facilities to open field testing. As knowledge and experience are gained, broadly applicable procedures and guidelines will be developed. Particular consideration will be given to the stability of engineered changes and the possibility that genetic elements might be transferred from one organism to another. Also important will be the development of data that will enable predictions of which organisms may become established in new ecosystems, and resulting environmental consequences.

USDA considers products developed through biotechnological techniques as no different from those products resulting from research using conventional techniques providing appropriate research review is conducted with established protocols. Agricultural biotechnology research activities require appropriate review to avoid untoward effects on human health and the environment.

USDA expects to rely on the existing network of scientific expertise in the agriculture research community. Thousands of plant selections, animal breeding lines, and microorganisms are tested annually at sites under varying climatic conditions through the Nation. This network of scientific expertise permits continual, open assessment of agricultural research and products of that research in the field. USDA has broad statutory authority to conduct and support research in wide ranging areas of agriculture. In addition to the authorities described in the matrix of Federal Laws related to biotechnology found in the Federal Register Notice of November 14, 1985 (50 FR 47174-47195) the Food Security Act of 1985 (Section 1404(2) of the National Agriculture Research, Extension, and Teaching Policy Act Amendments of 1985, Pub. L. No. 99-198), made the

Secretary of Agriculture responsible for establishing "appropriate controls with respect to the development and use of the application of biotechnology to agriculture." Through this authority, and pursuant to the Delegation of Authority Pertaining to Biotechnology published in the Federal Register on July 19, 1985 (50 FR 29367-68), the Assistant Secretary for Science and Education will complete development of a national system of agricultural biotechnology research oversight in much the same manner that agriculture has been a part for the last 10 years through the NIH-RAC.

The Assistant Secretary for Science and Education has initiated the establishment of the Agriculture Biotechnology and Recombinant DNA Advisory Committee (ABRAC), to be managed through an Office of Agriculture Biotechnology (OAB) which is a parallel to the National Institutes of Health Recombinant DNA Advisory Committee (NIT-RAC) and Office of Recombinant DNA Activities (ORDA). The OAB will serve as the focal point for developing and coordinating USDA policies and activities pertaining to biotechnology research and will perform related interagency and public liaison functions. OAB will also assist in carrying out the responsibilities assigned to the Assistant Secretary for Science and Education, including the development and implementation of policies and procedures, and guidelines for the conduct of laboratory and field research.

All federally-funded agriculture biotechnology research or research conducted at an entity receiving USDA funds will be subject to the USDA Guidelines for Biotechnology Research, which are published as a companion document to this policy statement, unless the specific research project is supported by and subject to the guidelines or regulations of another Federal agency. These Guidelines encompass the entire spectrum of degrees of containment in agricultural biotechnology research i.e.: (1) Contained laboratory experiments; (2) specialized isolation research (e.g., greenhouse, biotron); and (3) environmental research agricultural biotechnology release (e.g., controlled and segregated field plots). Research investigators not required to comply with USDA Guidelines will be encouraged to follow these Guidelines. To assure consistency, USDA adopted the model established by the NIH of providing such researchers with the opportunity to have their biotechnology research proposals reviewed as required by the Guidelines.

The USDA Guidelines for Biotechnology Research require that research organization use the Institutional Biosafety Committee (IBC) concept as established by NIH. This requirement assures that each research organization and its investigators employ a multidisciplinary team to assist in carrying out their responsibilities under the Guidelines. The IBC's, as described in the Guidelines, would consist of persons with relevant agricultural expertise in areas such as recombinant DNA technology, biological safety, physical containment, and ecology. Requests for review beyond IBC should be sent to the Office of Agriculture Biotechnology (OAB) through the Assistant Secretary of Science and Education, Room 324-A, Administration Bldg., Washington, D.C. 20250.

These Guidelines also would require compliance with existing statutes of the USDA involving the movement of regulated organisms that require the issuance of a permit. The movement of microorganism injurious to plants and animals as well as the movement of certain non-indigenous plants and animals would continue to follow long-established procedures for USDA approval. After review, a permit, if needed, may be issued that allows movement. It is the responsibility of the research scientists to obtain that permit.

The Assistant Secretary for Science and Education will complete establishment of a National Biological Impact Assessment Program (NBIAP) as indicated in the USDA

Guidelines for Biotechnology Research. NBIAP would serve to assist USDA in the evaluation and monitoring of biotechnology research and impact over time. Coordination of NBIAP will be provided through OAB.

IV. USDA Regulatory Policy Statements

The existing USDA regulatory authority for biotechnology was listed in the matrix of the December 31, 1984 Notice at 49 FR 50860-50874 and described in brief at 49 FR 50898-50899. The statutes considered most applicable to biotechnology applications are the Virus-Serum-Toxin Act (VSTA) of 1913 (21 U.S.C. 151-158), the Federal Plant Pest Act (FPPA) of May 23, 1957 (7 U.S.C. 150aa-150jj), the Plant Quarantine Act (PQA) of August 20, 1912 (7 U.S.C. 151-164, 166, 167), the Organic Act of September 21, 1944 (7 U.S.C. 147a), the Federal Noxious Weed Act (FNWA) of 1974 (7 U.S.C. 2801 *et seq.*), the Federal Seed Act (FSA) (7 U.S.C. 551 *et seq.*), the Plant Variety Protection Act (PVPA) (7 U.S.C. 2321 *et seq.*), the Federal Meat Inspection Act (FMIA) (21 U.S.C. 601 *et seq.*), and the Poultry Products Inspection Act (PPIA) (21 U.S.C. 451 *et seq.*).

. . .

V. Scientific Review Mechanisms

The manner in which both regulation and oversight of research in agriculture-related biotechnology evolves and is implemented in the United States will have a direct impact on the competitiveness of U.S. industry in both domestic and world markets. Inconsistent or unnecessary procedures for regulation and research will place the U.S. scientific effort and U.S. producers at a substantial disadvantage. It also is important that safeguards be built into biotechnological research processes, and that releases be based on careful evaluations while further experience is being gained. Therefore, USDA feels that such regulatory and research decisions must be based on the best science available.

While the responsibilities within USDA for biotechnology reside with the Assistant Secretary for Science and Education and the Assistant Secretary for Marketing and Inspection Services as the delegates of the Secretary of Agriculture, in carrying out their respective responsibilities based on the best science available, they would be able to take advantage of the expertise and perspectives within the Federal Government through a committee to be called the Committee on Biotechnology in Agriculture (CBA). The CBA, to be chaired by these two Assistant Secretaries, will function both as a policy body in the USDA and a bridge between its research and regulating structures.

Committee on Biotechnology in Agriculture

The objectives of the CBA will include:

To provide advice, when requested, on initiatives, proposals, and policy for agriculture-related regulation and research, and assist in the coordination of these activities;

To review scientific issues submitted by agencies within the Department;

To assist in identifying data gaps for basic research in agricultural biotechnology;

To foster public awareness of the scientific issues in biotechnology;

To provide Departmental support for participation in the FCCSET BSCC.

USDA expects that the CBA also will utilize existing cooperative entities (e.g., other Federal agencies, universities, State regulatory officials, the public sector, and industry) to acquire, when necessary, information for addressing those issues submitted to it. Such entities, when requested, can provide technical support for sound regulatory and research decisions regarding the use of biotechnology in agriculture and forestry. These entities offer a vast scientific resource upon which USDA can draw.

...

Department of Labor, Occupational Safety and Health Administration (OSHA), Agency Guidelines on Biotechnology

A. Background

The Occupational Safety and Health Administration (OSHA) published an announcement of guidelines on occupational safety and health in the Federal Register, Volume 50, Number 71, page 14483, April 12, 1985 with a request for public comment. All comments received supported the statement although the National Institute for Occupational Safety and Health (NIOSH) recommended increased surveillance because their research indicated gaps in current knowledge.

Biotechnology is the application of biological systems and organisms to technical and industrial processes. The technologies employed in this area include, but are not limited to:

(1) Classical genetic selection and/or breeding for purposes such as developing bakers yeast, conventional fermentation and vaccine development;

(2) The direct in vitro modification of genetic material, e.g., recombinant DA or gene splicing; and,

(3) Other novel techniques for modifying genetic material of living organisms, e.g., cell fusion and hybridoma technology.

Modern biotechnology is analogous to other conventional industrial processes and has great potential benefit to society and wide application to numerous industries. It is considered by some to have economic potential comparable to the microprocessor industry. Genetic engineering has a wide spectrum of applications of commercial importance, but many such applications are in the early stages of development or have been expressed only as concepts.

The Occupational Safety and Health Act of 1970 (OSH Act) grants the Secretary of Labor broad power to require employers to provide a safe and healthful workplace for their employees. Where other Federal agencies exercise their statutory authority to prescribe or enforce standards or regulations affecting occupational safety or health, OSHA is preempted by section 4(b)(1) of the Act.

Section 5(a)(1) of the Act requires employers to furnish their employees with a workplace "free from recognized hazards that are causing or are likely to cause death or serious physical harm." Section 5(a)(2) requires employers to comply with safety and health standards set by the Secretary. The Secretary in establishing standards to deal with toxic materials and harmful physical agents is required by the OSH Act to "set the standard which most adequately assures, to the extent feasible, on the basis of the best available evidence, that no employee will suffer material impairment of health or functional capacity even if such employee has regular exposure to the hazard dealt with by such standard for the period of his working life" (section 8(b)(5)). Under a recent Supreme Court decision permanent standards can be promulgated only upon a finding by the Secretary that the standard is reasonably necessary to remedy a significant risk of material health impairment. Finally, emergency temporary standards may be promulgated only upon a finding that employees are "exposed to grave danger." (section 8(c)(1).)

In view of the statutory criteria briefly outlined above and the currently known hazards from biotechnology processes there does not appear to be a need for new OSHA regulations. Furthermore, the biotechnology processes, whether present in laboratories, pilot projects or industrial plants, usually involve conventional chemicals and processes that are already covered by OSHA regulations. These conventional processes use solvents or products, some of which may be toxic or dangerous to employee health in certain dosages over certain periods of time. The potentially hazardous character of some aspects of biotechnology is primarily from the chemicals used and not the biotechnology products. Therefore, the regulations that effectively regulate chemical exposures will usually ensure that biohazards too will be controlled. However, when a process employing biotechnology alone or in combination with conventional chemicals and technology presents a significant hazard to employees which cannot be dealt with by existing standards or the general duty clause, OSHA will consider regulating in order to protect employees health. Increased industrial hygiene monitoring and medical surveillance will help to assure worker protection. At this time, no new regulations that would specifically cover biohazards are warranted.

OSHA endorses the BSCC definitions of "intergeneric (new) organism" and "pathogen" found in the preamble, believing they describe the microorganism appropriate for review when environmental or agricultural applications of microorganisms are contemplated. For contained commercial manufacturing processes, these definitions may also properly exclude from review certain microorganisms of known low risk.

OSHA is committed to the policy described in the section entitled "International Aspects" in the Office of Science and Technology Policy General Preamble, published in today's Federal Register.

B. Guidelines

As stated above, section 5(a) of the OSH Act requires that each employer:

(1) Shall furnish to each of his employees employment and a place of employment which are free from recognized hazards that are causing or are likely to cause death or serious physical harm to his employees;

(2) Shall comply with occupational safety and health standards under this Act.

Specific standards which may be applicable include:

—Specific air contaminants (29 CFR Part 1910, Subpart Z).

—Access to employee exposure and medical records (29 CFR 1910.20).

—Hazard communication (29 CFR 1910.1200).

—Exposure to toxic chemicals in laboratories (currently in draft and under development).

—Respiratory protection (29 CFR 1910.134) (currently being updated).

—Safety standards of a general nature, for example, general environmental, walking and working surfaces, fire protection, compressed gases, electrical safety, and material handling and storage contained in 29 CFR Part 1910 Subparts J, D, E and L, H, S and N).

Effective biological safety and health programs have been operative in a variety of laboratories for many years. Motivation and critical judgment are necessary in addition to specific safety and health knowledge to ensure protection of personnel, the public and the environment. All personnel directly involved in biotechnological projects should receive adequate instruction so that the potential biohazards can be understood and appreciated. Emergency plans should be formulated for each project where the chemicals used or biotechnical product produced pose a potential safety or health hazard. The plans should describe the procedures to be followed if an accident contaminates personnel or workplaces. If a research group is working with a known pathogen for which an effective vaccine is available, employees should be immunized, as appropriate.

Before biotechnological work is undertaken, it is important that management determine the potential hazards involved and the precautions to be taken. Program and support staff should then be advised of the real and potential hazards. Staff should be instructed and trained in the protection and techniques required to ensure safety and in the procedures for dealing with accidentally created hazards.

* * *

Other countries have taken different approaches to regulating ag-biotech products and production. Because such regulation may well determine whether U.S. ag-biotech producers have access to crucial overseas markets, the following excerpts outline the regulatory approach of the European Union as an example of one of the strictest such regimes.

The European Parliament and the Council of the European Union, Directive 2001/18/EC: of 12 March 2001 on the Deliberate Release into the Environment of Genetically Modified Organisms and Repealing Council Directive 90/220/EEC

2001 O.J. (L 106) 1

Part A
General Provisions

Article 1
Objective

In accordance with the precautionary principle, the objective of this Directive is to approximate the laws, regulations and administrative provisions of the Member States and to protect human health and the environment when:

—carrying out the deliberate release into the environment of genetically modified organisms for any other purposes than placing on the market within the Community,

—placing on the market genetically modified organisms as or in products within the Community.

Article 2
Definitions

For the purposes of this Directive:

(1) 'organism' means any biological entity capable of replication or of transferring genetic material;

(2) 'genetically modified organism (GMO)' means an organism, with the exception of human beings, in which the genetic material has been altered in a way that does not occur naturally by mating and/or natural recombination;

Within the terms of this definition:

(a) genetic modification occurs at least through the use of the techniques listed in Annex I A, part 1;

(b) the techniques listed in Annex I A, part 2, are not considered to result in genetic modification;

(3) 'deliberate release' means any intentional introduction into the environment of a GMO or a combination of GMOs for which no specific containment measures are used to limit their contact with and to provide a high level of safety for the general population and the environment;

(4) 'placing on the market' means making available to third parties, whether in return for payment or free of charge;

The following operations shall not be regarded as placing on the market:

—making available genetically modified microorganisms for activities regulated under Council Directive 90/219/EEC of 23 April 1990 on the contained use of genetically modified microorganisms[51] including culture collections,

—making available GMOs other than microorganisms referred to in the first indent, to be used exclusively for activities where appropriate stringent containment measures are used to limit their contact with and to provide a high level of safety for the general population and the environment, the measures should be based on the same principles of containment as laid down in Directive 90/219/EEC,

—making available GMOs to be used exclusively for deliberate releases complying with the requirements laid down in part B of this Directive;

(5) 'notification' means the submission of the information required under this Directive to the competent authority of a Member State;

(6) 'notifier' means the person submitting the notification;

(7) 'product' means a preparation consisting of, or containing, a GMO or a combination of GMOs, which is placed on the market;

(8) 'environmental risk assessment' means the evaluation of risks to human health and the environment, whether direct or indirect, immediate or delayed, which the deliberate release or the placing on the market of GMOs may pose and carried out in accordance with Annex II.

Article 3
Exemptions

1. This Directive shall not apply to organisms obtained through the techniques of genetic modification listed in Annex I B.

2. This Directive shall not apply to the carriage of genetically modified organisms by rail, road, inland waterway, sea or air.

Article 4
General obligations

1. Member States shall, in accordance with the precautionary principle, ensure that all appropriate measures are taken to avoid adverse effects on human health and the en-

51. OJ L 117, 8.5.1990, p. 1. Directive as amended by Directive 98/81/EC (OJ L 330 5.12.1998, p. 13).

vironment which might arise from the deliberate release or the placing on the market of GMOs. GMOs may only be deliberately released or placed on the market in conformity with part B or part C respectively.

2. Any person shall, before submitting a notification under part B or part C, carry out an environmental risk assessment. The information which may be necessary to carry out the environmental risk assessment is laid down in Annex III. Member States and the Commission shall ensure that GMOs which contain genes expressing resistance to antibiotics in use for medical or veterinary treatment are taken into particular consideration when carrying out an environmental risk assessment, with a view to identifying and phasing out antibiotic resistance markers in GMOs which may have adverse effects on human health and the environment. This phasing out shall take place by the 31 December 2004 in the case of GMOs placed on the market according to part C and by 31 December 2008 in the case of GMOs authorised under part B.

3. Member States and where appropriate the Commission shall ensure that potential adverse effects on human health and the environment, which may occur directly or indirectly through gene transfer from GMOs to other organisms, are accurately assessed on a case-by-case basis. This assessment shall be conducted in accordance with Annex II taking into account the environmental impact according to the nature of the organism introduced and the receiving environment.

4. Member States shall designate the competent authority or authorities responsible for complying with the requirements of this Directive. The competent authority shall examine notifications under part B and part C for compliance with the requirements of this Directive and whether the assessment provided for in paragraph 2 is appropriate.

5. Member States shall ensure that the competent authority organises inspections and other control measures as appropriate, to ensure compliance with this Directive. In the event of a release of GMO(s) or placing on the market as or in products for which no authorisation was given, the Member State concerned shall ensure that necessary measures are taken to terminate the release or placing on the market, to initiate remedial action if necessary, and to inform its public, the Commission and other Member States.

6. Member States shall take measures to ensure traceability, in line with the requirements laid down in Annex IV, at all stages of the placing on the market of GMOs authorised under part C.

Part B

Deliberate Release Of GMOs For Any Other Purpose Than For Placing On The Market

Article 5

1. Articles 6 to 11 shall not apply to medicinal substances and compounds for human use consisting of, or containing, a GMO or combination of GMOs provided that their deliberate release for any purpose other than that of being placed on the market is authorised by Community legislation which provides:

(a) for a specific environmental risk assessment in accordance with Annex II and on the basis of the type of information specified in Annex III without prejudice to additional requirements provided for by the said legislation;

(b) for explicit consent prior to release;

(c) for a monitoring plan in accordance with the relevant parts of Annex III, with a view to detecting the effects of the GMO or GMOs on human health or the environment;

(d) in an appropriate manner for requirements relating to treatment of new items of information, information to the public, information on the results of releases, and exchanges of information at least equivalent to those contained in this Directive and in the measures taken in accordance therewith.

2. Assessment of the risks to the environment presented by such substances and compounds shall be carried out in coordination with the national and Community authorities mentioned in this Directive.

3. Procedures ensuring conformity of the specific environmental risk assessment and equivalence with the provisions of this Directive must be provided for by the said legislation, which must refer to this Directive.

Article 6
Standard authorisation procedure

1. Without prejudice to Article 5, any person must, before undertaking a deliberate release of a GMO or of a combination of GMOs, submit a notification to the competent authority of the Member State within whose territory the release is to take place.

2. The notification referred to in paragraph 1 shall include:

(a) a technical dossier supplying the information specified in Annex III necessary for carrying out the environmental risk assessment of the deliberate release of a GMO or combination of GMOs, in particular:

(i) general information including information on personnel and training,

(ii) information relating to the GMO(s),

(iii) information relating to the conditions of release and the potential receiving environment,

(iv) information on the interactions between the GMO(s) and the environment,

(v) a plan for monitoring in accordance with the relevant parts of Annex III in order to identify effects of the GMO(s) on human health or the environment,

(vi) information on control, remediation methods, waste treatment and emergency response plans,

(vii) a summary of the dossier;

(b) the environmental risk assessment and the conclusions required in Annex II, section D, together with any bibliographic reference and indications of the methods used.

3. The notifier may refer to data or results from notifications previously submitted by other notifiers, provided that the information, data and results are non confidential or these notifiers have given their agreement in writing, or may submit additional information he considers relevant.

4. The competent authority may accept that releases of the same GMO or of a combination of GMOs on the same site or on different sites for the same purpose and within a defined period may be notified in a single notification.

5. The competent authority shall acknowledge the date of receipt of the notification and, having considered, where appropriate, any observations by other Member States

made in accordance with Article 11, shall respond in writing to the notifier within 90 days of receipt of the notification by either:

(a) indicating that it is satisfied that the notification is in compliance with this Directive and that the release may proceed; or

(b) indicating that the release does not fulfil the conditions of this Directive and that notification is therefore rejected.

6. For the purpose of calculating the 90 day period referred to in paragraph 5, no account shall be taken of any periods of time during which the competent authority:

(a) is awaiting further information which it may have requested from the notifier, or

(b) is carrying out a public inquiry or consultation in accordance with Article 9; this public inquiry or consultation shall not prolong the 90 day period referred to in paragraph 5 by more than 30 days.

7. If the competent authority requests new information it must simultaneously give its reasons for so doing.

8. The notifier may proceed with the release only when he has received the written consent of the competent authority, and in conformity with any conditions required in this consent.

9. Member States shall ensure that no material derived from GMOs which are deliberately released in accordance with part B is placed on the market, unless in accordance with part C.

Article 7
Differentiated procedures

1. If sufficient experience has been obtained of releases of certain GMOs in certain ecosystems and the GMOs concerned meet the criteria set out in Annex V, a competent authority may submit to the Commission a reasoned proposal for the application of differentiated procedures to such types of GMOs....

Article 8
Handling of modifications and new information

1. In the event of any modification of, or unintended change to, the deliberate release of a GMO or of a combination of GMOs which could have consequences with regard to risks for human health and the environment after the competent authority has given its written consent, or if new information has become available on such risks, either while the notification is being examined by the competent authority of a Member State or after that authority has given its written consent, the notifier shall immediately:

(a) take the measures necessary to protect human health and the environment;

(b) inform the competent authority in advance of any modification or as soon as the unintended change is known or the new information is available;

(c) revise the measures specified in the notification.

2. If information becomes available to the competent authority referred to in paragraph 1 which could have significant consequences with regard to risks for human health and the environment or under the circumstances described in paragraph 1, the competent authority shall evaluate such information and make it available to the public.

It may require the notifier to modify the conditions of, suspend or terminate the deliberate release and shall inform the public thereof.

Article 9
Consultation of and information to the public

1. Member States shall, without prejudice to the provisions of Articles 7 and 25, consult the public and, where appropriate, groups on the proposed deliberate release. In doing so, Member States shall lay down arrangements for this consultation, including a reasonable time-period, in order to give the public or groups the opportunity to express an opinion.

2. Without prejudice to the provisions of Article 25:

—Member States shall make available to the public information on all part B releases of GMOs in their territory;

—the Commission shall make available to the public the information contained in the system of exchange of information pursuant to Article 11.

Article 10
Reporting by notifiers on releases

After completion of a release, and thereafter, at any intervals laid down in the consent on the basis of the results of the environmental risk assessment, the notifier shall send to the competent authority the result of the release in respect of any risk to human health or the environment, with, where appropriate, particular reference to any kind of product that the notifier intends to notify at a later stage. The format for the presentation of this result shall be established in accordance with the procedure laid down in Article 30(2).

Article 11

Exchange of information between competent authorities and the Commission

1. The Commission shall set up a system of exchange of the information contained in the notifications. The competent authorities shall send to the Commission, within 30 days of its receipt, a summary of each notification received under Article 6. The format of this summary shall be established and modified if appropriate in accordance with the procedure laid down in Article 30(2).

2. The Commission shall, at the latest 30 days following their receipt, forward these summaries to the other Member States, which may, within 30 days, present observations through the Commission or directly. At its request, a Member State shall be permitted to receive a copy of the full notification from the competent authority of the relevant Member State.

3. The competent authorities shall inform the Commission of the final decisions taken in compliance with Article 6(5), including where relevant the reasons for rejecting a notification, and of the results of the releases received in accordance with Article 10.

4. For the releases of GMOs referred to in Article 7, once a year Member States shall send a list of GMOs which have been released on their territory and a list of notifications that were rejected to the Commission, which shall forward them to the competent authorities of the other Member States.

Part C
Placing on the Market of GMOs as or in Products

Article 12
Sectoral legislation

1. Articles 13 to 24 shall not apply to any GMO as or in products as far as they are authorised by Community legislation which provides for a specific environmental risk assessment carried out in accordance with the principles set out in Annex II and on the basis of information specified in Annex III without prejudice to additional requirements provided for by the Community legislation mentioned above, and for requirements as regards risk management, labelling, monitoring as appropriate, information to the public and safeguard clause at least equivalent to that laid down in this Directive.

2. As far as Council Regulation (EEC) No 2309/93 is concerned, Articles 13 to 24 of this Directive shall not apply to any GMO as or in products as far as they are authorised by that Regulation provided that a specific environmental risk assessment is carried out in accordance with the principles set out in Annex II to this Directive and on the basis of the type of information specified in Annex III to this Directive without prejudice to other relevant requirements as regards risk assessment, risk management, labelling, monitoring as appropriate, information to the public and safeguard clause provided by Community legislation concerning medicinal products for human and veterinary use.

3. Procedures ensuring that the risk assessment, requirements regarding risk management, labelling, monitoring as appropriate, information to the public and safeguard clause are equivalent to those laid down in this Directive shall be introduced, in a Regulation of the European Parliament and of the Council. Future sectoral legislation based on the provisions of that Regulation shall make a reference to this Directive. Until the Regulation enters into force, any GMO as or in products as far as they are authorised by other Community legislation shall only be placed on the market after having been accepted for placing on the market in accordance with this Directive.

4. During evaluation of the requests for the placing on the market of the GMOs referred to in paragraph 1, the bodies established by the Community under this Directive and by Member States for the purpose of implementing this Directive shall be consulted.

Article 13
Notification procedure

1. Before a GMO or a combination of GMOs as or in products is placed on the market, a notification shall be submitted to the competent authority of the Member State where such a GMO is to be placed on the market for the first time. The competent authority shall acknowledge the date of receipt of the notification and immediately forward the summary of the dossier referred to in paragraph 2(h) to the competent authorities of the other Member States and the Commission.

The competent authority shall without delay examine whether the notification is in accordance with paragraph 2 and shall, if necessary, ask the notifier for additional information.

When the notification is in accordance with paragraph 2, and at the latest when it sends its assessment report in accordance with Article 14(2), the competent authority shall forward a copy of the notification to the Commission which shall, within 30 days of its receipt, forward it to the competent authorities of the other Member States.

2. The notification shall contain:

(a) the information required in Annexes III and IV. This information shall take into account the diversity of sites of use of the GMO as or in a product and shall include information on data and results obtained from research and developmental releases concerning the impact of the release on human health and the environment;

(b) the environmental risk assessment and the conclusions required in Annex II, section D;

(c) the conditions for the placing on the market of the product, including specific conditions of use and handling;

(d) with reference to Article 15(4), a proposed period for the consent which should not exceed ten years;

(e) a plan for monitoring in accordance with Annex VII, including a proposal for the time-period of the monitoring plan; this time-period may be different from the proposed period for the consent;

(f) a proposal for labelling which shall comply with the requirements laid down in Annex IV. The labelling shall clearly state that a GMO is present. The words .this product contains genetically modified organisms. shall appear either on a label or in an accompanying document;

(g) a proposal for packaging which shall comprise the requirements laid down in Annex IV;

(h) a summary of the dossier. The format of the summary shall be established in accordance with the procedure laid down in Article 30(2).

If on the basis of the results of any release notified under part B, or on other substantive, reasoned scientific grounds, a notifier considers that the placing on the market and use of a GMO as or in a product do not pose a risk to human health and the environment, he may propose to the competent authority not to provide part or all of the information required in Annex IV, section B.

3. The notifier shall include in this notification information on data or results from releases of the same GMOs or the same combination of GMOs previously or currently notified and/or carried out by the notifier either inside or outside the Community.

4. The notifier may also refer to data or results from notifications previously submitted by other notifiers or submit additional information he considers relevant, provided that the information, data and results are non-confidential or these notifiers have given their agreement in writing.

5. In order for a GMO or combination of GMOs to be used for a purpose different from that already specified in a notification, a separate notification shall be submitted.

6. If new information has become available with regard to the risks of the GMO to human health or the environment, before the written consent is granted, the notifier shall immediately take the measures necessary to protect human health and the environment, and inform the competent authority thereof. In addition, the notifier shall revise the information and conditions specified in the notification.

Article 14
Assessment report

1. On receipt and after acknowledgement of the notification in accordance with Article 13(2), the competent authority shall examine it for compliance with this Directive.

2. Within 90 days after receipt of the notification the competent authority shall:

—prepare an assessment report and send it to the notifier. A subsequent withdrawal by the notifier shall be without prejudice to any further submission of the notification to another competent authority ...

3. The assessment report shall indicate whether:

(a) the GMO(s) in question should be placed on the market and under which conditions; or

(b) the GMO(s) in question should not be placed on the market.

The assessment reports shall be established in accordance with the guidelines laid down in Annex VI....

Article 18
Community procedure in case of objections

1. In cases where an objection is raised and maintained by a competent authority or the Commission in accordance with Articles 15, 17 and 20, a decision shall be adopted and published within 120 days in accordance with the procedure laid down in Article 30(2)....

Article 19
Consent

1. Without prejudice to requirements under other Community legislation, only if a written consent has been given for the placing on the market of a GMO as or in a product may that product be used without further notification throughout the Community in so far as the specific conditions of use and the environments and/or geographical areas stipulated in these conditions are strictly adhered to.

2. The notifier may proceed with the placing on the market only when he has received the written consent of the competent authority in accordance with Articles 15, 17 and 18, and in conformity with any conditions required in that consent.

3. The written consent referred to in Articles 15, 17 and 18 shall, in all cases, explicitly specify:

(a) the scope of the consent, including the identity of the GMO(s) to be placed on the market as or in products, and their unique identifier;

(b) the period of validity of the consent;

(c) the conditions for the placing on the market of the product, including any specific condition of use, handling and packaging of the GMO(s) as or in products, and conditions for the protection of particular ecosystems/environments and/or geographical areas;

(d) that, without prejudice to Article 25, the notifier shall make control samples available to the competent authority on request;

(e) the labelling requirements, in compliance with the requirements laid down in Annex IV. The labelling shall clearly state that a GMO is present. The words .This product contains genetically modified organisms. shall appear either on a label or in a document accompanying the product or other products containing the GMO(s);

(f) monitoring requirements in accordance with Annex VII, including obligations to report to the Commission and competent authorities, the time period of the monitoring plan and, where appropriate, any obligations on any person selling the product or any user of it, inter alia, in the case of GMOs grown, concerning a level of information deemed appropriate on their location.

4. Member States shall take all necessary measures to ensure that the written consent and the decision referred to in Article 18, where applicable, are made accessible to the public and that the conditions specified in the written consent and the decision, where applicable, are complied with.

Article 20
Monitoring and handling of new information

1. Following the placing on the market of a GMO as or in a product, the notifier shall ensure that monitoring and reporting on it are carried out according to the conditions specified in the consent. The reports of this monitoring shall be submitted to the Commission and the competent authorities of the Member States. On the basis of these reports, in accordance with the consent and within the framework for the monitoring plan specified in the consent, the competent authority which received the original notification may adapt the monitoring plan after the first monitoring period.

2. If new information has become available, from the users or other sources, with regard to the risks of the GMO(s) to human health or the environment after the written consent has been given, the notifier shall immediately take the measures necessary to protect human health and the environment, and inform the competent authority thereof....

Article 21
Labelling

1. Member States shall take all necessary measures to ensure that at all stages of the placing on the market, the labelling and packaging of GMOs placed on the market as or in products comply with the relevant requirements specified in the written consent referred to in Articles 15(3), 17(5) and (8), 18(2) and 19(3).

2. For products where adventitious or technically unavoidable traces of authorised GMOs cannot be excluded, a minimum threshold may be established below which these products shall not have to be labelled according to the provision in paragraph 1. The threshold levels shall be established according to the product concerned, under the procedure laid down in Article 30(2).

Article 22
Free circulation

Without prejudice to Article 23, Member States may not prohibit, restrict or impede the placing on the market of GMOs, as or in products, which comply with the requirements of this Directive.

Article 23
Safeguard clause

1. Where a Member State, as a result of new or additional information made available since the date of the consent and affecting the environmental risk assessment or reassessment of existing information on the basis of new or additional scientific knowledge, has detailed grounds for considering that a GMO as or in a product which has

been properly notified and has received written consent under this Directive constitutes a risk to human health or the environment, that Member State may provisionally restrict or prohibit the use and/or sale of that GMO as or in a product on its territory....

Part D
Final Provisions

Article 25
Confidentiality

1. The Commission and the competent authorities shall not divulge to third parties any confidential information notified or exchanged under this Directive and shall protect intellectual property rights relating to the data received.

2. The notifier may indicate the information in the notification submitted under this Directive, the disclosure of which might harm his competitive position and which should therefore be treated as confidential. Verifiable justification must be given in such cases.

3. The competent authority shall, after consultation with the notifier, decide which information will be kept confidential and shall inform the notifier of its decisions.

4. In no case may the following information when submitted according to Articles 6, 7, 8, 13, 17, 20 or 23 be kept confidential:

—general description of the GMO or GMOs, name and address of the notifier, purpose of the release, location of release and intended uses;

—methods and plans for monitoring of the GMO or GMOs and for emergency response;

—environmental risk assessment.

5. If, for whatever reasons, the notifier withdraws the notification, the competent authorities and the Commission must respect the confidentiality of the information supplied.

Article 26
Labelling of GMOs referred to in Article 2(4), second subparagraph

1. The GMOs to be made available for operations referred to under Article 2(4), second subparagraph, shall be subject to adequate labelling requirements in accordance with the relevant sections of Annex IV in order to provide for clear information, on a label or in an accompanying document, on the presence of GMOs. To that effect the words .This product contains genetically modified organisms. shall appear either on a label or in an accompanying document....

Article 28
Consultation of Scientific Committee(s)

1. In cases where an objection as regards the risks of GMOs to human health or to the environment is raised by a competent authority or the Commission and maintained in accordance with Article 15(1), 17(4), 20(3) or 23, or where the assessment report referred to in Article 14 indicates that the GMO should not be placed on the market, the relevant Scientific Committee(s) shall be consulted by the Commission, on its own initiative or at the request of a Member State, on the objection.

2. The relevant Scientific Committee(s) may also be consulted by the Commission, on its own initiative or at the request of a Member State, on any matter under this Directive that may have an adverse effect on human health and the environment....

Article 29
Consultation of Committee(s) on Ethics

1. Without prejudice to the competence of Member States as regards ethical issues, the Commission shall, on its own initiative or at the request of the European Parliament or the Council, consult any committee it has created with a view to obtaining its advice on the ethical implications of biotechnology, such as the European Group on Ethics in Science and New Technologies, on ethical issues of a general nature....

Article 31
Exchange of information and reporting

1. Member States and the Commission shall meet regularly and exchange information on the experience acquired with regard to the prevention of risks related to the release and the placing on the market of GMOs. This information exchange shall also cover experience gained from the implementation of Article 2(4), second subparagraph, environmental risk assessment, monitoring and the issue of consultation and information of the public.

Where necessary, guidance on the implementation of Article 2(4), second subparagraph, may be provided by the committee established under Article 30(1).

2. The Commission shall establish one or several register(s) for the purpose of recording the information on genetic modifications in GMOs mentioned in point A No 7 of Annex IV. Without prejudice to Article 25, the register(s) shall include a part which is accessible to the public. The detailed arrangements for the operation of the register(s) shall be decided in accordance with the procedure laid down in Article 30(2).

3. Without prejudice to paragraph 2 and point A No 7 of Annex IV,

(a) Member States shall establish public registers in which the location of the release of the GMOs under part B is recorded.

(b) Member States shall also establish registers for recording the location of GMOs grown under part C, inter alia so that the possible effects of such GMOs on the environment may be monitored in accordance with the provisions of Articles 19(3)(f) and 20(1). Without prejudice to such provisions in Articles 19 and 20, the said locations shall:

—be notified to the competent authorities, and

—be made known to the public

in the manner deemed appropriate by the competent authorities and in accordance with national provisions.

4. Every three years, Member States shall send the Commission a report on the measures taken to implement the provisions of this Directive. This report shall include a brief factual report on their experience with GMOs placed on the market in or as products under this Directive.

5. Every three years, the Commission shall publish a summary based on the reports referred to in paragraph 4.

6. The Commission shall send to the European Parliament and the Council, in 2003 and thereafter every three years, a report on the experience of Member States with GMOs placed on the market under this Directive.

7. When submitting this report in 2003, the Commission shall at the same time submit a specific report on the operation of part B and part C including an assessment of:

(a) all its implications, particularly to take account of the diversity of European ecosystems and the need to complement the regulatory framework in this field;

(b) the feasibility of various options to improve further the consistency and efficiency of this framework, including a centralised Community authorisation procedure and the arrangements for the final decision making by the Commission;

(c) whether sufficient experience has accumulated on the implementation of part B differentiated procedures to justify a provision on implicit consent in these procedures and on part C to justify the application of differentiated procedures; and

(d) the socioeconomic implications of deliberate releases and placing on the market of GMOs.

8. The Commission shall send to the European Parliament and the Council every year, a report on the ethical issues referred to in Article 29(1); this report may be accompanied, if appropriate, by a proposal with a view to amending this Directive.

Article 32
Implementation of the Cartagena Protocol on biosafety

1. The Commission is invited to bring forward as soon as possible and in any case before July 2001 a legislative proposal for implementing in detail the Cartagena Protocol on biosafety. The proposal shall complement and, if necessary, amend the provisions of this Directive.

2. This proposal shall, in particular, include appropriate measures to implement the procedures laid down in the Cartagena Protocol and, in accordance with the Protocol, require Community exporters to ensure that all requirements of the Advance Informed Agreement Procedure, as set out in Articles 7 to 10, 12 and 14 of the Cartagena Protocol, are fulfilled.

Article 33
Penalties

Member States shall determine the penalties applicable to breaches of the national provisions adopted pursuant to this Directive. Those penalties shall be effective, proportionate and dissuasive.

Article 34
Transposition

1. Member States shall bring into force the laws, regulations and administrative provisions necessary to comply with this Directive by 17 October 2002. They shall forthwith inform the Commission thereof....

Done at Brussels, 12 March 2001.

Commission of the European Communities, Report from the Commission to the Council and the European Parliament: on the Experience of Member States with GMOs Placed on the Market under Directive 2001/18/EC and Incorporating a Specific Report on the Operation of Parts B and C of the Directive

COM(2004) 575 final, SEC(2004) 1063 (August 31, 2004)

1. Background

On 17 April 2001, Directive 2001/18/EC of the European Parliament and of the Council on the deliberate release into the environment of genetically modified organisms (GMOs) and repealing Council Directive 90/220/EEC[52] entered into force. This Directive became applicable as of 17 October 2002.

According to Article 31(6) of this Directive, 'the Commission shall send to the European Parliament and the Council, in 2003 and thereafter every three years, a report on the experience of Member States with GMOs placed on the market under this Directive.' It should be noted that this first report relates only to 15 Member States given that the reporting period in question ended prior to the date of entry for accession countries (1 May 2004). Subsequent three-year reports will, however, include these additional Member States.

According to Article 31(7) of this Directive, "when submitting this report in 2003, the Commission shall at the same time submit a specific report on the operation of part B and part C including an assessment of: (a) all its implications, particularly to take account of the diversity of European ecosystems and the need to complement the regulatory framework in this field; (b) the feasibility of various options to improve further the consistency and efficiency of this framework, including a centralised Community authorisation procedure and the arrangements for the final decision making by the Commission; (c) whether sufficient experience has accumulated on the implementation of part B differentiated procedures to justify a provision on implicit consent in these procedures and on part C to justify the application of differentiated procedures; and (d) the socioeconomic implications of deliberate releases and placing on the market of GMOs".

In July 2003, the Commission funded a study[53] to gather information from four groups of stakeholders (15 Member States (MS), industry and research organisations, public interest groups and farmers' organisations), as a basis for this report. The final report of the study is available upon request.

In the following sections, the overall state of implementation is described, the experience of stakeholders in implementing the Directive is summarised and issues requiring further action are identified.

2. Overview of implementation

The Commission convenes twice-yearly meetings with the competent authorities (CAs) of the MS in order to exchange views on specific implementation issues. Since

52. OJ L 106, 17.4.2001 p. 1–39.

53. SBC (2004), 'Means to improve the consistency and efficiency of the legislative framework in the field of biotechnology', study contract number B4-3040/2003/359058/MAR/C4, carried out by Schenkelaars Biotechnology Consultancy (SBC), NL, in cooperation with Risk and Policy Analysts Ltd, UK, on behalf of the European Commission, April 2004.

April 2001, the date of entry into force of Directive 2001/18/EC, seven meetings have taken place. Working groups were established to develop the content of six implementing measures which have since been adopted by either the Commission or the Council in the framework of Directive 2001/18/EC. Two of these measures are specific to Part B of the Directive: (1) a standard format for summary notifications and (2) a standard format for reports on releases. Three are specific to Part C of the Directive: (1) a standard format for summary notifications; (2) guidelines for monitoring; and (3) the establishment of a register to record information related to genetic modifications. The sixth measure provides guidelines for environmental risk assessment concerning both Part B and Part C of the Directive.

Furthermore, Regulation 1830/2003[54] concerning the traceability and labelling of GMOs and the traceability of food and feed products produced from GMOs and amending Directive 2001/18/EC was adopted on 22 September 2003 and became fully applicable as of 15 April 2004. In the framework of this Regulation, and in relation to Article 19 of Directive 2001/18/EC, an additional implementing measure addressing the development and assignment of unique identifiers for GMOs was adopted on 14 January 2004.

Currently, additional working groups of CAs, chaired by the Commission, have been established to address specific issues such as herbicide resistance, Bt toxin, antibiotic resistance marker genes, post-market monitoring and ease of access to and exchange of information. In addition, as a result of the regular exchange of views among MS, the CAs have arrived at a common understanding on the implementation of specific articles of the Directive.

A full list of implementing measures and CA meetings is attached in Annex 1.

Regarding transposition of the Directive by the MS, it should be noted that, at the time of preparing this report, seven of the EU 15 MS and eight of the acceding countries had communicated transposition measures. Details are provided in Annex 2. The Commission has taken eight of the EU 15 States to court for non-transposition.

3. Number of applications for Part B and Part C releases

The number of Part B applications (by type of GMO) as of 26 February 2004 under Directive 2001/18/EC and its predecessor Directive 90/220/EEC[55] is presented in Annex 3, Table 1. Since the adoption of Directive 2001/18/EC, a slight increase in the number of summary notifications has occurred in France, Germany, Spain and the UK. In all other countries there has been a reduction or no change in the number of summary notifications.

Table 1 also highlights the fact that most experience with Part B applications has been with the authorisation of GM plants. Although a number of non-plant GMOs were authorised under Directive 90/220/EEC, very few have been authorised since Directive 2001/18/EC came into force.

Between January 2003 and March 2004, 24 Part C applications were submitted, as presented in Annex 3, Table 2. A number of these applications had originally been submitted under Directive 90/220/EEC (prior to 17 October 2002) and were complemented under Directive 2001/18/EC in accordance with Article 35 of the Directive. These applications are now at various stages of the authorisation process.

---

54. OJ L 268, 18.10.2003, p. 24–28.
55. OJ L 117, 8.5.1990, p. 15–27.

Although Part C of Directive 2001/18/EC covers all commercial releases, Regulation 1829/2003 on GM food and feed[56] now defines the procedures for placing GM food and feed (including crops for food or feed use) on the market. As of 18 April 2004 when the new Regulation became fully applicable, notifications submitted under Directive 2001/18/EC, concerning products for which feed use was included and for which an assessment report had not yet been provided, were to be transformed into applications under the new Regulation. Likewise, requests submitted under Regulation 258/97 on novel foods and novel food ingredients,[57] for which the initial assessment report had not been forwarded to the Commission as well as for all cases in which an additional assessment report had been requested, were to be transformed into applications under the new Regulation. Henceforth, applications for GMOs for food and feed use will be authorised under this Regulation. Thus, in future, the number of applications under Part C of Directive 2001/18/EC may be reduced as a consequence of the evolving legislative framework in the field of biotechnology.

4. Common issues relating to the operation of both Part B and Part C releases.

A number of issues are common to the operation of both Part B and Part C releases. These include:

- Pre-application discussions
- Environmental risk assessment (ERA)
- Public information and consultation
- Antibiotic Resistance Marker (ARM) Genes
- Implications for the diversity of European ecosystems
- Socio-economic implications
- Use of simplified and differentiated procedures

Details of the experience to date with these issues are provided in Annex 4.

5. Specific issues relating to Part C releases.

Two specific issues relate to Part C releases, as follows:

- The decision-making process
- Post-market monitoring and guidance

Details of the experience on these two issues are provided in Annex 5.

6. Improving the consistency and efficiency of the legislative framework.

The previous sections identify areas in the operation of Part B and Part C of Directive 2001/18/EC where progress has been made and implementation is running smoothly, and where work is already underway to develop further guidance (e.g. on antibiotic resistance marker genes and on monitoring) and to address outstanding issues (e.g. transposition). This section identifies issues at this stage of implementation of the Directive where further action could be envisaged to improve the consistency and efficiency of the overall legislative framework.

The current authorisation process (in terms of forms and guidance) is focused on GM plants. GM medicines and GM animals are also under development and their authorisa-

---

56. Regulation (EC) No 1829/2003 of the European Parliament and of the Council of 22 September 2003 on genetically modified food and feed, OJ L 268, 18.10.2003 p. 1–23.

57. OJ L 43, 14.2.1997, p. 1.

tion will require consideration of different issues. In order to allow research organisations, industry as well as MS CAs to address these issues in a harmonised way, it will be necessary to develop specific guidance on the risk assessment of non-plant GMOs.

Research relating to the safety of field releases has been part of the EU research programmes in biotechnology for over 20 years.[58] Further research sponsored by these programmes should be encouraged in areas such as: rates of gene flow and introgression in relation to the adventitious presence of GMOs in (non-GM) seeds, food and feed; the efficacy of measures to limit pollen flow; and the environmental impact of different methods of conventional farming against which to compare the findings from GM crop growing.

Some stakeholders have requested further guidance on the interaction between different pieces of legislation and how these will work in practice. For example, although Article 12.2 of Directive 2001/18/EC clearly states that GMOs for medical use are excluded from Part C of Directive 2001/18/EC, industry stakeholders believe that it may be necessary to submit applications under both the Deliberate Release Directive and the medical authorisation procedures, based on their experience for Part B applications.

Regarding the feasibility of a centralised Community authorisation procedure, industry stakeholders generally advocated this procedure. The experience of MS CAs with the centralised procedure under Regulation (EEC) No.2309/93[59] for the authorisation of medicinal products suggests that there is a need to clarify the obligations of the European Agency for the Evaluation of Medicinal Products (EMEA) when consulting national CAs, particularly with regard to the ERA. Experience has also shown that, for the purpose of cultivation, MS were not ready to accept the environmental risk assessment carried out by other MS, even if a common basis for such risks is foreseen in the Directive. As of 18 April 2004, Regulation 1829/2003 provides for a centralised procedure with the European Food Safety Authority (EFSA). In the light of experience to be acquired in the implementation of this Regulation, the Commission will consider the need for a centralised procedure under Directive 2001/18/EC.

7. Conclusions

This report is specifically concerned with Directive 2001/18/EC and the deliberate release of GMOs, although the wider legislative framework is also considered. The vast majority of GMOs that have been developed to date for deliberate release are transgenic crop plants, modified to be tolerant to certain herbicides or resistant to certain insect pests. Consequently, much of the available information and experience relates to GM crops.

Given that the Directive became fully applicable as of 17 October 2002, there is still relatively little experience of its implementation. The lack of transposition by a number of Member States also hinders implementation. Nevertheless, there is general agreement that the Directive, together with the recent Regulations on GM Food and Feed and Traceability and Labelling, help to increase confidence in the legislative framework and to increase the predictability of the decision-making process. In particular, in-

58. "A Review of Results: EC-sponsored research on safety of GMOS", European Commission, 2001, *available at* http://europa.eu.int/comm/research/quality-of-life/gmo/.

59. Council Regulation (EEC) No 2309/93 of 22 July 1993 laying down Community procedures for the authorization and supervision of medicinal products for human and veterinary use and establishing a European Agency for the Evaluation of Medicinal Products, OJ L 214, 24.8.1993, p. 1–21.

creased requirements for the environmental risk assessment address the possible longer term, direct, indirect, delayed and cumulative effects on the environment and wildlife of releasing and using GMOs.

Currently, most concerns relate to the need for guidance in interpreting elements of the Directive such as post-market monitoring, the phasing out of antibiotic resistance marker genes which may have adverse effects on human health and the environment, and non-plant GMOs. In addition, guidance is required on the interaction of the various pieces of legislation. The Commission and Member States are already working on guidance for post-market monitoring and antibiotic resistance marker genes.

Notes & Questions

1. Some have criticized the Coordinated Framework for Regulation of Biotechnology in the U.S. on the grounds that in practice it has not actually worked very well. Instead, such critics contend, for example, that the system addresses the risks in a "piecemeal, haphazard fashion" that results in "sizable gaps in coverage" and forces ag-biotech producers to "navigate a confusing maze of agencies and statutes, with resulting inefficiency and needlessly steep economic and opportunity costs...." John Charles Kunich, *Mother Frankenstein, Doctor Nature, and the Environmental Law of Genetic Engineering*, 74 S. Cal. L. Rev. 807 (2001). Should Congress instead pass a single statute addressed at regulating biotechnology?

2. The international regulation of ag-biotech products has also affected trade negotiations, often most pointedly between the U.S.—a strong ag-biotech producer—and other nations who resist the distribution of such products in their countries. Some may claim that there is a fair bit of protectionism at work in this resistance as well, with the other nations using anti ag-biotech sentiment and regulation as a bargaining chip in trade negotiations with the U.S. Even if this were true, is there anything necessarily wrong with that?

Chapter 9

Genetics in the Courtroom

As knowledge of genetics and DNA has grown, it increasingly has been employed as evidence in civil and criminal law. This chapter considers the many ways in which genetic testing and genetic information can be used in legal proceedings for purposes of identification, determinations of guilt, innocence, civil liability, and legal status. Part A reviews the standards of admissibility for scientific evidence, such as DNA, in state and federal courts. It serves as a prelude to Part B, which focuses on the use of DNA identification and genetic information in the context of criminal law. Part C looks at the growing controversies surrounding DNA repositories, registries and data banks. Part D explores the nascent use of genetic knowledge and information in civil liability cases. Finally, Part E considers the use of DNA as arbiter of identity in determining ancestry, ethnicity and species.

A. Scientific Evidence and Standards of Admissibility

Genetic science has bedeviled courts both in terms of complexity and pace of emerging knowledge. No sooner has one method of DNA analysis been recognized as admissible evidence than it is supplanted by a more precise, or improved, method. DNA identification techniques require significant ability to grasp scientific and statistical concepts and this presents challenges to judges and juries alike. Despite these complications, DNA evidence is steadily gaining credibility and is now viewed as the "gold standard" for scientific identification.

Further complicating the use of DNA evidence by the courts are the standards and requirements for admissibility. For many years, the standard for admissibility of the scientific evidence was based on the seminal case of Frye *v. United States.*

Frye v. United States

293 F. 1013 (1923)

[At issue in the case was the admissibility of evidence gleaned from administration of a systolic blood pressure deception test. This test postulated that the exertion and stress of a falsehood would result in a transient elevation of blood pressure. Careful monitoring of the blood pressure ergo could detect a lie versus truth. This evidence was excluded in a murder trial and defendant appealed, alleging the exclusion was in error.]

...

Counsel for defendant, in their able presentation of the novel question involved, correctly state in their brief that no cases directly in point have been found. The broad ground, however, upon which they plant their case, is succinctly stated in their brief as follows:

> The rule is that the opinions of experts or skilled witnesses are admissible in evidence in those cases in which the matter of inquiry is such that inexperienced persons are unlikely to prove capable of forming a correct judgment upon it, for the reason that the subject-matter so far partakes of a science, art, or trade as to require a previous habit or experience or study in it, in order to acquire a knowledge of it. When the question involved does not lie within the range of common experience or common knowledge, but requires special experience or special knowledge, then the opinions of witnesses skilled in that particular science, art, or trade to which the question relates are admissible in evidence.

Numerous cases are cited in support of this rule. Just when a scientific principle or discovery crosses the line between the experimental and demonstrable stages is difficult to define. Somewhere in this twilight zone the evidential force of the principle must be recognized, and while courts will go a long way in admitting expert testimony deduced from a well-recognized scientific principle or discovery, the thing from which the deduction is made must be sufficiently established to have gained general acceptance in the particular field in which it belongs.

...

* * *

The *Frye* test of "general acceptance" was the baseline standard for most of the twentieth century. However, as science progressed, a need for a more discriminatory standard evolved. This was partially satisfied by Federal Rule of Evidence 702:

> If scientific, technical, or other specialized knowledge will assist the trier of fact to understand the evidence or to determine a fact in issue, a witness qualified as an expert by knowledge, skill, experience, training, or education, may testify thereto in the form of an opinion or otherwise, if (1) the testimony is based upon sufficient facts or data, (2) the testimony is the product of reliable principles and methods, and (3) the witness has applied the principles and methods reliably to the facts of the case.

Rule 702 became the norm in federal courts and increasingly state jurisdictions began to adopt Rule 702, or some version of it, as well. In 1993, the *Frye* test became more fully eclipsed by *Daubert v. Merrell Dow Pharmaceuticals, Inc.*

Daubert v. Merrell Dow Pharmaceuticals, Inc.

509 U.S. 579 (1993)

Justice Blackmun delivered the opinion of the Court.

In this case we are called upon to determine the standard for admitting expert scientific testimony in a federal trial.

I

Petitioners Jason Daubert and Eric Schuller are minor children born with serious birth defects. They and their parents sued respondent in California state court, alleging that the birth defects had been caused by the mothers' ingestion of Bendectin, a prescription antinausea drug marketed by respondent. Respondent removed the suits to federal court on diversity grounds.

After extensive discovery, respondent moved for summary judgment, contending that Bendectin does not cause birth defects in humans and that petitioners would be unable to come forward with any admissible evidence that it does. In support of its motion, respondent submitted an affidavit of Steven H. Lamm, physician and epidemiologist, who is a well-credentialed expert on the risks from exposure to various chemical substances. Doctor Lamm stated that he had reviewed all the literature on Bendectin and human birth defects—more than 30 published studies involving over 130,000 patients. No study had found Bendectin to be a human teratogen (*i.e.*, a substance capable of causing malformations in fetuses). On the basis of this review, Doctor Lamm concluded that maternal use of Bendectin during the first trimester of pregnancy has not been shown to be a risk factor for human birth defects.

Petitioners did not (and do not) contest this characterization of the published record regarding Bendectin. Instead, they responded to respondent's motion with the testimony of eight experts of their own, each of whom also possessed impressive credentials. These experts had concluded that Bendectin can cause birth defects. Their conclusions were based upon "in vitro" (test tube) and "in vivo" (live) animal studies that found a link between Bendectin and malformations; pharmacological studies of the chemical structure of Bendectin that purported to show similarities between the structure of the drug and that of other substances known to cause birth defects; and the "reanalysis" of previously published epidemiological (human statistical) studies.

The District Court granted respondent's motion for summary judgment. The court stated that scientific evidence is admissible only if the principle upon which it is based is "'sufficiently established to have general acceptance in the field to which it belongs.'" The court concluded that petitioners' evidence did not meet this standard. Given the vast body of epidemiological data concerning Bendectin, the court held, expert opinion which is not based on epidemiological evidence is not admissible to establish causation. Thus, the animal-cell studies, live-animal studies, and chemical-structure analyses on which petitioners had relied could not raise by themselves a reasonably disputable jury issue regarding causation. Petitioners' epidemiological analyses, based as they were on recalculations of data in previously published studies that had found no causal link between the drug and birth defects, were ruled to be inadmissible because they had not been published or subjected to peer review.

The United States Court of Appeals for the Ninth Circuit affirmed. 951 F.2d 1128 (1991). Citing *Frye v. United States*, the court stated that expert opinion based on a scientific technique is inadmissible unless the technique is "generally accepted" as reliable in the relevant scientific community. The court declared that expert opinion based on a methodology that diverges "significantly from the procedures accepted by recognized authorities in the field ... cannot be shown to be 'generally accepted as a reliable technique.'"

...

We granted certiorari in light of sharp divisions among the courts regarding the proper standard for the admission of expert testimony.

In the 70 years since its formulation in the *Frye* case, the "general acceptance" test has been the dominant standard for determining the admissibility of novel scientific evidence at trial. Although under increasing attack of late, the rule continues to be followed by a majority of courts, including the Ninth Circuit.

...

The merits of the *Frye* test have been much debated, and scholarship on its proper scope and application is legion. Petitioners' primary attack, however, is not on the content but on the continuing authority of the rule. They contend that the *Frye* test was superseded by the adoption of the Federal Rules of Evidence. We agree.

...

Here there is a specific Rule that speaks to the contested issue. Rule 702, governing expert testimony, provides:

> If scientific, technical, or other specialized knowledge will assist the trier of fact to understand the evidence or to determine a fact in issue, a witness qualified as an expert by knowledge, skill, experience, training, or education, may testify thereto in the form of an opinion or otherwise.

Nothing in the text of this Rule establishes "general acceptance" as an absolute prerequisite to admissibility. Nor does respondent present any clear indication that Rule 702 or the Rules as a whole were intended to incorporate a "general acceptance" standard. The drafting history makes no mention of *Frye*, and a rigid "general acceptance" requirement would be at odds with the "liberal thrust" of the Federal Rules and their "general approach of relaxing the traditional barriers to 'opinion' testimony." Given the Rules' permissive backdrop and their inclusion of a specific rule on expert testimony that does not mention "'general acceptance,'" the assertion that the Rules somehow assimilated *Frye* is unconvincing. *Frye* made "general acceptance" the exclusive test for admitting expert scientific testimony. That austere standard, absent from, and incompatible with, the Federal Rules of Evidence, should not be applied in federal trials.

That the *Frye* test was displaced by the Rules of Evidence does not mean, however, that the Rules themselves place no limits on the admissibility of purportedly scientific evidence. Nor is the trial judge disabled from screening such evidence. To the contrary, under the Rules the trial judge must ensure that any and all scientific testimony or evidence admitted is not only relevant, but reliable.

The primary locus of this obligation is Rule 702, which clearly contemplates some degree of regulation of the subjects and theories about which an expert may testify. "*If scientific*, technical, or other specialized *knowledge will assist the trier of fact* to understand the evidence or to determine a fact in issue" an expert "may testify *thereto.*" (Emphasis added.) The subject of an expert's testimony must be "scientific ... knowledge." The adjective "scientific" implies a grounding in the methods and procedures of science. Similarly, the word "knowledge" connotes more than subjective belief or unsupported speculation. The term "applies to any body of known facts or to any body of ideas inferred from such facts or accepted as truths on good grounds." Webster's Third New International Dictionary 1252 (1986). Of course, it would be unreasonable to conclude that the subject of scientific testimony must be "known" to a certainty; arguably, there are no certainties in science.... ("Science is not an encyclopedic body of knowledge about the universe. Instead, it represents a *process* for proposing and refining theoretical explanations about the world that are subject to further testing and refinement" (emphasis in original)). But, in order to qualify as "scientific knowledge," an inference or assertion must be derived by the scientific method. Proposed testimony must be supported by appropriate validation—*i.e.*, "good grounds," based on what is known. In short, the requirement that an expert's testimony pertain to "scientific knowledge" establishes a standard of evidentiary reliability.

Rule 702 further requires that the evidence or testimony "assist the trier of fact to understand the evidence or to determine a fact in issue." This condition goes primarily to relevance. "Expert testimony which does not relate to any issue in the case is not relevant and, ergo, non-helpful." The study of the phases of the moon, for example, may provide valid scientific "knowledge" about whether a certain night was dark, and if darkness is a fact in issue, the knowledge will assist the trier of fact. However (absent creditable grounds supporting such a link), evidence that the moon was full on a certain night will not assist the trier of fact in determining whether an individual was unusually likely to have behaved irrationally on that night. Rule 702's "helpfulness" standard requires a valid scientific connection to the pertinent inquiry as a precondition to admissibility.

That these requirements are embodied in Rule 702 is not surprising. Unlike an ordinary witness, see Rule 701, an expert is permitted wide latitude to offer opinions, including those that are not based on firsthand knowledge or observation. See Rules 702 and 703. Presumably, this relaxation of the usual requirement of firsthand knowledge—a rule which represents "a 'most pervasive manifestation' of the common law insistence upon 'the most reliable sources of information,' ... —is premised on an assumption that the expert's opinion will have a reliable basis in the knowledge and experience of his discipline.

... Although the *Frye* decision itself focused exclusively on "novel" scientific techniques, we do not read the requirements of Rule 702 to apply specially or exclusively to unconventional evidence. Of course, well-established propositions are less likely to be challenged than those that are novel, and they are more handily defended. Indeed, theories that are so firmly established as to have attained the status of scientific law, such as the laws of thermodynamics, properly are subject to judicial notice under Federal Rule of Evidence 201.

Ordinarily, a key question to be answered in determining whether a theory or technique is scientific knowledge that will assist the trier of fact will be whether it can be (and has been) tested. "Scientific methodology today is based on generating hypotheses and testing them to see if they can be falsified; indeed, this methodology is what distinguishes science from other fields of human inquiry."

Another pertinent consideration is whether the theory or technique has been subjected to peer review and publication. Publication (which is but one element of peer review) is not a *sine qua non* of admissibility; it does not necessarily correlate with reliability, ... and in some instances well-grounded but innovative theories will not have been published. Some propositions, moreover, are too particular, too new, or of too limited interest to be published. But submission to the scrutiny of the scientific community is a component of "good science," in part because it increases the likelihood that substantive flaws in methodology will be detected. The fact of publication (or lack thereof) in a peer reviewed journal thus will be a relevant, though not dispositive, consideration in assessing the scientific validity of a particular technique or methodology on which an opinion is premised.

Additionally, in the case of a particular scientific technique, the court ordinarily should consider the known or potential rate of error, and the existence and maintenance of standards controlling the technique's operation.

Finally, "general acceptance" can yet have a bearing on the inquiry. A "reliability assessment does not require, although it does permit, explicit identification of a relevant scientific community and an express determination of a particular degree of acceptance within that community." Widespread acceptance can be an important factor in ruling particular evidence admissible, and "a known technique which has been able to attract only minimal support within the community," may properly be viewed with skepticism.

The inquiry envisioned by Rule 702 is, we emphasize, a flexible one. Its overarching subject is the scientific validity and thus the evidentiary relevance and reliability—of the principles that underlie a proposed submission. The focus, of course, must be solely on principles and methodology, not on the conclusions that they generate.

...

We conclude by briefly addressing what appear to be two underlying concerns of the parties and *amici* in this case. Respondent expresses apprehension that abandonment of "general acceptance" as the exclusive requirement for admission will result in a "free-for-all" in which befuddled juries are confounded by absurd and irrational pseudoscientific assertions. In this regard respondent seems to us to be overly pessimistic about the capabilities of the jury and of the adversary system generally....

Petitioners and, to a greater extent, their *amici* exhibit a different concern. They suggest that recognition of a screening role for the judge that allows for the exclusion of "invalid" evidence will sanction a stifling and repressive scientific orthodoxy and will be inimical to the search for truth.... It is true that open debate is an essential part of both legal and scientific analyses. Yet there are important differences between the quest for truth in the courtroom and the quest for truth in the laboratory. Scientific conclusions are subject to perpetual revision. Law, on the other hand, must resolve disputes finally and quickly. The scientific project is advanced by broad and wide-ranging consideration of a multitude of hypotheses, for those that are incorrect will eventually be shown to be so, and that in itself is an advance. Conjectures that are probably wrong are of little use, however, in the project of reaching a quick, final, and binding legal judgment—often of great consequence—about a particular set of events in the past. We recognize that, in practice, a gatekeeping role for the judge, no matter how flexible, inevitably on occasion will prevent the jury from learning of authentic insights and innovations. That, nevertheless, is the balance that is struck by Rules of Evidence designed not for the exhaustive search for cosmic understanding but for the particularized resolution of legal disputes.

...

To summarize: "General acceptance" is not a necessary precondition to the admissibility of scientific evidence under the Federal Rules of Evidence, but the Rules of Evidence—especially Rule 702—do assign to the trial judge the task of ensuring that an expert's testimony both rests on a reliable foundation and is relevant to the task at hand. Pertinent evidence based on scientifically valid principles will satisfy those demands....

Notes & Questions

1. In *Daubert*, the Supreme Court conclusively held that Federal Rule of Evidence 702 was the proper standard for admissibility of scientific evidence in federal courts. The Court also elaborated upon the test for admissibility under 702. Unlike *Frye*, the Federal Rule of Evidence 702 does not require general acceptance for the admissibility of scientific evidence. Once the judge is satisfied that the evidence is relevant and connected to a pertinent issue in the case (Federal Rules of Evidence 104 and 402, respectively), the judge is instructed to consider the following factors in determining admissibility:

(a) Whether the theory or technique in question can be, and has been, tested.

(b) Whether the theory or technique in question has been subject to peer review and publication.

(c) The theory or technique's known, or potential, error rate.

(d) The existence and maintenance of standards controlling the technique or theory's operation.

(e) Whether the theory or technique has attracted widespread acceptance within a relevant scientific community.

No one factor is dispositive; rather the judge must consider them all in totality in determining admissibility of the evidence. The judge has the discretion to look at the reliability and validity of the evidence, consider whether the expert testimony speaks to the reliability, and whether the evidence and testimony will assist the jury in coming to a decision in the case. Should the judge determine that while admissible, the evidence or expert witness could mislead the jury, unnecessarily confuse the issues, or cause unfair prejudice, the judge may exclude the expert or evidence on the ground that it is more prejudicial than probative. *See* Fed. R. Evid. 403. As a result of *Daubert* and the aforementioned Federal Rules of Evidence, the judge serves as a "gatekeeper" with respect to admissibility of scientific evidence and testimony. For additional reading on *Daubert* and its relationship to Federal Rule of Evidence 702, see Daniel A. Klein, *Reliability of Scientific Technique and Its Acceptance Within Scientific Community as Affecting Admissibility, at Federal Trial, of Expert Testimony as to Result of Test or Study Based on Such Technique—Modern Cases*, 105 A.L.R. Fed. 299 (2005); David G. Owen, *A Decade of Daubert*, 80 Denv. U. L. Rev. 345 (2002); Henry F. Fradella, et al., *The Impact of Daubert on Forensic Science*, 31 Pepp. L. Rev. 323 (2004); Christopher B. Mueller, *Daubert Asks the Right Questions: Now Appellate Courts Should Help Find the Right Answers*, 33 Seton Hall. L. Rev. 987 (2003); Hyongsoon Kim, *Adversarialism Defended: Daubert and the Judge's Role in Evaluating Expert Evidence*, 34 Colum. J. L. Soc. Probs. 223 (2001).

2. In the years following *Daubert*, the Supreme Court has decided two cases that further clarify scientific admissibility. The first of these, *General Electric Co. v. Joiner*, 522 U.S. 136 (1997), involved an electrician exposed to chemicals, notably a coolant containing polychlorinated biphenyls ("PCBs"), in his workplace. Joiner developed a particularly virulent form of lung cancer at the age of thirty-seven and sued his employer, arguing that the workplace exposure to PCBs caused the cancer. The trial court disallowed testimony regarding whether PCBs had the capacity to cause the specific type of lung cancer that affected Joiner. On appeal, the Eleventh Circuit reversed, arguing that the decision to exclude the testimony was subject to "a particularly stringent standard of review," because the testimony was outcome determinative. *Joiner v. General Elec. Co.*, 78 F. 3d 524, 529 (11th Cir. 1996). The Supreme Court disagreed with the Eleventh Circuit, holding that the standard of review the appellate court should have applied in reviewing the trial court's ruling was abuse of discretion. It specifically rejected the argument that a more stringent standard should be applied because the decision was outcome determinative.

Just two years after *Joiner*, the Supreme Court heard and decided *Kumho Tire Co. v. Carmichael*, 526 U.S. 137 (1999), a products liability case alleging that defective tires resulted in injuries and death for Carmichael's passengers. The trial court excluded the testimony of Carmichael's expert on the ground that his testimony failed the reliability test of *Daubert*. On appeal, the Eleventh Circuit reversed holding that the *Daubert* reliability approach applied to scientific evidence, not technical evidence like that of Carmichael's expert. The Supreme Court held that *Daubert* applies to all expert testimony, regardless of whether it is scientific, technical or other specialized knowledge. For a more extensive discussion of *Joiner* and *Kumho* and their impact, see D. Michael Risinger, et al., *The Daubert/Kumho Implications of Observer Effects in Forensic Science:*

Hidden Problems of Expectation and Suggestion, 90 CAL. L. REV. 1 (2002); Craig Lee Montz, *Trial Judges as Scientific Gatekeeper After Daubert, Joiner, Kumho Tire, and Amended Rule 702: Is Anyone Still Seriously Buying This?*, 33 UWLA L. REV. 87 (2001); Derek L. Mogck, *Are We There Yet?: Refining the Test for Expert Testimony Through Daubert, Kumho Tire and Proposed Federal Rule of Evidence 702*, 33 CONN. L. REV. 303 (2000); Catherine E. Brixen & Christine E. Meis, *Codifying the "Daubert Trilogy": The Amendment to Federal Rule 702*, 40 JURIMETRICS J. 527 (2000); David L. Faigman, et al., *Reply Essay—How Good is Good Enough?: Expert Evidence Under Daubert and Kumho*, 50 CASE W. RES. L. REV. 645 (2000); Michael H. Graham, *The Expert Witness Predicament: Determining "Reliable" Under the Gatekeeping Test of Daubert, Kumho, and Proposed Amended Rule 702 of the Federal Rules of Evidence*, 54 U. MIAMI L. REV. 317 (2000); Michael H. Gottesman, *From Barefoot to Daubert to Joiner: Triple Play or Double Error?*, 40 ARIZ. L. REV. 753 (1998); Andrew B. Gagen, *What is an Environmental Expert? The Impact of Daubert, Joiner and Kumho Tire on the Admissibility of Scientific Expert Evidence*, 19 UCLA J. ENVTL. L. & POL'Y 401 (2001).

3. In the wake of *Daubert v. Merrell Dow*, about half of the states have adopted a parallel standard, albeit often with some variation. For example, in Colorado, *Daubert* has been adopted in principle although the articulated focus of evidentiary inquiry is supposed to be the reliability and relevance of the science at issue, rather than application of the specific criteria articulated in *Daubert.* Fifteen jurisdictions have chosen to retain the *Frye* standard in principle, often elaborating upon it slightly. For example, Pennsylvania adheres to the *Frye* standard on the ground that it defers to the testimony of scientists and experts, rather than balancing a variety of factors, that may ultimately blur and undermine the integrity of the science. Yet another approach is that taken by Washington, in which there is a two-part test requiring first that the evidence meet the *Frye* standard and second, that the witness be qualified and helpful to the trier-of-fact. Wisconsin takes a similar tack with a three-part test focusing on relevance or the evidence at trial. Six states have not rejected the *Frye* test, but have chosen to apply the *Daubert* factors in addition to continuing to require general acceptance. Finally, four states have developed their own tests for admissibility. These states include Georgia (admissibility depends on whether a "scientific stage of verifiable certainty" has been reached), Utah (admissibility dependent upon "inherent reliability"), Wisconsin (relevance, unrelated to reliability) and Virginia (reliability through reliance on expert testimony.) For a complete summary, see Alice B. Lustre, *Post-Daubert Standards For Admissibility of Scientific and Other Expert Evidence in State Courts*, 90 A.L.R.5th 453 (2005); Clark Hedger, *Daubert and the States: A Critical Analysis of Emerging Trends*, 49 ST. LOUIS U. L.J. 177 (2004).

4. In the aftermath of the *Daubert* decision, there has been considerable scholarly comment devoted to whether the adoption of *Daubert* has resulted in admissibility standards that are more or less stringent than those provided by *Frye.* Critics of *Frye* note that general acceptance is ambiguous and allows an opportunity for admission of "junk science." Critics of *Daubert* allege that it liberates evidence from general acceptance, thus making "junk science" easier to admit. *Daubert* casts the judge in the role of "gatekeeper" and many argue that this role is assumed with more, or less, vigor, depending upon the judge. *See generally* Edward K. Cheng & Albert H. Yoon, *Does Frye or Daubert Matter? A Study of Scientific Admissibility Standards*, 91 VA. L. REV. 471 (2005); Pamela J. Jensen, *Frye versus Daubert: Practically the Same?*, 87 MINN. L. REV. 1579 (2003).

5. A number of scientific identification methods have confronted the evolving legal standards for admissibility of evidence, including fingerprint evidence, handwriting analysis, bite mark evidence, and voice spectrometry.

Although fingerprints have been a foundation in criminal identification and prosecution, science has provided forensic techniques to enhance and clarify fingerprints. These include using chemicals like ninhydrin and superglue, laser scanning technology for illumination, and digital enhancement. Most of these technologies have been found to be admissible. *See Com. v. Cintron*, 784 N.E.2d 617 (Mass. 2003) (photograph of bloody fingerprint enhanced by ninhydrin admissible, given that both before and after photographs taken of the print, assuring that the ninhydrin had not altered the print); *Cowans v. Bagley*, 236 F. Supp. 2d 841 (S.D. Ohio 2002) (superglue enhanced print reliable and admissible, despite fact that fingerprint expert could not fully explain the science behind the method); *United States v. Patterson*, 277 F.3d 709 (4th Cir. 2002) (laser scanned prints reliable given that deputy had extensive experience using the device, even though he was unable to speak to the reliability of device itself, only to the reliability of its depiction of the print); *State v. Hayden*, 950 P.2d 1024 (Wash. Ct. App. 1998) (digitally imaged handprint and fingerprint admissible despite fact that print would not have been recoverable absent the technology). *See also* Nathan Benedict, *Fingerprints and the Daubert Standard for Admission of Scientific Evidence: Why Fingerprints Fail and a Proposed Remedy*, 46 Ariz. L. Rev. 519 (2004); Kristin Romandetti, *Recognizing and Responding to a Problem with the Admissibility of Fingerprint Evidence Under Daubert*, 45 Jurimetrics J. 41 (2004); Robert Epstein, *Fingerprints Meet Daubert: The Myth of Fingerprint "Science" is Revealed*, 75 S. Cal. L. Rev. 605 (2002).

Handwriting analysis was viewed as technical in nature before the *Kumho* decision, but is increasingly considered using a *Daubert* approach. *See United States v. Velasquez*, 64 F.3d 844 (3d Cir. 1995) (handwriting experts were qualified and testimony met admissibility standards of 702); *United States v. King*, 532 F.2d 505 (5th Cir. 1976) (exclusion of handwriting expert justified given that expert training entirely the result of self-study); *United States v. Prime*, 363 F.3d 1028 (9th Cir. 2004) (*Daubert* applied finding that handwriting analysis has been tested, shown to have a high degree of accuracy, been subject to extensive peer review, and generally accepted, and therefore admissible).

Comparison of bite marks to suspect's dentition has also been the subject of analysis as scientific evidence. Such evidence has been taken from victims as well as from objects, such as bite marks on food items. In *Milone v. Camp*, 22 F.3d 693 (7th Cir. 1994), the court found that the probative value of bite mark evidence outweighed the risk of prejudice finding admissible the match of a bite mark in the victim's thigh to the defendant's dental impression, even though the science of forensic odontology was still in its infancy.

Voice spectrometry has also been used and much debated as a scientific method of identification. In *United States v. Franks*, 511 F.2d 25 (6th Cir. 1975), voiceprint evidence was admitted as generally accepted under *Frye*, but in *Reed v. State*, 391 A.2d 364 (Md. 1978), similar voiceprint evidence failed to pass muster as having achieved general acceptance. More recently, as voiceprint technology has advanced, it has satisfied the *Daubert* analysis. *See, e.g.*, *State v. Coon*, 974 P.2d 386 (Ala. 1999).

B. Genetics and Criminal Law

The somewhat variable standards applied to scientific evidence have influenced the admissibility of DNA evidence. This has been especially critical in criminal law where genetics has already had a significant effect on prosecution and defense, especially in the context of DNA identification of both perpetrator and victim. With respect to criminal defense, DNA has provided opportunity to refute guilt both initially and years after conviction. Post-conviction review has resulted in the freedom for numerous wrongfully convicted defendants, particularly through the efforts of the renowned Innocence Projects (discussed in Section 3 *infra*). Genetics has also been used as a potential defense and argument for mitigation of guilt and sentencing, although this body of case law is less developed.

Although much of the DNA chain is identical from person to person, certain distinctive, usually small sections are unique with respect to the alleles that compose them. No two individuals, save for identical twins, have exactly the same alleles at all polymorphic sites throughout their chromosomal DNA. In addition to the nuclear DNA that is organized into chromosomes, there is a quantum of DNA in the mitochondria of each human cell as well. Both nuclear and mitochondrial DNA has been used for identification purposes.

Several methods are available to analyze DNA. By discerning the genetic make-up at numerous sites on DNA samples, it is possible to prove a match with astonishingly high probability. The three most recognized analytic methods are polymerase chain reaction ("PCR") amplification, restriction fragment length polymorphism ("RFLP") analysis, and mitochondrial DNA ("mtDNA") analysis. These analytic methods exploit the polymorphisms in DNA that make individuals unique. All of them have been used in criminal law, most particularly with respect to identification of the perpetrator and victim, and the physical evidence connected to them.

PCR has the advantage of being able to be used when the sample is small; part of the process involves the replication and amplification of the DNA. It is also less expensive than RFLP. However, RFLP is considered more discriminatory and precise because the process generally scrutinizes more polymorphic sites. Mitochondrial DNA is not found in the nucleus of the cell, but in the surrounding cytoplasm. Mitochondria are considered the power plants of the cell, driving the functions of the cell that permit nuclear DNA to be expressed. Unlike nuclear DNA, mitochondrial DNA is organized in rings carrying genes composed of base pairs. MtDNA is passed from mother to progeny and allows matrilineage to be tracked back many centuries. All of these methods may suffer from undesirable artifacts as a result of laboratory inconsistencies or problems. This, coupled with the statistical probability issues, may give rise to concerns about the certainty of the DNA as scientific evidence and impact its admissibility.

1. DNA Evidence and the Prosecution: Identification of the Perpetrator

People v. Morganti

43 Cal.App.4th 643 (1996)

Hearle, J.

[In 1991, Ronald Turner was found dead in a locked hotel room in a burning California motel, with 26 stab wounds and a fractured skull. Investigators determined that the fire was the result of arson and also collected a leather glove with a small piece of hair inside, a section of linoleum imprinted with a bloody shoe print, and a bloodstained door chain from the motel unit. Defendant Morganti was convicted of second degree murder, personal use of a knife during commission of that crime, and arson of an inhabited structure. An accessory, Patterson, was also convicted. The trial court admitted blood evidence, including the results of an agglutination inhibition test (a process to detect specific genetic markers in blood) and a polymerase chain reaction analysis (a molecular biology technical procedure for exploiting genetic differences in DNA). Defendant appeals, challenging the admissibility of the DNA evidence.]

...

F. The Physical Evidence

A criminalist testified that the single hair found in the glove that was left at the crime scene was similar to Morganti's arm or hand hair. The criminalist also testified that the bloody shoe print left at the crime scene was made by a person wearing a Nike brand athletic shoe, based on the clear impression of the "swoosh" trademark.

Several tests were performed on bloodstain samples collected during the investigation. From these tests, the prosecution's expert was able to exclude certain individuals as sources of some of the stains and to identify others whose blood types were consistent with the stains.

The expert tested five distinct stains from Paterson's jeans. Morganti and Turner were excluded as potential donors of four out of the five stains. The genetic traits exhibited by the stains were consistent with Paterson and occur in one out of fourteen Caucasians. The expert opined that the fifth stain was not Morganti's blood, but was consistent with both Turner and Paterson.

A bloodstain found on a piece of tan upholstery in Morganti's pickup did not come from Morganti but could have been Paterson's or Turner's. A bloodstain found on a piece of gray upholstery in the Mercury Monarch did not come from Morganti or Paterson but could have been Turner's. The genetic traits exhibited by this stain occur in one out of one thousand seven hundred fifteen Caucasians.

A bloodstain found on the washbasin ... did not come from Morganti or Paterson, but could have been Turner's blood. The genetic traits exhibited by this stain occur in one out of sixty-one Caucasians.

A bloodstain on the door chain for the [motel unit] did not come from Turner or Paterson but could have been Morganti's blood. The genetic traits exhibited by this stain occur in one out of twenty-two Caucasians.

...

[Morganti alleged that he had met with the victim earlier at the motel unit earlier but denied having committing the murder and arson.]

Morganti admitted that the glove found at the crime scene was his and that he regularly carried a Kalinga knife. He claimed that the marks found on his arm were a spider bite and scratches he received while working in his yard on the night of the murder. Morganti also recalled touching the door chain on the motel unit but did not recall bleeding on it.

III. Discussion

A. *The Blood Evidence*

Morganti challenges the trial court's decision to admit evidence pertaining to two distinct types of tests that were performed to identify the sources of blood samples in this case: (1) a gamma marker (GM) blood analysis performed pursuant to the agglutination inhibition method (hereafter, the agglutination inhibition test); and (2) a type of DNA analysis known as polymerase chain reaction (hereafter, the PCR analysis). For reasons that follow, we conclude both types of blood evidence were properly admitted.

The admissibility of expert evidence pertaining to a new scientific technique is determined by applying the following analysis set forth by our Supreme Court in *People v. Kelly* (1976) 17 Cal.3d 24: "'(1) [T]he *reliability of the method* must be established, usually by expert testimony, and (2) the witness furnishing such testimony must be properly *qualified as an expert to give an opinion* on the subject. Additionally, the proponent of the evidence must demonstrate that correct scientific procedures were used in the particular case.'" (*People v. Leahy* (1994) 8 Cal.4th 587, 594 [34 Cal.Rptr.2d 663, 882 P.2d 321], quoting *People v. Kelly, supra*, 17 Cal.3d at p. 30, italics in original.)

With respect to the first prong of this test, "reliability" means that the technique "'must be sufficiently established to have gained general acceptance in the particular field in which it belongs.'" (*People v. Kelly, supra*, 17 Cal.3d at p. 30, italics omitted.) In determining whether there has been "general acceptance," "[t]he goal is not to decide the actual reliability of the new technique, but simply to determine whether the technique is generally accepted in the relevant scientific community." (*People v. Barney* (1992) 8 Cal.App.4th 798, 810 [10 Cal.Rptr.2d 731].) Courts "must consider the quality, as well as quantity, of the evidence supporting or opposing a new scientific technique. Mere numerical majority support or opposition by persons minimally qualified to state an authoritative opinion is of little value...." (*People v. Leahy, supra*, 8 Cal.4th at p. 612.)

With respect to the second prong of the *Kelly* test, regarding the expert(s)' qualifications, "[t]he trial court is given considerable latitude in determining the qualifications of an expert and its ruling will not be disturbed on appeal unless a manifest abuse of discretion is shown." (*People v. Kelly, supra*, 17 Cal.3d at p. 39; see also *People v. Cooper* (1991) 53 Cal.3d 771, 813 [281 Cal.Rptr. 90, 809 P.2d 865]; 3 Witkin, Cal. Evidence (3d ed. 1986) Introduction of Evidence at Trial, § 1844, pp. 1799–1800, and cases cited therein.)

The determination whether correct scientific procedures were used in a particular case is a "third-prong" of the *Kelly* test; it is not merely a question of evidentiary weight, but an element of the initial admissibility determination. (*People v. Axell* (1991) 235 Cal.App.3d 836, 862 [1 Cal.Rptr.2d 411]; *People v. Barney, supra*, 8 Cal.App.4th at pp. 822–824.)

1. *The Agglutination Inhibition Evidence*

Morganti challenges the admissibility of evidence relating to the agglutination inhibition tests performed on behalf of the prosecution in this case. He contends the tests excluded Turner as the source of the bloodstains found on Paterson's jeans and also excluded Paterson as the source of stains found on other "critical items." This argument is at least partially incorrect, since Turner was not excluded as a source of one of the stains on Paterson's jeans. In any event, we conclude the agglutination inhibition evidence was properly admitted.

a. *Prong One—General Acceptance*

"The agglutination inhibition process detects the presence of specific genetic markers in the bloodstream. Blood samples are dissolved in a saline solution and centrifuged to remove debris; a liquid remains. A chemical known as an 'agglutinator' is added to determine the presence of a specific genetic marker. If the marker is present, the agglutinator will chemically bind with it and neutralize. To discover whether this has occurred, antigen-coated indicator cells are added to the extract; these cells react only to the specific agglutinator used. There is no reaction if the agglutinator has neutralized. If it has not, however, the indicator cells clump together; and it is then known that the sample does not contain the particular genetic marker tested. Separate tests determine the presence of other genetic markers." (*People v. Yorba* (1989) 209 Cal.App.3d 1017, 1024, fn. 5 [257 Cal.Rptr. 641] (hereafter *Yorba*).)

Agglutination inhibition evidence was admitted in *Yorba*, *supra*, 209 Cal.App.3d 1017. "[O]nce a trial court has admitted evidence based upon a new scientific technique, and that decision is affirmed on appeal by a published appellate decision, the precedent so established may control subsequent trials, at least until new evidence is presented reflecting a change in the attitude of the scientific community." (*People v. Kelly*, *supra*, 17 Cal.3d at p. 32.) Thus, case-by-case adjudication as to the "general acceptance" prong of the *Kelly* test is not required once the scientific technique in question has been endorsed in a published appellate opinion. (*People v. Barney*, *supra*, 8 Cal.App.4th at pp. 824–825.)

Morganti concedes that agglutination inhibition testing was approved in *Yorba* but, nevertheless, maintains that *Yorba* was "improperly used by the trial judge ... to establish the reliability" of the particular agglutination inhibition method used in the present case. Morganti's long and convoluted argument boils down to this: agglutination inhibition testing involves the "working together" of two sets of cells, each of which has been separately mixed with foreign substances, to determine whether certain genetic markers are present. Different techniques can be used to achieve a "working together" of the cells. In this case, Seriological Laboratories (Seri) used a method referred to as the "Seri slide rotation method." Morganti contends, as he did below, that *Yorba* did not approve this specific method of working together the cells but only approved of agglutination inhibition testing generally. According to Morganti, the slide rotation method is not a generally accepted method of working together the cells.

The agglutination inhibition tests at issue in this case were performed by Gary Harmor, a forensic serologist who has been employed at Seri since that company's inception in 1978. Harmor testified at the *Kelly* hearing that there is more than one means by which to agitate or work together cells when performing this test: "The microtitre method Doctor Schanfield uses is a v-bottom plastic plate with wells in it, if you will, depressions in it. He puts all these reagents together and spins them to force the cells together. There's also a tube technology in which actually small glass test tubes are used the [reagents] are placed in the tube and the tubes are centrifuged and checked for clumping or no clumping of the cells. *With the slide technology that's been discussed and used in this case and Yorba the reactants are all placed in a flat plastic plate and then rotated by a machine to force the cells together.*" (Italics added.)

[The court reviews the use of the agglutination inhibition tests in the *Yorba* case and found that it was determined to be admissible and that the method used in the instant case was virtually identical.]

...

b. *Prong Two—Harmor's Expertise*

Morganti contends that Harmor should not have been accepted as an expert in this case because (1) he was not qualified to render an opinion as to whether agglutination inhibition is generally accepted in the scientific community, and (2) he was biased in favor of the prosecution.

Morganti underestimates the impact of published precedent. Once general acceptance of a scientific technique is established by precedent, it need not be established again under the second prong of the *Kelly* test. Of course an expert must always be qualified. But precedent eliminates the need, in a case such as this, for expert testimony *on the subject of the reliability of the scientific technique in question. People v. Leahy*, *supra*, 8 Cal.4th at p. 611.). Therefore, whether Harmor was qualified to testify as to the general acceptance of the agglutination inhibition test is not a relevant issue in our case.

We agree with the trial court that Harmor was sufficiently qualified to give expert testimony regarding the absorption inhibition testing he conducted in this case. Harmor, a forensic serologist, helped found Seri 15 years ago. He works as a consultant for both the prosecution, the defense and private parties. He has taught seminars on genetic markers used in forensic science and has published articles. Harmor has been performing absorption inhibition testing since 1979 and has used that test to locate GM markers since 1983. He has previously testified as an expert regarding GM testing between 30–35 times and has testified at no less than 6 *Kelly* hearings in California, one of which was the hearing in *Yorba*.

...

c. *Prong Three—Correct Scientific Procedures*

Morganti contends that *Kelly*'s third prong imposed on the prosecution the burden of proving general acceptance of the slide rotation method. In contrast, the People contend *Yorba* relieved the prosecution of having to prove anything under *Kelly*. Both parties are mistaken. Since the third prong of the *Kelly* test requires case specific proof that correct procedures were employed, it cannot be satisfied by relying on a published appellate decision. (*People v. Barney*, *supra*, 8 Cal.App.4th at p. 824.) But, when general acceptance is established by precedent, the "third-prong hearing" that must be conducted will not approach the "complexity of a full-blown" *Kelly* hearing. (*Id.* at p. 825.) "All that is necessary in the limited third-prong hearing is a foundational showing that correct scientific procedures were used." (*Ibid.*) The trial court properly found that the prosecution made the necessary foundational showing. Not only did Harmor testify that he followed established procedure or protocol, his testimony establishes that he followed the exact procedures that were deemed correct in *Yorba*.

2. *The PCR Analysis*

Morganti's second challenge involving the blood evidence pertains to a DNA analysis known as polymerase chain reaction or PCR. His objection to this evidence stems from the fact that PCR testing eliminated Paterson and Turner as possible sources of the bloodstain found on the door chain and identified Morganti as someone whose genetic traits were consistent with that stain.

PCR is "a molecular biology technical procedure for exploiting genetic differences in DNA," whereby small pieces of DNA are copied or amplified. The technique is employed when the DNA sample available is too small and/or degraded to perform a more common type of DNA analysis known as RFLP.

The PCR analysis performed in this case was used to amplify a specific gene known as the DQ alpha. The DQ alpha gene codes for proteins found on the surface of the white blood cell and is known to have alternate genetic forms, i.e., the gene does not look the same in all people. Six variations (or alleles) have been identified and labeled as 1.1, 1.2, 1.3, 2, 3 and 4. Because alleles are inherited in pairs, one from each parent, there are twenty-one possible combinations which are referred to as genotypes.

...

a. *Prong One—General Acceptance*
(i). *Standard of review*

Unlike agglutination inhibition testing, PCR has not been approved in published appellate precedent in California. The trial court in this case held a lengthy and extensive *Kelly* hearing and concluded that the PCR evidence was admissible. This court has previously recognized that, for purposes of appellate review, "'general acceptance' is best described as a mixed question of law and fact subject to limited de novo review." (*People v. Reilly* (1987) 196 Cal.App.3d 1127, 1134 [242 Cal.Rptr. 496].) "[W]e review the trial court's determination with deference to any and all supportable findings of 'historical' fact or credibility, and then decide as a matter of law, based on those assumptions, whether there has been general acceptance." (*Id.* at p. 1135.)

...

(ii). *The record*

In ruling that PCR analysis of the DQ alpha gene is generally accepted in the relevant scientific field, the trial court relied on expert testimony of two witnesses and extensive documentary evidence. The court found there is no significant controversy or dispute with respect to the reliability of this method and that the evidence did not indicate any flaw in the method or its use. Our review of the record confirms these findings....

Morganti also contends the documentary evidence establishes "less than full acceptance of the use of PCR in forensic testing, particularly in regard to criminal cases involving unknown blood on contaminated objects." As our Supreme Court has recently confirmed, *Kelly* does not demand absolute unanimity of views in the scientific community. (*People v. Leahy*, *supra*, 8 Cal.4th at pp. 611–612.) "'[I]f a fair overview of the literature discloses that scientists significant either in number or expertise publicly oppose [the technique] as unreliable, the court may safely conclude there is no such consensus at the present time.'" (*Id.* at p. 611, quoting *People v. Shirley*, *supra*, 31 Cal.3d at p. 56.) Our review of the literature in this record confirms there is no such significant public opposition.

(iii). *Judicial decisions*

PCR evidence has not been found admissible under *Kelly* in published California appellate precedent. But courts in other jurisdictions have concluded that PCR analysis of DQ alpha is generally accepted as reliable in the scientific community.

...

c. *Prong Three—Correct Scientific Procedures*

Morganti contends Harmor did not use correct scientific procedures. Many of his complaints challenge the quality of the testing rather than the correctness of the procedure used. '[T]he *Kelly/Frye* rule tests the fundamental validity of a new scientific methodology, not the degree of professionalism with which it is applied. Careless testing affects the weight of the evidence and not its admissibility, and must be attacked on cross-examination or by other expert testimony.' 'Once the court acts within its discretion and finds the witness qualified, as it did in this case, the weight to be given the testimony is for the jury to decide.'" (*People v. Cooper*, *supra*, 53 Cal.3d at p. 814.)

Accordingly, we focus on the correctness of the procedures that were used as opposed to the quality of the analyst's performance of those procedures. The Kit which was developed by Cetus Corporation to conduct PCR analysis of DQ alpha contains a "User's Guide" which was admitted into evidence in this case. Seri uses the Kit to do PCR testing. Both Blake and the FBI have used the Kit as well, and both approve of its use. Blake and Harmor both testified that the User's Guide contains the correct scientific procedures for conducting PCR analysis of DQ alpha. We have not been apprised of, nor do we find, any contrary evidence in this record. Harmor testified that he followed the procedure set forth in the User's Guide. Dr. Blake testified that he reviewed Harmor's work and that Harmor used scientifically correct procedures.

Morganti contends that, even if the User's Guide is scientifically correct, the procedure in this case was incorrect because Harmor (1) added extra TAQ enzyme to the bloodstain sample which was removed from the door chain at the crime scene after that sample failed to amplify, and (2) did not perform a "substrate" control for the door chain.

(i). *The additional TAQ*

The only technique Harmor employed that was not set forth in the User's Guide was the addition of extra "TAQ enzyme" when certain samples (such as the door chain sample) did not amplify. Harmor explained that, once DNA is extracted from a sample, it is added to a "cocktail" which comes in the Kit and then subjected to a series of procedures designed to cause amplification of the DNA. One reason the sample may not amplify is because "the stain itself has inhibitory substances present in it which cause either the TAQ enzyme not to function in the cocktail or block the DNA for the TAQ enzyme to actually copy the DNA." Harmor testified that, when the sample does not amplify, the analyst is faced with a choice: "At that point the analyst can assess whether or not it's worth another try on the evidence. Frequently bloodstains inhibit the PCR process. I believe the literature says it's because of the possibility of the E molecule interfering with the attachment of the TAQ enzyme onto the DNA primer and single strand. So, to overcome that, one analyst can dilute the sample, reduce the volume of sample added to the cocktail which would also reduce the amount of inhibitory substance and/or add additional TAQ enzyme which is purchased from Perkin-Elmer Corporation. This in effect would absorb the inhibitory substance, leave TAQ left over to copy the DNA."

... Although adding the TAQ enzyme to overcome inhibition is not prescribed in the User's Guide, taking such a step is not inconsistent with the procedures contained therein. Harmor testified that adding extra TAQ is an acceptable practice. Further, Blake testified that adding the TAQ is a "fairly standard strategy for overcoming inhibition difficulties," that it is discussed in the literature and is an acceptable, reliable methodology for amplification.

(ii). *The substrate control*

A substrate control is a PCR test performed on an unstained portion of the material from which bloodstain evidence is removed. The control is processed along with the stain evidence and tests "for any other stains that might not be visible that are present in the fabric or any interference the fabric might have with the actual PCR process and typing." Although Harmor always tries to obtain a substrate control, it is not unusual to be presented with evidence from which it is not possible to obtain one. The absence of such a control does not prohibit or affect the way he reports the results of the PCR analysis itself. In the present case, Harmor tried but was unable to perform a substrate control on the door chain because everywhere he tested on the chain turned out to be positive for blood.

...

We conclude that the scientific technique of PCR analysis of the DQ alpha gene is generally accepted in the relevant scientific community and that correct scientific procedures were employed to conduct that analysis in the present case. Morganti's remaining objection to admission of the DNA evidence pertains to the distinct issue of statistics.

3. *Statistics*

Once the PCR analysis is complete, there may or may not be a need to perform a statistical analysis. If the subject of the investigation is not compatible with the blood evidence, statistics or genetic frequency data is irrelevant. If the person has the same traits as the evidentiary specimen, then the question is how common or rare are those traits, i.e., what percentage of the population are potential donors of such a specimen. The People mistakenly contend that PCR statistical evidence is not subject to the *Kelly* analysis. "*Kelly*'s test of general acceptance in the scientific community applies not only to the techniques for laboratory analysis of the DNA material but also to the statistical calculations which indicate the likelihood that the crime scene sample of DNA would match with some individual other than the defendant." (*People v. Taylor*, *supra*, 33 Cal.App.4th at p. 266; see also *People v. Barney*, *supra*, 8 Cal.App.4th at p. 818.)

The PCR results in this case established that Paterson and the victim were not compatible with being sources of bloodstains found on the door chain at the crime scene, but that Morganti did have the same traits as the evidentiary specimen. Harmor used genetic frequency data to conclude that slightly over 4.5 percent or one in twenty-two people in the Caucasian population had the same traits as the evidentiary specimen. Morganti questions the reliability of this statistical conclusion.

...

The distinctions the trial court drew between RFLP and PCR statistics are amply supported by the record, especially in the testimony of Dr. Blake. The trial court also correctly observed that, in contrast to *People v. Barney*, no published literature or credible evidence was introduced into this record indicating any flaw or controversy with respect to the population frequency data used to evaluate PCR test results. The undisputed testimony of both Harmor and Blake establishes that no such controversy exists.

...

4. *Conclusions Regarding Admissibility of Blood Evidence*

We affirm the trial court's findings that both agglutination inhibition and PCR analysis of the DQ alpha gene are generally accepted as reliable techniques by the relevant scientific community. We also affirm the court's discretionary rulings regarding relevancy, witness credibility and expert qualifications. Finally, we affirm that correct scientific procedures were used to conduct the agglutination inhibition and PCR tests in this case. Therefore, evidence pertaining to these tests was properly admitted....

Sholler v. Commonwealth

969 S.W. 2d 706 (Ky. 1998)

Cooper, Justice

Appellant was convicted in the Kenton Circuit Court of two counts of robbery in the first degree, two counts of rape in the first degree, two counts of sodomy in the first degree, one count of burglary in the first degree, and of being a persistent felony offender in the first degree....

[Appellant's appeal alleges that the trial judge failed to strike two potential jurors for cause, erred in refusing to admit the testimony of a eyewitness misidentification expert, in allowing the jury to visit the crime scene, by requiring him to display his teeth to validate a witness' testimony, and allowed DNA evidence to be admitted without testimony from a statistical geneticist to support the science.]

...

II. DNA Expert.

Stacey Warnecke, a forensic scientist specializing in DNA testing, first testified that DNA testing satisfied the foundation requirements of *Daubert v. Merrell Dow Pharmaceuticals, Inc.*, 509 U.S. 579 (1993), as adopted in *Mitchell v. Commonwealth*, 908 S.W.2d 100 ([Ky.] 1995). She then testified that she determined from tests of the semen samples removed from K.B.'s eyebrow and thigh and of a blood sample obtained from Appellant that four of the five DNA strands of the semen samples matched those of Appellant's blood sample. She also testified that a "match" does not mean that Appellant must have been the source of the semen samples, but only that Appellant was not excluded as the source. If there had not been a "match," Appellant would have been excluded as the source.

Appellant claims Warnecke's testimony should have been suppressed in the absence of accompanying testimony from a population geneticist as to the statistical probabilities associated with a genetic "match." Of course, we do not know what that testimony would have been; but, based upon a reading of other cases, a population geneticist presumably would have testified that the probabilities of a DNA match between unrelated individuals would be, *e.g.*, ten to one, or ten million to one, or some other mathematical probability. *See United States v. Bonds,* 12 F.3d 540, 550 (6th Cir.1993), *aff'g United States v. Yee,* 134 F.R.D. 161 (N.D.Ohio 1991); *Harris v. Commonwealth,* 846 S.W.2d 678, 679 ([Ky.] 1992), *overruled on other grounds, Mitchell v. Commonwealth,* 908 S.W.2d 100 ([Ky.] 1995). Warnecke admitted that she was not qualified to testify to mathematical probabilities, but only to the fact that her testing did not exclude Appellant as a possible source of the semen samples obtained from K.B.'s body.

Appellant notes that the Supreme Judicial Court of Massachusetts has held that testimony of a genetic "match" cannot be introduced in the absence of proof of the significance of that conclusion. *Commonwealth v. Lanigan,* 596 N.E.2d 311 ([Mass.] 1992); *Commonwealth v. Curnin,* 565 N.E.2d 440 ([Mass.] 1991). However, there is no consensus on this issue. Some jurisdictions hold that evidence of mathematical probabilities based on DNA testing is inadmissible because of its prejudicial effect. *E.g., State v. Pennell,* 584 A.2d 513, 519–20 (Del.Super.Ct.1989); *State v. Schwartz,* 447 N.W.2d 422 (Minn.1989). "There is a real danger that the jury will use the evidence as a measure of the probability of the defendant's guilt or innocence ..." *Id.,* 447 N.W.2d at 428. In other jurisdictions, admissibility has been held to depend upon the degree of deviation in the database used to determine the mathematical probabilities. *Compare Caldwell v. State,* S.E.2d 436 (1990) and *Commonwealth v. Curnin, supra,* with *People v. Axell,* 1 Cal.Rptr.2d 411 (Cal.Ct.App.1991) and *People v. Castro,* N.Y.S.2d 985 (N.Y.Sup.Ct.1989). Still other jurisdictions hold that such evidence is admissible and the weight to be given to it is to be determined by the jury. *United States v. Bonds, supra; United States v. Gwaltney,* 790 F.2d 1378 (9th Cir.1986), *cert. denied,* 479 U.S. 1104 (1987); *Snowden v. State,* 574 So.2d 960, 966 (Ala.Crim.App.1990); *Hopkins v. State,* 579 N.E.2d 1297 (Ind.1991).

The Commonwealth claims that we resolved this issue when we held in *Commonwealth v. Petrey,* 945 S.W.2d 417 ([Ky.] 1997) that two witnesses are not required to satisfy the standard for admission of DNA evidence. *Id.* at 419. Actually, the issue addressed in *Petrey* was not whether DNA tests were admissible without concomitant evidence of statistical probabilities, but whether the Commonwealth's expert could testify to both the DNA test results and the foundation evidence required by *Daubert v. Merrell Dow Pharmaceuticals, Inc., supra,* and *Mitchell v. Commonwealth, supra.* The issue raised by Appellant in this case is one of first impression in this Commonwealth.

In fact, Warnecke's testimony did include an explanation of the significance of a DNA match, albeit to the limited extent that the results did not prove that Appellant was the source of the semen, but only that he could not be excluded as a possible source. We view Warnecke's testimony as similar to that of an expert who testifies that a defendant's blood type is the same as that of a blood sample found at a crime scene. *E.g., Wilhite v. Commonwealth,* 574 S.W.2d 304, 306 ([Ky.] 1978). Such does not mean that the crime scene blood was the defendant's blood, but only that the defendant is not excluded as the source of the crime scene blood. In that respect, the testimony is just another item of circumstantial evidence to be weighed by the jury.

To summarize, there was evidence that DNA testing is a recognized and accepted field of science and that Warnecke is an expert qualified to conduct such tests and report her results. The information she provided was both relevant and assisted the jury in determining whether Appellant could have been the perpetrator of these crimes. If Appellant desired additional evidence of statistical probabilities based on Warnecke's test results, he could have hired his own population geneticist to analyze the results and testify to those probabilities. There was no error in admitting the DNA test results with the accompanying explanation given by Warnecke.

...

Appellant claims reversal is required because of "cumulative error." Since we find no error occurred in Appellant's trial, there could have been no cumulative error....

United States v. Chase

No. F-7330-99, 2005 WL 757259 (D.C. Super. Jan. 10, 2005)

Patricia A. Broderick, Judge.

...

II. Introduction

On October 16, 1999, the Defendant was charged with Premeditated Murder, Felony Murder and Robbery of a Senior Citizen as a result of events allegedly occurring on July 8, 1996. The decedent allegedly was robbed and later was found beaten; he suffocated to death on a dead-end street, where witnesses saw the body, wrapped in a brown comforter, being dumped out of the back of a U-Haul truck.

Originally, the government sought to introduce evidence of the results of mitochondrial DNA (hereinafter referred to as "mtDNA") analysis conducted by the FBI Laboratory. The mtDNA analysis was conducted from hairs found at the scene of the incident, specifically on a handkerchief, comforter surrounding the victim's body and a towel found on the driver's seat of the victim's car. The results failed to exclude the Defendant and the Defendant's maternal relatives as potential contributors of some of the hairs tested by the laboratory.

The government sought to introduce evidence of the mtDNA analysis results, as well as testimony regarding the statistical significance of the results. Specifically, the government sought to introduce the testimony of Dr. Constance Fisher. Dr. Fisher was a Federal Bureau of Investigation (FBI) analyst who interpreted the mtDNA analysis. Dr. Fisher compared the mtDNA sequence obtained from the evidence in this case and from the Defendant with the FBI Scientific Working Group of DNA Analysis Methods, (hereinafter referred to as the "SWGDAM"), database.

The SWGDAM working group is a peer consensus group of forensic scientists and academics. Pursuant to federal mandate, the FBI Laboratory maintains the SWGDAM database. Dr. Budowle testified that the DNA Identification Act of 1994 gave the FBI the authority to set standards for DNA analysis in forensic crime labs, particularly government labs. To do that, an advisory group was formed to make recommendations and set standards. All forensic laboratories in the United States that conduct mitochondrial DNA testing use the SWGDAM database.

The Defendant opposed the introduction of the evidence and testimony, arguing that mtDNA was a new science without acceptance in the relevant scientific community, and that the database used to compare and explain the results was faulty and not acceptable under the relevant standards. Alternatively, the Defendant suggested that the Court could admit two evidentiary hairs that the Defendant had chosen to test pursuant to her rights under The Innocence Protection Act. These tests confirmed the results obtained by the FBI Laboratory with respect to the hairs on the comforter, handkerchief and towel on the driver's seat of the victim's car, but excluded the Defendant as the contributor of the other evidentiary hairs found on the scene. The exclusion evidence did not have to rely on the comparison to other sequences in the SWGDAM database to be statistically significant. The Defendant's alternative position was, therefore, that if the Court found that the science and technology of mtDNA was sufficiently accepted and thereby admissible, the Court should find that the database used to determine statistical comparisons was still faulty. Under this theory, the government's "inclusion" evidence would not be admissible, but the defendant's "exclusion" evidence would be.

III. *Frye* Hearing

The Court conducted a *Frye* hearing, inviting each of the parties to present witnesses as well as affidavits. The government presented the testimony of Dr. Constance Fisher, Dr. Terry Melton, Dr. Ranajit Chakraborty and Dr. Bruce Budowle. The defense presented the testimony of Dr. Frederika Kaestle, Dr. Terrence Speed, and Dr. Ricky Kittles. Additionally, both parties submitted voluminous scientific articles, book excerpts, and other written materials in support of their respective motions.

In a *Frye* Hearing, the test for admissibility of any novel scientific evidence at trial is whether the new technology or methodology has been sufficiently established to have "gained general acceptance in the particular field in which it belongs." *Frye [v. United*

States], 293 F. [1013, 1014 (1923)]. The same standard applies to the admissibility of expert testimony on a given subject under *Dyas v. U.S.*, 376 A.2d 827, 832 (D.C.1977) and *Ibn-Tamas v. U.S.*, 407 A.2d 626, 638 (D.C.1979).

As to the admissibility of DNA evidence specifically, the standard is set under *United States v. Porter*, (referred to as "*Porter II*") 618 A.2d 629 (D.C. 1992) (held that nuclear DNA evidence was generally accepted in the relevant scientific community). A party seeking to introduce evidence based upon new technology must demonstrate by a preponderance of the evidence, under the *Frye* test, that the relevant scientific community has generally accepted the technology. *Id.* at 633. *Porter II* noted that unanimity in the scientific community is not required to show general acceptance. *Id.* at 634. "[The] issue is consensus versus controversy over a particular technique,...." *Id.* (quoting *Jones v. United States*, 548 A.2d 35, 42 (D.C. 1988). *Frye* does not require unanimity. *Porter*, 618 A.2d at 634. The relevant scientific community within which a consensus must exist includes those "whose scientific background and training are sufficient to comprehend and understand the process and form a judgment about it." *Id.* Noting that "the probability of a coincidental match is an essential part of the DNA evidence," *Id.* at 640, *Porter II* holds that the statistical procedures for determining a match must pass muster under Frye. *Id.* at 631. In this regard, the *Porter II* Court required that probability estimates of any match be conservative. *Id.* at 642–643.

a. MtDNA is generally accepted in the scientific community.

Scientists first discovered Mitochondrial DNA in 1964. Since at least the early 1990s, forensic scientists began using it to identify the remains of victims of war, natural catastrophes and accidents.... mtDNA was used by the Human Genome Project and to study human evolutionary history. Notably, mtDNA was helpful in identifying the 9/11 victims at the World Trade Center. The FBI has been using mtDNA in casework since 1996, and since that time mtDNA has been used in thousands of cases.

The FBI started employing the technology in the early 1990s. The Court notes that none of the literature submitted on mtDNA questions the validity of mtDNA itself. MtDNA analysis is used for forensic purposes in regional laboratories in the United States, in approximately 50–100 laboratories within Europe and in other countries around the world. It is evident from a review of the literature, as well as the testimony during the *Frye* hearing, that mtDNA is generally accepted in the scientific community. Dr. Chakraborty ... testified that mtDNA and its underlying techniques are accepted in the scientific community. No one testified that it was not generally accepted in the scientific community. The literature submitted further showed that the science is accepted. Therefore, based on the testimony of the witnesses, affidavits of additional experts, written submission of the parties, and the numerous articles and appendices of the parties, it is clear that mtDNA is generally accepted in the scientific community.

b. The FBI's mtDNA methodology of mtDNA analysis is generally accepted in the scientific community.

The record before the Court, including the testimony of Dr. Fisher, shows that the FBI's methodology and procedures have been validated and in fact have been tested and retested.

...

In the years since mtDNA's emergence, the process has been subject to peer review and there are no published criticisms of the FBI's methodologies sufficient in number or degree of dissension to overcome its reliability. The FBI methodology uses sequence analysis that is generally accepted in the scientific community. The National Research Council, cited with approval in *Porter II* and other cases, approves this methodology for nuclear DNA. The literature suggests the same, reflecting that the use of [m]tDNA sequence analysis for forensic identity testing is robust and "validated".

One expert's testimony in particular, which the Court fully credits, could not be clearer on this point. Dr. Budowle testified that FBI mtDNA practices and protocols are similar to, if not exact, and consistent with all the other mtDNA practices and protocols in other laboratories around the world. According to Dr. Budowle, there is no document or consensus document that has generated concerning [m]tDNA for forensics, as there is for nuclear DNA, but there is no controversy. Dr. Budowle stated that there are other reports on mtDNA applications, but there probably will not be a consensus report because there is no "raging debate" about its application in the scientific arena. Additionally, Dr. Fisher, Dr. Chakraborty and Dr. Melton, all gave credible testimony, consistent with Dr. Budowle, that this science and methodology has scientific acceptance in the particular scientific community. Even one defense expert, Dr. Frederika Kaestle, testified that the underlying methodology and techniques of mtDNA sequencing, amplification, extraction and quantification are all accepted in the scientific community.

In sum, this Court finds, after consideration of the testimony of the witnesses, affidavits of additional experts, written submissions of the parties, and the numerous articles and appendices of the parties, that the methodologies used to conduct mtDNA analysis and the science of mtDNA are generally accepted in the particular scientific community.

... [The court went on to deem the methodology used to calculate the statistical evidence showing the probability of a match generally accepted in the scientific community.]

IV. Other Jurisdictions

Other courts and jurisdictions have found that mitochondrial DNA evidence is admissible. The following states have been noted for their rulings for admissibility based on *Frye* or *Frye*-Plus tests: Florida, *Magaletti v. State,* 847 So.2d 523 (Fla. App. 2003) (upholding, under *Frye,* trial court's admission of mtDNA evidence, finding that the state established the general acceptance of both the science and statistical methodology used in mtDNA analysis); Michigan, *People v. Holtzer,* 660 N.W.2d 405, 411 (Mich. App. 2003) (Southwick, P.J., concurring)(mtDNA testing found to be useful and reliable, and robust and validated, based on the "vast base of experience" of the forensic scientific community); Mississippi, *Adam v. State,* 794 So.2d 1049, 1060–1065 (Miss. Ct. App. 2001) (Frye-Plus test; holding that mtDNA sequence analysis is generally accepted in the scientific community and is reliable); New York, *People v. Ko,* 757 N.Y.S.2d 561, 563 (App. Div. 2003) ("mitochondrial DNA analysis has been found reliable by the relevant scientific community; issues regarding contamination go to the weight to be given such evidence) (citing *People v. Klinger,* 713 N.Y.S.2d 823 (N.Y.Co.Ct 2000)).

...

VI. Conclusion

Based on the motions, relevant case law under the *Frye* standard, and the entire record herein, this Court finds, under the *Frye* standard, that the particular relevant scientific community generally accepts the science of Mitochondrial DNA, the methodology employed by the FBI to analyze it and the SWGDAM database used to calculate probability estimates. The Court also finds the statistical analysis conservative and accepted by the scientific community. Furthermore, the Court finds that there is no reason to reopen the original *Frye* hearing as the defense has failed to provide any new persuasive information, and had ample time and opportunity to present its case during the *Frye* hearing.

State v. Leuluaialii

77 P.3d 1192 (Wash. Ct. App. 2003)

Grosse, J.

The methodology and technique for extracting and identifying deoxyribonucleic acid (DNA) in plants and animals is relatively well established, as is the methodology and technique for determining the probability and extent of a relationship between two samples of human DNA, including matching the DNA of a sample to a specific human being. However, the study of canine DNA has not progressed to the point of the study of human DNA sufficient to permit an expert to testify to a match between a sample and a specific dog. It was error for the trial court to have admitted such testimony, but an error that was harmless in the context of this case. Likewise, the erroneous instruction on accomplice liability was harmless.

...

Facts

In the early morning hours of December 9, 1996, Jay Johnson (Johnson) and Raquel Rivera (Rivera) were shot to death in their home. The victims' dog Chief received gunshot wounds and later died from complications related to the wounds. Johnson's and Rivera's assailants were searching for drugs and money and were members of a gang that included George Leuluaialii (Leuluaialii) and Kenneth Tuilefano (Tuilefano). Leuluaialii was charged and convicted of two counts of aggravated murder in the first degree, and one count of animal cruelty in the first degree. Tuilefano was charged and convicted of two counts of murder in the first degree.

...

The witnesses who observed the events testified that around 8:30 or 8:45 a.m. on the day in question, Leuluaialii, wearing a dark coat, something over his head, and carrying a gun, kicked in the victims' door and began shooting. Leuluaialii first shot the victims' dog Chief. He then entered the residence and more shots were heard being fired inside. There were also sounds of a woman screaming. Tuilefano, also wearing something over his head, followed Leuluaialii inside before any of the other individuals. [Other gang members claimed they entered the residence after this initial activity or not at all]. No one witnessed the shooting of Rivera. Tauiliili testified that when he entered the bedroom, Rivera had already been shot, and Johnson had been shot in the stomach.

Tauiliili stated he saw Leuluaialii holding a gun, kick and hit Johnson with the gun, and then saw Leuluaialii hand the gun to Tuilefano, telling him to "smoke this motherfucker." Niko [another gang member] testified that he saw Tuilefano shoot Johnson twice in the thigh.

Ballistic evidence revealed that Rivera was shot three times: once in the chin, once in the neck, and once in the hand. Autopsy results revealed that Johnson suffered two gunshot wounds to his abdomen and two to his legs. Although the murder weapon was not recovered, the State presented evidence that the bullets recovered from the victims' bodies were fired from the same gun used days earlier in an assault on an individual named Johnny Paik. Paik identified Leuluaialii in a police photo montage and in court as the person who shot at him. Fosi testified that he was with Leuluaialii during the assault, handed Leuluaialii the gun, and saw him shoot at someone matching Paik's description.

[Other gang members] testified that [they] searched the home for drugs and money. Tuilefano and Leuluaialii left the scene in a red Camaro which various witnesses saw parked near the victims' home around the time of the murders....

Both Tuilefano and Leuluaialii claimed that they were not present during the crimes. Although he did not testify in his defense, Tuilefano maintained that he never entered the victims' home and he did not participate in any of the crimes. Leuluaialii testified and denied being anywhere near the victims' home on the day of the murders. Leuluaialii's mother and father testified that on the morning of the murders he was asleep at home on the couch when they left for work, just before 5 a.m. and 8 a.m., respectively. His mother testified that when she called home between 8:45 a.m. and 9 a.m., Leuluaialii answered the phone and he sounded like he was still asleep. Leuluaialii claimed that he did not wake until 1 p.m.

...

To counter the appellants' claims that they were not present during the murder, the State provided the following physical evidence at trial:

- Leuluaialii's left shoe (SPD # 27) had characteristics that would have left the print on the victims' front door and could not be eliminated as a source of the print.
- Several hairs found on Leuluaialii's and Tuilefano's shoes (SPD # 27 and SPD # 34) had characteristics similar to Chief's hair.
- A single hair found on a jacket attributed to Leuluaialii's (SPD # 50) also had characteristics similar to Chief's hair.
- A piece of cloth similar to the hood or mask a witness testified that Leuluaialii wore was recovered at the scene.
- Human blood was found on Tuilefano's pants (SPD # 32) and on the jacket attributed to Tuilefano (SPD # 49).
- Both human blood and dog blood were found on the jacket attributed to Leuluaialii (SPD # 50).

The State also conducted DNA testing of the canine and human DNA evidence on several items of clothing with the assistance of three laboratories: PE Zoogen, a division of PE Applied Biosystems; Forensic Science Associates; and Cellmark Diagnostics (Cellmark). Prior to trial, Tuilefano filed a motion requesting a *Frye* hearing and an ER 702 hearing for the DNA testing done by Cellmark and PE Zoogen. Leuluaialii joined in Tuilefano's motion.

With regard to the canine DNA tested by PE Zoogen, the appellants primarily argued that no standardized testing was available for canine DNA and that a *Frye* hearing was necessary with regard to PE Zoogen's test. The appellants also argued that the polymerase chain reaction (PCR) DNA testing used by Cellmark utilized various loci not yet accepted in the scientific community, and the lab's procedures were unreliable and inadmissible under ER 702. Tuilefano focused on the DQ alpha loci used by Cellmark, but also included the LDLR, GYPA, HBGG, D7S8, and GC loci in his motion for a *Frye* hearing.

PE Zoogen tested three articles of clothing for the State which contained canine blood: two of three black jackets found in the Biltmore Hotel room attributed by the State to Tuilefano and Leuluaialii and Leuluaialii's pants. PE Zoogen used Chief's sample blood and 10 DNA markers in its testing. PE Zoogen's founder, Dr. Joy Halvorson, concluded that for all items tested at least 9 of the 10 markers matched the DNA found in various stains on the items. The two jackets attributed to Tuilefano and Leuluaialii had some stains that matched all 10 markers. Dr. Halvorson testified that with a 9-marker match, the probability of finding another dog with Chief's DNA profile was 1 in 18 billion; with a 10-marker match, the probability was 1 in 3 trillion. PE Zoogen used Chief's sample blood and 10 DNA markers, or loci, in its testing. Seven of the markers were developed by PE Zoogen in its mixed breed database which consisted of approximately 100 dogs, most of which came from a local dog shelter in Los Angeles. The other three were developed by the Fred Hutchinson Cancer Research Center in Seattle, Washington.

...

Tuilefano and Leuluaialii contested the results of both the canine and human DNA tests at trial and presented their own expert witnesses. Prior to closing argument, Tuilefano moved to strike all of the State's DNA evidence. Leuluaialii did not join in the motion. Tuilefano argued that various test results were inadmissible because the testing methods were not scientifically accepted; samples were mislabeled; various results were unreliable; and statistical probabilities were not given with some test results.

The court admitted Cellmark's test results, concluding that its PCR testing, and use of polymarkers, short tandem repeats (STRs), and the DQ alpha loci, were also generally accepted in the scientific community. The trial court ruled that the methodologies used in PE Zoogen's analysis of the canine DNA, utilizing PCR DNA testing of polymarkers on STRs sections of the canine DNA strand, was a method of DNA testing generally accepted in the scientific community. It concluded that a *Frye* hearing was not necessary. The court also found the appellants failed to make a prima facia showing that an ER 702 hearing was necessary for either the human or canine DNA evidence.

Discussion

1. *DNA Evidence.*

There is no dispute in this case with regard to the *Frye* standard or that it requires both accepted theory and a valid technique to implement that theory. There is also no serious dispute in this case but that the testing with regard to human DNA was done by means of accepted theory. The parties' positions diverge with regard to technique. However, as to technique, we believe the arguments about human DNA are better focused by reference to ER 702 and its two-part test: (1) does the witness qualify as an expert, and (2) will the testimony be helpful to the jury. Here, the appellants argue that the testing procedures for human DNA were so flawed as to be unreliable and thus should have been excluded as not helpful. However, a dispute over the validity of particular procedures generally goes to the weight of the evidence, not its admissibility. In short, the issue for the trial court was one of degree and focused on the showing made by the defense to support its request for an ER 702 hearing. On the record, we agree with the trial court that the dispute over human DNA evidence goes to weight not admissibility. While an ER 702 hearing would have been preferable, the defense showing on this point was scant.

But, with respect to the canine DNA evidence, we must differ with the trial court. The trial court ruled that the methodologies used in PCR testing, including the PCR testing used by PE Zoogen which analyzed STRs, were generally accepted in the scientific community and that no *Frye* hearing was needed. The trial court allowed the State's witness to testify that for all articles of clothing tested for canine blood, at least 9 of 10 loci matched Chief's DNA, and 10 loci matched on one article of clothing. The court then admitted the State's testimony that the probability of having the DNA come from another dog other than Chief was "1 in 3 trillion" for a 10 loci match, and "1 in 18 billion" for a 9 loci match.

The evidence here clearly involved novel scientific theory: the forensic identification with high statistical probabilities of a specific dog through analysis of canine DNA. There are no published United States cases that involve the use of canine DNA markers for forensic purposes or examine the validity of the specific markers used here. A *Frye* hearing was absolutely necessary in the present case.

This court reviews the trial court's decision to admit or exclude scientific evidence under *Frye* de novo. The reviewing court may consider other evidence not in the record, including scientific and law review articles and decisions from other jurisdictions, to determine whether (1) the scientific theory has general acceptance in the scientific community; (2) the techniques and experiments that currently exist can produce reliable results and are generally accepted by the scientific community; and (3) the laboratory performed the accepted scientific techniques in this case.

We have examined the record, existing case law on DNA evidence, scientific literature on the canine genome, and the documents submitted at our request by the parties. Based on this information, we are not convinced that forensic canine DNA identification is a theory that has received general acceptance in the scientific community, or that reliable techniques or experiments exist to identify individual canines for forensic purposes.

In *State v. Russell,* the defendant challenged the general acceptance of the PCR technique using a DQ alpha genetic marker system. The trial court heard testimony from experts that over 30 private and government laboratories were either in the process of implementing DQ alpha typing or already using it (including the Federal Bureau of Investigation (FBI)).

Following this testimony, the trial judge found the results of PCR testing at the HLA [human leukocyte antigen system] DQ alpha locus admissible under the *Frye* standard. The judge found that the underlying principle and techniques of PCR had been generally accepted by the scientific community, and added that DQ alpha testing and typing had gone sufficiently beyond the experimental stage to gain general acceptance in the scientific community.... The Supreme Court affirmed the trial court holding that the PCR amplification system for testing DNA at the HLA DQ alpha locus was generally accepted in the relevant scientific community. The PE Zoogen markers are in marked contrast.

In order to satisfy its concerns over the product rule as a means to estimate genetic profile frequencies, the Supreme Court looked to the extensive studies conducted worldwide by the FBI to demonstrate that human data bases are in Hardy-Weinberg and linkage equilibrium. We do not have such information for canines.

Although the general underlying principles of PCR testing of human DNA are accepted by the scientific community, all of the Washington cases that address the admissibility of DNA evidence recognize that human DNA and loci have been subjected to substantial testing and validation by the scientific community. Only a small percentage of the overall number of sites on the human DNA are variable, 0.1 to 0.3 percent of 3 billion, and scientific testing has resulted in the identification of highly variable, polymorphic portions of the DNA called loci or markers.

These loci contain alleles, or alternate forms of a gene at the specific loci. Scientific testing has also determined the relative probability estimates of these polymorphic markers and alleles in humans. Thus, the recurrence of several highly polymorphic markers in a tested human can be estimated with reasonable probabilities under the product rule.

To determine whether identifying a dog through canine DNA with the same forensic accuracy of identifying a human is accepted in theory and practice by the relevant scientific community and thus admissible here, the trial court should have established: (1) what was known about the nature and extent of genetic variation in canines; (2) whether the scientific community generally accepted that the specific loci used by PE Zoogen in the present case were highly polymorphic and appropriate for forensic use; and (3) whether the scientific community generally accepted that PE Zoogan's calculations of a random match were based on accurate probability estimates.

We have determined through our own examination of the record and the publications available in the scientific community that canines have genetic diversity similar to that observed in humans. Further, portions of the canine DNA are highly polymorphic and thus would yield polymorphic loci and alleles that might be appropriate for forensic use.

However, we were not able to conclusively determine whether all of the loci used in this case were polymorphic markers. More importantly, we also were not able to determine whether PE Zoogen's frequency estimates of its loci and alleles were accurate. The defense presented several expert witnesses who vehemently contested the validity of Zoogen's canine DNA markers. PE Zoogen indicated at trial that it would soon publish studies of its loci and their frequency estimates, but we have found no such studies and the State provided none despite a request by this court.

We recognize the State's contention that probability estimates in the trillions for human DNA markers are now accepted in court. Indeed, probability estimates of occurrences of various human DNA profiles may exceed the human population because of the extent of knowledge about human DNA and the frequency of certain polymorphic alleles. However, not as much is known about polymorphic loci in canine DNA and the probability of their occurrence as is known about human polymorphic loci. Current canine DNA testing and mapping focuses on the goals of paternity testing, pure breed testing, and cancer and disease research studies. There is little indication that polymorphic loci and alleles in canine DNA have been sufficiently studied such that probability estimates are appropriate for the forensic use applied in this case.

The lack of published studies on PE Zoogen's canine DNA markers and their probability estimates, and the disagreement of the experts at trial about their accuracy, leaves this court disinclined to accept the statistics given at trial. Further, we note the existence of a case from British Columbia that connected a defendant to a crime scene through the use of PE Zoogen's markers. PE Zoogen claimed, as here, that the markers used were highly polymorphic and estimated a 1-in-3 billion chance existed that the canine DNA tested on the defendant's pants came from any other dog than the dog killed at the crime scene.

Nine of the ten loci identified by PE Zoogen in the DNA of the dog in British Columbia were also found in Chief's DNA in the present case. Six of these loci were developed by PE Zoogen. Chief was a mixed breed dog with the predominant breed being pit bull or one of the bull terrier breeds, and the dog in the British Columbia case was a terrier, yet they had significant genetic similarities in terms of these nine markers. The

British Columbia case referenced in the article makes us question both the polymorphic nature of PE Zoogen's markers and the statistics used to estimate their frequency of occurrence in the canine population.

We are aware that canine DNA STR loci, like human STRs, may contain many separate identifiable alleles. Thus, identification of the same nine loci on two canine DNA samples may not be statistically improbable if the identified alleles within the loci differ. In fact, at least six of the PE Zoogen loci used here have since been characterized as multi-allele sites. Further, at least three of the loci used here are characterized as unlinked. This supports the possible conclusion that these three particular loci may be good candidates for probability estimates and studies. However, the lack of any studies to substantiate the statistical probabilities of PE Zoogen's loci and alleles used here, and thus their accuracy in identifying a specific dog with a "1 in 18 billion," or "1 in 3 trillion" probability, leaves us with little choice but to conclude that a *Frye* hearing was necessary.

In sum, the studies presently available on canine polymorphic loci, or the frequency of their occurrence in the canine population, are insufficient for specific markers to be accurate forensic indicators as they were used in the present case. Because PE Zoogen has not yet published sufficient data to show that its DNA markers and associated probability estimates are reliable, we would suggest that other courts tread lightly in these waters and closely examine canine DNA results before accepting them at trial.

2. *DNA Harmless Error.*

The error in admitting the canine DNA evidence was harmless. It was not an error of constitutional magnitude and we are convinced that the error did not affect the outcome of the trial within reasonable probabilities.

...

Notes & Questions

1. DNA analysis is a significant improvement over other biological identification techniques such as ABO blood and human leukocyte antigen ("HLA") typing. DNA offers far greater specificity and can affirmatively identify an individual, whereas the other techniques may have their greatest utility in ruling out identification. However, reliable DNA testing is dependent upon high levels of technical expertise and state of the art technology. Absent such expertise and technology, test results may be questionable. *See, e.g., United States v. Shea*, 159 F.3d 37 (1st Cir. 1998) (laboratory standards and procedures sufficient to ensure accuracy and reliability of results); *Ex parte Hutcherson*, 677 So. 2d 1205 (Ala. 1996) (admission of DNA evidence without first ascertaining that testing laboratory conformed to generally accepted standards of testing required reversal of conviction). Several sets of guidelines for laboratories have been issued and these guidelines are frequently cited in validating the DNA testing result. The FBI's Technical Working Group of DNA Analysis Methods ("TWGDAM"), mentioned in the *Chase* case has issued such guidelines, as has the Congressional Office of Technology Assessment, the American Association of Blood Banks ("AABB"), the National Academy of Sciences, the New York State Forensic DNA Analysis Panel, and the California Association of Crime Laboratory Directors ("CACLD").

2. Once the DNA from a crime scene is analyzed, be it by RFLP, PCR, or mtDNA methodology, the next question is whether or not it can be matched to the alleged perpetrator. This requires not only demonstrating a match between the two, but also docu-

menting the statistical significance of the match and the likelihood of mere coincidence. One method used is known as the "product rule," in which the frequency of DNA fragment lengths are calculated in relationship to a reference database comprised of individuals from the same racial and ethnic groups; then the individual frequencies of each DNA fragment length are multiplied together in order to calculate the frequency of the suspect's individual DNA fragment length. This procedure is applied across many DNA fragments, each independent of the other to calculate probability matches at numerous allele sites. The reference database is all important and there is ongoing concern that a database too focused on a subpopulation will lead to aberrant results.

To counter this problem, the National Research Council proposed that DNA forensic scientists identify a "ceiling" frequency for each tested allele determined from a reference database drawn from a group of randomly chosen samples in each of the representative populations in the United States. The "ceiling" frequency is the highest found in the subpopulations. This ceiling frequency methodology would have produced a conservative reading for matches that would offer greater certainty. However, the NRC's ceiling frequency approach was not accepted by experts in the field and was, in fact, roundly criticized. The NRC ultimately disbanded, leaving experts and courts to wrestle with establishing the statistical relevance of DNA matches.

As a result, numerous cases have focused on the statistical methods used in establishing the match. For example, in *Andrews v. State*, 533 So. 2d 841, *aff'd* 533 So. 2d 851 (Fla. Dist. Ct. App. 1988), testimony from a forensic scientist opined that there was less than a 1 in 800 million chance that anyone other than the defendant would have the same DNA profile using RFLP. The defense argued that the database used for comparison had only 710 samples. Defense failed to prevail largely because the American Association of Blood Banks had, in its guidelines, noted that a database of as few as 200 samples was enough to yield reliable statistical results. Similarly, in *People v. Brown*, 110 Cal. Rptr. 2d 750 (Ct. App. 2001), the court found that using an African-American database to calculate frequencies in comparison to those of rape defendant PCR determined genotype was adequate and statistically valid. *See generally* Lisa Carrabino, *The Admissibility of DNA Typing and Statistical Probability Evidence*, 29 Suffolk U. L. Rev. 473 (1995); James L. Ward, *The Admissibility of DNA Statistical Evidence Under* State v. Dinkins, 48 S.C. L. Rev. 93 (1996); Samuel Lindsey, et al., *Communicating Statistical DNA Evidence*, 43 Jurimetrics J. 147 (2003).

3. In *State v. Leuluaialii*, the court was faced with DNA from a canine, rather than human source, as evidence in a murder case. The court used the *Frye* standard, somewhat flavored with Rule 702 and determined that canine DNA had not yet reached general acceptance in the scientific community. The court is concerned that canine databases are not sufficiently developed to ensure that the statistical probabilities were accurate. Given the debate with respect to statistical relevance in the human database comparison, does the court's posture seem overly conservative?

2. Genetic Predisposition as a Defense

Although DNA identification in criminal prosecution has been widely used and increasingly accepted by courts, it has had far less utility in the defense context. From the identification standpoint, if a suspect's DNA does not match the critical evidence, it is unlikely that he or she would become a "defendant" in the first place. However, there has been much scholarly pondering over the possibility of a defense based on behavioral genetics. This theory keys off the idea that if genetics predispose an individual to violent, impulsive antisocial acts, then this predisposition should mitigate criminal culpability in much the same way as an insanity defense. This concept of a genetic defense led to a series of early cases based on a chromosomal abnormality.

State v. Roberts

544 P.2d 754 (Wash. Ct. App. 1976)

McInturff, Chief Judge

Anthony Roberts appeals from his conviction of grand larceny and taking and riding in a motor vehicle without the permission of the owner. The primary contentions of Mr. Roberts, who was a parolee, concern: (1) whether a parole officer, upon a phone call initiated by a parolee, must give Miranda warnings prior to listening to statements which are inculpatory; (2) whether statements made by a parolee to a parole officer are confidential and rise to the status of privileged communications; and (3) whether a continuance should be granted to ascertain if the defendant is the subject of a "47 XYY syndrome."

Mr. Roberts was an accessory to the theft of an automobile, camping equipment, and two guns in Moses Lake, Washington. After being persuaded by his girlfriend, he later telephoned his parole officer in Pasco, Washington, from the girlfriend's residence in Seattle. According to the parole officer:

> He indicated that he had done the most stupid thing a man could do on parole. I asked him what he had done and he said that he and a friend had burglarized a camper, taking a .22 rifle and .22 pistol, and that they had subsequently left the camper and had stolen an automobile. Tony went to great pains to explain that his friend, by the name of Wayne, had stolen the automobile, but that he had ridden in it to Seattle, and therefore was an accessory, because he knew the automobile was stolen.... Tony was calling, he said, realizing his parole would be revoked, and that prior to any revocation he simply wanted to set the record straight on what he had or had not done.

This, and other testimony by the parole officer, was admitted at trial after Mr. Roberts' unsuccessful motion to suppress. Mr. Roberts' motion for a continuance to allow additional psychiatric examination was also denied.

[The court found that Mr. Roberts' voluntary statements to his parole officer fell outside the protections of the Fifth Amendment and the rule of *Miranda*.]

47 XYY Syndrome

Defendant further assigns error to the refusal by the trial court to grant his motion for a continuance to allow additional psychiatric examination. It is the argument of defendant's counsel that defendant has characteristics of the "47 XYY syndrome," affecting mental competence. By denying the continuance, it is contended the trial court denied defendant this defense.

The "47 XYY syndrome" is a relatively recent defense theory which alleges mental incompetence due to a chromosome abnormality. The normal woman has a chromosome constellation containing two sex-determining chromosomes (XX), while the normal man has one X and one Y chromosome (XY). In some men, perhaps one in one thousand, a chromosome abnormality exists in which there is an XYY or "super male" constellation theorized to result in greater aggressive and anti-social behavior. There does in fact seem to be an incidence of the XYY defect among institutionalized men. However, the behavioral impact of this chromosome defect has not been precisely determined.

The XYY individual is said to often be extremely tall, with long limbs, facial acne, an aggressive behavior often directed toward property rather than persons, with no significant family history of mental illness or criminal activity. The XYY criminal also tends to be more resistant to conventional corrective training. "But ... presently available medical evidence is unable to establish a reasonably certain causal connection between the XYY defect and criminal conduct."

The granting or denying of a continuance lies within the sound discretion of the trial court and will not be disturbed on appeal, except for manifest abuse of discretion. In the absence of sound medical support of the XYY defense, the trial court did not abuse its discretion in denying defendant's motion for a continuance.

Judgment of the Superior Court is affirmed.

Turpin v. Mobley

502 S.E.2d 458 (Ga. 1998)

Fletcher, Presiding Justice.

Stephen Anthony Mobley was convicted of malice murder, armed robbery and other crimes in 1994 and sentenced to death for the murder.... In 1996, Mobley filed this habeas action, raising several claims, including ineffective assistance of counsel. The habeas court ruled that all of Mobley's claims other than ineffectiveness of trial counsel were either barred or defaulted. The habeas court then vacated Mobley's death sentence because Mobley's trial counsel had been ineffective in the preparation for and conduct of the sentencing phase....

The evidence adduced at trial showed that Mobley stole a .380 pistol from an acquaintance. On February 17, 1991, Mobley robbed a Domino's Pizza restaurant just after midnight. The only person in the restaurant was the manager, John Collins. After taking all the money in the cash register and back office, Mobley shot Collins in the back of the head as he was kneeling and facing away from Mobley. Over the next three weeks, Mobley committed six additional armed robberies of restaurants and dry-cleaning shops. The police arrested him after a high-speed chase as he was fleeing the last armed robbery. Mobley confessed to the armed robberies and the murder of John Collins, and a gun he tossed from his car during the chase, the .380 pistol he had previously stolen, matched the murder weapon.

...

Mobley's [new] claim of ineffective assistance of counsel is neither barred nor defaulted. An ineffective assistance of counsel claim does not need to be raised until trial counsel no longer represents the defendant. The record shows that Mobley's trial counsel represented him through his direct appeals, and his separate habeas counsel raised this claim at the first available post-conviction opportunity. Therefore, ineffective assistance of counsel remains a viable claim.

In order to prevail on a claim of ineffective assistance of counsel, Mobley must show both deficient performance and actual prejudice. To show deficient performance, he must demonstrate that his counsel's performance was not reasonable under the circumstances confronting his counsel at the time, without resorting to hindsight. Mobley's burden is high because his counsel is "strongly presumed to have rendered adequate assistance and made all significant decisions in the exercise of reasonable professional judgment." To show actual prejudice, he must demonstrate that "there is a reasonable probability (i.e., a probability sufficient to undermine confidence in the outcome) that, but for counsel's unprofessional errors, the result of the proceeding would have been different."

In its final order, the habeas court ruled that trial counsel had been ineffective in investigating and presenting mitigating evidence in the sentencing phase. Specifically, the habeas court found that trial counsel failed to uncover significant mitigating evidence regarding Mobley's alleged traumatic upbringing, failed to seek funds for an independent psychologist, failed to accept Mobley's father's funds to conduct a genetic test, and inadequately presented an unorthodox mitigating defense that attempted to show a possible genetic basis for Mobley's conduct. A claim of ineffective assistance of counsel is a mixed question of law and fact. The proper standard of review requires that we accept the habeas court's factual findings and credibility determinations unless clearly erroneous, but we independently apply the legal principles to the facts. We conclude that Mobley's counsel was not ineffective in the sentencing phase because trial counsel's mitigation strategy was reasonable and supported by adequate investigation and because Mobley cannot show actual prejudice.

A. *The investigation.*

Attorneys Dan Summer and Chuck Taylor were appointed to represent Mobley at his trial. Summer assumed the role of lead counsel. Summer is a former assistant district attorney and an experienced criminal defense attorney. At the time, he had served as co-counsel for the state on two capital trials. Summer made repeated attempts to persuade the district attorney to allow a guilty plea in exchange for multiple life sentences, but to no avail.

Having concluded that Mobley would be convicted due to the overwhelming evidence of his guilt, trial counsel focused on the sentencing phase and the development of mitigating evidence. Trial counsel interviewed Mobley's relatives, who told them that Mobley had been a difficult child who had frequent problems with lying, cheating, stealing, vandalizing, setting fires, and being cruel to animals. Trial counsel also subpoenaed all the records from the numerous schools and institutions that Mobley had attended and thoroughly reviewed all the records. The school and treatment records reveal numerous instances of Mobley's misbehavior, such as assaulting other students, using profanity to teachers, lying, stealing, and destroying property, and his resulting expulsions.

During his childhood, Mobley had been treated and evaluated by a number of psychologists and social workers. Trial counsel read all of these psychological records and consulted some of the mental health professionals who had treated Mobley. The psychological reports showed that Mobley had an average IQ and a conduct disorder manifested by a lack of a true values system. He was reported to be manipulative, self-centered and impulsive. Although some psychological reports early in Mobley's childhood suggested that he might have a learning disability or organic brain disorder, later reports found no evidence of either.

Mobley's counsel sought to find what they called "traditional mitigation evidence." They interviewed Mobley's mother, father, and sister, all of whom reported that there was no physical or sexual abuse in Mobley's childhood. Mobley's parents also denied any birth trauma or alcohol abuse. Mobley himself denied that he had ever been physically abused, sexually abused or neglected. Additionally, poverty was not a mitigating issue because Mobley's childhood standard of living had ranged from middle class to affluent. Trial counsel also found that Mobley had only one real friend, who was the owner of the car that he had used to commit the armed robberies (and who had told him that he could use the car to visit his family and look for a job).

The habeas court's final order faults trial counsel for failing to interview Mobley's maternal grandmother, who would have provided information that Mobley's mother had been a perfectionist who sometimes yelled at Mobley when he was a child, and often sent him to his room. The habeas court further notes that trial counsel failed to obtain his birth records, which showed that Mobley may have had some difficulty breathing when he was a newborn. In addition to the grandmother's testimony and the birth records, there was evidence presented that Mobley's parents had used inconsistent parenting styles in trying to deal with their difficult son. Mobley's father had tried spanking him, sometimes with a belt, but had given that up when it did not work. A psychologist testified that Mobley's family had been a "classic family of alcohol," but Mobley's father denied being an alcoholic or having a drinking problem.

The adequacy of a trial attorney's investigation into a defendant's background is judged by a standard of reasonableness. In the present case, Mobley's counsel thoroughly investigated the information reasonably available to them before making their strategy decisions. Trial counsel subpoenaed every available childhood psychological and school record and thoroughly reviewed them. They consulted doctors who had treated Mobley as a child for possible psychological mitigation evidence. They questioned most of the available Mobley family members, including Mobley himself, and all denied the existence of any "traditional mitigation evidence." We conclude that trial counsel's investigation was more than adequate and was reasonable under all the circumstances. In cases where we have held that lawyers failed to conduct an effective investigation, trial counsel either did no investigation or had obvious avenues of investigation available to them that reasonable counsel would have pursued and they did not pursue. The failure of trial counsel to uncover every possible favorable witness does not render their performance deficient. We recognize that post-conviction counsel will almost always be able to identify a potential mitigation witness that trial counsel did not interview or a record that trial counsel did not obtain.

Further, even if the mitigating evidence presented at the habeas evidentiary hearing had been presented at trial, Mobley has not shown actual prejudice. The facts presented at the habeas hearing, considered collectively, show no extenuating circumstances in Mobley's childhood, especially in light of Mobley's early violent behavior. Additionally, the state presented substantial evidence in aggravation, including his prior convictions, lack of remorse, boasting of the crime, contemptuous comments regarding the victim, and sexual assaults of other inmates while awaiting trial. The aggravating evidence presented by the state clearly showed Mobley's proclivity toward violence, future dangerousness, and utter lack of remorse over the murder. We conclude beyond a reasonable doubt that the limited additional mitigation evidence concerning Mobley's childhood presented at the evidentiary hearing would not have changed the outcome of Mobley's trial.

B. *Failure to seek funds for an independent psychologist.*

In its order, the habeas court found that Mobley's counsel were ineffective for failing to seek funds to hire an independent psychologist. The trial court had ordered a mental evaluation of Mobley and the state psychologist reported that Mobley was sharp-witted with above-average intelligence. Mobley had no delusions or hallucinations and was competent to assist in his defense.

The evidence shows that Mobley's counsel had reviewed all the previous psychological reports and had consulted several doctors who had treated Mobley as a child. In addition, trial counsel planned to call a psychologist who had treated Mobley when he was sixteen-years-old to testify on Mobley's behalf in the sentencing phase. Trial counsel considered hiring an expert psychologist but decided against it because the previous psychological reports from Mobley's childhood were not favorable to the mitigation case and any future tests were therefore unlikely to be favorable. Thus, the decision not to pursue an additional psychological examination was a reasonable strategic decision. Although other attorneys might have explored the mental issue further, we cannot conclude that trial counsel's psychological investigation and tactical judgment were outside the wide range of reasonably effective assistance.

C. *Failure to accept Mobley's father's funds for a genetic test.*

While searching for a reason to explain Mobley's behavior, Summer read an article about a researcher in the Netherlands who had studied a possible genetic basis for violent behavior. The study tracked several generations of a family that had a number of members with histories of violent and antisocial behavior, and the researcher discovered a possible link between this behavior and a point mutation in a structural gene for monoamine oxidase. According to the article, this study was the first time researchers had discovered a genetic disturbance directly related to violent or antisocial behavior.

Summer investigated the use of this genetic link to violence as a possible mitigation defense. He contacted a professor of genetics at Harvard Medical School and reviewed the case with her. She informed Summer that he needed to conduct a Mobley family history to determine if there was a prevalence of violent behavior that might suggest a genetic predisposition. Summer then spoke with Joyce Ann Elders, Mobley's father's cousin, who was considered the family historian. She revealed to Summer that a number of people in the last three generations of the Mobley family had exhibited aggressive and antisocial behavior. These people included a murderer, a rapist, an armed robber, several substance abusers, and several spouse abusers.

Summer then contacted the National Psycho Pharmacology Lab and a doctor at the Emory Nuclear Medicine Laboratory about the cost of preliminary testing to determine if Mobley had the same gene mutation as the people in the Netherlands study. Summer filed a "Motion for Continuance and Motion to Provide Funds for Expert Witness Assistance to Conduct Preliminary Analysis for MAOA Deficiency and other Genetic Analysis as Information Becomes Available" and supported the motion with his research, affidavits from doctors, and testimony from the family historian. After a hearing, the trial court denied Mobley funds to hire a geneticist and funds to conduct the genetic testing because the Netherlands family had a prevalence of mental retardation and Mobley's family did not. Mobley's father offered to pay for the genetic testing himself, but Summer declined. The habeas court has ruled that trial counsel was ineffective for failing to accept Mobley's father's offer to pay for the genetic test.

The evidence shows that trial counsel decided against going forward with the genetic test because (1) they believed that there was only a slim chance that the genetic test would reveal that Mobley had the same genetic defect as the people in the Netherlands study, (2) they intended to present a genetic defense without the geneticist, by using the family historian, and (3) they believed that the trial court's denial of funds might constitute reversible error and they wanted to preserve the issue for appeal. The first two reasons for declining the father's offer were reasonable conclusions. Trial counsel's desire to "preserve" the issue for appeal, however, was not a reasonable basis for the decision. We do not condone trial counsel foregoing a vigorous defense in the hope that a ruling might constitute error on appeal. If Mobley had prevailed on this issue on appeal, the reversal of the trial court would only result in a new trial in which counsel would have the assistance of a genetics expert, which is the same relief Mobley's father offered in the beginning.

Nevertheless, we conclude that the decision regarding the genetic test was a reasonable strategic decision and therefore did not constitute ineffectiveness by trial counsel. The presence of one flawed reason does not render counsel's otherwise reasonable strategic decision deficient performance. Additionally, Mobley was able to present the genetics theory and there has been no showing that a geneticist would have offered additional significant evidence. Therefore, even if the decision constituted deficient performance, Mobley has not demonstrated prejudice.

D. *The mitigation defense.*

The habeas court ruled that trial counsel presented an inadequate mitigation defense. Specifically, the habeas court found that, after being denied the funds for a geneticist, Mobley's counsel nonetheless persisted with presenting an unconventional genetic theory for Mobley's behavior, without the assistance of an expert witness. We disagree because this ruling fails to take into account the fact that the genetic defense was only one part of trial counsel's overall mitigation strategy.

Mobley's counsel's strategy in the penalty phase centered around the following theme: Mobley has a personality disorder that has affected his behavior since he was a child, this behavior may be the result of a genetic problem that he cannot control, the jury should show him mercy because people with personality disorders tend to "mellow out" as they age, and Mobley has accepted responsibility for his crimes by cooperating with the police and offering to plead guilty. Trial counsel adequately prepared the witnesses for their testimony and called Mobley's father as the first mitigation witness. He testified about Mobley's childhood problems and all the schools and juvenile institutions that Mobley had attended. He stated that a doctor had told him that his son would "mellow out" by age 40, and he also pleaded with the jury to spare his son's life. The next witness was Dr. J. Steven Ziegler, who had evaluated Mobley when he was almost seventeen years old. Dr. Ziegler testified that Mobley had a conduct disorder that would develop into a personality disorder and that a person who has this disorder displays antisocial personality characteristics. Dr. Ziegler further testified that people with conduct or personality disorders tend to display fewer problems as they age, and that there were some experimental drugs that had shown promise in treating people like Mobley. Next, Summer himself testified that Mobley had been willing to accept responsibility for his actions by pleading guilty and accepting the maximum years for each crime. The following witness was another lawyer, who testified that it would have been unprofessional for Summer to plead Mobley guilty without some type of assurance that death would not be imposed. Lastly, Joyce Ann Childers testified about the prevalence of people with criminal or behavioral problems in the last three Mobley family generations. She also testified that these people had tended to exhibit fewer aggressive tendencies ("mellow out") as they reached middle age. In his closing argument, Summer argued that Mobley's personality disorder had a genetic basis, that the jury should not sentence him to death for a disorder that may lessen with age, and that medical technology may be able to treat in the future.

The appropriate test for determining whether trial counsel was constitutionally effective is " 'whether some reasonable lawyer at the trial could have acted, in the circumstances, as defense counsel acted at trial.'" The purpose of an analysis of a defendant's Sixth Amendment right to effective counsel is not to grade trial counsel's performance, but is simply to ensure that the adversarial process at trial worked adequately. For this reason, we must be "highly deferential to those choices made by defense counsel in the conduct of a trial that are arguably dictated by a reasonable trial strategy."

Although the habeas court focused on trial counsel's genetic theory, it was only a part of the overall mitigation strategy. Further, a novel defense or mitigation theory is not unreasonable simply because it is unorthodox. We also do not believe that it was unreasonable for trial counsel to proceed with the introduction of the genetic theory without a geneticist, by using only the family historian. The simple argument that characteristics or traits, including violent behavior, may be passed from one family generation to another is not so technical that a layperson could not grasp it without the assistance of an expert. Therefore, we conclude that Mobley's counsel adopted a mitigation strategy that was not unreasonable under the circumstances.

Since the evidence at the habeas hearing does not support Mobley's burden, we reverse and reinstate the death sentence.

Von Dohlen v. State

602 S.E.2d 738 (S.C. 2004)

Justice Burnett:

We granted the petition for a writ of certiorari from Herman Henry "Bud" Von Dohlen (Petitioner) to consider whether the post-conviction relief (PCR) judge erred in denying Petitioner's request for a new sentencing proceeding. We reverse and grant Petitioner a new sentencing proceeding.

Factual and Procedural History

Petitioner, then age 35, averred in a signed confession to law enforcement investigators that he walked from the Berkeley County pawnshop he managed to a nearby dry cleaning shop to ask for change the morning of May 28, 1990. He stated shop employee Margaret McLean (Victim) refused to give him change and told him his brother, who recently had been murdered, deserved to die.

Petitioner returned to the pawnshop, loaded a rifle, and walked back to the shop. He stated he intended only to scare Victim for her alleged cruel and thoughtless comments. He forced Victim to disrobe to make the crime appear to be a rape. He stated the rifle discharged accidentally when Victim ran and caused a bar bolting the back door to strike Victim and the gun. Petitioner then shot Victim in the back of the head and decided to steal money from the store in order to make it appear to be a robbery.

The jury convicted Petitioner of murder and armed robbery, and recommended a sentence of death based on the aggravating circumstance of armed robbery. *See* S.C.Code Ann. §§ 16-3-20(A) and 16-3-20(C)(a)(1)(d) (Supp.1991). The trial judge sentenced Petitioner to death for murder on the jury's recommendation and twenty-five years for armed robbery. The convictions and sentences were affirmed on direct appeal. *State v. Von Dohlen,* 471 S.E.2d 689 (1996).

Petitioner filed a PCR application in 1997 and later amended it. The PCR judge denied the application after a hearing in 1999. We granted a writ of certiorari to consider two questions raised by Petitioner:

I. Does any evidence of probative value support the PCR judge's ruling that Petitioner's trial attorneys were not ineffective in failing to adequately prepare and present evidence during the penalty phase of the trial that Petitioner suffered from a major mental illness at the time of the murder?

II. Does any evidence of probative value support the PCR judge's ruling that Petitioner's trial attorneys were not ineffective in failing to object to the prosecutor's closing argument during the penalty phase of the trial that jurors should put themselves in Victim's shoes?

...

I. Expert Testimony about Petitioner's Major Mental Illness

During the penalty phase of the trial, witnesses testified Petitioner had been a good husband, married for seventeen years; a good father, with four children ages two through fourteen; and a dependable, likeable employee of grocery stores and pawnshops. Petitioner grew up in a very poor family and had been physically abused and emotionally neglected as a child. He had no prior criminal record. The violent murder was completely unexpected and out of character for a man who had never displayed violent tendencies.

Witnesses testified Petitioner's personality and demeanor underwent a dramatic change when—about two weeks before Victim's murder—Petitioner's brother was murdered by the brother's father-in-law. Petitioner became withdrawn, irritable, and depressed. He began abusing alcohol and Valium, an anti-anxiety medication.

At trial during the penalty phase, Dr. Michael Lampkin, a psychiatrist, testified Petitioner at the time of the murder suffered from "adjustment reaction with mixed features of emotions and conduct," as well as pathological intoxication from the abuse of alcohol and Valium. Adjustment reaction is a disorder in which a person's expression of grief exceeds what is normally expected. It is generally easily treatable and lasts no longer than three months. On cross-examination, Lampkin testified Petitioner did not have a chronic mental illness and did not dispute the solicitor's assertion that adjustment reaction disorder was "pretty small potatoes" in the spectrum of mental illnesses.

In the penalty phase closing arguments, the solicitor argued Petitioner did not suffer from any mental or emotional disturbance and that the murder was committed in "cold premeditation." The solicitor contended, "His brother Bill dying, a less than perfect childhood, vagaries, ups and downs of life that we all suffer. His own witness, Dr. Lampkin, said adjustment reaction as he called it, the stress. Divorce could bring it on, business problems can bring it on. These are things every person goes through. He could provide not one bit of excuse."

At the PCR hearing, Lampkin testified that if he had been provided with additional medical and psychiatric records that existed and were available before the trial, he would have diagnosed Petitioner as suffering at the time of the murder from "major depressive episodes with severe symptoms of anxiety and possible prepsychotic features," plus alcohol and Valium abuse.

Dr. Lampkin identified six items that changed his opinion: (1) the MMPI test administered to Petitioner in 1990 while at the William S. Hall Psychiatric Institute, a state hospital; (2) Petitioner's complete medical record from his four months at the Hall Institute, including nurses' notes with numerous references to Petitioner's depressed state, impaired memory, isolation, and hopelessness; (3) the medical records of Petitioner's father indicating he suffered from chronic depression and thus providing a genetic basis for Petitioner's chronic depression; (4) the medical records of Petitioner's brother, John, who attempted suicide shortly before Petitioner's trial, providing additional proof of a genetic predisposition for mental disorders; (5) an MCMI test administered to Petitioner in 1990 by Dr. Harold Morgan at the Hall Institute, revealing elevated scores for anxiety, depression, and delusional disorders; and (6) Petitioner's records prepared in 1990 by Dr. Don Hinnant, a psychologist, which revealed symptoms of major depression. All the records were potentially available to Petitioner's attorneys and expert witnesses before his trial in 1991.

Louisa Storen, a social worker who testified at trial about Petitioner's background and family, testified at the PCR hearing she asked Lampkin to review Petitioner's case shortly before trial to ensure she had not overlooked important issues. Storen provided a mostly oral summary of Petitioner's medical records and background to Lampkin. Storen did not expect Lampkin to testify at trial and, in a meeting lasting no more than thirty minutes, "what I remember was talking very fast, telegraphically trying to give him a bunch of information in a short period of time before he saw [Petitioner]."

At the PCR hearing, Dr. John DeWitt, a forensic psychiatrist, testified he treated Petitioner for 3 1/2 years beginning in August 1991, examining Petitioner fifty-two times. Petitioner suffered from a major mental illness at the time of Victim's murder—severe depression with psychotic and suicidal tendencies. Petitioner's mental condition in May 1990 was far more serious than the usually short-lived adjustment reaction disorder with which he was diagnosed.

Further, DeWitt testified Petitioner's severe depression was a condition to which he was predisposed by a family history of mental illness and alcohol or drug abuse, as well as a physically abusive childhood. The condition likely began in earnest when Petitioner was diagnosed with cancer in the 1980s. It was exacerbated by the suicide of his father in 1981, the murder of his brother two weeks before Victim's murder, and Petitioner's attempts at self-medication with alcohol and Valium. Severe depression can cause unpredictable, irrational, and chaotic behavior in people who never have exhibited such behavior, with personality and lifestyle changes so drastic it is "almost as if they had a brain transplant." Petitioner suffered a mental or emotional disturbance at the time of Victim's murder, and due to his altered mental state "[the murder] was not a volitional thing but out of his conscious awareness or control."

Petitioner contends his trial attorneys were ineffective in failing to adequately prepare and present evidence in the penalty phase of the trial that he suffered from severe, chronic depression, a major mental illness, at the time of the murder. The attorneys failed to provide to Lampkin medical records and relevant information that existed before trial. If they had done so, Lampkin would have reached the proper diagnosis and been able to correctly explain to jurors Petitioner's mental state and inability to control his actions on the date of the murder. There is a reasonable probability this information could prompt the jury to recommend a sentence of life in prison rather than death....

Petitioner has demonstrated his attorneys erred in failing to adequately investigate and prepare expert testimony about his mental condition as it existed at the time of the murder. While the attorneys exerted some effort, according to the testimony of Lampkin and DeWitt at the PCR hearing, it was insufficient. The absence of crucial medical records and related information which existed at the time of Petitioner's trial prevented Lampkin from conveying an accurate diagnosis and explanation of Petitioner's mental condition to the sentencing jury.

Furthermore, Petitioner has shown prejudice. There is a reasonable probability the outcome of the trial might have been different had the jury heard the available information about Petitioner's mental condition as it existed at the time of the murder. The PCR judge's decision is not supported by evidence of probative value.

[The court found that Von Dohlen's trial attorneys were sufficiently effective despite their decision to not object to certain aspects of the prosecutor's closing argument.]

Notes & Questions

1. The XYY chromosomal abnormality was first offered as a defense in a murder trial in France in 1968. The defendant, Daniel Hugon, alleged that his XYY karyotype produced uncontrollable violent behavior that induced him to commit the crime. This defense was ultimately unsuccessful and Hugon was convicted, although he received a sentence of only seven years. Later that same year, Richard Speck, who had brutally killed eight nurses in Chicago, was posited to have an XYY chromosomal makeup. Ultimately this would prove to be untrue. However, the Speck case was followed by a case in Australia, where a defendant allegedly was acquitted on the basis of his insanity and XYY chromosomal makeup. The acquittal was largely due to the former, and the latter was merely an incidental finding, but the concept of a "genetic defense" had been born. *See* Susan Horan, *The XYY Supermale and the Criminal Justice System: A Square Peg in a Round Hole*, 25 Loy. L.A. L. Rev. 1343 (1992). Several cases in the early 1970s alleged this defense, albeit with little success. *See People v. Tanner*, 91 Cal. Rptr. 656 (Ct. App. 1970) (finding the scientific support justifying XYY defense rudimentary and inconclusive). In the years following the spate of interest in the XYY defense, scientific evidence began to accumulate showing that XYY was not a definitive source of violent, aggressive or criminal behavior. *See* S. Borganonkar & S.A. Shah, *The XYY Chromosome Male—Or Syndrome*, 10 Prog. Med. Genet. 195 (1974). By 1976, when *State v. Roberts* was decided, the defense of the XYY chromosomal abnormality was waning in popularity.

2. Both *Turpin v. Mobley* and *Von Dohlen v. State* involve convicted murderers who seek to overturn their death sentences on the ground that ineffective counsel failed to investigate and introduce evidence of genetic predisposition to violence. These and other cases have postulated that because the convicted individual had a long history of violent, antisocial behavior, it must have been an inborn genetic predisposition. With growing knowledge of the genome, there is increased interest in such alleged predispositions. For example, the Human Genome Project maintains a website devoted to behavioral genetics. *See* Human Genome Project Information, Behavioral Genetics, http://www.ornl.gov/sci/techresources/Human_Genome/elsi/behavior.shtml. This website will direct you to a wealth of information on this topic. Notably, the linked Online Mendelian Inheritance in Man (OMIM) database contains biographic references and summaries of several genetically mediated traits including: relative hand skill (handedness); hand clasping pattern; arm folding preference; ability to move ears; tongue curling, folding, or rolling; musical perfect pitch; novelty seeking personality trait; stuttering; tobacco addiction; alcoholism; and homosexuality. In virtually all of these traits, although there are genetic factors, the precise gene-gene and gene-environment interactions are not yet identified and understood. Nevertheless, the idea of a "violence" or "risk-taking" gene continues to capture the attention—and imagination—of the popular media and the lay public.

Most scholars reviewing the evidence for a genetic propensity for violence and/or impulsive behavior have concluded that the science is not sufficiently developed to definitively determine the role of genetics. *See generally* Joseph E. Alper, *Biological Influences on Criminal Behavior: How Good is the Evidence?*, 310 BRITISH MED. J. 272 (1995); Charles C. Mann, *Behavioral Genetics in Transition*, 264 SCIENCE 1686 (1994). *But see* Amanda R. Evansburg, *"But Your Honor, It's in His Genes" The Case for Genetic Impairments as Grounds for a Downward Departure under the Federal Sentencing Guidelines*, 38 AM. CRIM. L. REV. 1565 (2001) (arguing that genetic predispositions, even if believed to be multifactorial in nature, should be grounds for a reduction in severity of sentence).

3. DNA, Wrongful Conviction, and Exoneration

DNA analysis ushered in a new era of post-conviction review. Prior to the use of DNA, innocent persons convicted of crimes were often unable to even begin to reopen their cases. With advances in DNA analysis, evidence—even old evidence—can be reexamined and analyzed at a level unimagined in past decades. In 1992, the pioneering "Innocence Project" was founded by Barry C. Scheck and Peter J. Neufield in New York. Its mission, and that of the numerous "Innocence Projects" since established, is to exonerate those wrongfully convicted using DNA testing. One such wrongfully convicted defendant was Larry Youngblood.

Arizona v. Youngblood

488 U.S. 51 (1988)

CHIEF JUSTICE REHNQUIST delivered the opinion of the Court.

Respondent Larry Youngblood was convicted by a Pima County, Arizona, jury of child molestation, sexual assault, and kidnaping [sic]. The Arizona Court of Appeals reversed his conviction on the ground that the State had failed to preserve semen samples from the victim's body and clothing. 734 P.2d 592 ([Ariz.] 1986). We granted certiorari to consider the extent to which the Due Process Clause of the Fourteenth Amendment requires the State to preserve evidentiary material that might be useful to a criminal defendant.

On October 29, 1983, David L., a 10-year-old boy, attended a church service with his mother. After he left the service at about 9:30 p.m., the boy went to a carnival behind the church, where he was abducted by a middle-aged man of medium height and weight. The assailant drove the boy to a secluded area near a ravine and molested him. He then took the boy to an unidentified, sparsely furnished house where he sodomized the boy four times. Afterwards, the assailant tied the boy up while he went outside to start his car. Once the assailant started the car, albeit with some difficulty, he returned to the house and again sodomized the boy. The assailant then sent the boy to the bathroom to wash up before he returned him to the carnival. He threatened to kill the boy if he told anyone about the attack. The entire ordeal lasted about 1 1/2 hours.

After the boy made his way home, his mother took him to Kino Hospital. At the hospital, a physician treated the boy for rectal injuries. The physician also used a "sexual assault kit" to collect evidence of the attack. The Tucson Police Department provided such kits to all hospitals in Pima County for use in sexual assault cases. Under standard procedure, the victim of a sexual assault was taken to a hospital, where a physician used the kit to collect evidence. The kit included paper to collect saliva samples, a tube for obtaining a blood sample, microscopic slides for making smears, a set of Q-Tip-like swabs, and a medical examination report. Here, the physician used the swab to collect samples from the boy's rectum and mouth. He then made a microscopic slide of the samples. The doctor also obtained samples of the boy's saliva, blood, and hair. The physician did not examine the samples at any time. The police placed the kit in a secure refrigerator at the police station. At the hospital, the police also collected the boy's underwear and T-shirt. This clothing was not refrigerated or frozen.

Nine days after the attack, on November 7, 1983, the police asked the boy to pick out his assailant from a photographic lineup. The boy identified respondent as the assailant. Respondent was not located by the police until four weeks later; he was arrested on December 9, 1983.

On November 8, 1983, Edward Heller, a police criminologist, examined the sexual assault kit. He testified that he followed standard department procedure, which was to examine the slides and determine whether sexual contact had occurred. After he determined that such contact had occurred, the criminologist did not perform any other tests, although he placed the assault kit back in the refrigerator. He testified that tests to identify blood group substances were not routinely conducted during the initial examination of an assault kit and in only about half of all cases in any event. He did not test the clothing at this time.

Respondent was indicted on charges of child molestation, sexual assault, and kidnaping [sic]. The State moved to compel respondent to provide blood and saliva samples for comparison with the material gathered through the use of the sexual assault kit, but the trial court denied the motion on the ground that the State had not obtained a sufficiently large semen sample to make a valid comparison. The prosecutor then asked the State's criminologist to perform an ABO blood group test on the rectal swab sample in an attempt to ascertain the blood type of the boy's assailant. This test failed to detect any blood group substances in the sample.

In January 1985, the police criminologist examined the boy's clothing for the first time. He found one semen stain on the boy's underwear and another on the rear of his T-shirt. The criminologist tried to obtain blood group substances from both stains using the ABO technique, but was unsuccessful. He also performed a P-30 protein molecule test on the stains, which indicated that only a small quantity of semen was present on the clothing; it was inconclusive as to the assailant's identity. The Tucson Police Department had just begun using this test, which was then used in slightly more than half of the crime laboratories in the country.

Respondent's principal defense at trial was that the boy had erred in identifying him as the perpetrator of the crime. In this connection, both a criminologist for the State and an expert witness for respondent testified as to what might have been shown by tests performed on the samples shortly after they were gathered, or by later tests performed on the samples from the boy's clothing had the clothing been properly refrigerated. The court instructed the jury that if they found the State had destroyed or lost evidence, they might "infer that the true fact is against the State's interest."

The jury found respondent guilty as charged, but the Arizona Court of Appeals reversed the judgment of conviction. It stated that "'when identity is an issue at trial and the police permit the destruction of evidence that could eliminate the defendant as the perpetrator, such loss is material to the defense and is a denial of due process.'" The Court of Appeals concluded on the basis of the expert testimony at trial that timely performance of tests with properly preserved semen samples could have produced results that might have completely exonerated respondent. The Court of Appeals reached this conclusion even though it did "not imply any bad faith on the part of the State." The Supreme Court of Arizona denied the State's petition for review, and we granted certiorari. 485 U.S. 903 (1988). We now reverse.

...

Our decisions in related areas have stressed the importance for constitutional purposes of good or bad faith on the part of the Government when the claim is based on loss of evidence attributable to the Government. In *United States v. Marion,* 404 U.S. 307 (1971), we said that "[n]o actual prejudice to the conduct of the defense is alleged or proved, and there is no showing that the Government intentionally delayed to gain some tactical advantage over appellees or to harass them." *Id.,* at 325; see also *United States v. Lovasco,* 431 U.S. 783, 790 (1977). Similarly, in *United States v. Valenzuela-Bernal, supra,* we considered whether the Government's deportation of two witnesses who were illegal aliens violated due process. We held that the prompt deportation of the witnesses was justified "upon the Executive's good-faith determination that they possess no evidence favorable to the defendant in a criminal prosecution." *Id.,* 458 U.S., at 872.

The Due Process Clause of the Fourteenth Amendment, as interpreted in *Brady,* makes the good or bad faith of the State irrelevant when the State fails to disclose to the defendant material exculpatory evidence. But we think the Due Process Clause requires a different result when we deal with the failure of the State to preserve evidentiary material of which no more can be said than that it could have been subjected to tests, the results of which might have exonerated the defendant. Part of the reason for the difference in treatment is found in the observation made by the Court in *Trombetta, supra,* 467 U.S., at 486, that "[w]henever potentially exculpatory evidence is permanently lost, courts face the treacherous task of divining the import of materials whose contents are unknown and, very often, disputed." Part of it stems from our unwillingness to read the "fundamental fairness" requirement of the Due Process Clause, see *Lisenba v. California,* 314 U.S. 219, 236 (1941), as imposing on the police an undifferentiated and absolute duty to retain and to preserve all material that might be of conceivable evidentiary significance in a particular prosecution. We think that requiring a defendant to show bad faith on the part of the police both limits the extent of the police's obligation to preserve evidence to reasonable bounds and confines it to that class of cases where the interests of justice most clearly require it, *i.e.,* those cases in which the police themselves by their conduct indicate that the evidence could form a basis for exonerating the defendant. We therefore hold that unless a criminal defendant can show bad faith on the part of the police, failure to preserve potentially useful evidence does not constitute a denial of due process of law.

In this case, the police collected the rectal swab and clothing on the night of the crime; respondent was not taken into custody until six weeks later. The failure of the police to refrigerate the clothing and to perform tests on the semen samples can at worst be described as negligent. None of this information was concealed from respondent at trial, and the evidence—such as it was—was made available to respondent's expert who declined to perform any tests on the samples. The Arizona Court of Appeals noted in its opinion—and we agree—that there was no suggestion of bad faith on the part of the police. It follows, therefore, from what we have said, that there was no violation of the Due Process Clause.

The Arizona Court of Appeals also referred somewhat obliquely to the State's "inability to quantitatively test" certain semen samples with the newer P-30 test. 734 P.2d, at

596. If the court meant by this statement that the Due Process Clause is violated when the police fail to use a particular investigatory tool, we strongly disagree. The situation here is no different than a prosecution for drunken driving that rests on police observation alone; the defendant is free to argue to the finder of fact that a breathalyzer test might have been exculpatory, but the police do not have a constitutional duty to perform any particular tests.

The judgment of the Arizona Court of Appeals is reversed, and the case is remanded for further proceedings not inconsistent with this opinion.

* * *

This 1988 Supreme Court case resulted in the reincarceration of Larry Youngblood. His conviction in 1985 was largely on the basis of eyewitness identification. The victim described the perpetrator as an African-American man with a disfigured eye. Youngblood fit this description. Although biological specimens had been collected from the victim, they had not been properly stored and had degraded too much to be used in the initial trial. This provided grounds for appeal on the ground that this biological evidence might have been exculpatory and because the police had failed to store it properly, Youngblood's rights to full due process had been abridged. Youngblood was released in 1988, only to be returned to prison after this Supreme Court determination.

In 2000, Youngblood's attorneys were successful in getting the original degraded specimens tested using improved DNA analysis that had not been available at the time of his conviction or the reinstatement of his conviction as a result of this Supreme Court case. The DNA test results exonerated Youngblood and he was released from prison in 2000. The DNA results did produce a match when fed into national criminal databases. This led to Walter Cruise, who was in prison in Texas for an unrelated crime. Cruise, an African-American blind in one eye, was ultimately convicted for the sexual assault of David L. and sentenced to twenty-four years in prison.

People v. Johnson

793 N.E.2d 591 (Ill. 2002)

Justice Fitzgerald delivered the opinion of the court:

...

On July 16, 1983, Patricia Payne and her boyfriend, Anthony Hackett, drove from their hometown of Emden, Illinois, and spent the day at Great America Amusement Park in Gurnee, Illinois. That day, Hackett bought a stuffed doll depicting the popular Tasmanian Devil character; he placed the receipt for the doll in his wallet. Around 10 p.m., Payne and Hackett left the park and, on the way home, they stopped Hackett's car along Interstate 55 in Will County to sleep. Hackett slept in the front seat; Payne slept in the back.

Around 1:30 a.m. on July 17, Payne awoke to tapping on the passenger-side window followed by gunshots which struck and killed Hackett. The assailant opened the passenger-side door and ordered Payne to give him Hackett's wallet and her purse. He then ordered Payne to crawl from the car and into a pickup truck parked nearby. The assailant climbed into the truck and drove down the interstate. While driving, the assailant sexually assaulted Payne; after exiting the interstate and stopping the truck, he raped her. The assailant again started to drive, but pulled the truck onto the shoulder of the road 10 minutes later. The assailant then stabbed Payne in the chest and dumped her from the truck. Payne was found on the grassy median an hour later at 5:30 a.m. by a passing motorist. She had no pulse or blood pressure, and she was rushed to a Joliet hospital, where doctors performed emergency surgery. Payne survived.

Later that morning, Special Agent John Meduga of the Illinois Department of Law Enforcement (now known as the Illinois State Police) spoke with Payne. Payne indicated to Meduga that her assailant was an African American man with no observable facial hair. Eight days later, Payne looked through approximately 1,500 mugshots and selected 42 photographs of persons with facial characteristics similar to her assailant, 34 of whom had facial hair. The record does not reveal whether the defendant's photograph was chosen by Payne. More than a month later, Payne looked through 137 mugshots, including one of the defendant, and selected four photographs of persons with facial hair and facial characteristics similar to her assailant. Payne did not choose the defendant's photograph.

The police investigation into these crimes stalled until Ann Shoemaker telephoned the Will County sheriff's office in February 1984. Shoemaker described an incident in which a dark pickup truck had passed her several times while she was driving one night in July 1983. She and a friend followed the truck and recorded its license plate number. On March 6, 1984, she gave this number to the police, who traced it to a truck owned by Sam Myers, the defendant's stepfather. After Myers signed a consent form, the police searched the truck and found Caucasian head hairs similar to Payne's hair, bloodstains, a steak knife, reddish brown fibers, and a sales receipt for a Tasmanian Devil stuffed doll. Based on these items, the police obtained a search warrant for Myers' residence, where the defendant lived. The police seized three .357 Magnum cartridges from a dresser in Myers' bedroom.

Also on March 6, 1984, Payne looked at five mugshots. The defendant's photograph was the only one among the five which Payne had seen on September 6, 1983. After several minutes, Payne tentatively identified the defendant as her assailant. On March 9, Payne viewed a six-person lineup. After each person in the lineup repeated commands that the assailant had given Payne on the night of her ordeal, Payne unmistakably identified the defendant as her assailant.

Initially, the Will County public defender was appointed to represent the defendant. On June 1, 1984, the day before the scheduled trial date, William Swano entered his appearance as the defendant's retained attorney. The trial court granted Swano three continuances, totaling 55 days, and set the trial date for July 26, 1984. The defendant moved for a change of venue, citing negative pretrial publicity in Will County, and the trial court transferred the case to Iroquois County. Following a jury trial, the defendant was convicted of the first degree murder of Hackett, as well as the aggravated kidnapping, deviate sexual assault, rape, and attempted murder of Payne. The defendant waived his right to a sentencing jury, and the trial court found the defendant eligible for the death penalty. The trial court further found no mitigating circumstances sufficient to preclude the death penalty and sentenced the defendant to death for Hackett's murder and to concurrent terms of 40 years' imprisonment for deviate sexual assault, rape, and attempted murder. On direct appeal, this court affirmed the defendant's convictions and sentences. See *People v. Johnson,* 499 N.E.2d 1355 ([Ill.] 1986).

The defendant then filed a *pro se* post-conviction petition in the Will County circuit court, alleging that he received ineffective assistance of counsel on direct appeal and in post-conviction proceedings. The trial court granted the State's motion to dismiss the petition. On appeal, we affirmed in part, reversed in part, and remanded. We held that the trial court properly dismissed the defendant's claim of ineffective assistance of appellate counsel, but that the trial court improperly dismissed the defendant's claim relating to his post-conviction attorney's performance. See *People v. Johnson,* 609 N.E.2d 304 ([Ill.] 1993).

On remand, the defendant filed a nine-count first amended post-conviction petition, which is the subject of this appeal. The State filed a motion to dismiss, and, in a written order, the trial court dismissed the defendant's amended petition without an evidentiary hearing. This appeal followed.

Analysis

[The defendant raised seven issues in this appeal. The first was whether his pending execution is unconstitutional because the State possessed forensic evidence which would help establish his innocence through DNA testing; other issues dealt with procedural issues and the adequacy of representation from his public defender.]

The Illinois Post-Conviction Hearing Act provides a procedural mechanism through which a criminal defendant can assert "that in the proceedings which resulted in his or her conviction there was a substantial denial of his or her rights under the Constitution of the United States or of the State of Illinois or both." 725 ILCS 5/122-1 (West 1998); see *People v. Coleman,* 701 N.E.2d 1063[, 1070] ([Ill.] 1998). In a post-conviction proceeding, the trial court does not redetermine a defendant's innocence or guilt, but instead examines constitutional issues which escaped earlier review. See *People v. Evans,* 708 N.E.2d 1158[, 1161] ([Ill.] 1999). A post-conviction petition is a collateral attack upon a prior conviction and sentence, not a substitute for or an addendum to a direct appeal. *People v. West,* 719 N.E.2d 664[, 669] ([Ill.] 1999). Consequently, any issues which were decided on direct appeal are barred by the doctrine of *res judicata;* any issues which could have been raised on direct appeal are forfeited. *West,* 719 N.E.2d [at 670].

[The Court disposed of several of the defendant's claims finding them without merit.]

DNA Testing

The defendant contends that his pending execution is unconstitutional because the State possesses forensic evidence which would establish his innocence. He asserts that DNA testing of a Vitullo rape kit completed at the hospital where Payne was treated would cast doubt on whether he raped Payne and, accordingly, whether he murdered Hackett.

In his petition, the defendant alleged that a vaginal swab taken during Payne's July 17, 1983, hospital examination was delivered to and retained by the State Police Crime Lab; this swab purportedly was never tested. The defendant claimed,

> [This swab] will have been maintained by the lab or evidence section in an acceptably preserved and uncontaminated state for DNA testing. Said swab would never be stored in a manner that would allow it to come into contact with foreign DNA. The swab has been subject to a chain of custody sufficient to establish that it has not been substituted, tampered with, replaced, or altered in any material respect.

The defendant further alleged that the only direct evidence in this case was Payne's identification testimony; thus, the central issue in this case was identification. The defendant then cited section 116-3 of the Code of Criminal Procedure of 1963 (725 ILCS

5/116-3 (West 1998)), which, he claimed, provides for such testing upon the allegations in his amended petition.

The defendant filed an appendix of exhibits supporting his petition, which included a form dated July 17, 1983, and entitled "Authorization for Release of Information and Evidence to Law Enforcement Agency" in which Payne authorized St. Joseph Hospital in Joliet, Illinois, to release "One sealed evidence kit," "Medical records," "Slides/Smears/Specimens," and "Sealed clothing bag(s)" to Special Agent Meduga. The appendix also contained a form signed by Illinois Department of Law Enforcement crime scene technician Melvin Trojanowski entitled "Evidence Receipt" which lists a "Vitullo Evidence Kit, marked Patricia Earl Payne, Received from S/A John Meduga" as agency exhibit 37. At trial, the State stipulated that defense exhibit 14 was the kit, which was later admitted into evidence. On the record before us, however, we cannot discern the condition of the Vitullo kit, and we do not know whether the kit contains any testable genetic material.

A claim of actual innocence based on newly discovered evidence may be raised in a post-conviction petition. See *People v. Washington,* 665 N.E.2d 1330[, 1337] ([Ill.] 1996); see also *People v. Bull,* 705 N.E.2d 824[, 840] ([Ill.] 1998) ("An important goal of the criminal justice process is the protection of the innocent accused against an erroneous conviction"). The supporting evidence must be new, material, noncumulative, and so conclusive that it would probably change the result on retrial. See *People v. Molstad,* 461 N.E.2d 398[, 401–02] ([Ill.] 1984), quoting *People v. Baker,* 158 N.E.2d 1[, 6] ([Ill.] 1959). The defendant has not provided evidence of his actual innocence, instead asserting that DNA testing would provide such evidence. Accordingly, the defendant raises the issue of whether DNA testing can be granted as post-conviction relief when it was unavailable at the time of his trial. The defendant contends that under either the fourteenth amendment of the United States Constitution or section 116-3, he may obtain the Vitullo kit for testing. We need not reach the constitutional issue, however, because section 116-3 provides an answer to the defendant's request. See *People v. Dunn,* 713 N.E.2d 568[, 571] ([Ill. App. Ct.] 1999).

Although section 116-3 was not in effect at the time the defendant filed his amended petition, it was in effect when the trial court entered its order. Section 116-3 provides:

> "(a) A defendant may make a motion before the trial court that entered the judgment of conviction in his or her case for the performance of fingerprint or forensic DNA testing on evidence that was secured in relation to the trial which resulted in his or her conviction, but which was not subject to the testing which is now requested because the technology for the testing was not available at the time of trial. Reasonable notice of the motion shall be served upon the State.
>
> (b) The defendant must present a prima facie case that:
>
> (1) identity was the issue in the trial which resulted in his or her conviction; and
>
> (2) the evidence to be tested has been subject to a chain of custody sufficient to establish that it has not been substituted, tampered with, replaced, or altered in any material aspect.
>
> (c) The trial court shall allow the testing under reasonable conditions designed to protect the State's interests in the integrity of the evidence and the testing process upon a determination that:
>
> (1) the result of the testing has the scientific potential to produce new, noncumulative evidence materially relevant to the defendant's assertion of actual innocence;

(2) the testing requested employs a scientific method generally accepted within the relevant scientific community." 725 ILCS 5/116-3 (West 1998).

Thus, in order to present a *prima facie* case for forensic testing, the defendant must show that identity was the central issue at trial and that the evidence to be tested was subject to a sufficiently secure chain of custody. The trial court then must determine whether this testing will potentially produce new, noncumulative evidence that is materially relevant to the defendant's actual-innocence claim.

...

Even if the State did not waive its current argument, we conclude that the defendant's petition made a *prima facie* case for DNA testing. The defendant has shown that identity was the central issue at trial. The defendant also has shown that the Vitullo kit was subject to a sufficiently secure chain of custody. Though the State contends that the defendant has presented no evidence of the kit's location since his 1984 trial, such evidence would not be available to the defendant. The Vitullo kit, as a piece of real evidence admitted at trial, would have remained in the custody of the circuit court clerk after the defendant's conviction.

The State further contends that a DNA test on the Vitullo kit does not have the potential to produce materially relevant evidence. We recently construed the term "materially relevant" in *People v. Savory,* 756 N.E.2d 804 ([Ill.] 2001). In *Savory,* the defendant was convicted of two murders in 1977. The appellate court held that the defendant's confession was inadmissible, reversed the convictions, and remanded for a new trial. At the defendant's second trial, the State presented significant evidence of the defendant's guilt, including a pair of the defendant's pants with a bloodstain whose type matched that of one of the victims. The defendant was again convicted of these murders in 1981. The appellate court affirmed the convictions. The defendant's post-conviction and *habeas corpus* petitions were denied, and in 1998, the defendant filed a motion for forensic testing under section 116-3. The defendant alleged that he did not commit the murders and that DNA testing would reveal the blood on his pants did not match that of one of the victims. The trial court denied this motion, concluding that favorable test results would not materially advance the defendant's actual-innocence claim. Even if the blood on the defendant's pants did not belong to the victim, the State's case would not be affected. The appellate court affirmed on different grounds, holding that the remedy under section 116-3 is available only in cases where a favorable test result would, by itself, completely vindicate the defendant.

After reviewing the language of section 116-3, we rejected the appellate court's restrictive reading of the term "materially relevant." *Savory,* 756 N.E.2d [at 810–11]. Instead, we held that evidence which is "materially relevant" to a defendant's actual-innocence claim need not, standing alone, exonerate the defendant; rather, it must tend to "significantly advance" his claim of actual innocence. *Savory,* 756 N.E.2d [at 810–11]. We stated, "if the legislature had intended to limit application of the statute to the instances in which a test result favorable to the defendant would, standing alone, lead to his complete vindication, it would have chosen a different way of expressing the statutory requirements." *Savory,* 756 N.E.2d [at 810–11]; accord *People v. Hockenberry,* 737 N.E.2d 1088[, 1093] ([Ill. App. Ct.] 2000) ("the application of the statute is not limited to those situations where additional scientific testing would result in total vindication"); *People v. Rokita,* 736 N.E.2d 205[, 212] ([Ill. App. Ct.] 2000) ("the plain and unambiguous language [of section 116-3] evinces no legislative intent to limit the use of scientific testing only to situations where the testing will result in total vindication or has the potential to exonerate the defendant").

...

Unlike evidence about the source of the bloodstain in *Savory,* evidence about the source of genetic material in the Vitullo kit was never presented at trial. That is, the defendant here does not seek merely to impeach the State's evidence. Instead, he seeks to present, for the first time, evidence about the genetic identity of Payne's assailant. Further, unlike the defendant in *Savory,* the defendant here never made damning admissions placing himself at the crime scene. The State presented a strong, but largely circumstantial, case; the only direct evidence of the defendant's guilt came from Payne's identification. A favorable result on a DNA test of the Vitullo kit would significantly advance the defendant's claim that he did not rape Payne, which, in turn, would significantly advance his claim that he did not murder Hackett. "If the available DNA evidence is capable of supporting such determination, there is no valid justification to withhold such relief if requested on postconviction review." *Dunn,* 713 N.E.2d [at 571]. The trial court erred in refusing to allow DNA testing of any testable genetic material in the Vitullo kit pursuant to section 116-3.

[The court went on to discuss remaining claims related to inadequacy of representation by counsel.]

...

Conclusion

The trial court erred in refusing to allow DNA testing of the Vitullo kit pursuant to section 116-3. The trial court also erred in dismissing without an evidentiary hearing the defendant's post-conviction claim that he received ineffective assistance from retained trial counsel William Swano. Finally, the trial court abused its discretion in refusing to order Swano's evidence deposition. The trial court properly dismissed the defendant's other post-conviction claims. For these reasons, we affirm in part, reverse in part, and remand to the circuit court for further proceedings.

Affirmed in part and reversed in part; cause remanded.

People v. Wise

752 N.Y.S.2d 837 (2002)

Charles J. Tejada, J.

On September 5, 2002, Kevin Richardson, Antron McCray, and Raymond Santana, the defendants, filed and served a Notice of Motion, pursuant to Criminal Procedure Law (CPL) 440.10(1)(g), Motion to Vacate Judgment, for an Order vacating their convictions after a jury trial of charges contained in Indictment Number 4762/89, upon the sole grounds of newly discovered evidence.... On September 9, 2002, and on September 24, 2002, Yusef Salaam and Kharey Wise, respectively, filed and served a Notice of Motion, pursuant to CPL 440.10(1)(g) for an order vacating each of their convictions after a jury trial of charges contained in Indictment Number 4762/89, also upon the sole grounds of newly discovered evidence. Each motion alleged that the newly discovered evidence is a statement from a convicted murderer and serial rapist and forensic DNA evidence. Those motions are hereby consolidated.

...

The convictions which the defendants seek to vacate are more than a decade old. Specifically, on August 18, 1990, a jury convicted McCray, Salaam and Santana, who were tried jointly on a 13-count indictment, of one count of Assault in the First Degree and Rape in the First Degree for the attack on a female victim, (hereinafter referred to as the female jogger or the Central Park jogger); Robbery in the First Degree and three counts of Assault in the Second Degree for the attack on John Loughlin; Assault in the Second Degree for the attack on David Lewis; and Riot in the First Degree. Since each defendant was less than 16 years of age, the trial court, set aside all their convictions except those for First Degree Robbery and Rape.

On December 11, 1990, a jury found Richardson guilty of each count of the indictment. Wise, who was tried jointly on a 13-count indictment with Richardson, was convicted of Assault in the First Degree and Sexual Abuse in the First Degree with respect to the attack on the Central Park jogger, and Riot in the First Degree. Because of Richardson's age, the trial court set aside all of Richardson's convictions except for Attempted Murder in the Second Degree, First Degree Robbery, Rape and Sodomy.

Yusef Salaam's convictions were affirmed by the Appellate Division (590 N.Y.S.2d 195) and by the Court of Appeals (629 N.E.2d 371). Antron McCray's convictions were also affirmed by the Appellate Division (604 N.Y.S.2d 93), and the Court of Appeals denied leave to appeal. The same holds true for Kharey Wise (612 N.Y.S.2d 117). Kevin Richardson's convictions were affirmed by the Appellate Division (608 N.Y.S.2d 627). Raymond Santana never perfected an appeal.

In deciding a motion for a new trial based on newly discovered evidence, Justice Irving Lang wrote, over a quarter of a century ago, that "The court recognizes that a jury verdict is not to be set aside but for the most compelling reasons. A jury verdict is the most desired, if not perfect, resolution of a case in our criminal justice system. But that verdict to have any meaning must be the result of a careful consideration of all the material facts." *People v. Maynard,* 363 N.Y.S.2d 384[, 398] (N.Y.Sup.Ct.1974). This statement embodies the spirit and the letter of CPL Article 440.

Article 440 recognizes that trials are human endeavors and that there are times when evidence is not discovered in time to be presented to a jury so that its verdict can be the result of a careful consideration of all material facts. When this occurs CPL Article 440 sets forth a procedure that allows a court to vacate a conviction and order a new trial in which the newly discovered evidence may be presented.

This procedure requires that the motion for a new trial "must be made in writing" and that it must contain "sworn allegations" and "information supporting or tending to support the allegations." The People may file an answer to the moving papers. The Court may also allow the defendants to file a reply to the People's answer. After all papers are filed, the court must consider "whether the motion is determinable without a hearing to resolve questions of fact." (McKinney's Cons. Laws of N.Y., Book 11A, Criminal Procedure Law § 440.30).

...

Given that defendants do not contest the People's version of the facts, a hearing to resolve questions of fact is not necessary. Moreover, "to grant such a hearing where the court is able to reach its conclusion on the papers alone would serve no end of justice but would only protract futile litigation."

...

A motion for a new trial based on newly discovered evidence is a statutory remedy and may be granted only in the sound discretion of the court. *People v. Patrick,* 183 N.Y. 52, 75 N.E. 963. The exercise of discretion requires a careful and dispassionate examination of the facts, as presented in the parties' papers and the application of the law to the facts.

This requires an examination of two aspects of the newly discovered evidence: (1) the conduct of the defendant; whether he could have discovered the evidence at the time of trial by due diligence, and whether after the discovery of the alleged new evidence, he made his motion with due diligence, and (2) the nature of the evidence; whether the new evidence is of sufficient character to create the probability it would have resulted in a more favorable verdict. "The evidence is viewed only in context of its effect on the previous outcome of the trial. It may be said that the rule of newly discovered evidence presupposes no suppression and an otherwise fair trial and, but for the new evidence, no further aspects of the trial need be considered." *Maynard,* 363 N.Y.S.2d [at 392]; *see also* CPL 440.10(1)(g).

The leading case on the issue of newly discovered evidence, *People v. Salemi,* 128 N.E.2d 377 ([N.Y.] 1955), sets the criteria for determining the sufficiency of the new evidence as: (1) it must be of such nature as would [probably] change the verdict should a new trial be granted; (2) it must have been discovered since the previous trial; (3) it must be of such nature that it could not have been discovered before the trial by the exercise of due diligence; (4) it must be material to the issue; (5) it must not be cumulative to the former issue; and (6) it must not be impeaching or contradictory of former evidence.

This criterion is not unique. Both sister state and federal courts follow similar criterion. *Berry v. State,* 10 Ga. 511, 527 (1851); Federal Rule of Criminal Procedure rule 33 (*see generally, United States v. Johnson,* 327 U.S. 106 (1946); *United States v. Diggs,* 649 F.2d 731 (9th Cir.1981).)

Examining first whether the new evidence was discovered since the previous trial and whether it was of such nature that it could not have been discovered before the trial by the exercise of due diligence, this Court makes the following conclusions.

It is uncontested that in January 2002, Matias Reyes, for the first time, informed law enforcement officials that he, alone, committed the rape and other crimes concerning the female jogger, for which several defendants were convicted, and that DNA testing confirms his participation in the rape. This evidence could not have been produced at trial in 1990, even with due diligence on defendants' part. It simply did not exist until 2002.

Each defendant's attorneys' affirmation is complete on its face. Each presents fully all the evidence, in the best possible light, that could be offered on the defendant's behalf, relating solely to the convictions concerning the female jogger. The moving papers allege a ground constituting a legal basis for the motion. Specifically, each defense attorney has affirmed, under a penalty of perjury, that the confession of Matias Reyes and DNA evidence relating to that evidence, would probably influence a jury to render a verdict more favorable to the defendants and each motion contains documentary proof, Reyes' notarized confession, to support this contention. Each motion was made with due diligence after the discovery of the newly discovered evidence.

The Peoples' Affirmation is complete on its face and also presents fully all the evidence, in the best possible light, that could be offered on the People's and on the defendants' behalf. Specifically, the People affirm, under a penalty of perjury, that the history of the prosecution of the defendants began on "April 19, 1989, when a series of incidents occurred in Central Park involving members of a group of more than 30 teenagers.... At approximately 9:05 p.m. [a man] was accosted by a band of youths on the East Drive. A few minutes later [another person] was assaulted and robbed. He was left unconscious. At approximately 9:12 to 9:15 p.m. a couple on a tandem bicycle was menaced. Moments later, a taxi cab driver had rocks hurled at his cab and was threatened when he got out of the car to investigate. Beginning at about 9:24 p.m. and continuing to about 9:45 p.m. a series of four male joggers were set upon on the jogging path at the northern end of the Central Park reservoir. Two of the male joggers escaped unharmed but two were assaulted. [One] was not seriously hurt, however, John Loughlin was knocked to the ground, kicked, punched, and beaten with a pipe and stick. He was knocked unconscious and sustained significant but not life threatening injuries."

The Peoples' affirmation further states that, "at approximately 1:30 a.m., an unconscious woman was found by two men walking on a foot path through Central Park. Police and medical personnel were summoned. The victim, a twenty-nine-year-old white woman who came to be known as the 'Central Park jogger,' was removed to the hospital. She had been badly beaten about the head, and suffered numerous bruises, scratches, and abrasions elsewhere on her body. Her t-shirt had been rolled into a ligature and used to tie her in a distinctive fashion. Subsequent investigation revealed that she had been raped and that her radio headset and keys were missing." "Raymond Santana and Kevin Richardson, as well as a number of other youths were apprehended at approximately 10:15 p.m., on April 19, 1989, after police officers responding to reports concerning some of the incidents spotted them on the western outskirts of the park. Antron McCray, Yusef Salaam and Kharey Wise were brought in for questioning on April 20, 1989, after they had been identified by other youths as having been present at or participated in some of the events in the park."

"Each of the defendants was questioned by detectives and made one or more statements. All five of the defendants implicated themselves in a number of the crimes which had occurred in the park. None of them admitted actually raping the Central Park jogger, but each gave an account of events in which he made himself an accomplice to the crime. Defendant Wise was 16 years old, defendants Salaam and McCray were 15 and defendants Richardson and Santana were 14."

The People further inform the Court that they first learned of the newly discovered evidence in February 2002, when the New York County "District Attorney's Office was notified that an inmate had come forward with a claim that he had attacked and raped the Central Park jogger, and that he had committed the attack alone. The inmate, Matias Reyes, had informed a Corrections Officer of his claim. On January 17, 2002, he was formally interviewed by an investigative supervisor from the Inspector General's office. Following this investigation, information about his contentions was forwarded to the District Attorney's office. Reyes is serving sentences totaling thirty-three and one-third years to life imprisonment for three rape/robberies, one rape/murder, and one robbery that he committed between June 11 and August 5, 1989." The sentences, which were imposed on November 1, 1991, "rested in part on DNA evidence taken from his victims and from the scenes of his crimes, which matched the DNA in a sample taken from him.... Upon learning of Reyes claims, efforts were made to locate the evidence from both cases, and the [Federal Bureau of Investigation] FBI laboratories were asked to make a comparison. On May 8, 2002, the District Attorney's office was notified that Reyes' DNA matched the DNA taken from the sock that had been found at the Central Park crime scene."

Further, as to what constitutes the newly discovered evidence, the People concede that "The newly discovered evidence in this case consists of the account of events provided by Matias Reyes, who states that he alone attacked and raped the Central Park jogger; DNA test results which conclusively establish that Reyes was the sole source of semen found on the sock at the crime scene and a cervical swab taken from the victim, as well as a pubic hair found on the same sock...."

The People also assert that there is additional newly discovered evidence, specifically "the record of prior, similar attacks committed by Reyes, including an assault and rape committed in Central Park two days before the jogger attack; and scientific test results undermining the probative value of evidence introduced in the defendants' trials."

The People also conducted forensic testing of DNA and hair samples to see whether the results corroborated Reyes' version of his involvement in the crimes involving the female jogger, and report in their Affirmation that, "After preliminary DNA results were received from the F.B.I. in May [2002], the District Attorney's Office retained a private laboratory to conduct additional forensic testing."

"The laboratory performed further tests in connection with those DNA samples which connected Reyes to the crime. The tests provided additional corroboration of Reyes' account. The private laboratory concurred with testimony given at the defendants' trials that the DNA on the sock found at the Central Park crime scene and the DNA on the cervical swab taken from the victim came from the same person. Thus, Reyes' DNA matched both."

"Moreover, the laboratory found additional, untested semen on the sock, which it tested using technology not in existence in 1989. The test established that Reyes was the source of the DNA to a factor of one in 6,000,000,000 people."

"The three hairs found on Kevin Richardson were reexamined following F.B.I. protocols for questioned hair samples. The hairs where first reexamine microscopically and then submitted for mitochondrial DNA testing. All had been mounted on slides for examination in 1989."

"The microscopic analysis of the hairs was performed by Special Agent Douglas Deedrick, formerly Chief of the Hair and Fibers Unit and currently Unit Chief of the Information and Evidence Section of the F.B.I. Agent Deedrick disagreed with the expert opinion offered at the original trials. His conclusion was the hairs were not suitable for comparison, and could not be used to link Richardson to the jogger."

Also, the People concede that, "All of that evidence meets the criteria set forth in the statute;" "A through and extensive investigation was undertaken at the time of the original proceedings in an effort to develop additional evidence. Nevertheless, the People's case at both trials rested almost entirely on the statements made by the defendants;" "DNA evidence was extracted from semen deposited on the jogger's sock, found near her at the crime scene. It did not match any of the defendants, or any other known sample. The same was true of DNA evidence extracted from a cervical swab; it did not match the defendants or any other known sample. Expert testimony at trial, however, established that the DNA from both the victim and the sock appeared to have come from the same source. Testimony also established that the DNA was not a mixture, it was from a single source, meaning that only one individual had ejaculated," and that, "Ultimately, there proved to be no physical or forensic evidence recovered at the scene or from the person or effects of the victim which connected the defendants to the attack on the jogger, or could establish how many perpetrators participated."

As to Reyes' statement, the People conducted an extensive investigation and they reported that, "That investigation has led to the conclusion that Reyes' account of the attack and rape is corroborated by, consistent with, or explanatory of objective, independent evidence in a number of important respects. Further, investigators have been unable to find any evidence that, as of 1989, Reyes, knew or associated with the defendants or any of the individuals known to have been in the park with them on the night of April 19."

The People also did a comparison of Reyes' criminal history to see if it contained any features which might serve as additional corroboration and reported to the Court that,

"Corroboration of Reyes' account of the crime is found both in the pattern of his other sexual attacks and in some of their specific facts. He consistently targeted and stalked Caucasian women, or women who appeared to be Caucasian. His crimes all involved conversation with his victims, either as a way of making initial contact or as a way of acquiring information that would enable him to steal more property. Frequently, conversation or a search of property alternated with outbursts of physical and sexual violence. All of his rapes or attempted rapes also involved robbery."

As to their assessment of the evidence presented at trial, the People conclude that the newly discovered evidence fatally weakens that evidence. Specifically, the People state that, "... an assessment of the likely impact of newly discovered evidence requires an honest appraisal of the strength or weakness of the case originally presented by the People. The defendants' statements in this case were sufficiently persuasive to result in the convictions of all five defendants on at least some of the charges against them, and, for that matter, persuasive enough to bring about those convictions before two separate juries. However, the confessions also had serious weaknesses." For example, the People state that, "... on the issue of who raped her, Richardson named Antron, Raymond, and Steve. McCray identified a tall, skinny black male, a Puerto Rican with a black hoodie, Clarence, and Kevin, and said that he himself simulated having sex with her. Santana claimed that Kevin raped her, after which Santana left the park. Salaam named Kevin, Kharey, and a couple of unknown males. And Kharey Wise named Steven, Raymond and Kevin. Kevin Richardson is the only name common with all the statements, with the exception of his own. It was, however, Richardson who first implicated members of the group in the rape, providing a possible motive for others to accuse him."

Most significantly, the People focus on the effect of the missing evidence in depriving the defendants from presenting an "alternative theory of the case." They state that, "... the jurors who originally heard the evidence were presented with no persuasive alternative theory of the case to consider. Certainly, no one would have thought that as the defendants and their group were making their way through Central Park, a serial rapist was also at large. The newly discovered evidence provides incontrovertible proof that he was." The theory that the newly discovered evidence would support was that, "A self-confessed and convicted serial rapist—who habitually stalked white women in their 20's; who attacked them, beat them, and raped them; who always robbed his victims, and frequently stole Walkmans; who tied one of his victims in a fashion much like the Central Park jogger; who lived on 102nd Street; who beat and raped a woman in Central Park two days before the attack on the transverse; whose DNA was the only DNA recovered inside and alongside the victim; whose narrative of events is corroborated in a number of significant ways; who had no connection to the defendants or their cohorts; and who committed all his sex crimes alone—has come forward to say that he alone stalked, attacked, beat, raped and robbed a white woman in her 20's, who was set upon on the 102nd Street transverse, was missing her Walkman, and was left tied in a way that has never before been explained."

...

With this further guidance and given the facts, as presented by the parties, this Court must apply the remaining Salemi factors to determine whether the new evidence is of such a character that it would create a probability that it would have resulted in a more favorable verdict. *People v. Maynard,* 363 N.Y.S.2d [at 392].

First, with respect to whether the newly discovered evidence is merely impeaching of or contradictory to the former evidence, this Court finds that although the defendants' made incriminating statements linking them to the crime scene, as established in the parties papers, none of the defendants admitted raping the jogger. Thus, Reyes' confession cannot be viewed as contradictory. Additionally, Reyes' confession cannot be considered cumulative either since the accounts given by the defendants differ on significant details, such as who initiated the attack, who knocked the victim down, who held her, who raped her, what weapons were used during the attack, and when, in the sequence of the events, the attack took place.

For example, as detailed in the People's Affirmation, on the issue of who knocked the jogger to the ground, Richardson said McCray, Santana and Steve did it. McCray said "everyone charged her." Santana said Kevin did it. Salaam said he did it and Wise named Santana and then said "Steve" did it. Similarly, on the issue of who raped the jogger, Richardson named McCray, Santana and "Steve." McCray said it was a tall skinny black man, a Puerto Rican with a black hoodie, Clarence and Kevin. And he said that he himself had simulated having sex with the jogger. Santana said Richardson raped her. Salaam named Richardson, Wise and a couple of unknown males. Wise named "Steven," Santana and Richardson.

Additionally, it is reported that Wise stated that the jogger's clothes had been cut off and that her legs had been cut with a knife. However, the record reveals that the jogger's clothes were not cut off and that there were no knife wounds on the jogger. Richardson said that her bra was ripped off, when in fact it was still on her when she was found. Santana described the jogger as naked when they left, although she was found with her jogging bra still on and her t-shirt tied around her head. None of the defendants accurately described where the attack on the jogger took place.

On the other hand, the People conclude that Reyes was accurate about specific details of the crimes against the jogger. He described the crime scene in detail and what the victim was wearing. He indicated that he used a heavy branch to attack her, which was consistent and explanatory of medical and crime scene evidence. Further, his account was corroborated by the fact that he had engaged in similar sexual attacks involving the targeting and stalking of Caucasian women or women who appeared to be Caucasian.

Consequently, Reyes' confession does not impeach nor contradict the evidence presented at trial.

The newly discovered evidence in this case not only consists of statements made by Reyes but by Reyes' DNA, which matched the DNA found on a sock at the Central Park crime scene and the DNA on the cervical swab taken from the victim. Pursuant to CPL §440.10(1)(g) and *People v. Salemi,* 128 N.E.2d [at 381], this evidence is certainly newly discovered in the traditional sense since it was not available at trial and could not have been discovered with due diligence. Moreover, it cannot be said that this evidence would be merely contradictory of the evidence already in the case since there was no DNA forensic evidence presented against the defendants at trial. Newly discovered evidence consisting of DNA analysis of semen and other secretions found on victim's clothing would not be merely cumulative to analysis offered at trial, in view of the significant potential which scientific evidence has to influence a jury.

Preliminary DNA results received from the FBI were confirmed by a private laboratory retained by the People to conduct additional forensic testing. That laboratory established that Reyes was the source of the DNA to a factor of one in 6,000,000,000 people. In addition, mitochondrial DNA testing established that Reyes was also the source of the pubic hair found on the sock in Central Park and confirmed that no one else's DNA was present in the samples taken from the victim or at the crime scene.

Given the facts as conceded by the People and found by the Court, it is virtually self evident that the newly discovered evidence, specifically, the confession of a self admitted murderer and serial rapist, corroborated by physical evidence including scientific testing establishing that he was the sole source of DNA evidence connected to the Central Park jogger's rape to a factor of one to 6,000,000,000, would create the probability that had such evidence been received at trial, the verdict would have been more favorable to the defendants.

However, that conclusion is not as readily apparent with respect to the convictions for Robbery in the First Degree. The victim of the robbery was John Loughlin. At first glance it would appear that this robbery is totally unrelated to the newly discovered evidence. Consequently, the sole issue remaining is whether a newly discovered confession and DNA evidence, related solely to the rape of the Central Park jogger, is material to the robbery of John Loughlin.

Since all the other Salemi factors have been established, the Court will now focus on the materiality of the new evidence to the robbery convictions.

Initially, it is noted that except for the argument presented in Yusef Salaam's motion that "the horrible nature of the assault/rape crime overwhelmed any possibility that he (and the other defendants) could receive a fair trial as to any and all of the charges," the defendants are silent as to a legal or factual basis that establishes materiality with respect to the newly discovered evidence and the robbery. Given the limited access that the defense attorneys had to the newly discovered evidence, this limited argument is understandable. However, this argument sets forth a compelling reason, in the interest of justice, as recognized by the People, for further examination of the effects of the newly discovered evidence on the robbery convictions.

"It is well recognized that the prosecution has a great advantage over the defendant in the fact-gathering process due to his superior manpower and access to other law enforcement facilities." *People v. Maynard,* 363 N.Y.S.2d [at 290].

The District Attorney has utilized his advantage on the People's and the defendants' behalf. The People's Affirmation is a reminder that, "the prosecutor is both an administrator of justice, and an advocate ..." and that, "the duty of the prosecutor is to seek justice, not merely to convict." (*see Code of Professional Responsibility, Standard 3-1.2: The Function of the Prosecutor*). Consequently, the People have presented a persuasive and compelling argument for the granting of the motion as to all convictions. The People demonstrate that based on their investigation and the defendants statements, they relied on a gang rampage/rape "single incident" theory to prosecute the defendants. Specifically, the People conclude that, "Under the extraordinary circumstances presented by this case, the People are constrained to consent to the defendants' motions with respect to the other charges of which they were convicted."

Further they concede that, "The People's theory was that [the Central Park jogger] was set upon by a number of young men, gang-raped by two or more of them, kicked and pummeled by the group, and beaten about the head with a pipe, a brick, and a rock."

They specify that, "It is commonplace for defendants to be charged in a single indictment with crimes of very different levels of gravity. The law permits it and correctly presumes that juries can and will follow instructions requiring that they weight evidence of guilt as to different counts separately. Thus, in and of itself, the relative seriousness of the jogger attack plainly would not merit setting aside the juries' verdicts as to other charges."

But they also point out that "In this case, however, other factors must also be weighed. The crimes the defendants were charged with were not widely separated by time or location, either from each other or from the attack on the jogger, all occurred within a single hour, at the northern end of Central Park. In effect, all were considered to be part of a single incident—a rampage in the park, as is reflected in the fact that the defendants were charged with Riot in the First Degree."

The People also demonstrate their commitment to a gang rampage/rape "single incident" theory in their closing argument to the juries and state that, "... the jurors in the trial of Kharey Wise and Kevin Richardson [...] should not lose sight of the 'overall pattern of the behavior ... [as] this group continued through the park for a period of approximately an hour attacking one after another after another person,'" and that "... this showed that the group acted with a joint purpose, that they were 'an entire group acting together in one violent outburst of destruction, or beating, or assaulting,'" and that "Similar references were made in summation in the earlier trial of McCray, Salaam and Santana."

Another basis for their conclusion as to the materiality of the new evidence to the robbery charge is their assessment that, "It was logical for the People to suggest that the defendants' culpability and criminal intent could be inferred from the pattern of conduct engaged in by the group of which they were a part. This would have been an inescapable inference for the jurors in any event. But the new evidence detailed above would, if credited, call into question the defendants' involvement in the most horrific crime in the pattern of incidents in the park—and indeed, the involvement of the larger group as well. Accordingly, it would likely have had a significant bearing, in the jurors' minds, on the defendants' culpability for those other crimes as well" and that, "the People's proof was limited by one fundamental fact: none of the victims could identify any of the defendants."

Moreover, the People state that, "... the admissions concerning the other crimes were contained in the same written and recorded statements as the admissions concerning the rape, and were largely obtained as part of the same process of questioning. As a consequence, the newly discovered evidence would probably raise questions about the reliability of those admissions similar to the questions raised about the defendants' confession to rape. There is some testimony that, in certain instances, admissions about other criminal incidents were made substantially before and apart from any statements about the rape. But that testimony alone, absent independent corroboration, would not have been sufficient to allay concerns about the defendants' confessions raised by the newly discovered evidence."

And the People finally concede that, "In sum, there was no significant evidence at trial establishing the defendants' involvement in the other crimes of which they stand convicted that would not have been substantially and fatally weakened by the newly discovered evidence in this matter," and that, "Assessing the newly discovered evidence is required solely in light of the proof introduced at the earlier trials, we conclude that there is a probability that the new evidence, had it been available to the juries, would have resulted in verdicts more favorable to the defendants, not only on the charges arising from the attack on the female jogger, but on the other charges as well."

Given the imperfection of the evidence before the jury, it is clear that the defendants' statements played a crucial role in the jury's verdict as to all convictions. These confessions were the quintessential evidence in the prosecution of the defendants. They laid the foundation for a course of action developed, followed, and relied on for the prosecution and conviction of the defendants. That course was based on a theory that the defendants were involved as a group in a single incident; a crime rampage, which included rape, robbery and other crimes. That theory also incorporated a logical 'guilt by association' to the crimes against the Central Park jogger inference. Although this theory cannot be said to have been unreasonable in 1990, given the evidence at the time of the trials, this Court finds that the newly discovered evidence, as conceded by the People, is so intertwined with all the crimes charged against the defendants and that it would so weaken the reliability of the confessions, that the newly discovered evidence would create a probability that had such evidence been received at trial, the verdict would have been more favorable to the defendants as to all the convictions.

Based on the foregoing, this Court concludes that if the statement and the forensic evidence, related to Matias Reyes, were available at the time of trial, there exist a reasonable probability that the verdicts in the defendants' trials would have been more favorable to defendants. Accordingly, defendants' motion to vacate judgment and order a new trial, based on newly discovered evidence, must be granted as to all of the remaining convictions.

Kathy Swedlow, *Don't Believe Everything You Read: A Review of Modern "Post-Conviction" DNA Testing Statutes*

38 Cal. W. L. Rev. 355 (2002)

...

This Article is organized around the basic parameters of, and sequential steps associated with, the various DNA testing statutes currently in existence....

II. Prerequisites to Filing

A. Who May File

All of the new statutes delineate who may file a petition for testing and, while some statutes enumerate the specific crimes or class(es) of felonies for which a petitioner must be convicted in order to file, generally speaking, petitioners seeking DNA testing will have been convicted of some sort of major felony.

Nonetheless, four distinct categories of individuals may be excluded from testing under certain situations, despite a felony conviction. First, while some of the new statutes do not specifically bar petitioners who have pleaded guilty from requesting testing, the vast majority do exclude such petitioners—despite extant DNA exonerations after guilty pleas and despite the Supreme Court's express recognition that innocent individuals can and do plead guilty—and only a handful of these statutes specifically include them. Only one state, Missouri, appears to both include and exclude petitioners who have pleaded guilty.

Second, many statutes refer only to individuals who seek complete exoneration, leaving aside those petitioners who may not assert their actual innocence but who instead seek to reduce or mitigate their sentencing exposure. Third and fourth, few of the current statutes address the situation of petitioners who are no longer in custody or those who seek to challenge one conviction while serving a sentence for a second conviction, regardless of whether the second conviction is related or unrelated. While some form of "custody" is normally a jurisdictional prerequisite in traditional post-conviction litigation, a good argument can be made that these testing statutes should not be similarly restricted, insofar as many of these statutes were enacted to correct systemic problems within the criminal justice system. In any event, in those jurisdictions where the testing statute is silent concerning custody, litigators may wish to be aware of their individual state's post-conviction requirements regarding custody.

B. Timing of Filing

While traditional post-conviction practice generally contemplates that a petitioner will pursue relief only after the conclusion of direct appeal, many of the new statutes allow a petitioner to seek relief at any time after conviction or sentencing, and only a minority of statutes anticipate that a petitioner will seek relief at the conclusion of direct appeal.

At first blush, this might not seem to be problematic: many of the current exonerations occurred years after the prisoner had exhausted his traditional legal remedies, and so it may seem inconsequential whether the request for testing be filed after conviction, sentencing, or direct appeal. However, in a case with a recent conviction, disastrous problems can arise if the petitioner's traditional rights are not protected during the pursuit of DNA testing.

...

C. Time Limits on Filing

Some of the new statutes mimic traditional post-conviction statutes insofar as they place time limits on the filing of applications for testing, i.e., they impose time limits based upon either the date of conviction or the date the petitioner's conviction becomes final. While a larger number of statutes impose no limits at all—allowing a petitioner to pursue relief under the statute at any time, assuming he is otherwise eligible—a handful of these new statutes contain sunset provisions, which provide that all applications for testing must be filed by a date certain. Finally, some jurisdictions appear to have adopted a hybrid approach, requiring evaluation of the particular statute's use after a particular period of time has elapsed.

D. Appointment of Counsel

Most statutes expressly provide for the appointment of counsel, but many do not have similar within-statute provisions. However, regardless of whether a particular statute provides for counsel or not, the mere fact that most petitioners will be seeking relief after the expiration of their direct appeal rights means that any right to counsel will necessarily be curtailed. The recent Illinois case of *People v. Love* [,727 N.E.2d 680 (Ill. App. Ct. 2000)] demonstrates how and why.

In Love, the petitioner sought DNA testing under the Illinois testing statute five years after his original conviction and one year after the conclusion of his state post-conviction proceedings. Despite the fact that the Illinois statute has no provision for the right to counsel, the trial court appointed counsel to assist Love. At a hearing on Love's motion for testing, at which Love was not present, the State argued that all of the blood evidence had been destroyed and that regardless, the issue of the destruction of the blood evidence had been previously litigated on direct appeal and in the previous post-conviction proceedings. When asked by the court whether a factual hearing needed to be convened to determine whether the blood evidence had been destroyed, Love's appointed counsel acquiesced, and the petition was dismissed.

On appeal, Love argued that his appointed counsel had been ineffective for not requesting a hearing. However, the appellate court disagreed, finding that because Love had no constitutional right to counsel, he had no accompanying right to the effective assistance of counsel. Moreover, because the Illinois testing statute did not even confer a statutory right to counsel, Love was not even entitled to a "reasonable level of assistance;" instead, all that Love was entitled to was the mere appointment of counsel, which he had received.

Similar problems can arise even when the petition for testing is filed during a time when the petitioner retains his Sixth Amendment rights. For example, in Nebraska, a petitioner may file his petition for testing at any time after conviction. While the Nebraska statute provides a statutory right to counsel for a petitioner requesting testing, counsel's appointment prior to the time when the petitioner's conviction becomes final will presumably be subject to Sixth Amendment effectiveness considerations.

However, what happens if the petition is dismissed before testing is ever ordered due, as the petitioner in Love alleged, to an error on the part of counsel? While the Nebraska testing statute is silent regarding the filing of successive testing petitions, Nebraska law makes clear that successive petitions filed under the traditional post-conviction statute will not be entertained "unless the motion affirmatively shows on its face that the basis relied upon for relief was not available at the time the movant filed the prior motion;" in other words, traditional successive petitions will be considered only under exceptional circumstances. Thus, the only chance of success—defined in terms of access to testing—for this petitioner may be either to hope that his direct appeal rights have been preserved so that he can request testing during those proceedings, or to hope that the court will consider a successive petition for testing.

III. Prerequisites to Testing

A. Standards for Testing

All of the statutes delineate standards for testing; the difference between the statutes rests mainly on how many different types of demonstrations the petitioner is required to make: depending on the jurisdiction, he may have to make as few as three, or as many as eight. Additionally, some statutes mandate testing upon a specific showing by the petitioner only, and others contemplate testing after a specific showing by the petitioner followed by additional findings by the court.

1. Materiality

All the statutes require some sort of demonstration of materiality by the petitioner, or a materiality finding by the court, prior to the issuance of an order for testing. The statutes differ, however, in the proof that a petitioner must offer to demonstrate materiality.

For example, the majority of statutes rest the materiality showing on a demonstration that the testing will produce "new" and "noncumulative" evidence. Under this version of materiality, the petitioner will have to show an enhancement in technology or that some item of evidence was collected during the crime investigation, but was never tested at the time of the original conviction.

...

B. Chain of Custody

In one form or another, virtually all of the statutes require proof of an unbroken chain of evidence, with some statutes placing the burden directly upon the petitioner and others merely requiring the court to make its own, independent determination. While most of the statutes envision a chain of custody to be established and found prior to testing, Michigan requires that the petitioner establish chain of custody as part of the motion for relief, i.e., after testing has been performed and after testing exonerates the petitioner. Both the Missouri and North Carolina statutes are silent concerning chain of custody issues; however, the Missouri statute does require that the petitioner allege under oath that the evidence to be tested is available and was secured in relation to the crime for which testing is requested.

In those jurisdictions where the petitioner bears the burden of demonstrating chain of custody as part of his pleading requirements, it is unclear how that burden can be met by a person who, by definition, has no access to the biological material he seeks to test. While one case from Illinois, *People v. Savory*, suggests that a petitioner should use his subpoena powers and/or should seek stipulations and affidavits from relevant state actors in order to show the chain of custody, this may not be a feasible solution in those instances where state actors are hostile to or skeptical of petitioner's claim.

Because those statutes which place the burden on the petitioner cast the burden in terms of a pleading requirement, the ordinary post-conviction petitioner—whose conviction became final years before he contemplated filing a motion for testing—will lack the jurisdiction of the court prior to the filing of his pleading to invoke his subpoena power. And, assuming state actors, for whatever reasons, are unwilling to enter into stipulations or sign affidavits regarding chain of custody issues, as the Savory Court suggested, it is unclear how the petitioner will be able to meet his burden.

C. Testing Which Was "Not Available" at the Time of Conviction

Many of these statutes allow for testing upon some sort of demonstration by the petitioner that such testing was "not available" at the time of trial or original conviction. While "not available" can refer to the actual existence of the scientific technology—and indeed, some of these statutes restrict the definition of "not available" to such a meaning—other definitions may be equally plausible. For instance, testing may not be available to a particular defendant because his counsel ineffectively failed to request such testing or because the trial court refused to release funding for the requisite tests. Or, testing may not have been geographically available to the defendant, insofar as the local laboratory in question may not have had the capabilities to perform the most sophisticated testing.

...

D. Identity as an Issue at Trial

While no statute currently has an express exclusion of defendants who have pleaded guilty, many require the petitioner to prove, as a prerequisite to testing, that "identity was an issue at trial." This provision logically includes those petitioners who claim that they were not present at the scene or who present certain kinds of antagonistic defenses, but would logically exclude petitioners who claim, for example, the defense of consent to a rape charge.

IV. Pre-testing Considerations

A. Discovery

In the normal course of litigation, a petitioner can file his petition and then request discovery of the materials necessary to amplify his claims. However, in the context of post-conviction requests for DNA testing, the opposite appears to be true: of the testing statutes in existence, not one makes mention of discovery, or even appears to contemplate that such a request may be filed. Thus, even in those jurisdictions in which a petitioner has the burden of demonstrating a chain of evidence, it is unclear what mechanism a petitioner may invoke to meet his burden.

Regardless, petitioners should note that many of these testing statutes are codified as sub-parts of traditional post-conviction statutes; accordingly, an argument can be made that a petitioner requesting testing enjoys the same right to discovery under relevant state law as afforded to a traditional post-conviction petitioner. Moreover, in all post-conviction proceedings, the state has a duty to disclose exculpatory evidence, even in the absence of any specific request for such material. And, given the recent recognition of a "due process right of access to ... genetic material for the limited purpose of DNA testing," petitioners may now argue that the right to discovery assumes constitutional dimensions, even in the face of the testing statute's silence regarding discovery.

B. Preservation of Evidence

At the heart of all of these DNA cases is the biological evidence. However, many of these statutes fail to adequately address the issue of evidence preservation, to the petitioner's detriment.

Generally speaking, these new statutes follow four main approaches to preservation, with several statutes hybridizing these approaches. First, and as a baseline, some statutes do not even contemplate preservation, which presumably means that the petitioner must expressly request preservation upon filing his request for testing. Second, in those instances where some sort of preservation is contemplated, the state can be required to preserve the evidence retroactively, quasi-retroactively, prospectively, or prospectively after the petitioner files his request for testing. Third, and in spite of any requirement for preservation, the state may be permitted to destroy biological evidence after meeting certain surreal requirements. Finally, in certain circumstances, the state may be penalized for destruction of evidence in violation of the statute.

While a statute that provides preservation mechanisms is quite obviously more desirable than one which does not, it is unclear how these preservation mechanisms, as currently drafted, will substantively affect post-conviction innocence cases. The most obvious question underlying these preservation provisions is whether they really work: if a state actor is inclined to destroy evidence, will a statute mandating preservation really prevent him from taking action?

Second, given the loopholes in the quasi-retroactive and prospective-upon-filing preservation approaches—which are included in a handful of the current statutes—the issue of "bad faith" destruction will rarely, if ever, arise.... Even more disturbing are those jurisdictions where the state is only required to preserve evidence after the petitioner has filed his request for testing; theoretically, all evidence in these jurisdictions could be destroyed in one fell swoop.

Moreover, the obvious loopholes associated with the preservation approaches currently in existence underscores the need for careful planning between traditional and new post-conviction remedies, because without such planning, a prisoner may be left without any evidence to test and without any statutory vehicle by which to challenge his conviction and/or sentence.

C. Laboratories

In general, the testing statutes follow three approaches to laboratories: those which mandate the use of state labs, those which contemplate the use of private labs, and those which are ambiguous as to whether state or private lab may be used.

While the most obvious problem associated with the use of state laboratories is the fact that so many of the recent exonerations are linked to abuse within government laboratories—begging the question of why a petitioner would want to pursue testing at a government facility—there are other problems as well. First and foremost, what if a state lab lacks the capabilities and/or talent to perform the testing in question? Insofar as the District of Columbia and Virginia link the meaning of "not available" to laboratory capabilities, petitioners may want to make in-court inquiries of their state lab facilities before blindly agreeing to have a state laboratory perform the testing. Second, petitioners will certainly want to investigate the lab's accreditation—not only that the lab is accredited, but what that accreditation actually means.

D. Costs of Testing

Cost is an issue addressed by most, but not all, of the testing statutes. Under most schemes, the petitioner is required to pay the cost of testing, unless he is indigent....

V. Standards for Relief

Surprisingly, less than half of the testing statutes address the issue of what should and will happen when testing exonerates. In those jurisdictions where the testing statute is silent regarding relief, a petitioner will presumably make some sort of request for relief after the testing exonerates him. However, it is unknown whether the petitioner will be required to make an additional evidentiary showing, as is required under the Maine and Michigan statutes, or whether some other set of requirements will be imposed.

For example, to obtain testing under the California statute, a petitioner must meet two substantive pleading requirements: he must explain "why the identity of the perpetrator was, or should have been, a significant issue in the case" and why, "in light of all the evidence, how the requested DNA testing would raise a reasonable probability that [his] verdict or sentence would be more favorable if the results of the DNA testing had been available at the time of the conviction." This showing is certainly far lower than the requirements of the Maine and Michigan statutes, which require, inter alia, a demonstration that "only the perpetrator of the crime" could be the source of the biological material. One can imagine a factual scenario where the petitioner could meet the California "reasonable probability" standard but not the more stringent "only the perpetrator" standard, which begs the question of the type of demonstration a California petitioner be required to make after testing excludes him? Certainly, the State would be expected to argue that the petitioner prove something more than a "reasonable probability."

...

VI. Retesting, Rehearing, and Appeal

In spite of shocking revelations about the state serologists in West Virginia, Oklahoma, and Illinois, and in spite of the fact that many testing statutes require use of state laboratories, no testing statute expressly allows a petitioner to petition for re-testing once he is included by the initial testing. However, in a handful of jurisdictions, the state is allowed to move for re-testing when the petitioner is excluded ...

VII. Successive Petitions

In the realm of post-conviction law, a "successive" petition is any petition filed under the same statute and after the first petition. While only some of the extant testing statutes contemplate the filing of successive petitions, and under what circumstances, there has been a growing trend in traditional post-conviction law to eliminate the availability of successive petitions. Thus, even though the majority of the testing statutes do not speak to successive petitions, traditional post-conviction concepts may inform the manner in which courts will address them.

...

VIII. Other Forms of Testing

Most, but not all, of the current statutes are limited specifically to DNA testing; however, some statutes also make mention of post-conviction testing of fingerprints. Given recent challenges to the admissibility of fingerprint testimony, it is unclear how this latter class of statute may fare in the future.

IX. Conclusion

Clearly, there is no such thing as a perfect testing statute. Partly, this is due to the extraordinary factual complexity of criminal cases, i.e., a testing statute may work wonderfully for one petitioner, but may prevent another petitioner from even filing his request. However, the lack of perfection in the extant testing statutes is largely attributable to their inability to address the complexities of state and federal post-conviction law. Petitioners seeking testing will thus want to familiarize themselves with relevant post-conviction law, both within their respective states and federally, to ensure that the trappings of traditional post-conviction litigation do not bar their opportunities both under the testing statutes, and in traditional post-conviction.

Notes & Questions

1. Since 1993, 162 wrongfully convicted persons have been exonerated through the Innocence Project's use of reexamined DNA evidence. *See* Innocence Project, http://www.innocenceproject.org/. In a study of exonerations done by Samuel Gross, et al., in 2004, researchers found that out of 328 exonerations between 1989 and 2003, 145 used DNA evidence in clearing the unjustly convicted individual. Most of these exonerations involved cases of murder (61%) or rape (37%); the remaining cases (2%) involved other crimes of violence (robbery, attempted murder, kidnapping) and drug and property crimes. Many of the convictions (64%) had been dependent upon eyewitness identification. This was especially true in rape cases in which nearly 90% of the convictions resulted from eyewitness identification. These cases had the benefit of retained DNA evidence. Although convictions for other violent crimes, such as robbery, may also result from mistaken eyewitness identification, biological evidence is usually not available to refute the eyewitness in these cases. For an exhaustive summary of exonerations, see Samuel R. Gross, et al., EXONERATIONS IN THE UNITED STATES: 1989 THROUGH 2003 (2004), http://www.soros.org/initiatives/justice/articles_publications/publications/exonerations_20040419/exon_report.pdf. For additional information on mistaken eyewitness identification and discussion of methods to improve reliability of such identification, see Gary L. Wells, et al., *Eyewitness Identification Procedures: Recommendations for Lineups and Photospreads*, 22 L. & HUM. BEHAV. 603–47 (1998).

2. The use of DNA in post-conviction review has been spectacular especially given that many of these exonerations have occurred without a legislative roadmap or judicial guidance. *See* Edward Connors, et al., CONVICTED BY JURIES, EXONERATED BY SCIENCE: CASE STUDIES IN THE USE OF DNA EVIDENCE TO ESTABLISH INNOCENCE AFTER TRIAL (1996), http://www.ncjrs.org/txtfiles/dnaevid.txt. Over the past decade, many states

have passed legislation addressing the use of DNA in post-conviction review, the preservation of DNA and biological evidence, and compensation for wrongful conviction. The Innocence Project maintains an up-to-date catalogue of these statutes on its website at http://www.innocenceproject.org/legislation/index.php.

As detailed in the excerpted article by Professor Swedlow, DNA testing statutes typically set forth the standards and procedures for post-conviction DNA testing and relief. A number of organizations have provided guidelines on standards for DNA testing and review of biologic evidence. *See, e.g.*, National Commission on the Future of DNA Evidence, Postconviction DNA Testing: Recommendations For Handling Requests, (1999), *available at* http://www.ojp.usdoj.gov/nij/pubs-sum/177626.htm; National Commission on the Future of DNA Evidence, Using DNA To Solve Cold Cases, (2002), *available at* http://www.ncjrs.org/pdffiles1/nij/194197.pdf.

There is tremendous variation in the statutes—in both breadth and specific content—from jurisdiction to jurisdiction. The Innocence Project has drafted a model law which attempts to provide guidance to state regulators. *See* Innocence Project, Model Statute for Obtaining Post Conviction DNA Testing, http://www.innocenceproject.org/docs/Model_Statute_Postconviction_DNA.pdf. However, like most model laws, while parts of it have been eagerly embraced by legislatures drafting post-conviction DNA testing law, most legislatures have drafted their laws in response to the perceived needs in their jurisdiction rather than moving toward uniformity.

3. A significant number of the DNA exonerations have involved a false confession by the alleged perpetrator(s). The recent study of exonerations by Gross, et al., found that in 51 (15%) of the 328 exonerations, the defendant(s) had confessed to the crime. Many of the exonerated who had falsely confessed were under age eighteen and/or had a mental disability. *See* Gross, et al., *supra* note 1. There are a variety of factors that may give rise to a false confession including police coercion, duress, and diminished capacity of the suspect. Such diminished capacity may result from mental disability, emotional immaturity, intoxication, or injury coupled with ignorance of the law. *See generally* Steven A. Drizen & Richard A. Leo, *The Problem of False Confessions in the Post-DNA World*, 82 N.C. L. Rev. 891 (2004).

People v. Wise is a famous case illustrating false confession. Mr. Wise and four others were convicted of having raped and assaulted the "Central Park Jogger." In this notorious case, the five teenage men were accused of rampaging through the park "wilding" and wreaking havoc with their violent behavior on an April night in 1989. The jogger, a twenty-eight year-old investment banker, was left unconscious and beaten, with her skull fractured; she was found in the early morning severely hypothermic and nearly dead from her injuries and loss of blood. Each of the five admitted, after a long interrogation to participating in the assault and rape of the Jogger. Although each young man's account was somewhat different as to time, location, and role of the participants, all confessed to some involvement. At trial, the Central Part jogger, who had survived her assault and traumatic brain injury, readily admitted that she had no memory of the assault and could not identify her assailants. None of the biological evidence collected was a confirmed match to any one of the alleged assailants. All five of the men were ultimately convicted. Mr. Wise, who was the oldest, at sixteen, was tried as an adult and sentenced to fifteen years in prison.

In early 2002, Matias Reyes admitted that he alone was responsible for the attack on the Central Park jogger. In fact, he had committed another rape in Central Park earlier that year that was quite similar to the attack on the Central Park Jogger. Using mitochondrial DNA testing, the police matched the Central Park Jogger biological specimens to Reyes. This corroborated Reyes' confession and simultaneously exonerated all five men who had been convicted. In late 2002, all five convictions were overturned. Mr. Wise had served eleven and a half years in prison before his exoneration.

C. DNA Repositories, Registries, and Data Banks

With the increase and dramatic success of using DNA identification in the criminal context, there has been an explosion in the number of DNA databanks, repositories and registries. This has, of course, provided opportunities for improved statistical validity as well as new opportunities to match criminals to unsolved crimes. On the flip side, there are questions with respect to requirements for inclusion, privacy rights, confidentiality risks, and use of the information for discriminatory purposes.

DNA databanks are maintained by states, the military and the federal government. The first state to establish a forensic databank was Virginia in 1989. However, by the end of the next decade, all states, as well as Puerto Rico, had followed Virginia's lead. The state laws generally require designated classes of convicted felons to provide blood and/or saliva samples to state labs for storage and/or profiling. There is substantial variation among the states with respect to what felonies, or even misdemeanors, should require inclusion of the convict's DNA in the databank. Several states require donation of a sample from a convict upon release or parole, even if no DNA was required at the time of the conviction. In many states, DNA samples, be they blood, saliva, or both, are maintained in state-based repositories. All states analyze the DNA sample, enter the resulting profile into a computerized database, and transfer the profile to the FBI for inclusion in the Combined DNA Identification System ("CODIS"). DNA profiles, as opposed to biological samples, are digitized records of short tandem repeats ("STR") of DNA at thirteen separate loci. These loci are not connected to known genetic traits or disorders, but rather are unique areas of "junk" DNA with unknown function at the cell level.

In 1994 Congress enacted the DNA Identification Act, an amendment to the Omnibus Crime Control and Safe Streets Act of 1968. *See* 42 U.S.C. § 14132. This legislation was built upon a pilot program begun by the FBI in 1990 that had collated data from fourteen states. The DNA Identification Act formalized the FBI's authority to establish a national DNA index for law enforcement purposes. In October 1998, the FBI's National DNA Index System ("NDIS") became operational and CODIS was established. CODIS is a database with three hierarchical levels (or tiers): local, state, and national. NDIS is the highest level in the CODIS hierarchy, and enables the laboratories participating in the CODIS Program to exchange and compare DNA profiles on a national level. All DNA profiles originate at the local level ("LDIS"), then flow to the state ("SDIS") and national levels. SDIS allows laboratories within states to exchange DNA profiles. The tiered approach allows state and local agencies to operate their databases according to their specific legislative or legal requirements. *See* Fed. Bureau of Investigation, CODIS Mission Statement & Background, *available at* http://www.fbi.gov/hq/lab/codis/program.htm.

CODIS organizes data into two indexes. The first, the Convicted Offender Index, contains the DNA profiles of convicted felons contributed by the states and the FBI. As of March, 2005, the Convicted Offender Index included data from 2,277,056 individuals. The second index, the Forensic Index, is comprised of profiles from samples taken as crime scene evidence, from unidentified human remains, and those contributed by family members of missing, as-yet undiscovered, victims of crime. As of March 2005, 103,402 profiles were included in the Forensic Index. CODIS profiles are comprised of a specimen identifier, the identity of the sponsoring laboratory, the laboratory personnel who developed the profile, and the actual DNA profile itself. The database contains only profiles, not biological samples. Nor does the CODIS database contain any criminal history information or social security numbers. The profiles are digitized data entered into a computer and the program is designed to facilitate the matching and linkage of DNA profiles to DNA evidence taken from crime scenes and similarly digitized. The DNA Identification Act authorized states to exchange profiles and search across the states through the database. All 50 states, as well as Puerto Rico, contribute to CODIS. When a match is determined, the laboratories that contributed the samples work together to validate the match before any identifying information is shared. CODIS has been instrumental in identifying the guilty and exonerating the innocent.

In addition to the databanks maintained by states and the FBI, the Department of Defense has a DNA Registry and Repository. This Repository and Registry was initiated during the Gulf War in 1991. It is now the largest DNA Databank in the world with well over 3.5 million specimens. All persons inducted into the military, on reserve or active duty, are required to provide blood and saliva samples to the DNA Repository. The stored samples consist of two bloodstain cards, one of which is stored in the serviceperson's medical record. The other bloodstain card and a buccal swab of saliva are stored in the DNA Repository. Each DNA card also includes the following identification information: social security number, date of birth, brand of service, fingerprint, bar code and signature. The card is stored in a vacuum-sealed bag and frozen at -20° Centigrade. The buccal swab is chemically preserved and stored at room temperature.

Unlike many of the states and CODIS, the DNA is not profiled until, and unless, the sample is accessed. The primary purpose of the stored DNA is for the identification of soldiers killed, or missing, in action. In earlier wars and armed conflicts, an appreciable number of military personnel were lost and/or never identified as a result of damage done by high velocity weapons, blasts, and deterioration before the remains were found. Since the Gulf War, there has not been a single "unknown" soldier and in fact, "unknown" soldiers from earlier wars have been identified using DNA analysis. Identification of casualties provides an opportunity for families to access death and life insurance benefits and also to achieve closure with respect to the death of their loved one.

Although access to the repository samples is tightly controlled, there is ongoing concern about the risks of maintaining the DNA in storage for the fifty-year timeframe of the Repository. This fifty-year storage parallels the length of storage for other military personnel records. It is possible to access samples in the Repository with a court order in the course of a felony prosecution. Most recently, a 2003 law has allowed law enforcement greater access to the military repository when investigating certain crimes. It is also possible, in some cases, to use the database to identify the remains of a former service person that has gone missing in civilian life. However, the specimens may not be used for any other genetic testing, including paternity testing without the consent of the serviceperson.

Even with the provisions for security in the military DNA repository and provisions for confidentiality of identifiable information in the state databases and CODIS, there have been a number of challenges to the databases. Many of these focus on who should be required to submit samples, when samples can be required, and when someone can refuse to submit a sample or expunge an existing sample or profile.

State v. Martinez

78 P.3d 769 (Kan. 2003)

The opinion of the court was delivered by GERNON, J.:

In this criminal appeal, Juan Pablo Martinez challenges the constitutionality of the Kansas statute which requires an individual to provide blood and saliva samples for a DNA database after a conviction of burglary....

Martinez was charged with one count each of felony aggravated burglary and misdemeanor theft. Martinez entered an *Alford* plea to one count of burglary pursuant to K.S.A. 21-3715. The district court sentenced Martinez to 24 months' probation and required him to provide blood and saliva samples for the DNA database in accordance with K.S.A.2001 Supp. 21-2511. Martinez appeals from the court's order requiring him to provide blood and saliva samples for the DNA database....

Martinez argues that forcing him to provide blood and saliva samples pursuant to K.S.A.2001 Supp. 21-2511 is a violation of his Fourth Amendment rights because a DNA sample is not reasonably related to the crime of burglary. Martinez argues that K.S.A.2001 Supp. 21-2511 is unconstitutional because it was amended to include burglary. Martinez argues that burglary does not involve DNA evidence like sex crimes and other violent crimes.

We recently addressed the constitutionality of K.S.A.2001 Supp. 21-2511 as it applies to the crime of burglary in State v. Maass, 64 P.3d 382 ([Kan.] 2003). In *Maass*, 64 P.3d [at 389], we upheld the statute applying the balancing test as set forth in *Jones v. Murray*, 962 F.2d 302 (4th Cir. 1992); *Rise v. Oregon*, 59 F.3d 1556 (9th Cir. 1995); *Schlicher v. Peters*, 103 F.3d 940 (10th Cir. 1996); *Boling v. Romer*, 101 F.3d 1336 (10th Cir. 1996); and *Gaines v. State*, 998 P.2d 166 ([Nev.] 2000), without considering the special needs doctrine. Although we are not overruling the *Maass* decision, we are clarifying the constitutional analysis, including the application of the special needs doctrine.

Case law clearly establishes that the extraction and analysis of bodily fluids, such as blood, saliva, urine, and semen, are searches in the context of the Fourth Amendment to the United States Constitution. *Skinner v. Ry. Labor Executives' Assn.*, 489 U.S. 602, 618 (1989) (blood and urine); *Schmerber v. California*, 384 U.S. 757, 767 (1966) (blood); *Schlicher*, 103 F.3d at 942–43 (blood and saliva); *Henry v. Ryan*, 775 F. Supp. 247, 253 (N.D. Ill. 1991) (saliva); *State v. Murry*, 21 P.3d 528[, 531] ([Kan.] 2001) (blood); *Crutchfield v. Hannigan*, 906 P.2d 184[, 186] ([Kan. Ct. App.] 1995) (urine); *State v. Williams*, 815 P.2d 569[, 577] ([Kan. Ct. App.] 1991) (semen). The United States Supreme Court, however, has not yet addressed whether the collection of blood and saliva for a DNA database is constitutional.

The Fourth Amendment does not protect against all searches and seizures, only those that are unreasonable. Whether a search or seizure is reasonable depends on the circumstances surrounding the search or seizure. *Skinner*, 489 U.S. at 619. Generally, a search or seizure is unreasonable if it is not accompanied by individualized suspicion. *City of Indianapolis v. Edmond*, 531 U.S. 32, 37 (2000). However, individualized suspicion is not an indispensable component of reasonableness. *Treasury Employees v. Von Raab*, 489 U.S. 656, 665 (1989).

The United States Supreme Court has recognized three exceptions to the general rule requiring individualized suspicion. *Edmond*, 531 U.S. at 37, 121 S.Ct. 447. When analyzing a search that lacks individualized suspicion, the first step in the constitutional analysis is to determine whether one of the three exceptions applies. If a case falls within one of the recognized exceptions, the next step in the analysis is to balance the need for the search with the invasion of the individual's rights. "Courts must consider the scope of the particular intrusion, the manner in which it is conducted, the justification for initiating it, and the place in which it is conducted." *Bell v. Wolfish*, 441 U.S. 520, 559 (1979).

The first exception to the rule requiring individualized suspicion recognizes the government's "'special needs, beyond the normal need for law enforcement.'" *Edmond*, 531 U.S. at 37 (citing *Vernonia School Dist. 47J v. Acton*, 515 U.S. 646 [1995] [validating the random drug-testing of high school athletes]; *Von Raab*, 489 U.S. 656 [upholding the drug testing of United States Customs employees for transfer or promotion]; *Skinner*, 489 U.S. 602 [approving the drug and alcohol testing of railroad employees]); see also *Ferguson v. City of Charleston*, 532 U.S. 67 (2001) (invalidating a program for drug testing pregnant mothers); *Griffin v. Wisconsin*, 483 U.S. 868 (1987) (upholding the search of a probationer's home without probable cause). In determining whether a special need exists, a court must closely review the scheme at issue to determine its primary purpose. *Ferguson*, 532 U.S. at 81.

The United States Supreme Court has established several different categories of special needs. The *Griffin* Court concluded that the government's responsibility to supervise probationers is a special need allowing probation officers to search a probationer's private dwelling without probable cause. 483 U.S. at 875–76. Finding a similar responsibility for supervising schoolchildren to be a special need, the *Vernonia School Dist. 47J* Court upheld a program of drug testing high school athletes. 515 U.S. at 664–65. In *Skinner*, the Supreme Court determined that the government's interest in regulating railroad employees to ensure safety is a special need and upheld a policy requiring railroad employees to submit to drug and alcohol screening. 489 U.S. at 620. The *Von Raab* Court found the government's substantial interest in deterring drug use and the promotion of drug users within the Customs Service to be a special need and validated a regulation requiring employees in certain positions to submit to drug testing. 489 U.S. at 666.

The second exception to the general rule requiring individualized suspicion involves limited administrative searches. *Edmond*, 531 U.S. at 37 (citing *New York v. Burger*, 482 U.S. 691 [1987] [upholding the administrative inspection of a closely regulated car-dismantling business]; *Michigan v. Tyler*, 436 U.S. 499 [1978] [validating the administrative inspection of fire-damaged building]; *Camara v. Municipal Court of City and County of San Francisco*, 387 U.S. 523 [1967] [approving an administrative inspection for compliance with city housing code]); see also *Wolfish*, 441 U.S. 520 (validating the strip search of inmates); *Pool v. McKune*, 987 P.2d 1073 ([Kan.] 1999) (upholding the use of plethysmograph testing for sex offenders).

The third exception to the rule requiring individualized suspicion involves motorist checkpoints. *Edmond*, 531 U.S. at 37 (invalidating a highway checkpoint for illegal narcotics); *Michigan Dept. of State Police v. Sitz*, 496 U.S. 444 (1990) (validating a sobriety checkpoint); *United States v. Martinez-Fuerte*, 428 U.S. 543 (1976) (validating an illegal alien checkpoint). This exception clearly has no application to the facts of this case.

However, it is interesting to note that although the *Edmond* Court recognized the checkpoint exception as a separate class, it blurred the line between the special needs exception and the checkpoint exception by invalidating a drug interdiction checkpoint because the government's primary purpose was crime control. 531 U.S. at 44.

Most of the courts that have reviewed the constitutionality of DNA collection and cataloging statutes have not categorized the analysis under one of the three exceptions to the general rule requiring individualized suspicion. Instead, these courts upheld the statutes by simply applying an interest balancing test. Our opinion in *Maass* follows the same approach. See 64 P.3d [at 389].

Although DNA collection and cataloging statutes do not fall within the special needs analysis previously articulated by the United States Supreme Court, some courts have reviewed DNA statutes using the special needs exception.... Some of these courts did not specifically analyze the special need involved. However, other courts concluded that the government's interest in solving past and future crimes and in deterring individuals from committing future offenses is a special need. This special need for DNA collection and cataloging statutes is distinguished from the "normal" need for law enforcement because the DNA samples prove "nothing by themselves regarding whether a donor has committed a crime" and, therefore, does not detect ordinary criminal wrongdoing.

This distinction is significant in light of the United States Supreme Court's decisions in *Ferguson* and *Edmond*. In *Ferguson*, the Court determined that the immediate objective for drug testing certain pregnant mothers was to "generate evidence for law enforcement purposes" rather than to treat drug addicted mothers and babies. Finding that the immediate objective was not a special need beyond the normal need for law enforcement, the *Ferguson* court struck down a municipal hospital's policy ordering that nonconsensual drug screens be performed on maternity patients who were suspected of using cocaine.

Likewise, in *Edmond*, 531 U.S. at 41–42, the Court concluded that the primary purpose for a narcotics checkpoint was to detect ordinary criminal wrongdoing and prosecute the offenders. Because the primary purpose was not beyond the normal need for law enforcement, the Court invalidated the checkpoint program.

The *Miles* court also considered the special needs doctrine when it analyzed a statute authorizing the collection and cataloging of DNA and determined that the government did not have a special need beyond the normal need for law enforcement. Relying on *Edmond* and *Ferguson*, the *Miles* court invalidated a federal statute requiring a former felon to provide a DNA sample. The Miles court distinguished case law upholding DNA statutes on the basis that they were either decided before *Edmond* and *Ferguson* or did not discuss the import of those decisions.

This court has a duty to uphold a statute under constitutional attack if there is any reasonable way to construe the statute as constitutionally valid. The United States Supreme Court has routinely validated the collection and analysis of bodily fluids as long as there was a special need beyond detecting criminal wrongdoing. Here, the State has a special need for accurately solving future crimes and, thereby, protecting the safety and welfare of Kansas citizens. This special need is beyond the normal need for law enforcement because it does not in and of itself detect criminal wrongdoing.

We disagree with the *Miles* court's analysis of *Edmond* and *Ferguson*. In determining that DNA collection was not beyond the normal need for law enforcement, the *Miles* court failed to consider the key distinction between DNA information and drug testing and checkpoint inspections. The key distinction is that the drug testing and the checkpoint inspections provide evidence of current or ongoing criminal wrongdoing. Based on the evidence obtained from the drug test and the checkpoint inspections, officers have probable cause to immediately arrest someone for a current or ongoing crime. With DNA information, however, there is no immediate possibility of finding probable cause to support an arrest. Like fingerprint and photograph identification information, the DNA information does not, in and of itself, detect or implicate any criminal wrongdoing. It is this distinction that removes the collection and cataloging of DNA information from the normal need for law enforcement. With this distinction in mind, we agree with the courts that have found the collection and cataloging of DNA information to be a special need beyond the normal need for law enforcement.

Having met the threshold requirement of establishing a special need as an exception to the general rule requiring individualized suspicion, we must balance the individual's rights against the State's legitimate interests by considering the scope of the intrusion, the manner in which the testing is conducted, the reason for the testing, and the place where the testing is conducted.

K.S.A.2001 Supp. 21-2511(a) provides for the collection and testing of a person's blood and saliva. The United States Supreme Court has previously determined that blood testing is commonplace and constitutes a minimal intrusion with virtually no risk. Saliva sampling is even less intrusive than blood sampling. K.S.A.2001 Supp. 21-2511(e) further requires that all of the blood sampling must be performed by qualified medical professionals in accordance with generally accepted medical practices. Although the statute does not specifically designate where the samples may be taken, it limits the available collection sites to those that comply with accepted medical practices, thereby minimizing the risk of infection. K.S.A.2001 Supp. 21-2511(c), (e). This method of collecting blood samples complies with the blood sampling approved by the United States Supreme Court in *Schmerber*, 384 U.S. at 771–72.

In balancing the reasons for the DNA testing, it is important to note that convicted felons, such as those specifically included in K.S.A.2001 Supp. 21-2511(a), are routinely fingerprinted and photographed for identification purposes. K.S.A.2001 Supp. 21-2511(b). Indeed, "it is elementary that a person in lawful custody may be required to submit to photographing and fingerprinting as part of routine identification processes. Other courts upholding DNA sampling and cataloging have also compared the process to fingerprinting and photographing persons legally in custody.

It is also significant that convicted criminals have a reduced expectation of privacy. Finding that a probationer's liberty is limited by the observance of special restrictions, the United States Supreme Court in *Griffin* upheld the search of a probationer's residence without probable cause by distinguishing between a probationer's expectation of privacy in his home and the general public's expectation of privacy in their homes....

Moreover, a person convicted of a crime has a reduced expectation of privacy in his or her identity. "Once a person is convicted of one of the felonies included as a predicate offense..., his identity has become a matter of state interest and he has lost any legitimate expectation of privacy in the identifying information derived from blood sampling."

The United States Supreme Court has recognized that dispensing with the warrant requirement may be necessary when it frustrates the government's purpose for the search. That principle applies in this case. The government cannot establish probable cause to collect DNA information when there is no indication that a crime has even been committed. The essential purpose for a warrant is "to protect privacy interests by assuring citizens subject to a search or seizure that such intrusions are not the random or arbitrary acts of government agents." Here, State authorities are not allowed to choose which offenders will provide samples but are directed by the statute to collect and catalog samples from all persons convicted of the listed crimes. K.S.A.2001 Supp. 21-2511. There is nothing random or arbitrary about the State's action in collecting DNA samples pursuant to K.S.A. 2001 Supp. 21-2511. Thus, a warrant is unnecessary to protect citizens from random or arbitrary DNA collection under the statute.

The State's justification for DNA testing is accurately solving future crimes to protect Kansas citizens from dangerous criminals. Weighing this substantial State interest against a convicted person's right to privacy, the balance must tip in favor of the State's substantial interest. The collection and cataloging of DNA information pursuant to K.S.A.2001 Supp. 21-2511 does not violate the Fourth Amendment's protection against unreasonable searches and seizures.

Martinez attempts to distinguish his case from others by pointing to the recent addition of burglary as one of the crimes set forth in the statute. He argues that DNA evidence is not likely to be used for solving future burglary crimes because the leaving of DNA is so incidental and the chances of police finding such DNA is so remote that there is no legitimate nexus between the two. This argument is without merit.

In *Bousman v. Dist. Ct. for Clinton County*, 630 N.W.2d 789, 801 (Iowa 2001), the Iowa Supreme Court held that the State must have probable cause before issuing an order requiring a suspect to submit DNA samples. (The holding does not address the application of a DNA collection and cataloging statute.) The case involved the investigation of a burglary that was accomplished by breaking a window. The burglar left drops of blood at the crime scene. Although not relevant to the constitutional analysis in this case, the *Bousman* case clearly identifies a situation in which DNA evidence may be used to determine who committed a burglary. It also highlights the potential for finding DNA evidence at burglary crime scenes by demonstrating that entry may be achieved through excessive force or breaking windows. Anytime there is excessive force or broken glass, there is the potential for injury and resulting blood evidence.

Martinez' argument is further diminished by the fact that other courts have upheld DNA collection and cataloging statutes that include burglary. The addition of burglary to the crimes included in K.S.A.2001 Supp. 21-2511 does not make the statute unconstitutional.

Affirmed.

United States v. Kincade

379 F.3d 813 (9th Cir. 2004)

O'Scannlain, Circuit Judge:

We must decide whether the Fourth Amendment permits compulsory DNA profiling of certain conditionally-released federal offenders in the absence of individualized suspicion that they have committed additional crimes.

I

A

Pursuant to the DNA Analysis Backlog Elimination Act of 2000 ("DNA Act"), Pub. L. No. 106-546, 114 Stat. 2726 (2000), individuals who have been convicted of certain federal crimes and who are incarcerated, or on parole, probation, or supervised release must provide federal authorities with "a tissue, fluid, or other bodily sample ... on which a[n] ... analysis of th[at sample's] deoxyribonucleic acid (DNA) identification information" can be performed. Because the Federal Bureau of Investigation ("the Bureau") considers DNA information derived from blood samples to be more reliable than that obtained from other sources (in part because blood is easier to test and to preserve than hair, saliva, or skin cells), Bureau guidelines require those in federal custody and subject to the DNA Act ("qualified federal offenders") to submit to compulsory blood sampling. *See* Nancy Beatty Gregoire, *Federal Probation Joins the World of DNA Collection,* 66 Fed. Probation 30, 31 (2002). Failure "to cooperate in the collection of that sample [is] ... a class A misdemeanor," punishable by up to one year's imprisonment and a fine of as much as $100,000. 42 U.S.C. § 14135a(a)(5); 18 U.S.C. §§ 3571 & 3581.

Once collected by a phlebotomist, qualified federal offenders' blood samples are turned over to the Bureau for DNA analysis—the identification and recording of an individual's "genetic fingerprint." Through the use of short tandem repeat technology ("STR"), the Bureau analyzes the presence of various alleles located at 13 markers (or loci) on DNA present in the specimen. These STR loci are each found on so-called "junk DNA"—that is, non-genic stretches of DNA not presently recognized as being responsible for trait coding—and "were purposely selected because they are not associated with any known physical or medical characteristics." H.R.Rep. No. 106-900(I). Because there are observed group variances in the representation of various alleles at the STR loci, however, DNA profiles derived by STR may yield probabilistic evidence of the contributor's race or sex. Even so, DNA profiles generated by STR are highly individuated: Due to the substantial number of alleles present at each of the 13 STR loci and wide-spread variances in their representation among human beings, the chance that two randomly selected individuals will share the same profile are infinitesimal—as are the chances that a person randomly selected from the population at large will present the same DNA profile as that drawn from crime-scene evidence.

Once STR has been used to produce an individual's DNA profile, the resulting record is loaded into the Bureau's Combined DNA Index System ("CODIS")—a massive centrally-managed database linking DNA profiles culled from federal, state, and territorial DNA collection programs, as well as profiles drawn from crime-scene evidence, unidentified remains, and genetic samples voluntarily provided by relatives of missing persons. 42 U.S.C. §§ 14132(a)–(b). As of March 2004, CODIS contained DNA profiles drawn from 1,641,076 offenders and 78,475 crime scenes. Fed. Bureau of Investigation, NDIS Statistics, *available at* http://www.fbi.gov/hq/lab/codis/clickmap.htm (last visited May 11, 2004). Of those profiles, 298,767 offender records and 10,270 forensic samples originated in the states comprising the Ninth Circuit. *See id.*

CODIS can be used in two different ways. First, law enforcement can match one forensic crime scene sample to another forensic crime scene sample, thereby allowing officers to connect unsolved crimes through a common perpetrator. Second, and of perhaps greater significance, CODIS enables officials to match evidence obtained at the scene of a crime to a particular offender's profile. In this latter capacity, CODIS serves as a potent tool for monitoring the criminal activity of known offenders. Through March 2004, Bureau data indicated that CODIS has aided some 16,160 investigations nationwide—1,710 within the Ninth Circuit. Fed. Bureau of Investigation, Investigations Aided, *available at* http://www.fbi.gov/hq/lab/codis/aidedmap.htm (last visited May 11, 2004).

B

On July 20, 1993, driven by escalating personal and financial troubles, decorated Navy seaman Thomas Cameron Kincade robbed a bank using a firearm in violation of 18 U.S.C. §§2113(a) & (d) and 18 U.S.C. §924(c)(1). He soon pleaded guilty to those charges and was sentenced to 97 months' imprisonment, followed by three years' supervised release. Among others, terms of his release required him to participate in an outpatient substance abuse program; not to commit another federal, state, or local crime; and to follow the instructions of his probation officer.

Shortly after his August 2000 release from federal prison, Kincade submitted a urine sample which tested positive for cocaine. A warrant was issued for his arrest in early October, and on November 13, the district court reinstated Kincade's original term of supervision. In April 2001, Kincade admitted relapsing into cocaine abuse and requested placement in a residential drug treatment program. No action was taken on his request, and on May 21 and May 28, 2001, Kincade again submitted cocaine-positive urine samples. As a result, the district court modified the terms of Kincade's supervised release on June 7, 2001 to include treatment in a residential drug program. Thereafter, Kincade appears to have begun making progress in reforming his life.

On March 25, 2002, Kincade's probation officer asked him to submit a blood sample pursuant to the DNA Act. He refused, eventually explaining that his objections were purely a matter of personal preference—in his words, "not a religious conviction." Kincade's probation officer suggested he contact his attorney for advice, and also explained that if he changed his mind he could submit a blood sample on April 16, 2002. On April 4, 2002, Kincade notified the Probation Office of his intention not to comply and, as promised, he refused to appear for DNA profiling on April 16. On May 7, 2002, Kincade's probation officer again contacted him in an effort to determine whether there was some way they could work through the issue. Kincade indicated that he would comply with the requirements of the DNA Act only if threatened with imposition of a significant term of incarceration. Lacking any alternative, Kincade's probation officer informed the district court that Kincade had refused to submit the blood sample required by the DNA Act. He also recommended revocation of Kincade's supervised release, and re-incarceration.

In briefing to the district court prior to a scheduled revocation hearing, Kincade challenged the constitutionality of the DNA Act on grounds that it violated the Ex Post Facto Clause, the Fourth Amendment, and separation of powers principles embodied in Article III and the Due Process Clause. On July 15, 2002, Kincade appeared at a revocation hearing before U.S. District Judge Dickran Tevrizian. After stating on the record that he was inclined to hold the DNA Act constitutional, Judge Tevrizian offered Kincade another opportunity to submit to DNA profiling in lieu of proceeding with the revocation hearing. Kincade consulted with counsel, who quickly informed the court that Kincade had again declined to reconsider his refusal to submit to DNA profiling.

Following argument, Judge Tevrizian rejected Kincade's constitutional challenges to the DNA Act. Concluding that Kincade had violated the terms of his supervised release by refusing to follow his Probation officer's lawful instruction to provide a blood sample, Judge Tevrizian sentenced Kincade to four months' imprisonment and two years' supervised release. Judge Tevrizian immediately stayed Kincade's sentence of imprisonment, and we expedited review of his appeal. On April 14, 2003—while this appeal was pending, and while Kincade was serving his additional supervised release—Kincade again tested positive for drug use. Consequently, Judge Tevrizian lifted his stay of Kincade's sentence and, once in custody, Kincade finally was forced to submit to DNA profiling. He persists in his challenge to the Act.

II

While "[i]t would be foolish to contend that the degree of privacy secured to citizens by the Fourth Amendment has been entirely unaffected by the advance of technology," *Kyllo v. United States,* 533 U.S. 27, 33–34 (2001), we begin—as always—with first principles.

A

Pursuant to the Fourth Amendment,"[t]he right of the people to be secure in their persons, houses, papers, and effects, against unreasonable searches and seizures, shall not be violated, and no Warrants shall issue, but upon probable cause, supported by Oath or affirmation, and particularly describing the place to be searched, and the persons or things to be seized." U.S. Const. amend. IV. "The touchstone of our analysis under the Fourth Amendment is always 'the reasonableness in all the circumstances of the particular governmental invasion of a citizen's personal security.'" *Pennsylvania v. Mimms,* 434 U.S. 106, 108–09 (1977) (quoting *Terry v. Ohio,* 392 U.S. 1, 19 (1968)).

Ordinarily, the reasonableness of a search depends on governmental compliance with the Warrant Clause, which requires authorities to demonstrate probable cause to a neutral magistrate and thereby convince him to provide formal authorization to proceed with a search by issuance of a particularized warrant. *United States v. United States Dist. Ct.,* 407 U.S. 297, 315–16 (1972); *see also Groh v. Ramirez,* 540 U.S. 551, [559] (2004). However, the general rule of the Warrant Clause is not unyielding. Under a variety of conditions, law enforcement may execute a search without first complying with its dictates. For instance, police may execute warrantless searches incident to a lawful arrest: It is reasonable for authorities to search an arrestee for weapons that might threaten their safety, or for evidence which might be destroyed. *See, e.g., Chimel v. California,* 395 U.S. 752, 762–63 (1969); *see also Thornton v. United States,* 541 U.S. 615 (2004). And even outside the context of a lawful arrest supported by probable cause, officers are likewise authorized to conduct a warrantless protective pat-down of individuals they encounter in the field so long as their concerns are justified by reasonable suspicion of possible danger. *See, e.g., Terry,* 392 U.S. at 27.

The Court has also sanctioned several general search regimes that are free from the usual warrant-and-probable cause requirements. Though not necessarily mutually-exclusive, three categories of searches help organize the jurisprudence. The first can be called "exempted areas." Included here are searches conducted at the border, in prisons, and at airports and entrances to government buildings.

The second category is typically labeled "administrative" searches, though it has not always been given that label. This class includes inspections of closely-regulated businesses, *see, e.g., Burger,* 482 U.S. at 702–04 ("[W]here the privacy interests of the owner are weakened and the government interests in regulating particular businesses are concomitantly heightened, a warrantless inspection of commercial premises may well be reasonable within the meaning of the Fourth Amendment."); *United States v. Biswell,* 406 U.S. 311, 317 (1972), and extends to other routine regulatory investigations. *See, e.g., Camara v. Mun. Ct. of S.F.,* 387 U.S. 523, 535–539 (1967) (authorizing municipal "area inspections" designed to monitor compliance with building safety codes).

A final category of suspicionless searches is referred to as "special needs," and in recent years, the Court has devoted increasing attention to the development of the accompanying analytical doctrine. *See Illinois v. Lidster,* 540 U.S. 419 (2004) (upholding a highway checkpoint designed to enable police to question citizens about a recent crime); *Bd. of Educ. v. Earls,* 536 U.S. 822 (2002) (upholding a program that subjected all students participating in extracurricular activities to submit to random, suspicionless drug testing); *Ferguson v. City of Charleston,* 532 U.S. 67 (2001) (invalidating a public hospital's non-consensual drug testing of maternity patients); *Edmond,* 531 U.S. at 48 (invalidating a roadside checkpoint designed to discover and interdict illegal drugs); *Vernonia Sch. Dist. 47J v. Acton,* 515 U.S. 646 (1995) (upholding a program subjecting student athletes to random, suspicionless drug testing); *see also Nat'l Treasury Employees Union v. Von Raab,* 489 U.S. 656 (1989) (upholding suspicionless drug testing of certain U.S. Customs officials); *Skinner,* 489 U.S. at 634 (upholding compulsory blood and urine tests of railroad employees involved in certain train accidents); *Griffin,* 483 U.S. at 879–80 (upholding a warrant-less search of a probationer's residence).

...

4

While these recent cases may seem to be moving toward requiring that *any* search conducted primarily for law enforcement purposes must be accompanied by at least some quantum of individualized suspicion, the Court signaled the existence of possible limitations in *United States v. Knights,* 534 U.S. 112 (2001). At issue there was a warrantless search of a probationer long suspected of having committed crimes targeting Pacific Gas & Electric ("PG & E") facilities. Shortly after Knights was placed on probation for an unrelated drug offense, an arson targeting a PG & E electrical transformer caused approximately $1.5 million in damage. *Id.* at 114–15.

...

To do so, it turned to the traditional totality of the circumstances test—balancing the invasion of Knights's interest in privacy against the State's interest in searching his home without a warrant supported by probable cause. Of central importance to our decision today, the Court explained that "Knights's status as a probationer subject to a search condition informs both sides of that balance." *Id.* at 119.... [T]he Court held, the government needs "no more than reasonable suspicion to conduct a search of [a] probationer's house." *Id.* at 121.

5

Having thus upheld a warrantless probation search designed purely to further law enforcement purposes, and having done so wholly outside the confines of special needs analysis, *Knights* suggests something of a departure from *Edmond* and *Ferguson* (and to a more limited extent *Griffin*). After all, each of those cases had assessed warrantless searches under a special needs rubric that demands some underlying motivation apart from the government's general interest in law enforcement. Yet even beyond declining to apply such analysis, *Knights* almost wholly ignored the Court's previous decisions in *Edmond* and *Ferguson.*

One possible distinction between *Knights,* on one hand, and *Edmond* and *Ferguson,* on the other, suggests a possible reconciliation: The search conducted in *Knights* was supported by reasonable suspicion, while the Court's most recent special needs cases have focused on suspicionless searches and seizures, such as the DNA profiling at issue here.... One might therefore be tempted to conclude that the quantum of suspicion supporting the search of Knights's apartment was what pushed the Court beyond special needs analysis.

We do not think so. The Court has long understood special needs analysis to be triggered not by a complete absence of suspicion, but by a departure from the Fourth Amendment's warrant-and-probable cause requirements. In *Griffin,* after all, the search upheld by the Court under special needs analysis was also supported by "reasonable grounds." ...

Moreover, *Knights* made clear the Court was not prepared to draw the line at a reasonable suspicion threshold—at least not when it comes to conditional releasees. To the contrary, it expressly left unresolved the question whether special needs analysis controlled suspicionless searches of probationers at all.... The only rational interpretation of *Knights's* express reservation is that—without regard to the Court's prior decisions in *Edmond* and *Ferguson*—it remains *entirely* an open question whether suspicionless searches of conditional releasees pass constitutional muster when such searches are conducted for law enforcement purposes.

B

We are not the first court called upon to address this unresolved issue. Confronted with challenges to the federal DNA Act and its state law analogues, our sister circuits and peers in the states have divided in their analytical approaches—both before and after the Supreme Court's recent special needs decisions. On one hand, the Second, Seventh, and Tenth Circuits, along with a variety of federal district courts and at least two state Supreme Courts, have upheld DNA collection statutes under a special needs analysis (though not always ruling out the possibility that the totality of the circumstances might validate the search absent some special need). *See Green v. Berge,* 354 F.3d 675, 679 (7th Cir.2004); *United States v. Kimler,* 335 F.3d 1132, 1146 (10th Cir.2003); *Roe v. Marcotte,* 193 F.3d 72, 79–82 (2d Cir.1999); *Vore v. U.S. Dep't of Justice,* 281 F.Supp.2d 1129, 1133–35 (D.Ariz.2003); *Miller v. U.S. Parole Comm'n,* 259 F.Supp.2d 1166, 1175–78 (D.Kan.2003); *United States v. Sczubelek,* 255 F.Supp.2d 315, 319–23 (D.Del.2003); *United States v. Reynard,* 220 F.Supp.2d 1142, 1165–69 (S.D.Cal.2002); *State v. Martinez,* 78 P.3d 769, 771–75 ([Kan.] 2003); *State v. Olivas,* 856 P.2d 1076, 1085–86 ([Wash.] 1993); *State v. Steele,* 802 N.E.2d 1127, 1132–37 ([Ohio] 2003); *In re D.L.C.,* 124 S.W.3d 354, 370–73 (Tex.App.2003); *State v. Surge,* 94 P.3d 345, [351] (Wash.Ct.App. July 12, 2004).

By contrast, the Fourth and Fifth Circuits, a Seventh Circuit Judge, numerous federal district courts, and a variety of state courts have approved compulsory DNA profiling under a traditional assessment of reasonableness gauged by the totality of the circumstances.

Finally, we observe that our own 1995 decision in *Rise v. Oregon,* 59 F.3d 1556 (9th Cir.1995), upheld the constitutionality of a state DNA collection statute by applying a pure totality of the circumstances analysis. Our resolution of the methodological question, left open by *Knights,* therefore squarely implicates the legitimacy of our own precedent and its method.

III

While not precluding the possibility that the federal DNA Act could satisfy a special needs analysis, we today reaffirm the continuing vitality of *Rise*—and hold that its reliance on a totality of the circumstances analysis to uphold compulsory DNA profiling of convicted offenders both comports with the Supreme Court's recent precedents and resolves this appeal in concert with the requirements of the Fourth Amendment.

...

Of course, the mere possibility that suspicionless searches of conditional releasees *may be* sustainable under a pure totality of the circumstances analysis is insufficient to establish that such searches *actually are* sustainable under such analysis. We begin our resolution of the issue by taking note of the well-established principle that parolees and other conditional releasees are not entitled to the full panoply of rights and protections possessed by the general public. Quite to the contrary, the Court has recognized that "those who have suffered a lawful conviction" are properly subject to a "broad range of [restrictions] that might infringe constitutional rights in free society," *McKune v. Lile,* 536 U.S. 24, 36 (2002), in no small part due to the extraordinary rate of recidivism among offenders. *See, e.g., Pa. Bd. of Prob. & Parole v. Scott,* 524 U.S. 357, 365 (1998); *Knights,* 534 U.S. at 120; *Griffin,* 483 U.S. at 875; *Crawford,* 372 F.3d at 1069–71 (Trott, J., concurring); *see also Ewing v. California,* 538 U.S. 11, 25–27 (2003); *Parke v. Raley,* 506 U.S. 20, 27 (1992) ("States have a valid interest in deterring and segregating habitual criminals."). Thus, conditional releasees may claim "only ... conditional liberty properly dependent on observance of special parole restrictions" that extend "substantially beyond the ordinary restrictions imposed by law on an individual citizen." *Morrissey,* 408 U.S. at 478 & 480 (1972); *Scott,* 524 U.S. at 365 ("[T]he State accords a limited degree of freedom in return for the parolee's assurance that he will comply with the often strict terms and conditions of his release. In most cases, the State is willing to extend parole only because it is able to condition it upon compliance with certain requirements.").

These restrictions generally "are meant to assure that the [conditional release term] serves as a period of genuine rehabilitation and that the community is not harmed by the [releasee]'s being at large. These same goals require and justify the exercise of supervision to assure that the restrictions are in fact observed." *Griffin,* 483 U.S. at 875. And whether they are initially legitimated as furthering a "special need," *id.* at 873–74, or recognized merely as serving the government's "'overwhelming interest' in ensuring that a [releasee] complies with those requirements and is returned to prison if he fails to do so," *Scott,* 524 U.S. at 365 (quoting *Morrissey,* 408 U.S. at 477), once such strictures are imposed and clearly noticed, they dramatically alter the relationship between the releasee and the government. For at bottom, they render all kinds of individual choices—choices that otherwise would be privately considered, privately determined, and privately undertaken—matters of legitimate government concern and investigation....

These transformative changes wrought by a lawful conviction and accompanying term of conditional release are well-recognized by the Supreme Court, which often has noted that conditional releasees enjoy severely constricted expectations of privacy relative to the general citizenry—and that the government has a far more substantial interest in invading their privacy than it does in interfering with the liberty of law-abiding citizens....

We believe that such a severe and fundamental disruption in the relationship between the offender and society, along with the government's concomitantly greater interest in closely monitoring and supervising conditional releasees, is in turn sufficient to sustain suspicionless searches of his person and property even in the absence of some non-law enforcement "special need"—at least where such searches meet the Fourth Amendment touchstone of reasonableness as gauged by the totality of the circumstances.

Let us be clear: Our holding in no way intimates that conditional releasees' diminished expectations of privacy serve to extinguish their ability to invoke the protections of the Fourth Amendment's guarantee against unreasonable searches and seizures. Where a given search or class of searches cannot satisfy the traditional totality of the circumstances test, a conditional releasee may lay claim to constitutional relief—just like any other citizen. Further, and without regard to the outcome of any such analysis, we reiterate Judge Trott's recent observation that conditional releasees likewise "retain [] a right of privacy against government searches and seizures that are arbitrary, a right of privacy against searches and seizures that are capricious, and a right of privacy against searches and seizures that are harassing."

We also wish to emphasize the limited nature of our holding. With its alarmist tone and obligatory reference to George Orwell's *1984,* Judge Reinhardt's dissent repeatedly asserts that our decision renders every person in America subject to DNA sampling for CODIS purposes, including "attendees of public high schools or universities, persons seeking to obtain drivers' licenses, applicants for federal employment, or persons requiring any form of federal identification, and those who desire to travel by airplane," "political opponents," "disfavored minorities," "all newborns," "passengers of vehicles," "arrestees,"—no, really, "the entire population." Nothing could be further from the truth—and we respectfully suggest that our dissenting colleague ought to recognize the obvious and significant distinction between the DNA profiling of law-abiding citizens who are passing through some transient status (e.g., newborns, students, passengers in a car or on a plane) and lawfully adjudicated criminals whose proven conduct substantially heightens the government's interest in monitoring them and quite properly carries lasting consequences that simply do not attach from the simple fact of having been born, or going to public school, or riding in a car.

B

With this framework in mind, we can now appraise the reasonableness of the federal DNA Act's compulsory DNA profiling of qualified federal offenders. In evaluating the totality of the circumstances, we must balance the degree to which DNA profiling interferes with the privacy interests of qualified federal offenders against the significance of the public interests served by such profiling. *See Brown v. Texas,* 443 U.S. 47, 50–51 (1979).

1

As we have recognized [above], compulsory blood tests implicate the individual's interest in bodily integrity—"a cherished value of our society." *Schmerber v. California,* 384 U.S. 757, 772 (1966). Nonetheless, it is firmly established that "the intrusion occasioned by a blood test is not significant, since such 'tests are a commonplace in these days of periodic physical examinations and experience with them teaches that the quantity of blood extracted is minimal, and that for most people the procedure involves virtually no risk, trauma, or pain.'" *Skinner,* 489 U.S. at 625 (quoting *Schmerber,* 384 U.S. at 771); *see also Winston,* 470 U.S. at 762 (observing "society's judgment that blood tests do not constitute an unduly extensive imposition on an individual's personal privacy and bodily integrity"); *Yin v. California,* 95 F.3d 864, 870 (9th Cir.1996) (Reinhardt, J.) ("In today's world, a medical examination that does not include either a blood test or urinalysis would be unusual.")....

At the same time, the DNA profile derived from the defendant's blood sample establishes only a record of the defendant's identity—otherwise personal information in which the qualified offender can claim no right of privacy once lawfully convicted of a qualifying offense (indeed, once lawfully arrested and booked into state custody). For, as we recognized in *Rise,* "[o]nce a person is convicted of one of the felonies included as predicate offenses under [the DNA Act], his identity has become a matter of state interest and he has lost any legitimate expectation of privacy in the identifying information derived from blood sampling.

Both Kincade and his supporting amici passionately protest that because the government does not destroy blood samples drawn for DNA profiling and because such samples therefore conceivably could be mined for more private information or otherwise misused in the future, any presently legitimate generation of DNA profiles is irretrievably tainted by the prospect of far more consequential future invasions of personal privacy. Judge Reinhardt's dissent likewise maintains that in light of the "nightmarish" possibilities CODIS portends, we must act immediately to halt the program—before the wolf enters the fold, rather than after.

The concerns raised by amici and by Judge Reinhardt in his dissent are indeed weighty ones, and we do not dismiss them lightly. But beyond the fact that the DNA Act itself provides protections against such misuse, our job is limited to resolving the constitutionality of the program before us, as it is designed and as it has been implemented. In our system of government, courts base decisions not on dramatic Hollywood fantasies, but on concretely particularized facts developed in the cauldron of the adversary process and reduced to an assessable record....

2

In contrast, the interests furthered by the federal DNA Act are undeniably compelling. By establishing a means of identification that can be used to link conditional releasees to crimes committed while they are at large, compulsory DNA profiling serves society's "'overwhelming interest' in ensuring that a parolee complies with th[]e requirements [of his release] and is returned to prison if he fails to do so." *Scott,* 524 U.S. at 365 (quoting *Morrissey,* 408 U.S. at 483). The deterrent effect of such profiling, *see, e.g., Roe,* 193 F.3d at 79; *Rise,* 59 F.3d at 1561 & n. 4; *Jones,* 962 F.2d at 311, similarly fosters society's enormous interest in reducing recidivism. As Judge Trott highlighted in his *Crawford* concurrence, rates of re-arrest among parolees and probationers are astounding, 372 F.3d at 1069–70 (Trott, J., concurring); the Supreme Court, too, has frequently stressed the pressing need to reduce recidivism among the offender population. *See, e.g., Ewing,* 538 U.S. at 25–27; *Smith v. Doe,* 538 U.S. 84, 103 (2003); *McKune,* 536 U.S. at 32–33; *Knights,* 534 U.S. at 120; *Griffin,* 483 U.S. at 875, 876, 878, 880. Finally, by contributing to the solution of past crimes, DNA profiling of qualified federal offenders helps bring closure to countless victims of crime who long have languished in the knowledge that perpetrators remain at large. Together, the weight of these interests is monumental.

These interests also are intimately related to the core purposes of conditional release: rehabilitating convicted offenders and sheltering society from future victimization. *See Knights,* 534 U.S. at 119; *Scott,* 524 U.S. at 365; *Griffin,* 483 U.S. at 875 & 880; *see also United States v. Jackson,* 189 F.3d 820, 824 (9th Cir.1999). As a deterrent, DNA profiling can help to steer conditional releasees toward law-abiding lives as productive members of our society, fostering the rehabilitative goal of our systems of conditional release. Such profiling likewise helps protect the society into which offenders are conditionally released by reducing crime attributable to the operation of limited release programs like probation and parole. *Rise,* 59 F.3d at 1561. And by laying a foundation for solving those crimes that are not successfully deterred by the collection of DNA profiles, the

DNA Act both provides a means to monitor such individuals' compliance with the terms of their release ... and helps minimize the pain and suffering recidivist offenders sow in our communities.

3

In light of conditional releasees' substantially diminished expectations of privacy, the minimal intrusion occasioned by blood sampling, and the overwhelming societal interests so clearly furthered by the collection of DNA information from convicted offenders, we must conclude that compulsory DNA profiling of qualified federal offenders is reasonable under the totality of the circumstances. Therefore, we today realign ourselves with every other state and federal appellate court to have considered these issues—squarely holding that the DNA Act satisfies the requirements of the Fourth Amendment.

IV

Because compulsory DNA profiling conducted pursuant to the federal DNA Act would have occasioned no violation of Kincade's Fourth Amendment rights, the judgment and accompanying sentence of the district court are

Affirmed.

Mayfield v. Dalton

109 F.3d 1423 (9th Cir. 1997)

Shroeder, Circuit Judge:

The plaintiffs-appellants in this case, John C. Mayfield and Joseph Vlacovsky, filed this action when they were on active duty in the Marine Corps. They challenged the constitutionality of a Department of Defense program to collect and store blood and tissue samples from all members of the armed forces for future DNA analysis (the "repository"). Mayfield and Vlacovsky argued that the compulsory taking of specimens without proper safeguards to maintain the privacy of the donor was a violation of the Fourth Amendment prohibition against unreasonable searches and seizures. *Mayfield v. Dalton*, 901 F.Supp. 300, 303 (D.Hawai'i 1995). In addition, they feared that information obtained from the repository samples, regarding the donors' propensities for hereditary diseases and genetic disorders, might be used to discriminate against applicants for jobs, insurance or benefit programs.

Refusing to comply with the program, Mayfield and Vlacovsky turned to the district court. They sought to represent a class of "'all military personnel serving on active duty in the United States Navy and/or the United States Marine Corps who have been or may be compelled to provide blood and/or other tissue samples for DNA identification or testing procedures under currently applicable Navy and/or Marine Corps policies, practices and/or regulations.'" The district court granted summary judgment in favor of the government and denied class certification.

On the merits, the district court first held that the DNA repository did not violate any constitutional rights because the taking of specimens without the service members' consent did not constitute an unreasonable seizure in violation of the Fourth Amendment. The court also stressed that the repository was instituted for the purpose of assisting in the identification of soldiers' remains, a purpose that plaintiffs-appellants did not challenge, and that other potential, more nefarious, uses were too speculative to be justiciable. The district court also held that Mayfield and Vlacovsky could not adequately represent all members of the class and therefore denied them class certification.

The district court's decision came down on September 8, 1995. In the intervening period between its decision and oral argument before this court, Mayfield and Vlacovsky have been honorably separated from active duty without ever having given any blood or tissue samples. The government suggests their claims may thus be moot. Mayfield and Vlacovsky counter that separation from active duty means that they are still contractually obligated to remain in the Marine Corps Reserves, and may thus be required to return to active duty in an emergency situation. Therefore, they argue, their case is not moot.

We agree with the government that Mayfield and Vlacovsky's challenge is moot because they are no longer subject to the DNA collection program, and face only a remote possibility that they may ever be subject to the repository policies they seek to challenge.... In this case, while there is a "possibility" that a national emergency might arise, and that the military might choose to recall Mayfield and Vlacovsky to active duty, the recall could happen only at some indefinite time in the future and then only upon the occurrence of future events now unforeseeable. "'[S]uch speculative contingencies afford no basis for our passing on the substantive issues'" presented in this case.

Not only are Mayfield and Vlacovsky unable to challenge the regulations that might have affected them in the past, they are also unable to challenge regulations that might apply to them in the future. Such a challenge to future application is not yet ripe.

Moreover, in the intervening time between the district court judgment and oral argument before this court, the military changed the repository in ways that appear to respond to some of plaintiffs-appellants' main concerns. As of April 1996, for example, the maximum length of time that the specimens will now be retained has been shortened from the originally challenged duration of 75 years to 50 years. In addition, upon the request of the donor, the military will now destroy individual specimen samples following the conclusion of the service member's military obligation. The changes made, which materially alter many aspects of the policy that Mayfield and Vlacovsky challenged in the district court, fortify our conclusion that the likelihood that these plaintiffs-appellants will ever be subject to the policy they challenged in the district court is too remote to make their suit justiciable.

We also conclude that the question presented does not fall within the category of harm "capable of repetition, yet evading review." In order for this exception to the mootness doctrine to apply, there must be a reasonable expectation that the same complaining party will be subject to the same injury again. There is no such "reasonable expectation" in this case. The second requirement for this mootness exception to apply is that the injury suffered must be of a type so inherently limited in duration that it is always likely to become moot before a federal court can fully review it. The injury claimed here is not so limited in duration.

Finally, Mayfield and Vlacovsky argue that even if their own claims are moot, the entire controversy is not moot, and the district court erred in refusing to certify their class.... The district court held, first, that Mayfield and Vlacovsky, who objected to the repository, could not properly represent a class comprised of all service members who were compelled to participate in the program because there were undoubtedly people among the broad class proposed by them who did not oppose the repository, and who, in fact, approved of it and wished the policies fully enforced. *Mayfield*, 901 F.Supp. at 305–306. Because Mayfield and Vlacovsky's interests would thus have been antithetical to the interests of such class members, Mayfield and Vlacovsky could not have adequately represented such class members.... We have here a conflict between the interests of the putative representative and members of the class.

To the extent that Mayfield and Vlacovsky may also have been seeking to represent a more limited class, consisting only of those service members who actually opposed the repository, the district court correctly held that plaintiffs-appellants failed to show that there existed others who could represent such a class....

Having determined that Mayfield and Vlacovsky's separation from active duty has mooted this appeal, we must now decide whether to vacate the district court's judgment. It has been our general practice to vacate the judgment below whenever a case becomes moot, so as to "prevent a judgment, unreviewable because of mootness, from spawning any legal consequences." ... In deciding whether to vacate a prior judgment in a case rendered nonjusticiable, the pivotal question is "whether the party seeking relief from the judgment below caused the [nonjusticiability] by voluntary action." If so, we generally remand with instructions to the district court to weigh the equities and determine whether it should vacate its own judgment. Because in this case it was not plaintiffs-appellants who mooted the appeal, ... vacatur is appropriate.

For the foregoing reasons, we vacate the judgment of the district court and remand with instructions to dismiss the case as moot.

Notes & Questions

1. As noted in the text, all fifty states have established DNA Databases and many of these also maintain DNA samples in repositories as well. Although the early DNA database statutes generally provided for the banking of profiles from violent offenders, the movement among states has been toward including more types of offenders and alleged offenders in the databases. In a survey done in mid 2004, thirty-four states had enacted statutes requiring that all those convicted of felonies be included in the state databank. Some states also require those convicted of misdemeanors, especially those misdemeanors associated with sexual and/or violent offenses, to submit DNA samples. Some states also include inchoate crimes such as attempts and conspiracy among those eligible for inclusion into the database.

In addition to the types of offenses that result in inclusion in the database, there is also the issue of whether, and when, juvenile offenders convicted of the crimes are eligible for inclusion. Twenty-eight states include juvenile offenders in the database if they have been convicted of equivalent qualifying offenses. However, twelve states restrict the scope of the qualifying offenses for juvenile offenses. Some require juveniles to submit to the DNA database only if they have been tried and convicted as adults. *See, e.g.*, N.M. Stat. § 29-16-3 (2005).

Four states provide for DNA samples to be taken from arrestees charged with certain felonies; Louisiana collects DNA from arrestees charged with any felony and California is scheduled to expand its approach to all felony arrestees in 2009. California is also the only state with law authorizing DNA collection from suspects who may—or may not—later be indicted for a qualifying offense. For additional information on state statute provisions with respect to inclusion in state DNA databases, see National Conference of

State Legislatures, DNA & Crime, *available at* http://www.ncsl.org/programs/health/genetics/dna.htm; National Conference of State Legislatures, State Laws on DNA Data Banks, Qualifying Offenses, Others Who Must Provide Sample, December 2004, *available at* http://www.ncsl.org/programs/health/genetics/DNAoffenses2004.htm. *See also* American Society of Law, Medicine & Ethics, Survey of DNA Database Statutes, *available at* http://www.aslme.org/dna_04/grid/index.php; American Society of Law, Medicine & Ethics, Survey of State DNA Database Statutes User's Guide, *available at* http://www.aslme.org/dna_04/grid/guide.php.

2. As detailed in *State v. Martinez*, many of the state database statutes have been challenged by plaintiffs alleging that they represent an unreasonable search and seizure and violates their Fourth Amendment rights. To date these challenges have been largely unsuccessful and databases have been found to be constitutional. *See, e.g.*, *Jones v. Murray*, 962 F.2d 302 (4th Cir. 1992) (applying a Virginia statute that included all convicted felons); *Shaffer v. Saffle*, 148 F.3d 1180 (10th Cir. 1998) (upholding Oklahoma statute requiring DNA samples from persons convicted of burglary); *Nicholas v. Goord*, No. 1:01-CV-07891, 2003 WL 256774 (S.D.N.Y. Feb. 6, 2003) (applying a New York statute that included burglary); *L.S. v. State*, 805 So. 2d 1004 (Fla. Dist. Ct. App. 2001) (upholding the Florida DNA statute as it applied to a juvenile that plead no contest to burglary); *Landry v. Attorney General*, 709 N.E.2d 1085 (Mass. 1999) (including burglary); *Gaines v. State*, 998 P.2d 166 (Nev. 2000) (upholding a Nevada DNA statute as it applied to a person convicted of burglary); *Doles v. State*, 994 P.2d 315 (Wyo. 1999) (including every person convicted of a felony).

In *Martinez*, the Kansas Supreme Court considered both the "special needs" exceptions to the Fourth Amendment and the "balancing test" approach that has also been used in evaluating questions of unreasonable search and seizure.

The "balancing test" approach is exemplified in *Michigan Department of State Police v. Sitz*, 496 U.S. 444 (1990). In this case, the court found that a highway checkpoint program, in which police briefly stopped all cars at the checkpoint, assessed drivers for signs of intoxication, and required possibly intoxicated drivers to submit to further testing, was not a violation of the Fourth Amendment. In coming to this conclusion the Court found that the State had an significant public interest in eradicating drunk driving that outweighed the minimal intrusion represented by the brief stopping of all cars at the checkpoint, and moreover, that the checkpoint program reasonably advanced the State's public policy interest.

The "special needs" concept was first discussed in *New Jersey v. T.L.O.*, 469 U.S. 325 (1985), a case that dealt with the right of school authorities to search the purse of a student caught smoking cigarettes in contravention of school policy. The search revealed not only tobacco cigarettes but evidence of use and sale of marijuana. The Court upheld the search on the basis that the reasonable suspicion of smoking justified the initial search; and the discovery of marijuana justified further searching of the student's personal effects. In effect, the Court balanced the governmental and private interests at play and validated the search on a less than probable cause standard given the overall public interest. Justice Blackmun concurred, but opined that such a relaxation of the standard should occur "only when we were confronted with 'a special law enforcement need for greater flexibility.'" 469 U.S. at 351. Two years later in *Griffin v. Wisconsin*, 483 U.S. 868 (1987), the majority adopted the "special needs" approach advocated by Blackmun. In *Griffin*, the Court upheld a search of a probationer's home on the basis of a regulation that allowed a search when there was a reasonable belief that the probationer possessed contraband. The Court found that supervision of those on probation constituted a "special need" of the State justifying the search, given that the probationer had a lesser expectation of privacy. The Court used this "special needs" approach in several subsequent cases. *See Chandler v. Miller*, 520 U.S. 305 (1997) (invalidating a statute requiring political candidates to submit to drug testing); *Veronia Sch. Dist. 47J v. Acton*, 515 U.S. 646 (1995) (upholding drug testing of students engaged in intercollegiate sports activities); *Bd. of Educ. v. Earls*, 536 U.S. 822 (2002) (upholding drug testing of student involved in school-sponsored extracurricular activities).

However, in *City of Indianapolis v. Edmond*, 531 U.S. 32 (2000), and *Ferguson v. City of Charleston*, 532 U.S. 67 (2001), the court began to recast the "special needs" approach by focusing on the underlying purpose of the search and considering whether the search was, in reality, part of a law enforcement aim. In *Edmond*, the question was whether a random stopping of motorists at a police checkpoint, accompanied with a drug-sniffing dog, constituted an illegal search. The Court held that because the checkpoint program's primary purpose was inseparable from crime control, the search violated the Fourth Amendment in that there was no probable cause or particularized suspicion. 531 U.S. at 47. In *Ferguson*, the Court held that obtaining blood and urine for drug testing from women presenting for prenatal care and then providing law enforcement with the positive test result violated the Fourth Amendment and did not qualify for a "special needs" exception. 532 U.S. at 84.

State v. Martinez demonstrates the convergence of the two approaches, a growing trend in DNA database case law. Here the Court first establishes that the required submission of DNA qualifies under a "special needs" analysis. Using *Edmond* and *Ferguson* as guidance, a suspicion-less search would pass muster under the Fourth Amendment if it met some "special need" beyond law enforcement. 78 P.3d at 771–72. If the primary purpose is law enforcement, the "special needs" approach gives way to the requirement for probable cause or particularized suspicion. In *Martinez*, the Court noted that the collection and cataloging of DNA information is a special need removed from immediate law enforcement needs, given that the samples themselves prove "nothing by themselves regarding whether a donor has committed a crime." 78 P.3d at 773. Having determined that the special need threshold was reached, the Court goes on to employ a "balancing test" and finds that the taking of the blood sample is minimally intrusive and that Martinez, like other felons covered under the statute, has a diminished expectation of privacy. 78 P. 3d 769. The public policy aim is to facilitate the solving of unsolved and future crimes and this outweighs Martinez's rights under the Fourth Amendment. This use of a "special needs" analysis followed by a "balancing test" is the prevalent approach used by both federal and state courts in deciding DNA database cases in the wake of *Edmond* and *Ferguson*. *See, e.g., United States v. Kimler*, 345 F.3d 1132 (10th Cir. 2003); *Velasquez v. Woods*, 329 F.3d 420 (5th Cir. 2003); *Vore v. Dep't of Justice*, 281 F. Supp. 2d 4542 (D. Ariz. 2003): *Nicholas v. Goord*, No. 1:01-CV-07891, 2003 WL 256774 (S.D.N.Y. Feb. 6, 2003); *Kellogg v. Travis*, 728 N.Y.S.2d 645 (N.Y. Sup. Ct. 2001) (applying a balancing test after special needs threshold met). *But see Padgett v. Ferrero*, 294 F. Supp. 2d 1338 (N.D. Ga. 2003); *L.S. v. State*, 805 So. 2d 1004 (Fla. Dist. Ct. App 2001) (using a balancing test without engaging in a "special needs" analysis).

3. The DNA Databank law in question in *United States v. Kincade* is the federal DNA Analysis Backlog Elimination Act of 2000, 42 U.S.C. § 14135; Pub. L. No. 106-546, 114 Stat. 2726. This law provides for inclusion of DNA from those convicted of qualifying federal crimes into the FBI's CODIS databank. Under the Act, collection of a DNA sample from individuals on probation, parole or supervised release is also authorized. Qual-

ifying federal offenses include violent crimes such as homicides, sex offenses, kidnapping, robbery, and conspiracies to commit such offenses.

The version of *United States v. Kincade* excerpted in the text is the *en banc* review of the case by the Ninth Circuit. This latest determination, Kincade II, "realigned" the Ninth Circuit with the prevailing view of other courts across the nation and vacated an earlier decision by a Ninth Circuit panel, *United States v. Kincade,* 345 F.3d 1095 (9th Cir. 2003) (*Kincade I*). The plurality opinion in *Kincade II* (five of the eleven judges) speaks to the "totality of the circumstances" in balancing Kincade's right to privacy with the State's interests and needs with respect to DNA banking. The opinion notes that several other Courts have used this totality of the circumstances, or balancing approach, to hold DNA banking constitutional without coupling it with a "special needs" analysis. A sixth judge on the panel concurred in the result reached by the plurality, but applied a "special needs" approach to do so. Five judges dissented in a strongly worded dissent:

> Today this court approves the latest installment in the federal government's effort to construct a comprehensive national database into which basic information concerning American citizens will be entered and stored for the rest of their lives—although no majority exists with respect to the legal justification for this conclusion. My colleagues claim to authorize merely the "compulsory DNA profiling of certain conditionally-released federal offenders," as authorized by the DNA Analysis Backlog Elimination Act of 2000. We would be lucky indeed if it were possible to so limit the effect of their opinions. For, under the rationales they espouse, especially the plurality's, all Americans will be at risk, sooner rather than later, of having our DNA samples permanently placed on file in federal cyberspace, and perhaps even worse, of being subjected to various other governmental programs providing for suspicion-less searches conducted for law enforcement purposes.

379 F.3d at 842–43. The strong dissent is not so surprising considering that the earlier Ninth Circuit opinion in the *Kincade I* case had found the DNA Act unconstitutional as applied to Kincade and other probationers.

The earlier Ninth Circuit decision, *Kincade I*, is one of the few cases that have found a DNA Databank law unconstitutional. In *Kincade I*, the Ninth Circuit held that the databank had no purpose or "special need" outside of law enforcement. The court reasoned that the convicts had already served their sentences and had been released on probation. As a result, under the court's analysis, they had recovered an expectation of privacy and requiring them to submit a sample absent probable cause or reasonable suspicion constituted an unreasonable search and seizure. The *Kincade I* panel found that neither the "special needs" nor the "balancing test" applied in this case. In coming to this determination, the Ninth Circuit relied upon *United States v. Miles*, 228 F. Supp. 2d 1130 (E.D. Cal. 2002), in which the federal district court determined that, in the wake of *Ferguson* and *Edmond*, the Supreme Court clearly required something more that the assertion of general law enforcement to justify a regime of suspicion-less searches. The *Miles* Court found that inclusion in CODIS could not be divorced from the primary purpose of law enforcement. Because there was no primary purpose "other than its use as a general law enforcement tool," *Miles* found that the DNA Act violated the Fourth Amendment.

4. *Mayfield v Dalton*, 901 F. Supp. 300, 303 (D. Haw. 1995), challenged the military DNA repository shortly after it was established during the Persian Gulf War. The Marines were charged with violating a superior's order for refusing to provide DNA specimens. The Marines claimed that taking DNA samples without their consent vio-

lated their Fourth Amendment rights. The military asserted that the DNA would only be used to identify the Marines' remains if necessary. In *Mayfield*, the federal district court held that the taking of DNA samples was not an unreasonable seizure, as it was a minimal intrusion on the Marines' diminished expectations of privacy. Although the District Court's opinion references the concept of special needs, it uses a balancing approach in addressing the Fourth Amendment claim. The court noted that the samples' benign purpose would primarily benefit the Marines' next of kin. Hypothetical concerns expressed by the Marines about possible future uses of the DNA did not present a justiciable case or controversy at the time the District Court decided *Mayfield*. The court also rebuffed the Marines' claim for class certification.

On appeal, the Ninth Circuit reaffirmed the reasoning taken by the District Court with respect to the Fourth Amendment issues and the class certification. By the time the Appeals Court reviewed the case, both Mayfield and Vlacovsky had been court-martialed for failing to obey orders. They received reprimands and were restricted to the base for one week. Both were subsequently honorably discharged from the service and were civilians when the Ninth Circuit heard the appeal. As noted in the opinion, by 1997, the Department of Defense had already begun to address some of the concerns raised by plaintiffs. The Ninth Circuit ultimately determined that the case was moot.

However, in 2003, a provision in the National Defense Authorization Act significantly broadened access to the DNA Repository by allowing access for law enforcement purposes. This provision, 10 U.S.C. §1565(a), allows law enforcement access with a court order and a covered purpose, defined as "an investigation or prosecution of a felony, or any sexual offence, for which no other source of DNA information is reasonably available." *Id.* The change, which allows access to the repository for law enforcement purposes, absent probable cause or particularized suspicion, followed a celebrated case in Fort Hood, Texas involving a soldier who had murdered one person and attempted to murder two others during a drunken spree. In the course of the murder investigation, military police found evidence related to a brutal rape of a woman soldier three months earlier. Although DNA had been found in the rape case, no access to the military DNA repository was available. After the murders, a Congressman from Texas sponsored the provision in §1565(a) that affords access for the investigation of such cases. *See* Patricia A. Ham, *An Army of Suspects: The History and Constitutionality of the U.S. Military's DNA Repository and Its Access for Law Enforcement Purposes*, Army Law., July–Aug. 2003, at 1.

5. In 1998, Iceland became the first nation to commit to building a national DNA database. The Health Sector Database Act provided for a centralized databank of DNA and health data with the aim of developing knowledge about and therapies for diseases afflicting the population. The database would be used by deCODE, a pharmaceutical firm, to develop medications and treatments for common diseases afflicting Icelanders. The Act provided for presumed consent, with an opt-out for those who did not want their DNA and health data included in the database. The Act was passed with strong affirmation by both the Parliament and population.

However, shortly after the databank samples began to be collected, the databank was challenged. The daughter of a deceased man alleged that inclusion of her father's DNA and health data in the database violated her rights of privacy with respect to her family health history, and ergo, her rights to be excluded from the database. She argued that her father's data would have health information that would essentially be as much hers, as her father's. Thus, her rights to privacy under Iceland's Constitution were abrogated. In 2003, the Icelandic Supreme Court held that the daughter's privacy rights in her father's information trumped the Health Sector Database Act. Gudmundsdottir v. State of Iceland, Icelandic Supreme Court, No.151/2003. The Supreme Court's decision derails the database as currently constructed.

6. Most recently, the Foundation for the National Institutes of Health has announced a partnership with Pfizer Global Research and Development to develop a database of genotypic and phenotypic information. This database, the Genetic Association Information Network (GAIN), ultimately would be publicly available with the goal of stimulating research on genetic determinants of common diseases. The GAIN project has raised concerns with respect to the rights of the subjects who contribute their samples and data to GAIN. GAIN anticipates that the subject samples and data will be contributed by other ongoing studies. The contributing studies will retain the subject identifiers. The GAIN project alleges that the data they will receive, devoid of identifiers, is not subject to the federal regulations governing human subjects research. *See* http://www.fnih.org/GAIN. Do you agree? What risks can you anticipate for these subjects? Is the public policy objective of gaining better knowledge of the genetic determinants of disease sufficient to justify risks to subjects in the GAIN database? What lessons might be learned from the Iceland experience?

There is a similar, but somewhat differently structured, program in the European Union. The Public Health Genomics European Network (PHGEN) seeks to address, with specific recommendations, future issues raised by the use and integration of genome-based knowledge into public health genomics. PHGEN brings together European experts to compile issues and priorities in public health genomics, including potential legal obstacles, as genetic tests, services, and products enter the cross-border market. Part of PHGEN's agenda is to address what controls should apply to biobanks. *See* http://www.phgen.nrw.

D. Genetics and Civil Liability

The role of genetics in civil actions to date has been primarily in the context of medical malpractice actions. Such actions include those brought as a result of inadequate or negligent prenatal testing and counseling as well as questions of duty to warn affected third parties. These cases are discussed in Chapters 7 and 2 respectively. There are also a variety of posited workplace actions related to use of genetic screening and testing; these are explored in Chapter 3. Scholars continue to explore the potential use of genetics in civil actions, both from the plaintiff and the defense perspectives. Many of these posited actions are grounded in existing case law involving "toxic" torts and exposure to environmental hazards.

Gary E. Marchant, *Genetic and Toxic Torts*

31 Seton Hall L. Rev. 949 (2001)

I. Genetic Markers of Susceptibility

A. Scientific Developments

One of the first pay-offs of the Human Genome Project and companion efforts to analyze the human genome is the identification of a growing number of genetic variations that affect individual susceptibility to foreign substances. The most common of these genetic variations, which exist in the human population at a frequency of at least one percent, are termed "polymorphisms." A consortium of pharmaceutical companies, known as the SNP Consortium, has mapped over one million "single nucleotide polymorphisms" ("SNPs"), which are common single-base pair genetic variations in human DNA. Many other genetic variants are present at much lower frequencies in the human genome, and some of these also have biological significance.

Many of the most frequent genetic polymorphisms that have been identified in the human gene pool appear to affect our individual susceptibility to disease from exposure to toxic substances. Our bodies metabolize foreign compounds that enter the body ("xenobiotics") through a series of enzymes coded by genes now known to be highly polymorphic (or variable) in humans. These enzymes convert the xenobiotic through a series of reactions into both reactive and inert metabolites as part of the process for detoxifying and removing the foreign compound from the body. The variations in the genes coding for these metabolic enzymes can greatly affect the dynamics of the metabolic process, increasing or decreasing the rates of detoxification and production of reactive intermediates and their associated risks. Each person will thus react to exposure to a particular substance in a different way depending on the set of metabolic gene variants they are born with.

For example, about ten percent of the Caucasian population carries a variant of one cytochrome p450 gene (CYP1A1) that increases the rate of metabolism of certain substances and thus the formation of reactive metabolites. This genetic variant has been associated with increased lung cancer risk in smokers in some (but not all) studies. In approximately fifty percent of the Caucasian population, a gene (GSTM1) coding for one in another set of metabolic enzymes (the glutathione S-transferases) is completely deleted, which is associated with an increased risk of bladder and lung cancer from exposure to several toxic substances normally detoxified by the GSTM1 enzyme.

The variations in the genes coding for metabolic enzymes can at least partly explain why only some individuals incur illness from particular toxic exposures, such as lung cancer from smoking. As a consequence of these same genetic variations, most pharmaceuticals are ineffective in some individuals and cause toxic side-effects in others. For example, the popular allergy drug Seldane was withdrawn from the market when it was found to cause, when taken with certain other drugs such as erythromycin, potentially fatal heart problems in people with a mutation in a particular gene coding for a metabolic enzyme in the cytochrome p450 family. Similarly, ten to fifteen percent of the approximately 2400 children in the United States who each year develop the deadly cancer, acute lymphoblastic leukemia have mutations of the thiopurine S-methyltransferase (TPMT) gene that causes them to metabolize the lifesaving drug used to treat the disease either too fast or slow, resulting respectively in either lack of therapeutic benefit or potentially lethal accumulation of the drug. Pre-treatment genetic testing is now being used to select the appropriate dosage for the medication depending on which versions of the gene the individual child carries. In addition to these polymorphisms in metabolism genes, individuals also differ in their response to foreign substances due to other genetic variations affecting functions such as DNA repair, cell cycle control, receptors, and immune function.

Notwithstanding the tremendous progress that has been made in understanding genetic susceptibility over the past few years, attempts to define the genetic susceptibility of an individual are nevertheless complicated by several factors. To begin with, most of the genes affecting susceptibility are probabilistic rather than deterministic in that they only increase the risk of disease and are neither necessary nor sufficient to cause disease.

The susceptibility genes are generally quite frequent in the population, but the increased (or decreased) risk in any one individual carrier is relatively modest. Moreover, research on genetic susceptibility markers often produces inconsistent results, with some studies finding a significant increased (or decreased) risk of disease from a particular gene-environment interaction, while other studies report no such effect.

Even when a susceptibility genetic marker has been unambiguously identified, its effects can vary across individuals for a variety of reasons. Some increases in susceptibility are dose-dependent, in that they primarily increase an individual's susceptibility to a toxic agent relative to the general population only at low or high doses. Certain associations appear to be ethnic-dependent, in that the susceptibility associated with a particular gene appears to be limited to particular ethnic groups and is not seen in other groups even when the same gene is present. The distribution of gene frequencies also varies significantly between different ethnic groups. Finally, individual susceptibility to potentially toxic agents is rarely determined by a single genetic locus, but rather is the combined influence of many different genes (as well as non-genetic factors). Thus, even if testing identifies a specific gene variant with a significant effect on individual susceptibility to a particular agent, the magnitude and nature of the susceptibility conferred by the gene may vary depending on the other gene variants present in a given individual.

Notwithstanding these complications, recent findings identifying and characterizing genetic markers of susceptibility demonstrate that there are substantial inter-individual differences in responses to, and risks from, toxic exposures. Perhaps even more important than the knowledge of the existence of frequent genetic heterogeneity within the population is the increasing capability to identify individuals who are more or less susceptible....

Thomas Parker Redick, *Twenty-First Century Toxicogenomics Meets Twentieth Century Mass Tort Precedent: Is There a Duty to Warn of a Hypothetical Harm to an "Eggshell" Gene?*

42 Washburn L.J. 547 (2003)

V. Fear of Cancer Claims in the Age of Toxicogenomics

Cancer fears have been compensable for many years in various jurisdictions for incidents involving intentional acts. Long before the biological mechanisms of carcinogenesis were well understood, fear of cancer claims made their appearance in the occasional case. Typically, a person's likelihood of developing cancer or other future illnesses as a result of toxic exposure is difficult to predict, as many forms of cancer involve long latency periods and development depends on interrelation of many factors.

Commentators saw the deluge coming and cautioned against arbitrary decisions based on bad facts. It is difficult to go a week without news of toxic exposure. Virtually everyone in society is conscious of the fact that the air they breathe, water, food and drugs they ingest, land on which they live, or products to which they are exposed are potential health hazards. Although few are exposed to all, few also can escape exposure to any.

With advances in diagnostic research involving the genetic triggers for cancer and the explosion of mass torts cases involving asbestos, however, "fear of cancer" cases began to emerge in the toxic tort arena.

The seminal case opening the door to medical monitoring for fear of cancer based upon genetic damage from a hazardous chemical is *Ayers v. Jackson Township*. In *Ayers*, over 300 plaintiffs alleging exposure to toxic substances in drinking water (leading to a "genetic switch" ready to turn cancerous in the future) were allowed to recover medical monitoring costs based on a largely unquantified excess risk substantiated by expert opinion about a reasonable likelihood of future illness.

As the permissible scope of recovery for fear of future illness expanded along with the research allowing expert opinions to create a reasonable fear of future illness, courts began expressing concern about opening the floodgates of litigation should such claims become widely available. As a result, the Supreme Court of California, in *Potter v. Firestone Tire & Rubber Co.*, made a policy decision: (1) to allow broad recovery for medical monitoring (with minimal and largely unspecified medical causation standards) where defendant acted with fraud or malice, while it simultaneously (2) limited recovery for future risks based on negligent conduct causing chemical exposure and resulting emotional distress lacking any physical injury.

The *Potter* decision involved exposure to residents living near a disposal site that was improperly used for disposal of Firestone's hazardous waste. From 1963 to 1980, Firestone operated a tire manufacturing plant near Salinas. In 1967, Firestone contracted with Salinas Disposal Service (SDS) and Rural Disposal, two companies operating the Crazy Horse Landfill. Firestone agreed to deposit its industrial waste in canisters provided by SDS located at the plant site, and SDS agreed to haul the waste to the Crazy Horse site.

At the outset of their contractual relationship, SDS informed Firestone that it did not allow dumping of toxic wastes at the landfill because groundwater would be contaminated. Firestone gave assurances it would not send toxics to the landfill; however, its plant manager still sent large quantities of liquid toxic waste to the landfill.

In May of 1977, Firestone's plant engineer in charge of environmental matters sent a memo to department heads about the proper disposal of liquid wastes, detailing legal disposal methods under California law. When compliance with proper procedures proved too costly, noncompliance became widespread. In 1984, the owners of property near the landfill discovered toxic chemicals in their home water wells and sued Firestone, seeking medical monitoring and damages for emotional distress, based upon their fear of future cancer.

The California Supreme Court in *Potter* set forth the following tests for fear of cancer claims: [I]n the absence of a present physical injury or illness, damages for fear of cancer may be recovered only if the plaintiff pleads and proves that:

> (1) as a result of the defendant's negligent breach of a duty owed to the plaintiff, the plaintiff is exposed to a toxic substance which threatens cancer; and
>
> (2) the plaintiff's fear stems from a knowledge, corroborated by reliable medical or scientific opinion, that it is more likely than not that the plaintiff will develop cancer in the future due to toxic exposure.

As an exception to the general rule, in the absence of physical injury or illness, damages for negligently inflicted emotional distress may be recovered without meeting the "more likely than not" threshold if the plaintiff pleads and proves that:

> (1) as a result of the defendant's negligent breach of a duty owed to the plaintiff, he or she is exposed to a toxic substance which threatens cancer;
>
> (2) the defendant, in breaching its duty to the plaintiff, acted with oppression, fraud or malice as defined in Civil Code section 3294; and

(3) the plaintiff's fear of cancer stems from a knowledge, corroborated by reliable medical or scientific opinion, that the toxic exposure caused by the defendant's breach of duty has significantly increased the plaintiff's risk of cancer and has resulted in an actual risk of cancer that is significant.

The court further stated that medical monitoring "costs are a compensable item of damages in a negligence action where the proofs demonstrate, through reliable medical expert testimony, that the need for future monitoring is a reasonably certain consequence of the plaintiff's toxic exposure and that the recommended monitoring is reasonable."

The standard of "more likely than not" (*i.e.*, 51% probability of future disease) for mere negligence is a very difficult one to meet given current scientific limits on predicting causation in particular individuals. Even with the advent of toxicogenomics, the risk of cancer actually occurring from genetic damage caused by carcinogens may never rise to over 50%. For example, the risk level for long term tobacco use, which has many known carcinogens, is generally considered to be less than 50%.

This 51% barrier to proof does not apply, however, in the context of the "malice" exception to the Potter doctrine, which allows recovery of medical monitoring for mere "significant risk" (a concept not well-defined in the decision or subsequent cases).

Once the plaintiff establishes that the defendant has acted with oppression, fraud or malice, the plaintiff must still demonstrate that his or her fear of cancer is reasonable, genuine and serious in order to recover damages. In determining what constitutes reasonable fear, ... it is not enough for a plaintiff to show simply an ingestion of a carcinogen or a significant increase in the risk of cancer. In addition, the plaintiff must show that his or her actual risk of cancer is significant before recovery will be allowed. Under this reasoning, a plaintiff's fear is not compensable when the risk of cancer is significantly increased, but remains a remote possibility.

While the plaintiffs asked for "doubling risk" as the standard for what is significant, the court in Potter did not define its scientific standard for "significant risk."

The *Potter* court also discussed at length the public policy concerns underlying its decision to deny easy recovery for mere negligent failure to warn. Recognizing the "indisputable fact that all of us are exposed to carcinogens every day," the court first noted that all of us are potential fear of cancer claimants.

Therefore, the more likely than not limit for mere negligence helps address the tremendous societal cost of otherwise allowing emotional distress compensation to a potentially unlimited class of plaintiffs.

A second policy concern weighing in favor of the 51% threshold was the unduly detrimental impact that unrestricted fear of cancer liability would have in the health care field. In particular, the supreme court recognized amicus curiae California Medical Association's point that "access to prescription drugs is likely to be impeded by allowing recovery of fear of cancer damages in negligence cases without the imposition of the heightened threshold." This explicit recognition of the benefits to many, despite harm to a few, may prove helpful in cases featuring idiosyncratic reactions (i.e., a rare toxicogenomic harm). It also stands as a judicial recognition of the threat to innovation in pharmaceuticals that "fear of future disease" cases pose.

The third policy concern considered is that allowing recovery to all victims who may reasonably fear cancer could ultimately work to the detriment of those who sustain actual physical injury and develop cancer as a result of toxic exposure. If the same recovery of $800,000 allowed to four plaintiffs in *Potter* were similarly allowed in large class actions, the numbers for this one type of injury alone would be staggering.

A fourth reason given by the supreme court focused on predictability and consistency of results. Here, the court noted that the more likely than not probability limitation establishes a sufficiently definite and predictable threshold for recovery to permit consistent application from case to case. Such a definite threshold may also contribute to early resolution or settlement of claims.

Finally, the court recognized that the more likely than not standard may foreclose compensation to individuals with genuine and objectively reasonable fears (*i.e.*, those who have undergone genetic testing and know themselves to be at risk from exposure to the compound in question). As a result, it is sometimes necessary to "limit the class of potential plaintiffs if emotional injury absent physical harm is to continue to be a recoverable item of damages in a negligence action."

While the court limited claims arising in negligence, it left the door open for any "significant" risks—including harm to a genetically susceptible subclass—that can prove a reckless or intentional failure to warn them, or a similarly reckless violation of regulations.

VI. Toxicogenomics and Typical Toxic Tort Defenses

Companies considering whether they have a duty to warn of a toxicogenomic hypothesis should evaluate the potential claims in light of existing defenses to toxic tort liability.

A. The "Doubling Risk" Defense

In recent years, epidemiology and the law have combined to create the doubling risk concept. This is the defense attorney's bright line for medical causation in tort law epidemiology. Many courts have embraced the idea. As noted above, plaintiffs' attorneys in *Potter* endorsed this standard for recovery under the malice exception's "significant risk" standard.

As a result, both defense experts and experts for plaintiffs will increasingly be moving toward use of genetic susceptibility data in proving toxic tort causation, to avoid application of the "doubling risk" standard for pretrial screening of toxic tort claims. A recent article in Jurimetrics by Sander Greenland and James Robins points toward a new approach that plaintiffs' experts could take in establishing causation, using "genotype stratification" to establish medical causation for susceptible groups. This appears to be a clever way to avoid a doubling risk defense to claims where medical causation is based on small increases in cancer risk because the courts generally require at least two times the background risk for a disease before they recognize increased risk under the more likely than not standard for medical causation.

Greenland and Robins suggest in a hypothetical that a relative risk of 2 may be subdivided into separate risk groups of 3 and 1.5 using toxicogenomic evidence. These experts point out that some subgroups making up the study population would be at 3 times relative risk, while others would be at 1.5 (under the doubling risk requirement). Greenland and Robins suggest that it would be unfair and arbitrary that some recover and others do not, simply because we do not fully understand the mechanism of causation.

Doubling risk as a judicial sorting device is admittedly crude, since a genetically susceptible person might fall through the cracks. Doubling risk motions can reward the unworthy in some cases, while denying recovery to the worthy in other cases. For example, doubling risk would require, for a group of 100,000 persons, some proof that a background incidence of 100 cancers has doubled to 200 probable cancers in the exposed population. The reason for this is simple—the court will not know which of the persons with cancer before it are imposters if there are only 150 cancers. About 100 of these cancers will be part of the "background incidence" of cancer, while 50 were possibly caused by the chemical in question. The odds of one person having the cancer caused by the chemical will be much less than 50%, not within the "preponderance of evidence" standard for proof.

With genetic susceptibility evidence, however, an expert can employ genotype stratification and separate the genetically susceptible into a subclass. From a group of 100,000 persons, there might be twenty-five genetically susceptible persons who can show excess risk (2x background) from chemical exposure. These people can show doubled risk if the class is narrowed by excluding those who are not genetically susceptible. Thus, even if the risk is still marginal (*i.e.*, just above the doubling risk for the genetically susceptible), it represents a risk that would have been lost in the haystack of the 100,000 people. As a result, this refinement in doubling risk analysis creates a fairer, more efficient system.

Genetic testing to establish a susceptible genotype could also be paired with the use of genetic tests revealing alleged biomarkers in damaged genes. DNA damage has an increasingly long and controversial history in toxic tort litigation. Pairing the damage with a genetic susceptibility, plaintiffs would present expert testimony of both the eggshell gene and the biomarker that could break it. For example, a genetic deficiency in the ability to repair DNA could provide a plaintiff with sufficient evidence to challenge existing limitations on recovery for fear of cancer in some jurisdictions.

Since *Potter* did not set a standard for cancer fears being "significant" under the malice exception, the plaintiffs in that case asked the court for a "doubling risk" standard for viable medical monitoring claims. As a result, the future medical monitoring case law may see the endorsement of doubling risk for particular genetic subclasses, who would then be entitled to medical monitoring.

Before a new, potentially toxic product is marketed, the company marketing the product should conduct studies to determine if doubling risk is exceeded for a particular subgroup of persons who will be exposed.

B. The Idiosyncratic Reaction Defense

A genetic susceptibility that is neither known nor readily knowable at the time of exposure provides an opportunity for alleging the idiosyncratic reaction defense to negligence and strict liability claims. Under this defense, the proximate cause of the injury is attributed to the unforeseeable idiosyncrasy or allergy of the plaintiff, not the defendant's failure to warn. The idiosyncratic reaction defense can provide defendants with a theory to avoid or significantly limit their liability by arguing that plaintiffs' injuries occurred because a particular plaintiff was especially and unforeseeably sensitive to a substance, chromium. Under both negligence and strict product liability failure to warn theory, a defendant need only warn about dangers that it knew or should have known about.

One of the essential elements of negligence liability is knowledge of the dangers involved. If the manufacturer actually knows or should know, in the exercise of reasonable care, of the dangerous character of the product, it is liable for failure to warn under negligence principles. A manufacturer or seller is "negligent if he fails to warn the ignorant of the hidden danger" in a product when he knows that the product might be dangerous to some members of the population (even if the susceptible group is a small minority of society).

Other courts have similarly recognized that a manufacturer may only be subject to liability for negligent failure to warn when it has "actual knowledge that its product might cause harm to an identifiable class of sensitive users or if, based on the state of scientific knowledge, it is chargeable with such knowledge." In *Adelman-Tremblay v. Jewel Cos.*, the plaintiff alleged injuries resulting from application of artificial fingernails with the defendant's kit. The Seventh Circuit, deciding the case under Wisconsin law, found that in a majority of jurisdictions in 1988 there was no duty to warn of the possibility of a rare and unusual allergic reaction. The inquiry should turn upon whether the defendant knew or should have known about the effect the product had on the plaintiff, and knowledge may be limited.

The rule barring the idiosyncratic consumer from recovery generally applies whether suit is brought under strict liability, breach of warranty, or negligence. The unusual susceptibility of the consumer was traditionally recognized as a complete defense where the manufacturer had no reason to know that a very few users of his product might be injured.

California's traditional idiosyncratic reaction defense is set forth in *Oakes v. E.I. Du Pont de Nemours & Co.* The court in Oakes affirmed the trial court's grant of a demurrer where the complaint failed to allege that the defendant knew or should have known that its weed killer could cause a reaction in allergic people. In *Oakes*, the manufacturer included a warning on the product to avoid exposure. The warning in *Oakes* stated the following: "Caution! May cause irritation of eyes, nose, throat, and skin. Avoid breathing dust or spray mist. Avoid contact with skin, eyes and clothing." The court found that the manufacturer was not required to include specific warnings of unknown potential risks or side effects. The defendant facing evidence of genetic susceptibility could be found to have had a duty to warn of known or knowable risks of allergies, but they did not have a duty to warn of unknown or unknowable potential idiosyncratic reactions.

In *Gober v. Revlon*, a Fourth Circuit case applying California law, the court found that a defendant manufacturer could be subject to liability if they knew (or should have known) about a potentially dangerous allergic reaction. The *Gober* court's decision to find liability for a susceptible subclass is premised upon the knowledge of the manufacturer that a class of persons could be allergic and exposed to a toxin without being warned about the risk of allergic reaction.

Several recent decisions in Illinois appear to be consistent with the *Oakes* holding. In *Goldman v. Walco Tool & Engineering Co.*, the plaintiff, a parts inspector for Caterpillar, was exposed to a rust preventative oil when he placed his hand in a bag containing the oil while inspecting a part manufactured by defendant. The plaintiff claimed multiple injuries resulted from the contact. Defendant received the oil from Mobil in 55-gallon drums with warning labels affixed to the drums. Defendant then used the oil in the packaging of their parts but placed no label on either the parts' bags containing the oil or the box in which the bags were shipped.

At trial, the defendant's expert opined that the plaintiff's condition was the result of an idiosyncratic reaction and that his medical problems were ongoing and genetic. The court distinguished this case from others involving the idiosyncratic reaction defense because this case involved an inherently dangerous chemical instead of an "over the counter" consumer product. While the court did not substantially change its analysis, it also noted that in recent years the rule of non-liability for idiosyncratic reactions has been relaxed. In ruling for the plaintiff, the court stated that the "duty to warn of a product's dangerous propensities is imposed upon a manufacturer or supplier where there is unequal knowledge, actual or constructive, and the defendant, possessed of such knowledge, knows or should know that harm might or could occur if no warning is given."

Illinois courts have traditionally found the idiosyncratic reaction defense viable. In *Presbrey v. Gillette*, the plaintiff claimed permanent injury from use of an antiperspirant manufactured by Gillette. The court held that the plaintiff was not entitled to recovery because the plaintiff's injury was an idiosyncratic reaction that would not occur in the average person. The manufacturer did not know, and it had no reason to know, that the plaintiff might be injured. Consequently, the court held that the manufacturer owed no prior duty to warn of a risk that was only remotely possible (*i.e.*, unknowable) and unknown to the manufacturer.

An Oregon case, however, demonstrates the difficulties a defendant may have in prevailing on summary judgment when asserting the idiosyncratic defense. In *Jones v. General Motors Corp.*, the plaintiff claimed injuries from an air contaminant stemming from a leak in the passenger area of his car. General Motors argued, among other things, that they were not liable for the plaintiff's injuries because his reaction was idiosyncratic. The court held that the defendant's idiosyncratic reaction defense is "itself a factual question."

The idiosyncratic nature of a reaction may be difficult to establish on summary judgment, if the plaintiff is successful at creating an issue of fact (*e.g.*, conflicting expert testimony about the idiosyncratic nature of the reaction). Thus, if there is any indication that genetic injury could plausibly be triggered by exposure to a toxic substance, there may be a fact issue requiring jury consideration. Over time, as more genetic links to chemicals are understood, genuine conflicts in expert testimony may increase, and the duty to warn subclasses known to be susceptible may increasingly be imposed as a result.

C. The "State of the Art" Defense: 'Tis Noble to Know What's "Knowable"

If a toxicogenomic harm was not known or knowable at the time the product was marketed and a plaintiff was foreseeably exposed, the court must consider "state of the art" evidence. Where a product liability defendant can show that the product was tested to a reasonably accepted industry standard that reflected the existing state of the scientific expertise (*i.e.*, the "state of the art"), this compliance with existing science can be raised as a defense when a future product risk causes harm. The policy reasons behind this are fairly clear—the courts are reluctant to make industry an insurer of products by holding companies liable for harms they could not have foreseen and corrected.

The California Supreme Court clarified the scope of the failure to warn theory of strict liability to allow state of the art evidence. In *Anderson v. Owens-Corning Fiberglas Corp.*, the court held that "[t]he rules of strict liability require a plaintiff to prove only that the defendant did not adequately warn of a particular risk that was known or knowable in light of the generally recognized and prevailing best scientific and medical knowledge available at the time of manufacture and distribution." This holding clearly applies to toxicogenomic knowledge, which is merely the next step in scientific understanding of medical causation of injury. As a result, courts following California's lead will initially consider toxicogenomic evidence of product harm to be insufficient to overcome a state of the art defense. However, this defense could fade as the toxicogenomic data becomes available at the time new products enter the market. Over time, the state of the art will include toxicogenomic evidence.

Moreover, some defendants may seek to introduce toxicogenomic evidence on their own initiative, if only to limit liability to a subclass of susceptible plaintiffs. Courts will presumably continue to allow defendants this option. Defendants would use toxicogenomic evidence as a shield to rule out causation, while plaintiffs might be denied the sword of toxicogenomic data to prove causation in particular cases.

The passage of time could also help to limit the scope of a duty to warn. In *Artiglio v. Corning Inc.*, the California Supreme Court held that too many years had elapsed between Dow Chemical's seminal toxicology research and activities on behalf of Dow Corning and the plaintiffs' alleged injuries. In *Artiglio*, plaintiffs argued that Dow Chemical, a bulk supplier that conducted early research on the silicone later used for breast implants, owed them a duty because Dow Chemical negligently undertook some efforts to ensure the safety of all of Dow Corning's silicone products. The court disagreed and found that Dow Chemical owed the plaintiffs no duty of care because the silicone research they did conduct was not of such breadth and magnitude to create a duty, and it occurred decades before the harm. Summary judgment for the defendant was upheld.

While the *Artiglio* decision featured a bulk supplier that was not on the front lines in marketing and testing the breast implants, there could be broader use of this decision outside the bulk supplier context. For genetic susceptibilities that are hypothetical and probabilistic in nature, long periods of time may pass between the first date when an ostensible gene for susceptibility is identified and the dates when disease is manifest and proof of causation is less probabilistic and more certain. After several human generations have come and gone, and data has accumulated confirming or disproving various hypothetical links, genetically supported proof of causation may become the dominant mode of proving causation in chemical exposure cases.

A well-documented review of potential adverse impacts can record this uncertainty and the enormous cost of warning the genetically susceptible. This review, twenty years hence, could provide evidence for a future summary judgment motion by the defense. As a result, proactive actions taken today to detect or rule out a duty to warn of toxicogenomic effects (including an offer of free genetic testing to those who are potentially susceptible) could foreclose future claims of a failure to warn the genetically susceptible, if those actions are well-documented.

D. "Substantial Factor" Causation: Contrasting California and Arizona

With the standards for "substantial factor" causation reaching into the lower regions of epidemiological risk and scientific certainty, strategic steps taken to rule out a duty to warn the genetically susceptible could become even more sensible over time.

The Ninth Circuit's decision in *Kennedy v. Southern California Edison Co.*, the "nuclear fleas" case, illustrates the potential for existing causation standards to create fertile ground for arguments based on "genotype stratification" theories. In a case involving alleged health effects from nuclear fleas (tiny particles of radioactive material) that allegedly packed a toxicogenomic punch, the Ninth Circuit applied California law to establish a medical causation standard for a radioactive substance. This wrongful death case arises from alleged radiation exposure from a nuclear power plant that allegedly caused Ellen Kennedy to develop terminal chronic myelogenous leukemia (CML), a rare blood cell cancer. The plaintiffs asserted that CML resulted from negligence on the part of Southern California Edison Company (Cal Edison) that led to her exposure to radiation at the San Onofre Nuclear Power Plant. Additionally, the plaintiffs sued Combustion Engineering, Inc., under a products liability cause of action, for the alleged faulty production of nuclear fuel rods. The theory of the case was that Joe Kennedy, Ellen Kennedy's husband, inadvertently brought home microscopic particles of radioactive material, known as nuclear fleas, from the power plant on his clothing, hair, tools, etc. The plaintiffs alleged that nuclear fleas, which contained radiation dosages in excess of the maximum allowable by federal regulations, caused Mrs. Kennedy's fatal cancer.

First, the court held that the district court erred in refusing to give a jury instruction under *Rutherford v. Owens-Illinois, Inc.*, in this single-defendant hazardous substance case. While this case involved two defendants, the court treated Cal Edison and Combustion Engineering as a single defendant with respect to the issue of alternative causes. While both defendants raised the defense that there were alternative possible causes of Mrs. Kennedy's cancer, neither argued that the other was an independent source of causation. The court found that with a Rutherford instruction, the jury could have found more than a "negligible probability" that Mrs. Kennedy's cancer was caused by radiation from the plant. However, the jury instructions, as given, stated that radiation from the plant need only have "contributed" to Mrs. Kennedy's risk of developing cancer. The court read Rutherford as requiring more. The court found that the plaintiffs' burden was to demonstrate that the exposure in reasonable medical probability was a substantial factor in contributing to the risk of cancer.

Second, the court held that the district court erred in dismissing claims under California product liability law. The plaintiffs presented evidence that the radioactive fuel fleas were released from Combustion Engineering's apparently defective fuel rods. Combustion Engineering argued that it was entitled to summary judgment on strict liability because this was an "isolated" transaction—it never marketed the fuel rods to the public and could not have foreseen that the rods would injure a non-employee of the plant like Mrs. Kennedy.

The court disagreed. It found that the record suggested that Combustion Engineering had supplied thousands of fuel rods on a continuing basis to the plant and several other nuclear plants. Therefore, Combustion Engineering's enterprise differed entirely in both quality and degree from the ad hoc and infrequent activities to which the "isolated transaction" exception has been previously deemed applicable. Based on *Elmore v. American Motors Corp.*, the court concluded that Combustion Engineering could have foreseen that the spouse of a nuclear-plant worker might fall within the foreseeable zone of danger posed by Combustion Engineering's products. As a result, it was error for the court to decide the issue as a matter of law.

The Kennedy case appears to state a broad notion of substantial factor causation. If applied to future cases involving genetic evidence, the standard for substantial factor causation could prove both detrimental to alternative cause arguments (since it will apparently be trumped by minor co-causal factors) and could allow the genetically susceptible plaintiff to argue for substantial factor causation based on slim percentage increases in background risk.

In contrast to the expansive view of causation taken in *Kennedy*, a superior court in Arizona addressing causation for the effects of TCE (an industrial solvent) applied "but for" causation to deny the plaintiffs' experts the opportunity to testify in a landmark *Daubert/Frye* motion that drew national attention. In *Lofgren v. Motorola, Inc.*, the plaintiffs alleged various theories to attempt to link their health problems, including cancers, to exposure to TCE. The court held that their experts did not have adequate scientific evidence to meet the "but for" causation standard in Arizona. Presumably evidence meeting the "but for" standard would also have to hurdle the next level of proximate cause—*i.e.*, where the foreseeability of harm is so remote, the courts decline to afford relief.

VII. "General Causation" Motions Under *Daubert/Frye* Standards

The impacts of genetic testing data flowing from the mapping of the human genome are already beginning. Any toxic tort counsel that retains cutting edge or world-class experts will find them making reference to emerging genetic theories in epidemiology, toxicology, and biostatistics. Over time, the evidence generated by the mapping of the human genome will expose many new links of causation that traditional epidemiology could not reach. The biotechnology industry will find new markets for its diagnostic tests. A new class of experts will provide the key to tracing new causation pathways, exonerating some suspects and implicating other suspects. Properly applied, using sound scientific techniques, toxicogenomic data could bring order to a chaotic, inefficient system of chemical regulation and liability. Improperly applied, it could increase the number of cases alleging "junk" science.

In federal courts in the United States, the Supreme Court has issued a series of decisions that make it quite clear that sound scientific methodologies are required to support an opinion that a chemical caused a particular disease. The *Daubert* doctrine was recently given a resounding 9–0 affirmance in a case reversing a trial court's decision to admit a series of fire causation experts. The gatekeeping role of the trial courts in keeping out spurious expert testimony is clearer than ever.

Plaintiffs' counsel would argue that there are some chinks in this *Daubert* armor where district courts appear to have let some dubious medical opinions in under a medical judgment exception to the scientific methodology requirements in *Daubert II*. In state courts, moreover, a patchwork quilt of decisions often allows doctors to present their medical experience-based opinions with minimal methodological foundation. California, because it follows the *Kelly-Frye* test of general acceptance for scientific opinions, has a line of cases that are not in accordance with the Daubert II decision on medical causation.

In the context of environmental mass torts, however, the courts of California have inherent power to require plaintiffs to make a prima facie case of actual injury before they require the court to engage in a long process of hearing evidence about injuries. In *Cottle v. Superior Court*, the following order was affirmed on appeal: "The court tentatively ordered the exclusion of 'all evidence, by lay or expert witnesses, that plaintiffs have or will suffer any particular injury or illness based on exposure to toxic substances in the Dunes' unless plaintiffs could demonstrate by May 31, 1991, that viable claims for personal injury existed."

Courts facing thousands of claims will generally use case management methods to require plaintiffs to show "general causation"—that the compound in question could possibly cause cancer (or other alleged effect) at the doses in question. This level of analysis sets aside the specific facts of particular plaintiffs, which complicate the question of causation considerably (e.g., they may have various alternative causes at issue for the harm they claim).

The adversarial process of tort litigation can lead juries to stray far afield from established scientific consensus, particularly in those state courts or federal circuits that allow medical opinions in without adequate regard for gatekeeper principles prevailing in federal courts. In some states that recognize both medical monitoring claims and the "medical judgment" exception to *Daubert*'s "gatekeeper doctrine," a physician expert may be allowed to propose the functional equivalent of a broad health insurance program (in the form of a medical monitoring award) payable in large part to his own medical group. If the floodgates are manned by physicians with an incentive to divert financial resources for medical monitoring to their own practices, this inherent bias could lead to runaway awards.

As noted above, epidemiology and the law have combined to create the doubling risk concept. To cross this threshold, plaintiffs are sometimes asked to prove that their risk is at least two times the background incidence of the disease allegedly caused by a chemical. In most toxic tort cases, the court will require an initial showing of general causation (*i.e.*, that scientific evidence shows an increased risk with valid scientific studies to support that conclusion). In many cases, doubling risk will get the standard. Once general causation is shown, specific proof of each plaintiff's case ("specific causation") can be addressed through discovery and trial.

For example, the defense expert would demonstrate that the increased cancer risk for that 90% of exposed persons is simply too low for the court to even consider medical causation. The remaining 10% of plaintiffs would have proved only general causation, *i.e.*, that they had enough exposure to be considered for specific causation. In many cases, modern epidemiology is insufficient in its specificity to demonstrate which of the various persons who have a greater than 2.0 relative risk could have cancer that was caused by the chemical exposure.

For companies trying to decide whether a warning is feasible, use of the doubling risk standard could provide a tool for initiating analysis of the duty to warn. If the genetically susceptible subgroup can be identified, and a warning is feasible (*e.g.*, website notifications), then warnings may be deemed necessary, with perfect hindsight, in some future lawsuit. The failure to warn today could open the door to a lawsuit tomorrow.

VIII. Conclusion

It is clear that the use of toxicogenomic data will be making many appearances in the courts and in debates over regulatory policy toward chemicals and radiation. There is no question that toxicogenomic evidence will sometimes be used without a solid scientific basis, as genome experts extend the boundaries of science into areas that are hypothetical (*i.e.*, "junk science"). With creative plaintiffs' attorneys guiding them, toxicogenomic experts could create a fearful new world where many people fear microscopic, largely hypothetical interactions of genes and chemicals.

For many, this fear of genes could lead to unintended adverse consequences. Decisions to sell a home near a waste facility or not to have children for fear of passing some genetic harm to them could be based on a largely unfounded fear manufactured by experts and counsel for purposes of litigation and money damages. In that sense, the toxicogenomic revolution could bring a Pandora's box scenario, releasing some unpleasant adverse consequences. Properly applied, however, toxicogenomic data will shine light on previously dark areas of medical causation, and bring everyone involved closer to the truth.

Bryson v. Pillsbury

573 N.W.2d 718 (Minn. Ct. App. 1998)

KALITOWSKI, JUDGE.

Appellant Nora Bryson challenges the district court's grant of summary judgment in favor of respondents Pillsbury Company, et al., arguing the district court erred because:

(1) Bryson submitted evidence that raised a genuine issue of material fact as to whether she suffered a present injury; and (2) Bryson presented sufficient evidence to establish her claim for damages based on her alleged increased risk of developing cancer.

Facts

Appellant Nora Bryson boarded her horse at the farm of an individual who, like Bryson, was an employee of respondent Pillsbury's subsidiary, Green Giant (company). On July 23, 1990, Bryson discovered that her horse had fallen into a pit filled with water from a storm. The pit, which was 20 feet by 20 feet with a 17-foot depth, had allegedly been used by the company to dispose of waste. Bryson entered the pit in an attempt to rescue the horse and, while in the pit, observed what she believed to be Captan-treated seeds floating in the water. Captan is a chemical treatment for seed that protects it from insects in the soil until germination.

Bryson and others succeeded in getting the horse out of the water. Later that day, Bryson broke out in a rash that covered her body. She presented evidence that she has subsequently developed additional rashes. Bryson, through her expert from the University of Minnesota, presented evidence that she suffered extensive chromosome breakage as a result of exposure to Captan and that, because of the chromosome breakage, she has an increased risk of developing cancer. The company made a motion for summary judgment arguing: (1) Bryson assumed the risk of harm by not leaving the pit when she saw the Captan-treated seeds; and (2) Bryson's alleged damages were too speculative. The district court denied the company's summary judgment motion on assumption of risk, but granted summary judgment in favor of the company stating that Bryson suffered no present injury and concluding that her claimed damages for future harm were too speculative as a matter of law.

Issues

1. Did Bryson present sufficient evidence to support her claim of a present injury?

2. Did Bryson present sufficient evidence to support her claim for damages based on her alleged increased risk of developing cancer?

Analysis

As an initial matter, the company moved to strike Bryson's reply brief arguing the brief raised new issues and theories on appeal. After a review of the parties' arguments, we conclude that Bryson's reply brief is proper and deny the company's motion.

On appeal from a district court's grant of summary judgment, this court determines: (1) whether any genuine issues of material fact exist; and (2) whether the district court erred in applying the law. *State by Cooper v. French,* 460 N.W.2d 2, 4 (Minn.1990). In making this determination, we "view the evidence in the light most favorable to the party against whom judgment was granted." *Fabio v. Bellomo,* 504 N.W.2d 758, 761 (Minn.1993).

I.

Bryson contends the district court erred in granting summary judgment, claiming she presented sufficient evidence to raise a genuine fact issue as to whether her chromosome damage constituted a present injury. The company asserts that because Bryson's claimed chromosome damage is asymptomatic, it does not constitute a legally compensable present injury. In a memorandum supporting its order for summary judgment, the district court, without reference to Bryson's allegations regarding present damages, stated: "In this matter there are no present injuries...." We conclude the district court erred by granting summary judgment where there is a genuine issue of disputed material fact regarding whether there was a present injury.

In *Werlein v. United States,* 746 F.Supp. 887, 901 (D.Minn.1990), *vacated in part on other grounds,* 793 F.Supp. 898 (D.Minn.1992), the United States District Court addressed a case in which the plaintiffs claimed that exposure to contaminated air and drinking water resulted in chromosome damage. The defendants argued that the plaintiffs did not suffer a present injury. *Id.* In denying the defendants' summary judgment motion, the court in *Werlein* stated that it could not rule as a matter of law that plaintiffs' alleged injuries are not "real" simply because they are subcellular. The effect of volatile organic compounds on the human body is a subtle, complex matter. It is for the trier of fact, aided by expert testimony, to determine whether plaintiffs have suffered present harm. *Id.*

The asymptomatic, subcellular damages claimed in *Werlein* are similar to the injury claimed by Bryson. Here, Bryson's expert witness presented evidence that Bryson's exposure to Captan resulted in chromosome breakage, and that such breakage is a "real and present physical and biologic injury." This testimony was disputed by the company, whose expert testified that "an elevated number of chromosome aberrations are not considered an 'injury' per se because they do not in and of themselves result in any physical impairment."

Following the reasoning of *Werlein,* we conclude the trier of fact should resolve this fact dispute.

Further, like the plaintiffs in *Werlein,* Bryson claims emotional distress damages and medical monitoring expenses because of her alleged chromosome damage. *Id.* at 901, 905. The court in *Werlein* determined that the existence and extent of these alleged damages also presented fact questions for the jury. *Id.* at 905–06. Again, following *Werlein,* we conclude that because there are genuine fact issues concerning the existence of Bryson's present injuries and damages, summary judgment on this claim is inappropriate.

II.

Bryson next argues that because she has offered expert evidence that she has a present injury, she need only present evidence that is "fair comment" on the medical implications of chromosome breakage to establish future damages resulting from her increased risk of cancer. Alternatively, Bryson argues that she has presented sufficient evidence to a reasonable medical certainty that entitles her to compensation for future damages as a result of her increased risk of cancer. The district court concluded that because Bryson can neither prove that her increased risk of future harm is more likely than not to occur, nor quantify her increased risk of developing cancer, her claimed damages for increased risk of future harm are too speculative as a matter of law. We agree.

A plaintiff must prove every element of a claim by a preponderance of the evidence. *Carpenter v. Nelson,* 101 N.W.2d 918, 921 ([Minn.] 1960). For Bryson to establish her claim for future damages, she must show: (1) that the future harm is more likely than not to occur; and (2) that her future damages are not too speculative. *Pietrzak v. Eggen,* 295 N.W.2d 504, 507 (Minn.1980). Bryson failed to present evidence on both issues.

We disagree with Bryson's contention that she need only present evidence that is "fair comment" on the medical implications of chromosome breakage. The term "fair comment" has been used to characterize expert medical testimony for purposes of determining the admissibility of evidence, not to provide the standard for proving future injury. *Dunshee v. Douglas,* 255 N.W.2d 42, 47 (Minn.1977). Here, Bryson's expert admitted that Bryson's increased risk of cancer could not be measured or quantified. Thus, the evidence presented by Bryson does not, as a matter of law, permit a factfinder to determine that Bryson is more likely than not to develop cancer.

Further, in *Faimon v. Winona State Univ.,* 540 N.W.2d 879, 884 (Minn.App.1995), this court affirmed the principle that plaintiffs may not recover damages that are too speculative. The determination of whether damages are too speculative or remote "should usually be left to the judgment of the trial court." *Jackson v. Reiling,* 249 N.W.2d 896, 897 ([Minn.] 1977). Because Bryson has presented no evidence to quantify her risk of developing cancer, we conclude the district court properly granted summary judgment in favor of the company on Bryson's claim for future damages.

Decision

The district court properly granted summary judgment in favor of the company on Bryson's claim for damages based on an alleged increased risk of future harm because: (1) Bryson has not presented evidence that it is more likely than not that she will develop cancer; and (2) Bryson's claimed damages for the increased risk of cancer are too speculative as a matter of law. We conclude, however, Bryson has presented sufficient evidence to establish a genuine issue of material fact concerning the existence of a present injury and damages as a result of the alleged injury. We, therefore, reverse and remand this claim for further proceedings.

Affirmed in part, reversed in part, and remanded; motion to strike denied.

Short, Judge (concurring in part, dissenting in part).

I concur insofar as the majority concludes the trial court properly granted summary judgment in favor of Pillsbury Company on Bryson's "risk of cancer" claim. I respectfully dissent on the narrow remand concerning Bryson's "chromosome breakage" claim because there is no evidence supporting an award of damages for present physical injury. *Compare Werlein v. United States,* 746 F.Supp. 887, 901 (D.Minn.1990) (holding summary judgment inappropriate where increased risk of harm damages are supported by evidence of present physical injury), *vacated in part on other grounds,* 793 F.Supp. 898 (D.Minn.1992) *with Reliance Ins. Co. v. Arneson,* 322 N.W.2d 604, 607 (Minn.1982) (concluding threat of future harm, not yet realized, will not satisfy damage requirement in negligence action). Mere allegations of emotional distress and possible medical monitoring expenses are insufficient to create a fact issue on whether Bryson now suffers from a present physical injury. *See* Minn. R. Civ. P. 56.05 (stating nonmoving party may not rest on pleading averments or denials, but must present specific facts showing genuine issue for trial); *Nicollet Restoration, Inc. v. City of St. Paul,* 533 N.W.2d 845, 848 (Minn.1995) (holding speculation and general assertions are not sufficient to create genuine issue of material fact for trial).

Even if an asymptomatic chromosome condition constitutes evidence of a present physical injury, Bryson also failed to offer any evidence that her alleged damages are capable of proof to a reasonable certainty. *See Fabio v. Bellomo,* 504 N.W.2d 758, 762–63 (Minn. 1993) (concluding, even if court were to adopt "loss of chance" theory in medical malpractice actions, summary judgment was appropriate on "loss of chance" theory because patient failed to present evidence that it was more probable than not that her cancer would recur or that she had diminished life expectancy); *see also Abuan v. General Elec. Co.,* 3 F.3d 329, 334 (9th Cir. 1993) (concluding plaintiff who seeks damages for increased risk of future illness or injury can recover only where toxic exposure more probably than not will lead to malady); *Laswell v. Brown*, 683 F.2d 261, 269 (8th Cir. 1982) (concluding lawsuit for personal injuries cannot be based only upon mere possibility of some future harm); *Thomas v. FAG Bearings Corp.*, 846 F. Supp. 1400, 1408 (W.D. Mo. 1994) (concluding claim for increased risk of cancer is not compensable unless reasonably certain to occur); *Ayers v. Township of Jackson*, 525 A.2d 287, 308 ([N.J.] 1987) (declining to recognize plaintiffs' cause of action for unquantified enhanced risk of disease because of speculative nature of an unquantified enhanced risk claim and difficulties inherent in adjudicating such claims). Under these circumstances, Bryson has no compensable injury and Pillsbury Company is entitled to judgment as a matter of law. I would affirm the trial court's grant of summary judgment.

Mark A. Rothstein, *Should Genetic Information Be Used to Predict Life Expectancy of Plaintiffs in Tort Cases?*

Hous. Lawyer, Sept.–Oct. 1996, at 49

Dr. Jane Smith is a 35 year-old neurosurgeon who entered private practice three years ago upon completion of her training. She has an annual income of $200,000. One day, while crossing the street from the doctors' parking lot to the hospital, she is run over by a Zippy Express delivery truck, whose unlicensed, intoxicated driver was speeding to a delivery and failed to stop for a red light. As a result of the accident, Dr. Smith has become quadriplegic and will be unable to perform surgery again.

In a negligence action against Zippy Express, a key component of Dr. Smith's economic damages is her lost income. Assuming she would have been able to work for 30 more years, with an income of $200,000 per year, this would amount to $6 million in current dollars, exclusive of projected earnings increases, merely for lost income.

Suppose, however, that Dr. Smith is in the unaffected, presymptomatic stage of Huntington's disease, amyotrophic lateral sclerosis, or some other late-onset genetic disorder. Further suppose that experts will testify that, in all likelihood, irrespective of the accident, she would not have been able to practice medicine beyond age 45 and that her life expectancy is 50 years. Applying traditional damages principles, this information would reduce her recovery for economic injury by at least $4 million.

Zippy Express and its insurers therefore would have a great economic incentive to discover information about Dr. Smith's genetic profile and to introduce this information at trial. Should the defendants be able to discover this information by obtaining access to Dr. Smith's medical records? Should they be able to obtain a court order directing Dr. Smith to submit to genetic testing? Should it matter whether genetic testing previously had been performed on Dr. Smith or whether there was something in her family or medical history to suspect a genetic disorder?

The preceding scenario and the resulting questions have the potential to become commonplace. Conceivably, in every case in which the plaintiff seeks to recover for permanent or long-term disability or lost future earnings, regardless of the legal theory of the case, the defendant could seek to discover the plaintiff's risk of premature incapacity or mortality by obtaining genetic records or performing genetic testing.

...

Damages for Lost Future Earnings

Special damages for quantifiable losses are based on the increased expenses and the lost income caused by the injury. The latter component, lost future earnings, is a function of income level and work life expectancy. A claim for lost future earnings or lost earning capacity is "an estimate of lost present ability to work in an appropriate occupation, now and in the future." Ordinarily, damages for lost future earnings are only relevant after the plaintiff proves that he or she has suffered a permanent injury. Thereafter, the evidence focuses on two issues: (1) the plaintiff's expected rate of earnings, and (2) the plaintiff's expected number of lost years of earning capacity.

Rate of earnings is relatively easy to compute. It is based on the plaintiff's abilities, training, experience, and preinjury earnings. Prospects for wage increases and loss of fringe benefits also are considered. Loss of future earnings is not all-or-nothing; thus, reduction of future earnings as well as inability to generate any earnings at all are recoverable.

Determining life expectancy is already more difficult, and it is likely to become increasingly complicated in the new era of genetics and predictive medicine. Currently, life expectancy is generally based initially on standard mortality tables. Although in Texas, mortality tables are not required in making a determination of life expectancy or work expectancy.

If the plaintiff at the time of the injury, already had been diagnosed with cancer, heart disease, or some other life-threatening illness this evidence is admissible to show a reduced life expectancy. The courts also have admitted a wide range of evidence of behavioral factors in attempting to prove that the plaintiff had a diminished life expectancy at the time of the injury. These factors include the plaintiff's use of drugs, alcohol, or cigarettes.

If evidence of cigarette smoking is admissible to show that the plaintiff's life expectancy is lessened because of the possibility of lung cancer, emphysema, or heart disease, then evidence that the plaintiff was genetically predisposed to such a disorder also would seem to be admissible. From the defendant's standpoint, the only issue is how to obtain access to such genetic information. The main ways include discovery of existing medical records, questioning the plaintiff at deposition, compelling a medical examination of the plaintiff, and questioning the plaintiff's physicians by interrogatories or depositions.

Although virtually all of the cases involve the defendant's attempt to introduce evidence of the plaintiff's shorter life expectancy, it is also possible for the plaintiff to introduce evidence of longevity. With genetic prediction becoming increasingly sophisticated, it may be possible to estimate increased longevity.

...

While it would violate public policy to permit unfettered access to genetic information and genetic examinations of personal injury plaintiffs at the whim of defendants, it also would be unfair to defendants to award compensatory damages for lost future earnings while the court excludes all evidence of the plaintiffs' preinjury or future health. Thus, it is necessary to find a middle ground, and this process involves drawing lines, making distinctions, and balancing interests.

There is a vital distinction between genetic evidence relevant to the issue of causation and genetic evidence relevant to the issue of damages. With adequate protective orders prohibiting redisclosure of the information, evidence of the plaintiff's genetic profile should be discoverable when it is relevant to the issue of causation. Thus, genetic testing may establish whether genetic or environmental factors caused the harm to the plaintiff. Nevertheless, before genetic testing is ordered to help establish the cause of the plaintiff's injuries, courts should require a clear showing of a basis in fact to suspect that the testing is necessary. A protective order also should be issued to limit the disclosure of the results.

Under established principles, if the plaintiff has a shortened life expectancy because of an already manifested illness, such as heart disease, cancer, or some genetic disorder, this fact is relevant and should be discoverable and admissible. A plaintiff with a life expectancy of one year would reap a windfall if the defendant were forced to pay lump sum damages based on a life expectancy of 30 years. What about the discovery of predictive health information, especially genetic information? With an asymptomatic plaintiff who is unaware of any genetic predisposition to a serious late-onset disorder, ordering compelled genetic testing would be tantamount to judicial sanctioning of a genetic fishing expedition. This testing would be extremely difficult to justify because it either would be wasteful and unrevealing or it would force the plaintiff to confront information he or she did not know previously and that he or she might not want to know.

Does the analysis change if the plaintiff previously underwent genetic testing in the clinical setting or otherwise knew (such as through family health history) of his or her genetic risks? In this situation, the plaintiff is not involuntarily confronted with new, possibly devastating information. Nonetheless, two other strong policies demand that the information not be discoverable. First, the plaintiff should be able to maintain the confidentiality of the information without disclosing such intimate medical information to litigants and counsel, as well as other individuals, such as family members, who may not have known of the original testing. Second, by permitting discovery, individuals may be deterred from seeking genetic testing or bringing possibly meritorious tort claims to avoid the disclosure of sensitive genetic information.

Discovery of general medical records should continue to be permitted even in the absence of any reason to suspect a serious disorder. This includes gathering medical records, questioning the plaintiff and the plaintiff's physicians at deposition, and upon an appropriate showing of good cause, compelling medical examination. Otherwise, plaintiffs with extant but nonobvious disorders would receive a windfall. Without new legislation, however, genetic information in general medical records could be revealed, with the attendant negative implications for public policy previously discussed. It must be emphasized, however, that if defendants cannot introduce evidence of genetic predictors of a reduced life expectancy, plaintiffs also should be precluded from introducing evidence of genetic predictors of longevity. In the absence of prior symptoms, both sides should continue to use standard mortality tables.

What are the costs and benefits of admitting or excluding genetic information? Using predictive genetic information in determining damages is outcome-neutral in the aggregate because, theoretically, over time, all plaintiffs will be awarded the same total amount of money from all defendants as they would have been awarded if calculations were based on mortality tables. Some plaintiffs will get more than average, some will get less. Defendants as a group will not save money. In fact, if one adds the costs of genetic testing and litigating the issue of life expectancy, defendants in the aggregate will be worse off if genetic information were utilized. Some defendants, however, will be much better off if they can obtain and use genetic information. In my view, the social gains achieved from attempting to have damage calculations more precisely determined do not offset the social costs of obtaining, divulging, and litigating predictive genetic information.

There are two relatively easy ways to limit the discovery of genetic information. The first way is a judicial solution, through an expansive reading and liberal use of protective orders pursuant to Rule 26(c) of the Federal Rules of Civil Procedure and analogous state rules of procedure. The second way would be to enact a specific genetic confidentiality statute, limiting or prohibiting access to genetic records and compelled testing. Although the specifics of these options, as well as other possibilities, are beyond the scope of this abbreviated article, each one needs to be considered. Genetic information has many valuable uses, but determining damages in civil litigation is not one of them.

Notes & Questions

1. Genetic susceptibility and genetic injury present cutting-edge issues as they enter the courtroom. Science is only just beginning to discover and explore the impact of a variety of toxins on the human genome. In the context of toxic tort litigation, genetics may come into play in two broad contexts. First are cases in which the plaintiffs argue that because of an inherited genetic susceptibility, they have been injured by exposure to a toxin. As noted in the excerpt from Professor Marchant's article, there are several known genetic anomalies that result in increased sensitivity to certain drugs and toxins. In these cases, the plaintiff will have to show that exposure to the toxic was more likely than not the cause of the injury. This can be an extremely difficult threshold for the plaintiff, especially given the multifactorial nature of most diseases. Even if that threshold can be overcome, the question will be whether the alleged tortfeasor could have known about the danger and had a duty to warn. If the defendant's anomalous susceptibility is so unusual and idiosyncratic, courts are unlikely to find that there was a duty to warn. Moreover, the plaintiff will have to be prepared to counter the arguments of alternate and multiple causations. The defense may argue that the genetic anomaly caused the disease independent of exposure to the toxin or that other environmental toxins and exposure could have triggered the susceptibility rather than the toxin at issue.

A second category of cases are those in which the plaintiff argues that exposure to a toxin actually damaged and changed their cellular genetics. This is a complex area of science that is just beginning to be studied and elucidated. Most of the research to date has focused on cytogenetic changes evidenced by breakage and changes in chromosomal structure in somatic cells. There are a few cases that have alleged such chromosomal injury, including *Pillsbury v. Bryson.* However, it is often difficult for the plaintiff to show that the chromosomal change is related to exposure to a critical dose of toxin. In addition, the plaintiff must prove that there is a definite harm or disease resulting from the chromosomal change—not just speculative fear. It is rare for fear of future or latent risk claims to succeed in the absence of a documented present injury.

For additional information on the emerging science and law related to genetic susceptibility and toxic injury, see Gary E. Marchant, *Genetic Susceptibility and Biomarkers in Toxic Injury Litigation*, 41 Jurimetrics J. 67 (2000); Susan R. Poulter, *Genetic Testing in Toxic Injury Litigation: The Path to Scientific Certainty or Blind Alley?*, 41 Jurimetircs J. 211 (2001); Gary E. Marchant, *Genetics and Toxic Torts*, 31 Seton Hall L. Rev. 949 (2001); Jon R. Pierce & Terrence Sexton, *Toxicogenomics: Towards the Future of Toxic Tort Causation*, 5 N.C. J.L. & Tech. 33 (2003).

2. The Redick article speaks to the complexity of toxicogenomics in the context of establishing injury and proving causation in a tort case. As Redick relates, such toxic tort cases are notoriously difficult to litigate. Injury is often so speculative that it fails to meet the typical tort standard of "more likely than not." Other non-genetic toxins such as tobacco and asbestos have provided a long line of cases demonstrating some of difficulties in proving that exposure to that, and only that, specific toxin resulted in disease.

Defendants in these toxic tort cases have several strategies available to them. Under the so-called "doubling risk" defense, the defense will argue that unless the exposure actually doubled the background risk for disease, then the increase in risk does not meet the standard of "more likely than not." However, this defense could become a two-edged sword if indeed genetic susceptibility becomes refined and specific enough to stratify the potential plaintiffs to yield a subset that can scientifically support a doubling of risk. Another theory likely to be used by defendants is the "state of the art" defense in which the defendant is not held liable for knowledge that he did not, and could not, have known by conducting accepted industry testing and quality controls. A somewhat more discrete version of "state of the art" is the idiosyncratic reaction defense. Under this defense, the argument is that such idiosyncrasy could not have been foretold or anticipated by the alleged tortfeasor and that there is no duty to warn against such an unusual and unknown adverse reaction. However, as Redick notes, as we become more knowledgeable about genetic toxins, the duty to warn expands and may eclipse both the "state of the art" and the idiosyncratic reaction defense. Another defense is the argument that the injury was not solely the result of exposure to the toxin but the result of many environmental and other factors, all of which combined to overcome the susceptible plaintiff. This defense was used with great effect in asbestos and coal-miner lung disease cases, where the plaintiffs were often smokers. Finally, a defendant may be able to flip the genetic susceptibility against the plaintiff and argue that the susceptibility would have resulted in disease regardless of the exposure to the alleged toxin.

For an excellent illustration of the complexity of toxic tort cases, see the prolonged litigation arising from the release of radioactive iodine by the Hanford Nuclear Reservation. This facility in southeastern Washington was built during World War II to manufacture high grade plutonium for the Manhattan Project and continued in operation for forty years. Radioactive iodine was released into the air during the 1940s and alleged resulted in adverse health effects for "downwinders." *See* Agency for Toxic Substances and Disease Registry, Are You a Hanford Downwinder?, http://www.atsdr.cdc.gov/hanford. Litigation began in 1991 when plaintiffs alleged that the emissions caused thyroid diseases and numerous cancerous conditions. Litigation continues to the present day as courts parse through the complex issue of causation in these "downwinder" cases. *See, e.g.*, The Hanford Downwinders Litigation Information Resource, http://www.downwinders.com/index.html; *see also* Eric Dejure Wilson, *Hope for Hanford Downwinders: The Ninth Circuit's Ruling in* In re Hanford Nuclear Reservation, 82 OR. L. REV. 581 (2003).

3. *Bryson v. Pillsbury* is one of a handful of cases alleging genetic injury as result of exposure to a toxic substance. Bryson argues that she suffers from both a present injury and a risk and fear of future illness as a result of exposure to Captan. Evidence of this future risk, she alleges, is inherent in the chromosomal damage she has suffered. The court allows Bryson an opportunity to make this—and only this—claim on remand. Note that the dissent would not even have allowed Bryson this limited opportunity. The dissenting judge expresses skepticism that asymptomatic chromosomal breaks are evidence of a present injury and capable of proof with reasonable certainty. For additional cases addressing present injury and future risks as a result of chromosome breakage, see *Cano v. Everest Mineral Corp.*, 362 F. Supp. 2d 814 (W.D. Tex. 2005) (excluding testimony by expert alleging that exposure to uranium resulted in cancer as evidenced by, among other things, chromosomal damage; testimony excluded as not sufficiently validated by science); *Good v. Fluor Daniel Corp.*, 222. F. Supp. 2d 1236 (E.D. Wash. 2002) (proposed expert testimony alleging that injurious exposure to radiation evidenced by chromosomal abnormalities excluded as not scientifically valid). *But see Bratford v.*

Susquehanna Corp., 586 F. Supp. 14 (D. Colo. 1984) (chromosomal damage indication of present injury and defendant's summary judgment motion denied); *In re TMI Litigation*, 193 F.3d 613 (3d Cir. 1999) (testimony regarding chromosomal aberrations not an accurate or reliable indicator of radiation exposure unless assayed within one to two years of irradiating dose; however, cytogenetic biomarkers might have been admitted as evidence had they been submitted prior to expiration of court's deadline). Should chromosomal breaks, without any known relationship to bodily function, qualify as a present injury? How would you make an argument for present injury? How would you refute it?

The *Bryson v. Pillsbury* court does not reverse the lower court's determination that risk of future illness and fear of it are too speculative to survive as cognizable claims. This is in keeping with numerous other cases that have addressed the issue of latent risks. Most courts limit any recognition of these claims to cases in which the plaintiff can easily demonstrate a present injury as well. Moreover, the plaintiff typically must show that the increased future risk is both substantial and ascertainable with relative certainty. *See Adams v. Johns Manville Sales Corp.*, 783 F.2d 589 (5th Cir. 1986) (present injury required to recover for alleged future risk of illness); *Ayers v. Township of Jackson*, 525 A.2d 287 (N.J. 1987) (no recovery when the risk of future disease cannot be quantified); *In re Paoli R.R. Yard PCB Litigation*, 916 F.2d 829 (3d Cir. 1990) (plaintiff must show that risk is significantly increased to get damages for monitoring for future disease).

4. Professor Rothstein's article posits that genetic information may be used by the courts to ascertain and modulate damages in civil tort cases. He argues that this would be patently unfair and suggests that discovery of such medical information should be precluded. Under Rule 35 of the Federal Rules of Civil Procedure, the Court may order a mental or physical exam in an action where the condition of a party is material to the controversy. To get such an exam, the other party must show that the information is not available elsewhere and that good cause warrants each examination. For an in-depth discussion of Rule 35 and genetic testing issues, see Anthony S. Niedwiecki, *Science Fact or Science Fiction? The Implications of Court Ordered Genetic Testing Under Rule 35*, 34 U.S.F. L. Rev. 295 (2000)

Courts have been struggling with this issue in the context of HIV over the past two decades. In *Sacramona v. Bridgestone/Firestone Inc.*, 152 F.R.D. 428 (D. Mass. 1993), the court refused to compel HIV testing because it was deemed an "extraordinary" measure, and the results would be so attenuated from the tort case that it was tantamount to a fishing expedition. However, in another case, *Pettyjohn v. Goodyear Tire & Rubber Co.*, No. 91-CV-2681, 1992 WL 105162 (E.D. Pa. 1992), the court allowed an HIV test because the plaintiff had placed his life expectancy in controversy by seeking future damage for the injury sustained at work. Moreover, courts frequently take into account alcoholism, drug use and life style issues in determining future damages. *See, e.g., Oxford v. Hamilton*, 763 S.W.2d 83 (Ark. 1989) (allowing jury to take into account the plaintiff's occupation, health habits, and other activities in determining future earnings and damages); *Smith v. Southland Corp.*, 738 F. Supp. 923 (E.D. Pa. 1990) (allowing the introduction of alcoholism for the question of life expectancy); *Ward v. Loomis Bros., Inc.*, 532 N.W.2d 807 (Iowa Ct. App. 1995) (marijuana use a factor in determining future earnings and the question of loss of value to estate). *But see McCarty v. Gappelberg*, 273 S.W.2d 943 (Tex. Civ. App. 1954) (personal-injury case remanded for retrial because defendant had introduced prejudicial evidence regarding plaintiff's alcohol history); *Krueger v. Gen. Motors Corp.*, 783 P.2d 1340 (Mont. 1989) (disallowing evidence of alleged habitual drug use because it was more prejudicial than probative).

In the hypothetical story of Jane Smith, would knowledge of her underlying genetic disease decrease the award amount given her shorter life span? Is this so unfair to Jane Smith? Isn't an award geared to a full life span an unjust enrichment for her? Alternatively, couldn't one argue that because her life span is shortened, each year of life is more precious to Jane Smith and should be valued at a higher rate? Is it fair for the defendant to pay less for his carelessness, merely because his victim had an inborn shorter lifespan? The hypothetical tortfeasor in the Rothstein hypothetical has been criminally negligent by driving while intoxicated. But assume that the tortfeasor is not an intoxicated, reckless Zippy Express driver, but rather a young father of three on his way home from work, and that Dr. Smith has crossed against the light because she is distracted having just received her genetic test results. The goal of the tort system is fair compensation and deterrence of negligence. Does having the tortfeasor pay more compensation than would be justified by the ascertainable, limited life span just and fair?

E. Genetic Identity: Ancestry, Race, Ethnicity, and Species Designation

An evolving area of interest is the role of genetics in identity in terms of determination of ancestry, race, ethnicity and even species definition. In the 1990s, the world's attention focused on the use of DNA to identify the remains of Russia's last czar and several of his family members. Executed during the Russian Revolution in 1918, the possible gravesite of the Romanov family was found in 1991, and the badly degraded remains were subject to extensive DNA testing. The results, published in NATURE GENETICS in 1994, revealed that the remains were those of the czar, czarina and three of their daughters. *See* Peter Gill, et al., *Identification of the Remains of the Romanov Family by DNA Analysis*, 6 NATURE GENETICS 130 (1994).

The saga of the search for the czar through genetic identification has given way to questions about genetic identity in the modern context. How is genetic identity established in terms of race, ethnicity and tribal membership? Is genetics likely to play a role in conclusively determining who is "in" and who is not with respect to membership in a minority group or tribe? Should genetics have an impact on the social construct of group membership? If so, how and why? Will genetic knowledge bring society renewed solidarity in light of our shared common genetic makeup or will it further separate us with renewed racism and ethnic pride? As scholars and ethicists ponder these questions, entrepreneurial companies already are offering genetic tests to determine ancestry and race/ethnicity. *See* Genelex Corporation, DNA Testing Leaders (2003), www.genelex.com. Only a few legal cases have emerged in this speculative new arena. One such case is the recent legal battle regarding the remains of the "Kennewick" man.

Bonnichsen v. United States

357 F.3d 962 (9th Cir. 2004)

GOULD, CIRCUIT JUDGE:

...

I

In July 1996, teenagers going to a boat race discovered a human skull and bones near the shore of the Columbia River just outside Kennewick, Washington. The remains were found on federal property under the management of the United States Army Corps of Engineers ("Corps") and, at the request of the county coroner, were removed for analysis by an anthropologist, Dr. James Chatters, pursuant to an Archaeological Resources Protection Act of 1979 ("ARPA"), 16 U.S.C. §§470aa–470mm, permit. Because of physical features such as the shape of the skull and facial bones, anthropologists at first thought the remains were those of an early European settler. But the anthropologists then found a stone projectile point embedded in the skeleton's upper hip bone. The object's design, when viewed with x-rays and CT scans of the hip, resembled a style that was common before the documented arrival of Europeans in the region. Further study of the remains revealed characteristics unlike those of a European settler, yet also inconsistent with any American Indian remains previously documented in the region. A minute quantity of metacarpal bone was radiocarbon dated. The laboratory estimated the age of the bones to be between 8340 and 9200 years old.

The skeleton attracted attention because some of its physical features, such as the shape of the face and skull, differed from those of modern American Indians. Many scientists believed the discovery might shed light on the origins of humanity in the Americas. On August 31, 1996, Dr. Douglas Owsley, Division Head for Physical Anthropology at the Smithsonian Institution in Washington, D.C., made arrangements for Dr. Chatters to bring this important find to the Smithsonian's National Museum of Natural History for further study.

Indian tribes from the area of the Columbia River opposed scientific study of the remains on religious and social grounds. Four Indian groups (the "Tribal Claimants") demanded that the remains be turned over to them for immediate burial. The Tribal Claimants based their demand on the Native American Graves Protection and Repatriation Act ("NAGPRA"), 25 U.S.C. §3001 et seq. The Corps agreed with the Tribal Claimants and, citing NAGPRA, seized the remains on September 10, 1996, shortly before they could be transported to the Smithsonian. The Corps also ordered an immediate halt to DNA testing, which was being done using the remainder of the bone sample that had been submitted earlier for radiocarbon dating. After investigation, the Corps decided to give the remains to the Tribal Claimants for burial. As required by NAGPRA, the Corps published a "Notice of Intent to Repatriate Human Remains" in a local newspaper on September 17, 1996, and September 24, 1996.

The scientists and others, including the Smithsonian Institution, objected to the Corps' decision, arguing that the remains were a rare discovery of national and international significance. In late September and early October 1996, several scientists asked Major General Ernest J. Herrell, Commander of the Corps' North Pacific Division, to allow qualified scientists to study the remains.

The scientists did not convince the Corps to permit them to study the remains, and commenced this litigation on October 16, 1996, in the United States District Court for the District of Oregon. In an opinion issued June 27, 1997, the district court denied the Corps' motion for summary judgment, finding that the Corps had "acted before it had all of the evidence," "did not fully consider or resolve certain difficult legal questions," and "assumed facts that proved to be erroneous." *Bonnichsen II*, 969 F.Supp. 628, 645 (D.Or.1997). The district court vacated the Corps' earlier decision on disposition of the remains and remanded the case to the Corps for further proceedings The district court also denied, without prejudice, Plaintiffs' motion to study the remains and directed the Corps to consider, on remand, "whether to grant [P]laintiffs' request [under ARPA] for permission to study the remains."

On March 24, 1998, the Corps and the Secretary of the Interior entered into an agreement that effectively assigned to the Secretary responsibility to decide whether the remains were "Native American" under NAGPRA, and to determine their proper disposition. The Department of the Interior then assumed the role of lead agency on this case.

Almost two years after this matter was remanded, the Secretary's experts began to examine the remains in detail. The experts estimated that Kennewick Man was 5" 9' to 5" 10' tall, 45 to 50 years of age when he died, and 15 to 20 years old when the projectile point became embedded in his hip. The experts could not determine, from non-destructive examination of the skeleton alone, when Kennewick Man lived. However, analysis of sediment layers where the skeleton was found supported the hypothesis that the remains dated back not less than 7600 years ago and Kennewick Man could have lived more than 9000 years ago (the date indicated by the initial radiocarbon dating of the skeleton). Further study of the sediment was recommended, but the Corps' decision to bury the discovery site in April 1998 prevented completion of those studies.

The experts compared the physical characteristics of the remains—e.g., measurements of the skull, teeth, and bones—with corresponding measurements from other skeletons. They concluded that Kennewick Man's remains were unlike those of any known present-day population, American Indian or otherwise.

The Secretary's experts cautioned, however, that an apparent lack of physical resemblance between the Kennewick Man's remains and present-day American Indians did not completely rule out the possibility that the remains might be biologically ancestral to modern American Indians. Moreover, although Kennewick Man's morphological traits did not closely resemble those of modern American Indian populations, the Secretary's experts noted that Kennewick Man's physical attributes are generally consistent with the very small number of human remains from this period that have been found in North America.

Relying solely on the age of the remains and the fact that the remains were found within the United States, on January 13, 2000, the Secretary pronounced Kennewick Man's remains "Native American" within NAGPRA's meaning. And on September 25, 2000, the Secretary determined that a preponderance of the evidence supported the conclusion that the Kennewick remains were culturally affiliated with present-day Indian tribes. For this reason, the Secretary announced his final decision to award Kennewick Man's remains to a coalition of the Tribal Claimants. The Corps and the Secretary also denied Plaintiffs' request to study the remains.

Plaintiffs filed an amended complaint in the district court challenging the Secretary's decisions. The district court again ruled in Plaintiffs' favor. As pertinent to this appeal, the district court vacated the Secretary's decisions as contrary to the Administrative Procedure Act, 5 U.S.C. § 706(2)(A) ("APA"), on the ground that the Secretary improperly concluded that NAGPRA applies. The district court also held that, because NAG-

PRA did not apply, Plaintiffs should have the opportunity to study Kennewick Man's remains under ARPA. Defendants and the Tribal Claimants appealed, and we stayed the district court's order granting Plaintiffs-scientists' study of the remains pending our decision herein.

II

[The court considered the validity of Plaintiff's standing and concluded that because it was likely that Plaintiffs' injury would be redressed by a favorable decision on the NAGPRA issue, the Plaintiffs had constitutional standing. The court also determined that it had jurisdiction over the Plaintiff's claims that NAGPRA was violated]

III

Our review of the Secretary's decision to transfer Kennewick Man to the Tribal Claimants is governed by the APA, which instructs courts to "hold unlawful and set aside agency action, findings, and conclusions found to be ... arbitrary, capricious, an abuse of discretion, or otherwise not in accordance with law." 5 U.S.C. § 706(2)(A).

NAGPRA vests "ownership or control" of newly discovered Native American human remains in the decedent's lineal descendants or, if lineal descendants cannot be ascertained, in a tribe "affiliated" with the remains. 25 U.S.C. § 3002(a). NAGPRA mandates a two-part analysis. The first inquiry is whether human remains are Native American within the statute's meaning. If the remains are not Native American, then NAGPRA does not apply. However, if the remains are Native American, then NAGPRA applies, triggering the second inquiry of determining which persons or tribes are most closely affiliated with the remains.

The parties dispute whether the remains of Kennewick Man constitute Native American remains within NAGPRA's meaning. NAGPRA defines human remains as "Native American" if the remains are "of, or relating to, a tribe, people, or culture that is indigenous to the United States." 25 U.S.C. § 3001(9). The text of the relevant statutory clause is written in the present tense ("of, or relating to, a tribe, people, or culture that is indigenous"). Thus the statute unambiguously requires that human remains bear some relationship to a presently existing tribe, people, or culture to be considered Native American.

It is axiomatic that, in construing a statute, courts generally give words not defined in a statute their "ordinary or natural meaning." *United States v. Alvarez-Sanchez*, 511 U.S. 350, 357 (1994); *see also Williams v. Taylor*, 529 U.S. 420 (2000) (holding that courts "give the words of a statute their ordinary, contemporary, common meaning, absent an indication Congress intended them to bear some different import") (internal quotation marks omitted).

In the context of NAGPRA, we conclude that Congress's use of the present tense is significant. The present tense "in general represents present time." R. Pence and D. Emery, A Grammar of Present Day English 262 (2d ed.1963). Congress, by using the phrase "is indigenous" in the present tense, referred to presently existing tribes, peoples, or cultures. We must presume that Congress gave the phrase "is indigenous" its ordinary or natural meaning. *Alvarez-Sanchez*, 511 U.S. at 357. We conclude that Congress was referring to presently existing Indian tribes when it referred to "a tribe, people, or culture that is indigenous to the United States." 25 U.S.C. § 3001(9) (emphasis added).

NAGPRA also protects graves of persons not shown to be of current tribes in that it protects disjunctively remains "of, or relating to" current indigenous tribes. Thus, NAGPRA extends to all remains that relate to a tribe, people, or culture that is indigenous to the United States, see 25 U.S.C. § 3001(9) (defining human remains as Native American if they are "of, *or relating to*, a tribe, people, or culture that is indigenous to the United States") (emphasis added).

Our conclusion that NAGPRA's language requires that human remains, to be considered Native American, bear some relationship to a presently existing tribe, people, or culture accords with NAGPRA's purposes. As regards newly discovered human remains, NAGPRA was enacted with two main goals: to respect the burial traditions of modern-day American Indians and to protect the dignity of the human body after death. NAGPRA was intended to benefit modern American Indians by sparing them the indignity and resentment that would be aroused by the despoiling of their ancestors' graves and the study or the display of their ancestors' remains. *See* H.R.Rep. No. 101-877, U.S.Code Cong. & Admin.News at 4367, 4369 (1990) ("For many years, Indian tribes have attempted to have the remains and funerary objects of *their ancestors returned to them*.") (emphasis added).

Congress's purposes would not be served by requiring the transfer to modern American Indians of human remains that bear no relationship to them. Yet, that would be the result under the Secretary's construction of the statute, which would give Native American status to any remains found within the United States regardless of age and regardless of lack of connection to existing indigenous tribes. The exhumation, study, and display of ancient human remains that are unrelated to modern American Indians was not a target of Congress's aim, nor was it precluded by NAGPRA.

NAGPRA was also intended to protect the dignity of the human body after death by ensuring that Native American graves and remains be treated with respect. *See* S.Rep. No. 101-473, at 6 (1990) ("The Committee believes that human remains must at all times be treated with dignity and respect."); H.R.Rep. No. 101-877, U.S.Code Cong. & Admin.News at 4367, 4372 (1990) ("Some Indian representatives testified that the spirits of *their ancestors* would not rest until they are returned to their homeland....") (emphasis added). Congress's purpose is served by requiring the return to modern-day American Indians of human remains that bear some significant relationship to them.

Despite the statute's language and legislative history, the Secretary argues that the district court's interpretation "improperly collapses" NAGPRA's first inquiry (asking whether human remains are Native American) into NAGPRA's second inquiry (asking which American Indians or Indian tribe bears the closest relationship to Native American remains). The Secretary is mistaken. Though NAGPRA's two inquiries have some commonality in that both focus on the relationship between human remains and present-day Indians, the two inquiries differ significantly. The first inquiry requires only a general finding that remains have a significant relationship to a presently existing "tribe, people, or culture," a relationship that goes beyond features common to all humanity. The second inquiry requires a more specific finding that remains are most closely affiliated to specific lineal descendants or to a specific Indian tribe. The district court's interpretation of NAGPRA preserves the statute's two distinct inquiries. Because the record shows no relationship of Kennewick Man to the Tribal Claimants, the district court was correct in holding that NAGPRA has no application.

...

Our conclusion that NAGPRA requires human remains to bear some relationship to a presently existing tribe, people, or culture to be considered "Native American" is also reinforced by how NAGPRA defines "sacred objects." NAGPRA defines "sacred objects" as "specific ceremonial objects which are needed by traditional Native American religious leaders for the practice of traditional Native American religions *by their present day adherents.*" 25 U.S.C. §3001(3)(C) (emphasis added). A literal reading of this definition reveals that any artifact to be deemed a "sacred object" must be connected to the practice of an American Indian religion by present-day peoples. This reading is consistent with our reading of "Native American"; that is, just as there must be a relationship between an artifact and a presently existing peoples for the artifact to be a "sacred object" under NAGPRA, there must be a relationship between a set of remains and a presently existing tribe, people, or culture for those remains to be "Native American" under NAGPRA.

Although NAGPRA does not specify precisely what kind of a relationship or precisely how strong a relationship ancient human remains must bear to modern Indian groups to qualify as Native American, NAGPRA's legislative history provides some guidance on what type of relationship may suffice. The House Committee on Interior and Insular Affairs emphasized in its report on NAGPRA that the statute was being enacted with modern-day American Indians' identifiable ancestors in mind. *See, e.g.*, H.R.Rep. No. 101-877, U.S.Code Cong. & Admin.News at 4367, 4372 (1990) ("Indian representatives testified that the spirits of *their ancestors* would not rest until they are returned to their homeland...." (emphasis added)); *id.* at 4369 ("For many years, Indian tribes have attempted to have the remains and funerary objects of *their ancestors* returned to them." (emphasis added)). Human remains that are 8340 to 9200 years old and that bear only incidental genetic resemblance to modern-day American Indians, along with incidental genetic resemblance to other peoples, cannot be said to be the Indians' "ancestors" within Congress's meaning. Congress enacted NAGPRA to give American Indians control over the remains of their genetic and cultural forbearers, not over the remains of people bearing no special and significant genetic or cultural relationship to some presently existing indigenous tribe, people, or culture.

The age of Kennewick Man's remains, given the limited studies to date, makes it almost impossible to establish any relationship between the remains and presently existing American Indians. At least no significant relationship has yet been shown. We cannot give credence to an interpretation of NAGPRA advanced by the government and the Tribal Claimants that would apply its provisions to remains that have at most a tenuous, unknown, and unproven connection, asserted solely because of the geographical location of the find.

IV

Finally, we address the Secretary's determination that Kennewick Man's remains are Native American, as defined by NAGPRA. We must set aside the Secretary's decision if it was "arbitrary" or "capricious" because the decision was based on inadequate factual support. *See* 5 U.S.C. §706(2)(A). We review the full agency record to determine whether substantial evidence supports the agency's decision that Kennewick Man is "Native American" within NAGPRA's meaning. Here, after reviewing the record, we conclude that the record does not contain substantial evidence that Kennewick Man's remains are Native American within NAGPRA's meaning.

The administrative record contains no evidence—let alone substantial evidence—that Kennewick Man's remains are connected by some special or significant genetic or cultural relationship to any presently existing indigenous tribe, people, or culture. An examination of the record demonstrates the absence of evidence that Kennewick Man and modern tribes share significant genetic or cultural features.

No cognizable link exists between Kennewick Man and modern Columbia Plateau Indians. When Kennewick Man's remains were discovered, local coroners initially believed the remains were those of a European, not a Native American, because of their appearance. Later testing by scientists demonstrated that the cranial measurements and features of Kennewick Man most closely resemble those of Polynesians and southern Asians, and that Kennewick Man's measurements and features differ significantly from those of any modern Indian group living in North America.

...

The Secretary also acknowledges that "there is very little evidence of burial patterns during the 9500-8500 period and significant temporal gaps exist in the mortuary record for other periods." So, even if we assume that Kennewick Man was part of a stable social group living in the area, it still would be impossible to say whether his group's burial practices were related to modern tribes' burial practices. The Secretary also noted that "the linguistic analysis was unable to provide reliable evidence for the 8500-9500 period."

...

Considered as a whole, the administrative record might permit the Secretary to conclude reasonably that the Tribal Claimants' ancestors have lived in the region for a very long time. However, because Kennewick Man's remains are so old and the information about his era is so limited, the record does not permit the Secretary to conclude reasonably that Kennewick Man shares special and significant genetic or cultural features with presently existing indigenous tribes, people, or cultures. We thus hold that Kennewick Man's remains are not Native American human remains within the meaning of NAGPRA and that NAGPRA does not apply to them. Studies of the Kennewick Man's remains by Plaintiffs-scientists may proceed pursuant to ARPA.

We remand to the district court for further proceedings consistent with this opinion.

Affirmed.

Eric Beckenhauer, Note, *Redefining Race: Can Genetic Testing Provide Biological Proof of Indian Ethnicity?*

56 Stan. L. Rev. 161 (2003)

Introduction

Kathy Lewis is destitute. A Chukchansi Indian from the foothills of Fresno, she lives in a two-room trailer with her daughter, mother, and brother. Her grandfather was born and raised on the nearby Table Mountain Rancheria, where she spent most of her childhood living in a shack. Like many other tribal members, she eventually left the economically stale rancheria to seek employment in a nearby town. But courtesy of the Indian Gaming Regulatory Act, the rancheria now boasts a full-scale casino with annual revenues topping $100 million. Hoping to share this new wealth with her brethren, she reapplies for membership in her former tribe. The tribe—now flush with gaming money—rejects her application, and tightens membership criteria for future applicants. Kathy Lewis is no longer welcome in a tribe where her grandfather was once Chief.

The Gros Ventre Indians call Robert Upham a mixed blood. Part Assiniboine, Nakota, Kootenai, and Salish Indian, he was raised on the Montana reservation of the Gros Ventre Indians, where four generations of his mother's family are buried. Though entirely Indian by heritage, his tribal membership is revoked because his blood lines have become too thin to merit acceptance by any one tribe. Equally devastating, Robert Upham is then denied the health and welfare benefits that accompany tribal membership.

The Western Mohegans, a band of about 330 Indians living on ancestral lands along the border of New York and Vermont, petition the United States government for status as a federally recognized tribe—a coveted designation granted to few, since it is accompanied by a panoply of federal benefits. Lacking adequate genealogical documentation to prove their ancestry to the government, they lobby Vermont legislators to endorse the reliability of DNA testing as a means of establishing ethnic identity. In the Vermont Assembly, a sympathetic representative sponsors a bill authorizing the state health commissioner to develop standards by which DNA testing can be used to "conclusively" identify individuals of Native American ancestry.

And on the expansive World Wide Web, GeneTree DNA Testing Center offers "Native American Verification Testing" from the comfort and convenience of home. For a mere $245, GeneTree will scan a cheek swab for DNA sequences purportedly unique to Native Americans, claiming that "DNA testing can definitively determine questions" regarding Native American ancestry. Other genetic testing laboratories quickly follow suit.

Can such genetic testing help Kathy Lewis, Robert Upham, and the Western Mohegans demonstrate they are Indian—or does it promise more than it delivers? And who decides who counts as Indian in the United States, anyway? The answers depend on who you ask, and why you are asking.

...

The two major methods used to ethnically identify Indians—blood quantum standards and descendancy requirements—though effective to a certain degree in controlling tribal growth and allocating scarce resources, are detrimental to Indians, regardless of whether employed by the federal government or implemented by individual tribes. Both present problems of proof: Since they require extensive and accurate record keeping, both methods are imperfect when records are incomplete or human error is likely. To the extent that they are overexclusive, both reduce the number of Indians and Indian tribes eligible for public funding and other essential services. And, inasmuch as they conflict with the premise that ethnicity is strictly a social and not a biological construct, both methods run contrary to modern sociobiological thought. Blood quantum requirements raise the additional problem that, given the inevitable march of time, they will be rendered useless since they threaten to vastly diminish tribal rolls by the end of this century. In Part II, this Note questions whether genetic testing can offer a superior definition of Indian ethnicity.

II. Can Genetic Testing Improve Ethnic Identification?

In the wake of the recently completed and widely publicized Human Genome Diversity Project (HGDP), the potential of genomics, while certainly enormous, has risen to near-mythic proportions. As modern genomic research becomes more commonplace, and as the promise of genetic therapy creeps toward reality, the public may become increasingly inclined to subscribe to a theory of genetic essentialism—basically, the notion that our genes determine who we are. As one group of scholars explains, "An unintended byproduct of the genomics revolution is a naive, almost religious faith in the power of genetics. The gene has become a powerful cultural icon; genetic explanations have a pride of place in the popular imagination."

In light of this increasingly common perception, it is interesting to consider one of the more surprising conclusions of the HGDP: Human beings share more than 99.9% of their DNA. Indeed, there is more genetic variation within a single race than there is among different races. This revelation has had critical implications for the meaning of race, which is now largely considered a social construct, rather than a biological reality. However, this is not to say that there is no genetic variation among ethnic groups, or that what little genetic variation exists is negligible. On the contrary, this genetic variation is responsible for the outwardly visible physical variation among ethnic groups—skin color, eye and nose shapes, and hair color, for example—that provide the usual bases for racial classifications.

It is important to note, however, that although stereotypical differences in outward physical characteristics are perhaps the most obvious manifestation of genetic variation among ethnic groups, they are not the only type of variation. Genetic variation among ethnic groups also exists within genes that code for nonoutward traits, such as blood type or predisposition to certain diseases, as well as within stretches of DNA that do not code for any expressed trait. These three types of variation among ethnic groups can be quantified in two traditional ways that allow us to describe an ethnic group in genetic terms: by the analysis of the relative prevalence of variants, and by the survey of unique private polymorphisms. A newer method, called ethnic-affiliation estimation, may also prove useful to genetically describe ethnic populations. The advantages—and limitations—of each of these three methods are assessed in this Part.

A. Prevalence of Variants Within Human Subpopulations

Most phenotypic variation among ethnic groups—such as differences in coloration and facial features—is controlled not by a single gene, but by many genes working in concert. For example, there is no single gene that determines height; rather, the products of many genes work together in complicated biochemical pathways to determine how short or tall a person will become. However, other physical traits are controlled by a single gene locus, making their analysis more straightforward; the ABO blood group system is a famous example of such a trait.

When a physical trait is exhibited by a population in two or more forms, the contrasting forms are called morphs or, more commonly, variants. For example, the ABO blood group system consists of four variants: types A, B, AB, and O. A population is said to be polymorphic ("many forms") for a trait if two or more variants are represented in high enough frequencies to be noticeable. Human subpopulations almost universally exhibit observable frequencies of at least two of the four ABO blood group variants; thus, they are said to be polymorphic for this trait.

Analysis of the differential prevalence of variants among human subpopulations enables us to make a descriptive statement, in genetic terms, about the characteristics of different ethnic groups. Although nearly all human subpopulations exhibit blood types A, B, AB, and O to some degree, the proportion of members falling into each category varies dramatically among subpopulations. For example, it is known that Armenians are about 50% type A, and that some South American native peoples are nearly 100% type O.

Such analyses often contribute to studies of migration, linguistics, and evolution. For example, when isolated populations exhibit a high proportion of a single variant, it is often the result of a founder effect (in which an entire population descends from a small number of ancestors) or a population bottleneck (in which some outside influence, often a natural disaster, greatly reduces the size of a population, essentially resulting in a novel founder effect). Likewise, evolutionists often supplant linguistic studies with genetic evidence of variation in order to decipher global patterns of migration. However, while these applications have proved helpful in estimating the arrival dates of indigenous peoples to the Americas, variant analysis is less helpful as a positive indicator of Indian descent so long as the variants used are common to other human subpopulations.

Regardless of the precision with which the relative prevalence of variants within a subpopulation can be determined, so long as those variants are also commonly present—to whatever degree—outside that subpopulation, no positive identification can be made on the basis of that trait. For example, even if 100% of a hypothetical North American Indian tribe were type O, the conclusion that a prospective member is descended from that tribe because he is also type O does not follow; since type O is a common variant, there are many type O individuals throughout the world that are not tribal descendants. Thus, so long as the variants analyzed are common to other human subpopulations, variant analysis will be virtually useless for identifying an individual as a member of a specific race.

B. Private Polymorphisms

Private polymorphisms are related to the polymorphic traits studied in variant analysis, but are more unusual, and thus more helpful, in genetically defining an ethnic group. A private polymorphism is a variation, often found in a noncoding region of a gene, that is common within a subpopulation but is otherwise rarely observed. Often, private polymorphisms are created when an ancestor passes a spontaneous mutation to his descendants, this mutation being unique to them. Private polymorphisms can arise throughout the human genome. However, due to their unique inheritance patterns and their ability to escape regular recombination processes, two specific portions of the genome are particularly conducive to the analysis of private polymorphisms: the Y chromosome and the mitochondrial DNA.

1. The Y chromosome.

The vast majority of the DNA in a human cell is found in the cell nucleus, subdivided into twenty-three pairs of molecules known as chromosomes; each pair consists of one maternal and one paternal chromosome. Chromosomes one through twenty-two are structurally similar to their pairs, and when a cell duplicates, these pairs often swap segments with one another in a process called recombination, resulting in paired chromosomes with new combinations of genes.

However, the twenty-third pair of chromosomes—the so-called sex chromosomes—may or may not be structurally similar, depending on the sex of the individual. The sex chromosomes in human females, typically two X chromosomes, are structurally similar and will recombine normally. But the sex chromosomes in human males, typically one X and one Y chromosome, are somewhat structurally dissimilar and are unlikely to recombine. Since Y chromosomes are transmitted strictly paternally, and since they escape regular recombination, any variation in the Y-chromosome sequence of an individual can result only from the accumulation of mutations as the Y chromosome is transmitted from father to son.

A group of geneticists and biochemists at Stanford University recently discovered a Y-chromosome polymorphism unique to indigenous populations in the Americas. By sequencing the Y chromosomes of 173 human subjects, the research team discovered a single base pair mutation, at the DYS199 locus, present in more than 90% of Central and South American subjects, 67% of Eskimo subjects, and 50% of North American Navajo subjects—but absent in all subjects outside the Americas. These data suggest that the DYS199 mutation originated either during the early stages of human habitation of the Americas, or shortly before that time, "in the ancestral population(s) from which all [indigenous] Americans may have originated."

Since this polymorphism is apparently private to indigenous American populations—that is, it is common among indigenous Americans, but otherwise nonexistent—it has the potential to affirmatively "mark" those of Indian descent, something that variant analysis fails to accomplish. However, few Y-chromosome private polymorphisms have so far been identified, likely because there is relatively little variability on the chromosome, most Y-chromosome DNA is quite stable and is unlikely to mutate, and many gene loci on the chromosome are not amenable to convenient analysis.

2. Mitochondrial DNA.

As mentioned above, most DNA in a human cell is found in the cell nucleus, packaged into the familiar forty-six chromosomes. But, a small amount of DNA also resides in the mitochondria, where it codes for the synthesis of proteins the mitochondria need to convert food into cellular energy. Since mitochondria are situated in the cytoplasm of the cell, and since the ovum always contributes much more cytoplasm to the human embryo than does the sperm, the mitochondria—and, thus, the mitochondrial DNA—come exclusively from the mother.

Several characteristics of mitochondrial DNA (mtDNA) make it an ideal subject for genetic analysis. Human mtDNA is a small, circular molecule present in 3000-5000 identical copies per cell. It is inherited strictly maternally and, like Y-chromosome DNA, it does not recombine. Thus, any variation in mtDNA sequence results from the accumulation of mutations as mtDNA is transmitted from a mother to her children.

Searches for private polymorphisms in mtDNA have been more successful than those in the Y chromosome, probably because the mitochondrial genome accumulates new mutations seven to ten times faster than the nuclear genome. As a result of its increased utility, mtDNA analysis has been used extensively to chronicle the migration of indigenous peoples throughout the Americas, often serving to corroborate previous linguistic groupings. Such studies generally conclude that American Indian mtDNA has evolved "into four discrete lineages, each characterized by a specific private polymorphism closely related to one also found in their hypothesized Asian ancestors." For example, an analysis of the Pima and Papago Indians of the southwestern United States has revealed that 41% of these indigenous populations harbor the rare polymorphism HincII morph 6, a variant found in only 2% of Asian subjects and absent in European and African subjects.

Like the recently discovered DYS199 mutation, mtDNA private polymorphisms allow scientists to identify individuals of Indian ancestry by the presence or absence of a single gene. Though polymorphisms like HincII morph 6 are not perfectly private, since they are not exclusively present in American Indians, their prevalence in non-American subpopulations is low enough to make them a powerful diagnostic tool. Further, since mtDNA private polymorphisms are more abundant and more easily studied than their Y-chromosome counterparts, the mitochondrial genome may continue to be a fruitful ground for research.

C. Ethnic-Affiliation Estimation with Population-Specific DNA Markers

The utility of private polymorphisms is limited by the extent to which they are private: A particular polymorphism, no matter how prevalent in the target population, is useless as a positive indicator of ethnicity if it is also common outside the target population. Thus, for ethnic identification by Y-chromosome and mtDNA analysis to be successful, the identification of rare polymorphisms is essential. Since there is actually very little genetic variation among ethnic groups, there may simply be few private polymorphisms awaiting discovery; more often, certain variants will be somewhat more prevalent in some populations than in others, but will not be perfectly private. Ethnic-affiliation estimation (EAE) is a developing statistical technique that analyzes variants that are significantly more prevalent in one subpopulation than in another—essentially, polymorphisms that are "private enough" for confident analysis—and then makes imperfect predictions of individual ethnic ancestry based on the presence or absence of such variants. By analyzing variants deemed useful in distinguishing between two populations, researchers claim to be able to reliably estimate the ethnic identity of an individual in one of those populations, with a success rate approaching 99% when the twenty most discriminating variants are used. Though studies have focused on distinguishing European American populations from African American and Hispanic American populations, researchers claim that similar sets of markers could be developed for other, less common U.S. populations such as American Indians.

Although EAE techniques show promise for identifying Indian ancestry by genetic makeup, they are not yet viable alternatives to private polymorphism identification for two reasons. First, the statistical methodology of EAE has been called seriously flawed, and may be subject to sampling bias. Though such challenges call into question the success of EAE, future fine-tuning is likely to make its methods sufficiently sophisticated to lead to "an assignment of the probability that someone ha[s] significant ancestry from certain broadly defined ethnic groups." Second, to assemble a collection of suitable genetic markers, EAE will require the harvesting and compilation of genetic data from thousands of Indians—an expensive and time-consuming proposition, especially in light of the numerous mtDNA markers already uncovered.

D. Limitations of DNA Analysis

Of the principal methods of ascribing genetic characteristics to specific ethnic groups, it is clear that: (1) variant analysis has little power to identify the ethnicity of individuals; (2) EAE, though more powerful than variant analysis, requires additional refinements and has not yet been successfully applied to Indian populations; and (3) identification of private polymorphisms, particularly via Y-chromosome and mtDNA analysis, is an accepted means to define the common genetic characteristics of an ethnic group, and an accurate means to determine whether an individual has some degree of Indian ancestry. However, the utility of private polymorphism analysis is subject to a number of limitations, which are best examined by asking whether the presence of a particular private polymorphism is "proof" of Indian ancestry, whether the absence of a particular private polymorphism is "disproof" of Indian ancestry, and whether the presence of such a polymorphism can indicate the degree of Indian ancestry.

1. Is presence of a private polymorphism proof of Indian ancestry?

In short, the answer is a qualified yes. The Y-chromosomal mutation at the DYS199 locus, discussed above, provides a neat illustration. This mutation is present, to varying degrees, in indigenous populations throughout the Americas, but in no other populations worldwide. Thus, absent laboratory error, an individual testing positive for this rare variant is certain to have indigenous ancestry—unless the Y chromosome of one of his paternal ancestors spontaneously mutated to generate an identical polymorphism (a "parallel mutation") at the DYS199 locus, an event that has a small, but not negligible, chance of occurring.

2. Is absence of a private polymorphism disproof of Indian ancestry?

Certainly not, for two reasons. First, akin to the parallel mutation described above, there is a small chance that the absence of a particular polymorphism could be the result of a second mutational event (a "reverse mutation") that abolished the preexisting variant. But a second, more important reason that the absence of a rare variant fails to disprove Indian descendancy is that the Y chromosome and mtDNA follow unique patterns of inheritance—and therein lies the most significant limitation of private polymorphism analysis. The modes of transmission of these particular DNA stretches—with the Y chromosome passing along strict paternal lines, and mtDNA along strict maternal lines—mean that having just one non-Indian ancestor can render these tests useless.

3. Can presence of a polymorphism indicate degree of Indian ancestry?

Again, the answer is an unqualified no.... [T]he presence of a Y-chromosomal mutation at the DYS199 locus of the tested individual suggests only that the father of his father's father carried the same mutation, and thus descended from indigenous stock; it says nothing about the ancestry of the tested individual's other three paternal grandparents. Likewise, the presence of the rare variant HincII morph 6 in the mtDNA of the tested individual suggests only that the mother of his mother's mother carried the same mutation, and thus descended from indigenous stock; it says nothing about the ancestry of the tested individual's other maternal grandparents. Therefore, it is apparent that an individual may test positively for either of these private polymorphisms, yet be as little as one-eighth Indian by blood. Conversely, an individual may test negatively for both of these private polymorphisms and be three-quarters Indian by blood.

[T]hese limitations are magnified as the number of generations increases. For example, looking back just three additional generations, an individual might test positively for either polymorphism while being but one sixty-fourth Indian by blood, a level of blood quantum accepted by only the most lenient tribes. Likewise, he might test negatively for both polymorphisms while being sixty-two sixty-fourths Indian by blood, nearly full-blooded by any measure. Given the high rate of intermarriage, and thus of genetic admixture, that occurs among Indians in the United States—and the economic resources at stake for being defined as an Indian—both Indian tribal governments and the U.S. government have cause to be skeptical of the utility of these tests.

E. Assessing the Utility of DNA Analysis

Thus, although the analysis of private polymorphisms by Y-chromosome and mtDNA testing is currently the best method to identify the ethnic ancestry of an individual, its limitations are clear. First, a positive test for either of these polymorphisms proves only that someone, at some point in the direct paternal or maternal lineage, descended from indigenous stock—the precise degree of ancestry cannot be determined. Second, no useful conclusion can be drawn from a negative test for either or both of these polymorphisms. Therefore, until EAE can be proven useful for Native American populations—that is, after its statistical methods have been refined and useful population-specific variants have been identified—DNA analysis will be of only marginal utility as an ethnic identifier.

Interestingly, the limitations of these forms of DNA analysis have not stopped private testing facilities from offering their services to the public—and from profiting from customer ignorance. Among the genetic testing services offered by GeneTree, a California-based DNA testing center, is "Native American Verification Testing." For a fee of $245, GeneTree will analyze DNA (obtained by a cheek swab) for the Y-chromosomal mutation at DYS199, and for an additional $245, will also scan for the series of mtDNA polymorphisms unique to Native American populations. Though the company's website acknowledges that both the Y chromosome and mtDNA are inherited only in limited patterns, it also advertises that "DNA testing can definitively determine questions" regarding Native American ancestry.

III. Attempts to Genetically Define Indians—and Native American Reaction

Unsurprisingly, attempts to genetically define Native Americans have garnered the attention of not just anthropologists and geneticists. At least one Indian tribe seeking federal recognition has tried to use DNA technology to establish a genetic link to other tribes. And, in response, at least one state government has considered legislation that would enable hopeful Indians to "conclusively" establish their ethnic identities.

A. Vermont House Bill 809

The Western Mohegans, a band of about 330 Indians living on ancestral lands along the border of New York and Vermont, once declined to sign a recognition treaty with the U.S. government. Now seeking state and federal recognition, the Mohegans—like others in their shoes—have found that they lack adequate genealogical documentation to prove their ancestry to the government, and have been denied status as a recognized tribe—and the benefits that accompany such recognition. In an attempt to establish a genetic link to the Mohican Indians of Wisconsin, a federally recognized tribe to which they claim ancestral ties, the Mohegans privately contracted to undergo DNA testing, the results of which they claim demonstrate such a genealogical relationship. To further their case for recognition, and to help other Indians who lack genealogical documentation, the Mohegans lobbied Vermont legislators to endorse the reliability of DNA testing as a means of establishing ethnic identity.

In the Vermont Assembly, sympathetic Representative Fred Maslack in early 2000 sponsored a bill that would have authorized the state health commissioner to develop standards by which DNA testing could be used to "conclusively" identify those of Native American ancestry, at their request and personal expense.

...

[A]side from the lackluster response of his Assembly colleagues to the proposed legislation, reaction from the community can fairly be characterized as nothing short of outrage. The Vermont Governor's Advisory Commission on Native American Affairs minced no words in its attack on H. 809, calling it "racist, unethical, and immoral." Journalists warned that the proposal smacked of eugenics. But by far, the loudest cries came from Native American activists. Their objections to Rep. Maslack's proposal—and to genetic testing in general—are surveyed in the balance of this Part.

B. Native American Objections to Genetic Definitions of Ethnicity

Rep. Maslack's proposal struck a chord with outspoken members of the Indian community.... Indian objections to genetic testing are generally threefold: (1) The term "Indian" represents a cultural identity that defies biological definition; (2) genetic descriptions of the term "Indian" threaten to usurp tribal sovereignty; and (3) condoning the use of genetic testing in this context will legitimize its abusive use in other contexts.

1. "Indian" is a culture—not a genotype.

Native Americans commonly argue that Indian status should be a cultural determination, not a biological one. Ethnic groups, they insist, are merely social constructs, and we must avoid reinforcing the assumption that ethnic identity is biologically determined. In this struggle, Native Americans have garnered widespread support from both activists and scientists. The Vermont Governor's Advisory Commission on Native American Affairs has warned that genetic testing threatens to reduce being Indian to a "racial type," instead of a "spiritual identity." Morris Foster, an anthropologist at the University of Oklahoma, cautions that "it is absurd to try to define what is essentially a social identity by using biological characteristics." And one researcher with the International Institute for Indigenous Resource Management in Denver suggests that scientists and policymakers who propose genetic testing as a means of ethnic identification "equate culture with race and assume that the characteristics of both can be detected biologically."

However, insofar as genetic testing is criticized for attempting to define a social identity using biological characteristics, it differs remarkably little from the use of blood quantum standards: both are undeniably biological measures. In addition, such objections largely reflect confused terminology, and highlight the need to exercise caution with hot-button words like ethnicity, race, and culture.

Because it lacked careful language, H. 809 fueled the fears of Indian tribes. By proposing that the results of DNA-HLA testing would serve as "conclusive proof" of Native American ancestry, and further, that test results would "determine the identity of an individual as a Native American," Rep. Maslack erred in suggesting that ethnic identity could be determined by genetic testing alone. However, this was probably not the bill's intent.

Under the commonly accepted premise that race and ethnicity are social constructs, not biological ones, no serious scientist (and hopefully, no legislator) would conflate a genetic inquiry into an individual's ancestral roots with a description of his present-day cultural ties. The DYS199 mutation does not make a man Indian—it merely suggests that one of his progenitors had indigenous roots. Further, even if DNA evidence could reveal that an individual is a full-blooded Indian, he is only politically Indian—and thus eligible for federal benefits—if granted citizenship by a federally recognized tribe.

2. Genetic definitions of "Indian" will usurp tribal sovereignty.

The autonomy to determine their own citizenship requirements instills in Indian tribes a sense of self-determination that is closely guarded. Genetic techniques for authenticating Indian heritage, whether promulgated by scientists or sanctioned by state governments, threaten to displace tribal definitions of citizenship with genetic ones, and usurp the sovereignty of tribes. Indeed, there is a common fear that by acquiescence to genetic definitions, tribes will eventually relinquish the right to define their populations. However, such a consequence seems unlikely, given the well-settled principle that Indian tribes, as sovereign governments, have the inherent power to establish their own membership criteria. This principle of self-determination has been specifically recognized by the Supreme Court, which has noted that a tribe's right to define its own membership criteria "has long been recognized as central to its existence as an independent political community." This principle seems unlikely to be challenged.

There is related concern that, although H. 809 offered genetic testing as an alternative method for establishing heritage, such testing may eventually become the sole method for doing so; thus an individual lacking the typical Native American genetic markers would be denied classification as Indian. Some of this worry stems from a simple misunderstanding of the proposal. One observer noted that the "ambiguity of the [proposed] legislation resulted in misinterpretations that the legislation was meant to require DNA analysis to prove an individual's tribal affiliation." Other commentators feared that the alternative might evolve into a requirement, noting that although "the current proposal does not contain wording that would negate other acceptable methods of identifying one's heritage, future application could do just that." This concern belies a misconception of the power of established methods of genetic analysis, and a lack of recognition of their limitations. Even the most accurate methods of genetic analysis of ethnicity—Y-chromosome and mtDNA private polymorphism analysis—cannot conclusively disprove Native American ancestry. And, despite their promise, statistical methods such as EAE will probably not be able to render more than an imperfect estimate of the degree of ethnic ancestry. The possibilities of genetics are not without limits, and these weaknesses will prevent genetic testing from becoming the sole indicator of ethnicity.

3. Condoning genetic testing in this context legitimizes scientific inquiry, and its consequences, in other contexts.

Several commentators have suggested that Indians have both a general aversion to the methods of scientific inquiry and a fear of its consequences. With respect to the methodology, observers have noted that this anti-science sentiment stems partly from feelings of intimidation engendered by the complexity of technology, partly from fear that scientific analysis is prone to error, and partly from traditionalist attitudes that characterize technology as the "anti-traditional, anti-spiritual ... earth-destroying work of the White man."

Further, the potential negative consequences of scientific inquiry have led many Indian communities to fear genetic research, and to distrust the motives of scientists. Anger abounds toward research perceived as an attempt to provide contrary answers to strongly held beliefs about the origin of Indian tribes, particularly when such questions are posed not by indigenous populations themselves, but by researchers. The assumption that Indian ancestry "will be 'discovered' and scientifically 'answered' is insulting to groups who already have strong beliefs regarding their origins."

...

When scientific inquiry frequently results in "truths" that contradict their traditions and religion, Indian tribes are naturally wary of condoning genetic research. Further, should they accept its validity for authenticating ancestral ties, they may be hard-pressed to reject its conclusions with respect to migration and evolution. Both scientists and policymakers should be responsive to these concerns.

Conclusion

Whether seeking tribal membership or federal recognition, welfare benefits or a sense of belonging, Indians in the United States face a bumpy road—one that is not becoming smoother. Federal acknowledgement is increasingly rare. Blood quantum requirements threaten to make enrollment plummet over the next century. And, for unenrolled Indians and Indians enrolled in unrecognized tribes, a lack of political affiliation can leave them feeling "less Indian."

Despite its mythical promises, genetic testing is no panacea. The reality is that genetic testing is of limited utility as an ethnic identifier: Because of the patterns of genetic inheritance, even the most advanced methods of genetic testing will fail to identify a huge proportion of those with Indian ancestry. And, the degree of Indian ancestry of those positively marked by rare polymorphisms is currently impossible to determine by genetic tests alone. Considering also the objections of Native Americans and the cost of genetic testing, one is left wondering whether, on balance, the prospect of genetic testing does Indians more harm than good.

However, though not useful as absolute indicators of ethnicity, genetic tests like mtDNA and Y-chromosome analysis will continue to uncover useful pieces of genealogical information that—in conjunction with anthropological studies and descendancy records—can help flesh out the nooks of Indian history. But to preserve and nurture even this measure of utility, scientists and legislators must tread lightly, use careful language, and be sensitive to the concerns of the ethnic and cultural groups they are trying to help.

Northwest Ecosystem Alliance v. United States Fish and Wildlife Service

No. CV 03-1505-PA, 2004 WL 1774559 (D. Or. Aug. 2, 2004)

PANNER, J.

...

Background

The western gray squirrel (Sciurus griseus griseus) ranges from central Washington to the Sierra Nevada Range in central California. For 13,000 years, the Columbia River has separated western gray squirrels in Washington from those in Oregon and California.

In Washington, the western gray squirrel once ranged from southern Puget Sound south to the Columbia River, east along the Columbia Gorge to the Southern Cascade Mountains, and north along the east side of the Cascades to Lake Chelan. During the last one hundred years, human encroachment and other factors have reduced the western gray squirrel's Washington range to three populations: the Puget Trough population in southern Puget Sound; the South Cascades population along the lower Columbia River; and the North Cascades population in north-central Washington. Field scientists have described the Washington populations of the western gray squirrel as secretive and reluctant to stray from the cover of trees, traits that may cause the squirrels to avoid urban areas.

The Puget Trough population lives mainly on the Fort Lewis Military Reservation, which includes the largest concentration of oak forests left in Puget Sound. The squirrels live in a transitional ecosystem of Oregon white oak and Douglas fir between upland Douglas fir forests and prairies. The Washington Department of Fish and Wildlife found that the long-term outlook for this population was not favorable.

The North Cascades population has had to adapt to habitats without oak trees. These squirrels rely on conifers, maples, berries, and cultivated walnut trees. The Washington Department of Fish and Wildlife found that the North Cascades population is isolated and vulnerable.

The South Cascades population is the largest in Washington. These squirrels forage from a variety of trees, including oak, fir, and pine. Squirrels from this population are larger than elsewhere, and have more extensive home ranges.

In January 2001, the FWS received plaintiffs' petition to list the Washington populations of the western gray squirrel as threatened or endangered, and to designate critical habitat under the Endangered Species Act.

In June 2003, the FWS issued its finding that the Washington populations were not "distinct population segments." The agency ruled that although the Washington populations were distinct from those in Oregon and California, the Washington populations were not significant to the subspecies as a whole.

Standards

Judicial review of an agency's action is governed by the Administrative Procedures Act. The court may set aside an agency's action if the action is "arbitrary, capricious, an abuse of discretion, or otherwise not in accordance with law...." 5 U.S.C. §706(a)(2)....

Discussion

I. The "Significance" Factor Is Valid

In 1978, Congress amended the Endangered Species Act's definition of "species" to include "any subspecies of fish or wildlife or plants, and *any distinct population segment* of any species of vertebrate fish or wildlife which interbreeds when mature." 16 U.S.C. §1532(16) (emphasis added). Congress did not define "distinct population segment," and the term has no accepted scientific meaning. *Center for Biological Diversity v. Lohn*, 296 F.Supp.2d 1223, 1234 (W.D.Wa.2003).

In 1996, the FWS and the National Marine Fisheries Service jointly issued a policy on interpreting "distinct population segment," which requires the agencies to evaluate:

> (1) Discreteness of the population segment in relation to the remainder of the species to which it belongs;
>
> (2) *The significance of the population segment to the species to which it belongs*; and
>
> (3) The population segment's conservation status in relation to the Act's standards for listing (i.e., is the population segment, when treated as if it were a species, endangered or threatened?).

61 Fed.Reg. 4722, 4725 (Feb. 7, 1996) (emphasis added). Here, plaintiffs challenge defendants' use of the second factor, significance.

The agencies use four considerations in determining significance:

> (1) Persistence of the discrete population segment in an ecological setting unusual or unique for the taxon,
>
> (2) Evidence that loss of the discrete population segment would result in a significant gap in the range of the taxon,
>
> (3) Evidence that the discrete population segment represents the only surviving natural occurrence of a taxon that may be more abundant elsewhere as an introduced population outside its historic range, or
>
> (4) Evidence that the discrete population segment differs markedly from other populations of the species in its genetic characteristics.

Id. The agencies' policy statement notes that "[b]ecause precise circumstances are likely to vary from case to case, it is not possible to describe prospectively all the classes of information that might bear on the biological and ecological importance of a discrete population segment." *Id.*

Plaintiffs contend that the "significance" requirement is not authorized by the statute. Plaintiffs argue that Congress chose not to use the term "significant" in describing "distinct population segment, while using the term in other provisions of the Endangered Species Act, e.g., 16 U.S.C. § 1532(6).

In *Center for Biological Diversity v. Lohn*, 296 F.Supp.2d [at] 1234–36, the court upheld the agencies' use of "significance" as a factor.... The Ninth Circuit has not addressed the validity of the significance requirement. *See National Ass'n of Home Builders v. Norton*, 340 F.3d 835 (9th Cir.2003). I agree with the cited district court decisions that the significance requirement is a reasonable interpretation of the term "distinct population segment."

Defendants move to reconsider my denial of their motion for partial judgment on the pleadings. I adhere to my previous ruling and deny defendants' motion to reconsider. In any event, the ruling in defendants' favor on the merits of this issue effectively moots defendants' motion to reconsider.

II. Applying the Significance Factor

Plaintiffs argue that even if the significance factor is a valid exercise of agency authority, defendants have improperly applied the test here. Plaintiffs note that the field office found that the Washington gray squirrel populations were significant, and the agency reversed that finding in its published finding. The field office found that the Washington population of western gray squirrel "differs markedly from other populations in its genetic characteristics." The field office cited evidence that loss of the Washington population would create "a significant gap in the range of the taxon," and that the Washington population was important to the species as a peripheral population.

Plaintiffs argue that the agency arbitrarily and capriciously rejected the field office's findings. Plaintiffs contend that the agency's final decision did not properly apply the second significance factor, which looks to "[e]vidence that loss of the discrete population segment would result in a significant gap in the range of the taxon." Plaintiffs argue that the final decision conceded that losing the Washington population would substantially modify the range of the subspecies, but nonetheless found that the loss was not sufficiently significant. Plaintiffs also contend that the Washington populations' isolation from the rest of the subspecies means that their loss would be significant.

Plaintiffs argue that the agency improperly disregarded evidence that the genetic makeup of the Washington populations differed markedly from other populations. The regional office found, based on a genetic analysis, that there were significant differences. The agency concluded that although the scientific findings "point towards significant genotypic differentiation between Washington populations and squirrel populations south of the Columbia River," the genetic differences did not show that the populations differed markedly. The finding states, "While there is clearly some genetic information that shows that the Washington populations are different from other populations (e.g., in the microsatellite DNA analyses no haplotype was shared across the Columbia River, also evidence suggests a long time interval since the Washington and California or Oregon populations diverged), at this time we do not believe them to be markedly so." The finding cites evidence of shared genetic characteristics.

I agree with defendants that the agency acted reasonably and that the decision was within its discretion. At oral argument, counsel for defendants noted that those making the final decision in agency headquarters are also scientists. The agency is not bound by the field office's findings. I cannot say that the agency's final decision was arbitrary or capricious.

Notes & Questions

1. The remains from the Russian Imperial family were tested using several methods of genetic analysis. This was partially because of the historical notoriety of the case, but also because the remains were substantially degraded. Portions of nine skeletons were recovered from the gravesite. The bones were evaluated with three different DNA tests. First, scientists analyzed genes unique to the X and Y chromosomes with the aim of establishing the gender of each set of skeletal remains. This revealed that five females and four males had been unearthed. Short tandem repeat ("STR") analysis proved that five of the skeletons came from one family and represented a mother, father and three daughters. Finally using mtDNA, scientists were able to show that the mother and father descended from their respective royal families. In the case of the czarina, Prince Philip of England contributed mtDNA to establish their common maternal ancestor. In the case of the czar, relatives related through his maternal ancestors were used to establish the identity of the remains. Remains of one daughter and the son of the czar and czarina have not been found.

As a genetic postscript to the Romanov story, DNA testing also disproved the claim of Anna Anderson Manahan that she was the long-lost Princess Anastasia, daughter of the czar and czarina. Manahan had emerged several years after the Russian Revolution, alleging that she had survived attempted execution and escaped Russia. Her story was immortalized in several movies and films. Manahan died several years before the Romanov graves were found, but surviving stored blood samples proved that she was not related to the Imperial family. *See* Ruth Levy Guyer, DNA's Role in Tales from the Crypt, Research in the News, http://science-education.nih.gov/nihHTML/ose/snapshots/multimedia/ritn/Romanov/Romanov1.html.

2. In *Bonnichsen v. United States*, the "Kennewick Man" case, the court was persuaded by anthropological evidence that the ancient human remains bore no relationship to a presently existing tribe, people, or culture. As a result, NAGPRA could not apply. As noted in the case, NAGPRA requires a two-part analysis. First, there must be a determination of whether the human remains are Native American within the statute's meaning. Second, if the remains are determined to be Native American, then the question is which of the possible tribes are most closely related to the remains. In the "Kennewick Man" case, the Ninth Circuit found that NAGPRA did not apply because the "Kennewick" remains were so old (approximately 9000 years old) that they could not be linked to existing Native American tribes or affiliated in any way. If the remains are not Native American, then NAGPRA does not apply. However, if the remains are Native American, then NAGPRA applies, triggering the second inquiry of determining which persons or tribes are most closely affiliated with the remains. The court notes that the legislative intent of NAGPRA was to respect the burial traditions of modern-day Native Americans by honoring the remains and gravesites of their ancestors. It determines that Congress's purposes would not be served by requiring the transfer to modern American Indians of human remains that bear no relationship to them.

Unfortunately, DNA has not shed any light on the genetic identity of the "Kennewick Man." In 1996 and in 2000, DNA testing was done on samples from the remains. In 1996, no DNA suitable for PCR amplification could be extracted from the samples. A second attempt, in 2000, focused on mitochondrial DNA, but was similarly unable to amplify the recovered DNA. They concluded that sufficient DNA was inaccessible using current analytic methods, and suggested that future novel techniques be tried when they become available. *See* D. Andrew Merriwether, et al., *Kennewick Man Ancient DNA Analysis: Final Report Submitted to the Department of the Interior, in* NATIONAL PARK

Service Archeology Program, Report on the DNA Testing Results of the Kennewick Human Remains from Columbia Park, Kennewick, Washington, *available at* http://www.cr.nps.gov/aad/kennewick/Merriwether_Cabana.htm.

3. The Beckenhauer article addresses the concept of verifying Native American heritage using DNA. As he discusses elsewhere in his article, determination of Native American and tribal status is a complex issue.

Federally recognized tribes have tribal sovereignty, but this is subject to oversight by Congress and complicated by a cascade of federally funded and administered social welfare programs. Under federal law, a tribe is recognized only when it meets seven criteria including: being identified as American Indian on a substantially continuous basis since 1900; comprised of a distinct community throughout its history to the present time; had an authority structure and maintained it from historical times to the present; documents or verification of membership criteria and governing procedures; membership confined to those who descend from a historical tribe or tribes that functioned as autonomous political entities; membership composed of persons who are not already members of an acknowledged North American Indian Tribe; and not the subject of prior Congressional legislation terminating or forbidding federal designation. Under federal law, a tribe can be deemed "American Indian" on the basis of enrollment lists, descendancy records, affidavits, and other information that would identify the tribe. *See* Federally Recognized Indian Tribe List Act of 1994, Pub. L. No. 103-454, 108 Stat. 4791, codified at 25 U.S.C. §§479a, 479a-1 (directing the Secretary of the Interior to annually publish a list of all federally recognized tribes); *see also* 25 C.F.R. §83 (2005); 43 Fed. Reg. 39361 (Sept. 5, 1978) (where the Department of the Interior first promulgated regulations establishing procedures by which Indian groups could establish their legal status as Indian tribes.). Over 500 tribes enjoy federal designation; they are able to exercise sovereignty and avail themselves of federal programs.

In addition to the federal recognition of tribes, there are confounding issues presented by tribal definitions regarding who can qualify for membership in a tribe, federally recognized or not. When individuals seek services under federally funded programs, eligibility is contingent on both federal recognition of the tribe and membership in the tribe. Criteria for tribal membership vary from tribe to tribe. Many tribes define membership on the basis of blood quantum, requiring a percentage of Indian blood for membership. This percentage varies from tribe to tribe, ranging from as much as 50% to as little as 3.125%. Tribes may also use descendancy as a criterion for membership. To establish descendancy, the tribal member must prove a lineal relationship to a current or ancestral member of the tribe. A substantial number of tribes require both a blood quantum and descendancy for eligibility as a tribal member. Given the complexity and difficulties inherent in both blood quantum and descendancy, one can easily contemplate the utility of genetic analysis.

However, Native Americans are historically suspicious, with good reason, of technologic innovations, including genetic research. Most recently, this suspicion has been fueled by a suit filed by the Havasupai tribe alleging that researchers at Arizona State University used tribal blood samples for unauthorized research purposes. For a discussion on this evolving case, see Chapter 5. Critics argue that being identified as a Native American is a cultural and social construct, not a scientific one. There is concern that genetics might be used to erode tribal sovereignty or to link a tribe to an ancestral group that is not consonant with the tribe's creation myth or spiritual tradition. This latter issue is one of the underlying complaints in the Havasupai case.

On a more material level, genetic analysis might well be used to demonstrate the absence of connection to a tribe, thus disqualifying an individual or group from federal benefits and tribal association. Alternatively it may be used to allow someone to opt-in to a tribe, when they would be unable to prove membership by blood quantum or descendancy. This may serve to dilute tribal wealth, especially given the new-found sources of revenues in the Indian gaming industry.

4. *Northwest Ecosystem Alliance v. United States Fish and Wildlife Service* is one of a number of cases focusing on species designation for purposes of protection as an endangered species. As evidenced in this case, genetics is already being used to determine whether an alleged endangered species is a "distinct population segment." Here the court uses DNA analysis of the Washington western gray squirrel to support its finding that the Fish and Wildlife Service had not erred in finding that the population was not sufficiently "distinct" to qualify for endangered species protection. It found that although the Washington western gray squirrel could be genetically differentiated from the populations south of the Columbia River, this genetic difference was insufficient as weighed against the shared genetic characteristics.

In contrast to *Northwest Ecosystem Alliance*, *Center for Biological Diversity v. Lohn*, 296 F. Supp. 2d 1223 (W.D. Wash. 2003) considered the status of the Southern Resident killer whale. The National Marine and Fisheries Services ("NMFS") had determined that the Southern Residents did not have markedly different genetic characteristics from other resident and transient killer whales. As a result, the NMFS found the Southern Resident whales were not entitled to protection as an endangered species. However, the court found that the NFMS had erred in comparing the genomic differences of Southern Residents vis-a-vis other Resident Whales to those between Resident and Transient Whale stocks. The latter comparison is between whales from two different taxons and therefore would have a greater magnitude of difference than two sub-species of whales in the same taxon. Moreover, the court recognized evidence that the Southern Residents have a unique social structure, language, rituals, behaviors, and knowledge that also contributed to their distinctiveness. The court ultimately remanded the case to NMFS for determination of whether the Southern Residents should be listed pursuant to the Endangered Species Act. *See Center for Biological Diversity v. Lohn*, 296 F. Supp. 2d at 1234.

Chapter 10

Genetics and Public Health: Past, Present, and Future

The government has an established history of undertaking programs to improve public health, safety, and general welfare. The classic examples are sanitation, fluoridation in the water, immunization and, in some circumstances, mandates to isolate or quarantine individuals or groups of individuals perceived to present health risks to the greater community. As our ability to translate genetic advances into tools that identify disease risk increases, so does the potential for genetics to further public health goals around disease prevention. The field of public health genetics has grown out of the realization that genetics will be an increasingly important public health tool.

This chapter provides an introduction to some of the ethical, legal, and social issues that accompany government efforts to use genetic advances as tools to promote and protect public health. It begins with an introduction to public health law, the body of law that bounds the government's ability to enforce public health programs, and the associated tension between government interest in public health and individual interests in autonomy, privacy, and liberty. It then moves into a discussion of the eugenics movement that flourished during the early part of the twentieth century and which, by some accounts, represents the first attempt in this country to use genetics to achieve public health objectives. It ends with a review of cases and materials surrounding three contemporary examples of genetics-based public health oriented programs—screening for sickle cell disease, prenatal screening, and newborn screening. These programs were selected to highlight some of the legal and policy issues confronting the future of public health genetics.

A. Public Health Law: Overview of Government Powers and Duties

Public health law has been defined as "the study of legal powers and duties of the state to assure the conditions for people to be healthy and the limitations on the power of the state to constrain the autonomy, privacy, liberty, proprietary or other legally protected interests of individuals for the protection or promotion of public health." Lawrence O. Gostin, Public Health Law: Power, Duty, Restraint 4 (University of California Press 2000). Part A of Chapter 10 provides a general overview of the legal framework that supports government interventions to identify and either minimize or prevent risks to the public's health.

Ellen Wright Clayton, *Genetics, Public Health, and the Law, in* Genetics and Public Health in the 21st Century: Using Genetic Information to Improve Health and Prevent Disease (M.J. Khoury, W. Burke, & E.J. Thomson, eds. 2000)

... Understanding where the government's power to protect the public health comes from is the first step in understanding what the government is and is not permitted to do in pursuit of this goal. Some modern political philosophers argue for a number of reasons that protection of the public health is an inherent function of the government. One set of arguments is that without healthy citizens, there can be no state, and that the community is harmed when some of its members are not well. Some argue, in fact, that the primary justification for government is its use of the so-called "police power" to promote the common good, including public health. Legal historians have demonstrated that protection of the public health has always been important in our country's governance and that the government has often acted quite broadly in pursuit of this goal. Many efforts of the current regulatory state, ranging from the provision of clean water to safety requirements for motor vehicles, are designed to protect individuals and are imposed without regarding to whether a particular person wants these protections or not....

A separate function of the government, but one that often overlaps to a significant degree with the exercise of the police power, is to protect individuals who cannot protect themselves in the state's role as *parens patriae.* Examples of individuals who are subject to this sort of protection include the mentally ill, who are unable to provide for their own needs, and young children who are abandoned, neglected, or abused by their parents. An important limitation of the *parens patriae* power is that is almost never invoked to protect competent adults.

A critical issue in the federal system is the allocation of authority among governments. The power to promote the public health was reserved to the states under the Tenth Amendment to the United States Constitution. On those rare occasions when the United States Supreme Court has addressed public health issues, the justices have stated that the states' powers in this area are very far-reaching.... The result is a complex interplay among different levels of government that changes over time.

The constraints of federalism are not the only limits on governmental actions undertaken to promote the public health. Efforts in this area can be pursued only if authorized by statutes and regulations. Put another way, there is no "common law" of public health so that judges may not uphold a public health activity in the absence of an authorizing statute or regulation. This means that all public health actions must survive the public scrutiny that accompanies the political process. The fact that growing and selling tobacco is still permitted and even subsidized in the face of overwhelming evidence of the adverse health consequences of this product is evidence of the impact of political considerations on the government's actions in the public health arena.

Although the government's policy powers are broad, several constitutionally protected individual rights have emerged as increasingly important restraints on governmental efforts to protect the public health. The *right to privacy,* a term that actually encompasses a number of different claims of the individual against the government, is the newest and the most ill-defined of these rights, being derived generally from the "penumbra" of various amendments to the Constitution. The first, and more widely discussed, aspect of the right to privacy is the "right to avoid disclosure of personal matters" by the government. The right to privacy, broadly viewed, also overlaps with other freedoms, such as the right to refuse "unreasonable searches and seizures."

The requirement of *due process* means that procedural protections must be in place to prevent inappropriate governmental interference with individuals. The specific procedures required vary directly with the importance of the individual interest that is being invaded. Thus, when the government is searching for evidence of a crime, it must obtain a search warrant before entering a person's house but not before watching that same person walk down a public street, a distinction justified because the home is more private than the street.

Finally, the provision ensuring individuals *equal protection* of the laws means both that the state may not make distinctions that have no basis in fact and that the state may not categorize individuals using certain suspect classifications, such as race and ethnicity, without compelling justification. To demonstrate both aspects of equal protection, the government could not permissibly mandate immunizations only for blacks and Hispanics, while exempting whites. There is no evidence that whites are already immune to vaccine-preventable diseases, and requiring only blacks and Hispanics to be immunized burdens and discriminates against those groups in ways that could promote unfounded negative stereotypes....

1. Case Examples: The Police Power

Jacobson v. Commonwealth of Massachusetts

197 U.S. 11 (1905)

Mr. Justice Harlan delivered the opinion of the court:

This case involves the validity, under the Constitution of the United States, of certain provisions in the statutes of Massachusetts relating to vaccination....

The board of health of the city of Cambridge, Massachusetts, on the 27th day of February, 1902, adopted the following regulation: 'Whereas, smallpox has been prevalent to some extent in the city of Cambridge, and still continues to increase; and whereas, it is necessary for the speedy extermination of the disease that all persons not protected by vaccination should be vaccinated; and whereas, in the opinion of the board, the public health and safety require the vaccination or revaccination of all the inhabitants of Cambridge; be it ordered, that all the inhabitants habitants of the city who have not been successfully vaccinated since March 1st, 1897, be vaccinated or revaccinated.'...

The above regulations being in force, the plaintiff in error, Jacobson, was proceeded against by a criminal complaint in one of the inferior courts of Massachusetts. The complaint charged that on the 17th day of July, 1902, the board of health of Cambridge, being of the opinion that it was necessary for the public health and safety, required the vaccination and revaccination of all the inhabitants thereof who had not been successfully vaccinated since the 1st day of March, 1897, and provided them with the means of free vaccination; and that the defendant, being over twenty-one years of age and not under guardianship, refused and neglected to comply with such requirement.

... [The defendant was ultimately found guilty of violating the compulsory vaccination law, was sentenced to pay a $5.00 fine and was committed to jail until the fine was paid.]

What, according to the judgment of the state court, are the scope and effect of the statute? What results were intended to be accomplished by it? These questions must be answered....

The authority of the state to enact this statute is to be referred to what is commonly called the police power,—a power which the state did not surrender when becoming a member of the Union under the Constitution. Although this court has refrained from any attempt to define the limits of that power, yet it has distinctly recognized the authority of a state to enact quarantine laws and 'health laws of every description;' indeed, all laws that relate to matters completely within its territory and which do not by their necessary operation affect the people of other states. According to settled principles, the police power of a state must be held to embrace, at least, such reasonable regulations established directly by legislative enactment as will protect the public health and the public safety....

It is equally true that the state may invest local bodies called into existence for purposes of local administration with authority in some appropriate way to safeguard the public health and the public safety. The mode or manner in which those results are to be accomplished is within the discretion of the state, subject, of course, so far as Federal power is concerned, only to the condition that no rule prescribed by a state, nor any regulation adopted by a local governmental agency acting under the sanction of state legislation, shall contravene the Constitution of the United States, nor infringe any right granted or secured by that instrument. A local enactment or regulation, even if based on the acknowledged police powers of a state, must always yield in case of conflict with the exercise by the general government of any power it possesses under the Constitution, or with any right which that instrument gives or secures....

We come, then, to inquire whether any right given or secured by the Constitution is invaded by the statute as interpreted by the state court. The defendant insists that his liberty is invaded when the state subjects him to fine or imprisonment for neglecting or refusing to submit to vaccination; that a compulsory vaccination law is unreasonable, arbitrary, and oppressive, and, therefore, hostile to the inherent right of every freeman to care for his own body and health in such way as to him seems best; and that the execution of such a law against one who objects to vaccination, no matter for what reason, is nothing short of an assault upon his person. But the liberty secured by the Constitution of the United States to every person within its jurisdiction does not import an absolute right in each person to be, at all times and in all circumstances, wholly freed from restraint. There are manifold restraints to which every person is necessarily subject for the common good. On any other basis organized society could not exist with safety to its members. Society based on the rule that each one is a law unto himself would soon be confronted with disorder and anarchy. Real liberty for all could not exist under the operation of a principle which recognizes the right of each individual person to use his own, whether in respect of his person or his property, regardless of the injury that may be done to others. This court has more than once recognized it as a fundamental principle that 'persons and property are subjected to all kinds of restraints and burdens in order to secure the general comfort, health, and prosperity of the state; of the perfect right of the legislature to do which no question ever was, or upon acknowledged general principles ever can be, made, so far as natural persons are concerned.' In *Crowley v. Christensen*, 137 U. S. 86, 89 (1890), we said: 'The possession and enjoyment of all rights are subject to such reasonable conditions as may be deemed by the governing authority of the country essential to the safety, health, peace, good order, and morals of the community. Even liberty itself, the greatest of all rights, is not unrestricted license to act according to one's own will. It is only freedom from restraint under conditions essential to the equal enjoyment of the same right by others. It is, then, liberty regulated by law.' In the Constitution of Massachusetts adopted in 1780 it was laid down as a fundamental principle of the social compact that the whole people covenants with each citizen, and each citizen with the whole people, that all shall be governed by certain laws for 'the common good,' and that government is instituted 'for the common good, for the protection, safety, prosperity, and happiness of the people, and not for the profit, honor, or private interests of any one man, family, or class of men.' The good and welfare of the commonwealth, of which the legislature is primarily the judge, is the basis on which the police power rests in Massachusetts.

Applying these principles to the present case, it is to be observed that the legislature of Massachusetts required the inhabitants of a city or town to be vaccinated only when, in the opinion of the board of health, that was necessary for the public health or the public safety. The authority to determine for all what ought to be done in such an emergency must have been lodged somewhere or in some body; and surely it was appropriate for the legislature to refer that question, in the first instance, to a board of health composed of persons residing in the locality affected, and appointed, presumably, because of their fitness to determine such questions. To invest such a body with authority over such matters was not an unusual, nor an unreasonable or arbitrary, requirement. Upon the principle of self-defense, of paramount necessity, a community has the right to protect itself against an epidemic of disease which threatens the safety of its members. It is to be observed that when the regulation in question was adopted smallpox, according to the recitals in the regulation adopted by the board of health, was prevalent to some extent in the city of Cambridge, and the disease was increasing. If such was the situation,—and nothing is asserted or appears in the record to the contrary,—if we are to attach, any value whatever to the knowledge which, it is safe to affirm, in common to all civilized peoples touching smallpox and the methods most usually employed to eradicate that disease, it cannot be adjudged that the present regulation of the board of health was not necessary in order to protect the public health and secure the public safety....

If the mode adopted by the commonwealth of Massachusetts for the protection of its local communities against smallpox proved to be distressing, inconvenient, or objectionable to some,—if nothing more could be reasonably affirmed of the statute in question,—the answer is that it was the duty of the constituted authorities primarily to keep in view the welfare, comfort, and safety of the many, and not permit the interests of the many to be subordinated to the wishes or convenience of the few. There is, of course, a sphere within which the individual may assert the supremacy of his own will, and rightfully dispute the authority of any human government,—especially of any free government existing under a written constitution, to interfere with the exercise of that will. But it is equally true that in every well-ordered society charged with the duty of conserving the safety of its members the rights of the individual in respect of his liberty may at times, under the pressure of great dangers, be subjected to such restraint, to be enforced by reasonable regulations, as the safety of the general public may demand. An American citizen arriving at an American port on a vessel in which, during the voyage, there had been cases of yellow fever or Asiatic cholera, he, although apparently free from disease himself, may yet, in some circumstances, be held in quarantine against his will on board of such vessel or in a quarantine station, until it be ascertained by inspection, conducted with due diligence, that the danger of the spread of the disease among the community at large has disappeared. The liberty secured by the 14th Amendment, this court has said, consists, in part, in the right of a person 'to live and work where he will'; and yet he may be compelled, by force if need be, against his will and without regard to his personal wishes or his pecuniary interests, or even his religious or political convictions, to take his place in the ranks of the army of his country, and risk the chance of being shot down in its defense. It is not, therefore, true that the power of the public to guard itself against imminent danger depends in every case involving the control of one's body upon his willingness to submit to reasonable regulations established by the constituted authorities, under the sanction of the state, for the purpose of protecting the public collectively against such danger....

Looking at the propositions embodied in the defendant's rejected offers of proof, it is clear that they are more formidable by their number than by their inherent value. Those offers in the main seem to have had no purpose except to state the general theory of those of the medical profession who attach little or no value to vaccination as a means of preventing the spread of smallpox, or who think that vaccination causes other diseases of the body. What everybody knows the court must know, and therefore the state court judicially knew, as this court knows, that an opposite theory accords with the common belief, and is maintained by high medical authority. We must assume that, when the statute in question was passed, the legislature of Massachusetts was not unaware of these opposing theories, and was compelled, of necessity, to choose between them. It was not compelled to commit a matter involving the public health and safety to the final decision of a court or jury. It is no part of the function of a court or a jury to determine which one of two modes was likely to be the most effective for the protection of the public against disease. That was for the legislative department to determine in the light of all the information it had or could obtain. It could not properly abdicate its function to guard the public health and safety. The state legislature proceeded upon the theory which recognized vaccination as at least an effective, if not the best-known, way in which to meet and suppress the evils of a smallpox epidemic that imperiled an entire population. Upon what sound principles as to the relations existing between the different departments of government can the court review this action of the legislature? If there is any such power in the judiciary to review legislative action in respect of a matter affecting the general welfare, it can only be when that which the legislature has done comes within the rule that, if a statute purporting to have been enacted to protect the public health, the public morals, or the public safety, has no real or substantial relation to those objects, or is, beyond all question, a plain, palpable invasion of rights secured by the fundamental law, it is the duty of the courts to so adjudge, and thereby give effect to the Constitution.

Whatever may be thought of the expediency of this statute, it cannot be affirmed to be, beyond question, in palpable conflict with the Constitution. Nor, in view of the methods employed to stamp out the disease of smallpox, can anyone confidently assert that the means prescribed by the state to that end has no real or substantial relation to the protection of the public health and the public safety. Such an assertion would not be consistent with the experience of this and other countries whose authorities have dealt with the disease of smallpox. And the principle of vaccination as a means to prevent the spread of smallpox has been enforced in many states by statutes making the vaccination of children a condition of their right to enter or remain in public schools....

Since, then, vaccination, as a means of protecting a community against smallpox, finds strong support in the experience of this and other countries, no court, much less a jury, is justified in disregarding the action of the legislature simply because in its or their opinion that particular method was—perhaps, or possibly—not the best either for children or adults.

Did the offers of proof made by the defendant present a case which entitled him, while remaining in Cambridge, to claim exemption from the operation of the statute and of the regulation adopted by the board of health? We have already said that his rejected offers, in the main, only set forth the theory of those who had no faith in vaccination as a means of preventing the spread of smallpox, or who thought that vaccination, without benefiting the public, put in peril the health of the person vaccinated. But there were some offers which it is contended embodied distinct facts that might properly have been considered. Let us see how this is.

The defendant offered to prove that vaccination 'quite often' caused serious and permanent injury to the health of the person vaccinated; that the operation 'occasionally' resulted in death; that it was 'impossible' to tell 'in any particular case' what the results of vaccination would be, or whether it would injure the health or result in death; that 'quite often' one's blood is in a certain condition of impurity when it is not prudent or safe to vaccinate him; that there is no practical test by which to determine 'with any degree of certainty' whether one's blood is in such condition of impurity as to render vaccination necessarily unsafe or dangerous; that vaccine matter is 'quite often' impure and dangerous to be used, but whether impure or not cannot be ascertained by any known practical test; that the defendant refused to submit to vaccination for the reason that he had, 'when a child,' been caused great and extreme suffering for a long period by a disease produced by vaccination; and that he had witnessed a similar result of vaccination, not only in the case of his son, but in the cases of others.

These offers, in effect, invited the court and jury to go over the whole ground gone over by the legislature when it enacted the statute in question. The legislature assumed that some children, by reason of their condition at the time, might not be fit subjects of vaccination; and it is suggested—and we will not say without reason—that such is the case with some adults. But the defendant did not offer to prove that, by reason of his then condition, he was in fact not a fit subject of vaccination at the time he was informed of the requirement of the regulation adopted by the board of health. It is entirely consistent with his offer of proof that, after reaching full age, he had become, so far as medical skill could discover, and when informed of the regulation of the board of health was, a fit subject of vaccination, and that the vaccine matter to be used in his case was such as any medical practitioner of good standing would regard as proper to be used. The matured opinions of medical men everywhere, and the experience of mankind, as all must know, negative the suggestion that it is not possible in any case to determine whether vaccination is safe. Was defendant exempted from the operation of the statute simply because of his dread of the same evil results experienced by him when a child, and which he had observed in the cases of his son and other children? Could he reasonably claim such an exemption because 'quite often,' or 'occasionally,' injury had resulted from vaccination, or because it was impossible, in the opinion of some, by any practical test, to determine with absolute certainty whether a particular person could be safely vaccinated?

It seems to the court that an affirmative answer to these questions would practically strip the legislative department of its function to care for the public health and the public safety when endangered by epidemics of disease. Such an answer would mean that compulsory vaccination could not, in any conceivable case, be legally enforced in a community, even at the command of the legislature, however widespread the epidemic of smallpox, and however deep and universal was the belief of the community and of its medical advisers that a system of general vaccination was vital to the safety of all.

We are not prepared to hold that a minority, residing or remaining in any city or town where smallpox is prevalent, and enjoying the general protection afforded by an organized local government, may thus defy the will of its constituted authorities, acting in good faith for all, under the legislative sanction of the state. If such be the privilege of a minority, then a like privilege would belong to each individual of the community, and the spectacle would be presented of the welfare and safety of an entire population being subordinated to the notions of a single individual who chooses to remain a part of that population. We are unwilling to hold it to be an element in the liberty secured by the Constitution of the United States that one person, or a minority of persons, residing in any community and enjoying the benefits of its local government, should have the power thus to dominate the majority when supported in their action by the authority of the state. While this court should guard with firmness every right appertaining to life, liberty, or property as secured to the individual by the supreme law of the land, it is of the last importance that it should not invade the domain of local authority except when it is plainly necessary to do so in order to enforce that law. The safety and the health of the people of Massachusetts are, in the first instance, for that commonwealth to guard and protect. They are matters that do not ordinarily concern the national government. So far as they can be reached by any government, they depend, primarily, upon such action as the state, in its wisdom, may take; and we do not perceive that this legislation has invaded any right secured by the Federal Constitution.

Before closing this opinion we deem it appropriate, in order to prevent misapprehension as to our views, to observe—perhaps to repeat a thought already sufficiently expressed, namely—that the police power of a state, whether exercised directly by the legislature, or by a local body acting under its authority, may be exerted in such circumstances, or by regulations so arbitrary and oppressive in particular cases, as to justify the interference of the courts to prevent wrong and oppression. Extreme cases can be readily suggested. Ordinarily such cases are not safe guides in the administration of the law. It is easy, for instance, to suppose the case of an adult who is embraced by the mere words of the act, but yet to subject whom to vaccination in a particular condition of his health or body would be cruel and inhuman in the last degree. We are not to be understood as holding that the statute was intended to be applied to such a case, or, if it was so intended, that the judiciary would not be competent to interfere and protect the health and life of the individual concerned....

Until otherwise informed by the highest court of Massachusetts, we are not inclined to hold that the statute establishes the absolute rule that an adult must be vaccinated if it be apparent or can be shown with reasonable certainty that he is not at the time a fit subject of vaccination, or that vaccination, by reason of his then condition, would seriously impair his health, or probably cause his death. No such case is here presented. It is the cause of an adult who, for aught that appears, was himself in perfect health and a fit subject of vaccination, and yet, while remaining in the community, refused to obey the statute and the regulation adopted in execution of its provisions for the protection of the public health and the public safety, confessedly endangered by the presence of a dangerous disease.

We now decide only that the statute covers the present case, and that nothing clearly appears that would justify this court in holding it to be unconstitutional and inoperative in its application to the plaintiff in error.

The judgment of the court below must be affirmed.

Notes & Questions

1. In the *Jacobson* case one of the challenges to the state's compulsory vaccination program focused on the underlying scientific merit of using vaccination as a means of preventing the spread of smallpox; a second focused on the health risks that accompany vaccinations, asserting that these risks outweigh the potential benefits. What did the Supreme Court conclude regarding the role courts should play in evaluating the underlying scientific merit of a public health intervention? Did the *Jacobson* court define a threshold for determining when the courts should second-guess a legislative body's determination regarding scientific or clinical merit? Should the state, or its local delegees (in this case the board of health of the city of Cambridge, Massachusetts) have a burden to demonstrate scientific merit? Should the state's burden of proof on this issue vary according to the nature and extent of a public health program's impact on individual interests?

Considering the following information regarding smallpox and the impact of vaccinations on mortality and morbidity, do you think compulsory vaccination programs for smallpox were based upon sound science?

> Smallpox is a serious, contagious and sometimes fatal infectious disease. There is no specific treatment for smallpox disease, and the only prevention is vaccination. There are two clinical forms of smallpox. Variola major is the severe and most common form, with a more extensive rash and higher fever. There are four types of variola major smallpox: ordinary (the most frequent type, accounting for 90% or more of cases); modified (mild and occurring in previously vaccinated persons); flat; and hemorrhagic (both rare and very severe). Historically, variola major has an overall fatality rate of about 30%; however, flat and hemorrhagic smallpox usually are fatal. Variola minor is a less common presentation and a much less severe disease, with death rates historically of 1% or less.
>
> The production and quality of vaccines available in the late 19th and early 20th centuries in Boston were unregulated by the government; they were largely safe but had known side effects. The case fatality rate (proportion of people with the disease who die from it) for vaccinated individuals in Boston was 11 percent; in unvaccinated people it was 22 percent. From 1901 to 1903 in Boston there were 1596 cases of smallpox, mostly in adults, since then the legislation requiring vaccination of children before entering public school was already in place. The population of Boston at that time was 560,900.

Smallpox Disease Overview, http://www.bt.cdc.gov/agent/smallpox/overview/disease-facts.asp; M.R. Albert, K.G. Ostheimer & J.G. Breman, *The Last Smallpox Epidemic in Boston and the Vaccination Controversy*, 344 New Eng. J. Med. 375 (2000).

Ex Parte Johnson

180 P. 644 (Cal. 1919)

Shaw, J.

. . .

The adoption of measures for the protection of the public health is universally conceded to be a valid exercise of the police power of the state, as to which the legislature is necessarily vested with large discretion not only in determining what are contagious and infectious diseases, but also in adopting means for preventing the spread thereof. The legislature in its discretion having determined the character of the disease in question, has imposed upon the health department of the city the duty, when having knowledge that one is afflicted therewith, of taking the necessary measures to prevent its spread.

In the absence of any showing to the contrary, we must, upon the evidence before us, assume that petitioner was, when subjected to quarantine regulations, and is now, afflicted with and suffering from gonococcus infection, which, by section 2979a of the Political Code (Stats. 1917, p. 171), is, with leprosy, smallpox, typhus fever, and a number of other diseases, declared to be contagious and infectious. The sole question thus presented is the right of proper authorities to isolate and place her in quarantine. By the section of the code just cited it is made the duty of the health officer, knowing the existence of any such contagious or infectious disease, to take such measures as may be necessary to prevent the spread thereof.

The isolation of one afflicted with a contagious or infectious disease is a reasonable and proper, indeed the usual, measure taken to prevent the increase and spread thereof.

It appears that petitioner was originally taken into custody without a warrant and, basing his argument upon such arbitrary action, counsel draws a lurid picture of what might result from maladministration of the law by those charged with the duty of enforcing it.

The fact that the authority so delegated may, in a given case, be abused is no legal reason for denying the power to quarantine summarily in a case where grounds therefor concededly exist. Possible maladministration of the law is no concern of petitioner, unless such administration thereof is shown to have affected her. Nor can her arrest without a warrant, after which and while being illegally held, an examination was made with her consent which disclosed the existence of the infection, avail her in this proceeding. Assuming the action of the police officer arbitrary and unjustified, she is not restrained of her liberty by reason thereof, but on account of a disease with which she was subsequently found to be afflicted, and in the ascertainment of which fact there appears to have been no arbitrary or unlawful action taken.

There is no merit in the contention that the infection with which petitioner is afflicted is noncommunicable except by actual contact, which contact in such cases must be predicated upon the assumption that an offense cognizable by law will be committed.

Assuming that grounds exist for petitioner's contention, no evidence tending to establish such fact has been presented and it is not a matter as to which the court may take judicial notice.

Counsel cites no authorities in support of the contention that one afflicted with a contagious disease cannot be subjected to quarantine regulations until it is first judicially established by some proceeding in court that he is so afflicted.

Manifestly to uphold such contention would render laws for the protection of the public health nugatory. The writ no doubt was granted upon the argument that petitioner was not, and never had been, afflicted with the infection, which if true would entitle her to be discharged from custody. The return and evidence taken at the hearing conclusively establish the fact to the contrary.

In our opinion, the return and evidence taken at the hearing show a legal cause for the detention of petitioner, and she is remanded to custody.

Notes & Questions

1. How does the public health intervention at issue in *Ex Parte Johnson* differ from the compulsory vaccination program involved in the *Jacobson* case? Are the implications for individual rights the same or different? *Ex Parte Johnson* involved the warrantless arrest and compulsory isolation of a woman suspected of having gonorrhea. In between the arrest and the quarantine she was examined and the diagnosis was confirmed. The court concluded the state's course of conduct was a "reasonable and proper" measure to prevent the spread of gonorrhea. Do you agree or disagree and why? Would it change your opinion if the woman was a prostitute? Did the mode of transmission for gonorrhea influence the court's analysis? To what extent should consideration of the natural history and epidemiology of the underlying disease play a role in deciding whether isolation and quarantine are "reasonable and proper" measures to prevent the increase and spread of an infectious disease (*e.g.*, smallpox is transmitted through casual contact and shared objects whereas transmission of gonorrhea requires sexual contact)?

In what ways are genetic diseases similar to infectious diseases? How are they different? Are there public health implications associated with the transmission of genetic disease that might warrant state intervention to protect or promote health and safety? If so, what might the intervention entail and what individual rights might be implicated?

Brown v. City School District of City of Corning

429 N.Y.S.2d 355 (1980)

Myron E. Tillman, Justice.

Plaintiff, Erving R. Brown, is seeking to enjoin Defendant, City School District of the City of Corning, New York, from preventing Ysreen Brown from attending classes at the Winfield Street School in Corning. Ysreen is presently a kindergarten student in that school, and has been attending classes since September 10, 1979. She has never received the immunizations required by Public Health Law, Section 2164. However, Plaintiff contends that the exemption contained in Public Health Law, Section 2164(9), relieves them of the obligation to obtain the required inoculations....

Subdivision 9 of Section 2164 of the Public Health Law provides: "This section shall not apply to children whose parent, parents, or guardian are bona fide members of a recognized religious organization whose teachings are contrary to the practices herein required, and no certificate shall be required as a prerequisite to such children being admitted or received into school or attending school."

The constitutionality of legislation making immunization and vaccination mandatory without religious exemption is not disputed. However, the New York State Legislature, decided to provide for religious exemption when it enacted the requirements for poliomyelitis vaccination in 1966. Legislative memoranda at that time revealed that the State Department of Education recommended against the religious exemption on the basis that any public health measure, in order to be effective, should provide for all children because of the danger to other children. The Department recommended that the present bill be approved, but that efforts be made in the next legislative session to make immunization against poliomyelitis compulsory for all children. The Legislature has declined to adopt this recommendation, notwithstanding later consideration on that point when the subdivision was renumbered in 1975. The Legislature has clearly indicated a desire to retain the statutory religious exemption....

The Plaintiff herein testified, and the proof showed, that he had never received immunization himself, that to the best of his knowledge his parents and grandparents had not received immunization for religious reasons.... Mr. Brown received his religious training from his parents, and he said that the Bible was the cornerstone of his training. He, himself, uses the Bible regularly in the religious instruction and training of his children. His faith is based on the Bible, which he views as a "message from God." He believes that man must live in harmony with the Bible, and he believes that man was born with a natural immunity. He testified that he does not fear disease and teaches his children to believe the same way. He believes that receiving manmade chemicals by inoculation or immunization will prevent him from attaining the hereafter, and he cites the Bible as support for his belief. These beliefs are actively practiced in Brown's home. He and his family have regular gatherings at which their religion and way of life is discussed, and the Bible is used to strengthen their faith. They are vigorously opposed to the ingestion of all drugs....

The Court's observation of the Plaintiff and his testimony convinced the Court of his genuineness and the sincerity of his religious beliefs.

The free exercise of religion is a fundamental right under the Constitution and, therefore, susceptible of restriction only to prevent "grave and immediate danger" to interests which the State may lawfully protect. In the case at bar, no "grave and immediate danger" was shown. Mr. Peter Crippen, the Immunization Program Coordinator for New York State Health Department, employed by the Federal Government, testified that he was unaware of any cases of diphtheria, measles, poliomyelitis, etc., in the Corning City School District. In addition, he testified that the geographic region in which the City of Corning is located has historically had the fewest number of cases indicting a danger of epidemic in the State of New York. Mr. Burdette B. Gleason, the Superintendent of Schools in the City of Corning School District, testified that there were four (4) children within the Corning City School District who have not been immunized (two of them on the basis of their religious beliefs).

The legislative history relative to the religious exemption from immunization reveals throughout a continuing intent to statutorily preserve, whenever possible, a coexistence of public health protection and recognition of the right of serious religious practice. Governments have reason to consider each concern as fundamental to the best welfare of their people.

The parent or guardian who comes before the Court claiming exemption under Section 2164(9) of the Public Health Law must satisfy the Court on two grounds. First, the Court must be satisfied as to the sincerity of the religious belief; and, secondly, that there is no present circumstance which, in the opinion of the public health authorities, represents a clear and present danger of the particular communicable disease. This hearing has satisfied both of the above tests, and the Court finds that the Plaintiff comes within the spirit and, in fact, is entitled by law to the exemption provided by Subdivision 9 of Section 2164 of the Public Health Law.

The Court grants the Plaintiff's application to preliminarily enjoin the Defendant from preventing Ysreen Brown from attending school.

Mason v. General Brown Central School District

851 F.2d 47 (N.Y. 1988)

George C. Pratt, Circuit Judge:

Plaintiffs C. Edgar Mason, individually and as guardian for his son, Jered Mason, and Karen L. Mason, appeal from a judgment entered in the United States District Court for the Northern District of New York after a bench trial before Howard G. Munson, Chief Judge, dismissing the complaint. Plaintiffs' action sought to compel defendants to permit plaintiffs' son, based on his own and his parents' religious beliefs, to attend public school without being immunized as required by New York law. Finding that plaintiffs' opposition to immunization was not religiously based, the trial court held (1) that plaintiffs were not entitled to a religious exemption as provided by N.Y. Pub. Health Law sec. 2164(9), and (2) that plaintiffs lacked standing to attack sec. 2164 on first amendment grounds.

Plaintiffs' appeal pivots on their claim that the district court erred in finding that plaintiffs' opposition to immunization was not religiously based. They contend that their commitment to living in a "natural order" is "over and above a level of scientific belief" and argue that the district court erroneously failed to recognize that their commitment to a lifestyle, based on what they perceive as a "genetic blueprint", rises to the level of religious belief. We reject these arguments and affirm.

C. Edgar and Karen L. Mason reside with their son Jered within the boundaries of the General Brown Central School District in Watertown, New York. The Masons advocate a "natural existence". They believe, for example, that the human body possesses the means of healing itself without medical intervention, and that, therefore, immunizations are unnecessary and indeed contrary to the "genetic blueprint" intended by nature. Similarly, they are convinced that any interference with natural neurological and physical functions results in decreased physical capacity and increased disease.

Although the record is unclear, Dr. Mason apparently developed these beliefs in the late 1970s while attending chiropractic school in Davenport, Iowa. While there, he became interested in and subsequently joined the Davenport Universal Life Church (DULC), organized by, and consisting mostly of, fellow chiropractors and chiropractic students in Davenport. The DULC is the Davenport local branch of the Universal Life Church (ULC). It has no membership requirements, no worship or other services, and no traditional doctrine. Instead, it advocates a "natural existence" with each member determining "the most effective means of expressing his/her life." Over the past several years since leaving Davenport for New York, the Masons have continued to cultivate their belief in this natural lifestyle: they grow some of their own food, eat as naturally as possible, exercise, meditate, and limit their television viewing.

In a letter dated April 16, 1985, addressed to the officers of the General Brown School District, the Masons explained their beliefs and requested that their son, Jered, be allowed to attend school without the immunizations mandated by N.Y.Pub. Health Law sec. 2164 (McKinney 1985). This section requires that all children be immunized against certain communicable diseases before they enter school, but provides an exemption to those who oppose immunization on religious grounds. N.Y. Pub. Health Law sec. 2164(9) (McKinney 1985). In support of their application for exemption, the Masons submitted a letter from the DULC, stating that Jered was a "member in good standing", and that the church opposed immunization because it defiled the human body.

After consideration, the school district refused to grant the exemption, finding that the required vaccinations were not in conflict with the family's religious beliefs. Plaintiffs appealed to the state Commissioner of Education, Gordon M. Ambach, who, while ultimately dismissing the Masons' appeal as untimely, also found that plaintiffs had presented "insufficient evidence" to establish that their religious tenets were inconsistent with immunization.

Thereafter, plaintiffs filed suit in federal district court seeking (1) a declaratory judgment that their beliefs fell within the purview of sec. 2164(9), (2) a declaration that the state statute is unconstitutional under the first amendment, and (3) damages, pursuant to 42 U.S.C. sec. 1983, in the amount of $1 million for violation of their constitutional rights as protected under the free exercise clause....

This appeal followed.

N.Y.Pub. Health Law sec. 2164(7) requires school officials to obtain from each child proof of immunization against certain communicable diseases before that child is allowed to enroll in school. The section also allows for exemption from this requirement: no immunization is required of a child whose parents "are bona fide members of a recognized religious organization whose teachings are contrary to the [immunization]." N.Y.Pub. Health Law sec. 2164(9) (McKinney 1985). New York courts have construed this exemption broadly, holding that it is sufficient if the child's parents have sincere religious beliefs opposed to immunization. Thus, put simply, in order to claim an exemption under sec. 2164(9) the Masons must show either (1) that they are members of a recognized religious organization whose teachings conflict with immunization, N.Y.Pub.Health Law sec. 2164(9) (McKinney 1985), or (2) that their opposition to immunization is a personal and "sincerely followed religious belief." The district court found that the Masons had failed to make a showing under either alternative, and we agree.

The Masons claim that, totally apart from their membership in any religious organization, they possess strong convictions concerning the necessity of a "natural existence". This belief, they contend, although based on chiropractic principles, rises "over and above a level of scientific belief" to form a "belief system which in its essence can be deemed religious."

There is no doubt, as the district court recognized, that "religious belief" encompasses more than the traditional Judeo-Christian, Moslem or Buddhist forms of worship. Indeed, we have held that the term "religious" has expanded beyond a strict belief in a deity to include the notion of a person's "ultimate concern." *Krishna Consciousness*, 650 F.2d 430, 441 (2d Cir. 1981); see also *United States v. Allen*, 760 F.2d 447, 450 (2d Cir.1985) ("an individual's most sincere beliefs do not necessarily fall within traditional religious categories"); *Seeger*, 380 U.S. 163, 165–66 (1965). As a consequence, to be religious, a belief need not necessarily contemplate an orthodox or traditional God; rather, it is sufficient if the belief "occupies a place in the life of its possessor parallel to that filled by the orthodox belief in God." *Seeger*, 380 U.S. at 166.

An individual's assertion that the belief he holds has reached this level does not, however, automatically mean that the belief is religious. To the contrary, "a threshold inquiry into the 'religious' aspect of particular beliefs and practices cannot be avoided", *Krishna Consciousness*, 650 F.2d at 433, if we are to determine what is in fact based on religious belief, and what is based on secular or scientific principles.

Recognizing these standards, the district court proceeded to evaluate the Masons' belief in a "genetic blueprint". It apparently had little doubt that this belief was sincere, but found that it was based, not on religious grounds, but on scientific and secular theories. This finding is not clearly erroneous.

There is ample evidence in the record suggesting that the plaintiffs' belief, taken on its own merits and considered under the standards illuminated above, is simply an embodiment of secular chiropractic ethics. Dr. Mason received his training from a school, and now is a member of a profession, that teaches a natural view of the human body and which rejects various types of drug and surgical intervention in favor of a belief that "health comes from within." At trial, he expressed his fear of the possible side effects from immunization in medical terms, agreeing that, to a large extent, his position was based on scientific evidence and personal theory. Indeed, when the trial court asked Mason to explain his objection to immunization, Mason candidly stated that it was primarily "biological": [E]ach of the substances that are required by the state law for a child to enter school have been shown to cause biological damage to the children that ... received the innoculation [sic]. In the case of polio, children have actually contracted polio directly because of the Savin [sic] oral vaccine. Diphtheria has been linked very heavily to encephalitis. It's been linked very heavily to hyperactivity in children. The measles and mumps vaccines are both a live virus vaccine which in those particular instances are directly injected into the bloodstream of the human organism that is receiving it and those types of live virus vaccines are violating the three natural defense mechanisms that your body already has in motion to prevent you from getting the disease in the first place.

We do not question that the Masons may have strong convictions so far as their belief in a "genetic blueprint" is concerned. These convictions are evidenced by the fact that the Masons have chosen to live in the country, to eat as naturally as possible, and to engage in many other health-oriented activities. However, this choice of lifestyle does not rise to the level of religion. Everyone makes basic choices about where to live, what to eat, and how to raise children. Merely because these decisions are important, and may be supported by strong conviction, does not render them religious. To the contrary, much like Thoreau's choice to isolate himself at Walden Pond, the beliefs are philosophical and personal, and as such, are neither protected by the religion clauses nor exempted under sec. 2164.

...

Notes & Questions

1. The *Brown* and *Mason* cases address the limits imposed upon the state's authority to promote public health by the federal constitution, and in particular the protection it offers to the free expression of individual religious beliefs. Although religious beliefs can warrant an exemption from compulsory vaccination programs, not all religious objections are treated equally. Based upon your review of these cases, what evidence do you think the courts require to uphold a religious exemption? Does the inquiry focus only on *bona fides* of the proffered religious beliefs or does it also take into account scientific or clinical evidence regarding the nature and extent of the public health threat? Today in the U. S. there is demonstrated "herd immunity" resulting from national vaccination efforts. This means that any one child is at very low risk provided those around her have been vaccinated. How should this influence the court's assessment of a religious exemption claim—or any claim that a compulsory vaccination program infringes upon an important individual right?

People v. Jillie

11 Cal. Rptr. 2d 107 (Cal. Ct. App. 1992)

Puglia, Presiding Justice.

... On January 31, 1991, Cheri Meyers was working in a video store in Red Bluff when defendant approached her, placed a note on the counter and told her, "Do everything I say on this note or your friend's life will be taken. You have twenty seconds to go and lock the door." The note stated, among other things, that if Meyers wanted to live for a long time she was to remove her clothing, orally copulate defendant and submit to being sodomized by him. Meyers began shaking and crying. Meyers's coworker summoned a postman from outside and he detained the defendant until the police arrived.

... [T]he trial court ordered defendant to submit to testing for the presence of AIDS antibodies. Defendant contends this was error.

Penal Code section 1202.1 provides: "(a) ... the court shall order every person convicted of a violation of a sexual offense listed in subdivision (d), whether or not a sentence or fine is imposed or probation is granted, to submit to a blood test for evidence of antibodies to the probable causative agent of acquired immune deficiency syndrome (AIDS). 'Each person tested under this section shall be informed of the results of the blood test. (b) ... the results of the blood test to detect antibodies to the probable causative agent of AIDS shall be transmitted by the clerk of the court to the Department of Justice. (c) ... the Department of Justice shall provide the results of a test or tests as to persons under investigation or being prosecuted under Section 647f or 12022.85, if the results are on file with the department, to the defense attorney upon request; and the results also shall be available to the prosecuting attorney upon request for the sole purpose of preparing counts for a subsequent offense under section 647f or sentence enhancement under Section 12022.85. (d) For the purposes of this section, sexual offenses include any of the following: (1) Rape in violation of Section 261. (2) Unlawful intercourse with a female under age 18 in violation of Section 261.5 (3) Rape of a spouse in violation of Section 262. (4) Sodomy in violation of Section 286. (5) Oral copulation in violation of Section 288a."

Defendant argues that because the offenses for which he was convicted, to wit, attempted sodomy and attempted forcible oral copulation, are not offenses specified in the statute, the statute is not applicable to him. The People urge the statute is ambiguous and should be construed to include attempts. We do not find the statute ambiguous. It expressly identifies the offenses within its scope, all of which are completed offenses. Had the Legislature meant to include attempts among the covered offenses, it could easily have done so as it has done in other instances, for example, Penal Code section 667.5, subdivision (c)(12) specifying attempted murder as one of several violent felonies, and Penal Code section 1192.7, subdivision (c)(27) making an attempt to commit any of the specifically listed felonies also a serious felony. Since the statute is clear and unambiguous, it is not necessary to resort to extrinsic aids for construction.

The order requiring defendant to submit to testing for AIDS antibodies is vacated. The superior court is directed to amend the abstract of judgment accordingly and to forward a certified copy thereof to the Department of Corrections. In all other respects the judgment is affirmed.

Notes & Questions

1. The police power is generally characterized as the inherent authority of the state to enact laws and adjudicate matters to protect, promote, and preserve public health, safety, and general welfare, even if in so doing it may restrict individual interests, both personal and economic. The selected cases highlight the tension between the state's duty to promote public health and certain personal interests. What are they? What alternative sources of legal authority potentially limit the state's exercise of police power? For a more in-depth introduction to these issues, *see* Lawrence O. Gostin, PUBLIC HEALTH LAW: POWER, DUTY, RESTRAINT 4 (2000).

2. The individual challenges to the public health programs involved in *Jacobson, Johnson, Brown*, and *Mason* predominantly involved what are generally referred to as "substantive due process claims." Substantive due process obligates the government to justify actions that limit or restrict individual interests in life, liberty or property. Thus, for example, the abrogation of individual choice regarding medical intervention that accompanies a compulsory vaccination program is justified on the basis of the state's police powers, which authorize interventions to promote public health. The case of *People v. Jillie* illustrates a procedural due process claim. What is it and how does it differ from the claims involved in the other cases in this section? For an in-depth overview of the derivation of substantive and procedural due process claims, as well as the distinctions between the two, *see* Lawrence O. Gostin, PUBLIC HEALTH LAW: POWER, DUTY, RESTRAINT 61–83 (2000).

2. Case Examples: Parens Patriae

Prince v. Massachusetts

321 U.S. 158 (1944)

Mr. JUSTICE RUTLEDGE delivered the opinion of the Court.

The case brings for review another episode in the conflict between Jehovah's Witnesses and state authority. This time Sarah Prince appeals from convictions for violating Massachusetts' child labor laws, by acts said to be a rightful exercise of her religious convictions.

When the offenses were committed she was the aunt and custodian of Betty M. Simmons, a girl nine years of age. Originally there were three separate complaints. They were, shortly, for (1) refusal to disclose Betty's identity and age to a public officer whose duty was to enforce the statutes; (2) furnishing her with magazines, knowing she was to sell them unlawfully, that is, on the street; and (3) as Betty's custodian, permitting her to work contrary to law. The Supreme Judicial Court reversed the conviction under the first complaint on state grounds; but sustained the judgments founded on the other two. They present the only questions for our decision. These are whether Sections 80 and 81, as applied, contravene the Fourteenth Amendment by denying or abridging appellant's freedom of religion and by denying to her the equal protection of the laws.

Sections 80 and 81 form parts of Massachusetts' comprehensive child labor law. They provide methods for enforcing the prohibitions of Section 69, which is as follows:

> 'No boy under twelve and no girl under eighteen shall sell, expose or offer for sale any newspapers, magazines, periodicals or any other articles of merchandise of any description, or exercise the trade of bootblack or scavenger, or any other trade, in any street or public place.'

Section 80 and 81, so far as pertinent, read:

> 'Whoever furnishes or sells to any minor any article of any description with the knowledge that the minor intends to sell such article in violation of any provision of sections sixty-nine to seventy-three, inclusive, or after having received written notice to this effect from any officer charged with the enforcement thereof, or knowingly procures or encourages any minor to violate any provisions of said sections, shall be punished by a fine of not less than ten nor more than two hundred dollars or by imprisonment for not more than two months, or both.' (Section 80)
>
> 'Any parent, guardian or custodian having a minor under his control who compels or permits such minor to work in violation of any provision of sections sixty to seventy-four, inclusive, ... shall for a first offence be punished by a fine of not less than two nor more than ten dollars or by imprisonment for not more than five days, or both; ...' (Section 81)

The story told by the evidence has become familiar. It hardly needs repeating, except to give setting to the variations introduced through the part played by a child of tender years. Mrs. Prince, living in Brockton, is the mother of two young sons. She also has legal custody of Betty Simmons who lives with them. The children too are Jehovah's Witnesses and both Mrs. Prince and Betty testified they were ordained ministers. The former was accustomed to go each week on the streets of Brockton to distribute 'Watchtower' and 'Consolation,' according to the usual plan. She had permitted the children to engage in this activity previously, and had been warned against doing so by the school attendance officer, Mr. Perkins. But, until December 18, 1941, she generally did not take them with her at night.

That evening, as Mrs. Prince was preparing to leave her home, the children asked to go. She at first refused. Childlike, they resorted to tears and, motherlike, she yielded. Arriving downtown, Mrs. Prince permitted the children 'to engage in the preaching work with her upon the sidewalks.' That is, with specific reference to Betty, she and Mrs. Prince took positions about twenty feet apart near a street intersection. Betty held up in her hand, for passersby to see, copies of 'Watch Tower' and 'Consolation.' From her shoulder hung the usual canvas magazine bag, on which was printed 'Watchtower and Consolation 5 cents per copy.' No one accepted a copy from Betty that evening and she received no money. Nor did her aunt. But on other occasions, Betty had received funds and given out copies.

Mrs. Prince and Betty remained until 8:45 p.m. A few minutes before this Mr. Perkins approached Mrs. Prince. A discussion ensued. He inquired and she refused to give Betty's name. However, she stated the child attended the Shaw School. Mr. Perkins referred to his previous warnings and said he would allow five minutes for them to get off the street. Mrs. Prince admitted she supplied Betty with the magazines and said, '(N)either you nor anybody else can stop me.... This child is exercising her God-given right and her constitutional right to preach the gospel, and no creature has a right to interfere with God's commands.' However, Mrs. Prince and Betty departed. She remarked as she went, 'I'm not going through this any more. We've been through it time and time again. I'm going home and put the little girl to bed.' It may be added that testimony, by Betty, her aunt and others, was offered at the trials, and was excluded, to show that

Betty believed it was her religious duty to perform this work and failure would bring condemnation 'to everlasting destruction at Armageddon.'

As the case reaches us, the questions are no longer open whether what the child did was a 'sale' or an 'offer to sell' within Section 69 or was 'work' within Section 81. The state court's decision has foreclosed them adversely to appellant as a matter of state law. The only question remaining therefore is whether, as construed and applied, the statute is valid. Upon this the court said: 'We think that freedom of the press and of religion is subject to incidental regulation to the slight degree involved in the prohibition of the selling of religious literature in streets and public places by boys under twelve and girls under eighteen and in the further statutory provisions herein considered, which have been adopted as a means of enforcing that prohibition.

Appellant does not stand on freedom of the press. Regarding it as secular, she concedes it may be restricted as Massachusetts has done. Hence, she rests squarely on freedom of religion under the First Amendment, applied by the Fourteenth to the states. She buttresses this foundation, however, with a claim of parental right as secured by the due process clause of the latter Amendment. These guaranties, she thinks, guard alike herself and the child in what they have done. Thus, two claimed liberties are at stake. One is the parent's, to bring up the child in the way he should go, which for appellant means to teach him the tenets and the practices of their faith. The other freedom is the child's, to observe these; and among them is 'to preach the gospel ... by public distribution' of 'Watchtower' and 'Consolation,' in conformity with the scripture: 'A little child shall lead them.'

If by this position appellant seeks for freedom of conscience a broader protection than for freedom of the mind, it may be doubted that any of the great liberties insured by the First Article can be given higher place than the others. All have preferred position in our basic scheme. All are interwoven there together. Differences there are, in them and in the modes appropriate for their exercise. But they have unity in the charter's prime place because they have unity in their human sources and functionings. Heart and mind are not identical. Intuitive faith and reasoned judgment are not the same. Spirit is not always thought. But in the everyday business of living, secular or otherwise, these variant aspects of personality find inseparable expression in a thousand ways. They cannot be altogether parted in law more than in life.

To make accommodation between these freedoms and an exercise of state authority always is delicate. It hardly could be more so than in such a clash as this case presents. On one side is the obviously earnest claim for freedom of conscience and religious practice. With it is allied the parent's claim to authority in her own household and in the rearing of her children. The parent's conflict with the state over control of the child and his training is serious enough when only secular matters are concerned. It becomes the more so when an element of religious conviction enters. Against these sacred private interests, basic in a democracy, stand the interests of society to protect the welfare of children, and the state's assertion of authority to that end, made here in a manner conceded valid if only secular things were involved. The last is no mere corporate concern of official authority. It is the interest of youth itself, and of the whole community, that children be both safeguarded from abuses and given opportunities for growth into free and independent well-developed men and citizens. Between contrary pulls of such weight, the safest and most objective recourse is to the lines already marked out, not precisely but for guides, in narrowing the no man's land where this battle has gone on.

The rights of children to exercise their religion, and of parents to give them religious training and to encourage them in the practice of religious belief, as against preponderant sentiment and assertion of state power voicing it, have had recognition here, most recently in *West Virginia State Board of Education v. Barnette*, 319 U.S. 624 (1943). Previously in *Pierce v. Society of Sisters*, 268 U.S. 510 (1925), this Court had sustained the parent's authority to provide religious with secular schooling, and the child's right to receive it, as against the state's requirement of attendance at public schools. And in *Meyer v. Nebraska*, 262 U.S. 390 (1923), children's rights to receive teaching in languages other than the nation's common tongue were guarded against the state's encroachment. It is cardinal with us that the custody, care and nurture of the child reside first in the parents, whose primary function and freedom include preparation for obligations the state can neither supply nor hinder. *Pierce v. Society of Sisters, supra.* And it is in recognition of this that these decisions have respected the private realm of family life which the state cannot enter.

But the family itself is not beyond regulation in the public interest, as against a claim of religious liberty. *Reynolds v. United States*, 98 U.S. 145 (1878); *Davis v. Beason*, 133 U.S. 333 (1890). And neither rights of religion nor rights of parenthood are beyond limitation. Acting to guard the general interest in youth's well being, the state as parens patriae may restrict the parent's control by requiring school attendance, regulating or prohibiting the child's labor, and in many other ways. Its authority is not nullified merely because the parent grounds his claim to control the child's course of conduct on religion or conscience. Thus, he cannot claim freedom from compulsory vaccination for the child more than for himself on religious grounds. The right to practice religion freely does not include liberty to expose the community or the child to communicable disease or the latter to ill health or death. The catalogue need not be lengthened. It is sufficient to show what indeed appellant hardly disputes, that the state has a wide range of power for limiting parental freedom and authority in things affecting the child's welfare; and that this includes, to some extent, matters of conscience and religious conviction.

But it is said the state cannot do so here. This, first, because when state action impinges upon a claimed religious freedom, it must fall unless shown to be necessary for or conducive to the child's protection against some clear and present danger; and, it is added, there was no such showing here. The child's presence on the street, with her guardian, distributing or offering to distribute the magazines, it is urged, was in no way harmful to her, nor in any event more so than the presence of many other children at the same time and place, engaged in shopping and other activities not prohibited. Accordingly, in view of the preferred position the freedoms of the First Article occupy, the statute in its present application must fall. It cannot be sustained by any presumption of validity. And, finally, it is said, the statute is, as to children, an absolute prohibition, not merely a reasonable regulation, of the denounced activity.

Concededly a statute or ordinance identical in terms with Section 69, except that it is applicable to adults or all persons generally, would be invalid. But the mere fact a state could not wholly prohibit this form of adult activity, whether characterized locally as a 'sale' or otherwise, does not mean it cannot do so for children. Such a conclusion granted would mean that a state could impose no greater limitation upon child labor than upon adult labor. Or, if an adult were free to enter dance halls, saloons, and disreputable places generally, in order to discharge his conceived religious duty to admonish or dissuade persons from frequenting such places, so would be a child with similar convictions and objectives, if not alone then in the parent's company, against the state's command.

The state's authority over children's activities is broader than over like actions of adults. This is peculiarly true of public activities and an [sic] matters of employment. A democratic society rests, for its continuance, upon the healthy, well-rounded growth of young people into full maturity as citizens, with all that implies. It may secure this against impeding restraints and dangers, within a broad range of selection. Among evils most appropriate for such action are the crippling effects of child employment, more especially in public places, and the possible harms arising from other activities subject to all the diverse influences of the street. It is too late now to doubt that legislation appropriately designed to reach such evils is within the state's police power, whether against the parents claim to control of the child or one that religious scruples dictate contrary action.

It is true children have rights, in common with older people, in the primary use of highways. But even in such use streets afford dangers for them not affecting adults. And in other uses, whether in work or in other things, this difference may be magnified. This is so not only when children are unaccompanied but certainly to some extent when they are with their parents. What may be wholly permissible for adults therefore may not be so for children, either with or without their parents' presence.

Street preaching, whether oral or by handing out literature, is not the primary use of the highway, even for adults. While for them it cannot be wholly prohibited, it can be regulated within reasonable limits in accommodation to the primary and other incidental uses. But, for obvious reasons, notwithstanding appellant's contrary view, the validity of such a prohibition applied to children not accompanied by an older person hardly would seem open to question. The case reduces itself therefore to the question whether the presence of the child's guardian puts a limit to the state's power. That fact may lessen the likelihood that some evils the legislation seeks to avert will occur. But it cannot forestall all of them. The zealous though lawful exercise of the right to engage in propagandizing the community, whether in religious, political or other matters, may and at times does create situations difficult enough for adults to cope with and wholly inappropriate for children, especially of tender years, to face. Other harmful possibilities could be stated, of emotional excitement and psychological or physical injury. Parents may be free to become martyrs themselves. But it does not follow they are free, in identical circumstances, to make martyrs of their children before they have reached the age of full and legal discretion when they can make that choice for themselves. Massachusetts has determined that an absolute prohibition, though one limited to streets and public places and to the incidental uses proscribed, is necessary to accomplish its legitimate objectives. Its power to attain them is broad enough to reach these peripheral instances in which the parent's supervision may reduce but cannot eliminate entirely the ill effects of the prohibited conduct. We think that with reference to the public proclaiming of religion, upon the streets and in other similar public places, the power of the state to control the conduct of children reaches beyond the scope of its authority over adults, as is true in the case of other freedoms, and the rightful boundary of its power has not been crossed in this case.

In so ruling we dispose also of appellant's argument founded upon denial of equal protection. It falls with that based on denial of religious freedom, since in this instance the one is but another phrasing of the other. Shortly, the contention is that the street, for Jehovah's Witnesses and their children, is their church, since their conviction makes it so; and to deny them access to it for religious purposes as was done here has the same effect as excluding altar boys, youthful choristers, and other children from the edifices in which they practice their religious beliefs and worship. The argument hardly needs more than statement, after what has been said, to refute it. However Jehovah's Witnesses may conceive them, the public highways have not become their religious property merely by their assertion. And there is no denial of equal protection in excluding their children from doing there what no other children may do....

The judgment is affirmed.

Roe v. Wade

410 U.S. 113 (1973)

Justice O'Connor delivered the opinion of the court.

...

We forthwith acknowledge our awareness of the sensitive and emotional nature of the abortion controversy, of the vigorous opposing views, even among physicians, and of the deep and seemingly absolute convictions that the subject inspires. One's philosophy, one's experiences, one's exposure to the raw edges of human existence, one's religious training, one's attitudes toward life and family and their values, and the moral standards one establishes and seeks to observe, are all likely to influence and to color one's thinking and conclusions about abortion. In addition, population growth, pollution, poverty, and racial overtones tend to complicate and not to simplify the problem....

Jane Roe, a single woman who was residing in Dallas County, Texas, instituted this federal action in March 1970 against the District Attorney of the county. She sought declaratory judgment that the Texas criminal abortion statutes were unconstitutional on their face, and an injunction restraining the defendants from enforcing the statutes.... She claimed that the Texas statutes were unconstitutionally vague and that they abridged her right of personal privacy, protected by the First, Fourth, Fifth, Ninth, and Fourteenth Amendments....

It perhaps is not generally appreciated that the restrictive criminal abortion laws in effect in a majority of states today are of relatively recent vintage. Those laws, generally proscribing abortion or its attempt at any time during pregnancy except when necessary to preserve the pregnant woman's life, are not of ancient or even of common-law origin. Instead, they derived from statutory changes effected, for the most part, in the latter half of the 19th century....

Three reasons have been advanced to explain historically the enactment of criminal abortion laws in the 19th century and to justify their continued existence.

It has been argued occasionally that these laws were the product of a Victorian social concern to discourage illicit sexual conduct. Texas, however, does not advance this justification in the present case, and it appears that no court or commentator has taken the argument seriously. The appellants and amici contend, moreover, that this is not a proper state purpose at all and suggest that, if it were, the Texas statutes are overbroad in protecting it since the law fails to distinguish between married and unwed mothers.

A second reason is concerned with abortion as a medical procedure. When most criminal abortion laws were first enacted, the procedure was a hazardous one for the woman. This was particularly true prior to the development of antisepsis. Antiseptic techniques, of course, were based on discoveries by Lister, Pasteur, and others first announced in 1867, but were not generally accepted and employed until about the turn of the century. Abortion mortality was high. Even after 1900, and perhaps until as late as the development of antibiotics in the 1940's, standard modern techniques such as dilation and curettage were not nearly so safe as they are today. Thus, it has been argued that a State's real concern in enacting a criminal abortion law was to protect the pregnant woman, that is, to restrain her from submitting to a procedure that placed her life in serious jeopardy.

Modern medical techniques have altered this situation. Appellants and various amici refer to medical data indicating that abortion in early pregnancy, that is, prior to the end of the first trimester, although not without its risk, is now relatively safe. Mortality rates for women undergoing early abortions, where the procedure is legal, appear to be as low as or lower than the rates for normal childbirth. Consequently, any interest of the State in protecting the woman from an inherently hazardous procedure, except when it would be equally dangerous for her to forgo it, has largely disappeared. Of course, important state interests in the areas of health and medical standards do remain. The State has a legitimate interest in seeing to it that abortion, like any other medical procedure, is performed under circumstances that insure maximum safety for the patient. This interest obviously extends at least to the performing physician and his staff, to the facilities involved, to the availability of after-care, and to adequate provision for any complication or emergency that might arise. The prevalence of high mortality rates at illegal 'abortion mills' strengthens, rather than weakens, the State's interest in regulating the conditions under which abortions are performed. Moreover, the risk to the woman increases as her pregnancy continues. Thus, the State retains a definite interest in protecting the woman's own health and safety when an abortion is proposed at a late stage of pregnancy,

The third reason is the State's interest—some phrase it in terms of duty—in protecting prenatal life. Some of the argument for this justification rests on the theory that a new human life is present from the moment of conception. The State's interest and general obligation to protect life then extends, it is argued, to prenatal life. Only when the life of the pregnant mother herself is at stake, balanced against the life she carries within her, should the interest of the embryo or fetus not prevail. Logically, of course, a legitimate state interest in this area need not stand or fall on acceptance of the belief that life begins at conception or at some other point prior to life birth. In assessing the State's interest, recognition may be given to the less rigid claim that as long as at least potential life is involved, the State may assert interests beyond the protection of the pregnant woman alone.

Parties challenging state abortion laws have sharply disputed in some courts the contention that a purpose of these laws, when enacted, was to protect prenatal life. Pointing to the absence of legislative history to support the contention, they claim that most state laws were designed solely to protect the woman. Because medical advances have lessened this concern, at least with respect to abortion in early pregnancy, they argue that with respect to such abortions the laws can no longer be justified by any state interest. There is some scholarly support for this view of original purpose. The few state courts called upon to interpret their laws in the late 19th and early 20th centuries did focus on the State's interest in protecting the woman's health rather than in preserving the embryo and fetus. Proponents of this view point out that in many States, including Texas, by statute or judicial interpretation, the pregnant woman herself could not be prosecuted for self-abortion or for cooperating in an abortion performed upon her by another. They claim that adoption of the 'quickening' distinction through received common law and state statutes tacitly recognizes the greater health hazards inherent in late abortion and impliedly repudiates the theory that life begins at conception.

It is with these interests, and the weight to be attached to them, that this case is concerned.

The Constitution does not explicitly mention any right of privacy. In a line of decisions, however, going back perhaps as far as *Union Pacific R. Co. v. Botsford*, 141 U.S.

250, 251 (1891), the Court has recognized that a right of personal privacy, or a guarantee of certain areas or zones of privacy, does exist under the Constitution. In varying contexts, the Court or individual Justices have, indeed, found at least the roots of that right in the First Amendment, in the Fourth and Fifth Amendments, in the penumbras of the Bill of Rights, in the Ninth Amendment, or in the concept of liberty guaranteed by the first section of the Fourteenth Amendment. These decisions make it clear that only personal rights that can be deemed 'fundamental' or 'implicit in the concept of ordered liberty,' are included in this guarantee of personal privacy. They also make it clear that the right has some extension to activities relating to marriage, procreation, contraception, family relationships, and child rearing and education.

This right of privacy, whether it is founded in the Fourteenth Amendment's concept of personal liberty and restrictions upon state action, as we feel it is, or, as the District Court determined, in the Ninth Amendment's reservation of rights to the people, is broad enough to encompass a woman's decision whether or not to terminate her pregnancy. The detriment that the State would impose upon the pregnant woman by denying this choice altogether is apparent. Specific and direct harm medically diagnosable even in early pregnancy may be involved. Maternity, or additional offspring, may force upon the woman a distressful life and future. Psychological harm may be imminent. Mental and physical health may be taxed by child care. There is also the distress, for all concerned, associated with the unwanted child, and there is the problem of bringing a child into a family already unable, psychologically and otherwise, to care for it. In other cases, as in this one, the additional difficulties and continuing stigma of unwed motherhood may be involved. All these are factors the woman and her responsible physician necessarily will consider in consultation.

On the basis of elements such as these, appellant and some amici argue that the woman's right is absolute and that she is entitled to terminate her pregnancy at whatever time, in whatever way, and for whatever reason she alone chooses. With this we do not agree. Appellant's arguments that Texas either has no valid interest at all in regulating the abortion decision, or no interest strong enough to support any limitation upon the woman's sole determination, are unpersuasive. The Court's decisions recognizing a right of privacy also acknowledge that some state regulation in areas protected by that right is appropriate. As noted above, a State may properly assert important interests in safeguarding health, in maintaining medical standards, and in protecting potential life. At some point in pregnancy, these respective interests become sufficiently compelling to sustain regulation of the factors that govern the abortion decision. The privacy right involved, therefore, cannot be said to be absolute. In fact, it is not clear to us that the claim asserted by some amici that one has an unlimited right to do with one's body as one pleases bears a close relationship to the right of privacy previously articulated in the Court's decisions. The Court has refused to recognize an unlimited right of this kind in the past. *Jacobson v. Massachusetts*, 197 U.S. 11 (1905) (vaccination); *Buck v. Bell*, 274 U.S. 200 (1927) (sterilization).

We, therefore, conclude that the right of personal privacy includes the abortion decision, but that this right is not unqualified and must be considered against important state interests in regulation....

Where certain 'fundamental rights' are involved, the Court has held that regulation limiting these rights may be justified only by a 'compelling state interest, and that legislative enactments must be narrowly drawn to express only the legitimate state interests at stake.

In the recent abortion cases, cited above, courts have recognized these principles. Those striking down state laws have generally scrutinized the State's interests in protecting health and potential life, and have concluded that neither interest justified broad limitations on the reasons for which a physician and his pregnant patient might decide that she should have an abortion in the early stages of pregnancy. Courts sustaining state laws have held that the State's determinations to protect health or prenatal life are dominant and constitutionally justifiable....

The pregnant woman cannot be isolated in her privacy. She carries an embryo and, later, a fetus, if one accepts the medical definitions of the developing young in the human uterus. See Dorland's Illustrated Medical Dictionary 478–479, 547 (24th ed. 1965). The situation therefore is inherently different from marital intimacy, or bedroom possession of obscene material, or marriage, or procreation, or education, with which Eisenstadt and Griswold, Stanley, Loving, Skinner and Pierce and Meyer were respectively concerned. As we have intimated above, it is reasonable and appropriate for a State to decide that at some point in time another interest, that of health of the mother or that of potential human life, becomes significantly involved. The woman's privacy is no longer sole and any right of privacy she possesses must be measured accordingly.

Texas urges that, apart from the Fourteenth Amendment, life begins at conception and is present throughout pregnancy, and that, therefore, the State has a compelling interest in protecting that life from and after conception. We need not resolve the difficult question of when life begins. When those trained in the respective disciplines of medicine, philosophy, and theology are unable to arrive at any consensus, the judiciary, at this point in the development of man's knowledge, is not in a position to speculate as to the answer.

It should be sufficient to note briefly the wide divergence of thinking on this most sensitive and difficult question. There has always been strong support for the view that life does not begin until live birth. This was the belief of the Stoics. It appears to be the predominant, though not the unanimous, attitude of the Jewish faith. It may be taken to represent also the position of a large segment of the Protestant community, insofar as that can be ascertained; organized groups that have taken a formal position on the abortion issue have generally regarded abortion as a matter for the conscience of the individual and her family. As we have noted, the common law found greater significance in quickening. Physicians and their scientific colleagues have regarded that event with less interest and have tended to focus either upon conception, upon live birth, or upon the interim point at which the fetus becomes 'viable,' that is, potentially able to live outside the mother's womb, albeit with artificial aid. Viability is usually placed at about seven months (28 weeks) but may occur earlier, even at 24 weeks. The Aristotelian theory of 'mediate animation,' that held sway throughout the Middle Ages and the Renaissance in Europe, continued to be official Roman Catholic dogma until the 19th century, despite opposition to this 'ensoulment' theory from those in the Church who would recognize the existence of life from the moment of conception. The latter is now, of course, the official belief of the Catholic Church. As one brief amicus discloses, this is a view strongly held by many non-Catholics as well, and by many physicians. Substantial problems for precise definition of this view are posed, however, by new embryological data that purport to indicate that conception is a 'process' over time, rather than an event, and by new medical techniques such as menstrual extraction, the 'morning-after' pill, implantation of embryos, artificial insemination, and even artificial wombs.

In areas other than criminal abortion, the law has been reluctant to endorse any theory that life, as we recognize it, begins before life birth or to accord legal rights to the unborn except in narrowly defined situations and except when the rights are contingent upon life birth. For example, the traditional rule of tort law denied recovery for prenatal injuries even though the child was born alive. That rule has been changed in almost every jurisdiction. In most States, recovery is said to be permitted only if the fetus was viable, or at least quick, when the injuries were sustained, though few courts have squarely so held. In a recent development, generally opposed by the commentators, some States permit the parents of a stillborn child to maintain an action for wrongful death because of prenatal injuries. Such an action, however, would appear to be one to vindicate the parents' interest and is thus consistent with the view that the fetus, at most, represents only the potentiality of life. Similarly, unborn children have been recognized as acquiring rights or interests by way of inheritance or other devolution of property, and have been represented by guardians ad litem. Perfection of the interests involved, again, has generally been contingent upon live birth. In short, the unborn have never been recognized in the law as persons in the whole sense....

Jefferson v. Spaulding

274 S.E. 2d 457 (Ga. 1981)

PER CURIUM.

On Thursday, January 22, 1981, the Griffin Spalding County Hospital Authority petitioned the Superior Court of Butts County, as a court of equity, for an order authorizing it to perform a caesarean section and any necessary blood transfusions upon the defendant, an out-patient resident of Butts County, in the event she presented herself to the hospital for delivery of her unborn child, which was due on or about Monday, January 26. The superior court conducted an emergency hearing on Thursday, January 22, and entered the following order:

> ...
>
> "Defendant is in the thirty-ninth week of pregnancy. In the past few weeks she has presented herself to Griffin Spalding County Hospital for pre-natal care. The examining physician has found and defendant has been advised that she has a complete placenta previa; that the afterbirth is between the baby and the birth canal; that it is virtually impossible that this condition will correct itself prior to delivery; and that it is a 99% certainty that the child cannot survive natural childbirth (vaginal delivery). The chances of defendant surviving vaginal delivery are no better than 50%.
>
> "The examining physician is of the opinion that a delivery by caesarean section prior to labor beginning would have an almost 100% chance of preserving the life of the child, along with that of defendant.
>
> "On the basis of religious beliefs, defendant has advised the Hospital that she does not need surgical removal of the child and will not submit to it. Further, she refuses to take any transfusion of blood.
>
> "The Hospital is required by its own policies to treat any patient seeking emergency treatment. It seeks authority of the Court to administer medical treatment to defendant to save the life of herself and her unborn child.
>
> "The child is, as a matter of fact, viable and fully capable of sustaining life independent of the mother (defendant). The issue is whether this unborn child has any legal right to the protection of the Court.
>
> "To abort this child would be a criminal offense in Georgia. Ga.Code Ann. ss 26-1201; 26-1202. A viable unborn child has the right under the U. S. Consti-

> tution to the protection of the State through such statutes prohibiting the arbitrary termination of the life of an unborn fetus. *Roe v. Wade*, 410 U.S. 113 (1973).
>
> "Because the life of defendant and of the unborn child are, at the moment, inseparable, the Court deems it appropriate to infringe upon the wishes of the mother to the extent it is necessary to give the child an opportunity to live.
>
> "Accordingly, the plaintiff hospitals are hereby authorized to administer to defendant all medical procedures deemed necessary by the attending physician to preserve the life of defendant's unborn child. This authority shall be effective only if defendant voluntarily seeks admission to either of plaintiff's hospitals for the emergency delivery of the child.
>
> "The Court has been requested to order defendant to submit to surgery before the natural childbirth process (labor) begins. The Court is reluctant to grant this request and does not do so at this time. However, should some agency of the State seek such relief through intervention in this suit or in a separate proceeding, the Court will promptly consider such request."

On Friday, January 23, the Georgia Department of Human Resources, acting through the Butts County Department of Family and Children Services, petitioned the Juvenile Court of Butts County for temporary custody of the unborn child, alleging that the child was a deprived child without proper parental care necessary for his or her physical health, and praying for an order requiring the mother to submit to a caesarean section. After appointing counsel for the parents and for the child, the court conducted a joint hearing in both the superior court and juvenile court cases and entered the following order on the afternoon of January 23:

> ...
>
> "This morning, the Georgia Department of Human Resources, acting through the Butts County Department of Family and Children Services, filed a complaint in the Juvenile Court of Butts County alleging deprivation and seeking temporary custody of Jessie Mae Jefferson's unborn child.
>
> "Because of the unusual nature of the relief sought in these cases and because the Juvenile Court of Butts County may not have the authority needed effectively to grant the relief sought, the Court consolidates these cases and renders the following judgment both as a Juvenile Court and under the broad powers of the Superior Court of Butts County. The Court readopts its findings contained in the Order dated January 22, 1981.
>
> "At the proceeding held today, Jessie Mae Jefferson and her husband, John W. Jefferson were present and represented by counsel, Hugh Glidewell, Jr. Richard Milam, Attorney at Law, represented the interests of the unborn child.
>
> "Based on the evidence presented, the Court finds that Jessie Mae Jefferson is due to begin labor at any moment. There is a 99 to 100 percent certainty that the unborn child will die if she attempts to have the child by vaginal delivery. There is a 99 to 100 percent chance that the child will live if the baby is delivered by Caesarean section prior to the beginning of labor. There is a 50 percent chance that Mrs. Jefferson herself will die if vaginal delivery is attempted. There is an almost 100 percent chance that Mrs. Jefferson will survive if a delivery by Caesarean section is done prior to the beginning of labor. The Court

finds that as a matter of fact the child is a human being fully capable of sustaining life independent of the mother.

"Mrs. Jefferson and her husband have refused and continue to refuse to give consent to a Caesarean section. This refusal is based entirely on the religious beliefs of Mr. and Mrs. Jefferson. They are of the view that the Lord has healed her body and that whatever happens to the child will be the Lord's will.

"Based on these findings, the Court concludes and finds as a matter of law that this child is a viable human being and entitled to the protection of the Juvenile Court Code of Georgia. The Court concludes that this child is without the proper parental care and subsistence necessary for his or her physical life and health.

"Temporary custody of the unborn child is hereby granted to the State of Georgia Department of Human Resources and the Butts County Department of Family and Children Services. The Department shall have full authority to make all decisions, including giving consent to the surgical delivery appertaining to the birth of this child. The temporary custody of the Department shall terminate when the child has been successfully brought from its mother's body into the world or until the child dies, whichever shall happen.

"Because of the unique nature of these cases, the powers of the Superior Court of Butts County are invoked and the defendant, Jessie Mae Jefferson, is hereby Ordered to submit to a sonogram (ultra sound) at the Griffin Spalding County Hospital or some other place which may be chosen by her where such procedure can be given. Should said sonogram indicate to the attending physician that the complete placenta previa is still blocking the child's passage into this world, Jessie Mae Jefferson, is Ordered to submit to a Caesarean section and related procedures considered necessary by the attending physician to sustain the life of this child.

"The Court finds that the State has an interest in the life of this unborn, living human being. The Court finds that the intrusion involved into the life of Jessie Mae Jefferson and her husband, John W. Jefferson, is outweighed by the duty of the State to protect a living, unborn human being from meeting his or her death before being given the opportunity to live." ...

Washington v. Harper

494 U.S. 210 (1990)

Justice Kennedy delivered the opinion of the Court.

The central question before us is whether a judicial hearing is required before the State may treat a mentally ill prisoner with antipsychotic drugs against his will. Resolution of the case requires us to discuss the protections afforded the prisoner under the Due Process Clause of the Fourteenth Amendment.

Respondent Walter Harper was sentenced to prison in 1976 for robbery. From 1976 to 1980, he was incarcerated at the Washington State Penitentiary. Most of that time, respondent was housed in the prison's mental health unit, where he consented to the administration of antipsychotic drugs. Antipsychotic drugs, sometimes called "neuroleptics" or "psychotropic drugs," are medications commonly used in treating mental disorders such as schizophrenia. As found by the trial court, the effect of these and similar drugs is to alter the chemical balance in the brain, the desired result being that the medication will assist the patient in organizing his or her thought processes and regaining a rational state of mind.

Respondent was paroled in 1980 on the condition that he participate in psychiatric treatment. While on parole, he continued to receive treatment at the psychiatric ward at Harborview Medical Center in Seattle, Washington, and was later sent to Western State Hospital pursuant to a civil commitment order. In December 1981, the State revoked respondent's parole after he assaulted two nurses at a hospital in Seattle.

Upon his return to prison, respondent was sent to the Special Offender Center (SOC or Center), a 144-bed correctional institute established by the Washington Department of Corrections to diagnose and treat convicted felons with serious mental disorders. At the Center, psychiatrists first diagnosed respondent as suffering from a manic-depressive disorder. At first, respondent gave voluntary consent to treatment, including the administration of antipsychotic medications. In November 1982, he refused to continue taking the prescribed medications. The treating physician then sought to medicate respondent over his objections, pursuant to SOC Policy 600.30....

As a matter of state law, the Policy itself undoubtedly confers upon respondent a right to be free from the arbitrary administration of antipsychotic medication. By permitting a psychiatrist to treat an inmate with antipsychotic drugs against his wishes only if he is found to be (1) mentally ill and (2) gravely disabled or dangerous, the Policy creates a justifiable expectation on the part of the inmate that the drugs will not be administered unless those conditions exist.

We have no doubt that, in addition to the liberty interest created by the State's Policy, respondent possesses a significant liberty interest in avoiding the unwanted administration of antipsychotic drugs under the Due Process Clause of the Fourteenth Amendment. Upon full consideration of the state administrative scheme, however, we find that the Due Process Clause confers upon respondent no greater right than that recognized under state law.

Respondent contends that the State, under the mandate of the Due Process Clause, may not override his choice to refuse antipsychotic drugs unless he has been found to be incompetent, and then only if the fact finder makes a substituted judgment that he, if competent, would consent to drug treatment. We disagree. The extent of a prisoner's right under the Clause to avoid the unwanted administration of antipsychotic drugs must be defined in the context of the inmate's confinement. The Policy under review requires the State to establish, by a medical finding, that a mental disorder exists which is likely to cause harm if not treated. Moreover, the fact that the medication must first be prescribed by a psychiatrist, and then approved by a reviewing psychiatrist, ensures that the treatment in question will be ordered only if it is in the prisoner's medical interests, given the legitimate needs of his institutional confinement. These standards, which recognize both the prisoner's medical interests and the State's interests, meet the demands of the Due Process Clause....

Applying these factors to the regulation before us, we conclude that the Policy comports with constitutional requirements. There can be little doubt as to both the legitimacy and the importance of the governmental interest presented here. There are few cases in which the State's interest in combating the danger posed by a person to both himself and others is greater than in a prison environment, which, "by definition," is made up of persons with "a demonstrated proclivity for antisocial criminal, and often violent, conduct." We confront here the State's obligations, not just its interests. The State has undertaken the obligation to provide prisoners with medical treatment consistent not only with their own medical interests, but also with the needs of the institution. Prison administrators have not only an interest in ensuring the safety of prison staffs and administrative personnel, but also the duty to take reasonable measures for the prisoners' own safety. These concerns have added weight when a penal institution, like the SOC is restricted to inmates with mental illnesses. Where an inmate's mental disability is the root cause of the threat he poses to the inmate population, the State's interest in decreasing the danger to others necessarily encompasses an interest in providing him with medical treatment for his illness.

SOC Policy 600.30 is a rational means of furthering the State's legitimate objectives. Its exclusive application is to inmates who are mentally ill and who, as a result of their illness, are gravely disabled or represent a significant danger to themselves or others. The drugs may be administered for no purpose other than treatment, and only under the direction of a licensed psychiatrist. There is considerable debate over the potential side effects of antipsychotic medications, but there is little dispute in the psychiatric profession that proper use of the drugs is one of the most effective means of treating and controlling a mental illness likely to cause violent behavior....

We hold that, given the requirements of the prison environment, the Due Process Clause permits the State to treat a prison inmate who has a serious mental illness with antipsychotic drugs against his will, if the inmate is dangerous to himself or others and the treatment is in the inmate's medical interest. Policy 600.30 comports with these requirements; we therefore reject respondent's contention that its substantive standards are deficient under the Constitution.

Having determined that state law recognizes a liberty interest, also protected by the Due Process Clause, which permits refusal of antipsychotic drugs unless certain preconditions are met, we address next what procedural protections are necessary to ensure that the decision to medicate an inmate against his will is neither arbitrary nor erroneous under the standards we have discussed above. The Washington Supreme Court held that a full judicial hearing, with the inmate being represented by counsel, was required by the Due Process Clause before the State could administer antipsychotic drugs to him against his will. In addition, the court held that the State must justify the authorization of involuntary administration of antipsychotic drugs by "clear, cogent, and convincing" evidence. We hold that the administrative hearing procedures set by the SOC Policy do comport with procedural due process, and conclude that the Washington Supreme Court erred in requiring a judicial hearing as a prerequisite for the involuntary treatment of prison inmates.

The primary point of disagreement between the parties is whether due process requires a judicial decision maker. As written, the Policy requires that the decision whether to medicate an inmate against his will be made by a hearing committee composed of a psychiatrist, a psychologist, and the Center's Associate Superintendent. None of the committee members may be involved, at the time of the hearing, in the inmate's treatment or diagnosis; members are not disqualified from sitting on the committee, however, if they have treated or diagnosed the inmate in the past. The committee's decision is subject to review by the Superintendent; if the inmate so desires, he may seek judicial review of the decision in a state court. Respondent contends that only a court should make the decision to medicate an inmate against his will....

Respondent's interest in avoiding the unwarranted administration of antipsychotic drugs is not insubstantial. The forcible injection of medication into a nonconsenting person's body represents a substantial interference with that person's liberty....

Notwithstanding the risks that are involved, we conclude that an inmate's interests are adequately protected, and perhaps better served, by allowing the decision to medicate to be made by medical professionals rather than a judge.... Respondent's own history of accepting and then refusing drug treatment illustrates the point. We cannot make the facile assumption that the patient's intentions, or a substituted judgment approximating those intentions, can be determined in a single judicial hearing apart from the realities of frequent and ongoing clinical observation by medical professionals.... Nor can we ignore the fact that requiring judicial hearings will divert scarce prison resources, both money and the staff's time, from the care and treatment of mentally ill inmates.

Under Policy 600.30, the decision maker is asked to review a medical treatment decision made by a medical professional. That review requires two medical inquiries: first, whether the inmate suffers from a "mental disorder"; and second, whether, as a result of that disorder, he is dangerous to himself, others, or their property. Under the Policy, the hearing committee reviews on a regular basis the staff's choice of both the type and dosage of drug to be administered, and can order appropriate changes. The risks associated with antipsychotic drugs are for the most part medical ones, best assessed by medical professionals. A State may conclude with good reason that a judicial hearing will not be as effective, as continuous, or as probing as administrative review using medical decision makers. We hold that due process requires no more.

A State's attempt to set a high standard for determining when involuntary medication with antipsychotic drugs is permitted cannot withstand challenge if there are no procedural safeguards to ensure the prisoner's interests are taken into account. Adequate procedures exist here. In particular, independence of the decision maker is addressed to our satisfaction by these procedures. None of the hearing committee members may be involved in the inmate's current treatment or diagnosis. The record before us, moreover, is limited to the hearings given to respondent. There is no indication that any institutional biases affected or altered the decision to medicate respondent against his will. The trial court made specific findings that respondent has a history of assaultive behavior which his doctors attribute to his mental disease, and that all of the Policy's requirements were met. The court found also that the medical treatment provided to respondent, including the administration of antipsychotic drugs, was at all times consistent "with the degree of care, skill, and learning expected of a reasonably prudent psychiatrist in the State of Washington, acting in the same or similar circumstances." In the absence of record evidence to the contrary, we are not willing to presume that members of the staff lack the necessary independence to provide an inmate with a full and fair hearing in accordance with the Policy. In previous cases involving medical decisions implicating similar liberty interests, we have approved use of similar internal decision makers. As we reasoned in *Vitek*, it is only by permitting persons connected with the institution to make these decisions that courts are able to avoid "unnecessary intrusion into either medical or correctional judgments."

Respondent contends that the Policy is nonetheless deficient because it does not allow him to be represented by counsel. We disagree. "[I]t is less than crystal clear why lawyers must be available to identify possible errors in medical judgment." *Walters v. National Association of Radiation Survivors*, 473 U.S. 305, 330 (1985). Given the nature of the decision to be made, we conclude that the provision of an independent lay adviser who understands the psychiatric issues involved is sufficient protection.

In sum, we hold that the regulation before us is permissible under the Constitution. It is an accommodation between an inmate's liberty interest in avoiding the forced administration of antipsychotic drugs and the State's interests in providing appropriate medical treatment to reduce the danger that an inmate suffering from a serious mental disorder represents to himself or others. The Due Process Clause does require certain essential procedural protections, all of which are provided by the regulation before us. The judgment of the Washington Supreme Court is reversed, and the case is remanded for further proceedings not inconsistent with this opinion.

DeShaney v. Winnebago

489 U.S. 189 (1989)

CHIEF JUSTICE REHNQUIST delivered the opinion of the Court.

Petitioner is a boy who was beaten and permanently injured by his father, with whom he lived. Respondents are social workers and other local officials who received complaints that petitioner was being abused by his father and had reason to believe that this was the case, but nonetheless did not act to remove petitioner from his father's custody. Petitioner sued respondents claiming that their failure to act deprived him of his liberty in violation of the Due Process Clause of the Fourteenth Amendment to the United States Constitution. We hold that it did not. The facts of this case are undeniably tragic. Petitioner Joshua DeShaney was born in 1979. In 1980, a Wyoming court granted his parents a divorce and awarded custody of Joshua to his father, Randy DeShaney. The father shortly thereafter moved to Neenah, a city located in Winnebago County, Wisconsin, taking the infant Joshua with him. There he entered into a second marriage, which also ended in divorce.

The Winnebago County authorities first learned that Joshua DeShaney might be a victim of child abuse in January 1982, when his father's second wife complained to the police, at the time of their divorce, that he had previously "hit the boy causing marks and [was] a prime case for child abuse." The Winnebago County Department of Social Services (DSS) interviewed the father, but he denied the accusations, and DSS did not pursue them further. In January 1983, Joshua was admitted to a local hospital with multiple bruises and abrasions. The examining physician suspected child abuse and notified DSS, which immediately obtained an order from a Wisconsin juvenile court placing Joshua in the temporary custody of the hospital. Three days later, the county convened an ad hoc "Child Protection Team"—consisting of a pediatrician, a psychologist, a police detective, the county's lawyer, several DSS caseworkers, and various hospital personnel—to consider Joshua's situation. At this meeting, the Team decided that there was insufficient evidence of child abuse to retain Joshua in the custody of the court. The Team did, however, decide to recommend several measures to protect Joshua, including enrolling him in a preschool program, providing his father with certain counselling services, and encouraging his father's girlfriend to move out of the home. Randy DeShaney entered into a voluntary agreement with DSS in which he promised to cooperate with them in accomplishing these goals.

Based on the recommendation of the Child Protection Team, the juvenile court dismissed the child protection case and returned Joshua to the custody of his father. A month later, emergency room personnel called the DSS caseworker handling Joshua's case to report that he had once again been treated for suspicious injuries. The caseworker concluded that there was no basis for action. For the next six months, the caseworker made monthly visits to the DeShaney home, during which she observed a number of suspicious injuries on Joshua's head; she also noticed that he had not been enrolled in school, and that the girlfriend had not moved out. The caseworker dutifully recorded these incidents in her files, along with her continuing suspicions that someone in the DeShaney household was physically abusing Joshua, but she did nothing more. In

November 1983, the emergency room notified DSS that Joshua had been treated once again for injuries that they believed to be caused by child abuse. On the caseworker's next two visits to the DeShaney home, she was told that Joshua was too ill to see her. Still DSS took no action.

In March 1984, Randy DeShaney beat 4-year-old Joshua so severely that he fell into a life-threatening coma. Emergency brain surgery revealed a series of hemorrhages caused by traumatic injuries to the head inflicted over a long period of time. Joshua did not die, but he suffered brain damage so severe that he is expected to spend the rest of his life confined to an institution for the profoundly retarded. Randy DeShaney was subsequently tried and convicted of child abuse.

Joshua and his mother brought this action under 42 U.S.C. sec. 1983 in the United States District Court for the Eastern District of Wisconsin against respondents Winnebago County, DSS, and various individual employees of DSS. The complaint alleged that respondents had deprived Joshua of his liberty without due process of law, in violation of his rights under the Fourteenth Amendment, by failing to intervene to protect him against a risk of violence at his father's hands of which they knew or should have known. The District Court granted summary judgment for respondents....

The Due Process Clause of the Fourteenth Amendment provides that "[n]o State shall ... deprive any person of life, liberty, or property, without due process of law." Petitioners contend that the State deprived Joshua of his liberty interest in "free[dom] from ... unjustified intrusions on personal security," by failing to provide him with adequate protection against his father's violence. The claim is one invoking the substantive rather than the procedural component of the Due Process Clause; petitioners do not claim that the State denied Joshua protection without according him appropriate procedural safeguards, but that it was categorically obligated to protect him in these circumstances.

But nothing in the language of the Due Process Clause itself requires the State to protect the life, liberty, and property of its citizens against invasion by private actors. The Clause is phrased as a limitation on the State's power to act, not as a guarantee of certain minimal levels of safety and security. It forbids the State itself to deprive individuals of life, liberty, or property without "due process of law," but its language cannot fairly be extended to impose an affirmative obligation on the State to ensure that those interests do not come to harm through other means.... Its purpose was to protect the people from the State, not to ensure that the State protected them from each other. The Framers were content to leave the extent of governmental obligation in the latter area to the democratic political processes.

Consistent with these principles, our cases have recognized that the Due Process Clauses generally confer no affirmative right to governmental aid, even where such aid may be necessary to secure life, liberty, or property interests of which the government itself may not deprive the individual.... As a general matter, then, we conclude that a State's failure to protect an individual against private violence simply does not constitute a violation of the Due Process Clause.

Petitioners contend, however, that even if the Due Process Clause imposes no affirmative obligation on the State to provide the general public with adequate protective services, such a duty may arise out of certain "special relationships" created or assumed by the State with respect to particular individuals. Petitioners argue that such a "special relationship" existed here because the State knew that Joshua faced a special danger of abuse at his father's hands, and specifically proclaimed, by word and by deed, its intention to protect him against that danger. Id., at 18–20. Having actually undertaken to protect Joshua from this danger—which petitioners concede the State played no part in creating—the State acquired an affirmative "duty," enforceable through the Due Process Clause, to do so in a reasonably competent fashion. Its failure to discharge that duty, so the argument goes, was an abuse of governmental power that so "shocks the conscience," as to constitute a substantive due process violation.

We reject this argument. It is true that in certain limited circumstances the Constitution imposes upon the State affirmative duties of care and protection with respect to particular individuals. In *Estelle v. Gamble*, 429 U.S. 97 (1976), we recognized that the Eighth Amendment's prohibition against cruel and unusual punishment, made applicable to the States through the Fourteenth Amendment's Due Process Clause, requires the State to provide adequate medical care to incarcerated prisoners. We reasoned that because the prisoner is unable "'by reason of the deprivation of his liberty [to] care for himself,'" it is only "'just'" that the State be required to care for him.

In *Youngberg v. Romeo*, 457 U.S. 307 (1982), we extended this analysis beyond the Eighth Amendment setting, holding that the substantive component of the Fourteenth Amendment's Due Process Clause requires the State to provide involuntarily committed mental patients with such services as are necessary to ensure their "reasonable safety" from themselves and others. As we explained: "If it is cruel and unusual punishment to hold convicted criminals in unsafe conditions, it must be unconstitutional [under the Due Process Clause] to confine the involuntarily committed—who may not be punished at all—in unsafe conditions."

But these cases afford petitioners no help. Taken together, they stand only for the proposition that when the State takes a person into its custody and holds him there against his will, the Constitution imposes upon it a corresponding duty to assume some responsibility for his safety and general well-being. In the substantive due process analysis, it is the State's affirmative act of restraining the individual's freedom to act on his own behalf—through incarceration, institutionalization, or other similar restraint of personal liberty—which is the "deprivation of liberty" triggering the protections of the Due Process Clause, not its failure to act to protect his liberty interests against harms inflicted by other means. The Estelle-Youngberg analysis simply has no applicability in the present case. Petitioners concede that the harms Joshua suffered occurred not while he was in the State's custody, but while he was in the custody of his natural father, who was in no sense a state actor. While the State may have been aware of the dangers that Joshua faced in the free world, it played no part in their creation, nor did it do anything to render him any more vulnerable to them. That the State once took temporary custody of Joshua does not alter the analysis, for when it returned him to his father's custody, it placed him in no worse position than that in which he would have been had it not acted at all; the State does not become the permanent guarantor of an individual's safety by having once offered him shelter. Under these circumstances, the State had no constitutional duty to protect Joshua. Judges and lawyers, like other humans, are moved by natural sympathy in a case like this to find a way for Joshua and his mother to receive adequate compensation for the grievous harm inflicted upon them. But before yielding to that impulse, it is well to remember once again that the harm was inflicted not by the State of Wisconsin, but by Joshua's father. The most that can be said of the state functionaries in this case is that they stood by and did nothing when suspicious circumstances dictated a more active role for them. In defense of them it must also be said that had they moved too soon to take custody of the son away from the father, they would likely have been met with charges of improperly intruding into the parent-child relationship, charges based on the same Due Process Clause that forms the basis for the present charge of failure to provide adequate protection.

The people of Wisconsin may well prefer a system of liability which would place upon the State and its officials the responsibility for failure to act in situations such as the present one. They may create such a system, if they do not have it already, by changing the tort law of the State in accordance with the regular lawmaking process. But they should not have it thrust upon them by this Court's expansion of the Due Process Clause of the Fourteenth Amendment.

Affirmed.

Notes & Questions

1. The selected cases in this section illustrate the nature and extent of one function of the state's role as *parens patriae*, which is to act as the guardian of persons who are legally incompetent or otherwise incapable of making their own decisions regarding personal health and safety. Thus, the selected cases involve state interventions to protect the health, safety, and welfare of minor children, prisoners, and, in certain circumstances, the potential life of the unborn. In these circumstances the state's decision to intervene can, and often does, interfere with individual autonomy, privacy or liberty and, as a result, the courts have developed standards and procedural requirements to safeguard individual interests from unfair or unreasonable intrusions. Based upon your review of the selected cases what are some of the standards and procedural requirements? How does the focus and scope of the state's *parens patriae* power differ from the police power?

A second function of the state's role as *parens patriae* is to safeguard the community's interest in health, safety, and welfare, a function that affords the state standing to sue in court to protect or promote community interests. Again, for a good discussion of the *parens patriae* power and cases illustrating the two principal functions of the state acting in this role *see* Lawrence O. Gostin, PUBLIC HEALTH LAW: POWER, DUTY, RESTRAINT (2000).

2. In *Roe v. Wade* the court concludes that the right of personal privacy encompasses the abortion decision. However, this right is not absolute and may be subject to interference by regulations advancing important state interests. What are the important state interests advanced by the abortion regulations? Whose health and welfare is the state, in its role as *parens patriae*, promoting through these regulations and what role, if any, do scientific advances play in redefining the nature or focus of the state's interests?

The court describes the ways in which state restrictions on the abortion decision might disadvantage or burden the pregnant woman. Does the description encompass the impact of carrying a pregnancy to term when prenatal screening has established the child will suffer from a genetic disease or disability? Should advances in prenatal genetic screening be a factor in the abortion debate? Does the nature or severity of the genetic diagnosis make a difference in your analysis? Consider the issue along the following spectrum of conditions: Tay-Sachs disease (a neurodegenerative disorder characterized by loss of motor skills beginning at three to six months of age and progressing to seizures, blindness, and eventual total incapacitation and death, usually before age four), Down Syndrome (a chromosomal abnormality which carries a near-certain risk of mental retardation, although the extent of the impairment is highly variable), hereditary deafness, gender, and Huntington disease. (For detailed information on these conditions visit the GeneTests (www.genetest.org), funded by the National Institutes of Health to provide current, authoritative information on genetic testing or the Genetics

& Genomics website maintained by the Centers for Disease Control (accessible through www.cdc.gov)).

The acceptable regulatory balance between a woman's right to choose and the state's competing interests in protecting maternal health and promoting potential fetal life has undergone significant scrutiny in the courts since the *Roe v. Wade* decision. Current precedent supports the right of state governments to promote fetal health and safety, provided such laws do not sacrifice maternal health or "unduly burden" women's procreative choices. *Planned Parenthood v. Casey*, 505 U.S. 833 (1992). The right of the state to protect the fetus becomes more "compelling" as the woman's pregnancy advances. As a result, the courts permit States to forbid abortion after fetal viability, provided continuation of the pregnancy does not threaten the pregnant woman's life or health. Thus far the courts have overruled state efforts to completely ban abortion prior to the point of viability, although the trend is to permit increasing regulation of the decision-making process. *See Stenberg v. Carhart*, 530 U.S. 914 (2000); the Federal Partial-Birth Abortion Ban Act of 2003, 18 U.S.C. § 1531; *Carhart v. Gonzales*, 413 F.3d 791 (8th Cir. 2005).

Historically the principal opposition to women's right to choose has come from the pro-life movement. whose agenda is focused on extending government protection to the fetus from the moment of conception, hence rendering pre-viability abortion illegal. How do advances in genetics impact a woman's right to choose? Consider the arguments of Ronald Green (among others) who uses the concept of fetal well-being to advocate for support of reproductive choice when he states, "Parents have a *prima facie* obligation not to bring a child into being deliberately or negligently with a health status likely to result in significantly greater disability or suffering, or significantly reduced life options relative to the other children with whom he/she will grow up." R. M. Green, *Prenatal Autonomy and the Obligation Not to Harm One's Child Genetically*, 25 J.L. Med. & Ethics 5 (1997). What impact does Green's argument have on the reproductive choice of parents who oppose abortion or oppose using prenatal testing and abortion to select against disabling traits that they are willing to embrace? *See* N. Press, *Assessing the Expressive Character of Prenatal Testing: the Choices Made or the Choices Made Available*, *in* Prenatal Testing and Disability Right 214 (E. Parens & A. Asch, eds., 2000).

How do advances in genetics impact the pro-life movement? Should the state's *parens patriae* powers be extended to protect the unborn pre-viable fetus—or the embryo—diagnosed with genetic disease? Alternatively, are there public health considerations that favor expanding public access to prenatal genetic diagnosis and selective termination procedures in an effort to prevent the transmission of genetic diseases associated with profound morbidity?

Prenatal diagnosis of Down Syndrome and neural tube defects became widely available in the early 1970s (H.L. Nadler & A.B. Gerbie, 282 New Eng. J. Med. 596 (1970), around the same time as the *Roe v. Wade* decision. However, even before *Roe v. Wade*, doctors were authorized to perform abortions for "medical" reasons. Therefore, the technologies that make prenatal genetic diagnosis possible have only been available in the context of legal abortion. If abortion laws were to continue to become more restrictive, or if *Roe v. Wade* were overturned, how would our thinking about and use of prenatal genetic diagnosis be impacted?

3. In the *Jefferson* case the court compelled a cesarean-section delivery over the religious objections of the pregnant woman because available medical evidence confirmed the presence of a complete placenta previa, a condition which posed a near certain risk of death to the child should the mother proceed with a vaginal delivery. The case

sparked considerable controversy because of its implications for evolving concepts of fetal personhood and a mother's duty to promote live birth. *See, e.g.*, J.L. Lenow, *The Fetus as a Patient: Emerging Rights as a Person*, 9 AM J. LAW. MED. 1 (1983); B.A. Leavine, COURT-ORDERED CESAREANS: CAN A PREGNANT WOMAN REFUSE? 29 HOUST. L.R. 185 (1992). Would the result in this case have changed if prenatal testing had established the child suffered from a profoundly disabling genetic disease or disability? Should it? Why or why not?

4. *DeShaney v. Winnebago* reflects the established principle that, while the Constitution reserves to the states the power to act to promote and protect public health, it does not impose an affirmative duty on the state or federal governments to protect citizens through the provision of services or otherwise. If the government chooses to act to promote public health or the welfare of the vulnerable, it has the authority to do so within the framework outlined in the foregoing cases and materials. However, failing to act does not generally give rise to liability even when the consequences of inaction are severe, as in *DeShaney*. "[O]ur cases have recognized that the Due Process Clause generally confers no affirmative right to governmental aid, even where such aid may be necessary to secure life, liberty or property interests of which the government itself may not deprive the individual." *DeShaney*, 489 U.S. at 196. How does this so-called negative theory of the Constitution reconcile with established public perceptions of the government's important role in promoting health and access to health care? In many states access to genetic services, which include genetic counseling, prenatal screening and diagnosis, clinical genetics services and ongoing surveillance is provided under the auspices of state departments of public health. What right do citizens who rely on these services have to demand or expect them to continue? In states where these services are not provided and not otherwise accessible to low-income families, what recourse is there for affected children and families to obtain care and treatment that necessitates training and expertise regarding genetics? The Supreme Court has previously upheld state statutes that prohibit the use of public funds, facilities or employees for abortion related services, including counseling that encourages a woman to consider abortion, unless the services are necessary to save the life of the mother. *Webster v. Reproductive Health Services*, 492 U.S. 490 (1989) (relying in part on *DeShanney*, 489 U.S. 189). Is there a sufficient nexus between prenatal genetic diagnosis and abortion services to justify withdrawal of public funding for prenatal genetic testing and counseling regarding the implications of test results?

B. The Eugenics Movement: Social Engineering in the Name of Public Health?

Martin S. Pernick, *Eugenics and Public Health in American History*

87 AM. J. PUBLIC HEALTH 1767 (1997)

Supporters of eugenics, the powerful early 20th-century movement for improving human heredity, often attacked that era's dramatic improvements in public health and medicine for preserving the lives of people they considered hereditarily unfit. However, American public health and eugenics had much in common as well. Surprisingly, the complex relationship between them has not often been studied. This paper sketches some of the key similarities and differences between eugenics and public health in the United States. Like such other turn-of-the-century catchwords as progressivism and efficiency, the term eugenics encompassed a large and shifting constellation of meanings. The term was first popularized by Charles Darwin's cousin Sir Francis Galton, who defined it as the science of improving heredity. American eugenicists sponsored a diverse range of activities, including statistically sophisticated analyses of disease inheritance, "better baby contests" modeled on rural livestock shows, forced sterilization of criminals and the retarded, selective ethnic restrictions on immigration, and even euthanasia for those deemed unfit to live. These and other programs were seen as eugenic because they all aimed at improving human heredity. But that common denominator also allowed many divergent responses to such key questions as[:] What does "improvement" mean? What does "heredity" mean? By what methods should heredity be improved? Who has the authority to answer the other questions? Disputes over these issues produced very different competing concepts of eugenics and its relationship to public health.

Many eugenicists regarded disease as nature's way of weeding out the unfit. Charles Davenport, America's foremost eugenic scientist, warned in 1915, "The artificial preservation of those whom the operation of natural agencies tends to eliminate ... may conceivably destroy the race." He considered it "anti-social" to "unduly restrict the operation of what is one of Nature's greatest racial blessings-death."

His comments exemplified the close kinship between eugenics and earlier Social Darwinist and Malthusian attacks on public health and social welfare programs, a link that remained powerful throughout the history of eugenics. A speaker at the 1914 National Conference on Race Betterment, the first major American eugenics conference, explained that "death is the normal process of elimination in the social organism, and ... in prolonging the lives of defectives we are tampering with the functioning of the social kidneys." A speaker at the last such American meeting, the Third International Congress on Eugenics in New York in 1932, echoed the same view: "The growth of sanitation, hygiene, and State medicine ... attempts to secure an ever increasing survival rate for the least competent types.... This interference with Natural Selection [is] disastrous." Leading eugenics popularizer Michael Guyer summarized the argument: "[O]ur improved methods of sanitation and care of the sick ... so eased the rigors of ... natural selection that decadent stocks ... are increasing relatively faster than normal stocks."

A second point of contention between public health and eugenics concerned the role of heredity in infectious diseases. Public health officials generally attributed the era's unprecedented decline in infections to the success of new preventive techniques based on bacteriology and immunology, from water filtration to vaccinations. In the case of tuberculosis, bacteriologists took particular pride in having disproved earlier beliefs that the disease was inherited. Yet many eugenicists continued to claim that infections, from tuberculosis to syphilis to infant diarrheas, were hereditary.

Historians often ridicule such claims as an unscientific repudiation of the germ theory. However, the struggle between eugenics and public health for jurisdiction over infectious diseases cannot be dismissed that simply. Eugenicists accepted that germs were necessary to cause infections, but they believed that hereditary resistance was the best way to cure and prevent them....

Rivalries such as this one were increasingly characteristic of early 20th century health sciences. The competition between microbiology and eugenics, like the era's many other similar disputes, was triggered by the emergence of professional specialization. As early as 1906, chemists, nutritionists, and bacteriologists battled over their mutually incompatible approaches to pure food, meat, and milk regulations. Germ-fighting techniques such as pasteurization and use of preservatives were attacked for destroying vitamins, altering taste, and adding toxic chemicals. Such controversies constituted both a struggle for professional power and a substantive contest over incompatible values fostered by the emergence of separate specialty professional cultures. Early 20th-century health scientists and Progressive Era social reformers expected specialization to be simply an efficient division of labor....

Yet at a deeper level, such conflicts were exacerbated, ironically, by a basic value the opponents shared: the faith that their common allegiance to the scientific method would eliminate such subjective sources of disagreement. To the extent that each side believed in the objective validity of its own science's methods, opposing conclusions could only be attributed to the opponents' bad science or bad faith.

While some advocates of each movement highlighted the differences between the two, others denied or minimized these disagreements. In fact, despite their controversies, eugenics and public health also had much in common. Public health agencies and eugenics organizations often overlapped in goals and methods, programs, and personnel. Many public health institutions included eugenics in their official duties....

This overlap in organizations resulted from important underlying similarities in values and ideas. Thus, many eugenics supporters rejected the claim that disease selectively killed the "unfit." They argued that hereditary resistance to disease was not a sign of overall genetic superiority and insisted that some highly advantageous traits were actually correlated with heightened susceptibility to particular diseases. The 1912 American translation of a book by Socialist eugenicist and child welfare pioneer Sigmund Engel attacked the "ultra Darwinian" view that spontaneous infant mortality was beneficial, noting that the leading childhood diseases killed the fit and the unfit alike. E. Blanche Sterling, a child hygiene worker for the Public Health Service, reminded the Third International Congress that "in laying so much stress on the fact that we are saving the unfit, the fact that we are also saving the fit seems to have been forgotten.... Very superior stock ... may have no immunity to certain serious diseases and it is our privilege to aid in preserving such strains." These views were especially common among women social reformers and child health advocates, for whom eugenics meant not simply "good genes" but "better babies." This debate over whether disease deaths were dysgenic combined scientific and value issues. The unresolved empirical questions included whether disease resistance was hereditary and whether any such hereditary resistance was positively or negatively correlated with other desirable traits. The value issues included which hereditary traits were judged to be beneficial and which traits should be valued most if disease susceptibility turned out to be correlated with something good, such as intelligence.

In addition, regardless of whether disease aided natural selection, many eugenicists opposed relying on nature's slow, cruel mechanism of Darwinian evolution. They considered eugenics to mean "artificial selection," the active intentional control of reproduction to achieve nature's goals by more efficient means. Pioneer eugenic popularizers Paul Popenoe and John Harvey Kellogg explained to the 1914 Race Betterment Conference that the death of "weaklings" constituted "Nature's way, the old method of natural selection." However, nature's methods were inefficient and inhumane; natural selection therefore "must be supplanted" by eugenic selection. Thus, eugenics and public health could cooperate instead of competing. Public health could continue to prevent the deaths of the unfit so long as eugenics prevented the unfit from passing on their defects.

Even those eugenicists who advocated death for the unfit sometimes won support from prominent public health officials. From 1915 to 1918, Chicago surgeon Harry Haiselden publicly permitted or hastened the deaths of at least six infants he diagnosed as eugenically defective. In the ensuing national debate, he won varying degrees of support from many public health figures, including visiting nurse pioneer Lillian Wald, Food and Drug Administration founder Harvey Wiley, antitoxin pioneer William H. Park, and public hygiene promoter Simon Baruch. Some supporters drew a parallel between eugenics euthanasia and the practice of killing infectious animals to protect public health.

Such arguments show that, even in the hotly contested arena of infection control, eugenics and public health could converge as well as compete. For a variety of reasons that illustrate how the meanings of both eugenics and public health were shaped by the interrelation of science and culture, eugenics sometimes was defined to include antibacterial measures.

First, it was widely believed that some of the damage done to people by infections could be biologically inherited by their descendants. In the 19th century, such beliefs had been based on the Lamarckian view that acquired traits could become hereditary. Thus, reform-minded 19th-century eugenicists urged the adoption of public health measures to prevent epidemics from becoming hereditary and to produce health improvements that might themselves be inherited. Such ideas retained support well into the early 20th century.

By the 1910s, however, scientists generally accepted August Weismann's opposite hypothesis—that environmentally caused changes in the body could not cause corresponding changes in the hereditary "germ plasm." Yet even Weismann's disciples believed that some infections were "germ poisons" that could damage the germ plasm in ways that could be inherited. In this view, catching malaria or typhoid did not cause your children to inherit those specific diseases, but the high fevers they produced might cause other kinds of birth defects that would be passed on. The scientific reasoning had changed, but the practical conclusion remained the same: that fighting infections could help reduce hereditary disease as well. Germs and genes also were seen as specific, reductionist causes of disease, more technical and less subjective than the broad array of personal and social conditions previously blamed for causing bad health. Progressive Era health reformers still sought to change individual behavior and social conditions, but both germs and genes provided precise targets for these reform efforts, thus making them seem more objective and efficient.

Second, broad linguistic and cultural associations linked heredity and contagion. Infections were caused by germs; inheritance was governed by germ plasm. In both cases, "germs" meant microscopic seeds. Both types of germs enabled disease to propagate and grow, to spread contamination from the bodies of the diseased to the healthy. The association was strengthened by the identification of blood as a medium of infection for diseases such as malaria, and by the introduction of blood tests for infections from typhoid to syphilis. Blood, the age-old metaphor for heredity, became identified as a vehicle for infection as well. Having "bad blood" meant you were contaminated and contaminating, whether the specific agent was a germ or the germ plasm.

Eugenics could even be expanded to include not just germ fighting but virtually all of public health. While eugenics aimed at improving heredity, the meaning of heredity could reach far beyond genetics. In both common usage and some scientific literature, calling a trait "hereditary" meant that "you got it from your parents," regardless of whether "it" was transmitted by genes or germs, precepts or probate. The Public Health Service film The Science of Life defined a man's heredity as "what he receives from his ancestors."

This expansive definition was based not on wrong science but on broader moral concerns. Attributing something to heredity meant holding the parents morally responsible for having caused it, not necessarily specifying the technical mechanism through which parental responsibility operated. By this definition of heredity, eugenics meant not just having good genes but also being a good parent, raising good children, or promoting good health for future generations. This version of eugenics was virtually synonymous with public health.

The similarities between infection and heredity also led to parallels in the methods of disease prevention adopted by public health and eugenics. Eugenicists urged the "segregation" of defectives in institutions, isolating them from society and from members of the opposite sex to prevent their reproduction and the consequent spread of hereditary disease. Such eugenic segregation directly echoed the centuries-old effort to stop the spread of infections through quarantine. The term segregation itself first was used medically in the mid-19th century to mean "selective isolation" or "quarantine." Infectious germs and bad germ plasm could also be stopped from spreading by a new method called sterilization. In both eugenics and bacteriology, to sterilize meant to eliminate the agents that reproduced disease.

Infection control also provided vital legal precedents for the two most important enactments of eugenic legislation. The eugenically based selective ethnic restrictions on immigration adopted by Congress in 1924 drew upon and made permanent earlier immigration restrictions adopted to fight infectious diseases, such as New York's 1892 selective quarantine of Russian Jewish immigrants during that year's typhus epidemic. Forcible sterilization of the unfit likewise drew on both the values and the example of infection control laws. The main legal precedent cited in *Buck v Bell*, the 1927 Supreme Court decision upholding involuntary eugenic sterilization, was *Jacobson v Massachusetts*, the 1905 case allowing mandatory smallpox vaccination. As Justice Oliver Wendell Holmes explained in *Buck v. Bell*, "The principle that sustains compulsory vaccination is broad enough to cover cutting the Fallopian." [*Buck v. Bell*, 274 U.S. 200 (1927)]....

Eugenics is notorious today for having promoted bigoted concepts of illness, in which race, class, ethnic, religious, and sexual prejudices determined who was defined as unfit. Eugenics leaders regularly portrayed African Americans and Native Americans as loathsome, disease-doomed races. Eugenicists also routinely ranked the genetic worth of various European "races." Harvey Wiley summed up what he alleged to be the overwhelming eugenic consensus when he told the readers of Good Housekeeping in 1922, "[I]t is universally acknowledged that descendants of the Scotch and Irish Presbyterians ... have always shown themselves to be a superior people." J. G. Wilson, a Public Health Service doctor in charge of examining immigrants on New York's Ellis Island, wrote in the 1913 Popular Science Monthly, "[T]he Jews are a highly inbred and psychopathically inclined race" whose defects are "almost entirely due to heredity." That Jews disagreed with his diagnosis simply confirmed its validity: "The general paranoid attitude of the race is shown in an almost universal tendency to fail to appreciate the point of view of the one who opposes them.

But eugenics was not unique among the health sciences in diagnosing social outcasts as diseased. Medical justifications for racial slavery predated Darwin and Galton, and even in its heyday, eugenics had no monopoly on scientific racism. Bacteriology, not just genetics, was also commonly used to label other races as diseased. Both eugenics and microbiology contributed to the assumptions about racial epidemiology that shaped the Public Health Service's decision to use African-American men for the Tuskegee study of untreated syphilis. By emphasizing heredity as the engine of human progress, eugenics expanded the medical importance of ancestry and race. But the identification of which specific races were good or bad was not intrinsic to eugenics. Instead, these diagnoses medicalized broader cultural biases. The specific values that shaped eugenic definitions of disease reflected the eugenicists' primarily White, native, middle-class, professional backgrounds, characteristics they shared with many other professionals, including many public health officials.

Cultural values thus deeply influenced past eugenics and public health proponents in their definitions of disease and their responses to it. The point is not that, in the benighted past, pure genetics or bacteriology were corrupted by extraneous social concerns. Rather, this history provides some particularly vivid examples of how cultural values have been integral to every effort to define and fight disease. Past eugenics and public health included values most thoughtful people now consider anathema. The problem, then, was not that past health sciences had values, but that they had bad values.

Racism and other social prejudices became part of both eugenics and public health in the past, not just because these values were prevalent among health professionals, but because health professionals convinced themselves that their sciences were purely objective. Helen Keller, the famed blind and deaf advocate for the disabled, captured the power of this faith when she urged letting doctors select which mentally impaired infants to let die. "A jury of physicians considering the case of an idiot would be exact and scientific. Their findings would be free from the prejudice and inaccuracy of untrained observation." This widely shared faith in objectivity did not succeed in eliminating subjective values from medicine, but it did serve to delegitimate the openly political and ethical debate that is necessary if a culture is to assess its value judgments intelligently.

In pointing out that there were similarities as well as differences between eugenics and public health, this paper refutes two comforting but simplistic notions: that eugenics was uniquely value laden, unscientific, and prejudiced; and that any science that is valid and well-intentioned can have nothing in common with eugenics. Some of what was done in the name of eugenics was also done in the name of infection control and public health. Eugenics was not an isolated movement whose significance is confined to the histories of genetics and pseudoscience. It is an important and cautionary part of past public health and of general medical history as well.

However, historical similarities are not moral equivalents. Their intertwined past certainly does not mean that public health was "as bad" as eugenics or that human genetics is "as good" as public health today. Past similarities between eugenics and public health serve as an alarm clock for all the health sciences, not as a lullaby for genetics.

City of Cleburne, Texas v. Cleburne Living Center

473 U.S. 432, 461–466 (1985)

Justice Marshall, dissenting.

... [T]he mentally retarded have been subject to a "lengthy and tragic history," of segregation and discrimination that can only be called grotesque. During much of the 19th century, mental retardation was viewed as neither curable nor dangerous and the retarded were largely left to their own devices. By the latter part of the century and during the first decades of the new one, however, social views of the retarded underwent a radical transformation. Fueled by the rising tide of Social Darwinism, the "science" of eugenics, and the extreme xenophobia of those years, leading medical authorities and others began to portray the "feeble-minded" as a "menace to society and civilization ... responsible in a large degree for many, if not all, of our social problems." A regime of state-mandated segregation and degradation soon emerged that in its virulence and bigotry rivaled, and indeed paralleled, the worst excesses of Jim Crow. Massive custodial institutions were built to warehouse the retarded for life; the aim was to halt reproduction of the retarded and "nearly extinguish their race." Retarded children were categorically excluded from public schools, based on the false stereotype that all were ineducable and on the purported need to protect nonretarded children from them. State laws deemed the retarded "unfit for citizenship."

Segregation was accompanied by eugenic marriage and sterilization laws that extinguished for the retarded one of the "basic civil rights of man"—the right to marry and procreate. Marriages of the retarded were made, and in some States continue to be, not only voidable but also often a criminal offense. The purpose of such limitations, which frequently applied only to women of child-bearing age, was unabashedly eugenic: to prevent the retarded from propagating. To assure this end, 29 States enacted compulsory eugenic sterilization laws between 1907 and 1931.

Prejudice, once let loose, is not easily cabined. As of 1979, most States still categorically disqualified "idiots" from voting, without regard to individual capacity and with discretion to exclude left in the hands of low-level election officials. Not until Congress enacted the Education of the Handicapped Act were "the door[s] of public education" opened wide to handicapped children. But most important, lengthy and continuing isolation of the retarded has perpetuated the ignorance, irrational fears, and stereotyping that long have plagued them....

* * *

Justice Marshall's dissent provides a chilling reminder of the misguided policies that arose during the Eugenics Movement and their devastating impact on the rights and civil liberties of the so-called "feeble-minded." Mentally handicapped individuals were not the only victims. Persons of color and alternative national origins, the poor or the "criminal" and those whose life-styles were at odds with prevailing social norms also suffered under the widespread legislative agenda the eugenicists propelled through state legislatures and, in the case of immigration restrictions, the U.S. Congress. This agenda included compulsory sterilization laws, antimiscegnation laws, and immigration restrictions that imposed restrictive immigration quotas and limited U.S. citizenship to white males. The following cases illustrate how a misunderstanding of the science of genetics influenced the implementation and enforcement of compulsory sterilization laws, beginning with the legendary case of *Buck v. Bell.*

Buck v. Bell

274 U.S. 200 (1927)

Mr. Justice Holmes delivered the opinion of the Court.

This is a writ of error to review a judgment of the Supreme Court of Appeals of the State of Virginia, affirming a judgment of the Circuit Court of Amherst County, by which the defendant in error, the superintendent of the State Colony for Epileptics and Feeble Minded, was ordered to perform the operation of salpingectomy upon Carrie

Buck, the plaintiff in error, for the purpose of making her sterile. The case comes here upon the contention that the statute authorizing the judgment is void under the Fourteenth Amendment as denying to the plaintiff in error due process of law and the equal protection of the laws.

Carrie Buck is a feeble-minded white woman who was committed to the State Colony above mentioned in due form. She is the daughter of a feeble-minded mother in the same institution, and the mother of an illegitimate feeble-minded child. She was eighteen years old at the time of the trial of her case in the Circuit Court in the latter part of 1924. An Act of Virginia approved March 20, 1924 (Laws 1924, c. 394) recites that the health of the patient and the welfare of society may be promoted in certain cases by the sterilization of mental defectives, under careful safeguard, etc.; that the sterilization may be effected in males by vasectomy and in females by salpingectomy, without serious pain or substantial danger to life; that the Commonwealth is supporting in various institutions many defective persons who if now discharged would become a menace but if incapable of procreating might be discharged with safety and become self-supporting with benefit to themselves and to society; and that experience has shown that heredity plays an important part in the transmission of insanity, imbecility, etc. The statute then enacts that whenever the superintendent of certain institutions including the above named State Colony shall be of opinion that it is for the best interest of the patients and of society that an inmate under his care should be sexually sterilized, he may have the operation performed upon any patient afflicted with hereditary forms of insanity, imbecility, etc., on complying with the very careful provisions by which the act protects the patients from possible abuse.

The superintendent first presents a petition to the special board of directors of his hospital or colony, stating the facts and the grounds for his opinion, verified by affidavit. Notice of the petition and of the time and place of the hearing in the institution is to be served upon the inmate, and also upon his guardian, and if there is no guardian the superintendent is to apply to the Circuit Court of the County to appoint one. If the inmate is a minor notice also is to be given to his parents, if any, with a copy of the petition. The board is to see to it that the inmate may attend the hearings if desired by him or his guardian. The evidence is all to be reduced to writing, and after the board has made its order for or against the operation, the superintendent, or the inmate, or his guardian, may appeal to the Circuit Court of the County. The Circuit Court may consider the record of the board and the evidence before it and such other admissible evidence as may be offered, and may affirm, revise, or reverse the order of the board and enter such order as it deems just. Finally any party may apply to the Supreme Court of Appeals, which, if it grants the appeal, is to hear the case upon the record of the trial in the Circuit Court and may enter such order as it thinks the Circuit Court should have entered. There can be no doubt that so far as procedure is concerned the rights of the patient are most carefully considered, and as every step in this case was taken in scrupulous compliance with the statute and after months of observation, there is no doubt that in that respect the plaintiff in error has had due process at law.

The attack is not upon the procedure but upon the substantive law. It seems to be contended that in no circumstances could such an order be justified. It certainly is contended that the order cannot be justified upon the existing grounds. The judgment finds the facts that have been recited and that Carrie Buck 'is the probable potential parent of socially inadequate offspring, likewise afflicted, that she may be sexually sterilized without detriment to her general health and that her welfare and that of society will be promoted by her sterilization,' and thereupon makes the order. In view of the general declarations of the Legislature and the specific findings of the Court obviously we cannot say as matter of law that the grounds do not exist, and if they exist they justify the result. We have seen more than once that the public welfare may call upon the best citizens for their lives. It would be strange if it could not call upon those who already sap the strength of the State for these lesser sacrifices, often not felt to be such by those concerned, in order to prevent our being swamped with incompetence. It is better for all the world, if instead of waiting to execute degenerate offspring for crime, or to let them starve for their imbecility, society can prevent those who are manifestly unfit from continuing their kind. The principle that sustains compulsory vaccination is broad enough to cover cutting the Fallopian tubes. *Jacobson v. Massachusetts*, 197 U. S. 11 [(1905)]. Three generations of imbeciles are enough.

But, it is said, however it might be if this reasoning were applied generally, it fails when it is confined to the small number who are in the institutions named and is not applied to the multitudes outside. It is the usual last resort of constitutional arguments to point out shortcomings of this sort. But the answer is that the law does all that is needed when it does all that it can, indicates a policy, applies it to all within the lines, and seeks to bring within the lines all similarly situated so far and so fast as its means allow. Of course so far as the operations enable those who otherwise must be kept confined to be returned to the world, and thus open the asylum to others, the equality aimed at will be more nearly reached.

Judgment affirmed.

In re Main

19 P.2d 153 (Okla. 1933)

Riley, Chief Justice.

Samuel W. Main, by his guardian, Richard H. Cloyd, appeals from a judgment of the district court of Oklahoma county, ... authorizing and directing Dr. D. W. Griffin, superintendent of the Central Oklahoma State Hospital of Norman, Okl. (a state hospital for insane) to have performed an operation of vasectomy ... so as to render the said Samuel W. Main sexually sterile.

These proceedings were pursuant to the provisions of article 3, ch. 26, Sess. Laws 1931, sections 5039–5044, Okl. Stats. 1931. This act provides for sexual sterilization by vasectomy and salpingectomy of certain patients in state institutions for the insane. Its application is limited to inmates of state institutions who are afflicted with hereditary forms of insanity that are recurrent, idiocy, imbecility, feeble-mindedness, or epilepsy, and to males under the age of 65 and females under the age of 47 years, and who are about to be discharged from such institutions. A condition precedent to the sterilization provided by the act is an affirmative finding, by the State Board of Public Affairs, based upon a hearing, that the inmate sought to be sexually sterilized is afflicted with an hereditary form of insanity that is recurrent, or that he is an idiot, imbecile, feeble-minded or epileptic, "and by the laws of heredity is the probable potential parent of socially inadequate off-spring likewise afflicted," and that the inmate may be sexually sterilized without detriment to his or her general health, and "that the welfare of the patient and of society will be promoted by such sterilization." ...

In the case at bar it is established beyond dispute that Samuel W. Main was received at the Central Oklahoma State Hospital, located at Norman, on January 4, 1932, upon commitment issued after a sanity hearing held on that date in the county court of Oklahoma county; that he is approximately thirty-nine years of age and has a wife and four children; that his wife at the time of hearing was pregnant; that prior to his commitment to the named state institution, he had been committed to state institutions of like character located at Osawatomie, Kan., and Patton, Cal. He was afflicted with a hereditary form of insanity that is recurrent. He was about to be discharged from the Central Oklahoma State Hospital.

The procedure provided by the act liberally afforded the patient consideration and protection of his rights, and in the case at bar there has been a scrupulous compliance with the provisions of the act, so that appellee has been accorded due process of law.

The appellant contends on this appeal that the lower court erred in finding that an operation of vasectomy and the resultant sterilization of Main would be without detriment to his general health.

The objection goes to the weight rather than the admissibility of the evidence. It is in effect that the doctors who testified that such an operation on Main would be beneficial rather than detrimental to his general health had not performed such an operation, but learned and scientific men can virtually know things without having experienced them.

In the case of *Buck v. Bell*, 130 S. E. 516 [(1927)], affirmed by the United States Supreme Court, it was said, with regard to evidence therein presented: "These operations do not impair the general health, or affect the mental or moral status of the patient, or interfere with his or her sexual desires or enjoyment. They simply prevent reproduction. In the hands of a skilled surgeon, they are 100 per cent successful in results."

In *Smith v. Command*, Wayne Probate Judge, 204 N. W. 140, 142 [(1925)], it was said: "These operations are the least radical known to medical science."

And quoting from authorities on penal reform it was said: "This operation is indeed very simple and easy to perform.... It requires about three minutes time to perform the operation, and the subject returns to his work immediately, suffering no inconvenience, and is in no way impaired for the pursuit of life, liberty, and happiness, but is effectively sterilized.... There is not only a diminution of the muscular and nervous fatigue, resulting from muscular exertion, but also a lessening of fatigue sensation and a decided increase of well being."

The record herein sustains the finding made, to wit that an operation of vasectomy and the resultant sterilization of this patient would be without detriment to his general health....

It is next contended that the Sterilization Act violates section 9 of article 2, Constitution of Oklahoma, which constitutional provision inhibits the infliction of cruel or unusual punishments.

The answer is that, "There is no element of punishment involved in the sterilization of feeble-minded persons." In this respect it is analogous to compulsory vaccination. Both are nonpunitive. It is therefore apparent that the constitutional inhibition against cruel or unusual punishment has no application to surgical treatment of feeble-minded persons, for the constitutional inhibition has reference to punishment after conviction of crimes. The record herein affords uncontradicted evidence to support the view of the trial court that vasectomy is not cruel, inhuman, unreasonable, or oppressive....

It is contended that the act violates section 7, art. 2, Constitution of Oklahoma, "in that it deprives a man of a part of his life, to-wit, the ability to produce life" or procreate. The constitutional inhibition provides: "No person shall be deprived of life, liberty, or property, without due process of law."

The phrase "without due process of law" is not without import in this connection. Therefore, assuming that the right to beget children is a natural and constitutional right, yet this right cannot be extended beyond the common welfare. Under the police power of the state and acting for the public good, the state may impose reasonable restrictions upon the natural and constitutional rights of its citizens. This statutory provision for sterilization of feeble-minded inmates of public institutions constitutes a reasonable restriction upon such natural and constitutional rights of such persons.

A like contention as to unconstitutionality of the act is based on the provisions of section 2, art. 2, Constitution of Oklahoma, which reads: "All persons have the inherent right to life, liberty, the pursuit of happiness, and the enjoyment of the gains of their own industry." The contention is without merit. In *Ex parte Tindall*, 229 P. 125, 126 [(1924)], this court held: "The term 'police power' comprehends the power to make and enforce all wholesome and reasonable laws and regulations necessary to the maintenance, upbuilding, and advancement of the public weal and protection of the public interests." ...

The attack is upon the procedure and the substantive law. The first is adequate and liberal—the latter is an enactment of public policy within the scope of the power of the Legislature.

Judgment affirmed.

Skinner v. State of Oklahoma ex rel. Williamson

316 U.S. 535 (1942)

Mr. Justice Douglas delivered the opinion of the Court.

This case touches a sensitive and important area of human rights. Oklahoma deprives certain individuals of a right which is basic to the perpetuation of a race—the right to have offspring. Oklahoma has decreed the enforcement of its law against petitioner, overruling his claim that it violated the Fourteenth Amendment. Because that decision raised grave and substantial constitutional questions, we granted the petition for certiorari.

The statute involved is Oklahoma's Habitual Criminal Sterilization Act. That Act defines an 'habitual criminal' as a person who, having been convicted two or more times for crimes 'amounting to felonies involving moral turpitude' either in an Oklahoma court or in a court of any other State, is thereafter convicted of such a felony in Oklahoma and is sentenced to a term of imprisonment in an Oklahoma penal institution. Machinery is provided for the institution by the Attorney General of a proceeding against such a person in the Oklahoma courts for a judgment that such person shall be rendered sexually sterile. Notice, an opportunity to be heard, and the right to a jury trial are provided. The issues triable in such a proceeding are narrow and confined. If the court or jury finds that the defendant is an 'habitual criminal' and that he 'may be rendered sexually sterile without detriment to his or her general health', then the court 'shall render judgment to the effect that said defendant be rendered sexually sterile by the operation of vasectomy in case of a male and of salpingectomy in case of a female. Only one other provision of the Act is material here and that is s 195 which provides that 'offenses arising out of the violation of the prohibitory laws, revenue acts, embezzlement, or political offenses, shall not come or be considered within the terms of this Act.'

Petitioner was convicted in 1926 of the crime of stealing chickens and was sentenced to the Oklahoma State Reformatory. In 1929 he was convicted of the crime of robbery with fire arms and was sentenced to the reformatory. In 1934 he was convicted again of robbery with firearms and was sentenced to the penitentiary. He was confined there in 1935 when the Act was passed. In 1936 the Attorney General instituted proceedings against him....

Several objections to the constitutionality of the Act have been pressed upon us. It is urged that the Act cannot be sustained as an exercise of the police power in view of the state of scientific authorities respecting inheritability of criminal traits. It is argued that due process is lacking because under this Act, unlike the act upheld in *Buck v. Bell* [274 U.S. 200 (1927)], the defendant is given no opportunity to be heard on the issue as to whether he is the probable potential parent of socially undesirable offspring. It is also suggested that the Act is penal in character and that the sterilization provided for is cruel and unusual punishment and violative of the Fourteenth Amendment. We pass those points without intimating an opinion on them, for there is a feature of the Act which clearly condemns it. That is its failure to meet the requirements of the equal protection clause of the Fourteenth Amendment. We do not stop to point out all of the inequalities in this Act. A few examples will suffice. In Oklahoma grand larceny is a felony. Okl.St.Ann. Tit. 21, s 1705 (s 5). Larceny is grand larceny when the property taken exceeds $20 in value. Embezzlement is punishable 'in the manner prescribed for feloniously stealing property of the value of that embezzled.' Hence he who embezzles property worth more than $20 is guilty of a felony. A clerk who appropriates over $20 from his employer's till and a stranger who steals the same amount are thus both guilty of felonies. If the latter repeats his act and is convicted three times, he may be sterilized. But the clerk is not subject to the pains and penalties of the Act no matter how large his embezzlements nor how frequent his convictions. A person who enters a chicken coop and steals chickens commits a felony; and he may be sterilized if he is thrice convicted. If, however, he is a bailee of the property and fraudulently appropriates it, he is an embezzler. Hence no matter how habitual his proclivities for embezzlement are and no matter how often his conviction, he may not be sterilized. Thus the nature of the two crimes is intrinsically the same and they are punishable in the same manner. Furthermore, the line between them follows close distinctions—distinctions comparable to those highly technical ones which shaped the common law as to 'trespass' or 'taking'. There may be larceny by fraud rather than embezzlement even where the owner of the personal property delivers it to the defendant, if the latter has at that time 'a fraudulent intention to make use of the possession as a means of converting such property to his own use, and does so convert it'. If the fraudulent intent occurs later and the defendant converts the property, he is guilty of embezzlement. Whether a particular act is larceny by fraud or embezzlement thus turns not on the intrinsic quality of the act but on when the felonious intent arose—a question for the jury under appropriate instructions.

It was stated in *Buck v. Bell*, supra, that the claim that state legislation violates the equal protection clause of the Fourteenth Amendment is 'the usual last resort of constitutional arguments.' Under our constitutional system the States in determining the reach and scope of particular legislation need not provide 'abstract symmetry'. They may mark and set apart the classes and types of problems according to the needs and as dictated or suggested by experience. It was in that connection that Mr. Justice Holmes, speaking for the Court in *Bain Peanut Co. v. Pinson*, 282 U.S. 499 [(1931)], stated, 'We must remember that the machinery of government would not work if it were not allowed a little play in its joints.'... Thus, if we had here only a question as to a State's classification of crimes, such as embezzlement or larceny, no substantial federal question would be raised. For a State is not constrained in the exercise of its police power to ignore experience which marks a class of offenders or a family of offenses for special treatment. Nor is it prevented by the equal protection clause from confining 'its restrictions to those classes of cases where the need is deemed to be clearest'....

But the instant legislation runs afoul of the equal protection clause, though we give Oklahoma that large deference which the rule of the foregoing cases requires. We are dealing here with legislation which involves one of the basic civil rights of man. Marriage and procreation are fundamental to the very existence and survival of the race. The power to sterilize, if exercised, may have subtle, farreaching and devastating effects. In evil or reckless hands it can cause races or types which are inimical to the dominant group to wither and disappear. There is no redemption for the individual whom the law touches. Any experiment which the State conducts is to his irreparable injury. He is forever deprived of a basic liberty. We mention these matters not to reexamine the scope of the police power of the States. We advert to them merely in emphasis of our view that strict scrutiny of the classification which a State makes in a sterilization law is essential, lest unwittingly or otherwise invidious discriminations are made against groups or types of individuals in violation of the constitutional guaranty of just and equal laws. The guaranty of 'equal protection of the laws is a pledge of the protection of equal laws.' When the law lays an unequal hand on those who have committed intrinsically the same quality of offense and sterilizes one and not the other, it has made as an invidious a discrimination as if it had selected a particular race or nationality for oppressive treatment. Sterilization of those who have thrice committed grand larceny with immunity for those who are embezzlers is a clear, pointed, unmistakable discrimination. Oklahoma makes no attempt to say that he who commits larceny by trespass or trick or fraud has biologically inheritable traits which he who commits embezzlement lacks. Oklahoma's line between larceny by fraud and embezzlement is determined, as we have noted, 'with reference to the time when the fraudulent intent to convert the property to the taker's own use' arises. We have not the slightest basis for inferring that that line has any significance in eugenics nor that the inheritability of criminal traits follows the neat legal distinctions which the law has marked between those two offenses. In terms of fines and imprisonment the crimes of larceny and embezzlement rate the same under the Oklahoma code. Only when it comes to sterilization are the pains and penalties of the law different. The equal protection clause would indeed be a formula of empty words if such conspicuously artificial lines could be drawn. In *Buck v. Bell*, supra, the Virginia statute was upheld though it applied only to feebleminded persons in institutions of the State. But it was pointed out that 'so far as the operations enable those who otherwise must be kept confined to be returned to the world, and thus open the asylum to others, the equality aimed at will be more nearly reached.' 274 U.S. page 208. Here there is no such saving feature. Embezzlers are forever free. Those who steal or take in other ways are not. If such a classification were permitted, the technical common law concept of a 'trespass' based on distinctions which are 'very largely dependent upon history for explanation' could readily become a rule of human genetics....

Reversed.

Mr. Chief Justice Stone concurring.

I concur in the result, but I am not persuaded that we are aided in reaching it by recourse to the equal protection clause.

If Oklahoma may resort generally to the sterilization of criminals on the assumption that their propensities are transmissible to future generations by inheritance, I seriously doubt that the equal protection clause requires it to apply the measure to all criminals in the first instance, or to none. Moreover, if we must presume that the legislature knows—what science has been unable to ascertain—that the criminal tendencies of any class of habitual offenders are transmissible regardless of the varying mental characteristics of its individuals, I should suppose that we must likewise presume that the legislature, in its wisdom, knows that the criminal tendencies of some classes of offenders are more likely to be transmitted than those of others. And so I think the real question we have to consider is not one of equal protection, but whether the wholesale condemnation of a class to such an invasion of personal liberty, without opportunity to any individual to show that his is not the type of case which would justify resort to it, satisfies the demands of due process.

There are limits to the extent to which the presumption of constitutionality can be pressed, especially where the liberty of the person is concerned and where the presumption is resorted to only to dispense with a procedure which the ordinary dictates of prudence would seem to demand for the protection of the individual from arbitrary action. Although petitioner here was given a hearing to ascertain whether sterilization would be detrimental to his health, he was given none to discover whether his criminal tendencies are of an inheritable type. Undoubtedly a state may, after appropriate inquiry, constitutionally interfere with the personal liberty of the individual to prevent the transmission by inheritance of his socially injurious tendencies. *Buck v. Bell*, 274 U.S. 200 [(1927)]. But until now we have not been called upon to say that it may do so without giving him a hearing and opportunity to challenge the existence as to him of the only facts which could justify so drastic a measure.

Science has found and the law has recognized that there are certain types of mental deficiency associated with delinquency which are inheritable. But the State does not contend—nor can there be any pretense—that either common knowledge or experience, or scientific investigation, has given assurance that the criminal tendencies of any class of habitual offenders are universally or even generally inheritable. In such circumstances, inquiry whether such is the fact in the case of any particular individual cannot rightly be dispensed with. Whether the procedure by which a statute carries its mandate into execution satisfies due process is a matter of judicial cognizance. A law which condemns, without hearing, all the individuals of a class to so harsh a measure as the present because some or even many merit condemnation, is lacking in the first principles of due process. And so, while the state may protect itself from the demonstrably inheritable tendencies of the individual which are injurious to society, the most elementary notions of due process would seem to require it to take appropriate steps to safeguard the liberty of the individual by affording him, before he is condemned to an irreparable injury in his person, some opportunity to show that he is without such inheritable tendencies. The state is called on to sacrifice no permissible end when it is required to reach its objective by a reasonable and just procedure adequate to safeguard rights of the individual which concededly the Constitution protects.

Mr. Justice Jackson, concurring.

I join the Chief Justice in holding that the hearings provided are too limited in the context of the present Act to afford due process of law. I also agree with the opinion of Mr. Justice Douglas that the scheme of classification set forth in the Act denies equal protection of the law. I disagree with the opinion of each in so far as it rejects or minimizes the grounds taken by the other....

I also think the present plan to sterilize the individual in pursuit of a eugenic plan to eliminate from the race characteristics that are only vaguely identified and which in our present state of knowledge are uncertain as to transmissibility presents other constitutional questions of gravity. This Court has sustained such an experiment with respect to an imbecile, a person with definite and observable characteristics where the condition had persisted through three generations and afforded grounds for the belief that it was transmissible and would continue to manifest itself in generations to come. *Buck v. Bell*, 274 U.S. 200 [(1927)].

There are limits to the extent to which a legislatively represented majority may conduct biological experiments at the expense of the dignity and personality and natural powers of a minority—even those who have been guilty of what the majority define as crimes. But this Act falls down before reaching this problem, which I mention only to avoid the implication that such a question may not exist because not discussed. On it I would also reserve judgment.

Poe v. Lynchburg Training School & Hospital

518 F. Supp. 789 (W.D. Va. 1981)

TURK, CHIEF JUDGE.

This case is filed as an individual and class action suit challenging the involuntary sterilization of a number of men and women by Virginia state officials acting pursuant to a statute enacted in 1924 by the Commonwealth of Virginia. The complaint also challenges the constitutionality of the purported refusal of appropriate Virginia state officials to notify all those persons who received such surgery as to their medical status and medical alternatives. In short, plaintiffs allege that many of those who were involuntarily sterilized are still unaware of the reason for their infertility as well as the medical ramifications of the procedure....

In 1924, the Commonwealth enacted legislation providing for the sexual sterilization of "mental defectives" in certain cases. 1924 Acts of Assembly, Chap. 394. As set forth in defendants' memorandum in support of the motion to dismiss, the statute specifically prescribed certain preliminary procedural steps including notification to the individual, or his or her parent, guardian, or committee as might be appropriate. Shortly after enactment of the statute, the constitutionality of the entire practice was tested in court, and the controversy eventually reached the United States Supreme Court. In *Buck v. Bell*, 274 U.S. 200 (1927), the United States Supreme Court held that the statute was not violative of any constitutionally guaranteed rights. However, in 1974, the involuntary sterilization statute was repealed. The parties agree that the Commonwealth has no statutory procedures permitting involuntary sterilization at the current time....

Stated briefly, plaintiffs seek as follows:

1. Entry of a judgment declaring that:

(a) the forced surgical sterilization of the sterilized class by Virginia state officials and agencies violated the Fourteenth Amendment, 42 U.S.C. § 1983, and the common law of Virginia; and

(b) defendants' subsequent failure to notify and prevent further harm to members of the sterilized class violates the Fourteenth Amendment, 42 U.S.C. s 1983, the Developmentally Disabled Assistance and Bill of Rights Act, and the common law of Virginia.

2. Entry of an Order enjoining defendants from authorizing or conducting any surgical sterilization without prior informed consent; and

3. Entry of an Order requiring defendants to provide adequate notice to all members of the sterilized class of the facts and circumstances of their involuntary surgical sterilization, including the effects and possible reversibility of the operations, and to provide such medical, surgical, and psychological assistance as is necessary to prevent further harm to members of the sterilized class, including operations to reverse the sterilization where possible....

Defendants' motion to dismiss for failure to state a claim is based on the assertions that the requested relief is barred by virtue of the Eleventh Amendment; that the complaint does not allege an actual case or controversy; and that the action is barred by virtue of the applicable statute of limitations....

The court has reached the conclusion that the motion must be granted in part and denied in part. Specifically, as to the different forms of relief sought by the complaint and as enumerated above, the court will enter an order granting the motion as to sections 1(a) and 2 of the prayer, and denying the motion as to sections 1(b) and 3....

Regardless of whatever philosophical and sociological valuation may be made regarding involuntary sterilizations in terms of current mores and social thought, the fact remains that the general practice and procedure under the old Virginia statute were upheld by the highest court in the land in *Buck v. Bell*, supra. It is no answer for the plaintiff to allude to changing patterns of social and constitutional thought as a ground for reopening the inquiry. Since 1974, well before the filing of the instant action, Virginia has had no involuntary sterilization statute. In short, this court has neither the authority nor the occasion to undertake an evaluation as to the constitutionality of the old Virginia statute permitting forced sterilizations....

Given the repeal of the involuntary sterilization statute, it is also apparent that plaintiffs are not entitled to an order, as sought in section 2 of the prayer, enjoining defendants from authorizing or conducting any surgical sterilization without prior informed consent. The complaint gives absolutely no indication that any of the defendants are likely to undertake such action in the future. Plaintiffs do not allege that there is any statutory or regulatory basis under which such action could be even conceivably undertaken. There is no reason to indicate that plaintiffs would, or could, be subjects of such action. Plaintiffs' allegations in this regard do not state the existence of a justiciable case or controversy and must accordingly be dismissed.

The court now directs its attention to those portions of plaintiffs' complaint and prayer dealing with defendants' alleged failure to notify plaintiffs of the fact of their sterilization and to otherwise provide information and assistance as might be appropriate. As suggested above, the old Virginia statute contained provisions which insured, at least in theory, that persons considered for involuntary sterilization, and their representatives, would be well advised prior to the surgery as to its purpose. Plaintiffs have alleged facts which indicate that in at least some instances, such notification was not provided and that potential candidates were affirmatively misled as to the purpose of the surgery. Plaintiffs contend that many such persons who were inadequately or inaccurately informed have suffered and continue to suffer medical, emotional, and mental problems, arising in large part from unsuccessful and uninformed attempts to deal with their infertility. Plaintiffs contend that defendants continue to refuse to notify and inform all those affected persons despite the fact that defendants now have reason to believe that some involuntarily sterilized persons were not properly notified at the time of their hospitalization. In short, plaintiffs contend that, in actual practice, the notification provisions of the statute were often not honored and that state officials have continued to perpetrate the deprivation through their subsequent refusal to notify all involuntarily sterilized persons as to their status. To the extent that the complaint sets forth such allegations, and to the extent of sections 1(b) and 3 of the prayer for relief, the court must conclude that the complaint states a claim.

As it must at this juncture, the court accepts as true all factual allegations of the complaint. Given those allegations, given the fundamental nature of personal interest involved, and considering the continuing anguish and discontent which could reasonably be inferred assuming that appropriate notification had been intentionally or negligently withheld, the court is unable to conclude as a matter of law that defendants are dispossessed of all continuing legal duty to plaintiffs. An exact determination as to the existence and extent of that duty must await more comprehensive development of the case, and indeed if such a duty does exist, it might well be that appropriate discharge of the duty would be inconsistent with the relief sought by plaintiffs....

An order in conformity will be entered this day. The case will be set for further proceedings upon petition of the parties.

Notes & Questions

1. *Buck v. Bell* was a test case pursued by leading eugenicists to obtain court approval of the Virginia sterilization law, the model law for their legislative agenda. It launched a movement across the U. S. to enact comparable laws, and by 1931 twenty-eight states had compulsory sterilization laws in place. Prior to World War II approximately 3000 operations were reported annually, probably an underestimate of the actual count. Although the practice of eugenics-based sterilizations declined after the war, it did not disappear completely, and by 1963 over 60,000 persons had been sterilized in various states pursuant to these laws. For more information on eugenics-based sterilization in the U.S. and in Nazi Germany, *see* Phillip R. Reilly, *Eugenics, Ethics, Sterilization Laws*, *in* ENCYCLOPEDIA OF ETHICAL, LEGAL AND POLICY ISSUES IN BIOTECHNOLOGY 204 (Thomas H. Murray & Maxwell J. Mehlman eds., 2000); Paul A. Lombardo, *Medicine, Eugenics and the Supreme Court: From Coercive Sterilization to Reproductive Freedom*, 13 J. CONTEMP. HEALTH L. & POL. 1 (1996); M.G. Silver, *Eugenics and Compulsory Sterilization Laws: Providing Redress for the Victims of a Shameful Era in United States History*, 72 GEO. WASH. L. REV. 862 (2004); A.N. Sofair & L.C. Kaldjian, *Eugenic Sterilization and a Qualified Nazi Analogy: The United States and Germany, 1930–1945*, 132 ANNALS OF INTERNAL MEDICINE 312 (2000). *See also* the cases and materials in Part C.

2. Obviously the "traits" at issue in the foregoing sterilization cases are not solely inherited but rather result from a complex mix of social, environmental, and genetic factors. Moreover, basic principles of Mendelian inheritance demonstrate that sterilization is not an effective means for eradicating inherited recessive traits such as "feeble-mindedness." What role did misunderstandings of the relevant science play in the eugenics movement? Consider the following analysis by Diane Paul and Hamish Spencer:

> Many textbooks suggest that eugenicists were guilty of an astoundingly simple mistake. According to conventional accounts, enthusiasts about eugenics thought they could eliminate mental deficiency by segregating or sterilizing affected individuals. But a basic understanding of the Hardy-Weinberg principle suffices to destroy that illusion.

> Eugenicists in the 1910s and 1920s attributed most mental defects to a recessive Mendelian factor (or in today's parlance, allele). But it is clear from the [Hardy-Weinberg equation] that if a trait is rare, most deleterious genes will be hidden in apparently normal carriers. Selection against those actually affected will thus be ineffective. Tables and formulas in many general biology and genetics textbooks serve to make the point that hundreds of generations are required before a rare deleterious trait would disappear.
>
> It is true that many eugenicists were muddled about genetics. But what about the host of respected geneticists ... who championed eugenics long after the implications of the Hardy-Weinberg principle were understood? The insight that selection is slow when genes are rare originated in 1917 and was popularized in the 1920s by J.B.S. Haldane in the United Kingdom and H.S. Hennings in the United States. Yet in the 1920s and 1930s, nearly all geneticists, including those traditionally characterized as opponents of eugenics, took it for granted that mental defectives should be prevented from breeding....
>
> It is often said that support for eugenics declined in the 1930s as scientific errors were exposed. But the eugenics movement grew stronger during the Depression. In the United States, the number of sterilizations increased....
>
> How then do we account for the popularity of the claim that eugenics was based on a technical error?.... In the first quarter of this century, nearly all geneticists were enthusiastic proponents of a movement that is now generally held in contempt.... So the history of the field is the source of some embarrassment (and defensiveness). It is far more comforting to think that eugenics' decline was also due to geneticists. The myth rights the historical balance....
>
> [Moreover if] eugenics is assumed to have rested on a technical error, it no longer raises thorny ethical questions. Geneticists can therefore condemn eugenics without questioning any of the aims of genetic testing.... Assuming eugenics is dead is one way to dispose of deep social, political and ethical questions. But it may not be the best one."

Diane B. Paul & Hamish G. Spencer, *The Hidden Science of Eugenics*, 374 NATURE 303 (1995).

3. The science underlying eugenics-based sterilization was not the only misunderstood aspect of the case against Carrie Buck. Paul Lombardo, among others, has written extensively regarding Carrie Buck's actual pedigree.

> In 1930 Doctor Bell reported that after her sterilization, Carrie Buck "was immediately returned to society and made good." That evaluation was only partially true. Although she was paroled as a domestic helper to a family in Bland, Virginia, she remained under the control of the Colony. Her discharge, like that of all sterilized Colony women, was conditioned on an annual visit to Doctor Bell for a physical examination. Had there been any complaints of ill behaviour, she could have been returned to the Colony at once.
>
> After Carrie left the Colony, she married and became a member of the Methodist Church in Bland where she sang in the choir as she had as a teenager in Charlottesville. After twenty-four years of marriage, her husband died and she traveled to Front Royal, Virginia, where she met and later married Charles Detamore. He took work in farms and orchards and Carrie assisted a local family in caring for an elderly relative....

> Throughout Carrie's adult life she regularly displayed intelligence and kindness that belied the "feeblemindedness" and "immorality" that were used as an excuse to sterilize her. She was an avid reader, and even in her last weeks was able to converse lucidly, recalling events from her childhood. Branded by Holmes as a second generation imbecile, Carrie provided no support for his glib epithet throughout her life.
>
> Carrie's daughter Vivian, like her mother, was wrongly accused. On the basis of a nurse's comment that she was "not quite normal," Vivan Buck was used to prove her mother's hereditary "defects." Although she lived barely eight years, she too disproved Holme's epigram. In her two years of schooling, she performed quite well, at one point earning a spot on the school "Honor Roll."
>
> Of the three generations, the least is known about Emma Buck. She died at the Colony, leaving few records of her life. She was, at worst, the "moron" that Priddy claimed; no one but Holmes charged her with imbecility. Her true shortcomings probably stemmed from poverty and perhaps promiscuity.

Paul A. Lombardo, *Three Generations, No Imbeciles: New Light on* Buck v. Bell, 60 N.Y.U. L. Rev. 30, 50–62 (1985). *See also* Paul A. Lombardo, *Facing Carrie Buck*, 33 The Hastings Center Report 14 (2003).

4. In *Skinner v. Oklahoma* the Supreme Court began to dismantle the legislative legacy of the eugenics movement, invalidating Oklahoma's compulsory sterilization law. The Court concluded the Oklahoma law was unconstitutional, but not because it impermissibly interfered with a constitutionally protected privacy right. What was the basis for the Court's ruling?

The Virginia compulsory sterilization statute was repealed by the state legislature in 1974. In light of this, what were plaintiffs in the *Poe* case trying to accomplish and to what extent were they successful? The case was actually filed with the support of the American Civil Liberties Union on behalf of 8000 women who had been involuntarily sterilized by the Lynchburg Training School, a state-run mental institution. Pursuant to a settlement reached in 1985 the state agreed to inform surviving women who had been involuntarily sterilized about what had been done and to provide access to counseling and medical treatment.

5. Is *Buck v. Bell* still good law? What impact, if any, does the Supreme Court's opinion in *Roe v. Wade* have on your analysis?

Relf v. Weinberger

372 F. Supp. 1196 (D.C. 1974)

Gesell, District Judge.

These two related cases, which have been consolidated with the consent of all parties, challenge the statutory authorization and constitutionality of regulations of the Department of Health, Education and Welfare (HEW) governing human sterilizations under programs and projects funded by the Department's Public Health Service and its Social and Rehabilitation Service. 39 Fed.Reg. 4730–34 (1974). Plaintiffs are the National Welfare Rights Organization (NWRO), suing on behalf of its 125,000 members, and five individual women, proceeding by class action on behalf of all poor persons subject to involuntary sterilization under the challenged regulations. Defendants are the Secretary of HEW, under whose authority the regulations were issued, 42 U.S.C. §216, and two high-level HEW officials charged with the administration of federal family planning funds.

The issues have been fully briefed and agued, and are now before the Court on separate motions for summary judgment by the respective plaintiffs and on the Secretary's motion for dismissal or summary judgment. Declaratory and injunctive relief is sought in both cases. The effective date of the regulations has been voluntarily deferred by the Secretary at the Court's request until March 18, 1974 to facilitate resolution of these issues.

Congress has authorized the funding of a full range of family planning services under two basic procedures. The Public Health Service administers federal grants to state health agencies and to public and private projects for the provision of family planning services to the poor, 42 U.S.C. §§300 et seq., 708(a), and the Social and Rehabilitation Service provides funds for such services under the Medicaid and Aid to Families of Dependent Children programs, 42 U.S.C. §§601 et seq., 1396 et seq....

Although there is no specific reference to sterilization in any of the family planning statutes nor in the legislative history surrounding their passage, the Secretary has considered sterilization to fall within the general statutory scheme and Congress has been made aware of this position. But until recently, there were no particular rules or regulations governing the circumstances under which sterilizations could be funded under these statutes.

Sterilization of females or males is irreversible. The total number of these sterilizations is clearly of national significance. Few realize that over 16 percent of the married couples in this country between the ages of 20 and 39 have had a sterilization operation. Over the last few years, an estimated 100,000 to 150,000 low-income persons have been sterilized annually under federally funded programs. Virtually all of these people have been adults: only about 2,000 to 3,000 per year have been under 21 years of age and fewer than 300 have been under 18. There are no statistics in the record indicating what percentage of these patients were mentally incompetent.

Although Congress has been insistent that all family planning programs function on a purely voluntary basis, there is uncontroverted evidence in the record that minors and other incompetents have been sterilized with federal funds and that an indefinite number of poor people have been improperly coerced into accepting a sterilization operation under the threat that various federally supported welfare benefits would be withdrawn unless they submitted to irreversible sterilization....

When such deplorable incidents began to receive nationwide public attention due to the experience of the Relf sisters in Alabama, the Secretary took steps to restrict the circumstances under which recipients of federal family planning funds could conduct sterilization operations. On August 3, 1973, the Department published in the Federal Register a notice of Guidelines for Sterilization Procedures under HEW Supported Programs. 38 Fed.Reg. 20930 (1973). The notice directed that the policies set forth in the guidelines be implemented through regulations to be issued by the departmental agencies administering programs which provide federal financial assistance for family planning services. Notices of proposed rule making were duly published in the Federal Register on September 21, 1973. 38 Fed.Reg. 26459 (1973). Interested persons were given an opportunity to participate in the rule making by submitting comments on the proposed regulations. Approximately 300 comments, including those of plaintiff NWRO, were received and reviewed by the Department. The final regulations here under attack were issued on February 6, 1974.

These regulations provide that projects and programs receiving PHS or SRS funds, whether for family planning or purely medical services, shall neither perform nor arrange for the performance of a nontherapeutic sterilization unless certain procedures are carried out. These vary depending upon whether the patient is, under state law, a legally competent adult, a legally competent person under the age of 18, a legally incompetent minor, or a mental incompetent. Briefly, they are as follows:

> (1) Legally competent adults must give their "informed consent" to sterilization. Such consent must be evidenced by a written and signed document indicating, inter alia, that the patient is aware of the benefits and costs of sterilization and of the fact that he may withdraw from the operation without losing federal benefits.
>
> (2) Legally competent persons under the age of 18 must also give such written consent. In these situations, a special Review Committee of independent persons from the community must also have determined that the proposed sterilization is in the best interest of the patient, taking into consideration (a) the expected mental and physical impact of pregnancy and motherhood on the patient, if female, or the expected mental impact of fatherhood, if male, and (b) the expected immediate and long-term mental and physical impact of sterilization on the patient. The Review Committee must also (a) review appropriate medical, social an psychological information concerning the patient, including the age of the patient, alternative family planning methods, and the adequacy of consent, and (b) interview the patient, both parents of the patient (if available), and such other persons as in its judgment will contribute pertinent information. However, parental consent is not required.
>
> (3) Legally incompetent minors must be afforded the above safeguards, and, in addition, a state court of competent jurisdiction must determine that the proposed sterilization is in the best interest of the patient.
>
> (4) The sterilization of mental incompetents of all ages must also be sanctioned by a Review Committee and a court. However, personal consent is not required—it is enough that the patient's "representative" requests sterilization. Although defendants interpret the term "representative" to mean a person empowered under state law to consent to the sterilization on behalf of the patient, no such definition appears in the regulations themselves.

Plaintiffs do not oppose the voluntary sterilization of poor persons under federally funded programs. However, they contend that these regulations are both illegal and arbitrary because they authorize involuntary sterilizations, without statutory or constitutional justification. They argue forcefully that sterilization of minors or mental incompetents is necessarily involuntary in the nature of things. Further, they claim that sterilization of competent adults under these regulations can be undertaken without insuring that the request for sterilization is in actuality voluntary. The Secretary defends the regulations and insists that only 'voluntary' sterilization is permitted under their terms....

For the reasons developed below, the Court finds that the Secretary has no statutory authority under the family planning sections of the Social Security or Public Health Services Acts to fund the sterilization of any person incompetent under state law to consent to such an operation, whether because of minority or of mental deficiency. It also finds that the challenged regulations are arbitrary and unreasonable in that they fail to implement the congressional command that federal family planning funds not be used to coerce indigent patients into submitting to sterilization. In short, federally assisted family planning sterilizations are permissible only with the voluntary, knowing and uncoerced consent of individuals competent to give such consent. This result requires an injunction against substantial portions of the proposed regulations and their revision to insure that all sterilizations funded under the family planning sections are voluntary in the full sense of that term and that sterilization of incompetent minors and adults is prevented.

The dispute with regard to minors and mental incompetents centers around two aspects of the statutory language. On the one hand, Congress included in every section mentioning family planning a requirement that such services be voluntarily requested. 42 U.S.C. §§ 300a-5, 602(a)(15), 708(a), 1396d(a)(4). On the other hand, these sections purport to offer family planning services to all poor people and two of them specifically include minors. 42 U.S.C. §§ 602(a)(15), 1396d(a)(4). The Secretary argues that this juxtaposition indicates that Congress intended that minors personally and incompetents through their representatives would be able to consent to sterilization under these sections. That conclusion is unwarranted.

Although the term 'voluntary' is nowhere defined in the statutes under consideration, it is frequently encountered in the law. Even its dictionary definition assumes an exercise of free will and clearly precludes the existence of coercion or force. Webster's Second New International Dictionary 2858 (2d ed. 1961). And its use in the statutory and decisional law, at least when important human rights are at stake, entails a requirement that the individual have at his disposal the information necessary to make his decision and the mental competence to appreciate the significance of that information....

The statutory references to minors and mental incompetents do not contradict this conclusion, for they appear only in the context of family planning services in general. Minors, for example, are not legally incompetent for all purposes, and many girls of Child-bearing age are undoubtedly sufficiently aware of the relevant considerations to use temporary contraceptives that intrude far less on fundamental rights. However, the Secretary has not demonstrated and the Court cannot find that Congress deemed such children capable of voluntarily consenting to an irreversible operation involving the basic human right to procreate. Nor can the Court find, in the face of repeated warnings concerning voluntariness, that Congress authorized the imposition of such a serious deprivation upon mental incompetents at the will of an unspecified "representative."

The regulations also fail to provide the procedural safeguards necessary to insure that even competent adults voluntarily request sterilization. Plaintiffs would require an elaborate hearing process prior to the operation to remedy this problem. The Secretary, however, has determined that the consent document procedure set forth in he existing regulations is adequate in most instances to insure a knowledgeable decision, and the Court finds that this determination is not unreasonable. In one respect, however, the consent procedure must be improved. Even a fully informed individual cannot make a 'voluntary' decision concerning sterilization if he has been subjected to coercion from doctors or project officers. Despite specific statutory language forbidding the recipients of federal family planning funds to threaten a cutoff of program benefits unless the individual submits to sterilization and despite clear evidence that such coercion is actually being applied, the challenged regulations contain no clear safeguard against this abuse. Although the required consent document must state that the patient can withdraw his consent to sterilization without losing other program benefits, there is nothing to prohibit the use of such coercion to extract the initial consent.

In order to prevent express or implied threats, which would obviate the Secretary's entire framework of procedural safeguards, and to insure compliance with the statutory language, the Court concludes that the regulations must also be amended to require that individuals seeking sterilization be orally informed at the very outset that no federal benefits can be withdrawn because of a failure to accept sterilization. This guarantee must also appear prominently at the top of the consent document already required by the regulations. To permit sterilization without this essential safeguard is an unreasonable and arbitrary interpretation of the congressional mandate.

Since these conclusions are based on statutory rather than constitutional grounds, the Court need not reach the question of whether involuntary sterilization could be funded by Congress. It is sufficient to note that there is no indication whatever that Congress intended to do so under the existing legislation, and such an intent will not be lightly assumed in light of the fundamental interests at stake. The present statutes were passed to facilitate only voluntary family planning and thus to assist the individual in the exercise of his voluntary right to govern his own procreation. Involuntary sterilization is not only distinguishable from these services, but diametrically so. It invades rather than compliments the right to procreate.

This controversy has arisen during a period of rapid change in the field of birth control. In recent years, through the efforts of dedicated proponents of family planning, birth control information and services have become widely available. Aided by the growing acceptance of family planning, medical science has steadily improved and diversified the techniques of birth prevention and control. Advancements in artificial insemination and in the understanding of genetic attributes are also affecting the decision to bear children. There are even suggestions in the scientific literature that the sex of children may soon be subject to parental control. And over this entire area lies the specter of overpopulation, with its possible impact upon the food supply, interpersonal relations, privacy, and the enjoyment of our 'inalienable rights.'

Surely the Federal Government must move cautiously in this area, under well-defined policies determined by Congress after full consideration of constitutional and far-reaching social implications. The dividing line between family planning and eugenics is murky. And yet the Secretary, through the regulations at issue, seeks to sanction one of the most drastic methods of population control—the involuntary irreversible sterilization of men and women—without any legislative guidance. Whatever might be the merits of limiting irresponsible reproduction, which each year places increasing numbers of unwanted or mentally defective children into tax supported institutions, it is for Congress and not individual social workers and physicians to determine the manner in which federal funds should be used to support such a program. We should not drift into a policy which has unfathomed implications and which permanently deprives unwilling or immature citizens of their ability to procreate without adequate legal safeguards and a legislative determination of the appropriate standards in light of the general welfare and of individual rights....

Notes & Questions

1. *Relf v. Weinberger* resulted from a highly-publicized case of involuntary sterilization involving the Relf sisters, three young black girls in Montgomery, Alabama. Two of the sisters, ages twelve and fourteen, were sterilized without their knowledge or consent after their illiterate mother placed her "x" on a surgical release form. The mother thought she was signing a release for her girls to continue receiving Depro Provera shots as part of a contraception study. The third sister, age seventeen, escaped sterilization but only by physically resisting. The defendants' appeal of the District Court's ruling was remanded for consideration of proposed modifications to the challenged regulations governing

human sterilization. The District Court rejected the proposed modifications (Relf v. Mathews, 403 F. Supp. 1235 (1975)), and the defendants again filed an appeal. The case was ultimately vacated as moot following the Secretary's decision to withdraw the pending regulations and propose a new framework that was more restrictive than the District Court's initial ruling required. *Relf v. Weinberger*, 565 F.2d 722 (D.C. Cir. 1977). Does the regulatory framework contemplated by the District Court offer adequate protection for the individual interests that are implicated in these types of cases?

2. What are the similarities and differences between the sterilization practices at issue in the *Relf* case and those under consideration in *Buck v. Bell*? What about the state's interests in each of the cases—are they similar or different?

Alexandra Minna Stern,
Sterilized in the Name of Public Health

95 Am. J. Public Health 1128 (2005)

...

... Home to an extensive eugenics movement that crisscrossed the domains of agriculture, education, medicine, and government, California was propitious terrain for the emergence of a far-reaching sterilization regimen. Eugenic ideas were espoused by influential professionals, such as Stanford University Chancellor David Starr Jordan, the Santa Rosa "plant wizard" Luther Burbank, and the Los Angeles politician Dr. John R. Haynes. In 1924, Charles M. Goethe, a Sacramento businessman, collaborated with University of California zoologist Samuel J. Holmes to found the Eugenics Section of the San Francisco-based Commonwealth Club of California.

Several years later, the agriculturalist and philanthropist Ezra S. Gosney, in consultation with the Eugenics Record Office (located in Cold Spring Harbor, NY), underwrote the Human Betterment Foundation to foment sterilization education and legislation. Gosney eventually selected Paul Popenoe, a date palm cultivator and social hygienist, to conduct a detailed study of sterilization. After collecting data and interviewing patients and staff at state homes and hospitals, he and Gosney coauthored *Sterilization for Human Betterment: A Summary of Results of 6000 Operations in California, 1909–1929*, which touted the immense value of reproductive surgery and rallied sterilization crusaders across the United States and Europe. This mission was furthered by the activities of the Eugenics Society of Northern California, the California Division of the American Eugenics Society, and the American Institute of Family Relations. In addition to these organizations, California's sterilization system was buoyed by the administration and involvement of the Department of Institutions, which managed state homes and hospitals, several of which were run by ardent superintendents who devised novel surgical techniques.

Because of the state's multi-faceted eugenics movement and the fact that it appreciably outpaced in absolute terms the other 32 states that passed sterilization laws at some point in the 20th century, California stands out when compared with the rest of the country. California carried out more than twice as many sterilizations as either of its nearest rivals, Virginia (approximately 8000) and North Carolina (approximately 7600). Furthermore, in many states, such as New Jersey and Iowa, sterilization laws were declared unconstitutional, judged to be "cruel and unusual punishment" or in violation of equal protection and due process. In contrast, California's statute—although reworked over the years—remained in effect without interruption from initial passage until repeal [in 1979].

One of the reasons for this longevity was that, from the outset, California defined sterilization not as a punishment but as a prophylactic measure that could simultaneously defend the public health, preserve precious fiscal resources, and mitigate the menace of the "unfit" and "feebleminded." California's prescience was acknowledged in 1927, when the most powerful judiciary in the land, the U.S. Supreme Court, ruled affirmatively on the constitutionality of Virginia's sterilization statute in *Buck v. Bell*, countenancing sterilization on behalf of the collective health of the citizenry. . . .

If utilitarian pursuit of the common good required mandatory vaccination to inoculate against communicable diseases, it also necessitated "immunizing" the hereditarily defective in order to prevent the spread of bad genes. Once seen as integral to health prophylaxis and as a cost-saving recourse, sterilization programs intensified at a clipped pace across the country in the 1930s. By 1932, twenty-seven states had laws on the books and procedures nationwide reached over 3900. Not only did operations increase markedly during this decade, but some states, such as Georgia and South Carolina, passed legislation for the first time.

In California, at least into the 1950s, compulsory sterilization was consistently described as a public health strategy that could breed out undesirable defects from the populace and fortify the state as a whole. Convinced of its efficacy, sterilization proponents pushed for implementation of the law beyond the walls of state institutions. For example, in his *Los Angeles Times* Sunday magazine column "Social Eugenics" (which ran from 1936 to 1941), Fred Hogue claimed that "in this country we have wiped out the mosquito carriers of yellow fever and are in a fair way to extinguish the malaria carriers: but the human breeders of the hereditary physical and mental unfit are only in exceptional cases placed under restraint." To rectify this situation, Hogue recommended broader intervention and argued that eugenic practices, above all sterilization, were essential to "the protection of the public health" and "the health security of the citizens of every State." [In the] second edition of their popular textbook *Applied Eugenics*, Popenoe and colleague Roswell H. Johnson underscored that "if persons whose offspring will be dysgenic are so lacking in intelligence, in foresight, or in self-control that they do not control themselves, the state must control them. Sterilization is the answer."

Rooted in this logic and shored up by *Buck v. Bell*, sterilizations rose dramatically in California in the 1930s, peaking at 848 in 1939 and 818 in 1941. By 1942, over 15 000 operations had been performed in the state, most since 1925. Even when per capita comparisons are made with states with much smaller populations, California's rates were always clustered at the top. Not until the 1940s, when California claimed about 60% of all operations nationwide, did a few states, such as Delaware, North Carolina, and Virginia, begin to consistently overtake California in either per capita or annual terms.

. . .

The final substantial year for California's sterilization program was 1951, with 255 operations performed. The following year, the number dropped considerably to 51, undoubtedly because of a revision to the statute inserting administrative requirements for physicians and safeguards for patients. This amendment, and another 1953 bill, deleted any references to syphilis (long since understood as microbial, not genetic, in etiology) and sexual perversion; instituted more demanding processes of notice, hearing, and appeal; and removed the terms "idiots" and "fools" from the law. By turning what had been a mere formality into a more taxing ordeal, these modifications deterred many physicians from requesting sterilization orders. Nevertheless, surgeries continued sporadically at every state institution into the 1970s.

In part, this legal modification reflected a shift in the criteria employed to sanction reproductive surgery, as an emphasis on parenting skills and welfare dependency began to supplant hereditary fitness and putative innate mental capacity as the determinants of an individual's social and biological drain on society. By this time, many eugenicists had conceded that earlier attempts to stamp out hereditary traits defined as recessive or latent, including alcoholism, immorality, and the catchall "feeblemindedness," had been proven futile by the Hardy-Weinberg equilibrium principle, which demonstrated that the overwhelming tendency of gene frequencies and ratios was to remain constant from one generation to the next. Thus, targeted interventions, such as sterilization, could not breed out defects; even if viable, they would show results only after thousands of years of regulated procreation. More and more, eugenicists traded in "unit characters" for polygenic inheritance and genetic predispositions. Accompanying this realignment was a heightened interest in the manipulation and management of human heredity through population control, which postwar eugenicists and their allies pursued through groups such as the Population Council, Population Reference Bureau, and Planned Parenthood.

On the basis of a revamped rationale of bad parenthood and population burden, sterilizations increased in the 1950s and 1960s in southern states such as North Carolina and Virginia. Concurrently, sterilization often regained a punitive edge and, preponderantly aimed at African American and poor women, began to be wielded by state courts and legislatures as a punishment for bearing illegitimate children or as extortion to ensure ongoing receipt of family assistance. By the 1960s, the protracted history of state sterilization programs in the United States, and the consolidation of a rationale for reproductive surgery that was linked to fears of overpopulation, welfare dependency, and illegitimacy, set the stage for a new era of sterilization abuse. In California, which never explicitly endorsed a punitive model, the state program was fairly quiescent by the mid-1950s. However, when federal backing for reproductive surgery began to be distributed in the late 1960s, the eugenic refrains of previous decades resurfaced. The reproductive tendencies of working-class Mexican-origin women were reviled in accordance with long-standing ideas of public health protection, along with more recent claims that these fecund female immigrants were worsening an already severe overpopulation problem.

...

The legacy of involuntary sterilization lingers in California. It is no coincidence, for instance, that the Golden State was home to Proposition 187, which was passed by a majority of votes in 1994 and strove to drastically restrict health, educational, and social services to "illegal aliens." Its intent and rhetoric strongly resembled that iterated by California eugenicists and the Department of the Institutions in the early 20th century in terms of who deserved access to health services during pregnancy (in this permutation, denial rather than the imposition of reproductive control), who was allowed to reproduce on American soil, and who should be deported. Discursively unoriginal, it targeted Mexicans, who were portrayed as infectious hyperbreeders, alien invaders, and vampires threatening to bankrupt the state. Because of its negation of basic rights to an entire class of individuals, Proposition 187 was swiftly contested in the courts and ruled unconstitutional in 1998.

If Proposition 187 demonstrates the perduring eugenic and fiscal logic of public health prophylaxis, then California's innovative prenatal testing program reveals the difficult ethical questions raised by contemporary instances of public health genetics. In

1986, California was first state to pass a law requiring that all pregnant mothers be offered MSAFP (maternal serum alpha-fetoprotein) screening to assess the likelihood of Down syndrome, spina bifida, and neural tube defects. Rather than making such testing compulsory, this law mandates that genetic counselors inform patients of the availability of MSAFP. As studies show, however, given societal pressure to use extant medical technologies in order to do the "best" for one's children, many women accede to prenatal testing even if, for linguistic or cultural reasons, the implications of testing or positive diagnosis are unclear.

Focusing on California, two medical anthropologists have described scenarios in which Mexican-origin women are, usually inadvertently, receiving incomplete or distorted information about genetic screening and its meanings. This situation is exacerbated by a dearth of minority and bilingual genetic counselors trained and prepared to translate complex scientific and technical information to diverse patient populations. However, it is also related to genetic professionals' desire to distance themselves from the coercive practices associated with eugenics, a psychological technique defined as "non-directiveness." Even if motivated by noble intentions, attaining such neutrality is not only unrealizable, given that social values are embedded in medical institutions and decisions, but often frustrates patients, especially those from newly arrived immigrant groups who expect expert advice from genetic practitioners.

With California at the forefront, the demographics of the United States are changing, and it is likely that within a century Whites will no longer constitute the nation's racial/ethnic majority. At the same time, genetic and reproductive technologies are proliferating and, although not necessarily offering therapy or cure, will generate information about the probabilities of genetic diseases that, in turn, will need to be communicated in a culturally sensitive manner. This is a great challenge for the 21st century; as a crucial component of tomorrow's public and reproductive health, it can be ethically enhanced by awareness of the ways in which history weighs on contemporary biomedicine and society.

Notes & Questions

1. Stern suggests that there is a common eugenic undercurrent throughout the history of sterilization practices in the U.S. Do you agree? Why or why not? What, if anything, does past history suggest regarding the potential eugenic implications associated with public health applications of genetic technologies? Like Stern, Diane Paul has used the California law mandating an offer of MSAFP screening to all pregnant women to stimulate a dialogue regarding the relationship between contemporary genetics and eugenics:

> Concerns about eugenics typically fall in one of three distinct classes. The first is fear of direct government programs.... How realistic is the fear of direct government intervention? In respect to coercive gene therapy, not very. Even if it were technically feasible, large-scale gene implantation would be an extraordinarily expensive kind of eugenics. And cost saving has always been the strongest motive for eugenics.... Cost benefit analysis could, however, produce a stimulus for "negative" eugenics. After all, the plus side of the cost-benefit ledger is represented by the number of terminations achieved for a specified condition. The more women who are screened, and affected fetuses aborted, the more efficient the genetic service. Hence cost-benefit arguments for state support of these programs provide an incentive to expand genetic testing and "maximize" the rate of terminations of pregnancy for 'costly' disorders.

> American states already sponsor many prenatal and newborn screening programs, including some that are mandatory. For example every state tests for phenylketonuria (PKU); parental consent is rarely required. Ultrasound screening is also routinely performed (without consent) on virtually every woman who sees a doctor early enough in her pregnancy. Cost-benefit considerations help explaining the vast expansion in the number of women who no undergo prenatal testing. They provide a powerful inducement to test more women, for more disorders, at an earlier age....
>
> Pressures to routinize screening will certainly increase with the development of tests that predict which individuals will bear offspring with genetic disorders. Individuals with the autosomal dominant gene for Huntington disease, polycystic kidney disease, and a rapidly growing list of other late-onset disorders can now be identified before they suffer symptoms and make reproductive decisions. Carriers of a number of autosomal recessive disorders, such as Tay Sachs disease, sickle cell anemia, and most recently, cystic fibrosis (CF), can also be identified. CF is the most common severe genetic disease affecting Caucasians, with an incidence of about 1 in 2500 live births. About 1 in 25 white persons (or more than eight million people) are asymptomatic carriers. The ability to screen for common autosomal recessive diseases offers a solution to the problem that has bedeviled eugenicists since the first decade of this century....

Diane B. Paul, *Is Human Genetics Disguised Eugenics? in* GENES AND HUMAN SELF-KNOWLEDGE: HISTORICAL AND PHILOSOPHICAL REFLECTIONS ON MODERN GENETICS 67–83 (R. Weir, S. Lawrence, & E. Fales, eds., 1994). Many would discount or disavow the suggestion that contemporary prenatal genetics has a negative eugenics undercurrent, arguing instead that using genetics to identify and avoid the disorders Paul describes represents a significant medical advance that promises to improve health and welfare for individuals and the population. Do you agree or disagree with the concerns expressed by Stern and Paul? Revisit this question after you review the following commentary presenting the disability rights critique of prenatal genetic testing.

Adrienne Asch, *Prenatal Diagnosis and Selective Abortion: A Challenge to Practice and Policy*

89 AM. J. PUBLIC HEALTH 1649 (1999)

...

Prenatal tests designed to detect the condition of the fetus include ultrasound, maternal serum ot-fetoprotein screening, chorionic villus sampling, and amniocentesis. Some (ultrasound screenings) are routinely performed regardless of the mother's age and provide information that she may use to guide her care throughout pregnancy; others, such as chorionic villus sampling or amniocentesis, do not influence the woman's care during pregnancy but provide information intended to help her decide whether to continue the pregnancy if fetal impairment is detected. Amniocentesis, the test that detects the greatest variety of fetal impairments, is typically offered to women who will be 35 years or older at the time they are due to deliver, but recently commentators have urged that the age threshold be removed and that the test be available to women regardless of age. Such testing is increasingly considered a standard component of prenatal care for women whose insurance covers these procedures, including women using publicly financed clinics in some jurisdictions.

These tests, which are widely accepted in the field of bioethics and by clinicians, public health professionals, and the general public, have nonetheless occasioned some apprehension and concern among students of women's reproductive experiences, who find that women do not uniformly welcome the expectation that they will undergo prenatal testing or the prospect of making decisions depending on the test results. Less often discussed by clinicians is the view, expressed by a growing number of individuals, that the technology is itself based on erroneous assumptions about the adverse impact of disability on life. Argument from this perspective focuses on what is communicated about societal and familial acceptance of diversity in general and disability in particular....

If public health frowns on efforts to select for or against girls or boys and would oppose future efforts to select for or against those who would have a particular sexual orientation, but promotes people's efforts to avoid having children who would have disabilities, it is because medicine and public health view disability as extremely different from and worse than these other forms of human variation. At first blush this view may strike one as self-evident. To challenge it might even appear to be questioning our professional mission. Characteristics such as chronic illnesses and disabilities (discussed together throughout this article) do not resemble traits such as sex, sexual orientation, or race, because the latter are not in themselves perceived as inimical to a rewarding life. Disability is thought to be just that to be incompatible with life satisfaction. When public health considers matters of sex, sexual orientation, or race, it examines how factors in social and economic life pose obstacles to health and to health care, and it champions actions to improve the well-being of those disadvantaged by the discrimination that attends minority status. By contrast, public health fights to eradicate disease and disability or to treat, ameliorate, or cure these when they occur. For medicine and public health, disease and disability is the problem to solve, and so it appears natural to use prenatal testing and abortion as one more means of minimizing the incidence of disability....

What many scholars, policymakers, and activists in the area of disability contend is that medically oriented understandings of the impact of disability on life contain two erroneous assumptions with serious adverse consequences: first, that the life of a person with a chronic illness or disability is forever disrupted, as one's life might be temporarily disrupted as a result of a back spasm, an episode of pneumonia, or a broken leg; second, that if a disabled person experiences isolation, powerlessness, unemployment, poverty, or low social status, these are inevitable consequences of biological limitation. Body, psyche, and social life do change immediately following an occurrence of disease, accident, or injury, and medicine, public health, and bioethics all correctly appreciate the psychological and physical vulnerability of patients and their families and friends during immediate medical crises. These professions fail people with disabilities, however, by concluding that because there may never be full physical recovery, there is never a regrouping of physical, cognitive, and psychological resources with which to participate in a rewarding life. Chronic illness and disability are not equivalent to acute illness or sudden injury, in which an active disease process or unexpected change in physical function disrupts life's routines. Most people with conditions such as spina bifida, achondroplasia, Down syndrome, and many other mobility and sensory impairments perceive themselves as healthy, not sick, and describe their conditions as givens of their lives—the equipment with which they meet the world. The same is true for people with chronic conditions such as cystic fibrosis, diabetes, hemophilia, and muscular dystrophy. These conditions include intermittent flare-ups requiring medical care and adjustments in daily living, but they do not render the person as unhealthy as most of the public—and members of the health profession—imagine....

The second way in which medicine, bioethics, and public health typically err is in viewing all problems that occur to people with disabilities as attributable to the condition itself, rather than to external factors. When ethicists, public health professionals, and policymakers discuss the importance of health care, urge accident prevention, or promote healthy lifestyles, they do so because they perceive a certain level of health not only as intrinsically desirable but as a prerequisite for an acceptable life....

Commitments to alleviate the difficulties arising from chronic illness and disability and efforts to promote healthy lifestyles throughout the population need not lead to a devaluation of the members of society who do not meet our typical understanding of health, but people with disabilities have indeed been subject to systematic segregation and second-class treatment in all areas of life. It is possible to appreciate the norm of two arms without being repelled by a woman with one arm; yet social science, autobiography, legislation, and case law reveal that people with both visible and "invisible" disabilities lose opportunities to study, work, live where and with whom they choose, attend religious services, and even vote....

If some forms of disability prevention are legitimate medical and public health activities, and if people with disabilities use the health system to improve and maintain their own health, there is an acknowledgment that the characteristic of disability may not be desirable. Although many within the disability rights movement challenge prenatal diagnosis as a means of disability prevention, no one objects to public health efforts to clean up the environment, encourage seat-belt use, reduce tobacco and alcohol consumption, and provide prenatal care to all pregnant women. All these activities deal with the health of existing human beings (or fetuses expected to come to term) and seek to ensure their well-being. What differentiates prenatal testing followed by abortion from other forms of disability prevention and medical treatment is that prenatal testing followed by abortion is intended not to prevent the disability or illness of a born or future human being but to prevent the birth of a human being who will have one of these undesired characteristics....

The medical professions justify prenatal diagnosis and selective abortion on the grounds of the costs of childhood disability—the costs to the child, to the family, and to the society. Some proponents of the Human Genome Project from the fields of science and bioethics argue that in a world of limited resources, we can reduce disability-related expenditures if all diagnoses of fetal impairment are followed by abortion.

On both empirical and moral grounds, endorsing prenatal diagnosis for societal reasons is dangerous. Only a small fraction of total disability can now be detected prenatally, and even if future technology enables the detection of predisposition to diabetes, forms of depression, Alzheimer disease, heart disease, arthritis, or back problems—all more prevalent in the population than many of the currently detectable conditions—we will never manage to detect and prevent most disability. Rates of disability increase markedly with age, and the gains in life span guarantee that most people will deal with disability in themselves or someone close to them. Laws and services to support people with disabilities will still be necessary, unless society chooses a campaign of eliminating disabled people in addition to preventing the births of those who would be disabled. Thus, there is small cost-saving in money or in human resources to be achieved by even the vigorous determination to test every pregnant woman and abort every fetus found to exhibit disabling traits....

Public health professionals must do more than they have been doing to change the climate in which prenatal tests are offered. Think about what people would say if prenatal clinics contained pamphlets telling poor women or African American women that they should consider refraining from childbearing because their children could be similarly poor and could endure discrimination or because they could be less healthy and more likely to find themselves imprisoned than members of the middle class or than Whites. Public health is committed to ending such inequities, not to endorsing them, tolerating them, or asking prospective parents to live with them. Yet the current promotion of prenatal testing condones just such an approach to life with disability....

In order to make testing and selecting for or against disability consonant with improving life for those who will inevitably be born with or acquire disabilities, our clinical and policy establishments must communicate that it is as acceptable to live with a disability as it is to live without one and that society will support and appreciate everyone with the inevitable variety of traits. We can assure prospective parents that they and their future child will be welcomed whether or not the child has a disability. If that professional message is conveyed, more prospective parents may envision that their lives can be rewarding, whatever the characteristics of the child they are raising. When our professions can envision such communication and the reality of incorporation and appreciation of people with disabilities, prenatal technology can help people to make decisions without implying that only one decision is right. If the child with a disability is not a problem for the world, and the world is not a problem for the child, perhaps we can diminish our desire for prenatal testing and selective abortion and can comfortably welcome and support children of all characteristics.

C. Public Health Genetics: Contemporary Applications and Future Issues

The use of genetic-based technology to conduct population screening is one of the clearest examples of public health genetics in practice. In population screening, large numbers of people who have no symptoms are tested to detect biological presence of disease before symptoms are apparent, thereby permitting early interventions to monitor and treat affected individuals and/or control person-to-person transmission of the disease. As our ability to use genetic testing to identify health risks and prevent disease increases, population-based genetic screening could well become a significant public health tool. Currently, genetic-based tests are used in screening programs to identify individuals at risk for relatively rare disorders that have significant morbidity or mortality without early intervention. Examples of these include state-mandated newborn screening programs for phenylketonuria; prenatal screening for neural tube defects, Down Syndrome and other trisomy-related disorders; and carrier screening to identify prospective parents who carry the genetic variants known to cause Tay-Sachs disease or sickle cell anemia. Consider, however, the prospect of using genetic-based screening to identify individuals at risk for common disorders such as heart disease, diabetes, and cancer. What ethical, legal, and social policy issues might accompany public health policy development in this area? Would it make a difference to your analysis if the screening is used in the adult population or for identifying disease risk in children? How important to your analysis is information regarding the presence or absence of interventions to treat the disease in question or ameliorate the risk of developing that disease? To assist you in answering these questions, we have selected cases and materials involving carrier screening, prenatal screening, and newborn screening. For additional background reading, *see* M.J. Khoury et al., *Population Screening in the Age of Genomic Medicine*, 348 NEW ENG. J. MED. 50 (2003); B.S. Wilfond & E.J. Thomson, MODELS OF PUBLIC HEALTH GENETIC POLICY DEVELOPMENT IN GENETICS AND PUBLIC HEALTH IN THE 21ST CENTURY 164 (M.J. Khoury, W. Burke, & E.J. Thomson, eds. 2000).

1. Carrier Screening

Howard Markel, *Scientific Advances and Social Risks: Historical Perspectives of Genetic Screening Programs for Sickle Cell Disease, Tay-Sachs Disease, Neural Tube Defects and Down Syndrome, 1970–1997*

Appendix 6, Final Report of the NIH-DOE Task Force on Genetic Testing (September 1997)

... It is difficult to pinpoint exactly why a collection of public health agencies, physicians, African-American activists, and the Federal and several state governments chose, from all the pressing medical and socioeconomic needs of the African-American community during the early 1970s, to focus on the implementation of mandatory sickle cell screening laws. Even now there is no definitive curative treatment for sickle cell anemia, a disease that affects one out of every 400 to 600 African-Americans, or 0.2 percent of that population. (One out of every 10 to 12 African-Americans are carriers of the trait.)

The majority of those screened for sickle cell in the early 1970s were school-aged children or young adults. If any of these individuals actually had sickle cell disease, they probably already had been clinically diagnosed. Because there was no definitive treatment to prevent damage, they were highly likely to have already been harmed. Nor, at that time, was there any safe and inexpensive means of making a prenatal diagnosis of sickle cell anemia in the developing fetus. (It was not until 1978 that Y. W. Kan developed the DNA limited marker test.) Since prenatal diagnosis was virtually not possible, and there were no curative therapies, what did the early sickle cell screening programs hope to accomplish? As Holtzman observed, the "compelling public health interest served by these laws is difficult to discern."

The early 1970s coincided with the peak of the Civil Rights movement, wider voter registration among African Americans, an increase in the number of African-American elected officials, and African-American activism ranging from that of clergy and church-based groups to the Black Panthers. In response to the maelstrom of social forces then engulfing the African-American community, President Richard Nixon issued a number of executive orders. A presidential initiative in 1971 increased federal support for the treatment of and research on, sickle cell anemia (approximately $6 million a year). That same year, U.S. Senate hearings on the establishment of a national sickle cell anemia program were initiated. Between 1970 and 1972, twelve states and the District of Columbia enacted mandatory sickle cell screening laws for African-American citizens. More often than not, however, these laws were written and passed without adequate attention to the stigmatizing of not only those people with the disease, but also of those who carried the sickle cell trait. As Reilly concluded in his analysis of the early sickle cell programs: "In retrospect it is clear that the haste with which these laws were drafted and passed contributed substantially to the acrimonious controversy that soon engulfed screening practices."

Several major criticisms of the early sickle cell screening programs have been identified. These criticisms include: 1) a lack of sensitivity to issues of race; 2) controversy surrounding the accuracy and validity of the early screening tests; and 3) inadequate protection of the patient's rights.

Race and Genetics. The most serious criticism of the early sickle cell screening programs has to do with the racial issues surrounding the disease. The initial programs were directed almost exclusively at African-Americans. The briefest review of some of the laws mandating these programs supports that a specific net was cast for African Americans. For example, the New York State law ordered that all persons "not of the Caucasian, Indian, or Oriental races" be tested for sickle cell trait before being allowed to obtain a marriage license. A subsequent New York State law required all urban (but not suburban or rural) schoolchildren to be screened with the tacit understanding that the overwhelming majority of African Americans living in New York at that time were urban dwellers. A similar law enacted in the District of Columbia went one step further in the process of genetic isolation by referring to the blood dyscrasia as a "communicable disease," a term traditionally reserved for infectious rather than inherited diseases and implying the need for quarantine or ostracism.,

The compulsory screening laws directed at only African Americans obscured the fact that ethnic groups other than blacks can carry the trait and suffer from sickle cell anemia (e.g., people of Mediterranean origins), an omission that ethicist John Fletcher characterized as "racial obfuscation." The national focus on a relatively rare genetic disease presented as "the most vital health issue" facing African Americans also presented several extremely negative political implications—a situation which was not lost on the black community. For example, Bryant Rollins, the executive editor of the Amsterdam News (New York City), noted that the federal government's award of a five-year $2.5 million grant to the Harlem Hospital for sickle cell research was far from ideal: "If you read the fine print, there is another side to this grant, the effect of which is to rob the Harlem community of $1 million in much needed funds" that might be better applied to the myriad social, economic, and health problems affecting it.

Misinterpretation of Test Results. A second criticism of the initial sickle cell screening programs was the potential for misinterpretation of the results. At some centers, the validity of the screening methods themselves became the subject of controversy. There were several documented reports of the misuse of the Sickledex test (which does not distinguish trait from homozygous affected) and of the poor quality of many of the laboratories performing the tests, sometimes under state mandates. Many of the state and local programs were based on an inadequate knowledge of the genetics of sickle cell disease and as a consequence many of the laws needlessly stigmatized carriers of the sickle cell trait as well as those with the illness. Perhaps most glaring was the apparent ease with which the diagnosis of a heterozygote "carrier status" of sickle cell anemia was used almost interchangeably with homozygote "disease status."

The ostracism of sickle cell carriers, unfortunately, became far more than a theoretical concern for African Americans and public health officials. One especially outrageous diatribe by the late scientist and Nobel laureate Linus C. Pauling published in a February, 1968 issue of the UCLA Law Review reflects this stigmatization process of sickle cell carriers: "There should be tattooed on the forehead of every young person, a symbol showing possession of the sickle cell gene [so as to prevent] two young people carrying the same seriously defective gene in single dose from falling in love with one another."

More seriously, by the early 1970s many African Americans were stigmatized by their carrier status in the form of being denied health and life insurance, employment opportunities, and even acceptance into the U.S. Air Force Academy. The African-American community soon perceived the psychosocial risks of the sickle cell screening programs and many persons expressed anger at being further discriminated against for simply being a carrier of sickle cell trait.,

Inadequate education and counseling at many of the early screening programs only contributed to the milieu of confusion, stigma, and what Abraham Bergman and his colleagues called "sickle cell 'nondisease.'" To make matters worse, many American physicians then were not well educated in the diagnosis and management of genetic diseases. For example, in a 1974 survey of 160 physicians' knowledge about sickle cell anemia, one in seven believed sickle cell trait to be indicative of a disease state; one in five found it difficult to clinically distinguish the trait from the disease, and one in two was unaware of the existence of the SC and the S-thal phenotypes.

Some community leaders responded by urging blacks to boycott the sickle cell screening programs. For example, in 1972, Ted Veal, a representative of the African-American activist group, the People's Health Council of New York, described the mandatory screening programs as "genocidal health practices" of the white medical establishment. Indeed, sickle cell screening programs of the early 1970s produced a negative label of disease for an easily identifiable social group that had a long history of being the victims of social discrimination. That made the screening markedly different and far more dangerous in a social context than those programs developed during the same time period for diseases without an ethnic or racial association.

Protection of the Patient's Rights. The third major objection to these early sickle cell screening programs was that in the rush to get the laws into print, many vital protective clauses were omitted, although we have since learned from hard experience to incorporate them. Features that might have tempered the harsh process of genetic stigmatization such as test result confidentiality, competent genetic counseling for people with the trait and the disease, adequate public education on issues of genetic diseases and carrier status, guaranteed medical benefits for those afflicted with sickle cell anemia, and uniform guidelines to ensure quality control of the testing and laboratory facilities were either not considered or were patently ignored by those drafting the original sickle cell legislation.,

The problems of this particular application of genetics to social policy began to be recognized soon after the enactment of the state laws described above. By late 1972, Congress passed the National Sickle Cell Anemia Control Act, which reflected a number of these concerns. Although these problems were not rectified immediately, the energetic efforts of the African-American and medical communities, in addition to numerous legislators, lawyers, and public policymakers, helped to modify and greatly improve use of sickle cell anemia screening technologies. For example, during the 1980s, it was found that newborn screening for sickle cell anemia was justified because of the ability of antibiotics to prevent serious and sometimes fatal infections in children with sickle cell anemia. In addition, newly developed pneumococcal vaccines have contributed to the reduction of early death due to susceptibility to pneumococcal infections. Many African-American parents recognized the value of the sickle cell newborn screen. Still, some clinicians continue to find evidence of fear and avoidance of all forms of sickle cell testing especially among those African-Americans with relatives who underwent testing during the 1970s. In a study conducted in Rochester, New York during the 1980s, less than half of the pregnant African-American women at risk of having affected fetuses utilized prenatal diagnosis technologies....

Genetic screening for Tay-Sachs disease began to be developed about the same time as the early sickle cell screening programs discussed above. Like sickle cell disease, Tay-Sachs was found to occur predominantly in one defined ethnic population—infants of Ashkenazi (East European) Jewish ancestry. Unlike sickle cell disease, however, which can vary greatly in clinical symptoms and severity from patient to patient, Tay-Sachs victims had no hope of productive life and faced irreversible and progressive neurodegeneration, dementia, and death during the first five years of life. Indeed, given the state of the art in medical care for Tay-Sachs disease during this period, the soundest public health approach to the problem was avoiding the birth of the affected fetus.

Ashkenazi Jews and African Americans had very different experiences with their genetic testing. In the first place, the reproductive choices for Tay-Sachs disease were less ambiguous when compared to sickle cell anemia; prenatal diagnosis for Tay-Sachs was possible. Then, too, there were striking social differences between them. The Jewish-American community was no stranger to discrimination, particularly in its relation to the application of genetic theory to social policy. Many of those enrolling in the Tay-Sachs screening programs of the 1970s were, literally, the grandchildren of the East European Jewish immigrants who were stigmatized during the 1920s and accused of importing inferior genes and "protoplasm" into the United States. Yet with the passage of time and acquisition of the confidence of assimilation, Jewish-Americans of the 1970s generally expressed fewer fears of discrimination than their African-American counterparts when confronted with these new screening technologies. There were some, however, who did not support Tay-Sachs screening.

This difference of perception may have been due to the social experiences of these two ethnic groups in the United States over the past two centuries. By the early 1970s, the lives of Jewish-Americans (both those originating from Germany and Eastern Europe) had, for the most part, markedly improved by all economic and social markers. Members of the African-American community, on the other hand, remained the target for a number of forms of discrimination and were actively fighting for basic civil rights. The latter group was particularly vulnerable to additional stigmatization in the form of a genetic label and less likely to view government or institutional involvement in health assessment as a positive development.

It is important that while the early Tay-Sachs programs were not extensively taken up by the entire Jewish-American community, many of their innovative features were subsequently found to be of great value. The same approach was used 25 years later to organize a study of heritable breast cancer in Ashkenazi Jews. Some of the earliest Tay-Sachs programs were organized at synagogues . In advance of implementing the screening programs, a series of productive meetings and discussion forums were held between physicians, ethicists, rabbis, and other members of the particular Jewish religious communities. As a result of these meetings, physicians and public health workers developed programs that focused on young Ashkenazi Jewish married couples who were considering having a child; other programs expanded this target group to include all unmarried members of the Ashkenazi Jewish community who were 18 years old or older.

Another positive feature of the early synagogue-based Tay-Sachs screening programs is that religious leaders and community volunteers worked side by side with physicians and genetics counselors to provide education at the screening site as well as to answer any questions the participants might have. Informed consents were routinely obtained and several steps were taken to ensure confidentiality. Those who tested positive for the carrier state were telephoned. Genetic counseling for individuals positive for Tay-Sachs was then offered, especially to those couples who both tested positive for the carrier state. In general, the woman in such couples underwent prenatal diagnostic testing of amniotic fluid when she became pregnant. The majority of those couples who were discovered to be carrying a fetus afflicted with Tay-Sachs disease elected to terminate the pregnancy.

This focus on religious institutions and communities was not entirely successful. Not all Jews were members of a synagogue and different areas in the United States and Canada embraced these programs at markedly different rates. For example, in Toronto, the Jewish community actively joined forces with the medical and public health communities to establish programs in the early 1970s, while in Montreal, the Jewish community did not. One impetus for the design of a well-known study was the lack of interest in Tay-Sachs screening among the Montreal Jewish community, leading the investigators to develop a study that "captured" Jewish high school students.

There are, of course, many different sectors of the Jewish-American community, divided along lines of religiosity (e.g., the Orthodox, Conservative, Reform movements, as well as non-practicing or secular Jews), place of geographic origin, economic status, and a number of other social factors that were recognized by the partnership of religious and community leaders and the medical establishment. One effort to address these differences was the Chevra Dor Yeshorim Program of New York City, designed to accommodate the cultural customs and religious beliefs of ultra-Orthodox Jews. Developed in partnership with members of the Orthodox-Hassidic Jewish community, which has a high risk of Tay-Sachs disease and strong opposition to abortion and contraception, this program relies on this community's practice of arranged marriages. When a Hassidic Jewish woman reaches 18 years of age or a man 20, the subject undergoes a blood test for Tay-Sachs disease. The laboratory handling the test assigns a code number to the sample and it is tested anonymously. The results are listed and stored by code number indefinitely. The subject is given only the code number but not the actual results of the test. At the time of a planned marriage, the shadchen, or matchmaker, is given the code numbers of the prospective bride and groom and presents them to the laboratory registry. If both partners are positive for the carrier state, the matchmaker is told that the match is not a good one and another match is arranged. If a couple does not use a matchmaker, they, too, may inquire of their status from the registry and make their decisions accordingly. A central aim of this plan is to keep the effects of genetic stigmatization to a minimum. Couples screening programs have been applied to cystic fibrosis (CF) in Scotland and England, and in Maine. The CF programs are similar to Chevra Dor Yeshorim in that only couples who were both positive for the trait are informed of the result; if only one partner is a carrier, s/he is not informed. The difference is that married couples are tested for CF. This program has since been applied to Orthodox Jewish communities elsewhere in the United States, Canada, Europe, and Israel.

As large populations were tested, problems surfaced concerning the reliability and validity of the available Tay-Sachs screening tools. For example, the earliest Tay-Sachs screening tests were plagued with an unacceptable rate of "false positives." Women concurrently using oral birth control pills were 50 percent or more likely to have a false-positive carrier test result. Other medications were discovered to be the cause of a false-negative carrier result. Fortunately, several research consortiums that were devoted to the prevention of Tay-Sachs disease conducted follow-up studies to identify and correct such problems in test validity.

The critically important, and potentially overlooked, lesson is that any genetic screening program must provide unrelenting vigilance in the implementation of such tests on large numbers of people, in addition to the careful surveillance of test development.

Since 1971, screening programs directed at the Ashkenazi Jewish population in the United States and Canada have led to a 90 percent reduction in Tay-Sachs disease. The Tay-Sachs screening programs are often recalled as a success in the blending of science, bioethics, and disease prevention. At the same time, several follow-up studies have documented that, although genetic counseling alleviated some of the anxieties experienced by the heterozygous, phenotypically normal Tay-Sachs carriers, there was evidence of residual unease among many of them simply at potentially being labeled a carrier.

Notes & Questions

1. How would you compare and contrast the two screening programs described by Markel? Were there either eugenic or discriminatory implications in either or both programs, and if so how were they mitigated? What role did scientific and medical understanding play in the outcome of each of these programs? What lessons do these two case studies offer that could potentially influence the development of public health genetic screening programs in the future?

2. Markel raises an important and controversial issue that is at the forefront of policy debates regarding research and practice in public health genetics—the relationship between race and genetics. *See, e.g.*, Richard S. Cooper et. al., *Race and Genomics*, 348 New Eng. J. Med. 1166 (2003); E.G. Burchard et al., *The Importance of Race and Ethnic Background in Biomedical Research and Clinical Practice*, 348 New Eng. J. Med. 1170 (2003); R.A. Kittles, *Race, Ancestry and Genes: Implications for Defining Disease Risk* 4 Annu. Rev. Genomics Hum. Genet. 33 (2003). Some argue that genetics research increasingly calls into question traditional notions of race as a biologic factor, proving for example the important role that social determinants play in racial disparities in health care and health outcomes. Others reach a very different interpretation of the available data, arguing that genetics research confirms that race is biologically rooted. How might these two different viewpoints influence policy focus and development in public health or health care generally?

3. Traditionally public health interventions are focused on measuring disease risk within a population and reducing that risk through early detection and prevention. In this context prevention measures are aimed at curtailing person-to-person transmission as opposed to preventing individual disease progression. What prevention measures might accompany genetic-based carrier screening programs?

2. Prenatal Screening

California Code Regulations, Title 17 § 6527

[Title 17: Public Health; Division 1, State Department of Health Services; Chapter 4, Preventive Medical Service; Subchapter 9, Heritable Diseases; Article 2, Testing of Pregnant Women for Heritable and Congenital Disorders]

§ 6527. Clinicians.

(a) Clinicians shall provide or cause to be provided to all pregnant women in their care before the 140th day of gestation, or before the 126th day from conception, as estimated by medical history or clinical testing, information regarding the use and availability of prenatal screening for birth defects of the fetus. This information shall be in a format to be provided or approved by the Department and shall be given at the first prenatal visit and discussed with each pregnant woman.

(b) The provisions of subsection (a) shall not apply if the pregnant woman has completed more than 140 days of gestation or 126 days post conception, as estimated by medical history or clinical testing, and this fact is entered in the medical record.

(c) Clinicians shall cause to be provided to all pregnant women who, after being provided with the information pursuant to subsection (a), voluntarily request prenatal screening for birth defects of the fetus, the opportunity, the circumstances of which are to be documented in the medical record, to read and sign an informed consent document in a format provided or approved by the Department.

(d) If the pregnant woman consents to testing, the clinician shall arrange for prenatal screening directly or by referral to another....

(g) For each woman in their care who was prenatally screened for birth defects of the fetus and who has an initial screening positive test, the clinician shall:

> (1) Inform the woman that authorized follow-up services are available at Expanded AFP Follow-up Vendors, and that the program participation fees or laboratory test fee covers the authorized services.
>
> (2) Report on the form provided by the Department for this purpose, within 30 calendar days of the end of the pregnancy, the outcome of pregnancy and status of each fetus, or infant resulting therefrom.

(h) The test results shall be confidential so that such information shall only be released with the knowledge and specific written consent of the woman tested. Persons authorized by the Department to conduct and monitor screening and/or to provide and monitor differential diagnostic follow-up services shall be provided information without necessity of specific written consent.

(i) Recognizing the strict gestational and time limits wherein prenatal detection of birth defects of the fetus is feasible, clinicians shall make every reasonable effort to schedule screening and differential diagnostic tests and procedures appropriately with respect to the gestational dates of the pregnant woman.

Galvez v. Frields

107 Cal. Rptr. 2d 50 (Cal. Ct. App. 2001)

Charles S. Vogel, P.J.

This is a medical malpractice case in which Nathaniel Galvez sues defendant Michael Frields, M.D., for wrongful life, contending that Frields failed to make reasonable efforts to ensure Nathaniel's mother, Michelle Sepulveda, was given a blood test to detect the presence of the neural tube defect from which Nathaniel suffers. Following a trial during which the trial court refused to give a jury instruction on negligence per se the jury found that Frields was not negligent in his care of Sepulveda. Nathaniel appeals and asserts as the sole claimed error the trial court's refusal to give the negligence per se instruction. We conclude that the court erred in refusing to give the proffered instruction. Such error was clearly prejudicial, and we therefore reverse and remand for a new trial....

Title 17 of the California Code of Regulations, section 6527, requires clinicians who provide prenatal care to advise all pregnant women in their care of the availability of the alpha-fetoprotein (AFP) test, which screens for neural tube defects in the fetus....

George Cunningham, M.D., chief of the Genetic Disease Branch of the California Department of Health Services (which administers the statewide program to screen for birth defects), participated in drafting the laws and regulations governing AFP testing. He testified at trial that neural tube defects are "a serious and common birth defect so it's to the individual family's interest and also to the State's interest to identify these defects prenatally so that if the woman chooses to terminate the pregnancy she has an opportunity to do that." A large majority of women who are told of the existence of a fetal neural tube defect elect to terminate their pregnancies.

AFP testing, which must be done between 15 and 19 completed weeks of pregnancy (or stated otherwise, between the beginning of the 16th week and the 20th week), involves drawing blood from the pregnant woman into a test tube provided by the state. The process of drawing the blood is no different from any other type of test requiring that blood be drawn. The blood sample does not have to be prepared for shipment; it is placed in the packaging provided by the state with a prepaid mailing label. The sample can be refrigerated if it cannot be mailed promptly. The time requirements imposed by the regulation are not in order to get an accurate result, rather they allow for follow-up diagnostic testing to be done while termination of the pregnancy is still feasible. The test results have to get back to the doctor; if the test is positive, the woman has to make an appointment at a prenatal center; an ultrasound is done; if amniocentesis (testing of the amniotic fluid) is done it takes two weeks to grow the cells and do the chromosome studies to confirm or deny the presence of a defect.

Cunningham said that the regulations require doctors to make reasonable efforts to make sure the woman is tested within the window. He acknowledged that there are different styles of practice, and that the Department of Health Services leaves the details as to how to do it up to individual practitioners. "[B]ut we expect they would make reasonable efforts if the woman says she wants to be tested to make sure some time in that period they got blood drawn." ...

Sepulveda learned she was pregnant in January 1994. Her first prenatal medical appointment was on February 8, 1994; she was seen by a prenatal counselor at Mullikin. The counselor weighed her, discussed pregnancy issues with her, and calculated that she was expected to give birth on October 3, 1994. The counselor gave Sepulveda the state-prepared booklet regarding the AFP test, and obtained from her signed consent to have the test performed. Sepulveda recalled talking to the counselor about a state test to determine if the baby was healthy, but she did not recall it being referred to by name. She did not read the booklet or the consent form she signed. She said that she was not told then or at any time what hours the AFP testing was done, or that the procedure was any different than with other blood tests. There was no evidence that the booklet given to Sepulveda had the laboratory hours for AFP testing written on it. A notation in Sepulveda's chart dated February 8, 1994, indicates that the window of time for her to have the AFP test performed was April 11 through May 17, 1994. On February 8, Sepulveda was given a laboratory requisition slip to have her blood drawn for a different test, and she had the blood drawn at that time. An appointment was scheduled for Sepulveda to be seen by Frields.

Frields saw Sepulveda on March 8, 1994. She was weighed and given a requisition slip to have a urinalysis performed and to have her blood drawn for laboratory tests. She took the requisition slip to the laboratory and had her blood drawn. Frields confirmed Sepulveda's due date.

At her next appointment on April 8, 1994, Sepulveda was weighed and had a urinalysis performed. Frields testified that he talked to her about having an ultrasound and her AFP test done in two weeks, based on the fact he noted in her chart: "Sono in 2 weeks and AFP in 2 weeks." An appointment was made for her to have the ultrasound done at the laboratory. He did not give her a laboratory requisition slip for the AFP test or instruct her to get one from the nursing staff.

The ultrasound was done on April 13, 1994, at 10:15 a.m., in the Mullikin laboratory. Sepulveda was then 15.2 weeks into her pregnancy, and was therefore within the AFP window. Sepulveda was not told she could or should have the AFP test done on that day, and it was not done.

When he ordered the ultrasound and when he reviewed the radiologist's report, Frields believed the April 13 ultrasound was capable of demonstrating the condition of the brain, spinal cord, and heart of the fetus. Frields's normal practice was to rely upon the radiologist's report and not review the ultrasound film. At deposition, he said he was confident that the ultrasound adequately performed a fetal organ survey and ruled out the degree of neural tube defect that was present in this fetus. He interpreted the radiologist's note that "[n]o fetal pathology is identified" to mean that the radiologist could see the spinal cord. The radiologist's report did not contain the notation made on the ultrasound technician's worksheet to "[f]ollow up to see fetal spine and organs." Had that notation been included in the radiologist's report, Frields would have interpreted it to mean that the anatomical survey of Sepulveda's fetus was incomplete, and he would have ordered another ultrasound. The defense's expert physician testified that a level one sonogram, which Sepulveda had undergone, could not be relied upon to rule out a neural tube defect of the kind involved here.

Sepulveda was again seen by Frields on May 6, 1994, at about 10:30 a.m. Frields knew there were only 11 days left to do the AFP test, and presumed Sepulveda wanted the test done. He knew her next appointment would be in June and the window of opportunity for performing the AFP test would be closed. He did not instruct anyone to make sure Sepulveda had the AFP test done. Sepulveda said that no one mentioned the AFP test to her that day.

Sepulveda's next appointment was on June 3, 1994. Frields was aware that she had not had the AFP test done. He did not discuss with her doing any alternative tests, such as another ultrasound or amniocentesis, and he did not order either test while Sepulveda was in her second trimester and termination of the pregnancy was still feasible. An obstetrical nurse at Mullikin testified that Sepulveda acknowledged that she had missed having the AFP test done due to personal problems. Sepulveda denied making that statement, having personal problems that would prevent the test being done, or otherwise discussing the test or the fact that she had missed it with anyone at Mullikin. She was unaware that she had missed the AFP test; she assumed that she would be given a form to have the test done and that whatever tests she needed and had agreed to had in fact been done.

On September 25, 1994, Sepulveda went to the hospital thinking she was having contractions and her amniotic fluid was leaking. Frields performed an ultrasound to see if there was sufficient amniotic fluid and immediately realized that the baby had an enlarged head, indicating hydrocephalus. Sepulveda was sent home. Her water broke and she went into labor the next morning. She was told her baby had spina bifida, a large hole in his back, and very little brain tissue. It was not expected that he would survive. Nathaniel was delivered that evening.

Despite the concurrence of various health care professionals that Nathaniel would not survive, and although Sepulveda followed their advice regarding performing or refraining from performing various medical procedures because he was expected to die, Nathaniel survived. He is profoundly disabled; he is paralyzed, although he has use of his left hand, he exhibits no purposeful movement, he is cortically blind, and he cannot speak or perform any basic function for himself.

Although the defense introduced evidence that Sepulveda is Catholic and that she would not have chosen to terminate the pregnancy, she testified unequivocally that had she known the fetus had a neural tube defect she would have terminated the pregnancy....

The trial court refused to give Nathaniel's requested jury instruction based on BAJI No. 3.45 regarding negligence per se, which stated: "If you find that a party to this action violated Section 6527 of Title 17, of the California Code of Regulations, the regulation set forth in Exhibit Number 16 and that such violation was a cause of injury to another, you will find that such violation was negligence unless such party proves by a preponderance of the evidence that he did what might reasonably be expected of a person of ordinary prudence, acting under similar circumstances, who desired to comply with the law. In order to sustain such burden of proof, such party must prove by a preponderance of the evidence that he was faced with circumstances which prevented compliance or justified noncompliance with the regulation." ...

The jury then found Frields was not negligent by a vote of nine to three. Judgment in favor of Frields was entered.

This appeal followed.

California recognizes an impaired child's right to recover damages for "wrongful life." The essence of a wrongful life action is that "if defendants had performed their jobs properly, [plaintiff] ... would not have been born at all." In such a case, an impaired child may recover special damages for the extraordinary expenses necessary to treat the hereditary ailment from which he or she suffers. Wrongful life is basically one form of a medical malpractice action.

As in ordinary medical malpractice cases, the plaintiffs in a wrongful life and wrongful birth case must establish the following basic elements: '(1) the duty of the professional to use such skill, prudence, and diligence as other members of his profession commonly possess and exercise; (2) a breach of that duty; (3) a proximate causal connection between the negligent conduct and the resulting injury; and (4) actual loss or damage resulting from the professional's negligence.'

Nathaniel contends the court erred in refusing to instruct the jury regarding negligence per se, using BAJI No. 3.45, which would have permitted the jury to find that an unreasonable failure to abide by the requirements of California Code of Regulations, title 17, section 6527, constituted negligence. The negligence per se doctrine is codified in Evidence Code section 669, under which negligence is presumed if the plaintiff establishes four elements: (1) the defendant violated a statute, ordinance, or regulation of a public entity; (2) the violation proximately caused death or injury to person or property; (3) the death or injury resulted from an occurrence of the nature of which the statute, ordinance, or regulation was designed to prevent; and (4) the person suffering the death or the injury to his person or property was one of the class of persons for whose protection the statute, ordinance, or regulation was adopted. The first two elements are normally questions for the trier of fact, while the latter two elements are determined by the trial court as a matter of law....

Frields contends that Nathaniel was not entitled to an instruction regarding negligence per se because he did not meet the third and fourth elements of the Evidence Code section 669 test; i.e., his injury did not result from an occurrence that the regulation was designed to prevent and he is not a member of the class of persons for whose protection the regulation was adopted. At trial, Frields concurred in Mullikin's contention that the protected class of persons is taxpayers who have to pay for the care of children born with neural tube defects, while on appeal he contends the protected class of persons is pregnant women. We reject this contention.

The essence of a wrongful life cause of action is that recovery is required where the defendant's negligence is the proximate cause of the child's need for extraordinary medical care and training. The ultimate concern is that the child exists and is entitled to legal recourse and compensation for such negligence. (*Gami v. Mullikin Medical Center* (1993) 22 Cal.Rptr.2d 819, citing *Turpin v. Sortini, supra,* 643 P.2d 954.)

In *Gami,* defendants negligently failed to inform a pregnant woman of the need for her to provide a second blood sample for AFP testing after the first blood sample she provided proved unsuitable for testing. "As a result of this negligence, [plaintiff's] mother did not have the opportunity to learn that [plaintiff] could have been afflicted with a neural tube defect" and the child was born with spina bifida. The appellate court held that the child was entitled to legal protection from the negligence of the health care providers, and could bring a wrongful life cause of action. (*Gami v. Mullikin Medical Center, supra,* 22 Cal. Rptr. 2d 819.) In so doing, the court rejected the defendants' contention that if anyone had suffered injury, it was the pregnant woman and not the child, because as a result of the alleged negligence, the mother did not have the opportunity to learn that the child was afflicted with a neural tube defect and was thereby deprived of the opportunity to have an abortion. According to defendants, only the mother had standing to seek damages based on the deprivation of her right to an abortion. The court rejected that notion, and so do we.

The regulations were, in fact, designed to prevent the birth of children with neural tube defects. By its very nature, genetic counseling is employed at least in part so that a mother may make an informed decision on whether to abort a genetically defective fetus. Cunningham, who took part in drafting the regulations at issue, stated that it was beneficial to everyone involved, including the taxpayers of this state, that neural tube defects be identified *prenatally.* The time constraints imposed by the regulation exist in order to allow for consideration of abortion while it is still feasible for the mother to make the choice to terminate the pregnancy during the second trimester. Subdivision (i) of section 6527 states: "Recognizing the strict gestational and time limits wherein prenatal detection of birth defects of the fetus is feasible, clinicians shall make every reasonable effort to schedule screening and differential diagnostic tests and procedures appropriately with respect to the gestational dates of the pregnant woman." It is undeniable that the regulations at issue were designed to give women like Sepulveda the option of avoiding the birth of a severely disabled child; to argue otherwise is simply disingenuous.

...

We conclude that the trial court erred in refusing to instruct the jury regarding negligence per se based on the regulation set forth in section 6527.... 'A judgment may not be reversed for instructional error in a civil case "unless, after an examination of the entire cause, including the evidence, the court shall be of the opinion that the error complained of has resulted in a miscarriage of justice." (Cal. Const., art. VI, § 13.)' Instructional error in a civil case is prejudicial '"[w]here it seems probable"' that the error prejudicially affected the verdict. (*LeMons v. Regents of University of California* (1978) 582 P.2d 946(4)27) It is not enough that there may have been a 'mere possibility' of prejudice ... the determination of prejudice depends heavily on 'the particular nature of the error, including its natural and probable effect on a party's ability to place his full case before the jury....'" (*Logacz v. Limansky, supra,* 84 Cal.Rptr.2d 257.)

It is clear from our review of the entire record that Nathaniel was not able to place his full case before the jury. As Frields correctly points out in his respondent's brief, the regulations at issue establish a standard of care. If properly instructed, the jury would have had the opportunity to find that Frields breached the applicable standard of care by violating the regulation. The evidence would have supported such a finding, but as we next explain, this jury was precluded from reaching that finding....

The judgment is reversed and the matter is remanded for a new trial on all issues. On remand, this case shall be assigned to a different trial judge. Plaintiff shall recover his costs on appeal.

Britell v. United States

72 F.3d 1370 (Cal. 2004)

Goodwin, Circuit Judge.

In January 1994, Britell and her husband, a Captain in the Air National Guard, were expecting their second child. A routine checkup about twenty weeks into her pregnancy revealed that Britell's fetus suffered from a rare condition called anencephaly; the diagnosis of anencephaly was confirmed by a second ultrasound. Faced with this horrific diagnosis, and the certain death of the fetus or newborn, the Britells consulted their family, doctors, grief counselors, psychiatrists, and their parish priest, all of whom agreed that the Britells should abort the fetus. On February 18, 1994, Britell had an abortion at the New England Medical Center—after thirteen hours of physically and emotionally painful labor, the fetus died during delivery. The diagnosis of anencephaly was confirmed.

After the abortion, the New England Medical Center sought payment for its services from Britell's insurer, the Civilian Health and Medical Program ("CHAMPUS"). In fulfilling its statutory mandate to "provid[e] an improved and uniform program of medical and dental care for members ... of the uniformed] services, and their dependents," CHAMPUS funds all "medically necessary services and supplies associated with maternity care." In the present case, however, CHAMPUS denied the claim based on 10 U.S.C.sec. 1093(a) and corresponding regulations. Section 1093(a) provides in relevant part that "[f]unds available to the Department of Defense may not be used to perform abortions except where the life of the mother would be endangered if the fetus is carried to term." The CHAMPUS regulations specifically provide that abortions performed in the case of "fetal abnormalities" including anencephaly are not covered by CHAMPUS. After the claim was denied by CHAMPUS, the New England Medical Center sued Britell in state court and obtained $4,000 through a settlement. Britell then filed suit against the United States in the United States District Court for the District of Massachusetts seeking "liquidated and unliquidated damages incurred when Defendant, pursuant to the Civilian Health and Medical Program of the Uniformed Services (hereinafter CHAMPUS'), 10 U.S.C. sec. 1093(a) and 32 C.F.R. sec. 199.4(e)(2), refused to pay or reimburse any portion of $4,500 in medical costs incurred by plaintiff Maureen

Britell relating to an abortion medical procedure performed upon her at New England Medical Center on February 18–19, 1994." In her complaint, Britell alleged that section 1093(a) "has no rational basis as applied to abortions performed where the fetus is suffering from a lethal anomaly, such as anencephaly (absence of all or significant part of the fetal brain)" and that "the section 1093 exclusion violates the Fifth Amendment of the United States Constitution." ...

Because the Supreme Court had previously held, in Harris v. McRae, 448 U.S. 297, 100 S.Ct. 2671, 65 L.Ed.2d 784 (1980), that the language of the Hyde Amendment language in the Medicaid statute prohibiting the use of federal funds to reimburse the cost of abortions "except where the life of the mother would be endangered if the fetus were carried to term") was facially constitutional under the Equal Protection Clause, Britell's challenge was narrow in scope. Britell argued that section 1093(a) was only unconstitutional "as applied" to her and similarly-situated pregnant women because the ban on CHAMPUS funding for abortions in cases of anencephaly does not further any of the legitimate state interests identified in McRae as supporting the facial constitutionality of congressional abortion funding restrictions. The government responded by arguing that there is no such thing as an "as applied" equal protection challenge to a statute whose facial constitutionality has been sustained, and that, in any event, the denial of funding in Britell's case passes muster under rational basis review because it encourages childbirth and is thus rationally related to the legitimate state interest in potential human life....

On appeal, the parties' arguments are essentially identical to those made before the district court. The government argues that Britell does not have a valid as-applied challenge and that McRae thus controls. Further, to the extent Britell's as-applied challenge is valid, the government argues that section 1093(a) is constitutional because the statute is rationally related to legitimate state interests, including the protection and promotion of potential human life. Britell, on the other hand, argues that the district court correctly held that her challenge is a valid as-applied challenge, and that as applied to her, section 1093(a) is unconstitutional because the distinction between medically necessary services and what she argues are medically necessary abortions in cases of anencephaly is not rationally related to any legitimate state interest....

With regard to the merits of Britell's appeal, the parties argue two core issues on appeal: (1) does the decision in McRae, upholding the facial validity of an abortion funding restriction identical to the one here, preclude Britell's as-applied challenge; and (2) if McRae does not preclude Britell's as-applied challenge, is the challenged statutory provision rationally related to a legitimate governmental interest? We address these issues in turn.

As to the first issue—whether Britell has a valid as-applied challenge to section 1093(a) despite the ruling of McRae—we find that this court need not reach the issue because, even if Britell has a valid as-applied challenge, Britell's equal protection challenge fails because section 1093(a) passes a rational basis review. Accordingly, we move directly to the second, outcome-determinative issue.

"The guarantee of equal protection under the Fifth Amendment is not a source of substantive rights or liberties, but rather a right to be free from invidious discrimination in statutory classifications and other governmental activity. It is well settled that where a statutory classification does not itself impinge on a right or liberty protected by the Constitution, the validity of classification must be sustained unless 'the classification rests on grounds wholly irrelevant to the achievement of [any legitimate governmental] objective.'" *Harris v. McRae*, 448 U.S. 297, 322 (1980) (quoting *McGowan v. Maryland*, 366 U.S. 420 (1961)). The presumption of constitutional validity does not exist, however, where the statutory classification is predicated on "suspect" criteria, e.g., race. *Id.*

In *McRae*, the Supreme Court determined that the Hyde Amendment, restricting Medicaid funding to abortions where the life of the mother is at risk, "places no governmental obstacle in the path of a woman who chooses to terminate her pregnancy," and does not "impinge[ ] on the constitutional protected freedom of choice recognized in Wade" because every woman has the same range of choice in deciding whether to obtain an abortion. *Id.* at 315–16. The Supreme Court also noted that the language of the Hyde Amendment "is not predicated on a constitutionally suspect classification" because the Supreme Court had "held repeatedly that poverty, standing alone is not a suspect classification." *Id.* at 322–23. In light of the uniformity between the language of the Hyde Amendment and that in section 1093(a), there can be no doubt that the classification drawn in section 1093(a) neither impinges on a fundamental right guaranteed by the Constitution nor is predicated on a suspect classification.

Accordingly, the remaining question is whether section 1093(a) is "rationally related to a legitimate governmental objective." Id. at 324. The government suggests several possible legitimate governmental objectives in justification of section 1093(a): (1) the protection and promotion of potential human life; (2) the creation of a bright-line rule that no birth defect justifies the use of federal funds for abortion; and (3) the accommodation of taxpayers who are strongly and sincerely opposed to abortion by not expending taxpayer funds on abortion. Because we find that section 1093(a) is rationally related to the first of these proffered interests, we need not address the other two suggested governmental interests.

In *McRae*, the Supreme Court found a rational relationship between the Hyde Amendment and the state's interest in protecting potential human life. The Supreme Court's analysis of the rational relationship bears repeating: The remaining question then is whether the Hyde Amendment is rationally related to a legitimate governmental objective. It is the Government's position that the Hyde Amendment bears a rational relationship to its legitimate interest in protecting the potential life of the fetus. We agree.

In *Wade*, the Court recognized that the State has an "important and legitimate interest in protecting the potentiality of human life." *Roe v. Wade*, 410 U.S. 113, 162 (1973). That interest was found to exist throughout a pregnancy, "grow[ing] in substantiality as the woman approaches term." *Id.*, at 162–163. Moreover, in *Maher*, the Court held that Connecticut's decision to fund the costs associated with childbirth but not those associated with nontherapeutic abortions was a rational means of advancing the legitimate state interest in protecting potential life by encouraging childbirth. *Maher v. Roe* 432 U.S. 464, 478–479 (1977).

It follows that the Hyde Amendment, by encouraging childbirth except in the most urgent circumstances, is rationally related to the legitimate governmental objective of protecting potential life. By subsidizing the medical expenses of indigent women who carry their pregnancies to term while not subsidizing the comparable expenses of women who undergo abortions (except those whose lives are threatened), Congress has established incentives that make childbirth a more attractive alternative than abortion for persons eligible for Medicaid. These incentives bear a direct relationship to the legitimate congressional interest in protecting potential life. Nor is it irrational that Congress has authorized federal reimbursement for medically necessary services generally, but not for certain medically necessary abortions. Abortion is inherently different from other medical procedures, because no other procedure involves the purposeful termination of a potential life. *McRae*, 448 U.S. at 324–26....

Recognizing, as she must, the long line of precedent supporting the government's argument that the state has a legitimate governmental interest in protecting potential human life, Britell argues that there is no legitimate governmental interest in protecting an anencephalic fetus because the fetus will never gain consciousness. Accordingly, Britell seeks a reading of the statute to require an additional exception to the abortion-funding ban in cases of anencephaly....

Supreme Court precedent makes clear that, from the very start of the pregnancy, there is a legitimate state interest in the potential human life.... The state has a legitimate interest in potential human life before anyone knows whether the fetus will be carried to term, or even reach viability, and this legitimate state interest exists even where the fetus I diagnosed with an abnormality or birth defect. Indeed, the Supreme Court has expressly noted that states have an "unqualified interest in the preservation of human life'... regardless of physical or mental condition." *Washington v. Glucksberg*, 521 U.S. 702 (1997).

For us to hold, as Britell urges, that in some circumstances a birth defect or fetal abnormality is so severe as to remove the state's interest in potential human life would require this court to engage in line-drawing of the most non-judicial and daunting nature. This we will not do. We agree with the government's argument that the type of line-drawing urged by Britell can create a slippery slope. It is not the role of the courts to draw lines as to which fetal abnormalities or birth defects are so severe as to negate the state's otherwise legitimate interest in the fetus' potential life. The district court opined that there was no slippery slope with regard to anencephaly because "anencephaly is a very distinctive physical condition with not just life-threatening, but fundamentally life-incompatible consequences for the fetus." *Britell II*, 204 F.Supp.2d at 198 (emphasis in original). We cannot agree. No reason has been presented, nor do we see one, to explain why consciousness (or extended life span) is the lynchpin of potential human life. Indeed, it could reasonably be argued that other birth defects or abnormalities, while different in their effects on the fetus, are also so severe as to negate the state's interest in potential human life. If that is the case, courts will be forced to determine on a condition-by-condition or abnormality-by-abnormality basis whether a fetus' condition is so severe as to eliminate the state's interest. Such line-drawing is something for which courts are ill-equipped, and is inconsistent with existing Supreme Court jurisprudence on what constitutes a "potential human life."

Without question, Congress could have drafted the abortion-funding ban of section 1093(a) differently, perhaps allowing exceptions in cases of severe birth defects or fetal abnormalities or even in cases where the health of the mother is at risk. Congress chose not to draw those lines, and we must respect that decision. Under rational basis review, "the constitutionality of state classifications ... cannot be determined on a person-by-person basis." *Kimel v. Fla. Bd. of Regents*, 528 U.S. 62, 85–86 (2000). Indeed, congressional line-drawing "inevitably requires that some persons who have an almost equally strong claim to favored treatment be placed on different sides of the line," such that there will almost certainly be "some harsh and apparently arbitrary consequences." *Mathews v. Diaz*, 426 U.S. 67, 83–84, 85–86 (1976). Put simply, "[p]erfection in making the necessary classifications is neither possible nor necessary." *Mass. Bd. of Retirement v. Murgia*, 427 U.S. 307, 314 (1976). And so it is that, even if Britell and the district court are correct that the funding ban of section 1093(a) is not perfect in that it does not allow for an exception in cases of anencephaly, Britell and the district court are incorrect that the statute fails under rational basis review. Supreme Court precedent makes clear that the state has a legitimate interest in any potential human life, even that of an anencephalic fetus. As much as in McRae, the language of section 1093(a) is rationally related to this state interest, and therefore section 1093(a) passes equal protection muster.... Accordingly, the district court's entry of judgment for Britell, must be reversed.

Notes & Questions

1. Prenatal genetic diagnosis is the most widespread application of genetic technology in medical care today. More than 50% of all pregnant women in the United States undergo maternal alpha-fetoprotein screening for metabolic markers associated with neural tube defects and chromosomal abnormalities such as Down Syndrome, and pregnancies in women of advanced maternal age (over thirty-five) are routinely screened using ultrasound and amniocentesis. *See* C.M. Powell, *The Current State of Prenatal Testing in the United States*, *in* PRENATAL TESTING AND DISABILITY RIGHTS 44–53 (E. Parens & A. Asch, eds. 2000). The California Statute requiring physicians to offer all pregnant women information on prenatal screening reflects a government policy to encourage widespread use of prenatal screening, at least for genetic conditions that are widely considered to be seriously disabling. What potential public health benefits flow from the practice of encouraging MSAFP screening? What preventive measures are available to combat genetic disease or disease risk identified through prenatal genetic screening? What ethical, legal, and social policy issues accompany the use of abortion as a tool for disease prevention or, stated differently, public health promotion? How might the access issues associated with current federal restrictions on public funding for abortion services influence the success of prenatal screening programs and the allocation of genetic-based disease burden across the population?

2. Revisit the notes and comments that accompany the case excerpt for *Roe v. Wade* and the excerpt of Stern's commentary on the history of sterilization programs in California and across the U. S. How does the use of prenatal genetic testing impact reproductive rights? Are there reasons to be concerned about the potential for hidden eugenic agendas?

3. Newborn Screening

Chapter 7 introduced the topic of newborn screening, both in the context of clinical care for the newborn and as a state-run public health program. In this chapter we revisit newborn screening in the public health context, using it as a case study to illustrate the types of challenges that accompany public health applications of genomic-based medicine and technology.

The discussion in Chapter 7 points out that newborn screening programs began in the 1960s with the introduction of a screening test for PKU and a system for collecting and storing blood samples on filter paper useable for laboratory analysis. Over the years newborn screening has evolved into a significant public health prevention program that operates in each of the fifty states and the District of Columbia (hereinafter collectively referred to as "states"). More than four million newborns are screened each year to identify those at risk for certain genetic and metabolic disorders that could threaten their life or have a serious adverse affect on long-term health. In addition, the states provide a range of associated services including parent and provider education, follow-up on abnormal screening tests, and ongoing surveillance and quality assurance. These programs are costly, with states spending over $120 million in 2001 alone. United States Government Accounting Office, Newborn Screening: Characteristics of State Programs (GAO-03-449; Mar. 2003).

The simultaneous evolution of genomics and technology, which has rapidly expanded the number and types of conditions that may be included in a screening panel, is slowly changing the face of newborn screening, raising numerous legal, ethical, and policy issues regarding the purpose of newborn screening programs, the scope of screening panels, disparities in access to screening and follow-up medical care, proper allocation of public health resources, and individual autonomy and parental rights to control health care decisions for their children. Deciding what the focus and structure of newborn screening will be in the future is a significant public health policy issue and the outcome of the newborn screening debate will influence the practice of public health genetics in the years to come. The following excerpt from the final report of the American Academy of Pediatrics (AAP) Task Force on Newborn Screening summarizes the evolution of newborn screening programs and the issues they face.

Report from the AAP Task Force on Newborn Screening, *Serving the Family From Birth to the Medical Home*

106 Pediatrics 389 (2000)

Newborn screening in the United States is a public health program aimed at the early identification of conditions for which early and timely interventions can lead to the elimination or reduction of associated mortality, morbidity, and disabilities. This screening takes place within the context of a newborn screening system, and involves the following components: screening, short-term follow-up, diagnosis, treatment/management, and evaluation. Inherent to each of these components is an education process.

The screening programs like these for the 4 million infants born each year in the United States have been heralded as successful and cost-effective. The newborn screening program's efficiency and effectiveness depends on the smooth integration of sample collection, laboratory testing, follow-up, diagnosis, timely treatment, and tracking of outcomes. The foundation and justification of newborn screening systems rest on the principles that testing procedures are readily available; technically feasible; economically sound; and clearly beneficial to affected newborns, their families, and to society. The universal acceptance of newborn screening for specified conditions over the past 3 decades attests to the undeniable benefits that flow from early testing and prompt, appropriate therapy. However, although newborn screening systems have succeeded in preventing morbidity and mortality, controversies, challenges, and opportunities continue.

The History of Newborn Screening

Newborn screening programs began in the early 1960s with the original work of Dr Robert Guthrie, who developed a screening test for phenylketonuria (PKU) and a system for collection and transportation of blood samples on filter paper. By 1962, Massachusetts launched a voluntary newborn PKU screening program that demonstrated the feasibility of mass genetic screening.

Initially, newborn screening for PKU was not a health department role or a legislated activity. Health professionals were slow to adopt the practice of screening for PKU, and the responsibility for screening was not defined (eg, should it be the responsibility of the hospital in which the infant was born, the mother's obstetrician, or the infant's pediatrician or primary care health professional). The American Academy of Pediatrics (AAP), acting as the professional association that develops policy for the care of children, raised concerns about the sensitivity and specificity of PKU screening tests, as well as the efficacy of early intervention for PKU. Out of these concerns, the need for further research about this testing was recognized, and the federal Children's Bureau (now the federal Maternal and Child Health Bureau [MCHB]) funded a collaborative study to address questions and concerns about the effectiveness of the PKU screening test.

At the same time, advocates for children remained concerned that children with undetected PKU were at high risk for mental retardation. The National Association for Retarded Citizens (now the ARC) proposed model legislation for creation of public programs to address low detection rates, and also conducted an extensive grass-roots lobbying effort to support passage of mandatory PKU screening legislation. Many state health departments supported the adoption of such legislation. The Kennedy Administration, with the guidance of the Presidential Advisory Commission on Mental Retardation, was also supportive. The Commission hired the Advertising Council, which mounted a public campaign for mandatory PKU screening. Other advocacy groups, such as the March of Dimes Birth Defects Foundation, mobilized volunteers to lobby for passage of legislation at the state level. As a result of this multidimensional advocacy campaign, most states passed laws in the early 1960s that mandated newborn screening for PKU. Forty-three states had formal statutes by 1973. State health departments, particularly their maternal and child health (MCH) programs (funded by Title V of the Social Security Act of 1935), assumed the central role in implementation of these new laws....

In 1976, federal legislation to support screening for genetic diseases was adopted, and in fiscal years 1979 and 1980, 34 state genetic service programs received federal funding. This support was welcomed by the states, as the cost of screening tests and the health departments' coordination of screening activities had not been completely covered by many state budgets.

As a result of the laws mandating PKU testing, and the establishment of health department newborn screening units that occurred in the 1960s and 1970s: Every newborn had an opportunity to be screened for PKU when laws were properly implemented; consequently, most were screened. Financial barriers to screening and diagnosis were removed, but families often had to pay for the special formula, special foods, and other related treatments. State newborn screening programs evolved, with the goal of providing safe screening tests and appropriate follow-up to every newborn.

During the 1980s, further systems development took place at the state and regional level. Newborn screening systems were set up by public health agencies to ensure coordination between the hospitals from which most specimens were received, the public health laboratory, the infant's pediatrician or primary care health professional to whom positive results were reported, and pediatric subspecialists to whom infants were referred for diagnosis and treatment. Together these entities comprised the backbone of newborn screening systems. Some state newborn screening systems also played a role coordinating follow-up; depending on their public health structure, medical care structure, and available resources. In many states, the Title V Children With Special Health Care Needs (CSHCN) programs performed this role.

In 1985, the Council of Regional Networks for Genetic Services (CORN) was developed in response to the need for an organization to facilitate state genetic program efforts through coordination and special initiatives. The CORN published newborn screening system guidelines that defined a 5-part system of screening, follow-up, diagnosis, treatment/management, and evaluation. These guidelines were not treatment guidelines or standards of care, but provided public health agencies with a detailed framework for a systems approach to newborn screening.

By 1985, 12 states had laws allowing charges or fees for screening tests. Today, a majority of the states have established newborn screening fees to be collected from the health care professional, birthing facility, third-party payer, or the parent of the newborn. Although newborn screening fees are collected in most states, financing the treatment of children identified with genetic conditions through newborn screening remains problematic. Eligible families in many states are ensured access to therapy, particularly when the special formula is deemed a prescription drug. Families deemed ineligible financially may be burdened by the cost of necessary treatments. However, when special PKU formula is classified as a food, many health insurers refuse to cover it at all; creating a problem for both eligible and ineligible families. . . .

Setting the Framework for State Newborn Screening Systems

Guidance for newborn screening systems have been in place for 2 decades. These guidelines are inextricably linked to ethical, legal, and social considerations and based on the premise that screening should be conducted only when science and technology can serve both the individual and public good. Three landmark reports emphasize the criteria that should be used to justify population-based newborn screening systems, and include: the National Academy of Sciences' (NAS) *Genetic Screening: Programs, Principles, and Research* in 1975; the Institute of Medicine (IOM) report, *Assessing Genetic Risks: Implications for Health and Social Policy* in 1994; and *Promoting Safe and Effective Genetic Testing in the United States: Final Report of the Task Force on Genetic Testing,* in 1997.

The NAS Report The 1975 NAS report set forth rigorous guidelines about the criteria for newborn screening including: evidence of substantial public benefit and acceptance (including acceptance by health care professionals); previous feasibility study; satisfactory test methods; appropriate laboratory facilities and quality control; resources for counseling, treatment, and follow-up; acceptable costs; effective education; informed consent; and the means to evaluate the effectiveness and success of each step. The National Research Council raised concerns about what it saw as the potential risks of inappropriate newborn screening. The NAS report was critical of how PKU screening had developed and suggested the establishment of patient advisory committees made up of individuals with medical and nonmedical expertise.

The IOM Report The 1994 IOM Committee on Assessing Genetic Risks recommended that:

"Newborn screening only take place 1) for conditions for which there are indications of clear benefit to the newborn, 2) when a system is in place for confirmatory diagnosis, and 3) when treatment and follow-up are available for affected newborns . . .

The Committee believes that mandatory offering of established tests (eg, PKU, congenital hypothyroidism) that lead to the diagnosis of a treatable condition, is appropriate. If there is no other way to ensure that affected newborns will be identified and have access to effective treatment (eg, in PKU, congenital hypothyroidism), then mandatory newborn screening is acceptable . . .

Mandatory newborn screening should only be undertaken if there is strong evidence of benefit to the newborn from effective treatment at the earliest possible age (eg, PKU and congenital hypothyroidism)." . . .

The Final Report of the Task Force on Genetic Testing The 1997 report entitled *Promoting Safe and Effective Genetic Testing in the United States: Final Report of the Task Force on Genetic Testing* pointed out that newborn screening should be of primary benefit to the infant identified. Like the IOM report, the Task Force on Genetic Testing report stated that it would be inappropriate to use traditional newborn screening solely to determine the carrier status of the infant. Moreover, the test should have analytical and clinical validity and utility. Interventions to improve the outcomes for an infant must be safe and effective....

New Challenges Facing Today's State Newborn Screening Systems

As a population-based public health activity, newborn screening systems are housed in state public health agencies. They operate under policies determined at the state level, and ideally, within the framework of the public health core functions of assessment, assurance, and policy development. States vary in public health infrastructure, newborn screening policy establishment, laboratory capacity, screening techniques, as well as in the laws that define the scope of services mandated in response to the identification of a condition. State newborn screening systems also vary in available system components, and in financing mechanisms to pay for these components.

Notably, the array of screening tests performed by each state varies and changes periodically. All state programs now include screening tests for PKU and congenital hypothyroidism. More than 40 programs screen for sickle cell disease and 48 screen for galactosemia. Some newborn screening systems include tests for congenital adrenal hyperplasia, homocystinuria, maple syrup urine disease, and biotinidase deficiency. A few states also include screening tests for cystic fibrosis, tyrosinemia, additional metabolic conditions, and/or other conditions such as congenital infections (i.e., HIV). Over half of the states now require all newborns be screened for hearing loss.

...

The mechanism for deciding which screening tests to include as part of a population-based newborn screening system varies among programs. Thus, the disorders screened for vary from state to state. These inconsistencies reflect differences in community values, in state political and economic environments, and in public health technical capabilities. Inequities regarding the selection of disorders for newborn screening panels are illustrated by sickle cell disease, a condition for which neonatal screening markedly reduces morbidity and mortality during early childhood. Nationally, sickle cell disease is the most prevalent condition included in newborn screening programs; however, disease prevalence within states varies more than 50-fold because of the widely differing ethnic populations of states. Currently, 41 states and the District of Columbia conduct universal screening for sickle cell disease. Three states conduct screening in infants of high-risk ethnic groups, and 6 states conduct no routine screening. These 9 states are among those with the lowest prevalence of sickle cell disease. Concerns about prevalence, cost-effectiveness, as well as concerns about the acceptability of screening to health professionals and the general public, have hindered implementation of this test despite an NIH-consensus conference recommendation for universal screening. In some cases, misperceptions about the benefits of screening, misperceptions about the prevalence of the disease in various ethnic groups, and/or the lack of effective advocacy for the disease have also contributed. Thus, while an African-American infant born in a state that does not universally screen for sickle cell disease has the same risk for sickle cell disease as an African-American infant born in a state with universal screening for sickle cell disease, the infant born in the non-screening state is denied the important benefit of screening. In this regard, it is interesting to note that the relatively low prevalence of sickle cell disease in each of the 9 states without universal screening for the disorder (estimated to be >1:40 000) is still higher than the prevalence of galactosemia (estimated to be about 1:60 000-80 000), a disorder included in the screening panels of all 9 states. This situation highlights the need for a more uniform national policy for the selection of newborn screening tests.

Because advances in science and technology are continually making it possible to screen for additional conditions, the decision about which tests to include in a newborn screening panel are complex. Moreover, in an era of accountability, decision-making is hampered by the lack of studies of and data about test validity and health outcomes. With existing variations between state newborn screening systems, a national model of the structure and function of newborn screening systems has not yet been embraced. Furthermore, there are no uniform guidelines for the periodic assessment of conditions for which screening is performed. As a result, infants across the country do not have equal access to newborn screening and its potential to prevent morbidity and mortality. The US Surgeon General, Dr David Satcher, has emphasized the need for the nation to address unequal access to health care, and the health disparities created by these inequalities. National standards are needed to promote greater comparability of newborn screening programs and address such inequities.

The work of David Hall and his colleagues in the United Kingdom provides useful guidance about creating equitable, sustainable, and effective newborn screening programs. Speaking in Washington, DC, on May 10, 1999, Dr Hall reminded the Task Force of the responsibility to do more than provide screening tests, saying: "If it is important enough to screen for, it is important enough to follow-up." He also spoke on the issues of quality assurance and adequate funding for newborn screening systems stating, "The balance is fine between good and harm in screening. Unless a screening program is a good one, it can do more harm than good."

In the United States, technological advances have had, and will continue to have a significant impact on the sensitivity, specificity, and scope of newborn screening. Pressure is mounting to deploy new diagnostic capabilities despite possessing limited knowledge of their risk and benefit, or their analytical or clinical validity and utility. Presently, tandem mass spectrometry offers, and shortly, DNA-based technology will offer the possibility of using one test or simpler tests to detect a larger group of genetic conditions. Furthermore, as the Human Genome Project is completed, the impetus and opportunity to translate genetic knowledge and technology into public health practice will increase. With these new technologies comes the ability to detect individuals affected by genetic conditions for which there is no clear advantage to early testing, no early or effective treatment, or no available treatment. How should we best use these emerging diagnostic capabilities in our newborn screening systems and, more generally, in improving the health outcomes of our children? ...

Notes & Questions

1. The purpose and scope of newborn screening programs is a critical issue in public health. The AAP Task Force's review of policy guidelines from the National Academy of Sciences, the Institute of Medicine and the NIH/DOE Task Force on Genetic Testing points out that the traditional approach to evaluating newborn screening tests emphasizes health benefits to the tested newborn, with the relevant criteria focusing on the

characteristics of the test (sensitivity, specificity, and predictive value) and the availability of a proven intervention. Preventing avoidable catastrophic health outcomes for newborns was an important justification for the states' initial decisions both to fund newborn screening and to make it mandatory. As the scope of newborn screening panels expands to include tests that have uncertain sensitivity, specificity or predictive value, and tests for conditions for which treatment is unavailable or conditions whose natural history and pathophysiology is not well characterized, the strength of these justifications is called into question.

Consider, for example, the full range of tests for metabolic disorders that can be accomplished using tandem mass spectrometry (MS/MS). Many of these tests are not fully understood or reveal abnormalities that are not fully understood. Should such tests be incorporated into a state-mandated, state-funded newborn screening program? As of 2005 only a handful of states had incorporated the full MS/MS panel in their mandated screening programs. Alternatively, consider DNA-based testing for cystic fibrosis, a devastating and relatively prevalent disease (the disease occurs in approximately one in 3,700 births). The test is well-characterized with appropriate sensitivity, specificity, and predictive value. However, there are no preventive measures currently available and the health benefits of early detection are controversial. Should states mandate CF screening for newborns? What difference would it make to your analysis to learn that disease prevalence varies across racial and ethnic groups (for example, prevalence is higher in non-Hispanic whites and lower in African Americans.)? As of 2005 8 states mandate newborn screening for CF.

2. The AAP Task Force expressed a number of concerns regarding newborn screening programs. Notable among them were the lack of national standards for test inclusion and the variability in state resources for program development—factors which in combination contributed to significant disparities in access to services for infants. AAP recommended that the federal government initiate a national process to develop and implement uniform newborn screening program standards and policies. In response, the Health Resources and Services Administration (HRSA) contracted with the American College of Medical Genetics (ACMG) to develop recommendations for a uniform newborn screening program. The resulting HRSA/ACMG report, published in the Federal Register on March 8, 2005, recommends that all states mandate screening and follow up for a core panel of twenty-nine conditions. An additional twenty-five conditions are designated as "secondary targets," which means they should be screened for, and the results should be reported to the family, follow-up through the state program is not required. *See* Newborn Screening: Toward a Uniform Screening Panel and System, *available at* http://mchb.hrsa.gov/screening.

These recommendations represent a significant expansion in the scope of newborn screening for a majority of the states, most of whom had previously screened for nine or fewer conditions, and require that state public health programs reassess newborn screening and make potentially difficult decisions regarding the scope of their panels, the range of services that will accompany screening tests, and what is the permissible impact of expanded screening on resource allocation across a range of other public health programs. What additional information would you need to know regarding the recommended panel of tests to help you assess whether the HRSA/ACMG recommendations should be embraced by state public health programs? The twenty-nine conditions recommended for the core screening panel include twenty metabolic disorders, three hemoglobinopathies, and six other genetic-based conditions including cystic fibrosis and congenital deafness. Of these, twenty-three are identified using MS/MS technology. How does the following recommendation from the ACMG/ASHG (American Society for Human Genetics) Test and Technology Transfer Committee Working Group influence your assessment:

> In summary, MS/MS can provide substantial benefits to patients and their families if thoughtfully integrated into newborn screening programs, provided that sufficient funding is made available to cover the costs of the additional and necessary personnel, medications and medical foods. Indeed, the expense and complexity of the instrumentation and the need for trained metabolic physicians to care for the additional patients could make it very difficult for states with small populations and/or few trained personnel to implement MS/MS, and development of regional laboratories and services may well be necessary to address this need.

ACMG/ASHG, *Statement Regarding Tandem Mass Spectrometry in Newborn Screening*, 2 Genetics in Med. 267 (2000).

What legal issues might accompany a decision to embrace expanded newborn screening? What legal issues might accompany a decision to reject the ACMG/HRSA recommendations?

3. The drive to expand newborn screening comes from a variety of sources, including disease advocacy groups and entrepreneurs who are eager to capture a share of an ever-increasing market. Interestingly, many biomedical researchers, who are committed to learning more about the genetic contributions to disease and developing interventions to prevent or ameliorate risk in the genetically susceptible, support the expansion of newborn screening programs because these programs provide a robust sample of human subjects for ongoing study and follow-up. Finally, parents of potentially affected children often champion expanded newborn screening in the belief that more knowledge will provide reassurance, inform reproductive planning decisions, and enable future planning for children who are affected. (The benefits and risks of genetic labeling are touched on in Chapter 7. *See, e.g.*, discussion of AAP statement regarding Ethical Issues with Genetic Testing in Pediatrics and ACMG/ASHG statement regarding Ethical, Legal and Psychosocial Implications of Genetic Testing in Children and Adolescents.) Are these goals consonant with the traditional focus of public health programs? Do these goals justify an exercise of state police power or *parens patriae* power to compel parents to submit their newborn to genetic screening?

4. For additional background and analysis of state newborn screening programs and the ethical and legal issues surrounding expanded goals for testing, *see* Ellen Wright Clayton, *Screening and Treatment of Newborns*, 29 Houst. L. Rev. 1 (1992); ACMG/ASHG, *Points to Consider: Ethical, Legal and Psychosocial Implications of Genetic Testing in Children and Adolescents*, 57 Am. J. Hum. Genet. 1233 (1995); Harvey L. Levy & Simone Albers, *Genetic Screening of Newborns*, 2000 Annu. Rev. Genomics Hum. Genet. 139 (2000); Robert M. Nelson et al., *Ethical issues with Genetic Testing in Pediatrics*, 107 Pediatrics 1451, 1455 (2001); Linda McCabe, Bradford Therrell & Edward McCabe, *Newborn Screening: Rationale for a Comprehensive, Fully Integrated Public Health System*, 77 Molecular Genet. and Metabolism 77 (2002).

Douglas County, Nebraska v. Anaya

694 N.W.2d 601 (Neb. 2005)

WRIGHT, J.

...

Rosa Ariel Anaya was born in the Anayas' home, without a physician present, on July 11, 2003. The birth was reported to the Department of Health and Human Services (DHHS) on July 17.

In August 2003, a DHHS employee received Rosa Anaya's birth certificate, checked DHHS' database, and determined that the testing for metabolic diseases required by §71-519 had not been performed. A certified letter was sent to the Anayas explaining the statute's requirements. Enclosed with the letter was a brochure detailing the screening process, which included drawing a small amount of blood from the heel of the infant to be tested. The Anayas declined to submit Rosa Anaya for the screening, stating that it was in direct conflict with their sincerely held religious beliefs that life is taken from the body if blood is removed from it and that a person's lifespan may be shortened if blood is drawn.

Douglas County brought an action seeking to compel the Anayas to comply with §71-519. At a hearing on September 26, 2003, Mary Anaya testified as to the Anayas' religious beliefs.

The Anayas subsequently filed a motion for judicial exemption from prosecution and dismissal of the petition. They alleged that it was impossible for them to comply with §71-519 because 70 days had passed since the birth was registered and DHHS regulations required that the testing be completed within 48 hours of the registration of the birth if the birth was not attended by a physician. They also claimed the statute violated the 14th Amendment to the U.S. Constitution.

The district court found that the State has a compelling state interest in the screening of infants for metabolic diseases and that the Anayas' religious beliefs did not outweigh the State's compelling interest that "these children can grow and develop to be free of a metabolic disease particularly in light of the minimal invasion of the blood test administration which is merely a pinprick to the child's heel." The court rejected the Anayas' claim that the issue was moot due to Rosa Anaya's age. Although testing procedures are most effective when administered shortly after birth, the court found that it was not too late to administer the test even if Rosa Anaya was 6 months of age or older. The court ordered the Anayas to comply with §71-519 by submitting Rosa Anaya for metabolic screening forthwith....

The Anayas argue that §71-519 infringes upon their First Amendment right to freely exercise their religion and that the district court erred in concluding that the State had shown a compelling interest which justifies the infringement....

The statute which the Anayas challenged provides:

> (1) All infants born in the State of Nebraska shall be screened for phenylketonuria, primary hypothyroidism, biotinidase deficiency, galactosemia, hemoglobinopathies, medium-chain acyl co-a dehydrogenase (MCAD) deficiency, and such other metabolic diseases as [DHHS] may from time to time specify....
>
> (2) ... If a birth is not attended by a physician and the infant does not have a physician, the person registering the birth shall cause such tests to be performed within the period and in the manner prescribed by [DHHS].

When Rosa Anaya was born, regulations prescribed by DHHS provided that if a birth was not attended by a physician and "the tests have not been performed within 48 hours of birth as otherwise required by these regulations, the person registering the birth must cause newborn screening tests for metabolic diseases to be performed within 48 hours of registration of the birth." 181 Neb. Admin. Code, ch. 2, §008 (2002).

The Anayas argue that because they have raised a free exercise of religion claim along with a parental substantive due process claim, they have a hybrid constitutional rights claim, which requires strict scrutiny review. Under a strict scrutiny review, the law must be justified by a compelling governmental interest and must be narrowly tailored to advance that interest. *See Church of Lukumi Babalu Aye, Inc. v. Hialeah*, 508 U.S. 520 (1993)....

In *Hialeah*, the Court ... held that to be found constitutional, a neutral law of general applicability does not require demonstration of a compelling governmental interest. "In addressing the constitutional protection for free exercise of religion, our cases establish the general proposition that a law that is neutral and of general applicability need not be justified by a compelling governmental interest even if the law has the incidental effect of burdening a particular religious practice." *Hialeah*, 508 U.S. at 531.

Federal courts have also discussed hybrid rights claims. In *Swanson By and Through Swanson v. Guthrie ISD I-L*, 135 F.3d 694 (10th Cir.1998), the federal court addressed an argument that a school policy violated a home-schooled student's free exercise rights and the parents' right to direct her education. The court stated: "[W]e believe that simply raising such a claim is not a talisman that automatically leads to the application of the compelling-interest test." *Id.* at 699. "[I]t cannot be true that a plaintiff can simply invoke the parental rights doctrine, combine it with a claimed free-exercise right, and thereby force the government to demonstrate the presence of a compelling state interest." *Id.* at 700.

In *Miller v. Reed*, 176 F.3d 1202, 1207 (9th Cir.1999), the court stated, "[W]e recently held that, to assert a hybrid-rights claim, 'a free exercise plaintiff must make out a "colorable claim" that a companion right has been violated—that is, a "fair probability" or a "likelihood," but not a certitude, of success on the merits.'" The court further stated that "a plaintiff does not allege a hybrid-rights claim entitled to strict scrutiny analysis merely by combining a free exercise claim with an utterly meritless claim of the violation of another alleged fundamental right or a claim of an alleged violation of a non-fundamental or non-existent right." *Id.* at 1208.

In rejecting the idea of strict scrutiny analysis for hybrid rights claims, the U.S. Court of Appeals for the Sixth Circuit has stated:

Such an outcome is completely illogical; therefore, at least until the Supreme Court holds that legal standards under the Free Exercise Clause vary depending on whether other constitutional rights are implicated, we will not use a stricter legal standard than that used in *Smith* to evaluate generally applicable, exceptionless state regulations under the Free Exercise Clause. *Kissinger v. Board of Trustees*, 5 F.3d 177, 180 (6th Cir.1993).

We conclude that the Anayas' assertion of a hybrid rights claim does not implicate a strict scrutiny review of §71-519. A party may not force the government to meet the strict scrutiny standard by merely asserting claims of violations of more than one constitutional right.

The second constitutional rights violation asserted by the Anayas seems to suggest that §71-519 violates their rights as parents to make decisions concerning the upbringing of their children. They rely upon *Pierce v. Society of Sisters*, 268 U.S. 510 (1925), and *Wisconsin v. Yoder*, 406 U.S. 205 (1972).

In *Pierce*, the Court held that a compulsory education law deprived parents of the right to select a school for their children. It held that the Oregon compulsory education statute "unreasonably interfere[d] with the liberty of parents and guardians to direct the upbringing and education of children under their control." *Pierce*, 268 U.S. at 534–35. The Court concluded that the challenged law served no state interest and therefore had no reasonable relation to any state purpose.

In *Yoder*, the Court held that a state could not compel Amish parents to require their children to attend formal high school and that the compulsory education law violated the 1st and 14th Amendments. The Court noted that no harm to the physical or mental health of the child was inferred but that when the health and safety of a child was involved, different considerations applied.

To be sure, the power of the parent, even when linked to a free exercise claim, may be subject to limitation under *Prince* [*v. Massachusetts*, 321 U.S. 158 (1944),] if it appears that parental decisions will jeopardize the health or safety of the child, or have a potential for significant social burdens. *Yoder*, 406 U.S. at 233–34. The Court did not conclude that strict scrutiny was required.

It is true that "the custody, care and nurture of the child reside first in the parents." *Prince v. Massachusetts*, 321 U.S. 158, 166 (1944). However, the Court has never held that parental rights to childrearing as guaranteed under the Due Process Clause of the 14th Amendment must be subjected to a strict scrutiny analysis. *See Troxel v. Granville*, 530 U.S. 57 (2000). "[T]he Supreme Court has yet to decide whether the right to direct the upbringing and education of one's children is among those fundamental rights whose infringement merits heightened scrutiny." *Brown v. Hot, Sexy and Safer Productions, Inc.*, 68 F.3d 525, 533 (1st Cir.1995). *Pierce* and *Yoder* do not support an inference that parental decisionmaking requires a strict scrutiny analysis.

The question is not whether the Anayas have set forth a hybrid rights claim but whether the law they have challenged is neutral and has general application.

This case is analogous to cases in which courts have upheld the State's right to require immunization of children. In *Boone v. Boozman*, 217 F.Supp.2d 938 (E.D. Ark. 2002), the court upheld the constitutionality of an immunization statute, finding that the free exercise claim challenged a neutral law of general applicability. The law applied to all school children except those whose health would be endangered by immunization. Because the law was neutral, heightened scrutiny was not required even though compulsory immunization might burden a plaintiff's right to free exercise.

The court stated, "It is well established that the State may enact reasonable regulations to protect the public health and the public safety, and it cannot be questioned that compulsory immunization is a permissible exercise of the State's police power." *Id.* at 954. Society's interest in protecting against the spread of disease takes precedence over parental rights and the right to free exercise of religion. *Id.*...

A law is neutral and of general applicability "if it does not aim to 'infringe upon or restrict practices because of their religious motivation,' and if it does not 'in a selective manner impose burdens only on conduct motivated by religious belief[.]'" *San Jose Christian College v. Morgan Hill*, 360 F.3d 1024, 1031 (9th Cir.2004), quoting *Church of Lukumi Babalu Aye, Inc. v. Hialeah*, 508 U.S. 520 (1993). Section 71-519 is a neutral law of general applicability. It is generally applicable to all babies born in the state and does not discriminate as to which babies must be tested. Its purpose is not directed at religious practices or beliefs. Pursuant to *Employment Div., Dept. of Human Res. v. Smith*, 494 U.S. 872 (1990), and its progeny, a neutral law of general applicability need not be supported by a compelling governmental interest even though it may have an incidental effect of burdening religion.

Section 71-519 does not contain a system of particularized exemptions that allow some children to be excused from testing. *See Kissinger v. Board of Trustees*, 5 F.3d 177 (6th Cir.1993). The statute does not unlawfully burden the Anayas' right to freely exercise their religion, nor does it unlawfully burden their parental rights. Section 71-519 cannot be construed as directly regulating religious-based conduct. There is no evidence that the State had an anti-religious purpose in enforcing the law. *See id.*

. . .

We conclude that the effect of §71-519 upon the constitutional claims the Anayas have asserted is properly analyzed under a rational basis review. Evidence was presented concerning the effects of the diseases that are tested for under the statute. Early diagnosis allows for prevention of death and disability in children. The State has determined that it is appropriate to test for these diseases soon after a child is born in order to address treatment options. The health and safety of the child are of particular concern, as are the potential social burdens created by children who are not identified and treated.

The State has an interest in the health and welfare of all children born in Nebraska, and the purpose of §71-519 is to protect such health and welfare. This is a rational basis for the law, and it is constitutional.

The Anayas argue that the case is moot because the testing was not performed within 48 hours of Rosa Anaya's birth or within 48 hours after the birth was registered. There is no merit to the Anayas' claim. One cannot refuse to comply with testing required within a particular timeframe and then claim that the case is moot because the time has passed.

Although the value of metabolic screening may decline as the child ages, the test results can prove helpful in preventing death or retardation later in development. The program manager for DHHS' newborn screening program testified that some of the conditions occur rapidly after birth and others occur later in childhood. Early diagnosis allows for prevention of death and disability in newborns and children. If a child is not born in a hospital and the testing is conducted outside the 48-hour timeframe, some of the benefit of treatment is reduced, but further damage can be prevented. It is not possible to determine if a child has any of these conditions by the appearance of the child.

A medical doctor testified concerning the diseases identified in §71-519. Phenylketonuria, referred to as "PKU," is an inherited metabolic condition due to a genetic absence of an enzyme. The condition creates an abnormal buildup of amino acid that interferes with the growth of nerve cells in the brain, which is critical in the very first weeks and months of an infant's life. Abnormal chemistry is present and can be diagnosed within hours of birth. Any damage occurs within the first few weeks of life, but clear evidence may not be seen until the second half of the first year. Treatment is a special diet that allows children to develop normally.

Hypothyroidism results in a loss of thyroid function and in newborns causes the brain not to develop, resulting in profound mental retardation and developmental delays. An infant with hypothyroidism would not grow well, and the condition would be obvious within a few weeks of birth.

Galactosemia is a condition due to a missing enzyme. Babies without the enzyme quickly become jaundiced and droopy, and they may have a bloodstream infection that kills them within days.

Biotinidase is an enzyme that helps to conserve a B vitamin. A person who lacks the enzyme can develop acidosis, blindness, mental retardation, seizures, and deafness. Treatment is inexpensive and inoffensive. Signs and symptoms of this disease do not manifest early or at a predictable time. A child who is deficient in biotinidase will probably become symptomatic during the first year, and a child who is partially deficient might become symptomatic during childhood or adolescence.

Hemoglobinopathies can result in diseases including thalassemia and sickle cell disease, which are readily diagnosable and at least partially correctable. Newborns with these diseases are susceptible to bloodstream infections during the first year of life. Symptoms include a low blood count and sometimes an enlarged spleen, which would generally be assessed by a physician.

MCAD, medium chain acyl-CoA dehydrogenase deficiency, is due to the absence of an enzyme that is responsible for burning body fat. MCAD may appear in the first few days or weeks of life or during a childhood illness with fever and vomiting. It can be seen in school-age children. Remedial measures include educating the parents and the child's physician as to the condition and the risks and giving the child a dietary supplement. An episode of severe flu-like symptoms can result in brain damage.

A moot case is one which seeks to determine a question which does not rest upon existing facts or rights, in which the issues presented are no longer alive. *State on behalf of Pathammavong v. Pathammavong*, 679 N.W.2d 749 (Neb. 2004). A case becomes moot when the issues initially presented in litigation cease to exist or the litigants lack a legally cognizable interest in the outcome of litigation. *Krajicek v. Gale*, 677 N.W.2d 488 (Neb. 2004)....

The testimony of expert witnesses demonstrated that there is value in testing a child even beyond the 48-hour period immediately after birth. Although some of the conditions would have already manifested themselves, others can develop later in life.

... The record demonstrates that even if metabolic screening is completed beyond the first 48 hours of life, it is still important for the health and welfare of the child. Steps can be taken to treat any condition detected. The district court was correct in finding that the issue is not moot.

The judgment of the district court is affirmed.

Creason v. State Department of Health Services

957 P.2d 1323 (Cal. 1998)

CHIN, JUSTICE.

This case presents two issues for our review: (1) whether the newborn screening program contained in the Hereditary Disorders Act imposed a mandatory duty on the Department to select accurate standards for testing for and reporting possible congenital hypothyroidism, breach of which duty could form the basis for a private cause of action against the state by plaintiffs; and (2) assuming an enforceable mandatory duty existed, whether the state was nonetheless immune from suit under the California Tort Claims Act. [W]e conclude (contrary to the opinion of the Court of Appeal in this case) that the state owed plaintiffs no mandatory duty with respect to its development of appropriate testing and reporting procedures, and that, in any event, the state was immune from plaintiffs' suit.

... The first amended complaint contains the following material allegations: Sierra was born on October 20, 1990. Shortly after her birth, and as required by state law, a "test specimen" of her blood was taken and sent to a state-contracted laboratory for analysis to determine the existence of certain genetic disorders, including congenital hypothyroidism. According to plaintiffs, "One purpose of such testing is to determine whether a newborn is producing sufficient thyroid hormone to ensure proper growth and development and to permit early medical intervention if necessary."

Plaintiffs further alleged that "Participation ... in the newborn screening and/or testing procedures was mandated under state law," and the test "was conducted solely by Defendant STATE and by STATE contracted or approved entities ... to ensure full public protection against the devastating effects of preventable hereditary disorders and to permit early detection and necessary medical intervention." According to plaintiffs, "Defendant State was under a mandatory duty to exercise reasonable diligence in the formulation of testing and reporting procedures such that accurate information was made available to parents and physicians of newborns ... in order to achieve the stated purposes" of state law.

Plaintiffs also alleged the testing laboratory, acting under state contract, informed plaintiffs and their physician the test was "negative" for congenital hypothyroidism. Several months later, plaintiffs discovered Sierra did not have a thyroid gland and suffered from congenital hypothyroidism. Plaintiffs alleged defendant breached its duty by failing to exercise reasonable care and diligence "in the formulation of testing and reporting procedures," resulting in the failure to detect plaintiff Sierra's congenital hypothyroidism. Although not specifically alleged, plaintiffs' implicit premise is that if Sierra's condition had been timely diagnosed, thyroid hormone could have been administered to prevent her injuries.

In addition to the allegations of the first amended complaint, plaintiffs' original complaint had alleged that on October 20, 1990, Sierra was tested for congenital hypothyroidism, that the test findings showed low counts on both the thyroid stimulating hormone (TSH) component and the thyroxin 4(T4) component of the test, and that defendant had previously determined that only those tests that resulted in a *high* TSH factor and a low T4 factor would be reported as "positive" to the child's parents and pediatrician. According to plaintiffs, defendant knew or should have known that children with a low count on both components of the test "are known to have congenital hypothyroidism...." Plaintiffs charged that defendant "so designed, created, managed, maintained, and operated said testing procedure ... so as to proximately cause Plaintiff, Sierra Creason's, congenital hypothyroidism to go undetected until approximately April 23, 1991...."

...

Based on those allegations in plaintiffs' pleadings, we may assume the gist of their action accuses defendant of adopting faulty testing standards that fail to report all possible cases of hypothyroidism. In other words, any negligence on defendant's part occurred not while testing Sierra but earlier, during the formulation of the standards designed for interpreting and reporting the results of the tests ultimately given. The question before us is whether the state had a mandatory duty to require its testing facilities to report the low TSH test values to parents and treating pediatricians as potentially indicative of hypothyroidism, rather than adopting testing standards deeming those values within a "Normal" or "Negative" range....

The California Tort Claims Act provides that a public entity is not liable for injury arising from an act or omission except as provided by statute. Under Government Code section 815.6, as we have construed IT, "a public entity is liable for an injury proximately caused by its failure to discharge a mandatory duty designed to protect against the risk of a particular kind of injury. Whether a particular statute is intended to impose a mandatory duty, rather than a mere obligation to perform a discretionary function, is a question of statutory interpretation for the courts.

In plaintiffs' view, the state breached a mandatory duty to devise accurate testing and reporting standards for hypothyroidism. Defendant asserts in response that, under the Hereditary Disorders Act, the formulation of appropriate standards for testing and reporting test results for hypothyroidism is a *discretionary* function that could not properly form the basis for public liability based on breach of a mandatory duty....

Several factors support the view that the Legislature did not intend to permit a private action for damages against the state for its negligence in formulating standards for testing or reporting potential hereditary disorders. First, the Legislature included language in the Hereditary Disorders Act strongly suggesting that the state's formulation of those standards is a discretionary, not a mandatory, function. In Health and Safety Code former section 150 (now § 124975), the Legislature set forth a variety of findings and declarations acknowledging the importance of screening for hereditary disorders and the entitlement of all persons to adequate health services. The section also observed, however, that specific legislation aimed at alleviating the problems associated with these disorders "may tend to be inflexible in the face of rapidly expanding medical knowledge, underscoring the need for *flexible approaches* to coping with genetic problems" and provided that state policy in this area should be "constantly reviewed to consider changing medical knowledge and ensure full public protection".

Following up on this theme of caution, flexibility, and constant review of changing medical knowledge, the Legislature vested the Director of Health Services (Director) with the duty to "establish such rules, regulations, *and standards* for hereditary disorders programs *as the director deems necessary* to promote and protect the public health and safety, in accordance with the principles established herein." This language points forcefully toward the conclusion that the Legislature left the selection of necessary and appropriate testing and reporting standards to the sound discretion of the Director, guided by certain "principles" that the Director should consider in drafting those standards.

One of these statutory principles, on which plaintiffs rely, is that "Clinical testing procedures ... be accurate, provide maximum information, and that the testing procedures selected produce results that are subject to minimum misinterpretation." Contrary to plaintiffs' argument, we think this provision creates no affirmative mandatory duty of care to other persons, but instead represents only a general principle or policy to guide the state's discretion in formulating appropriate testing and reporting standards. Similarly, a separate section sets forth the state policy of making "every effort to detect, as early as possible" preventable heritable or congenital disorders. This section charges the state with promoting a statewide testing program "in accordance with accepted medical practices." Tests under the program "shall be administered to each child ... *at such time as the state department has established appropriate regulations and testing methods.*" Once again, mandatory statutory language is tempered by reference to the state's discretion in formulating "appropriate" testing standards. Neither of the provisions on which plaintiffs rely imposes a duty to notify parents or physicians of test results showing particular TSH levels.

Read together, all these provisions indicate the Legislature intended that the Department, after considering the ever-increasing and changing information concerning heritable and congenital defects, as well as expert and public views on testing, would exercise discretion in selecting necessary and appropriate testing and reporting standards. We find it highly unlikely the Legislature intended that an asserted breach of the guiding principles or policies would afford a basis for state liability under Government Code section 815.6. The drafting of rules, regulations and standards by the governmental agency charged with that responsibility would unquestionably fall in the category of discretionary "basic policy decisions" for which governmental agencies usually are insulated from civil liability....

We conclude that the general statutory principles and policy goals plaintiffs cite in the present case ... fail to comprise a mandatory duty to select or impose any particular testing or reporting standard or component, and that the Director's allegedly negligent exercise of discretion in selecting a particular standard will not support a cause of action under Government Code section 815.6. The Hereditary Disorders Act's creation of a limited right of action for any individual "whose confidentiality has been breached" by a violation of the act, in the same section that imposed a duty on the Director to establish a testing program, supports this conclusion. The Legislature's failure to specify any other private cause of action arising under the act may indicate that none was intended.

Even had plaintiffs' complaint stated a cause of action against defendant for breach of a mandatory statutory duty to formulate accurate testing and reporting standards for hypothyroidism, plaintiffs could not prevail if defendant was immune from suit. If a specific immunity statute applies, it "cannot be abrogated by a statute which simply imposes a general legal duty or liability...." (*Caldwell v. Montoya, supra,* 897 P.2d 1320 [(Cal. 1995)].) Defendant contends that Government Code section 855.6 provides specific immunity in this case. We agree....

[T]he judgment of the Court of Appeal is reversed with directions to affirm the trial court order dismissing, without leave to amend, plaintiffs' action as against defendant State Department of Health Services.

KENNARD, JUSTICE, concurring.

This is indeed a tragic case. A diagnostic blood test performed under a state-mandated that screens California-born babies for certain inherited disorders showed that plaintiff Sierra Creason had tested "negative" for congenital hypothyroidism. A few months later, however, the family doctor determined that Sierra had no thyroid gland and that her condition had progressed to irreversible mental retardation. Although the state-mandated test here was properly performed under the testing procedure established by the State Department of Public Health (Department), plaintiffs allege that the Department negligently determined not to report certain test results as indicating possible hypothyroidism.

The majority holds, and I agree, that the Department is not liable for injuries resulting from congenital disorders that its testing program failed to detect in a particular case. In establishing the neonatal program at issue, the Legislature sought to reduce the "often costly, tragic, and sometimes deadly burdens to the health and well-being of the citizens of this state" (Health & Saf.Code, § 124975, subd. (b)) caused by hereditary disorders and to "contribute to the further understanding and accumulation of medical knowledge [about such disorders] that may lead to their eventual alleviation or cure" (*id.,* subd. (c)). Neonatal screening leads to preventive treatment of those children found to have hereditary disorders. In Sierra's case, tragically, the Department's test report failed to alert her parents and family doctor that Sierra suffered from hypothyroidism.

But to impose civil liability on the Department here and in any similar future case may well threaten the continuation of a generally beneficial statewide program that has screened millions of California babies for disabling congenital disorders. In a recent newsletter, the Department pointed out that between 1980 and 1995 approximately 99 percent of babies born in California were tested and that the screening of 7,443,147 infants detected 2,271 cases of congenital hypothyroidism. As the Law Revision Commission stressed in 1963, when it urged the Legislature to insulate government agencies from liability for mass public health screening programs, "Far more persons would suffer if government did not perform these functions at all than would be benefited by permitting recovery in those cases where the government is shown to have performed inadequately."

The facts of this case are heartrending, and the desire to afford the stricken child and her parents some measure of comfort and financial assistance is strong. But these considerations alone cannot dictate the outcome in this case. The Legislature's decision to provide a generally beneficial neonatal medical screening program without state liability is one we must respect. Nor is it a heartless decision, for if the alternative is not a program with liability but no program at all, more rather than fewer of these tragedies would result.

Notes & Questions

1. As the *Anaya* case demonstrates, the mandated nature of state newborn screening programs raises important legal issues regarding parental rights and religious autonomy. Nebraska is one of only five states that do not honor religious objections to testing (the other states are Arizona, Montana, South Dakota, and West Virginia). Given the goal of early disease detection, what are the pros and cons of compulsory screening? How important to your analysis is the presence of clearly defined, significant health benefits to the infant associated with early detection? If states move toward the expanded testing panel recommended by the HRSA/ACMG report, will the state continue to maintain authority to mandate the full range of screening tests? Mandated screening for hearing disorders is included in the HRSA/ACMG recommendations. Recall the earlier discussion of the disability rights perspective regarding genetic testing (*see* Chapter 2) How might members of the deaf community react to a state mandate requiring that their infants be screened for genetic markers associated with hearing impairment? Assume the *Anaya* court was analyzing an objection to newborn hearing screening advanced by parents who are active members of the deaf community and object to the stigma associated they believe is associated with genetic screening for hearing impairment and are also concerned that positive test results will result in pressure from the medical community to pursue treatment using cochlear implants (to which they are very opposed). How would the *Anaya* court rule? For additional background information regarding the deaf community's perspective on cochlear implants, *see, e.g.,* B.P. Tucker, *Deaf Culture, Cochlear Implants and Elective Disability*, 28 The Hastings Center Report 6 (1998).

2. As discussed in Chapter 7, most of the litigation surrounding newborn screening involves malpractice claims against providers who allegedly failed to order appropriate tests, order tests in a timely fashion, or correctly interpret and/or follow up on positive test results. The case of *Humana v. McKee* exemplifies this line of cases. The *Creason* case, on the other hand, involves allegations against the newborn screening program *per se.* Plaintiffs challenged the reasonableness of the testing and reporting standards for

congenital hypothyroidism (CH), one of several conditions on State of California's mandatory newborn screening panel. In essence they presented evidence that if a different threshold had been used for identifying and reporting "abnormal" test results their daughter would have been diagnosed with CH in sufficient time to intervene and avoid the profound mental retardation that accompanies untreated CH. The California Supreme Court affirmed a trial court decision dismissing plaintiff's claims, concluding the legislation authorizing the state's newborn screening program did not impose a duty upon the state to develop appropriate testing and reporting procedures and, moreover, even if it did, the state would be immune from suit. In so doing the Court supported the legislature's arguably broad delegation of discretion to the Director of Health Services to develop testing standards and reporting procedures for newborn screening tests and essentially insulated state newborn screening programs from liability for adopting outdated or incomplete testing and reporting procedures. How might this ruling impact the quality of newborn screening procedures in the future? Does the *Creason* opinion advance or hinder efforts to move toward more uniform national standards for newborn screening? Given the court's analysis, can you develop a newborn screening fact pattern that might expose the state to liability?

Index